CASES AND MATERIALS ON

ENVIRONMENTAL LAW

Tenth Edition

■ ■ ■

Daniel A. Farber
Sato Sho Professor of Law
University of California, Berkeley

Ann E. Carlson
Shirley Shapiro Professor of Environmental Law
UCLA School of Law

William Boyd
Professor
UCLA Institute of the Environment & Sustainability
UCLA School of Law

AMERICAN CASEBOOK SERIES®

WEST
ACADEMIC
PUBLISHING

American Casebook Series is a trademark registered in the U.S. Patent and Trademark Office.

ISBN: 978-1-64020-612-0

To Dianne
Dan Farber

To Carl, Hallie, and Ian
Ann Carlson

To Norrie, Eve, Mary Wallace, and Norrie
William Boyd

PREFACE

The Tenth Edition, like its predecessors, is designed to give students an understanding of federal environmental law and policy that is both broad and thematic as well as detailed and concrete. We have made some significant changes to this edition and updated it to reflect the fast-changing nature of environmental law. Environmental law has continued to be a significant part of the Supreme Court's docket. This edition provides revised treatment of the toxics materials to reflect recent legislative changes, and other chapters reflect important decisions such as UARG. Full attention is given to Obama Administrative initiatives and current efforts by the Trump Administration to roll them back.

As in the Ninth Edition, our opening chapters provide students with an understanding of the cross-cutting themes in environmental regulation, such as techniques of risk assessment, the controversial role of cost-benefit analysis, administrative procedure, environmental standing, property rights disputes, and the evolving contours of environmental federalism. When students begin to study specific regulatory schemes, they will already have a rich understanding of environmental policy and a grasp of the array of regulatory tools such as emissions trading systems. We have streamlined these introductory materials in this edition, however, to allow more focus on the intricacies of the major environmental statutes such as the Clean Air Act.

Climate change is an increasingly central area of environmental law. Although there now seems little immediate prospect of congressional action, litigation under the Clean Air Act continues, and states such as California remain active. In the meantime, each new issue of Science and Nature seems to demonstrate that climate change is happening earlier and more rapidly than scientific models have predicted. The future of climate change is now, and we are at a delicate, interesting and crucial moment in addressing the problem.

This edition reflects these developments. Because climate law is so dynamic, however, we recommend that readers consult the Berkeley/UCLA environmental law blog, LegalPlanet (www.legalplanet.wordpress.com), for the latest developments.

Special thanks are due to our families for giving us support and love during the writing process. And to our students, who challenge and inspire us to think about environmental issues in new and interesting ways. We also continue to owe a debt to Roger Findley and Jody Freeman for their contributions to earlier editions of this book.

DANIEL A. FARBER
ANN E. CARLSON
WILLIAM BOYD

July 2019

SUMMARY OF CONTENTS

TABLE OF CONTENTS

TABLE OF CASES

The principal cases are in bold type.

———

TABLE OF ACRONYMS

AB	Appellate Body (WTO)
ACE	Army Corps of Engineers
ADR	Alternative Dispute Resolution
AEC	Atomic Energy Commission
AEI	American Enterprise Institute
AFL-CIO	American Federation of Labor and Congress of Industrial Organizations
AFO	Animal Feeding Operation
AID	Agency for International Development
AISA	American Iron and Steel Institute
ALJ	Administrative Law Judge
AMC	American Mining Congress
AMI	American Meat Institute
ANILCA	Alaska National Interest Lands Conservation Act
APA	Administrative Procedure Act
APHIS	Animal Plant Health and Inspection Service
API	American Petroleum Institute
AQCR	Air Quality Control Regions
ARARs	Applicable or Relevant and Appropriate Requirements
ATA	American Trucking Association
AUM	Animal Unit Month
BACT	Best Available Control Technology
BADCT	Best Available Demonstrated Control Technology
BART	Best Available Retrofit Technology
BAT	Best Achievable Technology
BATEA	Best Available Technology Economically Achievable
BCT	Best Conventional Pollutant Control Technology
BDAT	Best Demonstrated Available Technology
BLM	Bureau of Land Management

BMP	Best Management Practices
BOD	Biochemical Oxygen Demand
BOD5	Biochemical Oxygen Demand measured over a 5-day period
BODS	Biochemical Oxygen-Demanding Substances
BPCTCA	Best Practicable Control Technology Currently Available
BPJ	Best Professional Judgment
BPCT	Best Practicable Control Technology
BRD	Biological Resources Division
BTUs	British Thermal Units
BWCA	Boundary Waters Canoe Area
BWCAW	Boundary Waters Canoe Area Wilderness
CAA	Clean Air Act
CAFE	Corporate Average Fuel Economy
CAFO	Concentrated Animal Feeding Operation
CARE	Citizens Against the Refinery's Effects
CARE	Concerned Area Residents for the Environment
CASAC	Clean Air Scientific Advisory Committee
CBA	Cost-Benefit Analysis
CBD	Convention on Biological Diversity
CBI	Confidential Business Information
CEQ	Council on Environmental Quality
CERCLA	Comprehensive Environmental Response, Compensation, and Liability Act
CFR	Code of Federal Regulations
CMA	Chemical Manufacturers Association
CO	Carbon Monoxide
CO_2	Carbon Dioxide
COCC	Columbia Organic Chemical Company
COD	Chemical Oxygen Demand
COLA	Cost of Living Adjustment
COP	Conference of the Parties
CPSC	Consumer Product Safety Commission

CRJ	Commission for Racial Justice
CSD	Commission on Sustainable Development
CSMA	Chemical Specialties Manufacturers Association
CSWG	Corporate Sunshine Working Group
CV	Contingent Valuation
CWA	Clean Water Act
CZMA	Coastal Zone Management Act
D_2O	Deuterium Oxide ("Heavy Water")
DAF	Dilution and Attenuation Factor
DBCP	Dibromochloropropane
DCO	Delayed Compliance Order
DDT	DichloroDiphenylTrichloroethane
DEP	Department of Environmental Protection
DES	Diethylstilbesterol
DF	Deterioration Factor
DHEC	Department of Health and Environmental Control
DMC	De Minimis Classification
DMRs	Discharge Monitoring Reports
DNA	Deoxyribonucleic Acid
DOI	Department of the Interior
DOJ	Department of Justice
DOT	Department of Transportation
DUs	Designated Uses
EA	Environmental Assessment
EC	European Community
ECJ	European Court of Justice
EDF	Environmental Defense Fund
EEC	European Economic Community
EEI	Edison Electric Institute
EGU	Electric Generating Unit
EIA	Environmental Impact Assessment
EIS	Environmental Impact Statement

ELI	Environmental Law Institute
EMSs	Environmental Management Systems
EP	Extraction Procedure
EP	Erythrocyte Protoporphyrin
EPA	Environmental Protection Agency
EPCRA	Emergency Planning and Community Right-to-Know Act
EQB	Environmental Quality Board
ESA	Endangered Species Act
ETP	Eastern Tropical Pacific
ETS	Environmental Transportation Systems
EU	European Union
EWG	The Environmental Working Group
FAA	Federal Aviation Administration
FACA	Federal Advisory Committee Act
FASB	Financial Accounting Standards Board
FBI	Federal Bureau of Investigation
FCC	Federal Communications Commission
FDA	Food and Drug Administration
FDD	Final Development Document
FDF	Fundamentally Different Factor
FEISS	Final Environmental Impact Statement Supplement
FERC	Federal Energy Regulatory Commission
FFDCA	Federal Food, Drug, and Cosmetic Act
FIFRA	Federal Insecticide, Fungicide, and Rodenticide Act
FIP	Federal Implementation Plan
FLPMA	Federal Land Policy and Management Act
FMC	Federal Maritime Commission
FOE	Friends of the Earth
FOIA	Freedom of Information Act
FONSI	Finding of No Significant Impact
FPA	Federal Power Act
FPAs	Final Project Agreements

FWPCA	Federal Water Pollution and Control Act
FWS	Fish and Wildlife Service
FY	Fiscal Year
GAAP	Generally Accepted Accounting Principles
GAO	General Accounting Office
GAP	Gap Analysis Program
GATT	General Agreement on Tariffs and Trade
GES	Global Environmental Facility
GHG	Greenhouse Gas
GIS	Geographic Information Systems
GM	General Motors
GM	Genetically Modified
GMOs	Genetically Modified Organisms
GNP	Gross National Product
GSA	General Services Administration
GWEN	Ground Wave Emergency Network
HC	Hydrocarbons
HCP	Habitat Conservation Plan
HREC	Hampton Roads Energy Company
HSWA	Hazardous and Solid Waste Amendments
HUD	Housing and Urban Development
HWIR	Hazardous Waste Identification Rule
ICC	Interstate Commerce Commission
ICR	Ignitable, Corrosive, and Reactive
ICS	Individual Control Strategies
IEPA	Illinois Environmental Protection Agency
I & M	Inspection and Maintenance
INS	Immigration and Naturalization Service
IPC	International Paper Company
IPCC	Intergovernmental Panel on Climate Change
IPM	Integrated Pest Management
IPM	Integrated Planning Model

ITC	Interagency Testing Committee
IWC	International Whaling Commission
JCAE	Joint Committee on Atomic Energy
JTU	Jackson Turbidity Unit
LAER	Lowest Achievable Emission Rate
LDRs	Land Disposal Restrictions
LEV	Low Emissions Vehicle
LIA	Lead Industry Association
LMFBR	Liquid Metal Fast Breeder Reactor
LULUs	Locally Undesirable Land Uses
LWK	Live Weight Killed
MACT	Maximum Achievable Control Technology
MCC	Metropolitan Correction Center
MCL	Maximum Contaminant Level
MCLG	Maximum Contaminant Level Goal
MGP	Manufactured Gas Plant
MMPA	Marine Mammal Protection Act
MOA	Memorandum of Agreement
MPRSA	Marine Protection, Research, and Sanctuaries Act
MSDS	Material Safety Data Sheets
MSHA	Mine Safety and Health Administration
MSW	Municipal Solid Waste
MTBE	Methyl Tertiary-Butyl Ether
MY	Model Year
NAACP	National Association for the Advancement of Colored People
NAAQS	National Ambient Air Quality Standards
NAFTA	North American Free Trade Agreement
NAS	National Academy of Sciences
NASA	National Aeronautics and Space Administration
NAZ	Nonattainment Zone
NBARs	Nonbinding Preliminary Allocations of Responsibility
NBII	National Biological Information Infrastructure

NBS	National Biological Service
NCCP	Natural Community Conservation Program
NCP	National Contingency Plan
NEPA	National Environmental Policy Act
NEPACCO	Northeastern Pharmaceutical and Chemical Company
NESHAP	National Emission Standards for Hazardous Air Pollutants
NFMA	National Forest Management Act
NGO	Nongovernmental Organization
NGPRP	Northern Great Plains Resources Program
NIEHS	National Institute of Environmental Health Sciences
NIMBY	"Not In My Back Yard"
NIPDWS	National Interim Primary Drinking Water Standards
NLEV	National Low Emission Vehicle
NO_2	Nitrogen Dioxide
NOAA	National Oceanographic and Atmospheric Agency
NODA	Notice of Data Availability
NO_x	Nitrogen Oxides
NPDES	National Pollutant Discharge Elimination System
NPL	National Priorities List
NRA	Negotiated Rulemaking Act
NRC	Nuclear Regulatory Commission
NRC	National Research Council
NRDC	Natural Resources Defense Council
NSPS	New Source Performance Standards
NSR	New Source Review
NWF	National Wildlife Federation
O_3	Ozone
OCPSF	Organic Chemicals, Plastics and Synthetic Fibers
OCS	Outer Continental Shelf
OCSLA	Outer Continental Shelf Lands Act
OMB	Office of Management and Budget
OSHA	Occupational Safety and Health Administration

OSWER	Office of Solid Waste and Emergency Response
OTAG	Ozone Transport Assessment Group
PANE	People Against Nuclear Energy
Pb	Lead
PBT	Persistent, Bioaccumulative, and Toxic
PCB	Polychlorinated Biphenyl
PEL	Permissible Exposure Limit
PG&E	Pacific Gas and Electric
PIRG	Public Interest Research Group
PM	Particulate Matter
POTWs	Publicly Owned Treatment Works
PPA	Plant Pest Act
ppm	parts per million
ppq	parts per quadrillion
ppt	parts per trillion
PRP	Potentially Responsible Party
PSD	Prevention of Significant Deterioration
PSNS	Pretreatment Standards for New Sources
PUD	Public Utility District
RACM	Reasonably Available Control Measures
RACT	Reasonably Available Control Technology
RAND	Research and Development (a think tank)
RCO	Responsible Corporate Officer
RCRA	Resource Conservation and Recovery Act
RECLAIM	Regional Clean Air Incentives Market
RFF	Resources for the Future
RPA	Renewable Resources Planning Act
RTCs	RECLAIM Trading Credits
SAB	Staff Accounting Bulletins
SAB	Scientific Advisory Board
SAP	Scientific Advisory Panel
SARA	Superfund Amendment and Reauthorization Act

SCRDI	South Carolina Recycling and Disposal, Inc.
SCS	Soil Conservation Service
SDWA	Safe Drinking Water Act
SEC	Securities and Exchange Commission
SEIS	Supplemental Environmental Impact Statement
SEPs	Supplemental Environmental Projects
SEPs	Supplemental Enforcement Plans
SIC	Standard Industrial Classification
SICEA	Steel Industry Compliance Extension Act
SIP	State Implementation Plan
SIPI	Scientists' Institute for Public Information
SIR	Supplemental Information Report
SO_2	Sulfur Dioxide
SPS	Sanitary and Phyto-Sanitary
SRF	State Revolving Fund
SWANCC	Solid Waste Agency of Northern Cook County
TC	Toxicity Characteristic
TCDD	2,3,7,8-Tetrachlorodibenzo-p-dioxin
TCLP	Toxicity Characteristic Leaching Procedure
TCP	2,4,5-Trichlorophenol
TCP	Transportation Control Plan
TMDLs	Total Maximum Daily Loads
TMI-1	Three Mile Island Unit 1 nuclear power plant
TMI-2	Three Mile Island Unit 2 nuclear power plant
TOC	Total Organic Carbon
TRI	Toxic Release Inventory
TRPA	Tahoe Regional Planning Agency
TSCA	Toxic Substances Control Act
TSD	Treatment, Storage, and Disposal
TSDFs	Treatment, Storage, and Disposal Facilities
TSS	Total Suspended Solids
TTHMs	Total Trihalomethanes

TVA	Tennessee Valley Authority
mg/m3	Micrograms per cubic meter (of air)
mg	Pb/dl Micrograms of lead per deciliter (of blood)
mg	Pb/m3 Micrograms of lead per cubic meter (of air)
U.N.	United Nations
UNDP	United Nations Development Programme
UNEP	United Nations Environment Programme
UNFCCC	United Nations Framework Convention on Climate Change
USDA	United States Department of Agriculture
USEPA	United States Environmental Protection Agency
USGS	United States Geological Survey
UST	Underground Storage Tank
VCP	Voluntary Cleanup Program
VOCs	Volatile Organic Compounds
WARC	Water and Air Resources Commission
WLAs	Wasteload Allocations
WQC	Water Quality Criteria
WQSs	Water Quality Standards
WQTP	Water Quality Trading Policy
WTO	World Trade Organization
WWTP	Wastewater Treatment Plant
ZEV	Zero Emission Vehicle

CASES AND MATERIALS ON

ENVIRONMENTAL LAW

Tenth Edition

CHAPTER 1

INTRODUCING ENVIRONMENTAL LAW

■ ■ ■

It may be helpful to begin with a roadmap of the book. Chapter 1 provides historical background on current environmental regulation and explores some basic themes. After that introduction, the casebook proceeds as follows:

- *Tools and Methods.* Chapter 2 provides an overview of tools and methods of environmental protection, including cost-benefit analysis, risk assessment, and tort liability.

- *A Statutory Case Study.* Chapter 3 begins our journey into environmental regulation with a detailed study of the Endangered Species Act. The ESA illustrates many of the themes, conflicts and approaches discussed in the first two chapters.

- *The Regulatory System.* The next two chapters focus on issues of process and structure. Chapter 4 considers the allocation of authority over environmental issues among various levels of government, with close attention to the constitutional issues raised by state and federal regulation. It also considers how the Takings Clause may constrain regulation of private property. Chapter 5 analyzes how environmental policy is made through the legislative and administrative process, and how courts interpret legislative choices while policing administrative actions.

- *Pollution Regulation.* Chapter 5 is followed by two chapters focusing on pollution. Chapter 6 covers air pollution, while Chapter 7 covers water pollution. These two chapters explain the operation of two central federal statutes—the Clean Air Act and the Clean Water Act. These complex statutes use a variety of tools and approaches to regulate the "externalities" of productive economic activity.

- *Toxic Chemicals.* The final two chapters focus on hazardous wastes and toxic chemicals, respectively. Chapter 8 covers RCRA and CERCLA, which together regulate the management of hazardous wastes and allocate liability for cleanups. Chapter 9 explains the regulation of toxic substances and genetically modified materials.

The journey begins with this introductory chapter. This introduction is intended to introduce you to the problem of environmental disruption and to important perspectives that shape our policy response. Section A provides an overview of the major themes and historical development of environmental law. Environmental law is not, of course, solely the result of some logical elaboration of neutral legal principles that establish timeless solutions for static problems.

Instead, environmental law is the product of a dynamic and often deeply political interaction between legislatures, government agencies, courts, and interest groups. In a way, the legal system is its own ecosystem. Understanding how these moving parts operate together illuminates why environmental laws take the shape that they do. Moreover, the field is interdisciplinary to its core; it depends on developments in biological and health sciences as well as economics, and our knowledge in these areas is constantly changing. The material in Section A explores these and other reasons why environmental law is special, and accounts for where we are in the field today.

Improving environmental quality involves pervasive collective action problems, which are explored in Section B. Environmental damage is often the result of a "tragedy of the commons," in which people face many incentives to exploit resources but few incentives to protect or preserve them. Section B uses global climate change (the greenhouse effect) as a case study of the difficulties of protecting the commons. No one owns the planetary atmosphere, or, to put it another way, everyone owns the atmosphere. This poses serious, but not necessarily insurmountable, challenges to efforts to control climate change.

A. ENVIRONMENTAL PROTECTION: AN OVERVIEW

As promised, we begin with a general overview of environmental law, focusing on some of the main themes throughout the course. We also provide a brief history of the field. Today's environmental regulations are the product of several decades of political development, rather than a deliberately designed and completely coherent system.

1. MAJOR THEMES

This book covers a wide range of environmental problems and issues— everything from automobile pollution to hazardous waste sites to biodiversity. Each of these problems has prompted a legal response, resulting in a complicated field comprised not only of common law and constitutional doctrines but also an array of federal statutes. Some of these laws are mind-boggling in their complexity. And even the relatively simple ones reveal unexpected nuances upon closer examination. All of this can be challenging to the novice. Indeed, the list of statutory acronyms alone can be intimidating to the newcomer: NEPA, CAA, RCRA, CERCLA, ESA—not to mention such lesser-known statutes as TSCA or FIFRA. (At the end of the book you will find a glossary identifying all these acronyms.) Each statute creates its own world of regulatory complexity, much like the tax code or the bankruptcy law.

To make matters even more challenging, environmental law overlaps in important ways with other areas of law, most notably constitutional law and administrative law, but also torts, criminal law, property law, and even international trade law. It is also highly interdisciplinary, with important contributions from economics as well as the sciences. All of this makes the course enormously interesting, but also difficult to distill and manage.

To help you tame this bewildering collection of statutes and legal doctrines, it is useful to focus on the perspectives and tools introduced in the first two chapters. They provide an anchor for the rest of the casebook. Fundamentally, despite all of the detail in the pages to come, we will be presented over and over again with four basic questions.

1.   *Who should set environmental policy?* We will frequently ask whether an administrative agency has exceeded the bounds of its legislative authorization. Sometimes we will also ask whether the states or the federal government should have authority, or whether the courts should take an active role in setting policy.

2.   *How should we make tradeoffs between environmental protection and cost?* Should we pursue environmental benefits at all costs, should we use cost-benefit analysis, or should we adopt some intermediate stance? Some crucial issues underlie these disputes, turning on whether we should adopt a utilitarian view of environmental law or view it as protecting basic rights to environmental quality.

3.   *What regulatory instruments should be used?* Conventional regulatory techniques include standards based directly on environmental goals, such as mandates to achieve certain levels of air quality, and standards based on technological feasibility. Alternatives to direct government regulation include tort liability, economic incentive programs, and negotiated outcomes. Whether any particular regulatory scheme has the right mix of instruments is often debatable.

4.   *How should we deal with scientific uncertainty?* The problem of scientific uncertainty crops up again and again: in determining when a possible risk must be discussed in an

environmental impact statement, in analyzing whether Congress unconstitutionally delegated too much discretion to the EPA to determine the "safe" level of air quality, in regulating toxic chemicals, in attempting to preserve endangered species. These problems are compounded because many of the effects in question are long-term and cannot be reliably gauged until decades in the future. We cannot wait until we have full information to regulate because the effects will already have occurred, but we must also keep in mind that we will have better information as science progresses.

5. *What are the distributional consequences of environmental harms and do environmental laws do anything to respond to these distributional concerns?* Not surprisingly, environmental harms do not affect all populations equally and evidence exists that some environmental problems disproportionately affect low income communities and communities of color. These distributional concerns have not always received the attention they deserve in the law.

In making sense of environmental law, it may help to have a grasp of the values that underlie environmental protection and the countervailing values that may act as constraints. The following excerpt provides a good overview.

JONATHAN CANNON, ENVIRONMENTALISM AND THE SUPREME COURT: A CULTURAL ANALYSIS
33 ECOLOGY L.Q. 363 (2006).[1]

The task here is to identify the basic set of tenets that characterize environmentalism, acknowledging from the outset that those calling themselves environmentalists hold divergent beliefs and values. In *Environmental Values in American Culture*, three anthropologists—Willett Kempton, James S. Boster, and Jennifer A. Hartley (collectively "Kempton")—distilled an interconnected set of values and beliefs identified with "American environmentalism."[18] These include beliefs that nature is a limited resource on which humans depend; that human-nature systems are interdependent, complex, and balanced; and that nature is to be valued for its own sake. In a separate study, sociologists Riley E. Dunlap and Kent D. Van Liere derived elements of an emerging "world view"—the "new

---

[1]   Copyright 2006 by the Regents of the University of California. Reprinted by permission.

[18]   Willett Kempton, James S. Boster & Jennifer A. Hartley, ENVIRONMENTAL VALUES IN AMERICAN CULTURE (1995). Kempton used "semistructured" interviews and form surveys of randomly selected "laypeople," such as workers at sawmills and dry cleaners, and "specialists" whose work or interests relate to the environment, such as Sierra Club members. Id. at 2.

environmental paradigm" (NEP).[20] The major dimensions of their NEP—recognizing the "limits to growth," preserving the "balance of nature," and rejecting "the anthropocentric notion that nature exists solely for human use"—were very similar to Kempton's findings. Recently Dunlap and Van Liere have added two additional elements to their NEP: rejection of human "exemptionalism" (that humans are not subject to natural constraints) and the potential for catastrophic environmental change or "ecocrisis."[21] The NEP strongly differentiates known environmentalists from the general public and is now the most widely used measure of environmental concern, although Dunlap has acknowledged that it "does not fully tap the richness of the construct [of environmentalism]."

In the discussion below I draw on the Kempton and Dunlap and Van Liere studies and other sources to elaborate aspects of environmentalism that have entered the Court's deliberations. I group these into three broad categories: the interdependence model, the urgency factor, and ecocentrism. These categories will serve as a useful framework when we turn to analyzing the cases.

1.   *Interdependence: The Ecological Paradigm*

Environmentalists share a belief that humans and things in nature are closely interconnected and that human intervention affecting one part of a human-natural system can be expected to have deleterious effects elsewhere in the system. I will refer to this central tenet variously as the "interdependence" or "ecological" model. The interdependence model combines elements of environmentalist beliefs detected by Kempton et al. and Dunlap et al., including concepts of nature as limited and of humans as dependent upon it and also of nature as interdependent such that disturbances are likely to cause other "multiply linked chain reactions." Associated with these holistic views Kempton et al. also found beliefs that the "interdependencies are so complex that the interactions are impossible for humans to predict" and thus warrant a general "proscription against human interference with nature." The interdependence model might be confirmed or refuted in particular cases by persuasive evidence of harmful secondary effects or their absence. Without such evidence, it operates for environmentalists as a kind of presumption or default rule.

Prophets of modern environmentalism repeatedly voiced the idea of a highly interdependent human-natural system. John Muir said: "When we try to pick out anything by itself, we find it hitched to everything else in

---

[20]   Riley E. Dunlap & Kent D. Van Liere, *The New Environmental Paradigm*, 9 J. ENVTL. EDUC. 10 (Summer 1978). The authors conducted surveys from two samples of Washington state residents in the summer of 1976. One group was based on names drawn from telephone directories across the state, and the other was based on names drawn from the mailing list of a statewide environmental organization. Id. at 11.

[21]   Riley E. Dunlap & Kent D. Van Liere, *Measuring Endorsement of the New Ecological Paradigm: A Revised NEP Scale*, 56 J. SOC. ISSUES 425, 432 (2000).

the universe." Aldo Leopold advanced the notion of a complexly interdependent "land organism" or "biotic community" which included humans as well as non-human nature. In *Silent Spring*, Rachel Carson described diverse harms to humans and wildlife from chemical poisons as "a problem of ecology, of interrelationships, of interdependence."

The idea of interdependence occurs in images of popular discourse such as the "web of life" (interconnecting strands supporting the larger structure) and "spaceship earth" (earth as a single system with interlocking parts essential for survival of the whole). It has also made its way into public policy. It is evident, for example, in the "purpose" provisions of federal statutes such as the National Environmental Policy Act (NEPA), the Endangered Species Act, and the Clean Water Act.

Although the interdependence model embodies a belief about the way the world works, it is often associated with a collective responsibility to care for the environment. Aldo Leopold's "land ethic" extends moral consideration to an expanded "community" that includes both humans and non-human nature. Leopold believed that this "extension of ethics" would take root as society came to understand its essential dependency on an increasingly beleaguered land organism. "All ethics . . . rest upon a single premise: that the individual is a member of a community of interdependent parts." In his influential account of the environmental movement, Philip Shabecoff quoted this sentence from Leopold with the comment that "[a]lmost all else in environmentalism proceeds from that premise."

2. *Urgency Factor*

A second element of environmentalism relevant to the analysis is the belief that the environment is in a serious state of decline. Kempton et al. do not separately identify this belief, but it is implicit in other elements of their environmentalism. Dunlap et al. make it explicit in their addition of "ecocrisis" to the NEP, and it is evident in numerous works in the environmentalist canon. This urgency factor may combine with the interdependence model, for which it can act as a kind of valence—spaceship earth with the rivets popping off. Or it may operate independently in areas where the interdependence model is of limited relevance, as in cases where environmental pollution poses direct health threats that do not depend on complex ecological relationships.

The urgency factor has left its mark on the law. In addition to the pesticide bans that followed Carson's book, numerous other federal regulatory measures have been prompted, or at least publicly justified, by environmental crises, such as Cleveland's Cuyahoga River catching on fire (Clean Water Act), seeping chemical wastes at Love Canal (Superfund), and the Exxon Valdez oil spill (Oil Pollution Act). Innovative or demanding provisions of these and other federal statutes are attributable to the perceived seriousness of the environmental problems they seek to remedy.

3. *Ecocentrism*

Another aspect of environmentalism that has entered the Court's deliberations is the extension of moral standing or reverence to the environmental other. In their interviews, Kempton et al. found three types of environmental values—religious, including feelings of spirituality not identified to a particular religion; anthropocentric, "concerned with only those environmental changes that affect human welfare;" and ecocentric, "which grant nature itself intrinsic rights." Environmentalism includes anthropocentric elements that emphasize non-commodity and existence values of nature and protection of environmental resources for future generations—so-called "weak anthropocentrism." But, strong forms of environmentalism are closely identified with ecocentric values and religious or spiritual regard for nature for its own sake.

NOTES

1.   Cannon also identifies four elements of the "dominant culture"— "support for private property rights, support for economic growth, faith in material abundance, and support for laissez faire government—had significant negative correlation with environmental concern." 33 ECOLOGY L. Q. at 372. He expanded upon these views, and analyzed thirty Supreme Court cases to determine the extent to which court decisions, oral arguments and judicial archives reflect different environmental ethoses among the Justices. *See* JONATHAN Z. CANNON, ENVIRONMENT IN THE BALANCE: THE GREEN MOVEMENT AND THE SUPREME COURT (2015).

2.   As you continue through the casebook, you will see large variations among judges in the extent to which they identify with environmentalist values or the dominant culture. To what extent do these value differences explain case outcomes?

3.   There is no single organizing principle that "explains" all of environmental law. As we will see throughout the book, environmental law is often a messy result of complex institutional dynamics and political conflict. However, the following excerpt discusses some principles that come up fairly often. Those principles may help you make sense of some of the confusing complexity of the specific legal doctrines.

DAN TARLOCK, IS THERE A THERE THERE IN ENVIRONMENTAL LAW?
19 J. LAND USE & ENVTL. LAW 213, 214, 248–254 (2004).[2]

As environmental law enters its fourth decade, it is now appropriate, if not imperative, to ask the question: what have environmentalism and environmental regulation contributed to the law? Gertrude Stein, the

---

[2] Copyright © 2004, Journal of Land Use. Reprinted by Permission. (internal citations omitted).

American expatriate writer, once described Oakland, California, where she spent much of her youth before fleeing to the East Coast and Paris, as a place where "there is no there there." In addition to stigmatizing the city of my birth, her quip haunts all efforts to legitimize new, especially contested, ideas and methods in modern culture, from twelve tone music to environmental protection. In this article, I leave the question of the merits of post-modern culture to others and address only the question, does Ms. Stein's famous epigram apply to environmental law? * * *

The dynamic process-making of environmental decisions means that we can only hope to structure decisions with principles that allow us to identify decisions as legitimate efforts to advance environmental goals, but do not lock us into consistent but dysfunctional decisions. I suggest the following candidate principles. They are a mix of how environmental law has evolved and how it should evolve.

A.   MINIMIZE UNCERTAINTY BEFORE AND AS YOU ACT

This principle is an expansion and correction of the more familiar first principle of environmental law that activities with potentially adverse environmental impacts, however defined, should be assessed before they are undertaken. It is codified in NEPA, but over time the original purpose of assessment—real risk and environmental damage minimization—has been lost. Assessment has too often become an end in and of itself rather than a means to obtain the necessary information for long-term, informed decision-making to achieve the necessary changes in the way that resources are used and managed. The duty to minimize uncertainty is a continuing one during all phases of an activity. For example, it will often require monitoring and adaptive management for activities that will last over a long period of time.

Adaptive management was developed in the late 1970s as a criticism of static or deterministic environmental assessment. The basic argument was that "a fixed review of an independently designed policy" was inconsistent with the experience of resource managers world-wide and with what has come to be called non-equilibrium ecology. The need for rigorous but flexible procedures to make decisions under conditions of uncertainty has a long intellectual pedigree. * * * Adaptive management is designed to close the gap between the available information and the information needed to make sound environmental decisions. It posits a continuous process of acquiring and evaluating scientific information through the practice of regulatory science.

B.   ENVIRONMENTAL DEGRADATION SHOULD BE A LAST RESORT AFTER ALL REASONABLE, FEASIBLE ALTERNATIVES HAVE BEEN EXHAUSTED

This principle casts another pillar of environmental law: an activity that is likely to cause the degradation of media and ecosystems environmental values should only be undertaken if there are no acceptable alternatives. A general non-degradation standard for all resources is not possible for economic and ethical reasons; human society does not, as some radical environmentalists have argued, have a duty to self-destruct. The most that we can do is to be highly skeptical of substantial departure from the baselines of environmental quality that we choose to establish. * * * My rule * * * is broader than the assertion of any duty to mitigate. It assumes that environmental values are of equal dignity to developmental ones, and thus mitigation may not always be an acceptable solution. Mitigation is generally a substitute for full compliance, and is in economic terms, a second best solution.

C. RISK CAN BE A LEGITIMATE INTERIM BASIS FOR PROHIBITION OF AN ACTIVITY

This principle attempts to strike a balance between the rejection of the due process-based common law background rule that mechanistic proof that an activity will cause demonstrable harm in the immediate future as a universal predicate for health and ecosystem protection regulation and the candidate replacement principle—the precautionary principle—endorsed in the 1992 Rio Declaration on Environment and Development. The principle that a high degree of certainty about the adverse impacts of a substance or activity is not a necessary prerequisite to limit it is well established in United States environmental law. The Constitution does not require mechanistic proof of cause in fact for pollution and toxic substance regulation because a lesser standard of proof is appropriate for public health based regulation because liability can be justified as a form of taxes imposed on those who directly profit from harmful activities and which is fairly spread over larger segments of the population.

The precautionary principle has, however, evolved, at least in the legal literature, from a limited tool to bridge the gap between current information and the societal desire to limit exposure to serious risk to a harder rule. Critics have begun to "demonize" it as incoherent and unfair compared to more rigorous decision methods such as risk analysis. The nub of the objection is the argument that once some potential, but uncertain risk of future environmental harm is established, it is legitimate to prohibit an activity that leads to "bad," "irrational" or inefficient choices.

It is essential to separate the soundness of the basic idea that society can choose to minimize risks in the face of scientific and other uncertainty from the question of implementation. The precautionary principle is firmly grounded in the scientific method. Many of the concerns can be addressed through burden of proof standards and the addition of a crucial element that is often missing in debates about the precautionary principle: a feedback loop to trigger reevaluation of the initial decision. Proponents of the precautionary principle have argued that opponents of precaution should bear the burden of rebutting the exercise of the principle, but given the risk that the precautionary principle could choke off a wide range of considerations, such as risk trade-offs, it seems more sensible to place the burden of justification on the government body that invokes it. This would ensure that alternative methods of minimizing the uncertainty, such as compensation, have been adequately explored, and that the principle is reserved for the most serious and largely irreversible risks. In addition, the idea that once the principle is invoked to minimize risk, the decision is permanent should be excised. The precautionary principle needs to be linked to the idea of adaptive management. The existence of monitoring and adaptive feedback mechanisms should be a major factor in validating the decision to limit an activity when the adverse impacts are uncertain.

D. POLLUTERS MUST CONTINUALLY UPGRADE WASTE REDUCTION AND PROCESSING TECHNOLOGY

Environmentalism dethroned engineers from the preeminent position they enjoyed for most of the twentieth century, but much of the progress in environmental protection has come from compelling polluters to install state-of-the-art technology. Sources of media pollution should be rolled back by the installation of progressively higher standards of technology established by the government. This principle incorporates two ideas: (1) technology has a major role to play in environmental protection; and (2) the level of technology required is a moving, not fixed, target.

E. ENVIRONMENTAL DECISIONMAKING SHOULD BE INCLUSIVE RATHER THAN EXCLUSIVE WITHIN THE LIMITS OF RATIONALITY

This final principle endorses the pluralistic nature of decision-making that has emerged from the efforts to force public and private actors to consider environmental values up to a point. Environmental law helped to undermine (but not overthrow) the New Deal model of the expert managerial or regulatory agency because outsiders offered a new perspective to the experts and helped to expose many of the unstated, crucial assumptions in purported "objective" analysis. The net result has been the development of hybrid forms of shared governance which depends as much on information disclosure to alter behavior as it does on command and control regulation.

Increased lay participation in decision making to promote transparency and a broadened perspective is a laudable, democratic objective, but transparency and public participation come with costs such as delay, the introduction of extraneous issues and the rejection of science-based solutions. However, environmental policy and law must remain bonded by science. The relevant question is always: how can we bridge the gap between what we want from science and what it can supply? The goals of public participation are to legitimate the application of science to an informed lay public and to allow an avenue for relevant scientific and non-scientific perspectives. They should never be allowed to substitute deals for scientifically credible outcomes.

CONCLUSION

This summing up of environmental law may strike many as disappointing because it dismisses the possibility of powerful, general transformative nature-centered rules, emerging to tame the drive to exploit and modify all planetary life support systems. Instead, it argues that environmental law will for the foreseeable future be a messy process of adapting the contingencies and limitations of science to "wicked" problems informed by rebuttable principles. This hard road seems inevitable because of the radical nature of the objectives of environmental law. If protection is to evolve into a permanent check on the full range of resource consumption decisions, it must be grounded in the enlightenment values of knowledge and reason.

NOTE

Tarlock's guiding principles have some traction in environmental law. For example, NEPA stresses consideration of alternatives in environmental impact statements. Both NEPA and administrative law contain some mechanisms for public participation. We will give considerable attention in this chapter and the next to how environmental law handles risk and uncertainty.

However, Tarlock's principles are also open to criticism. Some critics would argue that an overarching methodology of cost-benefit analysis should take the place of these five principles. This would provide a method of dealing with risks, considering alternatives, and establishing appropriate pollution control. We will consider this alternative approach in detail in Chapter 2.

Other critics might say that Tarlock's principles are too limited. The principles focus on specific problems—alternatives to a given project, pollution control for a given industry—rather than on systemic changes that might eliminate the need for certain projects or substitute new industrial processes that produce less pollution in the first place. Tarlock's principles also could be criticized for focusing on the short-run rather than on our obligations to later generations. Yet there are serious institutional difficulties to implementing more holistic, long-term solutions. As we examine particular environmental issues, ranging from global warming to hazardous waste disposal, consider whether more systemic solutions would be feasible.

Finally, Tarlock's principle of inclusion, while admirable, may be too limited in its focus. Consider the next excerpt:

GERALD TORRES, ENVIRONMENTAL JUSTICE: THE LEGAL MEANING OF A SOCIAL JUSTICE MOVEMENT

15 J. Law & Comm 397 (1996).

The environmental justice movement existed before there was a legal strategy designed to implement its goals. The movement began with several fairly commonplace observations. * * * The observations that community activists made were that poor and minority communities seemed to have worse environmental problems than wealthier and whiter neighborhoods and that environmental policy making seemed to exclude the interests of poor, non-white communities.

* * *

The claims were about both the structure of the environmental debate and the system of representation through which the interests of the civil rights constituency could be articulated.

By 1980 * * * images of Love Canal were refracted through the public imagination and created widespread fear concerning placement of toxic and hazardous waste sites. In 1982 a decision to locate a polychlorinated biphenyl landfill in a predominately black community led to public protests in North Carolina and triggered a request from Congressman Walter Fauntroy to the Government Accounting Office ("GAO") to investigate the socio-economic and racial composition of the communities surrounding hazardous waste landfills in the South. The GAO study revealed that three of the four major landfills were located in predominately black communities where citizens lived disproportionately below the poverty line.

The GAO findings led the United Church of Christ Commission on Racial Justice ("UCCCRJ") to conduct its own investigation. The UCCCRJ study, which was finished in 1987, came essentially to the same conclusions as the GAO study. The two studies showed that race was the most significant variable associated with the location of commercial waste facilities. has also been subject to scathing critique. * * *

B.   The Relationship of Environmental Justice
to Mainstream Civil Rights Issues

* * *

The first systematic study of the disparate impacts of environmental burdens was done by sociologist Robert Bullard in his book, Dumping in Dixie: Race, Class and Environmental Quality (1990). Two of his conclusions have become articles of faith in the discussion of the issue of environmental justice. First, Bullard claims that race is the factor that had the highest correlation between environmental burdens and sub-populations. Second, he claims that communities of color had been systematically excluded from decision-making processes in determining how environmental risks would be distributed.

* * *

E.   Proof?

* * *

As legal advocates began to compose complaints, questions of evidence became critically important. The type of proof demanded depended upon the legal theory underlying the claim. The first claims that were brought depended on demonstrable racial animus and they largely failed. There were complaints of disparate impacts based on both constitutional and statutory claims of racial discrimination. Regardless of the foundation, whether it be the Fourteenth Amendment or Title VI, the attacks on the unequal distribution of environmental burdens based solely on claims of racial discrimination foundered. Recent commentators have revealed an increased confidence in the uses of Title VI in light of the Executive Order 12898 [requiring, among other things, federal agencies to make environmental justice a core part of their mission]. Although that confidence has not yet been reflected in litigation victories, the concerns that animate it are reflected in the internal management of the agencies. This is a point to which I want to return.

II.   WHAT ARE THE MAJOR CRITICISMS OF THE CONCEPT?

There have been substantial criticisms of the concept of environmental justice. * * *

[A] market-based critique argues that locally undesirable land uses are attributable largely to the workings of the market.[1] The essence of the market suggests that poor people will be disadvantaged in relation to relatively better off people in the acquisition of goods. Environmental quality is merely a good that also is market sensitive. Thus, it should not be surprising that poor people, and poor black people as a subset of that economic class, suffer greater environmental burdens than do better off people. Poor people merely choose, and rationally so, to spend their scarce resources on other goods.

There is a "coming to the nuisance" argument that takes this theoretical insight into the workings of the market as a justification for the distribution of environmental burdens that civil rights activists have observed. In addition, as this criticism continues, review of the empirical studies indicate that many of the complained of burdens pre-date the current racial composition of the communities. The question thus becomes whether the site moved to the people or the people moved to the site.

Two additional general difficulties arise from this critique. First, by overlooking the extent to which market forces themselves have produced the results we see, totally apart from questions of racial animus, we may be misled by the observed disparities. Thus, the distribution might just be the revealed choices of people choosing to live close to one or another type of environmental problem for reasons we might disagree with, but with which we have no moral or legal basis to oppose. This choice might reflect a number of things. It might reflect the underlying land value and, because we are in a market and class society, it makes sense that poor people live where land is cheaper. However, the disparities might just reflect a desire to spend money on one thing rather than another.

The second general difficulty that this critique raises makes a simple point about the partiality of any analysis: the criticism of the choices the residents have made overlooks the benefits that might accrue to them. The principal benefit might be employment at the offending site. Thus, people might choose to live in a place because of the employment opportunities presented by the varieties of industrial or post-industrial facilities. * * *Professor Bullard, among others, responded to this specific criticism by noting that the methodology of the critics, tied as it is to census tract data, ignores the general historical evidence that predates the census and distorts the meaning of neighborhoods for purposes of analysis from the perspective of the residents themselves.

* * *

III. EVALUATION OF THE CRITICISMS?

* * *

First, some of the empirical work that is presently being done will answer the questions that have been raised regarding studies like the UCCCRJ report and the work of Professor Bullard. To suggest that they cannot emerge, or that the hypotheses are wrong, is to prejudge the issue, and broadside criticisms of that variety can wait to be tested.

Second, I believe the criticism of the proposed solutions as being overly paternalistic is basically misplaced. Even if we adopt the position that the revealed preferences of the affected populations ought not be displaced without some extraordinary justification, it is important to note from where the proposed solution that would have that effect is in fact coming. Most of the solutions that have been proposed have not arisen from the national leadership of the groups that are pushing this issue, but, in fact, have come from the people who feel themselves subject to the various problems. In addition, the concern about "racializing" a "non-race" issue also seems to be a concern that is largely hypothetical. Using an admittedly limited sample, I was able to observe during my time in the Justice Department, through meetings with a wide variety of grass root environmental justice activists, one interesting fact about the environmental justice issue. The concern over environmental quality that is at the core of the complaints about the inequity of environmental burdens generated interracial coalitions that other civil rights issues have been unable to generate. A look at issues like welfare reform, affirmative action, crime control, or many of the other issues that have arisen in the last few years in policy debate, will often reveal the existence of a racial divide at the level of policy formation. Environmental justice has, in fact, produced interracial coalitions largely because blacks and other minority communities have been the miner's canary for non-minority poor communities. While these inter- racial coalitions have arisen primarily in the South, they do suggest that mere references to the market are an insufficient policy response.

IV. WHAT ARE THE PROSPECTS FOR ENVIRONMENTAL JUSTICE?

One thing that seems clear is that the issues raised by the environmental justice movement are not going to go away. Arguments about environmental inequities will continue to inform both the civil rights and environmental protection debates. The explosion of scholarly attention to this issue, as well as continuing community activism, will ensure that the issue does not disappear. The exact form the issue will take is difficult to predict because of the heterogeneous integration of environmental justice concerns into the various local struggles. Apart from the promise in the grass root interracial coalitions there are hazards, as well.

* * *

The executive branch has . . . taken a leadership role in changing the way federal agencies respond to the issue raised by the environmental justice movement. In February 1994, the President signed Executive Order 12,898 entitled, "Federal Actions to Address Environmental Justice in Minority and Low-Income Populations." Under this Executive Order, federal agencies are supposed to make achievement of environmental justice part of their mission by identifying and addressing disproportionately high and adverse human health or environmental effects of their programs, policies, and activities. In addition, agencies are supposed to review their procedures to ensure that all portions of the population have a meaningful opportunity to participate in the development of, compliance with, and enforcement of federal laws, regulations and policies that affect human health or the environment regardless of race, color, national origin, or income.

* * *Agencies are organized and designed to fulfill the mission that Congress has assigned to them. In the course of fulfilling their missions, the agencies develop their own regulatory responses to the issues that come before them. The pattern of response and solution develops into the regulatory culture of the agency. That culture provides the framework for assessing and resolving the concerns generated by their statutory missions. In order to change the way agencies come to their conclusions and their proposals for action, their central mandate has to be altered sufficiently to affect their decision making structure and their conception of their mission. The principal model for achieving this kind of administrative genetic engineering is the National Environmental Policy Act ("NEPA").[48]

* * *

The intended effect of the Executive Order is based upon a theory of agency action and change. The theory behind the Executive Order presumes that it is possible to naturalize into the decision-making structure of the agencies a concern for the issues of environmental justice. That process, if the history of NEPA is a guide, is slow. But merely because change is slow does not mean that it is not occurring. . The rate of agency change may be frustrating to those who desire immediate action, but it also reflects the complex balancing of concerns that are part of every agency action, especially where there is a mandate expanding command to which the agency is responding.

* * *

V.   WHAT IS THE RELATIONSHIP BETWEEN ENVIRONMENTAL JUSTICE AND OTHER IMPORTANT THEMES IN ENVIRONMENTAL POLICY?

The emergence of the environmental justice movement and the constellation of issues surrounding it is linked to other important trends in environmental policy. Among the emerging ideals in environmental policy are sustainable development, ecosystem management, and pollution prevention. * * * By putting the issue of environmental justice into the broader debate over environmental quality, the relationship of the underlying issues to concepts such as sustainability becomes clear.

* * *In order to generate a set of policies that will produce a sustainable economic and environmental order, we need to ensure that the economic order does not produce an unstable political order. This is especially important in a society committed to liberal democratic values. Thus, the constitutional values of equal treatment, and the naturalization of those values into our common political discourse, requires that the unequal distribution of environmental burdens, whether through direct environmental insult or through unequal enforcement or provision of environmental goods, be justified independently of currently observable market results where there is the continuing residue of economic or political market failure.

---

[48]   42 U.S.C. sections 4321–4370d (1995).

Closely allied to the concept of sustainable development is the concept of ecosystem management. * * *It is "a strategy or plan to manage ecosystems to provide for all associated organisms, as opposed to a strategy or plan for managing individual species." * * *Like sophisticated conceptions of sustainable development, ecosystem management is designed to integrate planning to include diverse natural systems and their attendant social systems. The environmental justice movement can justifiably be seen as a part of this transformation in environmental management theory. It has raised issues about both the political sustainability of systems that ignore significant portions of the polity and about the reality of pollution control. Moreover, it has suggested that there is no "free" space to where we can displace the impacts of our industrial society. By changing the focus to the distributional impacts of the design and enforcement of environmental protection regimes, the environmental justice movement has merely highlighted the inter-connectedness of community life, the economy, and the natural world. * * *Even though the concept of ecosystem management has not advanced much beyond the area of forest and wildlife policy at the national level, aspects of the environmental justice movement reflect the power of this integrative ideal.

NOTE

Since Professor Torres wrote his article (based on a speech he delivered), the Executive Order to which he refers has remained in effect. Each year, EPA produces a report describing progress the country has made in implementing the EO and in reducing disparate environmental effects. *See* EPA, *Annual Environmental Justice Progress Reports*, https://www.epa.gov/environmental justice/annual-environmental-justice-progress-reports. Progress in cleaning up the nation's air has led to some of the most dramatic results, with the almost complete elimination of lead from the ambient air, and, as the chart on page 25, *infra* demonstrates, steep declines in the other major pollutants regulated under the Clean Air Act. Nevertheless, persistent problems remain, including in exposure to air pollution hotspots. *See, e.g.,* Ann E. Carlson, *The Clean Air Act's Blind Spot: Microclimates and Hotspot Pollution*, 65 UCLA L REV 1036 (2018). The drinking water crisis in Flint, Michigan—exposing a predominantly African American city with a high poverty level to lead see page—is another example of the disproportionate effects environmental problems can have on low-income communities of color. *See* Merrit Kennedy, *Lead-Laced Water in Flint: A Step-By-Step Look At the Makings of a Crisis,* NATIONAL PUBLIC RADIO (April 20, 2016), https://www.npr.org/sections/thetwo-way/2016/04/20/465545378/lead-laced-water-in-flint-a-step-by-step-look-at-the-makings-of-a-crisis. Recent research suggests that the Flint situation may reflect a more general problem of the disproportionate effects of drinking water violations. *See* Yolanda J. McDonald and Nicole E. Jones, *Drinking Water Violations and Environmental Justice in the United States, 2011–2015,* AMER. J. PUB. HEALTH (2018).

Professor Torres also pointed to NEPA as a potential legal solution to the problems raised by environmental justice advocates. NEPA is, as you will learn, limited to the review of new projects with which the federal government is involved, leaving many other potential harms without a remedy. One potential solution was Title VI of the Civil Rights Act, which was used by advocates to challenge the disparate impact of federal funding of projects like highways (many of which cut through low income communities). In *Alexander v. Sandoval*, 532 U.S. 275 (2001), however, the U.S. Supreme Court held that Title VI does not include a private right of action to enforce disparate impacts of federal agency actions.

All 50 states and the District of Columbia have some sort of law or regulation or policy addressing environmental justice, with almost all of the laws adopted after the federal government's Executive Order went into effect. *See* Robert Bullard, *Environmental Justice Milestones and Accomplishments: 1964–2014.* Whether those policies are effective is another question. Jessica Owley and Tonya Lewis examined New York's environmental justice statue and concluded that the state's policy is "largely symbolic." Tonya Lewis and Jessica Owley, *Symbolic Politics for Disempowered Communities: State Environmental Justice Policies*, 29 B.Y.U. J. PUB LAW 183 (2015).

As you consider the materials in the remaining chapters, keep environmental justice considerations in mind. Are the various laws designed to tackle different environmental problems (water, air, endangered species, toxic contamination, etc.) likely to produce just distributional effects? Are there ways you can imagine improving the likelihood of fair implementation? Are these environmental laws likely to allow for public participation of affected groups, including low income communities, including communities of color?

2.   THE HISTORY OF ENVIRONMENTAL LAW

Today's complex regulatory process did not emerge in an instant, like Athena springing from the forehead of Zeus. Instead, it is the product of a long and sometimes conflicted evolutionary process. The following excerpt provides an overview of the history.

RICHARD J. LAZARUS, THE GREENING OF AMERICA AND THE GRAYING OF UNITED STATES ENVIRONMENTAL LAW: REFLECTIONS ON ENVIRONMENTAL LAW'S FIRST THREE DECADES IN THE UNITED STATES
20 VA. ENVTL. L.J. 75 (2001).[3]

Those of us who have spent our professional lives as practicing lawyers, teachers, and scholars steeped in environmental law often lose

---

sight of the discipline's relative youth. Yet, prior to 1970, environmental protection law in the United States was essentially nonexistent. Of course, there were a few, isolated states pursuing fledgling efforts, and there were common law property and tort doctrines that some of the more activist judges were willing to invoke on behalf of environmental concerns in private and public lawsuits. But there was nothing even remotely resembling a comprehensive legal regime for regulating pollution of the air, water, or land. * * * What did the first generation of laws look like? There was, at the very outset, the National Environmental Policy Act ('NEPA'), literally signed into law on the first day of the decade, January 1, 1970. NEPA requires federal agency assessment of the environmental impacts of proposed federal agency action and possible alternatives. Although NEPA's essentially procedural requirement had a massive impact on governmental decision-making, the federal legislative enactments during the early 1970s that imposed substantive requirements were even more significant. Three of these substantive laws were the Clean Air Act of 1970, the Federal Water Pollution Control Act Amendments of 1972 (now, as further amended, referred to as the Clean Water Act), and the Endangered Species Act Amendments of 1973. These laws were dramatic, sweeping, and apparently uncompromising. Each of these laws imposed a series of specific statutory commands on polluting activities. They did not rely primarily on voluntary behavioral changes in response to mere exhortation. Nor did they turn, in the first instance, principally to financial incentives or otherwise seek to enlist market incentives to achieve their environmental protection objectives. They instead sought to identify classes and categories of polluting or environmentally destructive activities that threatened human health and the environment, and then to impose stringent standards on their performance.

The restrictions were generally not based on economic feasibility but rather on far more demanding norms. Some were based on technological standards designed not simply to replicate existing pollution control technology but rather, in effect, to force industry to develop new technology capable of substantially more reductions in existing levels of pollution. Other standards directly required that certain environmental or human health risks be eliminated regardless of either economic or technological feasibility, even if (in theory) compliance with such a standard could occur only upon shutdown of the polluting activity.

These first generation laws were also remarkably aspirational in scope and in their mandates. The standards, and corresponding deadlines for their accomplishment, were exceedingly ambitious, if not unrealistic. Indeed, as discussed below, although such ambitious laws necessarily made a strong symbolic societal statement regarding the importance of environmental protection and the need for fundamental change in humankind's relation to the natural environment, they also unwittingly triggered a pathological cycle of crisis, controversy, and public distrust, which has since hampered needed reform. * * *

It is, of course, far easier to set an ambitious goal than it is to meet one, and, almost as soon as these first generation laws were passed, it seemed as if they might well have a short half-life. Industry resisted their implementation, as did many state governments who concluded that the federal legislation improperly usurped state sovereignty.

The greatest challenge the laws faced, however, was the energy crisis of the mid-1970s. Industry promoted the notion, readily embraced by many politicians, that the energy needs of the nation were both more pressing than and inconsistent with environmental protection concerns. The country's need, for instance, to rely on abundant domestic supplies of coal, rather than petroleum imports, might require relaxing air pollution control requirements inconsistent with increased coal combustion. Likewise, the need to explore, extract, and transport domestic energy reserves of coal, petroleum, and natural gas would likely require relaxation of environmental restrictions that impeded or otherwise made such activities more costly.

The 'energy/environment' confrontation, however, ultimately fell far short of dismantling the first generation laws of the early 1970s. At the instigation of environmental citizen suits, courts insisted on strict implementation of those laws, resulting in a series of negotiated settlements between government and environmental interests, as well as judicial orders outlining schedules for agency compliance with statutory requirements. Although Congress amended the laws in certain respects, it did so without abandoning the law's basic structure and rigor. Congress extended some deadlines, fine-tuned some requirements to add incremental flexibility, and mostly relaxed standards only in terms of their application to the daily behavior of individual citizens (e.g., driving) rather than the conduct of industry.

Indeed, rather than abandon the first generation of environmental protection laws, Congress expanded upon them in the second half of the first decade. Congress enacted a new series of laws at least as ambitious and sweeping, and in some respects, even more so. These 'second generation laws' are distinguishable from the first generation largely because they tend to focus on a particular type of pollutant, rather than the identity of the particular environmental media in which pollutants are released. Hence, while the Clean Air Act, Clean Water Act, and Endangered Species Act focused on air, water, and wildlife (and habitat), the Toxic Substances Control Act ('TSCA') and Resource Conservation and Recovery Act ('RCRA') adopted in 1976, and the Comprehensive

Environmental Response, Compensation, and Liability Act ('CERCLA'), each focused on that subset of more dangerous, i.e., toxic or hazardous, pollutants and substances regardless of the environmental media in which they were found.

RCRA and TSCA were both classic, prospective, and comprehensive regulatory laws. They included both health-based provisions and technology-based provisions, with some consideration of costs versus benefits. The theoretical justification for these laws was the need to supplement the media-based laws, which risked simply chasing toxic pollutants from one medium to the next, with some laws that looked at the larger, overall picture. RCRA and TSCA were meant to close the 'last remaining loophole' in environmental law.

CERCLA likewise focused on 'hazardous' substances, but was fundamentally different in its orientation than any other previous legislation. It was a retrospective liability law, not a prospective regulatory enactment. CERCLA was designed to provide for cleanup of abandoned and inactive hazardous waste sites, and to assign liability to the responsible parties for those cleanup costs. * * *

CERCLA's liability scheme was wholly unprecedented when enacted, at least in terms of U.S. law. It assigns liability for cleanup costs not just to current owners and operators of the site, but to all past and previous owners of the site at the time of waste disposal. Also included within the liability net are any persons who generated the hazardous substances that were disposed on the site, as well as parties who transported substances to the site. Moreover, because liability is strict, and almost always joint and several (because the harm is indivisible), any one of these parties may be held liable for the entire cleanup cost. * * *

Modern environmental law's second decade in the United States began as tumultuously as the first but with a very different evolutionary spin. Immediately on the heels of congressional passage of CERCLA, the most far-reaching of all the environmental statutes, President Ronald Reagan took office. He favored a substantial cutback of environmental regulation and took concerted action to accomplish that end.* * *

Surprisingly, the popular President's efforts were not only stymied but actually prompted a legislative backlash that ultimately generated even more stringent environmental protection laws. The Reagan Administration's efforts at deregulation unwittingly fueled the public's pre-existing distrust of government—the legacy of the first decade's series of failed promises—especially the public's readiness to believe that the government might be compromising public health concerns in order to bolster the corporate profits of industry. The environmental community in the United States took effective advantage of public concern—vigorously promoting public outrage—and, as a result, substantially increased both their own financial resources and membership as well as their lobbying clout before Congress.

The Reagan Administration's short-term solution was to replace its initial head of the EPA, who had sought to decrease the agency's budget, with a highly regarded individual with strong environmental credentials. The long-term impact of the Administration's effort to cut back on federal environmental protection laws, however, was precisely the opposite from the Administration's original policy objective. Congress responded to the public's disapproval of deregulatory efforts by amending the federal environmental protection laws in a manner designed both to make them stronger and to reduce executive branch discretion to diminish their effectiveness in the future.

Hence, environmental laws that in the 1970s had conferred considerable discretion on the EPA regarding how best to meet strict environmental goals now commenced to dictate to the agency not only the statutory ends, but the precise means as well. Even those statutory amendments that retained some discretion in the EPA to develop environmental protection requirements in the first instance imposed strict deadlines on their promulgation. Furthermore, in the event those deadlines were not met, the amendments mandated the automatic triggering of stringent requirements, including absolute prohibitions on specified waste disposal activities.

From 1981 through 1990, Congress substantially amended virtually all of the major environmental protection laws. Congress amended the Endangered Species Act in 1982, the Resource Conservation and Recovery Act in 1984, CERCLA in 1986, the Clean Water Act in 1987, and the Clean Air Act in 1990. These detailed, prescriptive amendments converted what had been open-ended statutes, tens of pages in length, into statutes of several hundred pages in length. Congress had, in effect, deprived the executive branch of much of the environmental policymaking authority that the latter had historically enjoyed. Although the Clean Air Act included, for the first time, a major program dependent on market incentives (tradeable emission rights to control acid deposition), the statutes generally adhered to a 'command and control' regime of strict technology and health-based standards. * * *

Environmental law's third decade momentarily began with George [H.W.] Bush, the self-declared 'environmental President,' but quickly shifted in the early 1990s to an emphasis on regulatory retrenchment. His Vice President made environmental deregulation a major executive branch initiative, culminating in a formal moratorium on regulations, including several significant environmental protection programs.

The most remarkable challenge to federal environmental protection laws, however, came several years later in 1994, with the election of

Republican majorities to both the House and Senate of Congress. The Republicans campaigned on the basis of a program they dubbed as the 'Contract With America,' the full implications of which for environmental law became apparent only in the immediate aftermath of their election. The Contract targeted federal environmental protection programs more than any other area of the law for significant curtailment.

Republican majorities in both chambers moved swiftly on several legislative fronts to convert their agenda into positive law. They proposed legislation that would have replaced environmental standards based on minimum standards of human health and technology-forcing requirements. In their place would be environmental standards based on cost/benefit analyses, comparative risk assessment, and other economic efficiency criteria. Environmentalists have long complained that such standards inevitably decrease environmental protection by discounting environmental values not susceptible to monetary valuation and environmental risks not certain to occur. * * *

Remarkably, however, practically none of these varied proposals became law (although some proposals are still pending). The reform efforts dissipated almost as quickly they formed. In a reversal of roles, while the legislative branch in 1994 sought to reform environmental law, the executive branch sought to preserve it. In the 1980s, the executive branch had sought to obtain many similar changes, only to be rebuffed by Congress, but when Congress was instigating the reforms in 1994, the executive branch maintained the opposition.

The executive branch also used the same tactics against Congress that Congress had used against it a decade beforehand. Just as Congress had effectively exploited the public's distrust of government efforts to protect the environment in the 1980s to defeat that earlier reform effort, so too the executive branch now pursued an identical strategy to block Congress. The President, Vice President, and the EPA Administrator repeatedly characterized Congress as seeking to undermine public health and environmental quality at the behest of industry profits. The American public, always ready to perceive environmental protection in such stark terms, and prone to expect such a political sell-out, responded in a manner that ultimately deprived the legislative reform effort of its political strength. Hence, the third major effort in as many decades to dismantle the demanding framework of U.S. environmental law, like the two before it, fell flat.

NOTE ON U.S. ENVIRONMENTAL LAW SINCE 2000

One of the most important shifts in environmental policymaking in the years since Lazarus's account, which extends through the Clinton Administration, is that virtually all of it is taking place in the executive branch rather than in Congress. Each administration has a different focus, of course, and the policy swings between Republican and Democratic presidents can be quite jarring. Environmental policy took a sharp term away from the Clinton agenda when George W. Bush took office in 2001. Much of President Bush's environmental policy centered on energy issues. His energy plan came from a working group chaired by Vice President Cheney. The plan concluded that the United States would need about a third more oil by 2020. It called for building 1,000 to 2,000 additional power plants, expanding oil production on federal lands such as the Arctic National Wildlife Reserve, and streamlining the regulatory process for power plants. *See* Gary C. Bryner, *The National Energy Policy: Assessing Energy Policy Choices*, 73 U. COLO. L. REV. 341, 345–348 (2002). The Administration also disavowed the Kyoto agreement to control greenhouse gases, which would have required limitations on American use of fossil fuels. *Id.* at 388. At the same time, President Bush's rhetoric centered on the stewardship obligations of individual landowners. *See* Jonathan Cannon & Jonathan Riehl, *Presidential Greenspeak: How Presidents Talk About the Environment and What It Means*, 23 STAN. ENV. L. J. 195, 262–263 (2004).

Bush's approach to environmental policy centered on positive incentives and market mechanisms, along with efforts to emphasize environmental federalism. Barton H. Thompson, Jr., *The Bush Administration and Environmental Policy*, 32 ECOLOGY L. Q. 307, 335–347 (2005). He supported a congressional effort to replace much of the current Clean Air Act with an environmental trading mechanism. When this effort failed to advance in Congress, the EPA attempted to use its statutory authority under existing law to implement an ambitious trading system. EPA also encouraged trading in the area of water pollution. We will discuss these issues in detail later. While attempting to increase state regulatory authority in some areas, the Bush Administration also challenged state tort laws and environmental regulations that were deemed too burdensome on industry.

The election of Barack Obama marked yet another turn in environmental policy. The Obama Administration under EPA Administrators Lisa Jackson and Gina McCarthy issued important new rules to reduce mercury and other toxic pollutants from electric power plants, regulate greenhouse gas emissions that cause climate change, raise fuel efficiency requirements for cars, impose the first carbon limitations on new sources, and adopt a massive program to regulate greenhouse gases from existing power plants. The Administration also emphasized the benefits of renewable energy. See Jody Freeman, *Climate and Energy Policy in the Obama Administration*, 30 PACE ENV. L. REV. 375 (2012); Ann E. Carlson, *An Ode to the Clean Air Act*, 30 J LAND USE & ENV. LAW (2014) (describing use of Obama Administration's use of Clean Air Act to regulate greenhouse gases). But the Administration was also closely attuned to economic matters and heavily emphasized cost-benefit analysis, sometimes to the dismay of environmentalists. *See, e.g.,* Lisa Heinzerling, *Who Will Run the EPA?* 30 YALE J REG 39 (2013).

Donald Trump's election as President has swung the pendulum to the anti-regulatory end perhaps further than any other modern President. His Administration has to date worked to undo 78 environmental rules and regulations, many of them adopted by the Obama Administration. *See* Nadia Popovich, *et. al, 78 Environmental Rules on the Way Out Under Trump*, N.Y. TIMES (Updated Dec. 28, 2018). These include rolling back virtually all of the Obama climate regulations, changing rules governing the federal government's jurisdiction over wetlands, and dramatically reducing newly created national monuments. To date, the Trump Administration's efforts have faced strong headwinds in the courts. *See* Lisa Heinzerling, *Unreasonable Delays: the Legal Problems (So Far) of Trump's Deregulatory Binge*, 12 HARV. L & POL REV 13 (2018).

Under Presidents Clinton, Bush, Obama and Trump, the major source of policy changes has been the White House, not Congress. Congress has passed only one major piece of environmental legislation—an overhaul of chemical regulation explored in Chapter 9—since the Clean Air Act amendments passed in 1990. Since then, a legislative logjam has largely prevented new legislation. Increasingly acrid partisan politics and starkly different views of environmental regulation may be part of the reason, along with the reality that most Republican members of Congress deny that human-caused climate change is occurring.

The significance of U.S. environmental law is obvious if we measure it by pages of statutes, regulations, and court decisions. But, of course, that's not the point. The real question involves the impact of this legislation on improving the environment. At least in terms of air pollution, the results have been dramatic, as shown by the following table.

Percent Change in Air Quality

	1980 vs 2010	1990 vs 2010	2000 vs 2010	2010 vs 2017
Carbon Monoxide (CO)	−82	−73	−54	−13
Ozone (O_3) (8-hr)	−28	−17	−11	−6
Lead (Pb)	−90	−83	−62	−80
Nitrogen Dioxide (NO_2) (annual)	−52	−45	−38	−14
PM_{10} (24-hr)	—	−38	−29	0
$PM_{2.5}$ (annual)	—	—	−27	−18
$PM_{2.5}$ (24-hr)	—	—	−29	
Sulfur Dioxide (SO_2) (24-hr)	−76	−68	−48	−66

Source: EPA, Air Quality Trends, http://www.epa.gov/airtrends/aqtrends.html

B. THE ENVIRONMENT AS COMMONS

One of the principal reasons government steps in to regulate environmental problems is because of the nature of many environment resources. It is important to keep this underlying structural reality in mind when considering the material in this book—the air we breathe, the waters we drink, swim in, travel on and recreate in, and the animal species we seek to protect all raise problems of collective action, free riding, and other components of the problem of the tragedy of the commons, Because of the uncertainties associated with complex systems, responding to an environmental problem like global warming or toxic pollutants would be difficult in any event. But the difficulties are compounded by the need for collective action by multiple actors. Similarly, pollution typically comes from multiple sources and affects numerous individuals, and a solution must involve many individuals and firms. Environmental issues do not merely present scientific problems; they also present major problems of institutional design. This section considers these collective action problems and their possible solutions.

1. ENVIRONMENTAL PROTECTION AND THE DYNAMICS OF COLLECTIVE ACTION

Many medieval and early modern villages had a "commons" where all of the peasants were entitled to graze their animals. (To this day, Boston has a "commons" that now functions as a park.) This history became the basis for an important approach to conceptualizing environmental problems. In a classic article,[4] Garrett Hardin explained what he called the tragedy of the commons:

> The tragedy of the commons develops in this way. Picture a pasture open to all. It is to be expected that each herdsman will try to keep as many cattle as possible on the commons. Such an arrangement may work reasonably satisfactorily for centuries because tribal wars, poaching, and disease keep the numbers of both man and beast well below the carrying capacity of the land. Finally, however, comes the day of reckoning, that is, the day when the long-desired goal of social stability becomes a reality. At this point, the inherent logic of the commons remorselessly generates tragedy.

Rationally, each herdsman seeks to graze as many cattle as possible on the commons, because he gets the full benefit of selling each additional animal but suffers only a fraction of the harm to the pasture caused by the additional grazing. The result is individually rational but collectively tragic:

---

[4]   Garrett Hardin, *The Tragedy of the Commons*, 162 SCIENCE 1243, 1244–1245 (1968).

Adding together the component partial utilities, the rational herdsman concludes that the only sensible course for him to pursue is to add another animal to his herd. And another; and another * * *. But this is the conclusion reached by each and every rational herdsman sharing a commons. Therein is the tragedy. Each man is locked into a system that compels him to increase his herd without limit in a world that is limited. Ruin is the destination toward which all men rush, each pursuing his own best interest in a society that believes in the freedom of the commons. Freedom in a commons brings ruin to all.

As examples, Hardin pointed to overgrazing on federally owned Western lands by ranchers and overuse of the national parks by an increasing number of tourists. He also observed that pollution is a kind of "reverse" commons issue:

In a reverse way, the tragedy of the commons reappears in problems of pollution. Here it is not a question of taking something out of the commons, but of putting something in—sewage, or chemical, radio-active, and heat wastes into water; noxious and dangerous fumes into the air; and distracting and unpleasant advertising signs into the line of sight. The calculations of utility are much the same as before. The rational man finds that his share of the cost of the wastes he discharges into the commons is less than the cost of purifying his wastes before releasing them. Since this is true for everyone, we are locked into a system of "fouling our own nest," so long as we behave only as independent, rational, free-enterprisers.

The tragedy of the commons as a food basket is averted by private property, or something formally like it. But the air and waters surrounding us cannot readily be fenced, and so the tragedy of the commons as a cesspool must be prevented by different means, by coercive laws or taxing devices that make it cheaper for the polluter to treat his pollutants than to discharge them untreated. We have not progressed as far with the solution of this problem as we have with the first. Indeed, our particular concept of private property, which deters us from exhausting the positive resources of the earth, favors pollution. The owner of a factory on the bank of a stream—whose property extends to the middle of the stream—often has difficulty seeing why it is not his natural right to muddy the waters flowing past his door. The law, always behind the times, requires elaborate stitching and fitting to adapt it to this newly perceived aspect of the commons.[5]

The tragedy of the commons can be considered a special case of what game theorists call a prisoner's dilemma. This scenario gets its name from the following illustrative story.

Consider two prisoners, charged with being involved in the same crime but held in different rooms. The prosecutor gives each of them the following information: "(a) If neither of you confesses, I will charge you both with a lesser crime that I can easily prove, resulting in two-year sentences for each. (b) If you both confess, you will each get a three-year sentence. (c) If only one of you confesses, that person will get a one-year sentence and the other will get a four-year sentence." Each prisoner reasons as follows: "Either the other person will confess or not. If the other person does confess, I will get a three-year sentence if I confess but a four-year sentence if I don't. So if the other person confesses, I should do the same. If the other person doesn't confess, I will get a one-year sentence if I do confess and a two-year sentence if I don't, so the best move is to confess. Thus, no matter what the other person does, I will be better off if I confess." Following the same reasoning, the other prisoner also confesses, and they both get three-year sentences. This is the "rational" outcome. But notice that if the prisoners could somehow count on each other, neither would confess, and they would get only two-year sentences. So the individually rational set of actions leads to an inferior outcome in terms of their group welfare.

Climate change is perhaps the most serious illustration of this dilemma. Consider the situation of Freedonia, a hypothetical average country. If the rest of the world fails to address the greenhouse effect, Freedonia can do little on its own, and therefore shouldn't bother. If everyone else does take action to control the greenhouse effect, Freedonia can contribute only slight additional help but will have to spend a lot of money to do so. So if everyone else "does the right thing," Freedonia should take a "free ride" on their efforts rather than wasting its own resources to minimal effect. Thus, no matter what the rest of the world does, Freedonia is better off to do nothing. Reasoning the same way, every country in the world decides to take no action.

Yet, all might be better off if they could somehow make an enforceable deal to cooperate. But such deals are difficult to negotiate and enforce on the international level, because the prisoner's dilemma takes hold again: each individual country has an incentive to sit out the negotiations and let everyone else make a deal; once a deal is made, each country has an

---

[5]   For an overview of recent research relating to the commons problem and possible solutions, see Robert N. Stevins, *The Problem of the Commons Still Unsettled After 100 Years*, 101 AMER. ECON. REV. 81 (2011).

incentive to breach the agreement and allow others to bear the costs of carrying it out.

The upshot is that, in the absence of some mechanism for making and enforcing cooperative agreements, each nation may find inaction to be the only sensible individual choice, even though everyone also knows that collective inaction will only lead to disaster. Within individual nations, the central government can lead the way out of prisoner's dilemmas by forcing a cooperative solution. (As we will see in Chapter 4, however, even a strong central government, like that in the United States, may find practical and legal obstacles to solving the prisoner's dilemma.) In the international sphere, the problem is more difficult, but as we will see in the following note, some progress has been made.

The prisoner's dilemma poses a considerable barrier to international environmental regulation. Indeed, given the formidable barriers, we do not seem to have a good explanation for why international environmental regulation has been implemented *at all*:

> [T]he standard positive political theories provide an even weaker explanation of the origin of global environmental regulation than of national environmental regulation. The beneficiaries of global environmental quality are even more diffuse and latent than their national counterparts, suggesting an even greater public choice bias against regulation at the global level. Meanwhile, civic republican discourse is even more limited at the international level because of the vastly large scale of the polity, the greater diversity of cultures involved, and the more market-like rhetoric of international treaty negotiation. The origin of environmental regulation is thus even more difficult to explain at the global level than at the national level. Moreover, the voting rule for adopting international law requires the voluntary assent of every party to be bound, rather than the majoritarian voting rule provided for national legislation in most countries. The voluntary assent voting rule makes adopting regulation a cooperation game rather than a coercive enterprise, and thus raises the hurdles to be surmounted in order to adopt broadly applicable regulation. In sum, the establishment of global environmental regulation should be (nearly) impossible—a conclusion apparently belied by reality.

Jonathan Baert Wiener, *On the Political Economy of Global Environmental Regulation*, 87 GEO. L.J. 749, 750 (1999). For this reason, Wiener concludes, "current theories are inadequate to explain the origin and content of global environmental regulation."

Nevertheless, however, some communities do manage environmental resources collectively and sustainably despite these obstacles. Political Scientist Elinor Ostrom received the 2009 Nobel Prize in Economics for extensive empirical analysis of commons resources that are successfully managed by their users without external intervention. Generally speaking, Ostrom found—from her studies and those of other scholars—that successful commons management requires a relatively small number of users (her largest example involved 15,000 users) operating in a tight-knit community where social interactions contributed to the development of social norms of behavior that allowed for extensive cooperation to manage the commons resource. Relatively small groundwater basins and fisheries are good examples. *See* ELINOR OSTROM, GOVERNING THE COMMONS, THE EVOLUTION OF INSTITUTIONS FOR COLLECTIVE ACTION (1990). Commons resources that involve larger numbers of users and less social homogeneity are subject to the kinds of problems Garret Hardin and others identified. Government regulation, then, often becomes necessary to avoid the tragedy. We explore one example below.

2. APPLYING COMMONS ANALYSIS: FISHERIES

Fisheries are a paradigmatic commons problem. See Stephanie F. McWhinnie, *The Tragedy of the Commons in International Fisheries*, 57 J. ENV. ECON. & MANAGEMENT 321 (2009). The Magnuson Fishery Conservation and Management Act, involved an effort to "fence" the commons. Enacted in 1976, the Act extended the territorial limits of the United States from 6 to 200 miles into the oceans. 16 U.S.C. § 1801 Rule 3.4(b). After opposing such claims by other nations for years, the United States joined the trend in 1976 because fisheries off our Atlantic and Pacific coasts had been seriously depleted by foreign trawlers.

The Magnuson Act not only established a 200-mile exclusive economic zone of the United States, but also created regional fishery councils and charged them with rebuilding depleted fish stocks. The eight regional councils were dominated by local fishing interests and authorized to allocate to boat owners transferable rights to catch specified amounts of fish. In effect, collective fishing rights were privatized and distributed as windfalls to current boat owners, rather than, for example, being auctioned off to the highest bidders with proceeds going to the federal treasury.

The intent was that the councils would limit fishing rights sufficiently so that stocks would have the opportunity to recover. In some regions, at least, it did not work out that way. Excessive numbers of rights were allocated. The result was a catastrophic decline in the numbers of salmon in the Pacific Northwest and of cod, haddock, and flounder off the New England coast. *See* Timothy Egan, *Fishing Fleet Trawling Seas That Yield Many Fewer Fish,* N.Y. TIMES, Mar. 7, 1994, at A1. Late in 1994, upon recommendation of the New England Fishery Council, the U.S. Department of Commerce issued an emergency order closing three prime Atlantic fishing grounds, encompassing about 6,600 square miles of ocean, to virtually all commercial fishing. The order also banned the use, in other

New England waters, of nets with mesh sizes smaller than six inches. *See Three Depleted Fishing Grounds Ordered Closed*, L.A. TIMES, Dec. 8, 1994, at A18.

The Magnuson Act was reauthorized and amended by the 1996 Sustainable Fisheries Act, Pub. L. No. 104–297, 110 Stat. 3559 (1996). For an illuminating analysis of reasons for the failure of the 1976 Magnuson Act, and an explanation of some of the improvements and shortcomings of the 1996 Act, *see* David A. Dana, *Overcoming the Political Tragedy of the Commons: Lessons Learned from the Reauthorization of the Magnuson Act*, 24 ECOLOGY L.Q. 833 (1997). The statute gave rise to hundreds of lawsuits challenging fishing regulations for giving too little weight to economic impact. *See* Kristen M. Fletcher, *When Economics and Conservation Clash: Challenges to Economic Analysis in Fisheries Management*, 31 ENVTL. L. REP. 11,168 (2001).

The following case involves the implementation of the statute, particularly the vexing questions of how quotas should be allocated and who should be allowed to participate in the market

PACIFIC COAST FEDERATION V. BLANK

United States Court of Appeals, Ninth Circuit, 2012.
693 F.3d 1084.

CALLAHAN, CIRCUIT JUDGE:

In 2011, the National Marine Fisheries Service ("NMFS") and the Pacific Fishery Management Council ("Pacific Council" or "Council") adopted changes to the fishery management plan for the trawl sector of the Pacific Coast groundfish fishery. The changes, adopted as Amendments 20 and 21 to the Pacific Coast Groundfish Fishery Management Plan, are designed to increase economic efficiency through fleet consolidation, reduce environmental impacts, and simplify future decisionmaking. * * *

In 2007, Congress reauthorized the MSA and lifted the quota moratorium by adding a section that authorizes "limited access privilege programs." Under such programs, of which quota programs are a subset, fishery participants receive "privileges" (or, in the case of quota programs, "quota shares") to harvest a certain portion of the total catch allowed for a particular species. NMFS and the Fishery Management Councils must structure limited access programs in accordance with various requirements, some of which concern fishing communities and form the basis of the plaintiffs' arguments in this case. * * *

The Pacific groundfish fishery extends 200 miles into the Pacific Ocean, along the coasts of California, Oregon, and Washington, and includes more than 90 species of fish that dwell near the sea floor. Fishers use many different types of gear, including trawl nets (nets dragged by boats along the sea floor), traps, and longlines, but trawls dominate. The trawl sector consists of two fisheries, one targeting Pacific whiting (hake) and another targeting non-whiting species. The non-trawl sector includes fishers who use what is called "fixed gear," such as longlines and pots, and primarily targets sable-fish.

Every two years, the Pacific Council establishes catch limits, called "optimum yields" or "annual catch limits," which "represent an annual quantity of fish that the groundfish fishery as a whole may catch." Catch limits are divided among different sectors of the fishery, such as between trawlers and fixed gear fishers; these divisions are called "allocations." Prior to Amendments 20 and 21, the Council enforced catch limits primarily by regulating the number of fishing trips. The Council also used gear restrictions and seasonal and area closures. Through trip limits the Council was able to measure and restrict harvests, but it was not able to comprehensively measure or limit "bycatch," which refers to non-targeted (and often overfished) species that are incidentally caught and discarded. Indeed, before Amendments 20 and 21, bycatch was recorded on only one-quarter of non-whiting trawl fishing trips.

In mixed-stock fisheries like the Pacific groundfish fishery, harvests of healthy species are constrained by measures to protect overfished species, "even if those species are not targeted by any particular fishery." The result is sub-optimal harvests. Between 1999 and 2002, seven species were designated as overfished and have since had very low catch limits. The Council has made various efforts over the years to achieve optimum yields in the trawl fishery while reducing adverse impacts to these overfished species. Nonetheless, "biological, social, and economic concerns" have remained, and the fishery has continued to be viewed as "unsustainable."
* * *

In 2003, the Pacific Council set out to develop a program for better managing the Pacific groundfish fishery. * * *

In August 2010, NMFS approved Preferred Alternative 4b as Amendment 20, and various preferred alternatives as Amendment 21. NMFS issued regulations codifying the Amendments about two months later. Amendment 20 ("Trawl Rationalization") divides the trawl fishery into three sectors and then assigns a discrete number of fishing privileges within each sector. For the on-shore sector, privileges are initially allocated based on catch history and then become freely transferable after two years. Liberal transferability is expected to yield economic efficiency and bycatch reductions, but it also may force out participants from local fishing communities by consolidating privileges and making them more expensive. All trawl vessels must employ observers who measure the number of target fish caught and the number of non-target fish discarded as bycatch.

Finally, Amendment 20 includes various measures to reduce adverse impacts to fishing communities. * * *

Besides limiting Pacific halibut bycatch, Amendment 21 ("Intersector Allocation") does various things to support Amendment 20, the most important of which is to fix allocations of 19 groundfish stocks among the various trawl and non-trawl sectors. For other species, the Pacific Council will continue to assign allocations every two years. Amendments 20 and 21 were implemented on January 1, 2011. * * *

Section 1853a(c) of the MSA, entitled "Requirements for limited access privileges," contains various provisions related to fishing communities. * * * In developing participation criteria, the Pacific Council must consider factors such as traditional fishing practices, the "cultural and social framework relevant to the fishery," economic barriers to access, and economic and social impacts from the limited access program on fishery-dependent persons and businesses.

Section 1853a(c) also requires NMFS to "establish procedures to ensure fair and equitable initial allocations" of privileges. Such procedures must "include consideration of" current and past harvests, employment in the harvesting and processing sectors, investments in and dependent on the fishery, and "the current and historical participation of fishing communities." In addition, NMFS must "consider the basic cultural and social framework of the fishery," especially through "policies to promote the sustained participation of small owner-operated fishing vessels and fishing communities that depend on the fisheries" and "procedures to address concerns over excessive geographic or other consolidation in the harvesting or processing sectors of the fishery." * * *

The plaintiffs argue that the preceding provisions required NMFS to (1) develop criteria for ensuring that quota shares are distributed to fishing communities, and (2) adopt "other measures and policies" to ensure the sustained participation of fishing communities. NMFS responds that § 1853a(c) only required it to consider the sustained participation of fishing communities against other objectives, including by developing optional participation criteria or other measures, and that in any event Amendments 20 and 21 adequately serve to protect fishing communities.

NMFS is correct. The allocation provisions of § 1853a(c)(5) require NMFS, in developing "procedures to ensure fair and equitable initial allocations" of quota shares, to "includ[e] consideration of" four specific factors and to "consider" the "basic cultural and social framework of the fishery." These provisions do not require that fishing communities receive an allocation of quota or, as the district court explained, "even be made eligible to do so. Similarly, the plain language of § 1853a(c)(3) says that fishing communities must do certain things "[t]o be eligible" to participate in a fishery, including comply with "participation criteria for eligible communities" that NMFS develops. But this language does not mandate that NMFS actually develop participation criteria. In short, § 1853a requires NMFS to take fishing communities into account in fashioning a limited access program (something NMFS did); it does not require NMFS to guarantee communities any particular role in that program. Congress could have taken any number of steps to guarantee fishing communities a specific role, but it did not. * * *

The question remains whether NMFS met its obligations to consider fishing communities in fashioning Amendments 20 and 21. It did. NMFS recognized that fishing communities must be considered under the MSA; surveyed the current status of fishing communities (including observing that many are "faltering" under the status quo); described the effects of quota programs and other management tools on those communities; and explained how communities participated in the Pacific Council's decisions. In addition, NMFS proposed, and the Council adopted, various measures to mitigate the impacts of trawl rationalization on fishing communities, including, among other things: an adaptive management program under which up to ten percent of quota shares would be reserved for communities; a two-year moratorium on share transfers; a five-year review that includes a community advisory committee; and limits on the accumulation of shares by single entities. These measures will provide an "equitable initial allocation" of quota shares, "assist" entry-level participants and fishing communities, and prevent a single share holder from acquiring "excessive" shares. [Section 1853(a)(c) requires that the quota system "authorize limited access privileges to harvest fish to be held, acquired, used by, or issued under the system to persons who substantially participate in the fishery, including in a specific sector of such fishery, as specified by the Council."

The plaintiffs argue that § 1853a(c)(5) and (c)(7) require NMFS to restrict the authority to receive and hold quota shares to those who "substantially participate" in the fishery. NMFS, however, construes § 1853a(c)(1)(D) to be the sole provision setting forth who is excluded from acquiring quota shares, and § 1853a(c)(5)(E) to mean "that those who substantially participate in the fishery must be among those eligible to acquire [shares], but are not the only entities or person[s] who can receive [shares]." [The court concluded that the clear language of the statute supported the agency.]

The plaintiffs' final argument is one of policy: allowing persons who do not substantially participate in the fishery to acquire and hold quota shares leads to "liberal transferability," which in turn can result in "extreme or excessive fleet consolidation, regional shifts in fishing commerce, loss of fishing-related employment[,]" and other effects. However, as discussed above, NMFS was aware of these effects but decided to partially prioritize economic efficiency and fleet consolidation over the protection of existing fishery participants, a choice that required fewer restrictions on who could acquire and hold quota shares. The MSA did not preclude NMFS from making that choice. * * *

The MSA requires NMFS to consider fishing communities in fashioning a limited access program, not to guarantee them a particular role in the program. The MSA also requires NMFS to make fishing privileges available to those who substantially participate in a fishery, not to restrict such privileges to that group. NMFS satisfied these duties and complied with the MSA's National Standards. As for NEPA, NMFS appropriately studied Amendments 20 and 21 in separate EISs, considered an adequate range of alternatives, evaluated the Amendments' impacts on fish habitat and non-trawl communities, and considered and adopted appropriate mitigation measures.

NOTES

1.   This case highlights some features of environmental law that will become familiar as the course goes on. First, administrative agencies have the power to set environmental policies; the role of the courts is usually to police the agencies rather than to set policy on their own. Second, one key question in many cases is whether an agency has complied with the statute authorizing its action. Environmental law is intensely statutory, meaning that careful attention to the text of the enactment is often critical.

2.   *Pacific Coast Federation* also illuminates some of the issues involved in setting up a trading system to deal with an environmental problem. Such a system may be effective in dealing with overuse of a commons. (For a measured appraisal of the evidence on this point, see Holly Doremus, *Why International Catch Shares Won't Save Ocean Biodiversity*, 2 MICH. J. OF ENV. & ADMIN. L. 385, 399–405 (2013).) But critics commonly raise issues about the fairness of the system. In the preceding case, the agency admitted that the scheme might lead to industry consolidation by larger firms, to the detriment of some traditional fishing communities. Equity issues are not always front and center in environmental law, but many observers believe that environmental justice deserves more attention. What countervailing factors did NMFS view as outweighing the interests of fishing communities? Should it have given more weight to equity factors?

3.   THE CASE OF GLOBAL CLIMATE CHANGE

Collective action problems may be particularly severe for climate change, a classic commons problem. See Daniel H. Cole, *Climate Change and Collective Action*, 61 CURRENT LEGAL PROBLEMS 229 (2008). The collective action problems are truly daunting: climate change requires a coordinated response involving every country (or at least every major emitting country) on earth, a task made much harder because of the huge differences in development across the globe and the large economic interests involved in the extraction and sale of fossil fuels.

This section provides background on the climate change issue and the current policy choices facing the United States. We begin with a judicial opinion discussing the reliability of climate science and its admissibility as evidence. We explore the admission of expert testimony in more depth in Chapter 2, but here you should focus on how the court evaluates climate science in particular. The remainder of the section consists of two Notes— one summarizing scientific information about climate change, and the other discussing the current state of play in terms of policy. We take up the U.S. government's approach to the regulation of climate change in subsequent chapters, particularly in Chapter 8 on air pollution,

GREEN MOUNTAIN CHRYSLER PLYMOUTH DODGE JEEP v. CROMBIE

United States District Court, D. Vermont, 2007.
508 F.Supp.2d 295.

[This was a challenge to a state law restricting greenhouse gas emissions from vehicles. One issue before the Court involved the existence and strength of the state's regulatory interest. The state attempted to establish the harmfulness of climate change through expert testimony. The following portion of the opinion involves whether the key expert's testimony was sufficiently reliable to be admissible. Rule 702 of the Federal Rules of Evidence makes expert testimony admissible when it meets certain criteria: "(a) the expert's scientific, technical, or other specialized knowledge will help the trier of fact to understand the evidence or to determine a fact in issue; (b) the testimony is based on sufficient facts or data; (c) the testimony is the product of reliable principles and methods; and (d) the expert has reliably applied the principles and methods to the facts of the case."]

Plaintiffs did not produce any evidence to contradict Hansen's testimony on likely species extinctions and devastating regional impacts of global warming other than ice sheet disintegration. In addition, they do not address that testimony in their Motion. Therefore, the Court assumes that their motion seeks the exclusion of Hansen's testimony as to the concept of a "tipping point" and as to his predictions regarding ice sheet disintegration and sea level rise, but does not seek the exclusion of his testimony as to the effects of global warming on species extinction or regional impacts.

Hansen's testimony is based on sufficient facts and data and reliable methods, applied reliably to the facts. Hansen cited abundant data in support of his theories regarding climate change, including historical data gathered from a number of sources including measured temperatures, ice cores and ocean cores, as well as modeling results. He also cited substantial data regarding the likelihood of ice sheet disintegration, including satellite imagery and the GRACE satellite's gravitational field data showing recent losses of mass in Greenland and Antarctica, increases in ice quakes in Greenland, recent accelerations in ice streams flowing off Greenland, and historical data on sea level rise at other warm periods in paleo-climate history. As the '302 plaintiffs note in their motion to exclude Hansen's testimony, historical data is not a perfect predictor of what will happen in our current climate. [Eds.: "the '302 plaintiffs" were the plaintiffs in one of the consolidated cases having a docket number ending in 302.] The unprecedented nature of current human-made forcings means that history is not a perfect guide. However, that the situation is unprecedented does not mean that scientists may not testify reliably as to global warming's likely effects.

Plaintiffs' rebuttal expert, Dr. John Christy [the Alabama state climatologist], testified that Hansen's hypothesis regarding rapid sea level rise is unsupported by the scientific evidence. Christy critiqued the use of data from the GRACE satellite; while he agreed that the data was accurate, he noted that only a few years' worth of data are available. Since the GRACE data was only one of several sources supporting Hansen's conclusions, objections to that data are insufficient to render Hansen's testimony inadmissible. In addition, the Court, as the trier of fact, can take into account the short time period for which GRACE measurements exist. This limitation goes to the weight, rather than to the admissibility of Hansen's testimony.

As to sea level rise, Hansen acknowledges that no existing mathematical or scientific model can predict the sea level rise that will result from ice sheet disintegration, when it will occur, or the exact sea level rise it will cause. Under these circumstances, Hansen's use of his expertise to make a prediction based on climate history is not an unreasonable choice of methodology. Hansen's predictions need not be certainties to be admissible * * *, nor need his estimates of the timing and amount of sea level rise be exact to be admissible. The '302 plaintiffs refer to an "absence of any objective evidence" to support Hansen's opinion, but Hansen did reference substantial supporting evidence in his testimony, including several examples from climate history. The lack of a model to address ice sheet disintegration does not mean that evidence on that point is de facto unreliable.

The '302 plaintiffs repeatedly compare the IPCC's sea level rise predictions to Hansen's, arguing that Hansen's estimates are flawed because they are higher. The comparisons are misleading. The IPCC predicted a sea level rise of between eighteen and fifty-nine centimeters under a "business-as-usual" scenario. Although the IPCC takes into account runoff of snow and land-based ice from mountain glaciers, and continued ice sheet stream flow rates the same as those experienced from

1993–2003, in addition to thermal expansion, it does not address the possibility of ice sheet disintegration, which would cause much of the sea level rise that Hansen predicts. it is common and acceptable for trained experts to extrapolate from existing data, as Hansen has done in making predictions from available information on the Earth's climate history. Although a "court may conclude that there is simply too great an analytical gap between the data and the opinion proffered," there is no such gap here.
* * *

Hansen didn't testify to a screening test for a disease or genetic trait, which one would expect to have a particular error rate. Rather, he used various sources of evidence to make a prediction about the future of the Earth, a prediction which it is difficult to assign a defined error rate. As the conclusion which he reached is supported by evidence, the absence of a defined error rate does not render it inadmissible.

Plaintiffs argue at length that Hansen's theory is unreliable because it has not been tested by controlled scientific experimentation. It is difficult to imagine a conclusive test for any theory about the future climate effects of the world's current emissions of greenhouse gases. The appearance of Hansen's predicted large-scale impacts following a global temperature rise of two to three degrees Celsius would be the only entirely conclusive proof of his theories, but clearly it would be ridiculous to exclude his testimony on the grounds that this has not yet occurred. A prediction on this enormous scale must necessarily be tested by the extent to which it is confirmed by evidence such as the historical record and model results, rather than through testing. The same would be true of a theory on global warming offered by any expert. While the '302 plaintiffs complain that the theory has not been tested, their motion does not describe what sort of "controlled scientific experiment" they propose. The absence of controlled scientific testing does not undermine the reliability of Hansen's opinions given the nature of the predictions that he offers. * * *

There is widespread acceptance of the basic premises that underlie Hansen's testimony. Plaintiffs' own expert, Dr. Christy, agrees with the IPCC's assessment that in the light of new evidence and taking into account remaining uncertainties, most of the observed warming over the last fifty years is likely to have been due to the increase in GHG concentrations. Christy agrees that the increase in carbon dioxide is real and primarily due to the burning of fossil fuels, which changes the radiated balance of the atmosphere and has an impact on the planet's surface temperature toward a warming rate. Christy also agreed that climate is a nonlinear system, that is, that its responses to forcings may be disproportionate, and rapid changes would be more difficult for human beings and other species to adapt to than more gradual changes. He further agreed with Hansen that the regulation's effect on radiative forcing will be proportional to the amount of emissions reductions, and that any level of emissions reductions will have at least some effect on the radiative forcing of the climate.

The '302 plaintiffs contend that there is no support in the scientific community for Hansen's theories on sea level rise. Again, this is not accurate. At trial, Defendants introduced, in connection with Dr. Hansen's testimony, a peer-reviewed article by a group of scientists including Dr. Richard Alley, a top glaciologist, in which Dr. Alley and his coauthors conclude that "current knowledge cannot rule out a return to . . . conditions [in which ice sheets have contributed meters above modern sea level in response to modest warming] in response to continued GHG emissions. Moreover, a threshold triggering many meters of sea-level rise could be crossed well before the end of this century."

The '302 plaintiffs further argue that Hansen's testimony is inadmissible due to lack of evidence that the regulation will avoid triggering a tipping point. This objection to Dr. Hansen's testimony appears to rest on a misunderstanding of the opinion that he has offered.[6] Hansen does not argue that the change in GHG emissions that will result from the regulation challenged in this case will itself have the immense impact of preventing the Earth from reaching a "tipping point." Rather, he articulates a pressing need for the worldwide community to act in a comprehensive variety of arenas to reduce GHG emissions, as described in his "alternative scenario." He states that the reductions implied by the regulation at issue are consistent with that scenario. The fact that global warming will not be solved by changes in any one industry or by regulation of any one source of emissions in no way under-cuts the vital nature of the problem or the validity of partial responses; rather, it points to the necessity of responses, however incomplete when viewed individually, on any number of fronts.

The Court finds that Hansen's opinions are reliable for purposes of their admission into evidence.

CLIMATE SCIENCE AND IMPACTS OF CLIMATE CHANGE

The court's opinion refers to the IPCC as a source of evidence. In 2013 and 2014, the United Nation's Intergovernmental Panel on Climate Change issued its fifth assessment on climate change and by far its least equivocal. The IPCC consists of the IPCC Plenary (often referred to as "the Panel"), and three Working Groups with clearly defined mandates.[7] The Panel has sometimes been described as a body dominated more by politics than science because it is

---

[6]   Plaintiffs' expert Dr. Christy estimated that implementing the regulations across the entire United States would reduce global temperature by about 1/100th (.01) of a degree by 2100. Hansen did not contradict that testimony.

[7]   Intergovernmental Panel on Climate Change, *About IPCC: How the IPCC is Organized,* http://www.ipcc.ch/organization/organization.shtml.

open to national delegations from all United Nations Environment Programme (UNEP) and World Meteorological Organization (WMO) member states.[8]

The Panel elects the IPCC Chairman and members of the IPCC Bureau, who have significant authority in overseeing the assessment report process, and it decides on the scope and outline of all Reports. While lead authors and coordinating lead authors have exclusive responsibility for drafting the Reports, the IPCC process includes a review of both the first and second drafts. The first draft review is experts-only, but the review of the second draft includes both expert and governmental comments. IPCC procedures require lead authors to take "into account government and expert comments" when preparing a final draft.[9] In addition, the IPCC procedures require the national delegations from member states to provide line-by-line approval of each Assessment Report's Executive Summary and Summary for Policy Makers (SPM). IPCC procedures require consensus for *each line*.[10] As a result, the process is both deeply consensual and deeply political, leading some to be concerned that the reports understate risks in order to garner agreement. Others worry that the process for expert participation is too onerous and may lead some to refuse to participate. *See* Robert Stavins, *Onerous for Experts, IPCC Process in Danger of Becoming Politicized*, 34 ENV. FORUM 15 (2017).

At this writing, the Sixth Report is expected to be released in 2021. The Fifth Report made it clear that climate change is real: "Human influence on the climate system is clear, and recent anthropogenic emissions of greenhouse gases are the highest in history. Recent climate changes have had widespread impacts on human and natural systems." In 2018, the IPCC released a special report on whether the global community can keep temperature increases below 1.5 degrees C, a level the international community agreed to in adopting the Paris Agreement, which we explore later in the chapter. The report concluded that "Global warming is likely to reach 1.5 degrees C between 2030 and 2052 if it continues to increase at the current rate."

The IPCC findings rely heavily on climate modeling, so a basic understanding of modeling is helpful. Elizabeth Kolbert, an award-winning science journalist, gives a particularly clear explanation of the basics of climate modeling, discussing a particular model called GISS:

---

[8]   *See* Bernd Siebenhüner, *The Changing Role of Nation States in International Environmental Assessments—the Case of the IPCC*, 13 GLOBAL ENVIRONMENTAL CHANGE 113, 118 (2003) (characterizing the Plenary in terms of "political dominance" while describing the IPCC's subject-specific Working Groups which are open to government representatives but largely dominated by scientists, in terms of a "[b]alance between science and politics.") By comparison, the authors of the Working Group reports (which go into the IPCC Assessment Reports) are exclusively derived from the scientific community, and are characterized by "[S]cientific Dominance." *Id.*

[9]   *See* Intergovernmental Panel on Climate Change, *Principles Governing IPCC Work, Appendix A: Procedures for the Preparation, Review, Acceptance, Adoption, and Publication of IPCC Reports*, amended November 6–7, 2003, 4.2.4.2, 4.2.5.

[10]   If consensus is unattainable, dissenting views are noted in the report. *See* Knut H. Alfsen and Tora Skovdin, CENTER FOR INTERNATIONAL CLIMATE AND ENVIRONMENTAL RESEARCH POLICY NOTE 1998:3: *The Intergovernmental Panel and Climate*, 12–13.

Like all climate models, GISS's divides the world into a series of boxes. Thirty-three hundred and twelve boxes cover the earth's surface, and this pattern is repeated twenty times moving up through the atmosphere. . . . [I]n the world of the model, features such as lakes and forests and, indeed, whole mountain ranges are reduced to a limited set of properties, which are then expressed as numerical approximations. Time in this grid-world moves ahead for the most part in discrete, half-hour intervals, meaning that a new set of calculations is performed for each box for every thirty minutes that is supposed to have elapsed in actuality. Depending on what part of the globe a box represents, these calculations may involve dozens of different algorithms, so a model run [may involve] more than a quadrillion separate operations. A single run of the GISS model, done on a supercomputer, usually takes about a month.

The model calculates changes in each block based on fundamental laws and on "parameterizations." These parameterizations approximate complex physical processes with simpler equations that capture the physical results but without all the details of the process. See, ELIZABETH KOLBERT, FIELD NOTES FROM A CATASTROPHE: MAN, NATURE, AND CLIMATE CHANGE 99–101 (2006).

Because of improvements in modeling and data, the 2007 Report was able to eliminate some concerns that had previously been raised about climate change. In particular, four key issues were resolved. First, could evidence of warming be skewed because previously rural measurement sites have been swept into urban areas, which are warmer than their surroundings? The answer is no. While the urban heat-island effect, caused by the tendency of urban concrete and asphalt to absorb heat, is real, it is "a negligible influence" on overall temperature. Second, do satellite measurements show that the world is not really warming (unlike the ground level measurements)? Again, the answer is no. The previous discrepancy between earth-based and satellite-based temperature measurements has been resolved by improved satellite measurements, which are more in line with the earth-based results. Third, could warming be due to natural forces? Again, no. While natural forces such as volcanos and variations in solar intensity can influence climate and have done so in the past, these natural variations cannot produce the currently observed patterns of climate change. And fourth, is it plausible to think that small changes in the gas composition of the atmosphere could cause significant climate change? Yes, the evidence does show that the climate system is sufficiently sensitive to atmospheric composition to produce the observed climate change, as shown by the response to other disturbances such as the Mount Pinatubo eruption of 1990. Resolving these issues eliminates some of the residual uncertainty that had still clouded discussions of climate change, leaving little room for doubt that human-caused climate change is real and serious.

We have also seen improvements in the models since the issuance of the Fifth Report in 2013 and 2014. For example, several of the models can now at least partially incorporate changes in vegetation dynamics and land use changes, which have very important influences on climate, including through surface albedo and the evaporation of water. Some models are also now incorporating feedback effects among physical and chemical processes in the climate system. *See* IPCC, *AR5 Climate Change 2013: The Physical Science Basis, Chapter 9, Evaluation of Climate Models*, https://www.ipcc.ch/site/ assets/uploads/2018/02/WG1AR5_Chapter09_FINAL.pdf.

Although it is possible that the IPCC analysis overstates the likely warming effect, it is at least equally possible that the Report understates it. The high-end risks relating to climate change, while not considered to be likely, would impose extraordinary costs. For a controversial account of just how dire the effects of climate change could be, *see* David Wallace-Wells, *The Uninhabitable Earth*, NEW YORK MAGAZINE (July 9, 2017), http://nymag.com/ intelligencer/2017/07/climate-change-earth-too-hot-for-humans.html, *but see* Climate Feedback, *Scientists Explain What New York Magazine Article on "The Uninhabitable Earth" Gets Wrong*, https://climatefeedback.org/evaluation/ scientists-explain-what-new-york-magazine-article-on-the-uninhabitable-earth-gets-wrong-david-wallace-wells/.

Nevertheless, understatement of the risks of climate change is the more likely possibility for a number of reasons. Indeed, since the release of the 5th Assessment, scientists believe that the low end of predictions of average temperature increases seems less likely than it did when the 5th Assessment was released. *See* The Royal Society, *Climate Updates: What Have We Learnt Since the IPCC 5th Assessment Report?* https://royalsociety.org/~/media/policy/ Publications/2017/27-11-2017-Climate-change-updates-report.pdf. Scientists now know, for example, that the models do not account for slow but measurable increases in ocean surface warming, which means that the models are underestimating climate sensitivity to changes in greenhouse gas concentrations. *Id.* at 7. Methane concentrations have increased since the release of the report. Methane is a significantly more potent greenhouse gas than carbon dioxide. *Id.* at 8. In addition, there remains the possibility of "tipping points" or "threshold effects" that could dramatically increase the concentration of GHGs in the atmosphere, and result in "abrupt and irreversible change in the climate system." Daniel P. Schrag, *Confronting the Climate-Energy Connection,* ELEMENTS Vol. 3, 171–8, at 174 (June 2007). These include the potential for a rapid collapse of ice sheets in Greenland or the Antarctic, *see* Julienne Stroeve *et al.*, *Arctic Sea Ice Decline: Faster Than Forecast?* 34 GEOPHYSICAL RESEARCH LETTERS L09501 (2007). For a description of the latest data on potential sea level rise, including an assessment that the sea level projections in the 5th Assessment "will almost certainly worsen in the IPCC's next report" *see* Robinson Meyer, *A Terrifying Sea-Level Prediction Now Looks Far Less Likely: But Experts Warm That Our Overall Picture of Sea-level Rise Looks Far Scarier Today Than It Did Even Five Years Ago*, THE ATLANTIC (January 4, 2019). The empirical record to date of climate change effects also shows that surprises about climate change have usually been in the "wrong" direction. For example, it now appears that the arctic will be seasonally free of sea ice thirty years ahead of expectations. *See*

National Snow & Ice Data Center, *Arctic Sea Ice News & Analysis*, http://nsidc. org/arcticseaicenews/2018/09/no-endless-summer-in-the-arctic/ (showing steady declines). The arctic permafrost too appears to be melting faster than scientists had predicted, and because the permafrost contains both carbon dioxide and methane, its melting can have very serious amplifying effects on warming. *See* Craig Spence, *Exclusive: Some Arctic Ground No Longer Freezing—Even in Winter,* NAT GEOGRAPHIC (Aug 20, 2018), https://www. nationalgeographic.com/environment/2018/08/news-arctic-permafrost-may-thaw-faster-than-expected/. All of these data points suggest, then, that the effects of increasing temperatures are likely to be on the more dire end of predictions.

THE GLOBAL RESPONSE TO CLIMATE CHANGE

In an ideal world, the response to climate change might be a firm, prompt, coordinated legal effort. As the theory of the tragedy of the commons suggests, however, progress is likely to be difficult given the individual incentives countries fact to limit action to address the problem. And, indeed, international progress has been halting, though not insignificant. Though our focus in this book is on U.S. domestic rather than international law, the international global response is obviously important and has also influenced the U.S. response both positively and negatively. Future chapters address the domestic response, especially under the Clean Air Act, covered in Chapter 6. Here, we briefly describe the main international developments.

In 1992, the international community agreed to the United Nations Framework Convention on Climate Change (UNFCCC). See United Nations, *United Nations Framework Convention on Climate Change* (1992) https:// unfccc.int/resource/docs/convkp/conveng.pdf. The United States signed and ratified this agreement along with the other 196 countries that are members of the United Nations. The UNFCCC acknowledges the seriousness of climate change, calls for a joint effort to address the problem, and establishes the process that the global community has subsequently used to negotiate future agreements. Although developed countries such as the U.S. agreed in the original framework to limit their emissions in order to prevent dangerous levels of carbon in the atmosphere, the UNFCCC did not contain specific measures to implement this commitment.

In 1997, the global community adopted the first (and only) international treaty to establish binding commitments by some countries to limit greenhouse gas emissions. The Kyoto Protocol required developed countries (also known as Annex I countries) to reduce their emissions, using 1990 levels of greenhouse gases as a baseline. Developing countries, including China and India, had no such commitments. The Kyoto Protocol also embraced market mechanisms (like the fishing quotas we saw earlier) as a way to reach the treaty's emissions goals. The U.S. had insisted on the inclusion of these mechanisms but then failed to ratify the agreement because of concerns about the expense of limiting emissions and about the fact that the treaty did not require rapidly developing countries like China to commit to emissions reductions. The Kyoto Protocol was adopted in Kyoto, Japan, on 11 December 1997 and entered into force on 16 February 2005. The detailed rules for the implementation of the Protocol were adopted at COP 7 in Marrakesh, Morocco, in 2001, and are referred to as the "Marrakesh Accords." The Protocol's first commitment period started in 2008 and ended in 2012. Most, but not all, of the parties to the Protocol agreed to take on commitments in a second commitment period from 2013 to 2020. Although the Protocol covers too few of the world's major emitters to be considered a solution to the problem, it did lead some important developed countries—most notably those of the European Union—to develop programs to reduce their emissions, including by establishing the European Trading System. The ETS, as it is known, is the first and largest trading program for greenhouse gases in the world. Though it has had problems, it has been strengthened, remains in effect, and covers almost half of the EU's emissions. *See* European Commission, *EU Emissions Trading System (EU ETS), https://ec.europa.eu/clima/policies/ets_en.*

Efforts to enter into a new international agreement upon the expiration of the Kyoto Protocol sputtered along with little success until December of 2015. In that month, the countries of the world gathered in Paris, France and collectively ratified the Paris Agreement. The new international agreement commits the global community to attempt to limit temperature increases to under 2 degrees through a series of country commitments to limit their emissions. The Paris Agreement differs from many international treaties in that it does not contain binding commitments or numerical limits to which individual countries are subject. Instead, each country that is a party to the agreement makes its own "Nationally Determined Contribution," which outlines the emissions reductions to which the country commits. These are voluntary commitments—there is no real mechanism to bind any country to its NDC. Collectively, the more than 160 countries that submitted NDCs committed to emissions reductions that would not achieve the temperature target of below 2 degrees C; nevertheless, the NDCs are designed to get the global community on a trajectory to first halt the increase in emissions and then cut them dramatically by mid-century. The U.S. NDC committed the country to cuts of between 26 and 28 percent below 2005 levels by 2025; *see* The White House, *Fact Sheet: U.S. Reports Its 2025 Emissions Target to the UNFCC,* https://obamawhitehouse.archives.gov/the-press-office/2015/03/31/fact-sheet-us-reports-its-2025-emissions-target-unfccc. Two of the central components of the U.S. NDC, the Clean Power Plan and fuel efficiency standards for vehicles, are explored in more detail in Chapter 6. The Trump Administration has repudiated the Obama Administration's climate change commitments and announced its intention to withdraw from the Paris Agreement. *See, Statement by President Trump on the Paris Climate Accord* (June 1, 2017), https://www.whitehouse.gov/briefings-statements/statement-president-trump-paris-climate-accord/.

The parties to the UNFCC and to the Paris Agreement met again in Katowice, Poland in late 2018 and reached agreement on transparency mechanisms to track and monitor greenhouse gases emissions across the globe.

Though the Katowice accomplishments were modest, given that the U.S. has announced its withdrawal from the Paris Agreement, many observers considered the outcome a success. *See* United Nations, *At COP24, Countries Agree Concrete Way Forward to Bring the Paris Climate Deal to Life* (Dec. 15, 2018), https://news.un.org/en/story/2018/12/1028681.

One response to the Trump Administration's retrenchment on climate policy has been for states, municipalities and businesses to commit to reducing their own greenhouse gases. Many of these entities committed to the US. target of cutting their emissions by 26–28 percent by 2025. Some states went further. In California, efforts focusing specifically on climate change date back to 1988, when AB 4420 called for the first inventory of in-state greenhouse gas emissions. California has one of the most ambitious programs in the world, with its latest legislation committing the state to cut its emissions 40 percent below 1990 levels by 2030. The state has already met its goal of rolling back its emissions to 1990 levels by 2020. California has a Renewable Portfolio Standard requiring its utilities to get half their energy from renewable sources by 2030 and 100 percent clean energy by 2045. The utilities are on target to meet a 33 percent RPS by 2020. The state also has an aggressive zero emission vehicle program that 9 other states have adopted. See California Air Resources Board, *Climate Change Programs,* https://www.arb.ca.gov/cc/cc.htm. Additionally, a total of twenty states and the D.C. Circuit have statewide climate goals, 29 states have renewable energy policies, and 15 states have mandatory building codes that require appliance efficiency standards that exceed federal requirements. See Center for Climate and Energy Solutions, *State Climate Policy Maps*, https://www.c2es.org/content/state-climate-policy/. A number of northeast states entered the country's first cap-and-trade program to reduce emissions from the electric power sector in 2009; in 2017 states that are part of the Regional Greenhouse Gas Initiative agreed to cut power plant emissions by another 30 percent. *See The Regional Greenhouse Gas Initiative*, https://www.rggi.org. None of these programs collectively can replace U.S. policy or substitute for U.S. leadership on climate change issues. But they are an important way for parts of the United States that support international efforts on climate change to signal that much of the country disagrees with the U.S. decision to withdraw from Paris. Moreover, state policy experimentation and experience will be important to future federal efforts to reduce U.S. greenhouse gases.

Climate change is an issue that cuts across environmental law. Climate impacts will affect all ecosystems, imperiling biodiversity, and higher temperatures will impact water quality. Reducing carbon emissions will require extensive changes in the entire energy system, with significant consequences for emissions of conventional pollutants. Thus, you should not be surprised to find climate issues popping up in many of this book's chapters.

CHAPTER 2

APPROACHES TO RISK REGULATION

■ ■ ■

In Chapter 1, we explored several general perspectives on environmental protection. Much of this book consists of detailed examinations of particular regulatory schemes. This leaves something of a gap between the very general and the very specific in environmental law. This chapter will examine four different approaches to environmental hazards. The first approach asks whether significant risks exist and seeks to engage in the maximum feasible reduction of such risks. The second uses economics to gauge the appropriate level of risk reduction. The third focuses on how risks are distributed and seeks to remedy inequities. The final approach seeks to regulate indirectly by imposing liability for harms.

To provide some concreteness to the discussion that follows, a specific example may be helpful. Unfortunately, the environmental statutes we discuss in this book are too complicated to serve this purpose—that's the reason that we devote entire chapters to them. But, it may be helpful to consider the example of risk regulation under OSHA. As we will see, this is also the context in which the Supreme Court has considered risk issues.

OSHA is primarily concerned with protecting workers from accidents and from exposures to hazardous materials and conditions in the workplace. The statutory provision dealing expressly with toxic chemicals in the workplace is § 6(b)(5) of the Act, 29 U.S.C. § 655(d)(5). This section provides:

> The Secretary, in promulgating standards dealing with toxic materials or harmful physical agents under this subsection, shall set the standard which most adequately assures, to the extent feasible, on the basis of the best available evidence, that no employee will suffer material impairment of health or functional capacity even if such employee has regular exposure to the hazard dealt with by such standard for the period of his working life. * * * In addition to the attainment of the highest degree of health and safety protection for the employee, other considerations shall be the latest available scientific data in the field, the feasibility of the standards, and experience gained under this and other health and safety laws. Whenever practicable, the standard promulgated shall be expressed in terms of objective criteria and of the performance desired.

Another section of the Act, § 3(8), 29 U.S.C. § 652(8), is also relevant. This section simply defines an occupational safety and health standard as a regulation setting any one of a variety of requirements "reasonably necessary or appropriate to provide safe or healthful places of employment."

These OSHA provisions raise several questions that are common to all risk regulations:

1.   What kind of scientific evidence supports findings about risks such as carcinogens in the workplace? What should be done when the science is uncertain?

2.   What level of risk is needed to support a regulation? Does the agency need to be able to give a quantitative estimate of the risk, or is a serious concern enough? How big does the risk have to be?

3.   How does cost enter into the equation? May (or must) the agency compare the costs and benefits of the regulation? If not, is there some other approach to considering cost under the statute?

4.   Are there distributional issues that are implicated by these provisions? Should regulations take account of special vulnerabilities of certain workers?

These issues remain quite controversial, both in the occupational setting and for environmental law. Whether the subject is urban smog, toxic water pollution, endangered species protection, or climate change, these issues are pervasive in environmental law.

A. RISK-BASED APPROACHES

Environmental law is partly about preserving nature and partly about protecting human health from pollution and other hazards. Cancer risks have received particular attention in this regard. We will examine some of the techniques for determining the extent of these hazards and how much priority they should receive. Neither determination is as straightforward as one might expect. Instead, they involve difficult scientific and normative judgments.

Public health concerns in environmental law have often focused on potential environmental sources of cancer. Estimating environmental cancer risks involves multiple sources of evidence and a range of tools and methodologies across different disciplines. Epidemiology—statistical studies of the incidence of particular diseases across human populations—can provide information on cancer trends and correlations of specific cancers with particular groups of people. These studies are easiest to perform when identifiable occupational groups are exposed to high levels of some substance. The basic idea is simply to compare cancer rates in the occupational group with those in the general population. But in practice, this is much harder than it sounds. Cancer latency periods are often measured in decades, making it necessary to identify which people were exposed to what levels several decades earlier. People move in and out of particular occupations, making it difficult to track the exposed workers. Moreover, members of specific occupational groups usually differ from the general population in other ways such as diet, smoking, or alcohol use, and statistical controls are necessary to eliminate these confounding factors. For instance, if members of the occupational group tend to be heavy smokers, they will have an elevated lung cancer rate regardless of any occupational exposures. Finally, it is often necessary to extrapolate from the high levels of past occupational exposures to what are typically much lower levels of exposure that concern current regulators. This requires an estimate of the "dose-response curve," which is often controversial. The dose-response curve connects changes in exposure (dose) to changes in the incidence of cancer or some other disease (response). In cases of low-level exposures, current scientific knowledge often does not allow the shape of the curve to be estimated with precision, leading EPA and other regulatory agencies to use default approaches that are often criticized.

Instead of using an occupational group, epidemiologists can also study how disease levels vary with risk exposure among the general population. This avoids the need to assume a specific dose-response curve, but the problems of estimating exposure and eliminating confounding factors still remain. Because effects in the general population are typically much smaller, they can be hard to distinguish from random variations in the background rate or from the effects of confounding factors.

Another major source of evidence used to estimate cancer risks involves animal studies. Because these are controlled experiments, confounding factors can be eliminated. But other problems arise. Small groups of laboratory animals must be used because of the expense of the experiments. Hence, only very large effects can be detected. An experiment with thirty lab rats cannot detect a one in a thousand risk to the rats, let alone the even lower risk levels that are often of regulatory concern. Rather, the rate must be in the neighborhood of one in thirty, and even then could be missed by chance in some experiments. The only way to obtain these high rates is to use high doses, but then it is necessary to use a dose-response curve to estimate the effects of much lower human exposures. Moreover, mammals vary in their susceptibility to carcinogens: a substance that causes cancer in rats might not do so in humans, and vice versa.

Some of the materials that follow may seem rather abstract. But the practical stakes are high. Risk assessments translate into regulatory requirements. If the risk assessment results in risk estimates that are too high, large amounts of money may be spent on non-existent or trivial harms. If the risk estimates are too low, however, deaths that should have been avoided may occur.

There are many uncertainties in risk assessment. Some of the most important concern extrapolations from high doses to low doses and from animals to humans. EPA's method of handling these uncertainties has been the subject of considerable controversy. EPA's current approach to dealing with uncertainty and extrapolating from incomplete data is explained in the following excerpt.

ENVIRONMENTAL PROTECTION AGENCY, GUIDELINES FOR CARCINOGEN RISK ASSESSMENT AND SUPPLEMENTAL GUIDANCE FOR ASSESSING SUSCEPTIBILITY FROM EARLY-LIFE EXPOSURE TO CARCINOGENS
70 FR 17766 (2005).

1.3.   KEY FEATURES OF THE CANCER GUIDELINES

1.3.1.   Critical Analysis of Available Information as the Starting Point for Evaluation

* * * Use of health protective risk assessment procedures as described in these cancer guidelines means that estimates, while uncertain, are more likely to overstate than understate hazard and/or risk. * * *

In the absence of sufficient data or understanding to develop a robust, biologically based model, an appropriate policy choice is to have a single preferred curve-fitting model for each type of data set. Many different curve-fitting models have been developed, and those that fit the observed data reasonably well may lead to several-fold differences in estimated risk at the lower end of the observed range. In addition, goodness-of-fit to the experimental observations is not by itself an effective means of discriminating among models that adequately fit the data. To provide some measure of consistency across different carcinogen assessments, EPA uses a standard curve-fitting procedure for tumor incidence data. Assessments that include a different approach should provide an adequate justification and compare their results with those from the standard procedure. Application of models to data should be conducted in an open and transparent manner.

1.3.2.   Mode of Action

The use of mode of action in the assessment of potential carcinogens is a main focus of these cancer guidelines. This area of emphasis arose because of the significant scientific advances that have developed concerning the causes of cancer induction. Elucidation of a mode of action for a particular cancer response in animals or humans is a data-rich determination. Significant information should be developed to ensure that a scientifically justifiable mode of action underlies the process leading to cancer at a given site. In the absence of sufficiently, scientifically justifiable mode of action information, EPA generally takes public health—protective, default positions regarding the interpretation of toxicologic and epidemiologic data: Animal tumor findings are judged to be relevant to humans, and cancer risks are assumed to conform with low dose linearity.

Understanding of mode of action can be a key to identifying processes that may cause chemical exposures to differentially affect a particular population segment or lifestage. Some modes of action are anticipated to be mutagenic and are assessed with a linear approach. This is the mode of action of radiation and several other agents that are known carcinogens. Other modes of action may be modeled with either linear or nonlinear approaches after a rigorous analysis of available data under the guidance provided in the framework for mode of action analysis.

1.3.3.   Weight of Evidence Narrative

The cancer guidelines emphasize the importance of weighing all of the evidence in reaching conclusions about the human carcinogenic potential of agents. This is accomplished in a single integrative step after assessing all of the individual lines of evidence, which is in contrast to the step-wise approach in the 1986 cancer guidelines. Evidence considered includes tumor findings, or lack thereof, in humans and laboratory animals; an agent's chemical and physical properties; its structure-activity relationships (SARs) as compared with other carcinogenic agents; and studies addressing potential carcinogenic processes and mode(s) of action, either *in vivo* or *in vitro*. Data from epidemiologic studies are generally preferred for characterizing human cancer hazard and risk. However, all of the information discussed above could provide valuable insights into the possible mode(s) of action and likelihood of human cancer hazard and risk. The cancer guidelines recognize the growing sophistication of research methods, particularly in their ability to reveal the modes of action of carcinogenic agents at cellular and subcellular levels as well as toxicokinetic processes. Weighing of the evidence includes addressing not only the likelihood of human carcinogenic effects of the agent but also the conditions under which such effects may be expressed, to the extent that these are revealed in the toxicological and other biologically important features of the agent. * * *

1.3.4.   Dose-response Assessment

Dose-response assessment evaluates potential risks to humans at particular exposure levels. The approach to dose-response assessment for a particular agent is based on the conclusion reached as to its potential mode(s) of action for each tumor type. Because an agent may induce multiple tumor types, the dose-response assessment includes an analysis of all tumor types, followed by an overall synthesis that includes a characterization of the risk estimates across tumor types, the strength of the mode of action information of each tumor type, and the anticipated relevance of each tumor type to humans, including susceptible populations and lifestages (e.g., childhood).

Dose-response assessment for each tumor type is performed in two steps: assessment of observed data to derive a point of departure (POD), followed by extrapolation to lower exposures to the extent that is necessary. Data from epidemiologic studies, of sufficient quality, are generally preferred for estimating risks. When animal studies are the basis of the analysis, the estimation of a human-equivalent dose should utilize toxico-kinetic data to inform cross—species dose scaling if appropriate and if adequate data are available. Otherwise, default procedures should be applied. For oral dose, based on current science, an appropriate default option is to scale daily applied doses experienced for a lifetime in proportion to body weight raised to the $3/4$ power. * * *

The POD for extrapolating the relationship to environmental exposure levels of interest, when the latter are outside the range of observed data, is generally the lower 95% confidence limit on the lowest dose level that can be supported for modeling by the data. SAB (1997) [eds: SAB is EPA's Science Advisory Board] suggested that, "it may be appropriate to emphasize lower statistical bounds in screening analyses and in activities designed to develop an appropriate human exposure value, since such activities require accounting for various types of uncertainties and a lower bound on the central estimate is a scientifically-based approach accounting for the uncertainty in the true value of the ED10 [or central estimate]." However, the consensus of the SAB (1997) was that, "both point estimates and statistical bounds can be useful in different circumstances, and recommended that the Agency routinely calculate and present the point estimate of the ED10 [or central estimate] and the corresponding upper and lower 95% statistical bounds." For example, it may be appropriate to emphasize the central estimate in activities that involve formal uncertainty analysis that are required by OMB Circular A-4 (OMB, 2003) as well as ranking agents as to their carcinogenic hazard. Thus, risk assessors should calculate, to the extent practicable, and present the central estimate and the corresponding upper and lower statistical bounds (such as confidence limits) to inform decisionmakers.

The second step of dose-response assessment is extrapolation to lower dose levels, if needed. This extrapolation is based on extension of a biologically based model if supported by substantial data. Otherwise, default approaches can be applied that are consistent with current understanding of mode(s) of action of the agent, including approaches that assume linearity or nonlinearity of the dose-response relationship, or both. A default approach for linearity extends a straight line from the POD to zero dose/zero response. The linear approach is used when: (1) there is an absence of sufficient information on modes of action or (2) the mode of action information indicates that the dose response curve at low dose is or is expected to be linear. Where alternative approaches have significant biological support, and no scientific consensus favors a single approach, an assessment may present results using alternative approaches. A nonlinear approach can be used to develop a reference dose or a reference concentration. * * *

NOTES

1.   The dose-response curve for some chemical agents remains poorly understood. EPA has used a linear, non-threshold dose-response curve as a default for carcinogens—a decision that is viewed by some as overly conservative. Some evidence, for example, suggests a "u-shaped curve," in which very small doses might have a beneficial health effect. This effect, known as hormesis, has led to some to argue for a relaxation of risk regulations, while others have argued for more stringent regulation because of the possibility of obtaining health benefits by mandating "sub-threshold" doses. See Frank B. Cross, *Incorporating Hormesis in Risk Regulation*, 30 ENVTL. L. REP. 10778 (2000). Other studies suggest that one-time exposures to some chemicals may cause cancer, even at doses too small to create other toxic effects. *See* Edward J. Calabrese & Robyn Blain, *A Single Exposure to Many Carcinogens Can Cause Cancer*, 28 ENVTL. L. REP. 10254 (1998). Some of the practical difficulties in public health studies are explored in Carole Bass, *Solving a Massive Worker Health Puzzle*, SCIENTIFIC AMERICAN, March 2008, at 86. As an alternative, the National Research Council has recommended a focus on determining the pathways through which a given toxin operates, followed by cellular studies to determine the risks associated with each pathway. See Mark M. Duvall and Alexandra M. Wyatt, *Revising Regulatory Science*, THE ENVIRONMENTAL FORUM 30 (Nov./Dec. 2009).

2.   As discussed in more detail in Chapter 9, *infra*, attention has also increasingly focused on non-carcinogenic effects of exposures to hazardous substances, particularly disruption of the endocrine system and impacts on the developing brain. Since the early 1990s, a growing number of studies have indicated that estrogenic chemicals can cause biological effects at doses previously considered safe. In response, Congress mandated in the 1996 Food Quality Protection Act that EPA establish an endocrine disruptor screening program.   https://www.epa.gov/endocrine-disruption.   Likewise, mounting evidence of the neurodevelopmental and neurobehavioral impacts of industrial chemicals, pesticides, and ambient environmental pollution have led to calls for more stringent regulations. *See, e.g.,* Phillipe Grandjean and Philip J. Landrigan, *Developmental Neurotoxicity of Industrial Chemicals*, 368 LANCET 2167 (2006); Phillipe Grandjean and Philip J. Landrigan, *Neurobehavioral Effects of Developmental Toxicity*, 13 LANCET: NEUROLOGY 330 (2014); Philip J. Landrigan et al., *The Lancet Commission on Pollution and Health*, 391 LANCET 462 (2018).

3.   Risk assessment involves difficult scientific judgments, given the often-inconclusive nature of the data. One approach to improved decision making has been to mandate peer review of EPA's scientific findings:

> In recent years, lawmakers of all sorts have become interested in scientific peer review, and have the hope that scrutiny by independent experts can improve the quality of their own decision-making. As the phrase implies, peer review refers to the process of having work scrutinized by fellow experts, and it has long served as a quality control mechanism for the scientific community. Traditionally relegated to research funding and publication decisions, peer review recently has become of interest to regulatory agencies making decisions in the face of scientific uncertainty as well as to judges struggling to make sense of conflicting claims by expert witnesses. Although noteworthy, these applications remain fairly *ad hoc* to date.
>
> Peer review, in its broadest sense, represents the scientific community's effort to police itself and to assure a certain minimum level of quality so that scientists and others can rely on the results of reported scientific research. Peer review contributes to the advancement of science not merely through the screening of scientific work (its quality control function), but also by helping proponents of new hypotheses to improve their research and interpretations and by engaging others in a dialogue about important new discoveries. * * * As legal institutions often must do, peer review operates under constraints of limited time and information. Over the long haul, science may approach a gradual maturation of consensus, but the scientific community's various peer review techniques do not purport to anoint particular results as finally settling contested questions.

Lars Noah, *Peer Review and Regulatory Reform*, 30 ENVTL L. REP. 10606 (2000).

4.   Peer review may not be able to help with another problem, which is that scientists may be asked to address issues that are as much normative as scientific. Given the uncertainties in the available scientific information at any given time, the question of how to proceed is as much a value judgment as a scientific one. Yet Congress or the courts may require agencies to produce precise risk assessments, so the treatment of the uncertainties gets hidden in what is supposedly a purely scientific judgment. See Wendy E. Wagner, *Congress, Science, and Environmental Policy*, 1999 U. ILL. L. REV. 181 (1999). The following case involves a court's effort to grapple with the issue of uncertainty in a classic environmental context: release of a potentially dangerous substance into a water body.

RESERVE MINING CO. v. ENVIRONMENTAL PROTECTION AGENCY

United States Court of Appeals, Eighth Circuit, 1975.
514 F.2d 492.

BRIGHT, CIRCUIT JUDGE.

[Reserve Mining disposed of great quantities of mining byproducts by discharging them into Lake Superior. These materials contained asbestos, which is known to be a cause of cancer when inhaled. The district court enjoined further discharges, which meant the closing of the facility. On appeal, the Eighth Circuit began by considering two issues: "first, whether the ingestion of fibers, as compared with their inhalation, poses any danger whatsoever; and second, should ingestion pose a danger, whether the exposure resulting from Reserve's discharge may be said to present a legally cognizable risk to health."]

1.   Ingestion of Fibers as a Danger to Health

All epidemiological studies which associate asbestos fibers with harm to health are based upon inhalation of these fibers by humans. Thus, although medical opinion agrees that fibers entering the respiratory tract can interact with body tissues and produce disease, it is unknown whether the same can be said of fibers entering the digestive tract. If asbestos fibers do not interact with digestive tissue, they are presumably eliminated as waste without harmful effect upon the body.

The evidence bearing upon possible harm from ingestion of fibers falls into three areas: first, the court-sponsored tissue study, designed to measure whether asbestos fibers are present in the tissues of long-time Duluth residents; second, animal experiments designed to measure whether, as a biological phenomenon, fibers can penetrate the gastrointestinal mucosa and thus interact with body tissues; third, the increased incidence of gastrointestinal cancer among workers occupationally exposed to asbestos, and the hypothesis that this increase may be due to the ingestion of fibers initially inhaled.

a.   The Tissue Study

Recognizing the complete lack of any direct evidence (epidemiological or otherwise) on the issue of whether the ingestion of fibers poses a risk, the trial court directed that a tissue study be conducted to determine whether the tissues of long-time Duluth residents contain any residue of asbestos-like fibers.

The study sought to analyze by electron microscope the tissues of recently deceased Duluth residents who had ingested Duluth water for at least 15 years; that is, approximately since the beginning of Reserve's operations. As a "control" check on results, tissue samples were obtained from the deceased residents of Houston, Texas, where the water is free of asbestos fibers. Although this study was necessarily expedited, plaintiffs' principal medical witness, Dr. Selikoff, testified to the sound design of the study and expressed his belief that it would yield significant information.

One of the court-appointed experts, Dr. Frederick Pooley, in explaining the results of the study, stated that he found that the tissues of the Duluth residents were virtually free of any fibers which could be attributed to the Reserve discharge. Dr. Brown said of this study:

> It is my conclusion, from the tissue study, that residents of Duluth have not been found to have asbestiform fibers in their tissues when compared with Houston. * * *

* * * [P]laintiffs argued, and the district court agreed, that because the specimens of tissue represented only a microscopically minute body area, the actual presence of fibers may have been overlooked.

We note that this limitation had not seemed dispositive prior to the study when Dr. Selikoff commented:

> I would think we should find some fibers there. We're looking for needles in a haystack, but that's all right, we should find needles in the haystack with all the difficulties of the study, the technical difficulties, if we examine sufficiently large numbers of samples in some instances we should find some fibers there.

The district court decided, and we agree, that the study cannot be deemed conclusive in exonerating the ingestion of fibers in Lake Superior water as a hazard. The negative results must, however, be given some weight in assessing the probabilities of harm from Reserve's discharge into water. The results also weigh heavily in indicating that no emergency or imminent hazard to health exists. Thus, while this study crucially bears on the determination of whether it is necessary to close Reserve down immediately, the negative results do not dispose of the broader issue of whether the ingestion of fibers poses some danger to public health justifying abatement on less immediate terms.

b. Animal Studies and Penetration of the Gastrointestinal Mucosa

At a somewhat more theoretical level, the determination of whether ingested fibers can penetrate the gastrointestinal mucosa bears on the issue of harm through ingestion. If penetration is biologically impossible, then presumably the interaction of the fibers with body tissues will not occur.

This medical issue has been investigated through experiments with animals which, unfortunately, have produced conflicting results. For example, Reserve witness Dr. Davis reported on his experiment in feeding crocidolite and chrysotile asbestos to rats for varying periods of up to six months. He killed the rats at the end of the period and examined their gastrointestinal tissues for evidence of fibers. At the time of trial, light and electron microscopy has so far revealed no evidence of fibers in the tissues.

Plaintiffs, however, cited contrary studies. Research by George Westlake, in which rats were fed a diet including chrysotile fibers, indicated that fibers had traveled through the colon wall and accumulated in the area of the mesothelium. Pontrefact, who injected chrysotile fibers into the stomachs of rats, found that fibers had dispersed throughout the body tissues.

On this conflicting scientific evidence, Dr. Brown testified that the Westlake and Pontrefact studies provide some support for the hypothesis that asbestos fibers can penetrate the gastrointestinal mucosa.[46]

c. *Excess Gastrointestinal Cancer Among the Occupationally Exposed*

The affirmative evidence supporting the proposition that the ingestion of fibers poses a danger to health focuses on the increased rate of gastrointestinal cancer among workers occupationally exposed to asbestos dust. Plaintiffs' experts attribute this excess incidence of gastrointestinal cancer to a theory that the asbestos workers first inhaled the asbestos dust and thereafter coughed up and swallowed the asbestos particles.

The attribution of health harm from ingestion rests upon a theoretical basis. As Dr. Selikoff explained, there are several possible explanations for the increased evidence of gastrointestinal cancer, some of which do not involve ingestion. Moreover, as noted previously, the excess rates of gastrointestinal cancer are generally "modest" and substantially lower than the excess rates of mesothelioma and lung cancer associated with inhalation of asbestos dust. Also, the experts advised that an analysis of a small exposed population may produce statistically "unstable" results.

The existence of an excess rate of gastrointestinal cancer among asbestos workers is a matter of concern. The theory that excess cancers may be attributed to the ingestion of asbestos fibers rests on a tenable medical hypothesis. Indeed, Dr. Selikoff testified that ingestion is the "probable" route accounting for the excess in gastrointestinal cancer. The

---

[46] We note from the record that while attempts to induce tumors in experimental animals through the inhalation of fibers have succeeded, attempts to induce tumors by ingestion have generally failed. Reserve witness Dr. Smith ventured the opinion, based on such studies, that there is no proof that the ingestion of fibers causes cancer in man. The failure to induce animal tumors by ingestion cannot be dispositive on the issue of whether the ingestion of fibers poses a risk to humans. This is because, as a general matter, animal cancer susceptibility is not directly equivalent to human experience, and, more particularly, because the studies so far undertaken may be criticized for various shortcomings in experimental design. Thus, one of Reserve's own witnesses, Dr. Wright, testified that at least one of the studies may be criticized for using too few animals over too brief an experimental time.

occupational studies support the proposition that the ingestion of asbestos fibers can result in harm to health.

2.   Level of Exposure Via Ingestion

The second primary uncertainty with respect to ingestion involves the attempt to assess whether the level of exposure from drinking water is hazardous. Of course, this inquiry is handicapped by the great variation in fiber counts, and Dr. Brown's admonition that only a qualitative, and not a quantitative, statement can be made about the presence of fibers.

In spite of these difficulties, the district court found that the level of exposure resulting from the drinking of Duluth water was "comparable" to that found to cause gastrointestinal cancer in asbestos workers. The court drew this finding from an elaborate calculation by Dr. Nicholson in which he attempted to make a statistical comparison between the fibers probably ingested by an asbestos worker subject to an excess risk of gastrointestinal cancer with the probable number of amphibole fibers ingested by a Duluth resident over a period of 18 years. * * * As is evident, this calculation is beset by several uncertainties. * * * Reserve witness Dr. Gross performed a calculation similar to Dr. Nicholson's, but using somewhat different assumptions, and concluded that Duluth water would have to contain several hundred million fibers/liter and be ingested for 60 years before an exposure comparable with occupational levels would be reached.

The comparison has other weaknesses, for without regard to the comparability of the gross exposure levels, the dynamics of the exposure process are markedly different. The vagaries attendant to the use of assumptions rather than facts result in comparisons which are of dubious accuracy. Thus, Dr. Brown testified that, if Nicholson's calculations were correct, he would conclude only that the risk was non-negligible.

The Nicholson comparison, although evidentially weak, must be considered with other evidence. The record does show that the ingestion of asbestos fibers poses some risk to health, but to an undetermined degree. Given these circumstances, Dr. Brown testified that the possibility of a future excess incidence of cancer attributable to the discharge cannot be ignored:[50]

> * * * I would say that it is conceivable that gastrointestinal cancers can develop from the ingestion of asbestos, and what I don't know, Your Honor, is just how low that level of ingestion must be before the likelihood of GI cancer becomes so remote as to

---

[50]   Since Lake Superior affords water supplies to an estimated 200,000 people of Duluth and other North Shore Minnesota municipalities, as well as Superior, Wisconsin, we think it is essential that the facts regarding the present disease effects of the discharge be accurately stated. As our review below demonstrates, we conclude that there is no evidence on a scientific or medical basis showing that Duluth residents experience an excess rate of cancer attributable to Reserve's discharge.

be, for all intents and purposes, ignored as a real live possibility.
* * *

c.   Conclusion

The preceding extensive discussion of the evidence demonstrates that the medical and scientific conclusions here in dispute clearly lie "on the frontiers of scientific knowledge."

The trial court, not having any proof of actual harm, was faced with a consideration of (1) the probabilities of any health harm and (2) the consequences, if any, should the harm actually occur. * * *

In assessing probabilities in this case, it cannot be said that the probability of harm is more likely than not. Moreover, the level of probability does not readily convert into a prediction of consequences. On this record it cannot be forecast that the rates of cancer will increase from drinking Lake Superior water or breathing Silver Bay air. The best that can be said is that the existence of this asbestos contaminant in air and water gives rise to a reasonable medical concern for the public health. The public's exposure to asbestos fibers in air and water creates some health risk. Such a contaminant should be removed.

The district court found that Reserve's discharge into Lake Superior violated sections 1160(c)(5) and (g)(1) of the Federal Water Pollution Control Act (FWPCA). These two provisions authorize an action by the United States to secure abatement of water discharges in interstate waters where the discharges violate state water quality standards and "endanger * * * the health or welfare of persons." § 1160(g)(1).

In the context of this environmental legislation, we believe that Congress used the term "endangering" in a precautionary or preventive sense, and, therefore, evidence of potential harm as well as actual harm comes within the purview of that term. We are fortified in this view by the flexible provisions for injunctive relief which permit a court "to enter such judgment and orders enforcing such judgment as the public interest and the equities of the case may require." 33 U.S.C. § 1160(c)(5). * * *

Concededly, the trial court considered many appropriate factors in arriving at a remedy, such as a) the nature of the anticipated harm, b) the burden on Reserve and its employees from the issuance of the injunction, c) the financial ability of Reserve to convert to other methods of waste disposal, and d) a margin of safety for the public.

An additional crucial element necessary for a proper assessment of the health hazard rests upon a proper analysis of the probabilities of harm.

With respect to the water, these probabilities must be deemed low for they do not rest on a history of past health harm attributable to ingestion but on a medical theory implicating the ingestion of asbestos fibers as a causative factor in increasing the rates of gastrointestinal cancer among asbestos workers. With respect to air, the assessment of the risk of harm rests on a higher degree of proof, a correlation between inhalation of asbestos dust and subsequent illness. But here, too, the hazard cannot be measured in terms of predictability, but the assessment must be made without direct proof. But, the hazard in both the air and water can be measured in only the most general terms as a concern for the public health resting upon a reasonable medical theory. Serious consequences could result if the hypothesis on which it is based should ultimately prove true.

A court is not powerless to act in these circumstances. But an immediate injunction cannot be justified in striking a balance between unpredictable health effects and the clearly predictable social and economic consequences that would follow the plant closing.

In addition to the health risk posed by Reserve's discharges, the district court premised its immediate termination of the discharges upon Reserve's persistent refusal to implement a reasonable alternative plan for on-land disposal of tailings.

During these appeal proceedings, Reserve has indicated its willingness to deposit its tailings on land and to properly filter its air emissions. At oral argument, Reserve advised us of a willingness to spend 243 million dollars in plant alteration and construction to halt its pollution of air and water. Reserve's offer to continue operations and proceed to construction of land disposal facilities for its tailings, if permitted to do so by the State of Minnesota, when viewed in conjunction with the uncertain quality of the health risk created by Reserve's discharges, weighs heavily against a ruling which closes Reserve's plant immediately.

Indeed, the intervening union argues, with some persuasiveness, that ill health effects resulting from the prolonged unemployment of the head of the family on a closing of the Reserve facility may be more certain than the harm from drinking Lake Superior water or breathing Silver Bay air.

Furthermore, Congress has generally geared its national environmental policy to allowing polluting industries a reasonable period of time to make adjustments in their efforts to conform to federal standards.

We believe that on this record the district court abused its discretion by immediately closing this major industrial plant. In this case, the risk of harm to the public is potential, not imminent or certain, and Reserve says it earnestly seeks a practical way to abate the pollution. A remedy should be fashioned which will serve the ultimate public weal by insuring clean air, clean water, and continued jobs in an industry vital to the nation's welfare. * * *

Reserve shall be given a reasonable time to stop discharging its wastes into Lake Superior. A reasonable time includes the time necessary for Minnesota to act on Reserve's present application to dispose of its tailings at Milepost 7 (Lax Lake site), or to come to agreement on some other site acceptable to both Reserve and the state. Assuming agreement and designation of an appropriate land disposal site, Reserve is entitled to a reasonable turn-around time to construct the necessary facilities and accomplish a changeover in the means of disposing of its taconite wastes.

NOTES

1.   On the basis of a evidence discussed in the opinion, would a court be justified in finding by the preponderance of the evidence that waterborne asbestos fibers cause cancer? If not, how can the court justify forcing Reserve to spend $243 million to end the problem?

2.   Consider the aftermath of the case:

Reserve's dumping in Lake Superior ended on March 16, 1980—five years (almost to the day) after the Eighth Circuit's en banc opinion, . . . and *eleven and a half years* after the Stoddard Report recommended disposal at essentially the same location. Intransigence, in the end, bought Reserve eleven years of continued pollution and continued profits.

The epilogue is cruelly ironic. Over the years, from the original permit hearings to Milepost 7, Reserve had maintained that an end to dumping in the lake would be an end to its operations. In fact, Reserve profitably shifted to on-land disposal in 1980—only to shut down two years later in the general economic downturn of 1982. [Ultimately, the plant] was sold in bankruptcy to Cyprus Mineral Company in 1989, which reopened the facility at half capacity as Northshore Mining Company. Northshore is now a wholly owned subsidiary of Cleveland-Cliffs, coincidentally one of the original owners of Reserve.

John S. Applegate, *The Story of Reserve Mining: Managing Scientific Uncertainty in Environmental Regulation*, in RICHARD J. LAZARUS & OLIVER A. HOUCK, ENVIRONMENTAL LAW STORIES 70 (2005).

3.   The *Reserve* decision received strong endorsement from the D.C. Circuit's opinion in *Ethyl Corp. v. EPA*, 541 F.2d 1 (D.C. Cir. 1976) (en banc). That case involved § 211(c)(1)(A) of the Clean Air Act, authorizing EPA to regulate gasoline additives whose emission products "will endanger the public health or welfare." Acting pursuant to this power, EPA determined that lead additives in gasoline presented "a significant risk of harm" to the public health and issued orders limiting the use of such additives. In upholding EPA's regulations, the court stressed that risk management involves policy judgments rather than simply factual determinations. Thus, the court accorded substantial deference to the EPA's conclusion. As the court explained:

Questions involving the environment are particularly prone to uncertainty. Technological man has altered his world in ways never before experienced or anticipated. The health effects of such alterations are often unknown, sometimes unknowable. While a concerned Congress has passed legislation providing for protection of the public health against gross environmental modifications, the regulators entrusted with the enforcement of such laws have not thereby been endowed with a prescience that removes all doubt from their decision making. Rather, speculation, conflicts, and theoretical extrapolation typify their every action. How else can they act, given a mandate to protect the public health but only a slight or nonexistent data base upon which to draw?

Thus, the court concluded that a rigorous, step-by-step proof of cause and effect should not be demanded where a statute is precautionary in nature, the evidence is on the frontiers of scientific knowledge, and regulations are designed to protect the public health. Instead, EPA may apply its expertise to draw conclusions from "suspected, but not completely substantiated" relationships between facts, from trends among facts, from theoretical projections, and so forth.

This approach was followed in numerous lower court opinions. For example, in *Lead Industries Association, Inc. v. EPA,* 647 F.2d 1130 (D.C.Cir.1980), the D.C. Circuit upheld a primary air quality standard for lead that incorporated an "adequate margin of safety." In setting the margin of safety, EPA had given no consideration to feasibility or cost. Moreover, the evidence of harm was unclear. Nevertheless, the court held that feasibility and cost were irrelevant and that EPA had acted properly in setting the margin of safety. The court explained that use of a margin of safety is an important method of protecting against effects that have not yet been uncovered by research and effects whose medical significance is a matter of disagreement. As the court also explained, "Congress has recently acknowledged that more often than not the 'margins of safety' that are incorporated into air quality standards turn out to be very modest or nonexistent, as new information reveals adverse health effects at pollution levels once thought to be harmless." The court also reiterated the need for deference to EPA's expert judgments on these issues. Finally, the court held that the margin of safety requirement could be fulfilled by making conservative decisions at various points in the regulatory process, rather than by determining a safe level and adding a percentage to that as the "margin of safety."

In general, these lower court decisions demonstrated a high degree of deference to EPA's expert judgment. The lower courts, by and large, gave little weight to questions of cost and feasibility when dealing with toxic chemicals. Finally, these courts recognized that administrative action was justified without a showing that harmful effects were more likely than not. Instead, these courts concluded that regulatory intervention was justified whenever a reasonable likelihood of danger could be found.

As mentioned in the introduction to this chapter, the Supreme Court first took up these issues in the context of occupational health regulation. Contrast the Supreme Court's approach in the following case with that of the lower courts in *Reserve Mining* and *Ethyl Lead*.

INDUSTRIAL UNION DEPARTMENT, AFL-CIO V. AMERICAN PETROLEUM INSTITUTE

Supreme Court of the United States, 1980.
448 U.S. 607, 100 S.Ct. 2844, 65 L.Ed.2d 1010.

JUSTICE STEVENS announced the judgment of the Court and delivered an opinion in which THE CHIEF JUSTICE and JUSTICE STEWART join and in Parts I, II, III-A–C and E of which JUSTICE POWELL joins.

I.

[In sections I and II of the opinion, Justice Stevens set out the background of the case. The case involved an OSHA regulation governing exposure to benzene. The Secretary of Labor had found that benzene was a carcinogen and that no known safe level existed. Hence, he lowered the permissible exposure level for workers from 10 ppm (parts per million) to 1 ppm, which he considered the lowest feasible level. OSHA (the Occupational Safety and Health Administration, within the Department of Labor) estimated the total costs of compliance as including $266 million in capital investments, $200 million in first-year start-up costs, and $34 million in annual costs. About 35,000 employees would benefit from the regulation. There were two arguably relevant statutory provisions. Section 3(8) of the Act, 29 U.S.C. § 652(8), defined an occupational safety and health standard as a standard setting any one of a variety of requirements "reasonably necessary or appropriate to provide safe or healthful employment or places of employment." Section 6(b)(5) of the Act, 29 U.S.C. § 655(b)(5), required the Secretary to set a standard for any toxic materials "which most adequately assures, to the extent feasible, that no employee will suffer material impairment of health or functional capacity."]

III.

A.

[This section sets out the statutes and the contentions of the parties. Essentially, industry argued that § 3(8) required a cost-benefit analysis, while the Secretary argued that he was "required to impose standards that either guarantee workplaces that are free from any risk of material health impairment, however small, or that come as close as possible to doing so without ruining entire industries."]

If the purpose of the statute were to eliminate completely and with absolute certainty any risk of serious harm, we would agree that it would be proper for the Secretary to interpret §§ 3(8) and 6(b)(5) in this fashion.

But we think it is clear that the statute was not designed to require employers to provide absolutely risk-free workplaces whenever it is technologically feasible to do so, so long as the cost is not great enough to destroy an entire industry. Rather, both the language and structure of the Act, as well as its legislative history, indicate that it was intended to require the elimination, as far as feasible, of significant risks of harm.

B.

By empowering the Secretary to promulgate standards that are "reasonably necessary or appropriate to provide safe or healthful employment and places of employment," the Act implies that, before promulgating any standard, the Secretary must make a finding that the workplaces in question are not safe. But "safe" is not the equivalent of "risk-free." There are many activities that we engage in every day—such as driving a car or even breathing city air—that entail some risk of accident or material health impairment; nevertheless, few people would consider these activities "unsafe." Similarly, a workplace can hardly be considered "unsafe" unless it threatens the workers with a significant risk of harm.

Therefore, before he can promulgate *any* permanent health or safety standard, the Secretary is required to make a threshold finding that a place of employment is unsafe—in the sense that significant risks are present and can be eliminated or lessened by a change in practices. This requirement applies to permanent standards promulgated pursuant to § 6(b)(5), as well as to other types of permanent standards. For there is no reason why § 3(8)'s definition of a standard should not be deemed incorporated by reference into § 6(b)(5). The standards promulgated pursuant to § 6(b)(5) are just one species of the genus of standards governed by the basic requirement. That section repeatedly uses the term "standard" without suggesting any exception from, or qualification of the general definition; on the contrary, it directs the Secretary to select "*the* standard"—that is to say, one of various possible alternatives that satisfy the basic definition in § 3(8)—that is most protective. Moreover, requiring the Secretary to make a threshold finding of significant risk is consistent with the scope of the regulatory power granted to him by § 6(b)(5), which empowers the Secretary to promulgate standards, not for chemical and physical agents generally, but for "*toxic* chemicals" and "*harmful* physical agents." * * *

In the absence of a clear mandate in the Act, it is unreasonable to assume that Congress intended to give the Secretary the unprecedented power over American industry that would result from the Government's view of §§ 3(8) and 6(b)(5), coupled with OSHA's cancer policy. Expert testimony that a substance is probably a human carcinogen—either because it has caused cancer in animals or because individuals have contracted cancer following extremely high exposures—would justify the conclusion that the substance poses some risk of serious harm no matter how minute the exposure and no matter how many experts testified that they regarded the risk as insignificant. That conclusion would in turn justify pervasive regulation limited only by the constraint of feasibility. In light of the fact that there are literally thousands of substances used in the workplace that have been identified as carcinogens or suspect carcinogens, the Government's theory would give OSHA power to impose enormous costs that might produce little, if any, discernible benefit.

If the Government was correct in arguing that neither § 3(8) nor § 6(b)(5) requires that the risk from a toxic substance be quantified sufficiently to enable the Secretary to characterize it as significant in an understandable way, the statute would make such a "sweeping delegation of legislative power" that it might be unconstitutional under the Court's reasoning in *Schechter Poultry Corp. v. United States,* 295 U.S. 495, 539, 55 S. Ct. 837, 847, 79 L. Ed. 1570, and *Panama Refining Co. v. Ryan,* 293 U.S. 388, 55 S. Ct. 241, 79 L. Ed. 446. A construction of the statute that avoids this kind of open-ended grant should certainly be favored.

C.

[In this section of the opinion, Justice Stevens argues that this construction of the statute is supported by the legislative history.]

D.

Given the conclusion that the Act empowers the Secretary to promulgate health and safety standards only where a significant risk of harm exists, the critical issue becomes how to define and allocate the burden of proving the significance of the risk in a case such as this, where scientific knowledge is imperfect and the precise quantification of risks is therefore impossible. The Agency's position is that there is substantial evidence in the record to support its conclusion that there is no absolutely safe level for a carcinogen and that, therefore, the burden is properly on industry to prove, apparently beyond a shadow of a doubt, that there is a safe level for benzene exposure. The Agency argues that, because of the uncertainties in this area, any other approach would render it helpless, forcing it to wait for the leukemia deaths that it believes are likely to occur before taking any regulatory action.

We disagree. As we read the statute, the burden was on the Agency to show, on the basis of substantial evidence, that it is at least more likely than not that long-term exposure to 10 ppm of benzene presents a significant risk of material health impairment. Ordinarily, it is the proponent of a rule or order who has the burden of proof in administrative proceedings. *See* 5 U.S.C. § 556(d). In some cases involving toxic substances, Congress has shifted the burden of proving that a particular

substance is safe onto the party opposing the proposed rule.[61] The fact that
Congress did not follow this course in enacting OSHA indicates that it
intended the Agency to bear the normal burden of establishing the need for
a proposed standard.

In this case OSHA did not even attempt to carry its burden of proof.
The closest it came to making a finding that benzene presented a
significant risk of harm in the workplace was its statement that the
benefits to be derived from lowering the permissible exposure level from 10
to 1 ppm were "likely" to be "appreciable." The Court of Appeals held that
this finding was not supported by substantial evidence. Of greater
importance, even if it were supported by substantial evidence, such a
finding would not be sufficient to satisfy the Agency's obligations under the
Act.

The inadequacy of the Agency's findings can perhaps be illustrated
best by its rejection of industry testimony that a dose-response curve can
be formulated on the basis of current epidemiological evidence and that,
even under the most conservative extrapolation theory, current exposure
levels would cause at most two deaths out of a population of about 30,000
workers every six years. In rejecting this testimony, OSHA made the
following statement:

> In the face of the record evidence of numerous actual deaths
> attributable to benzene-induced leukemia and other fatal blood
> diseases, OSHA is unwilling to rely on the hypothesis that at most
> two cancers every six years would be prevented by the proposed
> standard. By way of example, the Infante study disclosed seven
> excess leukemia deaths in a population of about 600 people over a
> 25-year period. While the Infante study involved higher exposures
> than those currently encountered, the incidence rates found by
> Infante, together with the numerous other cases reported in the
> literature of benzene leukemia and other fatal blood diseases,
> makes it difficult for OSHA to rely on the [witness'] hypothesis to
> assure that statutorily mandated protection for employees. In any
> event, due to the fact that there is no safe level of exposure to
> benzene and that it is impossible to precisely quantify the
> anticipated benefits, OSHA must select the level of exposure
> which is most protective of exposed employees.

There are three possible interpretations of OSHA's stated reason for
rejecting the witness' testimony: (1) OSHA considered it probable that a

---

[61]   *See Envtl. Defense Fund v. EPA*, 548 F.2d 998, 1004, 1012–1018 (1976), *cert. denied*, 431
U.S. 925, 97 S.Ct. 2199, 53 L.Ed.2d 239, where the court rejected the argument that the EPA has
the burden of proving that a pesticide is unsafe in order to suspend its registration under the
Federal Insecticide, Fungicide and Rodenticide Act. The court noted that Congress had
deliberately shifted the ordinary burden of proof under the APA, requiring manufacturers to
establish the continued safety of their products.

greater number of lives would be saved by lowering the standard from 10 ppm; (2) OSHA thought that saving two lives every six years in a work force of 30,000 persons is a significant savings that makes it reasonable and appropriate to adopt a new standard; or (3) even if the small number is not significant and even if the savings may be even smaller, the Agency nevertheless believed it had a statutory duty to select the level of exposure that is most protective of the exposed employees if it is economically and technologically feasible to do so. Even if the Secretary did not intend to rely entirely on this third theory, his construction of the statute would make it proper for him to do so. Moreover, he made no express findings of fact that would support his 1 ppm standard on any less drastic theory. Under these circumstances, we can hardly agree with the Government that OSHA discharged its duty under the Act.

Contrary to the Government's contentions, imposing a burden on the Agency of demonstrating a significant risk of harm will not strip it of its ability to regulate carcinogens, nor will it require the Agency to wait for deaths to occur before taking any action. First, the requirement that a "significant" risk be identified is not a mathematical straitjacket. It is the Agency's responsibility to determine, in the first instance, what it considers to be a "significant" risk. Some risks are plainly acceptable and others are plainly unacceptable. If, for example, the odds are one in a billion that a person will die from cancer by taking a drink of chlorinated water, the risk clearly could not be considered significant. On the other hand, if the odds are one in a thousand that regular inhalation of gasoline vapors that are two percent benzene will be fatal, a reasonable person might well consider the risk significant and take appropriate steps to decrease or eliminate it. Although the Agency has no duty to calculate the exact probability of harm, it does have an obligation to find that a significant risk is present before it can characterize a place of employment as "unsafe."[62]

Second, OSHA is not required to support its finding that a significant risk exists with anything approaching scientific certainty. Although the Agency's findings must be supported by substantial evidence, 29 U.S.C. § 655(f), § 6(b)(5) specifically allows the Secretary to regulate on the basis of the "best available evidence." As several courts of appeals have held, this provision requires a reviewing court to give OSHA some leeway where its findings must be made on the frontiers of scientific knowledge. Thus, so long as they are supported by a body of reputable scientific thought, the

---

[62]   In his dissenting opinion, Mr. Justice Marshall states that "when the question involves determination of the acceptable level of risk, the ultimate decision must necessarily be based on considerations of policy as well as empirically verifiable facts. Factual determinations can at most define the risk in some statistical way; the judgment whether that risk is tolerable cannot be based solely on a resolution of the facts." We agree. Thus, while the Agency must support its finding that a certain level of risk exists by substantial evidence, we recognize that its determination that a particular level of risk is "significant" will be based largely on policy considerations. At this point we have no need to reach the issue of what level of scrutiny a reviewing court should apply to the latter type of determination.

Agency is free to use conservative assumptions in interpreting the data with respect to carcinogens, risking error on the side of over-protection rather than under-protection.[63]

Finally, the record in this case and OSHA's own rulings on other carcinogens indicate that there are a number of ways in which the Agency can make a rational judgment about the relative significance of the risks associated with exposure to a particular carcinogen.[64] * * *

E.

Because our review of this case has involved a more detailed examination of the record than is customary, it must be emphasized that we have neither made any factual determinations of our own, nor have we rejected any factual findings made by the Secretary. We express no opinion on what factual findings this record might support, either on the basis of empirical evidence or on the basis of expert testimony; nor do we express any opinion on the more difficult question of what factual determinations would warrant a conclusion that significant risks are present which make promulgation of a new standard reasonably necessary or appropriate. The standard must, of course, be supported by the findings actually made by the Secretary, not merely by findings that we believe he might have made.

In this case the record makes it perfectly clear that the Secretary relied squarely on a special policy for carcinogens that imposed the burden on industry of proving the existence of a safe level of exposure, thereby avoiding the Secretary's threshold responsibility of establishing the need for more stringent standards. In so interpreting his statutory authority, the Secretary exceeded his power.

IV.

[In this part of the opinion, the court remanded a standard governing skin contact with benzene, for similar reasons.]

The judgment of the Court of Appeals remanding the petition for review to the Secretary for further proceedings is affirmed.

---

[63] Mr. Justice Marshall states that, under our approach, the agency must either wait for deaths to occur or must "deceive the public" by making a basically meaningless determination of significance based on totally inadequate evidence. Mr. Justice Marshall's view, however, rests on the erroneous premise that the only reason OSHA did not attempt to quantify benefits in this case was because it could not do so in any reasonable manner. As the discussion of the Agency's rejection of an industry attempt at formulating a dose-response curve demonstrates, however, the Agency's rejection of methods such as dose-response curves was based at least in part on its view that nothing less than absolute safety would suffice.

[64] For example, in the coke oven emissions standard, OSHA had calculated that 21,000 exposed coke oven workers had an annual excess mortality of over 200 and that the proposed standard might well eliminate the risk entirely. In other proceedings, the Agency has had a good deal of data from animal experiments on which it could base a conclusion on the significance of the risk. For example, the record on the vinyl chloride standard indicated that a significant number of animals had developed tumors of the liver, lung and skin when they were exposed to 50 ppm of vinyl chloride over a period of 11 months. One hundred out of 200 animals died during that period.

It is so ordered.

CHIEF JUSTICE BURGER, concurring.

This case presses upon the Court difficult unanswered questions on the frontiers of science and medicine. The statute and the legislative history give ambiguous signals as to how the Secretary is directed to operate in this area. The opinion by Mr. Justice Stevens takes on a difficult task to decode the message of the statute as to guidelines for administrative action.

To comply with statutory requirements, the Secretary must bear the burden of "finding" that a proposed health and safety standard is "reasonably necessary or appropriate to provide safe or healthful employment and places of employment." This policy judgment entails the subsidiary finding that the pre-existing standard presents a "significant risk" of material health impairment for a worker who spends his entire employment life in a working environment where exposure remains at maximum permissible levels. The Secretary's factual finding of "risk" must be "quantified sufficiently to enable the Secretary to characterize it as significant in an understandable way." Precisely what this means is difficult to say. But because these mandated findings were not made by the Secretary, I agree that the 1 ppm benzene standard must be invalidated. However, I would stress the differing functions of the courts and the administrative agency with respect to such health and safety regulation.

The Congress is the ultimate regulator and the narrow function of the courts is to discern the meaning of the statute and the implementing regulations with the objective of ensuring that in promulgating health and safety standards the Secretary "has given reasoned consideration to each of the pertinent factors" and has complied with statutory commands. Our holding that the Secretary must retrace his steps with greater care and consideration is not to be taken in derogation of the scope of legitimate agency discretion. When the facts and arguments have been presented and duly considered, the Secretary must make a policy judgment as to whether a specific risk of health impairment is significant in terms of the policy objectives of the statute. When he acts in this capacity, pursuant to the legislative authority delegated by Congress, he exercises the prerogatives of the legislature—to focus on only one aspect of a larger problem, or to promulgate regulations that, to some, may appear as imprudent policy or inefficient allocation of resources. The judicial function does not extend to substantive revision of regulatory policy. That function lies elsewhere—in Congressional and Executive oversight or amendatory legislation; although to be sure the boundaries are often ill defined and indistinct.

Nevertheless, when discharging his duties under the statute, the Secretary is well admonished to remember that a heavy responsibility burdens his authority. Inherent in this statutory scheme is authority to refrain from regulation of insignificant or de minimis risks. * * * When the administrative record reveals only scant or minimal risk of material health impairment, responsible administration calls for avoidance of extravagant, comprehensive regulation. Perfect safety is a chimera; regulation must not strangle human activity in the search for the impossible.

JUSTICE POWELL, concurring in part and in the judgment.

I join Parts I, II, III A–C, and III-E of the plurality opinion.[1] The Occupational Safety and Health Agency relied in large part on its "carcinogen policy"—which had not been adopted formally—in promulgating the benzene exposure and dermal contact regulation at issue in these cases. For the reasons stated by the plurality, I agree that §§ 6(b)(5) and 3(8) must be read together. They require OSHA to make a threshold finding that proposed occupational health standards are reasonably necessary to provide safe workplaces. When OSHA acts to reduce existing national consensus standards, therefore, it must find that (i) currently permissible exposure levels create a significant risk of material health impairment; and (ii) a reduction of those levels would significantly reduce the hazard.

Although I would not rule out the possibility that the necessary findings could rest in part on generic policies properly adopted by OSHA, see Thomas O. McGarity, Substantive and Procedural Discretion in Administrative Resolution of Science Policy Questions: Regulating Carcinogens in EPA and OSHA, 67 Geo. L. J. 729, 754–759 (1979), no properly supported agency policies are before us in this case.[3] I therefore agree with the plurality that the regulation is invalid to the extent it rests upon the assumption that exposure to known carcinogens always should be reduced to a level proven to be safe or, if no such level is found, to the lowest level that the affected industry can achieve with available technology.

[Justice Powell concluded that the agency had failed to carry its burden and also had failed to give adequate consideration to cost.]

JUSTICE REHNQUIST, concurring in the judgment.

In considering these alternative interpretations, my colleagues manifest a good deal of uncertainty, and ultimately divide over whether

---

[1]   These portions of the plurality opinion primarily address OSHA's special carcinogen policy, rather than OSHA's argument that it also made evidentiary findings. I do not necessarily agree with every observation in the plurality opinion concerning the presence or absence of such findings. I also express no view on the question whether a different interpretation of the statute would violate the nondelegation doctrine of *Schechter Poultry Corp. v. United States*, 295 U.S. 495 (1935), and *Panama Refining Co. v. Ryan*, 293 U.S. 388 (1935).

[3]   OSHA has adopted a formal policy for regulating carcinogens effective April 12, 1980. 45 Fed. Reg. 5002 (Jan. 22, 1980). But no such policy was in effect when the agency promulgated its benzene regulation. Moreover, neither the factual determinations nor the administrative judgments upon which the policy rests are supported adequately on this record alone. Accordingly, we have no occasion to consider the extent to which valid agency policies may supply a basis for a finding that health risks exist in particular cases.

the Secretary produced sufficient evidence that the proposed standard for benzene will result in any appreciable benefits at all. This uncertainty, I would suggest, is eminently justified, since I believe that this case presents the Court with what has to be one of the most difficult issues that could confront a decision-maker: whether the statistical possibility of future deaths should ever be disregarded in light of the economic costs of preventing those deaths. I would also suggest that the widely varying positions advanced in the briefs of the parties and in the opinions of Mr. Justice Stevens, The Chief Justice, Mr. Justice Powell, and Mr. Justice Marshall demonstrate, perhaps better than any other fact, that Congress, the governmental body best suited and most obligated to make the choice confronting us in this case, has improperly delegated that choice to the Secretary of Labor and, derivatively, to this Court. * * *

If we are ever to reshoulder the burden of ensuring that Congress itself makes the critical policy decisions, this is surely the case in which to do it. It is difficult to imagine a more obvious example of Congress simply avoiding a choice which was both fundamental for purposes of the statute and yet politically so divisive that the necessary decision or compromise was difficult, if not impossible, to hammer out in the legislative forge. Far from detracting from the substantive authority of Congress, a declaration that the first sentence of § 6(b)(5) of the OSHA constitutes an invalid delegation to the Secretary of Labor would preserve the authority of Congress. If Congress wishes to legislate in an area which it has not previously sought to enter, it will in today's political world undoubtedly run into opposition no matter how the legislation is formulated. But that is the very essence of legislative authority under our system. It is the hard choices, and not the filling in of the blanks, which must be made by the elected representatives of the people. When fundamental policy decisions underlying important legislation about to be enacted are to be made, the buck stops with Congress and the President insofar as he exercises his constitutional role in the legislative process.

I would invalidate the first sentence of § 6(b)(5) of the Occupational Safety and Health Act of 1970 as it applies to any toxic substance or harmful physical agent for which a safe level, that is a level at which "no employee will suffer material impairment of health or functional capacity even if such employee has regular exposure to [that hazard] for the period of his working life[,]" is, according to the Secretary, unknown or otherwise "infeasible." Absent further congressional action, the Secretary would then have to choose, when acting pursuant to § 6(b)(5), between setting a safe standard or setting no standard at all.[8] Accordingly, for the reasons stated

---

[8]   This ruling would not have any effect upon standards governing toxic substances or harmful physical agents for which safe levels are feasible, upon extant standards promulgated as "national consensus standards" under § 6(a), nor upon the Secretary's authority to promulgate "emergency temporary standards" under § 6(c).

above, I concur in the judgment of the Court affirming the judgment of the Court of Appeals.

JUSTICE MARSHALL, with whom JUSTICE BRENNAN, JUSTICE WHITE, and JUSTICE BLACKMUN join, dissenting.

In cases of statutory construction, this Court's authority is limited. If the statutory language and legislative intent are plain, the judicial inquiry is at an end. Under our jurisprudence, it is presumed that ill-considered or unwise legislation will be corrected through the democratic process; a court is not permitted to distort a statute's meaning in order to make it conform with the Justices' own views of sound social policy.

Today's decision flagrantly disregards these restrictions on judicial authority. The plurality ignores the plain meaning of the Occupational Safety and Health Act of 1970 in order to bring the authority of the Secretary of Labor in line with the plurality's own views of proper regulatory policy. The unfortunate consequence is that the Federal Government's efforts to protect American workers from cancer and other crippling diseases may be substantially impaired.

The first sentence of § 6(b)(5) of the Act provides:

"The Secretary, in promulgating standards dealing with toxic materials or harmful physical agents under this subsection, shall set the standard which most adequately assures, to the extent feasible, on the basis of the best available evidence, that no employee will suffer material impairment of health or functional capacity even if such employee has regular exposure to the hazard dealt with by such standard for the period of his working life."

In this case the Secretary of Labor found, on the basis of substantial evidence, that (1) exposure to benzene creates a risk of cancer, chromosomal damage, and a variety of nonmalignant but potentially fatal blood disorders, even at the level of 1 ppm; (2) no safe level of exposure has been shown; (3) benefits in the form of saved lives would be derived from the permanent standard; (4) the number of lives that would be saved could turn out to be either substantial or relatively small; (5) under the present state of scientific knowledge, it is impossible to calculate even in a rough way the number of lives that would be saved, at least without making assumptions that would appear absurd to much of the medical community; and (6) the standard would not materially harm the financial condition of the covered industries. The Court does not set aside any of these findings. Thus, it could not be plainer that the Secretary's decision was fully in accord with his statutory mandate "most adequately [to] assure[ ] * * * that no employee will suffer material impairment of health or functional capacity."

The plurality's conclusion to the contrary is based on its interpretation of [section 3(8)], which defines an occupational safety and health standard as one "which requires conditions * * * reasonably necessary or appropriate to provide safe or healthful employment." According to the plurality, a standard is not "reasonably necessary or appropriate" unless the Secretary is able to show that it is "at least more likely than not" that the risk he seeks to regulate is a "significant" one. Nothing in the statute's language or legislative history, however, indicates that the "reasonably necessary or appropriate" language should be given this meaning. Indeed, both demonstrate that the plurality's standard bears no connection with the acts or intentions of Congress and is based only on the plurality's solicitude for the welfare of regulated industries. And the plurality uses this standard to evaluate not the agency's decision in this case, but a strawman of its own creation. * * *

The plurality's discussion of the record in this case is both extraordinarily arrogant and extraordinarily unfair. It is arrogant because the plurality presumes to make its own factual findings with respect to a variety of disputed issues relating to carcinogen regulation. It should not be necessary to remind the Members of this Court that they were not appointed to undertake independent review of adequately supported scientific findings made by a technically expert agency. And the plurality's discussion is unfair because its characterization of the Secretary's report bears practically no resemblance to what the Secretary actually did in this case. Contrary to the plurality's suggestion, the Secretary did not rely blindly on some draconian carcinogen "policy." If he had, it would have been sufficient for him to have observed that benzene is a carcinogen, a proposition that respondents do not dispute. Instead, the Secretary gathered over 50 volumes of exhibits and testimony and offered a detailed and evenhanded discussion of the relationship between exposure to benzene at all recorded exposure levels and chromosomal damage, aplastic anemia, and leukemia. In that discussion he evaluated, and took seriously, respondents' evidence of a safe exposure level. * * *

In recent years there has been increasing recognition that the products of technological development may have harmful effects whose incidence and severity cannot be predicted with certainty. The responsibility to regulate such products has fallen to administrative agencies. Their task is not an enviable one. Frequently no clear causal link can be established between the regulated substance and the harm to be averted. Risks of harm are often uncertain, but inaction has considerable costs of its own. The agency must decide whether to take regulatory action against possibly substantial risks or to wait until more definitive information becomes available—a judgment which by its very nature cannot be based solely on determinations of fact.

Those delegations, in turn, have been made on the understanding that judicial review would be available to ensure that the agency's determinations are supported by substantial evidence and that its actions do not exceed the limits set by Congress. In the Occupational Safety and Health Act, Congress expressed confidence that the courts would carry out this important responsibility. But in this case the plurality has far exceeded its authority. The plurality's "threshold finding" requirement is nowhere to be found in the Act and is antithetical to its basic purposes. "The fundamental policy questions appropriately resolved in Congress * * * are *not* subject to re-examination in the federal courts under the guise of judicial review of agency action." Surely this is no less true of the decision to ensure safety for the American worker than the decision to proceed with nuclear power.

Because the approach taken by the plurality is so plainly irreconcilable with the Court's proper institutional role, I am certain that it will not stand the test of time. In all likelihood, today's decision will come to be regarded as an extreme reaction to a regulatory scheme that, as the Members of the plurality perceived it, imposed an unduly harsh burden on regulated industries. But as the Constitution "does not enact Mr. Herbert Spencer's Social Statics," *Lochner v. New York,* 198 U.S. 45, 75, 25 S. Ct. 539, 546, 49 L. Ed. 937 (1905) (Holmes, J., dissenting), so the responsibility to scrutinize federal administrative action does not authorize this Court to strike its own balance between the costs and benefits of occupational safety standards. I am confident that the approach taken by the plurality today, like that in *Lochner* itself, will eventually be abandoned, and that the representative branches of government will once again be allowed to determine the level of safety and health protection to be accorded to the American worker.

NOTES

1.   According to the plurality, a one in a thousand risk "might well" be significant. As applied to the general population of the United States, such a risk level would mean approximately 325,000 deaths (based on a 2017 population of approximately 325 million people). How many additional deaths beyond that level would be required before the plurality would find a risk *clearly* significant?

2.   Much of the disagreement in *Industrial Union Department* seemed to stem from varying concepts of risk. The plurality seemed to identify risk with the actual mortality rate caused by existing conditions. The plurality apparently would require the Secretary to find that it is more likely than not that the mortality rate would be "significant." In other words, the Secretary sets a threshold and acts only if the mortality rate exceeds that threshold. Justice Marshall, on the other hand, believes the Secretary should act if there is a substantial likelihood, even though less than 50%, that the mortality rate caused by existing conditions is significant. As a result, in the "grey area"

where the evidence is too unclear to permit the Secretary to reach a definite conclusion about risk or safety, Marshall would allow regulation but Stevens apparently would not. For a critique of the plurality's treatment of this issue, *see* Howard A. Latin, *The "Significance" of Toxic Health Risks: An Essay on Legal Decisionmaking Under Uncertainty*, 10 ECOLOGY L.Q. 339, 339–56, 381–86, 394 (1982).

3.   OSHA had promulgated the benzene standard under its "Generic Cancer Policy"—a policy that was under development at the time and provided a framework for OSHA to discharge its responsibilities to regulate occupational exposures to carcinogens in a timely manner. Under the Generic Cancer Policy, OSHA took the position that if there was evidence that the substance in question caused cancer in animals, the agency would set the Permissible Exposure Limit at the lowest feasible level (the most stringent level allowed under the statute). One reason OSHA adopted this policy was because of the large number of chemicals it needed to regulate. Proceeding with a full-blown risk assessment for each chemical would take decades, and, in any event, was subject to significant uncertainty. As OSHA put it:

> if this proposal [the Generic Cancer Policy] or something like it is not promulgated, with present resources the output of standards to protect American workers from carcinogens will never be adequate and may collapse by means of the futility of the effort. Indeed, to follow the present system for each and every individual substance and hazard would be, we contend, beyond the abilities of any agency, no matter how large a staff it may have.

Identification, Classification, and Regulation of Carcinogens Posing a Potential Occupational Carcinogenic Risk, 42 Fed. Reg. 54,148, 54,154 (Oct. 4, 1977). The plurality in *Benzene* appeared to have little sympathy for OSHA's Generic Cancer Policy and the decision effectively ended OSHA's efforts to develop such a policy. For a discussion of OSHA's Generic Cancer Policy in the context of a broader history of risk assessment in health, safety, and environmental law, see William Boyd, *Genealogies of Risk: Searching for Safety, 1930s–1970s*, 39 ECOL. L. Q. 895, 962–63 (2012).

4.   The further history of the benzene standard is instructive. Under pressure from a public interest group, OSHA returned to the benzene issue in 1983. It made a protracted but ultimately unsuccessful attempt to use a negotiated rulemaking to set a new standard. One complication was industry's fear that, by determining that benzene exposure presented a "significant risk" under the Supreme Court's standards, any new rule would encourage tort litigation against the industry. Moreover, the Reagan White House allegedly intervened to assure industry that it would have veto power over any new standard. When the negotiations broke down, the steelworker's union went to court again to force OSHA to begin a new rulemaking. OSHA finally issued the new standard in 1987. The new standard, 1 ppm, was the same as the one that the Supreme Court had remanded. OSHA's documentation of its risk determination was more complete, however. OSHA estimated that reducing

the standard from 10 ppm to 1 ppm would result in somewhere between 40 and 140 fewer leukemia deaths among lifelong workers in the affected industries. The agency was able to rely on three major new studies that had not been available at the time of its original rulemaking. *See* Charles Caldart, *Negotiation as a Means of Developing and Implementing Environmental and Occupational Health and Safety Policy,* 23 HARV. ENVTL. L. REV. 141, 165–68 (1999). However, later studies suggest that even exposures below 1 ppm may have adverse health effects. *See Factory Study Shows Low Levels of Benzene Reduce Blood Cell Counts,* 306 SCI. 1665 (2004).

     5.   A year later, in *American Textile Mfrs Inst., Inc. v. Donovan,* 452 U.S. 490 (1981), the Court briefly considered the application of the *Benzene* standard. This case involved a disease called byssinosis, more commonly known as "brown lung" disease. The disease is primarily caused by the inhalation of cotton dust, a byproduct of textile manufacturing. One study showed that over 25% of the sample of cotton workers suffered at least some form of the disease, while 35,000 workers suffer from the most disabling form. In a footnote early in the opinion, the Court considered whether OSHA had complied with *Industrial Union Department* in promulgating a standard to govern cotton dust:

> OSHA amended its Cancer Policy to "carry out the Court's interpretation of the Occupational Safety and Health Act of 1970 that consideration must be given to the significance of the risk in the issuance of a carcinogen standard and that OSHA must consider all relevant evidence in making these determinations." 46 Fed. Reg. 4889, col. 3 (1981). Previously, although lacking such evidence as dose response data, the Secretary presumed that no safe exposure level existed for carcinogenic substances. Following this Court's decision, OSHA deleted those provisions of the Cancer Policy which required the "automatic setting of the lowest feasible level" without regard to determinations of risk significance.

> In distinct contrast with its Cancer Policy, OSHA expressly found that "exposure to cotton dust presents a significant health hazard to employees," and that "cotton dust produced significant health effects at low levels of exposure." In addition, the agency noted that "grade 1/2 byssinosis and associated pulmonary function decrements are significant health effects in themselves and should be prevented in so far as possible." In making its assessment of significant risk, OSHA relied on dose response curve data (the Merchant Study) showing that 25% of employees suffered at least Grade $^1/_2$ byssinosis at a 500 ug/m3 PEL, and that 12.7% of all employees would suffer byssinosis at the 200 ug/m 3PEL standard. Examining the Merchant Study in light of other studies in the record, the agency found that "the Merchant Study provides a reliable assessment of health risk to cotton textile workers from cotton dust." OSHA concluded that the "prevalence of byssinosis should be significantly reduced" by the 200 ug/m 3PEL. * * * It is difficult to

imagine what else the agency could do to comply with this Court's decision in *Industrial Union Department v. American Petroleum Institute.*

452 U.S. at 505–06 n.25, 101 S. Ct. at 2488–89 n.25. In the next section, we will consider the major issue in the *Cotton Dust* case: once a significant risk is identified, should the agency use cost-benefit analysis to determine the level of protection?

B. ECONOMIC APPROACHES

The economic perspective on environmental regulation has become increasingly influential, though it remains controversial. One of the major impacts of economic analysis has been the growing use of cost-benefit analysis (CBA). You may or may not find cost-benefit analysis an appealing technique, but there can be little question about its practical significance.

Shortly after taking office, President Reagan signed Executive Order 12,291, 46 Fed. Reg. 13,193 (1981), aimed at improving the efficiency of informal rulemaking by executive agencies. Section 2 directed that "major" regulations not be promulgated unless, "taking into account affected industries [and] the condition of the national economy," the potential benefits to society outweigh potential costs, and net benefits are at a maximum. Review of agency cost-benefit analyses was conducted by the Office of Management and Budget. In 1993, President Clinton issued Executive Order 12,866, maintaining the basic approach but attempting to streamline the process of OMB review. The rule was intended to reduce the number of regulations sent to OMB for approval and to make OMB's review more flexible. *See* Ellen Siegler, *Executive Order 12866: An Analysis of the New Executive Order on Regulatory Planning and Review*, 24 ENVTL. L. REP. 10070 (1994).

The George W. Bush Administration pursued cost-benefit analysis with particular fervor:

> [T]he battle continued to rage when President George W. Bush appointed John D. Graham, a strong proponent of cost-benefit analysis from the Harvard Center for Risk Analysis, to head the Office of Information and Regulatory Affairs (OIRA) in the Office of Management and Budget. This nomination was strongly supported by regulated industries and equally strongly opposed by public interest groups. From that position, to which he was confirmed in late 2001, Graham has overseen the centralized review process for health and safety regulations. To the chagrin of public interest groups and the joy of industry-funded think tanks, OIRA greatly stemmed the flow of health, safety and environmental regulation during the Bush Administration. Although EPA promulgated several important regulations, most

of which were required by statute, OSHA did not promulgate a single significant health standard during the entire four years.

Thomas O. McGarity, *The Story of the Benzene Case: Judicially Imposed Regulatory Reform Through Risk Assessment*, in RICHARD J. LAZARUS & OLIVER A. HOUCK, ENVIRONMENTAL LAW STORIES 169 (2005). Upon taking office, President Obama rescinded President Bush's executive orders on cost-benefit analysis. Essentially, the government then reverted to the Clinton-era version of the cost-benefit mandate. To the surprise of many observers, the Obama Administration turned out to be a staunch supporter of cost-benefit analysis, requiring rigorous documentation in support of proposed regulations.

President Donald J. Trump added two executive orders to supplement Executive Order 12,866. Executive Order 13,771 requires that "for every one new regulation issued, at least two prior regulations be identified for elimination." Executive Order 13,777 directs federal agencies to designate a regulatory reform officer to "oversee the implementation of regulatory reform initiatives," and to create a regulatory reform task force to evaluate existing regulations and make recommendations to the agency head regarding their repeal, replacement, or modification, consistent with applicable law. For discussion of the implementation of these orders, see Daniel Farber, *Regulatory Analysis in Anti-Regulatory Times* (forthcoming 2019), available at https://ssrn.com/abstract=3302206. Perhaps the most controversial aspect of the Trump administration's approach to cost-benefit analysis has been the EPA's efforts to reduce and even eliminate the use of "co-benefits " (that is, ancillary benefits, such as reductions of particulate matter, that result from a regulatory action directed at different pollutants), such as mercury or greenhouse gases. These issues are discussed in more detail in Chapter 6, *infra*.

Whether you feel favorable or hostile toward environmental economics, a basic understanding of cost-benefit analysis is important for any environmental lawyer. An examination of the details would obviously be well beyond the scope of this chapter, but the following brief notes will at least introduce you to some of the basic concepts. The "cost" side of CBA is relatively straightforward, since it normally involves immediate economic impacts that (at least in theory) are readily determined. But the "benefit" side can be more complex. We will consider two difficulties on the benefit side of the analysis: the difficulty of determining monetary measures for environmental benefits and the fact that these benefits often accrue in the future while costs are more immediate.

Valuation Issues. Let's suppose we wanted to do a cost-benefit analysis for a method of ending some form of water pollution. On the benefit side of the equation, we would need to assign values, based on willingness to pay, for the elimination of this source of pollution. Some of these values would be relatively easy to determine, given the necessary scientific information—for example, loss in profits to fishing boats caused by pollution. (At least, the calculations would be straightforward in theory, although in litigation expert witnesses may differ sharply with each other about these lost profit issues.)

For most of the regulations we will consider in this book, the big valuation issue is how to put a monetary value on reductions in mortality risks. Without worrying right now about the technicalities, we could assign monetary values to different levels of risk by looking at how much consumers are willing to pay for safer products, or how much income workers are willing to give up for safer jobs, or at how much travel time people are willing to sacrifice for the safety benefits of driving more slowly. All of these would be different ways of determining the market value of safety.

If people demand $1,000 in return for being exposed to a one in a thousand risk of death, it's conventional to say that the "value of life" is $1 million. This is a bit misleading, since they probably wouldn't be willing to commit suicide for that amount of money! To express this distinction, economists often speak of the value of a statistical (as opposed to individual) life. To assign a value of $1 million per statistical life is the same as saying that people would demand $1 in return for running a one-in-a-million chance of death.

Discounting Future Benefits. Often, the costs and benefits of a regulatory measure occur at different times. When the costs accrue today but the benefits are in the future, we need some method of taking the time factor into account. Global warming or endangered species provide obvious examples because the effects of our policy choices are multi-generational. Long-term delayed harms are ubiquitous, however, in environmental law. For this reason, discounting plays a key part in the economic analysis of environmental regulation.

The basic idea of discounting is simple. If we invest $1 today at a 7.2% interest rate, it will produce $2 in ten years. Turning this around, we can "discount" that $2 in ten years at the same interest rate, concluding that the "present value" of $2 receivable in ten years is $1 today. Making this adjustment allows us to compare different investments whose payoffs have varying time profiles. Thus, suppose we are comparing two different contracts. If one contract pays $1.50 today, using the same 7.2% interest rate as above, we know that it is a better deal than another which pays $2 in ten years, because we can take the $1.50, invest it, and have more than $2 in ten years. The shorthand way of saying this is that present value of the first contract is $1.50, while the present value of the other is only $1.

Over long time periods, the results of changes in discount rates are enormous, as Cass Sunstein explains, "[i]f a human life is valued at $8 million, and if an agency chooses a 10% discount rate, a life saved 100 years from now is worth only $581." Cass R. Sunstein, *Cost-Benefit Default Principles*, 99 MICH. L. REV. 1651, 1711 (2001). Thus, what seems at first blush to be a niggling technical issue turns out to have grave significance in evaluating long-term regulatory decisions. Discounting is particularly controversial in the multigenerational context. For a review of the debate, *see* Daniel A. Farber, *From Here to Eternity*, 2003 U. ILL. L. REV. 289 (2003).

In the setting of occupational health, both valuation and discounting are issues in cost-benefit analysis. Valuation involves the problem discussed above: setting the "price of a statistical life." Discounting is relevant because there is a lag time, often several decades, between exposure to a carcinogen and symptoms of cancer.

But should we use cost-benefit analysis at all in this setting? Begin by considering the following case, where the Supreme Court gave its view of the statute.

AMERICAN TEXTILE MANUFACTURERS INSTITUTE, INC. v. DONOVAN

Supreme Court of the United States, 1981.
452 U.S. 490, 101 S.Ct. 2478, 69 L.Ed.2d 185.

JUSTICE BRENNAN delivered the opinion of the Court.

The principal question presented in this case is whether the Occupational Safety and Health Act requires the Secretary, in promulgating a standard pursuant to § 6(b)(5) of the Act, to determine that the costs of the standard bear a reasonable relationship to its benefits. Relying on §§ 6(b)(5) and 3(8) of the Act, petitioners urge not only that OSHA must show that a standard addresses a significant risk of material health impairment, but also that OSHA must demonstrate that the reduction in risk of material health impairment is significant in light of the costs of attaining that reduction. Respondents on the other hand contend that the Act requires OSHA to promulgate standards that eliminate or reduce such risks "to the extent such protection is technologically and economically feasible." * * *

The starting point of our analysis is the language of the statute itself. § 6(b)(5) of the Act provides:

> The Secretary, in promulgating standards dealing with toxic materials or harmful physical agents under this subsection, shall set the standard which most adequately assures, *to the extent feasible,* on the basis of the best available evidence, that no employee will suffer material impairment of health or functional capacity even if such employee has regular exposure to the hazard dealt with by such standard for the period of his working life.

Although their interpretations differ, all parties agree that the phrase "to the extent feasible" contains the critical language in § 6(b)(5) for purposes of this case.

The plain meaning of the word "feasible" supports respondents' interpretation of the statute. According to Webster's Third New International Dictionary of the English Language, "feasible" means "capable of being done, executed, or effected." Accord, The Oxford English Dictionary 116 (1933) ("Capable of being done, accomplished or carried out"); Funk & Wagnalls New "Standard" Dictionary of the English Language 903 (1957) ("That may be done, performed or effected"). Thus, § 6(b)(5) directs the Secretary to issue the standard that "most adequately assures * * * that no employee will suffer material impairment of health," limited only by the extent to which this is "capable of being done." In effect then, as the Court of Appeals held, Congress itself defined the basic relationship between costs and benefits, by placing the "benefit" of worker health above all other considerations save those making attainment of this "benefit" unachievable. Any standard based on a balancing of costs and benefits by the Secretary that strikes a different balance than that struck by Congress would be inconsistent with the command set forth in § 6(b)(5). Thus, cost-benefit analysis by OSHA is not required by the statute because feasibility analysis is.[29] * * *

Even though the plain language of § 6(b)(5) supports this construction, we must still decide whether § 3(8), the general definition of an occupational safety and health standard, either alone or in tandem with § 6(b)(5), incorporates a cost-benefit requirement for standards dealing with toxic materials or harmful physical agents. § 3(8) of the Act provides:

> The term "occupational safety and health standard" means a standard which requires conditions, or the adoption or use of one or more practices, means, methods, operations, or processes, *reasonably necessary or appropriate* to provide safe or healthful employment and places of employment.

Taken alone, the phrase "reasonably necessary or appropriate" might be construed to contemplate some balancing of the costs and benefits of a standard. Petitioners urge that, so construed, § 3(8) engrafts a cost-benefit analysis requirement on the issuance of § 6(b)(5) standards, even if

---

[29] In this case we are faced with the issue whether the Act requires OSHA to balance costs and benefits in promulgating a *single* toxic material and harmful physical agent standard under § 6(b)(5). Petitioners argue that without cost-benefit balancing, the issuance of a single standard might result in a "serious misallocation of the finite resources that are available for the protection of worker safety and health," given the other health hazards in the workplace. This argument is more properly addressed to other provisions of the Act which may authorize OSHA to explore costs and benefits before deciding between issuance of several standards regulating different varieties of health and safety hazards, e.g., § 6(g) of the Act, 29 U.S.C. § 655(g); *see Industrial Union Department v. American Petroleum Institute, supra,* 448 U.S., at 644, 100 S.Ct., at 2865; see also Case Comment, 60 B.U.L.R. 115, 122, n. 52, or for promulgating other types of standards not issued under § 6(b)(5). We express no view on these questions.

§ 6(b)(5) itself does not authorize such analysis. We need not decide whether § 3(8), standing alone, would contemplate some form of cost-benefit analysis. For even if it does, Congress specifically chose in § 6(b)(5) to impose separate and additional requirements for issuance of a subcategory of occupational safety and health standards dealing with toxic materials and harmful physical agents; it required that those standards be issued to prevent material impairment of health *to the extent feasible.* Congress could reasonably have concluded that *health* standards should be subject to different criteria than *safety* standards because of the special problems presented in regulating them.

Agreement with petitioners' argument that § 3(8) imposes an additional and overriding requirement of cost-benefit analysis on the issuance of § 6(b)(5) standards would eviscerate the "to the extent feasible" requirement. Standards would inevitably be set at the level indicated by cost-benefit analysis, and not at the level specified by § 6(b)(5). For example, if cost-benefit analysis indicated a protective standard of 1000 ug/m 3PEL, while feasibility analysis indicated a 500 ug/m3 PEL, the agency would be forced by the cost-benefit requirement to choose the less stringent point. We cannot believe that Congress intended the general terms of § 3(8) to countermand the specific feasibility requirement of § 6(b)(5). Adoption of petitioners' interpretation would effectively write § 6(b)(5) out of the Act. We decline to render Congress' decision to include a feasibility requirement nugatory, thereby offending the well-settled rule that all parts of a statute, if possible, are to be given effect. Congress did not contemplate any further balancing by the agency for toxic material and harmful physical agents standards, and we should not "impute to Congress a purpose to paralyze with one hand what it sought to promote with the other."

[In the remaining portions of the opinion, the Court concluded that: (1) its construction of the statute was supported by the legislative history, and (2) the agency's finding that its cotton dust standard was feasible was supported by substantial evidence. Justice Stewart dissented from the substantial evidence holding. Justice Rehnquist, in an opinion joined by Chief Justice Burger, reiterated his view that the "feasibility" standard is no standard at all, and hence is unconstitutional.]

NOTES

1.   The upshot of the Court's two OSHA opinions is that risk and cost are separated: the agency first decides if there is currently a "significant risk," and then it regulates to decrease that risk to the extent feasible. From an economist's point of view, this leads to odd results, since a minor risk might be worth regulating if eliminating the risk is cheap enough, whereas a major risk might not be worth regulating if the solution would be disproportionately expensive (even though not enough to bankrupt the industry). The upshot of

the Court's decisions is that the final level of environmental quality depends in part on the current level of risk rather than achieving the risk level with the best tradeoff between costs and benefits.

But if we think in terms of incentives for regulators and industry, perhaps something can be said for the Court's approach: it screens minor risks out of the regulatory process entirely, thereby saving administrative resources and limiting the possibility of an industry being targeted for purely political reasons. It also gives industry an incentive to reduce risks voluntarily below the "significant" level so as to avoid more onerous regulations later. By using separate qualitative standards to assess risk and cost, rather than demanding calculation of a precise ratio, the Court's approach might be more responsive to the uncertainties surrounding risk regulation.

2. The *Benzene/Cotton Dust* approach was reaffirmed in *American Trucking Association* Chapter 5, page 338, *infra*. The Court held that the Clean Air Act's standard of "requisite to protect public health" was sufficiently clear to be a valid delegation of authority and that it precluded cost-benefit analysis. For some thoughts about the decision's implications, *see* Cass R. Sunstein, *Regulating Risks After* ATA, 2001 Sup. Ct. Rev. 1 (2001). On the other hand, in *Entergy Corp. v. Riverkeeper*, page 627, *infra,* the Supreme Court seemed willing to stretch statutory language in order to allow a form of cost-benefit analysis (determining whether costs were disproportionate to benefits).

3. Consider this critique of the feasibility approach:

If a standard with exceedingly high costs (or that would cause severe economic disruption) would also save thousands of lives, then society almost certainly would be better off even if the costs might seem unacceptably high. For example, government regulations eliminating lead from gasoline resulted in hundreds of millions of dollars in annual costs and appeared to threaten not only layoffs in the industrial firms that produced lead additives but also gasoline shortages during the transition to unleaded fuels. Nevertheless, these regulations also resulted in dramatic health benefits that substantially dwarfed the costs. If regulatory agencies had adhered to an approach that avoided all regulations that imposed costs exceeding a specified level or threatened economic dislocation, without any concern for the level of corresponding benefits, they may well have delayed or avoided phasing out lead additives in gasoline.

Cary Coglianese & Gary E. Marchant, *Shifting Sands: The Limits of Science in Setting Risk Standards,* 152 U. PA. L. REV. 1255, 1336 (2004). In addition, the authors observe, the feasibility approach allows agencies to "affirm standards that impose significant costs without proportional health protection benefits." They recommend cost-benefit analysis as a solution to these problems. See also Jonathan S. Masur and Eric A. Posner, *Against Feasibility Analysis,* 77 U. CHI. L. REV. 657 (2010). But this recommendation is also controversial. To explore this controversy, we begin with two articles providing contrasting viewpoints on the general question. Then we consider a third article focusing on the specific issue of climate change.

STEVE P. CALANDRILLO, RESPONSIBLE REGULATION: A SENSIBLE COST-BENEFIT, RISK VERSUS RISK APPROACH TO FEDERAL HEALTH AND SAFETY REGULATION
81 B.U. L. REV. 957 (2001).[1]

Federal health and safety regulations have saved or improved the lives of thousands of Americans, but protecting our citizens from risk entails significant costs. In a world of limited resources, we must spend our regulatory dollars responsibly in order to do the most we can with the money we have. Given the infeasibility of creating a risk-free society, this paper argues that a sensible cost-benefit, risk versus risk approach be taken in the design of U.S. regulatory oversight policy. The goal should always be to further the best interests of the nation, rather than to satisfy the narrow agenda of powerful industry or political forces. This entails designing safety regulations efficiently to maximize society's welfare, choosing the point where their marginal benefits equal their marginal costs—rather than simply asking whether total benefits exceed total costs in the aggregate. Federal regulatory oversight policy should also ask that proposed regulations compare the risks they reduce to the new risks they unintentionally create (substitution risks). Additionally, our citizens should be educated regarding systematic risk misperceptions, and regulatory agencies should make their risk assessments objectively. Moreover, most-likely scenarios must be addressed by responsible regulatory solutions, rather than the current practice of focusing on worst-case estimates. Finally, agencies should publish and justify their regulatory triggers and perform ex-post evaluations of their programs in an attempt to continuously improve the quality of regulatory design. * * *

"We live in a world of limited resources." "We can't place a dollar value on protecting human life or preserving our environment." Neither statement taken independently strikes the reader as particularly controversial—they both seem perfectly reasonable. Yet there is an inherent and unmistakable tension between the two, for no society has unlimited resources to devote to the protection of human health and the creation of a risk-free world. The questions become: Is it possible to balance the common sense concept of scarce public resources with our deep moral aversion to placing a dollar value on saving human lives? And, more importantly, how do we do it?

We would like to be able to protect every citizen from every harm in our society, but most understand this is neither possible nor financially

---

feasible. Federal environmental and safety regulations aimed at preventing harm have yielded tremendous benefits, but they carry staggering costs—on the order of half a trillion dollars annually! However, despite this reality, there is a startling disconnect between common sense notions of maximizing the effect of scarce resources and of actually putting that notion into practice in carrying out U.S. regulatory programs. Hypothetically, would it be worth tens of millions of dollars to save one person's life if President Bush were to tighten arsenic standards in drinking water to the level proposed by President Clinton in his last days in office? Or would that same money be better spent if it could save thousands of lives by providing subsidized food and prenatal care to low-income mothers and free vaccinations to their babies? If we allocated all our resources to preventing accidental deaths in one area, we would have nothing left over to spend to prevent cancer or to provide food, housing or medical care.

To a large degree, the problem is one of public perception. No politician wants to admit that "we can't save that elderly person's life or institute a proposed environmental protection program, because it will simply cost us too much money to do so." Yet, this cost-benefit rationale is inherent in countless personal decisions made every day, from what career to pursue to what city in which to reside. Similarly, in the regulatory arena, fiscal balancing of the costs against the benefits should play a role in responsible decisionmaking. The tradeoff between costs and results is always present, but we are sometimes gripped by a fear that prevents us from acknowledging it openly. This reluctance limits us as a society because it diverts resources from where they are most needed. Even worse, this diversion is not based on a well-articulated reason, but rather on a fear of the repercussions experienced by those who voice such opinions. For instance, can you imagine a Presidential candidate who said on election-day eve, "I want to do the greatest good for the greatest number, and that means I choose not to help you." Not likely.

This paper proposes that given the reality of limited public resources, America must efficiently reformulate its environmental and health regulatory policies in order to save and improve the most lives possible given the accompanying costs. This is not always going to be politically correct. It entails making tough choices and preferencing certain programs and policies over others, which necessarily implies that some causes will be sacrificed for the greater good. But I urge that given our reality, society must consider carefully how best to structure federal regulatory oversight policy—not how to make it perfect. Perfection is dangerous precisely because it cannot ever be achieved. This paper therefore concentrates on how to efficiently formulate government regulations under the constraint of limited resources, in the hope that such an approach will maximize the overall benefits to our society. * * *

[T]his paper outlines an alternative regulatory approach for America, proposing a sensible cost-benefit, risk versus risk approach to easing the tension between scarce public resources and the deontological value of protecting human lives. In analyzing this tradeoff, we as a caring, thoughtful society should require a cost-benefit analysis of all potential government regulation whether it is aimed at making our environment, air, water, food, or workplace safer. I take this cost-benefit notion one step further than most commentators by suggesting that not only should overall costs and benefits of potential programs be evaluated, but that government agencies must act to set the appropriate regulation at the level where marginal benefits equal marginal costs. Setting our regulatory triggers at this point will have a far greater impact on improving overall social welfare than an absolute cost-benefit comparison would. Most everyone in society should favor a form of regulation that maximizes the benefits minus the costs, and not one that merely asks whether the benefits exceed the costs in the aggregate. * * *

While the achievements made possible by executive oversight have been notable, the success of regulatory reform proposals may also implicitly depend upon rewriting the existing legislative mandates given to government agencies by Congress. Often, the relevant statutory authority governing the mission of U.S. regulatory agencies is oblivious to marginal cost-benefit assessments, or it may even prohibit such comparisons outright. For instance, the Occupational Safety and Health Administration ("OSHA") is charged with assuring "so far as possible [that] every working man and woman in the Nation [have] safe and healthful working conditions." This mandate ignores the fact that nothing can ever be made 100% safe, and that extreme safety precautions necessarily entail extreme costs. Instead, the congressional mandates given to federal regulatory bodies should require, or at a minimum, permit cost-benefit and risk-risk tradeoffs to be made. Such an approach will empower courts to enforce common sense notions about how to best allocate scarce public resources in order to benefit a greater number of our citizens than we do today. Modifying legislative mandates will also force regulatory decisionmakers to be accountable for the policy choices they make. * * *

Moreover, some have raised serious moral criticisms, openly deriding cost-benefit analysis as incurably insensitive to the intrinsic value of life.* * * This moral resistance also surfaces in the rhetoric of our politicians and in the language of our existing federal regulatory legislation. Our policies often eschew cost-benefit analysis as irresponsible and insensitive to the ultimate goal at hand, and instead opt for a world that should be made as safe as possible—whatever the costs may be.

I am the first to agree that there are serious problems that would make any marginal cost-benefit standard subject to potential manipulation and abuse. But that does not mean we should not try to improve upon what we currently have. The difficulty of measuring these values does not undermine the principle that responsible regulatory programs should focus their efforts where they can save the most lives given limited resources. We as a country would be foolhardy to choose to ignore cost, benefit and risk tradeoffs merely because of the difficulty in their assessment, because we would then be consciously deciding to do something less than the best we can. Thus, despite the valid concerns raised by critics, we must strive to conquer these problems if our ultimate goal is the betterment of society and the maximization of scarce resources.

Finally, we should bear in mind in conducting the foregoing regulatory oversight analysis that it is a matter of common sense that people weigh costs and benefits in making life decisions all the time. American businesses make cost-benefit and cost-effectiveness calculations daily. While individuals are understandably upset by public health and safety decisions that explicitly trade off lives for dollars, no one really wants to spend everything on safety. Policymakers should similarly be able to balance costs, benefits and risks openly in America's regulatory oversight policy. The choice is not between helping all of our citizens or helping none. Given limited resources, the government can only help some. This paper is therefore intended to provoke thought about how responsible, efficient regulatory policy can maximize the number and the value included within that "some."

NOTES

1. As we saw in the last section, estimating risk levels can be a difficult and uncertain exercise. How much of a problem is this for cost-benefit analysis? At what point do the uncertainties of cost-benefit analysis overwhelm its possible advantages?

2. For recent defenses of cost-benefit analysis, see John D. Graham, *Saving Lives Through Administrative Law and Economics*, 157 U. PA. L. REV. 395 (2008); W. Kip Viscusi, *Monetizing the Benefits of Risk and Environmental Regulation*, 33 FORDHAM URBAN L.J. 1003 (2006).

3. For an argument that cost-benefit analysis is compatible with an aggressive regulatory agenda, see RICHARD L. REVESZ & MICHAEL A. LIVERMORE, RETAKING RATIONALITY: HOW COST-BENEFIT ANALYSIS CAN BETTER PROTECT THE ENVIRONMENT AND OUR HEALTH (2008).

4. Quite apart from any practical problems with implementing cost-benefit analysis, some authors raise ethical objections to its use in risk management. These objections are the subject of the next article.

FRANK ACKERMAN AND LISA HEINZERLING, PRICING THE PRICELESS: COST-BENEFIT ANALYSIS OF ENVIRONMENTAL PROTECTION

150 U. PA. L. REV. 1553 (2002).[2]

Many analytical approaches to setting environmental standards require some consideration of costs and benefits. Even technology-based regulation, maligned by cost-benefit enthusiasts as the worst form of regulatory excess, typically entails consideration of economic costs. Cost-benefit analysis differs, however, from other analytical approaches in the following respect: it demands that the advantages and disadvantages of a regulatory policy be reduced, as far as possible, to numbers, and then further reduced to dollars and cents. In this feature of cost-benefit analysis lies its doom. Indeed, looking closely at the products of this pricing scheme makes it seem not only a little cold, but a little crazy as well.

Consider the following examples, which we are not making up. They are not the work of a lunatic fringe, but, on the contrary, they reflect the work products of some of the most influential and reputable of today's cost-benefit practitioners. We are not sure whether to laugh or cry; we find it impossible to treat these studies as serious contributions to a rational discussion.

Several years ago, states were in the middle of their litigation against tobacco companies, seeking to recoup the medical expenditures they had incurred as a result of smoking. At that time, W. Kip Viscusi—a professor of law and economics at Harvard and the primary source of the current $6.3 million estimate for the value of a statistical life—undertook research concluding that states, in fact, saved money as the result of smoking by their citizens.[2] Why? Because they died early! They thus saved their states the trouble and expense of providing nursing home care and other services associated with an aging population.

Viscusi didn't stop there. So great, under Viscusi's assumptions, were the financial benefits to the states of their citizens' premature deaths that, he suggested, 'cigarette smoking should be subsidized rather than taxed.'

Amazingly, this cynical conclusion has not been swept into the dustbin where it belongs, but instead recently has been revived: the tobacco company Philip Morris commissioned the well-known consulting group Arthur D. Little to examine the financial benefits to the Czech Republic of smoking among Czech citizens. Arthur D. Little International, Inc., found that smoking was a financial boon for the government—partly because, again, it caused citizens to die earlier and thus reduced government

---

[2]   W. Kip Viscusi, *Cigarette Taxation and the Social Consequences of Smoking* 47 (Nat'l Bureau of Econ. Research, Working Paper No. 4891, 1994), *available at* http://papers.nber.org/papers/w4891.pdf.

expenditure on pensions, housing, and health care. This conclusion relies, so far as we can determine, on perfectly conventional cost-benefit analysis.

There is more. In recent years, much has been learned about the special risks children face due to pesticides in their food, contaminants in their drinking water, ozone in the air, and so on. Because cost-benefit analysis has become much more prominent at the same time, there is now a budding industry in valuing children's health. Its products are often bizarre.

Take the problem of lead poisoning in children. One of the most serious and disturbing effects of lead contamination is the neurological damage it can cause in young children, including permanently diminished mental ability. Putting a dollar value on the (avoidable, environmentally caused) retardation of children is a daunting task, but economic analysts have not been deterred.

Randall Lutter, a frequent regulatory critic and a scholar at the AEI-Brookings Joint Center for Regulatory Studies, argues that the way to value the damage lead causes in children is to look at the amount parents of affected children spend on chelation therapy, a chemical treatment that is supposed to cause excretion of lead from the body.[7] Parental spending on chelation supports an estimated valuation of as low as $1100 per IQ point lost due to lead poisoning. Previous economic analyses by the EPA, based on the children's loss of expected future earnings, have estimated the value to be much higher—up to $9000 per IQ point. Based on his lower figure, Lutter claims to have discovered that too much effort is going into controlling lead: 'Hazard standards that protect children far more than their parents think is appropriate may make little sense'; thus, '[t]he agencies should consider relaxing their lead standards.'

In fact, Lutter presents no evidence about what parents think, only about what they spend on one rare variety of private medical treatment (which, as it turns out, has not been proven medically effective for chronic, low-level lead poisoning). Why should environmental standards be based on what individuals are now spending on desperate personal efforts to overcome social problems? * * *

What can it mean to say that saving one life is worth $6.3 million? Human life is the ultimate example of a value that is not a commodity and does not have a price. You cannot buy the right to kill someone for $6.3 million, nor for any other price. Most systems of ethical and religious belief maintain that every life is sacred. If analysts calculated the value of life itself by asking people what it is worth to them (the most common method

---

[7]   Randall Lutter, Valuing Children's Health: A Reassessment of the Benefits of Lower Lead Levels 3 (AEI-Brookings Joint Ctr. for Regulatory Studies, Working Paper No. 00–02, 2000), available at http://papers.ssrn.com/sol3/papers.cfm?abstract_id=243537.

of valuation of other environmental benefits), the answer would be infinite.
* * *

The standard response is that a value like $6.3 million is not actually a price on an individual's life or death. Rather, it is a way of expressing the value of small risks of death; for example, it is one million times the value of a one in a million risk. If people are willing to pay $6.30 to avoid a one in a million increase in the risk of death, then the 'value of a statistical life' is $6.3 million.

Unfortunately, this explanation fails to resolve the dilemma. It is true that risk (or 'statistical life') and life itself are distinct concepts. In practice, however, analysts often ignore the distinction between valuing risk and valuing life. Many regulations reduce risk for a large number of people and avoid actual death for a much smaller number. A complete cost-benefit analysis should, therefore, include valuation of both of these benefits. However, the standard practice is to calculate a value only for 'statistical' life and to ignore life itself.

The confusion between the valuation of risk and the valuation of life itself is embedded in current regulatory practice in another way as well. The Office of Management and Budget, which reviews cost-benefit analyses prepared by federal agencies pursuant to executive order, instructs agencies to discount the benefits of life-saving regulations from the moment of avoided death, rather than from the time when the risk of death is reduced. This approach to discounting is plainly inconsistent with the claim that cost-benefit analysis seeks to evaluate risk. When a life-threatening disease, such as cancer, has a long latency period, many years may pass between the time when a risk is imposed and the time of death. If monetary valuations of statistical life represented risk, instead of life, then the value of statistical life would be discounted from the date of a change in risk (typically, when a new regulation is enforced) rather than from the much later date of avoided actual death.

In acknowledging the monetary value of reducing risk, economic analysts have contributed to our growing awareness that life-threatening risk itself—and not just the end result of such risk, death—is an injury. But they have blurred the line between risks and actual deaths, by calculating the value of reduced risk while pretending that they have produced a valuation of life itself. The paradox of monetizing the infinite or immeasurable value of human life has not been resolved; it only has been glossed over. * * *

Finally, the economic valuation called for by cost-benefit analysis is fundamentally flawed because it demands an enormous volume of consistently updated information, which is beyond the practical capacity of our society to generate.

All attempts at valuation of the environment begin with a problem: the goal is to assign monetary prices to things that have no prices because they are not for sale. One of the great strengths of the market is that it provides so much information about real prices. For any commodity that actually is bought and sold, prices are communicated automatically, almost costlessly, and with constant updates as needed. To create artificial prices for environmental values, economists have to find some way to mimic the operation of the market. Unfortunately, the process is far from automatic, certainly not costless, and has to be repeated every time an updated price is needed. * * *

For the reasons we have discussed, there is nothing objective about the basic premises of cost-benefit analysis. Treating individuals solely as consumers, rather than as citizens with a sense of moral responsibility to the larger society, represents a distinct and highly contestable world view. Likewise, the use of discounting reflects judgments about the nature of environmental risks and citizens' responsibilities toward future generations that are, at a minimum, debatable. Because value-laden premises permeate cost-benefit analysis, the claim that cost-benefit analysis offers an 'objective' way to make government decisions is simply bogus.

Furthermore, as we have seen, cost-benefit analysis relies on a byzantine array of approximations, simplifications, and counterfactual hypotheses. Thus, the actual use of cost-benefit analysis inevitably involves countless judgment calls. People with strong, and clashing, partisan positions naturally will advocate that discretion in the application of this methodology be exercised in favor of their positions, further undermining the claim that cost-benefit analysis is objective.

Perhaps the best way to illustrate how little economic analysis has to contribute, objectively, to the fundamental question of how clean and safe we want our environment to be is to refer again to the controversy over cost-benefit analysis of the EPA's regulation of arsenic in drinking water. As Cass Sunstein has recently argued, the available information on the benefits of arsenic reduction supports estimates of net benefits from regulation ranging from less than zero up to $560 million or more.[44] The number of deaths avoided annually by regulation is, according to Sunstein, between zero and 112. A procedure that allows such an enormous range of different evaluations of a single rule is certainly not the objective, transparent decision rule that its advocates have advertised.

These uncertainties arise from the limited knowledge of the epidemiology and toxicology of exposure to arsenic as well as the controversial series of assumptions required for valuation and discounting of costs and (particularly) benefits. As Sunstein explains, a number of

---

[44]   Cass R. Sunstein, *The Arithmetic of Arsenic*, 90 GEO. L.J. 2255 (2002).

different positions, including most of those heard in the recent controversy over arsenic regulation, could be supported by one or another reading of the evidence.[46]

Some analysts might respond that this enormous range of outcomes is not possible if the proper economic assumptions are used—if, for example, human lives are valued at $6 million apiece and discounted at a five percent yearly rate (or, depending on the analyst, other favorite numbers). But these assumptions beg fundamental questions about ethics and equity, and one cannot decide whether to embrace them without thinking through the whole range of moral issues they raise. Yet once one has thought through these issues, there is no need then to collapse the complex moral inquiry into a series of numbers. Pricing the priceless merely translates our inquiry into a different, and foreign, language—one with a painfully impoverished vocabulary.

For many of the same reasons, cost-benefit analysis also generally fails to achieve the goal of transparency. Cost-benefit analysis is a complex, resource-intensive, and expert-driven process. It requires a great deal of time and effort to attempt to unpack even the simplest cost-benefit analysis. Few community groups, for example, have access to the kind of scientific and technical expertise that would allow them to evaluate whether, intentionally or unintentionally, the authors of a cost-benefit analysis have unfairly slighted the interests of the community or some of its members. Few members of the public can participate meaningfully in the debates about the use of particular regression analyses or discount rates which are central to the cost-benefit method.

The translation of lives, health, and nature into dollars also renders decision making about the underlying social values less rather than more transparent. As we have discussed, all of the various steps required to reduce a human life to a dollar value are open to debate and subject to uncertainty. However, the specific dollar values kicked out by cost-benefit analysis tend to obscure these underlying issues rather than encourage full public debate about them.

NOTES

1.   One question raised by Ackerman and Heinzerling is whether market valuations should be the basis for government policy. Arguably, the government's determination of the public interest might be based on different criteria than those that individuals use to make private choices. Is it rational for people to use different values as voters than as workers or consumers? Is it

---

[46]   Given this enormous range of uncertainty, it is hard to understand Sunstein's belief (expressed in the same article) that cost-benefit analysis is still useful for screening regulatory options. This could be true only if a significant number of serious proposals had costs that were many orders of magnitude greater than their benefits. As we have discussed, this is a widely held, but empirically false, view of environmental regulation.

paternalistic for the government to impose trade-offs (for example, more workplace safety but lower wages) that people would not voluntarily accept in the market?

2.   Is it morally offensive to put a dollar value on life? After all, we do make trade-offs between safety and cost all the time. Isn't cost-benefit analysis just a more systematic way of thinking about these trade-offs? Or does the use of cost-benefit analysis depersonalize our approach to these problems?

3.   An inter-agency task force provided a series of estimates of the "social cost of carbon" to guide government cost-benefit analyses. See http://epa.gov/oms/climate/regulations/scc-tsd.pdf. The estimates vary with the discount rate and the date. For instance, using a 5% discount rate, it would be worth spending hardly anything—only $4.70—to eliminate a ton of $CO2$ in 2015. On the other hand, with a 3% discount rate, the amount rises to $23.80, and at 2.5%, it rises again to $38.40. An alternative estimate, intended to give more weight to possibility of more extreme impacts, was $72.80 (at a 3% discount rate). The Trump Administration has disbanded the inter-agency taskforce and calculated the social cost of carbon to include only domestic, rather than global, costs. *See* Harvard Environmental and Energy Law Program, *The Social Cost of Carbon*, https://eelp.law.harvard.edu/2017/09/the-social-cost-of-carbon/. But how meaningful are these estimates? The following excerpt considers how cost-benefit analysis functions in the context of climate change policy.

DANIEL H. COLE, THE STERN REVIEW AND ITS CRITICS: IMPLICATIONS FOR THE THEORY AND PRACTICE OF BENEFIT-COST ANALYSIS
48 NAT. RESOURCES J. 53 (2008).[3]

In 2003, the United Kingdom's Chancellor of the Exchequer, Gordon Brown, appointed Nicholas Stern, an Oxford economist and former World Bank chief economist and senior vice president, as second permanent secretary at Her Majesty's (HM) Treasury. Two years later, Chancellor Brown asked Secretary Stern to head up an official governmental review of the economics of climate change. The UK Treasury published the Stern Review on the Economics of Climate Change on October 30, 2006.[2] It was not the first benefit-cost analysis (BCA) on climate change ever,[3] but it was the first such analysis to be issued with the imprimatur of a major government. Consequently, the Stern Review had unusually high political salience and potential to influence policy.

---

[3]   Copyright 2008 by Daniel H. Cole. Reprinted with permission of Natural Resources Journal, University of New Mexico School of Law.

[2]   Nicholas Stern, THE ECONOMICS OF CLIMATE CHANGE: THE STERN REVIEW (2007).

[3]   See, e.g., William R. Cline, THE ECONOMICS OF GLOBAL WARMING (1992); Robert O. Mendelsohn et al., *Country-Specific Market Impacts of Climate Change*, 45 CLIMATIC CHANGE 553 (2000); William D. Nordhaus & Joseph G. Boyer, WARMING THE WORLD: ECONOMIC MODELS OF GLOBAL WARMING (2000).

Unsurprisingly, politicians and NGOs that favor rapid and strong action to mitigate greenhouse gas emissions greeted the nearly 600-page Stern Review with uncritical adulation, while climate-change skeptics summarily bashed it. More serious academic critiques of the Review were not long in coming. Several well-respected economists have argued that the Review's assumptions, arguments, and recommendations are seriously flawed, even biased,[5] while others have read the Review more generously. In perhaps the most nuanced and interesting of all the reviews, Martin Weitzman deftly criticizes the Stern Review's assumptions and analysis, but goes on to suggest why, ultimately, the Review's conclusions might be sound.[7] Weitzman's analysis, in particular, has important implications for the practice of BCA as it applies to policies like climate change, which involve long time horizons, potentially catastrophic levels of harm, and very high levels of uncertainty.

One purpose of this article is to critically assess the Stern Review and its various reviews. Another is to explain that the disagreements over the quality of the Stern Review (among serious scholars without ostensible political or ideological agendas) largely reflect disagreements about how BCAs generally should—and should not—be done. To that end, the article focuses on the Stern Review's BCA from a process-oriented perspective and asks what producers and consumers of benefit-cost analyses can learn from the Stern Review and its critics about the theory and practice of benefit-cost analysis. The lessons are several, including many negative lessons about how benefit-cost analyses should not be done. Less obvious, but just as important, are one or two positive lessons from the Stern Review. The lessons, both positive and negative, relate to the selection of parameter values, including discount rates, and methods of estimating damages.* * *

In deriving its damage figures, the Stern Review employs standard economic assumptions from welfare economics theory, including the assumption of diminishing marginal utility of income in evaluating risks and future welfare. But then Stern deliberately courts controversy by choosing a very low pure rate of time preference (utility discount rate) of 0.1 percent per year. * * *

Based on its preferred parameter values, the Stern Review's analysis shows that under BAU (uncontrolled GHG emissions indefinitely into the future) the risks of climate change between 2100 and 2200 will be equivalent to about five percent of the gross global product each year, and possibly as high as 20 percent, "forever." As noted earlier, estimated

---

[5]   See, e.g., William D. Nordhaus, *A Review of the Stern Review on the Economics of Climate Change*, 45 J. ECON. LITERATURE 686 (2007); Partha Dasgupta, *Commentary: The Stern Review's Economics of Climate Change*, 199 NAT'L INST. ECON. Rev. 4 (2006); * * * Richard S.J. Tol, *The Stern Review of the Economics of Climate Change: A Comment*, 17 ENERGY & ENV'T 977 (2006) * * *.

[7]   *Martin Weitzman, A Review of the Stern Review on the Economics of Climate Change*, 45 J. ECON. LITERATURE 703, 717 (2007).

damages would be only one one-hundredth as large with different parameter values yielding r = 6 percent. [r is the discount rate, which includes the time preference and other factors.] This is not to say, however, that the Stern Review's parameter values were "wrong" or that its damage estimate is "too high." As the article later discusses, such conclusions involve ethical value judgments, which are inherently contestable. * * *

Next, the Stern Review authors assess the economics of mitigation/ stabilization. In accordance with IPCC TAR and more recent data, they find that stabilizing GHG concentrations at levels that would avoid very costly climate changes will require "deep emissions cuts of at least 25 percent by 2050," implying a nominal decline of 30 to 35 $GtCO_2$. To achieve that goal, emissions would peak during the next 10 to 20 years and then decline by between one percent and three percent per year. Stern Review estimates that cutting emissions 25 percent by 2050 would cost approximately one percent of annual global GDP (about $1 trillion in 2050), plus or minus three percent, and would stabilize concentration levels at between 500 to 550 ppm of carbon dioxide equivalent (CO_{2eq}). At concentration levels in that range, the most harmful effects of climate change would be averted. Stern calculates that by investing one percent of annual global GDP starting now and continuing potentially forever, the world could avert costs to annual global GDP of ten percent "forever." In the "worst case," climate change mitigation would yield net costs amounting to 3.4 percent of annual global GDP. In the "best case," climate change mitigation would add 3.9 percent net to annual global GDP. * * *

Compared to other studies, the Stern Review's discount rate is indeed very low, and its estimate of damages correspondingly high. Tol analyzed 28 published studies that provided 103 total estimates of the marginal damage costs of carbon dioxide emissions. The utility discount rates in those 28 studies generally ranged between one and three percent (with some cases of hyperbolic discounting). Tol's comparison found that the utility discount rate/pure rate of time preference starkly influences both the central estimate and the uncertainty:

> If we use a pure rate of time preference of 3 percent—corresponding to a social rate of discount of 4–5 percent, close to what most western governments use for most long-term investments—the combined mean estimate is $16/tC (ton of carbon), not exceeding $62/tC with a probability of 95 percent. Lower social rates of discount lead to higher estimates but particularly to greater uncertainty, but even for a 1 percent pure rate of time preference the combined mean is $51/tC. Even lower discount rates may be morally preferable, but are clearly out of line with common practice.

That last sentence is intriguing. If lower discount rates are "morally preferable" but "out of line with common practice," as Tol suggests they might be, which should be adjusted, the "morally preferable" discount rate or the "common practice"? As we shall see later, Weitzman presents a strong ethical argument that the discount rate should be made to comport to convention. But Weitzman also notes that structural uncertainties in climate change damage estimates might justify the selection of a very low discount rate (although he would prefer to deal with such structural uncertainties via the damage function, rather than the discount rate).

The Stern Review's estimate of $85/tCO$_{2eq}$ under BAU [business as usual] exceeded by more than a factor of five Tol's combined mean estimate from 28 previous studies. No wonder the Stern Review calls for quicker and steeper reductions in GHG emissions than any previous BCA. This is not to say, however, that the Stern Review's cost-estimate is necessarily wrong. Tol concedes that

> [t]he current generation of aggregate estimates may understate the true cost of climate change because they tend to ignore extreme weather events; exclude low probability/high consequence scenarios, such as a shut-down of the thermohaline circulation [basically the Gulf Stream] or a collapse of the West-Antarctic ice sheet; underestimate the compounding effect of multiple stresses; and ignore the costs of transition and learning.

Each of the factors missing from the earlier generation of aggregate estimates is present and accounted for in the Stern Review. That must justify a higher cost-estimate. How much higher? Tol does not tell us, but concludes that the Stern Review "overestimates the impacts of climate change, and therefore the benefits of emission reduction."

But why did the Stern Review authors choose such a low utility discount rate in the first place? Was their intent simply to manipulate cost estimates so as to justify more rapid and extreme measures to control GHG emissions? The Stern Review is replete with expressions of concern that earlier studies had underestimated the costs of climate change, but the authors do not attempt to justify the choice of a low discount rate based on that concern alone. Rather, they follow the lead of several other prominent economists such as Frank Ramsey, Amartya Sen, and Robert Solow in presenting affirmative and legitimate ethical reasons against anything higher than a minimal discount rate for estimating the costs of climate change. Ramsey famously argued that discounting is "ethically indefensible and arises merely from the weakness of the imagination." The late David Pearce argued that discounting is a "brute fact" because people are observed to discount for time and space in making individual investment/consumption decisions. But just because people are observed to do it does not make it right. Ramsey's point is that both the decision to discount and the choice of a social discount rate are not just matters of positive economics but normative ethics. Stern agrees with Ramsey that people should not discount for time and space. Indeed, the only reason the Stern Review uses a 0.1 percent pure rate of time preference, rather than a zero rate, is the risk of human extinction during the course of the current century.

The bottom-line question for present purposes is whether the Stern Review's pure rate of time preference is so low as to violate some presumed "best practice" standard. As a matter of theory and practice, this is a difficult question to answer. The choice of a social discount rate is inherently subjective and as Portney and Weyant have observed, "Those looking for guidance on the choice of discount rate could find justification [in the literature] for a rate at or near zero, as high as 20 percent, and any and all values in between." Thus, the Stern Review's choice of a discount rate close to zero does not seem invalid per se. That it deviates from the literature does not make it wrong, only deviant. We might conclude that deviance from an accepted norm would violate a duty of BCA producers not to impose their own values paternalistically on society. But it is not at all clear that such a norm (yet) exists. * * *

Although Weitzman strongly criticizes the Stern Review for its assumptions and analytical weaknesses, he is not as quick as other reviewers to denounce its conclusions or policy recommendations. To the contrary, he suggests that the Stern Review's value of r "may end up being more right than wrong when full accounting is made for the uncertainty of the discount rate itself, which arguably is the most important uncertainty of all in the economics of climate change" Why?

> The very same force of compound interest that makes costs and benefits a century from now seem relatively insignificant, and that additionally creates the "majority tilt" of a pain-postponing climate policy ramp of emissions reductions starting from a low gradual base [as in Nordhaus's model], also forces us to recognize the logic that over such long periods we should be using interest rates at the lower end of the spectrum of possible values.

Specifically, Weitzman suggests that uncertainty over which discount rates to use for the costs and benefits of climate change a century from now might reduce the value of r from six percent to as low as two percent, which is not far above the Stern Review's value of r. * * *

The "moral" drawn by Weitzman "is that the nature of the impacts of climate change determine[s] whether we should end up closer to using the risk-free rate or the economy-wide return on capital." But "trying to forecast costs and benefits of climate change scenarios a hundred years or so from now is more the art of inspired guesstimating by analogy than a science (imagine forecasting today's world a century ago)." Is Weitzman suggesting that "state of the art" economic analysis is not yet up to the task of dealing with a problem as potentially large and long-term as climate change? The last three sections of Weitzman's review of the Stern Review suggest that the answer to this question is a qualified yes.

The problem, in a nutshell, is the wide range of possible temperature increases under the IPCC's most current climate change models, including a five-percent possibility that temperature increases will equal or exceed 6 C° and a two-percent probability of increases equal to or greater than 8 C° within the next 100 to 200 years. Weitzman notes that "any honest economic modeler would have to admit" to complete uncertainty about the social, economic, and environmental effects of such a temperature increase because "such high temperatures have not existed for some tens of millions of years." * * * We don't even know how much we don't know about the probabilities. The structural uncertainties, Weitzman notes, are highly likely to matter more than the risk for "whomever wants to model optimal-expected-utility growth under endogenous greenhouse warming." * * *

Beyond the social discount rate and the factors that comprise it, concern about structural uncertainties might have broader implications about whether standard BCA remains the proper tool for making policy decisions concerning climate change. Structural uncertainties might, instead, favor the use of a "Safe Minimum Standards" (SMS) approach to regulatory decision making. SMS applies a relatively hard precautionary principle—harder, perhaps, than Weitzman's "generalized precautionary principle"—by establishing a floor "below which the flow of key ecosystem services should not be permitted to fall." The floor could be set to avoid the very kinds of potential discontinuities that complicate efforts to model climate change using traditional BCA. But just where should the floor be set? It would seem that the same structural uncertainties that vex conventional BCA would also create problems for SMS. The only difference is that SMS utilizes a hard precautionary principle according to which uncertainty would automatically support greater efforts at mitigation and stabilization. In other words, it builds in a higher level of risk aversion. Naturally, economists who prefer not to presume a high level of risk aversion would oppose the hard precautionary principle of SMS and would prefer BCA, either with or without Weitzman's presumably softer "generalized precautionary principle." Obviously, much work remains to be done to determine the best means of factoring risk aversion—in particular aversion to potentially catastrophic harms—into economic analyses. * * *

Anyone interested in BCA as a discipline should read both the Stern Review and its serious academic critics because they raise serious issues about the practice and practicability of BCA for long-run problems and policies with potentially severe consequences under high levels of Knightian uncertainty. Stern takes a strong position that such uncertainty is not an excuse for inaction, especially where the stakes are enormous, as is arguably the case with climate change. Whatever its analytical flaws, Stern is surely right about that most important point, as Weitzman notes.

NOTES ON COST-BENEFIT ANALYSIS AND CLIMATE CHANGE

1.   There are now about a dozen "integrated assessment" models that couple climate change predictions to economic analysis. These models differ in a number of dimensions: whether they focus on the energy sector or rely on a broad macroeconomic analysis, the degree to which they analyze localized versus average global impacts, and their treatment of uncertainty. The models differ in terms of three critical assumptions about the timing of abatement efforts, the types of policy instruments used, and the likelihood of technological innovation. Other relevant factors include the willingness of economic actors to substitute away from high carbon technologies and trends in energy efficiency.[4]

2.   There are similar difficulties in modeling the costs of mitigating and adapting to climate change. Most of the model results are in the range of two to five percent of GDP in 2050, but the range is from a four percent *gain* in GDP due to reduced use of carbon to a fifteen percent *loss* of GDP. A meta-analysis shows that key factors in explaining these differences are whether revenue from carbon taxes is recycled, what kinds of technological changes are assumed, whether shifts in energy sources have non-climate benefits, and whether the model includes international carbon trading, Many of the individual elements of the economic impact analysis are hotly disputed. For instance, economists hotly dispute the net effect of climate change on agriculture, with some finding an overall positive effect on U.S. agriculture (but with very large regional variations), while others find substantial negative effects.[5]

3.   The conventional account of the U.S. national interest regarding climate change may be incomplete. Our critique of the climate change winner perspective focuses, by contrast, on its curiously "isolationist" approach—its failure to consider, at least in any serious way, the possibility that many of the costs and burdens that other countries are likely to experience as a result of climate change will, to varying extents, spill over to the U.S. This could occur in the form of national security threats, which climate change will exacerbate in various regions of the world; economic spillovers, such as higher oil and other resource and commodity prices, supply shocks, demand shocks and disruption to financial markets; as well as spillovers that result from the spread of infectious disease and significant migration. A number of studies

---

[4]   Jason F. Shogren & Michael A. Toman, *How Much Climate Change is Too Much?*, *in* CLIMATE CHANGE ECONOMICS AND POLICY: AN RFF ANTHOLOGY 35, 42 (Michael A. Toman ed., 2001).

[5]   See Daniel A. Farber, *Modeling Climate Change and Its Impacts: Law, Policy, and Science*, 86 TEX. L. REV. 1655 (2008). For other critiques of the application of cost-benefit analysis to climate change, see Jonathan S. Masur and Eric A. Posner, *Climate Regulation and the Limits of Cost-Benefit Analysis*, 99 CAL. L. REV. 1557 (2011); Douglas A. Kysar, *Politics by Other Meanings*, 48 HOUS. L. REV. 43 (2011).

have now determined that climate change is likely to be a "threat multiplier" in precisely this way. For further discussion of these issues, see Andrew T. Guzman, OVERHEATED: THE HUMAN COST OF CLIMATE CHANGE (2013).

4.   Notwithstanding the formidable difficulties of estimating the costs of climate change, the U.S. government has attempted to do so. The Fourth National Climate Assessment, issued in November 2018, provided a range of different estimates of the costs of climate change for various sectors of the U.S. economy by the end of the 21st century. Under a scenario of moderate warming, the report estimated damages of $290 billion per year by 2090. More extreme warming resulted in damage estimates of $500 billion per year by 2090. See U.S. GLOBAL CHANGE RESEARCH PROGRAM, FOURTH NATIONAL CLIMATE ASSESSMENT, VOL. II: IMPACTS, RISKS, AND ADAPTATION IN THE UNITED STATES 1348–63 (Nov. 2018), https://www.globalchange.gov/nca4.

C. EQUITY-BASED APPROACHES

Risk-based approaches and economic approaches have one thing in common: they are both primarily interested in the cumulative degree of harm rather than on how the harm is distributed. As highlighted already by some of the introductory materials in Chapter 1, Environmental justice focuses on the distribution of environmental harms and the unevenness of environmental protection.

1. EVIDENCE OF UNEQUAL RISK LEVELS

RICHARD J. LAZARUS, PURSUING "ENVIRONMENTAL JUSTICE": THE DISTRIBUTIONAL EFFECTS OF ENVIRONMENTAL PROTECTION
87 NW. U. L. REV. 787, 792–96, 808, 812 (1993).[6]

Environmental protection confers benefits and imposes burdens in several ways. To the extent that the recipients of related benefits and burdens are identical, no problem of discrimination is presented (there may, of course, be other problems with the tradeoff). But identical recipients are rarely, if ever, the result. Hardly any laws provide Pareto optimality in the classic sense of making everyone better off and no one worse off. Virtually all laws have distributional consequences, including those laws designed to further a particular conception of the public interest. Problems of discrimination, therefore, may arise in the disparities between the distribution of benefits and their related burdens.[23]

---

[6]   Copyright © 1993 by Northwestern University, School of Law. Reprinted with permission.

[23]   Of course, the perception among developing nations of just such a disparity is what prompted many of them, during the recent United Nations Conference on the Environment and Development held in Rio De Janeiro, to demand monies from wealthier nations. The justification for these payments was to compensate the developing nations for the costs associated with their

The benefits of environmental protection are obvious and significant. A reduction in pollution decreases the public health risks associated with exposure to pollution. It also enhances public welfare by allowing greater opportunity for enjoyment of the amenities associated with a cleaner natural environment. Many would also contend that environmental protection furthers the human spirit by restoring balance between humankind and the natural environment. More pragmatically, environmental protection laws are the source of new jobs in pollution control industries. EPA recently estimated, for instance, that the recently amended Clean Air Act would result in the creation of 30,000 to 45,000 full-time equivalent positions during 1996–2000.

The burdens of environmental protection range from the obvious to the more subtle. They include the economic costs borne by both the producer and the consumer of goods and services that become more expensive as a result of environmental legislation. For consumers, product and service prices may increase; some may become unavailable because the costs of environmental compliance renders their production unprofitable; while other goods and services may be specifically banned because of their adverse impact on the natural environment. For those persons who produce goods and services made more costly by environmental laws, personal income may decrease, employment opportunities may be reduced or displaced, and certain employment opportunities may be eliminated altogether. Finally, environmental protection requires governmental expenditures, the source of which varies from general personal and corporate income taxes to special environmental taxes. These expenditures necessarily decrease public monies available for other social welfare programs.

The burdens of environmental protection, however, also include the redistribution of the risks that invariably occur with pollution control techniques that treat pollution following its production. For instance, air pollution scrubbers and municipal wastewater treatment facilities reduce air and water pollution, but only by creating a sludge that, when disposed, will likely impose risks on a segment of the population different than the segment which would have been exposed to the initial pollution in the air or water. Additionally, the incineration of hazardous wastes stored in drums and tanks converts a land disposal problem into an air pollution issue (leaving, of course, a sludge residue that presents a different land disposal problem), and thereby may change the identity of those in the general population exposed to the resulting pollution. Just transporting solid and hazardous wastes from one geographic area to another for treatment or storage results in a major redistribution of the risks associated with environmental protection. Indeed, such transportation,

---

taking action (for example, greater protection of tropical rain forests) that would provide environmental benefits to the entire world, including industrialized nations.

and the resulting shift of environmental risks, has been the recent subject of massive litigation, as various jurisdictions have sought to export their wastes or prevent the importation of waste from elsewhere.

Nor does the purported prevention of pollution, as opposed to its treatment, necessarily eliminate the distributional issue. "Pollution prevention" frequently depends upon production processes that reduce one kind of pollution by increasing another. For example, water pollution may increase as air pollution is decreased, or a decrease in the mining of one kind of natural resource may be limited or completely offset by the increase in mining of another. Such shifts in the type of pollution or activity allowed will almost invariably shift those risks arising with the "new" pollution or activity to different persons. Hence, pollution may decrease for society as a whole, yet simultaneously increase for certain subpopulations.

Racial minorities could therefore be disproportionately disadvantaged by environmental laws in a number of ways. For example, with regard to the benefits of environmental protection, the natural environments that are selected for protection may be less accessible, or otherwise less important, to minorities. This may be the result of priorities expressly established by statute, or by agency regulations or enforcement agenda.

Inequities in the ultimate distribution of environmental protection benefits may also result, paradoxically, from environmental improvement itself. A cleaner physical environment may increase property values to such an extent that members of a racial minority with fewer economic resources can no longer afford to live in that community. Indeed, the exclusionary impact of environmental protection can be more than just an incidental effect; it can be the raison d'etre, with environmental quality acting as a socially acceptable facade for attitudes that cannot be broadcast.

Minorities may at the same time incur a share of the burdens of environmental protection that are disproportionate to those benefits that they receive. Higher product and service prices may be regressive, as may some taxes depending on their form. Although whites are poorer in greater absolute numbers than nonwhites, the latter group is disproportionately poorer in terms of population percentages. Minorities may also more likely be the victims of reduced or eliminated job opportunities. Similarly, they may be less likely to enjoy the economic, educational, or personal positions necessary to exploit the new job opportunities that environmental protection creates. Finally, minorities may receive an unfair share of the environmental risks that are redistributed by environmental protection. Elimination of the risks in one location may result in the creation or increase of risks in another location where the exposure to minorities is greater. * * *

* * * Minority interests have traditionally had little voice in the various points of influence that strike the distributional balances necessary

to get environmental protection laws enacted, regulations promulgated, and enforcement actions initiated. The interest groups historically active in the environmental protection area include a variety of mainstream environmental organizations representing a spectrum of interests (conservation, recreation, hunting, wildlife protection, resource protection, human health), as well as a variety of commercial and industrial concerns. Until very recently, if at all, the implications for racial minorities of environmental protection laws have not been a focal point of concern for any of these organizations.

OMAR SALEEM, OVERCOMING ENVIRONMENTAL DISCRIMINATION: THE NEED FOR A DISPARATE IMPACT TEST AND IMPROVED NOTICE REQUIREMENTS IN FACILITY SITING DECISIONS

19 COLUMB. J. EVTL. L. 211, 213–19 (1994).[7]

In 1982, a predominately African-American community in Warren County, North Carolina, became the proposed site for a polychlorinated biphenyl (PCB) disposal facility. The decision to site the facility in Warren County ushered forth the first national African-American protest against hazardous waste siting practices. The local community, along with civil rights leaders, protested the siting of the facility. Despite efforts by the National Association for the Advancement of Colored People (NAACP) to secure a preliminary injunction to prohibit the siting of the facility—on the ground of racial discrimination—the facility was approved. The protest, however, led to a statewide review of hazardous waste siting procedures. North Carolina then passed a law barring additional sites in Warren County.

GAO Report

In response to the siting of the proposed facility in Warren County, Congressman Walter E. Fauntroy asked the Government Accounting Office (GAO) to determine the correlation between the location of hazardous waste landfills and the racial and economic status of the surrounding communities.[10] The GAO did so and found in pertinent part:

> There are four off-site hazardous waste landfills in [EPA] Region IV's eight States. Blacks make up the majority of the population in three of the four communities where the landfills are located. At least 26 percent of the population in all four communities have

---

[10]   U.S. General Accounting Office, *Siting of Hazardous Waste Landfills and Their Correlation With Racial and Economic Status of Surrounding Communities*, GAO/RCED-83–168 (June 1, 1983).

income below the poverty level and most of this population is Black.

An unrelated 1983 study presented similar data on the siting of solid waste facilities in Houston, Texas. The findings revealed solid waste facilities tended to be located in predominantly African-American neighborhoods.[12] Four years after the GAO report, the United Church of Christ Commission for Racial Justice (CRJ) published the report on toxic wastes and race in the United States.[13] The CRJ report, similar to the GAO report, examined the correlation between the location of hazardous waste landfills and the racial and economic status of surrounding communities. While the GAO report examined only the southeastern United States, the CRJ report examined the entire nation. The CRJ report concluded: "Race proved to be the most significant among variables tested in association with the location of commercial hazardous waste facilities. This represented a consistent national pattern." * * *

The GAO and CRJ reports nurtured a burgeoning movement that has been examining the functional relationship between race, poverty, and environmental hazards. The movement is called the "environmental justice movement." The term denotes an effort to broaden the goals of environmental protection to include providing a clean and safe environment where racial minorities and low-income people live and work. The movement seeks to identify and address "environmental racism" which has been defined to include "any policy, practice, or directive that differentially affects or disadvantages (whether intended or unintended) individuals, groups, or communities based on race or color [as well as] exclusionary and restrictive practices that limit participation by people of color in decision-making boards, commissions, and regulating bodies."[20]

EPA Actions and Reports

As part of their efforts, members of the environmental justice movement met with William K. Reilly, the U.S. Environmental Protection Agency [EPA] Administrator, in September 1990.[21] * * * As a result of this meeting the EPA subsequently formed the "Environmental Equity Workgroup" to "assess the evidence that racial minority and low-income communities bear a higher environmental burden than the general population, and consider what EPA might do about any identified

---

[12]   Robert D. Bullard, *Solid Waste and the Black Houston Community*, 53 SOC. INQUIRY 273 (1983).

[13]   United Church of Christ Commission for Racial Justice, Toxic Wastes and Race in the United States: A National Report on the Racial and Socio-Economic Characteristics of Communities With Hazardous Waste Sites (1987).

[20]   Robert Bullard, *The Threat of Environmental Racism*, 7 NAT. RESOURCES & ENV'T 23 (1993).

[21]   U.S. EPA, ENVIRONMENTAL EQUITY-REDUCING RISK FOR ALL COMMUNITIES 2 (June 1992).

disparities." The Workgroup consisted of senior-level officials from EPA regional offices and EPA headquarters. * * *

Although the GAO and CRJ reports were focal points, the movement is not limited to the siting of hazardous waste facilities. Other areas of concern include proposals to site incinerators, landfills, and nuclear waste facilities on Indian lands; farmworkers' exposure to pesticides; discharges from chemical plants; air pollution problems in minority communities; lead poisoning; workplace conditions; the exportation of hazardous waste to developing countries; placement of homes for the homeless; and international trade. * * *

In mid-1992 the EPA released its finding, which stated:

1.   There are clear differences between racial groups in terms of disease and death rates. There are also limited data to explain the environmental contribution to these differences * * *. The notable exception is lead poisoning.

2.   Racial minority and low-income populations experience higher than average exposures to selected air pollutants, hazardous waste facilities, contaminated fish, and agricultural pesticides in the workplace. Exposure does not always result in an immediate or acute health effect. High exposures, and the possibility of chronic effects, are nevertheless a clear cause for health concerns.

3.   Environmental and health data are not routinely collected and analyzed by income and race. Nor are data routinely collected on health risks posed by multiple industrial facilities, cumulative and synergistic effects, or multiple and different pathways of exposure * * *. However, risk assessment and risk management procedures can be improved to better take into account equity considerations.

4.   Great opportunities exist for EPA and other government agencies to improve communication about environmental problems with members of low-income and racial minority groups * * *.

5.   Since they have broad contact with affected communities, EPA's program and regional offices are well suited to address equity concerns * * *.

6.   Native Americans are a unique racial group that has a special relationship with the federal government and distinct environmental problems.[29]

---

[29]   Environmental Equity, supra note 21.

National Law Journal Findings

Beside government agencies, others were sparked into action by the efforts and advocacy of the environmental justice movement. For example, the *National Law Journal* examined the correlation between race and income and the EPA's enforcement of environmental laws. The resulting report revealed that not only are a disproportionate number of hazardous waste facilities located in low-income racial minority communities, but in addition, the EPA discriminates against minority communities in enforcing all federal environmental laws.[30] According to the *National Law Journal* report: 1) Penalties under hazardous waste laws at sites having the greatest proportion of white residents are 500% higher than penalties at sites with the greatest minority population, averaging $335,566 for white areas compared to $55,318 for minority areas. 2) The disparity under the toxic waste laws occurs by race alone, not income. 3) For all the federal environmental laws aimed at protecting citizens from air, water, and waste pollution, penalties in white communities are 46% higher than in minority communities. 4) Under the giant Superfund cleanup program, abandoned hazardous waste sites in minority areas take 20% longer to be placed on the national priority list than those in white areas. 5) In more than half of the ten autonomous regions that administer EPA programs around the country, action on cleanup at superfund sites begins 12% to 42% later at minority sites than at white sites. 6) At sites in minority communities, the EPA chooses "containment," the capping or walling off of a hazardous waste dump site, 7% more frequently than the cleanup method preferred under the law permanent "treatment"—to eliminate the waste or rid it of toxins. At sites in white neighborhoods, the EPA orders treatment 22% more often than containment.

NOTES

1.   Another study was reported in Vicki Been & Francis Gupta, *Coming to the Nuisance or Going to the Barrios? A Longitudinal Analysis of Environmental Justice Claims*, 24 ECOLOGY L.Q. 1 (1997). This study looked at the demographics of the 544 communities which in 1994 hosted active commercial hazardous waste treatment, storage, and disposal facilities (TSDFs). The authors looked first at the demographics of the communities at the time of the census taken immediately before they became hosts, then examined the demographic changes in each subsequent decade through the 1990 census. The authors summarized their findings as follows:

> [W]e found no substantial evidence that the facilities that began operating between 1970 and 1990 were sited in areas that were disproportionately African American. Nor did we find any evidence that these facilities were sited in areas with high concentrations of

---

[30]   Marianne Lavelle & Marcia Loyle, Unequal Protection—The Racial Divide in Environmental Law, NAT'L L.J., Sept. 21, 1992, at S1–S12.

the poor; indeed, the evidence indicates that poverty is negatively correlated with sitings. We did find evidence that the facilities were sited in areas that were disproportionately Hispanic at the time of the siting. The analysis produced little evidence that the siting of a facility was followed by substantial changes in a neighborhood's socioeconomic status or racial or ethnic composition. Finally, the analysis shows that the areas surrounding TSDFs currently are disproportionately populated by African Americans and Hispanics. *Id.* at 9.

2.   Thomas Lambert & Christopher Boerner, *Environmental Inequity: Economic Causes, Economic Solutions*, 14 YALE J. ON REG. 195 (1997), analyzed demographic characteristics around three types of industrial facilities and waste sites in and around St. Louis, Missouri: TSDFs, permitted solid waste landfills and incinerators, and inactive hazardous waste (CERCLA) sites. There were 167 facilities and sites in all. The authors found "no significant difference in poverty rates and percentages of minority residents between census tracts with active facilities (TSDFs, landfills, and incinerators) and those tracts without such facilities. Including inactive CERCLA waste sites in the data set, however, uncovered weak evidence that the percentages of poor and minority residents living near industrial and waste sites are significantly higher than the corresponding percentages living in tracts without facilities." The authors believed that they had "empirical support for the theory that housing values are closely related to existing environmental inequities, raising the possibility that siting decisions caused an influx of minority and poor residents, as opposed to the contrary causation assumptions made by environmental discrimination theorists." *Id.* at 203–204. As a solution to falling real estate values around facilities, the authors propose providing compensation to those who live near locally undesirable facilities so that, on balance, the surrounding property is not rendered less desirable. Possible forms of compensation include: (1) direct payments to affected landowners, (2) host fees which are paid into a community's general revenue fund to be used to finance a variety of public projects or to lower property taxes, (3) grants for improving local healthcare delivery and education, and (4) the provision of parks and other recreational amenities. *Id.* at 214.

3.   Another study, using more sophisticated statistical methods, considered both the effect of site location on housing values and the relationship between neighborhood composition and risk. It reached the following conclusions:

> [The statistical model] indicates that the price-risk tradeoff is higher for households in high-educated and high-income neighborhoods, and lower for households in neighborhoods with a high proportion of non-whites.* * * These results suggest that the welfare effects of risk reduction vary by neighborhood demographics, and a regulatory strategy based strictly on efficiency grounds would target these neighborhoods, increasing the concentration of environmental risk in low-educated, low-income, and high-nonwhite neighborhoods. * * *

By estimating the neighborhood characteristics that affect the level of risk exposure, I find that the level of risk is not a function of the income and education levels of the neighborhoods. Additionally, the level of risk is lower for neighborhoods with a large proportion of nonwhites. This could suggest that nonwhites have not been exposed to higher Superfund risks, or it could suggest that risk reduction efforts have been responsive to concerns of environmental racism. * * * Finally, this paper offers evidence that pollution is more likely in neighborhoods with a low propensity for collective action.

Ted Gayer, *Neighborhood Demographics and the Distribution of Hazardous Waste Risks: An Instrumental Variables Estimation*, 17 J. REG. ECON. 131, 152–53 (2000).

4.   Suppose that low-income and minority communities are exposed to higher levels of toxics, but that the cause is not bias or discrimination in the location of facilities. Should this unequal distribution of risks still be a concern? Or should we view the distribution as irrelevant, since someone else would be suffering the risks anyway? *See* Alice Kaswan, *Distributive Justice and the Environment*, 81 N.C. L. REV. 1031 (2003) (arguing that risk distribution should still be a concern).

2.   THE LEGAL IMPLEMENTATION OF ENVIRONMENTAL JUSTICE

In 1994, President Clinton signed Executive Order 12,898, Federal Actions to Address Environmental Justice in Minority Populations and Low-Income Populations, 59 FED. REG. 7629 (Feb. 16, 1994). The order provided that each federal agency "shall make achieving environmental justice part of its mission by identifying and addressing, as appropriate, disproportionately high and adverse human health or environmental effects of its programs, policies, and activities on minority populations and low-income populations in the United States and its territories and possessions." The Administrator of the EPA was directed to convene an interagency Federal Working Group on Environmental Justice, to assist each agency to develop an agency-wide environmental justice strategy. The Bush Administration left this order in effect but interpreted narrowly.

In 1995, EPA issued its environmental justice strategy, based on the principle that communities affected by decisions with environmental impacts should be actively involved in the decision-making process. The strategy calls for EPA to increase coordination with affected communities, state, tribal, and local governments, business, and nongovernmental organizations. To develop local knowledge bases necessary for effective participation in complex decision making, EPA would promote technical assistance programs and grants for minority and low-income areas. The Agency also would focus enforcement activities on minority and low-income areas suffering disproportionate environmental and health impacts. *See*

Terry Schnell & Kathleen Davis, *The Increased Significance of Environmental Justice in Facility Siting, Permitting*, 29 ENVTL. L. REP. 528, 529 (1998).

Pursuant to Executive Order 12,898 and Title VI of the Civil Rights Act of 1964, as amended, 42 U.S.C. §§ 2000d to 2000d–7, which prohibits discrimination under any program receiving federal financial assistance, EPA has begun to include environmental justice as a factor in its review of state permits under federally delegated programs pursuant to the Clean Air and Clean Water Acts and the Resource Conservation and Recovery Act. For further information about EPA's response to the executive order, *see* Denis Binder et al., *A Survey of Federal Agency Responses to President Clinton's Executive Order No. 12898 on Environmental Justice*, 31 ENVTL. L. REP. 11,133 (2001).

Environmental justice advocates saw Title VI of the 1964 Civil Rights Act as one of their most promising weapons. Title VI prohibits discrimination by recipients of federal funds, and the regulations under Title VI cover not only intentional discrimination but also actions having a disparate impact on minority groups. *See* Bradford C. Mank, *Is There a Private Cause of Action Under EPA's Title VI Regulations?: The Need to Empower Environmental Justice Plaintiffs*, 24 COLUM. J. ENVTL. L. 1 (1999). But the viability of private actions to enforce the Title VI regulations is doubtful. In *Alexander v. Sandoval*, 532 U.S. 275 (2001), the Court held that the Title VI regulations do not create a private cause of action. In dissent, however, Justice Stevens suggested that the decision had limited practical effect:

> [T]o the extent that the majority denies relief to the respondents merely because they neglected to mention 42 U.S.C. § 1983 in framing their Title VI claim, this case is something of a sport. Litigants who in the future wish to enforce the Title VI regulations against state actors in all likelihood must only reference § 1983 to obtain relief.

Id. at 1527. Soon afterwards, a federal appeals court rejected this theory. *See South Camden Citizens in Action v. New Jersey Dep't of Envtl. Prot.*, 274 F.3d 771 (3d Cir. 2001)*; see also Save Our Valley v. Sound Transit*, 335 F.3d 932 (9th Cir. 2003). The upshot is that evidence of intentional discrimination is critical. *See* Browne C. Lewis, *Changing the Bathwater and Keeping the Baby: Exploring New Ways of Evaluating Intent in Environmental Discrimination Cases*, 50 ST. LOUIS U.L.J. 469 (2006) (discussing the intent test and alternatives).

A related question involves the extent to which EPA has authority under various environmental statutes to consider environmental justice issues. For a discussion of the issue by two scholars advocating a broad interpretation of EPA's authority, *see* Richard J. Lazarus & Stephanie Tai,

Integrating Environmental Justice Into EPA Permitting Authority, 26 ECOLOGY L.Q. 617 (1999). According to a 2003 survey, of the 139 Title VI complaints received by EPA since 1993, seventy-five were rejected without investigation; twenty-six were accepted for investigation, but in none was timely evidence of discrimination found. The remaining thirty were still pending. Michael B. Gerrard, *EPA Dismissal of Civil Rights Complaints*, NY L.J., Nov. 28, 2003, at 3. Environmental justice received renewed emphasis, however, in the Obama Administration:

> Lisa Jackson, EPA's Administrator during President Obama's first term, has made environmental justice a key agency priority. The agency developed Plan EJ 2014 to guide the agency's achievement of environmental justice. The strategy is designed to better protect overburdened communities, empower those communities in environmental decision-making, and to establish stronger partnerships with the many governmental entities that likewise shape environmental outcomes, including tribal, state, and local governments. Substantively, the Plan encourages agencies to further integrate environmental justice in their rulemaking, permitting, compliance, and support for community-based programs. The Plan also recognizes that achieving environmental justice depends upon improving available tools, encouraging the development of scientific, legal, and information resources to support environmental justice outcomes, and fostering the development of mechanisms to channel those resources to disadvantaged communities. By encouraging all appropriate EPA programs to adopt an environmental justice initiative, the Plan also works to ensure that environmental justice is addressed throughout the agency.

Alice Kaswan, *Environmental Justice and Environmental Law*, 24 FORDHAM ENV. L. REV. 149 (2012–2013).

The Trump Administration has moved in a very different direction. President Trump's first EPA budget proposed to completely eliminate funding for the Agency's office of environmental justice. The head of the office, Mustafa Ali, who had been with the EPA since the 1990s, resigned in March of 2017. And, of course, ongoing efforts to relax, repeal, and/or replace existing regulations as well as cuts to enforcement in substantive programs dealing with air and water pollution, toxics, and hazardous substances could have significant environmental justice implications.

Another thrust of advocates of environmental justice is to provide opportunities for disadvantaged groups to participate in decision making in a meaningful way. Some possible approaches are discussed in Alejandro Esteban Camacho, *Mastering the Missing Voices: A Collaborative Model for Fostering Equality, Community Involvement and Adaptive Planning in*

Land Use Decisions, 24 STAN. ENV. L.J. 3 (2005); Sheila Foster, *Environmental Justice in an Era of Devolved Collaboration*, 26 HARV. ENV. L. REV. 459 (2002).

3.   EQUITY ISSUES AND GLOBAL CLIMATE CHANGE

Environmental justice is also relevant to climate change. Because, historically, the heaviest emissions have come from industrialized countries like the United States, while the heaviest impacts fall on poorer countries, claims for "climate justice" have already emerged. The following excerpt presents a critical appraisal of those claims.

ERIC POSNER AND CASS SUNSTEIN, CLIMATE JUSTICE
96 GEO. L.J. 1565 (2008).[8]

Let us assume, most starkly, that the United States would lose, on net, from a climate change agreement that is optimal from the standpoint of the world taken as a whole. As a matter of actual practice, the standard resolution of the problem is clear: The world should enter into the optimal agreement, and the United States should be given side-payments in return for its participation. The reason for this approach is straightforward. On conventional assumptions, the optimal agreement should be assessed by reference to the overall benefits and costs of the relevant commitments for the world. To the extent that the United States is a net loser, the world should act so as to induce it to participate in an agreement that would promote the welfare of the world's citizens, taken as a whole. With side-payments to the United States, of the kind that have elsewhere induced reluctant nations to join environmental treaties, an international agreement could be designed so as to make all nations better off and no nation worse off. Call this a form of international Paretianism. [Editor's note: A Pareto improvement is one that makes everyone involved better off than they would be otherwise.] Who could oppose an agreement based on international Paretianism?

Our puzzle is that almost everyone does so. No one is suggesting that the world should offer side-payments to the United States. Indeed, the United States is not even arguing for side-payments, perhaps on the ground that the argument would be regarded as preposterous. One reason involves distributive justice. The United States is the richest nation in the world, and many people would find it odd to suggest that the world's richest nation should receive compensation for helping to solve a problem faced by the world as a whole, and above all by poor nations. On this view, wealthy nations should be expected to contribute a great deal to solving the climate change problem; side-payments would be perverse. If ideas of distributive justice are at work, it might be far more plausible to suggest that nations

---

    8   Copyright 2008 by Eric Posner and Cass Sunstein. Reprinted by permission.

should pay China for agreeing to participate in a climate change agreement. And indeed, developing nations, including China, were given financial assistance as an inducement to reduce their emissions of ozone-depleting chemicals. Some people think that a climate change agreement should build on this precedent, and indeed the "Bali Roadmap" seems to do so, by suggesting financial assistance to developing nations. No one thinks that assistance to the United States, or to other wealthy countries, is in order.

But claims about distributive justice are only part of the story here. Corrective justice matters as well. The basic thought is that the largest emitters, above all the United States, have imposed serious risks on other nations. Surely it cannot be right for nations to request payments in return for ceasing to harm others. On the conventional view, wrongdoers should pay for the damage that they have caused and should be asked to stop. They should not be compensated for taking corrective action.

We shall raise serious questions about both accounts here. Rejecting international Paretianism, we agree that in many domains, resources should be redistributed from rich nations and rich people to poor nations and poor people. Such redistribution might well increase aggregate social welfare, since a dollar is worth more to a poor person than to a wealthy one; prominent nonwelfarist arguments also favor such redistribution. But significant greenhouse gas reductions are a crude and somewhat puzzling way of attempting to achieve redistributive goals. The arc of human history suggests that in the future, people are likely to be much wealthier than people are now. Why should wealthy countries give money to future poor people, rather than to current poor people? In any case, nations are not people; they are collections of people. Redistribution from wealthy countries to poor countries is hardly the same as redistribution from wealthy people to poor people. For one thing, many poor people in some countries will benefit from global warming, to the extent that agricultural productivity will increase and to the extent that they will suffer less from extremes of cold. For another thing, poor people in wealthy countries may well pay a large part of the bill for emissions reductions; a stiff tax on carbon emissions would come down especially hard on the poor.

The upshot is that if wealthy people in wealthy nations want to help poor people in poor nations, emissions reductions are unlikely to be the best means by which they might to do so. Our puzzle, then, is why distributive justice is taken to require wealthy nations to help poor ones in the context of climate change, when wealthy nations are not being asked to help poor ones in areas in which the argument for help is significantly stronger.

We also accept, for purposes of argument, the view that when people in one nation wrongfully harm people in another nation, the wrongdoers have a moral obligation to provide a remedy to the victims. It might seem to follow that the largest emitters, and above all the United States, have a special obligation to remedy the harms they have helped cause and certainly should not be given side-payments. But the application of standard principles of corrective justice to problems of climate change runs into serious objections. As we shall show, corrective justice arguments in the domain of climate change raise many of the same problems that beset such arguments in the context of reparations more generally. Nations are not individuals: they do not have mental states and cannot, except metaphorically, act. Blame must ordinarily be apportioned to individuals, and it is hard to blame all greenhouse gas-emitters for wrongful behavior, especially those from the past who are partly responsible for the current stock of greenhouse gases in the atmosphere.

Our principal submissions are that the distributive justice argument must be separated from the corrective justice argument, and that once the two arguments are separated, both of them face serious difficulties. If the United States wants to assist poor nations, reductions in greenhouse gas emissions are unlikely to be the best way for it to accomplish that goal. It is true that many people in poor nations are at risk because of the actions of many people in the United States, but the idea of corrective justice does not easily justify any kind of transfer from contemporary Americans to people now or eventually living in (for example) India and Africa.* * *

The current stock of greenhouse gases in the atmosphere is a result of the behavior of people living in the past. Much of it is due to the behavior of people who are dead. The basic problem for corrective justice is that dead wrongdoers cannot be punished or held responsible for their behavior, or forced to compensate those they have harmed. At first glance, holding Americans today responsible for the activities of their ancestors is not fair or reasonable on corrective justice grounds, because current Americans are not the relevant wrongdoers; they are not responsible for the harm.

Indeed, many Americans today do not support the current American energy policy and already make some sacrifices to reduce the greenhouse gas emissions that result from their behavior. They avoid driving, they turn down the heat in their homes, and they support electoral candidates who advocate greener policies. Holding these people responsible for the wrongful activities of people who lived in the past seems perverse. An approach that emphasized corrective justice would attempt to be more finely tuned, focusing on particular actors, rather than Americans as a class, which would appear to violate deeply held moral objections to collective responsibility. The task would be to distinguish between the contributions of those who are living and those who are dead.

The most natural and best response to this point is to insist that all or most Americans today benefit from the greenhouse gas emitting activities of Americans living in the past, and therefore it would not be wrong to require Americans today to pay for abatement measures. This argument is familiar from debates about slave reparations, where it is argued that Americans today have benefited from the toil of slaves 150 years ago. To the extent that members of current generations have gained from past wrongdoing, it may well make sense to ask them to make compensation to those harmed as a result. On one view, compensation can work to restore the status quo ante, that is, to put members of different groups, and citizens of different nations, in the position that they would have occupied if the wrongdoing had not occurred.

In the context of climate, however, this argument runs into serious problems. The most obvious difficulty is empirical. It is true that many Americans benefit from past greenhouse-gas-emissions, but how many benefit, and how much do they benefit? Many Americans today are, of course, immigrants or children of immigrants, and so not the descendants of greenhouse-gas-emitting Americans of the past. Such people may nonetheless gain from past emissions, because they enjoy the kind of technological advance and material wealth that those emissions made possible. But have they actually benefited, and to what degree? Further, not all Americans inherit the wealth of their ancestors, and even those who do would not necessarily have inherited less if their ancestors' generations had not engaged in the greenhouse-gas-emitting activities. The idea of corrective justice, building on the tort analogy, does not seem to fit the climate change situation.

Suppose that these various obstacles could be overcome and that we could trace, with sufficient accuracy, the extent to which current Americans have benefited from past emissions. As long as the costs are being toted up, the benefits should be as well, and used to offset the requirements of corrective justice. We have noted that climate change is itself anticipated to produce benefits for many nations, both by increasing agricultural productivity and by reducing extremes of cold. And if past generations of Americans have imposed costs on the rest of the world, they have also conferred substantial benefits. American industrial activity has produced products that were consumed in foreign countries, for example, and has driven technological advances from which citizens in other countries have gained. Many of these benefits are positive externalities, for which Americans have not been fully compensated. To be sure, many citizens in, say, India have not much benefited from those advances, just as many citizens of the United States have not much benefited from them. But what would the world, or India, look like if the United States had engaged in 10% of its level of greenhouse gas emissions, or 20%, or 40%? For purposes of corrective justice, a proper accounting would seem to be necessary, and it presents formidable empirical and conceptual problems.

In the context of slave reparations, the analogous points have led to interminable debates, again empirical and conceptual, about historical causation and difficult counterfactuals. But-for causation arguments, used in standard legal analysis and conventional for purposes of conventional justice, present serious and perhaps insuperable problems when applied historically. We can meaningfully ask whether an accident would have occurred if the driver had operated the vehicle more carefully, but conceptual and empirical questions make it difficult to answer the question whether and to what extent white Americans today would have been worse off if there had been no slavery—and difficult too to ask whether Indians would be better off today if Americans of prior generations had not emitted greenhouse gases. What kind of a question is that? In this hypothetical world of limited industrialization in the United States, India would be an entirely different country, and the rest of the world would be unrecognizably different as well.

Proponents of slave reparations have sometimes appealed to principles of corporate liability. Corporations can be immortal, and many corporations today benefited from the slave economy in the nineteenth century. Corporations are collectivities, not individuals, yet they can be held liable for their actions, which means that shareholders today are "punished" (in the sense of losing share value) as a result of actions taken by managers and employees long before the shareholders obtained their ownership interest. If innocent shareholders can be made to pay for the wrongdoing of employees who are long gone, why can't citizens be made to pay for the wrongful actions of citizens who lived in the past?

The best answer is that corporate liability is most easily justified on grounds other than corrective justice. Shareholder liability can be defended on the basis of consent or (in our view most plausibly) on the welfarist ground that corporate liability deters employees from engaging in wrongdoing on behalf of the corporate entity. A factor that distinguishes corporate liability is that purchasing shares is a voluntary activity and one does so with the knowledge that the share price will decline if a past legal violation comes to light, and this is reflected in the share price at the time of purchase. (One also benefits if an unknown past action enhances the value of the company.) But because the corporate form itself is a fiction, and the shareholders today are different from the wrongdoers yesterday, corporate liability cannot be grounded in corrective justice. Thus, it provides no analogy on behalf of corrective justice for the climate change debate. * * *

Many people do seem to be reducing their emissions on the basis of an assessment of roughly this kind. Those concerned about climate change rarely believe that they should altogether stop engaging in activities that produce greenhouse gases (a difficult task!); instead, they think that they should cut back on activities that generate unreasonable emissions of greenhouse gases in light of whatever benefits they produce. Some people go farther and purchase carbon offsets, but this type of activity seems, at present, supererogatory, whereas a case could be made today that a reasonable reduction of greenhouse gas emitting activities is morally required—that it represents an emerging community standard or norm.

Even if this is so, there is a problem with this argument, which is that the calculation given above assumes that everyone around the world, or at least hundreds of millions of people, are also cutting back on greenhouse-gas-producing activities. If many or most people fail to pay a carbon tax or (as we argue) fail to act as if they pay it by cutting back on less important activities that produce greenhouse gases, then the contribution of Americans who do this is quite small. And if this is the case, it cannot be considered negligent for Americans to fail to reduce their greenhouse-gas-emitting activities. Put differently, it is not negligent to fail to contribute to a public good if not enough others are doing similarly, so that the public good would not be created even if one did contribute. This is a "moral collective action problem," and however it should be assessed in moral terms, the failure to act when other people are not acting, so that positive action would generate no benefit, does not seem to constitute negligence.

NOTES

1.   How much of the responsibility for climate changes rests on past emissions? Although China overtook the United States as the world's largest emitter of CO_2 in 2007 and emitted 27% of global emissions in 2017 compared to 15% for the U.S., the United States is the largest historical contributor to the problem. *See* Justin Gillis and Nadja Popvich, *The U.S. Is the Biggest Carbon Polluter in History. It Just Walked Away From the Paris Climate Deal,* New York Times June 1, 2017, https://www.nytimes.com/interactive/2017/06/01/climate/us-biggest-carbon-polluter-in-history-will-it-walk-away-from-the-paris-climate-deal.html. Moreover, U.S. per capita emissions in 2017 (16.2 tons per person) were more than double those of China's (7 tons per person). And a large portion of China's emissions can be attributed to its manufacturing of goods for export, including exports to the U.S. market. These figures are taken from GLOBAL CARBON PROJECT, GLOBAL CARBON BUDGET 2018, http://www.globalcarbonproject.org/carbonbudget/index.htm. Note, finally, that this discussion focuses on CO_2 from energy and industrial sources. Attribution of responsibility for global emissions is more complex, and the U.S. role looks smaller if other greenhouse gases and non-industrial sources of CO_2 such as deforestation are included.

2.   One fundamental question is whether controlling greenhouse gases should be a considered a "redistributive mechanism," as Posner and Sunstein call it. It can only be considered *re*distributive if unrestricted emission—and therefore, unlimited climate change—is considered to be the baseline. Compared to this baseline of unrestricted emissions, restricting emissions makes poor countries better off and costs rich countries money, so it can be considered a redistribution of wealth. If, instead, we consider the baseline to be a world in which climate is stable, then the shoe is on the other foot. Starting

with that baseline, we would say that the U.S. and other wealthy emitters are redistributing income to themselves at the expense of poor countries by their on-going damage to the planetary climate system. If we start with this baseline, reducing emissions is not a redistribution of income; it merely leaves the distribution of income where it would be in the baseline state. The question, in other words, is whether we should think of pollution as a right—so that limitations on polluters are seen a redistribution of wealth to their victims— or whether we should view freedom from pollution as a right, which would imply that the polluters are unjustly prospering at the expense of others.

3.   Posner and Sunstein begin their article by expressing puzzlement by the lack of support for side-payments from impacted countries such as India to the United States as part of an international climate agreement. Do they make a persuasive argument for such side-payments? One might imagine such side payments, for example, in the form of "debt for carbon swaps," in which China would forgive U.S. debt in return for greater reductions in U.S. emissions. Does this seem like a plausible proposal?

4.   In 2017, President Trump followed through on a campaign promise and announced that the United States was abandoning the Paris Agreement on Climate Change, which was completed in 2015 under the United Nations Framework Convention on Climate Change and went into effect in 2016. The agreement now includes 184 countries as parties. Even though withdrawal as a formal matter cannot happen until 2020, the United States has effectively abandoned the agreement. *See* Gillis and Popvich, Note 1, *supra*.

5.   For 2018, preliminary data indicate that global carbon emissions will hit an all-time high. *See* GLOBAL CARBON PROJECT, Note 1, *supra.* U.S. energy-related CO2 emissions also increased by 3% in 2018—reversing several years of declining emissions. *See* U.S. ENERGY INFORMATION ADMINISTRATION, SHORT-TERM ENERGY OUTLOOK (December 11, 2018), https://www.eia.gov/outlooks/steo/report/renew_co2.php.

D.   TORT LAW AND THE ENVIRONMENT

The rest of this book will cover issues of instrument choice, regulatory design, and policy tradeoffs across a range of statutory domains dealing with various environmental problems. But it is useful to remember that the common law of torts provides an alternative (and much older) approach to environmental harms—one focused on liability for conduct that causes injury. This includes common law nuisance actions for air and water pollution, which will be discussed in chapters 6 and 7 respectively, as well as so-called toxic torts. In this section, we consider the common law of torts and related compensation schemes as tools for achieving environmental protection. Because these compensation schemes attempt to remedy the harm to victims, they may be more attractive from the perspective of environmental justice than conventional forms of regulation.

ALBERT C. LIN, BEYOND TORT: COMPENSATING
VICTIMS OF ENVIRONMENTAL TOXIC INJURY

78 S. CAL. L. REV. 1439, 1445–52 (2005).[9]

The paradigmatic traditional tort case involves a single identifiable plaintiff, a single identifiable defendant, and a readily determinable cause of the tortious event. For example, a pedestrian struck by a car can identify the driver of the car and the driver's negligence as the cause of the pedestrian's resulting injuries. Although the parties may dispute the driver's negligence or the harm suffered by the plaintiff, the judicial process is well equipped to determine such issues. Our judicial system is similarly able to handle classic strict liability claims, such as a dynamite explosion, a sudden flood from a reservoir, or even a catastrophic Bhopal-type accident. In such cases, cause and effect are readily identifiable. An environmental tort plaintiff, however, often faces far more formidable problems of proof. As an initial matter, courts generally apply a negligence standard rather than a strict liability standard to ordinary economic activities. Only where a polluter is engaged in abnormally dangerous activities do courts apply a strict liability standard. Furthermore, environmental tort plaintiffs must overcome the high hurdles of causation and latency of harm.

1.   Latency of Harm

Latency of harm complicates proving causation with any environmental disease that takes time to develop. For example, consider an individual who is diagnosed with cancer many years after an exposure to carcinogenic pollutants released from an industrial facility. Over the course of a lifetime, this individual has been exposed to numerous carcinogens through various pathways, including air, water, and food supply. In contrast to the paradigmatic tort plaintiff described above, this plaintiff's injury is latent, appearing some time after exposure. The length of the latency period may vary among individuals. Thus, even when a population is exposed simultaneously to a pollutant, incidences of disease occur over a period of time that can span several decades.

This latency and lack of simultaneity make evidence more difficult to gather. For example, victims may not have been aware of their first exposure to a toxic substance. Therefore, years later, they will likely be unable to prove the fact, timing, or extent of exposure. Exposure often occurs at low levels over extended periods of time. The passage of time not only complicates proof, but also increases the risk that a defendant will no longer be financially viable, assuming that the defendant can even be identified. Compounding plaintiffs' difficulties, statutes of limitations may

---

[9]   Copyright © 2005, University of Southern California. Reprinted with permission.

bar suit, although some jurisdictions have rules tolling the statutory period until the time when the injury is discovered.

2. Causation

An even greater barrier faced by plaintiffs is causation. Toxic tort plaintiffs typically must establish two types of causation. First, a plaintiff must prove general causation—that a substance is capable of causing the injury at issue. Second, a plaintiff must prove specific causation—that exposure to the substance in fact caused that plaintiff's injury. The scientific uncertainty that surrounds causation can make these burdens insurmountable.

A few diseases, such as asbestosis, are so-called "signature diseases"— diseases that are extremely rare in the general population, but far more prevalent in persons exposed to a particular substance. These illnesses can be traced to exposure to a specific substance. Illnesses involving environmental toxic exposure, however, often can result from multiple causes. For example, an individual instance of lung cancer might be attributed to exposure to tobacco smoke, exposure to pollutants from a nearby factory, or exposure to pollutants from traffic on a local highway. Separating the roles of the potential causal agents, which may interact in complex ways, is often problematic, if not impossible. Unlike our automobile accident example, there is usually no obvious evidence that a particular agent caused the plaintiff's harm in environmental tort cases.

a. General Causation

Much of the difficulty with environmental tort litigation is due to an insufficient scientific understanding of general causation. Essentially, the question is whether a certain chemical has the ability to cause a particular illness and, if so, to what extent. Reliable information regarding carcinogenic and other health effects is available for relatively few substances. For many substances, health effects are unknown. Molecular assays and animal bioassays provide some information on mutagenicity or carcinogenicity. Scientists, however, caution that this information cannot always be extrapolated in a reliable manner to estimate human cancer risks.

Courts tend to view epidemiological studies, which apply statistical techniques to explain variations in disease rates of human populations, as the most persuasive and acceptable type of general causation evidence in toxic tort cases. Yet the very use of such studies creates difficulties. * * * Detailed epidemiological data is available only for relatively few toxic substances. Furthermore, where such data is available, there may be uncertainty regarding the magnitude of the risk involved.

b. *Specific Causation*

Specific causation is also frequently uncertain with environmental toxic injuries. Epidemiological studies may establish that a substance can cause the type of harm suffered by a plaintiff, satisfying general causation. But a plaintiff must still demonstrate that the particular harm was in fact the result of exposure to a given substance. Epidemiological studies, however, can only attribute a proportion of the incidence of disease in a population to any particular source. They are not designed to prove specific causation. Specific causation requires a plaintiff to prove by a preponderance of the evidence that the defendant caused that particular plaintiff's harm. Many courts interpret the preponderance standard to require a relative risk ratio of 2.0 or greater—for example, a defendant's conduct more than doubled the plaintiff's risk of injury. This doubled-risk requirement, however, conflates two distinct burdens: the plaintiff's substantive burden of proof and the standard of persuasion applicable to that burden. Thus, if an epidemiological study indicates that exposure to a particular substance increases the incidence of a disease among those exposed by only forty percent, then a court will probably find that the plaintiff has failed to meet the burden of proving specific causation unless more direct evidence is offered.

Indeed, some courts demand particularistic proof of a causal connection—probabilistic proof is insufficient on its own. In such cases, it is insufficient even to prove that exposure to a substance more than doubled a plaintiff's risk of injury. In addition, if a particular disease-causing substance was generated by more than one source, a plaintiff may also have to demonstrate which of multiple potential defendants produced the substance responsible for the injury. But if a plaintiff is able to identify two or more tortfeasors who collectively released sufficient pollutants to cause the harm, courts may be willing to attach liability to each one. Courts may treat each as a causal agent under a "substantial factor" test, under a theory of joint and several liability, or under a theory of market share liability.

Resolution of all of these issues requires costly expert testimony. Here, environmental tort plaintiffs face another hurdle—the fairly rigorous standard for expert testimony mandated by *Daubert v. Merrell Dow Pharmaceuticals.*[52] In *Daubert*, the Supreme Court interpreted the Federal Rules of Evidence to require that the trial judge serve as a gatekeeper for scientific testimony. The Court identified several factors for trial courts to consider in determining the admissibility of scientific testimony. The

---

[52] *Daubert v. Merrell Dow Pharm., Inc.*, 509 U.S. 579 (1993). *Daubert* was itself a toxic tort case. On remand from the Supreme Court, the Ninth Circuit held that the plaintiffs' scientific evidence, which consisted of a reanalysis of epidemiological evidence, lab studies on animal tissues, and chemical structure analysis, was insufficiently reliable to be admitted under the Federal Rules of Evidence. *See also Daubert v. Merrell Dow Pharm., Inc.*, 43 F.3d 1311 (9th Cir. 1995).

Daubert standard has proven to be too strict for many toxic tort plaintiffs to meet—courts often find the proposed experts' testimony to be too unreliable to be admissible in light of scientific uncertainty and incomplete scientific knowledge.

NOTES

1. For recent discussion of *Daubert*, see David L. Faigman, *The Daubert Revolution and the Birth of Modernity: Managing Scientific Evidence in the Age of Science,* 46 U.C. DAVIS L. REV. 893 (2013).

2. Professor Lin recommends replacing the tort system with an administrative system:

> From an institutional analysis perspective, administrative systems have certain characteristics that make them a superior alternative for addressing the environmental toxic injury problem. Administrative systems typically employ specialized or expert decisionmakers who can conduct their own studies and consider a broad range of information. Administrative systems can also provide more continuous oversight and distribute compensation more fairly among a class of victims. In addition, administrative systems are, in theory, more politically accountable than the judicial system. This is not to suggest that setting compensation should be politicized; rather, the scientific uncertainty inherent in environmental toxic injuries necessitates making policy decisions. In an administrative system, that inescapably political judgment is subject to indirect democratic control.

3. Another problem in toxic tort litigation is establishing a link between a specific defendant and the release of the substance. For example, many hazardous waste generators may have shipped similar materials to the site in question. It may be quite difficult to establish whose containers leaked or in what quantities. We will see later in this book how that issue is handled in terms of liability under federal law, but federal law does not provide compensation for personal injuries, just clean-up costs.

A similar issue can arise in products liability cases. In *Sindell v. Abbott Laboratories*,[10] the plaintiff's mother was administered the drug diethylstilbesterol (DES) during pregnancy. Although DES was routinely given to prevent miscarriage, it is now known to cause a rare form of cancer in some daughters of women who took the drug. After developing such cancer, the plaintiff sued eleven of the more than 200 manufacturers of DES. The plaintiff was unable to identify the manufacturer of the particular DES which her mother took, but the court held that she had stated a cause of action against manufacturers of the drug using an identical formula. Resting this holding on a broad social policy, the court noted that the defendants were "better able to bear the cost of injury resulting from the manufacture of a defective product."

---

[10]   26 Cal.3d 588, 607 P.2d 924, 163 Cal.Rptr. 132, *cert. denied,* 449 U.S. 912 (1980).

The *Sindell* court then adopted a novel theory of liability by making each defendant liable for a share of the plaintiff's damages, based on its share of the DES market.

4.   As proportional liability illustrates, problems of proof are not simply a result of the state of available evidence but are also driven by substantive liability rules. For example, negligence may be quite difficult to prove, but tort law may or may not make fault a necessary element of the plaintiff's case. Thus, strict liability can ease the plaintiff's burden of proving liability. Similarly, it may be very hard to prove after the fact that a specific plaintiff's injury was caused by the defendant. Tort law might avoid such problems of proof by providing more limited compensation to everyone who is wrongfully exposed to the risk of injury from toxic chemicals, whether or not the risk materializes. The following two cases consider these issues, starting with the question of liability.

STATE V. VENTRON CORP.
Supreme Court of New Jersey, 1983.
94 N.J. 473, 468 A.2d 150.

POLLOCK, J.

This appeal concerns the responsibility of various corporations for the cost of the cleanup and removal of mercury pollution seeping from a forty-acre tract of land into Berry's Creek, a tidal estuary of the Hackensack River that flows through the Meadowlands. The plaintiff is the State of New Jersey, Department of Environmental Protection (DEP); the primary defendants are Velsicol Chemical Corporation (Velsicol), its former subsidiary, Wood Ridge Chemical Corporation (Wood Ridge), and Ventron Corporation (Ventron), into which Wood Ridge was merged. Other defendants are F.W. Berk and Company, Inc. (Berk), which no longer exists, United States Life Insurance Company, which was dismissed by the lower courts in an unappealed judgment, and Robert M. and Rita W. Wolf (the Wolfs), who purchased part of the polluted property from Ventron.

Beneath its surface, the tract is saturated by an estimated 268 tons of toxic waste, primarily mercury. For a stretch of several thousand feet, the concentration of mercury in Berry's Creek is the highest found in fresh water sediments in the world. The waters of the creek are contaminated by the compound methyl mercury, which continues to be released as the mercury interacts with other elements. Due to depleted oxygen levels, fish no longer inhabit Berry's Creek, but are present only when swept in by the tide and, thus, irreversibly toxified.

The contamination at Berry's Creek results from mercury processing operations carried on at the site for almost fifty years. * * *

After a fifty-five-day trial, the trial court determined that Berk and Wood Ridge were jointly liable for the cleanup and removal of the mercury;

that Velsicol and Ventron were severally liable for half of the costs; that the Wolfs were not liable * * *.

The Appellate Division substantially affirmed the judgment, but modified it in several respects, including the imposition of joint and several liability on Ventron and Velsicol for all costs incurred in the cleanup and removal of the mercury pollution in Berry's Creek. * * *

I

From 1929 to 1960, first as lessee and then as owner of the entire forty-acre tract, Berk operated a mercury processing plant, dumping untreated waste material and allowing mercury-laden effluent to drain on the tract. Berk continued uninterrupted operations until 1960, at which time it sold its assets to Wood Ridge and ceased its corporate existence.

In 1960, Velsicol formed Wood Ridge as a wholly-owned subsidiary for the sole purpose of purchasing Berk's assets and operating the mercury processing plant. In 1967, Wood Ridge subdivided the tract and declared a thirty-three-acre land dividend to Velsicol, which continued to permit Wood Ridge to dump material on the thirty-three acres. As a Velsicol subsidiary, Wood Ridge continued to operate the processing plant on the 7.1-acre tract from 1960 to 1968, when Velsicol sold Wood Ridge to Ventron.

Although Velsicol created Wood Ridge as a separate corporate entity, the trial court found that Velsicol treated it not as an independent subsidiary, but as a division. * * * Without spelling out all the details, we find that the record amply supports the conclusion of the trial court that "Velsicol personnel, directors, and officers were constantly involved in the day-to-day operations of the business of [Wood Ridge]."

In 1968, Velsicol sold 100% of the Wood Ridge stock to Ventron, which began to consider a course of treatment for plant wastes. * * *

Starting in the mid-1960s, DEP began testing effluent on the tract, but did not take any action against Wood Ridge. The trial court found, in fact, that the defendants were not liable under intentional tort or negligence theories.

Nonetheless, in 1970, the contamination at Berry's Creek came to the attention of the United States Environmental Protection Agency (EPA), which conducted a test of Wood Ridge's waste water. The tests indicated that the effluent carried two to four pounds of mercury into Berry's Creek each day. Later that year, Wood Ridge installed a waste treatment system that abated, but did not altogether halt, the flow of mercury into the creek. The operations of the plant continued until 1974, at which time Wood Ridge merged into Ventron. Consistent with N.J.S.A. 14A:10–6(e), the certificate of ownership and merger provided that Ventron would assume the liabilities and obligations of Wood Ridge. Ventron terminated the plant operations and sold the movable operating assets to Troy Chemical Company, not a party to these proceedings.

On February 5, 1974, Wood Ridge granted to Robert Wolf, a commercial real estate developer, an operation to purchase the 7.1-acre tract on which the plant was located, and on May 20, 1974, Ventron conveyed the tract to the Wolfs. The Wolfs planned to demolish the plant and construct a warehousing facility. In the course of the demolition, mercury-contaminated water was used to wet down the structures and allowed to run into the creek. The problem came to the attention of DEP, which ordered a halt to the demolition, pending adequate removal or containment of the contamination. DEP proposed a containment plan, but the Wolfs implemented another plan and proceeded with their project. DEP then instituted this action. * * *

II

Twenty-one years ago, * * * this Court adopted the proposition that "an ultrahazardous activity which introduces an unusual danger into the community . . . should pay its own way in the event it actually causes damage to others." *Berg v. Reaction Motors Div., Thiokol Chem. Corp.*, 37 *N.J.* 396, 410, 181 *A.*2d 487 (1962). * * *

In imposing liability on a landowner for an ultrahazardous activity, *Berg* adopted the test of the *Restatement of the Law of Torts* (1938). See id., §§ 519–20. Since *Berg,* the Restatement (Second) of the Law of Torts (1977) has replaced the "ultrahazardous" standard with one predicated on whether the activity is "abnormally dangerous." Imposition of liability on a landowner for "abnormally dangerous" activities incorporates, in effect, the *Rylands* test. RESTATEMENT (SECOND) § 520, comments (d) & (e). * * *

[T]he RESTATEMENT (SECOND) OF TORTS reformulated the standard of landowner liability, substituting "abnormally dangerous" for "ultrahazardous" and providing a list of elements to consider in applying the new standard. *Id.,* §§ 519–20. As noted, this standard incorporates the theory developed in *Rylands v. Fletcher.* Under the *Restatement* analysis, whether an activity is abnormally dangerous is to be determined on a case-by-case basis, taking all relevant circumstances into consideration. As set forth in the *Restatement*:

In determining whether an activity is abnormally dangerous, the following factors are to be considered:

(a) existence of a high degree of risk of some harm to the person, land or chattels of others;

(b) likelihood that the harm that results from it will be great;

(c) inability to eliminate the risk by the exercise of reasonable care;

(d) extent to which the activity is not a matter of common usage;

(e) inappropriateness of the activity to the place where it is carried on; and

(f) extent to which its value to the community is outweighed by its dangerous attributes.

RESTATEMENT (SECOND) OF TORTS § 520 (1977). * * *

We approve the trial court's finding that Berk, Wood Ridge, Velsicol, and Ventron are liable under common-law principles for the abatement of the resulting nuisance and damage. The courts below found that the Wolfs are not liable for the costs of cleanup and containment. DEP did not petition for certification on that issue, and we do not consider it on this appeal. Berk and Wood Ridge, not Mr. and Mrs. Wolf, polluted the environment. During their ownership, the Wolfs have not continued to dump mercury and they have been responsible for only a minimal aggravation of the underlying hazardous condition.

NOTES

1. RESTATEMENT (THIRD) OF TORTS: LIABILITY FOR PHYSICAL HARM (BASIC PRINCIPLES) § 20, "Abnormally Dangerous Activities," provides:

(a) A defendant who carries on an abnormally dangerous activity is subject to strict liability for physical harm resulting from the activity.

(b) An activity is abnormally dangerous if:

(1) the activity creates a foreseeable and highly significant risk of physical harm even when reasonable care is exercised by all actors; and

(2) the activity is not a matter of common usage.

Comment *g* to section 20 states that a risk of physical harm can be "highly significant" for either or both of two reasons: because the *likelihood* of harm is unusually high, even though the severity of expected harm is no more than ordinary; or because the *severity* of the harm could be enormous, although the likelihood of a harm-causing incident is low.

2. There has been recent discussion of efforts to retrieve the DNA of extinct species such as passenger pigeons, recreate the species, and release the animals into the environment. See *De-Extinction*, http://www.national geographic.com/deextinction/. Query: Would such efforts be subject to strict liability for any resulting damages?

AYERS V. TOWNSHIP OF JACKSON

Supreme Court of New Jersey, 1987.
106 N.J. 557, 525 A.2d 287.

STEIN, JUSTICE.

In this case we consider the application of the New Jersey Tort Claims Act [which limits the kinds of damages recoverable against public entities], N.J.S.A. 59:1–1 to 12–3, to the claims asserted by 339 residents of Jackson Township against that municipality.

The litigation involves claims for damages sustained because plaintiffs' well water was contaminated by toxic pollutants leaching into the Cohansey Aquifer from a landfill established and operated by Jackson Township. After an extensive trial, the jury found that the township had created a "nuisance" and a "dangerous condition" by virtue of its operation of the landfill, that its conduct was "palpably unreasonable,"—a prerequisite to recovery under *N.J.S.A.* 59:4–2—and that it was the proximate cause of the contamination of plaintiffs' water supply. The jury verdict resulted in an aggregate judgment of $15,854,392.78 [including $2,056,480 for emotional distress, $5,396,940 for deterioration of quality of life, and $8,204,500 for costs of future medical surveillance. The excerpts below focus on damages for increased risk exposure and medical surveillance]. * * *

In our view, an enhanced risk of disease caused by significant exposure to toxic chemicals is clearly an "injury" under the Act. In this case, neither the trial court nor the Appellate Division challenged the contention that the enhanced risk of disease was a tortiously-inflicted injury, but both concluded that the proof quantifying the likelihood of disease was insufficient to submit the issue to the jury. * * *

Among the recent toxic tort cases rejecting liability for damages based on enhanced risk is *Anderson v. W.R. Grace & Co.*, 628 *F.Supp.* 1219 (D. Mass. 1986). That case involved defendants' alleged chemical contamination of the groundwater in areas of Woburn, Massachusetts. Plaintiffs alleged that two wells supplying water to the City of Woburn drew upon the contaminated water, and that exposure to the contaminated water caused five deaths and severe personal injuries among plaintiffs. Among the claims for personal injuries dismissed before trial were plaintiff's claims for damages based on enhanced risk. Relying on the Massachusetts rule regarding prospective damages, the *Anderson* court reasoned that "recovery depends on establishing a 'reasonable probability' that the harm will occur." However, the *Anderson* court held that the plaintiffs failed to satisfy this threshold standard. They had not quantified their alleged enhanced risk: "Nothing in the present record indicates the magnitude of the increased risk or the diseases which plaintiffs may suffer." * * *

Other courts have acknowledged the propriety of the enhanced risk cause of action, but have emphasized the requirement that proof of future injury be reasonably certain. * * *

Additionally, several courts have permitted recovery for increased risk of disease, but only where the plaintiff exhibited some present manifestation of disease. * * *

Our disposition of this difficult and important issue requires that we choose between two alternatives, each having a potential for imposing unfair and undesirable consequences on the affected interests. A holding that recognizes a cause of action for unquantified enhanced risk claims exposes the tort system, and the public it serves, to the task of litigating vast numbers of claims for compensation based on threats of injuries that may never occur. * * *

Our dissenting colleague, arguing in favor of recognizing a cause of action based on an unquantified claim of enhanced risk, points out that "courts have not allowed the difficulty of quantifying injury to prevent them from offering compensation for assault, trespass, emotional distress, invasion of privacy or damage to reputation." Although lawsuits grounded in one or more of these causes of action may involve claims for damages that are difficult to quantify, such damages are awarded on the basis of events that have occurred and can be proved at the time of trial. In contrast, the compensability of the enhanced risk claim depends upon the likelihood of an event that has not yet occurred and may never occur—the contracting of one or more diseases the risk of which has been enhanced by defendant's conduct. It is the highly contingent and speculative quality of an unquantified claim based on enhanced risk that renders it novel and difficult to manage and resolve. * * *

In * * * our view, the speculative nature of an unquantified enhanced risk claim, the difficulties inherent in adjudicating such claims, and the policies underlying the Tort Claims Act argue persuasively against the recognition of this cause of action. Accordingly, we decline to recognize plaintiffs' cause of action for the *unquantified* enhanced risk of disease, and affirm the judgment of the Appellate Division dismissing such claims. We need not and do not decide whether a claim based on enhanced risk of disease that is supported by testimony demonstrating that the onset of the disease is reasonably probable could be maintained under the Tort Claims Act.

The claim for medical surveillance expenses stands on a different footing from the claim based on enhanced risk. It seeks to recover the cost of periodic medical examinations intended to monitor plaintiffs' health and facilitate early diagnosis and treatment of disease caused by plaintiffs' exposure to toxic chemicals. At trial, competent medical testimony was offered to prove that a program of regular medical testing and evaluation was reasonably necessary and consistent with contemporary scientific principles applied by physicians experienced in the diagnosis and treatment of chemically-induced injuries.

The Appellate Division's rejection of the medical surveillance claim is rooted in the premise that even if medical experts testify convincingly that medical surveillance is necessary, the claim for compensation for these costs must fall, as a matter of law, if the risk of injury is not quantified, or, if quantified, is not reasonably probable. This analysis assumes that the reasonableness of medical intervention, and, therefore, its compensability, depends solely on the sufficiency of proof that the occurrence of the disease is probable. We think this formulation unduly impedes the ability of courts to recognize that medical science may necessarily and properly intervene where there is a significant but unquantified risk of serious disease. * * *

Compensation for reasonable and necessary medical expenses is consistent with well-accepted legal principles. It is also consistent with the important public health interest in fostering access to medical testing for individuals whose exposure to toxic chemicals creates an enhanced risk of disease. The value of early diagnosis and treatment for cancer patients is well-documented. * * *

Although some individuals exposed to hazardous chemicals may seek regular medical surveillance whether or not the cost is reimbursed, the lack of reimbursement will undoubtedly deter others from doing so. An application of tort law that allows post-injury, pre-symptom recovery in toxic tort litigation for reasonable medical surveillance costs is manifestly consistent with the public interest in early detection and treatment of disease. * * *

Accordingly, we hold that the cost of medical surveillance is a compensable item of damages where the proofs demonstrate, through reliable expert testimony predicated upon the significance and extent of exposure to chemicals, the toxicity of the chemicals, the seriousness of the diseases for which individuals are at risk, the relative increase in the chance of onset of disease in those exposed, and the value of early diagnosis, that such surveillance to monitor the effect of exposure to toxic chemicals is reasonable and necessary. * * *

We find that the proofs in this case were sufficient to support the trial court's decision to submit the medical surveillance issue to the jury, and were sufficient to support the jury's verdict.

The medical surveillance issue was tried as if it were a conventional claim for compensatory damages susceptible to a jury verdict in a lump sum. The jury was so instructed by the trial court, and neither plaintiffs' nor defendant's request to charge on this issue sought a different instruction. * * *

The indeterminate nature of damage claims in toxic-tort litigation suggests that the use of court-supervised funds to pay medical-surveillance claims as they accrue, rather than lump-sum verdicts, may provide a more efficient mechanism for compensating plaintiffs. A funded settlement was used in the Agent Orange litigation. *In re "Agent Orange" Prod. Liab. Litig.,* 611 F.Supp. 1396, 1399 (E.D.N.Y. 1985), aff'd, 818 F.2d 194 (2d Cir. 1987). The use of insurance to fund future medical claims is frequently recommended by commentators. * * *

In our view, the use of a court-supervised fund to administer medical-surveillance payments in mass exposure cases, particularly for claims under the Tort Claims Act, is a highly appropriate exercise of the Court's equitable powers. * * *

Although there may be administrative and procedural questions in the establishment and operation of such a fund, we encourage its use by trial courts in managing mass-exposure cases. In litigation involving public-entity defendants, we conclude that the use of a fund to administer medical-surveillance payments should be the general rule, in the absence of factors that render it impractical or inappropriate. This will insure that in future mass-exposure litigation against public entities, medical-surveillance damages will be paid only to compensate for medical examinations and tests actually administered, and will encourage plaintiffs to safeguard their health by not allowing them the option of spending the money for other purposes. The fund mechanism will also foster the legislative objective of limiting the liability of public entities and facilitating the deduction from damage awards of collateral-source benefits.

However, we decline to upset the jury verdict awarding medical-surveillance damages in this case. Such a result would be unfair to these plaintiffs, since the medical-surveillance issue was tried conventionally, and neither party requested the trial court to withhold from the jury the power to return a lump-sum verdict for each plaintiff in order that relief by way of a fund could be provided. * * *

NOTES

1. The *Ayers* case distinguishes four kinds of claims related to potential future harms:

(a) Plaintiff has an *existing physical injury* that may worsen or develop into a more serious illness;

(b) Plaintiff has no existing injury or disease but, because of exposure to toxic substances, is at an *increased risk* of developing a particular disease, such as cancer, in the future;

(c)   Plaintiff, because of her susceptibility to the disease, suffers present *emotional distress*, usually fear or anxiety, which may or may not be accompanied by physical manifestations;

(d)   Plaintiff, again because of the enhanced risk of future serious illness, incurs or should incur present and future medical expenses for *surveillance* of the possible development of the disease.

The prevailing rule for cases in at least the first three categories is that increased risk of developing a future disease, such as cancer, as a consequence of exposure to toxic chemicals is not compensable unless plaintiff can establish that the probability of the future disease is greater than 50%. *See* Lisa Heinzerling & Cameron Hoffman, *Tortious Toxics*, 26 WM. & MARY L. REV. 67, 73 (2001). The fourth category is discussed below.

2.   *In re Paoli R.R. Yard PCB Litigation,* 916 F.2d 829 (3d Cir. 1990), held that a medical monitoring claimant must show (1) that she was significantly exposed to a proven hazardous substance through the negligent actions of defendant, (2) that as a proximate result of exposure she suffers an increased risk of contracting a serious latent disease, (3) that the increased risk makes medical examinations reasonably necessary, and (4) that monitoring and testing procedures exist which make early detection and treatment of the disease possible and beneficial.

In most medical monitoring cases plaintiffs have sought or courts have awarded a traditional common-law lump sum of monetary damages. In a few toxic exposure cases, however, litigants have pursued or courts have expressed their preference for periodic payment of future medical surveillance expenses out of a court-supervised trust fund or similar mechanism. *See* Amy B. Blumenberg, *Medical Monitoring Funds: The Periodic Payment of Future Medical Surveillance Expenses in Toxic Exposure Litigation*, 43 HASTINGS L.J. 661 (1992).

3.   The Supreme Court dealt with medical surveillance liability in *Metro-North Commuter R.R. Co. v. Buckley*, 521 U.S. 424 (1997), a case arising under the Federal Employers' Liability Act ("FELA").[11] The plaintiff had been exposed to asbestos as a pipe fitter while working for the railroad. After he learned that he faced an increased risk of cancer, he sought to recover damages for the resulting emotional distress and a lump-sum recovery for future medical check-ups. The Court noted a number of general concerns about allowing recovery for medical monitoring not connected with any existing injury, including the potentially wide scope of liability, the lower priority of claimants with monitoring costs versus those with already realized injury, the difficulty of identifying what extra monitoring is warranted by an exposure, and the possibility that monitoring expenses would be covered by health insurance or some other source. The Court's observations suggest some unease with medical monitoring damages in general.

---

[11]   Employers' Liability Acts (Federal Employers' Liability Act) (FELA), 45 U.S.C. § 51–60 (2007).

Ultimately, however, the Court's holding was narrow and rejected only what it considered to be a very broad rule of recovery of lump-sum damages:

> We have not tried to balance these, or other, competing considerations here. We point them out to help explain why we consider the limitations and cautions to be important—and integral—parts of the state-court decisions that permit asymptomatic plaintiffs a separate tort claim for medical monitoring costs. That being so, we do not find sufficient support in the common law for the unqualified rule of lump-sum damages recovery that is, at least arguably, before us here. And given the mix of competing general policy considerations, plaintiff's policy-based arguments do not convince us that the FELA contains a tort liability rule of that unqualified kind.

> This limited conclusion disposes of the matter before us. We need not, and do not, express any view here about the extent to which the FELA might, or might not, accommodate medical cost recovery rules more finely tailored than the rule we have considered.[12]

Some state courts have interpreted this limited holding as a broad rejection of medical monitoring expenses, but others continue to award such damages.[13]

In another setback for this theory of recovery, the court held in *In re Hanford Nuclear Reservation Litigation*, 534 F.3d 986 (9th Cir. 2008), that medical monitoring liability for radiation risks was precluded by a federal statute, the Price-Anderson Act.

---

[12] *Metro-North Commuter R.R. Co.*, 521 U.S. at 444. The Court's lack of sympathy to tort plaintiffs is fairly palpable here—not the willingness to dispose of the case on a ground that the court says is only "arguably present" in the case before it. In addition, as the dissent pointed out, the majority's discussion is extremely muddled:

It is not apparent why (or even whether) the Court reverses the Second Circuit's determination on Buckley's second claim. The Court of Appeals held that a medical monitoring claim is solidly grounded, and this Court does not hold otherwise. Hypothesizing that Buckley demands lump-sum damages and nothing else, the Court ruminates on the appropriate remedy without answering the anterior question: Does the plaintiff have a claim for relief? Buckley has shown that Metro-North negligently exposed him to "extremely high levels of asbestos," 79 F.3d, at 1341, and that this exposure warrants "medical monitoring in order to detect and treat [asbestos-related] diseases as they may arise." Id., at 1346. Buckley's expert medical witness estimated the annual costs of proper monitoring at $950. We do not know from the Court's opinion what more a plaintiff must show to qualify for relief.

Id. at 448 (Ginsburg, J., dissenting in part and concurring in the judgment).

[13] See Jamie A. Grodsky, Genomics and Toxic Torts: Dismantling the Risk-Injury Divide, 59 STAN. L. REV. 1671, 1712 (2007).

CHAPTER 3

ENDANGERED SPECIES

■ ■ ■

A. INTRODUCTION TO THE ENDANGERED SPECIES ACT

The ESA seeks to protect species at risk of extinction. To do this, Congress crafted powerful prohibitions and requirements. The statute provides for the listing of species as either "threatened" or "endangered." Once listed, the species are entitled to a variety of protections. These include a prohibition on any federal agency action likely to jeopardize their continued existence (so the ESA can block large infrastructure projects like dams and highways that are built, funded or sponsored by federal agencies), and a federal obligation to conserve the species and provide for their recovery. In addition, the Act prohibits anyone from "taking" listed endangered species, whether on public or private land. Because of these outright prohibitions and requirements, and their potential impact on private land, the ESA is very controversial. As you will see when you encounter the Clean Air Act, Clean Water Act, and hazardous waste laws in later chapters, the ESA is by comparison relatively simple and straightforward. Unlike the pollution laws, it is relatively free of technical jargon and detailed prescriptive standards. But it is far from mild-mannered.

The excerpt below explores the reasons for preserving endangered species. It is followed by some basic background on the ESA and then by the foundational Supreme Court opinion under the statute.

JOHN KUNICH, PRESERVING THE WOMB OF THE UNKNOWN SPECIES WITH HOTSPOTS LEGISLATION
52 HASTINGS L. J. 1149, 1162–69 (2001).[1]

* * * If the ESA or other pieces of legislation are to be given a chance of making a difference, people will need to understand the benefits they can expect to derive from the bargain. The reasons for humans to attempt to prevent the extinction of other creatures can be bundled into four main groups: (1) present practical value; (2) potential future practical value; (3) intangible value; and (4) moral duty. * * *

---

[1]   Copyright 2001. Reprinted by permission.

First, many species of plants and animals currently provide *Homo sapiens* with a variety of tangible, practical benefits of real value to people. A host of domesticated animals and crop plants are obvious examples, directly supplying nutrients for the human diet. * * * In addition to food, plants and animals are the producers of essentials such as cotton, wool, silk, leather, wood, paper, dyes, and their ancillary commodities. However, only twenty species provide ninety percent of the global food supply today, and three species (corn, wheat, and rice) contribute more than half of the total. Countless other species, currently known or unknown, could perhaps "be bred or provide genes to increase production in deserts, saline flats and other marginal habitats" to feed the world's expanding population in the future.

Plants are the source of many medicinal drugs, and about half of all prescription drugs in the United States come from wild organisms, of a total value estimated to exceed $14 billion per year. Our antibiotics, anti-cancer agents, pain killers, and blood thinners have been derived thus far from only a few hundred species, leaving the biochemistry and genetic components of millions of other species unexplored and untapped as a potentially colossal reservoir of new medicines and healing agents. * * *

The role of animals in medical and other scientific research has been of inestimable worth, and largely the contribution of otherwise insignificant or despised creatures such as the common mouse, rat, and fruit fly. Less obvious but still practical benefits come from creatures that facilitate the production of other plants or animals which in turn are consumed or otherwise used. This includes a vast array of insects, which pollinate many flowering plants, including fruit-bearing varieties, and which are the primary food source for many birds; it also includes annelids (earthworms) and other burrowing organisms which similarly play an unobtrusive yet vital role in aerating soil, making it suitable for producing plant life.

* * * In addition to all of the human-centered practical reasons for preserving species as individual species, there are tangible synergistic benefits produced by species interactions on an ecosystem level. The concept of "ecosystem services" is fairly new, but several enormously significant examples have been identified. These include the decomposition and detoxification of organic matter and other wastes, which is mostly performed by the smallest, least charismatic organisms in any ecosystem. * * * Other examples are generation and renewal of soil, mitigation of floods, purification of air and water, and partial stabilization of climate. * * *

Among the most fundamental of ecosystem services is the photosynthetic process of most plants, which not only fixes, or converts, solar energy into usable nutrients, but also converts carbon dioxide into oxygen, literally the life-breath of our species. And the exquisitely intricate natural system of checks and balances by which various species keep one another's populations—including those of pest and disease-causing organisms—within manageable limits is far more effective and safe than any pesticide program.

Most previously-identified species that provide obvious, practical benefits to humans are not in danger of extinction. In fact, many are actively safeguarded, raised, cultivated, and otherwise managed to maximize their productivity. There have been some cases of over-harvesting of such species, but for the most part this type of species is safe, due to our own self-interest. Of course, this presupposes that humans have (1) discovered the species and (2) learned of the benefits the species has to offer. In the case of the myriad unidentified species inhabiting the world's hotspots, neither of these presuppositions obtains.

The species that are less ostentatious about their value to people, moreover, may be even less fortunate. In some cases, for example, it is not even known which species of insects pollinate which useful plants, or which species are depended on by birds, fish, and other creatures for their sustenance, so humans may destroy or allow the destruction of these insects without realizing the consequences.

A second basic reason for humans to preserve species is that they may have future practical value to people. New uses are continually being discovered for living things, often transforming apparently inconsequential species into valuable assets. By definition, of course, it is impossible to know which or how many species fall into this category at any point in time. * * *

Each living species can be viewed as the end product of countless years of research and development, the culmination of eons of experimentation in nature's laboratory. * * * [W]ith the advent of genetic engineering, wherein it is increasingly possible to transfer genetic material from one taxonomic group to another (even across the kingdom barrier) to confer previously lacking biological traits, each species is potentially a significant genetic resource. * * *

It is possible, and even probable, that some currently "insignificant" species could take on a crucial role in the ecosystems of the future. Wild relatives of current crop species can be an invaluable source of genetic diversity in the event the monoculture cultivated plants fall prey to disease or other environmental conditions. And if environmental conditions change, through global warming, increased pollution, or other habitat alterations, some other species may possess traits that will prove preadapted to these new circumstances. Some species that occupy key positions in today's ecosystems may be unable to adapt, and unless other species are available to fill their niche, the ecosystems may suffer catastrophic degradation. The redundancy provided for by millions of years of natural selection cannot be fully understood and appreciated unless and until it is needed. It is not necessarily the large, obvious life forms that play these pivotal roles; in fact, the "lower" levels of the food web are the foundation upon which all other components of each ecosystem depend. * * *

* * * [S]ome species may be valuable precisely because they are endangered or threatened. A particularly vulnerable species within a given habitat may someday provide an early warning signal that there are problems that may eventually affect far more species. This has been termed the "canary in the mine" syndrome. * * *

A third main reason to preserve species is their intangible value. Although less practical, and less susceptible to being reduced to monetary worth, there is real wealth in living things. Many people find great beauty in nature, and nowhere else is the maxim more true that beauty is in the eye of the beholder. * * *

Other life forms also have intangible value as educational tools and entertainment sources. The persistent popularity of zoos, circuses, and televised nature programs is evidence of the deep-seated fascination other species hold for their human admirers. * * *

Finally, fourth, and least pragmatic, is the moral duty not to exterminate our fellow passengers on this planet. With its origins at least as ancient as the biblical injunction to "replenish" the earth as its caretakers, this moral duty has strong precedential support. Although most people accept the propriety of human use of other species for food, clothing, and other purposes, they likely would draw the line at exploiting these species into extinction.

* * * Additionally, people may want to preserve other species as a living legacy for their children and grandchildren, feeling it is wrong to deprive their posterity of a heritage their own ancestors had passed down for their enjoyment. * * *

M. LYNNE CORN, KRISTINA ALEXANDER, AND EUGENE H. BUCK, THE ENDANGERED SPECIES ACT: A PRIMER
Congressional Research Service (2012).

What Is the ESA?

The ESA is a comprehensive attempt to provide legal protection to identified species and to consider habitat protection as an integral part of that effort. It is administered primarily by the Fish and Wildlife Service (FWS), but also by the National Marine Fisheries Service (NMFS) for certain marine species. Under the ESA, individual species of plants and animals (both vertebrate and invertebrate) can be listed as either "endangered" or "threatened" according to assessments of the risk of their extinction. Once a species is listed, powerful legal tools are available to aid the recovery of the species and to protect its habitat. As of September 21, 2012, a total of 2,021 species of animals and plants had been listed as either endangered or threatened; 1,403 of these occur in the United States and its territories, and the remainder only in other countries. Of the U.S. species, 1,143 are covered by recovery plans.[2] The ESA was passed in 1973, but was preceded by simpler acts to conserve species in 1966 and 1969. It has been amended on numerous occasions since then: 1976, 1977, 1978, 1979, 1980, 1982, 1988, and 2003. The authorization for funding under the ESA expired on October 1, 1992, although Congress has appropriated funds in each succeeding fiscal year. ESA prohibitions and penalties remain in effect regardless of appropriations.

Why Is the ESA Controversial?

A stated purpose of the ESA is to "provide a means whereby the ecosystems upon which endangered species and threatened species depend may be conserved." While the ESA plays an important role in protecting species, it can also become a surrogate battleground in debates whose primary focus is the allocation of scarce or diminishing lands, waters, or resources. The surrogate role is especially likely because other laws often lack the strict substantive provisions that Congress included in the ESA * * *. There can be economic interests on multiple sides of some vanishing species issues. Like the miners' canaries signaling a scarce resource (safe air supply), declining species are often symptoms of resource scarcities and altered ecosystems. Examples of such resource controversies include the Tellico Dam (hydropower development and construction jobs versus farmland protection and tribal graves, as well as the endangered snail darter); Northwest timber harvest (protection of logging jobs and communities versus commercial and sport fishing, recreation, and ecosystem protection, as well as salmon and spotted owls); and oil development on the energy-rich plain around the northern mountain states (coal bed methane development, grazing rights, ground water protection, traditional ranching, and a petition for sage grouse listing). And the worldwide debate over the causes and effects of global climate change has found its avatar in the polar bear (carbon dioxide emission levels, shoreline erosion, melting glaciers, traditional jobs, agriculture, etc.).

Tensions over the ESA have increased as species have been added to the protected list, and as the greater demands of a growing economy and human population have affected species' habitats. Both Congress and the Executive Branch have sought to lessen these tensions by, among other things, tailoring application of the ESA for particular circumstances. The

---

[2]   [Editor's note] The numbers have expanded since this article was written. As of November 2018, the Fish and Wildlife Service's website listed 1660 endangered species as 594 threatened ones. https://ecos.fws.gov/ecp0/reports/box-score-report.

ESA's critics contend that neither the ESA nor administrative efforts go far enough in accommodating needs other than species conservation, while the ESA's defenders counter that it only balances what they see as an inherent bias toward development in other governmental laws and policies.

Debate on the ESA splits largely along demographic lines. While most demographic groups support species conservation to some degree, that support is stronger among urban and suburban populations and less so in rural areas, and is stronger among those along the coasts and less so in central and mountain states. Sport hunters and anglers seem divided on the issue. Native Americans, as a group often dependent on natural resources (e.g., fish), are frequently involved in ESA issues, most commonly siding with survival of listed species. Groups opposing strong protections for listed species usually assert that jobs will be lost if conservation measures are stringent, but those seeking strong protections often claim that jobs will be lost if they are not. It is also noteworthy that, while the debate often centers on jobs and biology, people on both sides claim ethical support for their positions, and many religious groups participate in the debate. In addition, some industries (e.g., logging and land development) generally see the ESA as a serious problem, while others (e.g., some commercial fishing and many recreation interests) see it as generally supporting their interests. * * *

* * * A major goal of the ESA is the recovery of species to the point at which the protection of the ESA is no longer necessary. If this is the standard, the ESA might be considered a failure, because only 28 species have been delisted due to recovery, as of September 21, 2012. Ten species have become extinct since their listing; five have been delisted due to scientific reclassification of the species; and eleven have been delisted due to improved data, changes in the law, or improved scientific understanding. In the case of the species now believed extinct, some were originally listed to protect any last remaining few that might have been alive at the time of listing. It can be quite difficult to prove whether extraordinarily rare species are simply that, or in fact are already extinct. For example, two bird species, the ivory-billed woodpecker and the Eskimo curlew, are both listed as endangered, though confirmed sightings are so rare or so far in the past that these birds may actually be extinct; proving a negative (i.e., that such species do not exist any longer) is quite difficult. Rare species are, by definition, hard to find.) * * *

Even so, because some scientific studies have demonstrated that most species are listed only once they are very depleted (e.g., median population of 407 animals for vertebrates listed as endangered according to one study), another measure of effectiveness might be the number of species that have stabilized or increased their populations, even if the species is not actually delisted. If this is the standard, the ESA could be considered a success, since a large number (41% of listed species according to one study) have improved or stabilized their population levels.

One could also ask what species might have become extinct if there were no ESA: some species (e.g., red wolves and California condors) might not exist at all without the ESA protection, and this too might be considered a measure of success, even though the species are still rare. The authors are unaware of comprehensive studies regarding the likely status of rare species were there no ESA, but some species (e.g., some salmon populations, Florida panthers, California condors, and plants of very narrow ranges) might have declined further, from exceptional rarity to extinction, if ESA did not exist.

The first ESA case to reach the Supreme Court, and the most famous, is excerpted below. It illustrates the potential power of the Act, as well as the Act's ability to provoke controversy.

TENNESSEE VALLEY AUTHORITY V. HILL

Supreme Court of the United States, 1978.
437 U.S. 153, 98 S.Ct. 2279, 57 L.Ed.2d 117.

MR. CHIEF JUSTICE BURGER delivered the opinion of the Court.

We begin with the premise that operation of the Tellico Dam will either eradicate the known population of snail darters or destroy their critical habitat. Petitioner does not now seriously dispute this fact. In any event, under § 4(a)(1) of the Act, the Secretary of the Interior is vested with exclusive authority to determine whether a species such as the snail darter is "endangered" or "threatened" and to ascertain the factors which have led to such a precarious existence. By § 4(d) Congress has authorized—indeed commanded—the Secretary to "issue such regulations as he deems necessary and advisable to provide for the conservation of such species." As we have seen, the Secretary promulgated regulations which declared the snail darter an endangered species whose critical habitat would be destroyed by creation of the Tellico Reservoir. Doubtless petitioner would prefer not to have these regulations on the books, but there is no suggestion that the Secretary exceeded his authority or abused his discretion in issuing the regulations. Indeed, no judicial review of the Secretary's determinations has ever been sought and hence the validity of his actions are not open to review in this Court. * * *

Starting from the above premise, two questions are presented: (a) would TVA be in violation of the Act if it completed and operated the Tellico Dam as planned? (b) if TVA's actions would offend the Act, is an injunction the appropriate remedy for the violation? For the reasons stated hereinafter, we hold that both questions must be answered in the affirmative.

It may seem curious to some that the survival of a relatively small number of three-inch fish among all the countless millions of species extant would require the permanent halting of a virtually completed dam for which Congress has expended more than $100 million. The paradox is not minimized by the fact that Congress continued to appropriate large sums of public money for the project, even after congressional Appropriations Committees were apprised of its apparent impact upon the survival of the snail darter. We conclude, however, that the explicit provisions of the Endangered Species Act require precisely that result.

One would be hard pressed to find a statutory provision whose terms were any plainer than those in § 7 of the Endangered Species Act. Its very words affirmatively command all federal agencies "to insure that actions authorized, funded, or carried out by them do not jeopardize the continued existence" of an endangered species or "result in the destruction or modification of habitat of such species. . . . " This language admits of no exception. * * * It has not been shown, for example, how TVA can close the gates of the Tellico Dam without "carrying out" an action that has been "authorized" and "funded" by a federal agency. Nor can we understand how such action will "insure" that the snail darter's habitat is not disrupted.[18] Accepting the Secretary's determinations, as we must, it is clear that TVA's proposed operation of the dam will have precisely the opposite effect, namely the eradication of an endangered species.

Concededly, this view of the Act will produce results requiring the sacrifice of the anticipated benefits of the project and of many millions of dollars in public funds. But examination of the language, history, and structure of the legislation under review here indicates beyond doubt that Congress intended endangered species to be afforded the highest of priorities. * * * [The Court then reviewed earlier federal legislation directed toward preserving endangered species, before turning to the ESA itself.]

---

[18] In dissent, MR. JUSTICE POWELL argues that the meaning of "actions" in § 7 is "far from 'plain,' " and that "it seems evident that the 'actions' referred to are not all actions that an agency can ever take, but rather actions that the agency is *deciding whether* to authorize, to fund, or to carry out." * * * Aside from this bare assertion, however, no explanation is given to support the proffered interpretation. This recalls Lewis Carroll's classic advice on the construction of language:

" 'When *I* use a word,' Humpty Dumpty said, in rather a scornful tone, 'it means just what *I* choose it to mean—neither more nor less.' " Through the Looking Glass, in The Complete Works of Lewis Carroll 196 (1939).

Aside from being unexplicated, the dissent's reading of § 7 is flawed on several counts. First, under its view, the words "or carry out" in § 7 would be superfluous since all prospective actions of an agency remain to be "authorized" or "funded." Second, the dissent's position logically means that an agency would be obligated to comply with § 7 only when a project is in the planning stage. But if Congress had meant to so limit the Act, it surely would have used words to that effect, as it did in the National Environmental Policy Act, 42 U.S.C. §§ 4332(2)(A), (C).

Despite the fact that the 1966 and 1969 legislation represented "the most comprehensive of its type to be enacted by any nation" up to that time, Congress was soon persuaded that a more expansive approach was needed if the newly declared national policy of preserving endangered species was to be realized. By 1973, when Congress held hearings on what would later become the Endangered Species Act of 1973, it was informed that species were still being lost at the rate of about one per year, * * * and "the pace of disappearance of species" appeared to be "accelerating." * * * Moreover, Congress was also told that the primary cause of this trend was something other than the normal process of natural selection:

> "[Man] and his technology has *[sic]* continued at an ever-increasing rate to disrupt the natural ecosystem. This has resulted in a dramatic rise in the number and severity of the threats faced by the world's wildlife. The truth in this is apparent when one realizes that half of the recorded extinctions of mammals over the past 2,000 years have occurred in the most recent 50-year period." * * *

That Congress did not view these developments lightly was stressed by one commentator:

> "The dominant theme pervading all congressional discussion of the proposed [Endangered Species Act of 1973] was the overriding need *to devote whatever effort and resources were necessary* to avoid further diminution of national and worldwide wildlife resources. Much of the testimony at the hearings and much debate was devoted to the biological problem of extinction. Senators and Congressmen uniformly deplored the irreplaceable loss to aesthetics, science, ecology, and the national heritage should more species disappear." * * *

The legislative proceedings in 1973 are, in fact, replete with expressions of concern over the risk that might lie in the loss of *any* endangered species. Typifying these sentiments is the Report of the House Committee on Merchant Marine and Fisheries on H.R. 37, a bill which contained the essential features of the subsequently enacted Act of 1973; in explaining the need for the legislation, the Report stated:

> "As we homogenize the habitats in which these plants and animals evolved, and as we increase the pressure for products that they are in a position to supply (usually unwillingly) we threaten their—and our own—genetic heritage.

> *"The value of this genetic heritage is, quite literally, incalculable.* * * *

> "Who knows, or can say, what potential cures for cancer or other scourges, present or future, may lie locked up in the structures of

plants which may yet be undiscovered, much less analyzed? . . . Sheer self-interest impels us to be cautious.* * * "

As the examples cited here demonstrate, Congress was concerned about the *unknown* uses that endangered species might have and about the *unforeseeable* place such creatures may have in the chain of life on this planet. * * *

In shaping legislation to deal with the problem thus presented, Congress started from the finding that "[the] two major causes of extinction are hunting and destruction of natural habitat." * * * Of these twin threats, Congress was informed that the greatest was destruction of natural habitats * * *. Virtually every bill introduced in Congress during the 1973 session responded to this concern by incorporating language similar, if not identical, to that found in the present § 7 of the Act. * * *

As it was finally passed, the Endangered Species Act of 1973 represented the most comprehensive legislation for the preservation of endangered species ever enacted by any nation. Its stated purposes were "to provide a means whereby the ecosystems upon which endangered species and threatened species depend may be conserved," and "to provide a program for the conservation of such . . . species. . . . " In furtherance of these goals, Congress expressly stated in § 2(c) that "all Federal departments and agencies *shall* seek *to conserve endangered species* and threatened species. . . . " Lest there be any ambiguity as to the meaning of this statutory directive, the Act specifically defined "conserve" as meaning "to use and the use of *all methods and procedures which are necessary* to bring *any endangered species* or threatened species to the point at which the measures provided pursuant to this chapter are no longer necessary." Aside from § 7, other provisions indicated the seriousness with which Congress viewed this issue: Virtually all dealings with endangered species, including taking, possession, transportation, and sale, were prohibited, except in extremely narrow circumstances. The Secretary was also given extensive power to develop regulations and programs for the preservation of endangered and threatened species. § 1533(d). Citizen involvement was encouraged by the Act, with provisions allowing interested persons to petition the Secretary to list a species as endangered or threatened, * * * and bring civil suits in United States district courts to force compliance with any provision of the Act, §§ 1540(c) and (g). * * *

Section 7 of the Act, which of course is relied upon by respondents in this case, provides a particularly good gauge of congressional intent. As we have seen, this provision had its genesis in the Endangered Species Act of 1966, but that legislation qualified the obligation of federal agencies by stating that they should seek to preserve endangered species only "*insofar as is practicable and consistent with* [*their*] *primary purposes. . . .* "

Likewise, every bill introduced in 1973 contained a qualification similar to that found in the earlier statutes. * * *

What is very significant in this sequence is that the final version of the 1973 Act carefully omitted all of the reservations described above. * * * [I]ndeed all phrases which might have qualified an agency's responsibilities had been omitted from the [House version of the] bill. * * *

* * * The Conference Report, H.R. Conf. Rep. No. 93–740 (1973), basically adopted the Senate bill, S. 1983; but the conferees rejected the Senate version of § 7 and adopted the stringent, mandatory language in H.R. 37. While the Conference Report made no specific reference to this choice of provisions, the House manager of the bill, Representative Dingell, provided an interpretation of what the Conference bill would require, making it clear that the mandatory provisions of § 7 were not casually or inadvertently included:

> "[Section 7] substantially [amplifies] the obligation of [federal agencies] to take steps within their power to carry out the purposes of this act. * * *

> "The purposes of the bill included the conservation of the species and of the ecosystems upon which they depend, and *every agency of government is committed* to see that those purposes are carried out. . . . [The] agencies of Government can no longer plead that they can do nothing about it. *They can, and they must. The law is clear.*"

It is against this legislative background that we must measure TVA's claim that the Act was not intended to stop operation of a project which, like Tellico Dam, was near completion when an endangered species was discovered in its path. While there is no discussion in the legislative history of precisely this problem, the totality of congressional action makes it abundantly clear that the result we reach today is wholly in accord with both the words of the statute and the intent of Congress. The plain intent of Congress in enacting this statute was to halt and reverse the trend toward species extinction, whatever the cost. This is reflected not only in the stated policies of the Act, but in literally every section of the statute. All persons, including federal agencies, are specifically instructed not to "take" endangered species, meaning that no one is "to harass, harm, pursue, hunt, shoot, wound, kill, trap, capture, or collect" such life forms. * * * Agencies in particular are directed * * * to "use . . . *all methods* and procedures which are necessary" to preserve endangered species. * * * In addition, the legislative history undergirding § 7 reveals an explicit congressional decision to require agencies to afford first priority to the declared national policy of saving endangered species. The pointed omission of the type of qualifying language previously included in endangered species legislation reveals a conscious decision by Congress to give endangered species priority over the "primary missions" of federal agencies. * * *

[I]t is clear Congress foresaw that § 7 would, on occasion, require agencies to alter ongoing projects in order to fulfill the goals of the Act. Congressman Dingell's discussion of Air Force practice bombing, for instance, obviously pinpoints a particular activity—intimately related to the national defense—which a major federal department would be obliged to alter in deference to the strictures of § 7. * * *

One might dispute the applicability of these examples to the Tellico Dam by saying that in this case the burden on the public through the loss of millions of unrecoverable dollars would greatly outweigh the loss of the snail darter. But neither the Endangered Species Act nor Art. III of the Constitution provides federal courts with authority to make such fine utilitarian calculations. On the contrary, the plain language of the Act, buttressed by its legislative history, shows clearly that Congress viewed the value of endangered species as "incalculable." Quite obviously, it would be difficult for a court to balance the loss of a sum certain—even $100 million—against a congressionally declared "incalculable" value, even assuming we had the power to engage in such a weighing process, which we emphatically do not. * * *

In passing the Endangered Species Act of 1973, Congress was also aware of certain instances in which exceptions to the statute's broad sweep would be necessary. Thus, § 10 creates a number of limited "hardship exemptions," none of which would even remotely apply to the Tellico Project. In fact, there are no exemptions in the Endangered Species Act for federal agencies, meaning that under the maxim *expressio unius est exclusio alterius*, we must presume that these were the only "hardship cases" Congress intended to exempt. * * *

Notwithstanding Congress' expression of intent in 1973, we are urged to find that the continuing appropriations for Tellico Dam constitute an implied repeal of the 1973 Act, at least insofar as it applies to the Tellico Project. In support of this view, TVA points to the statements found in various House and Senate Appropriations Committees' Reports* * *. Since we are unwilling to assume that these latter Committee statements constituted advice to ignore the provisions of a duly enacted law, we assume that these Committees believed that the Act simply was not applicable in this situation. But even under this interpretation of the Committees' actions, we are unable to conclude that the Act has been in any respect amended or repealed. [The Court emphasized that Congress often provides appropriations for projects despite on-going legal controversies, and that congressional rules provide that appropriations bills may not modify existing legislation.]

Having determined that there is an irreconcilable conflict between operation of the Tellico Dam and the explicit provisions of § 7 of the Endangered Species Act, we must now consider what remedy, if any, is appropriate. It is correct, of course, that a federal judge sitting as a chancellor is not mechanically obligated to grant an injunction for every violation of law. * * *

But these principles take a court only so far. Our system of government is, after all, a tripartite one, with each branch having certain defined functions delegated to it by the Constitution. While "[it] is emphatically the province and duty of the judicial department to say what the law is," *Marbury v. Madison*, 1 Cranch 137, 177 (1803), it is equally—and emphatically—the exclusive province of the Congress not only to formulate legislative policies and mandate programs and projects, but also to establish their relative priority for the Nation. Once Congress, exercising its delegated powers, has decided the order of priorities in a given area, it is for the Executive to administer the laws and for the courts to enforce them when enforcement is sought.

Here we are urged to view the Endangered Species Act "reasonably," and hence shape a remedy "that accords with some modicum of common sense and the public weal." * * * But is that our function? We have no expert knowledge on the subject of endangered species, much less do we have a mandate from the people to strike a balance of equities on the side of the Tellico Dam. Congress has spoken in the plainest of words, making it abundantly clear that the balance has been struck in favor of affording endangered species the highest of priorities, thereby adopting a policy which it described as "institutionalized caution."

Our individual appraisal of the wisdom or unwisdom of a particular course consciously selected by the Congress is to be put aside in the process of interpreting a statute. Once the meaning of an enactment is discerned and its constitutionality determined, the judicial process comes to an end. We do not sit as a committee of review, nor are we vested with the power of veto. The lines ascribed to Sir Thomas More by Robert Bolt are not without relevance here:

> "The law, Roper, the law. I know what's legal, not what's right. And I'll stick to what's legal. . . . I'm *not* God. The currents and eddies of right and wrong, which you find such plain-sailing, I can't navigate, I'm no voyager. But in the thickets of the law, oh there I'm a forester. . . . What would you do? Cut a great road through the law to get after the Devil? . . . And when the last law was down, and the Devil turned round on you—where would you hide, Roper, the laws all being flat? . . . This country's planted thick with laws from coast to coast—Man's laws, not God's—and if you cut them down . . . d'you really think you could stand

upright in the winds that would below then? . . . Yes, I'd give the Devil benefit of law, for my own safety's sake."

We agree with the Court of Appeals that in our constitutional system the commitment to the separation of powers is too fundamental for us to pre-empt congressional action by judicially decreeing what accords with "common sense and the public weal." Our Constitution vests such responsibilities in the political branches.

Affirmed.

MR. JUSTICE POWELL, with whom MR. JUSTICE BLACKMUN joins, dissenting.

In my view § 7 cannot reasonably be interpreted as applying to a project that is completed or substantially completed when its threat to an endangered species is discovered. Nor can I believe that Congress could have intended this Act to produce the "absurd result"—in the words of the District Court—of this case. If it were clear from the language of the Act and its legislative history that Congress intended to authorize this result, this Court would be compelled to enforce it. It is not our province to rectify policy or political judgments by the Legislative Branch, however egregiously they may disserve the public interest. But where the statutory language and legislative history, as in this case, need not be construed to reach such a result, I view it as the duty of this Court to adopt a permissible construction that accords with some modicum of common sense and the public weal. * * *

* * * [U]nder § 7 of the Endangered Species Act, at some stage of a federal project, and certainly where a project has been completed, the agency no longer has a reasonable choice simply to abandon it. When that point is reached, as it was in this case, the presumption against retrospective interpretation is at its strongest. The Court today gives no weight to that presumption. * * *

If the relevant Committees that considered the Act, and the Members of Congress who voted on it, had been aware that the Act could be used to terminate major federal projects authorized years earlier and nearly completed, * * * we can be certain that there would have been hearings, testimony, and debate * * *. The absence of any such consideration by the Committees or in the floor debates indicates quite clearly that no one participating in the legislative process considered these consequences as within the intendment of the Act. * * *

* * * [T]his view of legislative intent at the time of enactment is abundantly confirmed by the subsequent congressional actions and expressions. * * *

I have little doubt that Congress will amend the Endangered Species Act to prevent the grave consequences made possible by today's decision.

Few, if any, Members of that body will wish to defend an interpretation of the Act that requires the waste of at least $53 million, * * * and denies the people of the Tennessee Valley area the benefits of the reservoir that Congress intended to confer. There will be little sentiment to leave this dam standing before an empty reservoir, serving no purpose other than a conversation piece for incredulous tourists.

But more far reaching than the adverse effect on the people of this economically depressed area is the continuing threat to the operation of every federal project, no matter how important to the Nation. If Congress acts expeditiously, as may be anticipated, the Court's decision probably will have no lasting adverse consequences. But I had not thought it to be the province of this Court to force Congress into otherwise unnecessary action by interpreting a statute to produce a result no one intended.

MR. JUSTICE REHNQUIST, dissenting.

In the light of my Brother Powell's dissenting opinion, I am far less convinced than is the Court that the Endangered Species Act of 1973 * * * was intended to prohibit the completion of the Tellico Dam. But the very difficulty and doubtfulness of the correct answer to this legal question convinces me that the Act did *not* prohibit the District Court from refusing, in the exercise of its traditional equitable powers, to enjoin petitioner from completing the Dam. § 11(g)(1) of the Act * * * merely provides that "any person may commence a civil suit on his own behalf . . . to enjoin any person, including the United States and any other governmental instrumentality or agency . . . , who is alleged to be in violation of any provision of this chapter." * * *

NOTES

1.   In response to *TVA v. Hill,* Congress amended the Endangered Species Act by creating a special Endangered Species Committee, consisting of several cabinet level officers and other high-ranking officials. The Committee may grant an exemption to § 7's "no jeopardy" prohibition if it determines (by a vote of at least 5 to 2) that there are no reasonable alternatives to the agency action, that the benefits clearly outweigh those of compliance with the Act, and that the action is in the public interest and of at least regional significance. The Committee must also consider mitigation efforts. (These provisions are found in Endangered Species Amendment of 1978, § 7(e), (h), 16 U.S.C. § 1536(e), (h).)

The Committee unanimously denied an exemption for Tellico Dam, on the ground that reasonable alternatives to completion of the dam were available with acceptable cost-benefit ratios. The Committee also found that, despite the $100 million already invested in the dam, the benefits of completing the dam did not clearly outweigh the benefits of the alternatives. Essentially, the dam might easily fail to produce as much economic benefit as the farms it would flood.

Congress then passed a bill mandating completion of the dam. Does this further history show that the Supreme Court's decision was an exercise in futility, or does it show on the contrary that the Court was right to "remand" the problem to Congress? Should the Court have given a more "reasonable" interpretation to the ESA? Or would that have been inconsistent with the legislative mandate? *See* Daniel A. Farber, *Statutory Interpretation and Legislative Supremacy*, 78 GEO. L.J. 281, 294–298 (1989). For a retrospective view on *TVA v. Hill* by the lawyer who won the case, *see* Zygmunt J.B. Plater, *In the Wake of the Snail Darter*, 19 U. MICH. J.L. REFORM 805 (1986).

2.   As the first Endangered Species Act case before the Supreme Court, *TVA v. Hill* is (and was) viewed to be about as bad a set of facts as environmental plaintiffs could have imagined. The species in question was a small, neutral-colored fish whose existence was completely unknown before the project began, and the project itself was a nearly completed dam with, purportedly, important economic and political benefits. Though the litigation later uncovered the fact that the dam was a "pork barrel" project the benefits of which were suspect at best, this was not widely known at the outset. It was remarkable, then, that the Supreme Court ruled the way it did, adhering faithfully to the stringency of the law and setting aside the pragmatic aspects of the case as irrelevant. For further discussion of the case, see Elizabeth Garrett, *The Story of TVA v. Hill: Congress Has the Last Word in Statutory Interpretation*, in William N. Eskridge, Jr., Philip P. Frickey, and Elizabeth Garrett, STATUTORY INTERPRETATION STORIES (2011).

B. LISTING: SECTION 4

1. LISTING ENDANGERED AND THREATENED SPECIES

The first step in the statutory scheme of the Endangered Species Act is the listing of endangered or threatened species. Under § 4 of the Act, the Secretary of the Interior (in the case of land-based and freshwater species) or the Secretary of Commerce (in the case of marine species) shall:

determine whether any species is an endangered species or a threatened species because of any of the following factors:

(A) the present or threatened destruction, modification, or curtailment of its habitat or range;

(B) overutilization for commercial, recreational, scientific, or educational purposes;

(C) disease or predation;

(D) the inadequacy of existing regulatory mechanisms; or

(E) other natural or manmade factors affecting its continued existence.

16 U.S.C. § 1533(a) (2000).

The Act defines an "endangered species" as "any species which is in danger of extinction throughout all or a significant portion of its range. . . ." 16 U.S.C. § 1532(6) (2000). A "threatened species," on the other hand, is "any species which is likely to become an endangered species within the foreseeable future throughout all or a significant portion of its range." 16 U.S.C. § 1532(20).

In the listing of a species, the Secretary may not consider economic impacts. Rather, the Secretary must make the determination "solely on the basis of the best scientific and commercial data available to him." 16 U.S.C. § 1533(b)(1)(A). *See New Mexico Cattle Growers Ass'n v. United States Fish & Wildlife Serv.*, 248 F.3d 1277 (10th Cir. 2001) (holding that Service may not consider economic impacts in listing decision). *See also Center for Biological Diversity v. Badgley*, 335 F.3d 1097 (9th Cir. 2003) (holding decision not to list was based only on best available scientific and commercial data and therefore was not arbitrary or capricious).

In the designation of critical habitat, however, discussed *infra*, which is made at the same time as the listing of the species, the Secretary may consider other factors, including "the economic impact, the impact on national security, and any other relevant impact." 16 U.S.C. § 1533(b)(2).

The following case illustrates the issues pertaining to listing. The case is of particular interest since the threat to the species stemmed from climate change.

IN RE POLAR BEAR ENDANGERED SPECIES ACT LISTING AND SECTION 4(D) RULE LITIGATION—MDL NO. 1993

United States Court of Appeals, District of Columbia Circuit, 2013.
709 F.3d 1.

EDWARDS, SENIOR CIRCUIT JUDGE.

In 2005, the Center for Biological Diversity petitioned the Secretary of the Interior and the Fish and Wildlife Service ("FWS" or "agency") to list the polar bear under the Endangered Species Act ("ESA" or "Act"). When a species such as the polar bear is listed as either "threatened" or "endangered" under the Act, it is then subject to a host of protective measures designed to conserve the species. After a three-year rulemaking process, FWS found that, due to the effects of global climate change, the polar bear is likely to become an endangered species and face the threat of extinction within the foreseeable future.

A number of industry groups, environmental organizations, and states challenged the Listing Rule as either overly restrictive or insufficiently protective of the polar bear. These challenges were consolidated as a

Multidistrict Litigation case in the U.S. District Court for the District of Columbia. * * *

FWS cited three principal considerations in determining that polar bears should be listed as a threatened species. *First,* the polar bear depends on sea ice for its survival. *Second,* sea ice is declining. On this point, the Listing Rule states:

> Polar bears evolved to utilize the Arctic sea ice niche and are distributed throughout most ice-covered seas of the Northern Hemisphere. We find, based upon the best available scientific and commercial information, that polar bear habitat—principally sea ice—is declining throughout the species' range, that this decline is expected to continue for the foreseeable future, and that this loss threatens the species throughout all of its range. Therefore, we find that the polar bear is likely to become an endangered species within the foreseeable future throughout all of its range.

Third, climatic changes have and will continue to reduce the extent and quality of Arctic sea ice.

FWS concluded that these findings satisfied two of the statutory listing factors: (A) the threatened destruction of the species' habitat or range and (D) the inadequacy of existing regulatory mechanisms to preserve the species.

In aggregating data on climate change and sea ice, FWS relied on a variety of published studies and reports, including those of the Intergovernmental Panel on Climate Change ("IPCC"). FWS explained that:

> [t]he rapid retreat of sea ice in the summer and overall diminishing sea ice throughout the year in the Arctic is unequivocal and extensively documented in scientific literature. Further extensive recession of sea ice is projected by the majority of state-of-the-art climate models, with a seasonally ice-free Arctic projected by the middle of the 21st century by many of those models.

Noting that sea ice had reached a record low in the summer of 2007, FWS also explained that "[t]he observational record indicates that current summer sea ice losses appear to be about 30 years ahead of the ensemble of modeled values, which suggests that a transition towards a seasonally ice-free Arctic might occur sooner than the models indicate."

The agency's assessment of the species' dependence on sea ice derives from peer reviewed studies on polar bear biology and behavior, observed polar bear demographics, and population modeling. As noted above, FWS explained that the bears are highly dependent on sea ice, "including as a platform from which to hunt and feed upon seals; as habitat on which to seek mates and breed; as a platform to move to terrestrial maternity denning areas, and sometimes for maternity denning; and as a substrate on which to make long-distance movements." The Listing Rule anticipates that changes to the polar bear's habitat will soon pose an existential threat to the species:

Productivity, abundance, and availability of ice seals, the polar bear's primary prey base, would be diminished by the projected loss of sea ice, and energetic requirements of polar bears for movement and obtaining food would increase. Access to traditional denning areas would be affected. In turn, these factors would cause declines in the condition of polar bears from nutritional stress and reduced productivity. As already evidenced in the Western Hudson Bay and Southern Beaufort Sea populations, polar bears would experience reductions in survival and recruitment rates. The eventual effect is that polar bear populations would decline. The rate and magnitude of decline would vary among populations, based on differences in the rate, timing, and magnitude of impacts. However, within the foreseeable future, all populations would be affected, and the species is likely to become in danger of extinction throughout all of its range due to declining sea ice habitat.* * *

The Listing Rule rests on a three-part thesis: the polar bear is dependent upon sea ice for its survival; sea ice is declining; and climatic changes have and will continue to dramatically reduce the extent and quality of Arctic sea ice to a degree sufficiently grave to jeopardize polar bear populations. No part of this thesis is disputed and we find that FWS's conclusion—that the polar bear is threatened within the meaning of the ESA—is reasonable and adequately supported by the record.

The Listing Rule is the product of FWS's careful and comprehensive study and analysis. Its scientific conclusions are amply supported by data and well within the mainstream on climate science and polar bear biology. Thirteen of the fourteen peer reviewers to whom FWS submitted the proposed rule found that it generally "represented a thorough, clear, and balanced review of the best scientific information available from both published and unpublished sources of the current status of polar bears" and that it "justified the conclusion that polar bears face threats throughout their range." Only one peer reviewer dissented, "express[ing] concern that the proposed rule was flawed, biased, and incomplete, that it would do nothing to address the underlying issues associated with global warming, and that a listing would be detrimental to the Inuit of the Arctic." * * *

Appellants argue that FWS violated the APA [Administrative Procedure Act] and ESA by inadequately explaining how the predicted decrease in habitat would likely lead to such a dramatic population decline causing the species to be endangered within the next 45 years. * * *

Appellants' claim fails because FWS clearly explained how the anticipated habitat loss renders this particular species likely to become endangered. The agency considered and explained how the loss of sea ice harms the polar bear. The agency also considered the observed demographic trends in the areas where habitat loss has been most severe. For example, the Western Hudson Bay population—which "occurs near the southern limit of the species' range" in an area without year-round sea ice—has been in decline. Numerous experts predict that the sea ice loss in that area will soon weaken female polar bears to the point where reproduction levels become negligible. And climatologists anticipate that climatic changes will eventually affect all Arctic sea ice, causing FWS to predict "reduced numbers and reduced distributions of polar bears range-wide." * * *

Two of the Joint Appellants also argue that even if certain polar bear populations are threatened, FWS was wrong to conclude that the species is threatened throughout its range. They point to the agency's description of the Archipelago and Convergent ecoregions, both of which, FWS notes, are somewhat insulated from seasonal melting by various geophysical features. The ice in the far-northern Archipelago ecoregion is protected by "the buffering effects of the island archipelago complex, which lessens effects of oceanic currents and seasonal retractions of ice and retains a higher proportion of heavy more stable, multi-year sea ice." The Convergent ecoregion, because of generalized ice drift, "accumulates ice . . . as it is moved from the polar basin Divergent Ecoregion." As a result, this area "is characterized by heavy multiyear ice." Consequently, polar bear populations in both regions are not forecasted to decline as precipitously as those in the two more vulnerable ecoregions. Appellants seize on these projections to argue that the agency overreached by listing the entire species.

The agency considered comments along those lines and provided an adequate response. FWS acknowledged that receding sea ice may affect some polar bear populations later than others. However, the agency also explained that much of this region is

limited . . . in its ability to sustain a large number of polar bears because: (1) changes in the extent of ice and precipitation patterns are already occurring in the region; (2) the area is characterized by lower prey productivity (e.g., lower seal densities); and (3) polar bears moving into this area would increase competition among bears and ultimately affect polar bear survival. In addition, a small, higher-density population of polar bears in the Canadian Arctic would be subject to increased vulnerability to perturbations such as disease or accidental oil discharge from vessels. * * *

Appellants additionally challenge FWS's reliance on two polar bear population models developed by USGS. USGS submitted nine scientific reports to assist FWS in developing the Listing Rule. One of these reports presented two models of projected polar bear population trends. * * *

Citing these models' limitations, Appellants argue that FWS erred in relying on them. Appellants' chief criticism of the CM [one of the models] is its assumption that polar bear density will remain constant over time, which USGS itself conceded was "almost certainly not valid." Appellants argue that the BM [the other model] was also unreliable, pointing to FWS's own characterization of the BM "as an 'alpha' level prototype that would benefit from additional development and refinement."

"While courts routinely defer to agency modeling of complex phenomena," the agency must "explain[ ] the assumptions and methodology used in preparing the model and provide[ ] a complete analytic defense should the model be challenged." Appellants contend that FWS has not done so here. This argument is plainly meritless.

"That a model is limited or imperfect is not, in itself, a reason to remand agency decisions based upon it." FWS explained the methodology of the models within the Listing Rule itself, and FWS made available the full Amstrup Report for public comment before the final rule was promulgated. The Listing Rule acknowledges the limitations of these two models and repeatedly explains that the agency only used them for the limited purpose of confirming "the general direction and magnitude" of the population trends already forecast on the basis of other record evidence. * * *

The Act defines a threatened species as "any species which is likely to become an endangered species within the *foreseeable* future." FWS considered the particular circumstances of this listing decision and concluded that 45 years was the appropriate foreseeable time period. Appellants argue that FWS failed to justify its definition of "foreseeable" as a 45-year period.

The term "foreseeable" is not defined by statute or regulation. FWS determines what constitutes the "foreseeable" future on a case-by-case basis in each listing decision. Appellants apparently reject FWS's case-by-case approach and claim that " 'the foreseeable future' is the furthest period of time in which [FWS] can reliably assess, based on predicted conditions, whether the listing factors indicate that the species likely will become 'endangered.' " Appellants cite no legal authority suggesting that FWS was bound to follow their preferred definition. In any event, we conclude that, even applying Appellants' formulation, FWS's definition of foreseeability is reasonable.

FWS explained that "[t]he timeframe over which the best available scientific data allows us to reliably assess the effect of threats on the species is the critical component for determining the foreseeable future." "In the case of the polar bear, the key threat is loss of sea ice, the species' primary habitat." FWS looked at the most widely accepted climate models, as compiled by, among others, the IPCC. It found that there was general agreement in these models about warming and sea ice trends until about mid-century, at which point they diverge on the basis of uncertainties about, *inter alia,* population growth, technological improvements, and regulatory changes.

Appellants do not challenge the data underlying FWS's listing decision, but only FWS's interpretation of that data. That Appellants might have chosen a different period of foreseeability is of no moment so long as the agency's decision was justifiable and clearly articulated. Here, we find that FWS has not "relied on factors which Congress has not intended it to consider, entirely failed to consider an important aspect of the problem, [or] offered an explanation for its decision that runs counter to the evidence before the agency," nor is the agency's explanation "so implausible that it could not be ascribed to a difference in view or the product of agency expertise."

NOTES

1.   Climate change represents a global threat to biodiversity. See Daniel Farber, *Separated at Birth? Addressing the Twin Cases of Biodiversity and Climate Change*, 42 ECOLOGY L.Q. 841 (2015). Polar bears are not the only species to have been listed on this basis. For instance, in *Alaska Oil & Gas Ass'n v. Pritzker*, 940 F.3d 671 (9th Cir. 2016), the court upheld the listing of the Pacific bearded seal because of loss of sea ice. For analysis of these and other listing decisions, see Murray Feldamn and Andrew Mergen, *The Role of Climate Change in ESA Decisions*, 53 ROCKY MOUNTAIN L. FOUND. J. 67 (2016); Barry Kellman, *Climate Change in the Endangered Species Act: A Jurisprudential Dilemma*, 46 ENV. L. REP. 10845 (2016).

2.   Throughout the statutory text of the ESA, the relevant agency actor is typically the "Secretary." Within ESA cases, however, the courts typically refer to the U.S. Fish and Wildlife Service or the NOAA Fisheries Service (previously titled "the National Marine Fisheries Service" (NMFS)). In short form, the courts often will refer to these two agencies as the "Services." This can be confusing, but some brief history is helpful.

At the time of the Act's passage in 1973, the "Secretary" referred to the Secretary of Interior, whose department housed the U.S. Fish and Wildlife Service (FWS), and the Secretary of Commerce, whose department housed the National Marine Fisheries Service. As noted above, FWS is responsible for land-based and freshwater species, while NOAA Fisheries is responsible for all marine species and anadromous fish, which spend their lives in both fresh and saltwater. The reason for the divide between the two agencies is that, in 1970, President Nixon proposed a reorganization plan, under which the jurisdiction over marine fisheries would be transferred from the Department of Interior to the Department of Commerce. The two wildlife agencies under the departments often must work closely together, but the technical and legal divide still exists. For example, the agencies operate under different sets of regulations, and the agencies must be listed as individual parties where suit is brought against both.

For the purposes of this chapter, the terms "Secretary" or "Service" should be understood as referring to the respective wildlife agency being discussed.

3. As noted in the statutory text, *supra*, the Secretary must consider five factors under § 4(a)(1) in determining whether to list a species. If the Secretary determines that one or more of the five factors demonstrate that a species is endangered or threatened, she must list the species as such. In *Defenders of Wildlife v. Norton*, 258 F.3d 1136 (9th Cir. 2001), the Court overturned the Secretary's decision not to list the flat-tailed horned lizard, as the Secretary had failed to consider properly all five of the factors in determining whether the lizard was threatened or endangered. The Secretary earlier had recommended the lizard for listing but later withdrew the recommendation on the basis of new factors, claiming that, in spite of ongoing threats on private land, the lizard still had "large blocks of habitat with few anticipated impacts . . . on public lands throughout the range of th[e] species." Looking to the definition of endangered under § 3(6), "in danger of extinction throughout . . . a significant portion of its range," the court held that the Secretary, by excluding consideration of the private lands, failed properly to address this danger of extinction.

4. What is the "best available science" mandate that the statute references, *supra*? According to Holly Doremus, there is little to guide us on this point in the ESA itself, its legislative history, or the Services' regulations. The Services have, however, issued two policy statements that give more substance to the mandate.

> One deals with the use of information. It requires evaluation by biologists of all information used in listing, recovery planning, preparation of biological opinions, and issuance of permits, and documentation of that evaluation. It also directs agency biologists to prefer primary sources when possible and to affirmatively seek and impartially evaluate data contrary to the agency's official position or proposed actions.
>
> The second policy statement calls for the wildlife agencies to seek peer review of listing proposals by three independent specialists and to actively solicit peer review of draft recovery plans. In both cases, the final document must summarize the opinions of the reviewers, and the full opinions must be included in the administrative record. * * * In individual listing decisions, FWS has recognized that expert judgment plays a legitimate role in the analysis of data, and that internal technical review of the sort typical of many government reports carries indicia of reliability.

Holly Doremus, *The Purposes, Effects, and Future of the Endangered Species Act's Best Available Science Mandate*, 34 ENVTL. L. 397, 408–09 (2004). Doremus speculates that the "best available science" mandate serves any or all of four purposes: (1) the promotion of more accurate decision making; (2) increasing public trust and political credibility; (3) affecting judicial review, either by invoking special deference or, alternatively, by inviting more stringent review by giving the courts another standard to enforce; and (4) altering the decision-making process substantively one way or another.

5.   Under § 3(16) of the ESA, a species, for the purposes of listing decisions, is defined as "includ[ing] any subspecies of fish or wildlife or plants, and any distinct population segment of any species of vertebrate fish or wildlife which interbreeds when mature." 16 U.S.C. § 1532(16). Congress did not define this last term, "distinct population segment" (DPS), and accordingly, the definition and application of the DPS requirement has been a frequent subject in the litigation of listing decisions by the Services. In *Trout Unlimited v. Lohn*, 559 F.3d 946 (9th Cir. 2009), the court upheld a regulation requiring hatchery fish to be considered as part of the same evolutionarily significant unit (ESU), but making the endangered or threatened status of the fish turn on the viability of a natural, self-sustaining population, with the hatchery fish considered in terms of their possible positive or negative impacts on that goal. The court said that the debate about whether to include the hatchery fish in the ESU was "a good faith disagreement that is supported by science on both sides . . . In such situations we stay our hand." See also *Modesto Irrigation Dist. v. Guitierrez*, 619 F.3d 1024 (9th Cir. 2010) (upholding decision to place steelhead and rainbow trouts in distinct categories.) In contrast, in *In re Polar Bear Listing*, the converse argument was made: that the agency should have divided the polar bear into distinct population segments and found that only some segments were threatened. In a portion of the opinion not excerpted here, the court upheld the agency's determination that "there are no morphological or physiological differences across the range of the species that may indicate adaptations to environmental variations."

6.   Note that the polar bear was listed as threatened, not endangered. What is the difference? Statutorily, the main difference between these categories is that the § 9 prohibition on take, discussed *infra*, applies of its own force only to endangered species. That is, the statute does not contain an explicit prohibition against taking threatened species. The proviso to this comes in the text of § 4(d), which provides: "The Secretary may by regulation prohibit with respect to any threatened species any act prohibited under § 9(a)(1), in the case of fish or wildlife, or § 9(a)(2), in the case of plants, with respect to endangered species." 16 U.S.C.§ 1533(d) (2000).

Based on this authority, FWS has implemented a regulation that treats threatened species with the full force of § 9 unless otherwise noted. *See* 50 C.F.R. § 17.31 (2005). However, the Trump Administration has proposed eliminating this provision and requiring species-by-species orders regarding protection for threatened species This change would apply only to species listed in the future. See Fish and Wildlife Serv. And Dept. of Commerce, 83 Fed. Reg.

35193 (July 25, 2018). NOAA Fisheries has generally preferred to adopt a species-by-species approach in applying § 9 prohibitions to threatened species under its jurisdiction. To date, NOAA Fisheries has applied § 9 prohibitions to four main classes of threatened species: the Guadalupe fur seal, the Steller sea lion, anadromous fish, and sea turtles. *See* 50 C.F.R. pt. 223 (2005); *see also* Robert L. Fischman and Jaelith Hall-Rivera, *A Lesson for Conservation from Pollution Control Law: Cooperative Federalism for Recovery Under the Endangered Species Act*, 27 COLUM. J. ENVTL. L. 45, 63–64 (2002) (discussing the § 9 take prohibition and its application to threatened species). FWS has a much larger number of listings to manage and a very limited budget, so it may find it difficult to tailor rules for each species.

7.   If the polar bear is threatened by climate change, is any federal action that could lead to carbon emissions subject to consideration as a source of jeopardy? Could there be a minimum threshold of greenhouse gas emissions before ESA consultation is required? Consider the excerpt below.

J.B. RUHL, CLIMATE CHANGE AND THE ENDANGERED SPECIES ACT: BUILDING BRIDGES TO THE NO-ANALOG FUTURE
88 B.U.L. REV. 1 (2008).[3]

Like most other existing regulatory statutes, the ESA was not enacted with global climate change in mind, and the ESA alone will not arrest the causes or effects of our planet's no-analog future. But for the foreseeable future, until Congress or the states adopt statutes responding directly and comprehensively to climate change, the ESA is the nation's principal species conservation program. Even if the ESA cannot reverse climate change, pressure will be brought to bear on the FWS, just as it was on the EPA, to use its regulatory powers to "whittle away" at the problem.* * *

[The regulatory] authority [of the ESA] is only useful in circumstances where intervention is feasible and effective. For example, habitat loss, the leading cause of species decline, is often the result of easily identifiable human-induced factors susceptible to discrete and effective regulation. By contrast, invasive species, the runner-up in causes of species decline, typically present exceedingly complex causes and solutions, meaning there usually is no identifiable regulatory target.

In this respect, climate change presents a complicated scenario. To be sure, there is an easily identifiable regulatory target: greenhouse gas emissions. Leaving until later the question of how much discretion the ESA affords the FWS to regulate greenhouse gas emissions, there are obvious practical obstacles to this approach. First, regulating emissions in the United States alone is highly unlikely to sufficiently reduce global emission levels. Second, even if regulatory measures are implemented worldwide to

---

curtail emissions, the political reality is that the measures will impose phased-in reductions taking several decades to return to benchmark emission levels designed to stabilize or reduce greenhouse gas concentrations in the troposphere. Third, and most significantly, even if benchmark levels are attained in the near future, the physical dynamics of greenhouse gas effects on climate are such that climate change will continue on its present trajectory for a significant time period.* * *

[W]hat matters for most regulatory agencies is not how well we predict global trends such as surface temperature and sea levels, but what happens at the sub-global regional and local levels at which agencies act. * * * Yet even rather fundamental secondary effects questions, such as where it will rain more and less and how fast the ice will melt, remain open to wide variation in available models.

[F]or the FWS it often will be the case that what matters for a particular species is primarily a function of local ecological conditions and their effects on the species. The FWS, in other words, has to find models that predict the effects of global climate warming on a wide range of physical and biological cycles, "downscale" those effects to local ecological conditions, and then evaluate the effects of those local changes on the species of concern. Such specific downscaling efforts encounter the same nonlinear feedback properties that make climate change effects difficult to model and predict at mean global levels, but they operate with even more volatility at regional and local levels. Fundamentally, * * * the FWS has no models of this sort at its disposal because nobody has the experience or knowledge upon which to base them. Ultimately, they may simply be beyond our capacity. * * *

This is the no-analog future of the ESA. Some effects will be more predictable than others, such as that warmer waters will exceed the temperature limits of some fish species. But many effects will be difficult to predict, such as the cascade effects the loss of a top-level predator fish causes in its ecosystem. Where and when these effects will occur, their magnitude and duration, and the other effects they will set in motion are questions the FWS has only begun to confront.* * *

The effects of climate change * * * are unambiguously within the ambit of the listing criteria, leaving no room for the FWS to argue that it may leave climate change out of the listing calculus. Hence, like the EPA under the Clean Air Act, the FWS seems stuck with the challenge of identifying which species are endangered or threatened partly or primarily because of climate change. * * *

Although § 4 leaves no room for debate over whether the agency must integrate climate change effects in the listing decision, the statute provides considerable flexibility for how the agency does so. For example, a species is endangered if it is "in danger of extinction throughout all or a significant portion of its range" and is threatened if it "is likely to become an endangered species within the foreseeable future throughout all or a significant portion of its range." These are not precise concepts * * * the FWS may not be so hemmed in after all. Given the extent of agency expertise that must necessarily go into making such judgments, and given the uncertainty associated with downscaling global climate change effects to local species-specific ecological contexts, the FWS likely has considerable play in terms of matching different climate change threat scenarios with the ESA's endangered, threatened, not-threatened matrix. Indeed, the agency thus far has weaved between these terms and used its agency expertise and administrative discretion to find climate change a factor in some cases and not in others. * * *

Prosecuting a climate change case would be no mean feat either, given the generic effects of greenhouse gas emissions and the imprecision of downscaling models. Consider, for example, a scenario in which the pika is listed as endangered due to climate change. Who is taking the pika? Are greenhouse gas emissions from, say, a coal-fired power plant in Florida taking the pika? The plaintiff in such a case would have to show that the power plant emissions are the actual as well as proximate, foreseeable cause of the primary and secondary ecological effects which are in turn the actual as well as proximate, foreseeable cause of the pika's demise. Proving that would prove too much, however, as it would necessarily follow that *all* sources of greenhouse gases are taking the pika. This is an inherent feature of the take prohibition that makes it inapposite when take of a species occurs through large-scale, dispersed causal agents, such as water consumption and pollution—if *anyone* is taking the species, *everyone* is taking the species. Although nothing in the ESA prevents the FWS from attempting to prosecute such a case, it would be a daunting prosecutorial undertaking as well as likely political suicide. * * *

The take prohibition would prove more adept at enforcing discrete, identifiable actions that make it less likely a climate-threatened species will survive through the climate change transition. In particular, climate change is likely to present collisions between many species, climate-threatened or not, and human adaptations such as relocated agricultural and urban land uses, technological structures designed to impede sea level rise and floods, and new and intensified water diversions to sustain parched urban centers. Enforcement of the take prohibition in such settings, where proximate cause may be less difficult to establish, could help ensure that human adaptation measures do not disregard the interests of imperiled species. In this sense, § 9 would be used no differently from the way it is already used—climate change effects would simply be a reason to use it more vigilantly.* * *

The FWS has issued no official guidance on climate change with respect to the § 7 jeopardy consultation program, but it takes no stretch of imagination to fit climate change into this framework. Consider a project being carried out, funded, or authorized by a federal agency, the construction of which will remove habitat of a listed species and the operation of which will emit greenhouse gases. The removal of habitat and emission of greenhouse gases are clearly direct effects of the action added to the environmental baseline, both of which could have indirect effects that adversely affect the species. At some later time, the habitat removal could adversely affect the reproduction, numbers, or distribution of that species. Greenhouse gas emissions contribute to tropospheric warming, and the secondary effects of such warming could also, at some later time, adversely affect the species. Moreover, other state and private activities emitting greenhouse gases may also contribute to cumulative climate change effects that adversely affect the species. In short, greenhouse gas emissions and their climate change consequences both appear to be wrapped tightly into the framework for consultations under 7(a)(2).

To be sure, as with the listing decision, the FWS consultation decision depends on a three-part causal chain: greenhouse gas emissions cause tropospheric warming, which in turn causes secondary climate change effects, which in turn cause ecological changes that adversely affect the species. Although determining whether these downscale effects actually occur may be difficult to say in particular scenarios, the point is that they could occur. Unless the FWS intends on ruling out that possibility entirely—a difficult proposition after *Massachusetts v. EPA*—it stands to reason that consultations under § 7(a)(2) should consider the possible direct, indirect, and cumulative effects of greenhouse gas emissions and climate change.* * *

[T]he problem with fitting climate change into the consultation framework is that it exhibits more certainty at macro levels than at micro levels. Consider, for example, the proposed coal-fired power plant in Florida and its effects on the pika in the Sierra Nevada Mountains. It would seem quite a stretch to conclude that the power plant emissions will jeopardize the pika. Yet, at a macro level the analysis is rather straight forward: the power plant emits greenhouse gases (a direct effect of the action), greenhouse gases are reasonably certain to warm the troposphere (an indirect effect of the action), a warming troposphere is reasonably certain to adversely alter ecological conditions for the pika, and it is reasonably expected that such ecological changes will bring an end to the pika. At the micro level, however, it becomes difficult to link the *individual* plant's emissions as the jeopardizing agent for the pika, given that *all* greenhouse gas emissions worldwide are subject to the same macro analysis. Other than quantity of emissions, the FWS would have no reasoned basis for distinguishing between the power plant in Florida, a farm in Kansas, or an elementary school in Oregon. * * * Given these attributes of greenhouse gas emission effects on climate, it is difficult to conceive of how the agency would go about aggressively regulating greenhouse gas emissions through the jeopardy consultation program. The FWS does not have the pollution control expertise of the EPA, nor does any provision of the ESA explicitly provide authority to engage in emissions regulation. Given that all emission sources contribute to warming effects, the threat of jeopardy findings would have to be applied universally to all sources. * * * But is the FWS equipped to assume the role of nationwide regulator of farms, industrial facilities, auto emissions, and everything else? In short, the idea that *all* emission sources present jeopardy conditions to each and every climate-threatened species would prove too much, and likely render the ESA and the FWS political targets in the first degree.* * *

The ESA will be best served if the FWS adopts a cautious optimism that recognizes the limits of the ESA but keeps the statute relevant. . . . The job of the ESA is to help as many species as is reasonably possible get [to a point where the global community has achieved a stable climate outcome] with us—to serve as their bridge across the climate change transition into the no-analog future. Ironically, to do this will take some humility and restraint. Going for the jugular by regulating greenhouse gas emissions is *not* where the ESA can be of most help to imperiled species. There is little to be gained for the FWS or for climate-threatened species by having the agency go down this road. * * * Rather, the FWS can provide expert assistance to the agencies more appropriately charged with regulating greenhouse gas emissions, such as the EPA, by advising them about the effects of climate change on species.

As for its direct role in addressing climate change, the FWS can employ the ESA most effectively by identifying species threatened by climate change, identifying which of those can be helped through the ESA's habitat-based programs, and devising a management plan—one that uses regulatory action as well as recovery planning—to build each such species its bridge. Indeed, this strategy allows the FWS to dispense with the distinction between human-induced and natural climate variation. Climate change is climate change—it does not matter to the species what is causing it. What does matter to them is whether and in what shape they survive it.

NOTE ON CLIMATE CHANGE AND THE ESA

As Ruhl explains, administration of the Endangered Species Act in the face of climate change presents considerable challenges. Clearly, limiting the extent of climate change is a high priority, but the statute may not be well-adapted to address this problem directly, as Ruhl explains. There is some hope, however, that we may be able to save many species through a variety of techniques, including a reduction in other threats to habitat. See Christopher N. Johnson et al., *Biodiversity Losses and Conservation Responses in the*

Anthropocene, 356 SCIENCE 270 (2017); M.C. Urban et al., *Improving the Forecast for Biodiversity Under Climate Change*, 353 SCIENCE 1113 (2016).

But conventional techniques may not be enough to save some species. What then? If a large number of species are at risk, we may need to exercise triage, prioritizing those that can best be saved and letting the rest go. This would be quite contrary to the "Noah's Ark" principle of the ESA, which focuses on doing as much as possible for each individual species. Some species and subspecies may be saved, but only by "unnatural" interventions, such as transplanting them to new locations, interbreeding them hardier animals or plants, or even genetic engineering. But whether we should resort to these measures is highly controversial. If we resort to such techniques, can we still say we're preserving nature? And what do we mean by "nature"?

The Trump Administration has proposed regulations that would make it more difficult to list species on the basis of climate impacts and complicate listing decisions for species in general. Fish and Wildlife Service and National Oceanic and Atmospheric Administration, *Endangered and Threatened Wildlife and Plants; Revision of the Regulations for Listing Species and Designating Critical Habitat*, 83 Fed. Rep. 35193 (July 25, 2018). Notably, the proposal would redefine the relevant time horizon by tweaking the definition of "foreseeable." The revision would limit the time horizon to "only so far in the future as the Services can reasonably determine that the conditions potentially posing a danger of extinction in the foreseeable future are probable" based on the best available science. The agency must be able "to formulate a reliable prediction and avoid speculation and preconception." *Id.* at 35195–96, For comments on this and other proposed changes, see Eric Biber, *Comments on Proposed ESA Rule Changes,* Legal-Planet.org (Oct. 17, 2018), http://legal-planet.org/2018/10/17/comments-on-proposed-esa-rule-changes/.

2.   CRITICAL HABITAT

What happens after a listing? The listing of a species can be understood as the "trigger" of the Endangered Species Act. That is, once the Services list a species as endangered or threatened, the rest of the statutory requirements, prohibitions, and protections apply. Without a listing, a jeopardy determination cannot be made and the prohibition against take does not exist. Accordingly, for both those supporting the protection of endangered species and those for whom endangered species protection would be problematic, the § 4 determination is crucial.

As noted *supra*, the Secretary must, subject to important conditions, determine a species' critical habitat at the time of its listing. 16 U.S.C. § 1533(a)(3)(A). The Act defines "critical habitat" as:

the specific areas *within* the geographical area occupied by the species, at the time it is listed * * * on which are found those physical or biological features (I) essential to the conservation of the species and (II) which may require special management considerations or protection; and specific areas *outside* the geographical area occupied by the species at the time it is listed * * * upon a determination by the Secretary that such areas are essential for the conservation of the species.

16 U.S.C. § 1532(5)(A) (emphasis added).

Except in circumstances determined by the Secretary, "critical habitat shall not include the entire geographical area which can be occupied by the threatened or endangered species." 16 U.S.C. § 1532(5)(C).

Unlike the listing process, the critical habitat determination may involve considerations of "the economic impact, the impact on national security, and any other relevant impact." Indeed, the Secretary may choose not to designate an area as critical habitat:

if he determines that the benefits of such exclusion outweigh the benefits of specifying such area as part of the critical habitat, unless he determines, based on the best scientific and commercial data available, that the failure to designate such area as critical habitat will result in the extinction of the species concerned.

16 U.S.C. § 1533(b)(2).

The opinion that follows is a good illustration of the considerations that must go into the decision whether or not to designate critical habitat.

NORTHERN SPOTTED OWL V. LUJAN
United States District Court, W.D. Washington, 1991.
758 F.Supp. 621.

THOMAS S. ZILLY, UNITED STATES DISTRICT JUDGE.

[The saga of the spotted owl began in the late 1980s, when environmental groups petitioned for the listing of the owl, a bird whose habitat was (and is) the remaining stands of old-growth forest native to the Pacific Northwest. Because of continued and increasing logging of old-growth forests, the owl's habitat had been diminished greatly. In a previous stage of the litigation, the court had reversed an earlier decision by the Service not to list the spotted owl and remanded to the agency for further proceedings.]

On June 23, 1989, the Service proposed to list the northern spotted owl as a "threatened" species under the Endangered Species Act. *See* 54 Fed. Reg. 26,666 (1989). On June 26, 1990, the Service published its final rule confirming that listing decision. *See* 55 Fed. Reg. 26,114 (1990). In both the proposed and final listing rules, the Service expressly deferred designation of critical habitat for the spotted owl on grounds that it was not "determinable." * * *

Plaintiffs move this Court to order the federal defendants to designate "critical habitat" for the northern spotted owl. As defined under the ESA, "critical habitat" refers to geographic areas which are essential to the conservation of the spotted owl and which may require special management considerations or protection. 16 U.S.C. § 1532(5)(A)(i). Thus, even though more extensive habitat may be essential to maintain the species over the long term, critical habitat only includes the minimum amount of habitat needed to avoid short-term jeopardy or habitat in need of immediate intervention. Habitat not currently occupied by the spotted owl may be designated as critical only upon a determination by the Secretary of the Interior that such areas are essential to ensure the conservation of the species. 16 U.S.C. § 1532(5)(A)(ii). The Secretary must consult with other federal agencies to ensure that governmental actions do not "result in the destruction or adverse modification" of land designated as critical habitat. 16 U.S.C. § 1536(a)(2).

The initial determination of what areas constitute critical habitat is to be made on the basis of "the best scientific data available." 16 U.S.C. § 1533(b)(2). This requires identifying geographic areas containing the physical and biological features considered to be essential to the conservation of the species. *See* 50 C.F.R. § 424.12(b) (listing criteria for designating critical habitat). In addition, Congress directed the Secretary of the Interior to consider the probable economic or other impacts on human activities resulting from the critical habitat designation. The Secretary is expressly authorized to exclude any area from critical habitat if he determines that the benefits of such exclusion outweigh the conservation benefits, unless to do so would result in the extinction of the species. 16 U.S.C. § 1533(b)(2).

* * * The ESA requires the Secretary, "to the maximum extent prudent and determinable," to designate critical habitat *concurrently* with his decision to list a species as endangered or threatened. 16 U.S.C. § 1533(a)(3). When critical habitat is not determinable at the time of the final listing rule, the Secretary is authorized up to twelve additional months to complete the designation. 16 U.S.C. § 1533(b)(6)(C). The governing administrative regulations specify that the Secretary must state his reasons for not designating critical habitat in the proposed and final listing rules. 50 C.F.R. § 424.12(a).

* * * Plaintiffs charge that the Secretary has violated the Endangered Species Act and the Administrative Procedure Act by failing to designate critical habitat concurrently with the listing of the northern spotted owl. * * *

The language employed in § 4(a)(3) and its place in the overall statutory scheme evidence a clear design by Congress that designation of critical habitat coincide with the species listing determination. The linkage of these issues was not the product of chance; rather, it reflects the studied and deliberate judgment of Congress that destruction of habitat was the most significant cause of species endangerment. * * *

As originally enacted, the ESA admitted no exceptions to the requirement that the critical habitat designation occur concurrently with the listing determination. * * *

By its 1978 amendments, Congress expressly linked the timing of the critical habitat designation to the decision to list the species. A single exception to this duty was recognized when the habitat designation was not "prudent." * * *

* * * Under current regulations, a critical habitat designation is not "prudent" only if it is not in the best interest of the species.[3] * * *

In 1982, Congress expressed frustration at the slow pace of implementing the Endangered Species Act. Particular concern focused on the Secretary's critical habitat responsibilities as a source of delay. * * *

The solution adopted by Congress permits the Secretary to defer the habitat designation upon finding that critical habitat is not "determinable" at the time the Secretary proposes to list the species under the ESA or at the time of his final listing decision. 16 U.S.C. § 1533(b)(6)(C). In no event may the Secretary delay the designation of critical habitat for more than twelve months after publication of the final listing rule. * * * The authoring committee of the 1982 amendments, the House Committee on Merchant Marine and Fisheries, expressly emphasized the narrow nature of this exception:

> * * * The Committee feels strongly, however, that, where the biology relating to the status of the species is clear, it should not be denied the protection of the Act because of the inability of the Secretary to complete the work necessary to designate critical habitat. . . . *The Committee expects the agencies to make the strongest attempt possible to determine critical habitat within the time period designated for listing * * *.*

* * * The conference report to the 1982 amendments further emphasizes that designation is to occur at *the earliest possible time,* not to exceed twelve months after publication of the final listing rule. * * *

The conference report also states that the Secretary must "justify listing a species without designating critical habitat" to support it. * * *

---

[3]   The regulations of the Fish and Wildlife Service define only two situations when designation of critical habitat is not "prudent" within the meaning of 16 U.S.C. § 1533(a)(3):

> (i) The species is threatened by taking or other human activity, and identification of critical habitat can be expected to increase the degree of such threat to the species, or

> (ii) Such designation of critical habitat would not be beneficial to the species.

50 C.F.R. § 424.12(a)(1).

This legislative history leaves little room for doubt regarding the intent of Congress: The designation of critical habitat is to coincide with the final listing decision absent extraordinary circumstances. * * *

This Court rejects as incongruous the federal defendants' argument that § 4(b)(6)(C) authorizes an automatic extension of time merely upon a finding that critical habitat is not presently "determinable," even where no effort has been made to secure the information necessary to make the designation. To relieve the Secretary of any affirmative information gathering responsibilities would effectively nullify Congress' charge that the species listing and habitat designation occur concurrently, "to the maximum extent . . . determinable." 16 U.S.C. § 1533(a)(3). * * *

* * * The federal defendants fail to direct this Court to any portion of the administrative record which adequately explains or justifies the decision not to designate critical habitat for the northern spotted owl. Nowhere in the proposed or final rules did the Service state what efforts had been made to determine critical habitat. Nowhere did the Service specify what additional biological or economic information was necessary to complete the designation. Nowhere did the Service explain why critical habitat was not determinable. * * *

Indeed, the Service candidly acknowledged in its June 1989 proposed rule that it had not conducted the analyses required by § 4(b)(2). This Court interprets the Service's statement one year later that it "*will* evaluate the economic and other relevant impacts," absent any evidence of having done so, as tacitly reaffirming that the studies still had not been performed. * * *

More is required under the ESA and the Service's own regulations than the mere conclusion that more work needs to be done. * * * It cannot be established upon the record presented that the Service "considered the relevant factors" or that it "articulated a rational connection between the facts found and the choice made." * * * Accordingly, this Court must find the Service abused its discretion when it declined to designate critical habitat for the northern spotted owl. * * *

This Court is mindful of the prodigious resources dedicated by the Service to the spotted owl. The listing process required a truly remarkable effort by the Service given the volume of comments received and the complexity of the issues raised. The inter-agency consultations have consumed additional manpower and financial resources. * * *

In any event, such efforts, which the Court assumes have been on-going since prior to June 1989, do not relieve the Service of its statutory obligation to designate critical habitat concurrently with the species listing, or to provide a rational and articulated basis for concluding that critical habitat is not determinable. * * *

Common sense dictates that the spotted owl would be poorly served by a hastily crafted or uninformed habitat plan. Congress expressly provided for periodic revisions to critical habitat plans to avoid this result. *See* 16 U.S.C. § 1533(a)(3)(B). Accordingly, the Service is ordered to submit to the Court by March 15, 1991 a written plan for completing its review of critical habitat for the northern spotted owl. The Service is further ordered to publish its proposed critical habitat plan no later than forty-five days thereafter. The final rule is to be published at the earliest possible time under the appropriate circumstances. * * *

NOTES

1.   After listing the polar bear as threatened, the Fish and Wildlife Service also designated critical habitat. This designation was challenged in *Alaska Oil & Gas Ass'n v. Jewell*, 815 F.3d 544 (9th cir. 2016). The primary contention of the challengers was that the FWS had failed to show that all of the areas included had the "primary constituent elements"—the key features needed to support polar bears, such as suitable places for dens. The court rejected these claims. The court held the challengers had demanded "too high a standard of scientific proof" and that the agency had done the best it could given available scientific data.

2.   Is the consultation requirement in § 7 for a threat to existence of a species the same as for a threat to critical habitat? In *Sierra Club v. United States Fish & Wildlife Serv.*, 245 F.3d 434 (5th Cir. 2001), the Service had listed the Gulf sturgeon, but chose not to designate critical habitat for the fish, concluding that it was not prudent to do so, as the designation would not provide any additional benefit for the sturgeon beyond the basic consultation requirement. Environmental plaintiffs sued, challenging the decision and the regulation on which the Services based the decision. The problem, as plaintiffs saw it—and as the Fifth Circuit agreed—was that the regulation conflicted with the requirements of the ESA. The ESA requires consultation when a federal action will either jeopardize the existence of a listed species *or* will result in the "destruction or adverse modification" of the species' critical habitat. The court noted that these consultation standards were different, since critical habitat is meant to provide for the recovery—and not just the survival—of a species. In the Services' regulations, however, "destruction or adverse modification" was defined as "a direct or indirect alteration that appreciably diminishes the value of critical habitat for *both the survival and recovery of a listed species*." *Id.* at 439. Accordingly, the Services had set the consultation bar for critical habitat higher than what the ESA required.

The Ninth Circuit followed this decision on "the recovery goal of critical habitat." In *Gifford Pinchot Task Force v. United States Fish & Wildlife Serv.*, 378 F.3d 1059 (9th Cir. 2004), the court held the same regulation to be impermissible under the ESA, noting:

[T]he ESA was enacted not merely to forestall the extinction of species (i.e., promote a species survival), but to allow a species to recover to the point where it may be delisted. *See* 16 U.S.C. § 1532(3) (defining conservation as all methods that can be employed to "bring any endangered species or threatened species to the point at which the measures provided pursuant to this [Act] are no longer necessary") * * *. * * * By these definitions, it is clear that Congress intended that conservation and survival be two different (though complementary) goals of the ESA. * * * Clearly, then, the purpose of establishing "critical habitat" is for the government to carve out territory that is not only necessary for the species' survival but also essential for the species' recovery.

Congress, by its own language, viewed conservation and survival as distinct, though complementary, goals, and the requirement to preserve critical habitat is designed to promote both conservation and survival. Congress said that "destruction or adverse modification" could occur when sufficient critical habitat is lost so as to threaten a species' recovery even if there remains sufficient critical habitat for the species' survival.

Id. at 1070. *See also New Mexico Cattle Growers v. United States Fish & Wildlife Serv.*, 248 F.3d 1277 (10th Cir. 2001).

3. As noted above, one of the findings the Services can make in deciding not to list critical habitat is that the designation would not be "prudent." This springs from the requirement under § 4 of the ESA that the listing of a species must be accompanied by a designation of critical habitat "to the maximum extent prudent. . . ." *See* 16 U.S.C. § 1533(a)(3) (2000). What is prudence? In *Natural Resources Defense Council v. United States Dep't of Interior*, 113 F.3d 1121 (9th Cir. 1997), plaintiffs challenged the U.S. Fish and Wildlife Service's failure to list critical habitat for the coastal California gnatcatcher, a songbird unique to southern California. Though the ESA does not define prudence, the Service had based its findings on its own regulatory definition of what is *not* prudent: (i) The species is threatened by taking or other human activity, and identification of critical habitat can be expected to increase the degree of such threat to the species, or (ii) Such designation of critical habitat would not be beneficial to the species. *Id.* at 1125.

Based on this regulation, the Service claimed that the designation would not be prudent because (1) it would harm the species, since hostile landowners had a history of identifying and destroying gnatcatcher habitat; and (2) the designation would not appreciably benefit species, since most of the birds were located on private land, outside the ambit of § 7. The court rejected both of these bases, holding that the first violated the ESA requirement that the Service weigh the benefits against the risks of designation. In this case, the Service had performed no such weighing. As to the second basis, the court held that the Service impermissibly broadened the narrow statutory exception for imprudent designations by construing "no benefit" as no benefit to *most of* the species. This cut against the clear congressional intent that an imprudence designation should occur only "*in rare circumstances.*" *Id.* at 1126. Thus, even though most of the species' habitat was on private land, this fell far short of showing that the designation would have *no* benefit.

Affected landowners and resource interests are sensitive to the potential impacts on them of a designation of critical habitat. Not surprisingly, this is a fertile area of litigation. Also unsurprisingly, the Trump Administration has recently proposed regulations that would broaden the grounds for declining to define the critical habitat for the species and narrow the area to be included when defining critical habitat. See Fish and Wildlife Service and National Oceanic and Atmospheric Administration, *Endangered and Threatened Wildlife and Plants; Revision of the Regulations for Listing Species and Designating Critical Habitat*, 83 Fed. Rep. 35193 (July 25, 2018).

NOTE ON THE CONTINUING SPOTTED OWL CONTROVERSY

Following Judge Zilly's order to list critical habitat by April 30, 1991, the Fish and Wildlife Service surprised everyone when it designated 11.6 million acres of habitat on May 6, 1991. The designation included "6.5 million acres of [Forest Service] land, 1.4 million acres of [Bureau of Land Management] land, 0.7 million acres of state and tribal lands, and 3 million acres of private land." *See* Steven Lewis Yaffee, THE WISDOM OF THE SPOTTED OWL: POLICY LESSONS FOR A NEW CENTURY 132 (1994).

Two weeks after this contentious designation, Judge William Dwyer of the U.S. District Court for the Western District of Washington added to the controversy by permanently enjoining Forest Service timber sales in spotted owl habitat until the Forest Service completed a new spotted owl management plan and environmental analysis. *Id.* at 133; *see also Seattle Audubon Soc. v. Evans*, 771 F.Supp. 1081 (W.D. Wash. 1991).

The combination of these two related controversies led the Bush Administration to invoke the Endangered Species Committee provision of the Act. *See* 16 U.S.C. § 1536(e). As noted *supra,* the ESC was added to the Act in the 1978 in response to the Tellico Dam controversy, as a last resort to offer exemptions to those projects that could not comply with the terms of the Act. Because the Committee can officially sanction the demise of an endangered species, it has been colloquially termed the "God Squad." The God Squad is comprised of the Secretary of Agriculture, the Secretary of the Army, the Chairman of the Council of Economic Advisors, the Administrator of the Environmental Protection Agency, the Secretary of the Interior, the Administrator of the National Oceanic and Atmospheric Administration, and "one individual from each affected State" appointed by the President. 16 U.S.C. § 1536(e)(3).

An agency filing an ESC exemption application must satisfy several requirements under § 7(h):

(1) The Committee shall make a final determination whether or not to grant an exemption within 30 days after receiving the report of the Secretary pursuant to subsection (g)(5). The Committee shall grant

an exemption from the requirements of subsection (a)(2) for an agency action if, by a vote of not less than five of its members voting in person—

(A) it determines on the record, based on the report of the Secretary, the record of the hearing held under subsection (g)(4) and on such other testimony or evidence as it may receive, that—

(i) there are no reasonable and prudent alternatives to the agency action;

(ii) the benefits of such action clearly outweigh the benefits of alternative courses of action consistent with conserving the species or its critical habitat, and such action is in the public interest;

(iii) the action is of regional or national significance; and

(iv) neither the Federal agency concerned nor the exemption applicant made any irreversible or irretrievable commitment of resources prohibited by subsection (d); and

(B) it establishes such reasonable mitigation and enhancement measures, including, but not limited to, live propagation, transplantation, and habitat acquisition and improvement, as are necessary and appropriate to minimize the adverse effects of the agency action upon the endangered species, threatened species, or critical habitat concerned.

Any final determination by the Committee under this subsection shall be considered final agency action for purposes of [the Administrative Procedure Act].

16 U.S.C. § 1536(h)(1)(A).

Believing that its Northwest timber sales met these guidelines, the Bush Administration applied for an exemption from the Committee. This was, in fact, the first and only time the ESC has granted an exemption.

However, the saga did not end there. Throughout the Committee's deliberations, there were allegations of political interference by the White House. When the Committee finally handed down its decision to grant an exemption on May 14, 1992, environmental plaintiffs immediately filed suit in federal court. In *Portland Audubon Society v. Endangered Species Committee*, 984 F.2d 1534 (9th Cir. 1993), plaintiffs alleged that "improper ex parte contacts between the White House and members of the Committee tainted the decision-making process." The Ninth Circuit remanded the matter to the Committee for further proceedings, holding that the Committee was subject to the provisions of the Administrative Procedure Act and that, should the plaintiffs' allegations be true, the Committee would be in violation of the APA. For this reason, the court remanded for an evidentiary hearing by an administrative law judge.

In response to the ongoing litigation, as well as public demand for change in the management of Northwest forests, newly elected President Clinton convened a Forest Conference in 1993 and created a Forest Ecosystem Management Assessment Team (FEMAT) to study and develop a new, ecology-based management plan for the forests of the Northwest. In 1994, FEMAT's work resulted in the Northwest Forest Plan, which was the first ecosystem management plan for public lands. The Plan covered 24 million acres of public land in northern California, Oregon, and Washington, and had several conservation-based components. Among these were the creation of forest reserves, in which logging and roadbuilding were limited; the Aquatic Conservation Strategy, which protected salmon and other species in rivers and streams; and the Survey and Manage program, which required pre-logging inspections for lesser-known old-growth species on lands outside of the designated reserves. In *Seattle Audubon Soc'y v. Moseley*, 80 F.3d 1401 (9th Cir. 1996), the Ninth Circuit upheld the Plan and its accompanying EIS.

Beginning in 2002, the George W. Bush administration made attempts to roll back the protections under the Plan in several different ways: (1) lowering restrictions under the Aquatic Conservation Strategy; (2) initiating review of the ESA status of the spotted owl and marbled murrelet; (3) reverting to optional protections under Survey and Manage; and (4) settling a decade-old lawsuit with industry to reinterpret protections of the Bureau of Land Management's O & C lands.

In 2012, under court order, the government proposed a designation of critical habitat for the spotted owl. The White House immediately directed the Secretary of Interior to undertake a more intensive economic analysis of the proposal and to consider exempting private lands from the designation. Presidential Memorandum—Proposed Revised Habitat for the Spotted Owl: Minimizing Regulatory Burdens (February 28, 2012). The final rule designated almost ten million acres as critical habitat. For more information about the rule, including environmental and economic analyzes, see http://www.fws.gov/oregonfwo/species/data/northernspottedowl/CriticalHabitat/default.asp. The economic analysis concludes that the new critical habitat designation "is anticipated to have little incremental effects above and beyond the conservation measures already required as a result of its threatened status, and thus is expected to impose minimal additional regulatory burden."

Litigation over the spotted owl has continued apace. Much of it has focused on whether particular timber sales pose a threat to the owl or its critical habitat. See, e.g., *Conservation Congress v. U.S. Forest Serv.,* 720 F.3d 1048 (9th Cir. 2013). There is also continuing debate among scientists about the best way to preserve the owls. See Warren Cornwall, *Scientists Split on Oregon Old-Growth Forest Plan*, 353 SCIENCE 637 (2016).

C. CONSULTATION: SECTION 7

Section 7(a)(2) of the Act provides that:

> [e]ach Federal agency shall, in consultation with and with the assistance of the Secretary, insure that any action authorized, funded, or carried out by such agency (hereinafter in this section referred to as an "agency action") is not likely to jeopardize the continued existence of any endangered species or threatened species or result in the destruction or adverse modification of habitat of such species which is determined by the Secretary, after consultation as appropriate with affected States, to be critical, unless such agency has been granted an exemption for such action by the Committee pursuant to subsection (h) of this section. In fulfilling the requirements of this paragraph each agency shall use the best scientific and commercial data available.

16 U.S.C. § 1536(a)(2).

Accordingly, § 7(a)(2) is known as the "consultation" requirement of the ESA. The *TVA* case excerpted earlier showed the power of § 7. It would be a mistake to infer, however, that the action agency's only duty is to communicate with the Secretary. As *TVA v. Hill* illustrates, the consequences of a finding of jeopardy can be draconian. The next case explains the mechanics of the § 7 consultation process. Note that consultation is only required when the agency has some discretion in its decision. See *National Assn. of Home Builders v. Defenders of Wildlife*, 551 U.S. 644 (2007); *Karuk Tribe of California v. United States Forest Service*, 681 F.3d 1006 (9th Cir. 2012).

The Trump Administration has proposed amendments to the regulations governing the consultation process. See Department of the Interior and Department of Commerce, *Endangered and Threatened Wildlife and Plants: Revisions of Regulations for Interagency Cooperation*, 83 Fed. Reg. 35178 (July 25, 2018). Among other changes, the proposal would encourage the use of consultation about programs rather than individual actions, clarify (or arguably modify) the range of impacts the agency must consider, and eliminate the requirement of reconsultation when a new species is listed in an area covered by an existing land management plan. Some of these changes are contrary to existing caselaw, particularly in the Ninth Circuit. If they are incorporated into the final rule, litigation is sure to result.

THOMAS V. PETERSON

United States Court of Appeals, Ninth Circuit, 1985.
753 F.2d 754.

SNEED, CIRCUIT JUDGE

Plaintiffs sought to enjoin construction of a timber road in a former National Forest roadless area. The District Court granted summary judgment in favor of defendant R. Max Peterson, Chief of the Forest Service, and plaintiffs appealed. We affirm in part, reverse in part, and remand for further proceedings consistent with this opinion.

We conclude that: * * * The Endangered Species Act (ESA) requires the Forest Service to prepare a biological assessment to determine whether the road and the timber sales that the road is designed to facilitate are likely to affect the endangered Rocky Mountain Gray Wolf, and construction of the road should be enjoined pending compliance with the ESA. * * *

The Endangered Species Act Claim

The plaintiffs' third claim concerns the Forest Service's alleged failure to comply with the Endangered Species Act (ESA) in considering the effects of the road and timber sales on the endangered Rocky Mountain Gray Wolf.

The ESA contains both substantive and procedural provisions. Substantively, the Act prohibits the taking or importation of endangered species, *see* 16 U.S.C. § 1538, and requires federal agencies to ensure that their actions are not "likely to jeopardize the continued existence of any endangered species or threatened species or result in the destruction or adverse modification" of critical habitat of such species, *see* 16 U.S.C. § 1536(a)(2).

The Act prescribes a three-step process to ensure compliance with its substantive provisions by federal agencies. Each of the first two steps serves a screening function to determine if the successive steps are required. The steps are:

(1) An agency proposing to take an action must inquire of the Fish & Wildlife Service (FWS) whether any threatened or endangered species "may be present" in the area of the proposed action. *See* 16 U.S.C. § 1536(c)(1).

(2) If the answer is affirmative, the agency must prepare a "biological assessment" to determine whether such species "is likely to be affected" by the action. *Id.* The biological assessment may be part of an environmental impact statement or environmental assessment. *Id.*

(3) If the assessment determines that a threatened or endangered species "is likely to be affected," the agency must

formally consult with the FWS. *Id.* § 1536(a)(2). The formal consultation results in a "biological opinion" issued by the FWS. See *id.* § 1536(b). If the biological opinion concludes that the proposed action would jeopardize the species or destroy or adversely modify critical habitat, *see id.* § 1536(a)(2), then the action may not go forward unless the FWS can suggest an alternative that avoids such jeopardization, destruction, or adverse modification. *Id.* § 1536(b)(3)(A). If the opinion concludes that the action will not violate the Act, the FWS may still require measures to minimize its impact. *Id.* § 1536(b)(4)(ii)–(iii).

Plaintiffs first allege that, with respect to the Jersey Jack road, the Forest Service did not undertake step (1), a formal request to the FWS. The district court found that to be the case, but concluded that the procedural violation was insignificant because the Forest Service was already aware that wolves may be present in the area. The court therefore refused to enjoin the construction of the road. Plaintiffs insist, based on *TVA v. Hill*, 437 U.S. 153 (1978), that an injunction is mandatory once any ESA violation is found. Defendants respond, citing *Village of False Pass v. Clark*, 733 F.2d 605 (9th Cir. 1984), that *TVA* applies only to substantive violations of the ESA, and that a court has discretion to deny an injunction when it finds a procedural violation to be *de minimis*.

We need not reach this issue. The Forest Service's failure goes beyond the technical violation cited by the district court, and is not *de minimis*.

Once an agency is aware that an endangered species may be present in the area of its proposed action, the ESA requires it to prepare a biological assessment to determine whether the proposed action "is likely to affect" the species and therefore requires formal consultation with the FWS. *See supra.* The Forest Service did not prepare such an assessment prior to its decision to build the Jersey Jack road. Without a biological assessment, it cannot be determined whether the proposed project will result in a violation of the ESA's substantive provisions. A failure to prepare a biological assessment for a project in an area in which it has been determined that an endangered species may be present cannot be considered a *de minimis* violation of the ESA.

The district court found that the Forest Service had "undertaken sufficient study and action to further the purposes of the ESA." * * * Its finding was based on affidavits submitted by the Forest Service for the litigation. * * * These do not constitute a substitute for the preparation of the biological assessment required by the ESA. * * *

The district court, citing *Palila v. Hawaii Dept. of Land and Natural Resources*, 639 F.2d 495 (9th Cir. 1981), held that "[a] party asserting a violation of the Endangered Species Act has the burden of showing the proposed action would have some prohibited effect on an endangered species or its critical habitat," and found that the plaintiffs in this case had not met that burden. * * * This is a misapplication of *Palila*. That case concerned the ESA's prohibition of the "taking" of an endangered species, 16 U.S.C. § 1538(a)(1)(B), not the ESA's procedural requirements. Quite naturally, the court in *Palila* found that a plaintiff, in order to establish a violation of the "taking" provision, must show that such a "taking" has occurred. The holding does not apply to violations of the ESA's procedural requirements. A plaintiffs' burden in establishing a procedural violation is to show that the circumstances triggering the procedural requirement exist, and that the required procedures have not been followed. The plaintiffs in this case have clearly met that burden.

The Forest Service would require the district court, absent proof by the plaintiffs to the contrary, to make a finding that the Jersey Jack road is not likely to effect the Rocky Mountain Gray Wolf, and that therefore any failure to comply with ESA procedures is harmless. This is not a finding appropriate to the district court at the present time. Congress has assigned to the agencies and to the Fish & Wildlife Service the responsibility for evaluation of the impact of agency actions on endangered species, and has prescribed procedures for such evaluation. Only by following the procedures can proper evaluations be made. It is not the responsibility of the plaintiffs to prove, nor the function of the courts to judge, the effect of a proposed action on an endangered species when proper procedures have not been followed. *Cf. City of Davis v. Coleman*, 521 F.2d 661, 671 (9th Cir. 1975) (under NEPA, agency, not plaintiff, is responsible for investigating the environmental effects of a proposed action).

We therefore hold that the district court erred in declining to enjoin construction of the Jersey Jack road pending compliance with the ESA.

NOTES

1. The agency later attempted to delist the gray wolf. When this effort was frustrated, Congress intervened to delist gray wolves in the Northern Rockies except for Wyoming, an action upheld against constitutional challenge in *Center for Biological Diversity v. Salazar*, 672 F.3d 1170 (9th Cir. 2012). The FWS delisted the wolf in Wyoming on the ground that the state's conservation efforts would make extinction unlikely. The court upheld this decision in *Defenders of Wildlife v. Zinke*, 849 F.3d 1077 (D.C. Cir. 2017). The FWS also delisted the grey wolf in the Western Great Lakes region on the ground that it was no longer threatened or endangered in that part of its range, an action that was upheld in *Humane Society v. Zinke*, 865 F.3d 585 (D.C. Cir. 2017). Controversy has also swirled around efforts to save the red wolf. See Darryl Fears, *Can the Red Wolf Be Saved Again?*, WASH. POST (Feb. 6, 2018).

2. *Turtle Island Restoration Network v. U.S. Dept. of Commerce*, 878 F.3d 725 (9th Cir. 2017), presented an important question regarding the interplay of climate change and jeopardy assessments. This aspect of the case

involved the endangered loggerhead turtle, The agency found that the loggerhead was at high risk of extinction due to climate change and other threat, and that incidental takings from shallownet fishing would only result in small additional losses of population. The court reversed the agency, however, because its own models found that the incremental increase in population loss "would exacerbate the loggerheads' decline." *Id.* at 739. A proposed regulation by the Trump Administration would switch the burden of proof so that listing would be continued only if the agency could make an affirmative finding that the species was still endangered or threatened. Fish and Wildlife Service and National Oceanic and Atmospheric Administration, *Endangered and Threatened Wildlife and Plants; Revision of the Regulations for Listing Species and Designating Critical Habitat*, 83 Fed. Rep. 35193 (July 25, 2018).

3. What are the contents of a biological opinion? In discussing standing and jurisdictional issues under the ESA, Justice Scalia provides a concise synopsis in *Bennett v. Spear* (described in more detail in Chapter 5, *infra*).

> If an agency determines that action it proposes to take may adversely affect a listed species, it must engage in formal consultation with the Fish and Wildlife Service, as delegate of the Secretary, 50 CFR § 402.14 (1995), after which the Service must provide the agency with a written statement (the Biological Opinion) explaining how the proposed action will affect the species or its habitat, 16 U.S.C. § 1536(b)(3)(A). If the Service concludes that the proposed action will "jeopardize the continued existence of any [listed] species or result in the destruction or adverse modification of [critical habitat]," § 1536(a)(2), the Biological Opinion must outline any "reasonable and prudent alternatives" that the Service believes will avoid that consequence, § 1536(b)(3)(A). Additionally, if the Biological Opinion concludes that the agency action will not result in jeopardy or adverse habitat modification, or if it offers reasonable and prudent alternatives to avoid that consequence, the Service must provide the agency with a written statement (known as the "Incidental Take Statement") specifying the "impact of such incidental taking on the species," any "reasonable and prudent measures that the [Service] considers necessary or appropriate to minimize such impact," and setting forth "the terms and conditions . . . that must be complied with by the Federal agency . . . to implement [those measures]." § 1536(b)(4). 520 U.S. 154, 158 (1997).

Under § 4(b)(2) of the ESA, the agency must consider cost before designating critical habitat. In *Building Industry Ass'n v. U.S. Dep. of Commerce*, 792 F.3d 1027 (D.C. Cir. 2017), the court held that this provision does not require the agency to balance the economic impacts against the environmental benefits of designation, although the agency has discretion to exclude areas on this basis.

In *Hollis v. Lynch*, 827 F.3d 436 (5th Cir. 2016), the court upheld the designation of critical habitat for the dusky gopher frog to include private lands no longer inhabited by the toad. The Supreme Court granted cert. in *Weyerhaeuser Company v. United States Fish and Wildlife Service*, 2018 WL 4037489. The oral argument in October 2018 seemed to revolve around whether an area could be essential habitat for a species—or, perhaps, even "habitat" at all—if the species could not live there sustainably without habitat restoration. As this book goes to press, the opinion has not yet been issued. In the meantime, the proposed regulation cited in note 1 above would provide broader grounds for excluding private lands from critical habitat.

4. Aside from the core requirement of the consultation provision, two main qualifiers to note are that the requirement only applies to *actions* by *federal agencies*. While the definition of federal agencies is narrow and for the most part obvious, what defines an action is broader. As § 7(a)(2) itself states, the consultation requirement applies to "any action *authorized, funded, or carried out*" by a federal agency. 16 U.S.C. § 1536(a)(2) (emphasis added). Repeated litigation over the scope of this requirement has revealed a broad definition of federal actions.

In *Conner v. Burford*, 848 F.2d 1441, 1457–58 (9th Cir. 1988), the court held that, in preparing a biological opinion before the issuance of oil and gas leases, the agency action must be defined to encompass not only the leasing decision itself but also all post-leasing activities and their impacts. In *Tinoqui-Chalola Council of Kitanemuk & Yowlumne Tejon Indians v. United States Department of Energy*, 232 F.3d 1300 (9th Cir. 2000), the court held that the negotiation and execution of contracts constitutes an agency action. In *Turtle Island Restoration Network v. National Marine Fisheries Service*, 340 F.3d 969 (9th Cir. 2003), the court held that NMFS' issuance of fishing permits to boats clearly constituted agency action under the ESA.

National Ass'n of Home Builders v. Defenders of Wildlife, 551 U.S. 644 (2007) presented a difficult question of statutory construction involving § 7 and § 402(b) of the Clean Water Act. Section 402(b) sets forth nine statutory criteria a state must meet in order to receive permitting power under the CWA; so long as a state meets those criteria, the EPA must transfer the authority. Section 7, of course, creates a mandatory duty on the part of federal agencies to insure that federal action is not likely to jeopardize endangered or threatened species. The question raised in *National Homebuilders* was whether the EPA, in evaluating the State of Arizona's application for permitting authority, had to ensure under § 7 of the ESA that the transfer would not jeopardize the continued existence of endangered or threatened species or whether it simply had to find that Arizona met the nine CWA statutory criteria. The Court, in a 5–4 decision, held that as long as the nine statutory criteria are met, the EPA must transfer permitting authority. Since the EPA does not have discretion to deny permitting authority so long as the CWA statutory criteria are met, § 7 does not apply. Thus, it would seem, the ESA does not amend existing grants of agency authority to authorize them to consider impacts on an endangered species if they were not otherwise authorized to do so.

5. Section 7 applies with as much force to the "destruction or adverse modification" of critical habitat as it does to actions that may jeopardize the species. 16 U.S.C. § 1536(a)(2); *see also Gifford Pinchot Task Force v. United States Fish & Wildlife Serv.*, 378 F.3d 1059 (9th Cir. 2004) ("agency's finding that loss of critical habitat was not an 'adverse modification' because of the existence of suitable external habitat is arbitrary and capricious and is contrary to law.").

6. What happens after a jeopardy determination? The overwhelming majority of consultations under § 7(a)(2) result in a finding of 'no jeopardy' and, accordingly, only a minimal adjustment to the original plan of the federal action, such as scaling back a proposed timber cut, excluding particularly vital pieces of habitat from a plan, or adjusting the location or flow of a dam. In the small number of cases for which the determination is jeopardy or an injunction issues because of a failure of consultation, the on-the-ground results can be monumental. For example, in the aftermath of the listing of the Northern Spotted Owl, the designation of critical habitat, and President Clinton's Northwest Forest Plan, all noted *supra*, and the listing of other species such as the Marbled Murrelet, there has been a significant reduction in the annual timber cut in the Pacific Northwest.

The ESA can also have a dramatic effect on water supply and allocation, a matter of great political salience in the West where water supply remains a subject of intense conflict. Because of the ESA, water supply for irrigation or domestic consumption may need to be reduced—even during peak growing season—to leave sufficient in-stream flows for the survival and reproduction of endangered species. For example, in *National Wildlife Fed'n v. National Marine Fisheries Serv.*, 422 F.3d 782 (9th Cir. 2005), environmental plaintiffs won a preliminary injunction against the National Marine Fisheries Service (NMFS) due to the insufficiency of NMFS' biological opinions addressing the impact of the continuing operation of dams on salmon in the Columbia and Snake Rivers. The injunction required major releases of water through the spill gates of the dams rather than the hydroelectric turbines. Such spill would allow for the safe and easier passage of juvenile salmon in their downstream journey. Judge Redden found such spill to be necessary in order "to avoid irreparable harm to juvenile fall chinook" salmon. Though the agencies alleged that such spill would result in millions of dollars in lost revenue and electricity (indeed, among the appellants was the Bonneville Power Administration Customer Group), the Ninth Circuit affirmed the injunction. More recently, the Ninth Circuit upheld a Biological Opinion holding that failure to curtail water supplies to Central and Southern California would jeopardize fish in the California Bay Delta. The court faulted the lower court for engaging in overly intrusive review of the Biological Opinion. *San Luis & Delta-Mendota Water Authority v. Locke*, 776 F.3d 971 (9th Cir. 2014). As the court noted, some twenty-five million agricultural and residential water users depend on the water diverted from the Delta. *Id.* at 984. In contrast, the court held that a

Biological Opinion allowing a dam to be relicensed was arbitrary and capricious because the BiOp attributed all of the species decline to background provisions, even though large numbers of the species would be taken. *American Rivers v. FERC*, 895 F.3d 32 (D.C. Cir. 2018).

D. THE TAKE PROHIBITION: SECTION 9

Section 9 of the ESA, arguably the most controversial aspect of the statute, establishes the broad prohibition against "taking" endangered species. The text of the prohibition is brief, stating simply:

> with respect to any endangered species of fish or wildlife listed pursuant to section 4 of this Act it is unlawful for any person subject to the jurisdiction of the United States to—* * *
>
> (B) take any such species within the United States or the territorial sea of the United States;
>
> (C) take any such species upon the high seas * * *.

16 U.S.C. § 1538(a)(1) (2000).

Unlike § 7, which applies only to federal agencies, § 9 applies to "any person subject to the jurisdiction of the United States." Also unlike § 7, the take prohibition only applies to endangered species (though the current regulations of the Fish and Wildlife Service apply the prohibition to both threatened and endangered species).

To understand the take prohibition, it is necessary to consult § 3, the definitions section of the Act. Under § 3(19), "take" is defined as meaning "to harass, harm, pursue, hunt, shoot, wound, kill, trap, capture, or collect, or to attempt to engage in any such conduct." 16 U.S.C. § 1532(19) (2000). During the 1980s, a series of ESA cases were litigated in the U.S. District Court for the District of Hawaii and the Ninth Circuit concerning the Palila, an endangered bird native to Hawaii. To date, they remain the only line of cases in which a party was held liable under § 9 for failing to prevent a non-native species from destroying the habitat of an endangered species. In *Palila v. Hawaii Department of Land and Natural Resources*, 639 F.2d 495 (9th Cir. 1981) (*Palila I*) the Ninth Circuit addressed the question of whether the Hawaii Department of Land and Natural Resources could be held liable for failure to remove feral, non-native goats and sheep from the Palila's critical habitat. The Department had maintained a herd of the goats and sheep on the slopes of Mauna Kea, within the Palila's critical habitat, for the purposes of sport hunting. As the goats and sheep grazed on the slopes, the forest receded, thereby reducing the Palila's habitat. Though the Department fenced off about 25% of the forest, it chose not to remove the goats and sheep. In holding that this failure to remove the goats and sheep was a violation of § 9, the court noted that the regulatory definition of "harm" as "activity that results in significant environmental modification or degradation of the endangered animal's habitat." Since the goats and sheep were harming the Palila under this definition, and since the eradication of the goats and sheep was necessary to prevent this harm, the court held the Department to have violated § 9.

In the aftermath of *Palila I*, the Secretary of the Interior changed the definition of harm under 50 C.F.R. § 17.3. The new definition included the requirement that harm include significant habitat modification or degradation where it actually kills or injures wildlife by significantly impairing essential behavioral patterns, including breeding, feeding or sheltering." While the definition still allowed for harm via habitat modification or degradation, it added the seemingly more stringent requirement that such modification or degradation must actually kill or injure wildlife. In *Palila v. Hawaii Department of Land and Natural Resources*, 649 F.Supp. 1070 (D. Haw. 1986) (*Palila II*), the District Court for the District of Hawaii revisited the Palila controversy on the basis of defendants' argument that, under the new regulation, plaintiffs must show actual injury or death. The court refused to accept this regulation's narrow definition of harm. Instead, the court stated:

> A finding of "harm" does not require death to individual members of the species; nor does it require a finding that habitat degradation is presently driving the species further toward extinction. Habitat destruction that prevents the recovery of the species by affecting essential behavioral patterns causes actual injury to the species and effects a taking under § 9 of the Act.

Id. at 1075. Subsequently, the Ninth Circuit affirmed this holding. *Palila v. Hawaii Department of Land and Natural Resources*, 852 F.2d 1106 (9th Cir. 1988) (affirming district court and ordering removal of sheep).

The regulation's definition of "take" was challenged from the other side as too broad. In the case below, the Supreme Court considered whether the regulatory definition was a lawful interpretation of the Act.

BABBITT V. SWEET HOME CHAPTER OF COMMUNITIES FOR A GREAT OREGON

Supreme Court of the United States, 1995.
515 U.S. 687, 115 S.Ct. 2407, 132 L.Ed.2d 597.

[The plaintiffs were small landowners, logging companies, and families dependent on the logging industry in the Pacific Northwest and in the Southeast. They brought this action to challenge the Secretary of the Interior's regulation defining the term "take" under § 9 of the ESA. Section 9 makes it unlawful for any person to take endangered species, and defines "take" to mean "harass, harm, pursue," "wound," or "kill." The implementing regulation specifies that "harm" includes "significant habitat modification or degradation where it actually kills or injures wildlife." The plaintiffs alleged that application of the "harm" regulation to the red-cockaded woodpecker, an endangered species, and the northern spotted owl, a threatened species, covered by § 9 through regulation, had injured them economically. In an *en banc* opinion, the D.C. Circuit held that the word "harm" was limited to the direct application of force, partly because of its concern regarding the implications of the regulation in terms of the resulting extinction of "property rights."]

JUSTICE STEVENS delivered the opinion of the Court.

Because this case was decided on motions for summary judgment, we may appropriately make certain factual assumptions in order to frame the legal issue. First, we assume respondents have no desire to harm either the red-cockaded woodpecker or the spotted owl; they merely wish to continue logging activities that would be entirely proper if not prohibited by the ESA. On the other hand, we must assume arguendo that those activities will have the effect, even though unintended, of detrimentally changing the natural habitat of both listed species and that, as a consequence, members of those species will be killed or injured. Under respondents' view of the law, the Secretary's only means of forestalling that grave result—even when the actor knows it is certain to occur[9]—is to use his § 5 authority to purchase the lands on which the survival of the species depends. The Secretary, on the other hand, submits that the § 9 prohibition on takings, which Congress defined to include "harm," places on respondents a duty to avoid harm that habitat alteration will cause the birds unless respondents first obtain a permit pursuant to § 10.

The text of the Act provides three reasons for concluding that the Secretary's interpretation is reasonable. First, an ordinary understanding of the word "harm" supports it. The dictionary definition of the verb form of "harm" is "to cause hurt or damage to: injure." In the context of the ESA, that definition naturally encompasses habitat modification that results in actual injury or death to members of an endangered or threatened species.

Respondents argue that the Secretary should have limited the purview of "harm" to direct applications of force against protected species, but the dictionary definition does not include the word "directly" or suggest in any way that only direct or willful action that leads to injury constitutes "harm." Moreover, unless the statutory term "harm" encompasses indirect as well as direct injuries, the word has no meaning that does not duplicate the meaning of other words that § 3 uses to define "take." A reluctance to

---

[9]   As discussed above, the Secretary's definition of "harm" is limited to "act[s] which actually kil[l] or injur[e] wildlife." * * * We do not agree with the dissent that the regulation covers results that are not "even foreseeable * * * no matter how long the chain of causality between modification and injury." Respondents have suggested no reason why either the "knowingly violates" or the "otherwise violates" provision of the statute—or the "harm" regulation itself—should not be read to incorporate ordinary requirements of proximate causation and foreseeability.

treat statutory terms as surplusage supports the reasonableness of the Secretary's interpretation.

Second, the broad purpose of the ESA supports the Secretary's decision to extend protection against activities that cause the precise harms Congress enacted the statute to avoid. In *TVA v. Hill,* we described the Act as "the most comprehensive legislation for the preservation of endangered species ever enacted by any nation." Whereas predecessor statutes enacted in 1966 and 1969 had not contained any sweeping prohibition against the taking of endangered species except on federal lands, the 1973 Act applied to all land in the United States and to the Nation's territorial seas. As stated in § 2 of the Act, among its central purposes is "to provide a means whereby the ecosystems upon which endangered species and threatened species depend may be conserved * * *."

In *Hill,* we construed § 7 as precluding the completion of the Tellico Dam because of its predicted impact on the survival of the snail darter. Both our holding and the language in our opinion stressed the importance of the statutory policy. "The plain intent of Congress in enacting this statute," we recognized, "was to halt and reverse the trend toward species extinction, whatever the cost. This is reflected not only in the stated policies of the Act, but in literally every section of the statute." Although the § 9 "take" prohibition was not at issue in *Hill,* we took note of that prohibition, placing particular emphasis on the Secretary's inclusion of habitat modification in his definition of "harm." In light of that provision for habitat protection, we could "not understand how TVA intends to operate Tellico Dam without 'harming' the snail darter." Congress' intent to provide comprehensive protection for endangered and threatened species supports the permissibility of the Secretary's "harm" regulation.

Respondents advance strong arguments that activities that cause minimal or unforeseeable harm will not violate the Act as construed in the "harm" regulation. Respondents, however, present a facial challenge to the regulation. Thus, they ask us to invalidate the Secretary's understanding of "harm" in every circumstance, even when an actor knows that an activity, such as draining a pond, would actually result in the extinction of a listed species by destroying its habitat. Given Congress' clear expression of the ESA's broad purpose to protect endangered and threatened wildlife, the Secretary's definition of "harm" is reasonable.[13]

---

[13]   The dissent incorrectly asserts that the Secretary's regulation (1) "dispenses with the foreseeability of harm" and (2) "fail[s] to require injury to particular animals." As to the first assertion, the regulation merely implements the statute, and it is therefore subject to the statute's "knowingly violates" language, *see* 16 U.S.C. §§ 1540(a)(1), (b)(1), and ordinary requirements of proximate causation and foreseeability. Nothing in the regulation purports to weaken those requirements. To the contrary, the word "actually" in the regulation should be construed to limit the liability about which the dissent appears most concerned, liability under the statute's "otherwise violates" provision. The Secretary did not need to include "actually" to connote "but for" causation, which the other words in the definition obviously require. As to the dissent's second

Third, the fact that Congress in 1982 authorized the Secretary to issue permits for takings that § 9(a)(1)(B) would otherwise prohibit, "if such taking is incidental to, and not the purpose of, the carrying out of an otherwise lawful activity," 16 U.S.C. § 1539(a)(1)(B), strongly suggests that Congress understood § 9(a)(1)(B) to prohibit indirect as well as deliberate takings. The permit process requires the applicant to prepare a "conservation plan" that specifies how he intends to "minimize and mitigate" the "impact" of his activity on endangered and threatened species, 16 U.S.C. § 1539(a)(2)(A), making clear that Congress had in mind foreseeable rather than merely accidental effects on listed species. No one could seriously request an "incidental" take permit to avert § 9 liability for direct, deliberate action against a member of an endangered or threatened species, but respondents would read "harm" so narrowly that the permit procedure would have little more than that absurd purpose. "When Congress acts to amend a statute, we presume it intends its amendment to have real and substantial effect." Congress' addition of the § 10 permit provision supports the Secretary's conclusion that activities not intended to harm an endangered species, such as habitat modification, may constitute unlawful takings under the ESA unless the Secretary permits them.

We need not decide whether the statutory definition of "take" compels the Secretary's interpretation of "harm," because our conclusions that Congress did not unambiguously manifest its intent to adopt respondents' view and that the Secretary's interpretation is reasonable suffice to decide this case. The latitude the ESA gives the Secretary in enforcing the statute, together with the degree of regulatory expertise necessary to its enforcement, establishes that we owe some degree of deference to the Secretary's reasonable interpretation. * * *

When it enacted the ESA, Congress delegated broad administrative and interpretive power to the Secretary. The task of defining and listing endangered and threatened species requires an expertise and attention to detail that exceeds the normal province of Congress. Fashioning appropriate standards for issuing permits under § 10 for takings that would otherwise violate § 9 necessarily requires the exercise of broad discretion. The proper interpretation of a term such as "harm" involves a complex policy choice. When Congress has entrusted the Secretary with broad discretion, we are especially reluctant to substitute our views of wise policy for his. In this case, that reluctance accords with our conclusion, based on the text, structure, and legislative history of the ESA, that the Secretary reasonably construed the intent of Congress when he defined "harm" to include "significant habitat modification or degradation that actually kills or injures wildlife."

---

assertion, every term in the regulation's definition of "harm" is subservient to the phrase "an act which actually kills or injures wildlife."

In the elaboration and enforcement of the ESA, the Secretary and all persons who must comply with the law will confront difficult questions of proximity and degree; for, as all recognize, the Act encompasses a vast range of economic and social enterprises and endeavors. These questions must be addressed in the usual course of the law, through case-by-case resolution and adjudication.

JUSTICE O'CONNOR, concurring.

My agreement with the Court is founded on two understandings. First, the challenged regulation is limited to significant habitat modification that causes actual, as opposed to hypothetical or speculative, death or injury to identifiable protected animals. Second, even setting aside difficult questions of scienter, the regulation's application is limited by ordinary principles of proximate causation, which introduce notions of foreseeability. These limitations, in my view, call into question *Palila v. Hawaii Dept. of Land and Natural Resources*, 852 F.2d 1106 (C.A.9 1988) (*Palila II*), and with it, many of the applications derided by the dissent. Because there is no need to strike a regulation on a facial challenge out of concern that it is susceptible of erroneous application, however, and because there are many habitat-related circumstances in which the regulation might validly apply, I join the opinion of the Court.

In my view, the regulation is limited by its terms to actions that actually kill or injure individual animals. Justice Scalia disagrees, arguing that the harm regulation "encompasses injury inflicted, not only upon individual animals, but upon populations of the protected species." At one level, I could not reasonably quarrel with this observation; death to an individual animal always reduces the size of the population in which it lives, and in that sense, "injures" that population. But by its insight, the dissent means something else. Building upon the regulation's use of the word "breeding," Justice Scalia suggests that the regulation facially bars significant habitat modification that actually kills or injures hypothetical animals (or, perhaps more aptly, causes potential additions to the population not to come into being). Because "[i]mpairment of breeding does not 'injure' living creatures," Justice Scalia reasons, the regulation must contemplate application to "a population of animals which would otherwise have maintained or increased its numbers."

I disagree. As an initial matter, I do not find it as easy as Justice Scalia does to dismiss the notion that significant impairment of breeding injures living creatures. To raze the last remaining ground on which the piping plover currently breeds, thereby making it impossible for any piping plovers to reproduce, would obviously injure the population (causing the species' extinction in a generation). But by completely preventing breeding, it would also injure the individual living bird, in the same way that sterilizing the creature injures the individual living bird. To "injure" is, among other things, "to impair." One need not subscribe to theories of "psychic harm," to recognize that to make it impossible for an animal to reproduce is to impair its most essential physical functions and to render that animal, and its genetic material, biologically obsolete. This, in my view, is actual injury.

In any event, even if impairing an animal's ability to breed were not, in and of itself, an injury to that animal, interference with breeding can cause an animal to suffer other, perhaps more obvious, kinds of injury. The regulation has clear application, for example, to significant habitat modification that kills or physically injures animals which, because they are in a vulnerable breeding state, do not or cannot flee or defend themselves, or to environmental pollutants that cause an animal to suffer physical complications during gestation. Breeding, feeding, and sheltering are what animals do. If significant habitat modification, by interfering with these essential behaviors, actually kills or injures an animal protected by the Act, it causes "harm" within the meaning of the regulation. In contrast to Justice Scalia, I do not read the regulation's "breeding" reference to vitiate or somehow to qualify the clear actual death or injury requirement, or to suggest that the regulation contemplates extension to nonexistent animals.

JUSTICE SCALIA, with whom THE CHIEF JUSTICE and JUSTICE THOMAS join, dissenting.

I think it unmistakably clear that the legislation at issue here (1) forbade the hunting and killing of endangered animals, and (2) provided federal lands and federal funds for the acquisition of private lands, to preserve the habitat of endangered animals. The Court's holding that the hunting and killing prohibition incidentally preserves habitat on private lands imposes unfairness to the point of financial ruin—not just upon the rich, but upon the simplest farmer who finds his land conscripted to national zoological use. I respectfully dissent. * * *

The regulation has three features which, for reasons I shall discuss at length below, do not comport with the statute. First, it interprets the statute to prohibit habitat modification that is no more than the cause-in-fact of death or injury to wildlife. Any "significant habitat modification" that in fact produces that result by "impairing essential behavioral patterns" is made unlawful, regardless of whether that result is intended or even foreseeable, and no matter how long the chain of causality between modification and injury. See, e.g., *Palila v. Hawaii Dept. of Land and Natural Resources (Palila II)*, 852 F.2d 1106, 1108–1109 (C.A.9 1988) (sheep grazing constituted "taking" of palila birds, since although sheep do not destroy full-grown mamane trees, they do destroy mamane seedlings, which will not grow to full-grown trees, on which the palila feeds and nests).

Second, the regulation does not require an "act": the Secretary's officially stated position is that an omission will do. The previous version of the regulation made this explicit. * * * When the regulation was modified in 1981 the phrase "or omission" was taken out, but only because (as the final publication of the rule advised) "the [Fish and Wildlife] Service feels that 'act' is inclusive of either commissions or omissions which would be prohibited by § [1538(a)(1)(B)]." In its brief here the Government agrees that the regulation covers omissions (although it argues that "[a]n 'omission' constitutes an 'act' * * * only if there is a legal duty to act").

The third and most important unlawful feature of the regulation is that it encompasses injury inflicted, not only upon individual animals, but upon populations of the protected species. "Injury" in the regulation includes "significantly impairing essential behavioral patterns, including breeding." Impairment of breeding does not "injure" living creatures; it prevents them from propagating, thus "injuring" a population of animals which would otherwise have maintained or increased its numbers. What the face of the regulation shows, the Secretary's official pronouncements confirm. The Final Redefinition of "Harm" accompanying publication of the regulation said that "harm" is not limited to "direct physical injury to an individual member of the wildlife species," and refers to "injury to a population."

None of these three features of the regulation can be found in the statutory provisions supposed to authorize it. The term "harm" in § 1532(19) has no legal force of its own. An indictment or civil complaint that charged the defendant with "harming" an animal protected under the Act would be dismissed as defective, for the only operative term in the statute is to "take." If "take" were not elsewhere defined in the Act, none could dispute what it means, for the term is as old as the law itself. To "take," when applied to wild animals, means to reduce those animals, by killing or capturing, to human control. See, e.g., 11 *Oxford English Dictionary* (1933) ("Take ... To catch, capture (a wild beast, bird, fish, etc.)"); *Webster's New International Dictionary of the English Language* (2d ed. 1949) (take defined as "to catch or capture by trapping, snaring, etc., or as prey"); *Geer v. Connecticut*, 161 U.S. 519, 523, 16 S.Ct. 600, 602, 40 L.Ed. 793 (1896) ("[A]ll the animals which can be taken upon the earth, in the sea, or in the air, that is to say, wild animals, belong to those who take them") (quoting the Digest of Justinian); 2 W. Blackstone, *Commentaries* 411 (1766) ("Every man ... has an equal right of pursuing and taking to his own use all such creatures as are ferae naturae"). This is just the sense in which "take" is used elsewhere in federal legislation and treaty. And that meaning fits neatly with the rest of § 1538(a)(1), which makes it unlawful not only to take protected species, but also to import or export them; to possess, sell, deliver, carry, transport, or ship any taken species; and to transport, sell, or offer to sell them in interstate or foreign commerce. The taking prohibition, in other words, is only part of the regulatory plan of § 1538(a)(1), which covers all the stages of the process by which protected wildlife is reduced to man's dominion and made the object of profit. It is obvious that "take" in this sense—a term of art deeply embedded in the statutory and common law concerning wildlife—describes a class of acts (not omissions) done directly and intentionally (not indirectly and by accident) to particular animals (not populations of animals).

The Act's definition of "take" does expand the word slightly (and not unusually), so as to make clear that it includes not just a completed taking, but the process of taking, and all of the acts that are customarily identified with or accompany that process ("to harass, harm, pursue, hunt, shoot, wound, kill, trap, capture, or collect"); and so as to include attempts. § 1532(19). The tempting fallacy—which the Court commits with abandon—is to assume that once defined, "take" loses any significance, and it is only the definition that matters. The Court treats the statute as though Congress had directly enacted the § 1532(19) definition as a self-executing prohibition, and had not enacted § 1538(a)(1)(B) at all. But § 1538(a)(1)(B) is there, and if the terms contained in the definitional section are susceptible of two readings, one of which comports with the standard meaning of "take" as used in application to wildlife, and one of which does not, an agency regulation that adopts the latter reading is necessarily unreasonable, for it reads the defined term "take"—the only operative term—out of the statute altogether. * * *

NOTES

1.   Justice Scalia is the primary proponent of "textualism" in statutory interpretation. How persuasive is his argument that the ESA unambiguously precludes the agency's interpretation? The centerpiece of the dissent is his assertion that the word "take", as applied to wildlife, is "as old as the law itself," and means "to reduce those animals, by killing or capturing, to human control." How likely is it that Congress would have had in mind the meaning of the term "take" in game law? After all, the statute is not an amendment to other game or fishing laws, but instead is an aggressive addition to the corpus of federal environmental law, where the historic meaning of the word "take" might not immediately spring to mind. Moreover, while Justice Scalia is only willing to concede that the statutory definition of a taking "does expand the word slightly," surely a member of Congress who wanted to know what the word meant would have been more likely to look at the plain language of the definition section of the bill than to consult a treatise on game law.

Wouldn't it be peculiar to say that Mrs. O'Leary's cow didn't "harm" the people of Chicago when she kicked over the lantern that started the Chicago fire? (After all, she "only" modified their habitat!) Similarly, as a matter of ordinary English usage, doesn't someone who destroys the nesting grounds used by an endangered species or eliminates their food supply thereby harm them? Is Justice Scalia's interpretation really driven by the demands of the statutory text, or is he more motivated by his concern that the agency's interpretation "imposes unfairness to the point of financial ruin not just upon the rich, but upon the simplest farmer who finds his land conscripted to national zoological use"?

2.　　How much does *Sweet Home* narrow the regulatory definition through concepts such as proximate cause? For instance, if logging removes forest cover that helps protect an endangered bird from raptors, is the logging a proximate cause of harm? *See* Steven P. Quarles et al., Sweet Home *and the Narrowing of Wildlife 'Take' Under Section 9 of the Endangered Species Act*, 26 ENVTL. L. REP. 10,003, 10,012 (1996) (arguing against liability). The *Sweet Home* criteria may pose significant practical problems for developers:

> Questions of proximate cause and foreseeability are usually debatable. This uncertainty becomes more acute as the scale of activity and potential number of species members affected become smaller in scope. While we may know enough to conclude with reasonable certainty that a species as a whole is endangered, the localized effects of habitat loss on identifiable members of the species can be difficult to pinpoint. Even where a species' behavior characteristics and the habitat associated with them are well-defined, the effect of disturbance in or near areas of the habitat can be uncertain in terms of both predictability in advance and causal determination in retrospect. . . . Failure to investigate the potential effects of a project leaves the project fully exposed to subsequent liability should a take occur, with little basis for arguing unforeseeability given the absence of any effort to foresee. [But even] with intensive on-site studies it is usually difficult, if not impossible, to conclusively rule out all the possibilities.

J.B. Ruhl, *How to Kill Endangered Species, Legally: the Nuts and Bolts of Endangered Species Act 'HCP' Permits for Real Estate Development*, 5 ENVTL. LAW. 345, 361 (1999). For some examples of application of the proximate cause requirement, see *Aransas v. Shaw*, 756 F.3d 801, 829–822 (5th Cir. 801, 820–823 (2014) (grant of water permits did not foreseeably result in harm to whooping cranes); *Strahan v. Coxe,* 127 F.3d 155, 165 (1st Cir. 1997) (issuance of licenses for gillnets and lobster traps in certain areas foreseeably harmed whaltes; "causation here, while indirect, is not so removed that it extends outside the realm of causation as it is understood in the common law"); *Sierra Club v. Yeutter*, 926 F.2d 429, 432–433 (5th Cir. 1991) ("not unreasonable to conclude" that excessive timber cut harmed woodpeckers).

3.　　Should a property owner be deprived of the right to modify the habitat of an endangered species without compensation? Consider whether this would be a taking under current Supreme Court doctrine. *See Good v. United States*, 39 Fed. Cl. 81 (1997) (no taking unless all economic value is destroyed). *See also* Robert Meltz, *Where the Wild Things Are: The Endangered Species Act and Private Property*, 24 ENVTL. L. 369 (1994). On the other hand, if no compensation is offered, doesn't that give landowners an incentive to develop land quickly, eliminating possible endangered species, before legal restrictions can be imposed? *See* David A. Dana, *Natural Preservation and the Race to Develop*, 143 U. PA. L. REV. 655 (1995). For a policy argument in favor of building compensation payments into habitat conservation plans, see Barton H. Thompson, *The Endangered Species Act: A Case Study in Takings and Incentives*, 49 STAN. L. REV. 305 (1997).

4.   Under § 11(b) of the ESA, criminal liability is attached to "knowing" violations of § 9. *See* 16 U.S.C. § 1538(b). Such a knowing violation was the subject of *United States v. McKittrick*, 142 F.3d 1170 (9th Cir. 1998), in which the respondent was charged with knowingly taking an endangered gray wolf in violation of § 9(a)(1)(G) of the Act and regulations promulgated under that section. The court of appeals affirmed the conviction over respondent's allegation that he "did not realize what he was shooting," holding that "McKittrick need not have known he was shooting a wolf to 'knowingly violate[ ]' the regulations protecting the experimental population." 142 F.3d at 1173, 1177. As Congress had reduced in § 11 "the standard for criminal violations from 'willfully' to 'knowingly,' " the section "requires only that McKittrick knew he was shooting an animal, and that the animal turned out to be a protected gray wolf." *Id.* at 1177 (internal citations omitted). Is this standard for criminal liability defensible in this context?

5.   Is § 9 constitutional? We discuss federalism issues in more depth in the next chapter, but a brief discussion is appropriate here as well. In *Gibbs v. Babbitt*, 214 F.3d 483 (4th Cir. 2000) (Wilkinson, J.), the court rebuffed a constitutional challenge to a regulation under the ESA which prohibited the taking of red wolves on private lands. Yet there remain questions about how to categorize the underlying "regulated activity" in these cases for Commerce Clause purposes. In *GDF Realty Investments, Ltd. v. Norton*, 169 F.Supp.2d 648 (W.D. Tex. 2001), landowner plaintiffs alleged that § 9, as applied to habitat modifications on their properties, overstepped Congress' Commerce Clause authority. The case involved six species of listed invertebrates that resided entirely in underground caves ("Cave Species"). The court held that the activity regulated by § 9 in this case was the commercial development, which easily could be categorized as "activities that substantially affect interstate commerce." On appeal, the Fifth Circuit affirmed but rejected the lower court's rationale that commercial development was the regulated activity. Looking to the Supreme Court's then-recent decisions in *United States v. Morrison*, 529 U.S. 598 (2000) and *United States v. Lopez*, 514 U.S. 549 (1995), the court stated that, in performing an analysis of constitutionality under the Commerce Clause, a court must look to the conduct regulated by Congress (here, the taking of Cave Species) rather than the broader conduct implicated by the regulation (commercial development). Nevertheless, the court found that the aggregation of Cave Species takes together with those of all endangered species did implicate interstate commerce. *GDF Realty Investments, Ltd. v. Norton*, 326 F.3d 622 (5th Cir. 2003). *See also Rancho Viejo, LLC v. Norton*, 323 F.3d 1062 (D.C. Cir. 2003) (affirming dismissal of plaintiffs' Commerce Clause challenge to § 9); *cf. Rancho Viejo, LLC v. Norton,* 334 F.3d 1158 (D.C. Cir.

2003) (Roberts, J., dissenting) (noting the limiting necessity of looking only to the regulated activity and not beyond it).

E. INCIDENTAL TAKE STATEMENTS

The § 7 consultation process often concludes with the issuance of an incidental take statement (ITS), which allows for the otherwise prohibited taking of listed species, so long as the taking is incidental to the agency action and within the terms of the ITS.

The governing provision for the issuance of incidental take statements is § 7(b)(4) of the Act. If, after § 7 consultation, the Secretary concludes:

(A) the agency action will not violate [Section 7(a)(2)], or offers reasonable and prudent alternatives which the Secretary believes would not violate such subsection;

(B) the taking of an endangered species or a threatened species incidental to the agency action will not violate such subsection;
* * *

the Secretary shall provide the Federal agency and the applicant concerned, if any, with a written statement that—

(i) specifies the impact of such incidental taking on the species,

(ii) specifies those reasonable and prudent measures that the Secretary considers necessary or appropriate to minimize such impact, * * * [and]

(iv) sets forth the terms and conditions (including, but not limited to, reporting requirements) that must be complied with by the Federal agency or applicant (if any), or both, to implement the measures specified under clauses (ii) and (iii).

16 U.S.C. § 1536(b)(4) (2000). According to the Ninth Circuit, this provision applies only to endangered animals, not plants. See *Center for Biological Diversity v. Bureau of Land Management*, 833 F.3d 1136 (9th Cir. 2016).

This "written statement" has become known as an incidental take statement because it authorizes taking incidental to the permitted activity. Typically, the issuance of a Biological Opinion is accompanied by such an incidental take statement. Note that the restrictions in the Incidental Take Statement (ITS) must be clear and specific enough to be enforceable; normally this requires numerical limitations. See *Sierra Club v. U.S. Dept. of Interior*, 899 F.3d 260(4th Cir. 2018). An illustrative case concerning when an incidental take statement should be issued and what it must contain appears below.

ARIZONA CATTLE GROWERS' ASS'N V. UNITED STATES FISH AND WILDLIFE SERVICE

United States Court of Appeals, Ninth Circuit, 2001.
273 F.3d 1229.

WARDLAW, CIRCUIT JUDGE:

[The Fish and Wildlife Service had consulted with the Bureau of Land Management over the issuance of several grazing permits on BLM lands. Though the Service concluded that none of the permits would jeopardize the continued existence of listed species, it still chose to issue incidental take statements for all of the permits. Arizona Cattle Grower's Association challenged the issuance of the ITSs as arbitrary and capricious. The district court agreed with plaintiffs on all but one of the permits, whose issuance it held was not arbitrary and capricious. The Ninth Circuit affirmed. The opinion first considered whether an ITS is required even when the agency concludes that no take will occur.]

V.   Determining When the Fish and Wildlife Service Must Issue an Incidental Take Statement* * *

The Fish and Wildlife Service argues that the plain language of the statute and implementing regulations "expressly direct" it to issue an Incidental Take Statement in every case. * * *

* * * It is a "fundamental canon of statutory construction that the words of a statute must be read in their context and with a view to their place in the overall statutory scheme." Davis v. Mich. Dep't of Treasury, 489 U.S. 803, 809 * * * (1989). * * *

When read in context, it is clear that the issuance of the Incidental Take Statement is subject to the finding of the factors enumerated in the ESA. The statute explicitly provides that the written statement is subject to the consultation and the Secretary's conclusions. A contrary interpretation would render meaningless the clause stating that the Incidental Take Statement will specify "the impact of such incidental taking." 16 U.S.C. § 1536(b)(4)(C)(i) * * *. We therefore agree with ACGA that the plain language of the ESA does not dictate that the Fish and Wildlife Service must issue an Incidental Take Statement irrespective of whether any incidental takings will occur. * * *

The plain language of the implementing regulations also supports ACGA's argument. One regulation specifically instructs the Fish and Wildlife Service that its "responsibilities during formal consultation are . . . to formulate a statement concerning incidental take, if such take may occur." 50 C.F.R. § 402.14(g)(7) * * *. Moreover, the same regulation also instructs:

(1) In those cases where the Service concludes that an action (or the implementation of any reasonable and prudent alternatives)

and the resultant incidental take of listed species will not violate section 7(a)(2), . . . the Service will provide with the biological opinion a statement concerning incidental take that:

> (i)   Specifies the impact, i.e., the amount or extent, of such incidental taking on the species;

50 C.F.R. § 402.14(i)(1) (2001). Thus, consistent with the language of the statute, the regulations only require the issuance of an Incidental Take Statement when the "resultant incidental take of listed species will not violate section 7(a)(2)." *Id.* * * *.

Likewise, the legislative history supports this interpretation of the statute. If the sole purpose of the Incidental Take Statement is to provide shelter from § 9 penalties, as previously noted, it would be nonsensical to require the issuance of an Incidental Take Statement when no takings cognizable under Section 9 are to occur. * * *

* * * Accordingly, we hold that absent rare circumstances such as those involving migratory species, it is arbitrary and capricious to issue an Incidental Take Statement when the Fish and Wildlife Service has no rational basis to conclude that a take will occur incident to the otherwise lawful activity.

VI. Review of the Incidental Take Statements under the Arbitrary and Capricious Standard Pursuant to the APA

Because we reject the Fish and Wildlife Service's interpretation of the ESA and hold that it is not required to provide an Incidental Take Statement whenever it issues a Biological Opinion, we must now examine each Incidental Take Statement at issue under § 706. [Addressing each of the Incidental Take Statements issued by the Service, the court affirmed the district court's finding that the Service had not shown the existence of endangered species in any of the areas. Accordingly, the court affirmed the invalidation of the Incidental Take Statements.]

2.   The Anticipated Take Provisions

[The court next approached the incidental take statement for the "Cow Flat Allotment," which the district court had not set aside, addressing the question as to whether the Service had acted arbitrarily and capriciously in failing to specify a certain number amount of anticipated take in the statements. In lieu of such number amounts, the Service had used language requiring certain conditions on land use.]

In general, Incidental Take Statements set forth a "trigger" that, when reached, results in an unacceptable level of incidental take, invalidating the safe harbor provision, and requiring the parties to reinitiate consultation. Ideally, this "trigger" should be a specific number. *See, e.g., Mausolf v. Babbitt,* 125 F.3d 661 (8th Cir. 1997) (snowmobiling activity may take no more than two wolves); *Fund for Animals v. Rice*, 85 F.3d 535 (11th Cir. 1996) (municipal landfill may take fifty-two snakes during construction and an additional two snakes per year thereafter); *Mt. Graham Red Squirrel v. Madigan*, 954 F.2d 1441 (9th Cir. 1992) (telescope construction may take six red squirrels per year); *Ctr. for Marine Conservation v. Brown*, 917 F.Supp. 1128 (S.D. Tex. 1996) (shrimping operation may take four hawksbill turtles, four leatherback turtles, ten Kemp's ridley turtles, ten green turtles, or 370 loggerhead turtles). Here, however, the "trigger" took the form of several conditions. We must therefore determine whether the linking of the level of permissible take to the conditions set forth in the various Incidental Take Statements was arbitrary and capricious.

ACGA argues that the Incidental Take Statements fail to specify the amount or extent of authorized take with the required degree of exactness. Specifically, ACGA objected to the first condition:

> The service concludes that incidental take of loach minnow from the proposed action will be considered to be exceeded if any of the following conditions are met:
>
> [Condition 1] Ecological conditions do not improve under the proposed livestock management. Improving conditions can be defined through improvements in watershed, soil condition, trend and condition of rangelands (e.g., vegetative litter, plant vigor, and native species diversity), riparian conditions (e.g., vegetative and geomorphologic: bank, terrace, and flood plain conditions), and streamchannel conditions (e.g., channel profile, embeddedness, water temperature, and base flow) within the natural capabilities of the landscape in all pastures on the allotment within the Blue River watershed.

We have never held that a numerical limit is required. Indeed, we have upheld Incidental Take Statements that used a combination of numbers and estimates. * * *

Moreover, while Congress indicated its preference for a numerical value, it anticipated situations in which impact could not be contemplated in terms of a precise number. * * * In the absence of a specific numerical value, however, the Fish and Wildlife Service must establish that no such numerical value could be practically obtained.

We agree with the ACGA II court's conclusion that, "the use of ecological conditions as a surrogate for defining the amount or extent of incidental take is reasonable so long as these conditions are linked to the take of the protected species." * * * By "causal link" we do not mean that the Fish and Wildlife Service must demonstrate a specific number of takings; only that it must establish a link between the activity and the taking of species before setting forth specific conditions.

ACGA argues that it is entitled to more certainty than "vague and undetectable criteria such as changes in a 22,000 acre allotment's 'ecological condition.'" In response, the Fish and Wildlife Service argues that "the [Incidental Take Statement] provides for those studies necessary to provide the quantification of impacts which the Cattle Growers claim is lacking."

We disagree with the government's position. The Incidental Take Statements at issue here do not sufficiently discuss the causal connection between Condition 1 and the taking of the species at issue. Based on the Incidental Take Statement, if "ecological conditions do not improve," takings will occur. This vague analysis, however, cannot be what Congress contemplated when it anticipated that surrogate indices might be used in place of specific numbers. Moreover, whether there has been compliance with this vague directive is within the unfettered discretion of the Fish and Wildlife Service, leaving no method by which the applicant or the action agency can gauge their performance. * * *

Based upon the lack of an articulated, rational connection between Condition 1 and the taking of species, as well as the vagueness of the condition itself, we hold that its implementation was arbitrary and capricious. The terms of an Incidental Take Statement do not operate in a vacuum. To the contrary, they are integral parts of the statutory scheme, determining, among other things, when consultation must be reinitiated. Thus, even though the Fish and Wildlife Service was not arbitrary and capricious in issuing Incidental Take Statements for the Cow Flat Allotment, its failure to properly specify the amount of anticipated take and to provide a clear standard for determining when the authorized level of take has been exceeded is arbitrary and capricious. * * *

NOTES

1. Justice Scalia described the impact of a BiOp and ITS in *Bennett v. Spear*:

A Biological Opinion of the sort rendered here alters the legal regime to which the action agency is subject. When it "offers reasonable and prudent alternatives" to the proposed action, a Biological Opinion must include a so-called "Incidental Take Statement"—a written statement specifying, among other things, those "measures that the [Service] considers necessary or appropriate to minimize [the action's impact on the affected species]" and the "terms and conditions * * * that must be complied with by the Federal agency . . . to implement [such] measures." 16 U.S.C. § 1536(b)(4). Any taking that is in compliance with these terms and conditions "shall not be considered to be a prohibited taking of the species concerned." § 1536(o)(2). Thus, the Biological Opinion's Incidental Take Statement constitutes a permit authorizing the action agency to "take" the endangered or threatened species so long as it respects the Service's "terms and conditions." The action agency is technically free to disregard the Biological Opinion and proceed with its proposed action, but it does so at its own peril (and that of its employees), for "any person" who knowingly "takes" an endangered or threatened species is subject to substantial civil and criminal penalties, including imprisonment. *See* § 1540(a) and (b) (authorizing civil fines of up to $25,000 per violation and criminal penalties of up to $50,000 and imprisonment for one year); *see also Babbitt* v. *Sweet Home Chapter, Communities for Great Ore.*, 515 U.S. 687 (1995) (upholding interpretation of the term "take" to include significant habitat degradation).

The Service itself is, to put it mildly, keenly aware of the virtually determinative effect of its biological opinions.

520 U.S. 154, 169–70 (1997).

2.   The oil and gas industry has frequently received incidental take exemptions for its activities in the arctic. In *Center for Biological Diversity v. Salazar*, 695 F.3d 893 (9th Cir. 2012), the court found it sufficient that the FWS found that "a small number" of endangered walruses and polar bears would be affected, without providing quantitative estimate. The court's analysis involved the complex interplay between the MMPA and the ESA. Under § 101(a)(5)(A) of the MMPA, citizens who engage in a specified activity other than commercial fishing within a specified geographical region may request authorization for incidental take of "small numbers" of marine mammals pursuant to that activity for a period of no more than five years. The court rejected a regulation that merged the "small number" requirement into the independent statutory requirement of "negligible" impact, but found that the agency had treated the two factors independently in this particular case. The agency defined "small numbers" to mean small relative to the total population of the species. The court deferred to the agency's interpretation as reasonable. The court also held that the "agency need not quantify the number of marine mammals that would be taken under the regulations, so long as the agency reasonably determines through some other means that the specified activity will result in take of only 'small numbers' of marine mammals." The court reaffirmed the general view that under the ESA (as opposed to the MMPA) the permissible level of take should be expressed as a specific number whenever possible. In the case before it, however, the court upheld the use of a qualitative requirement combined with monitoring requirements because no better surrogate had been identified and because the MMPA requirement of "negligible impact" provided some of the same protection that a quantified take restriction would provide in the usual ESA case.

F. RECOVERY OF LISTED SPECIES: SECTION 4(f)

Section 4(f) of the ESA governs recovery planning for threatened and endangered species. The pertinent text provides:

(1) The Secretary shall develop and implement plans (hereinafter in this subsection referred to as "recovery plans") for the conservation and survival of endangered species and threatened species listed pursuant to this section, unless he finds that such a plan will not promote the conservation of the species. The Secretary, in developing and implementing recovery plans, shall, to the maximum extent practicable—* * *

> (B) incorporate in each plan—
>
>> (i) a description of such site-specific management actions as may be necessary to achieve the plan's goal for the conservation and survival of the species;
>>
>> (ii) objective, measurable criteria which, when met, would result in a determination, in accordance with the provisions of this section, that the species be removed from the list; and
>>
>> (iii) estimates of the time required and the cost to carry out those measures needed to achieve the plan's goal and to achieve intermediate steps toward that goal.

16 U.S.C. § 1533(f) (2000). The excerpt below uses an appealing metaphor to help explain the role of recovery planning compared to the other provisions of the ESA.

FEDERICO CHEEVER, THE ROAD TO RECOVERY: A NEW WAY OF THINKING ABOUT THE ENDANGERED SPECIES ACT
23 ECOLOGY L.Q. 1, 23–27 (1996).[4]

The Wranglers and the Herd

A homey metaphor may assist in comprehending the relationship between designated species and the provisions of the Endangered Species Act designed to protect them. One may conceive of the population of administratively listed species as a herd of sick and injured animals (each animal representing an entire species) crossing the apocalyptic landscape created by human destruction of the natural environment and subject to threats by a variety of human predators. This herd of beasts moving across the landscape is under the protection of an eccentric set of "wranglers" representing the protections created by the provisions of the Endangered Species Act.

The wrangler who represents the § 4 listing process gathers new animals into the herd when they are sufficiently sick or injured to require protection. As she does, she brands each either "endangered" or "threatened." Ideally, her only concern is whether the animals she

---

4   Copyright 1996. Reprinted by permission.

encounters meet the scientific criteria required for each brand. However, she has more work than she can reasonably handle, and has identified many animals apparently deserving the protection of the herd which she has not yet been able to brand. Once an animal is branded and placed in the herd, it is no longer the concern of the § 4 wrangler.

The wrangler who represents § 7 protects the entire herd—both threatened and endangered species. However, he only protects them from a specific type of threat—actions authorized, funded, or carried out by federal agencies—and he only protects them if the injury they suffer is potentially life-threatening, that is, likely to jeopardize the continued existence of the entire species. A non-federal actor might annihilate the herd and it would be of no concern to our § 7 wrangler. Federal actors or federally authorized actors may injure the herd members, prevent their return to health or harass them, and so long as the action does not significantly increase the chance of extinction it too would be of no concern to our § 7 wrangler.

The wrangler who represents § 9 will only protect some members of the herd, endangered species of fish and wildlife (threatened species of fish and wildlife may be protected by regulation and generally are), but will protect them against all threats, federally authorized or not, and protect them against all sorts of injury, whether it will jeopardize the continued existence of the species or not. Although potentially the most energetic of the wranglers, she has often been ignored until recently.

The § 7 wrangler is relatively incorruptible. He will discharge his duty to prevent jeopardy from federal actions unless expressly told not to do so by his superiors on the "God Committee." This is a rare occurrence indeed.

The § 9 wrangler is more open to persuasion, and may agree to stop protecting her charges against a certain threat if the predator in question obtains leave under one of two exemption processes created by the Endangered Species Act—§ 7(b)(4), under which a federal actor or federally authorized actor may obtain an exemption from the takings prohibition, or § 10(a), under which any actor may get an exemption from the taking prohibition. However, the § 9 wrangler's flexibility goes only so far. She will not allow you to get her into trouble with the § 7 wrangler by jeopardizing the continued existence of any species. Her caution is sufficiently great to lead her to reject exemptions from the taking prohibition by federal or non-federal actors. These three wranglers and their herd move across the landscape. As more species on or near the brink of extinction appear, they are branded "endangered" or "threatened" and added to the herd. The herd gets larger. As time goes by, a few branded animals die despite the wranglers' best efforts (no one is perfect), and a few recover from their wounds and injuries without assistance, but most continue on in the herd.

The Role of Recovery Planning: The Fourth Wrangler

Section 4(f) of the Endangered Species Act requires USFWS or NMFS to "develop and implement" documents called "recovery plans" for "the conservation and survival of endangered species and threatened species" unless the agency finds that "such a plan will not promote the conservation of the species." To the "maximum extent practicable" each plan should include "a description of such site—specific management actions as may be necessary to achieve the plan's goal," "objective measurable criteria which, when met, would result in a determination . . . that the species be removed from the list," and "estimates of the time required and the cost to carry out those measures needed to achieve the plan's goal."

The recovery planning section can be thought of as a fourth wrangler, charged with nursing the members of the herd back to health, thereby reducing the size of the herd and rendering protected species less susceptible to threats beyond the control of the section 7 and 9 wranglers. Indeed, all the wranglers, sitting around their evening fire, would agree that their ultimate goal is to nurse all the members of the herd back to health. For this reason, they might recognize that the recovery wrangler has a special status and should coordinate the actions of the company when disputes arise among them or when the extent of their specific duties is ambiguous.

Recovery planning could give the agencies charged with administering the Endangered Species Act more flexible authority to take actions to enhance the prospects of protected species without dealing with the immediate, inflexible, and sometimes politically charged threat from a planned project or program that may violate § 7 or 9. These benefits might also extend to other federal agencies with activities affected by species protection. As one commentator, discussing agency behavior under the Endangered Species Act, noted:

> Federal agencies ought to recognize that their interests lie in participating in [recovery] plan development. If the plans are binding, the agencies need to ensure that their discretion is explicitly preserved in the plan . . . If the plans are not binding, agencies should still find participation on recovery teams worthwhile to shape conservation activities that will occur on their geographic or functional turf. [Citation omitted.]

However, to date, this fourth member of the company has had little or no power to assist the herd or boss the other wranglers. Although the Endangered Species Act states that recovery or conservation of protected species and the ecosystems on which they depend is the central purpose of the Act, and USFWS informs us that "recovery planning under § 4(f) of the Act is the 'umbrella' that eventually guides all [Endangered Species Act] activities and promotes a species' conservation and eventual delisting," the recovery planning section and the concept of recovery it embodies have played an insignificant role in the legal protection of endangered and threatened species. The same agency that declares recovery planning the umbrella that eventually guides all activities also tells us that recovery plans are "guidance documents" and not "decision-making" documents. Although recovery plans are required by law to identify specific recovery actions and a specific time frame for implementing them, the agencies and courts agree that these "implementation schedules" are unenforceable. In 1993, researchers at the University of Idaho announced findings indicating that recovery plans for many species prescribed "management for extinction" rather than management for recovery by setting recovery goals so low that they could not significantly increase the chance of species survival. Not surprisingly, the size of the metaphorical herd continues to grow, and the health of its members does not often improve.

NOTES

1.   Recovery planning does not occupy a prominent role in the day-to-day implementation of the ESA and, consequently, it is not well understood. There has been relatively little litigation over recovery planning. Most decisions reviewing recovery plans concluded that they are highly discretionary and for guidance purposes only.

In *United States v. McKittrick*, 142 F.3d 1170 (9th Cir. 1998), defendant McKittrick was convicted of killing a gray wolf that was a member of an experimental population released in Yellowstone National Park. McKittrick argued that FWS's regulations establishing the experimental population were invalid under § 4(f), since the Secretary did not adopt a recovery plan giving priority to those species "most likely to benefit from such plans." *Id.* at 1176 (quoting 16 U.S.C. § 1533(f)). That is, since gray wolves were plentiful in Canada and Alaska, McKittrick alleged the reintroduction efforts to be a poor allocation of resources. The court disagreed, holding that the "Secretary has broad discretion to determine what methods to use in species conservation, * * * adoption of recovery plans is discretionary, * * * and the presence of healthy wolf populations in Canada and Alaska does not, in any event, make the recovery of U.S. populations any less crucial." *Id.*

Similarly, in *Fund for Animals v. Rice*, 85 F.3d 535 (11th Cir. 1996), the court rejected environmental plaintiffs' position that a recovery plan barred FWS from making a later "no jeopardy" finding. Plaintiffs had claimed that a recovery plan that the Service had developed in 1987 for the Florida Panther required that it preserve the species' habitat. Accordingly, by the Service's finding of "no jeopardy," which allowed for the construction of a landfill, the Service failed to implement the plan. The court strongly disagreed on several grounds, including that "the practical effect of the Plaintiffs' position would be to elevate the 1987 Recovery Plan into a document with the force of law." *Id.* at 547. Instead, the court noted, § 4(f) makes it clear that recovery plans are "for guidance purposes only," and that, with respect to recovery plans, the Act "breathes discretion at every pore." *Id.* (internal citations omitted). In *National Wildlife Federation v. Norton*, 386 F.Supp.2d 553, 568 (D. Vt. 2005), the court held that it would not overturn "the Secretary's decision to proceed with three recovery plans for the gray wolf rather than one comprehensive national plan," in spite of plaintiffs' allegation that the Secretary had violated § 4(f) in her failure to issue such a national recovery plan for the wolf.

2. Though courts have held the force of recovery plans to be discretionary, they have been more demanding with respect to the actual content of the plans. In *Defenders of Wildlife v. Babbitt*, 130 F.Supp.2d 121 (D.D.C. 2001), defendant FWS had downlisted the pronghorned antelope from endangered to threatened "without explaining the reasoning behind that determination or outlining where the record supports that determination." *Id.* at 133. The court found this to be inadequate, and held that the Service must either incorporate delisting criteria into its recovery plan or "provide an adequate explanation as to why the delisting criteria cannot practicably be incorporated at this time." *Id.* at 134. Similarly, in *Fund for Animals v. Babbitt*, 903 F.Supp. 96 (D.D.C. 1995), *amended by* 967 F.Supp. 6 (D.D.C. 1997), also addressing a downlisting, the court remanded a recovery plan in part because FWS had failed to include in the plan "objective, measurable criteria which, when met, would result in a determination, in accordance with the provisions of this section, that the species be removed from the list," as required by section 4(f)(1)(B)(ii) of the Act. What difference does it make if courts require "adequate plans" if they view them as discretionary and for guidance purposes only? Does the failure to enforce recovery plans undermine the other provisions of the ESA?

3. It can be controversial whether a species has recovered enough to be delisted. In *Greater Yellowstone Coalition, Inc. v. Servheen*, 665 F.3d 1015 (9th Cir. 2011), the court reversed the delisting of the Yellowstone grizzly because the agency had failed to reconcile the decision with the likely decline of the whitebark pine population, whose seeds are a key part of the grizzly's diet. The court rejected the agency's reliance on adaptive management to deal with any problems that might arise after delisting. "Just as it is not enough simply to invoke 'scientific uncertainty' as the basis for an agency's action, it is not enough to invoke 'adaptive management' as an answer to scientific uncertainty."

G. HABITAT CONSERVATION PLANS: SECTION 10

Under § 10 of the ESA, the Secretary may issue permits to private parties authorizing an otherwise prohibited taking, so long as the taking is "incidental to, and the not the purpose of, the carrying out of an otherwise lawful activity." 16 U.S.C. § 1539(a)(1)(B) (2000). In order to be eligible for such a permit, the applicant must submit a conservation plan specifying:

(i) the impact which will likely result from such taking;

(ii) what steps the applicant will take to minimize and mitigate such impacts, and the funding that will be available to implement such steps;

(iii) what alternative actions to such taking the applicant considered and the reasons why such alternatives are not being utilized; and

(iv) such other measures that the Secretary may require as being necessary or appropriate for purposes of the plan.

16 U.S.C. § 1539(a)(2)(A).

After the applicant submits the conservation plan, the Secretary must make certain findings before the issuance of the permit. These findings are that:

(i)   the taking will be incidental;

(ii) the applicant will, to the maximum extent practicable, minimize and mitigate the impacts of such taking;

(iii) the applicant will ensure that adequate funding for the plan will be provided;

(iv) the taking will not appreciably reduce the likelihood of the survival and recovery of the species in the wild; and

(v)   the measures, if any, required under subparagraph (A)(iv) will be met.

16 U.S.C. § 1539(a)(2)(B).

In practice, HCPs have become a mechanism for softening the impact of the otherwise stringent "take" prohibition. As a result, HCPs have much in common with Incidental Take Statements, except that HCPs are for private parties and ITSs are for agencies. A review of the history of HCPs demonstrates these similarities.

The HCP provision was introduced into the scheme of the ESA in the 1982 amendments. Per the amendments, private parties may apply for an "incidental take permit" under § 10 of the Act. The permits are issued by the Secretary upon approval of a "conservation plan" submitted by the private applicant under § 10(a)(2)(A). Once the Secretary approves the plan, the applicant is given limited immunity to § 9 "take" liability. As long as the applicant acts in accordance with the approved conservation plan (or, as we now know it, a Habitat Conservation Plan) and so long as the applicant satisfies the Secretary's findings noted *supra*, any incidental takings will not be subject to § 9 liability.

The use of HCPs was broadened during the Clinton administration with the development of the "No Surprises" policy. *See* Habitat Conservation Plans ("No Surprises") Rule, 63 Fed. Reg. 8,859 (1998). The

"No Surprises" Policy is essentially a guarantee to applicants that they will be obligated only to perform the mitigation required by the HCP and will not bear the burden or risk of misinformation or change. That is, if it becomes apparent after the issuance of an HCP that a listed species or its habitat is present on the permittee's land, or that the needs of the species are greater than initially thought, and this information was not known either to the government or the permittee, the permittee will not be "surprised" by additional liability beyond the terms of the HCP. Is the No Surprises policy the right balance of risks? Is it appropriate under the goals of the ESA? Is it necessary to provide HCP applicants with some degree of certainty?

Since their introduction, HCPs have been controversial, with supporters praising them as a desirable alternative to litigation—indeed as an instrument that can be *more* protective of species in some instances than the Act would otherwise be—and detractors claiming that they amount to the legalized killing of endangered species. The excerpt below captures the arguments for and against HCPs.

SHI-LING HSU, THE POTENTIAL AND PITFALLS OF HABITAT CONSERVATION PLANNING UNDER THE ENDANGERED SPECIES ACT
29 ENVTL. L. REP. 10592 (1999).[5]

The HCP concept stemmed from an early ESA conflict involving the rare mission blue butterfly's only habitat, which is located in the San Bruno hills south of San Francisco. Potential ESA restrictions had jeopardized plans to develop private property within the butterfly's habitat, and local environmental groups had threatened to use the ESA's citizen suit provision to derail development plans. After seeking out local environmental groups and local governments interested in the development plans, the developer initiated and obtained a negotiated agreement regarding habitat preservation for the mission blue butterfly. The FWS, which also participated in the negotiations, gave the agreement its blessing and sought to amend the ESA to legitimize these types of negotiated solutions. The mission blue butterfly plan thus became the first HCP formally recognized under the ESA with the passage of 1982 amendments to the ESA.

The duration of HCPs have varied. Individual landowners desiring to construct a single-family home on their lot are often issued permits lasting five years, which is sufficient time for them to construct their house. Logging companies, on the other hand, that plan their harvests over long periods of time sometimes have HCPs lasting 100 years. HCPs drew only modest interest in their earlier years, but experienced a dramatic upsurge

---

[5]   Copyright 1999. Reprinted by permission.

in interest in 1994. From 1982 to 1989, only three HCPs were approved and only three incidental take permits were issued. From 1990 to 1993, 22 HCPs were approved, but from 1994 to 1997, the number of HCPs skyrocketed to 193. As of January 31, 1998, the FWS had approved 230 HCPs. The upsurge in interest in HCPs has strained the FWS' resources, but citing a desire to engage in long-term, comprehensive, ecosystem-level planning, the FWS has embraced the HCP process. Affected landowners have also expressed enthusiasm for the HCP process, especially the increased regulatory certainty associated with HCPs. * * *

The FWS manifested its commitment to HCPs not only by processing significantly more HCPs than they ever had in the past, but also by further sweetening the deal for landowners. In August 1994, the FWS introduced the "No Surprises" policy. Under the No Surprises policy, the FWS may grant an assurance that if a permittee fully complies with the terms of an HCP that adequately covers a species, the FWS will not require the permittee to undertake any further mitigation measures deemed necessary in the future. Further mitigation measures may be deemed necessary in the future if it is determined that a species' habitat needs are greater than previously thought, if previously absent listed species migrate onto the landowner's property, or if species not currently listed become listed and trigger a series of habitat protection regulations. A landowner with an HCP but without a No Surprises assurance may face additional regulations under those circumstances. A No Surprises assurance guarantees that the landowner's liability to undertake mitigation measures is limited to those set forth in the HCP. A No Surprises assurance will typically require the landowner to undertake additional mitigation measures in the short term, but landowners have not been hesitant to seize a guarantee that barring the occurrence of extraordinary circumstances, the HCP represents an exhaustive list of obligations with respect to the species covered by the HCP.

One question, however, remains. Have HCPs been an effective tool for addressing these problems?

The criticisms of the HCP process are many. The most fundamental criticism is that HCPs allow the FWS to cede too much in the way of concessions to developers and loggers. The FWS has not used HCPs to aid in the recovery of listed species and has apparently settled for the more modest goal of only making sure that HCPs do not appreciably reduce the likelihood of survival and recovery of the species in the wild. In general, the FWS is criticized for implementing HCPs too generously by conceding to landowners far more than necessary in order to obtain their assent to an HCP. The evidence to support this assertion can be found in HCPs that seem to allow landowners to develop or log their property in substantially the same manner that they would in the absence of any ESA restrictions. * * *

It is premature to conclude, however, that this is simply a matter of the FWS giving away the store. Given the resources it has to work with, the FWS may simply be making the best of a bad situation. The FWS has shown more vigor in negotiations involving land that is more ecologically valuable. In cases where the quality of the habitat is poor, the FWS will strike a more generous bargain with the landowner than it will when the habitat is of high quality. For example, the FWS has been more willing to permit development in the portions of Alabama beach mouse habitat that has been heavily developed than in those portions where the habitat is rich and important. * * *

A second fundamental criticism of the HCP process pertains to the very long-term commitments that are being made by the FWS. While it is true that logging companies in particular need to plan for time horizons on the order of 100 years, it is also true that much can happen in 100 years. Wetlands were not even considered ecologically valuable until several decades ago. What might the FWS be agreeing to give away that will be deemed highly valuable 50 years from now? This is an especially compelling question in forest HCPs, where the complexity of the ecosystem interactions are still only beginning to be understood. Thus, there is a good reason that forest HCPs are the only class of HCPs for which "No Surprises" assurances are not automatically attached to the HCP as a matter of FWS policy.

A third criticism of HCPs is that it has curbed citizen participation in the ESA. Citizen participation has been perhaps most beneficial in the case of the ESA because many listings of endangered or threatened species have been made pursuant to citizen petitions. Professor Holly Doremus * * * points out three ways in which citizens are effectively shut out of the HCP process: (1) the early negotiations of HCPs take place between the FWS and the landowner, with no public input; (2) too little information is provided to the public too late in the process; and (3) citizen suits are effectively undermined by the issuance of an incidental take permit that eliminates the possibility that a landowner is operating in violation of the ESA. * * *

A final criticism of HCPs is that the precedent set by the HCP process poses some gaming problems for federal regulators in general. The success regulated parties have had in forcing the FWS to the bargaining table by threatening to sue or lobby for legislative reform and by shooting, shoveling, and shutting up invites further intimidation. While we may hope that our regulatory agencies can persist in representing broader interests, in many cases they will not. Moreover, the mere threat of litigation or legislative attack, even if unmeritorious, imposes costs upon agencies that must evaluate the seriousness of each attack. The resources required to put out such fires would almost certainly be better spent carrying out its regulatory duties.

Not all the news is bad for HCPs. The HCP program has also attracted many advocates, the most prominent of which is Secretary of the Interior Bruce Babbitt. Secretary Babbitt has long sought to avoid the logjam created by the litigation and political conflict over logging in the Pacific Northwest habitat of the northern spotted owl, which he characterized as a "national train wreck." HCPs represented such an opportunity. They are a mechanism for the FWS and landowners to avoid litigation and its attendant costs, both in terms of resources spent and the uncertainty introduced into the regulatory process. Litigation is particularly ominous if, as is often the case in the ESA, the only possible outcomes for a parcel of private property are: (1) the FWS regulates the property, and (2) the FWS doesn't regulate the property. The most efficient outcome is likely to be one in which there is some development or logging and some preservation because it is a rare case where complete development or logging or complete preservation are the most desirable outcomes from a societal standpoint. Thus, HCPs allow the FWS and landowners to escape from a binary world where either the FWS or the landowner is a winner, and the other is a loser.

HCPs also offer the opportunity to perform planning on a regional or ecosystem level. California's Natural Community Conservation Program (NCCP), which is also meant to facilitate planning on a regional level, offered the Secretary a model that could be coopted into the HCP mechanism. Indeed, the pilot NCCP programs in the San Diego area and in Orange County, California, are hailed as examples of how comprehensive planning can be done at the regional level and with the input of developers, environmental organizations, community groups, and local, state, and federal government. Ideally, planning on a regional or ecosystem level for multiple affected species and with multiple stakeholders participating in the process allows for broader and more comprehensive ecological considerations and helps to avoid litigation, providing more certainty for all parties. A broader planning scale also allows for the identification of the best areas for development and the best areas for conservation. In addition, such comprehensive plans, if done well, can effectively delegate significant authority to local governments to carry out some of the more ministerial aspects of habitat management. The city of Austin, Texas, and the county of Travis, Texas,—where Austin is located—are authorized to issue permits for development in certain areas of golden-cheeked warbler habitat, provided that certain mitigation measures are agreed to by the landowners, many of whom are individuals seeking to construct single-family homes on a single lot. The city of Austin and Travis County must also contribute to the acquisition of some prime golden-cheeked warbler habitat in an area known as the Balcones Canyonlands. Multiple species and regional HCPs are also being developed in Las Vegas, Nevada; St. George, Utah; and Western Riverside County, California.

Perhaps the most compelling argument in favor of HCPs is that they allow the FWS to make the best of a bad situation. Apart from the unfortunate need to mollify its political enemies, the FWS must solve its "shoot, shovel, and shut up" problem. There are two aspects to the problem: one regarding illegal behavior and one regarding legal behavior, but both can be addressed by HCPs. With respect to the problem of deterring the illegal killing of species, HCPs serve as a means of ameliorating the FWS' enforcement problem. If the FWS cannot compel lawful observance of the ESA, perhaps it can induce landowners to agree to it. This seems an unfortunate necessary evil, but given the resources of the FWS, it may be necessary.

NOTES

1.   HCPs vary greatly. The large majority are under 500 acres, and about an eighth are under one acre. But about 5% are over 100,000 acres, and a small minority are over a million acres. *See* 65 Fed. Reg. 35,248 (July 1, 2000). Does it matter whether these agreements cover a lot of territory, or whether they last five or fifty years?

2.   If an HCP is static, it may find itself overtaken by climate change and rendered ineffective. A review of existing HCPs revealed some significant shortcomings in this regard. "No surprises" provisions in HCPs may bar the government from seeking changes to deal with unanticipated changes except in extraordinary circumstances. But areas set aside for a species today may no longer be adequate in the future due to climate change. An analysis of thirty-five of the largest HCPs showed nearly half contained explicit references to climate change, depending on whether they negotiated before or during the Obama Administration. See Melinda Taylor and Holly Doremus, Habitat *Conservation Plans and Climate Change: Recommendations for Policy*, 45 ENV. L. REP. 10863 (2015). Taylor and Doremus make several recommendations. They suggest that new HCPs contain provisions to ensure flexibility depending on future climate developments. Existing HCPs pose a more difficult problem. The first step would be for the government to investigate whether existing species preserves are likely to be impaired by climate change. If so, the government should attempt to negotiate modifications in the HCP with land owners.

3.   Clearly, there are two very different perspectives on HCPs. Either they are a creative way to find win-win solutions and advance eco-system planning, or they are regrettable means to rescue an imperiled statute. Which seems more accurate? Would we be better off with full enforcement of the "take" prohibition, or do we need some entirely new approach to protecting biodiversity? As Alejandro Comacho pointed out, we would be in a better position to answer these questions if agencies had treated HCPs like an experiment, with systematic monitoring of the program's success. Alejandro E. Camacho, *Can Regulation Evolve? Lessons From a Study in Maladaptive Management*, 55 UCLA L. REV. 293 (2007).

4. HCPs resemble wetlands mitigation banking, in that they are an effort to prevent head-on collisions between land developers and environmental goals. They also share this characteristic with offset requirements under the Clean Air Act. Does this suggest something about future trends in environmental regulation? Based on HCPs and experiences with similar mechanisms, should we consider this trend an encouraging sign of regulatory creativity or a discouraging sign of lack of commitment? Should we make more extensive use of market-techniques in HCPs themselves? For a suggestion to that effect, see Jonathan Remy Nash, *Trading Species: A New Direction for Habitat Conservation Programs*, 31 COLUM. J. ENVT. L. 1 (2007).

5. The question of public participation in HCPs and more generally in regulatory contracts is a difficult one. On the one hand, without broad public participation, negotiations are likely to proceed much more smoothly. On the other hand, excluding the public sacrifices important democratic values of transparency and accountability. How we can best accommodate these conflicting values? Could we amend the HCP process to make it more "democratic"?

H. ASSESSING THE ESA

The Endangered Species Act has attracted a great deal of criticism since its inception. Not a political cycle goes by without threats to repeal or substantially amend the Act. Property rights advocates take aim at the law with zeal while environmentalists defend it with equal tenacity. Clearly, whether it is viewed more narrowly, as a statute designed to protect species, or more broadly, as a law aimed at preserving habitat and, ultimately biodiversity, the ESA is far from perfect. Some of the critiques focus on its initial design, while others focus on implementation and effectiveness. Still others reflect more ideological concerns. The excerpt below describes the dominant criticisms of the Act.

ERIC BIBER, THE APPLICATION OF THE ENDANGERED SPECIES ACT TO THE PROTECTION OF FRESHWATER MUSSELS: A CASE STUDY
32 ENVTL. L. 91, 140–47 (2002).[6]

Various explanations have been proposed for the lack of recovery success under the ESA. First, critics argue that the ESA, by attempting to conserve all species, effectively conserves none, because it spreads resources too thinly among too many listed species, resulting in underprotection for all, instead of fully recovering some species and allowing others to go extinct. What system of "triage" or prioritization should actually be used by the Act to determine which species to protect and which to allow to disappear, however, is less clear. Some critics argue

---

that only charismatic, popular species deserve protection; others call for focusing on species that are most likely to benefit from recovery efforts (maximal marginal recovery benefits from dollars spent); still others argue for focusing on species that are crucial to ecosystem functioning and survival; and others argue that priority should be given to species that have the most genetic information or taxonomic uniqueness, or that would protect entire ecosystems.

Second, the critics argue that the Act is counterproductive, at least when it comes to private lands. Because the Act is solely mandatory and prohibitive, at the very least it creates a disincentive for landowners to take proactive measures to conserve listed species. Increasing the numbers of listed species will result in the risk that landowners will face increased restrictions on their property through the § 9 take prohibition. At the worst, the punitive nature of the ESA toward private landowners engenders hostility and fear, which results in efforts by landowners to illegally and surreptitiously eliminate listed species from their property before the Service can enforce the law against them ("shoot, shovel, and shut up"), and a lack of cooperation (or outright anger) by landowners against the biologists seeking to recover the listed species. The horror stories and perceived threats against private property rights and extractive industries that the ESA has created has also contributed to the political opposition to the ESA. This critique of the ESA has produced a wave of suggestions for developing positive incentives for landowners under the ESA, including the use of tax credits and direct payments, the implementation of HCPs (with guarantees that agreements between the landowner and the government will not be overturned without payment ("No surprises")), and the "safe harbor" program, in which landowners are promised no additional land-use restrictions in return for proactively managing their property to encourage endangered species. Some of these suggestions have prompted actual administrative changes to the ESA's implementation.

A substantial number of the threats facing endangered species, however, are beyond the power of the ESA to address through its prohibitions on private actions. Some threats, particularly exotic species, are difficult or impossible for humans to correct. The task of controlling a species such as the zebra mussel, which is prolific in reproduction (producing millions or billions of offspring), and spreads by water currents and attachments to boats, seems impossible. Even where the threats may be feasibly dealt with, in many cases they will not be addressed by ESA regulation because the ESA does not (and probably could not) mandate positive actions by private or public actors. Thus, the ESA cannot eliminate the dams that currently have destroyed the vast majority of mussel habitat along the Tennessee and Cumberland Rivers in Kentucky and Tennessee, formerly the best and most diverse mussel communities in North America.

Similarly, for the control of exotic species, or the maintenance of natural disturbance patterns (such as fire) that are needed to maintain suitable habitats for certain species, even if such actions are achievable by humans, they often would require positive, proactive management by private and public landowners. Critics of the law argue that the punitive nature of the ESA, and its incentive structure, give rise to the inevitable result that no economically rational landowner will ever undertake such actions.

Another major criticism of the Act has been that it is too oriented on individual species and, as a result, inefficiently wastes time, money, and resources on attempting to save particular species as they become endangered, rather than attempting to protect entire functioning ecosystems and environments. By more proactively and holistically dealing with conservation threats, it is argued, the Act would more efficiently use its resources, saving whole communities of species from extinction rather than dealing with individual species one at a time. As one commentator argued, ecosystems all over the nation are quickly shrinking, but nothing is being done about them until they shrink far enough that a particular species in that ecosystem is listed under the Act: "the Endangered Species Act is treating the symptom and not the disease." [citation omitted.] Thus, there has been an avalanche of proposals to convert (or supplement) the ESA into an Endangered Ecosystems Act, which focuses on preserving whole ecosystems instead of individual species. The result, it is argued, would be more efficient, effective, and thoughtful conservation. To protect endangered species, we either must attempt to re-create or revive ecosystems ourselves, an enormously expensive proposition, or protect the ecosystems in the first place. Why not use ecosystem protection as the focus of the Act to begin with?

A fourth criticism of the effectiveness of the ESA is that conservation efforts under the Act often occur far too late. Indeed, one study found that the median population for a species of vertebrate animals at the time of listing was 1075 individuals, and for plants at the time of listing it was 120 individuals. Thus, by the time a species has been listed under the Act, its population is so low that recovery efforts may be unable to succeed, or will take extraordinary amounts of time and money to succeed. As a result, the ESA makes recovery and conservation efforts harder than they otherwise might be by delaying intervention until the threshold of "endangered" or "threatened" status has been reached. At that point, options have been foreclosed (by changes in land-use decisions, or falling population levels for the species) and expensive rescue efforts are the only possible solutions. Even if the populations of such species can be kept from falling any further, the encroachment of human development activities and the elimination of suitable habitat may mean that increasing the numbers or range of a species is impossible (at least given current economic and political constraints).

Finally, some commentators and environmental groups have argued that the Service's implementation of the law has been too weak, and that by changing key definitions of terms the Service has removed the effectiveness of some important legal tools within the ESA. For example, many environmentalists argue that critical habitat designation could be an extremely effective tool in the enforcement of the Act. * * * Arguably, a broader definition of adverse modification that included recovery would provide a much tougher critical habitat requirement under the ESA. A broader definition would have the potential to restrict far more federal actions, or to force the modification of those actions to provide much greater protection for listed species.

The fight over critical habitat designation is part of a larger critique of the ESA by a few commentators, who argue that (at least under current interpretation of the ESA by the Service) the ESA effectively manages species to avoid extinction rather than to promote recovery. Thus, all of the legal tools in § 7 (the jeopardy standard and the adverse modification standard, as applied through the consultation process) only prevent federal action that leads to jeopardy, not federal action that retards recovery (at least as currently interpreted by the Service). Similarly, the application of the § 9 take standards to the HCP process by the Service have allowed permits to be granted for projects as long as they do not jeopardize the survival of the species, rather than to require permitted projects to provide a net recovery benefit for the species. Thus, all of the pressure for recovering listed species is placed on an overburdened, underfunded recovery program rather than being built into the regulatory programs of sections 7 and 9.

NOTES

1. The Endangered Species Act remains highly controversial, particularly with development interests and property rights advocates. It remains to be seen whether they will succeed in making major changes to the statute.

2. One response to some of the rigidies of the ESA has been to postpone or decline listing a species when state conservation efforts seem to be sufficient to protect the species. This retains listing as a threat if states slacken in their conservation efforts. This technique has been used for species like the greater sage grouse and the lesser prairie chicken. If this approach works properly, it may help shift from the ESA's species-focused approach to one that is more ecosystem-oriented and perhaps more effective. But there is also the risk that state conservation efforts will ultimately provide less protection than the ESA. For a discussion of this approach, see *The ESA Today: Eco-Pragmatism and State Conservation Efforts*, 46 ENV. L. REP. 10827 (2016).

3. Other developments may challenge our current strategies to preserve biodiversity. In some locations, at least, climate change may make

it impossible for a species to survive. This raises the question of whether the species could be moved to a new location. Even the concept of extinction may be called into question, given some current efforts at de-extinction. Although it is an open question about the extent to which this will ever be practical, there is now serious discussion among some scientists of using advanced genetic engineering to bring back the passenger pigeon and the wooly mammoth from remaining genetic material. Assuming that such techniques became practical, would this change our attitude toward extinction? How much DNA would a living animal have to share with an extinct species to be considered a case of de-extinction? Does pursuing these options risk undermining support and resources for efforts to preserve currently endangered species?

CHAPTER 4

ENVIRONMENTAL PROTECTION
AND THE CONSTITUTION

■ ■ ■

The world is divided into political subunits. Although environmental problems themselves recognize no such boundaries, legal institutions are inherently tied to geography. Environmental institutions are still undergoing development at the international level. But the same is not true today *within* the U.S., which has long had an elaborate system of "cooperative federalism" to divide responsibility for environmental regulation between the federal government and the fifty states. Much of this chapter will be devoted to considering the extent to which the constitutional federalism restrictions limit regulation. The chapter closes with a discussion of constitutional protections for property as they impact environmental regulation.

We will begin our exploration of federalism by examining the policy debate over centralization in environmental regulation. We will then consider a key mechanism created by the U.S. Constitution in response to the difficulty of obtaining cooperation between states: empowering the federal government to take action on a national basis. Next, we will consider the possibility that state environmental regulations may be invalid under federal law. As we will see, state environmental regulations are increasingly challenged as violations of the Supreme Court's "dormant commerce clause" doctrine or as conflicting with federal regulatory requirements. We also explore the analogous problem at the international level, where trade agreements may impose similar restraints on environmental regulation by individual nations.

Another significant constitutional restriction on environmental protection relates to private property. Efforts to regulate land use in order to protect biodiversity or other environmental values may be challenged as "takings" of private property. Under some circumstances, the government may need to provide compensation if it wishes to prohibit environmentally harmful land uses.

A. UNIFORMITY VERSUS DIVERSITY IN ENVIRONMENTAL REGULATION

Most of this chapter focuses on the legal rules governing centralization and decentralization of environmental regulations—constitutional limits on federal regulation, commerce clause restraints on state regulation, and WTO limits on national regulation. In the midst of these quarrels over regulatory authority, it is easy to lose track of an equally important question: As a matter of policy, how much centralization is wise?

RICHARD L. REVESZ, THE RACE TO THE BOTTOM AND FEDERAL ENVIRONMENTAL REGULATION: A RESPONSE TO CRITICS

82 MINN. L. REV. 535 (1997).

My starting point is a rebuttable presumption in favor of decentralization. This presumption rests on three independent grounds. First, our country is large and diverse; it is therefore likely that different regions have different preferences for environmental protection. Environmental protection addresses an important resource-allocation question: as a society we can generally purchase additional environmental protection at some price, paid in the currency of jobs, wages, shareholders' profits, tax revenues, and economic growth. Given the existence of the states as plausible regulatory units, the tradeoffs reflecting the preferences of citizens of different regions should not be wholly disregarded in the regulatory process, absent strong reasons for doing so. * * *

Second, the benefits of environmental protection also vary throughout the country. For example, a stringent ambient [air quality] standard may benefit many people in densely populated areas but only a few elsewhere. Similarly, a particular level of exposure to a contaminant may be more detrimental if it is combined with exposure to other contaminants with which it has synergistic effects.

Third, the costs of meeting a given standard also differ across geographic regions. For example, a source may have a large detrimental impact on ambient air quality if it is directly upwind from a mountain or other topographical barrier. Similarly, a water polluter will have a far larger impact on water quality standards if it disposes its effluents in relatively small bodies of water. Climate might also play a role: certain emission or effluent standards may be easier (and cheaper) to meet in warmer weather.* * *

This presumption for decentralization should be overcome, however, if there is a systemic evil in letting states decide the level of environmental protection that will apply within their jurisdictions. In my work, I have explored in detail the two most prominent justifications for vesting responsibility over environmental regulation at the federal level: that interstate competition over environmental standards would result in a "race to the bottom," and that federal regulation is necessary to prevent interstate externalities.

The race-to-the-bottom rationale posits that states will try to induce geographically mobile firms to locate within their jurisdictions, in order to benefit from additional jobs and tax revenues, by offering them suboptimally lax environmental standards. The problem of interstate externalities arises because a state that sends pollution to another state obtains the labor and fiscal benefits of the economic activity that generates the pollution but does not suffer the full costs of the activity. Under these conditions, economic theory maintains that an undesirably large amount of pollution will cross state lines. * * *

My argument attacking the race-to-the-bottom justification proceeds in four steps. I start by pointing out that when states compete for industry through environmental standards, they are competing for the sale of a good: the right to locate within their jurisdictions. If competition for the sale of most goods is generally good, why should competition for the sale of this good be clearly bad? I show, moreover, why possible distinctions between a state as seller of location rights and sellers of traditional consumer products do not provide support for race-to-the-bottom claims.

Second, I analyze the leading economic model of the effects of interstate competition on the choice of environmental standards, which shows that inter-jurisdictional competition leads to the maximization of social welfare, rather than to a race to the bottom. In this model, Wallace Oates and Robert Schwab posit jurisdictions that compete for mobile capital through the choice of taxes and environmental standards. A higher capital stock benefits residents in the form of higher wages, but hurts them as a result of the foregone tax revenues and lower environmental quality needed to attract the capital.

Each jurisdiction makes two policy decisions: it sets a tax rate on capital and establishes an environmental standard. Professors Oates and Schwab show that competitive jurisdictions will set a net tax rate on capital of zero (the rate that exactly covers the cost of public services provided to the capital, such as police and fire protection). In turn, competitive jurisdictions will set an environmental standard that is defined by equating the willingness to pay for an additional unit of environmental quality with the corresponding change in wages. Professors Oates and Schwab show that these choices of tax rates and environmental standards are socially optimal.

Third, I acknowledge that, in particular instances, game-theoretic interactions among the states could lead to underregulation absent federal intervention. In such cases, federal minimum standards would be desirable. But it is equally plausible that in other instances the reverse would be true: that game-theoretic interactions among the states would lead to overregulation absent federal intervention. * * *

Fourth, I argue that even if states systematically enacted suboptimally lax environmental standards, federal environmental regulation would not necessarily improve the situation. If states cannot compete over environmental regulation because it has been federalized, they will compete along other regulatory dimensions, leading to suboptimally lax standards in other areas, or along the fiscal dimension, leading to the underprovision of public goods. Thus, the reduction in social welfare implicit in race-to-the-bottom arguments would not be eliminated merely by federalizing environmental regulation: the federalization of all regulatory and fiscal decisions would be necessary to solve the problem.

With respect to the interstate externality justification for federal environmental regulation, four features of my argument are worth emphasizing. First, the presence of interstate externalities provides a compelling argument for federal regulation under conditions in which * * * bargaining is unlikely to occur. Particularly with respect to air pollution, transaction costs are likely to be sufficiently high to prevent the formation of interstate compacts. It is difficult for such compacts to emerge in the absence of a clearly defined baseline concerning when upwind states have the right to send pollution downwind and in the absence of generally accepted mathematical models for translating a source's emissions into a quantity of ambient air quality degradation at all the places at which the emissions affect ambient air quality. Moreover, for different pollution sources, the range of affected states will vary; this shifting membership among the participants at the bargaining table makes it less likely that the emergence of conditions favoring cooperation will occur.

Second, the fact that interstate externalities provide a compelling justification for intervention does not mean that all federal environmental regulation can be justified on these grounds. For environmental problems such as the control of drinking water quality, there are virtually no interstate pollution externalities; the effects are almost exclusively local. Even with respect to problems for which there are interstate externalities, such as air pollution, the rationale calls only for a response specific to the problem. This may include a limit on the amount of pollution that can cross state lines, rather than across-the-board federal regulation.

Third, the environmental statutes have been an ineffective response to the problem of interstate externalities. For example, the core of the Clean Air Act—the statute designed to deal with the pollution that gives rise to the most serious problems of interstate externalities—consists of a series of federally prescribed ambient standards and emission standards. The federal emission standards do not effectively combat the problem of interstate externalities because they do not regulate the number of sources within a state or the location of the sources. Similarly, the various federal ambient air quality standards are not well-targeted to address the problem of interstate externalities. They are overinclusive because they require a state to restrict pollution that has only in-state consequences. But they are also underinclusive because a state could meet the applicable ambient standards but nonetheless export a great deal of pollution to downwind states (through tall stacks or a location near the interstate border). In fact, a state might meet its ambient standards precisely because it exports a large proportion of its pollution.

Fourth, in some ways the federal environmental statutes have exacerbated, rather than ameliorated, the problem of interstate externalities. Again, in the context of the Clean Air Act, the federal ambient standards give states an incentive to encourage sources within their jurisdiction to use taller stacks. In this way, states can externalize not only the health and environmental effects of the pollution but also the regulatory costs of complying with the federal ambient standards. Thus, not surprisingly, the use of tall stacks expanded considerably after the passage of the Clean Air Act in 1970. In 1970, only two stacks in the United States were higher than 500 feet. By 1985, more than 180 stacks were higher than 500 feet and twenty-three were higher than 1000 feet. While this method of externalizing pollution is now less of a problem as a result of stack height regulations that followed the 1977 amendments to the Clean Air Act, tall stacks remain a means by which excessive pollution can be sent to downwind states.

NOTES

1.   As the subtitle of this excerpt indicates, Revesz's critique of existing federal regulation has itself come in for a great deal of criticism.[1] Are you persuaded by Revesz's claim that state governments will not unduly lower their standards to attract industry? Given the nature of environmental problems, is it possible to draw a clear line between local environmental problems and spillover effects?

2.   If Revesz is right, should courts attempt to tilt the balance toward decentralization? Should they require a showing that federal regulation is

---

[1]   *See, e.g.*, Kirsten H. Engel, *State Environmental Standard-Setting: Is There a 'Race' and is It 'to the Bottom'?*, 48 HASTINGS L.J. 271 (1997); Daniel C. Esty, *Revitalizing Environmental Federalism*, 95 MICH. L. REV. 570 (1996); Joshua Sarnoff, *The Continuing Imperative (But Only from a National Perspective) for Federal Environmental Regulation*, 7 DUKE ENVTL. L. & POL'Y F. 225 (1997); Peter P. Swire, *The Race to Laxity and the Race to Undesirability: Explaining Failures in Competition Among Jurisdictions in Environmental Law*, 14 YALE J. ON REG. 67 (1996). *See also* Kirsten H. Engel & Scott R. Saleska, *'Facts Are Stubborn Things': An Empirical Reality Check in the Theoretical Debate Over the Race-To-The-Bottom in State Environmental Standard-Setting*, 8 CORNELL J.L. & PUB. POL'Y 55 (1998). On the other hand, a recent review of the economics literature found little support for the existence of a race to the bottom except in unusual circumstances. See Bruce G. Caruthers and Naomi R. Lamoreaux, *Regulatory Races: The Effects of Jurisdictional Competition on Regulatory Standards*, 54 J. ECON. LIT. 52 (2016).

tailored to spillover effects, to maintaining minimum national health standards, or to filling some other identifiable shortcoming in state regulation? Should they have a strong presumption that differences in state regulations are justified, even when such differences may cause some adverse economic effects? Or should the proper balance between federal and state regulation be left to the national political process to decide? For a recent discussion of the significance of spillover effects in environmental regulation, see Douglas R. Williams, *Toward Regional Governance in Environmental Law*, 46 AKRON L. REV. 1047 (2013).

3.   In a later article, Dean Revesz critiqued another justification for federal regulation, the idea that state governments are more prone to capture by industry groups. *See* Richard L. Revesz, *Federalism and Environment Regulation: A Public Choice Analysis*, 115 HARV. L. REV. 553 (2001). Besides contesting the theoretical validity of this idea, Revesz argued that state governments were doing a reasonably good job of regulating before the federal government entered the picture. He also suggested that they continue to be sources for innovative environmental measures today. William Buzbee argued, however, that the state-federal dichotomy Revesz set up fails to take into account the specific context of individual state and/or federal policies. *See* William W. Buzbee, *Contextual Environmental Federalism*, 14 N.Y.U. ENVTL L. J. 108 (2005). It also appears that state regulation was not effective in addressing environmental problems before the federal government stepped in, although this is subject to some dispute. See William L. Andreen, *Of Fables and Federalism: A Re-Examination of the Historical Rationale for Federal Environmental* Regulation, 42 ENV. L. 627 2012). On the other hand, dispersing authority among multiple decisionmakers such as states may mute the effects of federal regulatory rollbacks. See William W. Buzbee, *Federalism Hedging, Entrenchment, and the Climate Challenge*, 2017 WIS. L. REV. 1037 (2017).

If Revesz is correct in his criticisms of federal regulation, how do we account for its popularity? The following excerpt considers one possible answer and its implications for regulatory reform.

RICHARD B. STEWART, ENVIRONMENTAL QUALITY AS A NATIONAL GOOD IN A FEDERAL STATE
1997 U. CHI. LEGAL F. 199 (1997).

The problem exists of how to explain the dominance of federal environmental regulation in the face of public choice skepticism about the political efficacy of diffuse interests and the failure to develop a convincing welfare economic justification for the scope and scale of current federal programs.

I think we must simply conclude, as a matter of fact, that many Americans regard environmental quality as an important national good that transcends individual or local interest. This regard is the result of historical, cultural, and political contingencies that have yet to be fully or satisfactorily explained. The settlement and pioneer experiences; certain strands in American religious experience and sensibility; the acquisition and retention of the public lands, including many of exceptional scenic grandeur; and growing ambivalence towards technology and established economic and governmental institutions, along with other factors, all seem to have played a role in the emerging recognition of environmental quality and natural resource preservation as a national good.

Rather than attempting here to explain how Americans have come to regard environmental quality as a national good, I will simply posit it as fact that is reflected in various ways, including the following:

*Overwhelming support in public opinion polls for strong environmental measures.

*Widespread, sustained, effective political support for establishing, maintaining, implementing and enforcing far-reaching federal environmental regulatory programs.

*High levels of membership in and financial contributions to national environmental groups.

*Evidence of significant individual and constituent concern with and support for federal resource management and regulatory programs to secure environmental quality or preserve natural resources in other parts of the nation.

These manifestations are most powerful in the case of the Endangered Species Act, wilderness legislation, and other federal regulatory measures designed to protect natural resources of special rarity, beauty, or other significance. But public opinion and political support for other far-reaching forms of federal environmental regulation, including air and water pollution control and toxic waste regulation and cleanup suggest that these aspects of environmental quality are also regarded as part of the national good. This regard is probably to a considerable extent symbolic, but that in no way diminishes its political and social significance. To the extent that environmental protection is a symbolic good, public support for regulatory measures need not be based solely on environmental problems faced by individuals within their own locality, and can more readily be regarded as part of the national good.

If environmental quality is viewed as a national good, the benefits of environmental protection measures to deal with local pollution, toxic wastes, or habitat alteration are no longer individual and local but national and collective, undercutting the usual assumptions of the welfare economic/optimal environmental jurisdictional analysis, which generally defines environmental quality in terms of factors experienced directly by individuals (such as levels of pollution), making environmental policy a function of aggregate individual preferences, costs, and benefits. This analysis is methodologically "bottom up." It presumes that decentralized regulation is preferable because of variations in individual preferences and local circumstances. Centralized regulation is justified only if there are severe "decentralization failures" due to causes such as the "race to the bottom" or systematic state underprovision because of political distortions. To the extent, however, that environmental quality is regulated as a national good, a presumption in favor of a "top down" approach is logical: environmental programs should presumptively be federal unless "centralization failure" dictates decentralization.* * *

To say, however, that Americans regard and demand environmental quality as a national good is only a starting point for further analysis. Environmental quality is a highly complex and variable good that comes in many shapes and sizes. Scientific and technical complexity and uncertainty abound. Many different types of government measures can be deployed to promote environmental protection. The appropriate means for securing environmental quality is often complex and obscure. The media and political and policy entrepreneurs, including environmental groups and industrial, labor, and other organized commercial interests, play a key role in mobilizing and shaping public concern for environmental protection, defining the "problem," setting priorities, and advancing solutions.

The existing system of centralized federal command-and-control regulation and liability that has emerged out of this untidy tug and pull of factors and interests displays many grievous flaws. These include excessive rigidity and cost, barriers to innovation, lack of democratic political accountability, skewed priorities, excessive delay and transaction costs, and excessive legalization. Given the status of environmental quality as a national good, however, the appropriate response is not wholesale federal deregulation and devolution of regulatory responsibilities to lower levels of government. Advocates of dismantling the existing federal environmental regulatory system, including policy scholars and the more aggressive of House Republicans, have wholly failed to persuade. Accordingly, the question is how to advance the national commitment to environmental quality through new forms and structures that respond to the need for intelligent priority setting, avoid economic waste, reduce the dysfunctions of over-centralized regulation, and provide appropriate flexibility to deal with variations in local circumstances and accommodate values of local decisionmaking, which remain important. In short, the aim is not to dismantle but to reconstitute national environmental law and policy.

Some aspects of the centralization failures of our federal environmental regulatory system have been moderated by giving state regulators a substantial role in the implementation and enforcement of federal law. This development assumed increasing importance in the 1980s, once the basic apparatus of federal statutes and regulations had been established and attention shifted to implementation and enforcement. This arrangement avoids the need to create a more massive, duplicative federal administrative apparatus, takes advantage of state regulators' familiarity with local circumstances, and affords a degree of flexibility in adjusting regulatory requirements to those circumstances. Further, states generally enjoy the latitude to adopt measures more stringent than those required by federal law, and many have done so. These arrangements are not inconsistent with the status of environmental quality as a national good. The states no less than the federal government can be instruments for realizing national goals. Opinion polls indicate that the public wants both the federal and the state governments to play a substantial role in environmental protection, according a clear preference to neither. The public, consistent with Madison's view of the states and the federal government as competitors in promoting the public good, seems to favor this redundancy as providing greater assurance of effective environmental protection.

NOTES

1.   Unlike the European Union, the federal government does not have any explicit assignment of responsibility for environmental matters. If Stewart is right that Americans regard environmental quality as a national good, should this affect judicial interpretation of the commerce clause and other constitutional texts? Or should the Constitution be interpreted purely on the basis of the original understanding rather than the values of Americans today?

2.   Although their general approaches to environmental law are in many respects similar, Revesz and Stewart reach their shared conclusions from opposite directions. Revesz views environmental problems as presumptively local concerns, whereas Stewart views them as presumptively national concerns. Which presumption is more appealing?

3.   Stewart may be right that there is broad support for environmental quality as a national value, but there are also strong dissenting voices. For instance, in his effort to win the 2012 Republican nomination as a tea party candidate, former Congressman Ron Paul called for eliminating the EPA and handling environmental protection solely through state law damage suits by property owners. If anything, political polarization has increased substantially since then. Does this undermine Stewart's argument?

4.   As we will see in the second half of this book, it is a mistake to think of environmental regulation as either purely federal or purely state. In fact, both of levels of government are often involved in dealing with environmental problems, in part due to the structure of federal environmental law. Thus, much of environmental law is an exercise in cooperation, negotiation, or conflict between states and the federal government. See Erin Ryan, FEDERALISM AND THE TUG OF WAR WITHIN (2011).

B. THE SCOPE OF FEDERAL POWER

The federal government was formed to deal with problems that could not be solved without a unified response. Under the Articles of Confederation, federal action could only be taken with unanimous agreement of all states, which severely hindered the government's role. This made the states the equivalent of nations that can only cooperate based on unanimous consent; we saw in Chapter 1 that this creates serious difficulties. Thus, the Constitution is in part a solution to what economists call a collective action problem. See Robert D. Cooter and Neil Siegel, *Collective Action Federalism: A General Theory of Article I, Section 8*, 63 STAN. L. REV. 115 (2010). For a critique of this theory as an explanation of current doctrine, see Aziz Z. Huq, *Does the Logic of Collective Action Explain Federalism Doctrine?*, 66 STAN. L. REV. 217 (2014).

One of the basic assumptions of American constitutional law is that the federal government is a government of limited, delegated powers. Its authority was defined by the issues that at the time seemed to require a collective response. It does not always have the power even today to take whatever action it deems in the public interest. Instead, the federal government has a collection of specific powers: the power to regulate interstate commerce, the power to tax and spend, the power to enter treaties, etc. In this section, we will explore the scope of these federal powers and the extent to which they are limited by "states' rights." We begin with a case on the treaty power.

MISSOURI V. HOLLAND

Supreme Court of the United States, 1920.
252 U.S. 416, 40 S.Ct. 382, 64 L.Ed. 641.

MR. JUSTICE HOLMES delivered the opinion of the Court.

This is a bill in equity brought by the State of Missouri to prevent a game warden of the United States from attempting to enforce the Migratory Bird Treaty Act of July 3, 1918, and the regulations made by the Secretary of Agriculture in pursuance of the same. The ground of the bill is that the statute is an unconstitutional interference with the rights reserved to the States by the Tenth Amendment, and that the acts of the defendant done and threatened under that authority invade the sovereign right of the State and contravene its will manifested in statutes. * * *

On December 8, 1916, a treaty between the United States and Great Britain was proclaimed by the President. It recited that many species of birds in their annual migrations traversed certain parts of the United States and of Canada, that they were of great value as a source of food and in destroying insects injurious to vegetation, but were in danger of extermination through lack of adequate protection. It therefore provided for specified close seasons and protection in other forms, and agreed that the two powers would take or propose to their law-making bodies the necessary measures for carrying the treaty out. The above mentioned Act of July 3, 1918, entitled an act to give effect to the convention, prohibited the killing, capturing or selling of any of the migratory birds included in the terms of the treaty except as permitted by regulations compatible with those terms, to be made by the Secretary of Agriculture. Regulations were proclaimed on July 31, and October 25, 1918. It is unnecessary to go into any details, because, as we have said, the question raised is the general one whether the treaty and statute are void as an interference with the rights reserved to the States.

To answer this question it is not enough to refer to the Tenth Amendment, reserving the powers not delegated to the United States, because by Article II, § 2, the power to make treaties is delegated expressly, and by Article VI treaties made under the authority of the United States, along with the Constitution and laws of the United States made in pursuance thereof, are declared the supreme law of the land. If the treaty is valid there can be no dispute about the validity of the statute under Article I, § 8, as a necessary and proper means to execute the powers of the Government. The language of the Constitution as to the supremacy of treaties being general, the question before us is narrowed to an inquiry into the ground upon which the present supposed exception is placed.* * *

* * * [W]hen we are dealing with words that also are a constituent act, like the Constitution of the United States, we must realize that they have called into life a being the development of which could not have been foreseen completely by the most gifted of its begetters. It was enough for them to realize or to hope that they had created an organism; it has taken a century and has cost their successors much sweat and blood to prove that they created a nation. The case before us must be considered in the light of our whole experience and not merely in that of what was said a hundred years ago. The treaty in question does not contravene any prohibitory words to be found in the Constitution. The only question is whether it is forbidden by some invisible radiation from the general terms of the Tenth Amendment. We must consider what this country has become in deciding what that Amendment has reserved.

The State as we have intimated founds its claim of exclusive authority upon an assertion of title to migratory birds, an assertion that is embodied in statute. No doubt it is true that as between a State and its inhabitants the State may regulate the killing and sale of such birds, but it does not follow that its authority is exclusive of paramount powers. To put the claim of the State upon title is to lean upon a slender reed. Wild birds are not in the possession of anyone; and possession is the beginning of ownership. The whole foundation of the State's rights is the presence within their jurisdiction of birds that yesterday had not arrived, tomorrow may be in another State and in a week a thousand miles away. If we are to be accurate we cannot put the case of the State upon higher ground than that the treaty deals with creatures that for the moment are within the state borders, that it must be carried out by officers of the United States within the same territory, and that but for the treaty the State would be free to regulate this subject itself.

As most of the laws of the United States are carried out within the States and as many of them deal with matters which in the silence of such laws the State might regulate, such general grounds are not enough to support Missouri's claim. Valid treaties of course "are as binding within the territorial limits of the States as they are elsewhere throughout the dominion of the United States." No doubt the great body of private relations usually fall within the control of the State, but a treaty may override its power. * * *

Here a national interest of very nearly the first magnitude is involved. It can be protected only by national action in concert with that of another power. The subject-matter is only transitorily within the State and has no permanent habitat therein. But for the treaty and the statute there soon might be no birds for any powers to deal with. We see nothing in the Constitution that compels the Government to sit by while a food supply is cut off and the protectors of our forests and our crops are destroyed. It is not sufficient to rely upon the States. The reliance is vain, and were it otherwise, the question is whether the United States is forbidden to act. We are of the opinion that the treaty and statute must be upheld.

NOTES

1.   The Tenth Amendment states:

The powers not delegated to the United States by the Constitution, nor prohibited by it to the States, are reserved to the States respectively, or to the people.

Is this anything more than a "truism," that "all is retained which has not been surrendered," as the Court said in *United States v. Darby*, 312 U.S. 100, 124 (1941)? Did Justice Holmes give it any more meaning than this in *Holland v. Missouri*?

2.   Does federalism place any limit on the treaty power? As part of an air pollution treaty with Canada, could the federal government require officials in the State of Washington to engage in an extensive program of automobile inspections?

3.   The most important congressional power is the power to regulate interstate commerce, as the next case illustrates. As we will see, the issue remains controversial even today. The next case reflects the dominant approach from the New Deal to the 1990s. Courts today have carved out exceptions but still apply this approach frequently.

HODEL v. INDIANA

Supreme Court of the United States, 1981.
452 U.S. 314, 101 S.Ct. 2376, 69 L.Ed.2d 40.

JUSTICE MARSHALL delivered the opinion of the Court.

[In the Surface Mining Control and Reclamation Act of 1977, 30 U.S.C.A. §§ 1201–1328, Congress adopted a program of nationwide environmental standards for stripmining, with enforcement primarily in the hands of the states if they elect to exercise the authority. Generally, no person may conduct surface coal mining without a permit issued under a state or federal program. The Act specifies environmental protection performance standards which every permit must require. The coal mining operation must "restore the land affected to a condition capable of supporting the uses which it was capable of supporting prior to any mining, or higher or better uses of which there is reasonable likelihood," and use the best technology currently available to minimize environmental impacts. The statute also contains special provisions strictly regulating mining on "prime farmland." The issue before the Court in the following case was whether the surface mining statute exceeded the federal government's constitutional powers.]

The District Court gave two rationales for its decision on the Commerce Clause issue. The court first held that the six "prime farmland" provisions are beyond congressional power to regulate interstate commerce because they are "directed at facets of surface coal mining which have no substantial and adverse effect on interstate commerce." The court reached this conclusion by examining statistics in the *Report of the Interagency Task Force on the Issue of a Moratorium or a Ban on Mining in Prime Agricultural Lands (Interagency Report)* (1977). These statistics compared the prime farmland acreage being disturbed annually by surface mining to the total prime farmland acreage in the United States. The *Interagency Report* stated that approximately 21,800 acres of prime farmland were being disturbed annually and that this acreage amounted to .006% of the total prime farmland acreage in the Nation. This statistic and others derived from it, together with similar comparisons for Indiana, persuaded the court that surface coal mining on prime farmland has "an infinitesimal effect or trivial impact on interstate commerce." * * *

It is established beyond peradventure that "legislative Acts adjusting the burdens and benefits of economic life come to the Court with a presumption of constitutionality * * *." A court may invalidate legislation enacted under the Commerce Clause only if it is clear that there is no rational basis for a congressional finding that the regulated activity affects interstate commerce, or that there is no reasonable connection between the regulatory means selected and the asserted ends. * * *

In our view, Congress was entitled to find that the protection of prime farmland is a federal interest that may be addressed through Commerce Clause legislation. The *Interagency Report* provides no basis for the District Court's contrary view. That report dealt only with the question whether a complete moratorium or ban on surface coal mining on prime farmland was advisable as a matter of policy. The report neither purported to examine the full impact of surface mining on interstate commerce in agricultural commodities, nor concluded that the impact is too negligible to warrant federal regulation. More important, the court below incorrectly assumed that the relevant inquiry under the rational basis test is the volume of commerce actually affected by the regulated activity. * * *

We also conclude that the court below erred in holding that the prime farmland and 15 other substantive provisions challenged by appellees are not reasonably related to the legitimate goal of protecting interstate commerce from adverse effects attributable to surface coal mining. The court incorrectly assumed that the Act's goals are limited to preventing air and water pollution. * * *

Congress adopted the Surface Mining Act in order to ensure that production of coal for interstate commerce would not be at the expense of agriculture, the environment, or public health and safety, injury to any of which interests would have deleterious effects on interstate commerce. * * * The statutory provisions invalidated by the District Court advance these legitimate goals and we conclude that Congress acted reasonably in adopting the regulatory scheme contained in the Act.

The District Court also held that the 21 substantive statutory provisions discussed above violate the Tenth Amendment because they constitute "displacement or regulation of the management structure and operation of the traditional governmental function of the States in the area of land use control and planning * * *."

* * * [T]he sections of the Act under attack in this case regulate only the activities of surface mine operators who are private individuals and businesses, and the District Court's conclusion that the Act directly regulates the States as States is untenable. * * *

NOTES

1.   The Court applied a rational basis test to assess the validity of the statute. As a practical matter, does this test impose any significant constraints on Congress?

2.   It may be helpful to consider how the theories discussed in Section A apply in a specific case such as *Hodel*. Which of the following theories, if any, could justify federal regulation to protect prime farmland from strip mining: interstate environmental effects of strip mining such as water pollution, the economic impact of such strip mining on agricultural production, the potential

for a "race to the bottom" among state regulators of strip mining, or the greater expertise available to federal regulatory agencies than to state governments? On the other hand, are there reasons why, at least as a policy matter, we might prefer to leave the matter to state governments? For instance, are people in different states likely to have conflicting views about the importance of preserving prime farmland? Is it better for land use regulation to take place at a level of government more accessible to ordinary people?

1. THE REVIVAL OF LIMITS ON THE COMMERCE CLAUSE

As *Hodel* illustrates, Congress has not been shy about exercising the commerce power. Between 1965 and 1980, Richard Stewart reports, "Congress adopted sweeping new environmental, health, safety, and antidiscrimination regulatory statutes. There are at present over sixty major federal programs regulating business and non-profit organizations." Richard B. Stewart, *Madison's Nightmare*, 57 U. CHI. L. REV. 335, 339 (1990). In particular, Congress took the lead on environmental issues. *See* William W. Buzbee, *Brownfields, Environmental Federalism, and Institutional Determinism*, 21 WM. & MARY L. REV. 1 (1997) (discussing federal government's "first mover" status).

By the later 1980s, however, some conservative theorists were beginning to lay the groundwork for a retreat from this expansive view of federal power. The Supreme Court put its weight behind the effort to limit federal legislative power in *United States v. Lopez*, 514 U.S. 549 (1995). Chief Justice Rehnquist's opinion invalidated a federal ban on possession of firearms in the vicinity of schools (a subject on which the need for federal regulation does seem less than obvious). At the outset, Rehnquist invoked Madison's characterization of federal powers as "few and defined" while state powers are "numerous and indefinite." *Id.* at 549. Admittedly, he added, the scope of federal power had greatly increased in the post-New Deal era, partly because of the "great changes" in the economy and partly because of a desire to eliminate "artificial" restraints on federal power. *Id.* at 554. Rehnquist concluded, however, that the school gun law did not fall squarely within the post-New Deal judicial holdings, and he declined to further expand the scope of the commerce power.

The Court's pronouncements on the scope of federal power do not provide clear direction. In *Gonzales v. Raich*, 545 U.S. 1, 125 S.Ct. 2195,162 L.Ed.2d 1 (2005), the Court upheld the application of the federal Controlled Substances Act to cultivators of medical marijuana who cultivated the marijuana for home use consistent with a doctor's prescription under California's Compassionate Use Act. In so ruling, the Court made clear that "[w]e need not determine whether respondents' activities, taken in the aggregate, substantially affect interstate commerce in fact, but only whether a 'rational basis' exists for so concluding." Justice Stevens wrote the opinion of the Court, with Justices O'Connor, Rehnquist and Thomas dissenting. Notably, Justice Scalia concurred with the majority opinion. More recently, however, the Supreme Court held that the commerce power does not give Congress the power to require individuals to purchase health insurance, drawing a sharp line between prohibitions on conduct and mandates. *National Federation of Independent Business v. Sebelius*, 567 U.S. 519, 132 S. Ct. 2566, 183 L.Ed.2d 450 (2012).

Congress has used the commerce power as the basis for regulating air and water pollution, hazardous waste disposal, and a host of other environmental problems. For the present, at least, the bulk of federal environmental statutes resting on the commerce power still seems safe from constitutional attack. *See United States v. Olin Corp.*, 107 F.3d 1506 (11th Cir. 1997) (upholding application of federal law regarding leaking hazardous waste without proof that any off-site damage had occurred). But *Lopez* does leave open the possibility of attacking some particular federal environmental regulations, though *Raich* makes such attacks more difficult. Nevertheless, courts will still be asked to consider whether environmental laws that govern noncommercial activity in a traditional area of state concern and lack any evident interstate impact are constitutional.

One possible area of concern involves federal regulation of isolated wetlands. Such concerns are heightened by the following opinion.

SOLID WASTE AGENCY OF NORTHERN COOK COUNTY [SWANCC] v. UNITED STATES ARMY CORPS OF ENGINEERS

Supreme Court of the United States, 2001.
531 U.S. 159, 121 S.Ct. 675, 148 L.Ed.2d 576.

[page 685 of this casebook]

NOTES

1.   The majority opinion articulates an important rule of statutory interpretation in federalism cases: "Where an administrative interpretation of a statute invokes the outer limits of Congress' power, we expect a clear indication that Congress intended that result." This rule is "strongest where the administrative interpretation alters the federal-state framework by permitting federal encroachment upon a traditional state power." This canon may be relevant to other areas of environmental law, such as interpretation of the Endangered Species Act or the Clean Water Act, where federalism claims may be raised.

2.   More recently, the Supreme Court ruled on a case involving the statutory definition of navigable waters under the CWA as applied to wetlands, as well as Commerce Clause challenges to the application of the CWA to non-

adjacent wetlands. *Rapanos v. United States* [Chapter 7]. The Court rejected the government's broad definition of wetlands, but without discussing the constitutional issue.

3.   What about the Endangered Species Act? Does Congress have the power to protect a species that exists only in a single state? Consider the following case.

ALABAMA-TOMBIGBEE RIVERS COALITION V. KEMPTHORNE

United States Court of Appeals, Eleventh Circuit, 2007.
477 F.3d 1250.

CARNES, CIRCUIT JUDGE: Two fish, or not two fish? That is the question. More specifically, are the Alabama sturgeon and the shovelnose sturgeon separate species? The answer lies primarily in the field of taxonomy, which one observer has noted "is described sometimes as a science and sometimes as an art, but really it's a battleground." The battle over the Alabama sturgeon has been more like the Thirty Years War. A scientist first classified this small freshwater fish found in the Mobile River Basin of Alabama as endangered in 1976. Three decades and three trips to this Court later the fight over whether the Alabama sturgeon is an endangered species continues. On one side are various business interests, including the Alabama-Tombigbee Rivers Coalition, and on the other are the Fish and Wildlife Service and several federal officials involved with it.
* * *

The Coalition's third contention is that the Final Rule should be vacated because Congress has exceeded the power granted to it under the Commerce Clause by authorizing protection of the Alabama sturgeon, which the Coalition characterizes as an intrastate, noncommercial species. In the Coalition's view, protecting the Alabama sturgeon is not one of the three categories of activities Congress may regulate using its Commerce Clause powers. [*Lopez*] As the Supreme Court has recently summarized the law in this area, there are three permissible exercises of congressional authority over commerce: "First, Congress can regulate the channels of interstate commerce. Second, Congress has authority to regulate and protect the instrumentalities of interstate commerce, and persons or things in interstate commerce. Third, Congress has the power to regulate activities that substantially affect interstate commerce." *Gonzales v. Raich,* 545 U.S. 1, 17, 125 S.Ct. 2195, 2205, 162 L.Ed.2d 1 (2005) (citations omitted). The parties agree that the third category or power, regulating activities that substantially affect interstate commerce, is the one at issue here.

The Service counters that three circuits, in four published opinions issued since *Lopez,* have already upheld the constitutionality of Congress authorizing the Fish and Wildlife Service to list a purely intrastate species as endangered under the Endangered Species Act. *See GDF Realty Invs. v. Norton,* 326 F.3d 622 (5th Cir.2003); *Rancho Viejo, LLC v. Norton,* 323 F.3d 1062 (D.C.Cir.2003); *Gibbs v. Babbitt,* 214 F.3d 483 (4th Cir.2000); *Nat'l Ass'n of Home Builders v. Babbitt,* 130 F.3d 1041, 1052–54 (D.C.Cir.1997) [*NAHB*]. No circuit has held to the contrary. Meanwhile the Supreme Court has had the Endangered Species Act before it several times but has never questioned its constitutionality. Not only that, but last year in *Raich* the Supreme Court cited the prohibition on "takes" of eagles in the Bald and Golden Eagle Protection Act, which is a close cousin to the Endangered Species Act's "take" provision, as an example of "a rational (and commonly utilized) means of regulating commerce." * * *

In *Raich,* the Court upheld the application of provisions in the Controlled Substances Act criminalizing the manufacture, distribution, and possession of marijuana to intrastate growers and users of marijuana for medicinal purposes. In doing so, the Court explained the statement it had made in *Lopez* regarding the regulation of intrastate activity as part of a larger regulation of economic activity: "Our case law firmly establishes Congress' power to regulate purely local activities that are part of an economic 'class of activities' that have a substantial effect on interstate commerce." The courts "have never required Congress to legislate with scientific exactitude. When Congress decides that the 'total incidence' of a practice poses a threat to a national market, it may regulate the entire class."

This principle poses a problem for the Coalition's as-applied challenge, because "when 'a general regulatory statute bears a substantial relation to commerce, the *de minimis* character of individual instances arising under that statute is of no consequence.'" If the process of listing endangered species is "an essential part of a larger regulation of economic activity," then whether that process "ensnares some purely intrastate activity is of no moment." When Congress can and has regulated a class of activities, we "have no power to excise, as trivial, individual instances of the class." [*Raich*]

We agree with the three circuits that have concluded the Endangered Species Act is a general regulatory statute bearing a substantial relation to commerce. The Coalition does not argue to the contrary, nor could it do so persuasively. The Act prohibits all interstate and foreign commerce in endangered species. Although the true size of an illegal market is difficult to gauge, the United Nations Environment Programme estimates the illegal component of the worldwide trade in wildlife generates $5 billion to $8 billion in proceeds annually. Other reports state that the trade in wildlife products comprises the world's second largest black market, trailing only trade in illegal narcotics. The United States is not a bit player in this market. The Service conservatively estimates that Americans pay

$200 million annually for illegally caught domestic animals and $1 billion for those illegally caught in other countries.

The commercial impact of the Endangered Species Act is even greater than those large numbers suggest, because the economic value of endangered species extends far beyond their sale price. The House Report accompanying the Endangered Species Act explains that as human development pushes species towards extinction, "we threaten their—and our own—genetic heritage. The value of this genetic heritage is, quite literally, incalculable." Biodiversity's value is not ethereal; its preservation produces economic gain in even the most narrow sense. For example, species diversity is essential to medicine. Half of the most commonly prescribed medicines are derived from plant and animal species. Nine of the ten most commonly used prescription drugs in the United States are derived from natural plant products.

Genetic diversity is also important to improving agriculture and aquaculture. As the D.C. Circuit explained in *NAHB*, "the genetic material of wild species of plants and animals is inbred into domestic crops and animals to improve their commercial value and productivity." Of the explosive growth in this nation's farm production since the 1930s, genetic diversity is responsible "for at least one-half of the doubling in yields of rice, soybeans, wheat, and sugarcane, and a three-fold increase in corn and potatoes." The growing use of genetic modification in aquaculture, meanwhile, may prove essential to meeting the rising world demand for fish and fishmeal.

A species' simple presence in its natural habitat may stimulate commerce by encouraging fishing, hunting, and tourism. A Fish and Wildlife Service report found that in 2001 recreational anglers spent $35.6 billion, recreational hunters spent $20.6 billion, and wildlife watchers spent $38.4 billion. The report estimated direct expenditures only, and the total commercial impact of each activity may be greater still. A 1996 estimate found that recreational anglers alone had "a nationwide economic impact of about $108.4 billion, support[ed] 1.2 million jobs, and add[ed] $5.5 billion to Federal and State tax revenues." All of the industries we have mentioned—pharmaceuticals, agriculture, fishing, hunting, and wildlife tourism—fundamentally depend on a diverse stock of wildlife, and the Endangered Species Act is designed to safeguard that stock.

Just as it is apparent that the "comprehensive scheme" of species protection contained in the Endangered Species Act has a substantial effect on interstate commerce, it is clear that the listing process is "an essential part" of that "larger regulation of economic activity." [*Raich*] The decision to list a species as endangered or threatened is a necessary precondition to the protections afforded species under the Act. There would be no point to the Act if no species could be listed as endangered or threatened. * * *

There are several reasons for Congress' decision to regulate all endangered species, instead of only interstate ones. For one thing, Congress was concerned with "the unknown uses that endangered species might have." The extinction of species poses the risk that humanity may lose forever the opportunity to learn some of nature's secrets. Deforestation drove the rosy periwinkle, a delicate pink flower native to Madagascar, nearly to extinction before scientists discovered that it contained two substances now used to treat childhood leukemia and Hodgkin's lymphoma. Inside fragile living things, in little flowers or even in ugly fish, may hidden treasures lie. Because Congress could not anticipate which species might have undiscovered scientific and economic value, it made sense to protect all those species that are endangered. Because a species' scientific or other commercial value is not dependent on whether its habitat straddles a state line, Congress had good reason to include all species within the protection of the Act. It did not behave irrationally by taking the broader approach.

Congress also recognized "the unforeseeable place such creatures may have in the chain of life on this planet." As biologist Edward O. Wilson explained: "Every species is part of an ecosystem, an expert specialist of its kind, tested relentlessly as it spreads its influence through the food web. To remove it is to entrain changes in other species, raising the populations of some, reducing or even extinguishing others, risking a downward spiral of the larger assemblage." An insect with no apparent commercial value may be the favorite meal of a spider whose venom will soon emerge as a powerful and profitable anesthetic agent. That spider may in turn be the dietary staple of a brightly colored bird that people, who are notoriously biased against creepy crawlers and in favor of winsome winged wonders, will travel to see as tourists. Faced with the prospect that the loss of any one species could trigger the decline of an entire ecosystem, destroying a trove of natural and commercial treasures, it was rational for Congress to choose to protect them all.

Congress also reasoned that protection of an endangered species could "permit the regeneration of that species to a level where controlled exploitation of that species can be resumed. In such a case businessmen may profit from the trading and marketing of that species for an indefinite number of years, where otherwise it would have been completely eliminated from commercial channels. The Alabama sturgeon is potentially an example of that congressional hope. It was once harvested commercially, and over harvesting was one of the factors in the species' decline. The protection the Endangered Species Act affords may one day allow the replenishment of its numbers and eventual, controlled commercial exploitation of the fish. Indeed, this possibility underscores the fundamental irony in the Coalition's position. Under the Coalition's theory, Congress is free to protect a commercially thriving species that exists in abundance across the United States because it has economic worth, but once economic exploitation has driven that species so close to the brink of extinction that it desperately needs the government's protection, Congress is powerless to act. * * *

This case, like *Raich,* also turns on whether Congress had a rational basis for believing that regulation of an intrastate activity was an essential part of a larger regulation of economic activity. Unlike the statute involved in *Raich,* Congress did not rely on commodity pricing in justifying the Endangered Species Act. Instead, it made a determination that the most effective way to safeguard the commercial benefits of biodiversity was to protect all endangered species, regardless of their geographic range. That rational decision was within Congress' authority to make.

NOTES

1.   In *San Luis & Delta-Mendota Water Authority v. Salazar,* 638 F.3d 1163 (9th Cir. 2011), the court followed a similar analysis to uphold application of the ESA to the delta smelt, a fish found only in California. More recently, the Tenth Circuit upheld the application of the ESA to the Utah prairie dog, finding that the statute regulated a class of commercial and economic development activity, and that the long-term goal of the statute was to improve interstate commerce involving species by aiding their recovery. *People for the Ethical Treatment of Property v. U.S. Fish & Wildlife Serv.,* 852 F.3d 990 (10th Cir. 2017).

2.   Suppose Congress had enacted a separate law to protect the sturgeon rather than a broader protection of all endangered species. Would such a law pass constitutional muster even though it would not be part of a comprehensive regulatory scheme? Consider *United States v. Bramble,* 103 F.3d 1475 (9th Cir. 1996) (upholding a federal statute protecting the bald eagle).

3.   Putting aside constitutional issues, as a matter of policy, should protection of endangered species be a federal or state responsibility? Why?

4.   Could Congress use the *Raich* theory to support regulation of all wetlands, whether or not they are connected in any way with navigable streams?

5.   Although the Commerce Clause is the main source of regulatory power in federal environmental law, Congress has other relevant constitutional powers. The Property Clause gives Congress broad power to regulate activities on federal lands, which constitute roughly a third of the land area of the United States (mostly in the West and in Alaska). On the scope of this power, see Michael C. Blumm and Oliveir Jamin, *The Property Clause and Its Discontents: Lessons from the Malheur Occupation,* 43 ECOLOGY LQ 781(2016). The powers to tax and spend are also sweeping and allow Congress to place conditions on its spending, subject only to loose constitutional constraints. See Erin Ryan, *The Spending Power and Environmental Law after Sibelius,* 85 U. Colo. L. Rev. 1003 (2014).

2. STATE SOVEREIGNTY AND ENVIRONMENTAL LAW

For many years, the Tenth Amendment was considered to be nothing more than a reminder that the states retained whatever powers that had not been given to the federal government. In 1976, however, the Court resurrected the Amendment in *National League of Cities v. Usery,* 426 U.S. 833 (1976), striking down a law that extended the federal minimum wage to cover state employees.

Justice Blackmun had been the swing vote in *National League of Cities.* In *Garcia v. San Antonio Metropolitan Transit Authority,* 469 U.S. 528 (1985), he changed his mind, and became the decisive vote to overrule *National League of Cities.* Like the earlier case, *Garcia* involved the federal minimum wage law, this time as applied to public transit workers. Despairing of the effort to distinguish integral state functions from other state activities, the Court held that the political process is the primary shield of the states against Congress. At least in the absence of a clear breakdown in the political process, courts should not intervene. The dissenters in *Garcia* predicted a rapid demise for that case, but the Court (perhaps somewhat surprisingly) has never given any signal of interest in overruling *Garcia.*

The following case focuses on the narrower problem posed by statutes that impose affirmative mandates on state governments.

NEW YORK V. UNITED STATES
Supreme Court of the United States, 1992.
505 U.S. 144, 112 S.Ct. 2408, 120 L.Ed.2d 120.

JUSTICE O'CONNOR delivered the opinion of the Court.

[This case involves three provisions of the Low-Level Radioactive Waste Policy Amendments Act of 1985. Since 1979, only three disposal sites for low-level waste have been in operation. The statute is designed to create incentives for states to take responsibility for the waste they produce. Based largely upon a proposal of the National Governors' Association, the 1985 statute was a compromise between sited and unsited states (those containing or not containing disposal sites). The sited states agreed to accept waste for another seven years, and the unsited states agreed to handle their own waste by 1992. The statute provides several incentives to encourage states to tackle this problem. First, the sited states are authorized to charge gradually increasing fees for waste from unsited states. Second, states that miss certain deadlines may be charged higher surcharges and, eventually, may be denied access to disposal facilities altogether. Third, the so-called "take title" provision tells states that eventually they will literally own the problem themselves if they don't cooperate.

[New York joined no regional compact. It complied with the initial requirements of the statute by enacting legislation providing for the siting of a facility in the state. Residents of the two counties containing potential sites opposed the state's choice of location—a classic example of the NIMBY ("Not In My Back Yard") syndrome. Fearing that it could not comply with the statutory deadlines, New York and these two counties brought suit, contending that the statute is inconsistent with the Tenth Amendment and with the guarantee of a republican form of government in Article IV.]

Most of our recent cases interpreting the Tenth Amendment have concerned the authority of Congress to subject state governments to generally applicable laws. The Court's jurisprudence in this area has traveled an unsteady path. [Citing *National League of Cities* and *Garcia.*] This case presents no occasion to apply or revisit the holdings of any of these cases, as this is not a case in which Congress has subjected a State to the same legislation applicable to private parties.

This case instead concerns the circumstances under which Congress may use the States as implements of regulation; that is, whether Congress may direct or otherwise motivate the States to regulate in a particular field or a particular way. * * *

* * * While Congress has substantial powers to govern the Nation directly, including in areas of intimate concern to the States, the Constitution has never been understood to confer upon Congress the ability to require the States to govern according to Congress' instructions. The Court has been explicit about this distinction. "Both the States and the United States existed before the Constitution. The people, through that instrument, established a more perfect union by substituting a national government, acting, with ample power, *directly upon the citizens,* instead of the Confederate government, which acted with powers, greatly restricted, only upon the States."

This is not to say that Congress lacks the ability to encourage a State to regulate in a particular way, or that Congress may not hold out incentives to the States as a method of influencing a State's policy choices. Our cases have identified a variety of methods, short of outright coercion, by which Congress may urge a State to adopt a legislative program consistent with federal interests. Two of these methods are of particular relevance here.

First, under Congress' spending power, "Congress may attach conditions on the receipt of federal funds." Such conditions must (among other requirements) bear some relationship to the purpose of the federal spending; otherwise, of course, the spending power could render academic the Constitution's other grants and limits of federal authority. Where the recipient of federal funds is a State, as is not unusual today, the conditions attached to the funds by Congress may influence a State's legislative choices. * * *

Second, where Congress has the authority to regulate private activity under the Commerce Clause, we have recognized Congress' power to offer States the choice of regulating that activity according to federal standards or having state law pre-empted by federal regulation. This arrangement, which has been termed "a program of cooperative federalism," is replicated in numerous federal statutory schemes. * * *

By either of these two methods, as by any other permissible method of encouraging a State to conform to federal policy choices, the residents of the State retain the ultimate decision as to whether or not the State will comply. If a State's citizens view federal policy as sufficiently contrary to local interests, they may elect to decline a federal grant. If state residents would prefer their government to devote its attention and resources to problems other than those deemed important by Congress, they may choose to have the Federal Government rather than the State bear the expense of a federally mandated regulatory program, and they may continue to supplement that program to the extent state law is not preempted. Where Congress encourages state regulation rather than compelling it, state governments remain responsive to the local electorate's preferences; state officials remain accountable to the people.

By contrast, where the Federal Government compels States to regulate, the accountability of both state and federal officials is diminished. If the citizens of New York, for example, do not consider that making provision for the disposal of radioactive waste is in their best interest, they may elect state officials who share their view. That view can always be preempted under the Supremacy Clause if it is contrary to the national view, but in such a case it is the Federal Government that makes the decision in full view of the public, and it will be federal officials that suffer the consequences if the decision turns out to be detrimental or unpopular. But where the Federal Government directs the States to regulate, it may be state officials who will bear the brunt of public disapproval, while the federal officials who devised the regulatory program may remain insulated from the electoral ramifications of their decision. Accountability is thus diminished when, due to federal coercion, elected state officials cannot regulate in accordance with the views of the local electorate in matters not pre-empted by federal regulation.

[The Court upheld the Act's provision authorizing sited states to impose a surcharge on waste received from other states. These charges are intended to provide financial incentives for states to cooperate with the waste disposal scheme. The Court called this provision "an unexceptional exercise of Congress' power to authorize the states to burden interstate commerce." The Court upheld the provision under which the federal government collects a portion of this surcharge and places it into an escrow account, calling it "no more than a federal tax on interstate commerce." Also held valid was the provision under which states reaching a series of milestones in combating radioactive waste receive portions of these federally collected funds, which was considered an appropriate "conditional exercise of Congress' authority under the Spending Clause." The Court also upheld a provision authorizing states and regional compacts with disposal sites to increase the costs of access to those sites, and deny access altogether, to waste generated in states that do not meet federal guidelines. This was viewed as a "conditional exercise of Congress' commerce power." The Court then turned to the remaining provision, requiring states to take title to the waste if they fail to meet the 1996 deadline.]

The take title provision is of a different character. [It] offers States, as an alternative to regulating pursuant to Congress' direction, the option of taking title to and possession of the low level radioactive waste generated within their borders and becoming liable for all damages waste generators suffer as a result of the States' failure to do so promptly. In this provision, Congress has crossed the line distinguishing encouragement from coercion.

The take title provision appears to be unique. No other federal statute has been cited which offers a state government no option other than that of implementing legislation enacted by Congress. Whether one views the take title provision as lying outside Congress' enumerated powers, or as infringing upon the core of state sovereignty reserved by the Tenth Amendment, the provision is inconsistent with the federal structure of our Government established by the Constitution.

JUSTICE WHITE, with whom JUSTICE BLACKMUN and JUSTICE STEVENS join, concurring in part and dissenting in part.

Curiously absent from the Court's analysis is any effort to place the take title provision within the overall context of the legislation. * * * Congress could have pre-empted the field by directly regulating the disposal of this waste pursuant to its powers under the Commerce and Spending Clauses, but instead it *unanimously* assented to the States' request for congressional ratification of agreements to which they had acceded. * * * [T]he States wished to take the lead in achieving a solution to this problem and agreed among themselves to the various incentives and penalties implemented by Congress to insure adherence to the various deadlines and goals. The chief executives of the States proposed this approach, and I am unmoved by the Court's vehemence in taking away Congress' authority to sanction a recalcitrant unsited State now that New York has reaped the benefits of the sited States' concessions.

Ultimately, I suppose, the entire structure of our federal constitutional government can be traced to an interest in establishing checks and balances to prevent the exercise of tyranny against individuals. But these fears seem extremely far distant to me in a situation such as this. We face a crisis of national proportions in the disposal of low-level radioactive waste, and Congress has acceded to the wishes of the States by permitting local decisionmaking rather than imposing a solution from Washington. New York itself participated and supported passage of this legislation at both the gubernatorial and federal representative levels, and then enacted state laws specifically to comply with the deadlines and timetables agreed upon by the States in the 1985 Act. For me, the Court's civics lecture has a decidedly hollow ring at a time when action, rather than rhetoric, is needed to solve a national problem. * * *

NOTES

1.   *New York* seems to create something of a dilemma. On the one hand, individual states are clearly subject to a NIMBY problem. *See* Hamilton, *Political and Social Costs: Estimating the Impact of Collective Action on Hazardous Waste Facilities*, 24 RAND J. ECON. 101 (1993). They wish to have the benefits of using low-level radioactive materials for medical and other purposes, but would prefer to have the burden (political and otherwise) of disposing of the waste fall elsewhere. This is a classic collective action problem of the kind that motivated the formation of the national government.

One solution would be for each state to establish a quarantine, so that states would not be able to export their waste problems to each other. As we will see in the next section, however, this solution probably violates the dormant commerce clause. This leaves the states in what game theorists call a prisoner's dilemma; every state needs a place to dispose of the waste, but it is rational for each state to impose a ban on such sites, fearing that it will be flooded with waste from other states. *See* Paul E. McGreal, *The Flawed Economics of the Dormant Commerce Clause*, 39 WM. & MARY L. REV. 1191 (1998). This problem has led to a stalemate in terms of high-level nuclear waste disposes, as the selected waste disposal site has successfully blocked implementation of a national waste disposal system for high-level radioactive waste. See Bruce R. Huber, *Checks, Balances, and Nuclear Waste*, 48 Ariz. St. L.J. 1169 (2016).

Another method of solving this problem would be for the states to agree to behave responsibly in establishing disposal sites, rather than trying to free ride on each other. Obviously, there is an incentive for states to default on such an agreement. In order to avoid default, the states requested that Congress make the agreement legally binding on them. But the Court says that this violates federalism. Perhaps there are other ways to solve the collective action problem, but they did not occur: instead, reactor operators have been forced to store their waste on-site.

Query: Suppose that the states had embodied their agreement in an interstate compact, which would have required congressional approval to be enforceable. Would using this mechanism have avoided the *New York* holding? Could Congress simply replace its direct mandate with draconian funding cut-offs? Is some other mechanism available? Or is this dilemma simply an inescapable price of our federalist constitutional scheme?

2.   In *Board of Natural Resources v. Brown,* 992 F.2d 937 (9th Cir. 1993), the state of Washington challenged portions of the 1990 Forest Resources Conservation and Shortage Relief Act, 16 U.S.C.A. sections 620–620(j), which restricted the export of unprocessed timber from federal and state public lands in western states. The purpose of the restrictions was to preserve jobs at domestic sawmills in the face of reduced cutting in old-growth forests, due in part to efforts to protect the habitat of the Western Spotted Owl, an endangered species. The statute provided that "[e]ach state shall determine the species, grade, and geographic origin of unprocessed timber to be prohibited from export * * * and shall administer such prohibitions consistent with the intent of sections 620 to 620(j)," and that "the Governor * * * shall * * * issue regulations to carry out the purposes" of the Act. The court held that these provisions violated the Tenth Amendment as interpreted in *New York.*

Note that *Brown* expanded *New York* from a protection of the state legislature to a protection of state administrative officials. Although there is some reason to question whether this expansion is consistent with the original understanding of the Constitution (*see* Saikrishna Bangalore Prakash, *Field Office Federalism,* 79 VA. L. REV. 1957 (1993)), the Supreme Court ultimately ruled that Congress has no more power to commandeer state administrators than state legislators. *See Printz v. United States,* 521 U.S. 898 (1997) (striking down portions of a federal gun control statute on this basis). Recall, however, that while *New York* prohibits direct commandeering, it does allow Congress to use a battery of incentives to obtain state cooperation. As we will see in chapters 6 and 7, the Clean Air Act and the Clean Water Act rely heavily on state agencies to implement the federal programs, providing various incentives for states to participate.

3.   The problem of federal power discussed in this section has an analogue in the European Union. Unlike our constitution, however, the Maastricht treaty contains an explicit grant of power over environmental matters. This environmental authority is created by Article 130. The EU can also use its other regulatory powers, such as the general power to eliminate barriers to a unified economy, as a basis for environmental protection. (There are, however, some subtle differences in the legislative procedures involved with these various powers and in their preemptive effects on member states.) Should specific environmental regulatory authority be added to the U.S. Constitution or state constitutions?

C. COMMERCE CLAUSE RESTRICTIONS ON STATE POWER

In a unified national economy, the existence of a multitude of differing state pollution laws can impede the free flow of commerce. Yet the states have often taken the lead in the environmental area because of pressing local problems. This section deals with the need to accommodate these conflicting interests, which takes place under the auspices of the commerce clause.

The dormant commerce clause, like the grants of federal regulatory power discussed in the previous section, can be considered the solution to a collective action problem. Because out-of-state residents are not represented in the state legislature, the state may attempt to export the costs of regulation, while retaining the benefits. While the strategy makes sense for each state individually, it may leave the states worse off collectively. The federal courts step in to prevent this regulatory equivalent of the NIMBY syndrome.

The Commerce Clause, on its face, is a grant of power to Congress, not a restriction on state legislation. Yet, beginning with the period of the Marshall Court, the Supreme Court has always construed the Commerce Clause as preventing certain kinds of state regulation even when Congress has not spoken. Despite some indications to the contrary in the earliest cases, however, the states are not completely disabled from regulating interstate commerce. For instance, in *Huron Portland Cement Co. v. Detroit*, 362 U.S. 440 (1960), the Court upheld the application of an anti-smoke ordinance to ships that were temporarily docked in Detroit while engaged in transporting cement on the Great Lakes. Finding the ordinance to be "a regulation of general application," which did not discriminate against interstate commerce, the Court found no evidence that the regulation placed an "impermissible burden" on interstate commerce.

Huron Portland Cement illustrates one aspect of commerce clause doctrine, the undue burden test, which applies to *nondiscriminatory* state regulations. In applying this test, the Court will uphold a statute which effectuates a valid local purpose "unless the burden imposed on [interstate] commerce is clearly excessive in relation to the putative local benefits." *Pike v. Bruce Church, Inc.*, 397 U.S. 137, 142 (1970).

The *Pike* test does not apply, however, when a state law discriminates against interstate commerce rather than merely burdening it. In *City of Philadelphia v. New* Jersey, 437 U.S. 617 (1978), a state law prohibited disposal of out-of-state garbage in the state in order to conserve scarce landfill space. Regardless of whether the state's goal was environmental or protectionist, the Court held, "whatever New Jersey's ultimate purpose, it may not be accomplished by discriminating against articles of commerce coming from outside the State unless there is some reason, apart from their origin, to treat them differently." Subsequent cases make it clear that this test is almost impossible for a state to satisfy.

A final category of cases involves the state's own participation in the market. For example, in *Hughes v. Alexandria Scrap Corp.*, 426 U.S. 794 (1976), the state of Maryland gave a preference to local businesses and citizens in providing bonuses for recycling junked cars as scrap. The Court held that the dormant commerce clause does not apply when the state is acting as a market participant.

This three-part scheme may seem tidy, but applying it in practice is more difficult. *See* Daniel A. Farber & Robert E. Hudec, *Free Trade and the Regulatory State: A GATT's-Eye View of the Dormant Commerce Clause*, 47 VAND. L. REV. 1401 (1994). Consider two Supreme Court cases, which reach opposite results on facts that are at least superficially similar. Both cases involve what are called flow control ordinances. These ordinances provide a way for cities to ensure a steady flow of solid waste to a new facility that the city has financed. They do so by directing all waste generated within the city or county to the designated facility. Operators of other waste disposal sites sued, claiming that the ordinance discriminated in favor of the local facility as against out-of-state facilities.

In the first case, *C & A Carbone, Inc. v. Town of Clarkstown*, 511 U.S. 383, 114 S.Ct. 1677, 128 L.Ed.2d 399 (1994), the city had entered into an agreement with a private contractor to construct the facility, with the contractor to operate the city for five years (at which point the city would acquire it). The Court held that this ordinance violated the Commerce Clause;

> [T]he flow control ordinance is just one more instance of local processing requirements that we long have held invalid. The essential vice in laws of this sort is that they bar the import of the processing service. Out-of-state meat inspectors, or shrimp hullers, or milk pasteurizers, are deprived of access to local demand for their services. Put another way, the offending local laws hoard a local resource—be it meat, shrimp, or milk—for the benefit of local businesses that treat it.

> The flow control ordinance has the same design and effect. It hoards solid waste, and the demand to get rid of it, for the benefit of the preferred processing facility. The only conceivable distinction from the cases cited above is that the flow control ordinance favors a single local proprietor.

Such discrimination, the Court said, is "per se invalid, save in a narrow class of cases in which the municipality can demonstrate, under rigorous scrutiny, that it has no other means to advance a legitimate local interest."

The second case, *United Haulers Ass'n v. Oneida-Herkimer Solid Waste Management Auth.*, 550 U.S. 330, 127 S.Ct. 1786, 167 L.Ed.2d 655 (2007), was identical to *Carbone* except in one respect: the waste disposal site was owned and operated by the city from the start, rather than after a five-year period. The Court held that this was a permissible arrangement. It refused to classify the situation as a local processing requirement, because "any notion of discrimination assumes a comparison of substantially similar entities" and "States and municipalities are not private businesses—far from it. Unlike private enterprise, government is vested with the responsibility of protecting the health, safety, and welfare of its citizens." Hence, the court said, "it does not make sense to regard laws favoring local government and laws favoring private industry with equal skepticism." Instead of treating the ordinance as discriminatory, it instead applied the *Pike* balancing test. It then concluded that the ordinance was valid. After full discovery, the trial court did not find any disparate impact on out-of-state as opposed to in-state businesses. Moreover, on the positive side of the balance, the ordinance not only provided the counties "convenient and effective way to finance their integrated package of waste-disposal services," but also encouraged residents to recycle by raising the price of trash disposal.

Is government ownership of the facility in *United Haulers* a persuasive basis for distinguishing *Carbone*? Certainly, from the point of view of a municipality wishing to implement flow control, *United Haulers* allows it to achieve much the same end without much hindrance from the Dormant Commerce Clause. Is this a distinction without a real difference, or does public ownership create a greater degree of legitimacy for a local monopoly? For a defense of *United Haulers*, see Bradford Mank, *The Supreme Court's New Public-Private Distinction Under the Dormant Commerce Clause: Avoiding the Traditional versus Nontraditional Classification Trap*, 37 HASTINGS CONST. L.Q. 1 (2009).

Consider the impact of the dormant commerce clause on state climate change efforts. California has adopted a Low Carbon Fuel Standard. Various fuels such as gasoline and biofuels are rated based on the amount of carbon produced over their full life cycles. (For more on lifecycle analysis, see Stefanie Hellweg and Llorenç Milà Canals, *Emerging Approaches, Challenges, and Opportunities in Life Cycle* Assessment, 344 SCIENCE 1109 (2014).) For instance, the rating for ethanol produced from corn includes the carbon used to produce the electricity utilized to process the corn into biofuels. That amount depends on location: electricity produced in the Midwest uses much more coal than in other places (including California). Should the LCFS pass scrutiny under the dormant commerce clause?

ROCKY MOUNTAIN FARMERS UNION V. COREY

United States Court of Appeals, Ninth Circuit, 2015.
730 F.3d 1070.

GOULD, CIRCUIT JUDGE:

[This case involved California's low carbon fuel standard. The standard attempted to measure the carbon intensity of vehicle fuels based on a lifecycle analysis from production to combustion. The California Air Resources Board (CARB) had provided a set of default "pathways" in which location was a factor in calculating lifetime emissions, although producers could instead register their fuel based on the specific fuel's actual lifecycle emissions. A challenge was brought by out-of-state fuel producers. The excerpted portions of the case involve claims by ethanol producers. Ethanol is produced from a variety of feed stocks such as corn and sugar cane. The trial court found the standard to be discriminatory because it included geographic factors such as transportation distances and the carbon-intensity of the electricity used for processing the feedstocks. These factors disfavored some out-of-state producers, especially from the Midwest where coal is a favored fuel for generating the electricity used to process corn into ethanol. The trial court also found that the standard was impermissibly extra-territorial because it took into account carbon emissions that occurred outside of the state. In effect, the trial court thought, California was trying to regulate emissions outside of its own borders that were beyond its jurisdiction.]

Ethanol is an alcohol produced through fermentation and distillation of a variety of organic feedstocks. Most domestic ethanol comes from corn. Brazilian sugarcane dominates the import market. Ethanol production is a resource-intensive process, requiring electricity and steam. Steam is usually produced on site with coal or natural gas in dedicated boilers. The choices of type of feedstock, source of electricity, and source of thermal energy affect the carbon intensity of the fuel pathway. To illustrate, ethanol made with sugarcane, hydroelectricity, and natural gas would produce lower emissions than ethanol made from corn and coal. To determine the total carbon intensity values for each ethanol pathway, the CA–GREET model considers the carbon intensity of factors including: (1) growth and transportation of the feedstock, with a credit for the GHGs absorbed during photosynthesis; (2) efficiency of production; (3) type of electricity used to power the plant; (4) fuel used for thermal energy; (5) milling process used; (6) offsetting value of an animal-feed co-product called distillers' grains, that displaces demand for feed that would generate its own emissions in production; (7) transportation of the fuel to the blender in California; and (8) conversion of land to agricultural use.

In Table 6, CARB separates these factors into those that are correlated with location and those that are not, using a regional identifier as a shorthand for the factors correlated with location. The milling process, co-product, and source of thermal energy are not correlated with region, so they are labeled individually. Factors related to transportation, efficiency, and electricity are correlated with a plant's location in the Midwest, Brazil, or California. For example, California ethanol plants are newer and more efficient on average than those in the Midwest, using less thermal energy and electricity in the production process. Also, the electricity available on the grid in the Midwest produces more emissions in generation than electricity in California or Brazil because much of the electricity in the Midwest is generated by coal-fired power plants. By contrast, California receives most of its power from renewable sources and natural gas, and Brazil relies almost entirely on hydroelectricity.

Emissions from transporting the feedstock and the refined fuel are related to location, but they are not directly proportionate to distance traveled. Transportation emissions reflect a combination of: (1) distance traveled, including distance traveled inside California to the fuel blender; (2) total mass and volume transported; and (3) efficiency of the method of transport. California ethanol produces the most transportation emissions because California grows no corn for ethanol, so its producers import raw corn, which is bulkier and heavier than the refined ethanol shipped by producers in Brazil and the Midwest. * * *

Under the dormant Commerce Clause, distinctions that benefit in-state producers cannot be based on state boundaries alone. But a regulation is not facially discriminatory simply because it affects in-state and out-of-state interests unequally. If California is to assign different carbon intensities to ethanol from different regions, there must be "some reason, apart from their origin, to treat them differently."

Following this logic, the Supreme Court has consistently recognized facial discrimination where a statute or regulation distinguished between in-state and out-of-state products and no nondiscriminatory reason for the distinction was shown. * * *

Unlike these discriminatory statutes, the Fuel Standard does not base its treatment on a fuel's origin but on its carbon intensity. The Fuel Standard performs lifecycle analysis to measure the carbon intensity of all fuel pathways. When it is relevant to that measurement, the Fuel Standard considers location, but only to the extent that location affects the actual GHG emissions attributable to a default pathway. Under dormant Commerce Clause precedent, if an out-of-state ethanol pathway does impose higher costs on California by virtue of its greater GHG emissions, there is a nondiscriminatory reason for its higher carbon intensity value. Stated another way, if producers of out-of-state ethanol actually cause more GHG emissions for each unit produced, because they use dirtier electricity or less efficient plants, CARB can base its regulatory treatment on these emissions. If California is to successfully promote low-carbon-intensity fuels, countering a trend towards increased GHG output and rising world temperatures, it cannot ignore the real factors behind GHG emissions. * * *

[T]he dormant Commerce Clause does not guarantee that ethanol producers may compete on the terms they find most convenient. The Fuel Standard treats the electricity used by all producers the same way based on the real risks posed by different sources of generation. As with transportation, this is not a dormant Commerce Clause violation, even if the extent and carbon intensity of power on an electrical grid is related to the location of the grid. * * *.

We conclude: (1) that all sources of ethanol compete in the California market and are therefore relevant to comparison; (2) that all of the factors included in [the state's] lifecycle analysis are relevant to determining which forms of ethanol are similarly situated—not just those factors that are uncorrelated with location; (3) that the CA–GREET lifecycle analysis used by CARB, including the specific factors to which Plaintiffs object, does not discriminate against out-of-state commerce. We next address Plaintiffs' challenge to the regional categories and average values that form the default pathways in Table 6.

With Table 6, CARB provides a schedule of default pathways that regulated parties can use to meet the Fuel Standard's reporting requirements. As described, those default pathways are based on average values for each CA–GREET factor, and some of those factors are correlated with location. For those, CARB aggregates producers within California, the Midwest, and Brazil to measure average values. On Table 6, CARB lists each pathway with its regional identifier rather than separately listing each factor that is correlated with origin. Each source of ethanol may rely on a default pathway that incorporates average values for producers within its region that use the same mechanical methods and thermal-energy source and produce the same co-product. * * *

The Fuel Standard's regional categories for the default pathways show every sign that they were chosen to accurately measure and control GHGs and were not an attempt to protect California ethanol producers. For example, the two factors that the district court found were inextricably intertwined with origin support CARB's decision to set the boundaries of the regional categories as it did. Looking first at transportation emissions, we see that as of June 2011, there were no registered producers of corn ethanol from any state neighboring California. There was one in Idaho. Otherwise, every producer was located either in California, East of the Rocky Mountains, or in Brazil. Corn and ethanol from the Midwest must cross those mountains to reach California, raising emissions from transport and aggravating the difference between shipping raw corn and refined ethanol. This difference is enough to make transportation emissions for California even higher than those for Brazil, showing that it would make little sense to group California and the Midwest together. The three regions are distinct from each other, and within each region conditions are similar for each producer located there. From the perspective of transportation emissions, CARB's decision to align the regional categories as it did produced accurate carbon intensity values. This is the type of expert regulatory judgment that we expect state agencies to make in the public interest.

The regional electricity supplies provide a second nondiscriminatory reason for CARB's decision. As described, California's mix of electricity has a low carbon intensity, very different from the national average. This difference is likely to grow because California has instituted several measures to further decarbonize its electricity supply. Brazil's power grid is almost entirely hydroelectric, giving it an even lower carbon intensity than California's. These differences in electricity directly affect the goods produced with that electricity, so as the GHG emissions from California's electricity supply continue to decline, the difference in emissions attributable to ethanol made with electricity from California and the Midwest will grow. As with transportation, drawing the regional categories otherwise might only make CARB's assessment less accurate to the detriment of the public.

* * *

In addition to discrimination based on origin, the dormant Commerce Clause holds that any "statute that directly controls commerce occurring wholly outside the boundaries of a State exceeds the inherent limits of the enacting State's authority." *Healy v. Beer Inst.*, 491 U.S. 324, 336, 109 S.Ct. 2491, 105 L.Ed.2d 275 (1989). Under *Healy*, the "critical inquiry is whether the practical effect of the regulation is to control conduct beyond the boundary of the state." Id. (citing *Brown-Forman Distillers Corp. v. N.Y. State Liquor Auth.*, 476 U.S. 573, 579, 106 S.Ct. 2080, 90 L.Ed.2d 552 (1986)). To determine the practical effect of the regulation, we consider not only the direct consequences of the statute itself, but also "how the challenged statute may interact with the legitimate regulatory regimes of other States and what effect would arise if not one, but many or every, State adopted similar legislation." * * *

The Fuel Standard imposes no analogous conditions on the importation of ethanol. It says nothing at all about ethanol produced, sold, and used outside California, it does not require other jurisdictions to adopt reciprocal standards before their ethanol can be sold in California, it makes no effort to ensure the price of ethanol is lower in California than in other states, and it imposes no civil or criminal penalties on non-compliant transactions completed wholly out of state. The district court identified several factors that might encourage ethanol producers to adopt less carbon-intensive policies. For lifecycle analysis to be effective, it must consider all these factors and more. But California does not control these factors—directly or in practical effect—simply because it factors them into the lifecycle analysis. As the district court explained in a different order, the Fuel Standard "has no threshold [carbon intensity] requirement." It instead "encourages the use of cleaner fuels through a market system of credits and caps. * * *

The California legislature has determined that the state faces tremendous risks from climate change. With its long coastlines vulnerable to rising waters, large population that needs food and water, sizable deserts that can expand with sustained increased heat, and vast forests that may become tinderboxes with too little rain, California is uniquely vulnerable to the perils of global warming. The California legislature determined that GHG emissions from the production and distribution of transportation fuels contribute to this risk, and that those emissions are caused by the in-state consumption of fuels. Whether or not one agrees with the science underlying those views, those determinations are permissible ones for the legislature to make, and the Supreme Court has recognized that these risks constitute local threats.

To combat these risks, the California legislature and its regulatory arm CARB chose to institute a market-based solution that recognizes the costs of harmful carbon emissions. For any such system to work, two conditions must be met. First, the market must have full and accurate information about the real extent of GHG emissions. Second, the compliance costs of entering the market must not be so great as to prevent participation. Plaintiffs attack the lifecycle analysis and default pathways that fulfill these conditions, relying on archaic formalism to prevent action against a new type of harm. It has been sagely observed by Justice Jackson that the constitutional Bill of Rights is not a "suicide pact." Nor is the dormant Commerce Clause a blindfold. It does not invalidate by strict scrutiny state laws or regulations that incorporate state boundaries for good and non-discriminatory reason. It does not require that reality be ignored in lawmaking.

California should be encouraged to continue and to expand its efforts to find a workable solution to lower carbon emissions, or to slow their rise. If no such solution is found, California residents and people worldwide will suffer great harm. We will not at the outset block California from developing this innovative, nondiscriminatory regulation to impede global warming. If the Fuel Standard works, encouraging the development of alternative fuels by those who would like to reach the California market, it will help ease California's climate risks and inform other states as they attempt to confront similar challenges.

MURGUIA, CIRCUIT JUDGE, concurring in part and dissenting in part:

While I agree with the majority's conclusions concerning the crude oil regulations and preemption under the Clean Air Act, I respectfully dissent from the majority's conclusion that the Low Carbon Fuel Standard's ("LCFS") ethanol regulations do not facially discriminate against interstate commerce.

Determining whether a regulation facially discriminates against interstate commerce begins and ends with the regulation's plain language.

Discrimination "simply means differential treatment of in-state and out-of-state economic interests that benefits the former and burdens the latter." "[T]he purpose of, or justification for, a law has no bearing on whether it is facially discriminatory." Only after we find discrimination do we address, in our application of strict scrutiny, whether the reason for the discrimination is sufficiently compelling to justify the regulation.

I would therefore look only to the text of the LCFS to determine if it facially discriminates against out-of-state ethanol. Table 6 differentiates between in-state and out-of-state ethanol, according more preferential treatment to the former at the expense of the latter. Table 6 thus facially discriminates against out-of-state ethanol

The majority puts the cart before the horse and considers California's reasons for distinguishing between in-state and out-of-state ethanol before examining the text of the statute to determine if it facially discriminates. This approach is inconsistent with Supreme Court precedent, which instructs that we must determine whether the regulation is discriminatory before we address the purported reasons for the discrimination

Because the LCFS facially discriminates against interstate commerce, it is subject to strict scrutiny and is unconstitutional unless California can demonstrate that it: (1) serves a legitimate local purpose, and (2) that purpose could not be served as well by available nondiscriminatory means.

I would find that the LCFS serves the local purpose of reducing GHG emissions because California has a "legitimate interest in guarding against imperfectly understood environmental risks, despite the possibility that they may ultimately prove to be negligible." * * *

The nondiscriminatory alternative is apparent in the LCFS's current structure: Regulated parties may seek individualized pathways that use lifecycle analysis, but not Table 6's discriminatory carbon intensity values. These pathways are a reasonable, nondiscriminatory alternative that California could use to reduce lifecycle GHG emissions. This reasonable alternative, even if it is more difficult or costly to implement, means that California has failed to meet its burden of showing that discriminating against out-of-state ethanol is the only way to reduce lifecycle GHG emissions. * * *

The LCFS is the latest chapter in California's long history of innovative solutions to complicated environmental problems. But the current version of the LCFS facially discriminates against interstate commerce and California has failed to meet its onerous burden of demonstrating that a nondiscriminatory version of the regulation could not achieve its legitimate local interest of reducing GHG emissions. For this reason, I respectfully dissent.

ENERGY & ENVIRONMENTAL LAW INST. V. EPEL

United States Court of Appeals, Tenth Circuit, 2015.
793 F.3d 1169.

GORSUCH, CIRCUIT JUDGE.

Can Colorado's renewable energy mandate survive an encounter with the most dormant doctrine in dormant commerce clause jurisprudence? State law requires electricity generators to ensure that 20% of the electricity they sell to Colorado consumers comes from renewable sources. Under the law, too, this number will rise over time. It may be that Colorado's scheme will require Coloradans to pay more for electricity, but that's a cost they are apparently happy to bear for the ballot initiative proposing the renewable energy mandate passed with overwhelming support. So what does this policy choice by Coloradans affecting Colorado energy consumption preferences and Colorado consumer prices have to do with the United States Constitution and its provisions regarding interstate commerce? The Energy and Environment Legal Institute points out that Colorado consumers receive their electricity from an interconnected grid serving eleven states and portions of Canada and Mexico. Because electricity can go anywhere on the grid and come from anywhere on the grid, and because Colorado is a net importer of electricity, Colorado's renewable energy mandate effectively means some out-of-state coal producers, like an EELI member, will lose business with out-of-state utilities who feed their power onto the grid. And this harm to out-of-state coal producers, EELI says, amounts to a violation of one of the three branches of dormant commerce clause jurisprudence. * * *

It might be fair to describe the law as it's developed in this area a bit like the law as it's developed in antitrust, another pocket of federal jurisprudence characterized by a long and evolving history of almost common-law-like judicial decisionmaking. As there we find here a kind of "rule of reason" balancing test providing the background rule of decision with more demanding "per se " rules applied to discrete subsets of cases where, over time, the Court has developed confidence that the challenged conduct is almost always likely to prove problematic and a more laborious inquiry isn't worth the cost.

Before us in this case only the final, *Baldwin*, test is at issue. Yes, EELI asked the district court to invalidate Colorado's law under all three tests, *Pike*, *Philadelphia*, and *Baldwin*. Yes, the district court rejected all three arguments. But for reasons known only to it, EELI has appealed just the district court's disposition under *Baldwin*. So whether Colorado's law survives the *Pike* or *Philadelphia* tests may be interesting questions, but they are ones that will have to await resolution in some other case some other day.

Baldwin's extraterritoriality principle may be the least understood of the Court's three strands of dormant commerce clause jurisprudence. It is certainly the most dormant for, though the Supreme Court has cited Baldwin in passing a number of times, a majority has used its extraterritoriality principle to strike down state laws only three times

What do these three cases have in common? In *Baldwin*, New York prohibited out-state companies from selling milk in the State unless they purchased their milk from dairy farmers at the same price paid to New York dairy farmers—all to insulate the in-state dairy industry from price competition by out-of-state producers. In *Brown-Forman Distillers Corp. v. New York State Liquor Authority*, 476 U.S. 573, 106 S.Ct. 2080, 90 L.Ed.2d 552 (1986), New York law required liquor merchants to list their prices once a month and affirm that the prices they charged in New York were no higher than those they charged in other states. Because a seller couldn't lower price elsewhere without first doing so in New York on its monthly timetable, the scheme had the effect of preventing price competition out-of-state. In *Healy v. Beer Institute, Inc.*, 491 U.S. 324, 109 S.Ct. 2491, 105 L.Ed.2d 275 (1989), the Court struck down another price affirmation scheme that, due to its interaction with similar regulations elsewhere, again had the effect of inhibiting out-of-state price competition. In all three cases, then, the Court thus faced (1) a price control or price affirmation regulation, (2) linking in-state prices to those charged elsewhere, with (3) the effect of raising costs for out-of-state consumers or rival businesses.

In this light, you might ask whether the *Baldwin* line of cases is really a distinct line of dormant commerce clause jurisprudence at all. The usual telling of the law in this area suggests it is one of three separate strands of authority. But a careful look at the holdings in the three leading cases suggests a concern with preventing discrimination against out-of-state rivals or consumers. And given this, one might see Baldwin and its progeny as no more than instantiations of the Philadelphia anti-discrimination rule. In this vein it's worth noting that Baldwin was decided before the anti-discrimination rule solidified and might be said simply to have anticipated it. Indeed, one of the Court's earliest antidiscrimination cases, *Dean Milk Co. v. City of Madison*, conceived of *Baldwin* in just this way. *Healy* applied *Baldwin*'s rule only as an alternative holding to an application of anti-discrimination doctrine,—and only over the objection that the *Baldwin* analysis was therefore unnecessary. And you might even read *Brown-Forman*—where *Baldwin*'s rule seemed to do the most independent work—as treating *Baldwin* simply as an application of the anti-discrimination rule.

But whatever doctrinal pigeonhole you choose to place them in, we don't see how *Baldwin*, *Healy*, and *Brown-Forman* require us to strike down Colorado's mandate. For that mandate just doesn't share any of the three essential characteristics that mark those cases: it isn't a price control statute, it doesn't link prices paid in Colorado with those paid out of state, and it does not discriminate against out-of-staters. EELI doesn't even seriously attempt to suggest otherwise. While Colorado's mandate surely regulates the quality of a good sold to in-state residents, it doesn't directly regulate price in-state or anywhere for that matter. And state laws setting non-price standards for products sold in-state (standards concerning, for example, quality, labeling, health, or safety) may be amenable to scrutiny under the generally applicable Pike balancing test, or scrutinized for traces of discrimination under Philadelphia, but the Court has never suggested they trigger near-automatic condemnation under *Baldwin*.

In saying this much, we hardly mean to suggest non-price regulations don't impact price in or out of state. In today's interconnected national marketplace such a suggestion would be beyond naive. We readily recognize that state regulations nominally concerning things other than price will often have ripple effects, including price effects, both in-state and elsewhere. So, for example, when one or more states impose quality mandates manufacturers may find the cheapest way to comply isn't to produce a special product for them but to redesign their product as it's sold nationwide, with an increased cost felt by consumers everywhere. Still, without a regulation more blatantly regulating price and discriminating against out-of- state consumers or producers, *Baldwin's* near per se rule doesn't apply.

The reason, again, takes us to the question of certainty. In antitrust many agreements among market participants will affect price and all may be scrutinized under the rule of reason test. It's only when the parties' agreement involves "naked price fixing" or something else experience teaches to be clearly invidious that we will forgo that searching inquiry in favor of a shortcut and declare the agreement per se anticompetitive Similarly here, state regulations and standards across a wide spectrum may invite *Pike* balancing. But only price control or price affirmation statutes that link in-state prices with those charged elsewhere and discriminate against out-of-staters are considered by the Court so obviously inimical to interstate commerce that we will forgo that more searching inquiry in favor of *Baldwin* 's shortcut.

Our case illustrates the point. How can we have the sort of steadfast conviction the *Baldwin* Court did that interstate commerce will be harmed when, if anything, Colorado's mandate seems most obviously calculated to raise price for in-state consumers? EELI offers no story suggesting how Colorado's mandate disproportionately harms out-of-state businesses. To be sure, fossil fuel producers like EELI's member will be hurt. But as far as we know, all fossil fuel producers in the area served by the grid will be hurt equally and all renewable energy producers in the area will be helped equally. If there's any disproportionate adverse effect felt by out-of-state producers or any disproportionate advantage enjoyed by in-state producers, it hasn't been explained to this court. And it's far from clear how the mandate might hurt out-of-state consumers either. The mandate does have the effect of increasing demand for electricity generated using renewable sources and (under the law of demand) you might expect that to lead to higher prices for electricity of that sort for everyone in the market (here, presumably, everyone connected to the grid). But the mandate also reduces demand for and might be expected to reduce the price everyone in the market has to pay for electricity generated using fossil fuels. So the net price impact on out-of-state consumers is far from obviously negative and, for all we know, may tip in favor of those willing to shift usage toward fossil fuel generated electricity. To reach hastily for Baldwin 's per se rule, then, might lead to the decidedly awkward result of striking down as an improper burden on interstate commerce a law that may not disadvantage out-of-state businesses and that may actually reduce price for out-of-state consumers. * * *

NOTE

Consider the differing approaches these cases take to the extraterritoriality doctrine. The Ninth Circuit gives it somewhat broader scope than the Tenth Circuit opinion by now-Justice Gorsuch. Although in general the lower courts have applied the doctrine sparingly, there is considerable confusion about the applicable test. The doctrine is likely to resurface in future cases relating to climate change or renewable energy. Both carbon emissions and the electrical grid are large-scale systems that cross state lines, making it harder to distinguish between a state's legitimate internal sphere of action and impositions on activities in other states. For more discussion of these issues, see David M. Driesen, *Must the States Discriminate Against Their Own Producers under the Dormant Commerce Clause?*, 54 HOUSTON L. REV. 1 (2016); Jeffrey M. Schmitt, *Making Sense of Extraterritoriality: Why California's Progressive Global Warming and Animal Welfare Legislation Does Not Violate the Dormant Commerce Clause*, 39 HARV. ENVTL. L. REV. 423, 425 (2015); Danny Englese, *Tilting at Windmills: Finding an Alternative Dormant Commerce Clause Framework to Preserve Renewable Portfolio Standard Generator Location Requirements*, 47 ARIZ. ST. L.J. 983, 984 (2015).

D. FEDERAL PREEMPTION OF STATE STATUTES

The preceding material dealt with the validity of state regulation in the absence of federal regulation. Here we are concerned with the validity of state regulations in areas where Congress has acted. It is clear, of course, that in cases of direct conflict, the state statute must give way. The Supremacy Clause of the Constitution provides:

> This Constitution, and the Laws of the United States which shall be made in Pursuance thereof; and all Treaties made, or which shall be made, under the authority of the United States, shall be

the Supreme Law of the Land; and the Judges in every State shall be bound thereby, any Thing in the Constitution or Laws of any State to the Contrary notwithstanding.

The presence of a conflict between federal and state law, however, is often less than obvious.

The Supreme Court has set forth various factors that are to be considered in preemption cases. First, the federal regulatory scheme may be so pervasive and detailed as to suggest that Congress left no room for the state to supplement it. Or the statute enacted by Congress may involve a field in which the federal interest is so dominant that enforcement of state laws is precluded. Other aspects of the regulatory scheme imposed by Congress may also support the inference that Congress has completely foreclosed state legislation in a particular area. Even where Congress has not completely foreclosed state regulation, a state statute is void to the extent that it actually conflicts with a valid federal statute. Such a conflict can be found where compliance with both the federal and state regulations is impossible, or more often, where the state law interferes with the accomplishment of the full objectives of Congress.

These factors are obviously rather vague and difficult to apply. The Supreme Court has done little to create any more rigorous framework for analysis. Therefore, the only way to get some degree of understanding of the field is to examine particular cases in order to see what kinds of situations have been found appropriate for application of the preemption doctrine.

The Clean Air Act (CAA) presents some interesting preemption issues, particularly in connection with the regulation of mobile source emissions. Congress has preempted all states from regulating emissions from motor vehicle tailpipes under § 209 of the CAA with the exception of California. California may promulgate its own standards provided those standards are at least as protective of public health as the federal standards. Other states may opt into the California standards under § 177 as long as the standards are identical to California's. Many northeastern states have opted into the California standards, including standards California developed to require auto manufacturers to produce so-called zero and low emissions vehicles (ZEVs and LEVs).

California's ZEV and LEV regulations were struck down in *Central Valley Chrysler-Plymouth v. California Air Resources Board*, No. CV–F–02–5017, 2002 WL 34499459 (2002), on the ground that the regulations were preempted by the federal Energy Policy and Conservation Act. The case settled on appeal, though not before the Bush Administration filed an amicus brief arguing that California's regulations were preempted. Massachusetts and New York lost preemption challenges brought by auto manufacturers against regulations that opted into California's ZEV regulations on the grounds that California's regulations were contained in voluntary memoranda of agreements with the auto manufacturers, not in traditional regulations. *Association of Int'l Auto. Mfrs. v. Commissioner, Mass. Dept. of Envtl. Prot.*, 208 F.3d 1 (1st Cir. 2000); *American Auto. Mfrs. Ass'n v. Cahill*, 152 F.3d 196 (2nd Cir. 1998).

Below, we consider the Court's opinion in a preemption case involving mobile source emissions regulations promulgated by the South Coast Air Quality Management District (SCAQMD), the agency responsible for regulating the most polluted air district in the country, southern California. We will consider the state role in regulating vehicle emissions in more detail in Chapter 6.

ENGINE MANUFACTURERS ASS'N AND WESTERN STATES PETROLEUM ASS'N V. SOUTH COAST AIR QUALITY MANAGEMENT DISTRICT

Supreme Court of the United States, 2004.
541 U.S. 246, 124 S.Ct. 1756, 158 L.E.2d 529.

JUSTICE SCALIA delivered the opinion of the Court

[Although California has special status to issue its own mobile source emissions regulations, the SCAQMD does not. Instead, the local district is subject to the mobile source preemption provision of the CAA. At issue in the Supreme Court case were District "fleet rules" that required certain operators of vehicle fleets—street sweepers; fleets comprised of passenger cars, light and medium duty trucks; public transit vehicles and buses; solid waste collection vehicles; airport transport services; and heavy duty on-road vehicles—to purchase alternative fuel vehicles and low or zero emissions vehicles already approved by California's Air Resources Board (the state agency that generally sets policy on mobile source emissions) and already commercially available. The fleet rules were challenged on preemption grounds.] * * *

In August 2000, petitioner Engine Manufacturers Association sued the District and its officials, * * * claiming that the Fleet Rules are pre-empted by § 209 of the CAA, which prohibits the adoption or attempted enforcement of any state or local "standard relating to the control of emissions from new motor vehicles or new motor vehicle engines." The District Court granted summary judgment to respondents, upholding the Rules in their entirety. It held that the Rules were not "standard[s]" under § 209(a) because they regulate only the purchase of vehicles that are otherwise certified for sale in California. * * *

The Ninth Circuit affirmed the reasoning of the District Court.* * *

Section 209(a) of the CAA states:

"No State or any political subdivision thereof shall adopt or attempt to enforce any standard relating to the control of emissions from new motor vehicles or new motor vehicle engines subject to this part. No State shall require certification, inspection, or any other approval relating to the control of emissions * * * as condition precedent to the initial retail sale, titling (if any), or registration of such motor vehicle, motor vehicle engine, or equipment."

The District Court's determination that this express pre-emption provision did not invalidate the Fleet Rules hinged on its interpretation of the word "standard" to include only regulations that compel manufacturers to meet specified emission limits. This interpretation of "standard" in turn caused the court to draw a distinction between purchase restrictions (not pre-empted) and sale restrictions (pre-empted). Neither the manufacturer-specific interpretation of "standard" nor the resulting distinction between purchase and sale restrictions finds support in the text of § 209(a) or the structure of the CAA.

"Statutory construction must begin with the language employed by Congress and the assumption that the ordinary meaning of that language accurately expresses the legislative purpose." Today, as in 1967 when § 209(a) became law, "standard" is defined as that which "is established by authority, custom, or general consent, as a model or example; criterion; test." Webster's Second New International Dictionary 2455 (1945). The criteria referred to in § 209(a) relate to the emission characteristics of a vehicle or engine. To meet them the vehicle or engine must not emit more than a certain amount of a given pollutant, must be equipped with a certain type of pollution-control device, or must have some other design feature related to the control of emissions. This interpretation is consistent with the use of "standard" throughout Title II of the CAA (which governs emissions from moving sources) to denote requirements such as numerical emission levels with which vehicles or engines must comply, e.g., 42 U.S.C. § 7521(a)(1)(B)(ii), or emission-control technology with which they must be equipped, e.g., § 7521(a)(6).

Respondents, like the courts below, engraft onto this meaning of "standard" a limiting component, defining it as only "[a] *production* mandat[e] that require [s] *manufacturers* to ensure that the vehicles they produce have particular emissions characteristics, whether individually or in the aggregate." Brief for Respondent South Coast Air Quality Management District 13 (emphases added). This confuses standards with the means of enforcing standards. Manufacturers (or purchasers) can be made responsible for ensuring that vehicles *comply* with emission standards, but the standards themselves are separate from those enforcement techniques. While standards target vehicles or engines, standard-enforcement efforts that are proscribed by § 209 can be directed to manufacturers or purchasers.

The distinction between "standards," on the one hand, and methods of standard enforcement, on the other, is borne out in the provisions immediately following § 202. These separate provisions enforce the emission criteria—*i.e.,* the § 202 standards. Section 203 prohibits manufacturers from selling any new motor vehicle that is not covered by a "certificate of conformity." Section 206 enables manufacturers to obtain such a certificate by demonstrating to the EPA that their vehicles or engines conform to the § 202 standards. Sections 204 and 205 subject manufacturers, dealers, and others who violate the CAA to fines imposed in civil or administrative enforcement actions. By defining "standard" as a "production mandate directed toward manufacturers," respondents lump together § 202 and these other distinct statutory provisions, acknowledging a standard to be such only when it is combined with a mandate that prevents manufacturers from selling non-complying vehicles.

That a standard is a standard even when not enforced through manufacturer-directed regulation can be seen in Congress's use of the term in another portion of the CAA. As the District Court recognized, CAA § 246 (in conjunction with its accompanying provisions) requires state-adopted and federally approved "restrictions on the purchase of fleet vehicles *to meet clean-air standards.*" (emphasis added); * * * Clearly, Congress contemplated the enforcement of emission standards through purchase requirements.

Respondents contend that their qualified meaning of "standard" is necessary to prevent § 209(a) from pre-empting "far too much" by "encompass[ing] a broad range of state-level clean-air initiatives" such as voluntary incentive programs. * * * But it is hard to see why limitation to mandates on manufacturers is necessary for this purpose; limitation to mandates on manufacturers and purchasers, or to mandates on *anyone,* would have the same salvific effect. We need not resolve application of § 209(a) to voluntary incentive programs in this case, since all the Fleet Rules are mandates.

In addition to having no basis in the text of the statute, treating sales restrictions and purchase restrictions differently for pre-emption purposes would make no sense. The manufacturer's right to sell federally approved vehicles is meaningless in the absence of a purchaser's right to buy them. It is true that the Fleet Rules at issue here cover only certain purchasers and certain federally certified vehicles, and thus do not eliminate all demand for covered vehicles. But if one State or political subdivision may enact such rules, then so may any other; and the end result would undo Congress's carefully calibrated regulatory scheme.

A command, accompanied by sanctions, that certain purchasers may buy only vehicles with particular emission characteristics is as much an "attempt to enforce" a "standard" as a command, accompanied by sanctions, that a certain percentage of a manufacturer's sales volume must consist of such vehicles. We decline to read into § 209(a) a purchase/sale distinction that is not to be found in the text of § 209(a) or the structure of the CAA. * * *

The judgment is vacated, and the case is remanded for further proceedings consistent with this opinion.

NOTES

1.   Should it matter that the SCAQMD is located in California, a state that possesses special authority to regulate mobile source emissions under the CAA? Why do you think the state's Air Resources Board has not passed a fleet rule applicable to SCAQMD?

2.   The SCAQMD fleet rules were applicable only to the extent that low emissions vehicles were commercially available. Can you construct an argument about why this "commercially available" qualification should help insulate the fleet rules from legal attack? Put a different way, why would Congress prohibit the states from enacting separate motor vehicle emission standards? Are the fleet rules consistent or inconsistent with the statute's purpose?

3.   According to studies by the SCAQMD, mobile source emissions are the leading contributor to air toxics and air pollution by a large measure. Seventy-one percent of all toxic air contaminants, according to the district, come from diesel particulate. Another 20% of toxic air contaminants come from non-diesel mobile sources. *See* SCAQMD, MULTIPLE AIR TOXICS EXPOSURE STUDY IN THE SOUTH COAST AIR BASIN (2000), at ES-3, *available at* http://www.aqmd.gov/docs/default-source/air-quality/air-toxic-studies/mates-ii/mates-ii-contents-and-executive-summary.pdf. The fleet rules represented a significant part of the District's strategy to reduce mobile source pollution. On remand, SCAQMD reinstated those portions of the fleet rules that apply to state and local public agencies and private fleets under contract to those agencies, based on a federal district court opinion that such rules are not preempted. The reinstated portion of the rule was upheld in *South Coast Air Quality Management Dist. v. Western States Petroleum Association,* 498 F.3d 1031 (9th Cir. 2007).

METROPOLITAN TAXICAB BOARD OF TRADE
v. CITY OF NEW YORK

United States Court of Appeals, Second Circuit, 2010.
615 F.3d 152.

JOHN M. WALKER, JR., CIRCUIT JUDGE:

In December 2007, the City issued rules requiring that new taxicabs that were put into service on or after October 1, 2008 achieve at least 25 city miles per gallon of fuel, and those that were put into service beginning October 1, 2009 achieve 30 city miles per gallon (the "25/30 MPG rule"). In September 2008, the plaintiffs, including the Metropolitan Taxicab Board of Trade and several taxi fleet operators, sued the City, seeking to enjoin the 25/30 MPG rule on the basis that it violated preemption clauses in the EPCA [the Energy Policy and Conservation Act of 1975, which establishes the CAFÉ fuel efficiency standards for cars] and the CAA [Clean Air Act]. The district court granted a preliminary injunction after determining that the 25/30 MPG rule related to fuel economy standards and was thus preempted by the EPCA. The City did not appeal that decision.

On March 26, 2009, the City repealed the 25/30 MPG rule, and issued new rules that regulated taxicab "lease caps"—the maximum dollar amount per shift for which taxis can be leased—to provide incentives for reduced fuel usage and cleaner taxis. Under the new rules, the lease caps for hybrid and "clean diesel" taxis are raised by $3 per shift. At the same time, the new rules reduce the lease caps for non-hybrid, non-clean diesel vehicles, nearly all of which are Ford Crown Victorias, in three phases. * * * After the third phase is implemented, the lease cap difference between hybrids and Crown Victorias would be $15 per shift, reflecting the $3 upward adjustment for the hybrid lease caps and the $12 downward adjustment for the Crown Victoria lease caps. The new rules are designed to effectively shift fuel costs from taxi drivers, who currently pay for fuel, to fleet owners, who currently make vehicle purchasing decisions without the need to internalize fuel costs.

The plaintiffs amended their initial complaint to challenge these new rules and moved for a preliminary injunction against the enforcement of the Crown Victoria lease caps, again citing the preemption provisions of both the EPCA and the CAA. For obvious reasons, the plaintiffs did not challenge the $3 upward adjustment of the lease caps for hybrid taxis, which benefitted them, and that adjustment went into effect on May 1, 2009.

At an evidentiary hearing on the plaintiffs' motion, experts for both sides testified on the economic impact of the new rules on taxi fleet owners. The testimony of the plaintiffs' expert James Levinsohn tended to demonstrate that fleet owners would earn between $5,500 and $6,500 less per year for each Crown Victoria leased under the eventual $12 downward adjustment in comparison to leasing a hybrid under the $3 upward adjustment. The plaintiffs' expert estimated the current annual profit of leasing a Crown Victoria to be $8,518 per car per year. Thus, the lease cap reduction would lower profits by 65% to 75% for each Crown Victoria. The City did not challenge this estimated impact on plaintiffs' profits. The City's expert testified, however, that fleet owners could still make a "reasonable rate of return" on their purchase of a Crown Victoria notwithstanding the $12 downward adjustment. * * *

The EPCA preemption clause states:

> [A] State or a political subdivision of a State may not adopt or enforce a law or regulation related to fuel economy standards or average fuel economy standards for automobiles covered by an average fuel economy standard under this chapter. [49 U.S.C. § 32919(a).]

"Since [preemption] claims turn on Congress's intent, we begin as we do in any exercise of statutory construction with the text of the provision in question, and move on, as need be, to the structure and purpose of the Act in which it occurs" In the context of judging the scope of the preemption provision of the Employee Retirement Income Security Act ("ERISA), the Supreme Court has held that determining whether a state law relates to a preempted subject matter requires examining whether the challenged law contains a "reference" to the preempted subject matter or makes the existence of the preempted subject matter "essential to the law's operation." If the law contains such a reference or makes the existence of preempted subject matter essential to the law's operation, then that state law is preempted by the federal law.

As a threshold matter, we may rely on ERISA preemption precedents * * * because the pertinent language in that statute is virtually identical to the text in the preemption provision of the EPCA, which preempts state laws that are "related to fuel economy standards." For purposes of assessing preemption under the EPCA, the Supreme Court's discussions of the phrase "relate to" in ERISA cases is directly applicable.

Thus, our first inquiry in determining whether the new rules relate to "fuel economy standards," is whether they contain a reference to fuel economy standards or make fuel economy standards essential to the operation of those rules. We conclude that they do.

The new rules expressly rely on a distinction between hybrid and non-hybrid vehicles. The requirement that a taxi be a hybrid in order to qualify for the upwardly adjusted lease cap does nothing more than draw a distinction between vehicles with greater or lesser fuel-efficiency. The equivalency of the term "hybrid" with "greater fuel efficiency" for purposes of the new rules is self-evident. First, the EPCA specifically requires the separate consideration of "dual fueled" vehicles, including hybrids, in the determination of national fuel economy standards. Second, imposing reduced lease caps solely on the basis of whether or not a vehicle has a hybrid engine has no relation to an end other than an improvement in fuel economy across the taxi fleets operating in New York City.

Indeed, the City is unable to identify any plausible alternative reason for the imposition of such an engine-based rule. The City argues that the new rules "correct[ ] a structural problem with the standard vehicle lease arrangement that artificially insulates fleet owners from fuel costs." This proffered reason, however, still aims at the improvement of fuel economy, which underlies the "structural problem" relied upon by the City. This argument, moreover, ignores the City's mechanism for its structural correction, which is to shift costs solely on the basis of a vehicle's level of fuel efficiency, i.e., whether the vehicle is a hybrid. Indeed, the City's current list of approved vehicles includes every car approved for use under the now-repealed 25/30 MPG rule. The City's list of approved vehicles under the new rules, with the exception of wheelchair accessible vehicles (which are exempt from the lease cap adjustments) and the Crown Victoria, are either hybrids or achieve at least 25 miles per gallon. * * * The virtually complete overlap of the approved vehicles under the 25/30 MPG rule and the new rules underlines further that, in furtherance of the City's regulatory purpose, "hybrid" is simply a proxy for "greater fuel efficiency." In sum, the new rules are not applicable to gasoline costs in general, nor are they neutral to the fuel economy of the vehicles to which they apply. Rather, they are directly related to fuel economy standards because they rely on fuel economy, and on nothing else, as the criterion for determining the applicable lease cap.

NOTES

1. How plausible is it to assume that Congress necessarily means the same thing when it uses the same phrase in different, otherwise unrelated statutes? Or should the particular statutory context be decisive?

2. What do you think is the purpose of the CAFÉ preemption provision? Is that purpose served here? If the Clean Air Act does not of its own force preempt California law, should the EPA be able to do so? For a discussion of the issue of agency preemption, see David S. Rubenstein, *Delegating Supremacy?*, 65 VAND. L. REV. 1125 (2012).

3. Under the *SCAQMD* ruling, would the New York pricing scheme be preempted by the Clean Air Act?

4. If not for the city's price control regulation, the lessor of a hybrid would be able to charge the lessee more because of the better car mileage. Because of price control, however, the lessor was not able to do so, eliminating an incentive to buy hybrids that would exist in a competitive market. Under the Court's ruling, is there any way for the city to deal with this problem (apart from deregulating lease prices)?

5.   According to a 2015 empirical study, while voting in Supreme Court preemption cases was traditionally nonideological, there has been an increasing trend toward bloc voting in these cases. See Michael S. Greve, Jonathan Klick, Michael Petrino, and J.P. Sevilla, *Preemption in the Rehnquist and Roberts Courts: An Empirical Analysis*, 23 SUP. CT. ECON. REV. 353 (2015). Given judicial appointments since 2015, we expect this trend to continue.

NOTE ON STATE REGULATION OF GREENHOUSE GASES

As noted in Chapter 1, global warming is an example of a classic commons problem, one requiring an international response. In addition to (or in lieu of) an international agreement, one might expect a coherent federal response to emerge, in the form of a statute. Yet over the past several years an interesting phenomenon has occurred: many states have moved independently to address the problem. Since 2001, when the United States announced its intention to withdraw from the Kyoto Protocol, almost half the states have adopted measures to reduce their emissions of greenhouse gases (GHG) (of which carbon dioxide is the most prevalent). The measures range from the establishment of registries to track emissions by source to the enactment of renewable energy portfolio standards for utilities. Two of the most ambitious and interesting efforts include California's adoption of greenhouse gas emissions standards for mobile sources and a proposed cap and trade program known as the Regional Greenhouse Gas Initiative (RGGI) adopted by a consortium of northeastern states to limit GHG emissions from power plants.

The enactment of climate change initiatives to solve a global commons problem presents something of a puzzle. Why would States, who presumably have little incentive to reduce GHG emissions, nevertheless enact measures to do so? Possible explanations include concerns over potential localized effects of global warning (loss of snow pack, flooding, coastal erosion, increased air pollution); predicted cost savings from enacting measures to require energy efficiency; political and public concern over the lack of U.S. leadership on the issue; and political advantages for demonstrating environmental leadership. *See* Kirsten H. Engel, *Mitigating Global Climate Change in the United States: A Regional Approach*, 14 N.Y.U. ENVTL. L.J. 54 (2005). Once states begin moving toward decarbonization, the process may be self-sustaining, as policies promote the growth of green industry like renewable energy, which in turn strengthens the political base for further decarbonization. See Eric Biber et. al., *The Political Economy of Decarbonization A Research Agenda*, 82 BROOK. L. REV. 605 (2017).

The leadership exhibited by California and RGGI states may also be the product of unusual forms of federalism under the Clean Air Act. Under California's special CAA status to regulate mobile source emissions, the state is using its "superregulator" status to issue its greenhouse gas regulations, known by the name of the bill that enacted them, AB 1493. This special status may have created a regulatory dynamic that has led California to enact more environmentally stringent regulations than the state would have adopted in the absence of the CAA provision granting California its special role. *See* Ann

E. Carlson, *Federalism, Preemption, and Greenhouse Gas Emissions*, 37 U.C. DAVIS L. REV. 281 (2003)

AB 1493 faced legal challenges by auto manufacturers and by the Bush administration on the grounds that the regulations are preempted by the Energy Policy Conservation Act ("EPCA"), the CAA, and the foreign affairs clause of the U.S. Constitution. The EPCA preemption argument is that California's regulations impermissibly (though indirectly) set fuel economy standards and are therefore preempted by EPCA's provision preempting state regulation of fuel economy. Finally, the manufacturers argued that California's regulations interfere with the President's power to conduct foreign affairs by impinging upon his authority to negotiate greenhouse gas emissions reductions with other countries. If the regulations were upheld, ten states indicated their intent to follow California's lead, including Oregon and Washington. The district courts sided with California. The cases were then settled as part of an agreement over the adoption of federal restrictions on greenhouse emissions. This issue will be discussed in more depth in Chapter 6.

RGGI, while not the direct product of federal authority under the Clean Air Act, involves many of the states included in the Ozone Transport Commission (OTC), established by the 1990 Amendments to the CAA. As explained in Chapter 6, in 1999 the OTC adopted a successful cap and trade program to reduce ground level ozone. The states cooperated with each other in establishing the program, with EPA playing an important monitoring and coordinating role. The RGGI cap and trade program is based on the OTC experience and is designed to cap CO_2 emissions. For more information about RGGI, see http://www.rggi.org.

NOTE ON ENVIRONMENTAL REGULATION AND INTERNATIONAL TRADE

The primary subject of the preceding section was how to reconcile state environmental regulation and an open national economy. This issue is not unique to the United States. For example, the European Court of Justice [ECJ] has evolved its own set of doctrines analogous to the dormant commerce clause. Based on Articles 30 and 36 of the EEC Treaty, the ECJ has struck down regulations of member nations that act as trade barriers. The leading case is Commission v. Kingdom of Denmark, 1988 WL 765475, Case 302/86, 1988 E.C.R. 4607, which is better known as the "Danish beer case." Denmark had imposed rigorous requirements that beverage containers be not only recyclable but actually reused. The ECJ applied a balancing test akin to Pike to uphold much of the measure, while invalidating provisions that were unnecessarily burdensome for foreign manufacturers. The ECJ has also sometimes reached results interestingly different from U.S. law. For instance, it has allowed member states to ban the import of solid waste, on the theory that waste disposal is a responsibility of the member country generating the waste. For discussions of this case and other aspects of European Union law, see George

A. Bermann, Roger J. Goebel, William J. Davey and Eleanor M. Fox, Cases and Materials on European Union Law (3d ed. 2010).

For most American lawyers, let alone environmentalists and politicians, EU law is still an obscure subject. International trade, however, is another matter. Trade liberalization inevitably raises questions about environmental regulations. Because different countries, even more than different American states, have widely varying approaches to environmental regulation, tensions of various kinds are bound to arise.

So far, the tensions seem to fall into two major categories. First, as under the dormant commerce clause, there are situations in which stringent domestic regulations are attacked as trade barriers. The next Note will discuss the complicated international trade provisions applying to this situation. Second, there are situations in which a nation adopts trade measures, not as part of domestic regulations, but because of concerns about environmental degradation abroad. For example, the U.S. once imposed trade sanctions on Taiwan for refusing to halt the sale of tiger bones and rhinoceros horns. Thomas L. Friedman, *U.S. Puts Sanctions on Taiwan*, N.Y. TIMES, Apr. 12, 1994, at D6. Often, the reason for the trade measure is that the processes used to produce the goods, rather than the goods themselves, are environmentally questionable.

Because our focus in this book is domestic environmental law, we cannot explore the complex (not to mention spirited) debate in detail. We will, however, try to present those themes of trade law that most affect domestic regulation.

Unlike the constraints imposed on state government under the dormant commerce clause, the GATT restrictions imposed on member governments rest on an explicit mandate. GATT is a formal international agreement (now incorporated into the WTO) containing explicit prohibitions of certain kinds of protectionist trade barriers. The basic structure of the GATT agreement begins with "tariff bindings" setting a maximum rate for tariffs on an item-by-item basis. Then, to protect against other measures that would subvert the commercial opportunity created by tariff bindings, the GATT agreement adds a rather detailed code of rules prohibiting most other forms of trade barriers.[2]

---

[2]   The main provisions are the prohibition of non-tariff restrictions under GATT Article XI:1 and the prohibition of discriminatory internal taxes and regulations under the so-called "national treatment" rule of GATT Article III. The text of Article XI:1, which is subject to numerous exceptions, provides quite simply and broadly,

1.   No prohibitions or restrictions other than duties, taxes or other charges. . . shall be instituted or maintained by any contracting party on the importation of any product from the territory of any other contracting party or on the exportation or sale for export of any product destined for the territory of any other contracting party.

The key provision of the national treatment rule of GATT Article III are paragraphs 2 and 4:

4.   The products of the territory of any contracting party imported into the territory of any other contracting party shall be accorded treatment no less favourable than that accorded to like products of national origin in respect of all laws, regulations and requirements affecting their internal sale, offering for sale, purchase, transportation, distribution or use. * * *

Similar provisions are contained in NAFTA, which applies to trade among the United States, Canada, and Mexico.

The threat of interference with strict regulations has been accentuated by later changes in GATT. The two changes raising the most concern are the code on the Application of Sanitary and Phytosanitary Measures,[3] and the expanded rule on trade-restricting technical measures in the Standards Code.[4] Both texts were adopted in the Uruguay Round negotiations. Both make explicit that differentially burdensome regulations that deviate from internationally accepted standards may be subject to legal challenge. The result has been to heighten environmentalist concerns.

The application of GATT rules ultimately raises the same type of legal issues confronted by U.S. courts in dormant commerce clause cases. Like U.S. law, GATT allows consideration of the strength of a regulation's benefits. GATT's prohibitions are qualified by GATT Article XX, which authorizes exceptions whenever trade barriers are found to be required by other widely-accepted government regulatory objectives such as health, safety or law-enforcement.[5] Application of Article XX requires GATT tribunals to analyze the extent to which claimed regulatory objectives are served by a particular trade-restricting measure.

GATT law imposes the greatest restraints on trade-restricting measures that explicitly discriminate between domestic and foreign goods. Under GATT, such discriminatory measures are prima facie outlawed by Article III. The law has developed in a way that makes it very easy to find discrimination even if there is a legitimate regulatory justification for a distinction in treatment. However, Article XX permits even explicitly discriminatory measures when such discrimination is necessary to legitimate regulatory objectives. Article XX has been interpreted loosely, providing more room for claims of justification.

Like U.S. doctrine, GATT law also deals with facially neutral measures that may have a trade-restricting effect. For example, a different tax or regulatory burden may be placed on products with certain characteristics; it

---

[3]   GATT, DRAFT FINAL ACT EMBODYING THE RESULTS OF THE URUGUAY ROUND OF MULTILATERAL TRADE NEGOTIATIONS, MTN.TNC/W/FA, at L.35–L.52 (Dec. 20, 1991), (hereinafter GATT Doc.).

[4]   In particular, a new Article 2.2, contained in GATT Doc., *supra* note 3, at pages G.2 and G.3.

[5]   Article XX reads as follows:

Subject to the requirement that such measures are not applied in a manner which would constitute a means of arbitrary or unjustifiable discrimination between countries where the same conditions prevail, or a disguised restriction on international trade, nothing in this Agreement shall be construed to prevent the adoption or enforcement by any contracting party of measures:

(a)   necessary to protect public morals;

(b)   necessary to protect human, animal or plant life or health;* * *

(f)   imposed for the protection of national treasures of artistic, historic or archaeological value;

(g)   relating to the conservation of exhaustible natural resources if such measures are made effective in conjunction with restrictions on domestic production or consumption; * * *

"just happens" that all or most foreign products fall into the disadvantaged category. An example might be emission controls that impose less burdensome requirements for large-bore engines used in domestic automobiles than for small-bore engines normally used in foreign autos.

Recent decisions focus on the general anti-protectionism language of Articles III and XX. Article III:1 states that taxes and regulations "should not be applied to imported or domestic products so as to afford protection to domestic production." The "chapeau" to Article XX states that taxes and regulations must not be applied "in a manner which would constitute a means of arbitrary or unjustifiable discrimination between countries where the same conditions prevail" or be "a disguised restriction on international trade."

WTO decisions call for a "totality of the circumstances" analysis in applying such language. In one noteworthy decision, the WTO Appellate Body upheld a French ban on chrysotile asbestos imports. The Appellate Body held that, because of its health risks, chrysotile asbestos was not a "like product" to other products designed for the same uses. The Appellate Body rejected the argument that less restrictive regulations of asbestos use could have eliminated the health risk. See *WTO Appellate Body Upholds French Ban on Asbestos Imports*, 18 INT'L TRADE REP. DECISIONS (BNA) 426 (2001).Standards Code and the SPS Agreement explicitly adopt balancing tests.

The SPS Agreement and the Standards Code are like the *Pike* test under the dormant commerce clause: they allow a balancing of trade effects and regulatory benefits. But the basic GATT agreement is more awkwardly drafted: first trade effects are considered under Article III, then regulatory benefits are considered under Article XX, but the two are never compared with each other. Trade tribunals have sometimes engaged in complicated maneuvers in an attempt to avoid this dilemma.

Obviously, trade law is at least as complex as U.S. doctrines protecting free trade domestically. Indeed, it may be even less understandable to outsiders than the doctrines developed by the Supreme Court, and has only gotten more complex and opaque) over time. See Joel P. Trachtman, *WTO Trade and Environment Jurisprudence: Avoiding Environmental Catastrophe*, 58 HARV. INT'L L.J. 273 (2017) (surveying current doctrine). Despite these differences, however, WTO tribunals do seem to be wrestling with the same basic difficulty as the U.S. courts. On the one hand, they have a mandate to protect free trade, a goal that could be rapidly undermined unless protectionist regulations are kept under control. Moreover, their professional training and experience emphasize free trade as a value. On the other hand, neither WTO tribunals nor the U.S. courts have any authority to decide broad issues of public policy at the expense of other organs of government. Moreover, the judges themselves, like other citizens, are likely to be concerned about maintaining the effectiveness of environmental regulation.

Much of the preceding discussion has been most directly relevant to the situation in which domestic regulations are attacked as trade barriers. The use of trade sanctions to deal with extraterritorial environmental problems is even more controversial. In a case involving trade restrictions on tuna from Mexico due to the use of fishing methods dangerous to tuna, a GATT tribunal held that such trade measures target extra-jurisdictional conduct and are therefore invalid. But in a later round of the tuna dispute, the tribunal retreated from this position, and it has not found favor in later decisions. See Steve Charnovitz, *The Environment v. Trade Rules: Defogging the Debate*, 23 ENVTL. L. 475 (1993).

A few years later, the WTO decided a similar case, this time involving restrictions on shrimp imports. U.S. law requires shrimp trawlers to use "turtle exclusion devices" to prevent incidental killing of endangered sea turtles by shrimping vessels. Shrimp cannot be imported without a certification that the exporting country has a comparable regulatory program. A GATT panel held the U.S. ban illegal, on the ground that unilateral actions by individual member states would threaten to unravel the entire trade agreement, and thus violated the prohibition on "inappropriate" trade measures in the introductory section of Article XX (the "chapeau"). The Appellate Body invalidated the U.S. measure on narrower grounds relating to allegedly unfair methods of implementation. The implications of this decision and later decisions are discussed in Robert Howse, *The Appellate Body Rulings in the Shrimp/Turtle Case: A New Legal Baseline for the Trade and Environment Debate*, 27 COLUM. J. ENV. L. 491 (2002).

In 2012, a third round of disputes over U.S. restrictions on dolphin-unsafe tuna reached the WTO Appellate Body. This claim was brought under the Standards Code rather than the basic GATT agreement, and the Appellate Body made it clear that protecting animals outside of U.S. jurisdiction was a legitimate goal. See Trachtment, supra, 58 HARV. ENV. L. REV. at 298–299.

Should measures like the shrimp and tuna restrictions be seen as simple refusals to consume goods that are considered morally tainted by the importing country? Or should they be considered efforts at coercion of other governments? And is coercion in this context justified or merely cultural imperialism? Consider, for example, the trade sanctions against Taiwan for allowing sale of products derived from endangered species. Eco-globalism or neo-imperialism? For further discussion of the WTO issues, see Alessandra Arcuri, *Back to the Future: US-Tuna II and the New Environment-Trade Debate*, 3 EUR. J. RISK REG. 177 (2012).

Recall California's Low Carbon Fuel Standard, which rates fuels based on the amount of carbon used across the fuel's entire life cycle from production through combustion. Under this standard, foreign oil from some locations may have a higher rating than domestic U.S. oil. Does the LCFS violate WTO requirements? For discussion, see Cymie Payne, *Local Meets Global: The Low Carbon Fuel Standard and the WTO*, 34 N.C. J. INT'L L. & COMM'L REG. 891 (2009). For further discussion of the interplay between trade law and climate change policies, see Brian Chang, *Proposal for a Multilateral Border Carbon Adjustment Scheme that is Consistent with WTO Law*, 47 ENV. L. REP. 10829

(2017); Rick A. Waltman, *Renewable Energy Development for WTO Members*, 14 SANTA CLARA J. INT'L L. 543 (2016),

E. REGULATION AND PROPERTY RIGHTS

Environmental law challenges borders in the form of national or state jurisdiction. It also can challenge borders in terms of the ownership of a parcel, intruding on the owner's use of land because of potential environmental effects on others. In this section, we consider the interaction between traditional concepts of owner autonomy and newer ideas of ecological interdependence, as seen through the lens of legal doctrine.

1. THE TAKINGS CLAUSE

The takings clause is found in the 5th Amendment to the U.S. Constitution but long held to apply against the states via the due process clause of the 14th Amendment. Like federalism doctrines, it presents a limitation on governmental power to regulate. Modern takings doctrine originated in *Pennsylvania Coal Co. v. Mahon*, 260 U.S. 393 (1922). That case involved a Pennsylvania statute making it unlawful for coal companies to cause the collapse or subsidence of any public building, any street, or any private residence. The Mahons were bound by a covenant to allow a coal company, which had sold to the Mahons or their predecessor only the surface rights to their lot, to remove all the coal without liability. The effect of the statute was to annul this covenant. Pennsylvania law recognized three separate property rights: the right to use the surface, the ownership of the subsurface minerals, and the right to have the surface supported by the subsurface earth. The coal company claimed that the statute operated as a taking of both the second and third rights, which belonged to them under their deed with the Mahons. In perhaps the most important single decision under the takings clause, Justice Holmes held that the statute was indeed a taking. The heart of the opinion is to be found in the following famous passage:

> Government hardly could go on if to some extent values incident to property could not be diminished without paying for every such change in the general law. As long recognized, some values are enjoyed under an implied limitation and must yield to the police power. But obviously the implied limitation must have its limits, or the contract and due process clauses are gone.

But what are the boundaries of this "implied limitation" on property rights? Holmes gave the following explanation:

> One fact for consideration in determining such limits is the extent of the diminution. When it reaches a certain magnitude, in most if not in all cases there must be an exercise of eminent domain and compensation to sustain the act. So the question depends upon the

particular facts. The greatest weight is given to the judgment of the legislature, but it always is open to interested parties to contend that the legislature has gone beyond its constitutional power.

In applying this test, the Court stressed that the statute made coal mining in certain areas impractical and thus had "very nearly the same effect for constitutional purposes as appropriating or destroying it." The Court concluded that so long as "private persons or communities have seen fit to take the risk of acquiring only surface rights, we cannot see that the fact that the risk has become a danger warrants the giving to them greater rights than they bought." Justice Brandeis filed a strong dissent.

Trying to decide when a regulation has "gone too far" has been extremely difficult. *Penn Central Transportation Co. v. New York,* 438 U.S. 104 (1978), has probably been the Court's most significant effort at synthesis. *Penn Central* involved a New York historic preservation ordinance. Under the ordinance a special commission was empowered to designate buildings as landmarks, subject to administrative and judicial review. After designation, the exterior of a building had to be kept in good repair and exterior alterations had to be approved by the Commission. Development rights lost because of the landmark designation could be transferred to nearby plots of land, thereby allowing additional development on that land beyond the normal restrictions of the zoning and building codes. Penn Central owned Grand Central Terminal, a designated landmark. A plan by Penn Central to build a multistory office building perched above the terminal was rejected by the Commission. Penn Central then brought suit claiming that its property had been taken without compensation. It conceded, however, that the transferable development rights had some value and that the terminal was still capable of earning a reasonable return on its initial investment.

The Court began by reviewing the factors that had shaped prior decisions. The Court admitted that it had been unable to develop any "set formula" for determining when compensation was required. Instead, it referred to the prior cases as involving "essentially ad hoc, factual inquiries." The Court did point, however, to several relevant factors. The most important were (1) whether the regulation had "interfered with distinct investment backed expectations," and (2) whether the government had physically invaded the property or instead had simply enacted "some public program adjusting the benefits and burdens of economic life to promote the common good." In reviewing the specific regulation before it, the Court concluded that the purposes of the ordinance were permissible because the ordinance was "expected to produce a widespread public benefit and applicable to all similarly situated property." The Court then held that the regulation passed the *Pennsylvania Coal* test because it did not deprive the company of all use of the property, but instead allowed continuation of a past use, and more importantly, permitted the company to obtain a "reasonable return" on its investment. For discussion of how the *Penn Central* test has been implemented, see John D. Echeverria, *Making Sense of Penn Central*, 39 ENV. L. REP. 1047 (2009).

Since *Penn Central*, takings doctrine has burgeoned. Because space limitations preclude a review of all of the significant decisions, we will devote our attention to those with the greatest environmental significance.

In one significant development, the court has elaborated on the "physical occupation" branch of the takings doctrine. It seems clear that a public access easement on otherwise private property qualifies as a physical occupation. But such an easement may be a legitimate condition of a permit where it mitigates a project's impact. In two major decisions, the Court has articulated the necessary relationship between the project and the access condition. In *Nollan v. California Coastal Commission*, 483 U.S. 825 (1987), owners of beach property were required to dedicate an easement from the street to the beach, as a condition for a permit to demolish an existing house and build a new one. The Court held that this was a taking because of the absence of any "nexus" between the access condition and the construction project, which did not meaningfully impede existing public access to the beach. The Court took *Nollan* a step further in *Dolan v. City of Tigard*, 512 U.S. 374 (1994), by requiring the city to "make some sort of individualized determination" of "rough proportionality" between the permit condition and the impact of the project. Nearly a decade later, the Court expanded the scope of this rule to apply to all regulatory exactions (not just easements) and to denials of permits as well as issuances. *Koontz v. St. Johns River Water Management Dist.*, 133 S.Ct. 2586 (2013).

Another area of doctrinal development has involved direct restrictions on development. It is the subject of the next two cases. Be sure to take a close look at the lengthy footnote we have included from the first case.

LUCAS V. SOUTH CAROLINA COASTAL COUNCIL

Supreme Court of the United States, 1992.
505 U.S. 1003, 112 S.Ct. 2886, 120 L.Ed.2d 798.

JUSTICE SCALIA delivered the opinion of the Court.

In 1986, petitioner David H. Lucas paid $975,000 for two residential lots on the Isle of Palms in Charleston County, South Carolina, on which he intended to build single family homes. In 1988, however, the South Carolina Legislature enacted the Beachfront Management Act, which had the direct effect of barring petitioner from erecting any permanent habitable structures on his two parcels. A state trial court found that this prohibition rendered Lucas's parcels "valueless." This case requires us to decide whether the Act's dramatic effect on the economic value of Lucas's lots accomplished a taking of private property under the Fifth and Fourteenth Amendments requiring the payment of "just compensation." * * *

[O]ur decision in *Mahon* offered little insight into when, and under what circumstances, a given regulation would be seen as going "too far" for purposes of the Fifth Amendment. In 70-odd years of succeeding "regulatory takings" jurisprudence, we have generally eschewed any " 'set formula' " for determining how far is too far, preferring to "engag[e] in * * * essentially ad hoc, factual inquiries," [quoting *Penn Central*]. We have, however, described at least two discrete categories of regulatory action as compensable without case-specific inquiry into the public interest advanced in support of the restraint. The first encompasses regulations that compel the property owner to suffer a physical "invasion" of his property. * * *

The second situation in which we have found categorical treatment appropriate is where regulation denies all economically beneficial or productive use of land. As we have said on numerous occasions, the Fifth Amendment is violated when land-use regulation "does not substantially advance legitimate state interests *or denies an owner economically viable use of his land.*"[7]

We have never set forth the justification for this rule. Perhaps it is simply, as Justice Brennan suggested, that total deprivation of beneficial use is, from the landowner's point of view, the equivalent of a physical appropriation. * * * Surely, at least, in the extraordinary circumstance when *no* productive or economically beneficial use of land is permitted, it is less realistic to indulge our usual assumption that the legislature is simply "adjusting the benefits and burdens of economic life," [*Penn Central*], in a manner that secures an "average reciprocity of advantage" to

---

[7]   Regrettably, the rhetorical force of our "deprivation of all economically feasible use" rule is greater than its precision, since the rule does not make clear the "property interest" against which the loss of value is to be measured. When, for example, a regulation requires a developer to leave 90% of a rural tract in its natural state, it is unclear whether we would analyze the situation as one in which the owner has been deprived of all economically beneficial use of the burdened portion of the tract, or as one in which the owner has suffered a mere diminution in value of the tract as a whole. (For an extreme—and, we think, unsupportable—view of the relevant calculus, see *Penn Central Transportation Co. v. New York City,* 42 N.Y.2d 324, 333–334, 397 N.Y.S.2d 914, 920, 366 N.E.2d 1271, 1276–1277 (1977), aff'd, 438 U.S. 104, 98 S.Ct. 2646, 57 L.Ed.2d 631 (1978), where the state court examined the diminution in a particular parcel's value produced by a municipal ordinance in light of total value of the taking claimant's other holdings in the vicinity.) Unsurprisingly, this uncertainty regarding the composition of the denominator in our "deprivation" fraction has produced inconsistent pronouncements by the Court. The answer to this difficult question may lie in how the owner's reasonable expectations have been shaped by the State's law of property—*i.e.,* whether and to what degree the State's law has accorded legal recognition and protection to the particular interest in land with respect to which the takings claimant alleges a diminution in (or elimination of) value. In any event, we avoid this difficulty in the present case, since the "interest in land" that Lucas has pleaded (a fee simple interest) is an estate with a rich tradition of protection at common law, and since the South Carolina Court of Common Pleas found that the Beachfront Management Act left each of Lucas's beachfront lots without economic value.

everyone concerned. And the *functional* basis for permitting the government, by regulation, to affect property values without compensation—that "Government hardly could go on if to some extent values incident to property could not be diminished without paying for every such change in the general law"—does not apply to the relatively rare situations where the government has deprived a landowner of all economically beneficial uses.

On the other side of the balance, affirmatively supporting a compensation requirement, is the fact that regulations that leave the owner of land without economically beneficial or productive options for its use—typically, as here, by requiring land to be left substantially in its natural state—carry with them a heightened risk that private property is being pressed into some form of public service under the guise of mitigating serious public harm. As Justice Brennan explained: "From the government's point of view, the benefits flowing to the public from preservation of open space through regulation may be equally great as from creating a wildlife refuge through formal condemnation or increasing electricity production through a dam project that floods private property." The many statutes on the books, both state and federal, that provide for the use of eminent domain to impose servitudes on private scenic lands preventing developmental uses, or to acquire such lands altogether, suggest the practical equivalence in this setting of negative regulation and appropriation.

We think, in short, that there are good reasons for our frequently expressed belief that when the owner of real property has been called upon to sacrifice *all* economically beneficial uses in the name of the common good, that is, to leave his property economically idle, he has suffered a taking.* * *

It is correct that many of our prior opinions have suggested that "harmful or noxious uses" of property may be proscribed by government regulation without the requirement of compensation. For a number of reasons, however, we think the South Carolina Supreme Court was too quick to conclude that that principle decides the present case. The "harmful or noxious uses" principle was the Court's early attempt to describe in theoretical terms why government may, consistent with the Takings Clause, affect property values by regulation without incurring an obligation to compensate—a reality we nowadays acknowledge explicitly with respect to the full scope of the State's police power. * * *

The transition from our early focus on control of "noxious" uses to our contemporary understanding of the broad realm within which government may regulate without compensation was an easy one, since the distinction between "harm-preventing" and "benefit-conferring" regulation is often in the eye of the beholder. It is quite possible, for example, to describe in *either* fashion the ecological, economic, and aesthetic concerns that inspired the South Carolina legislature in the present case. One could say that imposing a servitude on Lucas's land is necessary in order to prevent his use of it from "harming" South Carolina's ecological resources; or, instead, in order to achieve the "benefits" of an ecological preserve. Whether one or the other of the competing characterizations will come to one's lips in a particular case depends primarily upon one's evaluation of the worth of competing uses of real estate. * * *

Where the State seeks to sustain regulation that deprives land of all economically beneficial use, we think it may resist compensation only if the logically antecedent inquiry into the nature of the owner's estate shows that the proscribed use interests were not part of his title to begin with. This accords, we think, with our "takings" jurisprudence, which has traditionally been guided by the understandings of our citizens regarding the content of, and the State's power over, the "bundle of rights" that they acquire when they obtain title to property. It seems to us that the property owner necessarily expects the uses of his property to be restricted, from time to time, by various measures newly enacted by the State in legitimate exercise of its police powers; "[a]s long recognized, some values are enjoyed under an implied limitation and must yield to the police power." [*Mahon.*] And in the case of personal property, by reason of the State's traditionally high degree of control over commercial dealings, he ought to be aware of the possibility that new regulation might even render his property economically worthless (at least if the property's only economically productive use is sale or manufacture for sale). In the case of land, however, we think the notion pressed by the Council that title is somehow held subject to the "implied limitation" that the State may subsequently eliminate all economically valuable use is inconsistent with the historical compact recorded in the Takings Clause that has become part of our constitutional culture.* * *

It seems unlikely that common-law principles would have prevented the erection of any habitable or productive improvements on petitioner's land; they rarely support prohibition of the "essential use" of land. The question, however, is one of state law to be dealt with on remand. We emphasize that to win its case South Carolina must do more than proffer the legislature's declaration that the uses Lucas desires are inconsistent with the public interest, or the conclusory assertion that they violate a common-law maxim such as *sic utere tuo ut alienum non laedas*. As we have said, a "State, by *ipse dixit,* may not transform private property into public property without compensation * * *." Instead, as it would be required to do if it sought to restrain Lucas in a common-law action for public nuisance, South Carolina must identify background principles of nuisance and property law that prohibit the uses he now intends in the circumstances in which the property is presently found. Only on this showing can the State fairly claim that, in proscribing all such beneficial uses, the Beachfront Management Act is taking nothing.

JUSTICE KENNEDY, concurring in the judgment.

In my view, reasonable expectations must be understood in light of the whole of our legal tradition. The common law of nuisance is too narrow a confine for the exercise of regulatory power in a complex and interdependent society. The State should not be prevented from enacting new regulatory initiatives in response to changing conditions, and courts must consider all reasonable expectations whatever their source. The Takings Clause does not require a static body of state property law; it protects private expectations to ensure private investment. I agree with the Court that nuisance prevention accords with the most common expectations of property owners who face regulation, but I do not believe this can be the sole source of state authority to impose severe restrictions. Coastal property may present such unique concerns for a fragile land system that the State can go further in regulating its development and use than the common law of nuisance might otherwise permit.

The Supreme Court of South Carolina erred, in my view, by reciting the general purposes for which the state regulations were enacted without a determination that they were in accord with the owner's reasonable expectations and therefore sufficient to support a severe restriction on specific parcels of property. The promotion of tourism, for instance, ought not to suffice to deprive specific property of all value without a corresponding duty to compensate. Furthermore, the means as well as the ends of regulation must accord with the owner's reasonable expectations. Here, the State did not act until after the property had been zoned for individual lot development and most other parcels had been improved, throwing the whole burden of the regulation on the remaining lots. This too must be measured in the balance.

JUSTICE BLACKMUN, dissenting.

[T]he Court justifies its new rule that the legislature may not deprive a property owner of the only economically valuable use of his land, even if the legislature finds it to be a harmful use, because such action is not part of the "long recognized" "understandings of our citizens." These "understandings" permit such regulation only if the use is a nuisance under the common law. Any other course is "inconsistent with the historical compact recorded in the Takings Clause." It is not clear from the Court's opinion where our "historical compact" or "citizens' understanding" comes from, but it does not appear to be history.

The principle that the State should compensate individuals for property taken for public use was not widely established in America at the time of the Revolution. * * *

Even into the 19th century, state governments often felt free to take property for roads and other public projects without paying compensation to the owners. As one court declared in 1802, citizens "were bound to contribute as much of [land], as by the laws of the country, were deemed necessary for the public convenience." * * *

In short, I find no clear and accepted "historical compact" or "understanding of our citizens" justifying the Court's new taking doctrine. Instead, the Court seems to treat history as a grab-bag of principles, to be adopted where they support the Court's theory, and ignored where they do not. If the Court decided that the early common law provides the background principles for interpreting the Taking Clause, then regulation, as opposed to physical confiscation, would not be compensable. If the Court decided that the law of a later period provides the background principles, then regulation might be compensable, but the Court would have to confront the fact that legislatures regularly determined which uses were prohibited, independent of the common law, and independent of whether the uses were lawful when the owner purchased. What makes the Court's analysis unworkable is its attempt to package the law of two incompatible eras and peddle it as historical fact.

NOTES

1.   After Hurricane Hugo, so many structures were damaged in the area of the Isle of Palms that the state relented on its ban on rebuilding existing houses. After further negotiations, South Carolina eventually bought the Lucas lots for over $1.5 million. The area has been flooded many times since the Supreme Court's ruling, and the inhabitants have constructed walls of two-ton and three-ton sandbags. Carol M. Rose, *The Story of Lucas: Environmental Land Use Regulation Between Developers and the Deep Blue Sea, in* RICHARD J. LAZARUS & OLIVER A. HOUCK, ENVIRONMENTAL LAW STORIES 268–69 (2005).

2.   One noteworthy aspect of *Lucas* is Justice Scalia's use of a narrowly construed "nuisance exception," at least in total takings cases. Justice Scalia's use of nuisance law has attracted attention from commentators, who have suggested that nuisance law has been far more fluid and adaptable than Scalia suggests. We will return later to the question of *Lucas*'s "categorical exemptions" from takings analysis.

3.   Footnote 7 of Justice Scalia's opinion discusses what has come to be known as the denominator problem: determining the relevant property interest in order to assess what percentage of its value has been lost due to a regulation. In general, owners will want to define the property interest narrowly, in order to make the percentage of loss as a high as possible, or better yet, be able to claim a total taking under *Lucas*. For instance, if a regulation prevent construction on part of a lot, the owner would like to say that this portion of the lot is a separate property interest that has been totally taken. Or if there is a temporary ban on construction, the owner would like to claim

that the ban operates as a total taking of a "time slice" of the property (akin to a possible leasehold interest).

The time-slice issue came before the Court a decade after *Lucas*. *Tahoe-Sierra Preservation Council, Inc. v. Tahoe Regional Planning Agency*, 535 U.S. 302 (2002), involved an effort to apply the *Lucas* rule to a building moratorium. The regional planning agency had imposed a building moratorium lasting almost three years while it considered new measures to preserve Lake Tahoe's water quality. The Court sided with the agency, whose position had been argued by John Roberts, the future Chief Justice. The Court stated that "[a]n interest in real property is defined by the metes and bounds that describe its geographic dimensions and the term of years that describes the temporal aspect of the owner's interest." The Court observed that delays of up to a year in processing permits as well as building moratoriums during planning efforts were common aspects of land use planning. Chief Justice Rehnquist dissented, joined by Justices Scalia and Thomas. Rehnquist argued that the government's action was equivalent to seizure of a multi-year lease of the property on its own behalf. In contrast, he contended, "short-term delays attendant to zoning and permit regimes are a long-standing feature of state property law and part of a landowner's reasonable investment-backed expectations." Writing separately, Justice Thomas (joined by Justice Scalia) expressed doubts about the entire "parcel as a whole" standard.

MURR V. WISCONSIN

Supreme Court of the United States, 2017.
___ U.S. ___, 137 S.Ct. 1933, 198 L. Ed.2d 497.

JUSTICE KENNEDY delivered the opinion of the Court.

[The Murr litigation began as a fairly routine zoning dispute. The Murrs were siblings whose parents had given them two adjoining lots on the bank of the St. Croix River, which Congress had designated a protected "wild and scenic river." The parents had first given them a lot containing a cabin (Lot F) and then an adjoining vacant lot (Lot E). The lots contained a 130-foot bluff, with land at the top fronting on a street and land on the bottom next to the river. The Murrs' cabin located on the bottomland frequently flooded, and they wanted to renovate it using funds from selling Lot E. Because of the protected nature of the river, the lots were subject to special zoning restrictions. They were denied a variance for their renovation plan. This left their request for a variance to sell Lot E, which became the central issue in the litigation. The reason the Murrs needed a variance to sell Lot E separately was that both lots were classified as substandard, being below the minimum buildable area required by the zoning ordinance. If the lots had been owned separately, each of them would be grandfathered in, since they existed before the passage of the building limits. But the grandfather clause did not apply when two adjoining lots were commonly owned.]

[When that variance was also denied, the Murrs started over again with a takings claim based on the restriction on separate use or sale of Lot E. The Murrs introduced evidence that Lot E was worth only $40,000 separately if the buyer could not build on the site. According to the state's appraiser, Lot F would be worth $373,000 as a separate improved lot, while apparently Lot E would be worth $398,000 on the same basis—yet the value of the two lots as a single buildable unit was $$698,000, only about ten percent below the combined value of two separate buildable lots, because of synergies between the lots.]

This case presents a question that is linked to the ultimate determination whether a regulatory taking has occurred: What is the proper unit of property against which to assess the effect of the challenged governmental action? Put another way, "[b]ecause our test for regulatory taking requires us to compare the value that has been taken from the property with the value that remains in the property, one of the critical questions is determining how to define the unit of property 'whose value is to furnish the denominator of the fraction.' "* * *

[N]o single consideration can supply the exclusive test for determining the denominator. Instead, courts must consider a number of factors. These include the treatment of the land under state and local law; the physical characteristics of the land; and the prospective value of the regulated land. The endeavor should determine whether reasonable expectations about property ownership would lead a landowner to anticipate that his holdings would be treated as one parcel, or, instead, as separate tracts. The inquiry is objective, and the reasonable expectations at issue derive from background customs and the whole of our legal tradition.

First, courts should give substantial weight to the treatment of the land, in particular how it is bounded or divided, under state and local law. The reasonable expectations of an acquirer of land must acknowledge legitimate restrictions affecting his or her subsequent use and dispensation of the property. A reasonable restriction that predates a landowner's acquisition, however, can be one of the objective factors that most landowners would reasonably consider in forming fair expectations about their property. In a similar manner, a use restriction which is triggered only after, or because of, a change in ownership should also guide a court's assessment of reasonable private expectations.

Second, courts must look to the physical characteristics of the landowner's property. These include the physical relationship of any distinguishable tracts, the parcel's topography, and the surrounding human and ecological environment. In particular, it may be relevant that the property is located in an area that is subject to, or likely to become subject to, environmental or other regulation.

Third, courts should assess the value of the property under the challenged regulation, with special attention to the effect of burdened land on the value of other holdings. Though a use restriction may decrease the market value of the property, the effect may be tempered if the regulated land adds value to the remaining property, such as by increasing privacy, expanding recreational space, or preserving surrounding natural beauty. A law that limits use of a landowner's small lot in one part of the city by reason of the landowner's nonadjacent holdings elsewhere may decrease the market value of the small lot in an unmitigated fashion. The absence of a special relationship between the holdings may counsel against consideration of all the holdings as a single parcel, making the restrictive law susceptible to a takings challenge. On the other hand, if the landowner's other property is adjacent to the small lot, the market value of the properties may well increase if their combination enables the expansion of a structure, or if development restraints for one part of the parcel protect the unobstructed skyline views of another part. That, in turn, may counsel in favor of treatment as a single parcel and may reveal the weakness of a regulatory takings challenge to the law.

State and federal courts have considerable experience in adjudicating regulatory takings claims that depart from these examples in various ways. The Court anticipates that in applying the test above they will continue to exercise care in this complex area. * * *

Under the appropriate multifactor standard, it follows that for purposes of determining whether a regulatory taking has occurred here, petitioners' property should be evaluated as a single parcel consisting of Lots E and F together.

First, the treatment of the property under state and local law indicates petitioners' property should be treated as one when considering the effects of the restrictions. As the Wisconsin courts held, the state and local regulations merged Lots E and F. The decision to adopt the merger provision at issue here was for a specific and legitimate purpose, consistent with the widespread understanding that lot lines are not dominant or controlling in every case. Petitioners' land was subject to this regulatory burden, moreover, only because of voluntary conduct in bringing the lots under common ownership after the regulations were enacted. As a result, the valid merger of the lots under state law informs the reasonable expectation they will be treated as a single property.

Second, the physical characteristics of the property support its treatment as a unified parcel. The lots are contiguous along their longest edge. Their rough terrain and narrow shape make it reasonable to expect their range of potential uses might be limited. The land's location along the river is also significant. Petitioners could have anticipated public regulation might affect their enjoyment of their property, as the Lower St.

Croix was a regulated area under federal, state, and local law long before petitioners possessed the land.

Third, the prospective value that Lot E brings to Lot F supports considering the two as one parcel for purposes of determining if there is a regulatory taking. Petitioners are prohibited from selling Lots E and F separately or from building separate residential structures on each. Yet this restriction is mitigated by the benefits of using the property as an integrated whole, allowing increased privacy and recreational space, plus the optimal location of any improvements.

The special relationship of the lots is further shown by their combined valuation. Were Lot E separately saleable but still subject to the development restriction, petitioners' appraiser would value the property at only $40,000. We express no opinion on the validity of this figure. We also note the number is not particularly helpful for understanding petitioners' retained value in the properties because Lot E, under the regulations, cannot be sold without Lot F. The point that is useful for these purposes is that the combined lots are valued at $698,300, which is far greater than the summed value of the separate regulated lots (Lot F with its cabin at $373,000, according to respondents' appraiser, and Lot E as an undevelopable plot at $40,000, according to petitioners' appraiser). The value added by the lots' combination shows their complementarity and supports their treatment as one parcel. * * *

Considering petitioners' property as a whole, the state court was correct to conclude that petitioners cannot establish a compensable taking in these circumstances. Petitioners have not suffered a taking under *Lucas*, as they have not been deprived of all economically beneficial use of their property. They can use the property for residential purposes, including an enhanced, larger residential improvement. The property has not lost all economic value, as its value has decreased by less than 10 percent.

Petitioners furthermore have not suffered a taking under the more general test of *Penn Central*. The expert appraisal relied upon by the state courts refutes any claim that the economic impact of the regulation is severe. Petitioners cannot claim that they reasonably expected to sell or develop their lots separately given the regulations which predated their acquisition of both lots. Finally, the governmental action was a reasonable land-use regulation, enacted as part of a coordinated federal, state, and local effort to preserve the river and surrounding land.* * *

Like the ultimate question whether a regulation has gone too far, the question of the proper parcel in regulatory takings cases cannot be solved by any simple test. Courts must instead define the parcel in a manner that reflects reasonable expectations about the property. Courts must strive for consistency with the central purpose of the Takings Clause: to "bar Government from forcing some people alone to bear public burdens which,

in all fairness and justice, should be borne by the public as a whole."
Treating the lot in question as a single parcel is legitimate for purposes of
this takings inquiry, and this supports the conclusion that no regulatory
taking occurred here.

GORSUCH took no part in the consideration or decision of this case.

CHIEF JUSTICE ROBERTS, with whom JUSTICE THOMAS and JUSTICE
ALITO join, dissenting.

The Murr family owns two adjacent lots along the Lower St. Croix
River. Under a local regulation, those two properties may not be "sold or
developed as separate lots" because neither contains a sufficiently large
area of buildable land. The Court today holds that the regulation does not
effect a taking that requires just compensation. This bottom-line conclusion
does not trouble me; the majority presents a fair case that the Murrs can
still make good use of both lots, and that the ordinance is a commonplace
tool to preserve scenic areas, such as the Lower St. Croix River, for the
benefit of landowners and the public alike.

Where the majority goes astray, however, is in concluding that the
definition of the "private property" at issue in a case such as this turns on
an elaborate test looking not only to state and local law, but also to (1) "the
physical characteristics of the land," (2) "the prospective value of the
regulated land," (3) the "reasonable expectations" of the owner, and (4)
"background customs and the whole of our legal tradition." Our decisions
have, time and again, declared that the Takings Clause protects private
property rights as state law creates and defines them. By securing such
established property rights, the Takings Clause protects individuals from
being forced to bear the full weight of actions that should be borne by the
public at large. The majority's new, malleable definition of "private
property"—adopted solely "for purposes of th[e] takings inquiry"—
undermines that protection.

I would stick with our traditional approach: State law defines the
boundaries of distinct parcels of land, and those boundaries should
determine the "private property" at issue in regulatory takings cases.
Whether a regulation effects a taking of that property is a separate
question, one in which common ownership of adjacent property may be
taken into account. Because the majority departs from these settled
principles, I respectfully dissent. * * *

As I see it, the Wisconsin Court of Appeals was wrong to apply a
takings-specific definition of the property at issue. Instead, the court
should have asked whether, under general state law principles, Lots E and
F are legally distinct parcels of land. I would therefore vacate the judgment
below and remand for the court to identify the relevant property using
ordinary principles of Wisconsin property law.

After making that state law determination, the next step would be to determine whether the challenged ordinance amounts to a "taking." If Lot E is a legally distinct parcel under state law, the Court of Appeals would have to perform the takings analysis anew, but could still consider many of the issues the majority finds important. The majority, for instance, notes that under the ordinance the Murrs can use Lot E as "recreational space," as the "location of any improvements," and as a valuable addition to Lot F. These facts could be relevant to whether the "regulation denies all economically beneficial or productive use" of Lot E. Similarly, the majority touts the benefits of the ordinance and observes that the Murrs had little use for Lot E independent of Lot F and could have predicted that Lot E would be regulated. These facts speak to "the economic impact of the regulation," interference with "investment-backed expectations," and the "character of the governmental action"—all things we traditionally consider in the *Penn Central* analysis

I would be careful, however, to confine these considerations to the question whether the regulation constitutes a taking. As Alexander Hamilton explained, "the security of Property" is one of the "great object[s] of government." The Takings Clause was adopted to ensure such security by protecting property rights as they exist under state law. Deciding whether a regulation has gone so far as to constitute a "taking" of one of those property rights is, properly enough, a fact-intensive task that relies "as much on the exercise of judgment as on the application of logic. But basing the definition of "property" on a judgment call, too, allows the government's interests to warp the private rights that the Takings Clause is supposed to secure.

JUSTICE THOMAS, dissenting.

I join THE CHIEF JUSTICE's dissent because it correctly applies this Court's regulatory takings precedents, which no party has asked us to reconsider. The Court, however, has never purported to ground those precedents in the Constitution as it was originally understood. In *Mahon*, the Court announced a "general rule" that "if regulation goes too far it will be recognized as a taking." But we have since observed that, prior to Mahon, "it was generally thought that the Takings Clause reached only a 'direct appropriation' of property, or the functional equivalent of a 'practical ouster of [the owner's] possession.' " In my view, it would be desirable for us to take a fresh look at our regulatory takings jurisprudence, to see whether it can be grounded in the original public meaning of the Takings Clause of the Fifth Amendment or the Privileges or Immunities Clause of the Fourteenth Amendment. See generally Rappaport, *Originalism and Regulatory Takings: Why the Fifth Amendment May Not Protect Against Regulatory Takings, but the Fourteenth Amendment* May, 45 SAN DIEGO L. REV. 729 (2008) (describing the debate among scholars over those questions).

NOTES

1.   James Krier and Stewart Sterk examined more than two thousand reported takings decisions from 1979 to 2012. James E. Krier and Stewart E. Sterk, *An Empirical Study of Implicit Takings*, 58 WM. & MARY L. REV. 35, 39 (2016). They found that under four percent of takings claims were based on *Lucas*, with about one percent succeeding. Krier and Sterk found that most of the opinions in those cases focused on whether a complete loss of value had occurred. Courts were divided on the issue that would ultimately reach the Court in *Murr* and on situations where inability to use the land was due to a combination of regulation and market forces. Krier and Sterk also found that *Penn Central* claims were markedly unsuccessful. Indeed, they said, "courts almost always defer to the regulatory decisions made by government officials, resulting in an almost categorical rule that *Penn Central*-type regulatory actions do not amount to takings." They found that owners won less than ten percent of *Penn Central* cases and that even this figure exaggerated the level of success, since it included decisions by lower courts that were reversed on appeal. Taking the sample of cases as a whole, Krier and Sterk found that diminution of value claims had only a five percent success rate. Claims had higher success when a regulation required out-of-pocket expenses or prohibited an existing property use. Thus, courts seemed to take the preregulatory status quo as the baseline, looking for loss of value compared to current use, rather than taking the property's potential value without regulation as the baseline.

2.   In the takings area, as in other fields of constitutional law, Justice Scalia pushed for the use of hard-edged rules as opposed to more flexible standards. At present, it appears that in the area of takings at least, this effort has stalled. Justice Brennan's *Penn Central* approach has seemingly been established as the general rule with only a few narrow exceptions. Balancing, it would appear, is triumphant. Is such balancing a return to substantive due process, allowing the Court to make its own determination of the reasonableness of a government regulation? Or does it reflect a desirable openness to regulatory context?

3.   *Murr* represents a serious blow to efforts to build upon Justice Scalia's opinion in *Lucas*. *Murr's* approach to the denominator issue obviously reduces the occasions on which an owner will be able to claim a total deprivation of value. Other aspects of *Murr* also help to limit *Lucas*. Justice Kennedy characterized the "nuisance exception" as broadly "recognizing the relevance of state law and land-use customs." Moreover, in discussing the relevance of a property's ecological features, he cited his own *Lucas* concurrence, quoting a statement that "[c]oastal property may present such unique concerns for a fragile land system that the State can go further in regulating its development and use than the common law of nuisance might otherwise permit." The dissents offered little solace to property rights advocates. Chief Justice Roberts seemed entirely at ease with the regulator-friendly *Penn Central* test. Nor did he seem unhappy with the majority's application of the test; his only concern was with the denominator issue. Justice Thomas's dissent was also unwelcome to property rights advocates, for

the article by Professor Ramsey casts doubt on the applicability of regulatory takings doctrine to the federal government. For commentary on *Murr* see Daniel A. Farber, *Murr v Wisconsin and the Future of Takings Law*, 2017 SUP. CT. REV. 115 (2017); Stewart E. Sterk, *Dueling Denominators and the Demise of Lucas*, 60 ARIZ. L. REV. 67, 68 (2018)

4.   So far, we have been considering the private owner's property interest in land. But under certain circumstances, the public may have a well-defined property interest in private land (a background principle of state law in terms of *Lucas*). We consider such property interests in the next subsection.

2. THE PUBLIC TRUST DOCTRINE

In *Lucas*, Justice Scalia pointed to nuisance law as a categorical exemption from takings claims. This subsection focuses on another doctrine that limits the rights of property owners.

ILLINOIS CENTRAL RAILROAD CO. V. ILLINOIS

Supreme Court of the United States, 1892.
146 U.S. 387, 13 S.Ct. 110, 36 L.Ed. 1018.

JUSTICE FIELD delivered the opinion of the court.

[In 1869 the Illinois legislature granted title to certain submerged lands under Lake Michigan to the Illinois Central Railroad. When the bill was introduced, it had conveyed these lands to the City of Chicago, but somehow before final passage the grantee had been changed to the railroad. In 1873, the State repealed the 1869 Act making the grant. Illinois sued to quiet title.]

The question, therefore, to be considered is whether the legislature was competent to thus deprive the State of its ownership of the submerged lands in the harbor of Chicago, and of the consequent control of its waters; or, in other words, whether the railroad corporation can hold the lands and control the waters by the grant, against any future exercise of power over them by the State.

That the State holds the title to the lands under the navigable waters of Lake Michigan, within its limits, in the same manner that the State holds title to soils under tide water, by the common law, we have already shown, and that title necessarily carries with it control over the waters above them whenever the lands are subjected to use. But it is a title different in character from that which the State holds in lands intended for sale. It is different from the title which the United States holds in the public lands which are open to preemption and sale. It is a title held in trust for the people of the State that they may enjoy the navigation of the waters, carry on commerce over them, and have liberty of fishing therein freed from the obstruction or interference of private parties. The interest of the people in the navigation of the waters and in commerce over them may be improved in many instances by the erection of wharves, docks and piers therein, for which purpose the State may grant parcels of the submerged lands; and, so long as their disposition is made for such purpose, no valid objections can be made to the grants. * * * The trust devolving upon the State for the public, and which can only be discharged by the management and control of property in which the public has an interest, cannot be relinquished by a transfer of the property. The control of the State for the purposes of the trust can never be lost, except as to such parcels as are used in promoting the interests of the public therein, or can be disposed of without any substantial impairment of the public interest in the lands and waters remaining. * * *

The harbor of Chicago is of immense value to the people of the State of Illinois in the facilities it affords to its vast and constantly increasing commerce; and the idea that its legislature can deprive the State of control over its bed and waters and place the same in the hands of a private corporation created for a different purpose, one limited to transportation of passengers and freight between distant points and the city, is a proposition that cannot be defended.

* * * It is hardly conceivable that the legislature can divest the State of the control and management of this harbor and vest it absolutely in a private corporation.

* * * The position advanced by the railroad company in support of its claim to the ownership of the submerged lands and the right to the erection of wharves, piers and docks at its pleasure, or for its business in the harbor of Chicago, would place every harbor in the country at the mercy of a majority of the legislature of the State in which the harbor is situated.

NOTES

1. *Illinois Central* holds that certain lands are held by the state in trust for the people, and that legislative actions are void (or at least voidable) if a court finds they violate the trust. With reference to the federal government, the Supreme Court has clearly endorsed only half of this doctrine:

> "All the public lands of the nation are held in trust for the people of the whole country." And it is not for the courts to say how that trust shall be administered. That is for Congress to determine. The courts cannot compel it to set aside the lands for settlement, or to suffer them to be used for agricultural or grazing purposes, nor interfere when, in the exercise of its discretion, Congress establishes a forest reserve for what it decides to be national and public purposes. In the same way and in the exercise of the same trust it may disestablish a reserve, and devote the property to some other national and public purpose. These are rights incident to proprietorship, to say nothing of the power of the United States as a sovereign over the property belonging to it.

Light v. United States, 220 U.S. 523, 537 (1911). (Note that Article IV, section 3 of the Constitution is a grant of plenary power to Congress to dispose of public lands.) *Light* seemingly implies that congressional actions that violate the public trust are nevertheless immune from judicial scrutiny.

2.   For a critique of *Illinois Central, see* Eric Pearson, Illinois Central *and the Public Trust Doctrine in State Law*, 15 VA. ENVTL. L. REV. 713 (1996). Pearson argues that the Court underestimated the amount of sovereign control which the state would retain even if title to the lake bed had actually passed to the railroad. He also argues that the state law was actually intended merely to authorize the railroad to operate a wharf, rather than permanently transferring title to property. For an exhaustive review of the history, *see* Joseph D. Kearney & Thomas W. Merrill, *The Origins of the American Public Trust Doctrine: What Really Happened in Illinois Central,* 71 U. CHI. L. REV. 799 (2004) (concluding that the railroad had legitimate reasons for seeking the legislation but probably used bribery to win).

MARKS V. WHITNEY

Supreme Court of California, In Bank, 1971.
6 Cal.3d 251, 98 Cal.Rptr. 790, 491 P.2d 374.

McCOMB, JUSTICE.

This is a quiet title action to settle a boundary line dispute caused by overlapping and defective surveys and to enjoin defendants (herein "Whitney") from asserting any claim or right in or to the property of plaintiff Marks. The unique feature here is that a part of Marks' property is tidelands acquired under an 1874 patent issued pursuant to the Act of March 28, 1868; a small portion of these tidelands adjoins almost the entire shoreline of Whitney's upland property. Marks asserted complete ownership of the tidelands and the right to fill and develop them. Whitney opposed on the ground that this would cut off his rights as a littoral owner and as a member of the public in these tidelands and the navigable waters covering them. He requested a declaration in the decree that Marks' title was burdened with a public trust easement; also that it was burdened with certain prescriptive rights claimed by Whitney.* * *

Appearing as *amici curiae* on the appeal are: the Attorney General, on behalf of the State Lands Commission, the Bay Area Conservation and Development Commission (BCDC) and as chief law enforcement officer of the state;[1] Sierra Club; and Westbay Community Associates.

---

[1]   California holds the state-wide public easement in tidelands and owns the submerged lands abutting the tidelands. The Legislature has vested in the State Lands Commission "All jurisdiction and authority remaining in the State as to tidelands and submerged lands as to which grants have been or may be made" and has given the commission exclusive administration and control of such lands. (Pub.Resources Code, section 6301.) BCDC is charged with specific duties concerning dredging and filling in San Francisco Bay (Gov.Code, sections 66600–66610). The Attorney General is presently involved in litigation involving lands in San Francisco Bay which were patented under the Act of March 23, 1868 and other statutes. The Attorney General asks this

Questions: First. *Are these tidelands subject to the public trust; if so, should the judgment so declare?*

Yes. Regardless of the issue of Whitney's standing to raise this issue the court may take judicial notice of public trust burdens in quieting title to tidelands. This matter is of great public importance, particularly in view of population pressures, demands for recreational property, and the increasing development of seashore and waterfront property. A present declaration that the title of Marks in these tidelands is burdened with a public easement may avoid needless future litigation.

[The court then traced the development of the public trust doctrine in California].

The public uses to which tidelands are subject are sufficiently flexible to encompass changing public needs. In administering the trust the state is not burdened with an outmoded classification favoring one mode of utilization over another. There is a growing public recognition that one of the most important public uses of the tidelands—a use encompassed within the tidelands trust—is the preservation of those lands in their natural state, so that they may serve as ecological units for scientific study, as open space, and as environments which provide food and habitat for birds and marine life, and which favorably affect the scenery and climate of the area. It is not necessary to here define precisely all the public uses which encumber tidelands.* * *

* * * It is within the province of the trier of fact to determine whether any particular use made or asserted by Whitney in or over these tidelands would constitute an infringement either upon the *jus privatum* of Marks or upon the *jus publicum* of the people. It is also within the province of the trier of fact to determine whether any particular use to which Marks wishes to devote his tidelands constitutes an unlawful infringement upon the *jus publicum* therein. It is a political question, within the wisdom and power of the Legislature, acting within the scope of its duties as trustee, to determine whether public trust uses should be modified or extinguished and to take the necessary steps to free them from such burden. In the absence of state or federal action the court may not bar members of the public from lawfully asserting or exercising public trust rights on this privately owned tidelands.

There is absolutely no merit in Marks' contention that as the owner of the *jus privatum* under this patent he may fill and develop his property, whether for navigational purposes or not; nor in his contention that his past and present plan for development of these tidelands as a marina have caused the extinguishment of the public easement. Reclamation with or

---

court to declare the existence of the public easement and to recognize the right of Whitney as a member of the public and as a littoral owner to have the existence of the easement in these tidelands declared in this action.

without prior authorization from the state does not *ipso facto* terminate the public trust nor render the issue moot.* * *

Second: *Does Whitney have "standing" to request the court to recognize and declare the public trust easement on Marks' tidelands?*

Yes. The relief sought by Marks resulted in taking away from Whitney rights to which he is entitled as a member of the general public. It is immaterial that Marks asserted he was not seeking to enjoin the public. The decree as rendered does enjoin a member of the public.

Members of the public have been permitted *to bring* an action to enforce a public right to use a beach access route; *to bring* an action to quiet title to private and public easements in a public beach; and *to bring* an action to restrain improper filling of a bay and secure a general declaration of the rights of the people to the waterways and wildlife areas of the bay. Members of the public have been allowed *to defend* a quiet title action by asserting the right to use a public right of way through private property. They have been allowed to assert the public trust easement for hunting, fishing and navigation in privately owned tidelands *as a defense* in an action to enjoin such use, and to navigate on shallow navigable waters in small boats.

Whitney had standing to raise this issue. The court could have raised this issue on its own.

NOTES

1.   The court says that the "trier of fact" should determine whether some particular proposed use conflicts with the public trust. Should this "trier of fact" be a judge or jury, or should it be an administrative agency such as the California Coastal Commission? Not all courts have taken such a dynamic view of the public trust. *See Bott v. Natural Res. Comm'n,* 327 N.W.2d 838 (Mich. 1982) (public trust does not protect access to recreational waters). For an overview of state doctrines, see Robin Kundis Craig, *A Comparative Guide to the Western States' Public Trust Doctrines,* 37 ECOLOGY L.Q. 53 (2010). A recent case by the Indiana Supreme Court holds that the public trust doctrine covers the bed of Lake Michigan up to the ordinary high way mark, giving the public the right to walk across the beach. *Gunderson v. State, Indiana Dep't of Nat. Res.,* 90 N.E.3d 1171 (Ind. 2018)

2.   A later California Supreme Court case considered the problem of legislative termination of the trust. Overruling two prior decisions, the court held that an 1870 act conveying title to submerged and tidal lands did not extinguish the public trust over those lands. *City of Berkeley v. Superior Ct.,* 606 P.2d 362 (Cal.1980). The court's holding was based on a strong presumption against termination of the trust. The court held, however, that its decision would not apply retroactively to individuals who had already reclaimed their land.

3.   What waters are within the scope of the public trust? In *Phillips Petroleum Co. v. Mississippi,* 484 U.S. 469 (1988), the Court ruled that the public trust extended to all tidal waters, not just navigable waters. The Court rejected the argument that this ruling would upset "settled expectations":

> We have recognized the importance of honoring reasonable expectations in property interests. But such expectations can only be of consequence where they are "reasonable" ones. Here, Mississippi appears to have consistently held that the public trust in lands under water includes "title to all the land under tidewater." Although the Mississippi Supreme Court acknowledged that this case may be the first where it faced the question of the public trust interest in non-navigable tidelands, the clear and unequivocal statements in its earlier opinions should have been ample indication of the State's claim to tidelands. Moreover, cases which have discussed the State's public trust interest in these lands have described uses of them not related to navigability, such as bathing, swimming, recreation, fishing, and mineral development. These statements, too, should have made clear that the State's claims were not limited to lands under navigable waterways. Any contrary expectations cannot be considered reasonable.

The Court observed that even in states where tidelands are privately held, public rights to use tidelands for fishing, hunting, and swimming have long been recognized, and might be undermined by limiting the public trust to navigable waters.

Hawaii has gone a step ahead of other states in extending the public trust doctrine to include groundwater. *In re Water Use Permit Applications for the Waiahole Ditch*, 9 P.3d 409, 445–447 (Haw. 2000). The court's theory was that "the common law distinctions between ground and surface water developed without regard to the manner in which 'both categories represent no more than a single integrated source of water with each element dependent upon the other for its existence.'" For a detailed discussion of the Waiahole Ditch opinion, see *Proceedings of the 2001 Symposium on Managing Hawai'i's Public Trust Doctrine*, 14 U. HAW. L. REV. 21, 43–50 (2001) (containing remarks by Jan Stevens).

4.   One of the most important modern applications of the public trust doctrine was *National Audubon Society v. Superior Court,* 658 P.2d 709 (Cal. 1983). At issue was the diversion by the City of Los Angeles of the streams feeding Mono Lake, which threatened to dry up the lake entirely. Under California water law, Los Angeles was entitled to the water as the first appropriator. The California Supreme Court held, however, that this system of prior appropriation must be reconciled with public trust doctrine, and mandated reconsideration of the water allocation in light of its detrimental environmental effects. Dave Owen argues that use of the public trust doctrine in California since *Lake Mono* has been cautious and incremental, and that various statutory and regulatory provisions have had more impact on

California water law than this judicial doctrine. Dave Owen, *The Mono Lake Case, The Public Trust Doctrine, and the Administrative State*, 45 U.C. DAVIS L. REV. 45 (2012).

5.   Can the public trust doctrine be used to compel government action to address climate change? Professor Lazarus argues that the climate change issue is far beyond judicial remedy:

> [A]ddressing sweeping problems like climate change will require our most creative thinking to craft political strategies and lawmaking institutions capable of breaking the logjam that has paralyzed our ability to make and maintain the laws necessary for the viability of future generations. Such complex lawmaking challenges are not going to be overcome in the first instance in any truly significant and long-lasting way by the judiciary relying on the public trust doctrine.

Richard J. Lazarus, *Judicial Missteps, Legislative Dysfunction, and the Public Trust Doctrine: Can Two Wrongs Make It Right?*, 45 ENVTL. L. 1139, 1161 (2015).

A federal district court held, however, that government inaction against climate change may violate its public trust obligations. According to the court, "[b]ecause a number of plaintiffs' injuries relate to the effects of ocean acidification and rising ocean temperatures, they have adequately alleged harm to public trust assets." See *Juliana v. United States*, 217 F. Supp. 3d 1224, 1241 (D. Or. 2016). The court also connected the public trust violation with the plaintiffs' substantive due process claim that the government's actions encouraging carbon emissions violated their constitutional right "to a climate system capable of sustaining human life." The court noted, however, that caution would be required in crafting a remedy:

> Should plaintiffs prevail on the merits, this Court would no doubt be compelled to exercise great care to avoid separation-of-powers problems in crafting a remedy. The separation of powers might, for example, permit the Court to direct defendants to ameliorate plaintiffs' injuries but limit its ability to specify precisely how to do so.

The Ninth Circuit rebuffed repeated efforts by the government to obtain mandamus to end the case. See *In re United States*, 895 F.3d 1101, 1104 (9th Cir. 2018). The Supreme Court denied a stay to the proceedings on November 2, 2018, though with a hint that the court of appeals might want to reconsider the issue now that the case was approaching trial.

The litigation has given rise to extensive scholarly discussion. See, e.g., Michael C. Blumm, *Two Wrongs? Correcting Professor Lazarus's Misunderstanding of the Public Trust Doctrine*, 46 ENVTL. L. 481, 482 (2016); Kassandra Castillo, *Climate Change & the Public Trust Doctrine: An Analysis of Atmospheric Trust Litigation*, 6 SAN DIEGO J. CLIMATE & ENERGY L. 221, 223 (2015)

6.   What is the effect of the public trust doctrine on takings claims under *Lucas* or the *Penn Central* test? The next excerpt argues that *Lucas* has had an unexpected effect on taking law by creating the concept of categorical exemptions such as public trust.

MICHAEL C. BLUMM AND LUCAS RITCHIE, *LUCAS'S* UNLIKELY LEGACY: THE RISE OF BACKGROUND PRINCIPLES AS CATEGORICAL TAKINGS DEFENSES
29 HARV. ENVTL. L. REV. 321, 321–366 (2005).[8]

The Supreme Court's decision in *Lucas v. South Carolina Coastal Council* is one of the most celebrated cases of the Rehnquist Court's property jurisprudence. Justice Scalia's opinion for a 6–3 Court declared that a regulation depriving a landowner of all economic value was a categorical constitutional taking of private property for public use requiring government compensation regardless of the public purpose served by the regulation. This new categorical rule was welcomed by private property advocates but denounced by defenders of government regulations.

But now, over a dozen years later, the legacy of the *Lucas* decision seems neither as revolutionary as its advocates hoped, nor as dire as its detractors feared. In fact, the *Lucas* legacy represents one of the starkest recent examples of the law of unintended consequences. For rather than heralding in a new era of landowner compensation or government deregulation, *Lucas* instead spawned a surprising rise of categorical defenses to takings claims in which governments can defeat compensation suits without case-specific inquiries into the economic effects and public purposes of regulations. *Lucas* accomplished this by establishing the prerequisite that a claimant must first demonstrate that its property interest was unrestrained by prior restrictions. The decision suggested that those restrictions had to be imposed by common law courts interpreting state nuisance and property law, but *Lucas* has not been interpreted by either the lower courts or the Supreme Court so narrowly.

Adding to the unanticipated consequences of the *Lucas* opinion was the fact that the categorical takings rule concerning economic wipeouts it established turned out to apply only to a very narrow class of takings cases, while the categorical defenses authorized by the decision are quite expansive in scope. In effect, the *Lucas* decision fundamentally revised all takings analysis by making the nature of the landowner's property rights a threshold issue in every takings case. Thus, although *Lucas* has proved to revolutionize takings jurisprudence, it did so in ways that hardly were anticipated, and which have proved to be much more protective of

---

government defendants than anyone imagined at the time of the decision.* * *

In 2002, the Ninth Circuit decided, in *Esplanade Properties, LLC v. City of Seattle*,[127] that a Washington landowner had no compensable interest in a proposal to construct structures in the navigable tidelands of Elliot Bay, an area regularly used by the public for various recreational activities, because the purpose "was inconsistent with the public trust that [the state] is obligated to protect."[128] Similarly, the Wisconsin Supreme Court recently upheld the denial of a state fill permit to complete the last phase of a marina on the bed and in the waters of Lake Superior, concluding that the public trust doctrine prevented the fill.[129] The developers were left with riparian rights of use and access only, which are "qualified, subordinate, and subject to the paramount interest of the state and the paramount rights of the public in navigable waters."[130] And in *Wilson v. Massachusetts*,[131] Massachusetts Court of Appeals ruled that the claimants' coastal landholdings were "impressed with a public trust," leaving them only limited rights to their beachfront property.[132] * * *

Closely related to the public trust doctrine are state common law natural use restrictions. The "natural use" doctrine maintains that landowners have no inherent property right to transform lands from their existing state. The leading case justifying application of natural use limits as part of the background principles of property law is *Just v. Marinette County*.[141] In *Just*, the Wisconsin Supreme Court rejected a takings challenge to the denial of a county permit required to fill a wetland, stating:

> An owner of land has no absolute and unlimited right to change the essential natural character of his land so as to use it for a purpose for which it was unsuited in its natural state and which injures the rights of others. * * * It seems to us that filling a swamp not otherwise commercially usable is not in and of itself an existing use, which is prevented, but rather is the preparation for some future use which is not indigenous to a swamp.[142]

Once mislabeled as a "phantom doctrine," *Just*'s natural use rationale was reaffirmed and expanded in scope by the Wisconsin Supreme Court fifteen years later in a case involving county-imposed wetland conservancy

---

[127] 307 F.3d 978 (9th Cir. 2002).

[128] *Id.* at 987.

[129] *See* R.W. Docks & Slips v. Wisconsin, 628 N.W.2d 781 (Wis. 2001).

[130] *Id.* at 788.

[131] 583 N.E.2d 894 (Mass. App. Ct. 1992), *aff'd*, 597 N.E.2d 43 (Mass. 1992).

[132] Id. at 901.

[141] 201 N.W.2d 761 (Wis. 1972); *see also* James M. McElfish, Jr., *Property Rights, Property Roots*, 24 Envtl. L. Rptr. (Envtl. L. Inst.) 10, 231, 10,244 (1994) (discussing *Just* and its relevance as a background principle).

[142] 201 N.W.2d at 768–70.

restrictions that precluded the claimant from developing ninety percent of its land.[144] The court ruled that the natural use principle applies regardless of "whether the regulated land is a wetland within a shoreland area, or land within a primary environmental corridor, or an isolated swamp."[145]

Other state courts have explicitly relied on *Just* to clarify that compensation is not due for restrictions placed on land that, in its natural and existing condition, is unsuitable for development. Jurisdictions approving the *Just* rationale include Florida, New Hampshire, South Dakota, South Carolina, Georgia, and New Jersey.

The natural use doctrine, at least as it concerns wetlands, seems to be well supported by English common law. * * * In fact, England's common law consistently upheld natural use-like limitations by promoting the "continuation of existing patterns of wetland ownership and use." Because American courts frequently look to English common law as authority for their decisions, government defendants may rely on relevant English common law analogues when making natural use arguments in state courts.* * *

At least two post-*Lucas* courts have endorsed state ownership of wildlife as a defense to takings challenges. In *New York v. Sour Mountain Realty, Inc.*,[208] New York's intermediate appellate court addressed a takings claim based on a county court injunction seeking removal of a landowner's fence, which precluded threatened snakes from important forage habitat. The court affirmed the injunction and denied claimant's takings challenge, determining that:

> The State, through the exercise of its police power, is safeguarding the welfare of an indigenous species that has been found to be threatened with extinction. . . . The State's interest in protecting its wild animals is a venerable principle that can properly serve as a legitimate basis for the exercise of its police power.[210]

The California Court of Appeals has also employed wildlife protections as a background principle to reject a takings challenge concerning the denial of a timber harvest permit in order to prevent threats to endangered species, including the marbled murrelet.[211] Importantly, the Court of

---

[144] See M & I Marshall & Isley Bank v. Town of Somers, 414 N.W.2d 824, 825 (Wis. 1987).

[145] *Id.* at 830. The court elaborated:

[A] parcel of land which consists of continuing wetland which is partly within and partly outside a shoreland area should be treated as if the entire wetland was located within a shoreland area. There would be little value to the wetland within the shoreland if the part of the wetland outside the shoreland area was allowed to be altered. Id. at 831.

[208] 714 N.Y.S.2d 78 (2000).

[210] *Id.* at 84.

[211] *See Sierra Club v. Dep't of Forestry & Fire Prot.*, 26 Cal. Rptr. 2d 338, 347 (Cal. Ct. App. 1993). The California Supreme Court denied review of this case without opinion on March 18, 1994, thereby upholding the appellate court's decision. However, in denying review, the Supreme Court also determined, pursuant to California Court Rules 976, 977, and 979, that the lower court

Appeals observed that "wildlife regulation of some sort has been historically a part of the preexisting law of property."[212]

These courts' observations that state wildlife protection can be a background principle of property law appear to be a reasonable application of *Lucas*. The full extent of the usefulness of this doctrine, however, will be determined as more courts encounter the issue.* * *

All of these observations lead to the conclusion that the background principles defense authorized in *Lucas* is alive and well and will continue to function as a useful tool for government defendants to defeat takings claims. Although the Supreme Court has not endorsed all of the many categorical defenses ushered in by the background principles inquiry, its ability to constrict background principles grounded in state law is quite limited, and the Court has explicitly approved federal defenses grounded on both common law and statutes.

NOTES

1. For a debate about this article's interpretation of the common law, see Michael C. Blumm & J.B. Ruhl, *Background Principles, Takings, and Libertarian Property: A Reply to Professor Huffman*, 37 ECOLOGY L. Q. 805 2010); James L. Huffman, *Background Principles and the Rule of Law: Fifteen Years After* Lucas, 35 ECOLOGY L.Q. 1 (2008); James L. Huffman, *Beware of Greens in Praise of the Common Law*, 58 CASE W. L. REV. 813 (2008). Some historical support for a wildlife exception can be found in John F. Hart, *Fish, Dams, and James Madison: Eighteenth-Century Species Protection and the Original Understanding of the Takings Clause*, 63 MD. L. REV. 287 (2004) (discussing "fish passage" laws that seriously restricted water mills). Hart also provides an interesting discussion of Madison's views:

> James Madison raised the prospect of mankind's "extirpating every useless production of nature." He felt it was:
>
>> Not probable that nature, after covering the earth with so great a variety of animal & vegetable inhabitants, and establishing among them so systematic a proportion, could permit one favorite offspring, by destroying every other, to render vain all her wise arrangements and contrivances.
>>
>> Destruction "not only of individuals, but of entire species," Madison insisted, was "forbidden . . . by the principles and laws which operate in various department's of her [that is, nature's] economy."

Id. at 291.

---

decision would not be officially published (even though it was previously published). Consequently, the *Sierra Club* decision cannot be cited in documents submitted to California courts.

[212] *Id.*

2.   Takings law is, of course, a significant part of constitutional doctrine in its own right. But it also provides a gauge of how our society draws the line between legitimate individual interests and the needs of others. *Lucas* provides some protection for core property interests. At the same time, the concept of category exemptions recognizes areas of overriding public interest. In the intermediate zone, the *Penn Central* test calls for a more individualized determination of legitimate investment-backed expectations, one that is sensitive to the reasonable foreseeability of future regulation when investments are made. No doubt, over coming decades, we will see shifts in these zones along with society's understanding of the legitimate limits of regulations.

3.   As with most areas of environmental law, climate change raises novel questions relating to the takings clause, as discussed in the following excerpt.

MEG CALDWELL AND CRAIG HOLT SEGALL, NO DAY AT THE BEACH: SEA LEVEL RISE, ECOSYSTEM LOSS, AND PUBLIC ACCESS ALONG THE CALIFORNIA COAST

34 ECOLOGY L.Q. 533 (2007).[6]

The sea is rising. All along the hundreds of miles of the California coast, global warming will cause higher water, more powerful storms, and increased coastal erosion. The California Coastal Commission and its predecessor regional commissions have worked to protect the state's coastal resources since the Commission's creation by voter initiative in 1972 and formalization in the California Coastal Act of 1976. Climate change-induced sea level rise presents the Commission—and all those who use and value the state's coastal resources—with a stark new set of challenges.

As sea level rises, pressure to armor the coast will grow. The bluffs and cliffs of the California coast may appear stable, but they are, in many places, riven with faults, joints, and fractures, and are often composed of unstable rock. Battering winter storms and high tides have and will continue to cause bluff collapse and the loss of structures built upon bluffs. Property owners, if allowed to do so, will attempt to forestall the inevitable with seawalls, rock revetments, and other barriers to the sea. But these walls, though temporarily freezing the coast in place, will have significant social and ecological costs. Beaches below the walls may be eroded away, or the thin ribbon of sand remaining will be blocked from the public by massive shoreline protection structures. Where estuarine marshes, which provide significant nursery habitat for many marine species, are threatened by sea level rise, coastal armoring will prevent marsh migration, leading to the eventual loss of ecosystem function. All along the

---

[6]   Copyright 2007 by the Regents of the University of California. Reprinted by permission.

coast, the dire effects of climate change may be amplified by the effects of shoreline armoring. * * *

How would rolling easements work in practice in California? Consider the scenario of a housing development slated to be built just above the beach. Below the low terrace where the housing is planned is a small strip of beach. As the sea rises and El Niño storms hammer the beach, the shoreline begins to erode towards the uplands. Without a rolling easement in place, the property owners would likely seek to erect some form of armoring, such as a seawall, revetment, or gunnite application to a bluff or cliff—perhaps covering the remaining beach with rock and concrete and certainly preventing the natural migration and survival of the beach. Similar scenarios apply to structures built slightly inland on marshlands and estuaries; there, storm waves will not often threaten but gradual sea level rise will cause the salt marsh to gradually migrate towards the buildings. If the buildings sit behind a bulkhead, the marsh will ultimately be unable to migrate and will drown beneath the rising waters. In the alternate case, where the state holds a rolling easement, the property owners do not own the right to prevent the shore from moving. Instead, they may use their property as normal until the sea reaches it. At this critical point, they must either move their structures or cede them to the ocean or advancing marshlands. Erosion will likely occur relatively slowly, over several decades. Thus this eventual end date will likely not appreciably reduce property values. It will, however, ensure that the coast will remain public and healthy at the reasonable cost of discouraging unwise overdevelopment of areas vulnerable to near-term erosion.

This general easement model does not rely upon any particular legal device: rather, it describes the ecological effects of allowing the shore to move rather than impeding that movement with an armoring device. The appropriate legal device to reach this ecological and social goal will vary, as discussed above, based upon the age of the structure in question and the potential ecological and social costs associated with allowing versus preventing armoring. Below, we discuss the array of tools that the Commission and the state can rely upon to allow the shoreline to migrate when appropriate. These tools are underlain by the central concept of the public trust doctrine, which both motivates and requires the state to protect its coastal resources that are under attack from the combined effect of sea level rise and development that impedes the natural and expected shore migration process. * * *

Could California impose a blanket rolling easement along its coastline without running into takings prohibitions and without being stymied by political opposition? The answer is probably yes, as a constitutional matter, but with serious practical caveats. Few judges, if any, will initially be comfortable with allowing structures built under one understanding of the law to yield to the sea, even if the public trust doctrine would appear to require this result. Because takings lawsuits are most likely if political processes break down, implementing easements in a savvy way is vital. Developing a mixed strategy, including the purchase of rolling easements from existing landowners in appropriate circumstances, will reduce political pressure and is the more equitable course. The cost of rolling easements for existing structures in sensitive areas has the potential to be relatively low if they are implemented within the context of a larger policy. As part of a general strategy * * * to deflect development away from highly sensitive areas, the imposition of rolling easements in undeveloped areas and requirements to mitigate permitted armoring can provide the lynch pin for sea level rise management.

James G. Titus of the EPA provides valuable analysis of the takings problems at issue.[166] Under the Supreme Court's decision in *Lucas v. South Carolina Coastal Council*, a taking will occur if a regulation "denies all economically beneficial or productive use of land." Even then, regulations that actualize title restrictions arising from "background principles of the State's law of property and nuisance" do not effect a taking. Under both prongs of analysis, rolling easements—even if imposed by the state without compensation—would probably not be a taking. As Titus argues, the common law of erosion and the public trust jointly act to "diminish the rights of coastal lowland owners, compared with the rights of noncoastal dryland owners." The public trust doctrine is a background principle of the common law and so would obviate a *Lucas* taking as applied in this case. The easement, simply put, has always been there: it is not an imposition on the property owner but part of the nature of his or her property.* * *

But even if a case did not involve this background principle, a state's direct imposition of a rolling easement would likely not cause the total loss of economically beneficial uses of land required for a *Lucas* taking. This is because rolling easements impose a future loss that will not occur for decades. Discounted for present value, a rolling easement will not significantly diminish property values. The change in value would be truly minimal for undeveloped land and would likely still be minor for most developed land, except those properties in almost immediate danger of loss.

NOTES

1. Under the "background principles" approach, would the constitutionality of rolling easements depend on the specific state's previous case law regarding coastal property rights? Could Congress create a uniform federal rule?

2. In *Stop the Beach Renourishment, Inc. v. Florida Department of Environmental Protection*, 130 S.Ct. 2592 (2010), the Court granted cert. to

---

[166] [James G. Titus, *Rising Seas, Coastal Erosion, and the Takings Clause: How to Save Wetlands and Beaches Without Hurting Property Owners*, 57 MD. L. REV. 1279, 1313 (1998).]

consider when, if ever, an action by a court (rather than a legislature) could be considered a taking. The Florida Supreme Court had rejected shoreline property owners' takings challenge to a state law authorizing the state to nourish beachfront areas with sand, and to assert public ownership of the created land area. A majority of the Supreme Court agreed that there could be no constitutional violation because, even *before* the Florida Supreme Court's decision, the owners had not had a property right to be free from beach renourishment. In a portion of his opinion joined only by a plurality, Justice Scalia advocated adoption of a theory of judicial takings. Justices Kennedy and Sotomayor argued in a partial concurrence that that "a judicial decision that eliminates or substantially changes established property rights" would violate due process, but not the takings clause. Justices Breyer and Ginsburg rejected both theories, while Justice Stevens did not participate in the case. For discussion of the various opinions, see Michael C. Blumm and Elizabeth B. Dawson, *The Florida Beach Case and the Road to Judicial Takings*, 35 ENV. L. & POL'Y REV. 713 (2011).

CHAPTER 5

JUDICIAL REVIEW AND ADMINISTRATIVE PROCESS

■ ■ ■

A. UNDERSTANDING THE ADMINISTRATIVE STATE

Because environmental statutes are generally implemented by administrative agencies, environmental regulation is inseparable from administrative law. The central focus of administrative law is ensuring that agencies act within the bounds of their legal mandates. The questions that arise in administrative law include: Is it constitutional for Congress to delegate this power to the agency? Does the statute authorize the agency to do what it did? Did the agency follow the appropriate procedures? Does the agency's decision—its actual policy choice—have enough factual support? One might approach nearly every environmental case with these questions in mind.

With the exception of private disputes over the costs of hazardous waste clean-ups, nearly all environmental litigation takes the form of challenges by a regulated firm, industry associations, environmental groups, or states, arguing that a federal agency has erred in executing the power delegated to it by Congress. To understand how such challenges work, and to grasp the importance of them to the development of environmental law, it is helpful to be familiar with the institutional context in which environmental law and policy are produced.

When Congress passes statutes, it typically enunciates general goals and then delegates much of the task of implementing those goals to administrative agencies. Congress could not possibly make every detailed decision regarding the implementation of every regulatory statute—for instance, determining the appropriate pollution control technologies for scores of industries. Managing such detailed decision-making would consume considerable time and resources, and members of Congress have other priorities to attend to (including policy-making tasks and constituency casework, but also including fundraising in order to pursue re-election). Institutional competence is another justification for delegating the details of implementation to an administrative agency. These agencies are staffed with experts, whereas Congress is full of generalist lawmakers, who are often relatively untrained and inexperienced in more than one or two regulatory areas. An agency like the EPA, which was specifically created for the purpose of administering environmental statutes and is staffed by trained scientists, economists and lawyers, is best situated to translate legislative policy choices into operational rules.

Though agencies are technically empowered merely to "implement" legislative policy, nearly everyone would agree that agencies to some are actively engaged in policymaking. Agency rules, once promulgated, have the force of law. Many agencies are authorized to issue administrative enforcement orders and to assess significant monetary penalties against violators of statutory or regulatory requirements, which are enforceable in civil court. Agencies also make policy through the resolution of specific matters in formal, trial-like adjudications presided over by administrative law judges (ALJs). (While these judges are not Article III judges with lifetime tenure, they share many of the same powers, including the authority to issue binding orders.) Agencies also have other, less formal methods to affect the behavior of private actors. Agencies may, for instance, issue interpretations of their own regulations through guidance documents, opinion letters and the like, which in practice guide the conduct of regulated entities. In other words, agency action has real consequences for the regulated community.

Reviewing courts are not the only institution playing an oversight role over agencies. Federal agencies must answer to congressional committees (in both the House and Senate) charged with overseeing their fidelity to legislative mandates. These committees can make life miserable for agency staff by, for example, ordering audits by the Government Accountability Office, requiring staff to appear at hearings on Capitol Hill, and cutting agency funding through the appropriations process. In addition to judicial and congressional oversight, the President also oversees the performance of environmental agencies. The heads of the key environmental agencies, such as the Administrator of EPA and the Secretary of the Interior, are appointed by the President and serve at the President's will.

Although courts are thus only part of the dynamic institutional setting in which environmental law is made, they nevertheless play a crucial role in overseeing the implementation of environmental statutes. Yet, in order to enlist courts in overseeing agency decisions, litigants must first satisfy the test for gaining access to judicial review, known as "standing." Meeting this test is crucial for environmental litigants who seek access to courts to vindicate what are sometimes non-economic and indirect interests in environmental values shared by many people. The cases below trace the history of standing law, and illustrate how it has expanded and contracted over time.

B. STANDING

In suits challenging actions by government agencies, often the first issue raised is whether the plaintiff has the right to file the suit at all. Those who wish to represent the public interest must prove they have standing. Standing doctrine stems in part from the constitutional requirement in Article III that federal courts hear only "cases or controversies," and in part from prudential principles developed by courts to restrict access to judicial review.

1. INJURY-IN-FACT

Traditionally, private suits against government were limited to vindicating "legal rights," meaning that the litigant had to allege injury to a "legally protected interest" granted by statute or the common law. Although the Sierra Club lost the case below, this landmark case represents a step toward more liberal standing law. The Court makes clear that non-economic environmental injuries, when properly pleaded, can satisfy the injury-in-fact test.

SIERRA CLUB v. MORTON

Supreme Court of the United States, 1972.
405 U.S. 727, 92 S.Ct. 1361, 31 L.Ed.2d 636.

[The Forest Service approved a plan by Walt Disney Enterprises, Inc., to build a $35 million resort in the Mineral King Valley, "an area of great natural beauty nestled in the Sierra Nevada Mountains." Construction of the huge resort-complex was opposed by the Sierra Club on the ground that the Forest Service had violated several federal statutes. The Sierra Club filed suit to enjoin approval of the Disney plan. It sued as a membership corporation with "a special interest in the conservation and the sound maintenance of the national parks, game refuges and forests of the country." As the Court noted, there was "no allegation in the complaint that members of the Sierra Club would be affected by the actions of [the respondents] other than the fact that the actions are personally displeasing or distasteful to them." The lower court had concluded: "We do not believe such club concern without a showing of more direct interest can constitute standing in the legal sense sufficient to challenge the exercise of responsibilities on behalf of all the citizens by two cabinet level officials of the government acting under congressional and constitutional authority."]

JUSTICE STEWART delivered the opinion of the Court.

The first question presented is whether the Sierra Club has alleged facts that entitle it to obtain judicial review of the challenged action. Whether a party has a sufficient stake in an otherwise justiciable controversy to obtain judicial resolution of that controversy is what has traditionally been referred to as the question of standing to sue. Where the party does not rely on any specific statute authorizing invocation of the judicial process, the question of standing depends upon whether the party has alleged such a "personal stake in the outcome of the controversy," as to ensure that "the dispute sought to be adjudicated will be presented in an adversary context and in a form historically viewed as capable of judicial resolution." Where, however, Congress has authorized public officials to perform certain functions according to law, and has provided by statute for judicial review of those actions under certain circumstances, the inquiry as to standing must begin with a determination of whether the statute in question authorizes review at the behest of the plaintiff.[3]

The Sierra Club relies upon § 10 of the Administrative Procedure Act (APA) which provides:

> A person suffering legal wrong because of agency action, or adversely affected or aggrieved by agency action within the meaning of a relevant statute, is entitled to judicial review thereof.

Early decisions under this statute interpreted the language as adopting the various formulations of "legal interest" and "legal wrong" then prevailing as constitutional requirements of standing. But, in *Association of Data Processing Service Organizations, Inc. v. Camp,* 397 U.S. 150, 90 S.Ct. 827, 25 L.Ed.2d 184, and *Barlow v. Collins,* 397 U.S. 159, 90 S.Ct. 832, 25 L.Ed.2d 192, decided the same day, we held more broadly that persons had standing to obtain judicial review of federal agency action under § 10 of the APA where they had alleged that the challenged action had caused them "injury in fact," and where the alleged injury was to an interest "arguably within the zone of interests to be protected or regulated" by the statutes that the agencies were claimed to have violated.[5]

In *Data Processing,* the injury claimed by the petitioners consisted of harm to their competitive position in the computer-servicing market through a ruling by the Comptroller of the Currency that national banks might perform data-processing services for their customers. In *Barlow,* the petitioners were tenant farmers who claimed that certain regulations of the Secretary of Agriculture adversely affected their economic position vis-a-vis their landlords. These palpable economic injuries have long been recognized as sufficient to lay the basis for standing, with or without a specific statutory provision for judicial review. Thus, neither *Data*

---

[3]   Congress may not confer jurisdiction on Art. III federal courts to render advisory opinions, or to entertain "friendly" suits, because suits of this character are inconsistent with the judicial function under Art. III. But where a dispute is otherwise justiciable, the question whether the litigant is a "proper party to request an adjudication of a particular issue," is one within the power of Congress to determine.

[5]   In deciding this case we do not reach any questions concerning the meaning of the "zone of interests" test or its possible application to the facts here presented.

Processing nor *Barlow* addressed itself to the question, which has arisen with increasing frequency in federal courts in recent years, as to what must be alleged by persons who claim injury of a noneconomic nature to interests that are widely shared. That question is presented in this case.

The injury alleged by the Sierra Club will be incurred entirely by reason of the change in the uses to which Mineral King will be put, and the attendant change in the aesthetics and ecology of the area. Thus, in referring to the road to be built through Sequoia National Park, the complaint alleged that the development "would destroy or otherwise adversely affect the scenery, natural and historic objects and wildlife of the park and would impair the enjoyment of the park for future generations." We do not question that this type of harm may amount to an "injury in fact" sufficient to lay the basis for standing under § 10 of the APA. Aesthetic and environmental well-being, like economic well-being, are important ingredients of the quality of life in our society, and the fact that particular environmental interests are shared by the many rather than the few does not make them less deserving of legal protection through the judicial process. But the "injury in fact" test requires more than an injury to a cognizable interest. It requires that the party seeking review be himself among the injured.

The impact of the proposed changes in the environment of Mineral King will not fall indiscriminately upon every citizen. The alleged injury will be felt directly only by those who use Mineral King and Sequoia National Park, and for whom the aesthetic and recreational values of the area will be lessened by the highway and ski resort. The Sierra Club failed to allege that it or its members would be affected in any of their activities or pastimes by the Disney development. Nowhere in the pleadings or affidavits did the Club state that its members use Mineral King for any purpose, much less that they use it in any way that would be significantly affected by the proposed actions of the respondents.[8]

The Club apparently regarded any allegations of individualized injury as superfluous, on the theory that this was a "public" action involving questions as to the use of natural resources, and that the Club's longstanding concern with and expertise in such matters were sufficient to give it standing as a "representative of the public." This theory reflects a misunderstanding of our cases involving so-called "public actions" in the area of administrative law. * * *

---

[8]   * * * In an amici curiae brief filed in this Court by the Wilderness Society and others, it is asserted that the Sierra Club has conducted regular camping trips into the Mineral King area, and that various members of the Club have used and continue to use the area for recreational purposes. These allegations were not contained in the pleadings, nor were they brought to the attention of the Court of Appeals. Moreover, the Sierra Club in its reply brief specifically declines to rely on its individualized interest, as a basis for standing. * * * Our decision does not, of course, bar the Sierra Club from seeking in the District Court to amend its complaint by a motion under Rule 15, Federal Rules of Civil Procedure.

The trend of cases arising under the APA and other statutes authorizing judicial review of federal agency action has been toward recognizing that injuries other than economic harm are sufficient to bring a person within the meaning of the statutory language, and toward discarding the notion that an injury that is widely shared is *ipso facto* not an injury sufficient to provide the basis for judicial review. We noted this development with approval in *Data Processing,* in saying that the interest alleged to have been injured "may reflect 'aesthetic, conversational, and recreational' as well as economic values." But broadening the categories of injury that may be alleged in support of standing is a different matter from abandoning the requirement that the party seeking review must himself have suffered an injury.

Some courts have indicated a willingness to take this latter step by conferring standing upon organizations that have demonstrated "an organizational interest in the problem" of environmental or consumer protection. It is clear that an organization whose members are injured may represent those members in a proceeding for judicial review. But a mere "interest in a problem," no matter how longstanding the interest and no matter how qualified the organization is in evaluating the problem, is not sufficient by itself to render the organization "adversely affected" or "aggrieved" within the meaning of the APA. The Sierra Club is a large and long-established organization, with a historic commitment to the cause of protecting our Nation's natural heritage from man's depredations. But if a "special interest" in this subject were enough to entitle the Sierra Club to commence this litigation, there would appear to be no objective basis upon which to disallow a suit by any other bona fide "special interest" organization however small or short-lived. And if any group with a bona fide "special interest" could initiate such litigation, it is difficult to perceive why any individual citizen with the same bona fide special interest would not also be entitled to do so.

The requirement that a party seeking review must allege facts showing that he is himself adversely affected does not insulate executive action from judicial review, nor does it prevent any public interests from being protected through the judicial process.[15] It does serve as at least a rough attempt to put the decision as to whether review will be sought in the hands of those who have a direct stake in the outcome. That goal would

---

[15]   In its reply brief, after noting the fact that it might have chosen to assert individualized injury to itself or to its members as a basis for standing, the Sierra Club states:

> The Government seeks to create a 'heads I win, tails you lose' situation in which either the courthouse door is barred for lack of assertion of a private, unique injury or a preliminary injunction is denied on the ground that the litigant has advanced private injury which does not warrant an injunction adverse to a competing public interest. Counsel have shaped their case to avoid this trap.

The short answer to this contention is that the "trap" does not exist. The test of injury in fact goes only to the question of standing to obtain judicial review. Once this standing is established, the party may assert the interests of the general public in support of his claims for equitable relief.

be undermined were we to construe the APA to authorize judicial review at the behest of organizations or individuals who seek to do no more than vindicate their own value preferences through the judicial process. The principle that the Sierra Club would have us establish in this case would do just that.

JUSTICE DOUGLAS, dissenting.

The critical question of "standing" would be simplified and also put neatly in focus if we fashioned a federal rule that allowed environmental issues to be litigated before federal agencies or federal courts in the name of the inanimate object about to be despoiled, defaced, or invaded by roads and bulldozers and where injury is the subject of public outrage. Contemporary public concern for protecting nature's ecological equilibrium should lead to the conferral of standing upon environmental objects to sue for their own preservation. *See* [Christopher D.] Stone, *Should Trees Have Standing? Toward Legal Rights for Natural Objects*, 45 S. CAL. L. REV. 450 (1972). This suit would therefore be more properly labeled as *Mineral King v. Morton.*

Inanimate objects are sometimes parties in litigation. A ship has a legal personality, a fiction found useful for maritime purposes. The corporation sole—a creature of ecclesiastical law—is an acceptable adversary and large fortunes ride on its cases. The ordinary corporation is a "person" for purposes of the adjudicatory processes, whether it represents proprietary, spiritual, aesthetic, or charitable causes.

So it should be as respects valleys, alpine meadows, rivers, lakes, estuaries, beaches, ridges, groves of trees, swampland, or even air that feels the destructive pressures of modern technology and modern life. The river, for example, is the living symbol of all the life it sustains or nourishes— fish, aquatic insects, water ouzels, otter, fisher, deer, elk, bear, and all other animals, including man, who are dependent on it or who enjoy it for its sight, its sound, or its life. The river as plaintiff speaks for the ecological unit of life that is part of it. Those people who have a meaningful relation to that body of water—whether it be a fisherman, a canoeist, a zoologist, or a logger—must be able to speak for the values which the river represents and which are threatened with destruction. * * *

Mineral King is doubtless like other wonders of the Sierra Nevada such as Tuolumne Meadows and the John Muir Trail. Those who hike it, fish it, hunt it, camp in it, frequent it, or visit it merely to sit in solitude and wonderment are legitimate spokesmen for it, whether they may be a few or many. Those who have that intimate relation with the inanimate object about to be injured, polluted, or otherwise despoiled are its legitimate spokesmen.

JUSTICE BLACKMUN, dissenting.

* * * I would permit an imaginative expansion of our traditional concepts of standing in order to enable an organization such as the Sierra Club, possessed, as it is, of pertinent, bona fide, and well-recognized attributes and purposes in the area of the environment, to litigate environmental issues. This incursion upon tradition need not be very extensive. Certainly, it should be no cause for alarm. It is no more progressive than was the decision in *Data Processing* itself. It need only recognize the interest of one who has a provable, sincere, dedicated, and established status. We need not fear that Pandora's box will be opened or that there will be no limit to the number of those who desire to participate in environmental litigation. The courts will exercise appropriate restraints just as they have exercised them in the past. Who would have suspected 20 years ago that the concepts of standing enunciated in *Data Processing* and *Barlow* would be the measure for today?

NOTES

1.   The trend toward liberalizing standing law was a key component in what Professor Richard Stewart has called the "interest representation" theory of administrative law, in which agencies are seen not as detached from politics, but as sites of interest group conflict. *See* Richard B. Stewart, *The Reformation of American Administrative Law,* 88 HARV. L. REV. 1669 (1975). According to this theory, courts ensure that agencies are accountable by requiring them to conduct a "surrogate political process," made possible by broad participation rights for interest groups and liberal access to judicial review. *Id.* at 1760–62.

2.   *United States v. Student Challenging Regulatory Agency Procedures (SCRAP)*, 412 U.S. 669 (1973), gave a liberal interpretation of the test for standing. The plaintiffs were law students challenging an increase the rates charged by railroads for transporting recycled materials. (At the time, railroad rates were regulated by a federal agency called the Interstate Commerce Commission, which no longer exists.) Their theory of standing was that higher rates would discourage recycling, resulting in more trash in local parks. The Court upheld their standing, rejecting the argument that the injury was too tenuous:

> The Government urges us to limit standing to those who have been "significantly" affected by agency action. But, even if we could begin to define what such a test would mean, we think it fundamentally misconceived. "Injury in fact" reflects the statutory requirement that a person be "adversely affected" or "aggrieved," and it serves to distinguish a person with a direct stake in the outcome of a litigation—even though small—from a person with a mere interest in the problem. We have allowed important interests to be vindicated by plaintiffs with no more at stake in the outcome of an action than a fraction of a vote, a $5 fine and costs, and a $1.50 poll tax.

       * * * While these cases were not dealing specifically with § 10 of the APA, we see no reason to adopt a more restrictive interpretation of "adversely affected" or "aggrieved." As Professor Davis has put it: "The basic idea that comes out in numerous cases is that an identifiable trifle is enough for standing to fight out a question of principle; the trifle is the basis for standing and the principle supplies the motivation." Kenneth C. Davis, *Standing: Taxpayers and Others*, 35 U. CHI. L. REV. 601, 613 (1968).

The Supreme Court, however, later referred to *SCRAP* as "[p]robably the most attenuated injury" conferring standing, and added that the *SCRAP* decision "surely went to the very outer limit of the law." *Whitmore v. Arkansas*, 495 U.S. 149, 159 (1990).

       3.   Beginning in 1970 with the Clean Air Act, Congress included citizen suit provisions in most of the major environmental statutes in order to allow ordinary citizens to bring suits to enforce these laws. *See, e.g.*, § 304 of the Clean Air Act, § 505 of the Clean Water Act, § 18 of the Toxic Substances Control Act (TSCA), § 7002 of the Resource Conservation and Recovery Act (RCRA), § 326 of the Emergency Planning and Community Right-To-Know Act, § 11(g) of the Endangered Species Act, and § 310 of CERCLA. An exception is the Federal Insecticide, Fungicide, and Rodenticide Act (FIFRA), which does not authorize citizen suits.

       Citizen suits have made it much easier for environmental organizations to play a key role in enforcing the nation's environmental laws. In the 1980s, when there was significant decline in federal enforcement of the environmental laws under the Reagan administration, more citizen suits were brought (especially by several national environmental organizations) to fill the void. These focused particularly on enforcement of the Clean Water Act because it was easy for plaintiffs to prove violations. Point-source dischargers were required to file discharge-monitoring reports, which were available to the public and could serve as prima facie evidence of noncompliance with permits. In addition, remedies available in Clean Water Act suits included not only injunctions against further violations but also the assessment of civil penalties payable to the government.

       However, citizen suit provisions still required the plaintiffs to demonstrate standing. In the 1990s, the Supreme Court began to restrict standing law considerably. The case below represents the Court's move toward a narrower interpretation of what is necessary to demonstrate injury in fact.

LUJAN V. DEFENDERS OF WILDLIFE

Supreme Court of the United States, 1992.
504 U.S. 555, 112 S.Ct. 2130, 119 L.Ed.2d 351.

JUSTICE SCALIA delivered the opinion of the Court with respect to Parts I, II, III-A, and IV, and an opinion with respect to Part III-B in which THE CHIEF JUSTICE, JUSTICE WHITE, and JUSTICE THOMAS join.

[As discussed in Chapter 3, the Endangered Species Act seeks to protect plant and animal species against human threats to their continuing existence. Endangered or threatened species are identified by a list compiled by the Secretary of the Interior. Section 7(a)(2) of the Act provides that each federal agency must, in consultation with the Secretary of Interior, ensure that "any action authorized, funded, or carried out by such agency * * * is not likely to jeopardize the continued existence of any endangered species or threatened species or result in the destruction or adverse modification of the habitat of such species." By regulation, the Secretary determined that § 7 applies only to species and habitats within the United States or the High Seas. USAID was not obligated to consult with the Secretary of Interior over whether the proposed overseas projects it was funding, would be likely to jeopardize listed species. The statute authorizes "citizen suits" to challenge violations of the Act. The plaintiffs obtained an injunction requiring the Secretary to promulgate a revised regulation applying § 7 extraterritorially.]

II

While the Constitution of the United States divides all power conferred upon the Federal Government into "legislative Powers," Art. I, § 1, "[t]he executive Power," Art. II, § 1, and "[t]he judicial Power," Art. III, § 1, it does not attempt to define those terms. To be sure, it limits the jurisdiction of federal courts to "Cases" and "Controversies," but an executive inquiry can bear the name "case" (the Hoffa case) and a legislative dispute can bear the name "controversy" (the Smoot-Hawley controversy). Obviously, then, the Constitution's central mechanism of separation of powers depends largely upon common understanding of what activities are appropriate to legislatures, to executives, and to courts. In The Federalist No. 48, Madison expressed the view that "[i]t is not infrequently a question of real nicety in legislative bodies whether the operation of a particular measure will, or will not, extend beyond the legislative sphere," whereas "the executive power [is] restrained within a narrower compass and * * * more simple in its nature," and "the judiciary [is] described by landmarks still less uncertain." One of those landmarks, setting apart the "Cases" and "Controversies" that are of the justiciable sort referred to in Article III "serv[ing] to identify those disputes which are appropriately resolved through the judicial process"—is the doctrine of standing. Though some of its elements express merely prudential considerations that are part of judicial self-government, the core component of standing is an essential and unchanging part of the case-or-controversy requirement of Article III.

Over the years, our cases have established that the irreducible constitutional minimum of standing contains three elements: First, the plaintiff must have suffered an "injury in fact"—an invasion of a legally-protected interest which is (a) concrete and particularized, and (b) "actual or imminent, not 'conjectural' or 'hypothetical.'" Second, there must be a causal connection between the injury and the conduct complained of—the injury has to be "fairly * * * trace[able] to the challenged action of the defendant, and not * * * th[e] result [of] the independent action of some third party not before the court." Third, it must be "likely," as opposed to merely "speculative," that the injury will be "redressed by a favorable decision."

III

We think the Court of Appeals failed to apply the foregoing principles in denying the Secretary's motion for summary judgment. Respondents had not made the requisite demonstration of (at least) injury and redressability.

A

Respondents' claim to injury is that the lack of consultation with respect to certain funded activities abroad "increase[s] the rate of extinction of endangered and threatened species." * * * To survive the Secretary's summary judgment motion, respondents had to submit affidavits or other evidence showing, through specific facts, not only that listed species were in fact being threatened by funded activities abroad, but also that one or more of respondents' members would thereby be "directly" affected apart from their "'special interest' in th[e] subject."

[The affidavits] alleged that two members, Kelly and Skilbred, had visited two project areas in the past and intended to return in the future to observe endangered species.

[The affidavits] plainly contain no facts * * * showing how damage to the species will produce "imminent" injury to Mss. Kelly and Skilbred. That the women "had visited" the areas of the projects before the projects commenced proves nothing. As we have said in a related context, "[p]ast exposure to illegal conduct does not in itself show a present case or controversy regarding injunctive relief * * * if unaccompanied by any continuing, present adverse effects." And the affiants' profession of an "inten[t]" to return to the places they had visited before—where they will presumably, this time, be deprived of the opportunity to observe animals of the endangered species—is simply not enough. * * *

Besides relying upon the Kelly and Skilbred affidavits, respondents propose a series of novel standing theories. The first, inelegantly styled "ecosystem nexus," proposes that any person who uses *any part* of a "contiguous ecosystem" adversely affected by a funded activity has standing even if the activity is located a great distance away. [But] a plaintiff claiming injury from environmental damage must use the area affected by the challenged activity and not an area roughly "in the vicinity" of it. It makes no difference that the general-purpose section of the ESA states that the Act was intended in part "to provide a means whereby the ecosystems upon which endangered species and threatened species depend may be conserved." To say that the Act protects ecosystems is not to say that the Act creates (if it were possible) rights of action in persons who have not been injured in fact, that is, persons who use portions of an ecosystem not perceptibly affected by the unlawful action in question.

Respondents' other theories are called, alas, the "animal nexus" approach, whereby anyone who has an interest in studying or seeing the endangered animals anywhere on the globe has standing; and the "vocational nexus" approach, under which anyone with a professional interest in such animals can sue. Under these theories, anyone who goes to see Asian elephants in the Bronx Zoo, and anyone who is a keeper of Asian elephants in the Bronx Zoo, has standing to sue because the Director of AID did not consult with the Secretary regarding the AID-funded project in Sri Lanka. This is beyond all reason. Standing is not "an ingenious academic exercise in the conceivable," but as we have said, requires, at the summary judgment stage, a factual showing of perceptible harm. It is clear that the person who observes or works with a particular animal threatened by a federal decision is facing perceptible harm, since the very subject of his interest will no longer exist. It is even plausible—though it goes to the outermost limit of plausibility—to think that a person who observes or works with animals of a particular species in the very area of the world where that species is threatened by a federal decision is facing such harm, since some animals that might have been the subject of his interest will no longer exist. It goes beyond the limit, however, and into pure speculation and fantasy, to say that anyone who observes or works with an endangered species, anywhere in the world, is appreciably harmed by a single project affecting some portion of that species with which he has no more specific connection. * * *

IV

The Court of Appeals found that respondents had standing for an additional reason: because they had suffered a "procedural injury." The so-called "citizen-suit" provision of the ESA provides, in pertinent part, that "any person may commence a civil suit on his own behalf (A) to enjoin any person, including the United States and any other governmental instrumentality or agency * * * who is alleged to be in violation of any provision of this chapter." The court held that, because § 7(a)(2) requires interagency consultation, the citizen-suit provision creates a "procedural righ[t]" to consultation in all "persons"—so that *anyone* can file suit in federal court to challenge the Secretary's (or presumably any other official's) failure to follow the assertedly correct consultative procedure, notwithstanding their inability to allege any discrete injury flowing from that failure. To understand the remarkable nature of this holding one must be clear about what it does *not* rest upon: This is not a case where plaintiffs are seeking to enforce a procedural requirement the disregard of which could impair a separate concrete interest of theirs (*e.g.,* the procedural requirement for a hearing prior to denial of their license application, or the procedural requirement for an environmental impact statement before a federal facility is constructed next door to them). Nor is it simply a case where concrete injury has been suffered by many persons, as in mass fraud or mass tort situations. Nor, finally, is it the unusual case in which Congress has created a concrete private interest in the outcome of a suit against a private party for the government's benefit, by providing a cash bounty for the victorious plaintiff. Rather, the court held that the injury-in-fact requirement had been satisfied by congressional conferral upon *all* persons of an abstract, self-contained, noninstrumental "right" to have the Executive observe the procedures required by law. We reject this view.

* * * To permit Congress to convert the undifferentiated public interest in executive officers' compliance with the law into an "individual right" vindicable in the courts is to permit Congress to transfer from the President to the courts the Chief Executive's most important constitutional duty, to "take Care that the Laws be faithfully executed," Art. II, § 3. It would enable the courts, with the permission of Congress, "to assume a position of authority over the governmental acts of another and co-equal department," and to become " 'virtually continuing monitors of the wisdom and soundness of Executive action.' " We have always rejected that vision of our role. * * *

JUSTICE BLACKMUN, with whom JUSTICE O'CONNOR joins, dissenting.

I part company with the Court in this case in two respects. First, I believe that respondents have raised genuine issues of fact—sufficient to survive summary judgment—both as to injury and as to redressability. Second, I question the Court's breadth of language in rejecting standing for "procedural" injuries. I fear the Court seeks to impose fresh limitations on the constitutional authority of Congress to allow citizen suits in the federal courts for injuries deemed "procedural" in nature. I dissent. * * *

I think a reasonable finder of fact could conclude from the information in the affidavits and deposition testimony that either Kelly or Skilbred will soon return to the project sites, thereby satisfying the "actual or imminent" injury standard. The Court dismisses Kelly's and Skilbred's general statements that they intended to revisit the project sites as "simply not enough." But those statements did not stand alone. A reasonable finder of fact could conclude, based not only upon their statements of intent to return, but upon their past visits to the project sites, as well as their professional backgrounds, that it was likely that Kelly and Skilbred would make a return trip to the project areas. Contrary to the Court's contention that Kelly's and Skilbred's past visits "prove nothing," the fact of their past visits could demonstrate to a reasonable factfinder that Kelly and Skilbred have the requisite resources and personal interest in the preservation of the species endangered by the Aswan and Mahaweli projects to make good on their intention to return again. * * * Similarly, Kelly's and Skilbred's professional backgrounds in wildlife preservation, also make it likely—at least far more likely than for the average citizen—that they would choose to visit these areas of the world where species are vanishing.

By requiring a "description of concrete plans" or "specification of *when* the some day [for a return visit] will be," the Court, in my view, demands what is likely an empty formality. No substantial barriers prevent Kelly or Skilbred from simply purchasing plane tickets to return to the Aswan and Mahaweli projects. This case differs from other cases in which the imminence of harm turned largely on the affirmative actions of third parties beyond a plaintiff's control. * * *

I fear the Court's demand for detailed descriptions of future conduct will do little to weed out those who are genuinely harmed from those who are not. More likely, it will resurrect a code-pleading formalism in federal court summary judgment practice, as federal courts, newly doubting their jurisdiction, will demand more and more particularized showings of future harm. * * *

* * * The Court expresses concern that allowing judicial enforcement of "agencies' observance of a particular, statutorily prescribed procedure" would "transfer from the President to the courts the Chief Executive's most important constitutional duty, to 'take Care that the Laws be faithfully executed,' Art. II, § 3." In fact, the principal effect of foreclosing judicial enforcement of such procedures is to transfer power into the hands of the Executive at the expense—not of the courts—but of Congress, from which that power originates and emanates. * * *

* * * The Court never has questioned Congress' authority to impose such procedural constraints on Executive power. Just as Congress does not violate separation of powers by structuring the procedural manner in which the Executive shall carry out the laws, surely the federal courts do not violate separation of powers when, at the very instruction and command of Congress, they enforce these procedures.

NOTES

1.   Can plaintiffs satisfy the majority in *Defenders* with careful drafting of the affidavits? *See* James McElfish, *Drafting Standing Affidavits After*

Defenders: In the Court's Own Words, 23 ENV. L. REP. 10026 (1993). What would the affidavits have had to say in *Defenders* in order to satisfy the Court's requirements?

2.   Environmental organizations frequently use member plaintiffs strategically to file lawsuits, without carefully developing evidence about how those plaintiffs actually use the resource in question. Stricter standards for alleging injury may have a salutary effect on the ability of environmental organizations to convince the court that the agency action complained of causes real harm to real people. *See* Ann E. Carlson, *Standing for the Environment*, 45 UCLA L. REV. 931 (1998). For an illustration of why plaintiffs must take care in establishing standing, *see Sierra Club v. EPA*, 292 F.3d 895, 902 (D.C. Cir. 2002), where a Sierra Club complaint disputing an EPA waste management regulation was dismissed when the Sierra Club failed to establish injury adequately, with the Court particularly (and disapprovingly) noting that the only member affidavit attesting to actual contamination from a particular plant was recycled from another, unrelated case, and had to do with an entirely different contaminant.

3.   Satisfying the "fairly traceable" requirement may be more difficult when the causation is behavioral rather than physical. In *Florida Audubon Society v. Bentsen*, 94 F.3d 658 (D.C. Cir. 1996) (en banc), the plaintiffs claimed that an environmental impact statement was required on the effects of a tax credit for a fuel additive. The plaintiffs alleged that the tax credit would increase corn and sugar production, resulting in increased agricultural cultivation and accompanying environmental harms in regions that border wildlife areas used by the plaintiffs. The court found this line of reasoning far too speculative. You may find it helpful to analogize to the proximate cause requirement in torts when trying to apply the "fairly traceable" test. See Luke Meier, *Using Tort Law to Understand the Causation Prong of Standing*, 80 FORDHAM L. REV. 1241 (2011). It is worth noting that, when the plaintiff challenges the procedure used to reach a decision (such as failure to prepare an environmental impact statement), rather than the substance of the decision, the "traceability" requirement is relaxed. The plaintiff needs only to show that the procedural error was connected to the agency's decision and that agency's decision would cause an injury to the plaintiff. See *Powder River Basin Resource Council v. Jewell*, 738 298 (D.C. Cir. 2013).

4.   In *Defenders*, a plurality would also have denied standing because the plaintiff's injury was not redressable. The issue of redressability arose more centrally in *Steel Co. v. Citizens for a Better Environment*, 523 U.S. 83 (1998), in which an environmental group sued a steel manufacturer under the Emergency Planning and Community Right-to-Know Act (EPCRA) for failing to file timely reports about toxic chemicals. By the time the suit was filed, however, the company had brought all of its reports up to date. The complaint requested a declaratory judgment, authorization to inspect the company's facilities and records, copies of the company's future compliance reports, civil penalties to be paid to the government, reimbursement of litigation costs and attorneys' fees, and a blanket plea for any other appropriate relief. The Court

denied standing because none of the requested remedies would redress the plaintiff's injury. Writing for the majority, Justice Scalia emphasized that civil penalties authorized by the statute were payable to the U.S. Treasury, not to the plaintiff: "[A]lthough a suitor may derive great comfort and joy from the fact that the United States Treasury is not cheated, that a wrongdoer gets his just deserts, or that the nation's laws are faithfully enforced, that psychic satisfaction is not an acceptable Article III remedy because it does not redress a cognizable Article III injury."

In *Steel Co.,* the Supreme Court denied standing for civil penalties to assess wholly past violations (noncompliance that has abated by the time of the suit). However, in the case excerpted below, the Court held that civil penalties for *ongoing* violations provide sufficient deterrence to support redressability. Of course, what constitutes an ongoing violation may not always be clear. For instance, in *Upstate Forever v. Kinder Morgan Energy Partners,* 887 F. 3d 637 (4th Cir. 2017), the plaintiffs sued about a discharge caused by a rupture pipe that had already been repaired; the court found an ongoing violation because leaked chemicals continued to flow through groundwater into a nearby stream. The following case also sheds light on when a continuing violation can be found and the extent to which the possibility of further violations affects the court's Article III jurisdiction.

FRIENDS OF THE EARTH, INC. v. LAIDLAW ENVIRONMENTAL SERVICES (TOC), INC.

Supreme Court of the United States, 2000.
528 U.S. 167, 120 S.Ct. 693, 145 L.Ed.2d 610.

[The plaintiffs sued defendant Laidlaw for repeatedly exceeding the effluent limits set by its National Pollutant Discharge Elimination System (NPDES) permit, granted under the Clean Water Act (CWA), for a wastewater treatment plant at its hazardous waste incinerator near Roebuck, South Carolina. Laidlaw had repeatedly dumped excessive levels of mercury into the Tyger River in violation of the permit. The District Court held that Friends of the Earth (FOE) had standing, noting that Laidlaw had continued to violate its permit after FOE filed suit. The Court assessed $405,800 in civil penalties against the company, but denied injunctive relief because Laidlaw had since come into "substantial compliance" with its permit requirements. On appeal, the Fourth Circuit assumed that FOE had standing, but held that the case had become moot under the *Steel Co.* decision, and that civil penalties payable to the government, the only remedy available, would not redress any injury plaintiff had suffered.]

JUSTICE GINSBURG delivered the opinion of the Court.

Laidlaw contends first that FOE lacked standing from the outset even to seek injunctive relief, because the plaintiff organizations failed to show that any of their members had sustained or faced the threat of any "injury in fact" from Laidlaw's activities. In support of this contention Laidlaw points to the District Court's finding, made in the course of setting the penalty amount, that there had been "no demonstrated proof of harm to the environment" from Laidlaw's mercury discharge violations.

The relevant showing for purposes of Article III standing, however, is not injury to the environment but injury to the plaintiff. To insist upon the former rather than the latter as part of the standing inquiry (as the dissent in essence does) is to raise the standing hurdle higher than the necessary showing for success on the merits in an action alleging noncompliance with an NPDES permit. Focusing properly on injury to the plaintiff, the District Court found that FOE had demonstrated sufficient injury to establish standing. * * *

[I]t is undisputed that Laidlaw's unlawful conduct—discharging pollutants in excess of permit limits—was occurring at the time the complaint was filed. * * * [T]he only "subjective" issue here is "[t]he reasonableness of [the] fear" that led the affiants to respond to that concededly ongoing conduct by refraining from use of the North Tyger River and surrounding areas. Unlike the dissent, we see nothing "improbable" about the proposition that a company's continuous and pervasive illegal discharges of pollutants into a river would cause nearby residents to curtail their recreational use of that waterway and would subject them to other economic and aesthetic harms. The proposition is entirely reasonable, the District Court found it was true in this case, and that is enough for injury in fact.

Laidlaw argues next that even if FOE had standing to seek injunctive relief, it lacked standing to seek civil penalties. Here the asserted defect is not injury but redressability. Civil penalties offer no redress to private plaintiffs, Laidlaw argues, because they are paid to the government, and therefore a citizen plaintiff can never have standing to seek them.

Laidlaw is right to insist that a plaintiff must demonstrate standing separately for each form of relief sought. But it is wrong to maintain that citizen plaintiffs facing ongoing violations never have standing to seek civil penalties.

We have recognized on numerous occasions that "all civil penalties have some deterrent effect." More specifically, Congress has found that civil penalties in Clean Water Act cases do more than promote immediate compliance by limiting the defendant's economic incentive to delay its attainment of permit limits; they also deter future violations. This congressional determination warrants judicial attention and respect. "The legislative history of the Act reveals that Congress wanted the district court to consider the need for retribution and deterrence, in addition to restitution, when it imposed civil penalties. . . . [The district court may] seek to deter future violations by basing the penalty on its economic impact."

It can scarcely be doubted that, for a plaintiff who is injured or faces the threat of future injury due to illegal conduct ongoing at the time of suit, a sanction that effectively abates that conduct and prevents its recurrence provides a form of redress. Civil penalties can fit that description. To the extent that they encourage defendants to discontinue current violations and deter them from committing future ones, they afford redress to citizen plaintiffs who are injured or threatened with injury as a consequence of ongoing unlawful conduct. * * *

We recognize that there may be a point at which the deterrent effect of a claim for civil penalties becomes so insubstantial or so remote that it cannot support citizen standing. The fact that this vanishing point is not easy to ascertain does not detract from the deterrent power of such penalties in the ordinary case. * * *

Laidlaw contends that the reasoning of our decision in *Steel Co.* directs the conclusion that citizen plaintiffs have no standing to seek civil penalties under the Act. We disagree. *Steel Co.* established that citizen suitors lack standing to seek civil penalties for violations that have abated by the time of suit. We specifically noted in that case that there was no allegation in the complaint of any continuing or imminent violation, and that no basis for such an allegation appeared to exist. In short, *Steel Co.* held that private plaintiffs, unlike the Federal Government, may not sue to assess penalties for wholly past violations, but our decision in that case did not reach the issue of standing to seek penalties for violations that are ongoing at the time of the complaint and that could continue into the future if undeterred. * * *

[The Court also found that the case was not moot, because the defendant had not shown it was "absolutely clear" that the wrongful behavior would not re-occur.]

JUSTICE SCALIA, with whom JUSTICE THOMAS joins, dissenting.

By accepting plaintiffs' vague, contradictory, and unsubstantiated allegations of "concern" about the environment as adequate to prove injury in fact, and accepting them even in the face of a finding that the environment was not demonstrably harmed, the Court makes the injury-in-fact requirement a sham. If there are permit violations, and a member of a plaintiff environmental organization lives near the offending plant, it would be difficult not to satisfy today's lenient standard.

* * * [B]y giving an individual plaintiff the power to invoke a public remedy, Congress has done precisely what we have said it cannot do: convert an "undifferentiated public interest" into an "individual right" vindicable in the courts. * * * A claim of particularized future injury has

today been made the vehicle for pursuing generalized penalties for past violations, and a threshold showing of injury-in-fact has become a lever that will move the world.

By permitting citizens to pursue civil penalties payable to the Federal Treasury, the Act does not provide a mechanism for individual relief in any traditional sense, but turns over to private citizens the function of enforcing the law. A Clean Water Act plaintiff pursuing civil penalties acts as a self-appointed mini-EPA. Where, as is often the case, the plaintiff is a national association, it has significant discretion in choosing enforcement targets. Once the association is aware of a reported violation, it need not look long for an injured member, at least under the theory of injury the Court applies today. And once the target is chosen, the suit goes forward without meaningful public control. The availability of civil penalties vastly disproportionate to the individual injury gives citizen plaintiffs massive bargaining power—which is often used to achieve settlements requiring the defendant to support environmental projects of the plaintiffs' choosing. Thus is a public fine diverted to a private interest. * * *

NOTES

1.   Does the dissent have a point that empowering private parties to enforce public laws is risky? Might self-appointed private attorneys general, with their own agendas, derail the enforcement agenda of public agencies? Some of the separate opinions in *Laidlaw* raise the constitutional question whether citizen suits intrude upon the President's authority under Article II to "take care that the laws be faithfully executed." *See* 528 U.S. at 197 (Kennedy, J., concurring); *id.* at 209 (Scalia, J., dissenting). A related issue is whether plaintiffs are performing an executive function and are therefore governed by the Appointments Clause. Or are citizen suits necessary and desirable because public agencies often fall short?

Does it affect your view that in *Laidlaw*, in order to preclude the citizen suit, the company arranged to have itself sued by the state environmental agency? Here is what happened: The CWA bars citizen suits if the EPA or a state agency has already commenced and is "diligently prosecuting" an enforcement action. Laidlaw's attorney drafted the state's complaint and paid its filing fee. Laidlaw then settled with the state agency for $100,000 in civil penalties and a promise to make "every effort" to comply in the future. It then continued to violate the effluent limits in its permit, and FOE sued. In finding that FOE had standing, the District Court held that the state enforcement action had not been "diligently prosecuted."

2.   In finding standing, the Court in *Laidlaw* relied on affidavits filed by members of the plaintiff organization. For instance, one member said he lived a half-mile from the river and would like to use it (and its surroundings) for recreational purposes, as he had when he was younger. But when he occasionally drove across a bridge over the river, it looked and smelled

polluted, and as a result he did not make use of the river "because of his concerns about Laidlaw's discharges." Other affidavits were similar.

In his dissent, Justice Scalia was incredulous that these allegations would suffice as a basis for standing, particularly given the absence of careful consideration of the injury issue by the lower courts. Justice Scalia's view was not unreasonable, given the relevant precedents (including several he himself had written). But the Court carefully distinguished prior cases on their facts.

MASSACHUSETTS V. EPA

Supreme Court of the United States, 2007.
549 U.S. 497, 127 S.Ct. 1438, 167 L.Ed.2d 248.

[States, local governments, and environmental organizations petitioned for review of EPA's denial of their petition, which had asked EPA to begin a rulemaking to regulate greenhouse gas emissions from motor vehicles under § 202(a)(1) of the Clean Air Act. A divided panel of the D.C. Circuit ruled in favor of the EPA, in part on the basis of questions about the petitioners' standing.]

JUSTICE STEVENS delivered the opinion of the Court.

A well-documented rise in global temperatures has coincided with a significant increase in the concentration of carbon dioxide in the atmosphere. Respected scientists believe the two trends are related. For when carbon dioxide is released into the atmosphere, it acts like the ceiling of a greenhouse, trapping solar energy and retarding the escape of reflected heat. It is therefore a species—the most important species—of a "greenhouse gas."

Calling global warming "the most pressing environmental challenge of our time," a group of States, local governments, and private organizations, alleged in a petition for certiorari that the Environmental Protection Agency (EPA) has abdicated its responsibility under the Clean Air Act to regulate the emissions of four greenhouse gases, including carbon dioxide. Specifically, petitioners asked us to answer two questions concerning the meaning of § 202(a)(1) of the Act: whether EPA has the statutory authority to regulate greenhouse gas emissions from new motor vehicles; and if so, whether its stated reasons for refusing to do so are consistent with the statute. * * *

Article III of the Constitution limits federal-court jurisdiction to "Cases" and "Controversies." Those two words confine "the business of federal courts to questions presented in an adversary context and in a form historically viewed as capable of resolution through the judicial process." It is therefore familiar learning that no justiciable "controversy" exists when parties seek adjudication of a political question, when they ask for an advisory opinion, or when the question sought to be adjudicated has been mooted by subsequent developments. This case suffers from none of these defects.

The parties' dispute turns on the proper construction of a congressional statute, a question eminently suitable to resolution in federal court. Congress has moreover authorized this type of challenge to EPA action. That authorization is of critical importance to the standing inquiry: "Congress has the power to define injuries and articulate chains of causation that will give rise to a case or controversy where none existed before." "In exercising this power, however, Congress must at the very least identify the injury it seeks to vindicate and relate the injury to the class of persons entitled to bring suit." We will not, therefore, "entertain citizen suits to vindicate the public's nonconcrete interest in the proper administration of the laws." * * *

To ensure the proper adversarial presentation, *Lujan* holds that a litigant must demonstrate that it has suffered a concrete and particularized injury that is either actual or imminent, that the injury is fairly traceable to the defendant, and that it is likely that a favorable decision will redress that injury. However, a litigant to whom Congress has "accorded a procedural right to protect his concrete interests,"—here, the right to challenge agency action unlawfully withheld—"can assert that right without meeting all the normal standards for redressability and immediacy." When a litigant is vested with a procedural right, that litigant has standing if there is some possibility that the requested relief will prompt the injury-causing party to reconsider the decision that allegedly harmed the litigant.

Only one of the petitioners needs to have standing to permit us to consider the petition for review. We stress here, as did Judge Tatel below, the special position and interest of Massachusetts. It is of considerable relevance that the party seeking review here is a sovereign State and not, as it was in *Lujan,* a private individual. * * *

When a State enters the Union, it surrenders certain sovereign prerogatives. Massachusetts cannot invade Rhode Island to force reductions in greenhouse gas emissions, it cannot negotiate an emissions treaty with China or India, and in some circumstances the exercise of its police powers to reduce in-state motor-vehicle emissions might well be preempted.

These sovereign prerogatives are now lodged in the Federal Government, and Congress has ordered EPA to protect Massachusetts (among others) by prescribing standards applicable to the "emission of any air pollutant from any class or classes of new motor vehicle engines, which in [the Administrator's] judgment cause, or contribute to, air pollution which may reasonably be anticipated to endanger public health or welfare." Congress has moreover recognized a concomitant procedural right to challenge the rejection of its rulemaking petition as arbitrary and capricious. Given that procedural right and Massachusetts' stake in protecting its quasi-sovereign interests, the Commonwealth is entitled to special solicitude in our standing analysis.

With that in mind, it is clear that petitioners' submissions as they pertain to Massachusetts have satisfied the most demanding standards of the adversarial process. EPA's steadfast refusal to regulate greenhouse gas emissions presents a risk of harm to Massachusetts that is both "actual" and "imminent." There is, moreover, a "substantial likelihood that the judicial relief requested" will prompt EPA to take steps to reduce that risk.

THE INJURY

The harms associated with climate change are serious and well recognized. Indeed, the NRC Report itself—which EPA regards as an "objective and independent assessment of the relevant science,"—identifies a number of environmental changes that have already inflicted significant harms, including "the global retreat of mountain glaciers, reduction in snow-cover extent, the earlier spring melting of rivers and lakes, [and] the accelerated rate of rise of sea levels during the 20th century relative to the past few thousand years. . . ."

Petitioners allege that this only hints at the environmental damage yet to come. According to the [declaration filed by] climate scientist Michael MacCracken, "qualified scientific experts involved in climate change research" have reached a "strong consensus" that global warming threatens (among other things) a precipitate rise in sea levels by the end of the century, "severe and irreversible changes to natural ecosystems," a "significant reduction in water storage in winter snowpack in mountainous regions with direct and important economic consequences," and an increase in the spread of disease. He also observes that rising ocean temperatures may contribute to the ferocity of hurricanes.

That these climate-change risks are "widely shared" does not minimize Massachusetts' interest in the outcome of this litigation. According to petitioners' unchallenged affidavits, global sea levels rose somewhere between 10 and 20 centimeters over the 20th century as a result of global warming. These rising seas have already begun to swallow Massachusetts' coastal land. Because the Commonwealth "owns a substantial portion of the state's coastal property," it has alleged a particularized injury in its capacity as a landowner. The severity of that injury will only increase over the course of the next century: If sea levels continue to rise as predicted, one Massachusetts official believes that a significant fraction of coastal property will be "either permanently lost through inundation or temporarily lost through periodic storm surge and flooding events." Remediation costs alone, petitioners allege, could run well into the hundreds of millions of dollars.

CAUSATION

EPA does not dispute the existence of a causal connection between man-made greenhouse gas emissions and global warming. At a minimum, therefore, EPA's refusal to regulate such emissions "contributes" to Massachusetts' injuries.

EPA nevertheless maintains that its decision not to regulate greenhouse gas emissions from new motor vehicles contributes so insignificantly to petitioners' injuries that the agency cannot be haled into federal court to answer for them. For the same reason, EPA does not believe that any realistic possibility exists that the relief petitioners seek would mitigate global climate change and remedy their injuries. That is especially so because predicted increases in greenhouse gas emissions from developing nations, particularly China and India, are likely to offset any marginal domestic decrease.

But EPA overstates its case. Its argument rests on the erroneous assumption that a small incremental step, because it is incremental, can never be attacked in a federal judicial forum. Yet accepting that premise would doom most challenges to regulatory action. Agencies, like legislatures, do not generally resolve massive problems in one fell regulatory swoop. They instead whittle away at them over time, refining their preferred approach as circumstances change and as they develop a more-nuanced understanding of how best to proceed. That a first step might be tentative does not by itself support the notion that federal courts lack jurisdiction to determine whether that step conforms to law.

And reducing domestic automobile emissions is hardly a tentative step. Even leaving aside the other greenhouse gases, the United States transportation sector emits an enormous quantity of carbon dioxide into the atmosphere—according to the MacCracken affidavit, more than 1.7 billion metric tons in 1999 alone. That accounts for more than 6% of worldwide carbon dioxide emissions. To put this in perspective: Considering just emissions from the transportation sector, which represent less than one-third of this country's total carbon dioxide emissions, the United States would still rank as the third-largest emitter of carbon dioxide in the world, outpaced only by the European Union and China. Judged by any standard, U.S. motor-vehicle emissions make a meaningful contribution to greenhouse gas concentrations and hence, according to petitioners, to global warming.

THE REMEDY

While it may be true that regulating motor-vehicle emissions will not by itself *reverse* global warming, it by no means follows that we lack jurisdiction to decide whether EPA has a duty to take steps to *slow* or *reduce* it. Because of the enormity of the potential consequences associated with man-made climate change, the fact that the effectiveness of a remedy might be delayed during the (relatively short) time it takes for a new motor-vehicle fleet to replace an older one is essentially irrelevant. Nor is it dispositive that developing countries such as China and India are poised to increase greenhouse gas emissions substantially over the next century: A reduction in domestic emissions would slow the pace of global emissions increases, no matter what happens elsewhere.

We moreover attach considerable significance to EPA's "agree[ment] with the President that 'we must address the issue of global climate change,'" and to EPA's ardent support for various voluntary emission-reduction programs. As Judge Tatel observed in dissent below, "EPA would presumably not bother with such efforts if it thought emissions reductions would have no discernable impact on future global warming."

In sum—at least according to petitioners' uncontested affidavits—the rise in sea levels associated with global warming has already harmed and will continue to harm Massachusetts. The risk of catastrophic harm, though remote, is nevertheless real. That risk would be reduced to some extent if petitioners received the relief they seek. We therefore hold that petitioners have standing to challenge the EPA's denial of their rulemaking petition. [The portion of the Court's opinion dealing with the merits is excerpted in Chapter 6.]

CHIEF JUSTICE ROBERTS, with whom JUSTICE SCALIA, JUSTICE THOMAS, and JUSTICE ALITO join, dissenting.

Before determining whether petitioners can meet [the normal test for standing] the Court changes the rules. It asserts that "States are not normal litigants for the purposes of invoking federal jurisdiction," and that given "Massachusetts' stake in protecting its quasi-sovereign interests, the Commonwealth is entitled to *special solicitude* in our standing analysis."

Relaxing Article III standing requirements because asserted injuries are pressed by a State, however, has no basis in our jurisprudence, and support for any such "special solicitude" is conspicuously absent from the Court's opinion. The general judicial review provision cited by the Court, affords States no special rights or status. * * * Under the law on which petitioners rely, Congress treated public and private litigants exactly the same.

Nor does the case law cited by the Court provide any support for the notion that Article III somehow implicitly treats public and private litigants differently. * * *

It is not at all clear how the Court's "special solicitude" for Massachusetts plays out in the standing analysis, except as an implicit concession that petitioners cannot establish standing on traditional terms. But the status of Massachusetts as a State cannot compensate for petitioners' failure to demonstrate injury in fact, causation, and redressability.

When the Court actually applies the three-part test, it focuses, as did the dissent below on the State's asserted loss of coastal land as the injury in fact. If petitioners rely on loss of land as the Article III injury, however, they must ground the rest of the standing analysis in that specific injury. * * * Without "particularized injury, there can be no confidence of 'a real need to exercise the power of judicial review' or that relief can be framed 'no broader than required by the precise facts to which the court's ruling would be applied.'"

The very concept of global warming seems inconsistent with this particularization requirement. Global warming is a phenomenon "harmful to humanity at large," and the redress petitioners seek is focused no more on them than on the public generally—it is literally to change the atmosphere around the world.

If petitioners' particularized injury is loss of coastal land, it is also that injury that must be "actual or imminent, not conjectural or hypothetical," "real and immediate," and "certainly impending."

As to "actual" injury, the Court observes that "global sea levels rose somewhere between 10 and 20 centimeters over the 20th century as a result of global warming" and that "[t]hese rising seas have already begun to swallow Massachusetts' coastal land." But none of petitioners' declarations supports that connection. [A]side from a single conclusory statement, there is nothing in petitioners' 43 standing declarations and accompanying exhibits to support an inference of actual loss of Massachusetts coastal land from 20th century global sea level increases. It is pure conjecture.

The Court's attempts to identify "imminent" or "certainly impending" loss of Massachusetts coastal land fares no better. One of petitioners' declarants predicts global warming will cause sea level to rise by 20 to 70 centimeters *by the year 2100*. [A]ccepting a century-long time horizon and a series of compounded estimates renders requirements of imminence and immediacy utterly toothless. * * *

Petitioners view the relationship between their injuries and EPA's failure to promulgate new motor vehicle greenhouse gas emission standards as simple and direct: Domestic motor vehicles emit carbon dioxide and other greenhouse gases. Worldwide emissions of greenhouse gases contribute to global warming and therefore also to petitioners' alleged injuries. Without the new vehicle standards, greenhouse gas emissions—and therefore global warming and its attendant harms—have been higher than they otherwise would have been; once EPA changes course, the trend will be reversed.

The Court ignores the complexities of global warming, and does so by now disregarding the "particularized" injury it relied on in step one, and using the dire nature of global warming itself as a bootstrap for finding causation and redressability. First, it is important to recognize the extent of the emissions at issue here. Because local greenhouse gas emissions disperse throughout the atmosphere and remain there for anywhere from 50 to 200 years, it is global emissions data that are relevant. According to one of petitioners' declarations, domestic motor vehicles contribute about 6 percent of global carbon dioxide emissions and 4 percent of global greenhouse gas emissions. The amount of global emissions at issue here is smaller still; [the applicable section] of the Clean Air Act covers only *new* motor vehicles and *new* motor vehicle engines, so petitioners' desired emission standards might reduce only a fraction of 4 percent of global emissions.

This gets us only to the relevant greenhouse gas emissions; linking them to global warming and ultimately to petitioners' alleged injuries next requires consideration of further complexities. As EPA explained in its denial of petitioners' request for rulemaking, "predicting future climate change necessarily involves a complex web of economic and physical factors * * *." Petitioners are never able to trace their alleged injuries back through this complex web to the fractional amount of global emissions that might have been limited with EPA standards. In light of the bit-part domestic new motor vehicle greenhouse gas emissions have played in what petitioners describe as a 150-year global phenomenon, and the myriad additional factors bearing on petitioners' alleged injury—the loss of Massachusetts coastal land—the connection is far too speculative to establish causation.

Redressability is even more problematic. To the tenuous link between petitioners' alleged injury and the indeterminate fractional domestic emissions at issue here, add the fact that petitioners cannot meaningfully predict what will come of the 80 percent of global greenhouse gas emissions that originate outside the United States. * * *

When dealing with legal doctrine phrased in terms of what is "fairly" traceable or "likely" to be redressed, it is perhaps not surprising that the matter is subject to some debate. But in considering how loosely or rigorously to define those adverbs, it is vital to keep in mind the purpose of the inquiry. The limitation of the judicial power to cases and controversies "is crucial in maintaining the tripartite allocation of power set forth in the Constitution." In my view, the Court today—addressing Article III's "core component of standing," * * * fails to take this limitation seriously.

NOTES

1.   State government litigation on environmental issues has become commonplace. See, e.g., *Delaware Dept. v. Natural Resources v. EPA*, 785 F.3d 1 (2015) (state challenges EPA industry emission standards that would increase air pollution in the state); *Indiana v. EPA*, 796 F.3d 803 (7th Cir. 2015) (state challenges EPA approval of a neighboring state's State Implementation Plan). Justice Stevens makes much of the sovereign status of the state and its implication for the state's claim of standing. The result may be to empower the states to challenge federal actions that would otherwise be immune from suit by private parties. Is this a healthy reinforcement of the states' role in the federalist system, or is it an invitation to litigate questions that are essentially political disagreements rather than live controversies? Putting that question aside, to what extent was the state's sovereign status determinative of the outcome?

2.   The Roberts dissent has some general language that seems unfavorable to claims of standing based on injuries caused by climate change. For instance, Roberts says that the "very concept of global warming" seems inconsistent with the particularization requirement in Article III because global warming is a phenomenon "harmful to humanity at large." On the other hand, he also criticizes the showing of standing made by these particular plaintiffs, such as what he views as insufficient evidence by the State of Massachusetts of impacts on its coastline. The latter problems, at least, might be avoided in future cases by more detailed evidence, particularly as climate science advances.

How would you respond to the Chief Justice's general concerns about the imminence and certainty of climate harm? Should standing law require such imminence or reflect a more precautionary approach? See Jonathan Remy Nash, *Standing and the Precautionary Principle*, 108 COLUM. L. REV. 494 (2008).

3.   Consider the following alternative standing argument that might have been made in *Massachusetts v. EPA*. Implementing regulation of CO_2 would almost certainly require improvements in fuel economy. By reducing the amount of gasoline burned, such restrictions would reduce the emissions of conventional pollutants from automobiles, thus assisting in the attainment of air quality standards designed to protect human health. This would be a relatively short-term, concrete impact that would have improved the health of residents in urban areas. Can you make an argument for why this would satisfy *Lujan*? (Consider *National Resources Defense Council v. EPA*, 464 F.3d 1 (D. C. Cir. 2006), holding that a lifetime risk of about one in 200,000 of developing a nonfatal skin cancer constituted injury in fact.) Assuming that this would have been a sound argument for standing, can you see why the plaintiffs might have chosen not to take this route in a marquee case? Would it make sense for plaintiffs to take a different tack in the future?

A NOTE ON CLIMATE-BASED STANDING

The Court had the opportunity to revisit the issue of standing in climate change cases in 2011. *American Elec. Power Co., Inc. v. Connecticut*, 131 S.Ct. 2527 (2011), was a public nuisance suit brought by several states, a city, and private land trusts against major carbon emitters. On the merits, the Court held that the federal common law of nuisance did not apply because it had been displaced by the regulatory scheme of the Clean Air Act. (Justice Sotomayor had participated in the lower court proceedings and therefore recused herself.) Prior to reaching the merits, the Court had to consider the issue of standing, but the treatment of the issue was somewhat cryptic:

> Four members of the Court would hold that at least some plaintiffs have Article III standing under Massachusetts, which permitted a State to challenge EPA's refusal to regulate greenhouse gas emissions, 549 U.S., at 520–526, 127 S.Ct. 1438; and, further, that no other threshold obstacle bars review.[6] Four members of the Court, adhering to a dissenting opinion in Massachusetts, 549 U.S., at 535, 127 S.Ct. 1438, or regarding that decision as distinguishable, would hold that none of the plaintiffs have Article III standing. We therefore affirm, by an equally divided Court, the Second Circuit's exercise of jurisdiction and proceed to the merits. See Nye v. United States, 313 U.S. 33, 44, 61 S.Ct. 810, 85 L.Ed. 1172 (1941).

The accompanying footnote read:

> [6]   In addition to renewing the political question argument made below, the petitioners now assert an additional threshold obstacle: They seek dismissal because of a "prudential" bar to the adjudication of generalized grievances, purportedly distinct from Article III's bar." [footnote by the Court]

It seems possible that at least one of the dissenters in *Massachusetts v. EPA* wanted to distinguish the case rather than overrule it. But this is necessarily speculative given the scant information provided by the Court's opinion.

Climate standing has continued to receive attention since *AEP*. In *Washington Environmental Council v. Bellon*, 732 F.3d 1131 (9th Cir. 2013), the plaintiffs contended that state agencies had failed to impose greenhouse gas restrictions on five oil refineries, which the plaintiffs claimed were required by the Clean Air Act. The court held that the plaintiffs lacked standing because the emissions in question were only five percent of the state's emissions. The court concluded that the refineries' contribution to climate failed to satisfy the "fairly traceable" causation requirement to the plaintiff's injuries from climate change. It distinguished *Massachusetts v. EPA* because the case before it did not involve the "special solicitude) owed to a sovereign state and did not involve a procedural right. In addition, unlike nationwide regulations of vehicle emissions, these five refineries did not make a meaningful contribution to global greenhouse gases. Three judges argued that the panel decision was too restrictive in its interpretation of *Massachusetts v. EPA*. See 741 F.3d at 1079–81 (Gould, J, dissenting); 741 F.3d at 1076–79 (Smith, J., concurring). For discussion of this and later climate-standing litigation, see Bradford C. Mank, *Article III Standing for Private Plaintiffs Challenging Greenhouse Gas Regulations*, 53 SAN DIEGO L. REV. 287 (2016).

It is easiest to establish standing when a government action involves a specific location, so it is possible to identify individuals who make continuing use of that area. But as the next case illustrates, plaintiffs can encounter difficulties when the locations uncertain.

SUMMERS V. EARTH ISLAND INSTITUTE

Supreme Court of the United States, 2009.
555 U.S. 488, 129 S.Ct. 1142, 173 L.Ed.2d 1.

[After the U.S. Forest Service approved the Burnt Ridge Project, a salvage sale of timber on 238 acres of fire-damaged federal land, several environmentalist organizations filed suit to enjoin the Service from applying its regulations exempting such small sales from the notice, comment, and appeal process it uses for more significant land management decisions. The District Court granted a preliminary injunction against the sale, and the parties then settled their dispute as to Burnt Ridge. Nevertheless, the Ninth Circuit held that the dispute about the regulations was still alive because the regulations applied to many other sites. It then held the regulations unlawful.]

JUSTICE SCALIA delivered the opinion of the Court.

The regulations under challenge here neither require nor forbid any action on the part of respondents. The standards and procedures that they prescribe for Forest Service appeals govern only the conduct of Forest Service officials engaged in project planning. "[W]hen the plaintiff is not himself the object of the government action or inaction he challenges, standing is not precluded, but it is ordinarily 'substantially more difficult' to establish." *Defenders of Wildlife*. Here, respondents can demonstrate standing only if application of the regulations by the Government will affect *them* in the manner described above. * * *

Respondents have identified no other application of the invalidated regulations that threatens imminent and concrete harm to the interests of their members. The only other affidavit relied on was that of Jim Bensman. He asserted, first, that he had suffered injury in the past from development on Forest Service land. That does not suffice for several reasons: because it was not tied to application of the challenged regulations, because it does not identify any particular site, and because it relates to past injury rather than imminent future injury that is sought to be enjoined.

Bensman's affidavit further asserts that he has visited many National Forests and plans to visit several unnamed National Forests in the future. Respondents describe this as a mere failure to "provide the name of each timber sale that affected [Bensman's] interests." It is much more (or much less) than that. It is a failure to allege that *any* particular timber sale or other project claimed to be unlawfully subject to the regulations will impede a specific and concrete plan of Bensman's to enjoy the National Forests. The National Forests occupy more than 190 million acres, an area larger than Texas. There may be a chance, but is hardly a likelihood, that Bensman's wanderings will bring him to a parcel about to be affected by a project unlawfully subject to the regulations. Indeed, without further specification it is impossible to tell *which* projects are (in respondents' view) unlawfully subject to the regulations. * * * Here we are asked to assume not only that Bensman will stumble across a project tract unlawfully subject to the regulations, but also that the tract is about to be developed by the Forest Service in a way that harms his recreational interests, and that he would have commented on the project but for the regulation. Accepting an intention to visit the National Forests as adequate to confer standing to challenge any Government action affecting any portion of those forests would be tantamount to eliminating the requirement of concrete, particularized injury in fact. * * *

The dissent proposes a hitherto unheard-of test for organizational standing: whether, accepting the organization's self-description of the activities of its members, there is a statistical probability that some of those members are threatened with concrete injury. Since, for example, the Sierra Club asserts in its pleadings that it has more than " '700,000 members nationwide, including thousands of members in California' " who " 'use and enjoy the Sequoia National Forest,' it is probable (according to the dissent) that some (unidentified) members have planned to visit some (unidentified) small parcels affected by the Forest Service's procedures and will suffer (unidentified) concrete harm as a result. This novel approach to the law of organizational standing would make a mockery of our prior cases, which have required plaintiff-organizations to make specific allegations establishing that at least one identified member had suffered or would suffer harm. * * *

JUSTICE KENNEDY, concurring.

I join in full the opinion of the Court. As the opinion explains, "deprivation of a procedural right without some concrete interest that is affected by the deprivation—a procedural right *in vacuo*—is insufficient to create Article III standing." The procedural injury must "impair a separate concrete interest."

This case would present different considerations if Congress had sought to provide redress for a concrete injury "giv[ing] rise to a case or controversy where none existed before." Nothing in the statute at issue here, however, indicates Congress intended to identify or confer some interest separate and apart from a procedural right.

JUSTICE BREYER, with whom JUSTICE STEVENS, JUSTICE SOUTER, and JUSTICE GINSBURG join, dissenting.

The Court holds that the Sierra Club and its members (along with other environmental organizations) do not suffer any "concrete injury" when the Forest Service sells timber for logging on "many thousands" of small (250-acre or less) woodland parcels without following legally required procedures—procedures which, if followed, could lead the Service to cancel or to modify the sales. Nothing in the record or the law justifies this counterintuitive conclusion. * * *

How can the majority credibly claim that salvage-timber sales, and similar projects, are unlikely to harm the asserted interests of the members of these environmental groups? The majority apparently does so in part by arguing that the Forest Service actions are not "imminent"—a requirement more appropriately considered in the context of ripeness or the necessity of injunctive relief. I concede that the Court has sometimes used the word "imminent" in the context of constitutional standing. But it has done so primarily to emphasize that the harm in question—the harm that was not "imminent"—was merely "conjectural" or "hypothetical" or otherwise speculative. Where the Court has directly focused upon the matter, *i.e.*, where, as here, a plaintiff has *already* been subject to the injury it wishes to challenge, the Court has asked whether there is a *realistic likelihood* that the challenged future conduct will, in fact, recur and harm the plaintiff. * * *

The Bensman affidavit does not say *which particular* sites will be affected by future Forest Service projects, but the Service itself has conceded that it will conduct thousands of exempted projects in the future. Why is more specificity needed to show a "realistic" threat that a project will impact land Bensman uses? To know, virtually for certain, that snow will fall in New England this winter is not to know the name of each particular town where it is bound to arrive. The law of standing does not require the latter kind of specificity. How could it?

NOTES

1. The key to environmental standing seems to be proof that a particular person would be at a particular affected place. The debate between the majority and the dissent is largely about how specific this allegation needs to be. But why is physical presence so critical to the existence of a "live dispute"? Given that the real disputes in these cases are between organizations and agencies rather than the individuals who end up being selected as plaintiffs, should it really matter whether the organization can come up with a detailed allegation about continued physical use of a particular location by a specific member?

2.   Justice Kennedy seemed to agree that a procedural injury is not enough by itself to create standing but he contended that Congress can specifically identify nonconventional types of injury. Environmental economists speak about "option values" associated with natural areas—the price that people might be willing to pay in the future to visit a place even though they have no specific plans to do so. Such option values are frequently used in cost-benefit analysis of projects or regulations. Under Kennedy's approach, could Congress specifically designate loss of option value as a cognizable injury? Would that create standing under Kennedy's approach?

3.   *Summers* also reiterates that injury must be imminent. A non-environmental case, *Clapper v. Amnesty International USA*, 133 S.Ct. 1138 (2013), substituted the phrase "certainly impending," which had been used but not emphasized in some earlier decisions. It remains to be seen whether this marks a significant shift in doctrine. Footnote 5 of the *Clapper* opinion concedes that "our cases do not uniformly require plaintiffs to demonstrate that it is literally certain that the harms they identify will come about," and "[i]n some instances, we have found standing based on a 'substantial risk' that the harm will occur, which may prompt plaintiffs to reasonably incur costs to mitigate or avoid that harm." However, the Court considered the claim of injury in *Clapper* too speculative: the plaintiffs had taken precautions against electronic surveillance by the government, but could not show that such surveillance was actually taking place or that a successful challenge to the particular statute in question would actually eliminate whatever surveillance might be taking place. Elsewhere in the opinion, the Court distinguished *Laidlaw* on the basis that the *Laidlaw* plaintiffs showed that the discharges actually had taken place; the only issue was about the reasonableness of their responses.

NOTE ON THE ZONE OF INTERESTS REQUIREMENT

The so-called "zone of interests" test is also known as the statutory (as opposed to Article III) test for standing. We can imagine a plaintiff who has demonstrated injury-in-fact, when the injury is both clearly caused by the defendant's illegal conduct and redressable by the court—yet the injury might be only coincidentally related to the reasons why the conduct is illegal. For instance, suppose the suit in *Sierra Club v. Morton* had been brought by a nearby ski resort, which wanted to keep Mineral King from being developed because the new resort would reduce its business. While satisfying the requirements of the injury-in-fact test (dollars out of pocket), causation (easily proved with expert witnesses), and redressability (no new resort, no competitive injury), there still seems to be something fishy about this lawsuit. After all, the environmental statutes aren't designed to protect competitors; they're designed to protect the environment. Is such a "coincidental" connection between the plaintiff's harm and a law designed for entirely different purposes enough to create standing? The doctrinal question in such cases is whether the litigant is "arguably within the zone of interests" protected by the statute. Answering this question typically involves an inquiry into legislative intent.

In *Bennett v. Spear*, 520 U.S. 154 (1997), the Court clarified the scope of this requirement. The Bureau of Reclamation informed the Fish and Wildlife Service that the operation of the Klamath Irrigation Project might harm two endangered species of fish (Lost River and shortnose suckers). The Service issued a Biological Opinion agreeing with the concern and recommending that the Bureau maintain minimum water levels in reservoirs. The Bureau then agreed to do so. The plaintiffs were irrigation districts and ranchers who claimed that the Biological Opinion violated various provisions of the ESA and the Administrative Procedure Act. The Ninth Circuit held that they lacked standing because their economic interests did not lie within the "zone of interests" protected by the ESA. There's a certain common sense appeal to this holding, because the plaintiffs were seeking to frustrate rather than advance an effort to protect endangered species.

In an opinion by Justice Scalia, the Court held that the zone of interests test did not apply to the citizen suit provisions of the ESA, which extended standing to the constitutional limit. Some of the plaintiff's claims, however, could only be brought under the Administrative Procedure Act and therefore were subject to this requirement. The Court concluded that the requirement was satisfied because the plaintiffs were within the zone of interests of the specific provision that they invoked, which was intended to prevent overzealous action by administrators in protecting endangered species at the expense of land owners:

> Whether a plaintiff's interest is "arguably * * * protected * * * by the statute" within the meaning of the zone-of-interests test is to be determined not by reference to the overall purpose of the Act in question (here, species preservation), but by reference to the particular provision of law upon which the plaintiff relies. * * *

> In the claims that we have found not to be covered by the ESA's citizen-suit provision, petitioners allege a violation of § 7 of the ESA, which requires, inter alia, that each agency "use the best scientific and commercial data available." Petitioners contend that the available scientific and commercial data show that the continued operation of the Klamath Project will not have a detrimental impact on the endangered suckers, that the imposition of minimum lake levels is not necessary to protect the fish, and that by issuing a Biological Opinion which makes unsubstantiated findings to the contrary the defendants have acted arbitrarily and in violation of § 1536(a)(2). The obvious purpose of the requirement that each agency "use the best scientific and commercial data available" is to ensure that the ESA not be implemented haphazardly, on the basis of speculation or surmise. While this no doubt serves to advance the ESA's overall goal of species preservation, we think it readily apparent that another objective (if not indeed the primary one) is to avoid needless economic dislocation produced by agency officials zealously but unintelligently pursuing their environmental objectives. * * * Petitioners' claim that they are victims of such a

mistake is plainly within the zone of interests that the provision protects. * * *

Bennett makes it clear that the "zone-of-interests" test is not part of Article III standing. Instead, as the Court clarified in a later case, it relates to whether the plaintiff is within the class of plaintiffs whom Congress has authorized to sue. See *Lexmark Int'l v. Static Control Components, Inc.,* 572 U.S. 118, 134 S. Ct. 1377, 199 L. Ed.2d 392 (2014).

Sierra Club v. EPA, 755 F.3d 968 (D.C. Cir. 2014), illustrates the application of the zone-of-interests test. EPA had issued a rule exempting certain waste from refineries from regulation under the Resource Conservation and Recovery Act. The rule was challenged by an association of suppliers of waste disposal and recycling technology. The association had an interest in promoting tougher regulation under RCRA to create business for its members, but the court held that this interest fell outside the zone of interests protected by the statue, which related to environmental protection and public health.

Because the zone-of-interests test is statutory rather than being based on Article III, plaintiffs may be able to establish other forms of injury rather than having to prove a link between carbon emissions and climate-related injuries. In *Wildearth Guardians v. U.S. Bureau of Land Management,* 870 F.3d 1222 (10th Cir. 2017), the plaintiffs challenged the issuance of coal leases because the agencies had failed to properly consider the impact of the leases on climate change. The court held that they had standing to bring this claim because they had aesthetic and recreational harms from the leases; those harms were fairly traceable to the leases; and the remedy they sought for this procedural issue would redress their harm by potentially leading the agency to reverse itself. Thus, it was unnecessary for the plaintiffs to show that their future harm from climate change would be traceable to the leases.

NOTE ON THE COMPLEXITY OF STANDING DOCTRINE

A closing thought: The Court's struggles with standing stem from the fact that the traditional function of lawsuits—that of vindicating private rights—is less central to the modern function of judicial review of agency decisions, which operates as much to uphold the public interest as to protect private rights. This mismatch between current function and traditional model clearly creates some intellectual tensions, which Justice Scalia seeks to resolve by endorsing the traditional model and branding the current function as illegitimate. Yet, unless the traditional model is applied very restrictively indeed, overturning *Sierra Club* and related cases, it may be impossible for the Court to return judicial review to its older function. See David Driesen, *Standing for Nothing: The Paradox of Demanding Concrete Context for Formalist Adjudication,* 89 CORNELL L. REV. 808 (2004), (questioning whether standing is too focused on the issue of concreteness, when plaintiffs' injuries do not actually provide much guidance in what are often actually reviews of wide-ranging policy issues).

Retired Judge Patricia Wald of the D.C. Circuit questioned whether the increasingly baroque law of standing has become dysfunctional. In *Humane Soc. of United States v. Babbitt*, 46 F.3d 93 (D.C. Cir. 1995), for example, the court rejected an effort by the Humane Society to prevent the transfer of Lota, an Asian elephant, from the Milwaukee Zoo. The transfer allegedly violated the Endangered Species Act. The court held that no one had standing to raise the question—not zoo visitors who claimed emotional harm or who wanted to learn about endangered elephants (there were others at the zoo), not those who wanted to see Lota in a conservation setting (too imprecisely defined). And besides, the court said, the government certificate only covered the transfer to the ultimate destination (an exhibition farm) rather than the departure from the Milwaukee Zoo (though it seems unlikely that the elephant would have left the zoo without having an approved final destination). Hence, the court said, the elephant's departure from the zoo was not "fairly traceable" to the government certificate for the transfer to the farm. Judge Wald is skeptical of the usefulness of this analysis:

> The descent in Talmudic refinements about whether one must be a student of the animal in that particular environment to bring suit, and whether the disputed permit covered the transport away from the zoo as well as to the animal exhibition would strike an ordinary person as the essence of caprice. * * * [A]s practical men and women of the law, I can only tell you to consult your zoology manual for details of the specialty fields of your putative plaintiffs and have them make their appointments well ahead of time at the local zoo. "Gotcha" is still the name of the standing game.

Patricia Wald, *Environmental Postcards from the Edge: The Year That Was and the Year That Might Be*, 26 ENVTL. L. REP. 10182 (1996).

A later case illustrating some of Judge Wald's concern about the standing inquiry is *ASPCA v. Ringling Bros. & Barnum & Bailey Circus*, 317 F.3d 334 (D.C. Cir. 2003). This presented somewhat similar circumstances to the *Humane Society* case, with a former animal handler at the circus challenging Ringling's alleged mistreatment of its elephants. The court found that he had standing, although not based on his status as a former employee. The judges felt that his status as a current and future audience member with a "personal attachment" to the animals (he had established an emotional rapport with the elephants and went back to see them after his employment) was enough to satisfy injury-in-fact, since he might observe evidence of the abuse of the elephants. After a full trial, however, the same court determined that his affection for animals was weaker than he had claimed, resulting in a denial of standing. See *American Society for the Preservation of Cruelty to Animals v. Feld Entertainment*, 659 F.3d 13 (D.C. Cir. 2011). Note that this ruling was some eleven years after the first effort to bring suit against the circus's practices. And this was not the last time a court would have to wrestle with the standing issue in animal welfare cases. See *Hill v. Coggins*, 867 499 (4th Cir. 2017) (plaintiffs had standing to challenge poor conditions for bears in zoo because they would see the bears for longer periods in a proper habitat).

Is it time for the Court to rethink standing doctrine before it becomes even more complex? Standing doctrine could be greatly simplified by adopting a place-based approach to standing. Under this approach, a plaintiff would have standing to contest environmental violations involving a specific geographic area, provided that the plaintiff has an appropriate personal connection to the area. *Massachusetts v. EPA* would be an easy case under this approach, because the state would clearly have the requisite connection with its own territory, given that sea level rise and other effects of climate change threatened the state's territory. For further discussion of this approach, see Daniel A. Farber, *A Place-Based Approach to Standing*, 55 UCLA L. REV. 1505 (2008). Would this approach be too great a modification of current doctrine to be plausible? Or, on the contrary, should a more radical approach be taken, perhaps by disconnecting standing from Article III entirely?

2. CITIZEN SUITS

While citizen suits are an important litigation tool, there remains controversy over whether they promote compliance with the law or hinder the ability of government officials to find the best balance between enforcement and flexibility. The following commentary discusses both viewpoints:

MARK SEIDENFELD AND JANNA SATZ NUGENT, "THE FRIENDSHIP OF THE PEOPLE": CITIZEN PARTICIPATION IN ENVIRONMENTAL ENFORCEMENT
73 GEO. WASH. L. REV. 269, 284–88, 301–02 (2005).[1]

Citizen suits have contributed to the EPA's ultimate goal of increasing compliance in the regulated community and, in many ways, have acted as sustenance to a starving agency. Plagued with the difficult task of detection, a lack of resources, and political constraints, the EPA has, to some extent, welcomed citizen suits to alleviate the tension created by demand for enforcement that outstrips the agency's supply.* * *

Citizen suit provisions contain notice requirements that were designed to protect the government's position as primary enforcer. First, at least sixty days prior to initiating a citizen suit, a person must notify the EPA, the violator, and under some statutes, the state where the violation occurred. This built-in "grace period" gives the EPA approximately two months to analyze the complaint and to decide whether to take over enforcement. If the government can show that it is already "diligently prosecuting" the alleged violation, the citizen suit is barred, although citizen groups may then intervene in the government's suit. The EPA cannot stop a citizen suit merely by commencing an administrative enforcement proceeding, although the EPA can bar such a suit by

---

[1]   Copyright 2005. Reprinted by permission.

commencing an administrative proceeding prior to notice of the citizen suit or if a citizen group fails to file suit within 120 days of the notice. Finally, once the citizen suit has commenced, a settlement agreement or consent order may not be entered until the DOJ and EPA receive a forty-five day notice. In theory, these notification requirements keep the crown on the sovereign enforcer: the EPA's diligent prosecution bars a citizen suit, and even its failure to prosecute does not forfeit its right to block a settlement negotiated by the private parties.

But reality often diverges from theory. The balance between public and private enforcement shifted in 1982 with the emergence of national and regional environmental groups that were well-funded and staffed. Public interest groups studied Discharge Monitoring Reports, which the Clean Water Act requires regulated entities to file, and initiated a plethora of citizen suits under that Act. A year later, private enforcement exceeded federal enforcement efforts, and has been the driving force of environmental litigation ever since. In some years, private enforcement has almost equaled overall government enforcement. * * *

Today, national and regional environmental groups like the Sierra Club, NRDC, and the Atlantic States Legal Foundation are responsible for filing a substantial number of citizen suits. As plaintiffs, the groups seek settlement agreements that provide compliance orders, SEPs [supplemental environmental projects], monetary penalties, and of course, attorneys' fees. This emphasis on financial reward has drawn criticism from those who see cost calculations as a sign of insincerity. At least one observer has noted that although groups may portray themselves as ardent defenders of the environment, they generally choose to prosecute when a company reports numerous violations to the EPA, thereby decreasing discovery costs and increasing the potential for large penalties. Supporters of interest groups' reliance on economic "rewards" insist that having violators pay such rewards offsets a corporation's calculated choice to violate environmental regulations. Moreover, even if the monetary rewards are aimed at self-preservation of the interest groups' business of private enforcement, long-term funding may greatly benefit the environment.

The propensity of the group to reach a reasonable settlement with the alleged violator varies, depending on the nature of the group bringing suit. When the plaintiff is a mass membership group, it might prefer the notoriety that comes from pressing for a big penalty to the certainty of a moderate settlement. When the plaintiff is a group dominated by a central staff, however, it may be more interested in obtaining attorneys' fees and payments to third-party groups controlled by the same staff than in either making a name for itself or improving the environment. It is even possible for a national interest group to derive publicity from having prevented the continuation of an ongoing violation while reaping the direct monetary payment of costs and fees.* * *

Although legislators authorizing the citizen suit provision under the 1970 Clean Air Act believed they were merely extending an established history of private compensation and qui tam actions, controversy has surrounded the power delegated to private citizens acting under environmental citizen suit provisions. Regulated entities cringe at the prospect of dual enforcement and worry that private enforcers will interfere with established relationships and understandings. For example, one of the major impediments to the efforts of states and EPA to induce companies to implement self-audit programs is the fear on the part of the companies that some overly zealous interest group will use the information they provide to sue them. Other members of the regulatory community share "widespread skepticism about both the motivations of private enforcers and their legitimacy as surrogates for government." Critics fear that private enforcers will replace the government's "leniency error," its failure to pursue actions that would produce public benefits, with the "zealousness error," which is created when pursuit of individual benefits imposes public costs. Even the federal courts have expressed concern that enforcement of the law is the proper province of the executive branch and not the citizenry generally.

But citizen suits are not necessarily maniacal exercises of power. Indeed, one of the benefits produced by citizen suits, namely, increased competition for enforcement, has far surpassed the effects originally envisioned. At the federal level, "the growth of private enforcement is acting as a competitive spur to government enforcers, prodding them to improve their management tools for measuring, securing, and overseeing compliance." Additionally, competition from private enforcers may have been the impetus for the EPA's innovative settlements and its reconciliation of policies and practices.

Citizen suits can also reinforce democratic values in our system of environmental regulation. Giving citizens a voice at the enforcement stage of the regulatory process can play an important role in keeping regulators publicly accountable. Although the Administrative Procedure Act affords citizens the opportunity to affect the content of regulation, the actual impact of regulation on the behavior of polluters depends on how those regulations are applied. An agency could alter the meaning of a regulation simply by construing it in a manner contrary to the understanding of the citizens who may have been involved in and even supported its promulgation, and "many interpretive issues arise only at the enforcement stage of a statute's implementation." Without the private right to file suit, agencies could simply elide the interpretive issue by refusing to attempt to enforce the regulation in a context that would raise the issue.

NOTES ON CITIZEN SUITS

1. A few studies have looked beyond the theoretical arguments for and against citizen suits to examine the on-the-ground reality of how citizen suits are used. In 1984, the Environmental Protection Agency commissioned the Environmental Law Institute to analyze the use of citizen suits under the Clean Air Act, Clean Water Act, Resource Conservation and Recovery Act, Toxic Substances Control Act, Safe Drinking Water Act, and Noise Control Act. ENVIRONMENTAL LAW INSTITUTE, CITIZEN SUITS: AN ANALYSIS OF CITIZEN ENFORCEMENT ACTIONS UNDER EPA-ADMINISTERED STATUTES (1984). This report presented a picture of early citizen suits as brought primarily under the Clean Water Act, often by large regional or national environmental organizations such as the Conservation Law Foundation of New England, the Sierra Club, and the Natural Resources Defense Council, and against large private defendants (in contrast to suits against public entities to force them to perform mandated statutory duties). Citizen suits were also being employed more often than either the EPA or the ELI had predicted, and the report hypothesized that this was due to perceived laxity of government enforcement efforts. It also recognized that the prevalence of CWA suits was due to the unique availability of reliable information about pollution discharges under that statute's reporting requirements. *See generally id.*

2. A later study examined citizen suits from 1995 to 2000, using Freedom of Information Act requests to gather information from the Department of Justice. Kristi M. Smith, *Who's Suing Whom?: A Comparison of Government and Citizen Suit Environmental Enforcement Actions Brought Under EPA-Administered Statutes, 1995–2000*, 29 COLUM. J. ENVTL. L. 359 (2004). This review found a significant change in the use of citizen suits, with large environmental organizations playing a far less prominent role, and more suits (about a third of the total in this time span) against public defendants. Individuals and organizations operating within a single state or smaller area brought the majority of suits within this period. Actions under the CWA were still the most common, although the study showed the number of CAA and RCRA suits increasing over the five years in question. *See id.* at 362, 382–92.

3. A more recent study examined Clean Water Act citizen suits from 2010 to 2016. The data contained some interesting patterns. First, the distribution of cases across the country was extremely uneven. With 219 cases, California ran away with the lead in citizen suits alleging CWA violations. The top dozen states by filing of complaints were California (219 cases), Washington (90 cases), Massachusetts (55 cases), West Virginia (36 cases), New York (24 cases), Tennessee (19 cases), Georgia (17 cases), New Hampshire (13 cases), Connecticut (13 cases), Oregon (11 cases), Alabama (10 cases), and North Carolina (7 cases). Regional rather than large national environmental groups filed most of the cases, with a significant number being filed by individuals. Finally, there were more than twice as many citizen suits as the number of judicial (rather than administrative) enforcement actions by EPA. Mark A. Ryan, *Clean Water Act Citizen Suits: What the Numbers Tell Us*, NAT. RESOURCES & ENV'T, Fall 2017, at 20, 22.

4.   As indicated at the beginning of this section, environmental statutes usually require that notice of intention to sue be given to the EPA, to the state in which the violation occurred, and to the alleged violator, at least 60 days prior to the filing of a citizen suit. In *Hallstrom v. Tillamook County,* 493 U.S. 20 (1989), the Supreme Court held that such notice requirements must be strictly interpreted and applied by the courts. *Hallstrom* presented the issue whether full compliance with the notice requirement in § 7002 of RCRA was a mandatory precondition to suit, or whether a failure to comply fully could be disregarded by the trial court at its discretion. In *Hallstrom,* plaintiffs were concerned that leachate from the defendant county's landfill was causing chemical and bacterial pollution of plaintiffs' soil and groundwater. Plaintiffs gave the defendant proper notice of their intent to sue but did not give notice to the federal EPA or to the state environmental agency until after the suit was filed. The federal district court found that the purpose of the notice requirement was to give the public agencies the opportunity to take over the enforcement of the statute from the private plaintiffs. Since neither the EPA nor the state agency showed any interest in taking action against the county, the court found that dismissing the action and forcing plaintiffs to refile would only waste judicial resources. After a trial on the merits, the district court found that defendant had violated RCRA. The Ninth Circuit held in favor of the county, rejecting the view that the notice requirement was procedural and therefore subject to waiver or equitable modification. The Supreme Court affirmed.

5.   What constitutes diligent prosecution sufficient to bar a citizen suit? In *Washington Public Interest Research Group v. Pendleton Woolen Mills,* 11 F.3d 883 (9th Cir. 1993), the EPA had issued a compliance order in 1988, stating that Pendleton was in violation of its NPDES permit. The order required Pendleton to prepare a report describing the causes of the violations and identifying the actions necessary to bring it into compliance. The order further required Pendleton to make those physical improvements identified as necessary. An amended compliance order included a threat of a sanction of $25,000 per day if Pendleton violated its terms. In 1990, WashPIRG notified EPA and Pendleton of its intent to bring suit against Pendleton for alleged permit violations. More than 60 days thereafter, WashPIRG filed a complaint seeking (1) a declaration establishing Pendleton's violations, (2) an injunction ordering Pendleton into compliance, and (3) civil penalties for Pendleton's violations from 1985 to the present. The district court entered summary judgment in favor of Pendleton, holding that the existence of EPA's action against Pendleton barred WashPIRG's citizen suit. The court of appeals reversed, holding that § 309(g)(6) of the Clean Water Act precludes citizen suits seeking civil penalties *only* if the EPA is diligently pursuing an administrative penalty action, and that the administrative compliance order which EPA had issued to Pendleton did not seek monetary penalties.

On the other hand, *Arkansas Wildlife Federation v. ICI Americas, Inc.,* 29 F.3d 376 (8th Cir. 1994), held that a citizen suit was jurisdictionally barred under the Clean Water Act because the state pollution control agency was diligently prosecuting, against the same defendant, an action under the state pollution control act. The bar to the citizen suit applied to *all* of ICI's past CWA violations, even though the original consent administrative order, which called for ICI to pay a civil penalty and to comply with applicable effluent limitations, did not cover all of ICI's violations. The court found that Arkansas had commenced a comparable action when it issued the original consent administrative order, prior to AWF's notice of intent to sue.

6.   Harmonizing citizen suits and governmental enforcement actions continues to prove troublesome. For a proposal to regularize the relationship between the two, *see* Jeffrey G. Miller, *Theme and Variations in Statutory Preclusions Against Successive Environmental Enforcement Actions by EPA and Citizens, Part One: Statutory Bars in Citizen Suit Provisions*, 28 HARV. ENVTL. L. REV. 401 (2004) (arguing for a narrow interpretation of the prosecution bar, applying it only when the state-undertaken enforcement will actually lead to compliance by regulated entity). Another coordination problem exists when the federal EPA "overfiles"—that is, files a federal enforcement action even though the state has already begun or completed its own enforcement effort.

7.   As noted, much of the most important environmental litigation is brought by public interest groups. Their ability to bring these suits is dependent on their access to funding. One of the most important sources of funding for these groups is the award of attorneys' fees authorized by many environmental statutes. The availability of fee awards and their size have been the subject of much litigation, both in the environmental area and elsewhere. Three basic rules are that (a) fees must be authorized by statute (*Alyeska Pipeline Service Co. v. Wilderness Society,* 421 U.S. 240 (1975)); (b) fees are available only to "prevailing parties" (*Buckhannon Board & Care Home, Inc. v. West Virginia Department of Health*, 532 U.S. 598 (2001)); and (c) the fee usually is calculated by multiplying a reasonable hourly rate times the number of hours reasonably invested in the suit.

C. LEGAL BASES FOR CHALLENGING AGENCY ACTION

1. CONSTITUTIONAL CHALLENGES

Once plaintiffs overcome the obstacles to court access, what claims may they bring? As an initial matter, plaintiffs may allege that a statute violates the non-delegation doctrine—the constitutional principle that forbids Congress from delegating legislative power to agencies. The Supreme Court has only rarely invalidated legislation on these grounds. Prior to *American Trucking* (excerpted below) there had been murmurs from individual Justices on the Court signaling the doctrine's potential revival. (Recall Justice Rehnquist's dissent in the *Benzene* case in Chapter 2, along with the plurality's discussion of the non-delegation doctrine.) *American Trucking* seems to lay that possibility to rest, however, though complaints by individual Justices about excessive delegation do surface from time to time.

WHITMAN v. AMERICAN TRUCKING ASSOCIATIONS, INC.

Supreme Court of the United States, 2001.
531 U.S. 457, 121 S.Ct. 903, 149 L.Ed.2d 1.

[Section 109(a) of the Clean Air Act requires the EPA Administrator to promulgate National Ambient Air Quality Standards (NAAQS) for each pollutant for which the agency has issued air quality criteria under § 108. Such standards and criteria are to be reviewed every five years. In 1997, when the EPA revised its standards for particulate matter (soot) and ozone (smog), a coalition of industry and states sued the agency for failing to use cost-benefit analysis in setting the new standards. In addition to holding that the EPA may not consider implementation costs in setting standards for NAAQS, the D.C. Circuit found that CAA § 109(b)(1) unconstitutionally delegated legislative power to the EPA Administrator because the EPA's interpretation of the statute offered no "intelligible principle" to limit agency discretion. However, rather than declaring the statute itself unconstitutional as a violation of the non-delegation doctrine, the circuit court remanded the issue and invited the EPA to adopt a more restrictive construction of the statute. The Supreme Court granted *certiorari* on petitions from both sides of the litigation.]

JUSTICE SCALIA delivered the opinion of the Court.

Section 109(b)(1) of the CAA instructs the EPA to set "ambient air quality standards the attainment and maintenance of which in the judgment of the Administrator, based on [the] criteria [documents of § 108] and allowing an adequate margin of safety, are requisite to protect the public health." The Court of Appeals held that this section as interpreted by the Administrator did not provide an "intelligible principle" to guide the EPA's exercise of authority in setting NAAQS. "[The] EPA," it said, "lack[ed] any determinate criteria for drawing lines. It has failed to state intelligibly how much is too much." The court hence found that the EPA's interpretation (but not the statute itself) violated the non-delegation doctrine. We disagree.

In a delegation challenge, the constitutional question is whether the statute has delegated legislative power to the agency. Article I, § 1, of the Constitution vests "[a]ll legislative Powers herein granted . . . in a Congress of the United States." This text permits no delegation of those powers, and so we repeatedly have said that when Congress confers decisionmaking authority upon agencies *Congress* must "lay down by legislative act an intelligible principle to which the person or body authorized to [act] is directed to conform." We have never suggested that an agency can cure an unlawful delegation of legislative power by adopting in its discretion a limiting construction of the statute. * * * The idea that an agency can cure an unconstitutionally standardless delegation of power by declining to exercise some of that power seems to us internally contradictory. The very choice of which portion of the power to exercise—that is to say, the prescription of the standard that Congress had omitted—would *itself* be an exercise of the forbidden legislative authority. Whether the statute delegates legislative power is a question for the courts, and an agency's voluntary self-denial has no bearing upon the answer.

We agree with the Solicitor General that the text of § 109(b)(1) of the CAA at a minimum requires that "[f]or a discrete set of pollutants and based on published air quality criteria that reflect the latest scientific knowledge, [the] EPA must establish uniform national standards at a level that is requisite to protect public health from the adverse effects of the pollutant in the ambient air." Requisite, in turn, "mean[s] sufficient, but not more than necessary." * * *

The scope of discretion § 109(b)(1) allows is in fact well within the outer limits of our non-delegation precedents. In the history of the Court we have found the requisite "intelligible principle" lacking in only two statutes, one of which provided literally no guidance for the exercise of discretion, and the other of which conferred authority to regulate the entire economy on the basis of no more precise a standard than stimulating the economy by assuring "fair competition." * * * And we have found an "intelligible principle" in various statutes authorizing regulation in the "public interest." In short, we have "almost never felt qualified to second-guess Congress regarding the permissible degree of policy judgment that can be left to those executing or applying the law."

It is true enough that the degree of agency discretion that is acceptable varies according to the scope of the power congressionally conferred. * * * [Congress] must provide substantial guidance on setting air standards that affect the entire national economy. But even in sweeping regulatory schemes we have never demanded, as the Court of Appeals did here, that statutes provide a "determinate criterion" for saying "how much [of the regulated harm] is too much." * * * It is therefore not conclusive for delegation purposes that, as respondents argue, ozone and particulate matter are "non-threshold" pollutants that inflict a continuum of adverse health effects at any airborne concentration greater than zero, and hence require the EPA to make judgments of degree. "[A] certain degree of discretion, and thus of lawmaking, inheres in most executive or judicial action." Section 109(b)(1) of the CAA, which to repeat we interpret as requiring the EPA to set air quality standards at the level that is "requisite"—that is, not lower or higher than is necessary—to protect the public health with an adequate margin of safety, fits comfortably within the scope of discretion permitted by our precedent.

We therefore reverse the judgment of the Court of Appeals remanding for reinterpretation that would avoid a supposed delegation of legislative power. It will remain for the Court of Appeals—on the remand that we direct for other reasons—to dispose of any other preserved challenge to the NAAQS under the judicial-review provisions contained in 42 U.S.C. § 7607(d)(9).

NOTES

1.   The D.C. Circuit opinion in *American Trucking* attracted significant criticism. *See, e.g.*, Richard Pierce, *The Inherent Limits on Judicial Control of Agency Discretion: The D.C. Circuit and the Non-Delegation Doctrine*, 52 ADMIN. L. REV. 63 (2000); Cass R. Sunstein, *Is the Clean Air Act Unconstitutional?* 98 MICH. L. REV. 303 (1999). The D.C. Circuit had adopted a novel view of the non-delegation doctrine, essentially arguing that a delegation that would otherwise be unconstitutional could be saved by the agency's construction of the statutory grant. The court wrote: "Where (as here) statutory language and an existing agency interpretation involve an unconstitutional delegation of power, but an interpretation without the constitutional weakness is or may be available, our response is not to strike down the statute but to give the agency an opportunity to extract a determinate standard on its own." *American Trucking Ass'ns v. EPA*, 175 F.3d 1027, 1038 (D.C. Cir. 1999). Should the agency be able to salvage an unconstitutional statute by restricting its own authority? On the one hand, this would accomplish the goal of ensuring that agencies do not exercise unconstrained discretionary power, which is one of the purposes of the non-delegation doctrine. See Lisa Schultz Bressman, *Disciplining Delegation After* Whitman v. American Trucking Ass'ns, 87 CORNELL L. REV. 452 (2002). On the other hand, perhaps this would do little to ensure that Congress makes the crucial policy decisions itself, another purpose of the doctrine. Indeed, allowing agencies to "save" overly broad delegations might encourage Congress to be careless in drafting statutes.

2.   The scholarly literature on the non-delegation doctrine is voluminous.[2] We think, however, that this literature may over-estimate the amount of vagueness in Congressional delegations. As we will see in the final four chapters of this book, agencies do enjoy significant discretion under the

---

[2]   *See, e.g.*, David Schoenbrod, POWER WITHOUT RESPONSIBILITY: HOW CONGRESS ABUSES THE PEOPLE THROUGH DELEGATION (1993) (arguing that delegation weakens democracy and urging federal courts to resurrect the non-delegation doctrine); Theodore J. Lowi, THE END OF LIBERALISM 93 (2d ed. 1979) (arguing that broad delegations are "policy without law"). *But cf.* Richard J. Pierce, Jr., *Political Accountability and Delegated Power: A Response to Professor Lowi*, 36 AM. U. L. REV. 391, 392 (1987) (arguing that judicial enforcement of the non-delegation doctrine would be a "terrible" response to broad delegations); Jerry L. Mashaw, *Prodelegation: Why Administrators Should Make Political Decisions*, 1 J.L. ECON. & ORG. 81, 83 (1985) (arguing that broad delegations increase administrative responsiveness); Thomas W. Merrill, *Rethinking Article I, Section I: From Nondelegation to Exclusive Delegation*, 104 COLUM. L. REV. 2097 (2004) (arguing that agencies should be allowed some legislative power, as long such authority stems exclusively from explicit statutory delegations by Congress, in order to take advantage of agencies' superior institutional capacity to make certain decisions).

major federal statutes, but the statutes are determinate enough that courts not infrequently invalidate agency actions as statutory violations.

2.   STATUTE-BASED CHALLENGES

Because non-delegation challenges are futile, the more common challenge to agency action attacks the procedural regularity and/or substantive lawfulness of an agency's decision. Litigants wishing to challenge agency decisions typically make at least two different arguments: First, that the agency missed or mishandled one of the procedural steps it is obligated to take under the applicable environmental statute or under the Administrative Procedure Act (APA) (which is the federal law generally applicable to all federal agency action). Second, that the agency made a substantive error, meaning that, although it observed all of the required procedures, the actual decision it made on the merits was unlawful. If a plaintiff prevails using either of these arguments, the court will invalidate the agency action. Sometimes, then, important victories turn on what might seem like rather technical claims that an agency mishandled a procedure, or that it missed a step in its reasoning.

If Congress wishes to provide for a different standard of review for a particular agency action, it can do so in the specific governing legislation. This would essentially trump the APA, which operates as a default. Indeed, it is important to remember that the legislation under which the agency derives its authority for the disputed action (for our purposes this would be a specific environmental law) is the first place to look to determine both which procedures the agency is obligated to follow, and what standard of review applies. Where that statute is silent, however, one must consult the APA.

At least in theory, however, courts pay different degrees of deference to different kinds of agency decisions. These degrees of deference are expressed as different "standards of review". The question of which of these standards ought to apply in any given instance of judicial review of agency action is called the "scope of review" issue. For example, courts generally review agency decisions of fact or policy using the "arbitrary or capricious" standard of review, whereas they review formal (trial type) adjudicative decisions using a "substantial evidence" standard of review because this is what the APA requires. Traditionally, courts were least deferential to agency interpretations of law. While in theory these standards of review are different—scrutinizing an agency's rationale for arbitrariness is seemingly more deferential than demanding the agency provide "substantial evidence" based on the hearing record—in practice, they can conflate into the same thing. This is a secret that administrative law professors reveal only toward the end of the semester, but it behooves us, in an environmental law course, to reveal it early. Indeed, critics of these different standards of review have argued that they devolve into a general and rather unprincipled test of "reasonableness" which allows courts to defer or not defer as they wish. Others claim that the differences are meaningful.

The scope-of-review issue cannot be fully understood without a grasp of the basics of administrative procedure, however. Indeed, effective environmental lawyers are necessarily very adept at administrative law. For our purposes, there are three important categories of administrative actions, all governed by the APA. The first category consists of "formal" adjudications. This type of procedure applies whenever the specific statute governing the agency action (e.g., the Endangered Species Act section 7(h) exemption provision) requires an issue to be "determined on the record after opportunity for an agency hearing." 5 U.S.C. § 554. The procedures required for a formal adjudication are essentially similar to those of a judicial trial. Administrative law judges preside over these quasi-trials and have considerable discretionary authority over the proceedings. In reviewing the agency's ruling following a formal adjudication, courts must uphold the action unless it is unsupported by "substantial evidence" or violates substantive limits on the agency's powers. This standard of review applies by virtue of the APA, which specifies a list of standards of review in 5 U.S.C. § 706(2)(A)–(E).

The second category of administrative action that is important for our purposes is informal rulemaking. Agencies like the EPA translate their legislative mandates into more specific requirements by promulgating regulations (also called "legislative rules"), which have the force and effect of legislation itself. Section 553 of the APA requires agencies to go through a notice-and-comment process when promulgating rules:

1.   The first step of informal rulemaking is publication of a notice in the Federal Register describing the proposed rule.

2.   The agency must then provide for an "opportunity to comment," during which interested parties have at least 30 days to respond to the proposed rule.

3.   Then, the agency must issue, in conjunction with its promulgation of the rule, a "concise general statement" of the rule's basis and purpose.

In practice, this simple-sounding procedure has become a highly contested, time-consuming and costly process. In a typical rulemaking involving a major environmental rule with significant implications, interested parties on all sides of the issue will participate in the comment process by submitting voluminous materials to the agency, which the agency then considers as it deliberates over the rule. The agency must usually comply with other analytic requirements imposed by other statutes or Executive Orders, such as cost-benefit analysis. The agency then develops an extremely detailed defense of its ultimate policy choice (which it publishes in the federal register as a rule), often carefully responding to objections from the comments and building its case with scientific data, all in order to withstand judicial review. The APA fails to specify clearly the scope of review for agency rules, but by default, "arbitrary or capricious" review applies. § 706(2)(A). There is also another kind of rulemaking procedure known as "formal rulemaking" which is akin to formal adjudication, but has virtually no practical importance.

The final category of agency action, and in a way the most important, is informal adjudication. Informal adjudications include the vast number of government actions that require neither a formal trial-type hearing (producing an order binding the instant parties) nor an informal notice-and-comment process (producing a rule affecting future conduct of regulated parties). Many important environmental decisions fall into this category, including many funding decisions, project approvals, and enforcement choices. The APA has little to say about the procedures to be used in these cases, and § 706 of the APA does not specify a standard of review for them. However, as we shall see in the case below, over time, courts have come to review these informal adjudications using the "arbitrary or capricious" standard. Thus, at a minimum, most agency decisions of any importance in environmental law will be subject to the arbitrary and capricious standard of review.

CITIZENS TO PRESERVE OVERTON PARK, INC. V. VOLPE

Supreme Court of the United States, 1971.
401 U.S. 402, 91 S.Ct. 814, 28 L.Ed.2d 136.

Opinion of the Court by JUSTICE MARSHALL, announced by JUSTICE STEWART.

The growing public concern about the quality of our natural environment has prompted Congress in recent years to enact legislation designed to curb the accelerating destruction of our country's natural beauty. We are concerned in this case with § 4(f) of the Department of Transportation Act of 1966, as amended, and § 18(a) of the Federal-Aid Highway Act of 1968, 82 Stat. 823, 23 U.S.C.A. § 138 (hereafter § 138). These statutes prohibit the Secretary of Transportation from authorizing the use of federal funds to finance the construction of highways through public parks if a "feasible and prudent" alternative route exists. If no such route is available, the statutes allow him to approve construction through parks only if there has been "all possible planning to minimize harm" to the park. [The plaintiffs contended that the Secretary violated these restrictions in approving the construction of an interstate highway through Overton Park, a 342-acre park in Memphis.]

A threshold question—whether petitioners are entitled to any judicial review—is easily answered. Section 701 of the Administrative Procedure

Act, 5 U.S.C.A. § 701, provides that the action of "each authority of the Government of the United States," which includes the Department of Transportation, is subject to judicial review except where there is a statutory prohibition on review or where "agency action is committed to agency discretion by law." In this case there is no indication that Congress sought to prohibit judicial review and there is most certainly no "showing of 'clear and convincing evidence' of a * * * legislative intent" to restrict access to judicial review. * * *

Similarly, the Secretary's decision here does not fall within the exception for action "committed to agency discretion." This is a very narrow exception. The legislative history of the Administrative Procedure Act indicates that it is applicable in those rare instances where "statutes are drawn in such broad terms that in a given case there is no law to apply."

Section 4(f) of the Department of Transportation Act and § 138 of the Federal-Aid Highway Act are clear and specific directives. Both the Department of Transportation Act and the Federal-Aid Highway Act provide that the Secretary "shall not approve any program or project" that requires the use of any public parkland "unless (1) there is no feasible and prudent alternative to the use of such land, and (2) such program includes all possible planning to minimize harm to such park * * *." This language is a plain and explicit bar to the use of federal funds for construction of highways through parks—only the most unusual situations are exempted.

Despite the clarity of the statutory language, respondents argue that the Secretary has wide discretion. They recognize that the requirement that there be no "feasible" alternative route admits of little administrative discretion. For this exemption to apply the Secretary must find that as a matter of sound engineering it would not be feasible to build the highway along any other route. Respondents argue, however, that the requirement that there be no other "prudent" route requires the Secretary to engage in a wide-ranging balancing of competing interests. They contend that the Secretary should weigh the detriment resulting from the destruction of parkland against the cost of other routes, safety considerations, and other factors, and determine on the basis of the importance that he attaches to these other factors whether, on balance, alternative feasible routes would be "prudent."

But no such wide-ranging endeavor was intended. It is obvious that in most cases considerations of cost, directness of route, and community disruption will indicate that parkland should be used for highway construction whenever possible. * * * Thus, if Congress intended these factors to be on an equal footing with preservation of parkland there would have been no need for the statutes.

Congress clearly did not intend that cost and disruption of the community were to be ignored by the Secretary. But the very existence of the statutes indicates that protection of parkland was to be given paramount importance. The few green havens that are public parks were not to be lost unless there were truly unusual factors present in a particular case or the cost or community disruption resulting from alternative routes reached extraordinary magnitudes. If the statutes are to have any meaning, the Secretary cannot approve the destruction of parkland unless he finds that alternative routes present unique problems.

Plainly, there is "law to apply" and thus the exemption for action "committed to agency discretion" is inapplicable. * * *

But the existence of judicial review is only the start: the standard for review must also be determined. For that we must look to § 706 of the Administrative Procedure Act, 5 U.S.C.A. § 706, which provides that a "reviewing court shall * * * hold unlawful and set aside agency action, findings, and conclusions found" not to meet six separate standards. In all cases agency action must be set aside if the action was "arbitrary, capricious, an abuse of discretion, or otherwise not in accordance with law" or if the action failed to meet statutory, procedural, or constitutional requirements. In certain narrow, specifically limited situations, the agency action is to be set aside if the action was not supported by "substantial evidence." And in other equally narrow circumstances the reviewing court is to engage in a *de novo* review of the action and set it aside if it was "unwarranted by the facts." * * *

[The Court rejected the plaintiff's arguments that either the "substantial evidence" test or the "*de novo* review" requirement applied.]

Even though there is no *de novo* review in this case and the Secretary's approval of the route of I-40 does not have ultimately to meet the substantial evidence test, the generally applicable standards of § 706 require the reviewing court to engage in a substantial inquiry. Certainly, the Secretary's decision is entitled to a presumption of regularity. * * * But that presumption is not to shield his action from a thorough, probing, in-depth review.

The court is first required to decide whether the Secretary acted within the scope of his authority. * * * This determination naturally begins with a delineation of the scope of the Secretary's authority and discretion. As has been shown, Congress has specified only a small range of choices that the Secretary can make. Also involved in this initial inquiry is a determination of whether on the facts the Secretary's decision can reasonably be said to be within that range. The reviewing court must consider whether the Secretary properly construed his authority to approve the use of parkland as limited to situations where there are no feasible alternative routes or where feasible alternative routes involve uniquely difficult problems. And the reviewing court must be able to find that the Secretary could have reasonably believed that in this case there are no feasible alternatives or that alternatives do involve unique problems.

Scrutiny of the facts does not end, however, with the determination that the Secretary has acted within the scope of his statutory authority. Section 706(2)(A) requires a finding that the actual choice made was not "arbitrary, capricious, an abuse of discretion, or otherwise not in accordance with law." To make this finding the Court must consider whether the decision was based on a consideration of the relevant factors and whether there has been a clear error of judgment.

* * * Although this inquiry into the facts is to be searching and careful, the ultimate standard of review is a narrow one. The court is not empowered to substitute its judgment for that of the agency.

* * * The lower courts based their review on the litigation affidavits that were presented. These affidavits were merely "*post hoc*" rationalizations * * * which have traditionally been found to be an inadequate basis for review. * * * And they clearly do not constitute the "whole record" compiled by the agency: the basis for review required by § 706 of the Administrative Procedure Act. * * *

Thus it is necessary to remand this case to the District Court for plenary review of the Secretary's decision. That review is to be based on the full administrative record that was before the Secretary at the time he made his decision. But since the bare record may not disclose the factors that were considered or the Secretary's construction of the evidence it may be necessary for the District Court to require some explanation in order to determine if the Secretary acted within the scope of his authority and if the Secretary's action was justifiable under the applicable standard.

The court may require the administrative officials who participated in the decision to give testimony explaining their action. Of course, such inquiry into the mental processes of administrative decisionmakers is usually to be avoided. *United States v. Morgan,* 313 U.S. 409, 422, 61 S.Ct. 999, 85 L.Ed. 1429 (1941). And where there are administrative findings that were made at the same time as the decision, as was the case in *Morgan,* there must be a strong showing of bad faith or improper behavior before such inquiry may be made. But here there are no such formal findings and it may be that the only way there can be effective judicial review is by examining the decisionmakers themselves. * * *

The District Court is not, however, required to make such an inquiry. It may be that the Secretary can prepare formal findings including the information required by DOT Order 5610.1 that will provide an adequate explanation for his action. Such an explanation will, to some extent, be a "*post hoc* rationalization" and thus must be viewed critically. If the District Court decides that additional explanation is necessary, that court should consider which method will prove the most expeditious so that full review may be had as soon as possible.

NOTES

1.   The Secretary ultimately decided to disapprove the highway, a decision that was upheld on appeal. *See Citizens to Preserve Overton Park, Inc. v. Brinegar*, 494 F.2d 1212 (6th Cir. 1974). Professor Strauss later wrote a detailed history of section 4(f) of the Transportation Act and the events leading up to *Overton Park*. He concluded that the Court misinterpreted the statute:

> Political controls, so far as one can tell, were the only controls Congress had considered; and in the instance, they were working well. A fuller appreciation for the Overton Park controversy, whether viewed from Washington, D.C., or Memphis, Tennessee, shows wide and effective engagement of a variety of political actors in the controversy. The effect of the Court's action * * * was to empower one of those actors to an extent that had not been contemplated. * * *

Peter L. Strauss, *Revisiting Overton Park: Political and Judicial Controls Over Administrative Actions Affecting the Community*, 39 UCLA L. REV. 1251 (1992). Professor Strauss suggested that the Court interfered in a well-functioning political process, just one that resulted in a loss for the citizen group. But should courts leave these decisions to the political process? Is there any reason to believe that environmental interests will be as powerful and well-resourced as other interests?

2.   As Justice Marshall points out, under the APA § 702, there is a category of agency action that is "committed to agency discretion." In *Heckler v. Chaney*, 470 U.S. 821 (1985), the Court held that an agency's decision to eschew enforcement action is unreviewable. The Court generally considers enforcement decisions unsuitable for judicial review, likening them to "prosecutorial" discretion and being loath to interfere with agency judgments. *See also Arnow v. United States Nuclear Regulatory Comm'n*, 868 F.2d 223 (7th Cir. 1989) (applying *Chaney* to an NRC enforcement decision). For a critique of *Chaney, see* Cass R. Sunstein, *Reviewing Agency Inaction After* Heckler v. Chaney, 52 U. CHI. L. REV. 653 (1985).

3.   When can a court review an agency's failure to act? In *Norton v. Southern Utah Wilderness Alliance*, 542 U.S. 55 (2004) (*SUWA*), the Court held that it could not review the Bureau of Land Management's refusal to regulate increased off-road vehicle use in an area under consideration for designation as wilderness even though a statute required the agency to manage such land so as not to compromise its wilderness character. The Court ruled that the land use plan in which the BLM promised to monitor vehicle use did not bind it to restrict use of the vehicles, and thus review of the BLM's implementation of the plan would allow a broad attack on policy rather than a challenge of a specific failure of an agency to perform a discrete and required action.

4.   The *Overton Park* approach to reviewing informal adjudication by an agency (in this case the Secretary's approval) was strongly reconfirmed in *Motor Vehicle Manufacturers Ass'n v. State Farm Mutual Automobile Insurance Co.*, 463 U.S. 29 (1983), in which the Court applied the "arbitrary or capricious" test to overturn an administrative decision to rescind a legislative rule. As background, the National Highway Traffic Safety Administration in 1981 rescinded an earlier decision requiring all new cars produced after September 1982 to be equipped with passive restraints (such as automatic seatbelts). After a detailed examination of the rulemaking record, the Court found the rescission to be arbitrary or capricious. The Court found that the agency failed to consider the possibility of modifying rather than rescinding the regulation and had been too quick to dismiss the safety benefits of automatic seatbelts. The agency had also failed to consider an obvious alternative: requiring air bags. *State Farm* remains the Supreme Court's clearest statement of what constitutes "arbitrary or capricious review," and it is routinely cited in environmental cases.

As an application of the *Overton Park / State Farm* standard, consider *Wildearth v. U.S. Bureau of Land Management*, 870 F.3d 1222 (10th Cir. 2017). The plaintiffs challenged approval of coal leases on federal lands. They argued that the government had violated the National Environmental Policy Act (NEPA) in its analysis of the climate change impacts of the leases. The government had concluded that the leases would have zero effect on carbon emissions because if the coal was not extracted there, it would simply be extracted elsewhere. The court held that the government's conclusion was arbitrary and capricious, because it was supported by no hard data and was based on an irrational assumption that a reducing the supply for a good would have no effect on demand.

5.   Agencies reverse their previous positions from time to time, often in connection with a change in presidents, as illustrated in the transition from Obama to Trump. Courts do not apply a higher standard of review to such reversals, but the agency is required to take into account the evidence and arguments that it had previously found persuasive, as well as any reliance by regulated parties or others on the prior rule. As illustrative recent cases, see *Mingo Logan Coal Co. v. EPA*, 829 F.3d 710 (D.C. Cir. 2016); *Alaska Forrest Ass'n v. State of Alaska*, 795 F.3d 956 (9th Cir. 2014). We expect to see many more cases in this category as the Trump Administration's deregulatory actions reach the courts.

6.   A major scholarly debate surrounds the kind of "hard look" review endorsed by *Overton Park* and *State Farm*. The following statement is typical of the view of the critics:

> The predictable result of stringent "hard look" judicial review of complex rulemaking is ossification. Because the agencies perceive that the reviewing courts are inconsistent in the degree to which they are deferential, they are constrained to prepare for the worst-case scenario on judicial review. This can be extremely resource-intensive

SEC. C   LEGAL BASES FOR CHALLENGING AGENCY ACTION   **349**

and time-consuming. Moreover, since the criteria for substantive judicial review are the same for repealing old rules as for promulgating new rules, the agencies are equally chary of revisiting old rules, even in the name of flexibility.

Thomas O. McGarity, *Some Thoughts on "Deossifying" the Rulemaking Process*, 41 DUKE L.J. 1385, 1419–20 (1992). Mark Seidenfeld responds that "experience as an agency lawyer leads me to believe that, without some external constraint on agency decisionmaking processes, staff members are apt to take shortcuts to avoid extra work, to yield to short-run political pressures that take time and energy to counter, or to alter a decision to make it easier to defend to their superiors." Mark Seidenfeld, *Demystifying Deossification: Rethinking Recent Proposals to Modify Judicial Review of Notice and Comment Rulemaking*, 75 TEX. L. REV. 483, 564 (1997).

An empirical study suggests that, at least for the ninety air toxics rules covered by the study, judicial review did not result in much improvement in outcomes. In fact, the existence of judicial review may have given regulated industries more leverage with the agency because of the ability to threaten expensive litigation. See Wendy Wagner, *Revisiting the Impact of Judicial Review on Agency Rulemakings*, 53 WM. & MARY L. REV. 1717 (2012).

A NOTE ON JUDICIAL REVIEW OF AGENCY PROCEDURES

In the early 1970s, a number of appellate courts appeared to find the APA's dichotomy between formal adjudication (with all its attendant "trial-type" procedural protections) and informal rulemaking (with only a guarantee of notice and comment) too confining. In several cases involving the review of agency rulemaking, courts required agencies to adopt procedures going beyond the basic statutory requirements in § 553 of the APA, thereby making the relatively low intensity process of informal rulemaking look more like the procedure-laden process of formal adjudication.

The hybrid rulemaking issue finally reached the Supreme Court in *Vermont Yankee Nuclear Power Corp. v. NRDC*, 435 U.S. 519 (1978). *Vermont Yankee* grew out of the long-standing controversy over nuclear waste disposal. Critics of atomic energy argued that nuclear energy plants should not be built until the disposal problem was solved. The Atomic Energy Commission consistently rejected this and other concerns about the safety of nuclear power. The issue before the Court was whether the agency had employed the proper procedures to consider this issue. If waste disposal had been considered during the proceeding to license a specific plant, a full trial-type hearing would have been required because the APA requires formal adjudication for licensing. By shifting consideration of the issue to a rulemaking process, could the agency escape all but the minimal "notice and comment" requirements?

The Court ruled that, beyond the requirements of the APA, it is up to the agency to decide whether to employ any additional procedures "[a]bsent constitutional constraints or extremely compelling circumstances." For instance, the Court said, "a totally unjustified departure from well settled agency procedures of long standing might require judicial correction."

Vermont Yankee thus appeared to close the door on judicial augmentation of the APA-required procedures. Yet despite *Vermont Yankee,* additional procedural restrictions have in effect been imposed on agencies through a broad construction of the specific APA provisions themselves. Further, a reviewing court may remand a matter to an agency because the agency's record is not sufficiently developed to enable the court to perform "whole record" review, as required by § 706. Indeed, on one reading, this is all the D.C. Circuit in *Vermont Yankee* was doing. Is remanding a decision to an agency on the basis of "whole record" review any different, in practice, from adding procedures to the § 553 minimum, as prohibited by *Vermont Yankee?*

Some political scientists argue that administrative procedures serve a political function by empowering interest groups to play an oversight role as agencies implement legislation. According to a school of thought known as "public choice theory," Congress can "stack the deck" by enfranchising those interest groups that benefited from the legislation to participate in agency decision making, replicating at the implementation phase the same political environment that gave rise to the initial legislative deal. Mathew D. McCubbins et al., *Structure and Process, Politics and Policy: Administrative Arrangements and the Political Control of Agencies,* 75 VA. L. REV. 431 (1989). From a public choice perspective, the role of courts is to enforce the original "deal" struck in the legislation. *But cf.* Jerry L. Mashaw, *Explaining Administrative Process: Normative, Positive, and Critical Stories of Legal Development,* 6 J.L. ECON. & ORG. 267 (1990) (arguing that procedural controls enfranchise not only favored interest groups but even disfavored ones); *see also* Jonathan R. Macey, *Separated Powers and Positive Political Economy: The Tug of War Over Administrative Agencies,* 80 GEO. L.J. 671 (1992) (arguing, in contrast to McCubbins, et al, that Congress uses procedure to enfranchise the legislative *losers*); David B. Spence, *Administrative Law and Agency Policymaking: Rethinking the Positive Theory of Political Control,* 14 YALE J. ON REG. 407 (1997).

There may be a point of diminishing returns in imposing procedural requirements, where the effect of adding them is to divert the agency from engaging in explicit rulemaking at all. In order to avoid the burden of heavy procedural demands, an agency may make rules through informal policy pronouncements such as guidance documents, or it may use case-by-case adjudication or even settlements to alter rules. Richard Lazarus reports:

> Another adverse effect of excessive oversight of EPA is that it has caused the agency to go "underground" in its lawmaking. To avoid overseers, EPA has increasingly resorted to less formal means of announcing agency policy determinations. Instead of promulgating rules pursuant to the Administrative Procedure Act, EPA now frequently issues guidance memoranda and directives. Also, many important agency rulings are not reflected in generic rulemaking, but

in individual permit decisions. OMB oversight is thereby avoided, and judicial review of agency action is limited.

Richard Lazarus, *The Tragedy of Distrust in the Implementation of Federal Environmental Law*, 54 L. & CONTEMP. PROBS. 311, 356 (Autumn, 1991).

So far, we have considered how courts review agency determinations of factual and policy matters. However, what is the standard of review for an agency's interpretations of law? Courts traditionally applied a multi-factored test for determining whether agency interpretations of law were entitled to deference (including a host of considerations, such as, whether the interpretation was contained in a "legislative rule" or an "interpretive rule;" whether the matter fell within the agency's area of expertise; whether the interpretation was supported by reasoned analysis, etc.) This issue of what degree of judicial deference to pay to agency interpretations of law is critical to environmental law because so many cases involve challenges to agency interpretations of the meaning of an environmental statute. In the landmark case excerpted below, the Supreme Court announced a more deferential approach to agency interpretations of law. As with *Overton Park* and *Vermont Yankee*, this administrative law decision comes in an environmental case.

CHEVRON, U.S.A. INC. V. NATURAL RESOURCES DEFENSE COUNCIL

Supreme Court of the United States, 1984.
467 U.S. 837, 104 S.Ct. 2778, 81 L.Ed.2d 694.

JUSTICE STEVENS delivered the opinion of the Court.

The question presented by this case is whether EPA's decision to allow States to treat all of the pollution-emitting devices within the same industrial grouping as though they were encased within a single "bubble" is based on a reasonable construction of the statutory term "stationary source." [The court of appeals had held the use of bubbles impermissible for nonattainment areas even though it found no explicit statutory language or legislative history on point.]

When a court reviews an agency's construction of the statute which it administers, it is confronted with two questions. First, always, is the question whether Congress has directly spoken to the precise question at issue. If the intent of Congress is clear, that is the end of the matter; for the court, as well as the agency, must give effect to the unambiguously expressed intent of Congress. If, however, the court determines Congress has not directly addressed the precise question at issue, the court does not simply impose its own construction on the statute, as would be necessary in the absence of an administrative interpretation. Rather, if the statute is silent or ambiguous with respect to the specific issue, the question for the court is whether the agency's answer is based on a permissible construction of the statute.

In light of these well-settled principles it is clear that the Court of Appeals misconceived the nature of its role in reviewing the regulations at issue. Once it determined, after its own examination of the legislation, that Congress did not actually have an intent regarding the applicability of the bubble concept to the permit program, the question before it was not whether in its view the concept is "inappropriate" in the general context of a program designed to improve air quality, but whether the Administrator's view that it is appropriate in the context of this particular program is a reasonable one. Based on the examination of the legislation and its history which follows, we agree with the Court of Appeals that Congress did not have a specific intention on the applicability of the bubble concept in these cases, and conclude that the EPA's use of that concept here is a reasonable policy choice for the agency to make. * * *

The Clean Air Act Amendments of 1977 are a lengthy, detailed, technical, complex, and comprehensive response to a major social issue. A small portion of the statute expressly deals with nonattainment areas. The focal point of this controversy is one phrase in that portion of the Amendments. * * *

The 1977 Amendments contain no specific reference to the "bubble concept." Nor do they contain a specific definition of the term "stationary source," though they did not disturb the definition of "stationary source" contained in § 111(a)(3), applicable by the terms of the Act to [all new sources in the New Source Performance Standards program]. Section 302(j), however, defines the term "major stationary source" as follows:

> Except as otherwise expressly provided the terms "major stationary source" and "major emitting facility" mean any stationary facility or source of air pollutants which directly emits, or has the potential to emit, one hundred tons per year or more of any air pollutant (including any major emitting facility or source of fugitive emissions of any such pollutant, as determined by rule by the Administrator).

Statutory Language

The definition of the term stationary source in § 111(a)(3) refers to "any building, structure, facility, or installation" which emits air pollution. This definition is applicable only to the NSPS program by the express terms of the statute; the text of the statute does not make this definition applicable to the permit program [for nonattainment areas]. Petitioners therefore maintain that there is no statutory language even relevant to ascertaining the meaning of stationary source in the permit program aside from § 302(j), which defines the term major stationary source. We disagree with petitioners on this point.

The definition in § 302(j) tells us what the word "major" means—a source must emit at least 100 tons of pollution to qualify—but it sheds virtually no light on the meaning of the term "stationary source." It does equate a source with a facility—a "major emitting facility" and a "major stationary source" are synonymous under § 302(j). The ordinary meaning of the term facility is some collection of integrated elements which has been designed and constructed to achieve some purpose. Moreover, it is certainly no affront to common English usage to take a reference to a major facility or a major source to connote an entire plant as opposed to its constituent parts. Basically, however, the language of § 302(j) simply does not compel any given interpretation of the term source.

Respondents recognize that, and hence point to § 111(a)(3). Although the definition in that section is not literally applicable to the permit program, it sheds as much light on the meaning of the word source as anything in the statute. As respondents point out, use of the words "building, structure, facility, or installation," as the definition of source, could be read to impose the permit conditions on an individual building that is a part of a plant. A "word may have a character of its own not to be submerged by its association." On the other hand, the meaning of a word must be ascertained in the context of achieving particular objectives, and the words associated with it may indicate that the true meaning of the series is to convey a common idea. The language may reasonably be interpreted to impose the requirement on any discrete, but integrated, operation which pollutes. This gives meaning to all of the terms—a single building, not part of a larger operation, would be covered if it emits more than 100 tons of pollution, as would any facility, structure, or installation. Indeed, the language itself implies a bubble concept of sorts: each enumerated item would seem to be treated as if it were encased in a bubble. While respondents insist that each of these terms must be given a discrete meaning, they also argue that § 111(a)(3) defines "source" as that term is used in § 302(j). The latter section, however, equates a source with a facility, whereas the former defines source as a facility, among other items.

We are not persuaded that parsing of general terms in the text of the statute will reveal an actual intent of Congress. We know full well that this language is not dispositive; the terms are overlapping and the language is not precisely directed to the question of the applicability of a given term in the context of a larger operation. To the extent any congressional "intent" can be discerned from this language, it would appear that the listing of overlapping, illustrative terms was intended to enlarge, rather than to confine, the scope of the agency's power to regulate particular sources in order to effectuate the policies of the Act.

Legislative History

In addition, respondents argue that the legislative history and policies of the Act foreclose the plantwide definition, and that the EPA's interpretation is not entitled to deference because it represents a sharp break with prior interpretations of the Act.

Based on our examination of the legislative history, we agree with the Court of Appeals that it is unilluminating. * * *. We find that the legislative history as a whole is silent on the precise issue before us. It is, however, consistent with the view that the EPA should have broad discretion in implementing the policies of the 1977 Amendments.

More importantly, that history plainly identifies the policy concerns that motivated the enactment; the plantwide definition is fully consistent with one of those concerns—the allowance of reasonable economic growth— and, whether or not we believe it most effectively implements the other, we must recognize that the EPA has advanced a reasonable explanation for its conclusion that the regulations serve the environmental objectives as well. Indeed, its reasoning is supported by the public record developed in the rulemaking process, as well as by certain private studies.

Our review of the EPA's varying interpretations of the word "source"— both before and after the 1977 Amendments—convince us that the agency primarily responsible for administering this important legislation has consistently interpreted it flexibly—not in a sterile textual vacuum, but in the context of implementing policy decisions in a technical and complex arena. The fact that the agency has from time to time changed its interpretation of the term source does not, as respondents argue, lead us to conclude that no deference should be accorded the agency's interpretation of the statute. An initial agency interpretation is not instantly carved in stone. On the contrary, the agency, to engage in informed rulemaking, must consider varying interpretations and the wisdom of its policy on a continuing basis. Moreover, the fact that the agency has adopted different definitions in different contexts adds force to the argument that the definition itself is flexible, particularly since Congress has never indicated any disapproval of a flexible reading of the statute.

Significantly, it was not the agency in 1980, but rather the Court of Appeals that read the statute inflexibly to command a plantwide definition for programs designed to maintain clean air and to forbid such a definition for programs designed to improve air quality. The distinction the court drew may well be a sensible one, but our labored review of the problem has surely disclosed that it is not a distinction that Congress ever articulated itself, or one that the EPA found in the statute before the courts began to review the legislative work product. We conclude that it was the Court of Appeals, rather than Congress or any of the decisionmakers who are authorized by Congress to administer this legislation, that was primarily responsible for the 1980 position taken by the agency.

Policy

The arguments over policy that are advanced in the parties' briefs create the impression that respondents are now waging in a judicial forum a specific policy battle which they ultimately lost in the agency and in the 32 jurisdictions opting for the bubble concept, but one which was never waged in the Congress. Such policy arguments are more properly addressed to legislators or administrators, not to judges.

In this case, the Administrator's interpretation represents a reasonable accommodation of manifestly competing interests and is entitled to deference: the regulatory scheme is technical and complex, the agency considered the matter in a detailed and reasoned fashion, and the decision involves reconciling conflicting policies. Congress intended to accommodate both interests, but did not do so itself on the level of specificity presented by this case. Perhaps that body consciously desired the Administrator to strike the balance at this level, thinking that those with great expertise and charged with responsibility for administering the provision would be in a better position to do so; perhaps it simply did not consider the question at this level; and perhaps Congress was unable to forge a coalition on either side of the question, and those on each side decided to take their chances with the scheme devised by the agency. For judicial purposes, it matters not which of these things occurred.

Judges are not experts in the field, and are not part of either political branch of the Government. Courts must, in some cases, reconcile competing political interests, but not on the basis of the judges' personal policy preferences. In contrast, an agency to which Congress has delegated policymaking responsibilities may, within the limits of that delegation, properly rely upon the incumbent administration's views of wise policy to inform its judgments. While agencies are not directly accountable to the people, the Chief Executive is, and it is entirely appropriate for this political branch of the Government to make such policy choices—resolving the competing interests which Congress itself either inadvertently did not resolve, or intentionally left to be resolved by the agency charged with the administration of the statute in light of everyday realities.

When a challenge to an agency construction of a statutory provision, fairly conceptualized, really centers on the wisdom of the agency's policy, rather than whether it is a reasonable choice within a gap left open by Congress, the challenge must fail. In such a case, federal judges—who have no constituency—have a duty to respect legitimate policy choices made by those who do.

NOTES

1. Is "*Chevron* deference" desirable? Apparently, it makes no difference to the Court whether Congress explicitly delegates interpretive power to an agency, simply fails to address it, or shunts it to the agency because members of Congress can't agree. Should the reason for the statutory ambiguity matter to the reviewing court? Is there any reason to believe that Congress prefers to have ambiguities resolved by administrators (potentially from the opposing political party) rather than courts? Conservative judges and commentators have recently expressed doubts about *Chevron*. For instance, Justice Gorsuch, while on the court of appeals, suggested that the doctrine be reconsidered because it distorts the separation of powers. In particular, he said that under *Chevron*, "courts are not fulfilling their duty to interpret the law and declare invalid agency actions inconsistent with those interpretations in the cases and controversies that come before them." *Gutierrez-Brizuela v. Lynch*, 834 F.3d 1142, 1153 (10th Cir. 2016) (Gorsuch, J., concurring). It remains to be seen whether the Court will limit the scope of *Chevron* or even overrule it.

2. While deferential on its face, the *Chevron* test has proved sufficiently malleable to enable reviewing courts to preserve a good deal of authority over determining statutory meaning. *See, e.g., FDA v. Brown & Williamson Tobacco Corp.*, 529 U.S. 120 (2000) (striking down at step one the FDA's assertion of regulatory authority over tobacco products as "drug delivery devices" within the meaning of the Food, Drug and Cosmetic Act). If the Court proceeds to step two, however, the "permissibility" inquiry is similar to arbitrary or capricious review: if the agency's interpretation is reasonable, it will typically be upheld. *See INS v. Aguirre-Aguirre*, 526 U.S. 415 (1999) (overruling the court of appeals for not accepting, at step two, the United States Board of Immigration Appeals' definition of "serious nonpolitical crime").

3. The reach of *Chevron* was also circumscribed by *United States v. Mead Corp.*, 533 U.S. 218 (2001). This opinion, on the validity of a Customs Service classification of day planners as "bound diaries" in deciding the correct tariff to be applied, held that *Chevron* deference should apply only where "Congress delegated authority to the agency generally to make rules carrying the force of law, and that the agency interpretation claiming deference was promulgated in the exercise of that authority." *Id.* at 226–27. In *Mead*, the Court decided that the procedures Congress set out for the Customs Service to make such rulings did not indicate any intention to grant the agency rulemaking authority, and thus the Customs ruling deserved less deference than it would be accorded under *Chevron*. *Id.* at 231–32. *Mead* moved from *Chevron*'s seemingly clear-cut two-step rule towards a more case-by-case approach. It invites courts to apply *Chevron* more narrowly and resurrects the never-resolved debate over how much deference agencies should receive. *See* Cass R. Sunstein, *Chevron Step Zero*, 92 VA. L. REV. 187 (2006) (arguing that *Chevron* should be applied more broadly than it was even before *Mead*, to allow decisions to be made by institutions more expert and more politically accountable than the courts). Note that *Chevron* deference applies even when the question is the agency's jurisdiction rather than the substance of its

decision. *City of Arlington, Tex. v. FCC*, 569 U.S. 290,133 S.Ct. 1863,185 L.Ed.2d 941 (2013).

D. THE NATIONAL ENVIRONMENTAL POLICY ACT

Observing the procedural requirements of the APA is intended to improve agency decision-making by making decisions both more rational and open to public scrutiny. There are, in addition to the APA, a number of other laws that seek to improve agency decision-making. One of the earliest and most significant is the National Environmental Policy Act, signed in 1970 by Richard Nixon and frequently cited as a landmark environmental law. NEPA is not a regulatory statute like the Clean Air Act or the Clean Water Act. It is not aimed at individuals or firms but instead at federal government agencies. To be sure, NEPA contains bold language. For example, the statute declares it to be the policy of the federal government to "use all practicable means and measures * * * to create the conditions under which man and nature can exist in productive harmony." § 101(a). The Act also states that "each person should enjoy a healthful environment." § 101(c). But its most important provision is a seemingly mild-mannered requirement that federal agencies file environmental impact statements (EISs) for major federal actions significantly affecting the human environment.

Specifically, § 102(2)(C) requires all agencies of the federal government to "include in every recommendation or report on proposals for legislation and other major Federal actions significantly affecting the quality of the human environment, a detailed statement by the responsible official" on the environmental impact of the proposed action and alternatives to the proposed action. Failure to comply with this requirement may bar an agency from moving forward. See *Oglala Sioux Tribe v. U.S. Nuclear Regulatory Commission*, 896 F.3d 520 (D.C. Cir. 2018), reversing a hearing officer's decision to leave a permit in effect after having found a serious NEPA violation.

Title II of NEPA establishes the Council on Environmental Quality (CEQ) in the Executive Office of the President, which Congress has charged chiefly with information gathering and disseminating responsibilities. The CEQ advises the President in preparation of annual environmental reports, gathers and publishes information on environmental trends, and reviews federal government programs to ensure that they are contributing to the achievement of NEPA's policy goals. § 204. In addition, the CEQ is tasked, by Executive Order, with issuing regulations to assist with the implementation of NEPA. *See* Executive Order No. 11514 (1970) as amended by Executive Order No. 11991 (1977).

The CEQ regulations, codified at 40 C.F.R. §§ 1500–1508, now contain detailed procedural requirements governing the entire EIS process, which are binding on all federal executive agencies. *See* 40 C.F.R. § 1500.3. Courts have held that CEQ regulations are entitled to "substantial deference." *See Andrus v. Sierra Club*, 442 U.S. 347 (1979). Many agencies have supplemented the CEQ regulations with EIS regulations of their own. The regulations have proved helpful to courts in interpreting NEPA's provisions and have provided guidance to agencies on how to perform their NEPA obligations. The Trump Administration asked for comments on possible improvements to the CEQ regulations in 2018 but has not yet proposed any amendments. *Update to the Regulations for Implementing the Procedural Provisions of the National Environmental Policy Act*, 83 FED. REG. 28591 (August. 20, 2018). This Advanced Notice of Proposed Rulemaking raised twenty questions about possible areas for change, including most of the issues covered in this chapter.

The process normally begins with an "environmental assessment" (EA), 40 C.F.R. §§ 1501.3–1501.4, prepared under procedures the agencies are required to develop themselves. § 1507.3. The EA is "a concise public document" that "[b]riefly provide[s] sufficient evidence and analysis" for deciding whether to produce an EIS, and that also considers alternatives to the proposed action, as required by § 102(2)(E) of NEPA. 40 C.F.R. § 1508.9. See *Western Watersheds Proj. v. Abbey*, 719 F.3d 1035 ((th Cir. 2013). If the agency decides not to prepare an EIS, it must make a "finding of no significant impact" (FONSI) available to the public. 40 C.F.R. § 1501.4(e)(1). This finding is subject to judicial review using the "arbitrary or capricious" standard. Courts have consistently held that a FONSI may be based on the impact as lessened by mitigation measures, subject to certain limitations. *See, e.g.*, *Atchafalaya Riverkeeper v. U.S. Department of the Interior*, 994 F.3d 692 (5th Cir. 2018) (mitigation banks for wetlands adequately compensated for harm caused by project.) Agencies need not do an EIS, or even an EA, if the activity in question merits a "categorical exclusion," a statutory exception for activities that have been previously determined neither individually nor cumulatively to have a significant effect on the human environment. 40 C.F.R. § 1508.4. *See also* Kevin H. Moriarty, Note, *Circumventing the National Environmental Policy Act: Agency Abuse of the Categorical Exclusion*, 79 NYU. L. REV. 2312 (2004) for more on the categorical exclusion process. The use of categorical exclusions has become increasingly common.

The first step in preparing an EIS is called "scoping." Scoping is intended: (a) to obtain early participation by other agencies and the public in planning the EIS, (b) to determine the scope of the EIS, and (c) to determine the significant issues to be discussed in the EIS. 40 C.F.R. § 1501.7(a).

The actual preparation of the EIS itself involves a draft EIS, a comment period, and a final EIS. 40 C.F.R. §§ 1503.1, 1503.4. Agencies with jurisdiction or special expertise relating to the project are required to comment. 40 C.F.R. § 1503.2. Major interagency disagreements are referred to CEQ, which can then take a variety of actions, including publication of recommendations or referral to the President. 40 C.F.R. §§ 1504.1, 1504.3(f). When an agency reaches a final decision on the project, it must prepare a "record of decision" summarizing its actions, and explaining why it rejected environmentally preferable alternatives and mitigation measures. 40 C.F.R. § 1503.3.

If you find this process confusing, you may want to consult a flow chart provided by CEQ, which appears at the end of this chapter.

We will begin by discussing the threshold requirements for performing an EIS rather than an EA. We then consider the scope, timing, and content of the EIS. The chapter then closes with a brief discussion of NEPA's past and future.

1. THRESHOLD REQUIREMENTS

NEPA requires the filing of an environmental impact statement in connection with "legislation and other major Federal actions significantly affecting the quality of the human environment."[3] Thus, an EIS is needed only when a project is "major," constitutes a "federal action," and has a "significant environmental impact." The following materials cover the scope of these threshold requirements. First, when is an impact "environmental" in nature?

METROPOLITAN EDISON CO. V. PEOPLE AGAINST NUCLEAR ENERGY
Supreme Court of the United States, 1983.
460 U.S. 766, 103 S.Ct. 1556, 75 L.Ed.2d 534.

JUSTICE REHNQUIST delivered the opinion of the Court.

The issue in these cases is whether petitioner Nuclear Regulatory Commission (NRC) complied with the National Environmental Policy Act, when it considered whether to permit petitioner Metropolitan Edison Co. to resume operation of the Three Mile Island Unit 1 nuclear power plant (TMI-1). The Court of Appeals for the District of Columbia Circuit held that the NRC improperly failed to consider whether the risk of an accident at TMI-1 might cause harm to the psychological health and community well-being of residents of the surrounding area. We reverse.

Metropolitan owns two nuclear power plants at Three Mile Island near Harrisburg, Pennsylvania. Both of these plants were licensed by the NRC

---

[3]   There are a few explicit statutory exclusions from NEPA, ranging from the important (the Alaska oil pipeline) to the bizarre (the San Antonio Freeway). *See* Frederick R. Anderson, *The National Environmental Policy Act, in* FEDERAL ENVIRONMENTAL LAW 273 (Erica L. Dolgin & Thomas G.P. Guilbert, eds. 1974). Note that many but not all EPA actions are also exempt. *See* § 511(c) of the Clean Water Act and 15 U.S.C.A. § 793.

after extensive proceedings, which included preparation of Environmental Impact Statements (EIS). On March 28, 1979, TMI-1 was not operating; it had been shut down for refueling. TMI-2 was operating, and it suffered a serious accident that damaged the reactor * * *.

After the accident, the NRC ordered Metropolitan to keep TMI-1 shut down until it had an opportunity to determine whether the plant could be operated safely. The NRC then published a notice of hearing specifying several safety related issues for consideration. The notice stated that the Commission had not determined whether to consider psychological harm or other indirect effects of the accident or of renewed operation of TMI-1. * * *

All the parties agree that effects on human health can be cognizable under NEPA, and that human health may include psychological health. The Court of Appeals thought these propositions were enough to complete a syllogism that disposes of the case: NEPA requires agencies to consider effects on health. An effect on psychological health is an effect on health. Therefore, NEPA requires agencies to consider the effects on psychological health asserted by PANE. PANE, using similar reasoning, contends that because the psychological health damage to its members would be caused by a change in the environment (renewed operation of TMI-1), NEPA requires the NRC to consider that damage. Although these arguments are appealing at first glance, we believe they skip over an essential step in the analysis. They do not consider the closeness of the relationship between the change in the environment and the "effect" at issue. * * *

To paraphrase the statutory language in light of the facts of this case, where an agency action significantly affects the quality of the human environment, the agency must evaluate the "environmental impact" and any unavoidable adverse environmental effects of its proposal. The theme of § 102 is sounded by the adjective "environmental": NEPA does not require the agency to assess *every* impact or effect of its proposed action, but only the impact or effect on the environment. If we were to seize the word "environmental" out of its context and give it the broadest possible definition, the words "adverse environmental effects" might embrace virtually any consequence of a governmental action that someone thought "adverse." But we think the context of the statute shows that Congress was talking about the physical environment—the world around us, so to speak. NEPA was designed to promote human welfare by alerting governmental actors to the effect of their proposed actions on the physical environment.

To determine whether § 102 requires consideration of a particular effect, we must look at the relationship between that effect and the change in the physical environment caused by the major federal action at issue. For example, if the Department of Health and Human Services were to implement extremely stringent requirements for hospitals and nursing homes receiving federal funds, many perfectly adequate hospitals and homes might be forced out of existence. The remaining facilities might be so limited or so expensive that many ill people would be unable to afford medical care and would suffer severe health damage. Nonetheless, NEPA would not require the Department to prepare an EIS evaluating that health damage because it would not be proximately related to a change in the physical environment.

Some effects that are "caused by" a change in the physical environment in the sense of "but for" causation, will nonetheless not fall within § 102 because the causal chain is too attenuated. For example, residents of the Harrisburg area have relatives in other parts of the country. Renewed operation of TMI-1 may well cause psychological health problems for these people. They may suffer "anxiety, tension and fear, a sense of helplessness," and accompanying physical disorders, because of the risk that their relatives may be harmed in a nuclear accident. However, this harm is simply too remote from the physical environment to justify requiring the NRC to evaluate the psychological health damage to these people that may be caused by renewed operation of TMI-1.

Our understanding of the congressional concerns that led to the enactment of NEPA suggests that the terms "environmental effect" and "environmental impact" in § 102 be read to include a requirement of a reasonably close causal relationship between a change in the physical environment and the effect at issue. This requirement is like the familiar doctrine of proximate cause from tort law. See generally W. Prosser, Law of Torts ch. 7 (4th ed. 1971).[7] The issue before us then is how to give content to this requirement. This is a question of first impression in this Court.

The federal action that affects the environment in this case is permitting renewed operation of TMI-1. The direct effects on the environment of this action include release of low-level radiation, increased fog in the Harrisburg area (caused by operation of the plant's cooling towers), and the release of warm water into the Susquehanna River. The NRC has considered each of these effects in its EIS, and again in the EIA. Another effect of renewed operation is a risk of a nuclear accident. The NRC has also considered this effect.[9]

---

[7]   In drawing this analogy, we do not mean to suggest that any cause-effect relation too attenuated to merit damages in a tort suit would also be too attenuated to merit notice in an EIS; nor do we mean to suggest the converse. In the context of both tort law and NEPA, courts must look to the underlying policies or legislative intent in order to draw a manageable line between those causal changes that may make an actor responsible for an effect and those that do not.

[9]   The NRC concluded that the risk of an accident had not changed significantly since the EIS for TMI-1 was prepared in 1972. We emphasize that in this case we are considering effects caused by the risk of an accident. The situation where an agency is asked to consider effects that will occur if a risk is realized, for example, if an accident occurs at TMI-1, is an entirely different case. The NRC considered, in the original EIS and in the most recent EIA for TMI-1, the possible effects of a number of accidents that might occur at TMI-1.

PANE argues that the psychological health damage it alleges "will flow directly from the risk of [a nuclear] accident." But a *risk* of an accident is not an effect on the physical environment. A risk is, by definition, unrealized in the physical world. In a causal chain from renewed operation of TMI-1 to psychological health damage, the element of risk and its perception by PANE's members are necessary middle links.[10] We believe that the element of risk lengthens the causal chain beyond the reach of NEPA.

Risk is a pervasive element of modern life; to say more would belabor the obvious. Many of the risks we face are generated by modern technology, which brings both the possibility of major accidents and opportunities for tremendous achievements. Medical experts apparently agree that risk can generate stress in human beings, which in turn may rise to the level of serious health damage. For this reason among many others, the question whether the gains from any technological advance are worth its attendant risks may be an important public policy issue. Nonetheless, it is quite different from the question whether the same gains are worth a given level of alteration of our physical environment or depletion of our natural resources. The latter question rather than the former is the central concern of NEPA. * * *

The Court of Appeals thought that PANE's contentions raised an issue of health damage, while those cases presented questions of fear or policy disagreement. We do not believe this line is so easily drawn. Anyone who fears or dislikes a project may find himself suffering from "anxiety, tension, fear, [and] a sense of helplessness." Neither the language nor the history of NEPA suggest that it was intended to give citizens a general opportunity to air their policy objections to proposed federal actions. The political process, and not NEPA, provides the appropriate forum in which to air policy disagreements.[12]

NOTES

1.   Does *PANE* suggest that psychological, social and economic impacts of a project are outside the scope of NEPA? At least one court of appeals has expressed serious doubts about whether socio-economic effects can ever be considered, even if some physical effects are also present. *See* Olmsted *Citizens for a Better Community v. United States*, 793 F.2d 201, 206 (8th Cir. 1986) (no

---

[10]   This risk can be perceived differently by different people. Indeed, it appears that the members of PANE perceive a much greater risk of another nuclear accident at Three Mile Island than is perceived by the NRC and its staff.

[12]   PANE's original contention seems to be addressed as much to the symbolic significance of continued operation of TMI-1 as to the risk of an accident. NEPA does not require consideration of stress caused by the symbolic significance individuals attach to federal actions. Psychological health damage caused by a symbol is even farther removed from the physical environment, and more closely connected with the broader political process, than psychological health damage caused by risk.

impact statement required for conversion of a mental hospital into a prison hospital). Also, Judge Posner has argued that aesthetic effects should rarely compel the completion of an impact statement, since they can be adequately described in the environmental assessment. *River Rd. Alliance, Inc. v. Corps of Eng'rs of U.S. Army*, 764 F.2d 445 (7th Cir. 1985). But other courts require discussion in the EIS of socioeconomic effects that are "interrelated" with physical effects. *See, e.g., Tongass Conserv. Soc. v. Cheney*, 924 F.2d 1137 (D.C. Cir. 1991) (Ginsburg, J.). For a summary of the post-*PANE* cases, *see* Jacquelyn Smith, *Consideration of Socioeconomic Effects Under NEPA and the EC Directive on Environmental Impact Assessment*, 1992 U. CHI. L. F. 355, 363.

2.   Once "environmental effects" are defined, the question still remains how to determine whether such effects are major and significant. The CEQ Regulations state that "[m]ajor reinforces but does not have a meaning independent of significantly." 40 C.F.R. § 1508.18. Note that even if an action is not "major" and therefore does not require an EIS, § 102(2)(E) of NEPA generally still requires agency consideration of alternatives. The CEQ Regulations defining a significant action says that " 'significantly' as used in NEPA requires consideration of both context and intensity":

(a)   *Context.* This means that the significance of an action must be analyzed in several contexts such as society as a whole (human, national), the affected region, the affected interests, and the locality. Significance varies with the setting of the proposed action. For instance, in the case of a site-specific action, significance would usually depend upon the effects in the locale rather than in the world as a whole. Both short-and long-term effects are relevant.

(b)   *Intensity.* This refers to the severity of impact. Responsible officials must bear in mind that more than one agency may make decisions about partial aspects of a major action. The following should be considered in evaluating intensity:

(1)   Impacts that may be both beneficial and adverse. A significant effect may exist even if the Federal agency believes that on balance the effect will be beneficial.

(2)   The degree to which the proposed action affects public health or safety.

(3)   Unique characteristics of the geographic area such as proximity to historic or cultural resources, park lands, prime farmlands, wetlands, wild and scenic rivers, or ecologically critical areas.

(4)   The degree to which the effects on the quality of the human environment are likely to be highly controversial.

(5)   The degree to which the possible effects on the human environment are highly uncertain or involve unique or unknown risks.

(6)   The degree to which the action may establish a precedent for future actions with significant effects or represents a decision in principle about a future consideration.

(7)   Whether the action is related to other actions with individually insignificant but cumulatively significant impacts. Significance exists if it is reasonable to anticipate a cumulatively significant impact on the environment. Significance cannot be avoided by terming an action temporary or by breaking it down into small component parts. * * *

40 C.F.R. 1508.27.

3.   *PANE* shares one feature in common with all other Supreme Court NEPA decisions: the government won. This may reflect in part a lack of enthusiasm for NEPA on the part of the Justices. It also reflects shrewd advocacy by the Solicitor General, including careful selection of cases for review and strategic concessions or abandonment of potentially losing arguments. See Richard Lazarus, *The National Environmental Policy Act in the U.S. Supreme Court: A Reappraisal and a Peek Behind the Curtains*, 100 GEO. L.J. 1507 (2012). Lazarus also noted that NEPA has had only one strong advocate within the Court, Justice Douglas, who was quite ineffective in his dealings with the other Justices on the issue.

HANLY V. KLEINDIENST [HANLY II]
United States Court of Appeals, Second Circuit, 1972.
471 F.2d 823, *cert. denied* 412 U.S. 908, 93 S.Ct. 2290, 36 L.Ed.2d 974 (1973).

MANSFIELD, CIRCUIT JUDGE.

[This case involved planning for a nine-story federal jail behind the U.S. Courthouse in Manhattan. In an earlier opinion, *Hanly v. Mitchell [Hanly I]*, 460 F.2d 640, cert. den. 409 U.S. 990 (1972), the court had remanded the agency's environmental assessment. According to the court, the EA needed to include factors relating to the "quality of life" for city residents, including crime, congestion, and the availability of drugs. (Query whether that holding survives the Supreme Court's later decision in *PANE*.) The GSA then began work on supplementing its assessment of environmental impacts.]

Following the remand a new threshold determination in the form of a 25-page "Assessment of the Environmental Impact" ("Assessment" herein) was made by the GSA and submitted to the district court on June 15, 1972. This document * * * reflects a detailed consideration of numerous relevant factors. Among other things, it analyzes the size, exact location, and proposed use of the MCC; its design features, construction, and aesthetic relationship to its surroundings; the extent to which its occupants and activities conducted in it will be visible by the community; the estimated effects of its operation upon traffic, public transit and parking facilities; its approximate population, including detainees and employees; its effect on the level of noise, smoke, dirt, obnoxious odors, sewage and solid waste removal; and its energy demands. It also sets forth possible alternatives, concluding that there is none that is satisfactory. Upon the basis of this Assessment the Acting Commissioner of the Public Building Service Division of the GSA, who is the responsible official in charge, concluded on June 7, 1972, that the MCC was not an action significantly affecting the quality of the human environment. * * *

In the absence of any congressional or administrative interpretation of the term, we are persuaded that in deciding whether a major federal action will "significantly" affect the quality of the human environment the agency in charge, although vested with broad discretion, should normally be required to review the proposed action in the light of at least two relevant factors: (1) the extent to which the action will cause adverse environmental effects in excess of those created by existing uses in the area affected by it, and (2) the absolute quantitative adverse environmental effects of the action itself, including the cumulative harm that results from its contribution to existing adverse conditions or uses in the affected area. Where conduct conforms to existing uses, its adverse consequences will usually be less significant than when it represents a radical change. Absent some showing that an entire neighborhood is in the process of redevelopment, its existing environment, though frequently below an ideal standard, represents a norm that cannot be ignored. For instance, one more highway in an area honeycombed with roads usually has less of an adverse impact than if it were constructed through a roadless public park.

Although the existing environment of the area which is the site of a major federal action constitutes one criterion to be considered, it must be recognized that even a slight increase in adverse conditions that form an existing environmental milieu may sometimes threaten harm that is significant. One more factory polluting air and water in an area zoned for industrial use may represent the straw that breaks the back of the environmental camel. Hence the absolute, as well as comparative, effects of a major federal action must be considered.

Chief Judge Friendly's thoughtful dissent, while conceding that we (and governmental agencies) face a difficult problem in determining the meaning of the vague and amorphous term "significantly" as used in § 102(2)(C), offers no solution other than to suggest that an impact statement should be required whenever a major federal action might be "arguably" or "potentially" significant and that such an interpretation would insure the preparation of impact statements except in cases of "true" insignificance. In our view this suggestion merely substitutes one form of semantical vagueness for another. * * *

* * * Now that the GSA has made and submitted its redetermination in the form of a 25-page "Assessment," our task is to determine (1) whether it satisfies the foregoing tests as to environmental significance, and (2) whether GSA, in making its assessment and determination, has observed "procedure required by law" as that term is used in § 10 of the APA, 5 U.S.C.A. § 706(2)(D). * * *

Appellants offer little or no evidence to contradict the detailed facts found by the GSA. For the most part their opposition is based upon a psychological distaste for having a jail located so close to residential apartments, which is understandable enough. It is doubtful whether psychological and sociological effects upon neighbors constitute the type of factors that may be considered in making such a determination since they do not lend themselves to measurement. However we need not decide that issue because these apartments were constructed within two or three blocks of another existing jail, The Manhattan House of Detention for Men, which is much larger than the proposed MCC and houses approximately 1,200 prisoners. Furthermore the area in which the MCC is located has at all times been zoned by the City of New York as a commercial district designed to provide for a wide range of uses, *specifically including "Prisons."*

Despite the GSA's scrupulous efforts the appellants do present one or two factual issues that merit further consideration and findings by the GSA. One bears on the possibility that the MCC will substantially increase the risk of crime in the immediate area, a relevant factor as to which the Assessment fails to make an outright finding despite the direction to do so in *Hanly I*. Appellants urge that the Community Treatment Program and the program for observation and study of nonresident out-patients will endanger the health and safety of the immediate area by exposing neighbors and passersby to drug addicts visiting the MCC for drug maintenance and to drug pushers and hangers-on who would inevitably frequent the vicinity of a drug maintenance center. If the MCC were to be used as a drug treatment center, the potential increase in crime might tip the scales in favor of a mandatory detailed impact statement. * * *

NOTES

1. Note the court's comment that "[a]bsent some showing that an entire neighborhood is in the process of redevelopment, its existing environment, though frequently below an ideal standard, represents a norm that cannot be ignored." This observation seems innocuous enough, and a similar view is echoed by courts that view compliance with local zoning as evidence against any significant impact. But the implications are potentially troubling. Recall the discussion of environmental justice in Chapter 2. Poor and minority neighborhoods are more likely to suffer already from a lack of environmental amenities, and from an excess of environmental harms. Hence, any given

project is less likely to be considered significant if it is located in such a neighborhood, rather than in a more affluent area. Is it unfair to suggest that the *Hanly* court would have been less troubled by a proposed jail in a low-income, primarily minority neighborhood? Because performing an EIS involves both expense and delay, there is consequently an incentive (other things being equal) to locate environmentally questionable projects in "bad" neighborhoods especially if there is a lack of organized political opposition. Is this "environmental racism" or merely realistic urban planning?

2.   Judge Posner has offered another interesting test for whether an impact is significant:

> The statutory concept of "significant" impact has no determinate meaning, and to interpret it sensibly in particular cases requires a comparison that is also a prediction: whether the time and expense of preparing an environmental impact statement are commensurate with the likely benefits from a more searching evaluation than an environmental assessment provides.

River Road Alliance Inc. v. Corps of Engineers, 764 F.2d 445 (7th Cir. 1985).

3.   Must agencies produce an EIS for environmental effects that they have no ability to prevent? Consider *Department of Transportation v. Public Citizen*, 541 U.S. 752 (2004), in which the Supreme Court reviewed the Department of Transportation's threshold determination that it did not have to produce an EIS for proposed rules regarding the effects of allowing trucks to enter the United States from Mexico. The rules were part of the Bush administration's effort to comply with the North American Free Trade Agreement (NAFTA). The decision to admit the trucks was made by the President, who is not covered by NEPA, although the trucks would not be able to enter until DOT adopted safety and inspection rules. The Court ruled that DOT did not have the authority to exclude the trucks, only to create safety conditions, so it was sufficient to assess the impacts of the safety program itself, such as emissions from diverting trucks for roadside inspections, rather than the overall effects of admitting the additional trucks.

4.   Besides the issues considered in the *Hanly* and *Public Citizen* cases, an additional threshold issue sometimes also arises: Is there a *federal* action? The CEQ Regulations state that an action is federal if it is "potentially subject to Federal control and responsibility," "including projects and programs entirely or partly financed, assisted, conducted, regulated, or approved by federal agencies." 40 C.F.R. § 1508.18. Another related problem arises when the federal government has failed to exercise its power to prevent actions by others. Courts have generally (but not always) held NEPA inapplicable. *See Defenders of Wildlife v. Andrus*, 627 F.2d 1238 (D.C. Cir. 1980); *Marbled Murrelet v. Babbitt*, 83 F.3d 1068 (9th Cir. 1996).

2. SCOPE AND TIMING OF THE EIS

NEPA is supposed to integrate environmental impact analysis into an agency's decision-making process, but at what point in an agency's deliberations should it be required to consider the environmental impacts of the alternatives it is considering? To environmentalists, the sooner the better, since early consideration may prevent the agencies from investing heavily in proposals that agencies may later come to realize impose heavy costs on the environment. Environmental plaintiffs worry that by the time the environmental impacts are assessed, administrative inertia and political momentum may carry the project to fruition despite a clear recognition of its potentially devastating effects on the environment. But to the agencies, the sooner they must prepare environmental assessments and environmental impact statements, the greater the burden on them will be, since they have yet to narrow down their choices. Conceivably, some options will be ruled out early in the decision-making process so it would be a waste of time to study their environmental impacts. And of course, some agencies will wish to wait as late as possible to file an EIS in order to stave off potential opposition as long as possible. Since the statute gives little guidance on the timing issue, courts have attempted to formulate a rule for the timing of environmental impact statements themselves.

An equally difficult question arises as to the true scope of the EIS required for a proposed federal action. The agency may want to define the project very narrowly to avoid the need for an EIS or at least minimize the scope of the impacts it must consider in an EIS. In the case of a highway, powerline, or pipeline, the agency may break a project into segments to minimize the need for environmental review. For instance, in *Delaware Riverkeeper Network v. FERC*, 753 F.3d 1304 (D.C. Cir. 2014), the agency had limited its environmental assessment to one segment of a series of related projects on the same pipeline. The court held this segmentation of the work to be arbitrary and capricious.

Segmentation is a relatively straightforward issue, but in more complex situations it can be hard to determine the boundaries of a project. This raises a number of questions. Suppose the responsible agency has no formal proposal for, say, granting oil leases, but is instead reviewing lease applications on a case-by-case basis. Here the worry is that the scope of each individual EIS for each individual license is too small in light of the cumulative impact. In this case, must the agency consider the existing leases and their cumulative environmental impact on a locale or region each time it considers a new lease application? Must the agency consider the potential *future* leases it might grant in the same region? Should courts impose a "constructive regional proposal" on an agency that appears to be pursuing an off-the-books regional policy, and allow citizen challenges to force the responsible agency to prepare an EIS for the region?

On the other hand, the agency may sometimes be defining the project too broadly, allowing it to justify local environmental impacts by pointing to benefits elsewhere. To what extent does the agency's own definition of the scope of its proposal determine the scope of the EIS? If an agency defines a proposal as national in scope, but the proposal is bound to have much heavier environmental impacts on a particular region of the country, should the agency be allowed to trade off the environmental impacts of its proposed action on that region by weighing it against the proposal's benefits elsewhere in the nation? Or should the courts closely scrutinize the purported scope of the proposal to see if, in light of its likely impacts, the agency should file a regional impact statement?

In the *Kleppe* case excerpted below, both timing and scope were at issue. The agency was found to have contemplated a regional plan at one point in its deliberations but didn't perform an EIS for that plan. It later adopted a national plan for which it did perform an EIS. First, then, did the agency delay too long before performing an EIS by waiting until adoption of a national plan to prepare an EIS? Second, by adopting a national plan that had profound *regional* impacts, was the scope of its resulting EIS too broad? Should the agency be allowed to define the scope of an EIS based purely on its own characterization of the reach of its plan? Here are the Court's answers.

KLEPPE V. SIERRA CLUB

Supreme Court of the United States, 1976.
427 U.S. 390, 96 S.Ct. 2718, 49 L.Ed.2d 576.

JUSTICE POWELL delivered the opinion of the Court.

Respondents, several organizations concerned with the environment, brought this suit in July 1973 in the United States District Court for the District of Columbia. The defendants in the suit, petitioners here, were the officials of the Department and other federal agencies responsible for issuing coal leases, approving mining plans, granting rights-of-way and taking the other actions necessary to enable private companies and public utilities to develop coal reserves on land owned or controlled by the Federal Government. Citing widespread interest in the reserves of a region identified as the "Northern Great Plains region," and an alleged threat from coal-related operations to their members' enjoyment of the region's environment, respondents claimed that the federal officials could not allow further development without preparing a "comprehensive environmental impact statement" under § 102(2)(C) [of NEPA] on the entire region. They sought declaratory and injunctive relief. * * *

The record and the opinions of the courts below contain extensive facts about coal development and the geographic area involved in this suit. The facts that we consider essential, however, can be stated briefly.

The "Northern Great Plains region" identified in respondents' complaint encompasses portions of four States—northeastern Wyoming, eastern Montana, western North Dakota and western South Dakota. There is no dispute about its richness in coal, nor about the waxing interest in developing that coal, nor about the crucial role the federal petitioners will play due to the significant percentage of the coal to which they control access. The Department has initiated, in this decade, three studies in areas either inclusive of or included within this region. The North Central Power Study was addressed to the potential for coordinated development of electric power in an area encompassing all or part of 15 States in the north central United States. It aborted in 1972 for lack of interest on the part of electric utilities. The Montana-Wyoming Aqueducts Study, intended to recommend the best use of water resources for coal development in southeastern Montana and northeastern Wyoming, was suspended in 1972 with the initiation of the third study, the Northern Great Plains Resources Program (NGPRP).

While the record does not reveal the degree of concern with environmental matters in the first two studies, it is clear that the NGPRP was devoted entirely to the environment. It was carried out by an interagency, federal-state task force with public participation, and was designed "to assess the potential social, economic and environmental impacts" from resource development in five States—Montana, Wyoming, South Dakota, North Dakota, and Nebraska. Its primary objective was "to provide an analytical and informational framework for policy and planning decisions at all levels of government" by formulating several "scenarios" showing the probable consequences for the area's environment and culture from the various possible techniques and levels of resource development. The final interim report of the NGPRP was issued August 1, 1975, shortly after the decision of the Court of Appeals in this case.

In addition, since 1973 the Department has engaged in a complete review of its coal leasing program for the entire Nation. * * * The purpose of the program review was to study the environmental impact of the Department's entire range of coal-related activities and to develop a planning system to guide the national leasing program. The impact statement, known as the "Coal Programmatic EIS," went through several drafts before issuing in final form on September 19, 1975—shortly before the petition for certiorari was filed in this case. * * *

The major issue remains the one with which the suit began: whether NEPA requires petitioners to prepare an environmental impact statement on the entire Northern Great Plains region. Petitioners, arguing the negative, rely squarely upon the facts of the case and the language of § 102(2)(C) of NEPA. We find their reliance well placed.

* * * Respondents can prevail only if there has been a report or recommendation on a proposal for major federal action with respect to the Northern Great Plains region. Our statement of the relevant facts shows there has been none; instead, all proposals are for actions of either local or national scope.

The local actions are the decisions by the various petitioners to issue a lease, approve a mining plan, issue a right-of-way permit, or take other action to allow private activity at some point within the region identified by respondents. Several courts of appeals have held that an impact statement must be included in the report or recommendation on a proposal for such action if the private activity to be permitted is one "significantly affecting the quality of the human environment" within the meaning of § 102(2)(C). The petitioners do not dispute this requirement in this case, and indeed have prepared impact statements on several proposed actions of this type in the Northern Great Plains during the course of this litigation. Similarly, the federal petitioners agreed at oral argument that § 102(2)(C) required the Coal Programmatic EIS that was prepared in tandem with the new national coal leasing program and included as part of the final report on the proposal for adoption of that program. Their admission is well made, for the new leasing program is a coherent plan of national scope, and its adoption surely has significant environmental consequences.

But there is no evidence in the record of an action or a proposal for an action of regional scope. The District Court, in fact, expressly found that there was no existing or proposed plan or program on the part of the Federal Government for the regional development of the area described in respondents' complaint. It found also that the three studies initiated by the Department in areas either included within or inclusive of respondents' region—that is, the Montana-Wyoming Aqueducts Study, the North Central Power Study, and the NGPRP—were not parts of any plan or program to develop or encourage development of the Northern Great Plains. That court found no evidence that the individual coal development projects undertaken or proposed by private industry and public utilities in that part of the country are integrated into a plan or otherwise interrelated. These findings were not disturbed by the Court of Appeals, and they remain fully supported by the record in this Court. * * *

[R]espondents have not attempted to support the Court of Appeals' decision. Instead, respondents renew an argument they appear to have made to the Court of Appeals, but which that court did not reach. Respondents insist that, even without a comprehensive federal plan for the development of the Northern Great Plains, a "regional" impact statement nevertheless is required on all coal-related projects in the region because they are intimately related.

There are two ways to view this contention. First, it amounts to an attack on the sufficiency of the impact statements already prepared by the petitioners on the coal-related projects that they have approved or stand ready to approve. As such, we cannot consider it in this proceeding, for the case was not brought as a challenge to a particular impact statement and there is no impact statement in the record. It also is possible to view the respondents' argument as an attack upon the decision of the petitioners not to prepare one comprehensive impact statement on all proposed projects in the region. This contention properly is before us, for the petitioners have made it clear they do not intend to prepare such a statement.

We begin by stating our general agreement with respondents' basic premise that § 102(2)(C) may require a comprehensive impact statement in certain situations where several proposed actions are pending at the same time. * * * By requiring an impact statement Congress intended to assure such consideration during the development of a proposal or—as in this case—during the formulation of a position on a proposal submitted by private parties. A comprehensive impact statement may be necessary in some cases for an agency to meet this duty. Thus, when several proposals for coal-related actions that will have cumulative or synergistic environmental impact upon a region are pending concurrently before an agency, their environmental consequences must be considered together.[20] Only through comprehensive consideration of pending proposals can the agency evaluate different courses of action.[21] * * *

Respondents conceded at oral argument that to prevail they must show that petitioners have acted arbitrarily in refusing to prepare one comprehensive statement on this entire region, and we agree. The determination of the region, if any, with respect to which a comprehensive statement is necessary requires the weighing of a number of relevant factors, including the extent of the interrelationship among proposed actions and practical considerations of feasibility. Resolving these issues requires a high level of technical expertise and is properly left to the informed discretion of the responsible federal agencies. Absent a showing of arbitrary action, we must assume that the agencies have exercised this

---

[20]   At some points in their brief respondents appear to seek a comprehensive impact statement covering contemplated projects in the region as well as those that already have been proposed. The statute, however, speaks solely in terms of *proposed* actions; it does not require an agency to consider the possible environmental impacts of less imminent actions when preparing the impact statement on proposed actions. Should contemplated actions later reach the stage of actual proposals, impact statements on them will take into account the effect of their approval upon the existing environment; and the condition of that environment presumably will reflect earlier proposed actions and their effects.

[21]   Neither the statute nor its legislative history contemplates that a court should substitute its judgment for that of the agency as to the environmental consequences of its actions. The only role for a court is to insure that the agency has taken a "hard look" at environmental consequences; it cannot "interject itself within the area of discretion of the executive as to the choice of the action to be taken." Natural Resources Defense Council v. Morton, 148 U.S. App. D.C. 5, 16, 458 F.2d 827, 838 (1972).

discretion appropriately. Respondents have made no showing to the contrary.

Respondents' basic argument is that one comprehensive statement on the Northern Great Plains is required because all coal-related activity in that region is "programmatically, geographically, and environmentally" related. Both the alleged "programmatic" relationship and the alleged "geographic" relationship resolve, ultimately, into an argument that the region is proper for a comprehensive impact statement because the petitioners themselves have approached environmental study in this area on a regional basis. Respondents point primarily to the NGPRP, which they claim—and petitioners deny—focused on the region described in the complaint. The precise region of the NGPRP is unimportant, [because it was only a background study]. As for the alleged "environmental" relationship, respondents contend that the coal-related projects "will produce a wide variety of cumulative environmental impacts" throughout the Northern Great Plains region. They described them as follows: diminished availability of water, air and water pollution, increases in population and industrial densities, and perhaps even climatic changes. Cumulative environmental impacts are, indeed, what require a comprehensive impact statement. But determination of the extent and effect of these factors, and particularly identification of the geographic area within which they may occur, is a task assigned to the special competency of the appropriate agencies. Petitioners dispute respondents' contentions that the interrelationship of environmental impacts is region-wide[25] and, as respondents' own submissions indicate, petitioners appear to have determined that the appropriate scope of comprehensive statements should be based on basins, drainage areas, and other factors. We cannot say that petitioners' choices are arbitrary. Even if environmental interrelationships could be shown conclusively to extend across basins and drainage areas, practical considerations of feasibility might well necessitate restricting the scope of comprehensive statements.

In sum, respondents' contention as to the relationships between all proposed coal-related projects in the Northern Great Plains region does not require that petitioners prepare one comprehensive impact statement covering all before proceeding to approve specific pending applications.[26]

---

[25] For example, respondents assert that coal mines in the region are environmentally interrelated because opening one reduces the supply of water in the region for others. Petitioners contend that the water supply for each aquifer or basin within the region—of which there are many—is independent. Moreover, petitioners state in their reply brief that few active or proposed mines in respondents' region are located within 50 miles of any other mine, and there are only 30 active or proposed mines in the entire 90,000 square miles of the region.

[26] Nor is it necessary that petitioners always complete a comprehensive impact statement on all proposed actions in an appropriate region before approving any of the projects. As petitioners have emphasized, and respondents have not disputed, approval of one lease or mining plan does not commit the Secretary to approval of any others; nor, apparently, do single approvals by the other petitioners commit them to subsequent approvals. Thus an agency could approve one pending project that is fully covered by an impact statement, then take into consideration the

As we already have determined that there exists no proposal for regionwide action that could require a regional impact statement, the judgment of the Court of Appeals must be reversed, and the judgment of the District Court reinstated and affirmed.

NOTES

1.   One fact of interest is that the Sierra Club made a deliberate decision not to challenge the sufficiency of the individual EISs, in part because to do so would require litigation in dozens of cases as additional leases were issued. *See* Richard A. Johnston, Kleppe v. Sierra Club: *An Environmental Planning Catch-22*, 1 HARV. ENVTL. L. REV. 182, 187–88 (1976).

2.   *Kleppe* states a simple rule: the scope and timing of the environmental review are dictated by the scope and timing of the proposal. But note that under some circumstances the agency may be required to consider synergistic effects between proposals, such as the impacts of multiple proposed amendments to a regulation. See *Western Watersheds Project v. Kraayenbrink*, 632 F.3d 472, 493–494 (9th Cir. 2011).

3.   The CEQ regulations address both the timing and scope issues. On the timing issue, the most important provision is 40 C.F.R. § 1508.23, which defines the term "proposal" as follows:

> "Proposal" exists at that stage in the development of an action when an agency subject to the Act has a goal and is actively preparing to make a decision on one or more alternative means of accomplishing that goal and the effects can be meaningfully evaluated. Preparation of an environmental impact statement on a proposal should be timed (section 1502.5) so that the final statement may be completed in time for the statement to be included in any recommendation or report on the proposal. A proposal may exist in fact as well as by agency declaration that one exists.

Section 1508.23 must be read together with two other sections. Section 1502.5 provides:

> An agency shall commence preparation of an environmental impact statement as close as possible to the time the agency is developing or is presented with a proposal (section 1508.23) so that preparation can be completed in time for the final statement to be included in any recommendation or report on the proposal. The statement shall be prepared early enough so that it can serve practically as an important contribution to the decisionmaking process and will not be used to rationalize or justify decisions already made * * *.

This section is reinforced by § 1501.2, which provides that "[a]gencies shall integrate the NEPA process with other planning at the earliest possible time

---

environmental effects of that existing project when preparing the comprehensive statement on the cumulative impact of the remaining proposals.

to insure that planning and decisions reflect environmental values, to avoid delays later in the process, and to head off potential conflicts." These regulations suggest a need to construe the definition of "proposal" in favor of early application.

The Regulations also provide explicit criteria on the scope issue:

2020 amendment deleted everything after this.

Scope consists of the range of actions, alternatives, and impacts to be considered in an environmental impact statement. The scope of an individual statement may depend on its relationships to other statements (sections 1502.20 and 1508.28). To determine the scope of environmental impact statements, agencies shall consider 3 types of actions, 3 types of alternatives, and 3 types of impacts. They include:

(a) Actions (other than unconnected single actions) which may be:

(1) Connected actions, which means that they are closely related and therefore should be discussed in the same impact statement. Actions are connected if they:

(i) Automatically trigger other actions which may require environmental impact statements.

(ii) Cannot or will not proceed unless other actions are taken previously or simultaneously.

(iii) Are interdependent parts of a larger action and depend on the larger action for their justification.

(2) Cumulative actions, which when viewed with other proposed actions have cumulatively significant impacts and should therefore be discussed in the same impact statement.

(3) Similar actions, which when viewed with other reasonably foreseeable or proposed agency actions, have similarities that provide a basis for evaluating their environmental consequences together, such as common timing or geography. An agency may wish to analyze these actions in the same impact statement. It should do so when the best way to assess adequately the combined impacts of similar actions or reasonable alternatives to such actions is to treat them in a single impact statement.

(b) Alternatives, which include: (1) No action alternative. (2) Other reasonable courses of actions. (3) Mitigation measures (not in the proposed action).

(c) Impacts, which may be: (1) Direct. (2) Indirect. (3) Cumulative.

40 C.F.R. § 1508.25. For instance, in considering the impact of a new source of air pollution, an agency must consider how it would add to (and interact chemically with) existing air pollution. See *Great Basin Resources v. Bureau of Land Management*, 844 1095, 1105 (9th Cir. 2016).

4. In *Weinberger v. Catholic Action of Hawaii*, 454 U.S. 139 (1981), the Navy was creating "nuclear ready" munitions storage facilities. The Court held

that the Navy only needed to consider the impacts of the construction and of operation of the facilities, not the potential issues relating to storage of nuclear weapons. Actual storage or non-storage of nuclear weapons at the facilities was classified, so the plaintiffs were unable to prove that there was a "proposal" to store the weapons. If such a classified proposal did exist, the Navy would be legally obligated to prepare a classified EIS, although plaintiffs would have no way of knowing whether the law was complied with.

5.   It is not unusual for an agency to perform a programmatic EIS covering a swathe of future actions, following up with EAs covering the remaining site-specific issues. This procedure creates the risk of a "shell game," since some issues may be deferred to later EAs where they can be dismissed as insignificant on a site-specific basis even though the cumulative effect is large. In *Pacific Rivers Council*, 689 F.3d 1012 (9th 2012), the court held that the court must consider environmental impacts as soon as it is reasonably possible to do so, meaning that they must be covered in the programmatic EIS if there is enough evidence available to make that feasible.

The following case considers a key issue in judicial review under NEPA: what is the standard of review?

MARSH V. OREGON NATURAL RESOURCES COUNCIL

Supreme Court of the United States, 1989.
490 U.S. 360, 109 S.Ct. 1851, 104 L.Ed.2d 377.

JUSTICE STEVENS delivered the opinion of the Court.

[This case involved the construction of the Elk Creek Dam. The EIS concluded that the dam would have no major effect on fish production, but that its effect on turbidity might occasionally impair fishing. The plaintiffs argued that a supplemental EIS was required because of two new documents: (1) the "Cramer Memorandum," an Oregon Department of Fish & Wildlife (ODFW) document suggesting that the dam would have a greater effect on downstream fishing, and (2) a U.S. Soil Conservation Service (SCS) soil survey that implied greater downstream turbidity than the EIS suggested. Applying a "reasonableness" standard, the Ninth Circuit held that these documents brought significant new information to light and that the Corps had failed to evaluate that information with sufficient care.]

The parties are in essential agreement concerning the standard that governs an agency's decision whether to prepare a supplemental EIS. They agree that an agency should apply a "rule of reason," and the cases they cite in support of this standard explicate this rule in the same basic terms. These cases make clear that an agency need not supplement an EIS every time new information comes to light after the EIS is finalized. To require otherwise would render agency decision making intractable, always awaiting updated information only to find the new information outdated by the time a decision is made. On the other hand, and as the Government concedes, NEPA does require that agencies take a "hard look" at the environmental effects of their planned action, even after a proposal has received initial approval. Application of the "rule of reason" thus turns on the value of the new information to the still pending decisionmaking process. In this respect the decision whether to prepare a supplemental EIS is similar to the decision whether to prepare an EIS in the first instance: If there remains "major Federal actio[n]" to occur, and if the new information is sufficient to show that the remaining action will "affec[t] the quality of the human environment" in a significant manner or to a significant extent not already considered, a supplemental EIS must be prepared.

[The Court stated that as "a classic example of a factual dispute the resolution of which implicates substantial agency expertise," this suit should be decided under an "arbitrary and capricious" standard rather than any less deferential test.] Because analysis of the relevant documents "requires a high level of technical expertise," we must defer to "the informed discretion of the responsible federal agencies." [*Kleppe*] Under these circumstances, we cannot accept respondents' supposition that review is of a legal question and that the Corps' decision "deserves no deference." Accordingly, as long as the Corps' decision not to supplement the FEISS was not "arbitrary or capricious," it should not be set aside.[23]

As we observed in [*Overton Park*], in making the factual inquiry concerning whether an agency decision was "arbitrary or capricious," the reviewing court "must consider whether the decision was based on a consideration of the relevant factors and whether there has been a clear error of judgment." This inquiry must "be searching and careful," but "the ultimate standard of review is a narrow one." When specialists express conflicting views, an agency must have discretion to rely on the reasonable opinions of its own qualified experts even if, as an original matter, a court might find contrary views more persuasive. On the other hand, in the context of reviewing a decision not to supplement an EIS, courts should not automatically defer to the agency's express reliance on an interest in finality without carefully reviewing the record and satisfying themselves that the agency has made a reasoned decision based on its evaluation of the significance—or lack of significance—of the new information. A contrary approach would not simply render judicial review generally meaningless, but would be contrary to the demand that courts ensure that

---

[23] Respondents note that several Courts of Appeals, including the Court of Appeals for the Ninth Circuit as articulated in this and other cases, have adopted a "reasonableness" standard of review, and argue that we should not upset this well-settled doctrine. This standard, however, has not been adopted by all of the Circuits. Moreover, as some of these courts have recognized, the difference between the "arbitrary or capricious" and "reasonableness" standards is not of great pragmatic consequence. Accordingly, our decision today will not require a substantial reworking of long-established NEPA law.

agency decisions are founded on a reasoned evaluation "of the relevant factors." * * *

[The Court went on to discuss the merits of the Cramer Memorandum and the SCS survey. Neither of these documents was brought up pretrial, nor was any concern expressed about the data they provided before litigation commenced, which cut against plaintiffs' insistence on the significance of the information they contained. The Court then reviewed the Corps' response to the information contained in these reports.]

The Court of Appeals attached special significance to two concerns discussed in the Cramer Memorandum: the danger that an increase in water temperature downstream during fall and early winter will cause an early emergence and thus reduce survival of spring chinook fry and the danger that the dam will cause high fish mortality from an epizootic disease. Both concerns were based partly on fact and partly on speculation. * * *

[Justice Stevens stated that the Corps had offered sufficient assurances on the water temperature issue with its explanation that the model used by the OFDW had not been validated and a demonstration that its results were unreliable. The Corps additionally contended that the Cramer Memorandum had not taken into account the full set of variables that would lessen the temperature increase or otherwise mitigate any of its adverse effects on downstream fish reproduction. The Court also accepted the Corps' argument that the hypothesis that the Lost Creek Dam had contributed to the outbreak of an epizootic disease that had killed off many fish in 1979 and 1980 was contradicted by later, inconsistent chinook mortality data, as well as the fact that water testing failed to reveal the diseased organisms thought to cause the epizootic disease in the outflow from the dam.]

In thus concluding that the Cramer Memorandum did not present significant new information requiring supplementation of the [Final Environmental Impact Statement Supplement] (FEISS), the Corps carefully scrutinized the proffered information. Moreover, in disputing the accuracy and significance of this information, the Corps did not simply rely on its own experts. Rather, two independent experts hired by the Corps to evaluate the ODFW study on which the Cramer Memorandum was premised found significant fault in the methodology and conclusions of the study. We also think it relevant that the Cramer Memorandum did not express the official position of ODFW. In preparing the memorandum, the authors noted that the agency had "adopted a neutral stand on Elk Creek Dam" and argued that new information raised the question whether "our agency should continue to remain neutral." The concerns disclosed in the memorandum apparently were not sufficiently serious to persuade ODFW to abandon its neutral position.

The Court of Appeals also expressed concern that the SCS survey, by demonstrating that the soil content in the Elk Creek watershed is different than assumed in the FEISS, suggested a greater turbidity potential than indicated in the FEISS. In addition, the court observed that ODFW scientists believe that logging and road-building in the Elk Creek watershed has caused increased soil disturbance resulting in higher turbidity than forecast by the FEISS. As to this latter point, the SIR simply concluded that although turbidity may have increased in the early 1980s due to logging, "watershed recovery appears to have occurred to reduce the turbidity levels back to those of the 1970s." The implications of the SCS soil survey are of even less concern. As discussed in the FEISS, water quality studies were conducted in 1974 and 1979 using computer simulation models. The 1974 Study indicated that turbidity in the Rogue River would increase by no more than one to three [Jackson Turbity Units] as a result of the Elk Creek Dam, and the 1979 study verified this result. These studies used water samples taken from Elk Creek near the proposed dam site and from near the Lost Creek Dam, and thus did not simply rely on soil composition maps in drawing their conclusions. Although the [Supplemental Information Report] did not expressly comment on the SCS survey, in light of the in-depth 1974 and 1979 studies, its conclusion that "the turbidity effects are not expected to differ from those described in the 1980 FEISS" surely provided a legitimate reason for not preparing a supplemental FEISS to discuss the subject of turbidity.

There is little doubt that if all of the information contained in the Cramer Memorandum and SCS survey was both new and accurate, the Corps would have been required to prepare a second supplemental EIS. It is also clear that, regardless of its eventual assessment of the significance of this information, the Corps had a duty to take a hard look at the proffered evidence. However, having done so and having determined based on careful scientific analysis that the new information was of exaggerated importance, the Corps acted within the dictates of NEPA in concluding that supplementation was unnecessary. Even if another decisionmaker might have reached a contrary result, it was surely not "a clear error of judgment" for the Corps to have found that the new and accurate information contained in the documents was not significant and that the significant information was not new and accurate. As the SIR demonstrates, the Corps conducted a reasoned evaluation of the relevant information and reached a decision that, although perhaps disputable, was not "arbitrary or capricious."

NOTES

1.   *Marsh* clearly endorses the rule of reason as the standard for agency implementation under NEPA and "arbitrary or capricious" as the test on judicial review. The combination would seem to give the agency a great deal of

leeway. And yet, the Court appraised the record very carefully to ensure that the agency took a "hard look" at the issue. Indeed, lower courts do not appear to have interpreted *Marsh* as a directive for lax judicial review.

2. Climate change is the granddaddy of environmental impacts. Yet no single federal project or regulation can be linked to any specific impact such as an incremental change in sea level. So do increased greenhouse emissions require an EIS (and if so, when)? The Ninth Circuit addressed that issue in the following case.

CENTER FOR BIOLOGICAL DIVERSITY V. NATIONAL HIGHWAY TRAFFIC SAFETY ADMINISTRATION

United States Court of Appeals, Ninth Circuit, 2007.
508 F.3d 508.

BETTY B. FLETCHER, CIRCUIT JUDGE.

In furtherance of the goal of energy conservation, Title V of the EPCA establishes automobile fuel economy standards. An "average fuel economy standard" (often referred to as a CAFE standard) is "a performance standard specifying a minimum level of average fuel economy applicable to a manufacturer in a model year." * * *

The impact of greenhouse gas emissions on climate change is precisely the kind of cumulative impacts analysis that NEPA requires agencies to conduct. Any given rule setting a CAFE standard might have an "individually minor" effect on the environment, but these rules are "collectively significant actions taking place over a period of time." 40 C.F.R. § 1508.7. * * * Thus, NHTSA must provide the necessary contextual information about the cumulative and incremental environmental impacts of the Final Rule in light of other CAFE rulemakings and other past, present, and reasonably foreseeable future actions, regardless of what agency or person undertakes such other actions. * * *

NHTSA's finding of no significant impact (FONSI) stated that the agency determined that its Final Rule "will not have a significant effect on the human environment." * * * In the Final EA, NHTSA explained that compared to the "baseline" alternative of extending the MY [Model Year] 2007 light truck CAFE standard through MYs 2008–2011, its evaluated alternatives would have a minor beneficial impact on various environmental resources. NHTSA concluded that "the final rule would produce, compared to U.S. emissions of CO2, a small decrease in emissions of CO2, the primary component of greenhouse gas emissions, under the selected alternative. . . . "

Petitioners argue that the evidence raises a substantial question as to whether the Final Rule may have a significant impact on the environment and that NHTSA failed to provide a convincing statement of reasons for why a small decrease (rather than a larger decrease) in the growth of CO2 emissions would not have a significant impact on the environment. Petitioners note that NHTSA has never evaluated the impacts of carbon emissions from light trucks or other vehicles, much less the effect of any reduction or increase in those emissions on climate change. Petitioners presented evidence that continued increase in greenhouse gas emissions may change the climate in a sudden and non-linear way. Without some analysis, it would be "impossible for NHTSA to know . . . whether a change in GHG emissions of 0.2% or 1% or 5% or 10% . . . will be a significant step toward averting the 'tipping point' " and irreversible adverse climate change.

We conclude that NHTSA's FONSI is arbitrary and capricious and the agency must prepare an EIS because the evidence raises a substantial question as to whether the Final Rule may have a significant impact on the environment. * * *

Petitioners have raised a "substantial question" as to whether the CAFE standards for light trucks MYs 2008–2011 "may cause significant degradation of some human environmental factor," particularly in light of the compelling scientific evidence concerning "positive feedback mechanisms" in the atmosphere.

Finally, Petitioners have satisfied several of the "intensity" factors listed in 40 C.F.R. § 1508.27(b) for determining "significant effect." For example, the Final Rule clearly may have an "individually insignificant but cumulatively significant" impact with respect to global warming. Evidence that Petitioners submitted in the record also shows that global warming will have an effect on public health and safety. Petitioners do not claim (nor do they have to show) that NHTSA's Final Rule would be the *sole* cause of global warming, and that is NHTSA's only response on this point.

Petitioners have also satisfied the "controversy" factor. * * * NHTSA received over 45,000 individual submissions on its proposal. * * *

In light of the evidence in the record, it is hardly "self-evident" that a 0.2 percent decrease in carbon emissions (as opposed to a greater decrease) is not significant. NHTSA's conclusion that a small reduction (0.2% compared to baseline) in the growth of carbon emissions would not have a significant impact on the environment was unaccompanied by any analysis or supporting data, either in the Final Rule or the EA.

Nowhere does the EA provide a "statement of reasons" for a finding of no significant impact, much less a "convincing statement of reasons." For example, the EA discusses the amount of CO_2 emissions expected from the Rule, but does not discuss the potential impact of such emissions on climate change. * * *

Thus, the FONSI is arbitrary and capricious.

The only reason NHTSA provided for why the environmental impact of the Final Rule would be insignificant is that it results in a decreased rate of growth of GHG emissions compared to the light truck CAFE standard for MY 2007. But simply because the Final Rule may be an improvement over the MY 2007 CAFE standard does not necessarily mean that it will not have a "significant effect" on the environment. NHTSA has not explained why its rule will not have a significant effect.

NOTES

1.   CEQ issued draft guidance in February 2010 about when greenhouse gas emissions relating to a project should be considered significant impacts:

> CEQ proposes to advise Federal agencies to consider, in scoping their NEPA analyses, whether analysis of the direct and indirect GHG emissions from their proposed actions may provide meaningful information to decision makers and the public. Specifically, if a proposed action would be reasonably anticipated to cause direct emissions of 25,000 metric tons or more of CO2-equivalent GHG emissions on an annual basis, agencies should consider this an indicator that a quantitative and qualitative assessment may be meaningful to decision makers and the public* * * * CEQ does not propose this as an indicator of a threshold of significant effects, but rather as an indicator of a minimum level of GHG emissions that may warrant some description in the appropriate NEPA analysis for agency actions involving direct emissions of GHGs. CEQ does not propose to make this guidance applicable to Federal land and resource management actions, but seeks public comment on the appropriate means of assessing the GHG emissions and sequestration that are affected by Federal land and resource management decisions.

The CEQ issued a modified draft guidance at the end of 2014. See Katherine Lee, *CEQ's Draft Guidance on NEPA Climate Analyses: Potential Impacts on Climate Litigation*, 45 ENV. L. REP. 10925 (2015). In August of 2016, the final guidance was issued. See Christina Goldfuss, *Final guidance for Federal Departments and Agencies on Climate Change in National Environmental Policy Act Reviews* (August 1, 2016). The Trump Administration quickly withdrew the guidance. See Donald J. Trump, *Presidential Executive Order on Promoting Energy Independence and Economic Growth* (March 28, 2017). But agencies must nevertheless consider climate impacts. For instance, in *Sierra Club v. FERC*, 867 F.3d 1357 (D.C. 2017), the court directed the agency to determine the amount of power-plant carbon emissions that would indirectly result from a new gas pipeline or explain why it was not feasible to do so. For a discussion of litigation on this issue as of 2016, see Barry Kellman, *NEPA Review of Climate Change*, 46 ENV. L. REP. 10378, 10381 (2016).

2.   The State of California, which has its own environmental assessment statute, the California Environmental Quality Act, (CEQA) is grappling with

a number of methodological questions including how to calculate increases in greenhouse gas emissions from projects subject to the statute and whether there is a threshold of emissions that triggers environmental review. See California Governor's Office of Planning and Research, *CEQA Guidelines and Greenhouse Gases*, http://www.opr.ca.gov/s_ceqaguidelines.php. On the possible use of CEQA as a model, see Dave Owen, *Climate Change and Environmental Assessment Law*, 33 COLUM. J. ENV. L. 57 (2008).

3.   As construed by the Supreme Court, NEPA is essentially a disclosure statute, with little capacity to force long-term planning or structural institutional changes. Are there other steps that should be taken to reorient federal land use planners, energy regulators, and others to integrate climate considerations into their planning? Would it make sense to impose a separate requirement for climate impact statements covering the effect of climate change on federal programs and projects?

3.   CONTENT OF THE IMPACT STATEMENT

So far, we have been largely concerned with what documents the agency must produce to satisfy NEPA, and when. We now turn to the question of what the EIS must contain. For instance, must an EIS that considers alternatives to the proposed action include detailed considerations of the environmental impacts of those alternatives? Must an EIS include alternatives that are beyond the power of the responsible agency to effect on its own without the cooperation of other agencies? Must the EIS consider alternatives that are extremely costly? How narrowly may the action agency define the project's purpose?

VERMONT YANKEE NUCLEAR POWER CORP. V. NATURAL RESOURCES DEFENSE COUNCIL, INC.

Supreme Court of the United States, 1978.
435 U.S. 519, 98 S.Ct. 1197, 55 L.Ed.2d 460.

[The bulk of this opinion dealt with procedural issues concerning a rulemaking about nuclear waste, but this portion of the opinion involved a reactor-license application by Consumers Power Company. A group called Saginaw intervened and submitted 119 environmental contentions, of which 17 related to the general topic of energy conservation. Saginaw participated in none of the hearings in the final stage of the proceedings. The licensing board declined to consider energy conservation issues. At about the time the administrative proceedings ended, the CEQ issued guidelines calling for agency consideration of energy conservation issues. The AEC refused to reopen the case, in part because of Saginaw's procedural default. The court of appeals reversed, holding that the AEC should have explored these issues *sua sponte*.]

JUSTICE REHNQUIST delivered the opinion of the Court.

There is little doubt that under the Atomic Energy Act of 1954 state public utility commissions or similar bodies are empowered to make the initial decision regarding the need for power. The Commission's prime area of concern * * * is public health and safety. * * *

NEPA, of course, has altered slightly the statutory balance, requiring "a detailed statement by the responsible official on * * * alternatives to the proposed action." But as should be obvious even upon a moment's reflection, the term "alternatives" is not self-defining. To make an impact statement something more than an exercise in frivolous boilerplate the concept of alternatives must be bounded by some notion of feasibility. As Court of Appeals for the District of Columbia Circuit has itself recognized:

> "There is reason for concluding that NEPA was not meant to require detailed discussion of the environmental effects of 'alternatives' put forward in comments when these effects cannot be readily ascertained and the alternatives are deemed only remote and speculative possibilities, in view of basic changes required in statutes and policies of other agencies—making them available, if at all, only after protracted debate and litigation not meaningfully compatible with the time-frame of the needs to which the underlying proposal is addressed."

Common sense also teaches us that the "detailed statement of alternatives" cannot be found wanting simply because the agency failed to include every alternative device and thought conceivable by the mind of man. Time and resources are simply too limited to hold that an impact statement fails because the agency failed to ferret out every possible alternative, regardless of how uncommon or unknown that alternative may have been at the time the project was approved.

With these principles in mind we now turn to the notion of "energy conservation," an alternative the omission of which was thought by the Court of Appeals to have been "forcefully pointed out by Saginaw in its comments on the draft EIS." Again, as the Commission pointed out, "the phrase 'energy conservation' has a deceptively simple ring in this context. Taken literally, the phrase suggests a virtually limitless range of possible actions and developments that might, in one way or another, ultimately reduce projected demands for electricity from a particular proposed plant." Moreover, as a practical matter, it is hard to dispute the observation that it is largely the events of recent years that have emphasized not only the need but also a large variety of alternatives for energy conservation. Prior to the drastic oil shortages imposed upon the United States in 1973, there was little serious thought in most government circles of energy conservation alternatives. Indeed, the Council on Environmental Quality did not promulgate regulations which even remotely suggested the need to consider energy conservation in impact statements until August 1, 1973. And even then the guidelines were not made applicable to draft and final statements filed with the Council before January 28, 1974. The Federal Power Commission likewise did not require consideration of energy conservation in applications to build hydroelectric facilities until June 19, 1973. And these regulations were not made retroactive either. All this occurred over a year and a half after the draft environmental statement for Midland had been prepared, and over a year after the final environmental statement had been prepared and the hearings completed.

We think these facts amply demonstrate that the concept of "alternatives" is an evolving one, requiring the agency to explore more or fewer alternatives as they become better known and understood. This was well understood by the Commission, which, unlike the Court of Appeals, recognized that the Licensing Board's decision had to be judged by the information then available to it. And judged in that light we have little doubt the Board's actions were well within the proper bounds of its statutory authority. Not only did the record before the agency give every indication that the project was actually needed, but there was nothing before the Board to indicate to the contrary.

We also think the court's criticism of the Commission's "threshold test" displays a lack of understanding of the historical setting within which the agency action took place and of the nature of the test itself. In the first place, while it is true that NEPA places upon an agency the obligation to consider every significant aspect of the environmental impact of a proposed action, it is still incumbent upon intervenors who wish to participate to structure their participation so that it is meaningful, so that it alerts the agency to the intervenors' position and contentions. This is especially true when the intervenors are requesting the agency to embark upon an exploration of uncharted territory, as was the question of energy conservation in the late '60s and early '70s. * * *

We have also made it clear that the role of a court in reviewing the sufficiency of an agency's consideration of environmental factors is a limited one, limited both by the time at which the decision was made and by the statute mandating review.

Neither the statute nor its legislative history contemplates that a court should substitute its judgment for that of an agency as to the environmental consequences of its actions * * *.

We think the Court of Appeals has forgotten that injunction here and accordingly its judgment in this respect must also be reversed.

NOTES

1.   Is the agency required only to consider *obvious* alternatives? Under *Marsh*, could the NRC have been required to prepare a supplemental EIS after

energy conservation emerged as an alternative? In applying *Vermont Yankee*, one problem is determining how obvious an alternative must be in order for the agency to have a duty to consider that alternative on its own initiative. One court has indicated that the alternative must be "reasonably apparent." *Roosevelt Campobello Int'l Park Comm'n v. EPA*, 684 F.2d 1041, 1047 (1st Cir. 1982). Is this a helpful formulation?

2.   When the project in question is proposed by a nonfederal party, the question arises whether that party can control the range of possible alternatives. In *Citizens Against Burlington, Inc. v. Busey*, 938 F.2d 190 (D.C. Cir. 1991), then-Judge Clarence Thomas wrote an opinion giving the project applicant considerable leeway. The case involved a decision by the city of Toledo to expand one of its airports. A NEPA suit was brought against the FAA, challenging the agency's approval of the project. The agency considered only the alternatives of approving the plan and doing nothing, rather than the possibilities of expanding the airport in other ways, changing flight patterns, or expanding other airports. FAA defined the goal for its action as "helping to launch a new cargo hub in Toledo and thereby helping to fuel the Toledo economy." It then eliminated all alternatives that did not promote that goal. Justice Thomas upheld this very narrow definition of alternatives under NEPA. In dissent, Judge Buckley said:

> By sanctioning the FAA's approach, the majority in effect allows a non-federal party to sort out alternatives based entirely on economic considerations, and then to present its preferred alternative as a take-it-or-leave-it proposition. If allowed to stand, today's decision will undermine the NEPA aim of "inject[ing] environmental considerations into the federal agency's decisionmaking process." The discussion of reasonable alternatives—"the heart of the environmental impact statement"—becomes an empty exercise when the only alternatives addressed are the proposed project and inaction.

Similar issues can arise even when the agency is the initiator of the action. The agency may define the project's purposes too broadly, making it impossible to determine what alternatives are relevant, or too narrowly, artificially favoring the chosen option. See *Sierra Club v. U.S. Forest Serv.*, 897 F.3d 582, 598–599 (4th Cir. 2018).

3.   The "rule of reason" test does not always operate to the advantage of the agency involved. In *Dubois v. United States Department of Agriculture*, 102 F.3d 1273 (1st Cir. 1996), the court held that the Service had failed to explore all reasonable alternatives for the proposed expansion of a ski facility, including the possibility of using an artificial pond rather than a natural one to store water for snowmaking. The agency had failed to discuss this option in the EIS, even though similar ponds had been used elsewhere in the vicinity. "After a searching and careful review of the record in the instant case," the court concluded, "we are not convinced that the Forest Service's decision was founded on a reasoned evaluation of the relevant factors, or that it articulated

a rational connection between the facts found and the choice made." *Id.* at 1289. Hence, the Forest Service's decision was arbitrary and capricious.

At times, courts inquire into the scientific foundations of a decision, usually an arena left to expert agencies, if the scientific analysis seems poorly supported. in *Center for Biological Diversity v. United States Forest Service*, 349 F.3d 1157 (9th Cir. 2003), the Court invalidated an EIS because of a Forest Service assumption in the draft impact statement about the scope of the habitat of a bird species to be affected by its action, criticizing the agency's failure to disclose and analyze the opposing viewpoint.

Another important issue in many NEPA cases is whether the agency has ignored important environmental impacts. A recurring question under NEPA has been how to treat uncertain but extremely negative outcomes. That issue is the subject of the next case.

ROBERTSON V. METHOW VALLEY CITIZENS COUNCIL

Supreme Court of the United States, 1989.
490 U.S. 332, 109 S.Ct. 1835, 104 L.Ed.2d 351.

[The plaintiffs challenged the Forest Service's issuance of special-use permits for a ski resort on national forest land. The EIS (entitled the Early Winters Alpine Winter Sports Study and referred to in the Court's opinion as the "Early Winters Study") considered the effect of the resort on wildlife and outlined possible mitigation measures. The Court of Appeals found the EIS inadequate for two reasons. First, the state Game department had predicted a 50% loss in the mule deer herd. The EIS adopted a 15% estimate, but admitted that the off-site effects of the resort were uncertain because they depended on the extent of private development. The EIS relied on mitigation measures to reduce the impact, but those measures had not been fully developed or tested. In light of this uncertainty, the Court of Appeals held that the EIS should have included a worst-case analysis. Second, the Court of Appeals held that the EIS was inadequate because it did not contain a complete mitigation plan to protect wildlife (and it lacked a plan to protect air quality).]

JUSTICE STEVENS delivered the opinion of the Court.

Simply by focusing the agency's attention on the environmental consequences of a proposed project, NEPA ensures that important effects will not be overlooked or underestimated only to be discovered after resources have been committed or the die otherwise cast. Moreover, the strong precatory language of § 101 of the Act and the requirement that agencies prepare detailed impact statements inevitably bring pressure to bear on agencies "to respond to the needs of environmental quality." 115 Cong. Rec. 40425 (1969) (remarks of Sen. Muskie).

Publication of an EIS, both in draft and final form, also serves a larger informational role. It gives the public the assurance that the agency "has indeed considered environmental concerns in its decisionmaking process," and, perhaps more significantly, provides a springboard for public comment. Thus, in this case the final draft of the Early Winters Study reflects not only the work of the Forest Service itself, but also the critical views of the Washington State Department of Game, the Methow Valley Citizens Council, and Friends of the Earth, as well as many others, to whom copies of the draft Study were circulated. Moreover, with respect to a development such as Sandy Butte, where the adverse effects on air quality and the mule deer herd are primarily attributable to predicted off-site development that will be subject to regulation by other governmental bodies, the EIS serves the function of offering those bodies adequate notice of the expected consequences and the opportunity to plan and implement corrective measures in a timely manner.

The sweeping policy goals announced in § 101 of NEPA are thus realized through a set of "action-forcing" procedures that require that agencies take a " 'hard look' at environmental consequences," and that provide for broad dissemination of relevant environmental information. Although these procedures are almost certain to affect the agency's substantive decision, it is now well settled that NEPA itself does not mandate particular results, but simply prescribes the necessary process. * * *

If the adverse environmental effects of the proposed action are adequately identified and evaluated, the agency is not constrained by NEPA from deciding that other values outweigh the environmental costs. In this case, for example, it would not have violated NEPA if the Forest Service, after complying with the Act's procedural prerequisites, had decided that the benefits to be derived from downhill skiing at Sandy Butte justified the issuance of a special use permit, notwithstanding the loss of 15 percent, 50 percent, or even 100 percent of the mule deer herd. Other statutes may impose substantive environmental obligations on federal agencies, but NEPA merely prohibits uninformed—rather than unwise— agency action.

To be sure, one important ingredient of an EIS is the discussion of steps that can be taken to mitigate adverse environmental consequences.[15]

---

[15]   CEQ regulations define "mitigation" to include:

(a) Avoiding the impact altogether by not taking a certain action or parts of an action.

(b) Minimizing impacts by limiting the degree or magnitude of the action and its implementation.

(c) Rectifying the impact by repairing, rehabilitating, or restoring the affected environment.

(d) Reducing or eliminating the impact over time by preservation and maintenance operations during the life of the action.

(e) Compensating for the impact by replacing or providing substitute resources or environments.

40 CFR § 1508.20 (1987).

The requirement that an EIS contain a detailed discussion of possible mitigation measures flows from both the language of the Act and, more expressly, from CEQ's implementing regulations. Implicit in NEPA's demand that an agency prepare a detailed statement on "any adverse environmental effects which cannot be avoided should the proposal be implemented," is an understanding that the EIS will discuss the extent to which adverse effects can be avoided. More generally, omission of a reasonably complete discussion of possible mitigation measures would undermine the "action-forcing" function of NEPA. Without such a discussion, neither the agency nor other interested groups and individuals can properly evaluate the severity of the adverse effects. An adverse effect that can be fully remedied by, for example, an inconsequential public expenditure is certainly not as serious as a similar effect that can only be modestly ameliorated through the commitment of vast public and private resources. Recognizing the importance of such a discussion in guaranteeing that the agency has taken a "hard look" at the environmental consequences of proposed federal action, CEQ regulations require that the agency discuss possible mitigation measures in defining the scope of the EIS, 40 CFR § 1508.25(b) in discussing alternatives to the proposed action, § 1502.14(f), and consequences of that action, § 1502.16(h), and in explaining its ultimate decision, § 1505.2(c).

There is a fundamental distinction, however, between a requirement that mitigation be discussed in sufficient detail to ensure that environmental consequences have been fairly evaluated, on the one hand, and a substantive requirement that a complete mitigation plan be actually formulated and adopted, on the other. In this case, the off-site effects on air quality and on the mule deer herd cannot be mitigated unless nonfederal government agencies take appropriate action. Since it is those state and local governmental bodies that have jurisdiction over the area in which the adverse effects need be addressed and since they have the authority to mitigate them, it would be incongruous to conclude that the Forest Service has no power to act until the local agencies have reached a final conclusion on what mitigating measures they consider necessary. Even more significantly, it would be inconsistent with NEPA's reliance on procedural mechanisms—as opposed to substantive, result-based standards—to demand the presence of a fully developed plan that will mitigate environmental harm before an agency can act.

We thus conclude that the Court of Appeals erred, first, in assuming that "NEPA requires that 'action be taken to mitigate the adverse effects of major federal actions,'" and, second, in finding that this substantive requirement entails the further duty to include in every EIS "a detailed explanation of specific measures which *will* be employed to mitigate the adverse impacts of a proposed action."

The Court of Appeals also concluded that the Forest Service had an obligation to make a "worst case analysis" if it could not make a reasoned assessment of the impact of the Early Winters project on the mule deer herd. Such a "worst case analysis" was required at one time by CEQ regulations, but those regulations have since been amended. Moreover, although the prior regulations may well have expressed a permissible application of NEPA, the Act itself does not mandate that uncertainty in predicting environmental harms be addressed exclusively in this manner. Accordingly, we conclude that the Court of Appeals also erred in requiring the "worst case" study.

In 1977, President Carter directed that CEQ promulgate binding regulations implementing the procedural provisions of NEPA. Pursuant to this presidential order, CEQ promulgated implementing regulations. Under § 1502.22 of these regulations—a provision which became known as the "worst case requirement"—CEQ provided that if certain information relevant to the agency's evaluation of the proposed action is either unavailable or too costly to obtain, the agency must include in the EIS a "worst case analysis and an indication of the probability or improbability of its occurrence." 40 CFR § 1502.22 (1985). In 1986, however, CEQ replaced the "worst case" requirement with a requirement that federal agencies, in the face of unavailable information concerning a reasonably foreseeable significant environmental consequence, prepare "a summary of existing credible scientific evidence which is relevant to evaluating the * * * adverse impacts" and prepare an "evaluation of such impacts based upon theoretical approaches or research methods generally accepted in the scientific community." 40 CFR § 1502.22(b) (1987). The amended regulation thus "retains the duty to describe the consequences of a remote, but potentially severe impact, but grounds the duty in evaluation of scientific opinion rather than in the framework of a conjectural 'worst case analysis.'" 50 Fed.Reg. 32237 (1985).

The Court of Appeals recognized that the "worst case analysis" regulation has been superseded, yet held that "[t]his rescission * * * does not nullify the requirement * * * since the regulation was merely a codification of prior NEPA case law." This conclusion, however, is erroneous in a number of respects. Most notably, review of NEPA case law reveals that the regulation, in fact, was not a codification of prior judicial decisions. The cases cited by the Court of Appeals ultimately rely on the Fifth Circuit's decision in *Sierra Club v. Sigler,* 695 F.2d 957 (1983). *Sigler,* however, simply recognized that the "worst case analysis" regulation codified the "judicially created principl[e]" that an EIS must "consider the probabilities of the occurrence of any environmental effects it discusses." *Id.,* at 970–971. As CEQ recognized at the time it superseded the regulation, case law prior to the adoption of the "worst case analysis" provision did require agencies to describe environmental impacts even in the face of substantial uncertainty, but did not require that this obligation necessarily be met through the mechanism of a "worst case analysis." CEQ's abandonment of the "worst case analysis" provision, therefore, is not inconsistent with any previously established judicial interpretation of the statute.

Nor are we convinced that the new CEQ regulation is not controlling simply because it was preceded by a rule that was in some respects more demanding. * * * Here, the amendment only came after the prior regulation had been subjected to considerable criticism. Moreover, the amendment was designed to better serve the twin functions of an EIS— requiring agencies to take a "hard look" at the consequences of the proposed action and providing important information to other groups and individuals. CEQ explained that by requiring that an EIS focus on reasonably foreseeable impacts, the new regulation "will generate information and discussion on those consequences of greatest concern to the public and of greatest relevance to the agency's decision," rather than distorting the decisionmaking process by overemphasizing highly speculative harms. In light of this well-considered basis for the change, the new regulation is entitled to substantial deference. Accordingly, the Court of Appeals erred in concluding that the Early Winters Study is inadequate because it failed to include a "worst case analysis."

NOTES

1. The BP Deepwater Horizon oil spill led to arguments that the "worst case" requirement should be reinstated. See Victor B. Flatt, *The "Worst Case" May Be the Best: Rethinking NEPA Law to Avoid Future Environmental Disasters*, 6 ENV. & ENERGY L. & POL'Y J. 1 (2011).

2. Note that the *Robertson* Court refers to section 101 as "precatory" and says that "NEPA itself does not mandate particular results, but simply prescribes the necessary process." *Robertson* seems to make it clear that NEPA is purely procedural and imposes no substantive restraint on the government. The courts of appeals had divided on the issue of substantive review under NEPA. In *Strycker's Bay Neighborhood Council, Inc. v. Karlen,* 444 U.S. 223 (1980), the Second Circuit had held that an agency's choice of a site for a housing project was unjustifiable under NEPA. The Supreme Court reversed. The opinion contained broad language about the procedural nature of NEPA, such as the following:

> [I]n the present case there is no doubt that [the agency] considered the environmental consequences of its decision to designate the proposed site for low-income housing. NEPA requires no more. 444 U.S. at 228.

A footnote, however, seemed to leave some possible room for substantive judicial review:

If we could agree with the dissent that the Court of Appeals held [the agency] had acted "arbitrarily" * * * we might also agree that plenary review is warranted. But the District Court expressly concluded that [the agency] had not acted arbitrarily or capriciously and our reading of the opinion of the Court of Appeals satisfies us that it did not overturn that finding. Instead, the Appellate Court required [the agency] to elevate environmental concerns over other, admittedly legitimate considerations. Neither NEPA nor the APA provides any support for such a reordering of priorities by review in court. 444 U.S. at 228 n.2.

3.   The *Robertson* Court did not refer to the *Strycker* footnote, but its description of § 101 as "precatory" seems to leave little room for substantive judicial review under NEPA. In adopting this view of NEPA, hasn't the Court overlooked the language of § 102(1)? How can the § 101 policies be completely precatory, when § 102 "directs that, to the fullest extent possible: (1) the policies, regulations, and public laws of the United States shall be interpreted and administered in accordance with the policies set forth in this chapter * * * "?

4. NEPA'S PAST AND FUTURE

NEPA has been widely imitated—at least fifteen states have adopted their own versions of NEPA, and EIS-type requirements have now been adopted in over thirty countries.

NEPA heightens the agency's normal duty to consider relevant factors in decision-making. Agencies must advert specifically to environmental factors that they might otherwise ignore. NEPA has had some other, less visible, impacts as well. First, the need to comply with the EIS requirement required agencies to reconsider their missions in light of the environmental impacts those missions caused. *See* DANIEL A. MAZMANIAN & JEANNE NIENABER, CAN ORGANIZATIONS CHANGE? (1979) (tracing history of resistance to NEPA by Army Corps of Engineers in light of its commitment to building large water-resource development projects). Second, even if NEPA is "merely procedural"—meaning that once the agency discloses environmental impacts fully it may proceed with its plans—the possibility of challenging a project because the agency failed to do an EIS, or because it produced an insufficient one, provides environmental groups some leverage to insist on mitigation as the price for settling NEPA lawsuits. NEPA thus has a "democratizing" effect on agency decision-making by affording groups that would normally be shut out of these decisions a seat at the bargaining table. Finally, NEPA litigation serves as an information-disclosure and political-rallying mechanism, which can help to generate political opposition to projects with negative environmental impacts. Whereas some developers and agency officials may view this use of NEPA as a form of extortion, environmental organizations tend to be unapologetic. They see this use of NEPA as good legal strategy and a legitimate second-best option: NEPA may be procedural as a legal matter, but it can still be useful as a political matter.

How effective has NEPA been in practice? According to the *Robertson* Court, NEPA's procedures are "almost certain to affect the agency's substantive decision." Among those who have studied NEPA, there have been a variety of opinions about the statute's effects. After a review of early airport runway-extension controversies, Professor Sax concluded that NEPA was simply ineffectual. Joseph L. Sax, *The (Unhappy) Truth about NEPA*, 26 OKLA. L. REV. 239 (1973). Other early commentators concluded that NEPA puts useful pressure on agencies to consider environmental issues, but is ultimately incapable of forcing them to do so. Roger C. Cramton & Richard K. Berg, *On Leading a Horse to Water: NEPA and the Federal Bureaucracy*, 71 MICH. L. REV. 511, 536 (1973). *See* Dinah Bear, *Some Modest Suggestions for Improving Implementation of the National Environmental Policy Act,* 43 NAT. RESOURCES J. 931, 935 (2003) for the more recent opinion by a former general counsel of the CEQ that NEPA is not sufficiently incorporated into the decision-making process of many agencies. On the other hand, clear instances exist of agencies substantially changing their actions in light of NEPA. Perhaps the best example is the Corps of Engineers' decision to broaden consideration of whether to issue dredge-and-fill permits to include full consideration of environmental factors, despite substantial opposition. *See Zabel v. Tabb,* 430 F.2d 199 (5th Cir. 1970).

The CEQ attempted in 1978 to determine the effects of NEPA litigation. A survey of 938 NEPA cases indicated the following results: (1) NEPA filings peaked in 1974; (2) a total of 202 government actions were delayed by a NEPA injunction, almost half of them for longer than one year; (3) none of the projects were halted by a permanent injunction; (4) 60 of the projects were abandoned after the NEPA action was filed. A later CEQ study found that NEPA has had a highly beneficial effect on EPA's construction grant program for wastewater treatment. *See* CEQ, TWENTIETH ANNUAL REPORT 31–37 (1990). In 2004, "156 NEPA cases were filed, and in only 11 of those cases did the judge grant an injunction. In 2002 150 NEPA cases were filed, and injunctions were issued in 27 of them. In 2003, 128 NEPA cases were filed, of which 6 resulted in injunctions." House Committee on Resources, Task Force on Improving the National Environmental Policy Act and Task Force on Updating the National Environmental Policy Act, *Initial Findings and Draft Recommendations* (2005). For the latest statistics on NEPA litigation trends and outcomes throughout the federal courts, *see* the Council on Environmental Quality's annual NEPA litigation surveys, available at https://ceq.doe.gov/ceq-reports/litigation.html.

Some of NEPA's impact may be invisible or hard to measure: agencies may shrink from proposing projects that they would have otherwise proposed absent NEPA requirements. So NEPA may eliminate the most environmentally damaging projects from consideration in the first place. For further discussion of NEPA's effects, *see* SERGE TAYLOR, MAKING BUREAUCRACIES THINK: THE ENVIRONMENTAL IMPACT STATEMENT STRATEGY OF ADMINISTRATIVE REFORM (1984); Dinah Bear, *NEPA at 19*, 19 ENVTL. L. REP. 10062 (1989).

The George W. Bush Administration curtailed NEPA review in several areas in the name of administrative efficiency. Executive Order 13,274 directed federal agencies to "expedite environmental reviews of high-priority transportation infrastructure projects." Exec. Order No. 13,274, 3 C.F.R. § 250 (2003). The Healthy Forests Restoration Act of 2003 "streamlined" the NEPA process by exempting individual Forest Service decisions about "fuel reduction" (*i.e.*, harvesting timber and clearing underbrush, on the theory that this will reduce the likelihood and severity of forest fires) from NEPA for the sake of swift action by the Forest Service in areas threatened by catastrophic wildfires. 16 U.S.C. §§ 6501–6591 (2003). Again citing efficiency concerns, the Forest Service issued a final rule in 2005 allowing a number of its other planning activities to be exempt from NEPA through categorical exclusions. National Forest System Land Management Planning, 70 FED. REG. 1023, 1030–34 (Jan. 5, 2005) (codified at 36 C.F.R. Part 219). In 2010, CEQ issued new guidance intended to curb overuse of categorical exclusions. https://www.energy.gov/nepa/downloads/guidance-federal-departments-and-agencies-establishing-applying-and-revising.

Some more basic changes were suggested for NEPA by a special task force convened by the CEQ in 2002 to find ways to make the statute more effective, more efficient, and timelier. The Task Force's final report suggested several ideas for improving NEPA's operation. Among the most prominent were promoting collaborative agreements; improving regulations for and use of programmatic documents; integrating adaptive management (particularly at the programmatic level); clarifying application of categorical exclusions; and creating more uniform and specific requirements for what to put in EAs, especially with regard to discussion of alternatives (in order to deal with the perceived lack of sufficient deference to EAs by courts). NEPA TASK FORCE, THE NEPA TASK FORCE REPORT TO THE COUNCIL ON ENVIRONMENTAL QUALITY: MODERNIZING NEPA IMPLEMENTATION vii–xvii (2003), *available at* https://www.energy.gov/sites/prod/files/2016/02/f29/finalreport.pdf. For a critique of the Task Force's recommendations, *see* Bradley C. Karkkainen, *Whither NEPA?*, 12 N.Y.U. ENVTL. L.J. 333 (2004). For a collection of thoughts about NEPA's past and future, see *NEPA at 40: How a Visionary Statute Confronts 21st Century Impacts*, 39 ENV. L. REP. 10575 (2009).

Under President Obama, CEQ issued new guidance urging agencies to make the EA/EIS process more efficient and the final documents more readable. CEQ has also published new guidance on mitigation and monitoring. The guidance calls on agencies to:

- commit to mitigation in decision documents when they have based environmental analysis upon such mitigation (by including appropriate conditions on grants, permits, or other agency approvals, and making funding or approvals for implementing the proposed action contingent on implementation of the mitigation commitments);

- monitor the implementation and effectiveness of mitigation commitments;

- make information on mitigation monitoring available to the public, preferably through agency web sites; and

- remedy ineffective mitigation when the Federal action is not yet complete.

76 FED. REG. 3843 (2011). It remains to be seen what changes, if any, the Trump Administration will make to the CEQ regulations.

NEPA provides a catch-all for environmental problems that are not covered by any specific substantive law like the Clean Air Act and for decisions that are not covered by the procedures of the Administrative Procedure Act. But as construed by the Supreme Court, it does not of its own force constrain the ultimate decisions. For such constraints, we must turn to the ESA or to the statutes governing pollution and toxic substances, which are the subjects of the remainder of this book.

Appendix: NEPA Flow Chart

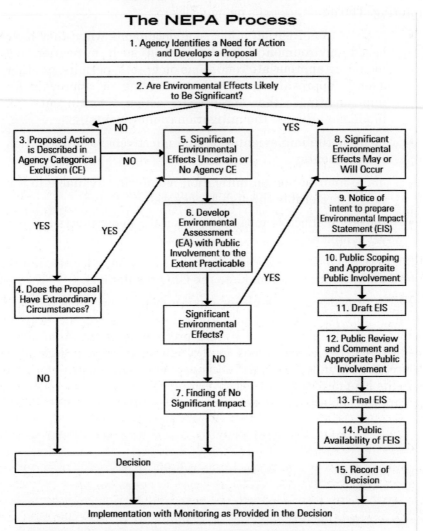

The NEPA Process

1. Agency Identifies a Need for Action and Develops a Proposal

2. Are Environmental Effects Likely to Be Significant?

NO — 3. Proposed Action is Described in Agency Categorical Exclusion (CE)

5. Significant Environmental Effects Uncertain or No Agency CE

YES — 8. Significant Environmental Effects May or Will Occur

4. Does the Proposal Have Extraordinary Circumstances?

6. Develop Environmental Assessment (EA) with Public Involvement to the Extent Practicable

9. Notice of intent to prepare Environmental Impact Statement (EIS)

10. Public Scoping and Appropraite Public Involvement

11. Draft EIS

Significant Environmental Effects?

12. Public Review and Comment and Appropriate Public Involvement

7. Finding of No Significant Impact

13. Final EIS

14. Public Availability of FEIS

Decision

15. Record of Decision

Implementation with Monitoring as Provided in the Decision

Significant new circumstances or information relevant to environmental concerns or substantial changes in the proposed action that are relevant to environmental concerns may necessitate preparation of a supplemental EIS following either the draft or final EIS or the Record of Decision (CEQ NEPA Regulations, 40 C.F.R. § 1502.9(c)).

From CEQ, A CITIZEN'S GUIDE TO THE NEPA: HAVING YOUR VOICE HEARD (2007), https://www.energy.gov/nepa/downloads/citizens-guide-nepa-having-your-voice-heard-ceq-2007

CHAPTER 6

AIR POLLUTION

■ ■ ■

Air pollution comes from many different sources, including stationary sources such as factories, power plants and dry cleaners. Mobile sources such as cars, trucks and buses also contribute significantly to air pollution. Some air pollutants are pervasive whereas others are local; some are harmful in large doses, some in smaller doses; and some are toxic. Air pollution causes adverse health effects, including impaired pulmonary and cardiac function. In some cases, exposure to air pollution can lead to premature death. Air pollution also impairs the health of ecosystems by adversely affecting trees, lakes, streams and other habitats. It can damage crops and animals, as well as buildings. Poor air quality can also have a negative aesthetic impact by reducing visibility in national parks and other wilderness areas, as well as in urban areas.

Why can't the market solve the problem of air pollution without government intervention? Surely people who care about air quality would be willing to pay for it. The problem is that air quality (like national defense) cannot be priced and reserved exclusively for those willing to pay. Clean air is a classic "public good" that will tend to be under-produced by the market. This market failure means that government intervention may be necessary to ensure sufficient production of air quality. Air pollution regulation may also be explained as a cost-internalizing mechanism that forces firms to pay for the real cost of production. In economic terms, air pollution can be understood as an externality of productive economic activity. Since firms do not pay for the air quality they degrade in the course of producing goods (as they would pay for labor and materials), they face an incentive to over-consume this free resource. Firms capture all of the economic benefit of dirtying the air without absorbing the full cost. Instead, most of the cost is borne by the wider community which suffers health and welfare effects caused by air pollution.

A. THE COMMON LAW

1. PRIVATE NUISANCE

The common law of nuisance has historically served as an indirect mechanism for compensating individuals harmed by pollution. As you read the case excerpted below, consider the relative strengths and weaknesses of using the common law to regulate air pollution.

BOOMER V. ATLANTIC CEMENT COMPANY
Court of Appeals of New York, 1970.
26 N.Y.2d 219, 309 N.Y.S.2d 312, 257 N.E.2d 870.

BERGAN, CIRCUIT JUDGE.

Defendant operates a large cement plant near Albany. These are actions for injunction and damages by neighboring land owners alleging injury to property from dirt, smoke and vibration emanating from the plant. A nuisance has been found after trial, temporary damages have been allowed but an injunction has been denied.

The public concern with air pollution arising from many sources in industry and in transportation is currently accorded ever wider recognition accompanied by a growing sense of responsibility in State and Federal Governments to control it. Cement plants are obvious sources of air pollution in the neighborhoods where they operate.

But there is now before the court private litigation in which individual property owners have sought specific relief from a single plant operation. The threshold question raised by the division of view on this appeal is whether the court should resolve the litigation between the parties now before it as equitably as seems possible; or whether, seeking promotion of the general public welfare, it should channel private litigation into broad public objectives.

A court performs its essential function when it decides the rights of parties before it. Its decision of private controversies may sometimes greatly affect public issues. Large questions of law are often resolved by the manner in which private litigation is decided. But this is normally an incident to the court's main function to settle controversy. It is a rare exercise of judicial power to use a decision in private litigation as a purposeful mechanism to achieve direct public objectives greatly beyond the rights and interests before the court.

Effective control of air pollution is a problem presently far from solution even with the full public and financial powers of government. In large measure adequate technical procedures are yet to be developed and some that appear possible may be economically impracticable.

It seems apparent that the amelioration of air pollution will depend on technical research in great depth; on a carefully balanced consideration of the economic impact of close regulation; and of the actual effect on public health. It is likely to require massive public expenditure and to demand more than any local community can accomplish and to depend on regional and interstate controls.

A court should not try to do this on its own as a by-product of private litigation and it seems manifest that the judicial establishment is neither equipped in the limited nature of any judgment it can pronounce nor prepared to lay down and implement an effective policy for the elimination of air pollution. This is an area beyond the circumference of one private lawsuit. It is a direct responsibility for government and should not thus be undertaken as an incident to solving a dispute between property owners and a single cement plant—one of many—in the Hudson River valley.

The cement making operations of defendant have been found by the court at Special Term to have damaged the nearby properties of plaintiffs in these two actions. That court, as it has been noted, accordingly found defendant maintained a nuisance and this has been affirmed at the Appellate Division. The total damage to plaintiffs' properties is, however, relatively small in comparison with the value of defendant's operation and with the consequences of the injunction which plaintiffs seek.

The ground for the denial of injunction, notwithstanding the finding both that there is a nuisance and that plaintiffs have been damaged substantially, is the large disparity in economic consequences of the nuisance and of the injunction. This theory cannot, however, be sustained without overruling a doctrine which has been consistently reaffirmed in several leading cases in this court and which has never been disavowed here, namely that where a nuisance has been found and where there has been any substantial damage shown by the party complaining an injunction will be granted.

The rule in New York has been that such a nuisance will be enjoined although marked disparity be shown in economic consequence between the effect of the injunction and the effect of the nuisance. * * *

* * * [T]o follow the rule literally in these cases would be to close down the plant at once. This court is fully agreed to avoid that immediately drastic remedy; the difference in view is how best to avoid it.

One alternative is to grant the injunction but postpone its effect to a specified future date to give opportunity for technical advances to permit defendant to eliminate the nuisance; another is to grant the injunction conditioned on the payment of permanent damages to plaintiffs which would compensate them for the total economic loss to their property present and future caused by defendant's operations. For reasons which will be developed the court chooses the latter alternative.

If the injunction were to be granted unless within a short period—e.g., 18 months—the nuisance be abated by improved methods, there would be no assurance that any significant technical improvement would occur.

The parties could settle this private litigation at any time if defendant paid enough money and the imminent threat of closing the plant would build up the pressure on defendant. If there were no improved techniques found, there would inevitably be applications to the court at Special Term for extensions of time to perform on showing of good faith efforts to find such techniques.

Moreover, techniques to eliminate dust and other annoying by-products of cement making are unlikely to be developed by any research the defendant can undertake within any short period, but will depend on the total resources of the cement industry nationwide and throughout the world. The problem is universal wherever cement is made.

For obvious reasons the rate of the research is beyond the control of defendant. If at the end of 18 months the whole industry has not found a technical solution a court would be hard put to close down this one cement plant if due regard be given to equitable principles.

On the other hand, to grant the injunction unless defendant pays plaintiffs such permanent damages as may be fixed by the court seems to do justice between the contending parties. All of the attributions of economic loss to the properties on which plaintiffs' complaints are based will have been redressed.

The nuisance complained of by these plaintiffs may have other public or private consequences, but these particular parties are the only ones who have sought remedies and the judgment proposed will fully redress them. The limitation of relief granted is a limitation only within the four corners of these actions and does not foreclose public health or other public agencies from seeking proper relief in a proper court.

It seems reasonable to think that the risk of being required to pay permanent damages to injured property owners by cement plant owners would itself be a reasonably effective spur to research for improved techniques to minimize nuisance.

The power of the court to condition on equitable grounds the continuance of an injunction on the payment of permanent damages seems undoubted. * * *

The judgment, by allowance of permanent damages imposing a servitude on land, which is the basis of the actions, would preclude future recovery by plaintiffs or their grantees * * *.

This should be placed beyond debate by a provision of the judgment that the payment by defendant and the acceptance by plaintiffs of permanent damages found by the court shall be in compensation for a servitude on the land.

JASEN, CIRCUIT JUDGE (dissenting).

It has long been the rule in this State, as the majority acknowledges, that a nuisance which results in substantial continuing damage to neighbors must be enjoined. * * * To now change the rule to permit the cement company to continue polluting the air indefinitely upon the payment of permanent damages is, in my opinion, compounding the magnitude of a very serious problem in our State and Nation today. * * *

I see grave dangers in overruling our long-established rule of granting an injunction where a nuisance results in substantial continuing damage. In permitting the injunction to become inoperative upon the payment of permanent damages, the majority is, in effect, licensing a continuing wrong. It is the same as saying to the cement company, you may continue to do harm to your neighbors so long as you pay a fee for it. Furthermore, once such permanent damages are assessed and paid, the incentive to alleviate the wrong would be eliminated, thereby continuing air pollution of an area without abatement.

It is true that some courts have sanctioned the remedy here proposed by the majority in a number of cases, but none of the authorities relied upon by the majority are analogous to the situation before us. In those cases, the courts, in denying an injunction and awarding money damages, grounded their decision on a showing that the use to which the property was intended to be put was primarily for the public benefit. Here, on the other hand, it is clearly established that the cement company is creating a continuing air pollution nuisance primarily for its own private interest with no public benefit.

This kind of inverse condemnation * * * may not be invoked by a private person or corporation for private gain or advantage. Inverse condemnation should only be permitted when the public is primarily served in the taking or impairment of property. * * * The promotion of the interests of the polluting cement company has, in my opinion, no public use or benefit.

Nor is it constitutionally permissible to impose servitude on land, without consent of the owner, by payment of permanent damages where the continuing impairment of the land is for a private use. * * * This is made clear by the State Constitution which provides that "[p]rivate property shall not be taken for public use without just compensation" (emphasis added). It is, of course, significant that the section makes no mention of taking for a private use. * * *

I would enjoin the defendant cement company from continuing the discharge of dust particles upon its neighbors' properties unless, within 18 months, the cement company abated this nuisance. * * *

I am aware that the trial court found that the most modern dust control devices available have been installed in defendant's plant, but, I submit, this does not mean that *better* and more effective dust control devices could not be developed within the time allowed to abate the pollution.

Moreover, I believe it is incumbent upon the defendant to develop such devices, since the cement company, at the time the plant commenced production (1962), was well aware of the plaintiffs' presence in the area, as well as the probable consequences of its contemplated operation. Yet, it still chose to build and operate the plant at this site.

NOTES

1.   Some additional facts about *Boomer* may be helpful in evaluating the case. The court's opinion focuses on air pollution. An examination of the appellate record, however, reveals that *Boomer* did not present simply a conventional pollution problem. Instead, the record suggests a severe but localized impact on neighboring lands, due less to the cement plant than to the operation of the quarry on the same site. In particular, neighbors complained of severe vibrations and heavy dust from blasting operations at the quarry. The main reason the trial judge declined to issue an injunction was not undue hardship to the cement company, but rather the central role of the plant in the local economy. Over half of the assessed value of the township involved the cement company's property—respondent had $45 million invested in the plant and employed more than 300 workers—so closing the plant would have had a devastating effect on the local government, economy, and school system. On remand, the trial judge calculated that the amount of the decline in fair market value for one of the parcels was $140,000 and then added a "kicker" of $35,000 to arrive at the damage award. The cement company's liability, including its settlement of the other pending cases, came to $710,000. For fuller details, *see* Daniel Farber, *Reassessing* Boomer: *Justice, Efficiency, and Nuisance Law,* in ESSAYS ON THE LAW OF PROPERTY AND LEGAL EDUCATION, IN HONOR OF JOHN E. CRIBBET (Michael H. Hoeflich & Peter Hay eds. 1988).

2.   Notice that private nuisance cases may only remedy the effects of pollution suffered by a single plaintiff, or a small handful of plaintiffs. What about the effect of air pollutants on communities further away? Or the effect of emissions on trees and streams that have no standing to sue for nuisance? There are other limitations to private nuisance cases as well. Many plaintiffs with meritorious claims may lack the resources to hire a lawyer. In addition, plaintiffs may be at a disadvantage when it comes to the legal test for nuisance. Many courts determine whether interference with use and enjoyment is unreasonable by applying a "gravity of harm" vs. "social utility of the conduct" balancing test. *See* RESTATEMENT OF TORTS (2d) § 826. Using this test, the harm suffered by plaintiffs like Mr. Boomer will likely seem small in comparison to the social utility of an industrial concern like the Atlantic Cement plant, which produces a valuable product, employs hundreds of workers, and pays substantial property taxes. Is there a way to apply this test that is not systematically biased against plaintiffs? Are there other tests for nuisance that do not require such balancing? *See* RESTATEMENT OF TORTS (2d) §§ 826, 829.

By awarding the plaintiff permanent damages instead of injunctive relief the *Boomer* court adapts nuisance law to accommodate the plaintiff's harm without shutting down a socially valuable industry. It may seem obvious that the choice between a damage remedy and an injunctive remedy has enormous practical importance in a case like *Boomer*. Yet this is less clear on further reflection. If Mr. Boomer is entitled to an injunction but has relatively small damages, it might make sense for him to enter into a settlement. Thus, he might choose to forego his injunction in exchange for cash. If so, the pollution will continue. Some economists have suggested, on similar grounds, that the existence or non-existence of liability, quite apart from the remedy, may have no effect on pollution levels. Assuming there are no transaction costs (a large assumption), parties will bargain to the efficient solution: if it is less costly to install pollution abatement controls or to shut down the plant than to compensate plaintiffs like Mr. Boomer, then the pollution will be controlled. Otherwise, it will continue, and Mr. Boomer will be compensated. The article below explains this thesis.

RONALD COASE, THE PROBLEM OF SOCIAL COST

3 J. L. ECON. 1, 1–8, 15–19 (1960).[1]

I propose to start my analysis by examining a case in which most economists would presumably agree that the problem would be solved in a completely satisfactory manner: when the damaging business has to pay for all damage caused *and* the pricing system works smoothly (strictly this means that the operation of a pricing system is without cost).

A good example of the problem under discussion is afforded by the case of straying cattle which destroy crops growing on neighbouring land. Let us suppose that a farmer and a cattle-raiser are operating on neighbouring properties. Let us further suppose that, without any fencing between the properties, an increase in the size of the cattle-raiser's herd increases the total damage to the farmer's crops. * * *

To simplify the argument, I propose to use an arithmetical example. I shall assume that the annual cost of fencing the farmer's property is $9 and that the price of the crop is $1 per ton. Also, I assume that the relation between the number of cattle in the herd and the annual crop loss is as follows:

---

[1]   Copyright © 1960, University of Chicago. Reprinted by permission.

Number in Herd (Steers)	Annual Crop Loss (Tons)	Additional Crop Loss per Additional Steer (Tons)
1	1	1
2	3	2
3	6	3
4	10	4

Given that the cattle-raiser is liable for the damage caused, the additional annual cost imposed on the cattle-raiser if he increased his herd from, say, 2 to 3 steers is $3 and in deciding on the size of the herd, he will take this into account along with his other costs. That is, he will not increase the size of the herd unless the value of the additional meat produced (assuming that the cattle-raiser slaughters the cattle), is greater than the additional costs that this will entail, including the value of the additional crops destroyed. * * * Given that the annual cost of fencing is $9, the cattle-raiser who wished to have a herd with 4 steers or more would pay for fencing to be erected and maintained, assuming that other means of attaining the same end would not do so more cheaply. * * *

I now turn to the case in which, although the pricing system is assumed to work smoothly (that is, costlessly), the damaging business is not liable for any of the damage which it causes. * * * I propose to show that the allocation of resources will be the same [optimal] as it was when the damaging business was liable for damage caused. * * *

* * * Suppose that the size of the cattle-raiser's herd is 3 steers (and that this is the size of the herd that would be maintained if crop damage was not taken into account). Then the farmer would be willing to pay up to $3 if the cattle-raiser would reduce his herd to 2 steers, up to $5 if the herd were reduced to 1 steer and would pay up to $6 if cattle-raising was abandoned. The cattle-raiser would therefore receive $3 from the farmer if he kept 2 steers instead of 3. This $3 foregone is therefore part of the cost incurred in keeping the third steer. Whether the $3 is a payment which the cattle-raiser has to make if he adds the third steer to his herd (which it would be if the cattle-raiser was liable to the farmer for damage caused to the crop) or whether it is a sum of money which he would have received if he did not keep a third steer (which it would be if the cattle-raiser was not liable to the farmer for damage caused to the crop) does not affect the final result. In both cases $3 is part of the cost of adding a third steer, to be included along with the other costs. If the increase in the value of production in cattle-raising through increasing the size of the herd from 2 to 3 is greater than the additional costs that have to be incurred (including the $3 damage to crops), the size of the herd will be increased. Otherwise, it will not. The size of the herd will be the same whether the cattle-raiser is liable for damage caused to the crop or not. * * *

It is necessary to know whether the damaging business is liable or not for damage caused since without the establishment of this initial delimitation of rights there can be no market transactions to transfer and recombine them. But the ultimate result (which maximizes the value of production) is independent of the legal position if the pricing system is assumed to work without cost. * * *

The argument has proceeded up to this point on the assumption * * * that there were no costs involved in carrying out market transactions. This is, of course, a very unrealistic assumption. In order to carry out a market transaction it is necessary to discover who it is that one wishes to deal with, to inform people that one wishes to deal and on what terms, to conduct negotiations leading up to a bargain, to draw up the contract, to undertake the inspection needed to make sure that the terms of the contract are being observed, and so on. These operations are often extremely costly, sufficiently costly at any rate to prevent many transactions that would be carried out in a world in which the pricing system worked without cost.

* * * Once the costs of carrying out market transactions are taken into account it is clear that such a rearrangement of rights will only be undertaken when the increase in the value of production consequent upon the rearrangement is greater than the costs which would be involved in bringing it about. When it is less, the granting of an injunction (or the knowledge that it would be granted) or the liability to pay damages may result in an activity being discontinued (or may prevent its being started) which would be undertaken if market transactions were costless. In these conditions the initial delimitation of legal rights does have an effect on the efficiency with which the economic system operates. One arrangement of rights may bring about a greater value of production than any other. But unless this is the arrangement of rights established by the legal system, the costs of reaching the same result by altering and combining rights through the market may be so great that this optional arrangement of rights, and the greater value of production which it would bring, may never be achieved. * * *

* * * An alternative solution is direct Government regulation. Instead of instituting a legal system of rights which can be modified by transactions on the market, the government may impose regulations which state what people must or must not do and which have to be obeyed. Thus, the government (by statute or perhaps more likely through an administrative agency) may, to deal with the problem of smoke nuisance, decree that certain methods of production should or should not be used (e.g., that smoke preventing devices should be installed or that coal or oil should not be burned) or may confine certain types of business to certain districts (zoning regulations). * * *

* * * But the governmental administrative machine is not itself costless. It can, in fact, on occasion be extremely costly. Furthermore, there is no reason to suppose that the restrictive and zoning regulations, made by a fallible administration subject to political pressures and operating without any competitive check, will necessarily always be those which increase the efficiency with which the economic system operates. Furthermore, such general regulations, which must apply to a wide variety of cases will be enforced in some cases in which they are clearly inappropriate. From these considerations it follows that direct governmental regulation will not necessarily give better results than leaving the problem to be solved by the market * * *. But equally there is no reason why, on occasion, such governmental administrative regulation should not lead to an improvement in economic efficiency. This would seem particularly likely when, as is normally the case with the smoke nuisance, a large number of people are involved and in which therefore the costs of handling the problem through the market * * * may be high.

NOTES

1.　As an exercise, explain how Coase would argue that the result in *Boomer* is irrelevant to the amount of pollution produced, in the absence of transaction costs. Use these two sets of figures:

Case 1: The company's profit from polluting is $3,000,000 per year; the total damage caused is $4,000,000.

Case 2: The company's profit from polluting is $3,000,000 per year; the total damage caused is $2,000,000.

What is the economically efficient result in each case (i.e., the result that would be favored by a cost-benefit analyst)? How might that result be reached if (a) only damage liability exists, (b) injunctions can be obtained, or (c) no liability exists? What effects do the various liability rules have on the distribution of wealth between the company's shareholders and its neighbors?

2.　The Coase Theorem has given rise to a considerable literature probing its validity and limitations. Some of the more important works are surveyed in Stewart J. Schwab, *Coase Defends Coase: Why Lawyers Listen and Economists Do Not*, 87 MICH. L. REV. 1171 (1989); Robert Cooter, *The Cost of Coase*, 11 J. LEGAL STUD. 1 (1982). For a more light-hearted look at Coase, *see* Daniel Farber, *The Case Against Brilliance*, 70 MINN. L. REV. 917, 918–20, 923–24 (1986). One particularly interesting (but fairly technical) critique of Coase can be found in Joseph Farrell, *Information and the Coase Theorem*, 1 J. ECON. PERSP. 113 (1987). An important empirical test of Coase was undertaken by John Donahue. He found that the initial assignment of incentive payments between employers and employees had substantial behavioral consequences, contrary to the predictions of the Coase Theorem. John Donahue, *Diverting the Coasean River: Incentive Schemes to Reduce Unemployment Spells*, 99 YALE L.J. 549 (1989). The upshot of all this literature can probably be summarized by saying that people will often (but not always) negotiate their way around legal rules to economically efficient outcomes.

3.   Although the "Coase Theorem" is one of the most famous results in law and economics, "The Problem of Social Cost" and Coase's other writings show that Coase regarded the zero-transaction-cost assumption as unrealistic and saw transaction costs as both inevitable and essential to understanding the structure of the economy. As he explained later, his aim in this article was to set up a simple thought experiment to help "make clear the fundamental role which transaction costs do, and should, play in the fashioning of the institutions which make up the economic system." Because of the "very peculiar properties" of a world without transaction costs, Coase concludes, "It would not seem worthwhile to spend much time investigating the properties of such a world." Ronald Coase, *The Firm, The Market, and the Law* 13–15 (1988). Coase observes that the world of zero transaction costs is not "Coasean," but rather the "world of modern economic theory, one which I was hoping to persuade economists to leave." *Id.* at 174. The failure of economists to consider transaction costs is, he believes, the major reason for their inability to account for real-world economic outcomes; consequently, their policy proposals are "the stuff that dreams are made of." *Id.* at 185. Given this widespread misinterpretation of what he intended by his theorem, in certain respects Coase ironically has more in common with some of his critics than with many of his supporters. *See* Daniel Farber, *Parody Lost/Paradigm Regained: The Ironic History of the Coase Theorem*, 83 VA. L. REV. 397 (1997).

4.   Because market transactions do have costs, the assignment of liability often affects both ultimate allocation of resources and distribution of income. Other authors have suggested, like Coase, that the courts might consider the economic efficiency and transaction costs of negotiating changes in established legal rights when selecting liability rules. For example, in the case of a factory whose smoke damages many homeowners, what kinds of transaction costs (informational, organizational, etc.) would be required to alter a legal rule under which: (a) the factory is not liable; (b) the factory is liable only for damage judgments; (c) the factory is liable to injunction at the behest of any injured homeowner? *See* Frank I. Michelman, *Pollution as a Tort: A Non-Accidental Perspective on Calabresi's Costs*, 80 YALE L.J. 647 (1971); Guido Calabresi & A. Douglas Melamed, *Property Rules, Liability Rules, and Inalienability: One View of the Cathedral*, 85 HARV. L. REV. 1089 (1972). Michelman says that in applying a "decentralist or transaction-organizing" version of nuisance law, a court may decide to impose liability on the polluter because it believes the polluter is the "cheapest cost avoider" or because it believes that the polluter is the "best briber." However, if the court acts on the latter ground, it should be wary of "injunctions with their heavy negotiation costs which may prevent the polluter from bribing effectively."

Calabresi and Melamed suggest a fourth legal rule in addition to those mentioned in the preceding paragraph: (d) the factory is liable to injunction, but only if plaintiff homeowners compensate the factory for its costs attributable to the injunction. Is this closer to rule (a) or (c)? For an illustration of rule (d), see the next case. A fifth rule, with seemingly limited practical application, has also been proposed: The factory decides whether or not to stay open, and if it closes, the neighbor pays damages measured by the social cost of the pollution. *See* James E. Krier & Stewart J. Schwab, *Property Rules and Liability Rules: The Cathedral in Another Light*, 70 N.Y.U. L. REV. 440 (1995).

2.   PUBLIC NUISANCE

In addition to private nuisance, plaintiffs may bring public nuisance claims to recover for harms suffered as a result of pollution. A public nuisance is an unreasonable interference with a right common to the general public, including public health and safety. Typically, the state brings a public nuisance action on behalf of its citizens and seeks injunctive relief. An example might be a state environmental agency bringing a public nuisance claim against a hazardous waste facility to enjoin operation of a site that, because of leaching chemicals, poses a threat to a community's drinking water supply.

For a private plaintiff to have standing to bring a public nuisance claim, the plaintiff must be able to show "special injury," which requires a difference in kind, and not just extent, of injury. More recently, courts and legislatures have liberalized this test. As a result, it can be fairly easy to satisfy. When reading the case below, consider how effective public nuisance is as a mechanism for air pollution regulation.

SPUR INDUSTRIES, INC. V. DEL E. WEBB DEVELOPMENT CO.

Supreme Court of Arizona, In Banc, 1972.
108 Ariz. 178, 494 P.2d 700.

[In 1957 Del Webb began construction of a retirement community called Sun City, west of Phoenix. By 1967 the development had moved close to Spur's feedlot, which had been in operation for several years before Webb came into the area.]

CAMERON, VICE CHIEF JUSTICE.

Del Webb's suit complained that the Spur feeding operation was a public nuisance because of the flies and the odor which were drifting or being blown by the prevailing south to north wind over the southern portion of Sun City. At the time of the suit, Spur was feeding between 20,000 and 30,000 head of cattle, and the facts amply support the finding of the trial court that the feed pens had become a nuisance to the people who resided in the southern part of Del Webb's development. The testimony indicated that cattle in a commercial feedlot will produce 35 to 40 pounds of wet manure per day, per head, or over a million pounds of wet manure per day for 30,000 head of cattle, and that despite the admittedly good feedlot management and good housekeeping practices by Spur, the resulting odor and flies produced an annoying if not unhealthy situation as far as the senior citizens of southern Sun City were concerned. There is no doubt that some of the citizens of Sun City were unable to enjoy the outdoor living which Del Webb had advertised and that Del Webb was faced with sales resistance from prospective purchasers as well as strong and persistent complaints from the people who had purchased homes in that area. * * *

The difference between a private nuisance and a public nuisance is generally one of degree. A private nuisance is one affecting a single individual or a definite small number of persons in the enjoyment of private rights not common to the public, while a public nuisance is one affecting the rights enjoyed by citizens as a part of the public. To constitute a public nuisance, the nuisance must affect a considerable number of people or an entire community or neighborhood.

Where the injury is slight, the remedy for minor inconveniences lies in an action for damages rather than in one for an injunction. Moreover, some courts have held, in the "balancing of conveniences" cases, that damages may be the sole remedy. *See Boomer v. Atlantic Cement Co. [supra,* page 398].* * *

It is clear that as to the citizens of Sun City, the operation of Spur's feedlot was both a public and a private nuisance. They could have successfully maintained an action to abate the nuisance. Del Webb, having shown a special injury in the loss of sales, had standing to bring suit to enjoin the nuisance. The judgment of the trial court permanently enjoining the operation of the feedlot is affirmed. * * *

In the so-called "coming to the nuisance" cases, the courts have held that the residential landowner may not have relief if he knowingly came into a neighborhood reserved for industrial or agricultural endeavors and has been damaged thereby. * * * Were Webb the only party injured, we would feel justified in holding that the doctrine of "coming to the nuisance" would have been a bar to the relief asked by Webb, and, on the other hand, had Spur located the feedlot near the outskirts of a city and had the city grown toward the feedlot, Spur would have to suffer the cost of abating the nuisance as to those people locating within the growth pattern of the expanding city. * * *

There was no indication in the instant case at the time Spur and its predecessors located in western Maricopa County that a new city would spring up, full-blown, alongside the feeding operation and that the developer of that city would ask the court to order Spur to move because of the new city. Spur is required to move not because of any wrongdoing on the part of Spur, but because of a proper and legitimate regard of the courts for the rights and interests of the public.

Del Webb, on the other hand, is entitled to the relief prayed for (a permanent injunction), not because Webb is blameless, but because of the damage to the people who have been encouraged to purchase homes in Sun City. It does not equitably or legally follow, however, that Webb, being entitled to the injunction, is then free of any liability to Spur if Webb has in fact been the cause of the damage Spur has sustained. It does not seem harsh to require a developer, who has taken advantage of the lesser land values in a rural area as well as the availability of large tracts of land on which to build and develop a new town or city in the area, to indemnify those who are forced to leave as a result.

Having brought people to the nuisance to the foreseeable detriment of Spur, Webb must indemnify Spur for a reasonable amount of the cost of moving or shutting down.

NOTES

1. *Spur* raises some interesting questions of tort law: Should the residents be estopped from seeking relief against Spur because they moved into an area despite conditions of which they should have been aware? About forty states make "coming to the nuisance" an affirmative defense to a private nuisance claim. Does this explain why Del Webb resorted to a public nuisance claim? What would a strict "coming to the nuisance" doctrine do to economic progress and growth?

2. Why doesn't the combination of private nuisance and public nuisance claims deal adequately with the problem of air pollution? Won't successful lawsuits deter industry from polluting? Or if it is cheaper to pay damages and keep polluting than to install pollution-control equipment, then isn't it rational and efficient to do just that, as per the Coase Theorem explored above? Is it problematic that the common law provides remedies after harm has occurred, rather than preventing harm in the first place?

3. Public and private nuisance claims may be argued using either an intentional or a negligence-based theory of liability. Using an intent theory, plaintiff must merely prove that the harm caused by defendant was "substantially foreseeable." Using a negligence theory, plaintiff must show that defendant behaved unreasonably in light of the risk of harm. The difference between the two is especially important in environmental cases. It is much harder to prevail on a nuisance claim using a negligence theory, because the conduct of the defendant and the precautions she has taken become relevant. In most pollution cases, it is easier to prove that intent is satisfied by substantial foreseeability (plaintiff surely knows that emissions or effluent from the daily operation of the factory will have to land somewhere). A negligence-based theory of nuisance might be appropriate in an instance where defendant was careless in maintaining equipment or training workers, causing an accident that results in environmental contamination. In addition, a nuisance claim may be brought based on a strict liability theory of liability. This may be appropriate when defendant is engaging in an abnormally

dangerous activity. Many judges are less than precise, however, in distinguishing analytically among the different bases of liability. For an explanation of the different theories of liability on which a nuisance claim can be maintained, *see* State of New York v. Schenectady Chemicals, Inc., 117 Misc.2d 960, 459 N.Y.S.2d 971 (1983).

Should nuisance law be used to regulate greenhouse gas emissions? During the administration of President George W. Bush, plaintiffs filed a number of nuisance cases in federal court against large emitters of greenhouse gases. The Supreme Court weighed in below.

AMERICAN ELECTRIC POWER CO., INC., ET AL. V. CONNECTICUT

Supreme Court of the United States, 2011.
564 U.S. 410, 131 S. Ct. 2527, 180 L.Ed.2d 435.

JUSTICE GINSBURG delivered the opinion of the Court.

We address in this opinion the question whether the plaintiffs (several States, the city of New York, and three private land trusts) can maintain federal common law public nuisance claims against carbon-dioxide emitters (four private power companies and the federal Tennessee Valley Authority). As relief, the plaintiffs ask for a decree setting carbon-dioxide emissions for each defendant at an initial cap, to be further reduced annually. The Clean Air Act and the Environmental Protection Agency action the Act authorizes, we hold, displace the claims the plaintiffs seek to pursue.

In *Massachusetts* v. *EPA*, 549 U. S. 497 (2007), this Court held that the Clean Air Act, 42 U. S. C. § 7401 *et seq.*, authorizes federal regulation of emissions of carbon dioxide and other greenhouse gases. * * * Responding to our decision in *Massachusetts*, EPA undertook greenhouse gas regulation. In December 2009, the agency concluded that greenhouse gas emissions from motor vehicles "cause, or contribute to, air pollution which may reasonably be anticipated to endanger public health or welfare," the Act's regulatory trigger. * * *

EPA and the Department of Transportation subsequently issued a joint final rule regulating emissions from light-duty vehicles, and initiated a joint rulemaking covering medium- and heavy-duty vehicles. EPA also began phasing in requirements that new or modified "[m]ajor [greenhouse gas] emitting facilities" use the "best available control technology." Finally, EPA commenced a rulemaking under § 111 of the Act, 42 U. S. C. § 7411, to set limits on greenhouse gas emissions from new, modified, and existing fossil-fuel fired power plants. * * *

The lawsuits we consider here began well before EPA initiated the efforts to regulate greenhouse gases just described. In July 2004, two groups of plaintiffs filed separate complaints in the Southern District of New York against the same five major electric power companies. The defendants, according to the complaints, "are the five largest emitters of carbon dioxide in the United States." Their collective annual emissions of 650 million tons constitute 25 percent of emissions from the domestic electric power sector, 10 percent of emissions from all domestic human activities, and 2.5 percent of all anthropogenic emissions worldwide.

By contributing to global warming, the plaintiffs asserted, the defendants' carbon-dioxide emissions created a "substantial and unreasonable interference with public rights," in violation of the federal common law of interstate nuisance, or, in the alternative, of state tort law. App. 103–105, 145–147. * * *

"There is no federal general common law," *Erie R. Co.* v. *Tompkins*, 304 U. S. 64, 78 (1938), famously recognized. In the wake of *Erie*, however, a keener understanding developed. *Erie* also sparked "the emergence of a federal decisional law in areas of national concern." Environmental protection is undoubtedly an area "within national legislative power," one in which federal courts may fill in "statutory interstices," and, if necessary, even "fashion federal law." * * * Recognition that a subject is meet for federal law governance, however, does not necessarily mean that federal courts should create the controlling law.* * *

It is an academic question whether, in the absence of the Clean Air Act and the EPA actions the Act authorizes, the plaintiffs could state a federal common law claim for curtailment of greenhouse gas emissions because of their contribution to global warming. Any such claim would be displaced by the federal legislation authorizing EPA to regulate carbon-dioxide emissions.

"[W]hen Congress addresses a question previously governed by a decision rested on federal common law," the Court has explained, "the need for such an unusual exercise of law-making by federal courts disappears." *Milwaukee II*, 451 U. S., at 314 (holding that amendments to the Clean Water Act displaced the nuisance claim recognized in *Milwaukee I*). Legislative displacement of federal common law does not require the "same sort of evidence of a clear and manifest [congressional] purpose" demanded for preemption of state law. *Id.*, at 317. " '[D]ue regard for the presuppositions of our embracing federal system ... as a promoter of democracy,' " *id.*, at 316, does not enter the calculus, for it is primarily the office of Congress, not the federal courts, to prescribe national policy in areas of special federal interest. *TVA* v. *Hill*, 437 U.S. 153, 194 (1978). The test for whether congressional legislation excludes the declaration of federal common law is simply whether the statute "speak[s] directly to [the] question" at issue.

We hold that the Clean Air Act and the EPA actions it authorizes displace any federal common law right to seek abatement of carbon-dioxide emissions from fossil-fuel fired power plants. *Massachusetts* made plain that emissions of carbon dioxide qualify as air pollution subject to regulation under the Act. 549 U. S., at 528–529. And we think it equally plain that the Act "speaks directly" to emissions of carbon dioxide from the defendants' plants.

Section 111 of the Act directs the EPA Administrator to list "categories of stationary sources" that "in [her] judgment . . . caus[e], or contribut[e] significantly to, air pollution which may reasonably be anticipated to endanger public health or welfare." § 7411(b)(1)(A). Once EPA lists a category, the agency must establish standards of performance for emission of pollutants from new or modified sources within that category. § 7411(b)(1)(B); see also § 7411(a)(2). And, most relevant here, § 7411(d) then requires regulation of existing sources within the same category.[7] For existing sources, EPA issues emissions guidelines, see 40 C. F. R. § 60.22, .23 (2009); in compliance with those guidelines and subject to federal oversight, the States then issue performance standards for stationary sources within their jurisdiction, § 7411(d)(1).* * *

If EPA does not *set* emissions limits for a particular pollutant or source of pollution, States and private parties may petition for a rulemaking on the matter, and EPA's response will be reviewable in federal court. See § 7607(b)(1); *Massachusetts*, 549 U. S., at 516–517, 529. As earlier noted, see *supra*, at 3, EPA is currently engaged in a § 7411 rulemaking to set standards for greenhouse gas emissions from fossil-fuel fired power plants. To settle litigation brought under § 7607(b) by a group that included the majority of the plaintiffs in this very case, the agency agreed to complete that rulemaking by May 2012. 75 Fed. Reg. 82392. The Act itself thus provides a means to seek limits on emissions of carbon dioxide from domestic power plants—the same relief the plaintiffs seek by invoking federal common law. We see no room for a parallel track.

The plaintiffs argue, as the Second Circuit held, that federal common law is not displaced until EPA actually exercises its regulatory authority, *i.e.*, until it sets standards governing emissions from the defendants' plants. We disagree.

As *Milwaukee II* made clear . . . the relevant question for purposes of displacement is "whether the field has been occupied, not whether it has been occupied in a particular manner." *Id.*, at 324. Of necessity, Congress

---

7   There is an exception: EPA may not employ § 7411(d) if existing stationary sources of the pollutant in question are regulated under the national ambient air quality standard program, §§ 7408–7410, or the "hazardous air pollutants" program, § 7412. See § 7411(d)(1).

selects different regulatory regimes to address different problems. Congress could hardly preemptively prohibit every discharge of carbon dioxide unless covered by a permit. After all, we each emit carbon dioxide merely by breathing.

The Clean Air Act is no less an exercise of the legislature's "considered judgment" concerning the regulation of air pollution because it permits emissions *until* EPA acts. See *Middlesex County Sewerage Authority* v. *National Sea Clammers Assn.*, 453 U. S. 1, 22, n. 32 (1981) (finding displacement although Congress "allowed some continued dumping of sludge" prior to a certain date). The critical point is that Congress delegated to EPA the decision whether and how to regulate carbon-dioxide emissions from power plants; the delegation is what displaces federal common law. Indeed, were EPA to decline to regulate carbon-dioxide emissions altogether at the conclusion of its ongoing § 7411 rulemaking, the federal courts would have no warrant to employ the federal common law of nuisance to upset the agency's expert determination. * * *

Indeed, this prescribed order of decisionmaking—the first decider under the Act is the expert administrative agency, the second, federal judges—is yet another reason to resist setting emissions standards by judicial decree under federal tort law. The appropriate amount of regulation in any particular greenhouse gas-producing sector cannot be prescribed in a vacuum: as with other questions of national or international policy, informed assessment of competing interests is required. Along with the environmental benefit potentially achievable, our Nation's energy needs and the possibility of economic disruption must weigh in the balance. * * *

It is altogether fitting that Congress designated an expert agency, here, EPA, as best suited to serve as primary regulator of greenhouse gas emissions. The expert agency is surely better equipped to do the job than individual district judges issuing ad hoc, case-by-case injunctions. Federal judges lack the scientific, economic, and technological resources an agency can utilize in coping with issues of this order. See generally *Chevron U. S. A. Inc.* v. *Natural Resources Defense Council, Inc.*, 467 U. S. 837, 865–866 (1984). Judges may not commission scientific studies or convene groups of experts for advice, or issue rules under notice-and-comment procedures inviting input by any interested person, or seek the counsel of regulators in the States where the defendants are located. Rather, judges are confined by a record comprising the evidence the parties present. Moreover, federal district judges, sitting as sole adjudicators, lack authority to render precedential decisions binding other judges, even members of the same court.

Notwithstanding these disabilities, the plaintiffs propose that individual federal judges determine, in the first instance, what amount of carbon-dioxide emissions is "unreasonable," App. 103, 145, and then decide what level of reduction is "practical, feasible and economically viable," App. 58, 119. These determinations would be made for the defendants named in the two lawsuits launched by the plaintiffs. Similar suits could be mounted, counsel for the States and New York City estimated, against "thousands or hundreds or tens" of other defendants fitting the description "large contributors" to carbon-dioxide emissions. Tr. of Oral Arg. 57.

The judgments the plaintiffs would commit to federal judges, in suits that could be filed in any federal district, cannot be reconciled with the decisionmaking scheme Congress enacted. The Second Circuit erred, we hold, in ruling that federal judges may set limits on greenhouse gas emissions in face of a law empowering EPA to set the same limits, subject to judicial review only to ensure against action "arbitrary, capricious, . . . or otherwise not in accordance with law." § 7607(d)(9).

NOTES

1. Would or should it make a difference if the plaintiffs seek damages rather than injunctive relief in a federal common law nuisance case? In Native Village of Kivalina v. ExxonMobil Corp, 696 F.3d 849 (9th Cir. 2012) the Ninth Circuit said no.

2. Should oil companies be held liable for damages from Hurricane Katrina on the grounds that their emissions contribute to global warming, which increases the risk of hurricanes? See Comer v. Murphy Oil, 607 F.3d 1049, 1053–55 (5th Cir. 2010). What problems might arise in trying to establish a claim for public nuisance for hurricane damages?

3. In North Carolina v. TVA, 615 F.3d 291 (4th Cir. 2010), the Fourth Circuit dismissed a public nuisance case seeking injunctive relief against four Tennessee Valley Authority power plants on the grounds that the Clean Air Act is a "carefully created system for accommodating the need for energy production and the need for clean air" that nuisance law would disrupt.

4. In 2017 and 2018, a number of municipalities and one state, Rhode Island, filed a new round of nuisance lawsuits under state, rather than federal, nuisance laws. The defendants in the cases are oil companies like ExxonMobile and Shell and the governments are seeking compensatory and punitive damages for damage caused by climate change. The new cases may fare better than the cases that have been dismissed in federal court in part because some states have nuisance statutes rather than relying only on common law (California is an example, see Cal. Civ. Code §§ 3479–3486.5), state courts are more accustomed to deciding common law claims (federal common law is relatively unusual), and the American Electric Power decision applied only to federal common law in holding that the Clean Air Act displaces federal common law nuisance claims for greenhouse gases. The lawsuits rely, too, on relatively new information that at least some of the oil company defendants knew about the risks of climate change as early as the 1960s, changed their

own internal operations as a result (by, for example, fortifying oil platforms that might be affected by storm surges and sea level rise), and nevertheless financed a campaign to create doubt among members of the public about whether climate change is occurring. For representative complaints *see* ClimateChangeLitigationDatabases: Common Law Claims, http://climatecase chart.com/case-category/common-law-claims/.

Do you think nuisance cases are an appropriate way to address the problem of climate change? What obstacles do you think plaintiffs will face in attempting to prove their cases? Will courts find that the Clean Air Act also displaces state nuisance claims?

5. For a robust debate about using nuisance to combat greenhouse gas emissions, *see* Benjamin Ewing & Douglas Kysar, *Prods and Pleas: Limited Government in an Era of Unlimited Harm*, 121 YALE L. JOUR. 121 (2011); Richard A. Epstein, *Beware of Prods and Pleas: A Defense of the Conventional Views on Tort and Administrative Law in the Context of Global Warming*, YALE LAW JOURNAL POCKET PART, (Dec. 2011); Jonathan Zasloff, *Courts in the Age of Dysfunction*, YALE LAW JOURNAL POCKET PART, (Feb. 2012).

6. The nuisance cases against oil companies are not the only novel form of litigation designed to combat greenhouse gas emissions. A group of 21 children has sued the federal government arguing that the government has a constitutional obligation to provide for a stable climate system and a public trust obligation to protect the global atmosphere. The case has to date withstood a motion to dismiss; an appeal of the district court's decision allowing the case to proceed is pending in the Ninth Circuit Court of Appeal. *See Juliana v. United States*, Case 6:15-cv-01577-AA (Oct. 2018), available at http://blogs2.law.columbia.edu/climate-change-litigation/wp-content/uploads/ sites/16/case-documents/2018/20181015_docket-615-cv-1517_opinion-and-order-1.pdf.

B. GOVERNMENT REGULATION OF AIR QUALITY

The market failure rationale mentioned in the introduction, together with the limitations of the common law as revealed by cases like *Boomer* and *Spur*, explain why government might seek to regulate pollution by statute. Still, important questions remain. To what extent, and with what mechanisms, should government try to improve air quality? Such choices are inevitably political. Government must determine the socially desirable level of air quality and then design regulatory mechanisms to achieve it. Controlling air pollution may require that we change how we produce goods. For example, we might substitute materials, switch to cleaner burning fuels, or package products differently. Controlling air pollution may require that we reduce our dependence on oil, and develop new technology to power motor vehicles. Ultimately controlling air pollution may require that we reduce consumption—a politically unpopular option in the United States.

The American approach to the problem of air pollution is largely command-and-control, which means that government sets the standards itself, and imposes emission limits directly on sources of pollution. Increasingly, however, EPA has used market mechanisms to address certain forms of air pollution but has faced some legal constraints, as we describe below. Typical command-and-control measures include mandatory emissions limits, technology and design requirements, and limitations on the use of certain materials or fuels. Permits are a common feature of command-and-control-regulation (although permits are used rather flexibly in practice to accommodate variations among firms and industrial classifications). One might think of permits as a license to pollute subject to certain conditions. In the typical case, firms subject to a permit requirement must disclose information to regulatory agencies in the application process, agree to emission-control measures, and comply with monitoring and record-keeping requirements. A failure to comply with permit requirements can lead to penalties and, in some cases, permit revocation.

A command-and-control approach can be costly and inefficient if the regulations are insufficiently sensitive to differences among firms. For example, a command-and-control regime that forced all firms to install the same technology, regardless of the age of the plants, would be inefficient. It is often more expensive for older plants to retrofit than for new plants to install state-of-the-art technology. In many cases, however, command-and-control regulation establishes performance standards and leaves it to firms themselves to determine how best to comply. For example, some firms might find it easier to comply with emission limits by switching to cleaner fuels, while others might prefer to curtail hours of production. To illustrate, firms located in or near western states with an abundance of low-sulfur coal might find it relatively cheap to substitute this fuel for comparatively more polluting high-sulfur coal. Firms located further east might find shipping costs prohibitive, and choose to meet emission limits by installing "scrubber" technology or by curtailing their hours of production. An alternative to performance standards is to cap emissions at an overall limit, allocate firms specific amounts of emission credits, and allow them to buy and sell emission credits beneath the cap. This way, older plants can purchase excess increments of pollution from newer firms that are able to reduce their emissions cheaply. If the net amount of pollution produced is lower, why should it matter if some firms pollute more than others?

Critics of command-and-control approaches have argued vigorously that market mechanisms such as these are superior to the "one size fits all" approach that they perceive command-and-control regulation to impose. *See, e.g.,* Bruce A. Ackerman & Richard B. Stewart, *Reforming Environmental Law: The Democratic Case for Market Incentives*, 13 COLUM. J. ENVTL. L. 171 (1988); Robert N. Stavins & Bradley W.

Whitehead, *Dealing with Pollution: Market-Based Incentives for Environmental Protection*, 34 ENVIRONMENT 7 (1992) (arguing that market-based incentives, properly managed, likely are the best approach to solving environmental problems). Defenders of command-and-control retort that market schemes may seem theoretically superior, but often fail to deliver their anticipated emissions reductions because of problems designing and monitoring the markets. In practice, some market schemes work quite well whereas others do not. *See* Jody Freeman and Charles D. Kolstad, eds., MOVING TO MARKETS IN ENVIRONMENTAL REGULATION: LESSONS FROM THIRTY YEARS OF EXPERIENCE (2006) (comparing market programs with command-and-control approaches and concluding, based on the empirical evidence, that both approaches can suffer from weaknesses in monitoring and enforcement). Uniform regulation arguably has many advantages over market approaches, including

> decreased information collection and evaluation costs, greater consistency and predictability of results, greater accessibility of decisions to public scrutiny and participation, increased likelihood that regulations will withstand judicial review, reduced opportunities for manipulative behavior by agencies in response to political or bureaucratic pressures, reduced opportunities for obstructive behavior by regulated parties, and decreased likelihood of social dislocation and "forum shopping" resulting from competitive disadvantages between geographical regions or between firms in regulated industries.

Howard Latin, *Ideal versus Real Regulatory Efficiency: Implementation of Uniform Standards and "Fine Tuning" Regulatory Reform*, 37 STAN. L. REV. 1267, 1271 (1985).

Of course, choosing the optimal regulatory instruments for purposes of achieving environmental policy goals is not a science. It depends on political feasibility as much as on technological capacity and economic analysis. In fact, there is a wide range of policy options for controlling air pollution: performance standards that leave to firms the decision about how to comply; design constraints; minimum technology requirements; pollution taxes; pollution prevention subsidies; market-trading schemes; restrictions on automobile trips; outright bans of certain fuels; or a combination of these measures. In short, regulation is a matter of design.

1. THE CLEAN AIR ACT

One could teach an entire course in environmental law by studying the Clean Air Act (CAA) alone (though we don't recommend it!). This 800-page statute tells the story of environmental regulation generally: bold legislative aspirations inevitably must be tempered in light of the difficulties of implementation. An underfunded and over-tasked agency subject to congressional, executive and judicial oversight must implement an enormously complicated set of congressional mandates and fill in the gaps left by vague or incomplete statutory language. The regulated community often resists implementation while environmentalists press for more rigorous enforcement, leading to a cacophony of lawsuits. Because of a combination of technical difficulty, complexity, and outright political resistance, compliance is partial, deadlines are missed and new problems, unanticipated by Congress when it originally passed the Act, arise. Periodically, Congress amends the law to extend deadlines and address new problems. Litigation ensues and the cycle continues.

The saga of the Clean Air Act also illustrates the themes we introduced in Chapters 1 and 2. Establishing air quality standards tends to turn on risk-based analyses that include scientific uncertainty; air pollution regulation in the United States explicitly prohibits cost-benefit analysis for some purposes while embracing it for others; and effective regulation requires a mix of approaches, including both prescriptive regulation and market mechanisms. Air pollution itself crosses physical boundaries, making it necessary—when conceiving of solutions—to cross conceptual boundaries between public and private institutions, or central and local control. And of course air pollution sometimes requires that we make trade-offs between environmental and economic goals. Air pollution can also have distributional consequences, with low income communities and communities of color living near sources that can cause serious health problems. For an analysis, *see* Ann E. Carlson, *The Clean Air Act's Blind Spot: Microclimates and Hotspot Pollution*, 65 UCLA L REV 1036 (2018). Finally, air pollution regulation is the product of the dynamic institutional environment we described in Chapter 5, one that includes Congress, the Executive branch, the judiciary, and powerful interest groups.

2. HISTORY OF CLEAN AIR LEGISLATION

Congress passed the Air Pollution Control Act, the first federal legislation aimed at curbing air pollution, in 1955. Traditionally, air pollution, like most environmental issues, had been a matter handled by the states. The 1955 legislation sought to assist states in their efforts by providing research support as well as technical and financial aid. This approach was largely ineffective in inducing states to act, however, and Congress finally opted to significantly enhance federal control over air pollution in the Clean Air Act Amendments of 1970. These have become known simply as the Clean Air Act (CAA). While the Act has been further amended since then (notably in 1977 and 1990), the heart of the 1970 legislation remains in place: Congress delegates to the EPA the task of setting National Ambient Air Quality Standards (NAAQS) for pervasive and harmful air pollutants known as "criteria pollutants", and requires states to devise State Implementation Plans (SIPs) to achieve those standards by statutory deadlines. This division of responsibility affords states the flexibility to mete out the pain of emissions reductions in a way that is sensitive to local conditions. These conditions are not just political but also geographical and cultural. Because of the variability among states in terms of their industrial base, geography, climate and tolerance for different kinds of regulation, state governments are thought to be in the best position to determine how to meet federal standards.

The Act stipulates minimum requirements for state plans to achieve federal standards, and the EPA must approve these plans. If the EPA disapproves a SIP, it may substitute a Federal Implementation Plan (FIP) instead. However, the political infeasibility and enormous cost of direct federal implementation means that this provision of the Act is rarely invoked, and leaves states with considerable authority to determine how the CAA plays out on the ground. The federal-state relationship is not, it bears noting, uniformly acrimonious. States frequently invoke the EPA's ultimate authority as the "gorilla in the closet" to provide political cover for state regulatory measures, and to exact concessions from regulated entities. At the same time, regional EPA offices frequently work cooperatively with their state counterparts. The Clean Air Act embodies environmental federalism by dividing authority between the federal and state governments in this way, creating an inter-dependent, though not entirely harmonious, partnership.

The 1970 legislation mandated attainment of NAAQS (with some exceptions) by 1975. It authorized the EPA to establish technology-based performance standards for all new sources of pollution, to regulate hazardous air pollutants at levels providing an "ample margin of safety," and to regulate tailpipe emissions from mobile sources. In the face of widespread non-compliance, Congress amended the Act in 1977 to extend the deadlines for achieving NAAQS to 1982, and provided a further extension to 1987 for "non-attainment" areas—those parts of the country with the most polluted air that were furthest from compliance with NAAQS. The 1977 Amendments also added provisions to prevent significant deterioration of air quality in parts of the country already in compliance with the NAAQS. The 1977 Amendments limited the extent to which air quality can degrade in these areas by establishing annual allowable increases in ambient concentrations.

Even the new deadlines proved too ambitious. While emissions from both stationary and mobile sources had been reduced considerably, many areas of the country still struggled to meet the NAAQS. As of 1989, 96 areas violated the ozone standard and 41 failed to meet the carbon monoxide limit. Env't Rep. (BNA) 815 (Aug, 24, 1990). For a combination of reasons, including the relative lack of scientific data and consensus on toxic exposure, the Act's toxics program had been a failure; the EPA had set standards for only seven toxic air pollutants.

In 1990, Congress significantly amended the Act. For nonattainment areas, it established new deadlines, with graduated requirements keyed to the severity of the nonattainment problem. Areas of the country furthest from compliance received more time to achieve NAAQS, but faced a greater regulatory burden in the interim. This graduated approach is sensitive to the ongoing difficulties that nonattainment areas still face in light of problems such as increasing population densities and the difficulties of controlling pollutants such as ozone (itself the product of a complicated chemical reaction involving more than one pollutant) emanating from a variety of hard-to-control stationary and non-stationary sources. The 1990 Amendments also created a new toxics program in light of the EPA's failure. Congress specifically listed 189 hazardous air pollutants (one has since been de-listed) and required the EPA to establish technology-based standards for all major sources (defined as sources producing 10 tons per year of any single listed hazardous pollutant, or 25 tons per year of any combination of such pollutants).

The 1990 Amendments also enhanced the EPA's enforcement power, affording the agency authority to issue administrative penalties up to $25,000 per day of violation and augmenting many of the Act's criminal sanctions. The Amendments added to the citizen-suit provision as well. Citizens may now bring suits against violators of the Act and against the EPA for failure to perform any non-discretionary duty. The Act provides for penalties and attorney's fees, and awards a $10,000 bounty to anyone providing information leading to a civil or criminal penalty.

Although the harm-based approach to setting national ambient standards, which are then implemented through regulations devised in state plans, remains the core of the Act, this approach has been supplemented by a variety of technology-based emissions standards that are directly imposed on individual sources of pollution, depending on where they are located, what they emit, when they were built, and whether they are considered "major" or not under the Act. These emission limits apply over and above measures states adopt in their SIPs to guarantee compliance with the NAAQS. A single stationary source of pollution may, therefore, be subject to a host of requirements. Until 1990, Congress did not require all major sources of air pollution to obtain permits; the onus was on the sources themselves to scour the statute, as well as the state plans, to determine all the measures they would have to take to comply. With the 1990 amendments, all major stationary sources must obtain a permit, which serves as the umbrella document containing all of the disparate requirements applicable to that source under all of the provisions of the statute. The Clean Air Act's original ambient-air regulatory approach thus has been supplemented by a permit-based approach like that adopted in the Clean Water Act. (These two laws have converged in various ways, even though they still differ in other respects. We will consider this comparison in more detail in Chapter 7.)

Thus far, the Clean Air Act has produced remarkable improvements in air quality and delivered far more in monetizeable benefits than it has cost. In order to monitor the achievements and failures of the Act, Congress added a provision as part of the 1990 Amendments requiring that the EPA periodically report on the overall costs and benefits of the legislation. The EPA has issued three such reports, retrospectively assessing the Clean Air Act's performance from 1970 to 1990, and prospectively appraising its costs and benefits from 1990 to 2020. EPA, Benefits and Costs of the Clean Air Act, https://www.epa.gov/clean-air-act-overview/benefits-and-costs-clean-air-act. All of these studies found that the benefits of the Clean Air Act have overwhelmingly outweighed its costs. Environmental Protection Agency, THE BENEFITS AND COSTS OF THE CLEAN AIR ACT, 1970 to 1990 (1997), *available at* https://www.epa.gov/clean-air-act-overview/benefits-and-costs-clean-air-act-1970-1990-retrospective-study (benefits quantified at between $6 and $50 trillion; direct compliance costs of only $0.5 trillion); Environmental Protection Agency, THE BENEFITS AND COSTS OF THE CLEAN AIR AT, 1990 to 2010 (1999), *available at* https://www.epa.gov/clean-air-act-overview/benefits-and-costs-clean-air-act-1990-2010-first-prospective-study (net benefit of $510 billion); THE BENEFITS AND COSTS OF THE CLEAN AIR ACT, 1990 to 2020 (2011), (available at https://www.epa.gov/clean-air-act-overview/benefits-and-costs-clean-air-act-1990-2020-second-prospective-study (quantifying net benefit of almost $2 trillion). In terms of absolute emissions, EPA data shows a steady decline in annual emissions of all criteria pollutants. Since 1970, concentrations of the six criteria pollutants have declined by an average of 73 percent even while the economy has grown by 324 percent. EPA, Clean Air Act, Progress Cleaning the Air And Improving People's Health, Detailed Summary, Clean Air Act Results, https://www.epa.gov/clean-air-act-overview/progress-cleaning-air-and-improving-peoples-health. Improvements in air quality are all the more impressive since vehicle miles driven and population have both increased dramatically over the past 49 years. Of course, significant challenges remain. The most easily attained air quality improvements have already been accomplished, mostly through the installation of relatively affordable technological controls. Taking the next steps will likely be more expensive. Many urban areas of the country are out of attainment with some of the NAAQS for a large portion of the year; mobile source emissions remain difficult to control given the political resistance to increased fuel efficiency standards and the prospect of gasoline or carbon taxes; interstate transport of ozone from upwind to downwind states continues to interfere with the ability of the downwind states to achieve compliance with ozone standards; and the rules for "new" and "modified" sources of air pollution are in flux and hotly contested in ongoing litigation. In addition, the emission of greenhouse gases that cause global warming have presented new challenges for air regulators.

3. HELPFUL DISTINCTIONS REGARDING THE CLEAN AIR ACT

It is easy to lose the forest for the trees when studying the CAA. To help organize your thinking as you read the materials in this chapter, keep in mind the following useful distinctions.

a. Harm-Based vs. Technology-Based Regulation

This distinction resurfaces in the next chapter on the Clean Water Act (and also can be useful in thinking through the Resource Conservation and Recovery Act, which we cover in Chapter 8). In the simplest terms, harm-based regulation is aimed at setting standards necessary to protect the public health, whereas technology-based regulation is aimed at setting standards that existing technology is capable of achieving. What is the difference in practice? When air standards are set at a level requisite to protect the public health, the question of whether technology can achieve these standards is secondary. The priority in the harm-based approach is to set concentration levels for pollutants (for example, so many parts per million of ozone in the ambient air) sufficiently low that people exposed to those pollutants will not become sick (setting aside the scientifically and politically contentious question of how to choose the class of people to protect, and how much to protect them). To comply with harm-based standards, industry might need to develop new technologies. In this sense, harm-based regulation can be *technology-forcing*.

Technology-based standards are necessarily derived from the technology that is currently available. Their primary focus is on the available equipment's emissions performance, not public health. As a result, they may be set too low to adequately protect the public health. On the other hand, standards set in this way may be more achievable precisely because the technology to achieve the standards already exists. Industry can be sure that it is in compliance with technology-based standards simply by adopting the same technology that the agency used to set the standards in the first place. The downside of a technology-based approach, according to critics, is that it may lock existing technology in place.

Technology-based standards are typically expressed as emission limits or concentrations (for example, so many parts per million of ozone; so many micrograms per cubic meter of lead; so many pounds per hour of sulfur dioxide). In simple terms, they tell a firm what amount or concentration of a pollutant they can produce, usually measured over some time period. However, these limits can be more or less stringent, depending on the technology used to set the standards. One way to understand the variance among different technology-based standards is to think in terms of the role that cost plays in choosing the technology. If cost plays a relatively large role, then the technology chosen to set the standard will likely be one that is already widely used in the industry. If it is widely used, most firms can adopt it without too much expense. If cost plays a relatively small role in the choice of technology, the agency might set the standard based on the state-of-the-art equipment, used by the industry leader. A standard based on this kind of technology would be expensive for most firms to meet; they might have to purchase new technology or take alternative, and presumably costly, steps to meet this stringent standard. Some firms might even go out of business, partly as a result of these costs. There are many technology-based standards in the CAA, including "Lowest Achievable Emission Rate" (LAER), "Best Demonstrated Achievable Technology" (BDAT), and "Maximum Achievable Control Technology" (MACT). Because these acronyms can sound so abstract, think of them in terms of a sliding scale of both stringency and cost. Another tip to keep in mind: frequently, different technology-based standards, like those mentioned above, differ only in theory, and conflate into the same level of control in practice.

b.   Stationary vs. Mobile Sources

Stationary sources include sources that don't move, such as oil refineries, power plants, pulp and paper mills, dry cleaners, and auto repair shops. Mobile sources include automobiles, trucks, and buses. The Act treats mobile sources differently than it does stationary sources. For now, try to imagine what makes it difficult to regulate automobiles versus stationary sources. Keep in mind that regulatory measures that might work well for stationary sources might not work well for mobile sources. Consider the example of an emission trading scheme, under which sources receive an initial allocation of pollution credits which they can then buy or sell. Such an approach may be easy to monitor if the trades occur between a handful of stationary sources, but impossible to monitor if trades occur between millions of cars crossing state lines.

c.   New vs. Existing Sources

Generally speaking, existing sources are treated more leniently than new sources: they are generally grandfathered into the statute by Congress and regulated less stringently. Determining whether a source is "new" is intuitive to some extent. A new source is one built after a given deadline (Congress has established different deadlines for different sections of the Act). For example, a power plant is considered a "new" source under section 111 if it is built *after* the EPA promulgates standards for that category of source (e.g., power plants) under section 111. The date on which the EPA issues the standards is the relevant deadline.

Whether a source is existing or new is not always so clear, however. For example, in a variety of provisions, the Act treats "modified" sources as new sources. In simple terms, a modification is defined as a change that increases, or has the potential to increase, emissions. So when a firm modifies its plant to update its technology (replacing or repairing a boiler for example), it might trigger "new source review" and the application of the more stringent provisions of the Act. In recent years, the question of whether "new" status is triggered has led to an explosion of litigation. Firms have argued that they should not be considered new sources when they are merely conducting "routine maintenance." As one might imagine, disputes over whether a given change amounts to routine maintenance, or is instead a modification triggering new source review, turn on highly technical questions regarding whether a given change either does or might increase emissions over the baseline emissions that the firm is already producing, or could potentially produce, if the firm were operating at full capacity. (As one might predict, this assessment is made even more complicated by debates about how to calculate baseline emissions.)

This quickly gets complicated. For now, remember this: being considered "new" as opposed to "existing" under the CAA is of monumental importance.

d. Attainment vs. Nonattainment Areas

Areas of the country that are already in compliance with the federal air pollution standards are considered "in attainment." Those areas of the country where the air quality does not yet meet NAAQS are considered nonattainment areas or nonattainment zones (NAZs). Congress added the nonattainment provisions to the Act in 1990, recognizing that its earlier deadlines for compliance with the NAAQS had not been met in every area of the country. The nonattainment provisions allow new stationary sources to be built in nonattainment zones, provided that states still make "reasonable further progress" toward attaining the NAAQS and provided that individual stationary sources comply with a number of stringent requirements. These amendments represent Congress's attempt to balance environmental and economic goals: Theoretically, had Congress not amended the statute to afford nonattainment zones more time to comply with NAAQS, industrial growth in these areas might have come to a standstill. Approving construction of any new industry in areas already badly out of attainment would, by definition, have amounted to a violation of the Act's requirement that states devise plans to meet NAAQS.

The 1990 Amendments require states to classify regions under their jurisdiction as either attainment or nonattainment (or "unclassifiable") areas for the pollutants for which the EPA has established NAAQS. In these Amendments, Congress provided a new set of deadlines for these areas to achieve compliance with NAAQS, and also established interim goals designed to ensure reasonable progress toward compliance over time. In the case of ozone, states must classify areas along a spectrum from "marginally" to "extremely" out of attainment. The more out of attainment an area, the more time Congress allows for that area to achieve compliance with the NAAQS for ozone. For example, a marginal nonattainment zone would have three years to achieve NAAQS, whereas an extreme nonattainment zone (the Los Angeles area and California's San Joaquin Valley are currently the only ones) had until 2010 before it had to comply. The 2015 revised ozone standard continues this approach, giving an extreme nonattainment zone, for example, 20 years from the designation date to comply. *See* 83 FR 10376, 10378 (March 9, 2018).

New or modified major sources of air pollution in nonattainment zones are subject to the most stringent regulation under the Act. Among other things, they must obtain a pre-construction permit, meet the most demanding technology-based emissions limits [known as "Lowest Achievable Emission Rate" (LAER)], and obtain offsetting reductions in emissions from other sources to counter-balance any new emissions they introduce into these relatively dirty areas of the country. The amount of offset required depends on the pollutant and the degree of nonattainment. The more polluted the area, the more a proposed new source will have to do to control its emissions. In addition to imposing requirements directly on stationary sources, it is important to stress that the Act's nonattainment provisions constrain the *state's* flexibility to design its implementation plans. Generally, states must do more in nonattainment zones than in other areas to demonstrate that they are making reasonable further progress toward attaining NAAQS.

e. Major vs. Non-Major Sources

Whether a stationary source of air pollution is "major" or not also affects how that source is treated under the Act. Generally, major sources of air pollution are regulated more stringently than non-major or "area" sources. The definition of "major," like the definition of "new," varies throughout the Act. The reason for the variability in this definition is, again, intuitive. In those parts of the country where the air is most polluted (those areas badly out of attainment with the federal ambient standards) it takes fewer emissions to qualify as a major source. For example, in a serious nonattainment zone, producing 50 tons of pollution per year makes a source major, whereas in an extreme nonattainment zone, major status is triggered by only 10 tons per year. Still another definition applies in those areas of the country that are in attainment with federal standards (either 100 tons per year of a listed pollutant or 250 tons per year of any pollutant). Another definition applies to "major" sources of hazardous air pollutants (either 10 tons per year of a single hazardous pollutant or 25 tons per year of any combination of hazardous pollutants). This detail can be overwhelming, but the key is to grasp that the definition of major varies, and that qualifying as a major stationary source matters because it usually means more stringent regulation.

4.   OVERVIEW OF THE CLEAN AIR ACT

TITLE I: ATTAINMENT AND MAINTENANCE OF NATIONAL AMBIENT AIR QUALITY STANDARDS

§ 108   Listing: The EPA must list "air pollutants" that, according to scientific evidence, may endanger the public health or welfare. Listing triggers the need to establish national primary and secondary standards.

§ 109   National Ambient Air Quality Standards (NAAQS): The EPA must promulgate health-based primary and secondary national ambient air quality standards for "criteria" pollutants (so named because the EPA prepares a "criteria" document comprised of scientific research for each pollutant). The six criteria pollutants for which the EPA has set standards are: sulfur dioxide, particulate matter, nitrogen dioxide, carbon monoxide, ozone, and lead. Primary standards are set at levels necessary to protect public health; secondary standards are set at standards necessary to protect public welfare, which includes crops, property, visibility and other effects not directly related to human health.

§ 110   State Implementation Plans (SIPs): Each state must establish a plan for the implementation, maintenance, and enforcement of the national standards within its jurisdiction or face sanctions. States must meet minimum statutory requirements in the design of their SIPs but otherwise have flexibility in choosing regulations, measures and methods that will result in the achievement of NAAQS. The EPA must approve or disapprove SIPs by statutory deadlines. If approved, SIPs become binding as a matter of both state and federal law and may be enforced by either state or federal officials. The EPA has the authority to disapprove a SIP if it fails to meet statutory requirements, and impose a federal implementation plan (FIP) instead.

§ 111   New Source Performance Standards (NSPS): The EPA must promulgate technology-based standards for new or modified major stationary sources of pollution. The standard reflects the degree of emission limitation and the percentage reduction achievable through application of the best technological system of continuous emission reduction ("Best Demonstrated Achievable Technology" or BDAT). The EPA establishes these standards on an industrial category basis. Sources built or modified after the EPA promulgates standards for that industrial category are considered new. In addition to whatever measures states adopt in their SIPs, these are the minimum technology-based emission limits imposed on all new stationary sources.

§ 112   National Emission Standards for Hazardous Air Pollutants (NESHAP): The EPA must set technology-based standards for 188 hazardous pollutants. The standard requires the maximum degree of reduction in emissions of the hazardous air pollutants, taking into consideration the cost of achieving such emission reduction and any non-air quality health and environmental impacts and energy requirements ("Maximum Achievable Control Technology" or MACT). The MACT standards apply to all major sources of hazardous air pollutants.

§ 113   Enforcement: Authorizes the EPA to issue administrative orders against any person not in compliance with the Act, and to issue administrative penalties of up to $25,000 per day of violation. The EPA may bring civil suit against violators. Violators are subject to both civil and criminal penalties. The EPA may also halt construction of any major stationary source in a state that is out of compliance with the rules governing the construction or modification of such sources.

§ 114   Information Disclosure and Inspection: The EPA may require sources to provide reports, maintain records, conduct sampling, and provide information to the EPA. The EPA may inspect any source. Any information obtained under this section is available to the public.

§§ 160–169A Prevention of Significant Deterioration (PSD): In areas that already meet or exceed the NAAQS, SIPs must contain provisions to prevent significant deterioration. The statute divides PSD areas into three classes (national parks and monuments must be Class I or II, for example), each with a separate increment of permissible pollution increases. These increments represent the extent to which the air quality for a given pollutant may be allowed to degrade over the baseline concentration of that pollutant in the air in the PSD area. The purpose of these provisions is to prevent air quality in areas with relatively clean air from falling below the concentration limits set by NAAQS. New or modified major sources in PSD areas must obtain pre-construction permits and comply with emission limits set according to "Best Available Control Technology" (BACT).

§ 171–178 Nonattainment Areas: A region that has not met the NAAQS is deemed a nonattainment area (also called a nonattainment zone or NAZ). New or modified major stationary sources in nonattainment areas must comply with stringent permitting requirements, including a showing that offsetting reductions from other sources will produce a net decrease in total emissions in the area, and achievement of the Lowest Achievable Emission Rate (LAER). Existing sources in nonattainment zones must comply with emission limits set according to Reasonably Available Control Technology (RACT). States must guarantee in their SIPs that they are making "reasonable further progress" toward compliance with NAAQS in nonattainment zones. For ozone, states must classify nonattainment areas according to the severity of the degree of non-attainment, along a spectrum ranging from marginal to extreme non-attainment. The worse the air quality, the longer the area has to achieve compliance with the ozone NAAQS. Nonattainment areas for ozone must implement different control measures depending on their classification. The worse the air quality, the more controls these areas must implement. Similar programs apply to areas that do not meet the NAAQS for carbon monoxide and particulate matter. Depending on the degree to which these areas exceed the carbon monoxide standard, they will be required to implement programs introducing oxygenated fuels and/or enhanced emission inspection programs, among other measures. Depending on their classification, areas exceeding the NAAQS for particulate matter must implement either reasonably available control measures or best available control measures, among other requirements.

TITLE II: MOBILE SOURCES

§§ 201–235 Emission Standards for Mobile Sources: The EPA is authorized to regulate fuels and fuel additives. Congress established stricter emissions standards for motor vehicles in the 1990 Amendments, and added new provisions on alternative fuels and "clean fuel" vehicles. Subject to EPA approval, California may set stricter emission limits than Congress, and other states may adopt California's standards.

TITLE III: GENERAL PROVISIONS

§ 304 Citizen Suits: Any person may file a civil action against any person alleged to have violated an emission standard, limit, or order under the Act, or against the EPA for failure to perform a non-discretionary duty.

§ 307 EPA Procedures and Judicial Review: Provides procedures governing the EPA rulemaking and judicial review. Judicial review is generally available in U.S. Courts of Appeals.

TITLE IV: ACID DEPOSITION

§§ 401–413: To address the problem of acid rain, these sections require rigorous controls on utilities to reduce the production of sulfur dioxide from new and existing plants. Congress created a market-based approach to address acid rain, establishing an overall cap on sulfur dioxide, authorizing the EPA to assign annual allocations of sulfur dioxide to firms based on their past emissions, and allowing firms to buy or sell allocations beneath the cap in a market regime.

TITLE V: PERMITS

§§ 501–507: All major stationary sources, and some others, must obtain an operating permit. Permit requirements include emission limits. The EPA may review state permits and has the authority to veto any permit not in compliance with the Act. Prior to the 1990 Amendments, sources were not obligated to have permits. There was no single document that contained all the control requirements that apply to a particular source. Source obligations were spread throughout the SIP, which made it very difficult for sources to know what compliance required.

The material in the following sections draws heavily on EPA documents available on the web. For more detail, students may wish to consult *The Plain English Guide to the Clean Air Act,* available at https://www.epa.gov/sites/production/files/2015-08/documents/peg.pdf. Other useful sources include ANN E. CARLSON & DALLAS BURTRAW, EDS, LESSONS FROM THE CLEAN AIR ACT: BUILDING DURABILITY AND ADAPTABILITY INTO CLIMATE AND ENERGY POLICY (forthcoming 2019); and ROBERT J. MARTINEAU, JR. & DAVID P. NOVELLO, THE CLEAN AIR ACT HANDBOOK (4th ed. 2017).

Technology-Based Control Standards under the CAA
(The Facts about BACTs, MACTs, and RACTs)

CAA Standards (in order of increasing stringency):

Standard:	Applies to:	Statute §:	Impact:
RACT (Reasonably Available Control Technology)	Existing sources in nonattainment areas	§ 172(c)(1)	Requires all such sources to use average existing technology (not cutting-edge "best" technology)
BDAT (Best Demonstrated Available Technology)	Stationary sources under NSPS (New Source Performance Standards)	§ 111(a)(1)	Specifically considers cost, but can require matching reductions of best-controlled similar source
BACT (Best Available Control Technology, sometimes given as BAT)	New major sources in PSD (prevention of significant deterioration) areas	§ 165(a)(4)	Requires maximum feasible pollution reduction, considering cost and other factors on case-by-case basis; must

			be at least as stringent as NSPS under § 111
MACT (Maximum Achievable Control Technology)	Major sources of hazardous air pollutants	§ 112(d)(2) § 112(d)(3)	Requires existing major sources to match best 12% of industry; new major sources to match best-controlled similar source
LAER (Lowest Achievable Emissions Reduction)	New or modified major stationary sources in nonattainment areas	§ 171(3) § 173(a)(2)	Requires most stringent existing emissions limit, whether achieved in practice or included in any SIP, for the applicable source category

C. THE BASICS OF THE CLEAN AIR ACT

1. AIR QUALITY STANDARDS

The Clean Air Act requires EPA to list pollutants that are 1) emitted from numerous and diverse sources and 2) emissions of which may endanger public health or welfare. After listing a pollutant, the EPA prepares "criteria documents" which consist of the scientific data indicating the health and welfare effects of the pollutant. The EPA must then establish an ambient standard for the pollutant, based on the health-based criteria documents. The standard is expressed as a maximum concentration limit for that pollutant in the surrounding air. The federal standard applies nationally, meaning that in no area of the country should the concentration of a listed pollutant exceed the federal standard.

These standards are not themselves directly enforceable. Instead they represent the air quality goals that states must achieve when designing SIPs. Subject to limitations provided in the Act, states directly regulate stationary sources and, to a more limited extent, mobile sources of air pollution, imposing the necessary reductions in emissions that will guarantee compliance with the NAAQS. The EPA must set both primary and secondary NAAQS. Primary standards are set at a level "requisite to protect public health," whereas secondary standards are set at a level "requisite to protect the public welfare." The EPA has promulgated primary and secondary NAAQS for only six pollutants: carbon monoxide, lead, nitrogen dioxide, ozone, particulate matter (divided into PM_{10} and $PM_{2.5}$—the numbers are in micrometers), and sulfur oxides. These six pollutants are known as "criteria pollutants." For all but two criteria pollutants (sulfur dioxide and the one year standard for PM_{10}), however, the primary and secondary standards are the same.

a. Criteria Pollutants

According to the EPA emissions of all criteria pollutants listed below "have decreased significantly since passage of the Clean Air Act in 1970." *See* the EPA's web page on air quality at https://www.epa.gov/air-trends/air-quality-national-summary. The following information regarding criteria pollutants is derived mostly from the EPA's helpful website on criteria air pollutants. *See* https://www.epa.gov/criteria-air-pollutants.

Carbon Monoxide (CO)

CO is a colorless, odorless, poisonous gas created from the incomplete combustion of fuels. Exhaust from cars produces the majority of CO.

- Source: burning of gasoline, natural gas, coal, oil, industrial processes

- Health Effects: reduces blood's ability to deliver oxygen to body cells and tissues; may be particularly hazardous to people with heart or circulatory problems and those with damaged lungs or breathing passages; at higher levels, exposure can impair vision, reduce work and learning capacity and affect coordination

Lead (Pb)

- Source: Historically leaded gasoline (which has been phased out), paint (houses, cars), smelters (metal refineries), manufacture and disposal of lead storage batteries

- Health Effects: accumulates in blood, bones and soft tissue, affecting brain and other nervous system function; high exposure may cause seizure and mental retardation; children are at elevated risk for central nervous system disorder

- Welfare Effects: Lead can harm wildlife and sharply reduce property values

Nitrogen Dioxide (NO₂)

NO_2 is a suffocating brownish gas, part of a family of poisonous and highly reactive gases including nitrous oxides (NO_x) that result from burning fuel at high temperatures. It reacts in the atmosphere to form corrosive nitric acid which contributes to acid rain. It plays a major role in the chemical reactions that produce ozone.

- Source: car exhaust, electric utilities, industrial boilers

- Health Effects: lung irritation, respiratory infection, children may be at higher risk of acute respiratory disease when exposed to high concentrations

- Welfare Effects: contributes to growth of algae and toxic conditions for fish in waterways; as precursor to acid rain, contributes to the acidification of lakes and forests

Ozone (O$_3$)

Ground level O$_3$, a poisonous form of pure oxygen, is the principal component of smog. It is the most pervasive and intractable of all the criteria pollutants because it is not directly emitted by sources, but rather results from a chemical reaction to which numerous sources contribute. Ozone is formed when volatile organic compounds (VOCs) like gasoline or other petroleum distillates and nitrous oxides react in sunlight. Ozone concentrations are affected by meteorological conditions as well as trends in VOCs and NO$_x$ emissions.

- Source: chemical reaction of volatile organic compounds, nitrous oxides and oxygen in sunlight

- Health Effects: damages lung tissue, decreases lung function, causes respiratory inflammation, asthma, eye irritation and stuffy nose, reduces resistance to colds and other infections, may accelerate aging of lung tissue

- Welfare Effects: responsible for $1–2 billion in crop damage per year nationally, damages plants making them more susceptible to disease, damages foliage in national parks and recreation areas and impairs habitat for endangered species, as well as reducing visibility.

Particulate Matter (PM)

PM includes solid and liquid particles in the atmosphere, some of which are visible as soot or smoke, others of which are too small to see with the naked eye. The health effects of PM$_{2.5}$ are particularly extreme.

- Source: burning of wood, diesel and other fuels; industrial plants; agriculture (plowing, burning of fields); unpaved roads

- Health Effects: impairs breathing and respiratory systems, irritates nose and throat, impairs body's ability to fight disease, aggravates existing pulmonary and cardiac disease, causes damage to lung tissue, carcinogenesis and premature death, and is especially dangerous to the elderly, children and people with chronic lung and heart disease

- Welfare Effects: particulates are the main source of haze that reduces visibility; ashes, soot, smoke and dust can discolor structures and other property including clothes and furniture

Sulfur Dioxide (SO₂)

- Source: burning of coal and oil, especially high sulfur coal burned by mid-western power plants; industrial processes (paper, metals)

- Health Effects: breathing difficulty, respiratory illness, impairs lung defenses, aggravates existing cardiovascular disease

- Welfare Effects: sulfur dioxide is an ingredient in acid rain, which can damage trees and lakes, corrode buildings and monuments, and reduce visibility

Volatile Organic Compounds (VOCs)

VOCs are not listed under the CAA as a criteria pollutant. However, they are a component of smog and are regulated as an ozone "precursor" under the Act.

- Source: released from burning of fuel (gasoline, oil, wood, coal, natural gas) or evaporation of solvents, paints, glues and other products used at work or at home. Cars are an important source of VOCs. VOCs include chemicals such as benzene, toluene, methylene chloride and methyl chloroform.

- Health Effects: In addition to contributing to smog, VOCs can cause serious health problems such as cancer

b. Listing Pollutants

The first step in the process of setting NAAQS is the decision by the EPA to list a pollutant based on scientific "criteria" documents indicating that pollutant's adverse impact on public health. The listing process triggers the need for the EPA to establish primary and secondary air standards, for which states must establish implementation plans. Thus, the decision to list or not list a pollutant is very consequential. In the case below, the EPA had refused to list lead as a pollutant despite overwhelming scientific evidence as to its health impacts. The agency had chosen instead to regulate the lead content of gasoline as its primary strategy of reducing lead emissions. An environmental group sued to force the listing.

NATURAL RESOURCES DEFENSE COUNCIL, INC. V. TRAIN
United States Court of Appeals, Second Circuit, 1976.
545 F.2d 320.

SMITH, CHIEF JUDGE.

The Environmental Protection Agency, ("EPA"), and its Administrator, Russell Train, appeal from an order of the United States District Court for the Southern District of New York, Charles E. Stewart, Jr., Judge, in an action under § 304 of the Clean Air Act, as amended, (a), requiring the Administrator of the EPA, within thirty days, to place lead on a list of air pollutants under § 108(a)(1) of the Clean Air Act ("the Act"). We affirm the order of the district court. * * *

The relevant part of § 108 reads as follows:

(a)(1) For the purpose of establishing national primary and secondary ambient air quality standards, the Administrator shall within 30 days after December 31, 1970, publish, and shall from time to time thereafter revise, a list which includes each air pollutant—

(A) which in his judgment has an adverse effect on public health or welfare;

(B) the presence of which in the ambient air results from numerous or diverse mobile or stationary sources; and

(C) for which air quality criteria had not been issued before December 31, 1970, but for which he plans to issue air quality criteria under this section.

Once a pollutant has been listed under § 108(a)(1), §§ 109 and 110 of the Act are automatically invoked. These sections require that for any pollutant for which air quality criteria are issued under § 108(a)(1)(C) after the date of enactment of the Clean Air Amendments of 1970, the Administrator must simultaneously issue air quality standards. Within nine months of the promulgation of such standards states are required to submit implementation plans to the Administrator. § 110(a)(1). The Administrator must approve or disapprove a state plan within four months. § 110(a)(2). If a state fails to submit an acceptable plan, the Administrator is required to prepare and publish such a plan himself. § 110(c). State implementation plans must provide for the attainment of primary ambient air quality standards no later than three years from the date of approval of a plan. § 110(a)(2)(A)(i). Extension of the three-year period for attaining the primary standard may be granted by the Administrator only in very limited circumstances, and in no case for more than two years. § 110(e).

The EPA concedes that lead meets the conditions of §§ 108(a)(1)(A) and (B)—that it has an adverse effect on public health and welfare, and that the presence of lead in the ambient air results from numerous or diverse mobile or stationary sources. The EPA maintains, however, that under § 108(a)(1)(C) of the Act, the Administrator retains discretion whether to list a pollutant, even though the pollutant meets the criteria of §§ 108(a)(1)(A) and (B). The Agency regards the listing of lead under § 108(a)(1) and the issuance of ambient air quality standards as one of numerous alternative control strategies for lead available to it. Listing of substances is mandatory, the EPA argues, only for those pollutants for which the Administrator "plans to issue air quality criteria." He may, it is contended, choose not to issue, *i.e., not* "plan to issue" such criteria, and decide to control lead solely by regulating emission at the source, regardless of the total concentration of lead in the ambient air. The Administrator argues that if he chooses to control lead (or other pollutants) under § 211, he is not required to list the pollutant under § 108(a)(1) or to set air quality standards. * * *

The issue is one of statutory construction. We agree with the district court and with appellees, National Resources Defense Council, Inc., et al., that the interpretation of the Clean Air Act advanced by the EPA is contrary to the structure of the Act as a whole, and that if accepted, it would vitiate the public policy underlying the enactment of the 1970 Amendments as set forth in the Act and in its legislative history. Recent court decisions are in accord, and have construed § 108(a)(1) to be mandatory if the criteria of subsections A and B are met.

Section 108(a)(1) contains mandatory language. It provides that "the Administrator *shall* . . . publish . . . a list. . . . " (emphasis added.) If the EPA interpretation were accepted and listing were mandatory only for substances "for which [the Administrator] plans to issue air quality criteria . . . ", then the mandatory language of § 108(a)(1)(A) would become mere surplusage. The determination to list a pollutant and to issue air quality criteria would remain discretionary with the Administrator, and the rigid deadlines of § 108(a)(2), § 109, and § 110 for attaining air quality standards could be bypassed by him at will. If Congress had enacted § 211 as an alternative to, rather than as a supplement to, §§ 108–110, then one would expect a similar fixed timetable for implementation of the fuel control section. The absence of such a timetable for the enforcement of § 211 lends support to the view that fuel controls were intended by Congress as a means for attaining primary air quality standards rather than as an alternative to the promulgation of such standards.

The EPA Administrator himself initially interpreted § 108(a)(1) as requiring inclusion on the initial list to be issued of those pollutants for which air quality criteria had not been issued but which he had already found in his judgment to have an adverse effect on public health or welfare and to come from sources specified in § 108(a)(1)(B).

We agree with Judge Stewart that it is to the initial list alone that the phrase "but for which he plans to issue air quality criteria" is directed, and that the Administrator must list those pollutants which he has determined meet the requisites set forth in section 108.

When a specific provision of a total statutory scheme may be construed to be in conflict with the congressional purpose expressed in an act, it becomes necessary to examine the act's legislative history to determine whether the specific provision is reconcilable with the intent of Congress. Because state planning and implementation under the Air Quality Act of 1967 had made little progress by 1970, Congress reacted by "taking a stick to the States in the form of the Clean Air Amendments of 1970. . . . " Train v. Natural Resources Defense Council, 421 U.S. 60. It enacted § 108(a)(1) which provides that the Administrator of the Environmental Protection Agency "shall" publish a list which includes each air pollutant which is harmful to health and originates from specified sources. Once a pollutant is listed under § 108(a)(1), §§ 109 and 110 are to be automatically invoked, and promulgation of national air quality standards and implementation thereof by the states within a limited, fixed time schedule becomes mandatory.

The EPA contention that the language of § 108(a)(1)(C) "for which [the Administrator] plans to issue air quality criteria" is a separate and third criterion to be met before § 108 requires listing lead and issuing air quality standards, thereby leaving the decision to list lead within the discretion of the Administrator, finds no support in the legislative history of the 1970 Amendments to the Act. * * *

While the literal language of § 108(a)(1)(C) is somewhat ambiguous, this ambiguity is resolved when this section is placed in the context of the Act as a whole and in its legislative history. The deliberate inclusion of a specific timetable for the attainment of ambient air quality standards incorporated by Congress in §§ 108–110 would become an exercise in futility if the Administrator could avoid listing pollutants simply by choosing not to issue air quality criteria. The discretion given to the Administrator under the Act pertains to the review of state implementation plans under § 110, and to § 211 which authorizes but does not mandate the regulation of fuel or fuel additives. It does not extend to the issuance of air quality standards for substances derived from specified sources which the Administrator had already adjudged injurious to health. * * *

The structure of the Clean Air Act as amended in 1970, its legislative history, and the judicial gloss placed upon the Act leave no room for an interpretation which makes the issuance of air quality standards for lead under § 108 discretionary. The Congress sought to eliminate, not perpetuate, opportunity for administrative foot-dragging. Once the conditions of §§ 108(a)(1)(A) and (B) have been met, the listing of lead and the issuance of air quality standards for lead become mandatory.

The order of the district court is affirmed.

NOTES

1.   The list of criteria pollutants for which national air quality standards have been set remains at six. Why do you think this is the case? The biggest change the EPA has made in recent years is dividing the particulate matter category into fine and course subsets ($PM_{2.5}$ and PM_{10}) in 1997. This decision was in response to the identification of health problems uniquely caused by

fine particles. *See* John H. Cushman, Jr., *Administration Issues Its Proposal for Tightening of Air Standards*, N.Y. TIMES, Nov. 28, 1996, at A1.

2.   By forcing the EPA to list lead as a criteria pollutant, the court is arguably interfering with the EPA's preferred regulatory strategy of addressing lead pollution by regulating fuel content, which the agency is authorized to do. This might be a much more cost-effective, technologically feasible and politically palatable approach. Should courts not defer to the agency when it comes to a policy choice such as this?

3.   Should greenhouse gases be listed as criteria pollutants? After all they come from numerous and diverse sources and endanger public health and welfare. The Center for Biological Diversity has petitioned the EPA to list GHGs as criteria pollutants, though the agency has not acted on the petition. *See* Center for Biological Diversity, Petition to Establish National Pollution Limits for Greenhouse Gases Pursuant to the Clean Air Act, https://www.biologicaldiversity.org/programs/climate_law_institute/global_warming_litigation/clean_air_act/pdfs/Petition_GHG_pollution_cap_12-2-2009.pdf.

c.   Setting Air Standards

The standard-setting process for criteria pollutants is, to say the least, complex. For a valuable explanation of the process, *see* William Boyd, *National Ambient Air Quality Standards*, in ANN E. CARLSON & DALLAS BURTRAW, EDS, LESSONS FROM THE CLEAN AIR ACT: BUILDING DURABILITY AND ADAPTABILITY INTO CLIMATE AND ENERGY POLICY (forthcoming 2019). The EPA relies on an independent science advisory panel to advise on the scientific data, but the science itself may lead to no clear conclusions about precisely where to set an ambient air standard. In studying the use of science to update air quality standards in the late nineties, Cary Coglianese and Gary Marchant concluded that the EPA frequently invoked science to cloak the value judgments implicit in the standard-setting process. Cary Coglianese & Gary E. Marchant, *Shifting Sands: The Limits of Science in Setting Risk Standards*, 152 U. PA. L. REV. 1255, 1260–61 (2004). Indeed, science cannot resolve the inherently political task of setting regulatory standards. Frequently, the science points only to a range in which risks due to air pollution increase. But risks to whom? Should we set air standards with children in mind? Asthmatics? The elderly? And how safe is safe? Should we seek to reduce risks to zero, no matter what the cost? Who should decide these things? Congress? Expert agency staff? And what role should courts play in this process?

The case below raises many of these questions. The Court's discussion of lead exposure, its implications for health, and the EPA's rationales for setting lead concentrations is long and technical. But it gives the reader a realistic flavor of the decision-making process that the EPA must go through when setting air standards. It also makes clear how challenging these decisions are for courts to review. Consider that many of the judges now reviewing air pollution regulations, such as these, were appointed to the bench before environmental law was an established field. Few of them ever took a course called "Environmental Law" in law school. As you read the excerpt, imagine yourself as a clerk to a judge having to decide this case.

LEAD INDUSTRIES, INC. V. EPA

United States Court of Appeals, District of Columbia Circuit, 1980.
647 F.2d 1130.

J. SKELLY WRIGHT, CHIEF JUDGE.

[Humans face lead exposure through ingestion or inhalation from food, water, air, dust, and peeling paint. Lead in sufficient concentrations can cause anemia, kidney damage, severe brain damage, or death. Traditionally, breathing atmospheric lead was the third largest source of human body lead. Initially the EPA sought to address this problem informally by reducing but not banning lead additives in gasoline. However, in 1975, the Natural Resources Defense Council and others successfully sued the EPA to force it to list lead as a criteria pollutant under CAA § 108 and promulgate national ambient air quality standards for it under § 109, which the EPA did. The Lead Industry Association, Inc. (LIA), the major nationwide lead industry trade association, and St. Joe Minerals Corporation (St. Joe), then petitioned for review of the EPA's health-based NAAQS for atmospheric lead, questioning whether (1) the EPA Administrator had acted within the scope of statutory authority, (2) the evidence adduced through the rulemaking process supported the NAAQS, and (3) procedural flaws required the EPA to reconsider its final determination on lead.]

II.   THE STATUTORY SCHEME

* * * Section 108 makes it clear that the term "air quality criteria" means something different from the conventional meaning of "criterion"; such "criteria" do not constitute "standards" or "guidelines," but rather refer to a document to be prepared by EPA which is to provide the basis for promulgation of air quality standards for the pollutant. This criteria document must "accurately reflect the latest scientific knowledge useful in indicating the kind and extent of all identifiable effects on public health or welfare which may be expected from the presence of such pollutant in the ambient air, in varying quantities." Section 108(a)(2).

At the same time as he issues air quality criteria for a pollutant, the Administrator must also publish proposed national primary and secondary air quality standards for the pollutant. Section 109(a)(2). National primary ambient air quality standards are standards "the attainment and maintenance of which in the judgment of the Administrator, based on such criteria and allowing an adequate margin of safety, are requisite to protect the public health." Section 109(b)(1). Secondary air quality standards "specify a level of air quality the attainment and maintenance of which in the judgment of the Administrator, based on such criteria, is requisite to protect the public welfare from any known or anticipated adverse effects associated with the presence of such air pollutant in the ambient air." Section 109(b)(2). Effects on "the public welfare" include "effects on soils, water, crops, vegetation, man-made materials, animals, wildlife, weather, visibility, and climate, damage to and deterioration of property, and hazards to transportation, as well as effects on economic values and on personal comfort and well-being." Section 302(h). The Administrator is required to submit the proposed air quality standards for public comment in a rulemaking proceeding, the procedure for which is prescribed by Section 307(d) of the Act.

Within six months of publication of the proposed standards the Administrator must promulgate final primary and secondary ambient air quality standards for the pollutant. Section 307(d)(10). Once EPA has promulgated national ambient air quality standards, responsibility under the Act shifts from the federal government to the states [to achieve the NAAQS].

III. THE LEAD STANDARDS RULEMAKING PROCEEDINGS

As required by statute, EPA's first step toward promulgating air quality standards for lead was to prepare a criteria document. The Lead Criteria Document was the culmination of a process of rigorous scientific and public review, and thus is a comprehensive and thoughtful analysis of the most current scientific information on the subject. * * *

A.   The Lead Criteria Document

* * * [T]he Criteria Document examined a large number of issues raised by the problem of lead in the environment. One of these was the effects of lead exposure on human health. The Criteria Document concluded that, among the major organ systems, the hematopoietic (blood-forming) and neurological systems are the areas of prime concern. * * *

The Criteria Document identified a variety of effects of lead exposure on the blood-forming system. * * * [It] concluded, after a review of various studies, that in children, a threshold level for anemia is about 40 µg Pb/dl, whereas the corresponding value for adults is about 50 µg Pb/dl. (The concentration of lead in the blood is measured in micrograms of lead per deciliter of blood—µg Pb/dl.)

The Criteria Document also examined other more subtle effects on the blood-forming system, associated with lower levels of lead exposure. The most pertinent of these "subclinical" effects for purposes of these cases is lead-related elevation of erythrocyte protoporphyrin (EP elevation). According to the Criteria Document, this phenomenon must, for a number of reasons, be regarded as an indication of an impairment of human health. * * * The Criteria Document reported that the threshold for EP elevation in children and women is at blood lead levels of 15–20 µg Pb/dl, and 25–30 µg Pb/dl in adult males. * * * The Criteria Document did not identify a particular blood lead level at which regulatory response was appropriate, but it did note with approval the 1975 guidelines issued by the Center For Disease Control, which use elevated EP at blood lead levels of 30 µg Pb/dl as the cut-off point in screening children for lead poisoning.

The Criteria Document also examined the effects of lead exposure on the central nervous system. Among the most deleterious effects of lead poisoning are those associated with severe central nervous system damage at high exposure levels. * * * After a review of various studies, the Criteria Document concluded that the blood lead threshold for these neurological effects of high level exposure is 80–100 µg Pb/dl in children, and 100–200 µg Pb/dl in adults.

The Criteria Document also went on to consider the evidence on whether lower level lead exposures can affect the central nervous system, particularly in children. It acknowledged that the issue is unsettled and somewhat controversial, but it was able to conclude, after a careful review of various studies on the subject, that "a rather consistent pattern of impaired neural and cognitive functions appears to be associated with blood lead levels below those producing the overt symptomatology of lead encephalopathy." The Criteria Document reported that "(t)he blood lead levels at which neurobehavioral deficits occur in otherwise asymptomatic children appear to start at a range of 50 to 60 µg/dl, although some evidence tentatively suggests that such effects may occur at slightly lower levels for some children."

In addition to examining the health effects of lead exposure, the Criteria Document also discussed other issues critical to the task of setting air quality standards for lead. One of these issues is the relationship between air lead exposure and blood lead levels—a relationship commonly referred to as the air lead/blood lead ratio. The Criteria Document acknowledged that derivation of a functional relationship between air lead exposure and blood lead levels is made difficult by the fact that the relationship is not a linear one; rather, the ratio tends to increase as air lead levels are reduced. The Document was nevertheless able to conclude, after a detailed examination of the relevant studies, that air lead/blood lead ratios fall within a range of 1:1 to 1:2 (µg Pb/m³ air):(µg Pb/dl blood) at the levels of lead exposure generally encountered by the population, i.e., blood lead levels increase by between 1 and 2 g Pb/dl of blood for every 1 µg Pb/m³ of air. (Air lead content is measured in micrograms of lead per cubic meter of air—µg Pb/m³.) * * * The Criteria Document looked into the question whether any sub-groups within the population are particularly vulnerable to the effects of lead exposure. It concluded that preschool-age children and pregnant women are particularly sensitive to lead exposure, the latter mainly because of the risk to the unborn child.

B. The Proposed Standards

Simultaneously with the publication of the Lead Criteria Document on December 14, 1977, the Administrator proposed a national primary ambient air quality standard for lead of 1.5 μg Pb/m^3 monthly average. He also proposed that the secondary air quality standard be set at the same level as the primary standard because the welfare effects associated with lead exposure did not warrant imposition of a stricter standard. In the preamble to the proposed standards the Administrator explained the analysis EPA had employed in setting the standards.

The Administrator first pointed out that a number of factors complicate the task of setting air quality standards which will protect the population from the adverse health effects of lead exposure. First, some sub-groups within the population have a greater potential for, or are more susceptible to the effects of, lead exposure. Second, there are a variety of adverse health effects associated with various levels of lead exposure. Third, the variability of individual responses to lead exposure, even within particular sub-groups of the population, would produce a range of blood lead levels at any given air lead level. Fourth, airborne lead is only one of a number of sources of lead exposure and the relative contribution from each source is difficult to quantify. Finally, the relationship between air lead exposure and blood lead levels is a complex one.

In response to the first problem the Administrator began by noting that protection of the most sensitive groups within the population had to be a major consideration in determining the level at which the air quality standards should be set. And he determined that children between the ages of 1 and 5 years are most sensitive to the effects of lead exposure both because the hematologic and neurologic effects associated with lead exposure occur in children at lower threshold levels than in adults, and because the habit of placing hands and other objects in the mouth subjects them to a greater risk of exposure. Next, the Administrator examined the various health effects of lead exposure and proposed that EP elevation should be considered the first adverse health effect of lead exposure because it indicates an impairment of cellular functions, and should be the pivotal health effect on which the lead standards are based. Accordingly, he proposed that the air lead standards be designed to prevent the occurrence of EP elevation in children. In order to accomplish this, and to address the problem of variable responses to lead exposure, the Administrator selected 15 μg Pb/dl, the lowest reported threshold blood lead level for EP elevation in children, as the target mean population blood lead level. He reasoned that setting the target mean population blood lead level at the lowest reported threshold blood lead level for EP elevation would ensure that most of the target population would be kept below blood lead levels at which adverse health effects occur. The Administrator also discussed the alternative approaches of basing the standard on more severe effects such as anemia, or attempting to decide the actual level of EP elevation which represents an adverse effect on health, and then making an adjustment to allow a margin of safety. He specifically invited comments on these alternative approaches. Finally, the Administrator outlined another approach to calculating the target mean population blood lead level involving the use of statistical techniques discussed in the Criteria Document.

[Extrapolating from estimates of the proportion of blood lead attributable to air sources on average across the nation, the Administrator calculated that the ambient air quality lead standard should be 1.5 µg Pb/dl.] * * *

D. The Final Air Quality Standards for Lead

The Administrator promulgated the final air quality standards on October 5, 1978, prescribing national primary and secondary ambient air quality standards for lead of 1.5 µg Pb/m³, averaged over a calendar quarter. Although the final standards were the same as the proposed standards (with the exception of the change in the averaging period from 30 to 90 days), the Administrator arrived at the final standards through somewhat different analysis. The preamble to the final standards reveals that the comments on the proposed standards had led the Administrator to reconsider his analysis. In particular, he seemed to feel that legitimate questions had been raised concerning the health significance of the early stages of EP elevation and about the threshold blood lead level for this condition. The Administrator's reexamination focused on two key questions: (1) What is the maximum safe individual blood lead level for children? and (2) what proportion of the target population should be kept below this blood lead level? Addressing the first issue required a review of the health effects of lead exposure discussed in the Criteria Document. The Administrator concluded that, although EP elevation beginning at blood lead levels of 15–20 µg Pb/dl is potentially adverse to the health of children, only when blood lead concentration reaches a level of 30 µg Pb/dl is this effect significant enough to be considered adverse to health. Accordingly, he selected 30 µg Pb/dl as the maximum safe individual blood lead level for children. The Administrator based this choice on three mutually supporting grounds. First, it is at this blood lead level that the first adverse health effect of lead exposure impairment of heme synthesis begins to occur in children. Second, a maximum safe individual blood lead level of 30 µg Pb/dl would allow an adequate margin of safety in protecting children against more serious effects of lead exposure anemia, symptoms of which begin to appear in children at blood lead levels of 40 µg Pb/dl, and central nervous system deficits which start to occur in children at blood lead levels of 50 µg Pb/dl. Third, the Administrator reasoned that the maximum safe individual blood lead level should be no higher than the blood lead level used by the Center for Disease Control in screening children for lead poisoning 30 µg Pb/dl.

Having determined the maximum safe individual blood lead level for the target population, the Administrator next focused on the question of what percentage of children between the ages of 1 and 5 years the standard should attempt to keep below this blood lead level. According to the 1970 census, there are approximately 20 million children under the age of 5 years in the United States, 12 million of them in urban areas and 5 million in inner cities where lead exposure may be especially high. The Administrator concluded that in order to provide an adequate margin of safety, and to protect special high risk sub-groups, the standards should aim at keeping 99.5% of the target population below the maximum safe individual blood lead level of 30 µg Pb/dl. . . . Using the lognormal statistical technique he had alluded to in the proposed standards, he calculated that a target mean population blood lead level of 15 µg Pb/dl (the same number as in the proposed standards, but arrived at through different analysis), would accomplish this task. [Once again, this resulted in a recommended] ambient air quality standard of 1.5 µg Pb/m³, the same as the proposed standard. * * *

V.   STATUTORY AUTHORITY

The petitioners' first claim is that the Administrator exceeded his authority under the statute by promulgating a primary air quality standard for lead which is more stringent than is necessary to protect the public health because it is designed to protect the public against "sub-clinical" effects which are not harmful to health. According to petitioners, Congress only authorized the Administrator to set primary air quality standards that are aimed at protecting the public against health effects which are known to be clearly harmful. They argue that Congress so limited the Administrator's authority because it was concerned that excessively stringent air quality standards could cause massive economic dislocation.

In developing this argument St. Joe contends that EPA erred by refusing to consider the issues of economic and technological feasibility in setting the air quality standards for lead. St. Joe's claim that the Administrator should have considered these issues is based on the statutory provision directing him to allow an "adequate margin of safety" in setting primary air quality standards. In St. Joe's view, the Administrator must consider the economic impact of the proposed standard on industry and the technological feasibility of compliance by emission sources in determining the appropriate allowance for a margin of safety. St. Joe argues that the Administrator abused his discretion by refusing to consider these factors in determining the appropriate margin of safety for the lead standards, and maintains that the lead air quality standards will have a disastrous economic impact on industrial sources of lead emissions.

This argument is totally without merit. St. Joe is unable to point to anything in either the language of the Act or its legislative history that offers any support for its claim that Congress, by specifying that the Administrator is to allow an "adequate margin of safety" in setting primary air quality standards, thereby required the Administrator to consider economic or technological feasibility. To the contrary, the statute and its legislative history make clear that economic considerations play no part in the promulgation of ambient air quality standards under Section 109.

Where Congress intended the Administrator to be concerned about economic and technological feasibility, it expressly so provided. For example, Section 111 of the Act directs the Administrator to consider economic and technological feasibility in establishing standards of performance for new stationary sources of air pollution based on the best available control technology. In contrast, Section 109(b) speaks only of protecting the public health and welfare. Nothing in its language suggests that the Administrator is to consider economic or technological feasibility in setting ambient air quality standards.

The legislative history of the Act also shows the Administrator may not consider economic and technological feasibility in setting air quality standards; the absence of any provision requiring consideration of these factors was no accident; it was the result of a deliberate decision by Congress to subordinate such concerns to the achievement of health goals. * * *

VI. HEALTH BASIS FOR THE LEAD STANDARDS

* * *

A.   Maximum Safe Individual Blood Lead Level

LIA attacks the Administrator's determination that 30 µg Pb/dl should be considered the maximum safe individual blood lead level for children, maintaining that there is no evidence in the record indicating that children suffer any health effects that can be considered adverse at this blood lead level. * * *

First, [LIA] contends that nothing in the record supports the suggestion that EP elevation at 30 µg Pb/dl is harmful to health, arguing that EP elevation is a mere "subclinical effect"—a biological response to lead exposure—which is without health significance, and noting that a number of its experts brought this matter to EPA's attention in their comments on the proposed standards. In LIA's view, the Administrator did not explain precisely how impairment of heme synthesis at blood lead levels of 30 µg Pb/dl adversely affects the health of children. Second, LIA challenges the Administrator's determination that a maximum safe individual blood lead level of 30 μg Pb/dl is justified by the need to allow an adequate margin of safety in protecting children against anemia and central nervous system deficits. It maintains that the evidence in the record does not support the Administrator's conclusion that the blood lead threshold for the symptoms of anemia in children is 40 μg Pb/dl. * * * Third, LIA contends that the preamble to the final regulations does not state the basis for the Administrator's finding that central nervous system deficits occur in children at blood lead levels of 50 μg Pb/dl, thereby precluding this court from being able to test the soundness of this determination. Finally, LIA argues that even if it were to concede that EPA's conclusions about the blood lead thresholds for anemia and central nervous system deficits are correct, there is still no explanation of why the Administrator concluded that a maximum individual safe blood level of 30 μg Pb/dl rather than 35 μg Pb/dl, for example is necessary to provide an adequate margin of safety against these effects.

Our review of the record persuades us that there is adequate support for each of the Administrator's conclusions about the health effects of lead exposure and, consequently, that LIA's challenges to the evidentiary support for these findings must be rejected. Under the statutory scheme enacted by Congress, the Criteria Document prepared with respect to each pollutant is to provide the scientific basis for promulgation of air quality standards for the pollutant. We have already noted that the Lead Criteria Document was the product of a process that allowed the rigorous scientific and public review that are essential to the preparation of a document "accurately reflect(ing) the latest scientific knowledge useful in indicating the kind and extent of all identifiable effects (of lead exposure) on (the) public health." In our view, the Criteria Document provides ample support for the Administrator's findings. * * *

To be sure, the Administrator's conclusions were not unchallenged; both LIA and the Administrator are able to point to an impressive array of experts supporting each of their respective positions. However, disagreement among the experts is inevitable when the issues involved are at the "very frontiers of scientific knowledge," and such disagreement does not preclude us from finding that the Administrator's decisions are adequately supported by the evidence in the record. * * *

B.   Margin of Safety

Both LIA and St. Joe argue that the Administrator erred by including multiple allowances for margins of safety in his calculation of the lead standards. Petitioners note that the statute directs the Administrator to allow an "adequate margin of safety" in setting primary air quality standards, and they maintain that as a matter of statutory construction the Administrator may not interpret "margin" of safety to mean "margins" of safety. In petitioners' view, the Administrator in fact did just this insofar as he made allowances for margins of safety at several points in his analysis. They argue that margin of safety allowances were reflected in the choice of the maximum safe individual blood lead level for children, in the decision to place 99.5 percent of the target population group below that blood lead level, in the selection of an air lead/blood lead ratio at 1:2, and in the Administrator's estimate of the contribution to blood lead levels that should be attributed to non-air sources. The net result of these multiple allowances for margins of safety, petitioners contend, was a standard far more stringent than is necessary to protect the public health. * * *

We agree with the Administrator that nothing in the statutory scheme or the legislative history requires him to adopt the margin of safety approach suggested by St. Joe. Adding the margin of safety at the end of the analysis is one approach, but it is not the only possible method. Indeed, the Administrator considered this approach but decided against it because of complications raised by the multiple sources of lead exposure. The choice between these possible approaches is a policy choice of the type that Congress specifically left to the Administrator's judgment. * * *

XI. CONCLUSION

The national ambient air quality standards for lead were the culmination of a process of rigorous scientific and public review which permitted a thorough ventilation of the complex scientific and technical issues presented by this rulemaking proceeding. Interested parties were allowed a number of opportunities to participate in exploration and resolution of the issues raised by the standard-setting exercise. EPA, and ultimately the public whose health these air quality standards protect, have benefited from their contribution. To be sure, even the experts did not always agree about the answers to the questions that were raised. Indeed, they did not always agree on what the relevant questions were. These disagreements underscore the novelty and complexity of the issues that had to be resolved, and both the EPA and the participants in the rulemaking proceeding deserve to be commended for the diligence with which they approached the task of coming to grips with these difficult issues.

We have accorded these cases the most careful consideration, combining as we must careful scrutiny of the evidence in the record with deference to the Administrator's judgments. We conclude that in this rulemaking proceeding the Administrator complied with the substantive and procedural requirements of the Act, and that his decisions are both adequately explained and amply supported by evidence in the record. Accordingly, we reject petitioners' claims of error. The regulations under review herein are

Affirmed.

NOTES

1.   What degree of deference should the court afford an agency in a complicated case such as this, where the agency must make policy decisions in the context of scientific uncertainty? On the applicable standard of review, the court said: "(A)fter our careful study of the record, we must take a step back from the agency's decision. We must look at the decision not as the chemist, biologist or statistician that we are qualified neither by training nor experience to be, but as a reviewing court exercising our narrowly defined duty of holding agencies to certain minimal standards of rationality. * * * We must affirm unless the agency decision is arbitrary or capricious." Do you think this is the appropriate standard of review?

2.   When the agency determines the maximum safe blood level for the target population, is it not making policy, rather than scientific judgments? Why choose children—arguably the most sensitive population—as the target population? And why set the maximum blood level where the agency did, if blood levels of lead can rise without manifesting any illness? Aren't reasonable people likely to differ about such judgments? Who should make these decisions, given how politically contentious they are? Congress, courts, or the agency? How should the balance be struck between flexibility to regulate and accountability of the decisionmaker?

3.   Basic scientific uncertainty still pervades the process of setting health-based limits. EPA set the lead NAAQS standard based on an assumption that 30 micrograms of lead per deciliter of blood was a conservative estimate of when adverse health effects might occur in children, while industry said the level ought to be at least 35. A recent report from the Advisory Committee on Childhood Lead Poisoning Prevention of the Centers for Disease Control and Prevention recommends medical monitoring of children with blood lead levels in excess of 5 micrograms and many scientists believe that no level of lead in blood is safe. *See Advisory Committee on Childhood Lead Poisoning Prevention of the Centers for Disease Control and Prevention,* LOW LEVEL LEAD EXPOSURE HARMS CHILDREN: A RENEWED CALL FOR PRIMARY PREVENTION (Jan 4, 2012), http://www.cdc.gov/nceh/lead/ACCLPP/Final_Document_030712.pdf.

4.   The EPA has an obligation under section 109(d) to review and, if necessary, revise the list of air pollutants every five years. The agency has been sued repeatedly by the American Lung Association for failing to do this. *See, e.g.,* American Lung Association v. Browner, 884 F.Supp. 345 (D. Ariz. 1994). The prevailing view from the courts is that the agency does not have a non-discretionary duty to revise the NAAQS, but it must take *some* action regarding review and revision by the statutory deadline. *See, e.g.,* Environmental Defense Fund v. Thomas, 870 F.2d 892 (2d Cir. 1989). In February, 2010, the EPA tightened the primary NAAQS for nitrous dioxide. *See* http://www.epa.gov/ttn/naaqs/standards/nox/fr/20100209.pdf. In 2015, it tightened the ozone standard after a lengthy court battle. *See* U.S. Environmental Protection Agency, Implementation of the 2015 National Ambient Air Quality Standard for Ozone: State Implementation Plan

Requirements,   https://www.epa.gov/ground-level-ozone-pollution/implement ation-2015-national-ambient-air-quality-standards-naaqs-ozone.

5.   Note the court's view that cost and technological feasibility should play no role in the setting of air standards under the Act. Before moving on to the next section where we take this up, what do you think of this analysis of § 109? Isn't cost a relevant consideration when establishing the lead standards if emissions reductions will be very burdensome for industry to achieve, perhaps even putting some firms out of business? Why have a public comment period if the agency is free to ignore all the evidence submitted about cost and technological feasibility?

d.   The Role of Cost in Standard Setting

In this section, we consider the appropriate role of cost in setting primary standards for air pollution. What did Congress mean when it required in § 109(b)(1) that primary standards be set which, "allowing an adequate margin of safety, are requisite to protect the public health?" In the case excerpted below, a coalition of states and industry groups challenged the EPA's 1997 revisions to the standards for ozone and particulate matter, arguing that the CAA requires the agency to consider cost when setting air standards, which the agency had not done. EPA's new standards updated the particulate matter and ozone NAAQS, dividing the former into fine and course particulates and amending the latter to be averaged over an eight hour rather than a one hour period. National Ambient Air Quality Standards for Particulate Matter, 62 Fed. Reg. 38,652 (July 18, 1997) (codified at 40 C.F.R. section 50); National Ambient Air Quality Standards for Ozone, 62 Fed. Reg 38,856 (July 18, 1997) (codified at 40 C.F.R. section 50).

The agency had revised the standards after a lengthy review process produced evidence that both acute and chronic health impacts could result from exposure to ozone and particulate matter at levels below those allowed by the existing standards.

WHITMAN V. AMERICAN TRUCKING ASSOCIATIONS, INC.
Supreme Court of the United States, 2001.
531 U.S. 457, 121 S.Ct. 903, 149 L.Ed.2d 1.

[The Court's treatment of the non-delegation issue raised in the case appears in Chapter 5 at page 338.]

JUSTICE SCALIA delivered the opinion of the Court.

Section 109(a) of the CAA, as added, 84 Stat. 1679, and amended, 42 U.S.C. § 7409(a), requires the Administrator of the EPA to promulgate NAAQS for each air pollutant for which "air quality criteria" have been issued under § 108, 42 U.S.C. § 7408. Once a NAAQS has been promulgated, the Administrator must review the standard (and the criteria on which it is based) "at five-year intervals" and make "such revisions . . . as may be appropriate." CAA § 109(d)(1), 42 U.S.C. § 7409(d)(1). These cases arose when, on July 18, 1997, the Administrator revised the NAAQS for particulate matter (PM) and ozone. * * *

In *Lead Industries Ass'n, Inc. v. EPA*, the District of Columbia Circuit held that "economic considerations [may] play no part in the promulgation of ambient air quality standards under Section 109" of the CAA. In the present cases, the court adhered to that holding * * * as it had done on many other occasions. * * *

Section 109(b)(1) instructs the EPA to set primary ambient air quality standards "the attainment and maintenance of which . . . are requisite to protect the public health" with "an adequate margin of safety." 42 U.S.C. § 7409(b)(1). Were it not for the hundreds of pages of briefing respondents have submitted on the issue, one would have thought it fairly clear that this text does not permit the EPA to consider costs in setting the standards. The language, as one scholar has noted, "is absolute." The EPA, "based on" the information about health effects contained in the technical "criteria" documents compiled under § 108(a)(2), 42 U.S.C. § 7408(a)(2), is to identify the maximum airborne concentration of a pollutant that the public health can tolerate, decrease the concentration to provide an "adequate" margin of safety, and set the standard at that level. Nowhere are the costs of achieving such a standard made part of that initial calculation.

Against this most natural of readings, respondents make a lengthy, spirited, but ultimately unsuccessful attack. They begin with the object of § 109(b)(1)'s focus, the "public health." When the term first appeared in federal clean air legislation—in the Act of July 14, 1955 (1955 Act), 69 Stat. 322, which expressed "recognition of the dangers to the public health" from air pollution—its ordinary meaning was "[t]he health of the community." Webster's New International Dictionary 2005 (2d ed. 1950). Respondents argue, however, that § 109(b)(1), as added by the Clean Air Amendments of 1970 (1970 Act), 84 Stat. 1676, meant to use the term's secondary meaning: "[t]he ways and means of conserving the health of the members of a community, as by preventive medicine, organized care of the sick, etc." Words that can have more than one meaning are given content, however, by their surroundings, * * * and in the context of § 109(b)(1) this second definition makes no sense. Congress could not have meant to instruct the Administrator to set NAAQS at a level "requisite to protect" "the art and science dealing with the protection and improvement of community health." *Webster's Third New International Dictionary* 1836 (1981). We therefore revert to the primary definition of the term: the health of the public.

Even so, respondents argue, many more factors than air pollution affect public health. In particular, the economic cost of implementing a very stringent standard might produce health losses sufficient to offset the health gains achieved in cleaning the air—for example, by closing down whole industries and thereby impoverishing the workers and consumers dependent upon those industries. That is unquestionably true, and Congress was unquestionably aware of it. * * * Section 110(f)(1) of the CAA permitted the Administrator to waive the compliance deadline for stationary sources if, *inter alia,* sufficient control measures were simply unavailable and "the continued operation of such sources is *essential . . . to the public health* or welfare." 84 Stat. 1683 (emphasis added). Other provisions explicitly permitted or required economic costs to be taken into account in implementing the air quality standards. * * * Subsequent Amendments to the CAA have added many more provisions directing, in explicit language, that the Administrator consider costs in performing various duties. * * * We have therefore refused to find implicit in ambiguous sections of the CAA an authorization to consider costs that has elsewhere, and so often, been expressly granted. * * *

Accordingly, to prevail in their present challenge, respondents must show a textual commitment of authority to the EPA to consider costs in setting NAAQS under § 109(b)(1). And because § 109(b)(1) and the NAAQS for which it provides are the engine that drives nearly all of Title I of the CAA, that textual commitment must be a clear one. Congress, we have held, does not alter the fundamental details of a regulatory scheme in vague terms or ancillary provisions—it does not, one might say, hide elephants in mouseholes. * * * Respondents' textual arguments ultimately founder upon this principle.

Their first claim is that § 109(b)(1)'s terms "adequate margin" and "requisite" leave room to pad health effects with cost concerns. * * * [W]e find it implausible that Congress would give to the EPA through these modest words the power to determine whether implementation costs should moderate national air quality standards. * * *

The same defect inheres in respondents' next two arguments: that while the Administrator's judgment about what is requisite to protect the public health must be "based on [the] criteria" documents developed under § 108(a)(2), *see* § 109(b)(1), it need not be based *solely* on those criteria; and that those criteria themselves, while they must include "effects on public health or welfare which may be expected from the presence of such pollutant in the ambient air," are not necessarily *limited* to those effects. Even if we were to concede those premises, we still would not conclude that one of the unenumerated factors that the agency can consider in developing and applying the criteria is cost of implementation. That factor is *both* so indirectly related to public health *and* so full of potential for canceling the conclusions drawn from direct health effects that it would surely have been expressly mentioned in §§ 108 and 109 had Congress meant it to be considered. Yet while those provisions describe in detail how the health effects of pollutants in the ambient air are to be calculated and given effect, *see* § 108(a)(2), they say not a word about costs.

Respondents point, finally, to a number of provisions in the CAA that *do* require attainment cost data to be generated. Section 108(b)(1), for example, instructs the Administrator to "issue to the States," simultaneously with the criteria documents, "information on air pollution control techniques, which information shall include data relating to the cost of installation and operation." 42 U.S.C. § 7408(b)(*l*). And § 109(d)(2)(C)(iv) requires the Clean Air Scientific Advisory Committee to "advise the Administrator of any adverse public health, welfare, social, economic, or energy effects which may result from various strategies for attainment and maintenance" of NAAQS. 42 U.S.C. § 7409(d)(2)(C)(iv). Respondents argue that these provisions make no sense unless costs are to be considered in setting the NAAQS. That is not so. These provisions enable the Administrator to assist the States in carrying out their statutory role as primary *implementers* of the NAAQS. It is to the States that the Act assigns initial and primary responsibility for deciding what emissions reductions will be required from which sources. * * * It would be impossible to perform that task intelligently without considering which abatement technologies are most efficient, and most economically feasible—which is why we have said that "the most important forum for consideration of claims of economic and technological infeasibility is before the state agency formulating the implementation plan," *Union Elec. Co. v. EPA* [*infra*, page 458]. Thus, federal clean air legislation has, from the very beginning, directed federal agencies to develop and transmit implementation data, including cost data, to the States. * * * That Congress chose to carry forward this research program to assist States in choosing the means through which they would implement the standards is perfectly sensible, and has no bearing upon whether cost considerations are to be taken into account in formulating the standards.

It should be clear from what we have said that the canon requiring texts to be so construed as to avoid serious constitutional problems has no application here. No matter how severe the constitutional doubt, courts may choose only between reasonably available interpretations of a text. * * * The text of § 109(b), interpreted in its statutory and historical context and with appreciation for its importance to the CAA as a whole, unambiguously bars cost considerations from the NAAQS-setting process, and thus ends the matter for us as well as the EPA. We therefore affirm the judgment of the Court of Appeals on this point.

JUSTICE BREYER, concurring in part and concurring in the judgment.

[I agree] that the Clean Air Act does not permit the Environmental Protection Agency to consider the economic costs of implementation when setting national ambient air quality standards under § 109(b)(1) of the Act.

But I would not rest this conclusion solely upon § 109's language or upon a presumption, such as the Court's presumption that any authority the Act grants the EPA to consider costs must flow from a "textual commitment" that is "clear." * * * In order better to achieve regulatory goals—for example, to allocate resources so that they save more lives or produce a cleaner environment—regulators must often take account of all of a proposed regulation's adverse effects, at least where those adverse effects clearly threaten serious and disproportionate public harm. Hence, I believe that, other things being equal, we should read silences or ambiguities in the language of regulatory statutes as permitting, not forbidding, this type of rational regulation.

In this case, however, other things are not equal. Here, legislative history, along with the statute's structure, indicates that § 109's language reflects a congressional decision not to delegate to the agency the legal authority to consider economic costs of compliance.

For one thing, the legislative history shows that Congress intended the statute to be "technology forcing." Senator Edmund Muskie, the primary sponsor of the 1970 Amendments to the Act, introduced them by saying that Congress' primary responsibility in drafting the Act was not "to be limited by what is or appears to be technologically or economically feasible," but "to establish what the public interest requires to protect the health of persons," even if that means that *industries will be asked to do what seems to be impossible at the present time.*" * * *

The Senate directly focused upon the technical feasibility and cost of implementing the Act's mandates. And it made clear that it intended the Administrator to develop air quality standards set independently of either. * * *

Indeed, this Court, after reviewing the entire legislative history, concluded that the 1970 Amendments were "expressly designed to force regulated sources to develop pollution control devices that *might at the time appear to be economically or technologically infeasible.*" Union Elec. Co. v. EPA (emphasis added). And the Court added that the 1970 Amendments were intended to be a "drastic remedy to . . . a serious and otherwise uncheckable problem." Subsequent legislative history confirms that the technology-forcing goals of the 1970 Amendments are still paramount in today's Act. * * *

To read this legislative history as meaning what it says does not impute to Congress an irrational intent. Technology-forcing hopes can prove realistic. Those persons, for example, who opposed the 1970 Act's insistence on a 90% reduction in auto emission pollutants, on the ground of excessive cost, saw the development of catalytic converter technology that helped achieve substantial reductions without the economic catastrophe that some had feared. * * *

At the same time, the statute's technology-forcing objective makes regulatory efforts to determine the costs of implementation both less important and more difficult. It means that the relevant economic costs are speculative, for they include the cost of unknown future technologies. It also means that efforts to take costs into account can breed time-consuming and potentially unresolvable arguments about the accuracy and significance of cost estimates. Congress could have thought such efforts not worth the delays and uncertainties that would accompany them. In any event, that is what the statute's history seems to say. * * * And the matter is one for Congress to decide.

Moreover, the Act does not, on this reading, wholly ignore cost and feasibility. * * * [T]he Act allows regulators to take those concerns into account when they determine how to implement ambient air quality standards. Thus, States may consider economic costs when they select the particular control devices used to meet the standards, and industries experiencing difficulty in reducing their emissions can seek an exemption or variance from the state implementation plan. * * *

The Act also permits the EPA, within certain limits, to consider costs when it sets deadlines by which areas must attain the ambient air quality standards. * * * And Congress can change those statutory limits if necessary. Given the ambient air quality standards' substantial effects on States, cities, industries, and their suppliers and customers, Congress will hear from those whom compliance deadlines affect adversely, and Congress can consider whether legislative change is warranted. * * *

Finally, contrary to the suggestion of the Court of Appeals and of some parties, this interpretation of § 109 does not require the EPA to eliminate every health risk, however slight, at any economic cost, however great, to the point of "hurtling" industry over "the brink of ruin," or even forcing "deindustrialization." * * * The statute, by its express terms, does not compel the elimination of *all* risk; and it grants the Administrator sufficient flexibility to avoid setting ambient air quality standards ruinous to industry.

Section 109(b)(1) directs the Administrator to set standards that are "requisite to protect the public health" with "an adequate margin of safety." But these words do not describe a world that is free of all risk—an impossible and undesirable objective. * * * Nor are the words "requisite" and "public health" to be understood independent of context. We consider football equipment "safe" even if its use entails a level of risk that would make drinking water "unsafe" for consumption. And what counts as "requisite" to protecting the public health will similarly vary with background circumstances, such as the public's ordinary tolerance of the particular health risk in the particular context at issue. The Administrator can consider such background circumstances when "decid[ing] what risks are acceptable in the world in which we live."

The statute also permits the Administrator to take account of comparative health risks. That is to say, she may consider whether a proposed rule promotes safety overall. A rule likely to cause more harm to health than it prevents is not a rule that is "requisite to protect the public health." * * *

The statute ultimately specifies that the standard set must be "requisite to protect the public health" "*in the judgment of the Administrator,*" § 109(b)(1) (emphasis added), a phrase that grants the Administrator considerable discretionary standard-setting authority.

The statute's words, then, authorize the Administrator to consider the severity of a pollutant's potential adverse health effects, the number of those likely to be affected, the distribution of the adverse effects, and the uncertainties surrounding each estimate. * * * They permit the Administrator to take account of comparative health consequences. They allow her to take account of context when determining the acceptability of small risks to health. And they give her considerable discretion when she does so.

This discretion would seem sufficient to avoid the extreme results that some of the industry parties fear. After all, the EPA, in setting standards that "protect the public health" with "an adequate margin of safety," retains discretionary authority to avoid regulating risks that it reasonably concludes are trivial in context. Nor need regulation lead to deindustrialization. Preindustrial society was not a very healthy society; hence a standard demanding the return of the Stone Age would not prove "requisite to protect the public health."

Although I rely more heavily than does the Court upon legislative history and alternative sources of statutory flexibility, I reach the same ultimate conclusion. Section 109 does not delegate to the EPA authority to base the national ambient air quality standards, in whole or in part, upon the economic costs of compliance.

NOTES

1. The Supreme Court's holding that the agency may not consider cost when setting air standards was greeted with a collective sigh of relief by environmentalists. That they were so worried about the possibility of a different outcome, however, signifies the ascendance of cost-benefit analysis in scholarly as well as judicial circles over the last twenty years. In recent years, however, despite worries that cost-benefit analysis would limit environmental protection, sophisticated analyses have shown that regulations under the CAA frequently deliver benefits far in excess of costs. For a defense of the use of cost-benefit analysis from authors who believe (and show) that cost-benefit

analysis often helps justify environmentally protective regulations, *see* RICHARD REVESZ AND MICHAEL LIVERMORE, RETHINKING RATIONALITY: HOW COST-BENEFIT ANALYSIS CAN BETTER PROTECT THE ENVIRONMENT AND OUR HEALTH (2008). (On the limitations of cost-benefit analysis for setting health protective air standards in particular, *see* Lisa Heinzerling, *The Clean Air Act and the Constitution*, 20 ST. LOUIS U. PUB. L. REV. 121 (2001).

2.　The Clean Air Act still allows for consideration of cost in the NAAQS process, as Justice Breyer's concurrence points out, only later, at the implementation stage, when states design their SIPs for meeting the NAAQS. What practical difference does this make? If cost ultimately affects the design of the implementation plans, does cost ultimately constrain the manner and rate at which states comply with national air standards? As practitioners close to the ground know, standards are just numbers: they are arguably meaningless until implemented. If implementation is where the action is, doesn't cost ultimately, if indirectly, control the stringency of air standards?

D. MAJOR PROVISIONS OF THE CAA

Once a pollutant is designated a criteria pollutant subject to a NAAQS, a number of additional provisions kick in. We turn next to these additional provisions. Their application is not always, however, limited to criteria pollutants: the PSD and NSPS standards outlined in the next section, for example, under some circumstances apply to any pollutant regulated under the act. As a result, the application of these provisions has huge implications for the regulation of greenhouse gases, an issue we explore in detail beginning at page 530, *infra*. Hazardous Air Pollutants are treated in a separate section of the Act and we describe the operation of Section 112 here as well.

1.　STATE IMPLEMENTATION PLANS

Section 110 of the CAA assigns to states the responsibility for devising implementation plans that will achieve the federal NAAQS. The SIP process is onerous. In developing a SIP, states must first determine the extent to which air quality in the state's air quality regions violates the NAAQS. It must then calculate the emissions reductions necessary to achieve compliance with NAAQS and, finally, it must allocate the reductions among the sources of emissions. This final step requires knowing something about the emissions currently produced by the variety of stationary sources in the state, and predicting what the technological and economic impact of imposing reductions on them would likely be. States must also take into account the contributions that mobile sources make to the failure to meet NAAQS. Though the contribution of mobile sources to air pollution can be substantial, states are severely restricted in their ability to regulate these sources. For example, under the mobile source provisions of the law, emissions standards for automobiles are set by Congress, with a secondary role given to the EPA. Only California may, with an EPA waiver, adopt stricter standards, and other states may adopt California standards.

Even after the 1990 amendments, the SIP process remains central to the Act's structure, but it has been significantly supplemented by a variety of other provisions (including those applicable to PSD and nonattainment areas) that limit the states' discretion and impose additional burdens directly on stationary sources.

Section 110(a)(2) establishes minimum requirements for SIPs. Among other things, SIPs must:

(A) include enforceable emission limitations and other control measures, means or techniques (including economic incentives such as fees, marketable permits, and auctions of emissions rights) * * * as may be necessary or appropriate to meet the applicable requirements of this Act;

(B) provide for the establishment and operation of appropriate devices, methods, systems, and procedures necessary to—

(i) monitor, compile, and analyze data on ambient air quality, and

(ii) upon request, make such data available to the Administrator;

(C) include a program to provide for the enforcement of the measures described in subparagraph A * * * including a permit program as required by parts C and D [the PSD and nonattainment provisions of the Act]

(D) contain adequate provisions—

(i) prohibiting * * * any source or other type of emissions activity within the State from emitting any air pollutant in amounts which will—

(I) contribute significantly to nonattainment in, or interfere with maintenance by, any other State with respect to any such national primary or secondary ambient air quality standard

(E) provide (i) necessary assurances that the State * * * will have adequate personnel, funding, and authority * * * to carry out such implementation plan

Section 110(a) also requires states to revise plans as may be necessary, impose a variety of monitoring and record-keeping requirements on stationary sources, and perform air quality modeling.

Section 110(k) requires the EPA to establish criteria for plan completeness, determine whether those criteria have been met, and approve plans that meet all the applicable requirements. The EPA may call for plan revisions whenever "the Administrator finds that the applicable implementation plan for any area is substantially inadequate to attain or maintain the relevant national ambient air quality standard, to mitigate adequately the interstate pollutant transport * * *, or to otherwise comply with any requirement of this chapter" [§ 110(k)(5)].

If a state fails to submit a plan to the EPA, or if the EPA determines that the plan does not meet the minimum statutory criteria, and the state does not correct the deficiency, the EPA must promulgate a federal implementation plan [§ 110(c)].

The cases below establish the basic principle that the EPA must approve a state plan if it will attain the NAAQS. The agency may not reject a plan because it is weaker than the agency thinks feasible or less rigorous than a previous state plan. Nor may it reject a plan because it is too stringent to be economically or technologically feasible. Thus, so long as the national standards are met, the state may use any mix of controls it wishes, no matter how lax or how strict.

UNION ELECTRIC CO. V. EPA

Supreme Court of the United States, 1976.
427 U.S. 246, 96 S.Ct. 2518, 49 L.Ed.2d 474.

JUSTICE MARSHALL delivered the opinion of the Court.

After the Administrator of the Environmental Protection Agency (EPA) approves a state implementation plan under the Clean Air Act, the plan may be challenged in a court of appeals within 30 days, or after 30 days have run if newly discovered or available information justifies subsequent review. We must decide whether the operator of a regulated emission source, in a petition for review of an EPA-approved state plan filed after the original 30-day appeal period, can raise the claim that it is economically or technologically infeasible to comply with the plan. * * *

Petitioner is an electric utility company servicing the St. Louis metropolitan area, large portions of Missouri, and parts of Illinois and Iowa. Its three coal-fired generating plants in the metropolitan St. Louis area are subject to the sulfur dioxide restrictions in the Missouri implementation plan. Petitioner did not seek review of the Administrator's approval of the plan within 30 days, as it was entitled to do under § 307(b)(1) of the Act, * * * but rather applied to the appropriate state and county agencies for variances from the emission limitations affecting its three plants. Petitioner received one-year variances, which could be extended upon reapplication. The variances on two of petitioner's three plants had expired and petitioner was applying for extensions when, on

May 31, 1974, the Administrator notified petitioner that sulfur dioxide emissions from its plants violated the emission limitations contained in the Missouri plan. Shortly thereafter petitioner filed a petition in the Court of Appeals for the Eighth Circuit for review of the Administrator's 1972 approval of the Missouri implementation plan.

Section 307(b)(1) allows petitions for review to be filed in an appropriate court of appeals more than 30 days after the Administrator's approval of an implementation plan only if the petition is "based solely on grounds arising after such 30th day." Petitioner claimed to meet this requirement by asserting, *inter alia,* that various economic and technological difficulties had arisen more than 30 days after the Administrator's approval and that these difficulties made compliance with the emission limitations impossible. * * *

We reject at the outset petitioner's suggestion that a claim of economic or technological infeasibility may be considered upon a petition for review based on new information and filed more than 30 days after approval of an implementation plan even if such a claim could not be considered by the Administrator in approving a plan or by a court in reviewing a plan challenged within the original 30-day appeal period. * * * Regardless of when a petition for review is filed under § 307(b)(1), the court is limited to reviewing "the Administrator's action in approving * * * [the] implementation plan * * *." Accordingly, if new "grounds" are alleged, they must be such that, had they been known at the time the plan was presented to the Administrator for approval, it would have been an abuse of discretion for the Administrator to approve the plan. To hold otherwise would be to transfer a substantial responsibility in administering the Clean Air Act from the Administrator and the state agencies to the federal courts.

Since a reviewing court—regardless of when the petition for review is filed—may consider claims of economic and technological infeasibility only if the Administrator may consider such claims in approving or rejecting a state implementation plan, we must address ourselves to the scope of the Administrator's responsibility. The Administrator's position is that he has no power whatsoever to reject a state implementation plan on the ground that it is economically or technologically infeasible, and we have previously accorded great deference to the Administrator's construction of the Clean Air Act. After surveying the relevant provisions of the Clean Air Act Amendments of 1970 and their legislative history, we agree that Congress intended claims of economic and technological infeasibility to be wholly foreign to the Administrator's consideration of a state implementation plan.

As we have previously recognized, the 1970 Amendments to the Clean Air Act were a drastic remedy to what was perceived as a serious and otherwise uncheckable problem of air pollution. The Amendments place the primary responsibility for formulating pollution control strategies on the States, but nonetheless subject the States to strict minimum compliance requirements. These requirements are of a "technology-forcing character," * * * and are expressly designed to force regulated sources to develop pollution control devices that might at the time appear to be economically or technologically infeasible.

This approach is apparent on the face of § 110(a)(2). The provision sets out eight criteria that an implementation plan must satisfy, and provides that if these criteria are met and if the plan was adopted after reasonable notice and hearing, the Administrator "shall approve" the proposed state plan. The mandatory "shall" makes it quite clear that the Administrator is not to be concerned with factors other than those specified, and none of the eight factors appears to permit consideration of technological or economic infeasibility. * * *

In sum, we have concluded that claims of economic or technological infeasibility may not be considered by the Administrator in evaluating a state requirement that primary ambient air quality standards be met in the mandatory three years. And, since we further conclude that the States may submit implementation plans more stringent than federal law requires and that the Administrator must approve such plans if they meet the minimum requirements of § 110(a)(2), it follows that the language of § 110(a)(2)(A) provides no basis for the Administrator ever to reject a state implementation plan on the ground that it is economically or technologically infeasible. Accordingly, a court of appeals reviewing an approved plan under § 307(b)(1) cannot set it aside on those grounds, no matter when they are raised.

Our conclusion is bolstered by recognition that the Amendments do allow claims of technological and economic infeasibility to be raised in situations where consideration of such claims will not substantially interfere with the primary congressional purpose of prompt attainment of the national air quality standards. Thus, we do not hold that claims of infeasibility are never of relevance in the formulation of an implementation plan or that sources unable to comply with emission limitations must inevitably be shut down.

Perhaps the most important forum for consideration of claims of economic and technological infeasibility is before the state agency formulating the implementation plan. So long as the national standards are met, the State may select whatever mix of control devices it desires, and industries with particular economic or technological problems may seek special treatment in the plan itself. Moreover, if the industry is not exempted from, or accommodated by, the original plan, it may obtain a variance, as petitioner did in this case; and the variance, if granted after notice and a hearing, may be submitted to the EPA as a revision of the plan. Lastly, an industry denied an exemption from the implementation plan, or denied a subsequent variance, may be able to take its claims of economic or technological infeasibility to the state courts. * * *

* * * Congress plainly left with the States, so long as the national standards were met, the power to determine which sources would be burdened by regulation and to what extent. Technology forcing is a concept somewhat new to our national experience and it necessarily entails certain risks. But Congress considered those risks in passing the 1970 Amendments and decided that the dangers posed by uncontrolled air pollution made them worth taking. Petitioner's theory would render that considered legislative judgment a nullity, and that is a result we refuse to reach.

NOTE

The opinion stresses that there are several points in the SIP regulatory process, at both federal and state levels, where problems of economic and technological infeasibility may properly be considered. Among the most important adjustment mechanisms are variances, exemptions, and enforcement orders. *See, e.g.*, section 118 (exemptions for federal facilities); section 113 (d) (enforcement orders); and section 110(f) and (g) (temporary energy or economic authority). Are there any limits to such exceptions, however? *See* section 110(a)(3)(C). The Supreme Court has affirmed that a state does not have unlimited discretion in implementing the Clean Air Act, especially if it attempts to exploit flexibility in mechanisms that are traditionally the prerogative of the EPA. *See Alaska Dep't of Envtl. Conservation* v. *EPA*, 540 U.S. 461 (2004) (holding that the EPA has authority to ascertain reasonableness of state agency's determination of Best Achievable Control Technology).

Union Electric holds that considerations of feasibility do not justify overturning a SIP as too burdensome. The case below explores the EPA's flexibility to disapprove a SIP that grants variances when the SIP would otherwise meet applicable statutory requirements.

TRAIN V. NATURAL RESOURCES DEFENSE COUNCIL, INC.

Supreme Court of the United States, 1975.
421 U.S. 60, 95 S.Ct. 1470, 43 L.Ed.2d 731.

JUSTICE REHNQUIST delivered the opinion of the Court.

No one can doubt that Congress imposed upon the Agency and States a comprehensive planning task of the first magnitude which was to be accomplished in a relatively short time. In the case of the States, it was soon realized that in order to develop the requisite plans within the statutory nine-month deadline, efforts would have to be focused on determining the stringent emission limitations necessary to comply with national standards. This was true even though compliance with the standards would not be necessary until the attainment date, which normally would be three years after Agency approval of a plan. The issue then arose as to how these stringent limitations, which often could not be satisfied without substantial research and investment, should be applied during the period prior to that date.

One approach was that adopted by Florida, under which the plan's emission limitations would not take effect until the attainment date. Under this approach, no source is subject to enforcement actions during the preattainment period, but all are put on notice of the limitations with which they must eventually comply. * * *

Georgia chose the Agency's preferred approach. Its plan provided for immediately effective categorical emission limitations, but also incorporated a variance procedure whereby particular sources could obtain individually tailored relief from general requirements. This variance provision was one of the bases upon which the Agency's approval of the Georgia plan was successfully challenged by respondents in the Court of Appeals. It is the only aspect of that court's decision as to which the Agency petitioned for certiorari.

The Agency's approval of Georgia's variance provision was based on its interpretation of § 110(a)(3), which provides that the Agency shall approve any revision of an implementation plan which meets the § 110(a)(2) requirements applicable to an original plan. The Agency concluded that § 110(a)(3) permits a State to grant individual variances from generally applicable emission standards, both before and after the attainment date, so long as the variance does not cause the plan to fail to comply with the requirements of § 110(a)(2). * * *

* * * [The position of respondent NRDC and] individual respondents who reside in affected air quality control regions within the State of Georgia, is that variances applicable to individual sources may be approved only if they meet the stringent procedural and substantive standards of § 110(f). This section permits one-year postponements of any requirement of a plan, subject to conditions which will be discussed below. * * *

* * * Since a variance would normally implicate only the § 110(a)(2)(A) requirement that plans provide for attainment and maintenance of national ambient air standards, treatment as revisions would result in variances being readily approved in two situations: first, where the variance does not defer compliance beyond the attainment date; and second, where the national standards have been attained and the variance is not so great that a plan incorporating it could not insure their continued maintenance. Moreover, a § 110(a)(3) revision may be granted on the basis of hearings conducted by the State, whereas a § 110(f) postponement is available only after the Agency itself conducts hearings.

There is thus considerable practical importance attached to the issue of whether variances are to be treated as revisions or as postponements * * *. This practical importance reaches not merely the operator of a particular source who believes that circumstances justify his receiving a variance from categorical limitations. It also reaches the broader issue of whether Congress intended the States to retain any significant degree of control of the manner in which they attain and maintain national standards, at least once their initial plans have been approved * * *. To explain our conclusion as to Congress' intent, it is necessary that we consider the revision and postponement sections in the context of other provisions of the amended Clean Air Act, particularly those which distinguish between national ambient air standards and emission limitations. * * *

The Agency is plainly charged by the Act with the responsibility for setting the national ambient air standards. Just as plainly, however, it is relegated by the Act to a secondary role in the process of determining and enforcing the specific, source-by-source emission limitations which are necessary if the national standards it has set are to be met. Under § 110(a)(2), the agency is *required* to approve a state plan which provides for the timely attainment and subsequent maintenance of ambient air standards, and which also satisfies that section's other general requirements. The Act gives the Agency no authority to question the wisdom of a State's choices of emission limitations if they are part of a plan which satisfies the standards of § 110(a)(2), and the Agency may devise and promulgate a specific plan of its own only if a State fails to submit an implementation plan which satisfies those standards. § 110(c). Thus, so long as the ultimate effect of a State's choice of emission limitations is in compliance with the national standards for ambient air, the State is at liberty to adopt whatever mix of emission limitations it deems best suited to its particular situation.

This analysis of the Act's division of responsibilities is not challenged by respondents insofar as it concerns the process of devising and promulgating an initial implementation plan. Respondents do, however, deny that the States have such latitude once the initial plan is approved. Yet the third paragraph of § 110(a), and the one immediately following the paragraphs which specify that States shall file implementation plans and that the Agency shall approve them if they satisfy certain broad criteria, is the section which *requires* the Agency to "approve any revision of an implementation plan" if it "determines that it meets the requirements" of § 110(a)(2). On its face, this provision applies to *any* revision, without regard either to its breadth of applicability, or to whether it is to be effective before or after the attainment date; rather, Agency approval is subject only to the condition that the revised plan satisfy the general requirements applicable to original implementation plans. Far from evincing congressional intent that the Agency assume control of a State's emission limitations mix once its initial plan is approved, the revision section is to all appearances the mechanism by which the States may obtain approval of their developing policy choices as to the most practicable and desirable methods of restricting total emissions to a level which is consistent with the national ambient air standards.

In order to challenge this characterization of § 110(a)(3), respondents principally rely on the contention that the postponement provision, § 110(f), is the only mechanism by which exceptions to a plan's requirements may be obtained, under any circumstances. Were this an accurate description of § 110(f), we would agree that the revision authority does not have the broad application asserted by the Agency. Like the Ninth Circuit, however, we believe that § 110(f) serves a function different from that of supervising state efforts to modify the initial mix of emission limitations by which they implement national standards.

In our view, § 110(f) is a safety valve by which may be accorded, under certain carefully specified circumstances, exceptions to the national standards themselves. That this is its role is strongly suggested by the process by which it became a part of the Clean Air Act. [The Court analyzed legislative history and other portions of the Act supporting its interpretation.]

* * *

We believe * * * that Congress, consistent with its declaration that, "Each State shall have the primary responsibility for assuring air quality" within its boundaries, § 107(a), left to the States considerable latitude in determining specifically how the standards would be met. This discretion includes the continuing authority to revise choices about the mix of emission limitations. We therefore conclude that the Agency's interpretation of §§ 110(a)(3) and 110(f) was "correct," to the extent that it can be said with complete assurance that any particular interpretation of a complex statute such as this is the "correct" one. * * *

NOTES

1.   Section 116 authorizes states, with a few limitations, to regulate air pollution more stringently than required under the CAA. Is it fair to say, therefore, that although Congress has "federalized" environmental law by passing regulatory statutes, states still enjoy considerable flexibility to regulate air pollution?

2.   Because *Train* requires that a variance (in the form of a "plan revision") result in NAAQS compliance (or at least a move in that direction), these variances are theoretically unavailable in nonattainment areas. Nevertheless, in response to heavy demand from industry, states continue to issue such "variances" in large numbers, even though they are invalid under

federal law. Only occasionally does the EPA exercise its power to enforce the SIP in these circumstances. For a fuller explanation, and two interesting case studies, *see* Marc Melnick & Elizabeth Willes, *Watching the Candy Store: EPA Overfiling in Local Air Pollution Variances*, 20 ECOLOGY L.Q. 207 (1993).

———————

In addition to granting variances to ease the burden on stationary sources that have a difficult time complying with emission limits, states may also resort to creative calculations in order to ease regulatory burdens. Consider Virginia's use of its discretion in the case below, to conclude that new sources of pollution will result in no net increase in pollution.

CITIZENS AGAINST THE REFINERY'S EFFECTS, INC. V. EPA

United States Court of Appeals, Fourth Circuit, 1981.
643 F.2d 183.

HALL, CIRCUIT JUDGE.

Citizens Against the Refinery's Effects (CARE) appeals from a final ruling by the Administrator of the Environmental Protection Agency (EPA) approving the Virginia State Implementation Plan (SIP) for reducing hydrocarbon pollutants. The plan requires the Virginia Highway Department to decrease usage of a certain type of asphalt, thereby reducing hydrocarbon pollution by more than enough to offset expected pollution from the Hampton Roads Energy Company's (HREC) proposed refinery. We affirm the action of the administrator in approving the state plan.

The Clean Air Act establishes National Ambient Air Quality Standards (NAAQS) for five major air pollutants. 42 U.S.C. § 7409. The EPA has divided each state into Air Quality Control Regions (AQCR) and monitors each region to assure that the national standard for each pollutant is met. 42 U.S.C. § 7407. Where the standard has not been attained for a certain pollutant, the state must develop a State Implementation Plan designed to bring the area into attainment within a certain period. 42 U.S.C. § 7410. In addition, no new source of that pollutant may be constructed until the standard is attained. 40 CFR § 51.18 (1973).

The Clean Air Act created a no-growth environment in areas where the clean air requirements had not been attained. EPA recognized the need to develop a program that encouraged attainment of clean air standards without discouraging economic growth. Thus the agency proposed an Interpretive Ruling in 1976 which allowed the states to develop an "offset program" within the State Implementation Plans. The offset program, later codified by Congress in the 1977 Amendments to the Clean Air Act, permits the states to develop plans which allow construction of new pollution sources where accompanied by a corresponding reduction in an existing pollution source. 42 U.S.C. § 7502(b)(6) and § 7503. In effect, a new emitting facility can be built if an existing pollution source decreases its emissions or ceases operations as long as a positive net air quality benefit occurs.

If the proposed factory will emit carbon monoxide, sulfur dioxide, or particulates, the EPA requires that the offsetting pollution source be within the immediate vicinity of the new plant. The other two pollutants, hydrocarbons and nitrogen oxide, are less "site-specific," and thus the ruling permits the offsetting source to locate anywhere within a broad vicinity of the new source.

The offset program has two other important requirements. First, a base time period must be determined in which to calculate how much reduction is needed in existing pollutants to offset the new source. This base period is defined as the first year of the SIP or, where the state has not yet developed a SIP, as the year in which a construction permit application is filed. Second, the offset program requires that the new source adopt the Lowest Achievable Emissions Rate (LAER) using the most modern technology available in the industry.

HREC proposes to build a petroleum refinery and offloading facility in Portsmouth, Virginia. Portsmouth has been unable to reduce air pollution enough to attain the national standard for one pollutant, photochemical oxidants, which is created when hydrocarbons are released into the atmosphere and react with other substances. Since a refinery is a major source of hydrocarbons, the Clean Air Act prevents construction of the HREC plant until the area attains the national standard.

In 1975, HREC applied to the Virginia State Air Pollution Control Board (VSAPCB) for a refinery construction permit. * * * The VSAPCB, in an effort to help HREC meet the clean air requirements, proposed to use the offset ruling to comply with the Clean Air Act.

On November 28, 1977, the VSAPCB submitted a State Implementation Plan to EPA which included the HREC permit. The Virginia Board proposed to offset the new HREC hydrocarbon pollution by reducing the amount of cutback asphalt used for road paving operations in three highway districts by the Virginia Department of Highways. By switching from "cutback" to "emulsified" asphalt, the state can reduce hydrocarbon pollutants by the amount necessary to offset the pollutants from the proposed refinery.

Notices of the proposed plan were published * * *. Numerous comments were received, including several from CARE. The EPA administrator carefully considered the comments and approved the Virginia offset plan on January 31, 1980.

CARE raises four issues regarding the state plan. First, they argue that the geographic area used as the base for the offset was arbitrarily determined and that the area as defined violates the regulations. Second, CARE contends that EPA should have used 1975 instead of 1977 as the base year to compare usage of cutback asphalt. Third, CARE insists that the offset plan should have been disapproved since the state is voluntarily reducing usage of cutback asphalt anyway. Fourth, CARE questions the approval of the plan without definite Lowest Achievable Emissions Rates (LAER) as required by the statute. We reject the CARE challenges to the state plan.

CARE contends that the state plan should not have been approved by EPA since the three highway-district area where cutback usage will be reduced to offset refinery emissions was artificially developed by the state. The ruling permits a broad area (usually within one AQCR) to be used as the offset basis.

The ruling does not specify how to determine the area, nor provide a standard procedure for defining the geographic area. Here the Virginia Board originally proposed to use four highway districts comprising one-half the state as the offset area. When this was found to be much more than necessary to offset pollution expected from the refinery, the state changed it to one highway district plus nine additional counties. Later the proposed plan was again revised to include a geographic area of three highway districts.

The agency action in approving the use of three highway districts was neither arbitrary, capricious, nor outside the statute. First, Congress intended that the states and the EPA be given flexibility in designing and implementing SIPs. Such flexibility allows the states to make reasoned choices as to which areas may be used to offset new pollution and how the plan is to be implemented. Second, the offset program was initiated to encourage economic growth in the state. Thus a state plan designed to reduce highway department pollution in order to attract another industry is a reasonable contribution to economic growth without a corresponding increase in pollution. Third, to be sensibly administered the offset plan had to be divided into districts which could be monitored by the highway department. Use of any areas other than highway districts would be unwieldy and difficult to administer. Fourth, the scientific understanding of ozone pollution is not advanced to the point where exact air transport may be predicted. Designation of the broad area in which hydrocarbons may be transported is well within the discretion and expertise of the agency.

Asphalt consumption varies greatly from year to year, depending upon weather and road conditions. Yet EPA must accurately determine the volume of hydrocarbon emissions from cutback asphalt. Only then can the agency determine whether the reduction in cutback usage will result in an offset great enough to account for the new refinery pollution. To calculate consumption of a material where it constantly varies, a base year must be selected. In this case, EPA's Interpretive Ruling establishes the base year as the year in which the permit application is made. EPA decided that 1977 was an acceptable base year. CARE argues that EPA illegally chose 1977 instead of 1975.

Considering all of the circumstances, including the unusually high asphalt consumption in 1977, the selection by EPA of that as the base year was within the discretion of the agency. Since the EPA Interpretive Ruling allowing the offset was not issued until 1976, 1977 was the first year after the offset ruling and the logical base year in which to calculate the offset. Also, the permit issued by the VSAPCB was reissued in 1977 with extensive additions and revisions after a full hearing. Under these circumstances, 1977 appears to be a logical choice of a base year.

For several years, Virginia has pursued a policy of shifting from cutback asphalt to the less expensive emulsified asphalt in road-paving operations. The policy was initiated in an effort to save money, and was totally unrelated to a State Implementation Plan. Because of this policy, CARE argues that hydrocarbon emissions were decreasing independent of this SIP and therefore are not a proper offset against the refinery. They argue that there is not, in effect, an actual reduction in pollution.

The Virginia voluntary plan is not enforceable and therefore is not in compliance with the 1976 Interpretive Ruling which requires that the offset program be enforceable. The EPA, in approving the state plan, obtained a letter from the Deputy Attorney General of Virginia in which he stated that the requisites had been satisfied for establishing and enforcing the plan with the Department of Highways. Without such authority, no decrease in asphalt-produced pollution is guaranteed. In contrast to the voluntary plan, the offset plan guarantees a reduction in pollution resulting from road-paving operations.

[The Court then deferred to the EPA's calculation of Lowest Achievable Emission Rate.]

CONCLUSION

In approving the state plan, EPA thoroughly examined the data, requested changes in the plan, and approved the plan only after the changes were made. There is no indication that the agency acted in an arbitrary or capricious manner or that it stepped beyond the bounds of the Clean Air Act. We affirm the decision of the administrator in approving the state plan.

NOTES

1.   One might get the impression from reading section 110 of the CAA, and from the cases above, that a SIP is a single, coherent document filed on one occasion by the state and reviewed by the EPA in one, or a few, sittings. SIPs are not that simple, however. Like the legendary Loch Ness Monster, SIPs may exist, but people rarely get more than a glimpse of them. One EPA administrator put it this way: "I don't even think I can lift this, but I will try. The box is full. The box is simply the 1979 amendment to the Illinois SIP. We couldn't bring the whole SIP. Nobody could read the whole SIP. Nobody even knows what is in one at this point." When the same administrator was asked how many boxes it would take to carry the SIP from California, he replied, "They would measure it in truckloads." JOHN-MARK STENSVAAG & CRAIG N. OREN, CLEAN AIR ACT: LAW AND PRACTICE 14–4 to 14–5 (1990).

A SIP is best thought of as a collection of regulations, instruments, and measures that a state adopts over time and submits sequentially to the EPA for approval. When considered together as a package, these measures must assure the EPA that the state will make progress toward, and ultimately achieve, compliance with NAAQS by deadlines established in the Act. The SIP process is technically complex, disjointed, and hard to follow, even for experts. Part of the difficulty is that different aspects of a SIP receive approval on a rolling basis. The EPA might approve part of a SIP while sending another part back to the state for revision. It is no exaggeration to say that the SIP approval process is rife with uncertainty and based to a significant extent on both guesswork and hope. Can you imagine a less cumbersome and costly way for states to implement NAAQS?

2.   SIPs have been subject to criticism as a less than ideal method for attaining air quality. Arnold W. Reitze, Jr., in a comprehensive review of the Clean Air Act's evolution, highlighted a number of possible reasons for the failure of SIPs to attain air quality standards in many areas: growth in the population and energy use nullifying the progress that has been made in reducing emissions; fear of the costs of the CAA preventing strict application; falling short of reductions goals in the transportation sector, along with a faster-than-projected increase in vehicle miles traveled and a shift towards high-emitting vehicles such as SUVs; suburban sprawl resulting from a disconnect between transportation and land use planning; unreliable and/or expensive models used to demonstrate that SIPs would lead to attainment, at times resting on overly optimistic assumptions; slower than expected phasing out of "grandfathered" emissions sources predating the imposition of control technologies; transport of ozone from "upwind" states in the west to "downwind" states in the east; lack of negative consequences for local officials when air quality targets are not met, leaving no incentives for them to impose costly control measures; inadequacy of EPA sanctions; and the lack of any milestone program to identify and address state missteps. Arnold W. Reitze, Jr., *Air Quality Protection Using State Implementation Plans—Thirty-Seven Years of Increasing Complexity*, 15 VILL. ENVTL. L.J. 209, 358–66 (2004) (noting that "approximately 133 million people in 2001 lived in counties that violated

one or more NAAQS"). Reitze points to federally-mandated measures as an increasingly large and important part of SIPs in terms of actually achieving emissions reductions (e.g., mobile source measures such as inspection and maintenance for motor vehicles, reformulated gasoline, and conformity planning; and the acid rain program) and predicts more such federal measures as the major cause of emissions reductions in the future. *See id.* at 366.

2. HAZARDOUS AIR POLLUTANTS

Hazardous air pollutants are those known or suspected to cause cancer and serious illness, such as reproductive effects or birth defects. Large stationary sources like chemical factories, incinerators and coal-burning power plants produce toxic pollutants. So do small sources such as dry cleaners and auto paint shops. When automobiles burn gasoline, they emit toxics, such as formaldehyde and benzene, from their tailpipes. Natural events, such as forest fires, may also release toxics into the air. However, most toxic air pollution is generated by man-made sources.

Once toxic pollution is emitted, wind can carry it far from its original source. Some toxics degrade either slowly or not at all. Metals can remain in the environment forever. Depending on the intensity and duration of exposure, humans exposed to toxics may suffer an increased risk of cancer and other serious health effects, including damage to their neurological, reproductive, respiratory and immune systems. Accidental releases of large quantities of air toxics can kill many people. This was brought home to the American public when, in 1984, a U.S.-owned pesticide manufacturing plant in Bhopal, India released methyl isocyanate, killing approximately 4,000 people and injuring more than 200,000. Toxic pollutants can also cause serious damage to wildlife that may ingest them. The regulation of air toxics not only responds to these kinds of harms, but may also help to reduce concentrations of criteria pollutants such as smog and ozone because some toxics are also volatile organic compounds that contribute to the formation of smog or particulate matter.

In the 1990 Amendments to the CAA, Congress overhauled the toxics program created by the 1970 legislation. The previous version of the Act had required the EPA to set emission limits for air toxics individually, based on their health risks, with an "ample margin of safety." After the 1970 provisions were passed, disagreements erupted over precisely what level of regulation this required, and whether it could include considerations of cost and technological feasibility. The EPA was still relatively inexperienced with risk assessment at this time, and scientists and policy experts could not agree on risk assessment methodologies and assumptions. Nor could they agree on how much data was necessary to support a given level of regulation. As a result of these difficulties, by the late eighties, the EPA had listed only seven air toxics.

In the 1990 Amendments, Congress itself listed 189 hazardous air pollutants (selected on the basis of their potential to be hazardous to health or the environment) and required the EPA to use a technology-based approach to set emissions standards for all major sources. The EPA established standards for each category of source (there are now 175 categories of industrial and commercial sources that emit one or more toxic air pollutants) and classifies sources as major (large) or area (small) sources within each category.

Under the 1990 Amendments, the EPA must set emissions standards for all major toxic sources, using Maximum Available Control Technology (MACT). MACT standards are based on emissions levels that are already being achieved by the better-controlled and lower-emitting sources in each industry. MACT standards come in two varieties: more stringent or less stringent. New major sources must meet the more stringent MACT standard covering their category, defined as the standard of emissions control achieved by the best-controlled similar source through any of the following: clean processes, control devices, work practices, or other methods. Existing sources must meet the less stringent MACT standard, defined as the emissions limit achieved by the best performing 12 percent of sources in that source category. In setting MACT standards, the EPA does not generally require sources to adopt particular technologies. Instead, sources may achieve the required performance level in whatever way is most cost-effective for them. Of course, some sources may find it easiest and most cost-effective to simply adopt the technology that the EPA used to set the standard. The MACT standards are *minimum* standards. The EPA is authorized to impose more stringent standards on individual source categories.

Major sources are defined as sources that emit 10 or more tons per year of any of the listed toxic air pollutants, or 25 or more tons per year of a combination of air toxics. Examples include chemical plants, steel mills, oil refineries and hazardous waste incinerators. Toxics might be emitted through stacks or vents, or they might be "fugitive" emissions that escape from industrial processes without passing through the normal exhaust system. Area sources are smaller sources of air toxics, defined as producing fewer than 10 tons per year of a single air toxic or fewer than 25 tons of any mixture of air toxics. Examples of area sources include dry cleaners and gas stations. Collectively, these emissions can cause serious risks, especially when high numbers of area sources are located in densely populated areas.

MACT standards generally apply to all sources, but the EPA may limit their applicability to major sources and impose on areas sources the separate, and less stringent, requirement of "generally available control technologies or management practices." The EPA need not list all categories of area sources, and it need not establish emission standards for unlisted sources. As of November, 2018, the EPA had issued 139 air toxics MACT standards under § 112 of the CAA. These standards affect over 160 categories of industrial sources. *See* U.S. Environmental Protection Agency, *National Emissions Standards for Hazardous Air Pollutants (NESHAP)*, https://www.epa.gov/stationary-sources-air-pollution/national-emission-standards-hazardous-air-pollutants-neshap-9.

The case below explains the different treatment of major and area sources, and explores the EPA's definition of "major source" for purposes of the NESHAP provisions in § 112 of the Act. The agency had defined the term broadly, leading industry groups to sue.

NATIONAL MINING ASSOCIATION V. EPA

United States Court of Appeals, District of Columbia Circuit, 1995.
59 F.3d 1351.

[Various companies and associations petitioned for review of the EPA order implementing the 1990 Amendments to the CAA requiring identification of "major sources" of hazardous air pollutants. Because major sources are potentially subject to stricter control than area sources, petitioners sought to limit the circumstances under which facilities would be deemed major. Among other things, they challenged the EPA's decision to aggregate all hazardous air emissions within a plant site (instead of counting separately emissions from equipment in similar industrial categories) in determining whether a source was major.]

PER CURIAM:

This is a petition for review of an order of the Environmental Protection Agency implementing the 1990 amendments to § 112 of the Clean Air Act. Petitioners are General Electric Company and four trade associations: (1) National Mining Association, which represents companies that produce metal, coal, and minerals, and that manufacture mining equipment; (2) American Forest and Paper Association, which represents companies that make pulp, paper, paperboard, and solid wood; (3) Chemical Manufacturers Association, which represents companies that manufacture industrial chemicals; and (4) American Petroleum Institute, which represents companies engaged in the petroleum industry. * * *

In 1990, as part of its comprehensive overhaul of the Clean Air Act, Congress revised § 112 of the Act, which regulates emissions of hazardous air pollutants. Dissatisfied with EPA's health-based regulation of hazardous air pollutants under the 1970 program, Congress replaced this approach with a detailed, technology-based regulatory scheme. The 1990 amendments to § 112 establish an initial list, which EPA may periodically revise, of 189 hazardous air pollutants. 42 U.S.C. § 7412(b)(1)–(3). EPA must publish a list of "categories and subcategories" of "major sources" and certain "area sources" that emit these pollutants. 42 U.S.C. § 7412(c). For each listed "category or subcategory of major sources and area sources" of hazardous air pollutants, § 112(d) of the Act directs EPA to promulgate emission standards. 42 U.S.C. C7412(d)(1).

Under the Act, "major sources" of hazardous air pollutants are potentially subject to stricter regulatory control than are "area sources." For example, major sources must comply with technology-based emission standards requiring the maximum degree of reduction in emissions EPA deems achievable, often referred to as "maximum achievable control technology" or MACT standards. 42 U.S.C. § 7412(d)(1)–(2). In order to obtain an operating permit under title V of the Act, §§ 501–507, major sources must comply with extensive monitoring, reporting and record-keeping requirements. 42 U.S.C. §§ 7661–7661(f). Further, § 112(g) generally conditions the modification, construction or reconstruction of a major source on the source's meeting MACT emission limitations. 42 U.S.C. § 7412(g).

"Area sources" of hazardous air pollutants are not necessarily subject to such stringent regulation. EPA need not list all "categories and subcategories" of area sources, 42 U.S.C. § 7412(c)(3), and it does not have to establish emission standards for unlisted area sources, 42 U.S.C. § 7412(d)(1). For listed area sources, EPA may choose to promulgate emission standards requiring only "generally available control technologies or management practices." 42 U.S.C. § 7412(d)(5). These standards can be less rigorous than those required for major sources under 42 U.S.C. § 7412(d)(1). Area sources are not subject to title V permitting requirements, or to § 112(g)'s restrictions on modification, construction and reconstruction of their facilities. * * *

[The EPA promulgated a rule setting emissions standards for listed source categories as required by § 112(e)].

Among other things, the general provisions rule implements § 112(a)(1)'s definition of "major source." The rule defines "major source" in terms nearly identical to those in § 112(a)(1) of the Clean Air Act:

> Major source means any stationary source or group of stationary sources located within a contiguous area and under common control that emits or has the potential to emit considering controls, in the aggregate, 10 tons per year or more of any hazardous air pollutant or 25 tons per year or more of any combination of hazardous air pollutants, unless the Administrator establishes a lesser quantity, or in the case of radionuclides, different criteria from those specified in this sentence.

A "stationary source" is "any building, structure, facility or installation which emits or may emit any air pollutant." An "area source [is] any stationary source . . . that is not a major source." The preambles to the proposed and final rules, and other definitions adopted in the final rule explain in greater detail how EPA plans to identify major sources.

Petitioners challenge three aspects of EPA's implementation of the definition of "major source." First, National Mining Association and American Forest and Paper Association (collectively referred to as "National Mining Association") and General Electric question EPA's requiring the aggregation of all hazardous air emissions within a plant site—instead of only those emissions from equipment in similar industrial categories—in a § 112 major source determination. * * *

General Electric and National Mining Association have similar arguments against the final rule's implementation of § 112(a)(1). Both maintain that EPA may not, in determining whether a site is a major source, include emissions from all facilities on a contiguous plant site under common control. These petitioners assert that, for purposes of major source determinations, EPA may aggregate emissions from different facilities on a contiguous plant site under common control only when the facilities fall within a similar industrial classification. General Electric says EPA must aggregate emissions on a "source category" basis * * *.

* * * Congress intended, according to EPA, "that all portions of a major source be subject to MACT [emission standards] regardless of the number of source categories into which the facility is divided." "Thus, the EPA will set one or more MACT standards for a major source, and sources within that major source will be covered by the standard(s), regardless of whether, when standing alone, each one those regulated sources would be major." * * *

If § 112(a)(1) is viewed in isolation, EPA's reading of the provision is not simply consistent with the provision; it is nearly compelled by the statutory language. Section 112(a)(1) states that a "group of stationary sources" need meet only three conditions to be termed a "major source": (1) sources within the group must be "located within a contiguous area"; (2) they must be "under common control"; and (3) in the aggregate, they must emit or, considering controls, have the potential to emit 10 or more tons per year of a single hazardous air pollutant or 25 or more tons per year of any combination of hazardous air pollutants. * * *

Petitioners ask us to look beyond the language of § 112(a)(1). In the first of several loosely connected arguments, General Electric recites fragments from § 112's other provisions, including: (1) § 112(c)(1), which directs EPA to publish "a list of all categories and subcategories of major sources and area sources"; (2) § 112(d)(1), which directs EPA to establish emission standards "for each category or subcategory of major sources and area sources"; and (3) § 112(j)(2), which describes what an operator of a "major source in [a] category" must do if EPA does not promulgate an emission standard for that "category of major sources." From these portions of § 112, General Electric leaps to the conclusion that "major source must be defined 'with reference to' (and cannot be broader than) the source category defined by EPA for § 112 regulation."

General Electric's logic is hard to grasp. Rather than supporting General Electric, the provisions the company invokes, read in full and in context, tend to support EPA's implementation of "major source" without reference to source categories. Section § 112 directs EPA to perform certain tasks on a category-wide basis—it is to identify categories of major and area sources of hazardous air pollutants (§ 112(c)(1)), and it must promulgate category-wide emission standards for these sources (§ 112(d)(2)). It by no means follows that because the statute in several provisions uses the terms "major source" and "category" in the same sentence—which is all General Electric's argument amounts to—EPA must read a source category restriction into § 112(a)(1)'s definition of "major source." Nor does § 112(c) somehow prohibit EPA from applying § 112(d)'s MACT emission limitations "to minor sources in a listed category of major sources without complying with the statutory requirements for listing area sources." *See* Brief for General Electric at 18. Section 112(c) simply requires the listing of all major sources and those area sources presenting adverse health or environmental effects. 42 U.S.C. § 7412 (c)(1), (3). Neither § 112(c) nor § 112(d) says anything about EPA's including "minor sources" in a "listed category of major sources." * * *

In sum, EPA's definition of "major source" without respect to source categories * * * is reasonable, as is its requirement that fugitive emissions be included in a source's aggregate emissions in determining whether the source is major. We therefore deny the petition for review with respect to these issues. * * *

[The Court granted review with respect to the agency's decision to calculate a source's potential emissions only by considering federally enforceable emission limits, which, petitioners claimed, would systematically over-estimate potential emissions because facilities are subject to state emissions limits as well.]

NOTES

1.   What would the consequences be had the Court agreed with General Electric's interpretation of "major source" in this case?

2.   *National Mining Association* illustrates how crucial seemingly technical definitions can be. The agency's regulations interpreting statutory terms like "major" and "new" can determine which sources are regulated and to what extent. Since this is so consequential, why doesn't Congress clarify such things beyond any reasonable doubt, so that the need for these costly lawsuits would disappear? Does Congress just overlook these issues, or is it purposely delegating their resolution to the EPA? What difference would it

make if the answer were the former rather than the latter? When considering this question, you may wish to refresh your memory of the Supreme Court's holding and rationale for deferring to the agency interpretation in *Chevron, supra,* at page 351.

3.   In 2012, after endless legislation and litigation battles, EPA issued a final rule to regulate emissions of mercury from existing sources. *See* http://www.gpo.gov/fdsys/pkg/FR-2012-02-16/pdf/2012-806.pdf. Under President George W. Bush, EPA had established a cap-and-trade program to regulate mercury emissions from power plants; the D.C. Circuit struck down the program as inconsistent with Section 112. *See New Jersey v. EPA,* http://www.cadc.uscourts.gov/internet/opinions.nsf/68822E72677ACBCD85257440004707 36/$file/05-1097a.pdf (2008). A central concern about using cap-and-trade to regulate mercury emissions is that it might create "hot spots" if emitters chose to buy allowances to cover their emissions rather than reduce them. Can you see why?

The 2012 rule was challenged by a group of states, interest group and businesses, leading to the following ruling:

MICHIGAN V. EPA

Supreme Court of the United States, 2015.
576 U.S. ___, 135 S.Ct. 2699, 192 L.Ed.2d 674.

JUSTICE SCALIA delivered the opinion of the Court.

The Clean Air Act directs the Environmental Protection Agency to regulate emissions of hazardous air pollutants from power plants if the Agency finds regulation "appropriate and necessary." We must decide whether it was reasonable for EPA to refuse to consider cost when making this finding.

I

The Clean Air Act establishes a series of regulatory programs to control air pollution from stationary sources (such as refineries and factories) and moving sources (such as cars and airplanes). 69 Stat. 322, as amended, 42 U.S.C. §§ 7401–7671q. One of these is the National Emissions Standards for Hazardous Air Pollutants Program—the hazardous-air-pollutants program, for short. Established in its current form by the Clean Air Act Amendments of 1990, 104 Stat. 2531, this program targets for regulation stationary-source emissions of more than 180 specified "hazardous air pollutants." § 7412(b).

For stationary sources in general, the applicability of the program depends in part on how much pollution the source emits. A source that emits more than 10 tons of a single pollutant or more than 25 tons of a combination of pollutants per year is called a major source. § 7412(a)(1). EPA is required to regulate all major sources under the program. § 7412(c)(1)–(2). A source whose emissions do not cross the just-mentioned thresholds is called an area source. § 7412(a)(2). The Agency is required to regulate an area source under the program if it "presents a threat of adverse effects to human health or the environment . . . warranting regulation." § 7412(c)(3).

At the same time, Congress established a unique procedure to determine the applicability of the program to fossil-fuel-fired power plants. The Act refers to these plants as electric utility steam generating units, but we will simply call them power plants. Quite apart from the hazardous-air-pollutants program, the Clean Air Act Amendments of 1990 subjected power plants to various regulatory requirements. The parties agree that these requirements were expected to have the collateral effect of reducing power plants' emissions of hazardous air pollutants, although the extent of the reduction was unclear. Congress directed the Agency to "perform a study of the hazards to public health reasonably anticipated to occur as a result of emissions by [power plants] of [hazardous air pollutants] after imposition of the requirements of this chapter." § 7412(n)(1)(A). If the Agency "finds . . . regulation is appropriate and necessary after considering the results of the study," it "shall regulate [power plants] under [§ 7412]." *Ibid.* EPA has interpreted the Act to mean that power plants become subject to regulation on the same terms as ordinary major and area sources, see 77 Fed.Reg. 9330 (2012), and we assume without deciding that it was correct to do so.

And what are those terms? EPA must first divide sources covered by the program into categories and subcategories in accordance with statutory criteria. § 7412(c)(1). For each category or subcategory, the Agency must promulgate certain minimum emission regulations, known as floor standards. § 7412(d)(1), (3). The statute generally calibrates the floor standards to reflect the emissions limitations already achieved by the best-performing 12% of sources within the category or subcategory. § 7412(d)(3). In some circumstances, the Agency may also impose more stringent emission regulations, known as beyond-the-floor standards. The statute expressly requires the Agency to consider cost (alongside other specified factors) when imposing beyond-the-floor standards. § 7412(d)(2).

EPA completed the study required by § 7412(n)(1)(A) in 1998, 65 Fed.Reg. 79826 (2000), and concluded that regulation of coal- and oil-fired power plants was "appropriate and necessary" in 2000, *id.,* at 79830. In 2012, it reaffirmed the appropriate-and-necessary finding, divided power plants into subcategories, and promulgated floor standards. The Agency found regulation "appropriate" because (1) power plants' emissions of mercury and other hazardous air pollutants posed risks to human health and the environment and (2) controls were available to reduce these emissions. 77 Fed.Reg. 9363. It found regulation "necessary" because the imposition of the Act's other requirements did not eliminate these risks.

Ibid. EPA concluded that "costs should not be considered" when deciding whether power plants should be regulated under § 7412. *Id.,* at 9326.

The Agency issued a "Regulatory Impact Analysis" alongside its regulation estimating that the regulation would force power plants to bear costs of $9.6 billion per year. *Id.,* at 9306. The Agency could not fully quantify the benefits of reducing power plants' emissions of hazardous air pollutants; to the extent it could, it estimated that these benefits were worth $4 to $6 million per year. *Ibid.* The costs to power plants were thus between 1,600 and 2,400 times as great as the quantifiable benefits from reduced emissions of hazardous air pollutants. The Agency continued that its regulations would have ancillary benefits—including cutting power plants' emissions of particulate matter and sulfur dioxide, substances that are not covered by the hazardous-air-pollutants program. Although the Agency's appropriate-and-necessary finding did not rest on these ancillary effects, *id.,* at 9320, the regulatory impact analysis took them into account, increasing the Agency's estimate of the quantifiable benefits of its regulation to $37 to $90 billion per year, *id.,* at 9306. EPA concedes that the regulatory impact analysis "played no role" in its appropriate-and-necessary finding. Brief for Federal Respondents 14.

* * *

The Court of Appeals upheld the Agency's decision not to consider cost, with Judge Kavanaugh concurring in part and dissenting in part. *White Stallion Energy Center, LLC v. EPA,* 748 F.3d 1222 (2014) (*per curiam*). . . .

II

* * *

Agency action is lawful only if it rests "on a consideration of the relevant factors." (citations omitted).

EPA's decision to regulate power plants under § 7412 allowed the Agency to reduce power plants' emissions of hazardous air pollutants and thus to improve public health and the environment. But the decision also ultimately cost power plants, according to the Agency's own estimate, nearly $10 billion a year. EPA refused to consider whether the costs of its decision outweighed the benefits. The Agency gave cost no thought *at all,* because it considered cost irrelevant to its initial decision to regulate.

EPA's disregard of cost rested on its interpretation of § 7412(n)(1)(A), which, to repeat, directs the Agency to regulate power plants if it "finds such regulation is appropriate and necessary." The Agency accepts that it *could* have interpreted this provision to mean that cost is relevant to the decision to add power plants to the program. But it chose to read the statute to mean that cost makes no difference to the initial decision to regulate.

* * *

We review this interpretation under the standard set out in *Chevron U.S.A. Inc. v. Natural Resources Defense Council, Inc.,* 467 U.S. 837, 104 S.Ct. 2778, 81 L.Ed.2d 694 (1984). *Chevron* directs courts to accept an agency's reasonable resolution of an ambiguity in a statute that the agency administers. Even under this deferential standard, however, * * * EPA strayed far beyond those bounds when it read § 7412(n)(1) to mean that it could ignore cost when deciding whether to regulate power plants.

A

The Clean Air Act treats power plants differently from other sources for purposes of the hazardous-air-pollutants program. Elsewhere in § 7412, Congress established cabined criteria for EPA to apply when deciding whether to include sources in the program. It required the Agency to regulate sources whose emissions exceed specified numerical thresholds (major sources). It also required the Agency to regulate sources whose emissions fall short of these thresholds (area sources) if they "presen[t] a threat of adverse effects to human health or the environment . . . warranting regulation." § 7412(c)(3). In stark contrast, Congress instructed EPA to add power plants to the program if (but only if) the Agency finds regulation "appropriate and necessary." § 7412(n)(1)(A). One does not need to open up a dictionary in order to realize the capaciousness of this phrase. In particular, "appropriate" is "the classic broad and all-encompassing term that naturally and traditionally includes consideration of all the relevant factors." 748 F.3d, at 1266 (opinion of Kavanaugh, J.). Although this term leaves agencies with flexibility, an agency may not "entirely fai[l] to consider an important aspect of the problem" when deciding whether regulation is appropriate. *State Farm, supra,* at 43, 103 S.Ct. 2856. Read naturally in the present context, the phrase "appropriate and necessary" requires at least some attention to cost. One would not say that it is even rational, never mind "appropriate," to impose billions of dollars in economic costs in return for a few dollars in health or environmental benefits. In addition, "cost" includes more than the expense of complying with regulations; any disadvantage could be termed a cost. EPA's interpretation precludes the Agency from considering *any* type of cost—including, for instance, harms that regulation might do to human health or the environment. The Government concedes that if the Agency were to find that emissions from power plants do damage to human health, but that the technologies needed to eliminate these emissions do even more damage to human health, it would *still* deem regulation appropriate. No regulation is "appropriate" if it does significantly more harm than good.

There are undoubtedly settings in which the phrase "appropriate and necessary" does not encompass cost. But this is not one of them. Section 7412(n)(1)(A) directs EPA to determine whether "*regulation* is appropriate and necessary." (Emphasis added.) Agencies have long treated cost as a centrally relevant factor when deciding whether to regulate. Consideration of cost reflects the understanding that reasonable regulation ordinarily requires paying attention to the advantages *and* the disadvantages of agency decisions. It also reflects the reality that "too much wasteful expenditure devoted to one problem may well mean considerably fewer resources available to deal effectively with other (perhaps more serious) problems." *Entergy Corp. v. Riverkeeper, Inc.,* 556 U.S. 208, 233, 129 S.Ct. 1498, 173 L.Ed.2d 369 (2009) (BREYER, J., concurring in part and dissenting in part). [*see Entergy, supra* at page 627] against the backdrop of this established administrative practice, it is unreasonable to read an instruction to an administrative agency to determine whether "regulation is appropriate and necessary" as an invitation to ignore cost.

Statutory context reinforces the relevance of cost. The procedures governing power plants that we consider today appear in § 7412(n)(1), which bears the caption "Electric utility steam generating units." In subparagraph (A), the part of the law that has occupied our attention so far, Congress required EPA to study the hazards to public health posed by power plants and to determine whether regulation is appropriate and necessary. But in subparagraphs (B) and (C), Congress called for two additional studies. One of them, a study into mercury emissions from power plants and other sources, must consider "the health and environmental effects of such emissions, technologies which are available to control such emissions, *and the costs of such technologies.*" § 7412(n)(1)(B) (emphasis added). This directive to EPA to study cost is a further indication of the relevance of cost to the decision to regulate.

* * *

EPA has not explained why § 7412(n)(1)(B)'s reference to "environmental effects . . . and . . . costs" provides "direct evidence that Congress was concerned with environmental effects," but not "direct evidence" that it was concerned with cost. *Chevron* allows agencies to choose among competing reasonable interpretations of a statute; it does not license interpretive gerrymanders under which an agency keeps parts of statutory context it likes while throwing away parts it does not.

* * *

D

Our reasoning . . . establishes that it was unreasonable for EPA to read § 7412(n)(1)(A) to mean that cost is irrelevant to the initial decision to regulate power plants. The Agency must consider cost—including, most importantly, cost of compliance—before deciding whether regulation is appropriate and necessary. We need not and do not hold that the law unambiguously required the Agency, when making this preliminary estimate, to conduct a formal cost-benefit analysis in which each advantage and disadvantage is assigned a monetary value. It will be up to the Agency to decide (as always, within the limits of reasonable interpretation) how to account for cost.

* * *

We hold that EPA interpreted § 7412(n)(1)(A) unreasonably when it deemed cost irrelevant to the decision to regulate power plants. We reverse the judgment of the Court of Appeals for the D.C. Circuit and remand the cases for further proceedings consistent with this opinion.

JUSTICES KAGAN, BREYER, GINSBURG and SOTOMAYOR, dissenting;

* * * *At the outset, EPA determined that regulating plants' emissions of hazardous air pollutants is "appropriate and necessary" given the harm they cause, and explained that it would take costs into account in developing suitable emissions standards. Next, EPA divided power plants into groups based on technological and other characteristics bearing significantly on their cost structures. It required plants in each group to match the emissions levels already achieved by the best-performing members of the same group—benchmarks necessarily reflecting those plants' own cost analyses. EPA then adopted a host of measures designed to make compliance with its proposed emissions limits less costly for plants that needed to catch up with their cleaner peers. And with only one narrow exception, EPA decided not to impose any more stringent standards (beyond what some plants had already achieved on their own) because it found that doing so would not be cost-effective. After all that, EPA conducted a formal cost-benefit study which found that the quantifiable benefits of its regulation would exceed the costs up to nine times over—by as much as $80 billion each year. Those benefits include as many as 11,000 fewer premature deaths annually, along with a far greater number of avoided illnesses.

Despite that exhaustive consideration of costs, the Court strikes down EPA's rule on the ground that the Agency "unreasonably . . . deemed cost irrelevant." On the majority's theory, the rule is invalid because EPA did not explicitly analyze costs at the very first stage of the regulatory process, when making its "appropriate and necessary" finding. And that is so even though EPA later took costs into account again and again and . . . so on. The majority thinks entirely immaterial, and so entirely ignores, all the subsequent times and ways EPA considered costs in deciding what any regulation would look like.

That is a peculiarly blinkered way for a court to assess the lawfulness of an agency's rulemaking. I agree with the majority—let there be no doubt about this—that EPA's power plant regulation would be unreasonable if "[t]he Agency gave cost no thought *at all*." (emphasis in original). But that is just not what happened here. Over more than a decade, EPA took costs into account at multiple stages and through multiple means as it set emissions limits for power plants. And when making its initial "appropriate and necessary" finding, EPA knew it would do exactly that—knew it would thoroughly consider the cost-effectiveness of emissions standards later on. That context matters. The Agency acted well within its authority in declining to consider costs at the opening bell of the regulatory process given that it would do so in every round thereafter—and given that the emissions limits finally issued would depend crucially on those accountings. Indeed, EPA could not have measured costs at the process's initial stage with any accuracy. And the regulatory path EPA chose parallels the one it has trod in setting emissions limits, at Congress's explicit direction, for every other source of hazardous air pollutants over two decades. The majority's decision that EPA cannot take the same approach here—its micromanagement of EPA's rulemaking, based on little more than the word "appropriate"—runs counter to Congress's allocation of authority between the Agency and the courts. Because EPA reasonably found that it was "appropriate" to decline to analyze costs at a single stage of a regulatory proceeding otherwise imbued with cost concerns, I respectfully dissent.

NOTES

1.   Would it make a difference in EPA's analysis if it considered cost before or after deciding to issue regulations? On April 25, 2016, EPA issued a supplemental finding holding that it is "appropriate and necessary" to regulate mercury from the electric power sector. *See* 81 FR 24420. 20 states and industry groups immediately appealed the finding. *Murray Energy v. EPA,* No. 16–1127 (D.C. Cir). The Trump Administration subsequently asked the court to suspend briefing in the case while it evaluated the rule. EPA is now proposing to rescind the "appropriate and necessary" finding on the grounds that the Obama Administration inappropriately considered co-benefits from reducing particulate and other conventional pollutants in deciding whether to regulate. Instead, EPA's new proposal would consider only those benefits that come directly from regulating mercury and other hazardous pollutants at the "appropriate and necessary" stage. Because the quantified direct benefits (between $4 and $6 million) are so much lower than the costs to implement pollution controls (between $7 and $9 billion), EPA says there is a "gross imbalance" between the costs on industry of compliance versus the benefits to human health and environment. Although the agency proposes rescinding the "appropriate and necessary" finding, it does not propose rescinding the rule. *See* U.S. EPA, *Regulatory Actions—Final Mercury and Air Toxics Standards (MATS) for Power Plants, EPA Proposes Revised Cost Finding for MATS and Completes Risk and Technology Revie* (Dec. 27, 2018), https://www.epa.gov/mats/regulatory-actions-final-mercury-and-air-toxics-standards-mats-power-plants. For an analysis of the Trump Administration strategy, *see* Ann Carlson, *The Curious Case of EPA's Mercury Cost-Benefit Decision*, LEGAL PLANET (Dec. 30, 2018), http://legal-planet.org/2018/12/30/the-curious-case-of-epas-mercury-cost-benefit-decision/. Do you think the new proposal—considering only direct

costs at the "appropriate and necessary" stage and finding no need to regulate—is a reasonable interpretation of the statute under *Chevron*? Notably, the utility industry has not requested reconsideration of the MAT standard, although the coal industry has done so.

2.   Is the opinion in *Michigan v. EPA* consistent with the *Chevron* doctrine? Does the Court's opinion signal that it will defer less frequently to agency interpretations of ambiguous statutory provisions? Should the Court have decided the case under Step 1 of Chevron rather than Step 2? For a sense of newly-confirmed Justice Brett Kavanaugh's view of the Chevron Doctrine, *see* Brett Kavanaugh, *Fixing Statutory Interpretation*, 129 HARV. L. REV. 2118 (2016). Justice Neil Gorsuch also criticized the doctrine when he served as a circuit court judge on the 10th Circuit. *Guitierrez-Brezuela v. Lynch*, 834 F.3d 1142 (10th Cir. 2016)

3.   PSD AREAS

The 1970 Clean Air Act did not address areas of the country that were already in compliance with NAAQS or, that exceeded them. This hole in the statutory scheme was first addressed in litigation, when the Sierra Club challenged the EPA's approval of SIPs that allowed power plant emissions to degrade the air in these relatively clean regions. A district judge rejected the EPA's decision, and that outcome was upheld by the D.C. Circuit and then the Supreme Court in 1973. *Sierra Club* v. *Ruckelshaus*, 344 F.Supp. 253 (D.D.C. 1972), aff'd by an equally divided court, *Fri v. Sierra Club*, 412 U.S. 541 (1973). This meant the EPA could not approve implementation plans that permitted increases in air pollution in these relatively clean areas unless Congress amended the CAA. Congress did just that in the 1977 amendments to the Act, by adding non-degradation, or "prevention of significant deterioration," (PSD) provisions. BRUCE A. ACKERMAN & WILLIAM T. HASSLER, CLEAN COAL/DIRTY AIR 28–29 (1981); *see also* Robert L. Glicksman, *The Value of Agency—Forcing Citizen Suits To Enforce Non-Discretionary Duties*, 10 WIDENER L. REV. 353, 358–61 (2004).

Under § 107 of the Act, states must classify areas as in attainment, out of attainment or unclassifiable. For areas that are either in attainment or are unclassifiable, SIPs must contain provisions to prevent significant deterioration [§ 110 (a)(2)(j)]. The statute divides PSD areas further into three classes (national parks and monuments must be Class I or II, for example), each with a separate increment of permissible pollution increases. These increments represent the extent to which the air quality for a given pollutant may be allowed to degrade over the baseline concentration of that pollutant in the air in the PSD area. The increments are calculated as a percentage of the NAAQS. For example, the maximum permissible increase annually in the amount of particulate matter in a

Class I PSD area is 2 percent of the NAAQS for particulate matter. Section 163 establishes allowable increments for sulfur dioxide and particulates.

New or modified major sources in PSD areas must meet technology-based emissions limits set using Best Available Control Technology (BACT) and obtain pre-construction permits (§ 165). BACT standards may be no less stringent than New Source Performance Standards (NSPS), which are applicable to all new sources under § 111 and which are set according to BDAT. Sources in PSD areas are subject to NAAQS as a ceiling under § 163 (b)(4). So, even if a source could technically emit more of a pollutant without exceeding the annual allowable increment, it may not do so if those emissions will result in ambient levels that would exceed the NAAQS. In addition, although only new major sources must obtain permits, *all* sources produce emissions that count toward the annual increment. States may need to impose limits on existing sources in PSD areas to avoid falling below the NAAQS, even though these provisions of the CAA do not directly require existing sources to obtain permits or meet technology-based standards.

Under the PSD provisions, "major emitting facilities" are subject to the BACT standards and must obtain pre-construction permits. The term "major emitting facility" is defined in Section 7479(1) and applies generally to facilities that emit, or have the potential to emit, 100 tons per year for types sources delineated in the section or 250 tons per year for sources not delineated in the statute. The provision applies to sources that emit "any air pollutant." In *Massachusetts v. EPA*, *infra* at page 530, the Supreme Court made clear that air pollutant includes carbon dioxide and other greenhouse gas emissions. As described in more detail *infra*, EPA has issued PSD provisions for new sources of greenhouse gas emissions. Does the term "major emitting facility" work for greenhouse gas emitters?

4. THE NONATTAINMENT PROBLEM

As we have seen, the 1970 Act afforded states considerable flexibility, through the SIP process, to achieve compliance with the NAAQS as they thought best. Subsequent amendments to deal with the problem of nonattainment have limited that flexibility, however. For example, the 1977 Amendments required all SIPs to provide for the implementation of "reasonably available control measures" (RACM) in nonattainment zones, including the application of "reasonably available control technology" (RACT) at all existing major stationary sources with the potential to emit 100 tons per year of the regulated pollutant or its precursors. Prior to this amendment, states could shelter existing sources from the imposition of such controls. The 1977 Amendments also required states to adopt a permit program for new major stationary sources in nonattainment zones and required states to impose on such sources a stringent technology-based standard known as "lowest achievable emission rate" (LAER). States were forbidden from permitting these new sources unless the new emissions could be offset by a decrease in emissions from existing sources in the same area or another area that contributes to the first area's non-attainment problem and itself has an equal or worse non-attainment problem, and only then if states could ensure "reasonable further progress" toward attainment. The EPA has issued an interpretive rule on its offset policy, which stipulates that only offsets of the same pollutant are acceptable, and that the baseline for determining credit for offsets consists of the SIP limits in effect at the time of the application. Credits may be granted for reductions achieved by a variety of methods, including shutdowns, reduction of hours of operation below baseline levels, and switching to cleaner fuels. All emissions reductions claimed as credits must be federally enforceable. *See* 40 C.F.R. Pt. 51, App. S, §§ IV.A, IV.C.

Between 1977 and 1990, without the benefit of congressional action, the EPA addressed the problem of nonattainment by issuing "SIP calls" to states, demanding SIP revisions for nonattainment areas. States were asked to demonstrate that they were adopting measures that would ensure attainment by the deadlines in the Act, and to guarantee steady progress toward compliance in the interim. The case below illustrates the difficult position the EPA found itself in prior to the 1990 Amendments.

DELANEY V. EPA

United States Court of Appeals, Ninth Circuit, 1990.
898 F.2d 687.

WIGGINS, CIRCUIT JUDGE.

Residents of Maricopa and Pima counties, Arizona, petition this court to vacate as arbitrary or capricious the Environmental Protection Agency's approvals of the counties' Clean Air Act implementation plans. * * *

The Clean Air Act, as amended in 1970, mandated that states as expeditiously as practicable, but not later than December 31, 1975, reduce the levels of certain ambient pollutants to comply with the National Ambient Air Quality Standards set by the EPA. Preliminarily, each state had to develop a state implementation plan to achieve this goal.

After many areas of the country failed to attain some or all of the national ambient air quality standards on time, Congress amended the Act in 1977, providing new deadlines for nonattainment areas. The 1977 amendments required states to submit by January 1, 1979, for each of their nonattainment areas, a revised implementation plan that provided for implementation of all reasonably available control measures to attain the relevant national ambient air quality standards as expeditiously as practicable, but not later than December 31, 1982. If a state did not submit an adequate revised state implementation plan by the 1979 deadline, the EPA had to promulgate its own federal implementation plan. The 1977 amendments provided only one exception: If a state demonstrated in its revised implementation plan that the carbon monoxide or ozone ambient air quality standard could not be attained by the close of 1982 despite implementation of all reasonably available control measures, the state could have until the end of 1987 to attain the relevant air quality standard in that nonattainment area. In that case, the state had to submit a second revised implementation plan to the EPA by July 1, 1982.

In 1978, the EPA designated large areas of both Maricopa and Pima counties as nonattainment areas for carbon monoxide. In 1979, Arizona submitted revised implementation plans for both areas. In 1983, the EPA approved the plans subject to certain conditions. Neither area, however, satisfied the EPA's conditions or attained the carbon monoxide standard by the 1982 deadline. Arizona failed in its attempt to extend both areas' attainment deadlines to 1987, but submitted additional revised plans for the areas to attain by the 1987 deadline anyway. The EPA rejected these additional revised plans and we upheld that decision.

When Arizona thereafter failed to submit adequate plans for Maricopa and Pima counties, petitioners filed suit in the Arizona district court. That court ordered the EPA to promulgate implementation plans for both counties by March 30, 1988 (later extended to August 10, 1988), unless before this date Arizona submitted, and the EPA approved, adequate state plans. *McCarthy v. Thomas*, No. 85–344 (D. Ariz. August 10, 1987). Arizona submitted, and the EPA ultimately approved (with revisions), state implementation plans for both counties on August 10, 1988. Petitioners now challenge these approvals. * * *

Because the Clean Air Act amendments of 1977 made the 1982 compliance deadline absolute (with the one exception noted above), the amendments did not specify an additional deadline for nonattainment areas that failed to obtain revised implementation plan approval and national ambient air quality standard compliance by the 1982 deadline. In this circumstance, the EPA adopted the policy that it should evaluate the adequacy of the Maricopa and Pima county plans based on whether they provide for attainment by three years from the date it approved those plans, August 10, 1991. Petitioners contend that the EPA's policy is arbitrary or capricious. Now that the 1977 amendments' deadline for compliance has passed, petitioners assert, Pima and Maricopa Counties must attain the carbon monoxide ambient air quality standard as soon as possible utilizing every available control measure.

The EPA contends that Congress expressed no clear intent on the attainment deadline that the EPA should apply in evaluating the Maricopa and Pima plans because the 1977 amendments did not specify a deadline for nonattainment areas that failed to obtain revised state implementation plan approval and national ambient air quality standard compliance by the

1982 deadline. The EPA argues that this amounts to a "statutory gap." As a result, the EPA believes, we must uphold its policy of allowing compliance within three years of state implementation plan approval because it is a reasonable construction of the 1977 amendments.

The EPA argues that if Congress had considered that some nonattainment areas would not meet the deadline specified in the 1977 Amendments, Congress would have intended that the EPA administratively establish a new three year attainment period from the date of implementation plan approval deadline, like those provided in the Clean Air Act amendments of 1970. The EPA contends that this result is consistent with the language, history, and overall purposes of the Act. The EPA contends that Congress knew some states would not attain by the 1982 deadline and did not intend that states implement draconian measures. * * *

Although we recognize the EPA's predicament, we cannot accept the EPA's position. As the EPA itself recognizes, Congress explicitly declined to allow extensions of the deadline because it believed an absolute deadline to be necessary. * * *

We, and the EPA, are bound by the statutory scheme until Congress alters that scheme. * * *

When Congress has explicitly set an absolute deadline, congressional intent is clear. It is a semantic game to claim that once a state fails to meet an absolute deadline, a statutory gap is created because Congress has not provided a back-up deadline for its explicitly absolute deadline. If Congress had been more lenient and allowed a one-year fall back extension, the EPA would be bound by that directive. The EPA cannot extract leeway from a statute that Congress explicitly intended to be strict. * * *

CONCLUSION

We grant the petition for review. We vacate the EPA's approvals of Maricopa and Pima counties' Clean Air Act implementation plans. We direct the EPA to disapprove these plans and to promulgate federal implementation plans consistent with this opinion within six months.

NOTES

1.   Wasn't the agency's approach here eminently reasonable? What happened to the idea, per *Chevron, supra*, page 351, that a court should defer to an agency's reasonable interpretation of an ambiguous statutory provision? Are the relevant statutory provisions in this case really as clear-cut as the Court suggests?

2.   What are the practical consequences of the EPA disapproving a SIP and issuing a FIP? The agency does not seem to be trying hard to avoid this eventuality here. Why?

In the 1990 Amendments, Congress added a new set of nonattainment provisions, further limiting the states' discretion with regard to SIPs and imposing greater burdens on stationary sources in these areas. For ozone, Congress divided areas into categories meant to reflect the severity of the nonattainment problem. Congress then established compliance deadlines on a graduated basis, with more time given to those areas further out of attainment. Control requirements also follow this graduated approach: the further out of attainment, the more controls that area must adopt. For example, an ozone nonattainment area may be classified as marginally, moderately, seriously, severely or extremely out of attainment. The new deadlines were expressed in terms of the number of years after 1990 afforded to the area to comply with NAAQS. Marginal areas had three years beyond 1990 to comply, serious areas had nine years, and extreme areas (currently only Los Angeles and the San Joaquin Valley) were given twenty years. In addition, every area except marginal nonattainment areas were required to reduce emissions of volatile organic compounds (which contribute to ozone) by 15% by 1996, with further reductions of 3% to be achieved annually thereafter. Additional restrictions apply as well. For example, in areas classified as serious or worse, gas stations are required to install special hose-and-nozzle controls on gas pumps to capture fuel vapors.

The provisions relating to pollutants other than ozone are generally similar, but the EPA is afforded somewhat more discretion. For example, the carbon monoxide provisions require the use of reformulated gasoline. Reformulated gasoline typically contains additives such as ethanol (made from corn) or Methyl Tertiary-Butyl Ether (MTBE) that increase the amount of oxygen available for combustion, thereby decreasing emissions of carbon monoxide.

Areas out of attainment for a criteria pollutant for which Congress has not specified a deadline must comply with NAAQS within five years of being classified as a nonattainment area. The EPA may extend this deadline, though not indefinitely. States must adopt revisions to their SIPs for nonattainment areas which include the imposition of RACT for existing sources; a permit program for new sources as prescribed by section 173; provisions to ensure reasonable further progress toward attainment; and any other measures that may be necessary to ensure attainment. EPA has decided that for the new, 2015 ozone standard, the deadlines that applied to ozone nonattainment in the 1990 amendments will extend to nonattainment to comply with the 2015 standard. That means, for example, that extreme non-attainment areas will have 20 years from attainment designations to comply with the standard. *See* 83 FR 10376, 10378 (March 9, 2018).

Next, we return to the *American Trucking* case, (*supra,* page 338) regarding the role of cost in CAA standard-setting). After the Supreme Court concluded that the EPA could not consider cost in setting NAAQS, the Court reviewed the EPA's determination about how to implement the revised standards in nonattainment zones. Before delving into the complicated excerpt below, refresh your memories about the standard of review courts use to review agency interpretations of law by reviewing the *Chevron* case, *supra,* page 351. This part of the *American Trucking* case is a rare example of the Supreme Court refusing to defer to an agency interpretation of law once it reaches Step Two of the *Chevron* test. Do not confuse step one and two of the *Chevron* test with the issue in the case, which involves "Subpart 1" and "Subpart 2" of Part D of the CAA.

The Court's discussion, below, of whether Subpart 1 or Subpart 2 of Part D of the statute controls the implementation of a revised air standard is confusing for non-experts. Subpart 1 establishes general requirements for nonattainment areas (those areas classified as not meeting applicable air standards) and Subpart 2 contains more specific provisions for attaining primary standards (health-based standards, which are involved here) for particular pollutants. Meeting the EPA's revised ozone standard could impose a heavy burden on nonattainment zones already struggling with attaining the old ozone standard. The agency's implementation plan thus had to address what to do about areas that would be classified as "nonattainment" zones for the new standard.

The question is whether the agency has discretion to implement its revised (and more stringent) ozone standard under Subpart 1's general provisions governing nonattainment zones, or whether the more specific timetables in Subpart 2 apply. There are important differences between the two subparts. Subpart 1 requires areas to demonstrate attainment of primary standards within five to ten years following the area's designation as nonattainment. However, areas are exempt from this deadline for pollutants for which specific timetables are established elsewhere in Part D. Some of Subpart 2's provisions thus override the provisions of Subpart 1. Subpart 2 classifies nonattainment areas for ozone into five classes—from Marginal through Extreme—and establishes detailed attainment deadlines for each class.

The EPA had reasoned that Subpart 2's deadlines are tied to the standard for ozone established prior to 1990, when Congress enacted Subpart 2. The agency thus concluded that Subpart 1's attainment deadlines, rather than the specific deadlines for ozone contained in Subpart 2, would apply to its revised standard. As a result, each area classified as a nonattainment zone for the new standard would have to submit a plan demonstrating how it would achieve attainment by Subpart 1's five to ten year deadline. This could pose a hardship for nonattainment areas, by forcing them to attain the new, tougher standard *even before* the specific deadlines in Subpart 2 would require them to reach attainment of the less stringent existing standard. However, this effect can be ameliorated: under Subpart 1, the EPA retains considerable flexibility to extend deadlines, whereas under Subpart 2, the timetables are specific and extensions are more limited. The EPA's strategy in adopting its implementation plan, and this understanding of Part D, were based on the idea that attainment of the new ozone standard would be achieved mostly though adopting a program to reduce emissions of nitrogen oxides that cross state lines. The Supreme Court, in the excerpt below, struggles to discern Congress' intent on the matter, focusing on whether Subpart 2 was meant to cover all areas designated as nonattainment, even those designated as nonattainment in response to a *revised* standard, or whether Subpart 2 is limited to those areas designated as nonattainment only for those standards already in effect when Congress enacted Subpart 2 in 1990. Applying *Chevron*, the Court ultimately concludes that the statute is ambiguous, but that the agency's view of Part D is unreasonable.

[The analysis of Part D above draws heavily on Craig N. Oren, *Run Over by* American Trucking *Part II: Can EPA Implement Revised Air Quality Standards?*, 30 Envtl. L. Rep. 10034 (2000).]

WHITMAN V. AMERICAN TRUCKING ASSOCIATIONS, INC.

Supreme Court of the United States, 2001.
531 U.S. 457, 121 S.Ct. 903, 149 L.Ed.2d 1.

* * *

Our approach to the merits of the parties' dispute is the familiar one of *Chevron U.S.A. Inc. v. Natural Resources Defense Council, Inc.* If the statute resolves the question whether Subpart 1 or Subpart 2 (or some combination of the two) shall apply to revised ozone NAAQS, then "that is the end of the matter." But if the statute is "silent or ambiguous" with respect to the issue, then we must defer to a "reasonable interpretation made by the administrator of an agency." We cannot agree with the Court of Appeals that Subpart 2 clearly controls the implementation of revised ozone NAAQS, because we find the statute to some extent ambiguous. We conclude, however, that the agency's interpretation goes beyond the limits of what is ambiguous and contradicts what in our view is quite clear. We therefore hold the implementation policy unlawful. * * *

So, does Subpart 2 provide for classifying nonattainment ozone areas under the revised standard? It unquestionably does. The backbone of the subpart is Table 1, * * * which defines five categories of ozone nonattainment areas and prescribes attainment deadlines for each. Section 7511(a)(1) funnels all nonattainment areas into the table for classification, declaring that "[e]ach area designated nonattainment for ozone . . . shall be classified at the time of such designation, under table 1, by operation of law." And once an area has been classified, "the primary standard attainment date for ozone shall be as expeditiously as practicable but not later than the date provided in table 1." The EPA argues that this text is not as clear or comprehensive as it seems, because the title of § 7511(a) reads "Classification and attainment dates for 1989 nonattainment areas," which suggests that Subpart 2 applies only to areas that were in nonattainment in 1989, and not to areas later designated nonattainment under a revised ozone standard. The suggestion must be rejected, however, because § 7511(b)(1) specifically provides for the classification of areas that *were* in attainment in 1989 but have subsequently slipped into nonattainment. It thus makes clear that Subpart 2 is *not* limited solely to 1989 nonattainment areas. * * *

* * * [However,] Subpart 2's method for calculating attainment dates * * * make[s] no sense for areas that are first classified under a new standard after November 15, 1990. If, for example, areas were classified in the year 2000, many of the deadlines would already have expired at the time of classification.

These gaps in Subpart 2's scheme prevent us from concluding that Congress clearly intended Subpart 2 to be the exclusive, permanent means of enforcing a revised ozone standard in nonattainment areas. The statute is in our view ambiguous concerning the manner in which Subpart 1 and Subpart 2 interact with regard to revised ozone standards, and we would defer to the EPA's reasonable resolution of that ambiguity. We cannot defer, however, to the interpretation the EPA has given.

Whatever effect may be accorded the gaps in Subpart 2 as implying some limited applicability of Subpart 1, they cannot be thought to render Subpart 2's carefully designed restrictions on EPA discretion utterly nugatory once a new standard has been promulgated, as the EPA has concluded. The principal distinction between Subpart 1 and Subpart 2 is that the latter eliminates regulatory discretion that the former allowed. While Subpart 1 permits the EPA to establish classifications for nonattainment areas, Subpart 2 classifies areas as a matter of law based on a table. * * * Whereas the EPA has discretion under Subpart 1 to extend attainment dates for as long as 12 years, under Subpart 2 it may grant no more than 2 years' extension. * * * Whereas Subpart 1 gives the EPA considerable discretion to shape nonattainment programs, Subpart 2 prescribes large parts of them by law. * * * To use a few apparent gaps in Subpart 2 to render its textually explicit applicability to nonattainment areas under the new standard utterly inoperative is to go over the edge of reasonable interpretation. The EPA may not construe the statute in a way that completely nullifies textually applicable provisions meant to limit its discretion.

The EPA's interpretation making Subpart 2 abruptly obsolete is all the more astonishing because Subpart 2 was obviously written to govern implementation for some time. Some of the elements required to be included in SIP's under Subpart 2 were not to take effect until many years after the passage of the Act. A plan reaching so far into the future was not enacted to be abandoned the next time the EPA reviewed the ozone standard—which Congress knew could happen at any time, since the technical staff papers had already been completed in late 1989. Yet nothing in the EPA's interpretation would have prevented the agency from aborting Subpart 2 the day after it was enacted. Even now, if the EPA's interpretation were correct, some areas of the country could be required to meet the new, more stringent ozone standard in *at most* the same time that Subpart 2 had allowed them to meet the old standard. Compare § 7502(a)(2) (Subpart 1 attainment dates) with § 7511(a) (Subpart 2 attainment dates). Los Angeles, for instance, "would be required to attain the revised NAAQS under Subpart 1 no later than the same year that marks the outer time limit for attaining Subpart 2's one-hour ozone standard." An interpretation of Subpart 2 so at odds with its structure and manifest purpose cannot be sustained.

We therefore find the EPA's implementation policy to be unlawful, though not in the precise respect determined by the Court of Appeals. After our remand, and the Court of Appeals' final disposition of this case, it is left to the EPA to develop a reasonable interpretation of the nonattainment implementation provisions insofar as they apply to revised ozone NAAQS.

To summarize our holdings in these unusually complex cases: (1) The EPA may not consider implementation costs in setting primary and secondary NAAQS under § 109(b) of the CAA. (2) Section 109(b)(1) does not delegate legislative power to the EPA in contravention of Art. I, § 1, of the Constitution. (3) The Court of Appeals had jurisdiction to review the EPA's interpretation of Part D of Title I of the CAA, relating to the implementation of the revised ozone NAAQS. (4) The EPA's interpretation of that Part is unreasonable.

The judgment of the Court of Appeals is affirmed in part and reversed in part, and the cases are remanded for proceedings consistent with this opinion.

It is so ordered.

NOTES

1.   Given the technical nature of the CAA, the ambiguity left by Congress on how Subparts One and Two interact in the case of revised standards, and the fact that Congress has assigned the implementation of this law to the EPA, shouldn't the Court defer to this agency's expert interpretation? Is the *Chevron* inquiry into legislative intent even sensible in

a case like this? The CAA, like other environmental statutes, simply may be "too unwieldy to receive the consideration in Congress that it requires. * * * Given the detail of the statute, it is hard to believe that anyone in Congress made a conscious decision to leave the issue unaddressed. Rather, the intricacy of the statute simply overwhelmed the legislative process." Craig N. Oren, *Run Over by American Trucking Part II,* 30 Envtl. L. Rep. 10034, 10048 (2000).

2.   Remanding the timetable for implementation to the agency is potentially more consequential than it appears on its face. While the case was pending before the Supreme Court, George W. Bush was elected President. As a result, while the original implementation plan was the product of Carol Browner's EPA under President Clinton—the EPA that had developed and promulgated the new standards—the new implementation plan fell to the new Bush Administration, whose first EPA Administrator, Christine Todd Whitman, resigned, partly in frustration with the Administration's policies. Do such personnel changes make a difference to implementation? Should they?

The final version of the 8-hour ozone standard ended up amalgamating Subparts 1 and 2, separating areas by their level of air quality under the 1-hour standard. Areas with ozone levels below the minimum covered by the classifications of Subpart 2 will be subject to the Subpart 1 deadlines, allowing them more flexibility, while those with ozone levels putting them under Subpart 2 will be categorized according to its more prescriptive designations, with corresponding deadlines. 40 C.F.R. sections 51.902–.904; *see also* Final Rule To Implement the 8-Hour Ozone National Ambient Air Quality Standard—Phase 1, Part II, 69 Fed. Reg. 23,951, 23,956–61 (Apr. 30, 2004) (explaining the rationale for choosing that regulatory scheme).

3.   The Supreme Court remanded the case to the D.C. Circuit, leaving open the possibility that the lower court might invalidate the revised standards under "arbitrary or capricious" review. The appellate court upheld the EPA's new NAAQS for ozone and fine particulate matter on remand, finding ample evidence to justify them. *See American Trucking Ass'ns, Inc.* v. *EPA,* 283 F.3d 355 (D.C. Cir. 2002).

4.   The EPA adopted a new ozone standard in 2015. It recently issued regulations giving non-attainment areas the same number of years contained in the 1990 amendments to come into attainment with the 2015 standards. *See* 83 FR 10376, 10378 (March 9, 2018). Is the agency correct in doing so given Part II of the American Trucking decision?

5. NEW SOURCE PERFORMANCE STANDARDS

Section 111 of the CAA authorizes the EPA to establish technology-based standards for new sources, which the EPA promulgates on a category-by-category basis. Examples include petroleum refineries, asphalt and concrete plants, sewage treatment plants, and synthetic organic chemicals manufacturing operations. These standards apply to all new sources, defined as any source built or modified after the EPA promulgates the standard applicable to that type of source. Modification is defined in § 111(a)(4) as any "physical change in, or change in the method of operation of, a stationary source which increases the amount of any air pollutant emitted by such source or which results in the emission of any air pollutant not previously emitted." The technology-based standard the EPA must use is the "degree of emission limitation achievable through the application of the best system of emission reduction which (taking into account the cost * * *) * * * has been adequately demonstrated" [BDAT] [§ 111 (a)(1)]. The emission limits themselves are generally expressed as concentrations or emission rates. These standards are not limited to major facilities. They represent the basic, minimum controls imposed on all new sources, regardless of whether they are major or not, and regardless of where they are located. However, some new source standards might not be terribly stringent because they were set by the EPA years ago, when technology was not as effective at controlling emissions as it is today.

As with the PSD provisions, the NSPS provisions apply to sources that emit "any air pollutant." CAA Sec. 111(3), 42 U.S.C. Sec 7411(3). Even more importantly, Section 111(d) requires the Administrator to establish regulations for *existing sources* for the emission of pollutants that are not criteria or hazardous air pollutants. States must develop plans similar to SIPS to regulate such existing sources. These provisions have huge implications for the regulation of greenhouse gases, as we describe below.

6. NEW SOURCE REVIEW[3]

New Source Review (NSR) refers to pre-construction review and permitting for all new or modified major stationary sources in PSD and nonattainment areas. As described above, Section 165 requires preconstruction permits for new and modified sources in PSD areas. Section 173 of the Act requires permits for "new or modified major stationary sources" in all nonattainment areas. The EPA has provided detailed rules for implementing this requirement. 40 C.F.R. §§ 51.160–51.166 Although NSR is not explicitly required by the Act for PSD areas, the EPA has required it as part of its overall scheme for maintaining air quality. 40 C.F.R. §§ 52.21–52.24. Ideally, NSR provides for the installation of pollution controls in new facilities as they are constructed, and also in facilities predating the Act, which were "grandfathered" in without any initial technology requirement, as they modernize their equipment. Thus any new or modified sources in both attainment and non-attainment areas require NSR, though the standard for the technology that must be installed is more stringent in non-attainment areas.

[3]   We are grateful to Peter Wyckoff, Counsel, Pillsbury Winthrop Shaw Pittman for generously sharing his insights on the NSR program.

a. What Does NSR Require?

If a source triggers NSR, it must comply with certain technology-based standards—for PSD areas, the best available control technology (BACT), and for nonattainment areas, the lowest achievable emissions rate (LAER). The permitting authority decides on a case-by-case basis what control technology these standards demand. The mandated "top-down" BACT analysis, a fairly rigorous test, requires the permittee to rank available ("demonstrated") technologies and use the most stringent choice unless it can convince the permitting authority that "technical considerations, or energy, environmental, or economic impacts justify a conclusion that the most stringent technology is not 'achievable' in that case." ROBERT J. MARTINEAU, JR. & DAVID P. NOVELLO, THE CLEAN AIR ACT HANDBOOK 157–58 (2d ed. 2004).

Additionally, a PSD source undergoing NSR must perform an "air quality impacts analysis" showing that its new emissions, along with other emissions from the source, will not significantly impact ambient air quality. For criteria pollutants, this requires a demonstration that the emissions will not cause or contribute to violation of any relevant NAAQS or PSD increment. 40 C.F.R. § 51, app. W. The demonstration must utilize dispersion modeling, a computer modeling method that is notoriously poor; yet here serves as the basis for important decisions about environmental controls and economic growth.

Other than the different technology required by NSR, and the definition of major source (discussed below), there are only a few differences between NSR in PSD and nonattainment areas. The other pertinent distinctions are the pollutants covered (nonattainment NSR focuses on criteria pollutants whereas PSD covers "any air pollutant") and the increase thresholds for triggering NSR. Rolf R. von Oppenfeld et al., *A Primer on New Source Review and Strategies for Success,* 32 Envtl. L. Rep. 11091 (2002).

b. Triggering NSR

i. *"Major Stationary Source"*

The default definition of "major stationary sources," in § 302(j), is any source that emits or has the potential to emit 100 tons or more per year of any air pollutant regulated under the Act. A major source for PSD areas is one from a specified list of source categories that has the potential to emit 100 tons per year of a pollutant covered by the Act, any source with the potential to emit 250 tons per year of a regulated pollutant, or an otherwise non-major source undergoing a physical change where the change will by itself increase the potential to emit enough to satisfy the definition of major source (*e.g.,* a plant emitting 90 tons per year of sulfur dioxide that plans to make a change that will increase its potential to emit sulfur dioxide by

260 tons per year). 40 C.F.R. § 51.21(b)(1). In nonattainment zones, the threshold for a major source varies with the severity of nonattainment—not surprisingly, the more out of attainment an area is, the lower the threshold for the definition of major source. For example, a major source in a serious nonattainment area is one that emits, or has the potential to emit, at least 70 tons per year of PM 10, 42 U.S.C. § 7513(b)(3) and 50 tons per year for volatile organic compounds, 42 U.S.C. § 7511a(c). A list of the thresholds for major source in nonattainment areas by pollutant can be found at 40 C.F.R. § 51.165(a)(iv)(A), http://www.ecfr.gov/cgi-bin/text-idx?c=ecfr&sid=5f2b25d1de7e11a0da1dbe1ebd0ce9a1&rgn=div8&view=text&node=40:2.0.1.1.2.6.8.6&idno=40. As with PSD areas, a source undergoing modification qualifies if the potential to emit from the physical change would itself exceed the emissions limit for a major source. *See* CAA §§ 182, 187, 189.

A source may avoid qualifying as major by accepting enforceable limits on its potential to emit that keep it under the PSD major source threshold. One ongoing debate has been whether those limits must be legally federally enforceable to constitute a valid cap; the regulation states that in calculating a source's potential to emit "under its physical and operational design," an emissions limitation "shall be treated as part of its design if the limitation or the effect it would have on emissions is federally enforceable." 40 C.F.R. §§ 51.165, 52.21. Traditionally, this meant the restriction had to be contained in a permit issued under a federal program, but that requirement was rejected by the D.C. Circuit in 1995. Chemical Mfrs. Ass'n v. EPA, 70 F.3d 637 (D.C. Cir. 1995) (mem.) (vacating the EPA regulations based on National Mining Ass'n v. EPA, 59 F.3d 1351 (D.C. Cir. 1995)). Subsequently, the EPA has interpreted "federally enforceable" to mean only that the limit must be "enforceable as a practical matter," with the permit including provisions for monitoring, record-keeping, and reporting so as to allow the EPA to verify compliance. Prevention of Significant Deterioration (PSD) and Nonattainment New Source Review (NSR), 67 Fed. Reg. 80,186, 80,190–91 (Dec. 31, 2002). Even so, this mechanism requires a certain sacrifice of flexibility by a permittee, and may be less desirable than avoiding the application of NSR altogether.

ii. "Modified Source"

Because of the burdensome requirements imposed on a source once it falls under NSR, there has been an extended and heated debate regarding almost every ambiguity in the CAA's dictates. The most contested of these questions has been about what constitutes a "modified source." The Act defines modification as "any physical change in, or change in the method of operation of, a stationary source which increases the amount of any air pollutant emitted by such source or which results in the emission of any air pollutant not previously emitted." § 111(a)(4). The EPA's major task has been to elucidate the meaning of "any physical change . . . or change in the method of operation." Since Congress did not intend for every single change in a major source to engage the cumbersome machinery of NSR, the EPA has adopted several exclusions from the domain of changes that would trigger NSR. These exceptions include: Routine Maintenance, Repair, and Replacement (RMRR); an increase in hours of operation or in production rate; and Plantwide Applicability Limits (exempting sources from NSR as long as they stay below a certain cap on facility emissions). 40 C.F.R. § 52.21. In addition, the EPA has determined that a change does not qualify as a modification for the purposes of NSR unless it triggers a "significant" emissions increase, qualifying as a "major modification."

Since firms are understandably eager to take advantage of these exclusions and avoid the onerous emissions limitations that come with NSR, not to mention the administrative delays and expenses of the process itself, the details of their implementation play a large role in shaping the application of NSR. The most contentious debate has been centered around the definition of the "significant increase" and "routine maintenance, repair, and replacement" provisions.

This debate is complicated by the fact that much of the old, polluting equipment at issue has lasted far longer than anyone predicted when clean air regulation began. For the history of Clean Air Act grandfathering and a powerful critique, *see* RICHARD REVESZ AND JACK LIENKE, STRUGGLING FOR AIR: POWER PLANTS AND THE WAR ON COAL (2016).

Given the complexity of NSR, isn't there a simpler way to address the problem of grandfathered facilities? Is this really something that the EPA should be managing by rulemaking or by settlements with large emitters? The latter appear to be increasingly popular but they are relatively low-visibility mechanisms for making policy. Should Congress step in to make decisions of this magnitude?

iii. The Interaction of NSPS and NSR

One might reasonably ask what role NSPS standards play, since all "new" sources (whether in PSD areas or non-attainment zones) must go through New Source Review. Why have both NSPS and the BACT or LAER standards for PSD and nonattainment?

First, NSPS, like the MACT standards for hazardous air pollutants, are the result of an intensive examination by agency and consultant engineers of particular classes of equipment, focusing on stack and fugitive emissions, available controls, costs, and alternative compliance regimes (which have made quantum leaps in recent years with continuous emissions monitoring). Essentially, these standards are detailed equipment-specific blueprints of "Good Air Pollution Control Management"—what engineers would consider sensible air pollution control measures or "good housekeeping" for particular pieces of equipment. Compared to the approach in setting BACT standards under the PSD provisions, the NSPS approach is very specific and tailored to specific equipment, and it incorporates state-of-the-art monitoring requirements. By contrast, BACT standards are the product of a dialogue between the permit applicant and the (usually state) government; the resources spent on BACT standards are a fraction of those devoted by the EPA to NSPS and MACT standards. And BACT standards tend to focus only on emission limits rather than the most advanced compliance and monitoring regimes. In short, BACT standards piggy-back on the work done in setting NSPS and MACT standards.

Second, the rules for PSD/NSR are different than those for NSPS: they allow more "netting out" of review. NSPS focuses on new or modified "affected facilities" which essentially covers discrete emitting units, and there is no de minimus threshold for calculating what counts as a "modification." By contrast, PSD/NSR is plantwide, offering opportunities to "minor" or "net" out of review, and there are appreciable "significance" thresholds for the determination of what counts as modification. It is possible then, for a new piece of equipment—a mid-sized boiler, say—to escape PSD/NSR and yet still be covered by the NSPS standards. NSPS thus serves as a backstop to PSD/NSR.

7.   TITLE V PERMITS

Prior to the 1990 Amendments, a variety of provisions of the CAA required some stationary sources to obtain a permit. For example, new major stationary sources in both NAZ (§ 173) and PSD areas (§ 165) had to obtain pre-construction permits. Sometimes, sources had to comply with the permit requirements under both of these provisions. This is because no area of the country is out of attainment for all six NAAQS. This means that stationary sources that are in nonattainment zones for one pollutant will by definition be in PSD areas for other pollutants (recall that an area of the country that is *in* attainment for a criteria pollutant is subject to the Act's PSD requirements designed to prevent deterioration of air quality below levels set by NAAQS). Thus, prior to 1990, many sources already had to comply with the permit requirements of *both* the NAZ and the PSD programs. In addition, prior to 1990, some states, such as California, had already adopted a general permit program. For example, California's South Coast Air Quality Management District (SCAQMD) already required operating permits for any equipment that may emit air contaminants (which are defined very broadly). This rule did not establish a threshold of a minimum quantity of emissions.

However, Title V of the 1990 Amendments added an entirely new and more comprehensive permit program to the CAA. The program applies to all major sources [as defined under various provisions of the CAA, including the air toxics provisions (§ 112), and the NAZ provisions (§§ 171–193) and those sources that fit the default definition of major stationary source and major emitting facility in § 302(j)]. Permits also apply to all "affected" sources as defined in Title IV's acid rain provisions; all sources subject to § 111 NSPS; all sources of air toxics regulated under § 112 (including area sources); all sources required to have permits under the PSD and nonattainment provisions of Titles C and D; and any other sources designated by EPA regulations as requiring a permit. Clearly, almost every stationary source regulated under one or another CAA provision will be included in the Title V requirements. Permits contain enforceable emission limits and impose monitoring requirements on permit holders [§§ 504(a) and (b)]. All permitted sources must pay substantial permit fees as well (§ 502). Compliance with the requirements of a Title V permit is deemed to be compliance with the CAA [§ 504(f)].

Title V is administered by the states, which had to amend their SIPs to establish a permit program. The EPA promulgated the rules implementing the Title V permit program in 1992. The rules specify what state permit programs must contain. State-issued permits must incorporate terms and conditions to assure compliance with "applicable requirements under the Act" and impose monitoring and record-keeping requirements on permit-holders, among other things.

Title V has been widely touted as a means of streamlining air quality regulation for individual sources by placing all applicable requirements into a single permit. It was also thought that a general permit requirement would make compliance information more accessible to the public. In theory, the permit requirement is a procedural change, not a substantive one. However, because permits can translate general requirements into detailed and rigid specifications, they may reduce the flexibility of sources to make changes in operations that affect emissions. In addition, for thousands of stationary sources that previously had no obligation to obtain a permit, the permitting process itself can be onerous and costly. Perhaps most significantly, the new monitoring requirements imposed on stationary sources as part of the Title V permit program enable the EPA to press for more stringent monitoring, which, "in effect, cause the underlying emissions control requirements to become more stringent." The new reporting requirements may also make sources more vulnerable to citizen suits. *See* Ivan Tether and Robert S. Nicksin, *New Frontiers for the Push and Pull of Federalism—Implementation of the Clean Air Act's Operating Permit Program in Southern California*, 29 Envtl. L. Rep. 10757, 10763 (1999). That new susceptibility to citizen suits was partially confirmed and partially diluted in *New York Public Interest Research Group v. Johnson*, where the Second Circuit held that the EPA must issue a notice of violation to a plant that the state environmental agency had found to be in violation of Title V, but affirmed the state and federal agencies' previously recognized discretion in using their expertise to decide whether such a violation has in fact occurred. 427 F.3d 172 (2d Cir. 2005) (citing *New York Pub. Interest Research Group v. Whitman*, 321 F.3d 316 (2d Cir. 2003), for the proposition that the agency retains discretion in determining non-compliance).

Electric power companies and industry trade associations scored a victory on this issue, when the D.C. Circuit set aside the EPA's 1998 guidance document directing state permitting authorities to conduct wide-ranging sufficiency reviews and to enhance the monitoring required in individual permits beyond that contained in state or federal emissions standards, where states found existing monitoring requirements inadequate. The Court reasoned that the guidance documents effectively broadened the EPA's underlying rule requiring only periodic monitoring, which the agency could not do without going through the required rulemaking procedure. *See* Appalachian Power Co. v. EPA, 208 F.3d 1015 (D.C. Cir. 2000). The EPA began to promulgate just such a rule in 2002, but then suddenly reversed itself in the final rule, adopting the position that states may not impose requirements beyond the minimum periodic monitoring necessary to confirm a source's compliance with permit requirements. However, the D.C. Circuit found that the EPA's "flip-flop" had not allowed proper notice and opportunity for public comment on this interpretation, and thus vacated the rule. *Environmental Integrity Project v. EPA*, 425 F.3d 992, 997 (D.C. Cir. 2005).

Prior to the adoption of Title V, clean air regulation differed from clean water regulation because under the permit system of water quality, only permitted discharges were allowed, while under clean air regulation, emissions were generally allowed unless specifically prohibited by rules and regulations. Title V thus adopts the "only if permitted" model from the clean water context. See Chapter 7.

E. MOBILE SOURCE, SPILLOVERS AND OTHER SPECIAL PROVISIONS OF THE CLEAN AIR ACT

1. MOBILE SOURCES

Along with stationary sources, mobile sources are the other major cause of air pollution. Motor vehicles are responsible for up to half of the VOCs and nitrogen oxides that form smog, and they produce more than half of all air toxics. In addition, motor vehicles produce up to 90 percent of the carbon monoxide in the urban air. Cars were also the primary source of lead emissions until lead was phased out of gasoline in accordance with § 211(n) of the Act. Motor vehicles pose different problems than do stationary sources because of their vastly greater numbers, and because they cross the borders of states and air regions alike.

The Act regulates mobile sources primarily by requiring standards for tailpipe emissions (which targets the auto industry rather than individual car owners) and by regulating fuels to make them cleaner. As described in *Massachusetts v. EPA*, page 530, *infra,* Section 202(a)(1) requires the EPA to promulgate regulations prescribing emission standards "applicable to the emission of any air pollutant from any class or classes of new motor vehicles or new motor vehicle engines which in [the EPA's] judgment cause or contribute to air pollution which may reasonably be anticipated to endanger public health or welfare." These emission standards apply for the "useful life" of the vehicle, which is defined in the 1990 Amendments to be ten years or 100,000 miles, whichever comes first. [§ 202(d)(1)]. The EPA has promulgated separate standards for different classes of vehicles, including passenger vehicles, light duty trucks, heavy duty vehicles and motorcycles. *See* 40 C.F.R. part 86.

Congress has reserved for the federal government the primary role in setting tailpipe emissions standards, leaving a secondary role to the EPA and pre-empting the states (with the exception of California) from setting more stringent standards. Section 209 of the CAA reserves to the federal government exclusive authority to regulate motor vehicle emissions but specifically allows California to adopt its own standards if California determines that its standards will be no less protective of the public health than the federal standards and if the state applies for a waiver from the EPA. States may adopt these standards under § 177, providing they are "identical" to California's. In addition, SIPs may contain a variety of transportation controls and inspection and maintenance programs, which more directly affect vehicle owners, though Congress has curtailed these measures over the years because they are politically contentious and difficult to implement.

Pollution from cars has improved tremendously in the last 30 years. Today's cars produce 99 percent less pollution than cars in the 1960s, and leaded gas has been phased out entirely. The progress is all the more impressive because air pollution has declined even as the number of car miles and car trips per person have gone up dramatically. In 1970, Americans traveled 1 trillion miles in motor vehicles (known as VMTs for vehicle miles travelled). By 2018 that number exceeded 3 trillion miles. For a chart depicting VMTs for the past 40 years and year-to-year changes, *see* U.S. Department of Energy, Energy Efficiency & Renewable Energy, Alternative Fuels Data Center, *Maps and Data—Annual Vehicle Miles Traveled in the U.S.*, https://afdc.energy.gov/data/.

a. History of Mobile Source Provisions

Section 202 of the 1970 Amendments to the Act originally required auto makers to reduce emissions of hydrocarbons and carbon monoxide 90% from average emissions for model year 1970. The new standard was to be effective for model year 1975. Congress also required auto makers to reduce nitrogen oxide emissions in the 1976 models 90% from average emissions in 1971 models. Perhaps surprisingly, these rather dramatic reductions were not calculated based on scientific data. Nor were they based on economic analysis nor on an assessment of technological feasibility. Rather, they were based on the assumption that since air pollution concentrations exceeded NAAQS by five times in the most polluted areas, tailpipe emissions should be reduced by 80% (plus 10% because of increased vehicle use), and this would make air quality sufficiently safe. *See* JAMES E. KRIER & EDMUND URSIN, POLLUTION AND POLICY: A CASE ESSAY ON CALIFORNIA AND FEDERAL EXPERIENCE WITH MOTOR VEHICLE AIR POLLUTION, 1940–1975 at pp. 206–7 (1977).

Congress knew when it passed these mandatory emissions reductions that they would be "technology-forcing." Yet although Congress itself set the 90 per cent reduction, it delegated to the EPA the task of translating that mandate into an emissions standard expressed in terms of "grams per mile" for each of the regulated pollutants. To do this, the EPA had to calculate the baseline average emissions of model year 1971, then reduce that figure by 90 percent as required by the Act. For example, the EPA calculated the 1970 baseline for hydrocarbons as 4.1 grams per mile and subsequently required auto makers to reduce it to .41 grams per mile by 1975. Section 202 also provided that the EPA could grant a one-year non-renewable waiver under certain conditions, including that the manufacturer had made "all good efforts" to achieve the standards. The auto manufacturers sought a waiver in 1972, anticipating that they would not be able to meet the new standards because the technology to do so did not yet exist. The EPA denied the waiver, and the D.C. Circuit reviewed the denial in the case below.

INTERNATIONAL HARVESTER CO. V. RUCKELSHAUS

United States Court of Appeals, District of Columbia Circuit, 1973.
478 F.2d 615.

LEVENTHAL, CIRCUIT JUDGE.

The tension of forces presented by the controversy over automobile emission standards may be focused by two central observations:

(1) The automobile is an essential pillar of the American economy. Some 28 percent of the nonfarm workforce draws its livelihood from the automobile industry and its products.

(2) The automobile has had a devastating impact on the American environment. As of 1970, authoritative voices stated that "[a]utomotive pollution constitutes in excess of 60% of our national air pollution problem" and more than 80 percent of the air pollutants in concentrated urban areas.
* * *

On December 31, 1970, Congress grasped the nettle and amended the Clean Air Act to set a statutory standard for required reductions in levels of hydrocarbons (HC) and carbon monoxide (CO) which must be achieved for 1975 models of light duty vehicles. Section 202(b) of the Act added by the Clean Air Amendments of 1970, provides that, beginning with the 1975 model year, exhaust emission of hydrocarbons and carbon monoxide from "light duty vehicles" must be reduced at least 90 percent from the permissible emission levels in the 1970 model year. * * *

Congress was aware that these 1975 standards were "drastic medicine," designed to "force the state of the art." There was, naturally, concern whether the manufacturers would be able to achieve this goal. Therefore, Congress provided, in Senator Baker's phrase, a "realistic escape hatch"; the manufacturers could petition the Administrator of the EPA for a one-year suspension of the 1975 requirements, and Congress took the precaution of directing the National Academy of Sciences to undertake an ongoing study of the feasibility of compliance with the emission standards. * * * Under section 202(b)(5)(D) of the Act, the Administrator is authorized to grant a one-year suspension only if he determines that (i) such suspension is essential to the public interest or the public health and welfare of the United States, (ii) all good faith efforts have been made to meet the standards established by this subsection, (iii) the applicant has established that effective control technology, processes, operating methods, or other alternatives are not available or have not been available for a sufficient period of time to achieve compliance prior to the effective date of such standards, and (iv) the study and investigation of the National Academy of Sciences conducted pursuant to subsection (c) of this section and other information available to him has not indicated that technology, processes, or other alternatives are available to meet such standards. * * *

At the outset of his Decision, the Administrator determined that the most effective system so far developed was the noble metal oxidizing catalyst. * * *

[At that point tests of cars using catalytic converter technology had shown only one model that achieved the necessary standard. The Administrator alleged, however, that the test data did not fully reflect the variables that would determine real-world auto emissions, and that given certain adjustments of the data based on predictions about future real-world conditions such as changes in fuel composition, calculations of the effect of equipment deterioration, regulatory requirements for catalyst replacement, and other variables, 1975 models would in fact be able to achieve the mandated emissions reductions.]

With the data submitted and the above assumptions, the Administrator concluded that no showing had been made that requisite technology was not available. The EPA noted that this did not mean that the variety of vehicles produced in 1975 would be as extensive as before. According to EPA, "Congress clearly intended to require major changes in the kinds of automobiles produced for sale in the United States after 1974" and there "is no basis, therefore, for construing the Act to authorizing suspension of the standards simply because the range of performance of cars with effective emission control may be restricted as compared to present cars." As long as "basic demand" for new light duty motor vehicles was satisfied, the applicants could not establish that technology was not available. * * *

["While the case was on appeal, the National Academy of Sciences (NAS) completed a report on the issue pursuant to its obligation under section 202(b)(5)(D) of the Clean Air Act, and concluded that "the technology necessary to meet the requirements of the Clean Air Act Amendments . . . is not available at this time." After the report had been issued, the court remanded the case to allow EPA to comment on it.]

The Administrator apparently relied, however, on the report to bolster his conclusion that the applicants had not established that technology was unavailable. The same NAS Report had stated:

> * * * the status of development and rate of progress made it possible that the larger manufacturers will be able to produce vehicles that will qualify, provided that provisions are made for catalyst replacement and other maintenance, for averaging emissions of production vehicles, and for the general availability of fuel containing suitably low levels of catalyst poisons.

The Administrator pointed out that two of NAS's provisos—catalytic converter replacement and low lead levels—had been accounted for in his analysis of the auto company data, and provision therefore had been insured through regulation. * * *

The most authoritative estimate in the record of the ecological costs of a one-year suspension is that of the NAS Report. Taking into account such "factors as the vehicle-age distribution among all automobiles, the decrease in vehicle miles driven per year, per car as vehicle age increases, the predicted nationwide growth in vehicle miles driven each year" and the effect of emission standards on exhaust control, NAS concluded that:

> * * * the effect on total emissions of a one-year suspension with no additional interim standards appears to be small. The effect is not more significant because the emission reduction now required of model year 1974 vehicles, as compared with uncontrolled vehicles (80 percent for HC and 69 percent for CO), is already so substantial. * * *

On balance the record indicates the environmental costs of a one-year suspension are likely to be relatively modest. This must be balanced against the potential economic costs—and ecological costs—if the Administrator's prediction on the availability of effective technology is incorrect. * * *

If in 1974, when model year 1975 cars start to come off the production line, the automobiles of Ford, General Motors and Chrysler cannot meet the 1975 standards and do not qualify for certification, the Administrator of EPA has the theoretical authority, under the Clean Air Act, to shut down the auto industry, as was clearly recognized in congressional debate. We cannot put blinders on the facts before us so as to omit awareness of the reality that this authority would undoubtedly never be exercised. [More realistically, the court said, the standards would be later relaxed if they turned out to be wrong, but this too would cause problems.]

* * * The record before us suggests that there already exists a technological gap between Ford and General Motors, in Ford's favor. General Motors did not make the decision to concentrate on what EPA found to be the most effective system at the time of its decision—the noble metal monolithic catalyst. Instead it relied principally on testing the base metal catalyst as its first choice system. * * *

The case is haunted by the irony that what seems to be Ford's technological lead may operate to its grievous detriment, assuming the relaxation-if-necessary approach * * *. If in 1974, when certification of production vehicles begins, any one of the three major companies cannot meet the 1975 standards, it is a likelihood that standards will be set to permit the higher level of emission control achievable by the laggard. This will be the case whether or not the leader has or has not achieved compliance with the 1975 standards. Even if the relaxation is later made industry-wide, the Government's action, in first imposing a standard not generally achievable and then relaxing it, is likely to be detrimental to the leader who has tooled up to meet a higher standard than will ultimately be required.

In some contexts high achievement bestows the advantage that rightly belongs to the leader of high quality. In this context before us, however, the high achievement in emission control results, under systems presently available, in lessened car performance—an inverse correlation. The competitive disadvantage to the ecological leader presents a forbidding outcome—if the initial assumption of feasibility is not validated, and there is subsequent relaxation—for which we see no remedy. * * *

This case inevitably presents, to the court as to the Administrator, the need for a perspective on the suspension that is informed by an analysis which balances the costs of a "wrong decision" on feasibility against the gains of a correct one. These costs include the risks of grave maladjustments for the technological leader from the eleventh-hour grant of a suspension, and the impact on jobs and the economy from a decision which is only partially accurate, allowing companies to produce cars but at a significantly reduced level of output. Against this must be weighed the environmental savings from denial of suspension. The record indicates that these will be relatively modest. * * *

Another consideration is present, that the real cost to granting a suspension arises from the symbolic compromise with the goal of a clean environment. We emphasize that our view of a one-year suspension, and the intent of Congress as to a one-year suspension, is in no sense to be taken as any support for further suspensions. This would plainly be contrary to the intent of Congress to set an absolute standard in 1976. * * *

We approach the question of the burden of proof on the auto companies with the previous considerations before us.

It is with utmost diffidence that we approach our assignment to review the Administrator's decision on "available technology." The legal issues are intermeshed with technical matters, and as yet judges have no scientific aides. Our diffidence is rooted in the underlying technical complexities, and remains even when we take into account that ours is a judicial review, and not a technical or policy redetermination. * * *

The Act makes suspension dependent on the Administrator's determination that:

> the applicant has established that effective control technology, processes, operating methods, or other alternatives are not available or have not been available for a sufficient period of time to achieve compliance prior to the effective date of such standards * * *.

Clearly this requires that the applicants come forward with data which showed that they could not comply with the contemplated standards. The normal rules place such a burden on the party in control of the relevant information. It was the auto companies who were in possession of the data about emission performance of their cars.

The submission of the auto companies unquestionably showed that no car had actually been driven 50,000 miles and achieved conformity of emissions to the 1975 standards. The Administrator's position is that on the basis of the methodology outlined, he can predict that the auto companies can meet the standards, and that the ability to make a prediction saying the companies can comply means that the petitioners have failed to sustain their burden of proof that they cannot comply. * * *

The number of unexplained assumptions used by the Administrator, the variance in methodology from that of the Report of the National Academy of Sciences, and the absence of an indication of the statistical reliability of the prediction, combine to generate grave doubts as to whether technology is available to meet the 1975 statutory standards. We say this, incidentally, without implying or intending any acceptance of petitioners' substitute assumptions. These grave doubts have a legal consequence. This is customarily couched, by legal convention, in terms of "burden of proof." We visualize the problem in less structured terms although the underlying considerations, relating to risk of error, are related. As we see it the issue must be viewed as one of legislative intent. And since there is neither express wording nor legislative history on the precise issue, the intent must be imputed. The court must seek to discern and reconstruct what the legislature that enacted the statute would have contemplated for the court's action if it could have been able to foresee the precise situation. It is in this perspective that we have not flinched from our discussion of the economic and ecological risks inherent in a "wrong decision" by the Administrator. We think the vehicle manufacturers established by a preponderance of the evidence, in the record before us, that technology was not available, within the meaning of the Act, when they adduced the tests on actual vehicles; that the Administrator's reliance on technological methodology to offset the actual tests raised serious doubts and failed to meet the burden of proof which in our view was properly assignable to him, in the light of accepted legal doctrine and the intent of Congress discerned, in part, by taking into account that the risk of an "erroneous" denial of suspension outweighed the risk of an "erroneous" grant of suspension. We do not use the burden of proof in the conventional sense of civil trials, but the Administrator must sustain the burden of adducing a reasoned presentation supporting the reliability of EPA's methodology. * * *

[T]he parties should have opportunity on remand to address themselves to matters not previously put before them by EPA for comment * * *.

[Meanwhile] the Administrator may consider possible use of interim standards short of complete suspension. The statute permits conditioning of suspension on the adoption, by virtue of the information adduced in the suspension proceeding, of interim standards, higher than those set for 1974.

NOTES

1.   For an argument that the court's decision in *International Harvester* flouted the statutory mandate, *see* Daniel Farber, *Statutory Interpretation and Legislative Supremacy*, 78 GEO. L.J. 281, 298–300 (1989).

2.   *International Harvester* turned out to be only the first of a series of delays in meeting new car standards. On remand in *International Harvester,* the Administrator granted the suspension and imposed interim emission standards more lenient than the ninety percent reduction, although allowing California to impose a more rigorous standard. In 1974 Congress amended the

Act to postpone the final compliance deadlines until 1977, with another "escape hatch" to 1978. In 1975 the Administrator granted another one year suspension. In the 1977 Clean Air Act Amendments, Congress postponed final compliance until 1981, with provision for reductions in the interim and for limited opportunities to obtain additional waivers. *See* James A. Henderson, Jr. & Richard N. Pearson, *Implementing Federal Environmental Policies: The Limits of Aspirational Commands*, 78 COLUM. L. REV. 1429, 1447 (1978). The 1981 standards were also the subject of waivers given to "financially troubled" automakers. *See* 12 Env't Rep. (BNA) 1398 (1981). Car makers did, eventually, meet the standards, though not on the timetable Congress originally specified.

3.   Suppose the court of appeals had allowed the EPA to deny the suspension; what options would Congress have had if it appeared the industry could not meet the standards on time? What remedial options would Congress have that are not available to a court?

4.   Is the following a fair assessment of Judge Leventhal's opinion: The statutory requirement to reduce auto emissions 90 percent, read literally, is a "rule" rather than a "goal." However, when this provision is read as if it were conditioned by the express commitment of Congress to amend the requirements if the manufacturers make a real effort to comply, the section does not constitute a strict rule, but instead a flexible goal. There was no congressional intention to apply the 90 percent requirement in the future; Congress was not about to shut down Detroit and had not concluded that accomplishing the 90 per cent reduction was feasible. For these very reasons, the leading judicial interpretation of the 90 per cent requirement dealt with the requirement primarily as a question of policy rather than one of rule interpretation. *See* David Schoenbrod, *Goals Statutes or Rules Statutes: The Case of the Clean Air Act*, 30 UCLA L. REV. 740, 786 (1983).

5.   The 90 percent emission reduction requirement imposed by the 1970 Clean Air Act was an example of "technology forcing" standards, that is, standards that can be met only through development of new technology not in existence at the time the standards are prescribed. Note that the vehicle manufacturers applied for suspensions at almost the earliest possible date (early in 1972), and that the EPA Administrator found against them on all four statutory points except the one concerning "good faith efforts" to meet the standard. In retrospect, wasn't it inevitable, given the language of the statute, that the companies would not meet the 1975 deadline and that either Congress, the Administrator or the court would forgive them? *See* James A. Henderson & Richard N. Pearson, *Implementing Federal Environmental Policies: The Limits of Aspirational Commands*, 78 COLUM. L. REV. 1429, 1445–1453 (1978). What does this say about how realistic Congress tends to be when it passes environmental statutes? Is Congress aware that its laws will be partially implemented, and that, routinely, statutory deadlines will be missed? If Congress is aware of this and continues to set ambitious legislative goals, are members of Congress just not so smart? Or might there be a method to their madness? Why doesn't Congress worry that it will be blamed by the public for passing ineffective laws?

In a more recent attempt at technology-forcing, the EPA, following its duty under CAA section 129(a)(3) to promulgate standards that "reflect the greatest degree of emission reduction achievable" based on the Administrator's projection of what cost-effective technology will be available in the future, issued a rule drastically reducing standards for emissions from diesel engines beginning in 2007. 66 Fed. Reg. 5002 (Jan. 18, 2001). Hearing an industry challenge to the EPA's prediction, the D.C. Circuit upheld all of the standards, finding that the EPA had successfully "identif[ied] the major steps for improvement and give[n] plausible reasons for its belief that the industry will be able to solve those problems in the time remaining," and was not obliged to "provide detailed solutions to every engineering problem." National Petrochemical & Refiners Ass'n v. EPA, 287 F.3d 1130 (D.C. Cir. 2002). Compare the EPA's role here (determining what technology will be available and setting emissions requirements accordingly) versus in *International Harvester* (where Congress had already set the standards, and the agency only decided whether industry would get an extra year to comply). Which method seems best suited to force industry to utilize new emissions-control technology: when Congress puts its foot down and mandates reductions no matter what, or when the agency uses its expert knowledge to judge when technologies are feasible enough to require their implementation? Does either of these mechanisms seem likely to induce the adoption of technology that is expensive but achieves significant emissions reductions? Do you think industry would adopt new technologies as they became available without being required to by the EPA? Would a positive incentive (e.g. research subsidies, tax breaks for environmentally-friendly products) be more efficient in influencing manufacturers' behavior?

The 1990 Amendments to the Clean Air Act added extensive new provisions relating to mobile sources and imposing even stricter standards for new cars: .25 g/m for hydrocarbons; 3.4 g/m of carbon monoxide and .4 g/m of nitrogen dioxide. Manufacturers could phase in the new standards: 40 per cent of the 1994 cars were required to meet this standard; 80 per cent of 1995 cars were required to meet it, and 100 per cent had to comply thereafter. The EPA has since updated these standards twice, as required by CAA section 202(g)(1). The agency's current program is known as the "Tier 3" program, and requires fleet averages to meet strict emissions standards that are implemented gradually from 2017 to 2025. The standards apply to passenger cars, light and medium duty trucks and some heavy duty trucks and treat the vehicle and the fuel as one integrated system. *See* U.S. Environmental Protection Agency, *Final Rule for Control of Air Pollution from Motor Vehicles: Tier 3 Motor Vehicle Emission and Fuel* Standards, https://www.epa.gov/regulations-emissions-vehicles-and-engines/final-rule-control-air-pollution-motor-vehicles-tier-3. The emphasis on mobile source regulation partly stems from the recognition that the transportation sector offers the opportunity for relatively manageable emissions cuts, compared to the economic costs of squeezing more reductions out of already heavily-regulated stationary sources. Henry A. Waxman et al., *Cars, Fuels, and Clean Air: A Review of Title II of the*

Clean Air Act Amendments of 1990, 21 ENVTL. L. 1947, 1950 (1991). Mobile sources are also the leading source of air pollution in many urban areas.

b. California's Special Status in Emissions Regulation

The 1990 Amendments left intact California's special status to impose tighter emissions standards. Many states have adopted California's standards, and the auto industry regularly launches a legal challenge to try and prevent it. In one instance, a majority of states comprising the "ozone transport commission" (a commission of mid-Atlantic and Northeastern states established under § 184 to address interstate migration of ozone) sought uniform adoption of the California standards regionally. The EPA promulgated a rule mandating that 12 states and the District of Columbia adopt the California standards. *See* 60 Fed. Reg. 4712 (Jan. 24, 1995). In *Virginia v. EPA*, 108 F.3d 1397 (D.C. Cir. 1997), the D.C. Circuit struck down the rule. The Court held that the EPA has no authority under § 110 (the SIP provision of the Act) to *require* adoption of particular control measures such as California's auto emission standards. However, states can still adopt them voluntarily. Complex negotiations followed, involving California, the Northeastern states, and the EPA. The result was an agreement that substantially harmonized the California and national requirements, arguably allowing the EPA to partially leapfrog the pre-2004 statutory freeze on new national standards mandated by the 1990 amendments to the Act. *See* 62 Fed. Reg. 31,192 (June 6, 1997).

California also instituted an ambitious Low Emissions Vehicle (LEV) program that has been plagued by delays and controversy. The program had required 2 per cent of all new vehicles in California to be electric-powered Zero Emission Vehicles (ZEV), with that percentage increasing yearly to 10 per cent by 2003. Auto manufacturers argued that they could not meet these targets because the demand for ZEVs had not yet developed. While the state dropped the sales quotas, it entered private memoranda of agreements (MOAs) with automakers under which automakers agreed to supply a certain number of ZEVs to California markets for the 1998–2000 model years. In 2002, California's ZEV regulations were temporarily enjoined in *Central Valley Chrysler-Plymouth v. California Air Resources Board*, No. CV–F–02–5017, 2002 WL 34499459 (2002), on the grounds that the regulations were preempted by the federal Energy Policy and Conservation Act, which governs fuel economy standards. The case settled while still on appeal, however, mooting that decision and instituting a new program that was in effect from 2003–2008. In 2008 CARB modified the ZEV program to promote plug-in hybrids and to combine its conventional air pollutant program with its program to regulate greenhouse gases (described in more detail below). *See* California Environmental Protection Agency, Air Resources Board, *Zero Emissions Vehicles*, http://www.arb.ca.gov/msprog/zevprog/zevprog.htm.

As noted earlier, § 177 of the CAA allows other states to adopt California's standards, providing they are "identical." And although the 1990 Amendments prohibited the EPA from adopting new emission standards until model-year 2004, the agency adopted a voluntary national Low Emission Vehicle (LEV) program, under which manufacturers could voluntarily agree to adopt stricter emission standards for new cars sold in the Northeastern states beginning in 1998. In the end, New York adopted California's ZEV-sales requirement anyway, and the Second Circuit upheld it as being in compliance with section 177. *See* Motor Veh. Mfrs. Ass'n v. New York State Dept. of Envtl. Conservation, 17 F.3d 521 (2d Cir. 1994). When California repealed its sales quotas for model years 1998–2000, however, automakers challenged the New York requirements on the ground that they now violated the requirement that they be "identical" to the California program. The Second Circuit agreed, holding that § 209 pre-empted the non-identical program. American Auto. Mfrs. Ass'n v. Cahill, 152 F.3d 196, 200–01 (2d Cir. 1998).

In another instance, Massachusetts, which previously had copied California's LEV program, amended the ZEV portion of its LEV program to duplicate some, but not all, portions of the new MOAs that California had reached with automakers. The Auto Manufacturers' Association sued, arguing that the Massachusetts regulations were preempted by the Act because the California agreements were not a traditional "standard" and the Massachusetts program was not "identical" in any event. After lengthy litigation, in which the First Circuit Court of Appeals took the unusual step of invoking the doctrine of "primary jurisdiction" to refer the matter to the EPA, the Court ultimately held for the auto manufacturers. *See* Association of Int'l. Auto. Mfrs., Inc. v. Commissioner, Massachusetts Dep't. of Envtl. Prot., 208 F.3d 1 (1st Cir. 2000). The result is that the Section 177 states that choose to follow California's program must adopt the program in its entirety, not deviate from it in any respect.

Despite the setback to its LEV program, California continues to blaze the trail on automobile emissions regulation generally. On November 5, 1999, the California Air Resources Board voted to impose stricter emission standards for new automobiles sold in California, to be phased in over a three year period starting in 2004. The standards required sport utility vehicles, minivans and pickups to meet the same emission standards as passenger cars. *See In the News: California Emissions Standards*, 29 Envtl. L. Rep. 10055 (1999). Since that time, the state has tightened standards several times, with its current program called the LEV III program. The federal Tier 3 standards are largely (though not completely) now harmonized with the California LEV III standards. *See* MECA, *Regulatory Background on the U.S. Mobile Source Emission Control Program: USA EPA Tier 3 and California LEV III Rulemakings,* http://www.meca.org/regulation/epa-tier-3-and-california-lev-iii-rulemakings. California's Zero

Emission Vehicle program is a distinct requirement that is not followed by the federal government. It is described in more detail *infra* at page 510.

As described in more detail in Chapter 4, in 2000, the South Coast Air Quality Management District (a subdivision of the California government responsible for air quality in the Los Angeles area) adopted the "Fleet Rules," which required local companies with large fleets of vehicles, such as taxicab and street sweeping companies, to purchase certain numbers of low-emissions or alternative-fuel vehicles, essentially phasing out older, dirtier vehicles. The Engine Manufacturers' Association sued the District, asserting that the prohibition in § 209(a) on any state "adopt[ing] or attempt[ing] to enforce any standard relating to the control of emissions from new motor vehicles or new motor vehicle engines" included within its compass this attempt to regulate vehicle purchases based on emissions limitations. The Supreme Court agreed with this view, holding that the purchase restriction qualified as an attempt to enforce an emissions standard, and was thus preempted by federal regulation. Engine Mfrs. Ass'n v. South Coast Air Quality Mgmt. Dist., 541 U.S. 246 (2004). The District subsequently reinstated large portions of the Fleet Rules as they applied to state or local public agencies and private fleets under contract to those agencies, following a 2004 federal district court decision finding that those applications of the rules, as valid procurement requirements, were not preempted by the Clean Air Act. *See* South Coast Air Quality Management District, *Clean Fleet Vehicle Rules* (July 20, 2005), http:// www.aqmd.gov/docs/default-source/Regulations/Fleet-Rules/fleetrule advisory-july202005.pdf?sfvrsn=0.

Most recently, California has focused on reducing greenhouse gases from vehicles. We describe those efforts at page 543, *infra*.

c.   **Clean Fuels**

In addition to these new emission standards, the 1990 amendments contain new provisions for alternative fuels aimed at changing the composition of gasoline in heavily polluted cities. There seem to be two reasons for this program. First, the changed tailpipe standards have only a gradual impact on pollution levels, since they affect only new cars. Second, leaks from the system may defeat even the best exhaust treatment equipment. *See Gasoline: The Unclean Fuel?*, 246 SCIENCE 199 (1989). The new provisions require the nine worst nonattainment areas to sell only reformulated gasoline [§ 211(k)]. These nonattainment areas, collectively, account for about 30 per cent of the gasoline consumed in the United States. The Act also requires states with serious or worse nonattainment classifications to amend their SIPs to implement a clean fuel program [§ 182(c)(4)]. The EPA is also required to adopt a pilot clean-fuel vehicle program in California [§ 249(a)].

The changes in fuel composition are designed to reduce ozone and carbon monoxide levels in the most smog-ridden cities. Reformulated gasoline has certain features that help to ameliorate pollution, including reduced hydrocarbon emissions and sulfur content. Reformulated gasoline need not contain oxygenated fuel additives such as ethanol or MTBE, but these additives help to meet the reformulated fuel requirements by promoting more efficient combustion of fuel. The oxygenates help to convert CO into CO_2, reducing CO emissions as required by the Act. Ironically, it does so at the price of producing CO_2, which contributes to global warming! This is an example of how trying to address one environmental problem can exacerbate others.

Moreover, federal requirements specify that gasoline must contain a minimum weight of oxygenated fuel but leaves the choice of oxygenate to the states. In another example of how environmental regulation can have unanticipated secondary effects, California's choice of MTBE as its oxygenate led to groundwater contamination from leaking underground storage tanks. California chose MTBE because it was readily available, had high octane value, and also reduced toxic emissions from tail pipes. Yet MTBE has leached out of underground storage tanks at gas stations and migrated into the drinking water supply. While MTBE has not been found to be a carcinogen, it has a strong taste and odor, making water undrinkable. As a result, the Governor of California ordered that the oxygenate be phased out. *See* Executive Order D–5–99 (Mar. 25, 1999). California is now faced with the dilemma of how to achieve the mandated oxygen level without using MBTE. (Ethanol could be used as an alternative to MBTE to achieve the proper oxygen content, but that would require almost the entire supply of ethanol produced in the United States, and according to California studies would interfere with achievement of the state's particulate matter and ozone NAAQS.) In 1999, the state sought a waiver of the requirement under CAA § 211(m)(3)(A), which allows it to be set aside if the EPA finds that compliance with the mandated oxygen content will "prevent or interfere with the attainment by the area of a national primary ambient air quality standard." The EPA denied the waiver based on its independent findings that the ramifications for California's ozone attainment were unclear, and never reached the issue of PM attainment. Davis v. EPA, 348 F.3d 772, 777–78 (9th Cir. 2003). That denial was vacated by the Ninth Circuit in 2003 because of the EPA's failure to consider the effect on California's attainment of the particulate matter NAAQS. *Id.* at 784–85. However, on remand the agency once again denied the waiver, claiming that any adverse effect on particulate matter levels would not in fact delay the attainment date. EPA, California Oxygen Waiver Decision (June 2005), *available at* http://www.epa.gov/otaq/regs/fuels/rfg/420s05005.pdf.

The reformulated gasoline requirements have spawned a significant amount of litigation. One important rule was overturned in *American Petroleum Inst. v. EPA*, 52 F.3d 1113 (D.C. Cir. 1995) (striking down a requirement that thirty percent of oxygen in reformulated fuel be derived from renewable sources such as ethanol). Manufacturers complain that some state fuel standards will in effect require stricter emissions standards for cars. *See* Motor Vehicle Mfrs. Ass'n v. New York State Dep't of Envtl. Conservation, 79 F.3d 1298 (2d Cir. 1996) (finding this claim to be unripe). Industry has challenged the authority of states to regulate fuel oxygenation, arguing that the Clean Air Act preempts state authority to require a minimum oxygenate standard greater than 2.7 per cent. Recently, the Ninth Circuit rejected this argument, holding that the statutory preemption provisions focused on the regulation of fuel additives, rather than oxygenate standards, and that states are required under the Act to set minimum oxygen content for fuel in carbon monoxide non-attainment areas in order to meet the NAAQS. *See* Exxon Mobil Corp. v. EPA, 217 F.3d 1246 (9th Cir. 2000).

California has also embarked on an ambitious program to regulate the carbon content of fuel. The state's Low Carbon Fuel Standard is designed to lower the carbon intensity of the state's fuels by 10 percent by 2020. *See* California Environmental Protection Agency, *Low Carbon Fuel Standard*, http://www.arb.ca.gov/fuels/lcfs/lcfs.htm. The Ninth Circuit has upheld the LCFS against Commerce Clause and other challenges twice. *See Rocky Mountain Farmers Union v. Corey*, No. 17-16881 (9th Cir. 2019); *Rocky Mountain Farmers Union v. Corey*, 730 F.3d 1070 (9th Cir. 2013), *cert denied* (2014).

d.   Inspection and Maintenance Programs and Transportation Controls

As long as we drive gasoline-powered motor vehicles, emissions control will be an essential part of air pollution regulation. And no matter how good the controls are when the car is manufactured, they will do little to reduce air pollution unless they remain effective over the life of the car. The EPA has required increasingly strict inspection and maintenance (I & M) programs for this reason, though their implementation has been plagued by delays. *See* Arnold W. Reitze, Jr. & Barry Needleman, *Control of Air Pollution from Mobile Sources Through Inspection and Maintenance Programs*, 30 HARV. J. ON LEG. 409 (1993); GAO, *Delays in Motor Vehicle Inspection Programs Jeopardize Attainment of the Ozone Standard* (GAO/RCED 98–175, June 1998).

I & M programs are unpopular because, unlike direct regulation of stationary sources or emission standards imposed on the auto industry, they tend to inconvenience consumers. For example, states may require "smog checks" before people can register their cars. However I & M programs can be more effective than the alternatives. One study found that repairs to a single high-polluting car would reduce emissions more than fuel alterations in all eighty-four vehicles in the test group combined. Stuart P. Beaton et al., *On-Road Vehicle Emissions: Regulations, Costs, and Benefits*, 268 SCIENCE 991, 992 (1995). A more recent study found that the I & M program implemented in Los Angeles reduces air pollution hydrocarbons by 14–24 percent. *See* D.S. Eisenger, *Evaluating Inspection and Maintenance Programs: a Policy-making Framework*, 55 J AIR WASTE MGMT ASSN 147 (2005).

Transportation Control Plans (TCPs), which Congress demanded of the states in the original 1970 Amendments, are also politically unpopular and difficult to implement. In theory, TCPs include things like parking surcharges, limits on driving days and pre-construction review of stationary sources that tend to attract large numbers of cars (e.g., malls, stadiums). Section 110 of the 1970 Amendments originally required SIPs to include "land use and transportation controls" if the Act's other controls would not result in compliance with the NAAQS by mandatory deadlines. The prospect of requirements such as these caused such an outcry from the states that Congress amended § 110 to eliminate or badly weaken the EPA's ability to demand things like parking surcharges in SIPs. The history of both TCPs and the I & M program has been rocky. Congress has eliminated the most controversial aspects of these requirements, only to reinstate them in part later, and to threaten states with sanctions for failing to adopt them. Most recently, Congress has required TCPs in serious, severe and extreme nonattainment areas. *See* § 182(c)(5), § 182(d)(1) and § 182(e).

NOTES

Why is it so difficult to implement TCPs? What would you think about a proposal to limit drivers to driving on only certain days of the week which has been adopted in Mexico City. Or, congestion taxes and other measures to reduce traffic into urban areas, as London has done? What about increasing parking fees or tolls? How might such a regime work? Instead of punitive measures, what about providing more positive incentives akin to special car-pool lanes, or preferred parking? And what role should public transportation play in controlling both air pollution and greenhouse gases? Note that some of the highest polluting and fastest growing urban centers have weak or non-existent public transportation systems e.g., Phoenix, Dallas and Atlanta.

2. INTERSTATE AIR POLLUTION

a. Overview

Air pollution is particularly troublesome because it migrates. As a result, pollution produced by stationary and mobile sources in one state can affect air quality in other states. What are the mechanisms by which the law deals with such "spillovers"? We discuss common law remedies for interstate spillovers in the next chapter, because the leading cases on the matter involve water pollution.

Here we focus on how the CAA, and not the common law, addresses inter-state pollution. The issue has been handled only with great difficulty, because the statutory scheme is largely geared toward a state-by-state approach to achieving air standards. When air pollution fails to respect state lines, institutional innovation is required to deal with the spillover effects. These institutional innovations are particularly troublesome legislatively because it is clear in advance who will be the winners (downwind states) and losers (upwind states). This creates a "zero sum" political situation in which conflict is guaranteed, consensus is difficult, and deadlock is likely. Thus, even in the context of a federal union with strong centralized government, interjurisdictional spillovers are difficult to control.

The principal provisions of the Clean Air Act aimed at interstate pollution are §§ 110(a)(2)(D) and 126. Section 110(a)(2)(D) requires that SIPs contain adequate provisions prohibiting emissions that will significantly interfere with another's state nonattainment problem. CAA § 126 provides a mechanism whereby downwind states may petition the EPA to directly regulate upwind sources of pollution. Under § 126(b), a downwind state "may petition the Administrator for a finding that any major source or group of stationary sources emits or would emit any air pollutant in violation" of CAA § 110(a)(2)(D).

Notwithstanding these provisions, for the first three decades of the CAA the EPA largely failed to address the problem of transboundary pollution. Several states invoked these sections of the Act in petitions to, and suits against, the EPA, without tangible results. In *New England Legal Foundation v. Costle,* 475 F.Supp. 425 (D. Conn. 1979), *aff'd* 632 F.2d 936 (2d Cir. 1980) and 666 F.2d 30 (2d Cir. 1981)), Connecticut plaintiffs sued the EPA Administrator and a New York public utility, seeking declaratory and injunctive relief from air pollution allegedly originating in New York and New Jersey. The EPA was claimed to have failed in its statutory duty to insist on revisions to New York and New Jersey SIPs, in order to abate transport of pollutants to Connecticut. The court held that the EPA had no "mandatory duty at this time" and dismissed all causes of action against the Administrator. In another case, *Connecticut v. EPA*, 656 F.2d 902 (2d Cir. 1981), New York had submitted for EPA approval a revision in its air pollution plan allowing a utility company to burn high sulfur oil for one year, and Connecticut and New Jersey had responded by filing protest petitions under section 126(b). With the court's approval, the EPA approved the state plan revision before ruling on the § 126 petitions.

b. Interstate Ozone and NOx

Nitrogen oxides (NOx) emissions in other regions results in the creation of ozone, which is transported hundreds of miles into the Northeast. This long-range transport made it impossible for the Northeast states to attain the federally mandated air quality standard for ozone. Under the EPA's own interpretation of the statute, however, ozone transport was no excuse for nonattainment, *see* Southwestern Penn. Growth Alliance v. Browner, 121 F.3d 106 (3d Cir. 1997). As noted above, the EPA avoided the imposition of sanctions against the downwind states, doing nothing to solve the problem. The 1990 amendments established a special mechanism for dealing with such spillovers. Section 176(A)(a) grants the EPA authority to establish "transport regions" when interstate transport of pollutants from one or more states contributes significantly to the failure to meet NAAQS in another state. The EPA must establish an "Interstate Transport Commission" for each transport region, consisting of various representatives designated by the statute. The Commission must evaluate interstate transport of pollutants, assess mitigation strategies and make recommendations to the EPA to ensure all SIPs comply with the requirements of the Act. Congress specifically provided for a Northeast Ozone Transport Region (including Connecticut, Delaware, Maine, Maryland, Massachusetts, New Hampshire, New Jersey, New York, Pennsylvania, Rhode Island, Vermont, and the District of Columbia), since ozone attainment had been a particularly challenging issue in this region. Each state had a representative on the Northeast Ozone Transport Commission, a body with the objective of evaluating possible regional solutions to ozone pollution. In 1994, the Commission reached agreement on the NOx Budget Program, a proposal to set up a cap-and-trade system among major NOx sources within its member states in order to achieve the requisite reductions in emissions. James McKinley, Jr., *Agreement Is Reached on Pollution*, N.Y. TIMES, Oct. 2, 1994, at 33. Subsequent evaluations of the program indicate that it achieved substantial cuts in NOx emissions. *See* Environmental Protection Agency, *Ozone Transport Commission*, http://www.epa.gov/airmarkets/progress/docs/otcreport.pdf.

However, it became clear in the 1990s that ozone from upwind states was also significantly hindering eastern states from meeting their air quality standards. Representatives from thirty-seven states and the District of Columbia, along with industry representatives, environmental groups, and EPA officials, had formed the Ozone Transport Assessment Group (OTAG) in 1995 to analyze this next obstacle to ozone attainment. Using comprehensive modeling of ozone transport and the effects of various proposed remedies, OTAG was able to determine that the major source of NOx transported to the eastern states was large fossil fuel fired combustion units, especially electric generating units, in twenty-two southern and Midwestern states. OTAG's analysis, as well as other independent sources, showed that the regional cap-and-trade system would not suffice to meet ozone standards because of ozone coming from upwind sources.

[The above is drawn mainly from Bart E. Cassidy, *Litigation Rages Regarding Interstate Air Pollution*, LEG. INTELLIGENCER, Apr. 12, 1999.]

In response, eight northeastern states petitioned the EPA in 1997 to make a formal finding under § 126 that certain sources (mainly in the Midwest) were significantly contributing to their own nonattainment of ozone standards. John H. Cushman, Jr., *Northeast States Pressuring E.P.A. To Move on Smog*, N.Y. TIMES, Aug. 8, 1997, at A1. In response, the EPA issued a rule in 1998 (with implementation beginning in 2003) mandating that 22 states and the District of Columbia revise their SIPs to require sufficient reductions in NO_x emissions to mitigate the interstate transport of ozone (the "NO_x SIP call"); the states had the option to participate in the Northeast's NO_x trading program (newly renamed the NOx Budget Trading Rule. This action set off a vociferous debate over whether upwind states should significantly reduce their emissions solely to assist other states in meeting their air quality targets, or whether downwind states should have to further reduce their own emissions, economically disadvantaging them compared to the less stringently controlled Midwest and South, when they might not ever be able to attain air quality standards without reductions by upwind contributors. In two legal challenges to the rule the mandated reductions were largely upheld on appeal to the D.C. Circuit, although the Court agreed with certain states that the EPA findings with respect to their contributions of NO_x, and certain of the agency's calculations, were not sufficiently supported. *See* Michigan v. EPA, 213 F.3d 663 (D.C. Cir. 2000; Appalachian Power Co. v. EPA, 249 F.3d 1032 (D.C. Cir. 2001). In *Michigan*, the court upheld the EPA's methodology for determining which upwind sources were "significant contributors" to downwind air pollution in other states. The court also upheld the EPA's determination that significant contributors "need only reduce their ozone by the amount achievable with 'highly cost-effective controls.'" Highly cost-effective controls were defined as those controls that could be undertaken for less than $2000 per ton.

With these two cases largely validating its approach, EPA succeeded in its NOx Budget Trading Program in establishing a cap-and-trade program for NOx emissions that included 22 states in most of the Midwestern and eastern parts of the country under the auspices of reducing interstate air pollution.

Based on the success of the NOx Budget Trading program, in 2005, the Bush administration proposed replacing the program with the Clean Air Interstate Rule, which would go into effect in 2009. The rule controlled not only NOx emissions but also sulfur dioxide emissions previously covered by Title IV of the CAA, which established a cap-and-trade program to reduce emissions that create acid rain (see Section E 1 (c), *infra,* for a further description.) CAIR was challenged by several states and regulated parties on a variety of grounds. The U.S. Court of Appeals for the D.C. Circuit struck down CAIR in *North Carolina v. EPA,* 531 F.3d 896 (D.C. Cir. 2008).

EPA issued a revised program, called the Transport Rule, in 2011 in response to the *North Carolina* decision. A number of states and power plants sued to invalidate the new Rule. The Supreme Court took up the challenge and issued the following decision.

EPA v. EME HOMER CITY GENERATION

United States Supreme Court, 2014.
572 U.S. 489, 134 S.Ct. 1584, 188 L.Ed.2d 775.

JUSTICE GINSBURG delivered the opinion of the Court.

These cases concern the efforts of Congress and the Environmental Protection Agency to cope with a complex problem: air pollution emitted in one State, but causing harm in other States. Left unregulated, the emitting or upwind State reaps the benefits of the economic activity causing the pollution without bearing all the costs. Conversely, downwind States to which the pollution travels are unable to achieve clean air because of the influx of out-of-state pollution they lack authority to control. To tackle the problem, Congress included a Good Neighbor Provision in the Clean Air Act (Act or CAA). That provision, in its current phrasing, instructs States to prohibit in-state sources "from emitting any air pollutant in amounts which will . . . contribute significantly" to downwind States' "nonattainment . . ., or interfere with maintenance," of any EPA-promulgated national air quality standard. 42 U.S.C. § 7410(a)(2)(D)(i).

Interpreting the Good Neighbor Provision, EPA adopted the Cross-State Air Pollution Rule (commonly and hereinafter called the Transport Rule). The rule calls for consideration of costs, among other factors, when determining the emission reductions an upwind State must make to improve air quality in polluted downwind areas. The Court of Appeals for the D.C. Circuit vacated the rule in its entirety. . . .

In *Chevron U.S.A. Inc. v. Natural Resources Defense Council, Inc.,* we reversed a D.C. Circuit decision that failed to accord deference to EPA's reasonable interpretation of an ambiguous Clean Air Act provision. Satisfied that the Good Neighbor Provision does not command the Court of Appeals' cost-blind construction, and that EPA reasonably interpreted the provision, we reverse the D.C. Circuit's judgment.

I

A

* * *

...Curtailing interstate air pollution poses a complex challenge for environmental regulators. . . . identifying the upwind origin of downwind air pollution is no easy endeavor. Most upwind States propel pollutants to more than one downwind State, many downwind States receive pollution from multiple upwind States, and some States qualify as both upwind and downwind. The overlapping and interwoven linkages between upwind and downwind States with which EPA had to contend number in the thousands.

B

* * *

* * * The [CAA], in its current form, requires SIPs to "contain adequate provisions . . . prohibiting . . . any source or other type of emissions activity within the State from emitting any air pollutant in amounts which will . . . contribute significantly to nonattainment in, or interfere with maintenance by, any other State with respect to any . . . [NAAQS]." 42 U.S.C. § 7410(a)(2)(D)(i) (2006 ed.). The controversy before us centers on EPA's most recent attempt to construe this provision.

C

Three times over the past two decades, EPA has attempted to delineate the Good Neighbor Provision's scope by identifying when upwind States "contribute significantly" to nonattainment downwind. In 1998, EPA issued a rule known as the "NOx SIP Call." That regulation limited NOx emissions in 23 upwind States to the extent such emissions contributed to nonattainment of ozone standards in downwind States. In *Michigan v. EPA*, 213 F.3d 663 (2000), the D.C. Circuit upheld the NOx SIP Call, specifically affirming EPA's use of costs to determine when an upwind State's contribution was "significan[t]" within the meaning of the statute.

In 2005, EPA issued the Clean Air Interstate Rule, or CAIR. The D.C. Circuit initially vacated CAIR as arbitrary and capricious [but] the court decided to leave the rule in place, while encouraging EPA to act with dispatch in dealing with problems the court had identified. See *North Carolina v. EPA*, 550 F.3d 1176, 1178 (C.A.D.C.2008) (*per curiam*).

The rule challenged here—the Transport Rule—is EPA's response to the D.C. Circuit's *North Carolina* decision. Finalized in August 2011, the Transport Rule curtails NOx and SO2 emissions of 27 upwind States to achieve downwind attainment of three different NAAQS: the two 1997 NAAQS previously addressed by CAIR [NOx and SO2], and the 2006

NAAQS for $PM_{2.5}$ levels measured on a daily basis. See 76 Fed.Reg. 48208–48209.

Under the Transport Rule, EPA employed a "two-step approach" to determine when upwind States "contribute[d] significantly to nonattainment," and therefore in "amounts" that had to be eliminated. At step one, called the "screening" analysis, the Agency excluded as *de minimis* any upwind State that contributed less than one percent of the three NAAQS to any downwind State "receptor," a location at which EPA measures air quality. If all of an upwind State's contributions fell below the one-percent threshold, that State would be considered not to have "contribute[d] significantly" to the nonattainment of any downwind State. States in that category were screened out and exempted from regulation under the rule.

The remaining States were subjected to a second inquiry, which EPA called the "control" analysis. At this stage, the Agency sought to generate a cost-effective allocation of emission reductions among those upwind States "screened in" at step one.

The control analysis proceeded this way. EPA first calculated, for each upwind State, the quantity of emissions the State could eliminate at each of several cost thresholds. Cost for these purposes is measured as cost per ton of emissions prevented, for instance, by installing scrubbers on powerplant smokestacks. EPA estimated, for example, the amount each upwind State's NO_X emissions would fall if all pollution sources within each State employed every control measure available at a cost of $500 per ton or less. The Agency then repeated that analysis at ascending cost thresholds.

Armed with this information, EPA conducted complex modeling to establish the combined effect the upwind reductions projected at each cost threshold would have on air quality in downwind States. The Agency then identified "significant cost threshold[s]," points in its model where a "noticeable change occurred in downwind air quality, such as . . . where large upwind emission reductions become available because a certain type of emissions control strategy becomes cost-effective." For example, reductions of NO_X sufficient to resolve or significantly curb downwind air quality problems could be achieved, EPA determined, at a cost threshold of $500 per ton (applied uniformly to all regulated upwind States). "Moving beyond the $500 cost threshold," EPA concluded, "would result in only minimal additional . . . reductions [in emissions]."

Finally, EPA translated the cost thresholds it had selected into amounts of emissions upwind States would be required to eliminate. For each regulated upwind State, EPA created an annual emissions "budget." These budgets represented the quantity of pollution an upwind State would produce in a given year if its in-state sources implemented all pollution controls available at the chosen cost thresholds. If EPA's projected improvements to downwind air quality were to be realized, an upwind State's emissions could not exceed the level this budget allocated to it, subject to certain adjustments not relevant here.

Taken together, the screening and control inquiries defined EPA's understanding of which upwind emissions were within the Good Neighbor Provision's ambit. In short, under the Transport Rule, an upwind State "contribute[d] significantly" to downwind nonattainment to the extent its exported pollution both (1) produced one percent or more of a NAAQS in at least one downwind State (step one) and (2) could be eliminated cost-effectively, as determined by EPA (step two). Upwind States would be obliged to eliminate all and only emissions meeting both of these criteria.

For each State regulated by the Transport Rule, EPA contemporaneously promulgated a Federal Implementation Plan allocating that State's emission budget among its in-state sources.[10] For each of these States, EPA had determined that the State had failed to submit a SIP adequate for compliance with the Good Neighbor Provision.

* * *

D

* * *

EPA's actions, the appeals court held, exceeded the Agency's statutory authority. . .

[The D.C. Circuit held that States should first have been able to develop their own SIPs addressing cross-border pollution rather than have a Federal Implementation Plan imposed upon them].

The D.C. Circuit also held that the Agency's two-part interpretation of the Good Neighbor Provision ignored three "red lines . . . cabin[ing the] EPA's authority." First, the D.C. Circuit interpreted the Good Neighbor Provision to require upwind States to reduce emissions in "a manner proportional to their contributio[n]" to pollution in downwind States. The Transport Rule, however, treated all regulated upwind States alike, regardless of their relative contribution to the overall problem. It required all upwind States "screened in" at step one to reduce emissions in accord with the uniform cost thresholds set during the step two control analysis. Imposing these uniform cost thresholds, the Court of Appeals observed, could force some upwind States to reduce emissions by more than their "fair share."

---

[10] These FIPs specified the maximum amount of pollution each in-state pollution source could emit. Sources below this ceiling could sell unused "allocations" to sources that could not reduce emissions to the necessary level as cheaply. This type of "cap-and-trade" system cuts costs while still reducing pollution to target levels.

According to the Court of Appeals, EPA had also failed to ensure that the Transport Rule did not mandate upwind States to reduce pollution unnecessarily. The Good Neighbor Provision, the D.C. Circuit noted, "targets [only] those emissions from upwind States that 'contribute significantly *to nonattainment*'" of a NAAQS in downwind States. Pollution reduction beyond that goal was "unnecessary over-control," outside the purview of the Agency's statutory mandate. *Ibid.* Because the emission budgets were calculated by reference to cost alone, the court concluded that EPA had done nothing to guard against, or even measure, the "over-control" potentially imposed by the Transport Rule. See *ibid.*

Finally, by deciding, at the screening analysis, that upwind contributions below the one-percent threshold were insignificant, EPA had established a "floor" on the Agency's authority to act. Again pointing to the rule's reliance on costs, the Court of Appeals held that EPA had failed to ensure that upwind States were not being forced to reduce emissions below the one-percent threshold.

We granted certiorari to decide whether the D.C. Circuit had accurately construed the limits the CAA places on EPA's authority.

II

A

As the State respondents put it, a FIP allocating a State's emission budget "must issue *after* EPA has quantified the States' good-neighbor obligations [in an emission budget] and given the States a reasonable

* * *

B

[The Court first held that EPA was correct in imposing FIPs on states because the agency had found state SIPS to be inadequate and states had not corrected the deficiencies in their SIPs within two years. It rejected the D.C. Circuity's argument that EPA first should have provided data deficient states to allow them to address the deficiency, reasoning that the statute requires no such data provision.]

* * *

III

A

The D.C. Circuit also held that the Transport Rule's two-step interpretation of the Good Neighbor Provision conflicts with the Act.

* * *

B

We routinely accord dispositive effect to an agency's reasonable interpretation of ambiguous statutory language. *Chevron* . . . is the pathmarking decision.

* * *

When "Congress has not directly addressed the precise [interpretative] question at issue," we cautioned, a reviewing court cannot "simply impose its own construction o[f] the statute." Rather, the agency is charged with filling the "gap left open" by the ambiguity. Because " 'a full understanding of the force of the statutory policy . . . depend [s] upon more than ordinary knowledge' " of the situation, the administering agency's construction is to be accorded "controlling weight unless . . . arbitrary, capricious, or manifestly contrary to the statute." . . .

We conclude that the Good Neighbor Provision delegates authority to EPA at least as certainly as the CAA provisions involved in *Chevron*. The statute requires States to eliminate those "amounts" of pollution that "contribute significantly to *nonattainment* " in downwind States. 42 U.S.C. § 7410(a)(2)(D)(i) (emphasis added). Thus, EPA's task is to reduce upwind pollution, but only in "amounts" that push a downwind State's pollution concentrations above the relevant NAAQS. As noted earlier, however, the nonattainment of downwind States results from the collective and interwoven contributions of multiple upwind States. The statute therefore calls upon the Agency to address a thorny causation problem: How should EPA allocate among multiple contributing upwind States responsibility for a downwind State's excess pollution?

A simplified example illustrates the puzzle EPA faced. Suppose the Agency sets a NAAQS, with respect to a particular pollutant, at 100 parts per billion (ppb), and that the level of the pollutant in the atmosphere of downwind State A is 130 ppb. Suppose further that EPA has determined that each of three upwind States—X, Y, and Z—contributes the equivalent of 30 ppb of the relevant pollutant to State A's airspace. The Good Neighbor Provision, as just observed, prohibits only upwind emissions that contribute significantly to downwind *nonattainment*. EPA's authority under the provision is therefore limited to eliminating a *total* of 30 ppb, *i.e.,* the overage caused by the collective contribution of States X, Y, and Z.

How is EPA to divide responsibility among the three States? Should the Agency allocate reductions proportionally (10 ppb each), on a per capita basis, on the basis of the cost of abatement, or by some other metric? The Good Neighbor Provision does not answer that question for EPA. Under *Chevron,* we read Congress' silence as a delegation of authority to EPA to select from among reasonable options.

Yet the Court of Appeals believed that the Act speaks clearly, requiring EPA to allocate responsibility for reducing emissions in "a manner proportional to" each State's "contributio[n]" to the problem. Nothing in the text of the Good Neighbor Provision propels EPA down this path. Understandably so, for as EPA notes, the D.C. Circuit's proportionality approach could scarcely be satisfied in practice. ("[W]hile it is possible to determine an emission reduction percentage if there is a single downwind [receptor], most upwind states contribute to multiple downwind [receptors] (in multiple states) and would have a different reduction percentage for each one.").

To illustrate, consider a variation on the example set out above. Imagine that States X and Y now contribute air pollution to State A in a ratio of one to five, *i.e.,* State Y contributes five times the amount of pollution to State A than does State X. If State A were the only downwind State to which the two upwind States contributed, the D.C. Circuit's proportionality requirement would be easy to meet: EPA could require State Y to reduce its emissions by five times the amount demanded of State X.

The realities of interstate air pollution, however, are not so simple. Most upwind States contribute pollution to multiple downwind States in varying amounts. Suppose then that States X and Y also contribute pollutants to a second downwind State (State B), this time in a ratio of seven to one. Though State Y contributed a relatively larger share of pollution to State A, with respect to State B, State X is the greater offender. Following the proportionality approach with respect to State B would demand that State X reduce its emissions by seven times as much as State Y. Recall, however, that State Y, as just hypothesized, had to effect five times as large a reduction with respect to State A. The Court of Appeals' proportionality edict with respect to *both* State A and State B appears to work neither mathematically nor in practical application. Proportionality as to one downwind State will not achieve proportionality as to others. Quite the opposite. And where, as is generally true, upwind States contribute pollution to more than two downwind receptors, proportionality becomes all the more elusive.

Neither the D.C. Circuit nor respondents face up to this problem.

* * *

Persuaded that the Good Neighbor Provision does not dictate the particular allocation of emissions among contributing States advanced by the D.C. Circuit, we must next decide whether the allocation method chosen by EPA is a "permissible construction of the statute." *Chevron.* As EPA interprets the statute, upwind emissions rank as "amounts [that] . . . contribute significantly to nonattainment" if they (1) constitute one percent or more of a relevant NAAQS in a nonattaining downwind State and (2) can be eliminated under the cost threshold set by the Agency. In other words, to identify which emissions were to be eliminated, EPA considered both the magnitude of upwind States' contributions and the cost associated with eliminating them.

The Industry respondents argue that, however EPA ultimately divides responsibility among upwind States, the final calculation cannot rely on costs. The Good Neighbor Provision, respondents and the dissent emphasize, "requires each State to prohibit only those *'amounts'* of air pollution emitted within the State that 'contribute significantly' to another State's nonattaintment." The cost of preventing emissions, they urge, is wholly unrelated to the actual "amoun[t]" of air pollution an upwind State contributes. Because the Transport Rule considers costs, respondents argue, "States that contribute identical 'amounts' . . . may be deemed [by EPA] to have [made] substantially *different* " contributions.

But, as just explained, the Agency cannot avoid the task of choosing which among equal "amounts" to eliminate. The Agency has chosen, sensibly in our view, to reduce the amount easier, *i.e.,* less costly, to eradicate, and nothing in the text of the Good Neighbor Provision precludes that choice.

Using costs in the Transport Rule calculus, we agree with EPA, also makes good sense. Eliminating those amounts that can cost-effectively be reduced is an efficient and equitable solution to the allocation problem the Good Neighbor Provision requires the Agency to address. Efficient because EPA can achieve the levels of attainment, *i.e.,* of emission reductions, the proportional approach aims to achieve, but at a much lower overall cost. Equitable because, by imposing uniform cost thresholds on regulated States, EPA's rule subjects to stricter regulation those States that have done relatively less in the past to control their pollution. Upwind States that have not yet implemented pollution controls of the same stringency as their neighbors will be stopped from free riding on their neighbors' efforts to reduce pollution. They will have to bring down their emissions by installing devices of the kind in which neighboring States have already invested.

Suppose, for example, that the industries of upwind State A have expended considerable resources installing modern pollution-control devices on their plants. Factories in upwind State B, by contrast, continue to run old, dirty plants. Yet, perhaps because State A is more populous and therefore generates a larger sum of pollution overall, the two States' emissions have equal effects on downwind attainment. If State A and State B are required to eliminate emissions proportionally (*i.e.,* equally*)*, sources in State A will be compelled to spend far more per ton of reductions because they have already utilized lower cost pollution controls. State A's sources will also have to achieve greater reductions than would have been required had they not made the cost-effective reductions in the first place. State A, in other words, will be tolled for having done more to reduce pollution in the past. EPA'S cost-based allocation avoids these anomalies.

Obligated to require the elimination of only those "amounts" of pollutants that contribute to the nonattainment of NAAQS in downwind States, EPA must decide how to differentiate among the otherwise like contributions of multiple upwind States. EPA found decisive the difficulty of eliminating each "amount," *i.e.,* the cost incurred in doing so. Lacking a dispositive statutory instruction to guide it, EPA's decision, we conclude, is a "reasonable" way of filling the "gap left open by Congress." *Chevron.*

C

The D.C. Circuit stated two further objections to EPA's cost-based method of defining an upwind State's contribution. Once a State was screened in at step one of EPA's analysis, its emission budget was calculated solely with reference to the uniform cost thresholds the Agency selected at step two. The Transport Rule thus left open the possibility that a State might be compelled to reduce emissions beyond the point at which every affected downwind State is in attainment, a phenomenon the Court of Appeals termed "over-control." Second, EPA's focus on costs did not foreclose, as the D.C. Circuit accurately observed, the possibility that an upwind State would be required to reduce its emissions by so much that the State no longer contributed one percent or more of a relevant NAAQS to any downwind State. This would place the State below the mark EPA had set, during the screening phase, as the initial threshold of "significan[ce]."

We agree with the Court of Appeals to this extent: EPA cannot require a State to reduce its output of pollution by more than is necessary to achieve attainment in every downwind State or at odds with the one-percent threshold the Agency has set. If EPA requires an upwind State to reduce emissions by more than the amount necessary to achieve attainment in *every* downwind State to which it is linked, the Agency will have overstepped its authority, under the Good Neighbor Provision, to eliminate those "amounts [that] contribute . . . to nonattainment." Nor can EPA demand reductions that would drive an upwind State's contribution to every downwind State to which it is linked below one percent of the relevant NAAQS. Doing so would be counter to step one of the Agency's interpretation of the Good Neighbor Provision. See 76 Fed.Reg. 48236 ("[S]tates whose contributions are below th[e] thresholds do not significantly contribute to nonattainment . . . of the relevant NAAQS.").

Neither possibility, however, justifies wholesale invalidation of the Transport Rule. First, instances of "over-control" in particular downwind locations . . . may be incidental to reductions necessary to ensure attainment elsewhere. Because individual upwind States often "contribute significantly" to nonattainment in multiple downwind locations, the emissions reduction required to bring one linked downwind State into attainment may well be large enough to push other linked downwind States over the attainment line. As the Good Neighbor Provision seeks attainment in *every* downwind State, however, exceeding attainment in one State cannot rank as "over-control" unless unnecessary to achieving attainment in *any* downwind State. Only reductions unnecessary to downwind attainment *anywhere* fall outside the Agency's statutory authority.

Second, while EPA has a statutory duty to avoid over-control, the Agency also has a statutory obligation to avoid "under-control," *i.e.,* to maximize achievement of attainment downwind. For reasons earlier explained, a degree of imprecision is inevitable in tackling the problem of interstate air pollution. Slight changes in wind patterns or energy consumption, for example, may vary downwind air quality in ways EPA might not have anticipated. The Good Neighbor Provision requires EPA to seek downwind attainment of NAAQS notwithstanding the uncertainties. Hence, some amount of over-control, *i.e.,* emission budgets that turn out to be more demanding than necessary, would not be surprising. Required to balance the possibilities of under-control and over-control, EPA must have leeway in fulfilling its statutory mandate.

* * *

If any upwind State concludes it has been forced to regulate emissions below the one-percent threshold or beyond the point necessary to bring all downwind States into attainment, that State may bring a particularized, as-applied challenge to the Transport Rule, along with any other as-applied challenges it may have. Satisfied that EPA's cost-based methodology, on its face, is not "arbitrary, capricious, or manifestly contrary to the statute," *Chevron,* we uphold the Transport Rule. The possibility that the rule, in uncommon particular applications, might exceed EPA's statutory authority does not warrant judicial condemnation of the rule in its entirety.

In sum, we hold that the CAA does not command that States be given a second opportunity to file a SIP after EPA has quantified the State's interstate pollution obligations. We further conclude that the Good Neighbor Provision does not require EPA to disregard costs and consider exclusively each upwind State's physically proportionate responsibility for each downwind air quality problem. EPA's cost-effective allocation of emission reductions among upwind States, we hold, is a permissible, workable, and equitable interpretation of the Good Neighbor Provision.

* * *

It is so ordered.

JUSTICES SCALIA and THOMAS, dissenting:

Too many important decisions of the Federal Government are made nowadays by unelected agency officials exercising broad lawmaking authority, rather than by the people's representatives in Congress. With the statute involved in the present cases, however, Congress did it right. It specified quite precisely the responsibility of an upwind State under the Good Neighbor Provision: to eliminate those *amounts of pollutants* that it contributes to downwind problem areas. But the Environmental Protection Agency was unsatisfied with this system. Agency personnel, perhaps correctly, thought it more efficient to require reductions not in proportion to the *amounts of pollutants* for which each upwind State is responsible, but on the basis of how *cost-effectively* each can decrease emissions.

Today, the majority approves that undemocratic revision of the Clean Air Act. The Agency came forward with a textual justification for its action, relying on a farfetched meaning of the word "significantly" in the statutory text. That justification is so feeble that today's majority does not even recite it, much less defend it. The majority reaches its result ("Look Ma, no hands!") without benefit of text, claiming to have identified a remarkable "gap" in the statute, which it proceeds to fill (contrary to the plain logic of the statute) with cost-benefit analysis—and then, with no pretended textual justification at all, simply extends cost-benefit analysis beyond the scope of the alleged gap.

I would affirm the judgment of the D.C. Circuit that EPA violated the law both in crafting the Transport Rule and in implementing it.

NOTES

1. Is the *EME Homer* opinion consistent with *Whitman v. American Trucking, supra* at page 449, in its holding that EPA can take into account costs in setting state emissions budgets? Does *Michigan v. EPA, supra* at page 476, affect the analysis? What would a regulatory regime to address interstate air pollution that did not take into account cost look like? For a detailed analysis of the opinion, see Daniel A. Farber, *Unpacking EME Homer: Cost, Proportionality, and Emissions Reductions*, 4 MICH. J. ENV. & ADMIN. L. 2 (2015).

2. How, if at all, does the Transport Rule address the problem of the exemption of existing stationary sources from regulation? Put a different way, is it likely that some existing stationary sources that have largely been exempt from regulation will need to reduce their emissions in response to the Transport Rule?

3. Justice Scalia's dissent parallels, in many respects, the D.C. Circuit Court of Appeals decision below striking down the Transport Rule. The author of the Court of Appeals decision—overturned by the majority—was now Justice Brett Kavanaugh.

3. GREENHOUSE GAS EMISSIONS AND THE CLEAN AIR ACT

Without a doubt, the most contentious and important recent developments in the interpretation of the Clean Air Act involve the regulation of greenhouse gases. In Massachusetts v. EPA, the Supreme Court took up the question of whether greenhouse gases constitute pollutants under the act and EPA's responsibility to regulate them. (The standing portion of the case is included in Chapter 5 on page.) The opinion is excerpted below.

MASSACHUSETTS V. EPA
United States Supreme Court, 2007.
549 U.S. 497, 127 S.Ct. 1438, 167 L.Ed.2d 248.

JUSTICE STEVENS delivered the opinion of the Court in which KENNEDY, SOUTER, GINSBURG, and BREYER, JJ., joined.

I

Section 202(a)(1) of the Clean Air Act . . . provides:

"The [EPA] Administrator shall by regulation prescribe (and from time to time revise) in accordance with the provisions of this section, standards applicable to the emission of any air pollutant from any class or classes of new motor vehicles or new motor vehicle engines, which in his judgment cause, or contribute to, air pollution which may reasonably be anticipated to endanger public health or welfare. . . ."

The Act defines "air pollutant" to include "any air pollution agent or combination of such agents, including any physical, chemical, biological, radioactive . . . substance or matter which is emitted into or otherwise enters the ambient air." § 7602(g). "Welfare" is also defined broadly: among other things, it includes "effects on . . . weather . . . and climate." § 7602(h).

When Congress enacted these provisions, the study of climate change was in its infancy. In 1959, shortly after the U. S. Weather Bureau began monitoring atmospheric carbon dioxide levels, an observatory in Mauna Loa, Hawaii, recorded a mean level of 316 parts per million. This was well above the highest carbon dioxide concentration—no more than 300 parts per million—revealed in the 420,000-year-old ice-core record. By the time Congress drafted § 202(a)(1) in 1970, carbon dioxide levels had reached 325 parts per million.

In the late 1970's, the Federal Government began devoting serious attention to the possibility that carbon dioxide emissions associated with human activity could provoke climate change. In 1978,

Congress enacted the National Climate Program Act, 92 Stat. 601, which required the President to establish a program to "assist the Nation and the world to understand and respond to natural and man-induced climate processes and their implications," *id.*, § 3. President Carter, in turn, asked the National Research Council, the working arm of the National Academy of Sciences, to investigate the subject. The Council's response was unequivocal: "If carbon dioxide continues to increase, the study group finds no reason to doubt that climate changes will result and no reason to believe that these changes will be negligible. . . . A wait-and-see policy may mean waiting until it is too late."

Congress next addressed the issue in 1987, when it enacted the Global Climate Protection Act * * *. Finding that "manmade pollution—the release of carbon dioxide, chlorofluorocarbons, methane, and other trace gases into the atmosphere—may be producing a long-term and substantial increase in the average temperature on Earth,"

* * * Congress directed EPA to propose to Congress a "coordinated national policy on global climate change," § 1103(b), and ordered the Secretary of State to work "through the channels of multilateral diplomacy" and coordinate diplomatic efforts to combat global warming, § 1103(c). Congress emphasized that "ongoing pollution and deforestation may be contributing now to an irreversible process" and that "[n]ecessary actions must be identified and implemented in time to protect the climate." § 1102(4).

Meanwhile, the scientific understanding of climate change progressed. In 1990, the Intergovernmental Panel on Climate Change (IPCC), a multinational scientific body organized under the auspices of the United Nations, published its first comprehensive report on the topic. Drawing on expert opinions from across the globe, the IPCC concluded that "emissions resulting from human activities are substantially increasing the atmospheric concentrations of . . . greenhouse gases [which] will enhance the greenhouse effect, resulting on average in an additional warming of the Earth's surface."

Responding to the IPCC report, the United Nations convened the "Earth Summit" in 1992 in Rio de Janeiro. The first President Bush attended and signed the United Nations Framework Convention on Climate Change(UNFCCC), a nonbinding agreement among 154 nations to reduce atmospheric concentrations of carbon dioxide and other greenhouse gases for the purpose of "prevent[ing] dangerous anthropogenic [i.e., human-induced] interference with the [Earth's] climate system." * * * The Senate unanimously ratified the treaty.

Some five years later—after the IPCC issued a second comprehensive report in 1995 concluding that "[t]he balance of evidence suggests there is a discernible human influence on global climate"—the UNFCCC signatories met in Kyoto, Japan, and adopted a protocol that assigned mandatory targets for industrialized nations to reduce greenhouse gas emissions. Because those targets did not apply to developing and heavily polluting nations such as China and India, the Senate unanimously passed a resolution expressing its sense that the United States should not enter into the Kyoto Protocol. * * *. President Clinton did not submit the protocol to the Senate for ratification.

* * *

VI

On the merits, the first question is whether § 202(a)(1) of the Clean Air Act authorizes EPA to regulate greenhouse gas emissions from new motor vehicles in the event that it forms a "judgment" that such emissions contribute to climate change. We have little trouble concluding that it does. In relevant part, § 202(a)(1) provides that EPA "shall by regulation prescribe . . . standards applicable to the emission of any air pollutant from any class or classes of new motor vehicles or new motor vehicle engines, which in [the Administrator's] judgment cause, or contribute to, air pollution which may reasonably be anticipated to endanger public health or welfare." * * *. Because EPA believes that Congress did not intend it to regulate substances that contribute to climate change, the agency maintains that carbon dioxide is not an "air pollutant" within the meaning of the provision.

The statutory text forecloses EPA's reading. The Clean Air Act's sweeping definition of "air pollutant" includes "any air pollution agent or combination of such agents, including any physical, chemical . . . substance or matter which is emitted into or otherwise enters the ambient air. . . ." § 7602(g). On its face, the definition embraces all airborne compounds of whatever stripe, and underscores that intent through the repeated use of the word "any." Carbon dioxide, methane, nitrous oxide, and hydrofluorocarbons are without a doubt "physical [and] chemical . . . substance[s] which [are] emitted into . . . the ambient air." The statute is unambiguous.[26]

---

[26] In dissent, JUSTICE SCALIA maintains that because greenhouse gases permeate the world's atmosphere rather than a limited area near the earth's surface, EPA's exclusion of greenhouse gases from the category of air pollution "agent[s]" is entitled to deference under Chevron * * *EPA's distinction, however, finds no support in the text of the statute, which uses the phrase "the ambient air" without distinguishing between atmospheric layers. Moreover, it is a plainly unreasonable reading of a sweeping statutory provision designed to capture "any physical, chemical . . . substance or matter which is emitted into or otherwise enters the ambient air." 42 U. S. C. § 7602(g). JUSTICE SCALIA does not (and cannot) explain why Congress would define "air pollutant" so carefully and so broadly, yet confer on EPA the authority to narrow that definition

Rather than relying on statutory text, EPA invokes postenactment congressional actions and deliberations it views as tantamount to a congressional command to refrain from regulating greenhouse gas emissions. Even if such post enactment legislative history could shed light on the meaning of an otherwise-unambiguous statute, EPA never identifies any action remotely suggesting that Congress meant to curtail its power to treat greenhouse gases as air pollutants. That subsequent Congresses have eschewed enacting binding emissions limitations to combat global warming tells us nothing about what Congress meant when it amended § 202(a)(1) in 1970 and 1977. And unlike EPA, we have no difficulty reconciling Congress' various efforts to promote interagency collaboration and research to better understand climate change with the agency's pre-existing mandate to regulate "any air pollutant" that may endanger the public welfare. * * * Collaboration and research do not conflict with any thoughtful regulatory effort; they complement it.

EPA's reliance on Brown & Williamson Tobacco Corp. is similarly misplaced. In holding that tobacco products are not "drugs" or "devices" subject to Food and Drug Administration (FDA) regulation pursuant to the Food, Drug and Cosmetic Act (FDCA) we found critical at least two considerations that have no counterpart in this case.

First, we thought it unlikely that Congress meant to ban tobacco products, which the FDCA would have required had such products been classified as "drugs" or "devices." Here, in contrast, EPA jurisdiction would lead to no such extreme measures. EPA would only regulate emissions, and even then, it would have to delay any action "to permit the development and application of the requisite technology, giving appropriate consideration to the cost of compliance," § 7521(a)(2). However much a ban on tobacco products clashed with the "common sense" intuition that Congress never meant to remove those products from circulation * * * there is nothing counterintuitive to the notion that EPA can curtail the emission of substances that are putting the global climate out of kilter.

Second, in Brown & Williamson we pointed to an unbroken series of congressional enactments that made sense only if adopted "against the backdrop of the FDA's consistent and repeated statements that it lacked authority under the FDCA to regulate tobacco." We can point to no such enactments here: EPA has not identified any congressional action that conflicts in any way with the regulation of greenhouse gases from new motor vehicles. Even if it had, Congress could not have acted against a regulatory "backdrop" of disclaimers of regulatory

whenever expedient by asserting that a particular substance is not an "agent." At any rate, no party to this dispute contests that greenhouse gases both "ente[r] the ambient air" and tend to warm the atmosphere. They are therefore unquestionably "agent[s]" of air pollution.

authority. Prior to the order that provoked this litigation, EPA had never disavowed the authority to regulate greenhouse gases, and in 1998 it in fact affirmed that it had such authority. * * * There is no reason, much less a compelling reason, to accept EPA's invitation to read ambiguity into a clear statute.

EPA finally argues that it cannot regulate carbon dioxide emissions from motor vehicles because doing so would require it to tighten mileage standards, a job (according to EPA) that Congress has assigned to [the Department of Transportation (DOT) under a different statute]. But that DOT sets mileage standards in no way licenses EPA to shirk its environmental responsibilities. EPA has been charged with protecting the public's "health" and "welfare," * * * a statutory obligation wholly independent of DOT's mandate to promote energy efficiency. * * * The two obligations may overlap, but there is no reason to think the two agencies cannot both administer their obligations and yet avoid inconsistency.

While the Congresses that drafted § 202(a)(1) might not have appreciated the possibility that burning fossil fuels could lead to global warming, they did understand that without regulatory flexibility, changing circumstances and scientific developments would soon render the Clean Air Act obsolete. The broad language of § 202(a)(1) reflects an intentional effort to confer the flexibility necessary to forestall such obsolescence. * * * Because greenhouse gases fit well within the Clean Air Act's capacious definition of "air pollutant," we hold that EPA has the statutory authority to regulate the emission of such gases from new motor vehicles.

VII

The alternative basis for EPA's decision—that even if it does have statutory authority to regulate greenhouse gases, it would be unwise to do so at this time—rests on reasoning divorced from the statutory text. While the statute does condition the exercise of EPA's authority on its formation of a "judgment," 42 U. S. C. § 7521(a)(1), that judgment must relate to whether an air pollutant "cause[s], or contribute[s] to, air pollution which may reasonably be anticipated to endanger public health or welfare," *ibid.* Put another way, the use of the word "judgment" is not a roving license to ignore the statutory text. It is but a direction to exercise discretion within defined statutory limits. If EPA makes a finding of endangerment, the Clean Air Act requires the agency to regulate emissions of the deleterious pollutant from new motor vehicles. *Ibid.* (stating that "[EPA] shall by regulation prescribe . . . standards applicable to the emission of any air pollutant from any class of new motor vehicles"). EPA no doubt has significant latitude as to the manner, timing, content, and coordination of its regulations with those of other agencies. But once EPA has responded to a petition for rulemaking, its reasons for action or inaction must conform to the authorizing statute. Under the clear terms of the Clean Air Act, EPA can avoid taking further action only if it determines that greenhouse gases do not contribute to climate change or if it provides some reasonable explanation as to why it cannot or will not exercise its discretion to determine whether they do. *Ibid.* To the extent that this constrains agency discretion to pursue other priorities of the Administrator or the President, this is the congressional design.

EPA has refused to comply with this clear statutory command. Instead, it has offered a laundry list of reasons not to regulate. For example, EPA said that a number of voluntary executive branch programs already provide an effective response to the threat of global warming, 68 Fed. Reg. 52932, that regulating greenhouse gases might impair the President's ability to negotiate with "key developing nations" to reduce emissions, *id.*, at 52931, and that curtailing motor-vehicle emissions would reflect "an inefficient, piecemeal approach to address the climate change issue," *ibid.*

Although we have neither the expertise nor the authority to evaluate these policy judgments, it is evident they have nothing to do with whether greenhouse gas emissions contribute to climate change. Still less do they amount to a reasoned justification for declining to form a scientific judgment. In particular, while the President has broad authority in foreign affairs, that authority does not extend to the refusal to execute domestic laws. In the Global Climate Protection Act of 1987, Congress authorized the State Department—not EPA—to formulate United States foreign policy with reference to environmental matters relating to climate. See § 1103(c), 101 Stat. 1409. EPA has made no showing that it issued the ruling in question here after consultation with the State Department. Congress did direct EPA to consult with other agencies in the formulation of its policies and rules, but the State Department is absent from that list. § 1103(b).

Nor can EPA avoid its statutory obligation by noting the uncertainty surrounding various features of climate change and concluding that it would therefore be better not to regulate at this time. See 68 Fed. Reg. 52930–52931. If the scientific uncertainty is so profound that it precludes EPA from making a reasoned judgment as to whether greenhouse gases contribute to global warming, EPA must say so. That EPA would prefer not to regulate greenhouse gases because of some residual uncertainty—which, contrary to JUSTICE SCALIA's apparent belief [referring to Justice Scalia's dissent] is in fact all that it said, see 68 Fed. Reg. 52929 ("We do not believe . . . that it would be either effective or appropriate for EPA to establish [greenhouse gas] standards for motor vehicles at this time" (emphasis added))—is irrelevant. The statutory question is whether sufficient information exists to make an endangerment finding.

In short, EPA has offered no reasoned explanation for its refusal to decide whether greenhouse gases cause or contribute to climate change. Its action was therefore "arbitrary, capricious, . . . or otherwise not in accordance with law." 42 U. S. C. § 7607(d)(9)(A). We need not and do not reach the question whether on remand EPA must make an endangerment finding, or whether policy concerns can inform EPA's actions in the event that it makes such a finding. We hold only that EPA must ground its reasons for action or inaction in the statute.

VIII

The judgment of the Court of Appeals is reversed, and the case is remanded for further proceedings consistent with this opinion.

JUSTICE SCALIA, with whom THE CHIEF JUSTICE, JUSTICE THOMAS, and JUSTICE ALITO join, dissenting.

I

A

* * * As the Court recognizes, the statute "condition[s] the exercise of EPA's authority on its formation of a 'judgment.'" * * * There is no dispute that the Administrator has made no such judgment in this case. * * *

The question thus arises: Does anything require the Administrator to make a "judgment" whenever a petition for rulemaking is filed? Without citation of the statute or any other authority, the Court says yes. Why is that so? When Congress wishes to make private action force an agency's hand, it knows how to do so.* * * Where does the CAA say that the EPA Administrator is required to come to a decision on this question whenever a rulemaking petition is filed? The Court points to no such provision because none exists.

Instead, the Court invents a multiple-choice question that the EPA Administrator must answer when a petition for rulemaking is filed. The Administrator must exercise his judgment in one of three ways: (a) by concluding that the pollutant does cause, or contribute to, air pollution that endangers public welfare (in which case EPA is required to regulate); (b) by concluding that the pollutant does not cause, or contribute to, air pollution that endangers public welfare (in which case EPA is not required to regulate); or (c) by "provid[ing] some reasonable explanation as to why it cannot or will not exercise its discretion to determine whether" greenhouse gases endanger public welfare, ante, at 30, (in which case EPA is not required to regulate).

I am willing to assume, for the sake of argument, that the Administrator's discretion in this regard is not entirely unbounded— that if he has no reasonable basis for deferring judgment he must grasp the nettle at once. The Court, however, with no basis in text or precedent, rejects all of EPA's stated "policy judgments" as not "amount[ing] to a reasoned justification," * * * effectively narrowing the universe of potential reasonable bases to a single one: Judgment can be delayed only if the Administrator concludes that "the scientific uncertainty is [too] profound." * * * The Administrator is precluded from concluding for other reasons "that it would . . . be better not to regulate at this time." * * * Such other reasons—perfectly valid reasons—were set forth in the agency's statement.

"We do not believe . . . that it would be either effective or appropriate for EPA to establish [greenhouse gas] standards for motor vehicles at this time. As described in detail below, the President has laid out a comprehensive approach to climate change that calls for near-term voluntary actions and incentives along with programs aimed at reducing scientific uncertainties and encouraging technological development so that the government may effectively and efficiently address the climate change issue over the long term.

. . . "[E]stablishing [greenhouse gas] emission standard for U. S. motor vehicles at this time would . . . result in an inefficient, piecemeal approach to addressing the climate change issue. The U. S. motor vehicle fleet is one of many sources of [greenhouse gas] emissions both here and abroad, and different [greenhouse gas] emission sources face different technological and financial challenges in reducing emissions. A sensible regulatory scheme would require that all significant sources and sinks of [greenhouse gas] emissions be considered in deciding how best to achieve any needed emission reductions.

"Unilateral EPA regulation of motor vehicle [greenhouse gas] emissions could also weaken U. S. efforts to persuade developing countries to reduce the [greenhouse gas] intensity of their economies. Considering the large populations and growing economies of some developing countries, increases in their [greenhouse gas] emissions could quickly overwhelm the effects of [greenhouse gas] reduction measures in developed countries. Any potential benefit of EPA regulation could be lost to the extent other nations decided to let their emissions significantly increase in view of U. S. emissions reductions. Unavoidably, climate change raises important foreign policy issues, and it is the President's prerogative to address them." [excerpted from EPA's petition denial.]

The Court dismisses this analysis as "rest[ing] on reasoning divorced from the statutory text." "While the statute does condition the exercise of EPA's authority on its formation of a 'judgment,' . . . that judgment must relate to whether an air pollutant 'cause[s], or contribute[s] to, air pollution which may reasonably be anticipated to endanger public health or welfare.' " True but irrelevant. When the Administrator makes a judgment whether to regulate greenhouse gases, that judgment must relate to whether they are air pollutants that "cause, or contribute to, air pollution which may reasonably be anticipated to endanger public health or welfare." the statute says nothing at all about the reasons for which the Administrator may defer making a judgment—the permissible reasons for deciding not to grapple with the issue at the present time. Thus, the various "policy" rationales, * * * that the Court criticizes are not "divorced from the statutory text," except in the sense that the statutory text is silent, as texts are often silent about permissible reasons for the exercise of agency discretion. The reasons the EPA gave are surely considerations executive agencies regularly take into account (and ought to take into account) when deciding whether to consider entering a new field: the impact such entry would have on other Executive Branch programs and on foreign policy. There is no basis in law for the Court's imposed limitation.

EPA's interpretation of the discretion conferred by the statutory reference to "its judgment" is not only reasonable, it is the most natural reading of the text. The Court nowhere explains why this interpretation is incorrect, let alone why it is not entitled to deference under Chevron. As the Administrator acted within the law in declining to make a "judgment" for the policy reasons above set forth, I would uphold the decision to deny the rulemaking petition on that ground alone.

B

Even on the Court's own terms, however, the same conclusion follows. As mentioned above, the Court gives EPA the option of determining that the science is too uncertain to allow it to form a "judgment" as to whether greenhouse gases endanger public welfare. Attached to this option (on what basis is unclear) is an essay requirement: "If," the Court says, "the scientific uncertainty is so profound that it precludes EPA from making a reasoned judgment as to whether greenhouse gases contribute to global warming, EPA must say so." But EPA has said precisely that—and at great length, based on information contained in a 2001 report by the National Research Council (NRC) entitled Climate Change Science: An Analysis of Some Key Questions:

"As the NRC noted in its report, concentrations of [greenhouse gases (GHGs)] are increasing in the atmosphere as a result of human activities (pp. 9–12). It also noted that '[a] diverse array of evidence points to a warming of global surface air temperatures' (p.16). The report goes on to state, however, that '[b]ecause of the large and still uncertain level of natural variability inherent in the climate record and the uncertainties in the time histories of the various forcing agents (and particularly aerosols), a [causal] linkage between the buildup of greenhouse gases in the atmosphere and the observed climate changes during the 20th century cannot be unequivocally established. The fact that the magnitude of the observed warming is large in comparison to natural variability as simulated in climate models is suggestive of such a linkage, but it does not constitute proof of one because the model simulations could be deficient in natural variability on the decadal to century time scale' (p. 17).

"The NRC also observed that 'there is considerable uncertainty in current understanding of how the climate system varies naturally and reacts to emissions of [GHGs] and aerosols' (p. 1). As a result of that uncertainty, the NRC cautioned that 'current estimate of the magnitude of future warming should be regarded as tentative and subject to future adjustments (either upward or downward).' *Id.* It further advised that '[r]educing the wide range of uncertainty inherent in current model predictions of global climate change will require major advances in understanding and modeling of both (1) the factors that determine atmospheric concentrations of [GHGs] and aerosols and (2) the so-called "feedbacks" that determine the sensitivity of the climate system to a prescribed increase in [GHGs].' *Id.*

"The science of climate change is extraordinarily complex and still evolving. Although there have been substantial advances in climate change science, there continue to be important uncertainties in our understanding of the factors that may affect future climate change and how it should be addressed. As the NRC explained, predicting future climate change necessarily involves a complex web of economic and physical factors including: Our ability to predict future global anthropogenic emissions of GHGs and aerosols; the fate of these emissions once they enter the atmosphere (e.g., what percentage are absorbed by vegetation or are taken up by the oceans); the impact of those emissions that remain in the atmosphere on the radiative properties of the atmosphere; changes in critically important climate feedbacks (e.g., changes in cloud cover and ocean circulation); changes in temperature characteristics (e.g., average temperatures, shifts in daytime and evening temperatures); changes in other climatic parameters (e.g., shifts in precipitation, storms); and ultimately the impact of such changes on human health and welfare (e.g., increases or decreases in agricultural productivity, human health impacts). The NRC noted, in particular, that '[t]he understanding of the relationships between weather/climate and human health is in its infancy and therefore the health consequences of climate change are poorly understood' (p. 20). Substantial scientific uncertainties limit our ability to assess each of these factors and to separate out those changes resulting from natural variability from those that are directly the result of increases in anthropogenic GHGs.

"Reducing the wide range of uncertainty inherent in current model predictions will require major advances in understanding and modeling of the factors that determine atmospheric concentrations of greenhouse gases and aerosols, and the processes that determine the sensitivity of the climate system." [excerpted from EPA's petition denial.]

I simply cannot conceive of what else the Court would like EPA to say.

II

A

Even before reaching its discussion of the word "judgment," the Court makes another significant error when it concludes that "§ 202(a)(1) of the Clean Air Act authorizes EPA to regulate greenhouse gas emissions from new motor vehicles in the event that it forms a 'judgment' that such emissions contribute to climate change." Ante, at 25 (emphasis added). For such authorization, the Court relies on what it calls "the Clean Air Act's capacious definition of 'air pollutant.'"

"Air pollutant" is defined by the Act as "any air pollution agent or combination of such agents, including any physical, chemical, . . . substance or matter which is emitted into or otherwise enters the ambient air." 42 U. S. C. § 7602(g). The Court is correct that "[c]arbon dioxide, methane, nitrous oxide, and hydro fluorocarbons," * * * fit within the second half of that definition: They are "physical, chemical, . . . substance[s] or matter which [are]emitted into or otherwise ente[r] the ambient air." But the Court mistakenly believes this to be the end of the analysis. In order to be an "air pollutant" under the Act's definition, the "substance or matter [being] emitted into . . . the ambient air" must also meet the first half of the definition—namely, it must be an "air pollution agent or combination of such agents." The Court simply pretends this half of the definition does not exist.

The Court's analysis faithfully follows the argument advanced by petitioners, which focuses on the word "including" in the statutory definition of "air pollutant." As that argument goes, anything that follows the word "including" must necessarily be a subset of whatever precedes it. Thus, if greenhouse gases qualify under the phrase following the word "including," they must qualify under the phrase preceding it. Since greenhouse gases come within the capacious phrase "any physical, chemical, . . . substance or matter which is emitted into or otherwise enters the ambient air," they must also be "air pollution agent[s] or combination[s] of such agents," and therefore meet the definition of "air pollutant[s]."

That is certainly one possible interpretation of the statutory definition. The word "including" can indeed indicate that what follows will be an "illustrative" sampling of the general category that precedes the word. Often, however, the examples standing alone are broader than the general category, and must be viewed as limited in light of that category. The Government provides a helpful (and unanswered) example: "The phrase 'any American automobile, including any truck or minivan,' would not naturally be construed to encompass a foreign-manufactured [truck or] minivan." * * * The general principle enunciated—that the speaker is talking about American automobiles—carries forward to the illustrative examples (trucks and minivans), and limits them accordingly, even though in isolation they are broader. Congress often uses the word "including" in this manner.

In short, the word "including" does not require the Court's (or the petitioners') result. It is perfectly reasonable to view the definition of "air pollutant" in its entirety: An air pollutant can be "any physical, chemical, . . . substance or matter which is emitted into or otherwise enters the ambient air," but only if it retains the general characteristic of being an "air pollution agent or combination of such agents." This is precisely the conclusion EPA reached: "[A] substance does not meet the CAA definition of 'air pollutant' simply because it is a 'physical, chemical, . . . substance or matter which is emitted into or otherwise enters the ambient air.' It must also be an 'air pollution agent.' " * * * Once again, in the face of textual ambiguity, the Court's application of Chevron deference to EPA's interpretation of the word "including" is nowhere to be found.[2]

Evidently, the Court defers only to those reasonable interpretations that it favors.

B

Using (as we ought to) EPA's interpretation of the definition of "air pollutant," we must next determine whether greenhouse gases are

---

[2]   Not only is EPA's interpretation reasonable, it is far more plausible than the Court's alternative. As the Court correctly points out, "all airborne compounds of whatever stripe," * * * would qualify as "physical, chemical, . . . substance[s] or matter which [are] emitted into or otherwise ente[r] the ambient air," * * *. It follows that everything airborne, from Frisbees to flatulence, qualifies as an "air pollutant." This reading of the statute defies common sense.

"agent[s]" of "air pollution." If so, the statute would authorize regulation; if not, EPA would lack authority.

Unlike "air pollutants," the term "air pollution" is not itself defined by the CAA; thus, once again we must accept EPA's interpretation of that ambiguous term, provided its interpretation is a "permissible construction of the statute." [citing Chevron] In this case, the petition for rulemaking asked EPA for "regulation of [greenhouse gas] emissions from motor vehicles to reduce the risk of global climate change." Thus, in deciding whether it had authority to regulate, EPA had to determine whether the concentration of greenhouse gases assertedly responsible for "global climate change" qualifies as "air pollution." EPA began with the commonsense observation that the "[p]roblems associated with atmospheric concentrations of CO2," * * * bear little resemblance to what would naturally be termed "air pollution" [and that EPA's prior use of the CAA's general regulatory provisions address air pollution problems that occur primarily at ground level or near the surface of the earth].

In other words, regulating the buildup of CO2 and other greenhouse gases in the upper reaches of the atmosphere, which is alleged to be causing global climate change, is no taking to regulating the concentration of some substance that is polluting the air.

We need look no further than the dictionary for confirmation that this interpretation of "air pollution" is eminently reasonable. The definition of "pollute," of course, is "[t]o make or render impure or unclean." Webster's New International Dictionary 1910 (2d ed. 1949). And the first three definitions of "air" are as follows: (1) "[t]he invisible, odorless, and tasteless mixture of gases which surrounds the earth"; (2) "[t]he body of the earth's atmosphere; esp., the part of it near the earth, as distinguished from the upper rarefied part"; (3) "[a] portion of air or of the air considered with respect to physical characteristics or as affecting the senses." EPA's conception of "air pollution"— focusing on impurities in the "ambient air" "at ground level or near the surface of the earth"—is perfectly consistent with the natural meaning of that term.

In the end, EPA concluded that since "CAA authorization to regulate is generally based on a finding that an air pollutant causes or contributes to air pollution," the concentrations of CO2 and other greenhouse gases allegedly affecting the global climate are beyond the scope of CAA's authorization to regulate. "[T]he term 'air pollution' as used in the regulatory provisions cannot be interpreted to encompass global climate change." Once again, the Court utterly fails to explain why this interpretation is incorrect, let alone so unreasonable as to be unworthy of Chevron deference.

The Court's alarm over global warming may or may not be justified, but it ought not distort the outcome of this litigation. This is a straightforward administrative-law case, in which Congress has passed a malleable statute giving broad discretion, not to us but to an executive agency. No matter how important the underlying policy issues at stake, this Court has no business substituting its own desired outcome for the reasoned judgment of the responsible agency.

NOTES

1.   After a long and protracted battle, the EPA issued an endangerment finding in April, 2009 holding that greenhouse gas emissions in the atmosphere threaten the public health and welfare "of current and future generations." U.S. Environmental Protection Agency, *Overview of EPA's Proposed Endangerment and Cause or Contribute Findings for Greenhouse Gases Under the Clean Air Act* (April 17, 2009). The Obama Administration then followed the endangerment finding with two sets of regulations to cut greenhouse gases from vehicles. The first set grew out of California's efforts to regulate GHGs from passenger cars. The effort began when the state passed Assembly Bill 1493, authorizing the state's Air Resources Board to establish standards for emissions of carbon dioxide (CO_2). *See* California Air Resources Board, Climate Change, http://www.arb.ca.gov/cc/cc.htm#Background, for more information about regulations implementing the law, which were to take effect in January 2006 for model years 2009 and thereafter. California could not implement its regulations without a waiver from the federal government. After a long and convoluted battle that included several federal lawsuits and an initial denial of the waiver by the Bush Administration, on June 30, 2009 the EPA finally granted the California waiver. California and the U.S. then issued harmonized greenhouse gas regulations for 2012–2016 model years, regulations that also harmonized fuel economy standards (known as I standards) under the Energy Policy and Conservation Act. The standards set a fleet average of 35.5 miles per gallon by the 2016 year. The federal government and California together then issued a set of standards for the 2017–2025 model years, with a 2025 fleet average standard of 55.5 mph. *See* U.S. EPA, *Regulations for Emissions from Vehicles and Engines, Final Rule for Model Year 2017 and Later Light Duty Vehicle Greenhouse Gas Emissions and Corporate Average Fuel Economy Standards.* The Trump Administration has since proposed freezing the second set of standards at 2020 levels and revoking the California waiver to issue greenhouse gas standards and for its Zero Emission Vehicle program. U.S. EPA, *U.S. EPA and DOT Propose Fuel Economy Standards for MY 2021–2026 Vehicles.* The Administration claims that the new standards would be uneconomical and cause an increase in traffic deaths, both claims that have been heavily criticized. *See, e.g.,* Robinson Meyer, *The Trump Administration Flunked Its Math Homework*, THE ATLANTIC (Oct. 31, 2018), https://www. theatlantic.com/science/archive/2018/10/trumps-clean-car-rollback-is-riddled- with-math-errors-clouding-its-legal-future/574249/. For an explanation of how the proposal to revoke California's waiver is part of a broader attack on

California climate policy, *see* Ann Carlson, *The Trump Administration's Assault on California's Global Climate Leadership,* 112 AJIL UNBOUND 269 (2018), HTTPS://WWW.CAMBRIDGE.ORG/CORE/JOURNALS/AMERICAN-JOURNAL-OF-INTERNATIONAL-LAW/ARTICLE/TRUMP-ADMINISTRATIONS-ASSAULT-ON-CALIFORNIAS-GLOBAL-CLIMATE-LEADERSHIP/B8E9E27819772B52B9515E518C C289F6. At the time this book went to press the Trump Administration proposal to freeze the standards and revoke California's waiver had not yet been finalized.

2.   Is *MA v. EPA* consistent with *FDA v. Brown & Williamson?* In that case, the Food, Drug and Cosmetics Act (FDCA) defined a "drug" as "any article (other than food) intended to affect the structure or any function of the human body." At least facially, nicotine surely met that definition. Yet in interpreting the FDCA, the Court emphasized a canon of construction that statutes should not be construed to give agencies authority over questions of great "economic and political" significance unless Congress has spoken clearly (known as the "major questions" canon). Scholars have referred to this outcome as "democracy-forcing" because it sends the matter back to democratically elected officials for a clear statement. The EPA was arguably in a far stronger position than was the FDA in *Brown & Williamson*: both *Chevron* and the "major questions" canon pulled in the same direction, toward deference to the agency. Yet the Court did not engage in democracy-forcing in *MA v. EPA*. It did not defer to the EPA, which would have required Congress to more clearly authorize GHG regulation if it wanted the EPA to act. How can you reconcile the two cases? Was there a relevant difference in congressional activity in the two fields of tobacco regulation and climate change? Or was *Brown & Williamson* simply an aberrational case, involving an ad hoc doctrinal move that turned out to have no traction? Was *Brown v. Williamson* "democracy forcing" or simply "industry protecting"? After *MA v. EPA*, has *Brown v. Williamson* been limited to its facts (that is, overruled in all but name)?

3.   The EPA's endangerment finding has enormous implications for the regulation of greenhouse gas emissions. One possibility is that EPA should issue NAAQS for greenhouse gases. Can you see why? Does the endangerment finding mean that the EPA will now be required, under *NRDC v. Train,* to list carbon dioxide and other greenhouse gas emissions as a criteria pollutant under Section 108(a)(1)? Does it matter that the U.S. cannot, on its own, reduce greenhouse gas emissions dramatically enough to solve the problem of global climate change?

Instead, EPA has used the PSD and NSPS sections of the act to regulate greenhouse gases. For an explanation of how the endangerment finding set off a cascade of regulations once made, *see* Ann E. Carlson, *An Ode to the Clean Air Act,* 30 J LAND USE & ENV LAW 119 (2014). Recall that the PSD and NSPS sections apply not just to criteria pollutants but to "any air pollutant" regulated under the CAA. Once EPA issued its finding that greenhouse gas emissions endanger public health and welfare as required, it next issued what are known as the "Timing and Tailoring rules." A huge number of businesses challenged those rules and the endangerment finding and were joined by some states opposed to greenhouse gas regulation, including Texas. The D. C. Circuit upheld the endangerment finding in *Coalition for Responsible Regulation v. EPA*, 684 F.3d 102 (D.C. Circuit, 2012); the U.S. Supreme Court issued the following opinion about the Timing and Tailoring Rules.

UTILITY AIR REGULATORY GROUP V. EPA
United States Supreme Court, 2014.
573 U.S. 302, 134 S.Ct. 2427, 189 L.Ed.2d 372.

JUSTICE SCALIA announced the judgment of the Court and delivered the opinion of the Court with respect to Parts I and II.

Acting pursuant to the Clean Air Act, the Environmental Protection Agency recently set standards for emissions of "greenhouse gases" (substances it believes contribute to "global climate change") from new motor vehicles. We must decide whether it was permissible for EPA to determine that its motor-vehicle greenhouse-gas regulations automatically triggered permitting requirements under the Act for stationary sources that emit greenhouse gases.

I.   Background

A.   Stationary-Source Permitting

The Clean Air Act regulates pollution-generating emissions from both stationary sources, such as factories and powerplants, and moving sources, such as cars, trucks, and aircraft. . . .

* * *

Stationary sources in areas designated attainment or unclassifiable are subject to the Act's provisions relating to "Prevention of Significant Deterioration" (PSD). §§ 7470–7492. EPA interprets the PSD provisions to apply to sources located in areas that are designated attainment or unclassifiable for *any* NAAQS pollutant, regardless of whether the source emits that specific pollutant. * * *

It is unlawful to construct or modify a "major emitting facility" in "any area to which [the PSD program] applies" without first obtaining a permit. §§ 7475(a)(1), 7479(2)(C). To qualify for a permit, the facility must not cause or contribute to the violation of any applicable air-quality standard, § 7475(a)(3), and it must comply with emissions limitations that reflect the "best available control technology" (or BACT) for "each pollutant subject to regulation under" the Act. § 7475(a)(4). The Act defines a "major emitting facility" as any stationary source with the potential to emit 250 tons per year of "any air pollutant" (or 100 tons per year for certain types of sources). § 7479(1). It defines "modification" as a physical or operational change that causes the facility to emit more of "any air pollutant." § 7411(a)(4).

[The Court also explained the requirements of Title V, requiring general permits for all major sources].

B. EPA's Greenhouse-Gas Regulations

In 2007, the Court held that Title II of the Act "authorize[d] EPA to regulate greenhouse gas emissions from new motor vehicles" if the Agency "form[ed] a 'judgment' that such emissions contribute to climate change." *Massachusetts v. EPA,* 549 U.S. 497, 528, 127 S.Ct. 1438, 167 L.Ed.2d 248 (quoting § 7521(a)(1)). In response to that decision, EPA embarked on a course of regulation resulting in "the single largest expansion in the scope of the [Act] in its history." Clean Air Act Handbook, at xxi.

* * * *Under EPA's view, once greenhouse gases became regulated under any part of the Act, the PSD and Title V permitting requirements would apply to all stationary sources with the potential to emit greenhouse gases in excess of the statutory thresholds: 100 tons per year under Title V, and 100 or 250 tons per year under the PSD program depending on the type of source. Because greenhouse-gas emissions tend to be "orders of magnitude greater" than emissions of conventional pollutants, EPA projected that numerous small sources not previously regulated under the Act would be swept into the PSD program and Title V, including "smaller industrial sources," "large office and residential buildings, hotels, large retail establishments, and similar facilities." The Agency warned that this would constitute an "unprecedented expansion of EPA authority that would have a profound effect on virtually every sector of the economy and touch every household in the land," yet still be "relatively ineffective at reducing greenhouse gas concentrations."

In 2009, EPA announced its determination regarding the danger posed by motor-vehicle greenhouse-gas emissions. * * *

Next, EPA issued its "final decision" regarding the prospect that motor-vehicle greenhouse-gas standards would trigger stationary-source permitting requirements. (hereinafter Triggering Rule). EPA announced that beginning on the effective date of its greenhouse-gas standards for motor vehicles, stationary sources would be subject to the PSD program and Title V on the basis of their potential to emit greenhouse gases. * * *

EPA then announced steps it was taking to "tailor" the PSD program and Title V to greenhouse gases. (hereinafter Tailoring Rule). Those steps were necessary, it said, because the PSD program and Title V were designed to regulate "a relatively small number of large industrial sources," and requiring permits for all sources with greenhouse-gas emissions above the statutory thresholds would radically expand those programs, making them both unadministrable and "unrecognizable to the Congress that designed" them. EPA nonetheless rejected calls to exclude greenhouse gases entirely from those programs, asserting that the Act is not "ambiguous with respect to the need to cover [greenhouse-gas] sources under either the PSD or title V program." Instead, EPA adopted a "phase-in approach" that it said would "appl[y] PSD and title V at threshold levels that are as close to the statutory levels as possible, and do so as quickly as possible, at least to a certain point."

The phase-in, EPA said, would consist of at least three steps. During Step 1, from January 2 through June 30, 2011, no source would become newly subject to the PSD program or Title V solely on the basis of its greenhouse-gas emissions; however, sources required to obtain permits anyway because of their emission of conventional pollutants (so-called "anyway" sources) would need to comply with BACT for greenhouse gases if they emitted those gases in significant amounts, defined as at least 75,000 tons per year CO_2e. During Step 2, from July 1, 2011, through June 30, 2012, sources with the potential to emit at least 100,000 tons per year CO_2e of greenhouse gases would be subject to PSD and Title V permitting for their construction and operation and to PSD permitting for modifications that would increase their greenhouse-gas emissions by at least 75,000 tons per year CO_2e. At Step 3, beginning on July 1, 2013, EPA said it might (or might not) further reduce the permitting thresholds (though not below 50,000 tons per year CO_2e), and it might (or might not) establish permanent exemptions for some sources. Beyond Step 3, EPA promised to complete another round of rulemaking by April 30, 2016, in which it would "take further action to address small sources," which might (or might not) include establishing permanent exemptions.

. . . After the decision below, EPA issued its final Step 3 rule, in which it decided not to lower the thresholds it had established at Step 2 until at least 2016.

* * *

II. Analysis

This litigation presents two distinct challenges to EPA's stance on greenhouse-gas permitting for stationary sources. First, we must decide whether EPA permissibly determined that a source may be subject to the PSD and Title V permitting requirements on the sole basis of the source's potential to emit greenhouse gases. Second, we must decide whether EPA permissibly determined that a source already subject to the PSD program because of its emission of conventional pollutants (an "anyway" source) may be required to limit its greenhouse-gas emissions by employing the "best available control technology" for greenhouse gases.

* * *

We review EPA's interpretations of the Clean Air Act using the standard set forth in *Chevron U.S.A. Inc. v. Natural Resources Defense Council, Inc.* Under *Chevron*, we presume that when an agency-administered statute is ambiguous with respect to what it prescribes,

Congress has empowered the agency to resolve the ambiguity. The question for a reviewing court is whether in doing so the agency has acted reasonably and thus has "stayed within the bounds of its statutory authority."

A. The PSD and Title V Triggers

We first decide whether EPA permissibly interpreted the statute to provide that a source may be required to obtain a PSD or Title V permit on the sole basis of its potential greenhouse-gas emissions.

1

EPA thought its conclusion that a source's greenhouse-gas emissions may necessitate a PSD or Title V permit followed from the Act's unambiguous language. The Court of Appeals agreed and held that the statute "compelled" EPA's interpretation. We disagree. The statute compelled EPA's greenhouse-gas-inclusive interpretation with respect to neither the PSD program nor Title V.

The Court of Appeals reasoned by way of a flawed syllogism: Under *Massachusetts,* the general, Act-wide definition of "air pollutant" includes greenhouse gases; the Act requires permits for major emitters of "any air pollutant"; therefore, the Act requires permits for major emitters of greenhouse gases. The conclusion follows from the premises only if the air pollutants referred to in the permit-requiring provisions (the minor premise) are the same air pollutants encompassed by the Act-wide definition as interpreted in *Massachusetts* (the major premise). Yet no one—least of all EPA—endorses that proposition, and it is obviously untenable.

The Act-wide definition says that an air pollutant is "any air pollution agent or combination of such agents, including any physical, chemical, biological, [or] radioactive . . . substance or matter which is emitted into or otherwise enters the ambient air." § 7602(g). In *Massachusetts,* the Court held that the Act-wide definition includes greenhouse gases because it is all-encompassing; it "embraces all airborne compounds of whatever stripe." 549 U.S., at 529, 127 S.Ct. 1438. But where the term "air pollutant" appears in the Act's operative provisions, EPA has routinely given it a narrower, context-appropriate meaning.

That is certainly true of the provisions that require PSD and Title V permitting for major emitters of "any air pollutant." Since 1978, EPA's regulations have interpreted "air pollutant" in the PSD permitting trigger as limited to *regulated* air pollutants. . . And since 1993 EPA has informally taken the same position with regard to the Title V permitting trigger, a position the Agency ultimately incorporated into some of the regulations at issue here. Those interpretations were appropriate: It is plain as day that the Act does not envision an elaborate, burdensome permitting process for major emitters of steam, oxygen, or other harmless airborne substances. It takes some cheek for EPA to insist that it cannot possibly give "air pollutant" a reasonable, context-appropriate meaning in the PSD and Title V contexts when it has been doing precisely that for decades.

Nor are those the only places in the Act where EPA has inferred from statutory context that a generic reference to air pollutants does not encompass every substance falling within the Act-wide definition. Other examples abound:

- The Act authorizes EPA to enforce new source performance standards (NSPS) against a pre-existing source if, after promulgation of the standards, the source undergoes a physical or operational change that increases its emission of "any air pollutant." § 7411(a)(2), (4), (b)(1)(B). EPA interprets that provision as limited to air pollutants *for which EPA has promulgated new source performance standards.* 36 Fed.Reg. 24877 (1971), codified, as amended, 40 C.F.R. § 60.2; 40 Fed.Reg. 58419 (1975), codified, as amended, 40 C.F.R. § 60.14(a).

- The Act requires a permit for the construction or operation in a nonattainment area of a source with the potential to emit 100 tons per year of "any air pollutant." §§ 7502(c)(5), 7602(j). EPA interprets that provision as limited to pollutants *for which the area is designated nonattainment.* 45 Fed.Reg. 52745 (1980), promulgating 40 C.F.R. § 51.18(j)(2), as amended, § 51.165(a)(2).

* * *

Although these limitations are nowhere to be found in the Act-wide definition, in each instance EPA has concluded—as it has in the PSD and Title V context—that the statute is not using "air pollutant" in *Massachusetts'* broad sense to mean any airborne substance whatsoever.

Massachusetts did not invalidate all these longstanding constructions. That case did not hold that EPA must always regulate greenhouse gases as an "air pollutant" everywhere that term appears in the statute, but only that EPA must "ground its reasons for action *or inaction* in the statute," 549 U.S., at 535, 127 S.Ct. 1438 (emphasis added), rather than on "reasoning divorced from the statutory text," *id.,* at 532, 127 S.Ct. 1438. EPA's inaction with regard to Title II was not sufficiently grounded in the statute, the Court said, in part because nothing in the Act suggested that regulating greenhouse gases under that Title would conflict with the statutory design. Title II would not compel EPA to regulate in any way that would be "extreme," "counterintuitive," or contrary to " 'common sense.' " *Id.,* at 531, 127 S.Ct. 1438. At most, it would require EPA to take the modest step of adding greenhouse-gas standards to the roster of new-motor-vehicle emission regulations. *Ibid.*

Massachusetts does not strip EPA of authority to exclude greenhouse gases from the class of regulable air pollutants under other parts of the Act where their inclusion would be inconsistent with the statutory scheme. The Act-wide definition to which the Court gave a "sweeping" and "capacious" interpretation, *id.,* at 528, 532, 127 S.Ct. 1438, is not a command to regulate, but a description of the universe of substances EPA may *consider* regulating under the Act's operative provisions. *Massachusetts* does not foreclose the Agency's use of statutory context to infer that certain of the Act's provisions use "air pollutant" to denote not every conceivable airborne substance, but only those that may sensibly be encompassed within the particular regulatory program.

* * *

To be sure, Congress's profligate use of "air pollutant" where what is meant is obviously narrower than the Act-wide definition is not conducive to clarity. One ordinarily assumes " 'that identical words used in different parts of the same act are intended to have the same meaning.' " *Environmental Defense v. Duke Energy Corp.,* 549 U.S. 561, 574, 127 S.Ct. 1423, 167 L.Ed.2d 295 (2007). In this respect (as in countless others), the Act is far from a *chef d'oeuvre* of legislative draftsmanship. But we, and EPA, must do our best, bearing in mind the " 'fundamental canon of statutory construction that the words of a statute must be read in their context and with a view to their place in the overall statutory scheme.' " *FDA v. Brown & Williamson Tobacco Corp.,* 529 U.S. 120, 133, 120 S.Ct. 1291, 146 L.Ed.2d 121 (2000). As we reiterated the same day we decided *Massachusetts,* the presumption of consistent usage " 'readily yields' " to context, and a statutory term—even one defined in the statute—"may take on distinct characters from association with distinct statutory objects calling for different implementation strategies." *Duke Energy, supra,* at 574, 127 S.Ct. 1423.

We need not, and do not, pass on the validity of all the limiting constructions EPA has given the term "air pollutant" throughout the Act. We merely observe that taken together, they belie EPA's rigid insistence that when interpreting the PSD and Title V permitting requirements it is bound by the Act-wide definition's inclusion of greenhouse gases, no matter how incompatible that inclusion is with those programs' regulatory structure.

* * *

2

Having determined that EPA was mistaken in thinking the Act *compelled* a greenhouse-gas-inclusive interpretation of the PSD and Title

V triggers, we next consider the Agency's alternative position that its interpretation was justified as an exercise of its "discretion" to adopt "a reasonable construction of the statute." Tailoring Rule 31517. We conclude that EPA's interpretation is not permissible.

Even under *Chevron* 's deferential framework, agencies must operate "within the bounds of reasonable interpretation." *Arlington,* 569 U.S., at ___, 133 S.Ct., at 1868. And reasonable statutory interpretation must account for both "the specific context in which . . . language is used" and "the broader context of the statute as a whole." *Robinson v. Shell Oil Co.,* 519 U.S. 337, 341, 117 S.Ct. 843, 136 L.Ed.2d 808 (1997). A statutory "provision that may seem ambiguous in isolation is often clarified by the remainder of the statutory scheme . . . because only one of the permissible meanings produces a substantive effect that is compatible with the rest of the law." *United Sav. Assn. of Tex. v. Timbers of Inwood Forest Associates, Ltd.,* 484 U.S. 365, 371, 108 S.Ct. 626, 98 L.Ed.2d 740 (1988). Thus, an agency interpretation that is "inconsisten[t] with the design and structure of the statute as a whole," *University of Tex. Southwestern Medical Center v. Nassar,* 570 U.S. ___, ___, 133 S.Ct. 2517, 2529, 186 L.Ed.2d 503 (2013), does not merit deference.

EPA itself has repeatedly acknowledged that applying the PSD and Title V permitting requirements to greenhouse gases would be inconsistent with—in fact, would overthrow—the Act's structure and design. In the Tailoring Rule, EPA described the calamitous consequences of interpreting the Act in that way. Under the PSD program, annual permit applications would jump from about 800 to nearly 82,000; annual administrative costs would swell from $12 million to over $1.5 billion; and decade-long delays in issuing permits would become common, causing construction projects to grind to a halt nationwide. The picture under Title V was equally bleak: The number of sources required to have permits would jump from fewer than 15,000 to about 6.1 million; annual administrative costs would balloon from $62 million to $21 billion; and collectively the newly covered sources would face permitting costs of $147 billion. Moreover, "the great majority of additional sources brought into the PSD and title V programs would be small sources that Congress did not expect would need to undergo permitting." EPA stated that these results would be so "contrary to congressional intent," and would so "severely undermine what Congress sought to accomplish," that they necessitated as much as a 1,000-fold increase in the permitting thresholds set forth in the statute.

Like EPA, we think it beyond reasonable debate that requiring permits for sources based solely on their emission of greenhouse gases at the 100- and 250-tons-per-year levels set forth in the statute would be "incompatible" with "the substance of Congress' regulatory scheme." *Brown & Williamson,* 529 U.S., at 156, 120 S.Ct. 1291. A brief review of the relevant statutory provisions leaves no doubt that the PSD program and

Title V are designed to apply to, and cannot rationally be extended beyond, a relative handful of large sources capable of shouldering heavy substantive and procedural burdens.

Start with the PSD program, which imposes numerous and costly requirements on those sources that are required to apply for permits. Among other things, the applicant must make available a detailed scientific analysis of the source's potential pollution-related impacts, demonstrate that the source will not contribute to the violation of any applicable pollution standard, and identify and use the "best available control technology" for each regulated pollutant it emits. § 7475(a)(3), (4), (6), (e). The permitting authority (the State, usually) also bears its share of the burden: It must grant or deny a permit within a year, during which time it must hold a public hearing on the application. § 7475(a)(2), (c). Not surprisingly, EPA acknowledges that PSD review is a "complicated, resource-intensive, time-consuming, and sometimes contentious process" suitable for "hundreds of larger sources," not "tens of thousands of smaller sources."

Title V contains no comparable substantive requirements but imposes elaborate procedural mandates. It requires the applicant to submit, within a year of becoming subject to Title V, a permit application and a "compliance plan" describing how it will comply with "all applicable requirements" under the Act; to certify its compliance annually; and to submit to "inspection, entry, monitoring, . . . and reporting requirements." §§ 7661b(b)–(c), 7661c(a)–(c).

* * *

The fact that EPA's greenhouse-gas-inclusive interpretation of the PSD and Title V triggers would place plainly excessive demands on limited governmental resources is alone a good reason for rejecting it; but that is not the only reason. EPA's interpretation is also unreasonable because it would bring about an enormous and transformative expansion in EPA's regulatory authority without clear congressional authorization. When an agency claims to discover in a long-extant statute an unheralded power to regulate "a significant portion of the American economy," *Brown & Williamson,* 529 U.S., at 159, 120 S.Ct. 1291, we typically greet its announcement with a measure of skepticism. We expect Congress to speak clearly if it wishes to assign to an agency decisions of vast "economic and political significance." *Id.,* at 160, 120 S.Ct. 1291; see also *MCI Telecommunications Corp. v. American Telephone & Telegraph Co.,* 512 U.S. 218, 231, 114 S.Ct. 2223, 129 L.Ed.2d 182 (1994); *Industrial Union Dept., AFL-CIO v. American Petroleum Institute,* 448 U.S. 607, 645–646, 100 S.Ct. 2844, 65 L.Ed.2d 1010 (1980) (plurality opinion). The power to require permits for the construction and modification of tens of thousands, and the operation of millions, of small sources nationwide falls comfortably within the class of authorizations that we have been reluctant to read into ambiguous statutory text. Moreover, in EPA's assertion of that authority, we confront a singular situation: an agency laying claim to extravagant statutory power over the national economy while at the same time strenuously asserting that the authority claimed would render the statute "unrecognizable to the Congress that designed" it. Since, as we hold above, the statute does not compel EPA's interpretation, it would be patently unreasonable—not to say outrageous—for EPA to insist on seizing expansive power that it admits the statute is not designed to grant.

3

EPA thought that despite the foregoing problems, it could make its interpretation reasonable by adjusting the levels at which a source's greenhouse-gas emissions would oblige it to undergo PSD and Title V permitting. Although the Act, in no uncertain terms, requires permits for sources with the potential to emit more than 100 or 250 tons per year of a relevant pollutant, EPA in its Tailoring Rule wrote a new threshold of *100,000* tons per year for greenhouse gases.

* * *

We conclude that EPA's rewriting of the statutory thresholds was impermissible and therefore could not validate the Agency's interpretation of the triggering provisions. An agency has no power to "tailor" legislation to bureaucratic policy goals by rewriting unambiguous statutory terms. Agencies exercise discretion only in the interstices created by statutory silence or ambiguity; they must always " 'give effect to the unambiguously expressed intent of Congress.' " *National Assn. of Home Builders v. Defenders of Wildlife,* 551 U.S. 644, 665, 127 S.Ct. 2518, 168 L.Ed.2d 467 (2007) (quoting *Chevron,* 467 U.S., at 843, 104 S.Ct. 2778). It is hard to imagine a statutory term less ambiguous than the precise numerical thresholds at which the Act requires PSD and Title V permitting. When EPA replaced those numbers with others of its own choosing, it went well beyond the "bounds of its statutory authority." *Arlington,* 569 U.S., at ___, 133 S.Ct., at 1868 (emphasis deleted).

* * *

Were we to recognize the authority claimed by EPA in the Tailoring Rule, we would deal a severe blow to the Constitution's separation of powers. Under our system of government, Congress makes laws and the President, acting at times through agencies like EPA, "faithfully execute[s]" them. U.S. Const., Art. II, § 3; see *Medellín v. Texas,* 552 U.S. 491, 526–527, 128 S.Ct. 1346, 170 L.Ed.2d 190 (2008). The power of executing the laws necessarily includes both authority and responsibility to resolve some questions left open by Congress that arise during the law's administration. But it does not include a power to revise clear statutory terms that turn out not to work in practice.

In the Tailoring Rule, EPA asserts newfound authority to regulate millions of small sources—including retail stores, offices, apartment buildings, shopping centers, schools, and churches—and to decide, on an ongoing basis and without regard for the thresholds prescribed by Congress, how many of those sources to regulate. We are not willing to stand on the dock and wave goodbye as EPA embarks on this multiyear voyage of discovery. We reaffirm the core administrative-law principle that an agency may not rewrite clear statutory terms to suit its own sense of how the statute should operate. EPA therefore lacked authority to "tailor" the Act's unambiguous numerical thresholds to accommodate its greenhouse-gas-inclusive interpretation of the permitting triggers. Instead, the need to rewrite clear provisions of the statute should have alerted EPA that it had taken a wrong interpretive turn. Agencies are not free to "adopt . . . unreasonable interpretations of statutory provisions and then edit other statutory provisions to mitigate the unreasonableness." App. 175, 2012 WL 6621785, *16 (Kavanaugh, J., dissenting from denial of rehearing en banc). Because the Tailoring Rule cannot save EPA's interpretation of the triggers, that interpretation was impermissible under *Chevron*.

B.   BACT for "Anyway" Sources

For the reasons we have given, EPA overstepped its statutory authority when it decided that a source could become subject to PSD or Title V permitting by reason of its greenhouse-gas emissions. But what about "anyway" sources, those that would need permits based on their emissions of more conventional pollutants (such as particulate matter)? We now consider whether EPA reasonably interpreted the Act to require those sources to comply with "best available control technology" emission standards for greenhouse gases.

1

To obtain a PSD permit, a source must be "subject to the best available control technology" for "each pollutant subject to regulation under [the Act]" that it emits. § 7475(a)(4). The Act defines BACT as "an emission limitation based on the maximum degree of reduction of each pollutant subject to regulation" that is "achievable . . . through application of production processes and available methods, systems, and techniques, including fuel cleaning, clean fuels, or treatment or innovative fuel combustion techniques." § 7479(3). BACT is determined "on a case-by-case basis, taking into account energy, environmental, and economic impacts and other costs." *Ibid.*

Some petitioners urge us to hold that EPA may never require BACT for greenhouse gases—even when a source must undergo PSD review based on its emissions of conventional pollutants—because BACT is fundamentally unsuited to greenhouse-gas regulation. BACT, they say, has traditionally been about end-of-stack controls "such as catalytic converters or particle collectors"; but applying it to greenhouse gases will make it more about regulating energy use, which will enable regulators to control "every aspect of a facility's operation and design," right down to the "light bulbs in the factory cafeteria." Brief for Petitioner Energy-Intensive Manufacturers Working Group on Greenhouse Gas Regulation et al. in No. 12–1254, But see Brief for Calpine Corp. as *Amicus Curiae* 10 ("[I]n Calpine's experience with 'anyway' sources, the [greenhouse-gas] analysis was only a small part of the overall permitting process").

EPA has published a guidance document that lends some credence to petitioners' fears. It states that at least initially, compulsory improvements in energy efficiency will be the "foundation" of greenhouse-gas BACT, with more traditional end-of-stack controls either not used or "added as they become more available." PSD and Title V Permitting Guidance for Greenhouse Gases 29 (Mar. 2011) (hereinafter Guidance); see Peloso & Dobbins, Greenhouse Gas PSD Permitting: The Year in Review, 42 Tex. Env. L.J. 233, 247 (2012) ("Because [other controls] tend to prove infeasible, energy efficiency measures dominate the [greenhouse-gas] BACT controls approved by the states and EPA"). But EPA's guidance also states that BACT analysis should consider options *other than* energy efficiency, such as "carbon capture and storage." Guidance 29, 32, 35–36, 42–43. EPA argues that carbon capture is reasonably comparable to more traditional, end-of-stack BACT technologies, *id.,* at 32, n. 86, and petitioners do not dispute that.

Moreover, assuming without deciding that BACT may be used to force some improvements in energy efficiency, there are important limitations on BACT that may work to mitigate petitioners' concerns about "unbounded" regulatory authority. For one, BACT is based on "control technology" for the applicant's "proposed facility," § 7475(a)(4); therefore, it has long been held that BACT cannot be used to order a fundamental redesign of the facility. For another, EPA has long interpreted BACT as required only for pollutants that the source itself emits, see 44 Fed.Reg. 51947 (1979); accordingly, EPA acknowledges that BACT may not be used to require "reductions in a facility's demand for energy from the electric grid." Guidance 24. Finally, EPA's guidance suggests that BACT should not require every conceivable change that could result in minor improvements in energy efficiency, such as the aforementioned light bulbs. *Id.,* at 31. The guidance explains that permitting authorities should instead consider whether a proposed regulatory burden outweighs any reduction in emissions to be achieved, and should concentrate on the facility's equipment that uses the largest amounts of energy. *Ibid.*

2

The question before us is whether EPA's decision to require BACT for greenhouse gases emitted by sources otherwise subject to PSD review is, as a general matter, a permissible interpretation of the statute under *Chevron*. We conclude that it is.

The text of the BACT provision is far less open-ended than the text of the PSD and Title V permitting triggers. It states that BACT is required "for each pollutant subject to regulation under this chapter" (*i.e.,* the entire Act), § 7475(a)(4), a phrase that—as the D.C. Circuit wrote 35 years ago—"would not seem readily susceptible [of] misinterpretation." *Alabama Power Co. v. Costle,* 636 F.2d 323, 404 (1979). Whereas the dubious breadth of "any air pollutant " in the permitting triggers suggests a role for agency judgment in identifying the subset of pollutants covered by the particular regulatory program at issue, the more specific phrasing of the BACT provision suggests that the necessary judgment has already been made by Congress. The wider statutory context likewise does not suggest that the BACT provision can bear a narrowing construction: There is no indication that the Act elsewhere uses, or that EPA has interpreted, "each pollutant subject to regulation under this chapter" to mean anything other than what it says.

Even if the text were not clear, applying BACT to greenhouse gases is not so disastrously unworkable, and need not result in such a dramatic expansion of agency authority, as to convince us that EPA's interpretation is unreasonable. We are not talking about extending EPA jurisdiction over millions of previously unregulated entities, but about moderately increasing the demands EPA (or a state permitting authority) can make of entities already subject to its regulation. And it is not yet clear that EPA's demands will be of a significantly different character from those traditionally associated with PSD review. In short, the record before us does not establish that the BACT provision as written is incapable of being sensibly applied to greenhouse gases.

We acknowledge the potential for greenhouse-gas BACT to lead to an unreasonable and unanticipated degree of regulation, and our decision should not be taken as an endorsement of all aspects of EPA's current approach, nor as a free rein for any future regulatory application of BACT in this distinct context. Our narrow holding is that nothing in the statute categorically prohibits EPA from interpreting the BACT provision to apply to greenhouse gases emitted by "anyway" sources.

However, EPA may require an "anyway" source to comply with greenhouse-gas BACT only if the source emits more than a *de minimis* amount of greenhouse gases. As noted above, the Tailoring Rule applies BACT only if a source emits greenhouse gases in excess of 75,000 tons per year CO_2e, but the Rule makes clear that EPA did not arrive at that number by identifying the *de minimis* level. See nn. 1, 3, *supra.* EPA may establish an appropriate *de minimis* threshold below which BACT is not required for a source's greenhouse-gas emissions. We do not hold that 75,000 tons per year CO_2e necessarily exceeds a true *de minimis* level, only that EPA must justify its selection on proper grounds. Cf. *Alabama Power, supra,* at 405.

To sum up: We hold that EPA exceeded its statutory authority when it interpreted the Clean Air Act to require PSD and Title V permitting for stationary sources based on their greenhouse-gas emissions. Specifically, the Agency may not treat greenhouse gases as a pollutant for purposes of defining a "major emitting facility" (or a "modification" thereof) in the PSD context or a "major source" in the Title V context. To the extent its regulations purport to do so, they are invalid. EPA may, however, continue to treat greenhouse gases as a "pollutant subject to regulation under this chapter" for purposes of requiring BACT for "anyway" sources. The judgment of the Court of Appeals is affirmed in part and reversed in part.

It is so ordered.

NOTES

1.   Why didn't EPA just categorically exempt small emitters of greenhouse gases from the PSD provisions on the grounds that Congress could not have intended to apply the provisions so broadly or on the grounds of administrative convenience? *See* NRDC v. Costle, 568 F.2d 1369 (D.C. Circ 1977), excerpted at page 602, *infra.* Could EPA have simply delayed indefinitely regulating small sources and succeeded in doing so even if sued?

2.   Do you agree with Justice Scalia's application of Chevron, Step 1, to the interpretation of the PSD threshold levels and the definition of air pollutant?

3.   What is the import of the plurality's reliance on *Brown v. Williamson?* Consider this question in light of legal challenges to the Obama Administration's Clean Power Plan, described below in paragraph 5.

4.   The PSD provisions are not the only CAA sections triggered by the endangerment finding. The NSPS provisions, like the PSD provisions, apply to "any air pollutant." *See* Section 111 of the CAA. Can you trace the basis for the triggering of NSPS for greenhouse gas emissions?

5.   In 2014, EPA, after a protracted legal and political battle, issued NSPS for both new and existing electric generating units (EGUs or, more conventionally, power plants) to limit greenhouse gas emissions. The rules for new power plants would have essentially banned the regulatory approval of coal-fired power plants by setting an emissions limit equivalent to efficient natural gas plants, one that existing technology for new coal plants couldn't easily meet. The much larger regulatory program, however, would have regulated greenhouse gases from *existing* power plants. Section 111(d) of the

CAA requires states to submit plans similar to SIPs that establish "standards of performance" for "an existing source of any air pollutant" that is not regulated as a criteria pollutant. 42 U.S.C. § 7411(d). "Standard of performance" is defined as a standard "which reflects the degree of emission limitation achievable through the application of the best system of emission reduction which ... the Administrator determines has been adequately demonstrated." 42 U.S.C. § 7411(a)(1). In issuing existing power plant regulations, (the Clean Power Plan), the Obama EPA treated the "best system of emission reduction" as the electric grid itself. It set targets for individual states to meet through their plans based not only on traditional controls on existing power plants but also by including reductions that could occur by going "beyond the fenceline" of the power plant to include reductions that could be achieved by switching to cleaner fuels (e.g., coal to natural gas) and to renewable fuels. When fully implemented, the CPP was expected to reduce GHGs from the electricity sector by 32 percent below 2005 levels. For a more detailed explanation of the CPP, *see* U.S. EPA Archived Documents, *Overview of the Clean Power Plan*, https://archive.epa.gov/epa/sites/production/files/2015-08/documents/fs-cpp-overview.pdf. The CPP was challenged immediately by a coalition of states and industry groups. *State of West Virginia v. EPA*, No. 15–1363 (D.C. Circuit Court of Appeals). In what many observers considered to be an extraordinary move, the U.S. Supreme Court stayed the implementation of the CPP pending resolution of its legality. *See* U.S. Supreme Court, *Order in Pending Case, Chamber of Commerce. v EPA* (2016), https://www.supremecourt.gov/orders/courtorders/020916zr3_hf5m.pdf. Although the case is still pending in the D.C. Circuit Court of Appeal, the Trump Administration has withdrawn the rule and issued a new proposed rule in its place.

6. The new Trump Administration proposed rule under Section 111(d) is called the "Affordable Clean Energy" (ACE) Rule. It sets the best system of emission reduction based only on "inside the fenceline" reductions, in other words those reductions that can occur only from controlling emissions directly from individual power plants. *See* U.S. Environmental Protection Agency, *Proposal: Affordable Clean Energy (ACD) Rule*, https://www.epa.gov/stationary-sources-air-pollution/proposal-affordable-clean-energy-ace-rule. The proposed rule would result in far fewer emissions reductions than the CPP (indeed perhaps emissions increases) and may well cost industry as much as CPP compliance would. *See* 83 Fed. Reg. at 44786, Table 9.

7. Relying on the *Chevron* doctrine, what arguments would you make in support of EPA's Clean Power Plan proposal? What role do you think *Brown v. Williamson* could play if the CPP reached the U.S. Supreme Court? Do you think the new proposed ACE rule is based on a permissible interpretation of Section 111d?

The Clean Power Plan and the fuel economy standards formed the heart of the Obama Administration's submission to the United Nations Framework Convention on Climate Change to comply with its obligation to submit a Nationally Determined Contribution (NDC) under the Paris Agreement. For an explanation of how the Paris Agreement works and the role of NDCs *see* Chapter 1 at page 44 *infra*. The Trump Administration announced in 2017 that is withdrawing the U.S. from the Paris Agreement and repudiating the U.S. commitments contained in its NDC.

4. MARKET MECHANISMS TO CONTROL AIR POLLUTION

The Clean Power Plan would have allowed states to set up regional, market-based programs to reduce emissions from the electricity sector. The Transport Rule described in UARG v. EPA, *supra* at page 545 also uses market mechanisms to reduce air pollutants from power plants. And the NO_x trading scheme that preceded the Transport Rule, described *supra* at page 517, embodies a market based approach to air pollution—it is a "cap and trade" system under which government establishes the upper limit of pollution (in this case in the form of pollution "budgets"), but then relies on the states to manage the necessary reductions. Although cap-and-trade programs were once thought to be dubious—even immoral—because they essentially allocate "rights" to pollute, they have now become fairly common. They are especially widespread around the world to address greenhouse gases, including in California and in the Regional Green House Gas Initiative, a cap-and-trade program to reduce greenhouse gases from the power sector in the northeastern United States. Cap-and-trade systems can provide flexibility and produce cheaper emissions reductions than conventional regulation but can also pose unique problems, and differ from prescriptive regulatory regimes in important ways. We explore these systems in the materials below.

a. Banking, Bubbles, and Offsets

Long before developing the NOx trading program, the EPA first experimented with a variety of smaller-scale market mechanisms in the New Source Review provisions of the Clean Air Act. These techniques include "bubbles," "netting" and "offsets." For example, offsets apply only within a single nonattainment area (or areas with equal or worse nonattainment problems that contribute to the first area's nonattainment), while bubbles cover only a single multi-source plant. The first excerpt below offers a helpful overview of some of these regulatory devices and an early evaluation of them. The second focuses specifically on the bubble rule adopted by the EPA in the famous *Chevron* case, excerpted in Chapter 5, *supra*, page 351.

ROBERT W. HAHN & GORDON L. HESTER, MARKETABLE PERMITS: LESSONS FOR THEORY AND PRACTICE
16 ECOLOGY L.Q. 361 (1989).[2]

Offsets are used by new and modified sources in nonattainment areas and by certain specified sources in attainment areas. The Clean Air Act specifies that no new emission sources would be allowed in areas that did not meet the original 1975 air quality deadlines. Concern that this provision would stifle economic growth prompted EPA to institute the offset rule in 1976. This rule requires new and modified emission sources in these areas to obtain emission credits from sources in the same area to offset their new emissions. The sources are still subject to the most stringent emission limits. Offsets may be obtained through internal or external trades. [O]ffset transactions are controlled at the state level.

Bubbles, first allowed in 1979, are used by existing sources in attainment or nonattainment areas. The name derives from the concept of placing an imaginary bubble over a multi-source plant. The levels of emission controls applied to different sources in a bubble may be adjusted to reduce control costs so long as the aggregate limit is not exceeded. In effect, emission credits are created by some sources within the plant and used by others. Originally, all bubbles had to be submitted by the states to EPA for approval. In 1981 EPA began to approve "generic bubble rules" that enabled states to approve bubbles. Several states now have such rules.

Banking, which was first allowed in 1979, provides a mechanism for firms to save emission credits for future use. EPA has established guidelines for banking programs, but states must set up and administer the rules governing banking. * * *

[L]evels of activity in the three programs have varied widely. * * * An estimated 2,000 offset transactions have taken place, of which only about ten percent have been external. Fewer than 150 bubbles have been approved, only two of which are known to have involved external trades. About twice as many bubbles have been approved by states under generic rules than have been approved at the federal level. In fact, the general pattern seems to be that programs controlled at the state level are much more active than those controlled at the federal level. Banking, however, was not received well by either state regulators or firms. The figures listed for banking are an estimate of the number of times firms have withdrawn banked credits for sale or use. There has been little such activity.

* * * Federally approved bubbles have resulted in savings estimated at $300 million, while state bubbles have resulted in an estimated $135

---

[2]   Copyright © 1989, Ecology Law Quarterly. Reprinted by permission.

million in cost savings.[77] * * * [O]ffsets result in no direct emission control cost savings because the use of offsets does not allow a firm to avoid any emission limits. However, since a firm using offsets is allowed to locate major new emission sources in nonattainment areas, presumably there is some economic advantage to the firm, or it would locate in an attainment area where offsets are not required. The willingness of firms to go to the expense of obtaining offsets indicates that they derive some net gain from doing so, but the extent of this gain cannot be estimated. Cost savings from banking also cannot be estimated, but are necessarily small given the number of transactions that have occurred.

[T]he effects [of trading] on environmental quality have been, on the whole, insignificant. * * * Offsets, which require trading ratios greater than 1:1, will naturally lead to reduced emissions. For bubbles, the lack of systematic data collection leaves the question of effects on environmental quality unresolved, but early reports indicated that aggregate effects may be slightly positive. Emission credits for a few of these transactions have been created by lowering permitted emission levels, but not making any actual reduction in emissions. Such transactions have an adverse environmental effect in the sense that emission reductions that would otherwise have been required were foregone. However, their aggregate effect on air quality in local areas is thought to be inconsequential. Banking has probably had a very slight positive effect, since banked credits represent emission reductions that have not been used to offset emission increases. However, because there has been little banking activity, this effect is also very small.

The performance evaluation of emissions trading activities reveals a mixed bag of accomplishments and disappointments. The program has clearly afforded many firms flexibility in meeting emission limits. This flexibility has resulted in significant aggregate cost savings—in the billions of dollars—without significantly affecting environmental quality. However, these cost savings have been realized almost entirely from internal trading. They fall far short of the potential savings that could be realized if there were more external trading.

A variety of factors affect the performance of emissions trading. High transaction costs are the single most important determinant of program performance. A large part of these costs result from regulatory restrictions on trading and from administrative requirements that prolong the approval of trades.

---

[77] All cost savings figures are for the lives of the different programs, and are not adjusted for inflation. It is interesting to note that although more state bubbles have been approved than federal, the average cost savings for federal bubbles is much higher.

JODY FREEMAN, THE STORY OF CHEVRON: ENVIRONMENTAL LAW AND ADMINISTRATIVE DISCRETION

ENVIRONMENTAL LAW STORIES 171 (Richard Lazarus & Oliver Houck eds. 2005).[3]

* * *

II.   The Debate over the Bubble Approach

The bubble rule at issue in *Chevron* did not appear overnight. As the EPA began implementing the CAA in the early seventies, the agency began to consider the merits of using the bubble in a variety of CAA programs. This was part of a larger move toward adopting emissions trading, a policy tool that was quickly swept up in the politics of environmental regulation.

In theory, the bubble concept seems completely unobjectionable. It simply treats all the polluting units in a firm as if there were a tent over them, with a single hole for emissions, and allows firms to distribute emissions reductions among the individual units in whichever manner they choose. The bubble concept is a way of affording firms flexibility to make operational decisions about how to reach a given regulatory target in the cheapest way possible, providing they meet the target. Why does this benefit firms? Given the cost of technology, it can be much more expensive to squeeze the last increment of pollution control out of a new piece of equipment than to take other steps—such as shutting down an older and less efficient unit, switching fuels, or finding other practices to change at the facility that will yield improvements in air quality. The bubble allows firms to choose their poison.

To see the potential benefits of such an approach, consider what Mike Levin, Assistant Administrator in EPA's Office of Planning and Management (OPM) at the time, often did in cafeterias around the country to illustrate it.

> Take a salt shaker and a pepper shaker. Assume that command and control regulation typically requires uniform reductions from each emission point within an industrial category. If the shakers each are stacks at (say) a refinery, and each currently is allowed to (and does) emit 250 tons per year (TPY) of volatile organic compounds, a new rule would require each to reduce by 100 TPY. But let's say it will cost 5 times as much to reduce 100 tons at Salt as at Pepper because, for example, there's not enough room to install control equipment there, or because Salt's location is much hotter, so it will have to install condensers & refrigeration to make control equipment work reliably.

> Why not allow Pepper (or Pepper plus another unregulated refinery source emitting the same pollutants) to reduce by 200

---

tons instead? Costs might not only be reduced fivefold in this case, but industry resistance to issuance of the rule in the first place could be reduced. So would foot-dragging on compliance, or applications for "variances" on grounds of cost-effectiveness (which if granted, would require little or no reduction at Salt). More important, the rule suddenly seems reasonable, because it allows adjustment for site-specific variations that regulators knew nothing about. Still more important, it encourages regulated sources to come forward with superior and more efficient reduction options than they had previously had reason to seek or disclose. Regulators can use this information to secure further reductions with less friction on a system-wide basis, as long as they do so without directly penalizing the sources that came forward this way. Over time, regulators' jobs get easier, and more real reductions are secured.

Understood in these terms, bubbles seem eminently sensible. Indeed, as an abstract policy idea, the bubble concept garnered praise from everyone: EPA officials, representatives of industry, and even environmentalists. Yet the disagreement lay in details of the *application* of the bubble concept by EPA in nonattainment zones. There is a vast difference between using a bubble to help existing sources achieve compliance under approved state plans, and using it to allow offsets between units in non-attainment zones, as the EPA's bubble rule did.

To appreciate the "dark side" of the bubble consider these objections: as implemented by EPA in nonattainment zones, the bubble allowed firms to retire or modify old units and apply the resulting emission credits to new or modified units. And this would occur without requiring the firm to install pollution control technology that would force an even greater reduction in emission levels over time. Allowing this kind of offsetting essentially enables firms to perpetuate existing emission levels indefinitely. They "bank" the excess pollution from old units, converting existing pollution levels into an entitlement going forward. The public never sees the air quality benefit of retired units with this approach. Over time, the bubble could also result in firms capturing future credits for what are called "anyway" tons—tons of pollution that would have been retired anyway, as firms, in the regular course of business, replace old equipment with new units.

Moreover, when examined closely, the EPA's application of the bubble in fact allowed firms to calculate a net *increase* in pollution as if it were equivalent to no net increase. This was the result of the agency's definition of what constituted a "significant increase" for purposes of triggering NSR. Under the agency's definition, for example, a forty-ton increase in emissions would not be considered significant. So using bubbles in nonattainment zones would actually allow air quality to degrade in areas of the country where health risks were perceived to be greatest.

Perhaps the most fundamental objection to the bubble was that companies were evading controls that were obviously intended to apply when new capital commitments were made, by opportunistically seizing the inevitable "headroom" between the actual operation of existing sources and the regulatory requirements applicable to them. What the regulatory reforms sought to do was to capture that extra "headroom" and give it back to the companies instead of the public. The result for non-attainment zones then, was the exact opposite effect of what Congress seemed to require. Finally, industry's argument that NSR would retard modernization was dubious: pollution control costs, it was argued, are only one factor in a firm's investment decisions.

Leading the opposition to the bubble on these grounds was the Natural Resources Defense Council (NRDC), which had emerged by the mid-seventies as a forceful advocate for the environment (and which, of course, ultimately ended up as the plaintiff in *Chevron*). In the NRDC's view, widespread adoption of the bubble would at worst reduce, and at best delay, the air quality gains that would otherwise have been made under NSR.

Perhaps surprisingly, many states opposed the bubble idea as well. They worried that this new policy idea would provide industry with new opportunities to litigate, potentially interfering with the states' attempts to revise their SIPs, and generally undermining ongoing enforcement efforts. Moreover, a number of states believed they already had the authority to use bubbles, and some were already doing so; they thought they possessed the flexibility that the EPA wanted to bestow upon them.

The divide over bubbles also pervaded the agency itself. Scratch the surface of *Chevron* and one finds not a united EPA seeking policy flexibility and judicial deference, but a struggle within the agency based on two very different views of the law. On one side were regulatory reformers like Mike Levin, who believed that the promise of market mechanisms—in terms of cost savings, ease of administration, and incentives to modernization—outweighed the inflated predictions about what command and control strategies would otherwise achieve. They argued that chasing every small emissions increase was a misallocation of resources that would cost firms dearly for little air quality gain. Command and control regulation was reaching its limits in terms of effectiveness. Bubbles would simply afford states flexibility as they wrote SIPs, and the SIPs could be relied upon to guarantee compliance with NAAQS.

On the other side were many career employees in the agency, both in the Office of Air Quality Planning and Standards (OAQPS) and the enforcement office, who believed that most of the progress on air pollution had been, and would continue to be, the result of forcing firms to apply technology to their sources (as in the New Source Performance Standards Program). * * *

Beyond the matter of whether the bubble policy was a lawful interpretation of the statutory term "stationary source"—the key legal issue in *Chevron*—there remains the question of whether the bubble concept is good policy. At the time, there was little empirical evidence one way or the other; the likely effect of the bubble's widespread adoption was a matter of pure speculation. So the policy debate turned mostly on a normative argument about whether using such a strategy would be, in theory, superior to the alternative of the unit-by-unit approach required by command and control. One's view of this depends heavily on one's beginning assumptions about the appropriate baseline from which to make comparisons. In the debate over whether the EPA's bubble strategy would advance or retard progress toward the federal air quality standards, a key question was, and still is, "What, realistically, would NSR have *otherwise* required?"

This kind of conflict over baselines arises often in environmental regulation, especially in the context of air regulation. Should we assume that a command and control program will be perfectly implemented, and then compare the anticipated results to a market approach? Or is it more realistic to assume incomplete implementation, and to consider the cost and administrative expense associated with the command and control approach, when comparing it to the market alternative? And what are the transaction costs and compliance rates of the market alternative?

Whether trading of this sort, in any of its applications, is good policy, is not a "snapshot" issue. That is, any attempt at a real world answer must take account of how the policy has evolved over time, whether it has been reformed in light of criticism (in the case of the bubble, to eliminate the opportunity for "phony" paper trades). And, most importantly, answering this question requires continually comparing the trading option to the (also evolving and also imperfect) alternatives. Would we have been better off without the bubble? Would cap-and-trade programs—now the preferred policy tool for addressing greenhouse gas regulation—have developed even if *Chevron* had come out the other way? The answer is unclear.

NOTE

Some environmentalists have complained that bubbles and offsets make little contribution to progress on pollution control. For example, Professor Rodgers notes concerns that many offsets are for improvements already required in SIPs, and offsets are rarely available to new sources but are instead used by the owners of existing sources who wish to expand or build new facilities. WILLIAM H. RODGERS, ENVIRONMENTAL LAW 217–18 (2d ed. 1994). Are they still preferable to command-and-control regulation? In which instances would you resort to one over the other?

b.   Intra-State Trading Regimes

Congress has sought to encourage states to adopt market mechanisms in their state implementation plans. For example, § 110 specifically authorizes states to adopt economic incentives such as fees, marketable permits, and auctions of emissions rights among the "enforceable emission limits" states must impose in their SIPs. There are also examples of intra-state trading schemes. Yet these measures can be difficult to design. California's South Coast Air Quality Management District adopted Rule 1610, creating the Regional Clean Air Incentives Market (RECLAIM), a "cap and trade" program under which stationary sources like oil refineries were given initial allowances of RECLAIM Trading Credits (or RTCs), which they could either consume or sell to other facilities. RECLAIM was expected to apply initially to about 400 facilities, accounting for between two-thirds and three-quarters of the emissions from stationary sources with permits. The initial allocation was set based on maximum emissions during 1989–1992, with an adjustment to control the total emissions from all sources. The amount of pollution represented by an RTC was to decline steadily each year. For a detailed description of the program, *see* Daniel P. Selmi, *Transforming Economic Incentives from Theory to Reality: The Marketable Permit Program of the South Coast Air Quality Management District*, 24 Envtl. L. Rep. 10695 (1994).

By 1998, more than $42 million in trades had taken place among the 330 facilities in the program (as of 2011 there are 276 facilities in the program). In the early years of the program, emission reductions fell far short of their targets, and the retrofitting anticipated by the program was been minimal. A November, 2002 EPA report evaluating RECLAIM's performance since its inception, concluded that the program had produced far fewer emission reductions than were projected at time of adoption. The report is available at http://www.epa.gov/region9/air/reclaim/reclaim-report.pdf. Most critically, problems with program design, including the failure to establish a robust market and no provision to allow for the banking of allowances, led to a major crisis in the program during the 2000–01 electricity crisis when allowance prices spiked dramatically and the cap was breached. The South Coast Air Quality Management District then revised the program rules in response to the crisis. *See* South Coast Air Quality Management District, *Over a Dozen Years of RECLAIM Implementation: Lessons Learned from California's First Air Pollution Cap-and-Trade Program* (June 2007), http://www.aqmd.gov/docs/default-source/reclaim/policy-paper/policy-paper-part-1.pdf.

Critics of RECLAIM argue that the initial allocation of credits were so plentiful and cheap that the market could not work effectively to incentivize emission reductions. *See* Gary Polakovic, *Innovative Smog Plan Makes Little Progress*, L.A. TIMES, Apr. 17, 2001, B1. In addition, the scheme has attracted criticism from the environmental justice movement because it proposed to include trades between stationary and mobile sources emissions, potentially creating "hot spots" that concentrate pollution in low-income and minority neighborhoods. *See* Richard T. Drury et al., *Pollution Trading and Environmental Injustice: Los Angeles' Failed Experiment in Air Quality Policy*, 9 DUKE ENVTL. L. & POL'Y F. 231 (1999); Vivien Foster & Robert W. Hahn, *Designing More Efficient Markets: Lessons from Los Angeles Smog Control*, 38 J. L. & ECON. 19 (1995). Another article accused RECLAIM of stifling technological innovation by forcing companies to hurriedly install pollution-control technologies at the outset of the program rather than allowing them to explore developing options. Curtis A. Moore, *RECLAIM: Southern California's Failed Experiment with Air Pollution Trading*, 34 Envtl. L. Rep. 10261 (2004). Moore also criticized the lack of actual emissions reductions under the RECLAIM regime, the lack of any emissions floor to act as a safety net, and the lack of transparency in the program as leading to non-compliance and outright cheating. *Id.*

Despite the criticisms, RECLAIM remained in effect for many years and stabilized and improved in its effectiveness since the 2000–01 energy crisis. For a review *see* South Coast Air Quality Management District, *Over a Dozen Years of RECLAIM Implementation: Lessons Learned from California's First Air Pollution Cap-and-Trade Program* (June 2007), http://www.aqmd.gov/docs/default-source/reclaim/policy-paper/policy-paper-part-1.pdf. For more background on the program, *see* South Coast Air Quality Management District, *RECLAIM*, http://www.aqmd.gov/home/programs/business/business-detail?title=reclaim. In January, 2018, SCAQMD began to transition RECLAIM away from a market based program to a command and control program. *See* SCAQMD Advisor, *Sunset of Reclaim Program*, (March/April 2018), http://www.aqmd.gov/docs/default-source/publications/aqmd-advisor/march-april-2018-advisor.pdf.

c. Acid Rain

In addition to using bubbles, banking and offsets, in the late eighties, the EPA successfully phased lead out of gasoline using a program that relied in part on a market based trading approach. *See* Richard Newell & Kristian Rogers, *The Market-Based Lead Phasedown, in* MOVING TO MARKETS IN ENVIRONMENTAL REGULATION: LESSONS FROM THIRTY YEARS OF EXPERIENCE (C. Kolstad & J. Freeman eds., 2006). Yet the first wide-scale domestic experiment with a cap and trade system was attempted in the acid rain provisions of the 1990 amendments to the Clean Air Act. The program is widely viewed as a success and as a model for other tradeable permit regimes.

Indeed, it was in connection with the problem of acid rain that interstate air pollution spillover effects initially gained widespread public attention. The dimensions of the transport problem were suggested in an article by an EPA official, discussing the clockwise movement of plumes from Ohio Valley power plants through Illinois, Iowa and Minnesota, over the Great Lakes and Canada, down through New England, and out over the Atlantic. *Ruckelshaus Defends Reagan on Acid Rain, Says House, Senate Measures Would Not Work*, 14 Env't Rep. (BNA) 2205 (Apr. 6, 1984). The problem of ozone transport was exacerbated by firms building tall stacks which were designed to disperse pollution more widely in order to meet air pollution standards near the source.

The EPA estimated that sulfur oxides and nitrogen oxides account for 14 per cent (27.4 million metric tons) and 12 per cent, respectively, of total air pollution in the United States. Although other pollutants also are precursors to acid rain, these two oxides are the major contributors. Sulfur oxides are emitted primarily from stationary sources, such as smelters and power plants, which burn coal as a fuel. Nitrogen oxides come from stationary sources using fossil fuels (56 per cent) and from motor vehicles (40 per cent). After being discharged into the atmosphere, the most common sulfur and nitrogen oxides, sulfur dioxide (SO_2) and nitric oxide (NO), can be chemically converted by oxidation into sulfuric and nitric acids, which may return to the earth as components of rain or snow. Early studies of acid rain concluded that the problem was serious:

> Hundreds of lakes in North America and Scandinavia have become so acidic that they can no longer support fish life. More than 90 lakes in the Adirondack Mountains in New York State are fishless because acidic conditions have inhibited reproduction. Recent data indicate that other areas of the United States, such as northern Minnesota and Wisconsin, may be vulnerable to similar adverse impacts.

> While many of the aquatic effects of acid precipitation have been well documented, data related to possible terrestrial impacts are just beginning to be developed. Preliminary research indicates that the yield from agricultural crops can be reduced as a result of both the direct effects of acids on foliage, and the indirect effects resulting from the leaching of minerals from soils. The productivity of forests may be affected in a similar manner.

EPA, *Acid Rain* 2 (Research Summary, 1979). In addition, acid deposition is contributing to the destruction of stone monuments and statuary throughout the world. The 2,500 year old Parthenon and other classical buildings on the Acropolis in Athens, Greece, have shown much more rapid decay in this century as a result of the city's high air pollution levels. Research is underway to clarify the role of acid rain in the destruction.

Under the Reagan Administration, acid rain became a highly controversial, heavily politicized issue. The Administration's position was that no action on the acid rain problem was advisable until a considerable amount of further study. Hence, the Administration opposed congressionally proposed control programs and refused to take action in cooperation with the Canadians on the problem. *Canada Announces New Effort to Cut Acid Rain*, N.Y. TIMES, March 8, 1984. (Note the resemblance to the George W. Bush administration's approach to greenhouse gases and climate change.)

The political deadlock was broken during the first Bush Administration with the passage of the 1990 Amendments. Congress entirely bypassed the existing mechanism for resolving interstate disputes and established a new system to reduce sulfur dioxide emissions nationwide. In Title IV, Congress created a "cap and trade" market system for addressing sulfur dioxide emissions. Congress set the absolute ceiling on emissions by electric utilities nationwide at 8.9 million tons, and authorized the EPA to allocate annual emissions in tons per year to firms. Firms are allowed to transfer (buy and sell) allocations beneath the cap. Each allowance is equal to one ton of emissions. Firms that are able to reduce their emissions can sell unused allocations, which is intended to create incentives to develop better emission-control technology.

The sulfur trading program introduced in the 1990 Amendments was divided into two phases. In Phase I, extending from 1995 to 1999 and covering only a minority of the nation's steam-electric generating units, over one hundred plants (listed in the Act) were required to meet a standard of 2.5 pounds of SO_2 per million British Thermal Units (BTUs). The 111 utility power plants in question were those that in 1990 emitted more than 2.5 pounds of SO_2 per million BTUs. (For example, generator #1 at the Colbert plant in Alabama received a Phase I allowance of 13,570 tons.) This standard had to be attained by 1995, except that plants using scrubbers to meet the standards had until 1997. This provision was intended to encourage the use of scrubbers and thereby continue at least part of the market for eastern high-sulfur coal. The Phase I allowances were expected to reduce SO_2 emissions by about 10 million tons per year.

Phase II, which began in January, 2000 and applies to virtually all steam-electric utility units in the country, required utilities to reduce emissions by an additional 50 per cent. Large, poorly controlled plants were required to reduce emissions to 1.2 million lbs/mBTUs. A complex formula applies to smaller plants. While total emissions could not exceed 8.9 million tons annually, the EPA had a half million extra allowances in reserve for the first ten years. A further forty thousand allowances could be given to high-growth states. The allowances were allocated largely on the basis of past emissions and fuel consumption, with extra allowances for a variety of purposes. For example, from 1995 to 1999, an extra 200,000 allowances were allocated to power plants in Illinois, Indiana, and Ohio.

In part, the system of allocations embodies the efficiency concerns of economists. It seems to have been manipulated in the interests of regional equity, however, so that utilities that were required to engage in heavy investments would be able to recoup part of their expenses. The initial allocations were large enough that some of these utilities would find it feasible to control emissions more than required to stay within their initial allowance, thereby allowing them to sell excess allowances. At least some of these excess allowances would have to be purchased by new utility plants in order to operate.

By the end of the 1990s, the EPA and many other observers claimed the trading program was a major success. For several years, the Chicago Board of Trade has conducted an annual auction of sulfur dioxide emission allowances on behalf of the EPA, and during the March 2002 auction, the average purchase price for each of the 125,000 currently usable allowances sold at auction was around $167. *See* Michael Bologna, *Results of Sulfur Dioxide Auction Suggest Companies Anticipate Gentler Enforcement*, 33 Env't Rep. (BNA) 678 (2002). There is general agreement that the sulfur dioxide emissions trading program substantially reduced total emissions at a fraction of original estimates of control costs. A study by Resources for the Future found "compelling evidence that the program's benefits far exceed its costs." Indeed, the EPA used the sulfur dioxide program as a model for its emission trading system for NO_x, which it implemented in 1999 by rule, pursuant to CAA § 126. Nevertheless, a 2012 report from the influential policy group Resources for the Future concluded that, "although the program appears to have been successful on nearly all dimensions, a substantial source of its cost-effectiveness was an unanticipated consequence of the deregulation of railroad rates in the late 1970s and early 1980s." *See* Richard Schmalensee and Robert Stavins, *The SO₂ Allowance Trading System: The Ironic History of a Grand Policy Experiment*, Resources for the Future Discussion Paper (2012), https://www.nber.org/papers/w18306.pdf. Further analysis by RFF suggests that the cost savings from the Acid Rain Trading Program are lower than initially estimated (on the order of $210–$240 million annually) and that health costs compared to more traditional regulation much higher. *See* H. Ron Chan, *et al.*, *The Impact of Trading on the Costs and Benefits of the Acid Rain Program*, Resources for the Future Discussion Paper (2017), https://www.nber.org/papers/w21383.pdf.

Recently, because the Acid Raid trading program includes statutory caps that have been met, additional reductions in SO₂ have occurred through the Transport Rule and the predecessor cross-state rules described in the UARG case.

Whatever the trading program's relative success at reducing the cost of total cuts in sulfur emissions, the program has drawn criticism because of the political process that led to its adoption in 1990.

To begin with, Congress never really discussed the level of emissions reduction to seek:

> Review of the history of the 1990 Amendments reveals that reasoned deliberation did not occur. Indeed, in sharp contrast to the expectations of emissions trading proponents, Congress deliberately refused to debate the emissions limitation as the Amendments made their way through the legislature. The legislation, originally proposed by the Bush administration, called for a reduction in sulfur dioxide emissions of approximately ten million tons from 1980 levels. This directive remained unchanged from the time the 1990 Amendments were first proposed to the time they were enacted into law. The Senate did, however, add the 8.9 million ton cap on emissions, apparently in order to ensure the achievement of the ten million ton reduction.

Lisa Heinzerling, *Selling Pollution, Forcing Democracy*, 14 STAN. ENVTL. L.J. 300, 323–24 (1995). This absence of debate was all the more striking because a key study estimated that reducing emissions by eight million tons would be equally effective and perhaps cost only half as much. *Id.* at 326. What Congress did debate was how to allocate the allowances:

> It is difficult to imagine what lies behind these special bonuses and exemptions [under the Act], other than the kind of special interest deal that proponents of emissions trading had hoped their system would preempt. The criteria for special bonuses and exemptions are, indeed, so disparate as to invite the conclusion that the only master strategy at work in the allocation of allowances under the 1990 Amendments was the satisfaction of powerful interests. As two commentators have observed, "It would appear that the Senators saw little distinction between the Clean Air Act and a fight over which defense installation to close, or an appropriation for public works projects. The pork tastes as good, from whichever barrel it comes." It is easy to see, for example, the hand of the eastern coal industry, which mines mostly high-sulfur coal, in the incentives to install scrubbers and clean-coal technology.

Id. at 330. *But cf.* Paul L. Joskow & Richard Schmalensee, *The Political Economy of Market-Based Environmental Policy: The U.S. Acid Rain Program*, 41 J.L. & ECON. 37 (1998) (statistical study of voting patterns finding only limited influence by "special interests").

Such criticism aside, the widely acknowledged success of the SO_2 Allowance Trading Program has helped to build enthusiasm for more widespread adoption of cap and trade programs. As we outlined in Chapter 1, international and state efforts to attack greenhouse gas emissions have relied heavily on cap-and-trade. And EPA has attempted, increasingly, to use cap-and-trade to attack interstate air pollution and its recent success in the *UARG* case will allow those attempts to continue.

d. Design of Cap-and-Trade Systems

Should the type of pollutant matter in deciding whether to use cap and trade to regulate? Is it appropriate to allow trading in toxic pollutants like mercury, even when there is a risk of creating concentrations or "hot spots" that might affect some sub-populations more than others? Are greenhouse gases better suited for cap and trade?

As just noted, recently cap and trade systems have emerged as the preferred policy option for domestic regulation of greenhouse gases. What are the key design questions? Consider the following issues, summarized by a leading Harvard economist:

> The first question might be: What should be the scope of coverage? Which sources and industries should be included? This was a major issue of discussion and debate when the European Union's Emissions Trading System was being designed but it is not necessarily the right place to begin. Just posing this question limits the possibilities and omits what may be some of the best options. Instead, we might ask: What should be the point of regulation? The possibilities include downstream sources (i.e., CO_2 emitting sources), which would require issuing CO_2 emission permits. This would be very similar to the SO_2 allowance trading. Alternatively, we might regulate upstream sources (i.e., producers and importers of fossil fuels). In this scenario, carbon rights would be linked with the carbon content of fossil fuels. This approach would be similar to the EPA's lead trading regime, which was part of the lead phase down in the 1980s—a very successful program that removed leaded gasoline from the market in five years with low transaction costs and cost savings of $250 million per year. There are, in addition, various midstream alternatives.

> When choosing among the alternative points of regulation we should consider the following criteria: First, breadth of coverage. If the point of regulation were downstream generators, CO_2 emission permits would likely include electricity generators and likely exclude motor vehicles, home furnaces, etc. If the point of regulation were upstream producers, a carbon rights system could provide complete coverage of CO_2 emissions. However, non-combustion uses of fuels would be affected, suggesting a need for compensating credits. And what about carbon management (i.e., the separation and removal of CO_2 from stack gases)? An upstream system provides no incentive for this, again suggesting the need for credits. What about biological carbon sequestration, perhaps through an integrated trading system? This would be

much more difficult, but possible and quantitatively important. Second, we should consider the number of regulated entities included in the market. Smaller numbers ease the burden of monitoring and enforcement but could raise competitiveness concerns if the market were very small.

The third relevant criteria is the monitoring regime. Effective monitoring is required for market confidence, but continuous emissions monitoring is very costly. The fourth consideration is the number and type of greenhouse gases to include. This is a design issue itself, and it can affect choice of point of regulation. Should the scheme include only carbon dioxide or others as well? Should the system allow for inter-gas trading?

This brings us to the next design question: What should be the point of allocation? The point of allocation need not be the same as the point of regulation. These are separate design issues. For example, upstream regulation in theory can be combined with mid-stream or downstream allocation of the tradeable permits. Possibilities for point of allocation include downstream sources (e.g., CO_2 emission sources) or sources even further downstream (e.g., electricity users) or upstream producers (e.g., producers and importers of fossil fuels). Note that the point of allocation combined with the nature of the allocation affects the distribution of the cost burden.

The third design question is: What should be the rules for allocation? Should permits or carbon rights be auctioned, given away without charge, or a mix? The political advantages of freely allocating emission rights can lead to efficiency problems. Usually, costs under a tradeable permit regime are independent of initial allocation, so allocation can be left to political process (which is why such systems are so politically attractive). However, the execution of a tradeable permit program—like any such regulatory constraint—can exacerbate distortions & drive up costs. And in contrast to an auctioned permit system—which generates revenues for government—a freely-allocated permit system provides no opportunity for reducing or eliminating the distortions by cutting existing distorting taxes. Further, in the presence of some types of transaction costs, the post-trading outcome is sensitive to the initial allocation. So, a successful attempt to establish a politically viable program through initial (free) allocation can increase costs. There are other issues that arise when choosing the rules for allocation, including the choice of the baseline emissions and baseline year, and the specific allocation cross-sectionally, and over time.

Fourth, what about temporal flexibility? Among the rules that govern trading, those that affect temporal flexibility are exceptionally important. Should the regime allow banking, which entitles the holder to save emission permits for a future time period? Banking has been key in both the lead trading program and the ongoing sulfur dioxide program. But programs that are phased in over time can create emissions leakage from regulated to unregulated sources. There is also the matter of borrowing (using emission permits from a future period). Borrowing can in theory increase cost-effectiveness of a program. The rules for banking and borrowing and for the length of compliance periods (e.g., 1 year in the sulfur dioxide program and five years in the Kyoto Protocol) should depend upon the nature of the environmental problem and the potential solutions. And finally, what kind of enforcement regime is required? Market based instruments such as cap and trade systems are not *deregulation*, but rather can amount to more enlightened regulation. Government enforcement is still required. Stiff penalties provide effective incentives for compliance, but excessive penalties are not credible. For example, in the sulfur dioxide program, the penalty is $2,900 per ton of excess emissions (compared with marginal abatement costs that have been 10% of that); the result is near perfect compliance. The sulfur dioxide program also requires emissions offsets in subsequent years. If this is eliminated, the penalty is a tax on "excess emissions," and we have a "safety valve" on costs. Whether to use such a safety valve is another major design issue. So, reasonable penalties are necessary, but it is wise to avoid prior approval by government for trades because it can drive up transaction costs.

Another worry is whether permits in a cap and trade system might be used as barriers to entry by incumbent firms. In theory, firms with market power in either the permit market or respective product markets can withhold permits from the market, driving up price, and keeping out competition. What to do? The solution in the sulfur dioxide allowance trading program was a zero-revenue annual auction of about 3 per cent of the allowances (i.e., the government is a seller of last resort). While such anti-competitive behavior can be a problem in theory, it has not been a problem to date in either the lead or sulfur dioxide programs. Ultimately the appropriate agency to address this may not be the EPA, but the anti-trust division at the Department of Justice.[4]

---

[4] Based on material presented by Professor Robert N. Stavins, Director of the Environmental Economics Program, Harvard University, Address at the Harvard Law School

Although emissions trading for greenhouse gases has yet to develop into national legislation, several Northeastern states have confronted these design questions and agreed to a carbon cap and trade system among regional power plants known as the Regional Greenhouse Gas Initiative. *See* http://www.rggi.org. And California has now adopted the most ambitious greenhouse gas cap-and-trade program in the country and perhaps globally. These are two of the many state initiatives on greenhouse gas regulation.

Though some criticize state and local initiatives as too limited, or as interfering with the development of a coherent national approach, others praise them. Consider the following appraisal of regional trading systems such as the one created by the Northeastern states:

> This fragmented "bottom-up" approach to carbon trading is not simply a stiff smile to be painted on the wreckage of grander visions for global trading. Rather, it is pragmatic and effective. The architects of global trading were blinded by the theoretical benefits that could arise from trading among diverse economies; a universal system, they thought, would also prevent free riding. However, global institutions are too weak to monitor and enforce what is, in effect, a new monetary system. Global agreements are also vulnerable to exit when commitments become inconvenient (such as when the United States abandoned the Kyoto process). A system that originates from the top takes the speed of its least ambitious nation.
>
> The strength of a bottom-up approach is its ability to tap stronger national and regional institutions for governance. . . . The EU, although it now has 25 members, initially applied its carbon trading scheme to just the subset of 15 members that have the longest history of cooperation. . . .

David G. Victor, Joshua C. House, & Sarah Joy, *A Madisonian Approach to Climate Policy,* 309 SCIENCE 1820 (2005).

Conference on New Prospects for Climate Change Regulation: Learning from Experience: An Overview of Greenhouse Gas Trading Design Issues (Mar. 10, 2006).

CHAPTER 7

WATER POLLUTION

■ ■ ■

A. BACKGROUND

1. HISTORICAL CONTEXT

Until just after the Second World War, the federal government played a minor role in the regulation of water pollution. The federal Rivers and Harbors Act of 1899 prohibited the discharge of refuse matter into the navigable waters of the United States, but its primary goal was to ensure that dumping did not interfere with navigation and commerce. At this time and well into the twentieth century, water pollution (like air pollution) was viewed as a state and local matter. Private plaintiffs relied on common law nuisance suits and other state-created causes of action to recover for harms related to water contamination. Again, as with air pollution, these remedies were based on property rights, and were limited in their capacity to comprehensively address the contamination of the nation's waterways by widespread industrial and domestic discharge of waste.

In 1948, Congress passed the Federal Water Pollution Control Act (FWPCA). Unlike the Refuse Act, the FWPCA was aimed specifically at reducing pollution in interstate waterways. However, the federal government declined to take the primary regulatory role, instead providing funding to the states for research and for the development of state programs to address pollution control. In the 1965 Amendments to the FWPCA, Congress strengthened its role, requiring states to establish water quality standards subject to federal approval for all water bodies in their jurisdiction, and to develop state implementation plans.

Even as amended, however, the law proved largely ineffective. In the 1965 Act, Congress had adopted an ambient approach to water pollution by requiring states to set water quality standards for receiving bodies. These water quality standards could vary with respect to different water bodies and their existing level of pollution so that a river heavily polluted by industry could have much lower standards than a pristine lake. In its ambient focus, the 1965 act resembled the modern Clean Air Act. An ambient approach with bodies of water is more complex than with air, though. Consider why. There are thousands of bodies of water potentially subject to regulation rather than a relatively confined number of air basins; determining "appropriate" or "safe" levels of ambient pollutants for each of them is difficult. These water bodies vary dramatically in size, use, fresh v. salt water and so forth. The Pacific Ocean is dramatically different from a small creek. Setting the standards can be quite complex as a result. Setting ambient standards requires scientific data to determine the effects of different pollutants under different conditions. Yet the data may not be sufficient to assist in establishing safe levels. Moreover, even assuming standards can be set, achieving them can be challenging. Regulators must work backwards from water quality standards to controls, identifying dischargers responsible for the failure of the water body to meet standards and then allocating to each a share of the pollutant reductions necessary to ameliorate the problem. And of course each body of water requires its own set of standards and controls. Keep these differences between the regulation of air pollution and water pollution in mind as you work through the material in the chapter.

The 1965 legislation contained no regulatory mechanism enabling states to readily identify and individually regulate the multiple sources that might have contributed to the ambient water quality problem. As a result, even assuming states had the political will to regulate water quality (and most did not), enforcement of ambient water quality standards proved nearly impossible. *See generally* Drew Caputo, *A Job Half Finished: The Clean Water Act After 25 Years,* 27 ENVTL. L. REP. 10,574 (1997). Given the difficulty of tracing pollutants from the receiving body back to the responsible source(s), individual sources could, presumably, dispute the findings that they contributed to water quality problems and resist the imposition of cuts. Moreover, federal enforcement capacity was weak. While the federal government was authorized to set water quality standards and file implementation plans where states failed to do so, the Act did not authorize federal officials to impose the implementation plan on states.

In the end, as implemented by the states, the FWPCA's ambient approach did not lead to significant improvement in water quality. Instead, it tended to lock in existing uses and reinforce the status quo. Water bodies that were designated for industrial use were allowed to meet far lower standards than those designated for recreational use. This meant that, typically, waterways were permitted to languish if they had historically been used as a dumping ground for wastewater from industrial facilities.

Indeed, through the late 1960s water pollution continued largely unabated. Cities routinely dumped raw sewage, and industrial plants sent a variety of pollutants including toxics, into the surface waters of the United States. Urban and agricultural runoff choked rivers and streams, as did runoff from resource extraction operations like coal mining and logging. Perhaps the most enduring image of this era is that of Ohio's Cuyohoga River bursting into flames in 1969 because it was so badly polluted with oil and industrial waste. Because of incidents like this, public awareness of the dangers of water pollution began to grow.

In the 1972 Amendments to the FWPCA (then renamed the Clean Water Act), Congress acted forcefully, taking the lead in regulating pollution in the nation's waterways. Congress established federal standards to be implemented by states and backed up the new regime with sanctions. The Amendments relegated the ambient approach of the earlier legislation to secondary status in favor of a new national permit system (the national pollution discharge elimination system, or NPDES) that would impose technology-based effluent limits on all "point sources" of water pollution. The Amendments required the newly created EPA to establish technology-based performance standards for different categories of dischargers and for different types of pollutants. These standards would be set based on technology then available and already in use. Cost was to be taken into consideration to varying degrees when setting these standards, depending on the category of source (existing or new) and the nature of the pollutant.

Prior to the adoption of the modern Clean Water Act, just as with air quality violations, common law nuisance sometimes helped resolve disputes over interstate water pollution. The next section addresses the interplay between the CWA and common law nuisance.

B.   THE CLEAN WATER ACT AND THE COMMON LAW

Prior to passage of the 1972 Clean Water Act, states sought recourse in the federal courts to resolve disputes over interstate water pollution. In the typical case, a downstream state would complain that its population was suffering adverse health effects because of sewage pumped into a river from the upstream state. The courts grappled with these cases in the absence of congressional action to address the problem. In *Illinois v. Milwaukee*, 406 U.S. 91 (1972) [*Milwaukee I*], the Supreme Court held that interstate pollution violated the federal common law and that nuisance actions could be brought in federal court to redress the violation. The passage of the CWA raised obvious questions about how to coordinate the nuisance action with the extensive requirements contained in the new law.

MILWAUKEE V. ILLINOIS [MILWAUKEE II]
Supreme Court of the United States, 1981.
451 U.S. 304, 101 S.Ct. 1784, 68 L.Ed.2d 114.

JUSTICE REHNQUIST delivered the opinion of the Court.

When this litigation was first before us we recognized the existence of a federal "common law" which could give rise to a claim for abatement of a nuisance caused by interstate water pollution. *Illinois v. Milwaukee,* 406 U.S. 91, 92 S. Ct. 1385, 31 L. Ed. 2d 712 (1972). Subsequent to our decision, Congress enacted the Federal Water Pollution Control Act Amendments of 1972. We granted certiorari to consider the effect of this legislation on the previously recognized cause of action. * * *

Federal courts, unlike state courts, are not general common law courts and do not possess a general power to develop and apply their own rules of decision. The enactment of a federal rule in an area of national concern, and the decision whether to displace state law in doing so, is generally made not by the federal judiciary, purposefully insulated from democratic pressures, but by the people through their elected representatives in Congress. * * *

When Congress has not spoken to a particular issue, however, and when there exists a "significant conflict between some federal policy or interest and the use of state law,"[7] the Court has found it necessary, in a "few and restricted" instances, to develop a federal common law. Nothing in this process suggests that courts are better suited to develop national policy in areas governed by federal common law than they are in other areas, or that the usual and important concerns of an appropriate division of functions between the Congress and the federal judiciary are inapplicable. * * *

Contrary to the suggestions of respondents, the appropriate analysis in determining if federal statutory law governs a question previously the subject of federal common law is not the same as that employed in deciding if federal law pre-empts state law. In considering the latter question "we start with the assumption that the historic police powers of the States were not to be superseded by the Federal Act unless that was the clear and manifest purpose of Congress." While we have not hesitated to find pre-emption of state law, whether express or implied, when Congress has so indicated, or when enforcement of state regulations would impair "federal superintendence of the field," our analysis has included "due regard for the presuppositions of our embracing federal system, including the principle of diffusion of power not as a matter of doctrinaire localism but as a promoter of democracy." Such concerns are not implicated in the same fashion when the question is whether federal statutory or federal common law governs, and accordingly the same sort of evidence of a clear and manifest purpose is not required. Indeed, as noted, in cases such as the present "we start with the assumption" that it is for Congress, not federal courts, to

---

[7]   In this regard we note the inconsistency in Illinois' argument and the decision of the District Court that both federal and state nuisance law apply to this case. If state law can be applied, there is no need for federal common law; if federal common law exists, it is because state law cannot be used.

articulate the appropriate standards to be applied as a matter of federal law.[9]

We conclude that, at least so far as concerns the claims of respondents, Congress has not left the formulation of appropriate federal standards to the courts through application of often vague and indeterminate nuisance concepts and maxims of equity jurisprudence, but rather has occupied the field through the establishment of a comprehensive regulatory program supervised by an expert administrative agency. The 1972 amendments to the Federal Water Pollution Control Act were not merely another law "touching interstate waters" of the sort surveyed in *Illinois v. Milwaukee* and found inadequate to supplant federal common law. Rather, the amendments were viewed by Congress as a "total restructuring" and "complete rewriting" of the existing water pollution legislation considered in that case. Congress' intent in enacting the amendments was clearly to establish an all-encompassing program of water pollution regulation. *Every* point source discharge is prohibited unless covered by a permit, which directly subjects the discharger to the administrative apparatus established by Congress to achieve its goals. The "major purpose" of the amendments was "to establish a *comprehensive* long-range policy for the elimination of water pollution." No Congressman's remarks on the legislation were complete without reference to the "comprehensive" nature of the amendments. * * * The establishment of such a self-consciously comprehensive program by Congress, which certainly did not exist when *Illinois v. Milwaukee* was decided, strongly suggests that there is no room for courts to attempt to improve on that program with federal common law.

Turning to the particular claims involved in this case, the action of Congress in supplanting the federal common law is perhaps clearest when the question of effluent limitations for discharges from the two treatment plants is considered. The duly issued permits under which the city commission discharges treated sewage from the Jones Island and South Shore treatment plants incorporate, as required by the Act, *see* § 402(b)(1), the specific effluent limitations established by EPA regulations pursuant to § 301 of the Act. There is thus no question that the problem of effluent limitations has been thoroughly addressed through the administrative scheme established by Congress, as contemplated by Congress. This being so there is no basis for a federal court to impose more stringent limitations than those imposed under the regulatory regime by reference to federal common law, as the District Court did in this case. * * *

---

[9]   Since the States are represented in Congress but not in the federal courts, the very concerns about displacing state law which counsel against finding pre-emption of *state* law in the absence of clear intent actually suggest a willingness to find congressional displacement of *federal* common law. Simply because the opinion in *Illinois v. Milwaukee* used the term "pre-emption," usually employed in determining if federal law displaces state law, is no reason to assume the analysis used to decide the usual federal-state questions is appropriate here.

Respondents argue that congressional intent to preserve the federal common law remedy recognized in *Illinois v. Milwaukee* is evident in §§ 510 and 505(e) of the statute. Section 510 provides that nothing in the Act shall preclude States from adopting and enforcing limitations on the discharge of pollutants more stringent than those adopted under the Act. It is one thing, however, to say that States may adopt more stringent limitations through state administrative processes, or even that States may establish such limitations through state nuisance law, and apply them to in-state discharges. It is quite another to say that the States may call upon *federal* courts to employ *federal* common law to establish more stringent standards applicable to out-of-state dischargers. Any standards established under federal common law are federal standards, and so the authority of States to impose more stringent standards under § 510 would not seem relevant. Section 510 clearly contemplates state authority to establish more stringent pollution limitations; nothing in it, however, suggests that this was to be done by federal court actions premised on federal common law.

Subsection 505(e) provides:

"Nothing *in this section* shall restrict any right which any person (or class of persons) may have under any statute or common law to seek enforcement of any effluent standard or limitation or to seek any other relief (including relief against the Administrator or a state agency)" (emphasis supplied).

Respondents argue that this evinces an intent to preserve the federal common law of nuisance. We, however, are inclined to view the quoted provision as meaning what it says: that nothing in § 505, the citizen suit provision, should be read as limiting any other remedies which might exist.

Subsection 505(e) is virtually identical to subsections in the citizen suit provisions of several environmental statutes. The subsection is common language accompanying citizen suit provisions and we think that it means only that the provision of such suit does not revoke other remedies. It most assuredly cannot be read to mean that the Act as a whole does not supplant formerly available federal common law actions but only that the particular section authorizing citizen suits does not do so. No one, however, maintains that the citizen-suit provision pre-empts federal common law. * * *

We therefore conclude that no federal common law remedy was available to respondents in this case. The judgment of the Court of Appeals is therefore vacated, and the case remanded for proceedings consistent with this opinion.

JUSTICE BLACKMUN, with whom JUSTICE MARSHALL and JUSTICE STEVENS join, dissenting.

Nine years ago, this Court unanimously determined that Illinois could bring a federal common-law action against the city of Milwaukee, three other Wisconsin cities, and two sewerage commissions. At that time, Illinois alleged that the discharge of raw and untreated sewage by these Wisconsin entities into Lake Michigan created a public nuisance for the citizens of Illinois. The Court remitted the parties to an appropriate federal district court, "whose powers are adequate to resolve the issues."

Illinois promptly initiated the present litigation, and pursued it through more than three years of pretrial discovery, a six-month trial that entailed hundreds of exhibits and scores of witnesses, extensive factual findings by the District Court and an exhaustive review of the evidence by the Court of Appeals. Today, the Court decides that this nine-year judicial exercise has been just a meaningless charade, inasmuch as, it says, the federal common law remedy approved in *Illinois v. Milwaukee* was implicitly extinguished by Congress just six months after the 1972 decision. Because I believe that Congress intended no such extinction, and surely did not contemplate the result reached by the Court today, I respectfully dissent. * * *

[The Clean Water Act] sets forth certain effluent limitations. As did the Court of Appeals, a court applying federal common law in a given instance may well decline to impose effluent limitations more stringent than those required by Congress, because the complainant has failed to show that stricter standards will abate the nuisance or appreciably diminish the threat of injury. But it is a far different proposition to pronounce, as does the Court today, that federal courts "*lack authority* to impose more stringent effluent limitations under federal common law than those imposed" under the statutory scheme. The authority of the federal courts in this area was firmly established by the decision in *Illinois v. Milwaukee*. In delineating the legitimate scope of the federal common law, the Court there expressly noted the relevance of state standards, adding that "a State with high water-quality standards *may well ask that its strict standards be honored* and *that it not be compelled to lower itself* to the more degrading standards of a neighbor." (Emphasis added.) The Act attributes comparable respect to the strict effluent limitation levels imposed by individual States. § 510. Since both the Court and Congress fully expected that neighboring States might differ in their approaches to the regulation of the discharge of pollutants into their navigable waters, it is odd, to say the least, that federal courts should now be deprived of the common law power to effect a reconciliation of these differences. * * *

NOTES

1. In *Milwaukee II,* the defendant was in compliance with the requirements of the Clean Water Act. In *Middlesex County Sewerage Authority v. National Sea Clammers Ass'n*, 453 U.S. 1 (1981), the Court extended *Milwaukee II* by holding that even a defendant who is violating the Act is immune from federal nuisance liability. The lower courts have also given

Milwaukee II an expansive reading. *See, e.g.*, Conner v. Aerovox, Inc., 730 F.2d 835 (1st Cir. 1984) (Clean Water Act preempts federal maritime law).

2.   On remand, the Seventh Circuit held that application of Illinois nuisance law to the interstate pollution originating in Wisconsin was also preempted by the Clean Water Act. Illinois v. Milwaukee, 731 F.2d 403 (7th Cir. 1984), *cert. denied* 469 U.S. 1196 (1985). This issue reached the Supreme Court in the next case.

INTERNATIONAL PAPER COMPANY V. OUELLETTE

Supreme Court of the United States, 1987.
479 U.S. 481, 107 S.Ct. 805, 93 L.Ed.2d 883.

[The defendant operated a pulp and paper mill on the New York side of Lake Champlain. Its discharge pipe ran from the mill through the water toward Vermont, ending just before the state line that divides the lake. The plaintiffs owned or rented land on the Vermont shore. They filed suit in state court for compensatory and punitive damages, as well as an injunction requiring the defendant to restructure part of its water treatment system. The action was removed to federal district court. The trial court held that Vermont nuisance law was applicable and was not preempted by the Clean Water Act. The Second Circuit affirmed, relying on the savings clauses in sections 505(e) and 510.]

JUSTICE POWELL delivered the opinion of the court. * * *

To begin with, the plain language of the provisions on which respondents rely by no means compels the result they seek. Section 505(e) merely says that "nothing *in this section*," i.e., the citizen-suit provisions, shall affect an injured party's right to seek relief under state law; it does not purport to preclude pre-emption of state law by other provisions of the Act. Section 510, moreover, preserves the authority of a State "with respect to the waters (including boundary waters) of such State." This language arguably limits the effect of the clause to discharges flowing *directly* into a State's own waters, i.e., discharges from within the State. The savings clause then, does not preclude pre-emption of the law of an affected State.

Given that the Act itself does not speak directly to the issue, the Court must be guided by the goals and policies of the Act in determining whether it in fact pre-empts an action based on the law of an affected State. After examining the CWA as a whole, its purposes and its history, we are convinced that if affected States were allowed to impose separate discharge standards on a single point source, the inevitable result would be a serious interference with the achievement of the "full purposes and objectives of Congress." Because we do not believe Congress intended to undermine this carefully drawn statute through a general saving clause, we conclude that the CWA precludes a court from applying the law of an affected State against an out-of-state source.

In determining whether Vermont nuisance law "stands as an obstacle" to the full implementation of the CWA, it is not enough to say that the ultimate goal of both federal and state law is to eliminate water pollution. A state law also is pre-empted if it interferes with the methods by which the federal statute was designed to reach this goal. In this case the application of Vermont law against IPC would allow respondents to circumvent the NPDES permit system, thereby upsetting the balance of public and private interests so carefully addressed by the Act.

By establishing a permit system for effluent discharges, Congress implicitly has recognized that the goal of the CWA—elimination of water pollution—cannot be achieved immediately, and that it cannot be realized without incurring costs. The EPA Administrator issues permits according to established effluent standards and water quality standards, that in turn are based upon available technology, and competing public and industrial uses. The Administrator must consider the impact of the discharges on the waterway, the types of effluents, and the schedule for compliance, each of which may vary widely among sources. If a State elects to impose its own standards, it also must consider the technological feasibility of more stringent controls. Given the nature of these complex decisions, it is not surprising that the Act limits the right to administer the permit system to the EPA and the source States.

An interpretation of the saving clause that preserved actions brought under an affected State's law would disrupt this balance of interests. If a New York source were liable for violations of Vermont law, that law could effectively override both the permit requirements and the policy choices made by the source State. The affected State's nuisance laws would subject the point source to the threat of legal and equitable penalties if the permit standards were less stringent than those imposed by the affected State. Such penalties would compel the source to adopt different control standards and a different compliance schedule from those approved by the EPA, even though the affected State had not engaged in the same weighing of the costs and benefits. This case illustrates the problems with such a rule. If the Vermont Court ruled that respondents were entitled to the full amount of damages and injunctive relief sought in the complaint, at a minimum IPC would have to change its methods of doing business and controlling pollution to avoid the threat of ongoing liability. In suits such as this, an affected state court also could require the source to cease operations by ordering immediate abatement. Critically, these liabilities would attach even though the source had complied fully with its state and federal permit obligations. The inevitable result of such suits would be that Vermont and other States could do indirectly what they could not do directly—regulate the conduct of out-of-state sources.

Application of an affected State's law to an out-of-state source also would undermine the important goals of efficiency and predictability in the permit system. The history of the 1972 amendments shows that Congress intended to establish "clear and identifiable" discharge standards. As noted above, under the reading of the saving clause proposed by respondents, a source would be subject to a variety of common-law rules established by the different States along the interstate waterways. These nuisance standards often are "vague" and "indeterminate." The application of numerous States' laws would only exacerbate the vagueness and resulting uncertainty. * * *

Our conclusion that Vermont nuisance law is inapplicable to a New York point source does not leave respondents without a remedy. The CWA precludes only those suits that may require standards of effluent control that are incompatible with those established by the procedures set forth in the Act. The saving clause specifically preserves other state actions, and therefore nothing in the Act bars aggrieved individuals from bringing a nuisance claim pursuant to the law of the *source* State. By its terms the CWA allows States such as New York to impose higher standards on its own point sources, and in *Milwaukee II* we recognized that this authority may include the right to impose higher common-law as well as higher statutory restrictions.

An action brought against IPC under New York nuisance law would not frustrate the goals of the CWA as would a suit governed by Vermont law. First, application of the source State's law does not disturb the balance among federal, source-state, and affected-state interests. Because the Act specifically allows source States to impose stricter standards, the imposition of source-state law does not disrupt the regulatory partnership established by the permit system. Second, the restriction of suits to those brought under source-state nuisance law prevents a source from being subject to an indeterminate number of potential regulations. Although New York nuisance law may impose separate standards and thus create some tension with the permit system, a source only is required to look to a single additional authority, whose rules should be relatively predictable. Moreover, States can be expected to take into account their own nuisance laws in setting permit requirements.

IPC asks the Court to go one step further and hold that all state-law suits also must be brought in source-state *courts.* As petitioner cites little authority or justification for this position, we find no basis for holding that Vermont is an improper forum. Simply because a cause of action is pre-empted does not mean that judicial jurisdiction over the claim is affected as well; the Act pre-empts laws, not courts. In the absence of statutory authority to the contrary, the rule is settled that a district court sitting in diversity is competent to apply the law of a foreign State.

NOTES

1. If the Court had gone the other way regarding application of Vermont law, wouldn't we have come full circle? *Milwaukee I* established federal common law to replace state nuisance law; *Milwaukee II* preempted the federal common law; an affirmance in *Ouellette* would have resurrected the multitude of state laws the Court had buried in *Milwaukee I.* Of course, the answer may be that the mistake was made earlier in the chain—some of the Justices would have argued that the crucial mistake was *Milwaukee II.* But given the *Milwaukee* opinions, a contrary result in the final case of the trilogy would have been decidedly peculiar.

2. Does *Ouellette* apply to air pollution? *See* Her Majesty The Queen In Right of the Province of Ontario v. City of Detroit, 874 F.2d 332 (6th Cir. 1989) (allowing an action by Ontario under the Michigan Environmental Protection Act to enjoin the construction of Detroit's proposed garbage burner). A dissent argued that *Ouellette* allows state law injunctions if a source's pollution causes damage, but not an injunction before the source is constructed. Id. at 346–347 (Boggs, J., dissenting). The Supreme Court has addressed whether federal common law nuisance applies to greenhouse gas emissions in *American Electric Power v. Connecticut,* 131 S. Ct. 2527 (2011), excerpted *supra* at page 411. In the last several years, local and state governments have filed a new round of nuisance cases in state court under state nuisance law against oil producers for failing to control greenhouse gases. One line of defense for the oil companies is that the federal Clean Air Act preempts state nuisance claims. *See supra* at pages 415–416.

3. *Milwaukee II* invokes attractive concepts of judicial competence, legislative supremacy, and federalism. In light of *Ouellette,* has the Court actually furthered any of these goals? For a negative answer, see Daniel Farber & Philip Frickey, *In the Shadow of the Legislature: The Common Law in the Age of the New Public Law,* 89 MICH. L. REV. 875 (1991). Note that *Ouellette* provides a cause of action for violating the *source* state's standards but no forum for complaints based on a *receiving* state's desire to have higher water quality. As we shall see later when we consider *Arkansas v. Oklahoma,* the CWA's provisions regarding state obligations to maintain water quality may provide a mechanism for redressing this problem.

C.   MODERN REGULATION OF WATER POLLUTION

1.   FEDERAL STATUTES GOVERNING WATER POLLUTION

The CWA is not the only federal statute regulating water pollution. It is supplemented by other statutes targeted at specific problems. The Safe Drinking Water Act, 42 U.S.C. §§ 300f et seq. (1974) regulates contaminants in drinking water supplied by public water systems and requires the EPA to set national drinking water regulations that incorporate enforceable maximum contaminant levels or treatment techniques. The Ocean Dumping Act, 33 U.S.C. §§ 1401–1445 (1972) prohibits the unpermitted dumping of wastes in the area seaward of the inner boundary of the U.S. territorial sea. The Oil Pollution Act, 33 U.S.C. §§ 2701–2761 (1990) imposes minimum design standards on vessels operating in U.S. waters and makes owners of vessels discharging oil liable for cleanup costs. The CWA is the most comprehensive federal law regulating water pollution, however, and we take it up in detail below.

2. OVERVIEW OF THE CLEAN WATER ACT

As previously described, the NPDES system was envisioned as the heart of the CWA and was meant to comprehensively cover discharges by "point sources": section 301 prohibits the discharge of any pollutant into the navigable waterways of the United States by any "point source" without an NPDES permit. The CWA requires these permitted point sources to install up-to-date technology to reduce their pollution discharges—the technology varies based on the type of pollutant and whether the source is new or existing—and to meet numerical limitations contained in their NPDES permits that available technology can achieve. A key question, then, is what constitutes a point source since Congress drew a distinction between point sources, which could not discharge without a permit, and other producers of water pollution called "nonpoint" sources. Point sources are largely comprised of industrial polluters and municipal treatment works from which effluent flows through a discrete conveyance, such as a pipe. Nonpoint sources consist primarily of facilities or operations from which waste travels via runoff without passing through pipes. Examples include cropland, livestock feedlots, and drainage from waste disposal sites as well as mining and logging operations. We will return to this distinction.

The CWA does contain provisions to address water pollution on an ambient basis but the regulatory focus in the first 15 years of the Act's existence was largely on the permitting system. In the early years of the Act, the CWA also provided extensive funding for constructing and improving municipal sewage treatment plants so that sewage would be controlled to certain standards before effluent could be discharged into water bodies. The Act requires publicly owned treatment works (POTWs), which process sewage, to perform "secondary treatment" before discharging waste into water bodies.

The ambient provisions of the CWA are designed in some sense as a "backstop" to the NPDES permitting system. Section 303(d) of the Act requires states to designate water body uses (typically through narrative descriptions like "swimmable," "fishable," "drinkable,") and to establish water quality standards (sometimes narrative, sometimes numerical) to support those uses. Section 302 of the Act authorizes EPA to tighten permit requirements where water quality is too polluted to meet water quality standards. The idea, then, is that the permit system should produce pollution reductions necessary to achieve water quality standards. If the reductions prove insufficient to achieve those standards, the permits can be strengthened. Section 303(d) contains a further backstop, however. For those bodies of water that fail to meet water quality standards, states are required to establish "Total Maximum Daily Loads," numerical limits on the total amount of a given pollutant that can be discharged into a water body from all sources. If a TMDL is set, then permit limitations of pollutants cannot, in total, add up to more than the TMDL.

This system, with NPDES at its heart and WQS and TMDLs as backup, should in theory produce water bodies that are clean enough for their designated uses. The theory, however, leaves out an important piece of the puzzle: non-point sources. Moreover, it assumes that the policies contained in the CWA are actually being implemented. Yet the system of TMDLs remained largely dormant for the first 25 years of the statute's existence until litigation began to force states to set TMDLs. Thus while the combination of the NPDES system and the financing of municipal waste water treatment plants led to significant improvements in water quality, the lack of regulation of non-point sources and the failure to implement TMDLs for impaired water bodies has left significant gaps in our regulatory system. In 1987 Congress stepped in to begin to address the non-point source problem, though it did not impose direct controls on non-point sources, and in 1996 the courts stepped in to begin to force states to set TMDLs. This background should be helpful in making sense of the materials that follow.

a. Pollutants Covered by the CWA

The CWA subjects different categories of pollutants—"conventional" pollutants, toxic pollutants, and "non-conventional" pollutants—to different technology-based standards. Permitees that discharge different types of pollutants are required to install technology that meets the standard (e.g., the "best available technology.") The treatment produces an alphabet soup of acronyms but several overarching comments are especially important here:

1)   conventional pollutants, specified in Section 304(a)(4), include total suspended solids, biochemical oxygen demand, fecal coliform, and Ph, and are subject to one set of technology standards;

2)   Toxic pollutants are regulated under Section 307 of the statute, which references a list of pollutants to be regulated. 126 toxic pollutants (including pesticides, lead, and mercury) are on what is called the Priority List and subject to a stronger set of technology-based standards than conventional pollutants; their regulatory history has evolved as described below;

3) non-conventional pollutants are those pollutants that are neither conventional nor toxic and include chlorine and ammonia;

4) toxic and non-conventional pollutants are treated the same with respect to which technology-based standards apply while conventional pollutants are subject to a somewhat less stringent standard.

The various categories of pollutants come from a variety of sources. Municipal sewage plants produce oxygen-depleting nutrients, pathogens, and fecal coliform. Industrial sources like chemical and power plants, pulp and paper mills, food processors, metal manufacturers and so forth are the more likely source of toxic chemicals, including benzene, cyanide, and methyl chloride, and heavy metals like zinc, mercury and lead. These are not the only sources of regulated pollutants, however—many largely unregulated non-point sources like agriculture discharge pollutants like pesticides into water bodies. And some pollutants, such as greenhouse gases, can cause large water pollution problems like ocean acidification that to date are not regulated under the Clean Water Act.

Figure 1: Legal Categories of Pollutants under the CWA

Conventional Pollutants

Pollutants often found in municipal sewage, and for which municipal secondary treatment plants are typically designed such as BOD, TSS, fecal coliform bacteria, oil and grease, and pH.

Nonconventional Pollutants

All pollutants that are not included in the list of conventional or toxic pollutants, including pollutants such as chemical oxygen demand (COD), total organic carbon (TOC), nitrogen, and phosphorus.

Toxic Pollutants

Pollutants or combinations of pollutants, including disease-causing agents, which after discharge and upon exposure, ingestion, inhalation or assimilation into any organism, either directly from the environment or indirectly by ingestion through food chains, will, on the basis of information available to the Administrator of the EPA, cause death, disease, behavioral abnormalities, cancer, genetic mutations, physiological malfunctions, (including, among others, DDT, PCBs, dioxins, and other chlorinated hydrocarbons; mercury, cadmium, lead, and other toxic metals).

b. Effluent Limitations and Technology-Based Standards Under the NPDES System

Section 301 of the Clean Water Act prohibits discharges of pollutants from point sources without a permit. The permitting system, called the NPDES, was established in the 1972 Amendments to the FWPCA. It was aimed at the ambitious, and in retrospect wildly unrealistic, goal of eliminating all discharges of all pollutants into U.S. waters by 1985, and making all waters safe for swimming and indigenous fish and wildlife by

1983. (Surprisingly, even today, the statute still contains these long-passed deadlines.) As with the CAA, the CWA subjects permittees to technology-based standards, standards that EPA uses to set effluent limits (for example, numerical concentrations) according to technology that is, typically, currently available and used by at least some members of the industrial category to which it applies. The original technology-based approach to regulating pollutants established in the 1972 amendments did not distinguish between pollutant types. All existing sources of pollutants, no matter what the type, were subject to the Best Practicable Control Technology (BPT). The 1977 amendments changed not only the technology standards to which pollutants were subject but subjected different pollutants to different standards and timelines. Some categories of polluters, however, are still subject to BPT where EPA has yet to update permit requirements. Here is generally the way the system works:

> *For conventional pollutants,* a new standard, "best conventional pollutant control technology" (BCT), was established. It was to be achieved by July 1, 1984. In establishing effluent limitations for conventional pollutants, the EPA is to consider, among other things, "the reasonableness of the relationship between the costs of attaining a reduction in effluents and the effluent reduction benefits derived." By contrast, balancing is not required in formulating technology-based standards (described below) for toxic and nonconventional pollutants. §§ 304(a)(4) and (b)(4).

> *For toxic pollutants,* Best Available Technology (BAT) standards for an initial list of 126 "priority pollutants" were to be achieved by July 1, 1984 (or, for pollutants not on the original list, within three years after EPA adoption of applicable effluent limitations), with no exceptions allowed. § 301(b)(2)(C)–(D).

> *For nonconventional pollutants,* effluent limitations based on BAT were to be achieved by July 1, 1987, but the EPA was authorized to modify these standards on a case-by-case basis. §§ 301(b)(2)(F) and 301(g).

> *For all new sources, regardless of which pollutants they discharge,* the installation of the best demonstrated available technology (BDAT) is required through New Source Performance Standards (NSPS).

At least in theory, the standards for each of these categories vary in terms of stringency, with the least stringent applied in the 1972 amendments (BPT) to all existing sources; the next stringent (BCT) applied to existing sources of conventional pollutants by 1984; the next most stringent for existing sources of toxic and non-conventional pollutants by 1984 and 1987 (BAT), and the most stringent for new sources (BDAT). Related to stringency, the standards vary with respect to the role cost plays in setting them. For example, the EPA may be obligated to factor cost into its analysis when setting effluent standards for existing point sources under BPT, whereas it might only need to "consider" cost when setting New Source Performance Standards (NSPSs) according to BDAT. These differences seem subtle, and in practice they can shrink to nothing, but they can theoretically result in the EPA choosing (or declining to choose) a particularly expensive and highly effective technology for setting standards. This in turn might make a big difference to the ultimate limits imposed on dischargers in their permits. Figure 2 below describes the technology-based standards by weakest to strongest. It includes "Best Management Practices," the weakest of the standards and the one applied to the management of stormwater, described *infra* at page 619.

Figure 2: CWA Technology-Based Standards in Order of Increasing Stringency

Standard:	Applies to:	Statute §:	Impact:
BMP (Best Management Practices)	Nonpoint sources	§ 319(a)(1)(C) § 319(b)(2)(A)	Requires states to identify best management practices where state water quality standards are not met due to nonpoint sources; determines state eligibility for federal technical assistance and program planning funds, but creates no directly enforceable standards
BPT (Best Practicable Technology [currently available])	Existing sources	§ 301(b)(1)(A) § 304(b)(1)(A) § 304(b)(1)(B)	Requires sources to meet standards set by average of best performers in source category; EPA must weigh costs v. benefits but deferential standard, no 'knee of curve' test is required
Standard:	Applies to:	Statute §:	Impact:
BCT (Best Conventional [pollutant control] Technology)	Existing sources producing conventional pollutants (e.g., BOD, silt, fecal bacteria) but unable to meet BAT	§ 301(b)(2)(E) § 304(b)(4)(A) § 304(b)(4)(B)	Includes explicit CBA requirement; intended to be more rigorous than BPT while awaiting BAT, but has collapsed into BPT in practice
BAT (Best Available Technology [economically achievable])	Existing Sources	§ 301(b)(2)(A) § 304(b)(2)(A) § 304(b)(2)(B)	The Agency may require such sources to match emissions performance of single best performer in the applicable source category; requires consideration of cost, but not weighing; for toxics, may include zero discharge standard (§ 307(a)(2))

BDAT (Best Demonstrated Available Technology)	New sources (built after promulgation of applicable new source standard by EPA)	§ 306(a)(1)	Requires best control technology demonstrated and available at time of construction; explicitly allows consideration of process changes and zero discharge, cost consideration is mandatory, but as in BAT it does not require a balancing, and the Administrator has broad discretion in factoring in cost.

Finally, as a general matter, as with the CAA, it is important to remember that new sources are regulated more stringently than existing sources and that less dangerous substances are controlled to a lesser extent than more dangerous ones. For example, toxic water pollutants (e.g., mercury and PCBs) are controlled to a greater extent than "conventional" water pollutants (e.g., oxygen-depleting substances, sediment, nutrients and pH).

The final factor to keep in mind is, simply, time. The initial deadlines established by Congress in the 1972 Act expired before the EPA could promulgate effluent standards for all categories and incorporate them into the industrial discharge permits required by the NPDES. As a result, in the 1977 Amendments to the Act and again in the 1987 Amendments, Congress extended the deadlines for dischargers to come into compliance, and relaxed or abandoned some requirements. For example, Congress abandoned the health-based approach it had adopted in 1972 to control toxic pollutants in favor of the technology-based approach it had already adopted for other pollutants and specified which toxic chemicals (through the publishing of the "Priority List,") would be subject to initial regulation. The Priority List can be found here. U.S. EPA, *Priority Pollutant List*, https://www.epa.gov/sites/production/files/2015-09/documents/priority-pollutant-list-epa.pdf.

In 1987, Congress again amended the law to extend the deadline for achieving both BCT and BAT limits to March 31, 1989. Specifically, dischargers were to achieve BCT for conventional pollutants by 1989 (an extension of 5 years), BAT for nonconventional pollutants by 1989 (an extension of 2 years) and BAT for toxic pollutants by 1989 (an extension of 5 years). New sources were to achieve BDAT. Such sources are "new" and subject to NSPS requirements (a) if construction of the source began after an applicable standard was promulgated, or (b) if construction commenced after proposal of a standard but before promulgation, where promulgation occurred within the required 120 days following proposal. *See* 40 C.F.R. § 122.2 (2002); NRDC v. EPA, 822 F.2d 104 (D.C. Cir. 1987); *cf.* Pennsylvania Dep't of Envtl. Res. v. EPA, 618 F.2d 991 (3d Cir. 1980).

The chart below illustrates the categories of pollutants, the application of technology based standards, and the various deadlines imposed and then extended under various amendments to the CWA.

Figure 3: Effluent Limits, Dates of Compliance
by Pollutant Category

CWA Overall Goals Since 1972:

Goal: Eliminate discharge of pollutants into navigable national waterways by 1985. § 101(a)(1)
Interim Goal: Wherever attainable protect fish, shellfish and wildlife and provide for recreation in and on the water by 1983. § 101(a)(2)

I. Aim High 1972 FWCPA Amendments	**II. Extend & Weaken** 1977 Amendments and name change to CWA	**III. Extend & Simplify** 1987 Amendments

Existing Sources

All non-toxic pollutants:

BPT by 1977

BAT by 1983

Conventional: BCT by 1984

BCT by 1989

Nonconventional BAT by 1987

Toxic Discharges

EPA to list toxins, then issue **health-based standards** to achieve "ample margin of safety"

BAT by 1984
(No longer health-based: EPA could opt for zero discharge of a toxin if necessary)

BAT as soon as possible but no later than 1989

New Sources

EPA to set BDAT standards by 1974 for categories of sources

BDAT

BDAT by 1989

c.   Water Quality Standards and Nonpoint Source

Congress retained the ambient water quality standards from the 1965 Act as a backup to the new "end-of-pipe" effluent standards and the NPDES system. Under § 303(b), states were required to establish water quality standards (WQS) that consist of three components: designated uses (DUs) for intrastate water bodies, water quality "criteria" (WQC) that will protect those uses, and anti-backsliding provisions. States set WQS subject to EPA approval under § 303(c). The WQS provisions strengthen the technology-based provisions of the Act via § 302(a), which requires that permits issued to point sources contain more stringent effluent limits when necessary to prevent a failure to achieve WQS. In addition, under § 303(d), states must identify waters that fail to meet WQS and establish total maximum daily loads (TMDLs) the receiving water can tolerate without falling below WQS. Indirectly, the TMDL process can lead to controls for nonpoint sources, though there is no mandatory language in § 303(d) to this effect.

Congress came to recognize, however, that these water quality provisions were not working as well as envisioned, partly because states were publishing narrative water quality criteria (a particular body of water should, for example, be available for recreational uses) instead of numerical limits on particular pollutants. In 1987, Congress amended the Act to require that states adopt numerical criteria for toxic pollutants. In addition, Congress required states to identify controls they would impose on point and nonpoint sources in order to achieve WQS. Section 304(*l*) requires states to designate toxic "hot spots" where BAT limits are insufficient to satisfy WQS, to identify the responsible sources and pollutants, and then to specify control strategies. Congress also added § 319, which requires states to identify waters that fail to achieve WQS because of nonpoint sources, and to develop management plans subject to EPA approval that include the application of "best management practices." These management plans are not made enforceable against nonpoint sources, however.

The 1987 Amendments also required point sources discharging stormwater runoff from construction sites, industrial facilities, and municipal storm sewers to obtain permits by 1992 (later extended to 1994). Permits for effluent from construction and industrial sites were to meet BCT and BAT standards, and discharges from urban storm sewers were to meet standards achievable by best management practices (BMPs). Finally, the 1987 Amendments strengthened federal enforcement power by adding provisions for administrative penalties (up to $10,000 per day of violation) and augmenting civil and criminal penalties (up to $25,000, and $50,000 plus up to 15 years in prison, respectively).

The NPDES system and the WQS/TMDL program are meant, then, to work in concert with each other. Figure 4, below, illustrates the relationship between the two programs.

Figure 4: Structure of the Clean Water Act

NPDES Program

Water Quality Standards

EPA establishes Technology Based Controls for Point Source Discharges

NPDES Permitting Program

Point Source Discharges of Conventional Pollutants BCT; NSPS/BDAT for New Sources

Point Source Discharges of Non-Conventional Pollutants BAT; NSPS/BDAT for New Sources

Point Source Discharges of Priority Pollutants (Toxics) BAT; NSPS/BDAT for New Sources

EPA guidance to states for ambient water quality standards (numeric limits for priority pollutants)

States establish water quality standards; EPA approves; standards/criteria incorporated into NPDES permits

States prepare (and EPA approves) list of impaired waters – feeds into TMDL program

Total Maximum Daily Load (TMDL) Program
States required to establish TMDLs for impaired waters; States and/or EPA incorporate TMDL requirements into NPDES permits for point sources; TMDLs also apply to non-point sources

Publicly Owned Treatment Works (POTWs) – receive discharges from "indirect sources" - Must have NPDES Permit

Indirect Sources - industrial discharges to POTWs must meet pretreatment requirements for priority pollutants

Non-Point Sources

d. Federal Authority to Regulate Water Pollution: "Waters of the United States"

One final issue is important in understanding the overall structure of the CWA: to what waters does the act apply? Though the question may seem straightforward, it has proved to be anything but.

Federal regulatory jurisdiction under the CWA applies to the discharge of a "pollutant" from a "point source" into "waters of the United States." The definition of "discharge of pollutant" includes the addition of any pollutant to the "navigable waters" or to the "waters of the contiguous zone or the ocean from any point source. . . ." § 502(12). The term "navigable waters" means "the waters of the United States, including the territorial seas." § 502(7). This jurisdiction describes both the EPA's authority to impose the NPDES system and the effluent controls under § 301 on dischargers, and it also describes a separate and important program: the Army Corps of Engineers' authority to issue dredge and fill permits under § 404. Section 404 is meant to protect wetlands, as we explore below.

The meaning of "waters of the United States" has been tested repeatedly in the federal courts, with the result that it has come to be very broadly defined, allowing for expansive federal regulatory control. As it turns out, waters subject to federal regulation need not be navigable. The Supreme Court has held that Congress chose to define the waters covered by the Act broadly.

> Although the Act prohibits discharges into 'navigable waters,' the Act's definition of 'navigable waters' as 'the waters of the United States' makes it clear that the term 'navigable' as used in the Act is of limited import. In adopting this definition of 'navigable waters,' Congress evidently intended to repudiate limits that had been placed on federal regulation by earlier water pollution control statutes and to exercise its powers under the Commerce Clause to regulate at least some waters that would not be deemed 'navigable' under the classical understanding of that term.

United States v. Riverside Bayview Homes, Inc., 474 U.S. 121, 133 (1985). In *Riverside,* the Court held that "waters of the United States" included wetlands adjacent to other bodies of water over which the government has jurisdiction. The Court deferred to the Army Corps' determination that such wetlands fall within the Act's reach because "wetlands adjacent to lakes, rivers, streams, and other bodies of water may function as integral parts of the aquatic environment even when the moisture creating the wetlands does not find its source in the adjacent bodies of water." 474 U.S. at 133. In *Riverside*, respondent's property was part of a wetland that abutted a navigable waterway and respondent was therefore required to obtain a § 404 permit. In SWANCC v. United States Army Corps of Engineers, however, the Court cast doubt on the applicability of the CWA to isolated non-navigable water bodies. 531 U.S. 159 (2001), excerpted at page 685. In a subsequent decision, Rapanos v. United States, the Court issued a plurality decision authored by Justice Scalia and a concurring opinion by Justice Anthony Kennedy that further complicated the question of jurisdiction. 547 U.S. 715 (2006), excerpted at page 691. We cover in detail the jurisdictional complexities of the CWA in the context of wetlands permits at page 679. But for now, be aware that the EPA's definition of "waters of the United States is contested and the subject of new rulemaking by the Trump Administration. The exact dividing line between "waters of the United States" and other waters, according to the CWA, can be hard to determine, especially with regard to smaller streams, ephemeral waterbodies, and wetlands not adjacent to other "waters of the United States."

We conclude the overview of the CWA with a description of the individual provisions of the CWA and a chart translating the U.S. Code Sections of the Act with the bill section numbers—the provision are often referred to by their bill section numbers (e.g., Section 404) rather than the code sections. We also offer observations on the similarities and differences between the Clean Water Act and the Clean Air Act before turning to particular controversies in the implementation of the CWA.

e.   Statutory Overview of the Clean Water Act

The section below provides a brief overview of important provisions of the CWA to give you a general sense of the overall statute.

TITLE II: Grants for Construction of Treatment Works

§ 208 Areawide Waste Treatment Management: Requires states to identify areas with substantial water quality control problems and to engage in areawide planning, including identification of both point source and nonpoint source contributions.

TITLE III: Standards and Enforcement

§ 301 Effluent Limitations: Prohibits the discharge of any pollutant by any person, except as permitted by the Act. Sets effluent limits for point sources. Requires that point sources of conventional pollutants apply the best conventional pollutant control technology (BCT) and that point sources of nonconventional pollutants comply with effluent limitations requiring best available technology economically achievable (BAT). Also prohibits the discharge into navigable waters of any radiological, chemical, or biological warfare agent, high-level radioactive waste, or medical waste.

§ 302 Water Quality Related Effluent Limits: Authorizes the Administrator to tighten effluent limitations for point sources when necessary to prevent interference with the attainment or maintenance of water quality standards.

§ 303 Water Quality Standards and Total Maximum Daily Loads (TMDLs): Requires states to adopt water quality standards for intrastate waters subject to EPA approval. Authorizes the EPA to establish water quality standards when states fail to do so or when state standards fail to meet federal requirements. Requires states to identify waters where effluent limits are not stringent enough to implement applicable water quality standards and to establish the total maximum daily load (TMDL) of pollutants for such waters at a level necessary to implement applicable water quality standards.

§ 304 Federal Water Quality Criteria and Guidelines: Requires the EPA to adopt water quality criteria and guidelines for effluent standards, pretreatment programs at publicly owned sewage treatment works (POTWs), and state permit programs. States may depart from EPA criteria.

§ 306 New Source Performance Standards: Requires the EPA to specify technology-based performance standards for industrial categories based on best demonstrated control technology.

§ 307 Toxic and Pretreatment Effluent Standards: Establishes list of toxic pollutants (consisting of 126 "priority" pollutants) and authorizes the EPA to revise list. Requires toxic pollutants to meet effluent limits based on best available technology economically achievable for the applicable category or class of point source. Requires the EPA to establish pretreatment standards for industrial discharges of toxics into POTWs.

§ 309 Enforcement: Authorizes the EPA to issue compliance orders and administrative penalties and to seek civil and criminal penalties for violation of the Act.

§ 319 Nonpoint Source Management Programs: Requires states and tribes to identify waters that do not meet water quality standards due to nonpoint source pollution, to identify nonpoint sources responsible, and to prepare management plans including best management practices and control measures to reduce loadings from nonpoint sources.

TITLE IV: Permits and Licenses

§ 401 Certification: Requires applicants for federal licenses or permits conducting any activity which may result in any discharge into navigable waters to obtain certification from the state in which discharge will originate ensuring that discharge will comply with CWA requirements. Authorizes states to impose conditions, including effluent limits, on applicant for certification.

§ 402 National Pollutant Discharge Elimination System: Establishes the national pollutant discharge elimination system (NPDES) to be administered by the EPA or by states and tribes with EPA-approved programs. The NPDES is the vehicle for imposing § 301-mandated technology-based discharge limits on all point sources. Section 402(p) applies to stormwater pollution.

§ 404 Dredge and Fill Permits: Authorizes U.S. Army Corps of Engineers to issue permits to control the discharge of dredged or fill material into navigable waterways.

TITLE V: General Provisions

§ 505 Citizen Suits: Authorizes citizen suits against violators of effluent standards or compliance orders and against the EPA for failure to perform a non-discretionary duty.

§ 509 Administrative Procedure and Judicial Review: Provides for judicial review of specified EPA actions in the U.S. Courts of Appeals.

§ 510 State Authority: Authorizes states to adopt more stringent standards than those required by the Act.

§ 518 Indian Tribes: Authorizes the EPA to treat Indian tribes as states for purposes of specified portions of the Act, providing tribes have governmental authority and capacity to implement requirements of the Act.

As with many complex federal statutes, the CWA is divided into Section numbers. The Section numbers do not, however, correspond with the U.S. Code Section numbers. Clean Water Act experts typically refer to the Act's section numbers rather than the code section numbers but legal research often requires the latter. The Table below, from Claudia Copeland, *Clean Water Act: A Summary of the Law*, Congressional Research Service (2010), https://usace.contentdm.oclc.org/digital/collection/p16021coll5/id/230/ shows the corresponding Code Sections and CWA section numbers of important provisions:

Major U.S. Code Sections of the Clean Water Act (codified generally as 33 U.S.C., Chapter 26, Sections 1251–1387)		
33 U.S.C.	**Section Title**	**Clean Water Act (as amended)**
Subchapter I	**Research and Related Programs**	
1251	Declaration of goals and policy	Sec. 101
1262	Definitions and authorizations	Sec. 112
1265	In-place toxic pollutants	Sec. 115
Subchapter III	**Standards and Enforcement**	
1311	Effluent Limitations	Sec. 301
1312	Water quality related effluent limitations	Sec. 302
1313	Water quality standards and implementation plans	Sec. 303
1314	Information and guidelines	Sec. 304

1315	Water quality inventory	Sec. 305
1316	National standards of performance	Sec. 306
1317	Toxic and pretreatment effluent standards	Sec. 307
1318	Inspections, monitoring, and entry	Sec. 308
1319	Federal enforcement	Sec. 309
1320	International pollution abatement	Sec. 310
1326	Thermal discharges	Sec. 316
1329	Nonpoint source management programs	Sec. 319
Subchapter IV	**Permits and Licenses**	
1341	Certification	Sec. 401
1342	National pollutant discharge elimination system	Sec. 402
1343	Ocean discharge criteria	Sec. 403
1344	Permits for dredged or fill material	Sec. 404
1345	Disposal of sewage sludge	Sec. 405
1346	Coastal recreation water quality monitoring and notification	Sec. 406
Subchapter V	**General Provisions**	
1361	Administration	Sec. 501
1362	General definitions	Sec. 502
1365	Citizen suits	Sec. 505
1369	Administrative procedure and judicial review	Sec. 509
1370	State authority	Sec. 510
1371	Other affected authority	Sec. 511
1376	General authorization	Sec. 517
1377	Indian tribes	Sec. 518

Note: This table only shows the major code sections. For more detail, the reader should consult the official printed version of the U.S. Code.

D.   ISSUES IN THE IMPLEMENTATION OF THE CWA

1. POINT SOURCES

Because the CWA treats point sources and non-point sources so differently, the determination of what constitutes a point-source is very consequential. Not surprisingly, the definition of the term has been the subject of substantial litigation. In the cases below, the courts grapple with this issue.

a.   Conventional and Non-Conventional (Non-Toxic) Pollutants

NRDC v. COSTLE
United States Court of Appeals, District of Columbia Circuit, 1977.
568 F.2d 1369.

LEVENTHAL, CIRCUIT JUDGE.

Section 402 of the FWPCA provides that under certain circumstances the EPA Administrator "may . . . issue a permit for the discharge of any pollutant" notwithstanding the general proscription of pollutant discharges found in § 301 of the Act. The discharge of a pollutant is defined in the FWPCA as "any addition of any pollutant to navigable waters from any point source" or "any addition of any pollutant to the waters of the contiguous zone or the ocean from any point source other than a vessel or floating craft." 33 U.S.C. § 1362(12). In 1973 the EPA Administrator issued regulations that exempted certain categories of "point sources" of pollution from the permit requirements of § 402. The Administrator's purported authority to make such exemptions turns on the proper interpretation of § 402.

A "point source" is defined in § 502(14) as "any discernible, confined and discrete conveyance, including but not limited to any pipe, ditch, channel, tunnel, conduit, well, discrete fissure, container, rolling stock, concentrated animal feeding operation, or vessel or other floating craft, from which pollutants are or may be discharged."

The 1973 regulations exempted discharges from a number of classes of point sources from the permit requirements of § 402, including all silvicultural point sources; all confined animal feeding operations below a certain size; all irrigation return flows from areas of less than 3,000 contiguous acres or 3,000 noncontiguous acres that use the same drainage system; all nonfeedlot, nonirrigation agricultural point sources; and separate storm sewers containing only storm runoff uncontaminated by any industrial or commercial activity. The EPA's rationale for these exemptions is that in order to conserve the Agency's enforcement resources for more significant point sources of pollution, it is necessary to exclude these smaller sources of pollutant discharges from the permit program.

The National Resources Defense Council, Inc. (NRDC) sought a declaratory judgment that the regulations are unlawful under the FWPCA. Specifically, NRDC contended that the Administrator does not have authority to exempt any class of point source from the permit requirements of § 402. It argued that Congress in enacting §§ 301, 402 of the FWPCA intended to prohibit the discharge of pollutants from *all* point sources unless a permit had been issued to the discharger under § 402 or unless the point source was explicitly exempted from the permit requirements by statute. The District Court granted NRDC's motion for summary judgment. It held that the FWPCA does not authorize the Administrator to exclude any class of point sources from the permit program. The EPA has appealed to this court. * * *

The appellants argue that § 402 not only gives the Administrator the discretion to grant or refuse a permit, but also gives him the authority to exempt classes of point sources from the permit requirements entirely. They argue that this interpretation is supported by the legislative history of § 402 and the fact that unavailability of this exemption power would place unmanageable administrative burdens on the EPA. * * *

Under the EPA's interpretation the Administrator would have broad discretion to exempt large classes of point sources from any or all requirements of the FWPCA. This is a result that the legislators did not intend. Rather they stressed that the FWPCA was a tough law that relied on explicit mandates to a degree uncommon in legislation of this type. * * *

There are innumerable references in the legislative history to the effect that the Act is founded on the "basic premise that a discharge of pollutants without a permit is unlawful and that discharges not in compliance with the limitations and conditions for a permit are unlawful." Even when infeasibility arguments were squarely raised, the legislature declined to abandon the permit requirement. * * *

The wording of the statute, legislative history, and precedents are clear: the EPA Administrator does not have authority to exempt categories of point sources from the permit requirements of § 402. * * *

II. ADMINISTRATIVE INFEASIBILITY

The appellants have stressed in briefs and at oral argument the extraordinary burden on the EPA that will be imposed by the above interpretation of the scope of the NPDES program. The specter of millions of applications for permits is evoked both as part of appellants' legislative history argument—that Congress could not have intended to impose such burdens on the EPA—and as an invitation to this court to uphold the regulations as deviations from the literal terms of the FWPCA necessary to permit the agency to realize the general objectives of that act. * * *

A. Uniform National Effluent Limitations

* * *

EPA contends that certain characteristics of runoff pollution make it difficult to promulgate effluent limitations for most of the point sources exempted by the 1973 regulations:

> The major characteristic of the pollution problem which is generated by runoff . . . is that the owner of the discharge point . . . has no control over the quantity of the flow or the nature and amounts of the pollutants picked up by the runoff. The amount of flow obviously is unpredictable because it results from the duration and intensity of the rainfall event, the topography, the type of ground cover and the saturation point of the land due to any previous rainfall. Similar factors affect the types of pollutants which will be picked up by that runoff, including the type of farming practices employed, the rate and type of pesticide and fertilizer application, and the conservation practices employed. . . .

> An effluent limitation must be a precise number in order for it to be an effective regulatory tool; both the discharger and the regulatory agency need to have an identifiable standard upon which to determine whether the facility is in compliance. That was the principal [sic] of the passage of the 1972 Amendments. * * *

As noted in *NRDC v. Train*, the primary purpose of the effluent limitations and guidelines was to provide uniformity among the federal and state jurisdictions enforcing the NPDES program and prevent the "Tragedy of the Commons" that might result if jurisdictions can compete for industry and development by providing more liberal limitations than their neighboring states. The effluent limitations were intended to create floors that had to be respected by state permit programs.

But in *NRDC v. Train* it was also recognized that permits could be issued before national effluent limitations were promulgated and that permits issued subsequent to promulgation of uniform effluent limitations could be modified to take account of special characteristics of subcategories of point sources. * * *

* * * In [*Train*] this court fully appreciated that technological and administrative constraints might prevent the Administrator from developing guidelines and corresponding uniform numeric effluent limitations for certain point sources anytime in the near future. The Administrator was deemed to have the burden of demonstrating that the failure to develop the guidelines on schedule was due to administrative or

technological infeasibility. Yet the underlying teaching was that technological or administrative infeasibility was a reason for adjusting court mandates to the minimum extent necessary to realize the general objectives of the Act. It is a number of steps again to suggest that these problems afford the Administrator the authority to exempt categories of point sources from the NPDES program entirely. * * *

In sum, we conclude that the existence of uniform national effluent limitations is not a necessary precondition for incorporating into the NPDES program pollution from agricultural, silvicultural, and storm water runoff point sources. The technological or administrative infeasibility of such limitations may result in adjustments in the permit programs, as will be seen, but it does not authorize the Administrator to exclude the relevant point source from the NPDES program.

B.   Alternative Permit Conditions under § 402(a)

EPA contends that even if it is possible to issue permits without national effluent limitations, the special characteristics of point sources of runoff pollution make it infeasible to develop restrictions on a case-by-case basis. EPA's implicit premise is that whether limitations are promulgated on a class or individual source basis, it is still necessary to articulate any limitation in terms of a numerical effluent standard. That is not our understanding.

Section 402 provides that a permit may be issued upon condition "that such discharge will meet either all applicable requirements under sections 301, 302, 306, 307, 308 and 403 of this Act, *or prior to taking of necessary implementing actions relating to all such requirements, such conditions as the Administrator determines are necessary to carry out the provisions of this Act.*" 33 U.S.C. § 1342(a) (Supp. V 1975) (emphasis added). This provision gives EPA considerable flexibility in framing the permit to achieve a desired reduction in pollutant discharges. The permit may proscribe industry practices that aggravate the problem of point source pollution.

EPA's counsel caricatures the matter by stating that recognition of any such authority would give EPA the power "to instruct each individual farmer on his farming practices." Any limitation on a polluter forces him to modify his conduct and operations. * * * Of course, when alternative techniques are available, Congress intended to give the discharger as much flexibility as possible in choosing his mode of compliance. We only indicate here that when numerical effluent limitations are infeasible, EPA may issue permits with conditions designed to reduce the level of effluent discharges to acceptable levels. This may well mean opting for a gross reduction in pollutant discharge rather than the fine-tuning suggested by numerical limitations. But this ambitious statute is not hospitable to the concept that the appropriate response to a difficult pollution problem is not to try at all.

It may be appropriate in certain circumstances for the EPA to require a permittee simply to monitor and report effluent levels; EPA manifestly has this authority. Such permit conditions might be desirable where the full extent of the pollution problem is not known.

C.   General Permits

Finally, EPA argues that the number of permits involved in the absence of an exemption authority will simply overwhelm the Agency. Affidavits filed with the District Court indicate, for example, that the number of silviculture point sources may be over 300,000 and that there are approximately 100,000 separate storm sewer point sources. We are and must be sensitive to EPA's concerns of an intolerable permit load. But the District Court and the various parties have suggested devices to mitigate the burden—to accommodate within a practical regulatory scheme Congress's clear mandate that all point sources have permits. All that is required is that EPA make full use of its interpretational authority. The existence of a variety of options belies EPA's infeasibility arguments.

Section 402 does not explicitly describe the necessary scope of a NPDES permit. The most significant requirement is that the permit be in compliance with limitation sections of the Act described above. As a result NRDC and the District Court have suggested the use of area or general permits. The Act allows such techniques. Area-wide regulation is one well-established means of coping with administrative exigency. * * *

There is also a very practical difference between a general permit and an exemption. An exemption tends to become indefinite: the problem drops out of sight, into a pool of inertia, unlikely to be recalled in the absence of crisis or a strong political protagonist. In contrast, the general or area permit approach forces the Agency to focus on the problems of specific regions and requires that the problems of the region be reconsidered at least every five years, the maximum duration of a permit.

NOTES

1.   The 1972 FWPCA Amendments undeniably placed a massive administrative burden upon the EPA. Within six months after the new enactment, the EPA had received nearly 33,000 NPDES permit applications, and this number almost doubled by mid-1974. *See* PERCIVAL ET AL., ENVIRONMENTAL REGULATION 680 (4th ed. 2003). Because this task was clearly beyond the resources of the fledgling federal agency, the NPDES permit system was designed to shift much of the burden to the states, which would hold primary responsibility for permitting, monitoring, and enforcement under section 402, while the EPA would only supervise state actions. *See* JACKSON B. BATTLE & MAXINE I. LIPELES, WATER POLLUTION 18–19 (3d ed. 1998). Yet many

states were slow to establish NPDES permitting programs. Three states, along with the District of Columbia and U.S. territories such as Guam and Puerto Rico, still had none in 2018, and nine other states only adopted programs between 1990 and 2018. *See* the EPA's website for information on the NPDES program, *available at* https://www.epa.gov/npdes.

2.   Is NRDC v. Costle consistent with Coalition for Responsible Regulation v. EPA, 684 F. 3d 102 (D.C. Circ. 2012), excerpted *supra* at page 557?

3.   After this case, Congress in 1987 specifically amended the definition of "point source" to exclude "agricultural stormwater discharges and return flows from irrigated agriculture." *See* 33 U.S.C. § 1362(14). Can you justify this exemption?

4.   Because of the ambiguity of the term, the Second Circuit has ruled that a human being cannot be a "point source." *See* United States v. Plaza Health Labs., Inc., 3 F.3d 643 (2d Cir. 1993), *cert. denied*, 512 U.S. 1245 (1994) (individual who dropped vials of blood from blood-testing laboratory into Hudson River not criminally liable under CWA). The next case further probes the ambiguity in the definition of "point source."

SIERRA CLUB V. ABSTON CONSTRUCTION COMPANY

United States Court of Appeals, Fifth Circuit, 1980.
620 F.2d 41.

RONEY, CIRCUIT JUDGE.

In this suit to enforce portions of the Federal Water Pollution Control Act Amendments of 1972 against coal strip miners, the issue is whether pollution carried in various ways into a creek from defendant coal miners' strip mines is "point source" pollution controlled by the Act. * * *

Defendants Abston Construction Co., Mitchell & Neely, Inc., Kellerman Mining Co. and The Drummond Co. (hereinafter miners) operate coal mines near Daniel Creek, a tributary of the Black Warrior River, in Tuscaloosa County, Alabama. They each employ the strip mining technique, whereby rock material above the coal—the overburden—is removed, thereby exposing the coal that is close to the land surface. When the overburden is removed, it is pushed aside, and forms "spoil piles." During the mining operations, and thereafter if the land is not reclaimed by replacing the overburden, the spoil piles are highly erodible. Rainwater runoff or water draining from within the mined pit at times carried the material to adjacent streams, causing siltation and acid deposits. In an effort to halt runoff, the miners here occasionally constructed "sediment basins," which were designed to catch the runoff before it reached the creek. Their efforts were not always successful. Rainfall sometimes caused the basins to overflow, again depositing silt and acid materials into Daniel Creek. * * *

The parties do not dispute the ultimate fact that these pollutants appeared in the creek due to excess rainfall. Nor is there any disagreement the activities would be prohibited if the pollutants had been pumped directly into the waterways. The parties differ only on the legal responsibility of the miners for controlling the runoff and the legal effect of their efforts to control the runoff.

Plaintiff may prevail in its citizen suit only if the miners have violated some effluent limitations under the Act. 33 U.S.C.A. § 1365(a)(1)(A). Those limitations, in turn, apply only to "point sources" of pollution, as defined in the Act.

> The term "point source" means any discernible, confined and discrete conveyance, including but not limited to any pipe, ditch, channel, tunnel, conduit, well, discrete fissure, container, rolling stock, concentrated animal feeding operation, or vessel or other floating craft, from which pollutants are or may be discharged. 33 U.S.C.A. § 1362(14).

Nonpoint sources, on the other hand, are not due to be controlled.

Thus, the issue is whether defendants' activities amounted to the creation of point sources of pollution. The district court ruled they did not. On the facts before it, the district court found the pollution had not resulted "from any affirmative act of discharge by the defendants." Instead, any water and other materials that were deposited in Daniel Creek were carried by natural forces, mostly erosion caused by rainwater runoff, even though such erosion was "facilitated by the acts of defendants of creating pits and spoil banks in the course of their mining operations."

A preliminary question here is whether the Act may be applied to mining activities at all. The district court, although holding the miners here did not create point sources of pollution, conceded, correctly, we think, that "some strip mine operations may involve the discharge of pollutants in ways which would trigger application of the Act's enforcement provisions." * * *

The district court correctly concluded that mining activities, although embracing at times nonpoint sources of pollution that were intended only to be studied by the EPA, may also implicate point sources of pollution, expressly covered by the Act's effluent limitations.

As to whether the activities here fall under the definition of point sources of pollution, three positions are asserted: plaintiff's, defendants', and a middle ground presented by the Government. We adopt the Government's approach.

Plaintiff would merely require a showing of the original sources of the pollution to find a statutory point source, regardless of how the pollutant found its way from that original source to the waterway. According to this argument, the broad drainage of rainwater carrying oily pollutants from a road paralleling a waterway, or animal pollutants from a grazing field contiguous to the waterway, would violate the Act. * * *

Defendants, on the other hand, would exclude from the point source definition any discharge of pollutants into the waterway through ditches and gullies created by natural erosion and rainfall, even though the pollutant and the base material upon which the erosion could take place to make gullies was created by the mine operation, and even though the miners' efforts may have permitted the rainwater to flow more easily into a natural ditch leading to the waterway. * * *

The United States, which participated in the case as amicus curiae, takes a middle ground: surface runoff collected or channeled by the operator constitutes a point source discharge. Simple erosion over the material surface, resulting in the discharge of water and other materials into navigable waters, does not constitute a point source discharge, absent some effort to change the surface, to direct the waterflow or otherwise impede its progress. Examples of point source pollution in the present case, according to the Government, are the collection, and subsequent percolation, of surface waters in the pits themselves. Sediment basins dug by the miners and designed to collect sediment are likewise point sources under the Government's view even though the materials were carried away from the basins by gravity flow of rainwater.

We agree with the Government's argument. Gravity flow, resulting in a discharge into a navigable body of water, may be part of a point source discharge if the miner at least initially collected or channeled the water and other materials. A point source of pollution may also be present where miners design spoil piles from discarded overburden such that, during periods of precipitation, erosion of spoil pile walls results in discharges into a navigable body of water by means of ditches, gullies and similar conveyances, even if the miners have done nothing beyond the mere collection of rock and other materials. The ultimate question is whether pollutants were discharged from "discernible, confined, and discrete conveyance(s)" either by gravitational or nongravitational means. Nothing in the Act relieves miners from liability simply because the operators did not actually construct those conveyances, so long as they are reasonably likely to be the means by which pollutants are ultimately deposited into a navigable body of water. Conveyances of pollution formed either as a result of natural erosion or by material means, and which constitute a component of a mine drainage system, may fit the statutory definition and thereby subject the operators to liability under the Act. * * *

Under the view of the law adopted here, there remain genuine issues of material fact. * * * Earl Bailey, a Sierra Club vice president and a professor at the University of Alabama, testified by affidavit that he observed,

> gullies and ditches running down the sides of steep spoil piles created by Abston Construction Company. The sedimentation and pollutants are carried through these discernible, confined and discrete conveyances to Daniel Creek.

Bailey's observations of ditches and gullies were confirmed by Philip Abston, president of the Abston Construction Co., who noted that the gullies would carry water and sediment toward the creek.

Dwight Hicks, who served as defendant Drummond Co.'s manager of reclamation and environmental control, testified that in some areas, drainage basins were constructed to catch sediment flowing down the outer edges of the spoil piles. * * *

An affidavit filed by Garry Drummond, president of defendant Drummond Co. in support of its motion for summary judgment, contains starkly contrasting language.

> Neither company has engaged in the operation of any discernible, confined and discrete conveyance, including but not limited to any pipe, ditch, channel, tunnel, conduit, well, discrete fissure, container, rolling stock, concentrated animal feeding operation or vessel or other floating craft from which pollutants are or may be discharged.

> Neither company has discharged any pollutant including surface water runoff into Daniel Creek or the tributaries of the same during the period of operation as noted hereinabove. * * *

Thus, additional findings are necessary to determine the precise nature of spoil basins constructed by defendant Drummond. In light of Hicks's statement that a "standpipe and an emergency spillway" were constructed to guard against spoil basin overflow, we note that a "pipe" from which pollutants are discharged may be a point source of pollution. 33 U.S.C.A. § 1362(14). This design could likewise fit under the *Earth Sciences* finding that "the escape of liquid from [a] confined system is from a point source," [*United States v. Earth Sciences, Inc.*, 599 F.2d 368, 374 (10th Cir. 1979)], since the affidavits and depositions suggest that water and other materials escaped from the mines and sediment basins, eventually finding their way to Daniel Creek. Furthermore, factual findings are lacking insofar as the sediment basins and other devices may be characterized as encompassing "container(s), . . . from which pollutants are or may be discharged." 33 U.S.C.A. § 1362(14).

While defendants have denied taking any direct action resulting in the discharge of pollutants into Daniel Creek, Bailey described "(m)ine spoil pushed into Daniel Creek so as to block the waterway." Even under the district court's requirement that the alleged polluters take some "affirmative act" before a finding of point source pollution is warranted, the activity described by Bailey suggests a discharge of pollutants into the creek. In considering this issue, the district court should deem controlling § 502(12) of the Act, which, as pointed out by the *Earth Sciences* court, defines discharge as "any addition of any pollutant to navigable waters. . . ." 33 U.S.C.A. § 1362(12).

Although the point source definition "excludes unchanneled and uncollected surface waters," *Appalachian Power Co. v. Train*, 545 F.2d 1351, 1373 (4th Cir. 1976), surface runoff from rainfall, when collected or channeled by coal miners in connection with mining activities, constitutes point source pollution. * * *

REVERSED AND REMANDED.

NOTES

1.   Does the court's definition of point source pollution create a disincentive to some environmentally beneficial collection and control efforts? Is there anything mine operators like Abston Construction Company can do—or not do—in the future to help prevent a court from characterizing their mine wastes as point sources subject to heightened regulatory requirements? Or does the court's broadened definition of point sources mean that any pile of mine spoil automatically becomes a point source?

2.   Where should the line between point and nonpoint sources be drawn? Is it fair to make businesses and individuals responsible for pollution resulting at least in part from circumstances beyond their control? The next case discusses another situation where human conduct and natural weather events interacted to cause pollution, and the court grapples with the relationship between these inputs in deciding where to draw this line.

CONCERNED AREA RESIDENTS FOR THE ENVIRONMENT V. SOUTHVIEW FARM

United States Court of Appeals, Second Circuit, 1994.
34 F.3d 114, *cert. denied,* 514 U.S. 1082, 115 S.Ct. 1793, 131 L.Ed.2d 721 (1995).

OAKES, SENIOR CIRCUIT JUDGE.

This is a citizen's suit under the Clean Water Act of 1977 ("CWA" or the "Act"), with some state law claims for nuisance, negligence and trespass. The suit arises on account of the liquid manure spreading operations of a large dairy farm in western New York. * * *

The appeal by plaintiffs involves only the five CWA violations and raises anew the question what is a "point source" within the meaning of 33 U.S.C. § 1362(14) * * *. The appeal also concerns whether the liquid manure spreading operations fell within the "agricultural stormwater discharges" exception to point source discharges under the Act. 33 U.S.C. § 1362(14).

We now hold that the liquid manure spreading operations are a point source within the meaning of CWA section 1362(14) because the farm itself falls within the definition of a concentrated animal feeding operation ("CAFO") and is not subject to the agricultural exemption.

I.   Background

Plaintiffs, who refer to themselves collectively as Concerned Area Residents For the Environment ("CARE"), are a group of land owners who live near Southview Farms, a dairy farm in the town of Castile, in Wyoming County, New York. Defendants are the farm itself, and Richard H. Popp, an individual. Southview Farm is one of the largest dairy farms in the State of New York. It employs twenty-eight full-time and nine part-time employees. As of 1992, it owned 1,100 crop acres and had an animal population of 1,290 head of mature cows with over 900 head of young cattle, heifers and calves, making a total of 2,200 animals.

Unlike old-fashioned dairy farms, Southview's operations do not involve pasturing the cows. Instead, the cows remain in their barns except during the three times per day milking procedure. Also unlike old-fashioned dairy farms where the accumulated manure was spread by a manure spreader, Southview's rather enormous manure operations are largely performed through the use of storage lagoons and liquid cow manure. The storage lagoons number five on the main farm property ("A Farm"). One four-acre manure storage lagoon has a capacity of approximately six-to-eight million gallons of liquid cow manure.

In connection with this particular manure storage lagoon, Southview has installed a separator which pumps the cow manure over a mechanical device which drains off the liquid and passes the solids out through a compressing process. The solids that remain are dropped into bins for transport while the liquid runs by gravity through a pipe to the four-acre manure storage lagoon. This separated liquid was apparently used for the purpose of washing down the barns where the cows are housed.

Insofar as application of the manure as fertilizer to the land is concerned, there is a center pivot irrigation system for spreading liquid manure over the fields. The diameter of the circle of this irrigation system can be modified to conform to the field on which the application is being made. A series of pipes connects the pivot to the liquid manure storage lagoons. The pivot is self-propelled with the height of the arc from the manure spray being somewhere between 12 and 30 feet.

Southview also spreads its manure with a hard hose traveler which is a long piece of plastic tubing on a large reel. The traveler can be unwound and has a nozzle on the end which can send liquid manure 150 feet in either direction making a 300-foot-wide swath for purposes of fertilizing farm fields. The height of the arc from the projected spray is "a couple of feet higher" than that of the center pivot irrigator. Since 1988, a piping system consisting of a six-inch aluminum pipe and running under both the state highway and a town road to a lagoon on at least one Southview Farm other than the "A Farm," has transported liquid manure from the storage lagoon to various locations without the use of vehicles.

Southview also uses conventional manure spreading equipment including spreaders pulled by tractors and self-propelled vehicles which, generally speaking, have a 5,000 gallon capacity for liquid manure. These vehicles were used to spread manure from the smaller lagoons on the "A Farm" which do not receive liquid manure processed through the separation system. Southview's manure spreading record reflects the application of millions of gallons of manure to its fields. * * *

IV. Discussion

The CWA provides that, absent a permit and subject to certain limitations, "the discharge of any pollutant by any person shall be unlawful." 33 U.S.C. § 1311(a); see *Plaza Health*, 3 F.3d at 645. A pollutant includes "solid waste, . . . sewage, . . . biological materials, . . . and agricultural waste discharged into water" and thus includes the manure in this case. 33 U.S.C. § 1362(6). A "discharge" is "any addition of any pollutant to navigable waters from any point source." 33 U.S.C. § 1362(12). The term "point source" includes "any discernible, confined and discrete conveyance, including but not limited to any . . . concentrated animal feeding operation. . . . This term does not include agricultural stormwater discharges and return flows from irrigated agriculture." 33 U.S.C. § 1362(14). Our basic questions on review then are whether the defendants discharged the manure pollutant from any point source into navigable waters and whether the agricultural stormwater exemption or any other limitation applies.

The plaintiff-appellants' contentions relate to [the following] specific CWA violations which the jury found but the district court overturned * * *:

(1) A July 13, 1989, violation on field 104 on the so-called Wyant Farm, located to the east of Middle Reservation Road and bordering on Letchworth State Park through which the Genesee River runs. As to this violation, two of the plaintiffs observed liquid manure flowing into and through a swale on the Wyant Farm and through a drain tile leading directly into a stream which ultimately flows into the Genesee River. * * *

(3) September 26, 1990, and April 15, 1991, violations as to which the appellants claim that the district court erroneously set aside the jury verdicts because no reasonable juror could find that the discharges were not excepted under the Act as agricultural stormwater discharges.

It is at this point that the United States amicus position and the position of the appellants tend to coincide, if not directly meet. It is significant to note, as previously stated, that the cows are not put out to pasture. The fields to which the manure is applied, as above indicated, are used for crops. The United States appears as amicus curiae in support of the appellants on the basis that, because the Southview operations involve more than 700 cattle, it is a facility which is defined in the regulations under the Act as a CAFO, and therefore one type of "point source" under the Act, thereby requiring a permit for discharges which was not obtained in this instance. As we have stated, the Act defines the term "point source" as including "any . . . concentrated animal feeding operation." 33 U.S.C. § 1362(14). In this connection, the district court concluded that, as a matter of law, Southview was not a CAFO because crops are grown on a portion of the farm. The United States contends that Southview is a CAFO as a matter of law because crops are not grown in the feed lot in which the milking cows are confined. * * *

A. July 13, 1989, Violation on Field 104

The July 13 violation, found by the jury but overturned by the district court, as we have said, occurred on field 104 on the Wyant property which shares the boundary line with Letchworth State Park. Field 104 contains a slew or swale which tends to collect liquid manure spread by Southview's tankers and conveys it through a pipe in a stonewall and through the stonewall itself into a ditch which runs for some length on the Southview property before it reaches the boundary of the state park.

On July 13, 1989, appellants Kirk Bly and Philip Karcheski observed the manure collecting in the slew or swale and flowing into the ditch which in turn flowed off of the Southview property into Letchworth State Park property, and, in turn, joined a stream which ultimately flowed into the Genesee River.

The district court held and appellees contend that the July 13 discharge was not a point source discharge because the liquid simply and quite naturally flowed to and through the lowest areas of the field, and that the pollutants reached the stream that flows into the Genesee "in too diffuse a manner to create a point source discharge." The district court also suggested that the pollutants were not "collected" by human activity but in fact the opposite occurred in that the manure was dispersed over the ground.

The appellants argue that, given the testimony and the photographic evidence before the court, even if the liquid manure flowing from field 104 into the swale could be characterized as "diffuse run-off," as the district court characterized it, the manure pollutant was nevertheless thereafter channelled or collected sufficiently to constitute a discharge by a point source. Alternatively, the appellants contend that the appellees' liquid-manure-spreading vehicles themselves may be treated as point sources because 33 U.S.C. § 1362(14) defines a point source to include a "container" or "rolling stock." They point out that a number of district court cases have found vehicles to be within the definition of point sources. See, e.g., *Avoyelles Sportsmen's League, Inc. v. Marsh*, 715 F.2d 897, 922 (5th Cir. 1983) (bulldozers and backhoes constitute point sources under the CWA) * * *. They urge that by pumping the liquid manure from Southview's various lagoons into manure spreading tankers and other vehicles before discharging the liquid manure on to its various fields, Southview has "collected by human effort" the pollutant discharged into the navigable waters.

We agree with the appellants on both counts. We believe that the swale coupled with the pipe under the stonewall leading into the ditch that leads into the stream was in and of itself a point source. As this court has previously noted, the definition of a point source is to be broadly interpreted. [S]ee also *Sierra Club v. Abston Constr. Co.*, 620 F.2d 41, 45–46 (5th Cir.1980) (defendants were engaged in strip mining operations and placed their overburden in highly erodible piles which were then carried away by rain water through naturally created ditches); *United States v. Earth Sciences, Inc.*, 599 F.2d 368, 374 (10th Cir.1979) (discharge from a large capacity reserve sump serving a gold extraction process could be a point source even though "the source of the excess liquid is rainfall or snow melt"). In *Sierra Club*, the Fifth Circuit held that a defendant is not relieved from liability simply because it does not actually construct the conveyances "so long as they are reasonably likely to be the means by which the pollutants are ultimately deposited into a navigable body of water." *Sierra Club*, 620 F.2d at 45; *see also United States v. Oxford Royal Mushroom Prods., Inc.*, 487 F.Supp. 852, 854 (E.D.Pa.1980) (discharge resulting from spraying overabundance of water onto surface of an irrigation field which, in turn, ran off into a nearby stream through a break in a berm around the field may constitute discharge from a point source). Here, the liquid manure was collected and channelized through the ditch or depression in the swale of field 104 and thence into the ditch leading to the stream on the boundary of the Southview property as it adjoins Letchworth State Park. Nothing in *Plaza Health* is to the contrary. There the court simply refused to treat a human being as a "point source" under the criminal provisions of the Act by virtue of the rule of lenity. Plaza Health, 3 F.3d at 649.

Moreover, we agree with the appellants that, alternatively, the manure spreading vehicles themselves were point sources. The collection of liquid manure into tankers and their discharge on fields from which the manure directly flows into navigable waters are point source discharges under the case law. * * *

C. September 26, 1990, and April 15, 1991, Violations

We believe the district court also erred in setting aside the jury's verdict on the September 26, 1990, and April 15, 1991, violations on the basis that "no reasonable juror could find that these discharges were not excepted under the Act as agricultural stormwater discharges." The district court drew this conclusion even though it had given explicit instructions to the jury on the availability of the "agricultural stormwater" exemption under 33 U.S.C. § 1362(14).

We agree with appellants that, while the statute does include an exception for "agricultural stormwater discharges," there can be no escape from liability for agricultural pollution simply because it occurs on rainy days. * * *

We think the real issue is not whether the discharges occurred during rainfall or were mixed with rain water run-off, but rather, whether the discharges were the result of precipitation. Of course, all discharges eventually mix with precipitation run-off in ditches or streams or navigable waters so the fact that the discharge might have been mixed with run-off cannot be determinative. Accordingly, we must uphold the verdict to the extent that the jury had a reasonable basis to find that the discharges on September 26, 1990, and April 15, 1991, were not the result of rain, but rather simply occurred on days when it rained. * * *

[The Court concluded that the jury could properly find that the run-off was primarily caused by the over-saturation of the fields rather than the rain and that sufficient quantities of manure were present so that the run-off could not be classified as "stormwater."] * * *

2. CAFO Exception to Nonpoint Source Provisions

The New York Farm Bureau, Inc., and American Farm Bureau Federation, as amici curiae, ("Farm Bureau amici"), argue that agricultural activities are regulated as "nonpoint sources" under the Clean Water Act and are not subject to citizens' suits enforcement. * * * The Farm Bureau amici point out that nonpoint sources "were addressed by Congress through the Section 208 planning process * * *." Thus when Congress enacted the 1972 Amendments, it considered and chose to exempt agricultural activities under the Section 208 nonpoint source provisions *except in the case of [CAFOs]."* Brief of Farm Bureau Amici at 7 (emphasis added).

It is understood that the 1972 framework remains in place and that the revision made in 1977 to the point source definition excluded "return flows from irrigated agriculture," 33 U.S.C. § 1362(14) * * *.

* * * [T]he United States amicus points out that the Clean Water Act by definition includes in the term "point source," "any discernible, confined and discrete conveyance, including but not limited to, any . . . concentrated animal feeding operation. . . ." 33 U.S.C. § 1362(14). The regulatory

definition of a CAFO is found at 40 C.F.R. 122.23(b) (1994). This provision defines CAFO as an animal feeding operation ("AFO") that meets the criteria of appendix B, which, as pertinent here denotes that the AFO contains more than 700 mature dairy cattle. 40 C.F.R. 122.23(b). The preambles to the regulations indicate that if an AFO exceeds the relevant number of animal units provided in Appendix B Supp. to Part 122 at (a), the AFO is presumably a CAFO, unless "the only time a discharge of pollutants into navigable waters occurs is during a 25 year, 24-hour rainfall event." * * * 41 Fed. Reg. 11458, 11458 (final regulations) * * *. Given that it is undisputed that the feed lot at Southview confines more than 700 mature dairy cattle, and there is no claim that the run-offs in question were caused by a 25-year, 24-hour rainfall event, we face the question whether the fact that crops are grown on the fields, even though the cattle at Southview are not pastured on those fields, prevents Southview from being an AFO.

An AFO is defined in the regulations as "a lot or facility . . . where the following conditions are met:

> (i)   Animals . . . have been, are, or will be stabled or confined and fed or maintained for a total of 45 days or more in any 12-month period, and, (ii) crops, vegetation forage growth, or post-harvest residues are not sustained in the normal growing season over any portion of the lot or facility.

40 C.F.R. 122.23 (b)(1). There appears to be no doubt that Southview's feed lot meets the criteria of sub-paragraph (i). The district court held that Southview was not an AFO because crops are grown on fields adjacent to the feed lot in which the milking cows are penned; therefore, according to the court, Southview does not meet the criteria of sub-paragraph (ii). * * *

V. Conclusion

In short, we conclude with the United States as amicus, that Southview has an animal feeding lot operation with a tremendous number of cattle in a concentrated feeding facility in which no vegetation is grown; that operation in and of itself is a point source within the Clean Water Act and not subject to any agricultural exemption thereto. * * *

NOTES

1.   What balance of human and natural inputs should be sufficient to constitute a point source, which is subject to much heavier regulation, enforcement, and possible penalties than a nonpoint source? Is the solution to this line-drawing dilemma just to regulate nonpoint sources more like point sources, notwithstanding the comparative difficulty of controlling nonpoint pollution?

2.   To what degree should businesses or individuals be responsible for the weather? The EPA regulations, in presuming a sufficiently large AFO to be a CAFO, and, therefore, a point source, unless discharge only occurs during a 25-year, 24-hour rainfall event, sharply limits polluters' ability to claim an "Act of God" and avoid liability. Rather, AFOs are responsible for predictable outcomes of their activities except under weather conditions so severe as to happen on average only once every 25 years. Is this an appropriate standard?

3.   In the modern United States, where the overwhelming majority of the population consists of urban dwellers, most lawyers and law students did not grow up on farms and know little about agriculture. Yet, as noted in the government reports on water quality excerpted at the beginning of this chapter, agricultural operations cumulatively constitute one of the nation's largest and most difficult to control sources of water pollution. Potential pollution problems from agriculture have grown as agricultural operations, like Southview Farms, have expanded to an industrial scale. Is there any good reason to continue to exempt such farms from regulation? If not, what explains Congress' reluctance to regulate them?

4.   In *South Florida Water Mgmt. Dist. v. Miccosukee Tribe of Indians*, 541 U.S. 95 (2004), the U.S. Supreme Court addressed an interesting question about what constituted the "addition" of a pollutant to a water body within the meaning of the Act. The question was whether petitioner's longstanding practice of pumping accumulated water from a water collection canal (which collects ground water and rain water from urban and agricultural development) to a water conservation area (an undeveloped wetland) within the Florida Everglades constitutes an addition of a pollutant from a point source, where the water contains a pollutant but the pumping station source itself adds no pollutants to the water being pumped. (In this case, the pumping moves phosphorous-laden water from the canal to the wetland but does not independently add a pollutant.) The Supreme Court, per Justice O'Connor, held that NPDES permits are required for point sources that do not themselves generate pollutants but that merely convey them. However, the court remanded the case for further proceedings regarding the parties' factual dispute over whether the canal and the water conservation area are meaningfully distinct water bodies. If not, there would be no "addition" of a pollutant from one water body to another within the meaning of the CWA, triggering the need for an NPDES permit. The Court essentially reaffirmed the *Miccosukee Tribe* case in *Los Angeles County Flood Control District v. NRDC*, 133 S.Ct. 710 (2013) stating that, "[T]he flow of water from an improved portion of a navigable waterway into an unimproved portion of the same waterway does not qualify as a discharge of pollutants under the CWA." Oddly, however, the Court appears to have decided the case based on an erroneous understanding of the facts in the case. For an explanation, *see* Sean Hecht, *Supreme Court Overturns Ninth Circuit Decision that Held L.A. County Flood Control District liable for stormwater pollution in a Poorly-Reasoned, but Narrow, Decision*, LEGAL PLANET (Jan. 8, 2013), http://legalplanet.wordpress. com/2013/01/08/supreme-court-overturns-ninth-circuit-decision-that-held-l-a-

county-flood-control-district-liable-for-stormwater-pollution-in-a-poorly-reasoned-but-narrow-decision/.

5.   The Ninth Circuit recently held that groundwater that has been contaminated by the injection of effluent disposal from a municipal wastewater treatment system on the Island of Maui must obtain an NPDES permit. The groundwater wells reach the Pacific Ocean and pollutants from the effluent have been traced to several of the wells. The court found that the wells constitute a point source under the CWA. *Hawai'i Wildlife Fund v. County of Maui* (No. 15–17447), http://www.scotusblog.com/wp-content/uploads/2018/09/18-260-opinion-below.pdf. The 4th Circuit held similarly in *Kinder Morgan Energy v. Upstate Forever*, where a gasoline pipeline ruptured and allegedly leaked gasoline into groundwater aquifers, causing what the court found to be a discharge subject to permitting under the CWA. As this book went to press, the U.S. Supreme Court granted certiorari in the cases. United States Supreme Court, *Order List: 586*, (February 19, 2019). The Solicitor General's brief had argued for the grant of the petition on the grounds, in part, that there is a conflict in the circuits, with the 6th Circuit holding in *Kentucky Waterways Alliance v. Kentucky Utilities Co.,* 905 F.3d 925 (6th Cir. 2018) that the operator of a coal-fired power plant that stored coal ash in ponds that leaked into groundwater, which subsequently leaked into a lake, did not constitute a discharge prohibited by the CWA without a permit.

b.   Stormwater Pollution and Point Sources

Though the CWA focuses extensively on those sources of pollution that are discharged out of discreet pipes, by virtually all accounts, one of the largest sources of water pollution across the country is stormwater pollution. During rain storms, water picks up various contaminants—metals, pesticides, trash, sediments, motor oil, algae-promoting nutrients—and carries those contaminants into streams, rivers, lakes and oceans. *See* Environmental Def. Ctr. v. EPA, 344 F.3d 832, 840–41 (9th Cir. 2003). In many urban areas, stormwater is discharged through storm sewers or drains that carry the contaminants directly into bodies of water. Despite the diffuse nature of stormwater pollution, these storm drains are considered point sources under the Clean Water Act. NRDC v. Costle, 568 F.2d 1369, 1379 (D.C. Cir. 1977) *(supra,* page 602.) Despite the fact that storm drains have long been defined as point sources, for years regulation of the problem was close to non-existent. In 1987, Congress amended the Clean Water Act to add § 402(p) to govern "Municipal and Industrial Stormwater Discharges." Section 402(p) requires NPDES permits for stormwater discharges "associated with industrial activity" and discharges from medium and large municipal separate storm sewer systems. § 402(p)(2)(B)(C)(D). Permits may also be required for stormwater discharges that violate water quality standards or are significant contributors of pollutants. § 402(p)(2)(E). Yet these sources remain extremely difficult to regulate. Virtually every person in a municipal area is a source of stormwater pollution—individuals who use outdoor pesticides, wash their cars, change their oil or leave trash cans uncovered contribute, and countless small businesses, construction sites, parking lots and roadways are sources of stormwater pollution.

These sources are now all theoretically captured by Section 402(p) even though the runoff looks less like a traditional point source with a discreet pipe or other channel because the pollution drains into a storm drain system, which is considered a point source. Many states are regulating municipal storm systems with general statewide stormwater permits and have taken a similar approach with industrial sources. For a map of regulated municipal separate stormwater systems (known as MS4s) and background on municipal permits, *see* U.S. EPA, *Stormwater Discharges from Municipal Sources*, https://www.epa.gov/npdes/storm water-discharges-municipal-sources. Sources of stormwater pollution that lie outside of municipal stormwater systems can also be regulated as point sources.

NOTES

1. How is the operator of a municipal stormwater system subject to section 402(p) supposed to regulate all of the diffuse sources that drain into the system? Many cities have decried the stormwater provisions for imposing huge, unfunded costs on them. Some states now require, as part of their NPDES permitting systems, municipalities to establish extensive and expensive programs to reduce stormwater pollution from businesses and households within their jurisdictions, to conduct extensive educational outreach, to sample and monitor water bodies into which storm systems drain and to clean their storm drain collection systems. For an overview of the stormwater permitting system in California, *see* John H. Minan, *Municipal Storm Water Permitting in California*, 40 SAN DIEGO L. REV. 245 (2003); Sean Hecht, *Stormwater Regulation, in* 2004 S. CAL. ENVTL. REPORT Card 31 (2004).

2. In 2015, EPA issued an updated general industrial permit for industrial permittees operating in states that do not administer their own stormwater programs. *See* EPA NPDES Stormwater Multi-Sector General Permit for Industrial Activities, available at https://www.epa.gov/npdes/storm water-discharges-industrial-activities. By regulation, EPA in its Industrial Stormwater Rule, requires that ten categories of stormwater discharges "associated with industrial activity" be permitted under the NPDES system (construction activities have a separate permit). Categories include heavy manufacturing, coal and mineral mining, hazardous waste treatment and so forth. *See*, U.S. Environmental Protection Agency, *NPDES, Stormwater Discharges from Industrial Activities, https://www.epa.gov/npdes/storm water-discharges-industrial-activities*. EPA has specifically included a special regulation for silvicultural activity (logging), 40 CFR 122.27 and has interpreted that regulation to exempt from permitting runoff from logging roads. In *Decker v. Northwest Environmental Defense Center*, environmental

groups sued a logging company for violating the CWA by channeling stormwater through drains and into adjacent rivers and streams. The Supreme Court deferred to EPA's interpretation of the Industrial Stormwater Rule as exempting runoff from logging roads from the NPDES permitting system and found no CWA violation. Decker v. Northwest Environmental Defense Center,133 S.Ct. 1326 (2013). See also W. Whitlock, A. Cavender, T. Zakim and A. Forsten, *Supreme Court Reverses 9th Circuit on Logging Roads, Deferring to EPA on Its Industrial Stormwater Rule,* Pillsbury Client Alert (April 5, 2013) http://www.pillsburylaw.com/siteFiles/Publications/Alert20130405ELUNR TheSupremeCourtReversestheNinth.pdf

3.   In addition to the silvicultural exemption for logging roads, the largest remaining loophole in nonpoint source and stormwater pollution is for pollution from agricultural operations. As described above, return flows from irrigated agriculture are exempt from the definition of point sources and "agricultural stormwater discharges" are also exempt. 33 U.S.C. § 1362(14). Agricultural runoff is the single largest source of water pollution of streams, rivers and lakes. Why do you think Congress exempted agricultural runoff in the first place and why does the exemption remain in place?

c.   Litigation over the Setting of Technology-Based Effluent Limits

The 1972 amendments to the FWPCA were not unequivocal about exactly how the permitting system and technology-based effluent limitations were to be implemented. Would the standards be set nationwide for each industrial category of source, or would the standards be set on a plant-by-plant basis by the issuer of each permit? Certain chemical companies challenged the EPA's authority to issue regulations for classes of existing point sources under § 301 of the FWPCA. They argued that § 301 only provides guidance for any agency (state or federal) *issuing permits* on a plant-by-plant basis under § 402 (NPDES), so the EPA Administrator had overstepped statutory authority in setting effluent limits for entire categories of point source polluters. Moreover, these companies argued that the new source regulations under § 306, which required BDAT standards for seemingly all new plants without exception, must be read as allowing for some variances for individual plants. In the case below, the Supreme Court sided with the Administrator on both challenges and held that the Administrator, not the permit issuing authorities, must set the technology-based limits for classes of facilities under § 301, and that § 306 applies to all new sources without exception and without variances for individual facilities.

E. I. DU PONT DE NEMOURS & CO. V. TRAIN

Supreme Court of the United States, 1977.
430 U.S. 112, 97 S.Ct. 965, 51 L.Ed.2d 204.

MR. JUSTICE STEVENS delivered the opinion of the Court.

Inorganic chemical manufacturing plants operated by the eight petitioners in Nos. 75–978 and 75–1473 discharge various pollutants into the Nation's waters and therefore are "point sources" within the meaning of the Federal Water Pollution Control Act (Act), as added and amended by § 2 of the Federal Water Pollution Control Act Amendments of 1972. The Environmental Protection Agency has promulgated industry wide regulations imposing three sets of precise limitations on petitioners' discharges. The first two impose progressively higher levels of pollution control on existing point sources after July 1, 1977 and after July 1, 1983, respectively. The third set imposes limits on "new sources" that may be constructed in the future.

These cases present [the following questions of statutory construction]: whether the EPA has the authority under § 301 of the Act to issue industry wide regulations limiting discharges by existing plants; * * * [and] whether the new-source standards issued under § 306 must allow variances for individual plants. * * *

The Statute

* * *

The first steps required by the Act are described in § 304, which directs the Administrator to develop and publish various kinds of technical data to provide guidance in carrying out responsibilities imposed by other sections of the Act. Thus, within 60 days, 120 days, and 180 days after the date of enactment, the Administrator was to promulgate a series of guidelines to assist the States in developing and carrying out permit programs pursuant to § 402. §§ 304(h), (f), (g). Within 270 days, he was to develop the information to be used in formulating standards for new plants pursuant to § 306. § 304(c). And within one year he was to publish regulations providing guidance for effluent limitations on existing point sources. Section 304(b) goes into great detail concerning the contents of these regulations. They must identify the degree of effluent reduction attainable through use of the best practicable or best available technology for a class of plants. The guidelines must also "specify factors to be taken into account" in determining the control measures applicable to point sources within these classes. A list of factors to be considered then follows. The Administrator was also directed to develop and publish, within one year, elaborate criteria for water quality accurately reflecting the most current scientific knowledge, and also technical information on factors necessary to restore and maintain water quality. § 304(a). The title of § 304 describes it as the "information and guidelines" portion of the statute.

Section 301 is captioned "effluent limitations." Section 301(a) makes the discharge of any pollutant unlawful unless the discharge is in compliance with certain enumerated sections of the Act. The enumerated sections which are relevant to this case are § 301 itself, § 306, and § 402. A brief word about each of these sections is necessary.

Section 402 authorizes the Administrator to issue permits for individual point sources, and also authorizes him to review and approve the plan of any State desiring to administer its own permit program. These permits serve "to transform generally applicable effluent limitations . . . into the obligations (including a timetable for compliance) of the individual discharger[s]. . . . " EPA v. California ex rel. State Water Resources Control Board, 426 U.S. 200, 205. Petitioner chemical companies' position in this litigation is that § 402 provides the only statutory authority for the issuance of enforceable limitations on the discharge of pollutants by existing plants. It is noteworthy, however, that although this section authorizes the imposition of limitations in individual permits, the section itself does not mandate either the Administrator or the States to use permits as the method of prescribing effluent limitations.

Section 306 directs the Administrator to publish within 90 days a list of categories of sources discharging pollutants and, within one year thereafter, to publish regulations establishing national standards of performance for new sources within each category. Section 306 contains no provision for exceptions from the standards for individual plants; on the contrary, subsection (e) expressly makes it unlawful to operate a new source in violation of the applicable standard of performance after its effective date. The statute provides that the new-source standards shall reflect the greatest degree of effluent reduction achievable through application of the best available demonstrated control technology.

Section 301(b) defines the effluent limitations that shall be achieved by existing point sources in two stages. By July 1, 1977, the effluent limitations shall require the application of the best practicable control technology currently available; by July 1, 1983, the limitations shall require application of the best available technology economically achievable. The statute expressly provides that the limitations which are to become effective in 1983 are applicable to "categories and classes of point sources"; this phrase is omitted from the description of the 1977 limitations. While § 301 states that these limitations "shall be achieved," it fails to state who will establish the limitations.

Section 301(c) authorizes the Administrator to grant variances from the 1983 limitations. Section 301(e) states that effluent limitations established pursuant to § 301 shall be applied to all point sources.

To summarize, § 301(b) requires the achievement of effluent limitations requiring use of the "best practicable" or "best available" technology. It refers to § 304 for a definition of these terms. Section 304 requires the publication of "regulations, providing guidelines for effluent limitations." Finally, permits issued under § 402 must require compliance with § 301 effluent limitations. Nowhere are we told who sets the § 301 effluent limitations, or precisely how they relate to § 304 guidelines and § 402 permits.

The Regulations

The various deadlines imposed on the Administrator were too ambitious for him to meet. For that reason, the procedure which he followed in adopting the regulations applicable to the inorganic chemical industry and to other classes of point sources is somewhat different from that apparently contemplated by the statute. Specifically, as will appear, he did not adopt guidelines pursuant to § 304 before defining the effluent limitations for existing sources described in § 301(b) or the national standards for new sources described in § 306. This case illustrates the approach the Administrator followed in implementing the Act.

EPA began by engaging a private contractor to prepare a Development Document. This document provided a detailed technical study of pollution control in the industry. The study first divided the industry into categories. For each category, present levels of pollution were measured and plants with exemplary pollution control were investigated. Based on this information, other technical data, and economic studies, a determination was made of the degree of pollution control which could be achieved by the various levels of technology mandated by the statute. The study was made available to the public and circulated to interested persons. It formed the basis of "effluent limitation guideline" regulations issued by EPA after receiving public comment on proposed regulations. These regulations divide the industry into 22 subcategories. Within each subcategory, precise numerical limits are set for various pollutants. The regulations for each subcategory contain a variance clause, applicable only to the 1977 limitations.

Eight chemical companies filed petitions in the United States Court of Appeals for the Fourth Circuit for review of these regulations. The Court of Appeals rejected their challenge to EPA's authority to issue precise, single-number limitations for discharges of pollutants from existing sources. It held, however, that these limitations and the new plant standards were only "presumptively applicable" to individual plants. We granted the chemical companies' petitions for certiorari in order to consider the scope of EPA's authority to issue existing-source regulations. We also granted the Government's cross-petition for review of the ruling that new-source standards are only presumptively applicable. For convenience, we will refer to the chemical companies as the "petitioners."

The Issues

The broad outlines of the parties' respective theories may be stated briefly. EPA contends that § 301 (b) authorizes it to issue regulations establishing effluent limitations for classes of plants. The permits granted under § 402, in EPA's view, simply incorporate these across-the-board limitations, except for the limited variances allowed by the regulations themselves and by § 301(c). The § 304(b) guidelines, according to EPA, were intended to guide it in later establishing § 301 effluent-limitation regulations. Because the process proved more time consuming than Congress assumed when it established this two-stage process, EPA condensed the two stages into a single regulation.

In contrast, petitioners contend that § 301 is not an independent source of authority for setting effluent limitations by regulation. Instead, § 301 is seen as merely a description of the effluent limitations which are set for each plant on an individual basis during the permit-issuance process. Under the industry view, the § 304 guidelines serve the function of guiding the permit issuer in setting the effluent limitations. * * *

We think § 301 itself is the key to the problem. The statutory language concerning the 1983 limitations, in particular, leaves no doubt that these limitations are to be set by regulation. Subsection (b)(2)(A) of § 301 states that by 1983 "effluent limitations for categories and classes of point sources" are to be achieved which will require "application of the best available technology economically achievable for such category or class." These effluent limitations are to require elimination of all discharges if "such elimination is technologically and economically achievable for a category or class of point sources." This is "language difficult to reconcile with the view that individual effluent limitations are to be set when each permit is issued." American Meat Institute v. EPA, 526 F.2d 442, 450 (1975). The statute thus focuses expressly on the characteristics of the "category or class" rather than the characteristics of individual point sources. Normally, such class wide determinations would be made by regulation, not in the course of issuing a permit to one member of the class.

The question of the form of § 301 limitations is tied to the question whether the Act requires the Administrator or the permit issuer to establish the limitations. Section 301 does not itself answer this question, for it speaks only in the passive voice of the achievement and establishment of the limitations. But other parts of the statute leave little doubt on this score. Section 304(b) states that "[f]or the purpose of adopting or revising effluent limitations ... the Administrator shall" issue guideline regulations; while the judicial-review section, § 509(b)(1), speaks of "the Administrator's action ... in approving or promulgating any effluent limitation or other limitation under section 301. . . ." And § 101 (d) requires us to resolve any ambiguity on this score in favor of the Administrator. It provides that "[e]xcept as otherwise expressly provided in this Act, the Administrator of the Environmental Protection Agency ... shall administer this Act." In sum, the language of the statute supports the view that § 301 limitations are to be adopted by the Administrator, that they are to be based primarily on classes and categories, and that they are to take the form of regulations. * * *

The remaining issue in this case concerns new plants. Under § 306, EPA is to promulgate "regulations establishing Federal standards of performance for new sources. . . ." § 306(b)(1)(B). A "standard of performance" is a "standard for the control of the discharge of pollutants which reflects the greatest degree of effluent reduction which the Administrator determines to be achievable through application of the best available demonstrated control technology, ... including, where practicable, a standard permitting no discharge of pollutants." § 306(a)(1). In setting the standard, "[t]he Administrator may distinguish among classes, types, and sizes within categories of new sources ... and shall consider the type of process employed (including whether batch or continuous)." § 306(b)(2). * * *

* * * It is clear that Congress intended these regulations to be absolute prohibitions. The use of the word "standards" implies as much. So does the description of the preferred standard as one "permitting no discharge of pollutants." (emphasis added.) It is "unlawful for any owner or operator of any new source to operate such source in violation of any standard of performance applicable to such source." § 306(e) (emphasis added). In striking contrast to § 301(c), there is no statutory provision for variances, and a variance provision would be inappropriate in a standard that was intended to insure national uniformity and "maximum feasible control of new sources." S. Rep. No. 92–414, page 58 (1971), Leg. Hist. 1476.

That portion of the judgment of the Court of Appeals * * * requiring EPA to provide a variance procedure for new sources is reversed. In all other aspects, the judgment of the Court of Appeals are affirmed.

It is so ordered.

NOTES

1. Practically speaking, what would have happened if the Court had agreed with petitioners that the EPA could not set effluent standards by industrial category? Aren't standards tailored to specific facilities always better than standards set by industrial category? Can you imagine why, despite their posture in this case, industry groups might in another circumstance argue against the individualized plant-by-plant approach to setting standards?

2. As illustrated above in Figure 2, *supra,* page 592, the EPA was charged with setting technology-based effluent limits at various levels of

stringency to eventually meet the ambitious goal of zero discharge from point sources into the nation's navigable waterways. The EPA had to set and justify each limit for each category of plant or facility it devised, and these limits were vigorously challenged by regulated industries—which argued that the EPA was imposing costs far out of proportion with the intended benefits—*and* by environmentalists, who argued the standards were too lenient to satisfy the statutory mandates. The agency found itself, in this instance, between a rock and a hard place, able to please no one. The Court turned out to be the agency's ally in this case, but this does not always occur. Imagine what it must be like to get up every day and face the overwhelming administrative obstacles that confront agency officials: an unimplementable statute, inadequate funding, an impatient Congress, a meddlesome President, interfering courts, angry interest groups, etc. Does this make you sympathetic to government agencies?

The next case addresses an important question under the CWA. Under what circumstances does cost play a role in setting regulations and how should EPA consider costs v. benefits?

ENTERGY CORP. v. RIVERKEEPER, INC., ET AL.

Supreme Court of the United States, 2009.
129 S.Ct. 1498, 173 L.Ed.2d 369.

SCALIA, J., delivered the opinion of the Court.

JUSTICE SCALIA delivered the opinion of the Court.

These cases concern a set of regulations adopted by the Environmental Protection Agency (EPA or agency) under § 316(b) of the Clean Water Act, 33 U. S. C. § 1326(b). 69 Fed. Reg. 41576 (2004). Respondents—environmental groups and various States—challenged those regulations, and the Second Circuit set them aside. The issue for our decision is whether, as the Second Circuit held, the EPA is not permitted to use cost-benefit analysis in determining the content of regulations promulgated under § 1326(b).

I

Petitioners operate—or represent those who operate—large powerplants. In the course of generating power, those plants also generate large amounts of heat. To cool their facilities, petitioners employ "cooling water intake structures" that extract water from nearby water sources. These structures pose various threats to the environment, chief among them the squashing against intake screens (elegantly called "impingement") or suction into the cooling system ("entrainment") of aquatic organisms that live in the affected water sources. Accordingly, the facilities are subject to regulation under the Clean Water Act, 33 U. S. C. § 1251 *et seq.*, which mandates:

"Any standard established pursuant to section 1311 of this title or section 1316 of this title and applicable to a point source shall require that the location, design, construction, and capacity of cooling water intake structures reflect the best technology available for minimizing adverse environmental impact." § 1326(b).

Sections 1311 and 1316, in turn, employ a variety of "best technology" standards to regulate the discharge of effluents into the Nation's waters.

The § 1326(b) regulations at issue here were promulgated by the EPA after nearly three decades in which the determination of the "best technology available for minimizing [cooling water intake structures'] adverse environmental impact" was made by permit-issuing authorities on a case-by-case basis, without benefit of a governing regulation.

In 1995, the EPA entered into a consent decree which, as subsequently amended, set a multiphase timetable for the EPA to promulgate regulations under § 1326(b). In the first phase the EPA adopted regulations governing certain new, large cooling water intake structures. These regulations were upheld in large part by the Second Circuit in *Riverkeeper, Inc.* v. *EPA*, 358 F. 3d 174 (2004).

The EPA then adopted the so-called "Phase II" rules at issue here. They apply to existing facilities that are point sources, whose primary activity is the generation and transmission (or sale for transmission) of electricity, and whose water-intake flow is more than 50 million gallons of water per day, at least 25 percent of which is used for cooling purposes. Over 500 facilities, accounting for approximately 53 percent of the Nation's electric-power generating capacity, fall within Phase II's ambit.

To address those environmental impacts, the EPA set "national performance standards," requiring Phase II facilities (with some exceptions) to reduce "impingement mortality for all life stages of fish and shellfish by 80 to 95 percent from the calculation baseline"; a subset of facilities must also reduce entrainment of such aquatic organisms by "60 to 90 percent from the calculation baseline." Those targets are based on the environmental improvements achievable through deployment of a mix of remedial technologies, which the EPA determined were "commercially available and economically practicable."

In its Phase II rules, however, the EPA expressly declined to mandate adoption of closed-cycle cooling systems or equivalent reductions in impingement and entrainment, as it had done for new facilities subject to the Phase I rules. It refused to take that step in part because of the "generally high costs" of converting existing facilities to closed-cycle operation, and because "other technologies approach the performance of this option. Thus, while closed-cycle cooling systems could reduce impingement and entrainment mortality by up to 98 percent, (compared to the Phase II targets of 80 to 95 percent impingement reduction), the cost of rendering all Phase II facilities closed-cycle-compliant would be approximately $3.5 billion per year, nine times the estimated cost of compliance with the Phase II performance standards. Moreover, Phase II facilities compelled to convert to closed-cycle cooling systems "would produce 2.4 percent to 4.0 percent less electricity even while burning the same amount of coal," possibly requiring the construction of "20 additional 400-MW plants . . . to replace the generating capacity lost." *Id.,* at 41605. The EPA thus concluded that "[a]lthough not identical, the ranges of impingement and entrainment reduction are similar under both options. . . . [Benefits of compliance with the Phase II rules] can approach those of closed-cycle re-circulating at less cost with fewer implementation problems."

II

In setting the Phase II national performance standards and providing for site-specific cost-benefit variances, the EPA relied on its view that § 1326(b)'s "best technology available" standard permits consideration of the technology's costs, and of the relationship between those costs and the environmental benefits produced. That view governs if it is a reasonable interpretation of the statute—not necessarily the only possible interpretation, nor even the interpretation deemed *most* reasonable by the courts.

As we have described, § 1326(b) instructs the EPA to set standards for cooling water intake structures that reflect "the best technology available for minimizing adverse environmental impact." The Second Circuit took that language to mean the technology that achieves the greatest reduction in adverse environmental impacts at a cost that can reasonably be borne by the industry. That is certainly a plausible interpretation of the statute. The "best" technology—that which is "most advantageous," Webster's New International Dictionary 258 (2d ed. 1953)—may well be the one that produces the most of some good, here a reduction in adverse environmental impact. But "best technology" may also describe the technology that *most efficiently* produces some good. In common parlance one could certainly use the phrase "best technology" to refer to that which produces a good at the lowest per-unit cost, even if it produces a lesser quantity of that good than other available technologies.

Respondents contend that this latter reading is precluded by the statute's use of the phrase "for minimizing adverse environmental impact." Minimizing, they argue, means reducing to the smallest amount possible, and the "best technology available for minimizing adverse environmental impacts," must be the economically feasible technology that achieves the greatest possible reduction in environmental harm. But "minimize" is a term that admits of degree and is not necessarily used to refer exclusively to the "greatest possible reduction." For example, elsewhere in the Clean Water Act, Congress declared that the procedures implementing the Act "shall encourage the drastic minimization of paperwork and interagency decision procedures." 33 U. S. C. § 1251(f). If respondents' definition of the term "minimize" is correct, the statute's use of the modifier "drastic" is superfluous.

Other provisions in the Clean Water Act also suggest the agency's interpretation. When Congress wished to mandate the greatest feasible reduction in water pollution, it did so in plain language: The provision governing the discharge of toxic pollutants into the Nation's waters requires the EPA to set "effluent limitations [which] shall require the *elimination* of discharges of all pollutants if the Administrator finds . . . that such elimination is technologically and economically achievable," § 1311(b)(2)(A) (emphasis added). See also § 1316(a)(1) (mandating "where practicable, a standard [for new point sources] permitting *no discharge* of pollutants" (emphasis added)). Section 1326(b)'s use of the less ambitious goal of "minimizing adverse environmental impact" suggests, we think, that the agency retains some discretion to determine the extent of reduction that is warranted under the circumstances. That determination could plausibly involve a consideration of the benefits derived from reductions and the costs of achieving them. It seems to us, therefore, that the phrase "best technology available," even with the added specification "for minimizing adverse environmental impact," does not unambiguously preclude cost-benefit analysis.

Respondents' alternative (and, alas, also more complex) argument rests upon the structure of the Clean Water Act. The Act provided that during its initial implementation period existing "point sources"—discrete conveyances from which pollutants are or may be discharged, 33 U. S. C. § 1362(14)—were subject to "effluent limitations . . . which shall require the application of the *best practicable control technology* currently available." § 1311(b)(1)(A) (emphasis added). (We shall call this the "BPT" test.) Following that transition period, the Act initially mandated adoption, by July 1, 1983 (later extended to March 31, 1989), of stricter effluent limitations requiring "application of the *best available technology economically achievable* for such category or class, which will result in reasonable further progress toward the national goal of eliminating the discharge of all pollutants." § 1311(b)(2)(A) ([T]he "BATEA" test.) Subsequent amendment limited application of this standard to toxic and nonconventional pollutants, and for the remainder established a (presumably laxer) test of "best conventional-pollutant control technology." § 1311(b)(2)(E). (We shall call this "BCT.") Finally, § 1316 subjected certain categories of new point sources to "the greatest degree of effluent reduction which the Administrator determines to be achievable through application of the *best available demonstrated control technology.*" § 1316(a)(1);

§ 1316(b)(1)(B). (We shall call this the "BADT" test.) The provision at issue here, applicable not to effluents but to cooling water intake structures, requires, as we have described, "the *best technology available for minimizing adverse environmental impact*," § 1326(b) (emphasis added). (We shall call this the "BTA" test.)

The first four of these tests are elucidated by statutory factor lists that guide their implementation. To take the standards in (presumed) order of increasing stringency: In applying the BPT test the EPA is instructed to consider, among other factors, "the total cost of application of technology in relation to the effluent reduction benefits to be achieved." § 1314(b)(1)(B). In applying the BCT test it is instructed to consider "the *reasonableness of the relationship* between the costs of attaining a reduction in effluents and the effluent reduction benefits derived." § 1314(b)(4)(B). And in applying the BATEA and BADT tests the EPA is instructed to consider the "cost of achieving such effluent reduction." §§ 1314(b)(2)(B), 1316(b)(1)(B). There is no such elucidating language applicable to the BTA test at issue here.

The Second Circuit, in rejecting the EPA's use of cost-benefit analysis, relied in part on the propositions that (1) cost-benefit analysis is precluded under the BATEA and BADT tests; and (2) that, insofar as the permissibility of cost-benefit analysis is concerned, the BTA test (the one at issue here) is to be treated the same as those two. It is not obvious to us that the first of these propositions is correct, but we need not pursue that point, since we assuredly do not agree with the second. It is certainly reasonable for the agency to conclude that the BTA test need not be interpreted to permit only what those other two tests permit. Its text is not identical to theirs. It has the relatively modest goal of "minimizing adverse environmental impact" as compared with the BATEA's goal of "eliminating the discharge of all pollutants." And it is unencumbered by specified statutory factors of the sort provided for those other two tests, which omission can reasonably be interpreted to suggest that the EPA is accorded greater discretion in determining its precise content.

This extended consideration of the text of § 1326(b), and comparison of that with the text and statutory factors applicable to four parallel provisions of the Clean Water Act, lead us to the conclusion that it was well within the bounds of reasonable interpretation for the EPA to conclude that cost-benefit analysis is not categorically forbidden. Other arguments may be available to preclude such a rigorous form of cost-benefit analysis as that which was prescribed under the statute's former BPT standard, which required weighing "the total cost of application of technology" against "the . . . benefits to be achieved." But that question is not before us.

In the Phase II requirements challenged here the EPA sought only to avoid extreme disparities between costs and benefits. The agency limited variances from the Phase II "national performance standards" to circumstances where the costs are "significantly greater than the benefits" of compliance. In defining the "national performance standards" themselves the EPA assumed the application of technologies whose benefits "approach those estimated" for closed-cycle cooling systems at a fraction of the cost: $389 million per year, as compared with (1) at least $3.5 billion per year to operate compliant closed-cycle cooling systems, (or $1 billion per year to impose similar requirements on a subset of Phase II facilities, (2) significant reduction in the energy output of the altered facilities. And finally, EPA's assessment of the relatively meager financial benefits of the Phase II regulations that it adopted—reduced impingement and entrainment of 1.4 billion aquatic organisms with annualized use benefits of $83 million, and non-use benefits of indeterminate value,— when compared to annual costs of $389 million, demonstrates quite clearly that the agency did not select the Phase II regulatory requirements because their benefits equaled their costs.

In the last analysis, even respondents ultimately recognize that some form of cost-benefit analysis is permissible. They acknowledge that the statute's language is "plainly not so constricted as to require EPA to require industry petitioners to spend billions to save one more fish or plankton." This concedes the principle—the permissibility of at least some cost-benefit analysis—and we see no statutory basis for limiting its use to situations where the benefits are *de minimis* rather than significantly disproportionate.

* * *

We conclude that the EPA permissibly relied on cost-benefit analysis in setting the national performance standards and in providing for cost-benefit variances from those standards as part of the Phase II regulations. The judgment of the Court of Appeals is reversed, and the cases are remanded for further proceedings consistent with this opinion.

JUSTICE STEVENS, with whom JUSTICE SOUTER and JUSTICE GINSBURG join, dissenting.

Section 316(b) of the Clean Water Act (CWA), 33 U. S. C. § 1326(b), which governs industrial powerplant water intake structures, provides that the Environmental Protection Agency (EPA or Agency) "shall require" that such structures "reflect the best technology available for minimizing adverse environmental impact." The EPA has interpreted that mandate to authorize the use of cost-benefit analysis in promulgating regulations under § 316(b). For instance, under the Agency's interpretation, technology that would otherwise qualify as the best available need not be used if its costs are "significantly greater than the benefits" of compliance. 40 CFR § 125.94(a)(5)(ii)(2008).

Like the Court of Appeals, I am convinced that the EPA has misinterpreted the plain text of § 316(b). Unless costs are so high that the best technology is not "available," Congress has decided that they are outweighed by the benefits of minimizing adverse environmental impact. Section 316(b) neither expressly nor implicitly authorizes the EPA to use cost-benefit analysis when setting regulatory standards; fairly read, it prohibits such use.

I

As typically performed by the EPA, cost-benefit analysis requires the Agency to first monetize the costs and benefits of a regulation, balance the results, and then choose the regulation with the greatest net benefits. The process is particularly controversial in the environmental context in which a regulation's financial costs are often more obvious and easier to quantify than its environmental benefits. And cost-benefit analysis often, if not always, yields a result that does not maximize environmental protection.

For instance, although the EPA estimated that water intake structures kill 3.4 billion fish and shellfish each year, the Agency struggled to calculate the value of the aquatic life that would be protected under its § 316(b) regulations, *id.* To compensate, the EPA took a shortcut: Instead of monetizing all aquatic life, the Agency counted only those species that are commercially or recreationally harvested, a tiny slice (1.8 percent to be precise) of all impacted fish and shellfish. This narrow focus in turn skewed the Agency's calculation of benefits. When the EPA attempted to value all aquatic life, the benefits measured $735 million. But when the EPA decided to give zero value to the 98.2 percent of fish not commercially or recreationally harvested, the benefits calculation dropped dramatically— to $83million. *Id.,* at 41666. The Agency acknowledged that its failure to monetize the other 98.2 percent of affected species " 'could result in serious misallocation of resources,' " because its "comparison of complete costs and incomplete benefits does not provide an accurate picture of net benefits to society."

Because benefits can be more accurately monetized in some industries than in others, Congress typically decides whether it is appropriate for an agency to use cost-benefit analysis in crafting regulations. Indeed, this Court has recognized that "[w]hen Congress has intended that an agency engage in cost-benefit analysis, it has clearly indicated such intent on the face of the statute." Accordingly, we should not treat a provision's silence as an implicit source of cost-benefit authority, particularly when such authority is elsewhere expressly granted and it has the potential to fundamentally alter an agency's approach to regulation. Congress, we have noted, "does not alter the fundamental details of a regulatory scheme in vague terms or ancillary provisions—it does not, one might say, hide elephants in mouse holes." [citations omitted].

NOTES

1.   Has Justice Scalia, in ruling that the EPA may use cost-benefit analysis, abandoned his commitment to a "texualist" approach to statutory interpretation, under which agencies (and the Court) are to follow literally what a statute says even if the results may be extreme?

2.   Are there, paradoxically, positive implications for greenhouse gas emissions reductions in the Court's ruling?

3.   Under the Court's ruling, can the EPA on remand adopt new regulations that are more environmentally protective than those challenged in the *Entergy* case?

d.   Toxics

In 1972, Congress required the EPA to list toxics (which were broadly defined) and to set health-based standards for their discharge, without regard to cost or technological feasibility. § 307. What followed was primarily delay. The EPA was already reeling under the administrative burdens of both its CWA and CAA obligations, and health-based standard setting proved especially difficult. As Professor Olivor Houck puts it,

> EPA simply found itself with more power than it knew how to exercise. The science of toxicity was too rudimentary to allow it to set levels for all but the best documented and most celebrated toxins, e.g., PCBs, DDT, and endrin, for which the levels approached zero. Further, the looming, omnipresent factors of economic and technological feasibility could be neither included nor ignored. The statute appeared to preclude them and, as a practical matter, if they were included, derivation of the resulting standard would be difficult to distinguish from standards set as best practicable technology and best available technology. On the other hand, the prospects of requiring a technology that did not exist, or forcing an entire industry—pesticide manufacture, steel manufacture—to close, was unthinkable. EPA was paralyzed.

Oliver A. Houck, *The Regulation of Toxic Substances Under the Clean Water Act*, 21 ENVTL. L. REP. 10528 (1991).

The NRDC filed suit challenging the EPA's failure to establish effluent standards for toxics as required by the statute. *See* NRDC v. Costle, 561 F.2d 904 (D.C. Cir. 1977) *modified sub nom.* NRDC v. Costle. The suit eventually settled, with the NRDC, the EPA and a variety of industrial intervenors entering a consent decree known as the "Flannery Decree" (so-named for the presiding judge). The Consent Decree established a schedule for EPA promulgation of effluent limits for 65 pollutants (known as "priority pollutants") and 21 industry categories. The Flannery Decree was incorporated into the 1977 Amendments to the Act in § 307(a)(1) with the list of priority pollutants growing to 126 and the number of industry categories expanded to 34. Thus was the initial health-based approach to toxics supplanted by a technology-based approach.

However, the new technology-based approach proved challenging as well. Houck explains:

> The development of technology standards was the most Herculean task ever imposed on an environmental agency. EPA had literally to master the economics, engineering, and technology of every industrial process in the most industrialized and fastest-growing economy in world history. It had to learn state-of-the-art and potential alternative technologies for each process. It had to be able to defend its technology-forcing conclusions against the most experienced engineers, economists and lawyers money could buy. Every draft standard EPA proposed was subject to intense scrutiny, lobbying, and opposition from the affected industry and, within the limits of its resources, at least one organization. Nearly every final standard was immediately taken to court. * * *

> By early 1983, most of EPA's proposals for regulation of the priority pollutants of the consent decree industries had been developed in at least draft form. The transaction costs of the process, however, were already noticeable . . . for several of the high-volume toxic discharges, the Agency was extending compliance deadlines to 1988 but was also retreating from stringent BAT proposals in its earlier draft proposals and adopting, instead, more relaxed requirements equal to or no better than BPT. * * *

> By the latter half of the 1980s, EPA's technology standards program was limited to grinding out guidelines for the remaining consent decree categories. No additional categories had been proposed. No additions to the list of regulated "priority pollutants" were proposed. No revisions were proposed to upgrade standards from those set, in some case, 10 years before.

Houck, *id.*

Congress amended the Act to add a provision requiring the agency a) to develop a plan for scheduling annual review and revision of existing guidelines, b) to identify unregulated industrial source categories, and c) and to issue standards by 1991 (later extended to 1994). However, well into the 1990s, many industrial facilities discharging toxic pollutants remained outside the federal BAT standards and most of the existing BAT standards were fast becoming obsolete. Even today, the standards for a number of industries have not been updated since the 1970s and existing users remain subject to BPT, rather than BAT standards. For a list of effluent guidelines by industry, including the date of adoption, *see* U.S. EPA,

Effluent Guidelines: Industrial Effluent Guidelines, Existing Regulations, https://www.epa.gov/eg/industrial-effluent-guidelines.

e.   New Source Performance Standards

CHEMICAL MANUFACTURERS ASSOCIATION V. EPA
United States Court of Appeals, Fifth Circuit, 1989.
870 F.2d 177, *cert. denied,* 495 U.S. 910, 110 S.Ct. 1936, 109 L.Ed.2d 299 (1990).

Acting under the mandate of the Clean Water Act (CWA), the Environmental Protection Agency (EPA), has promulgated final regulations limiting the discharge of pollutants into the nation's navigable waters by manufacturing plants in the organic chemicals, plastics, and synthetic fibers (OCPSF) industries. The regulations, which the statute requires to be implemented beginning March 31, 1989, cover both direct discharge and indirect discharge through publicly-owned treatment works (POTWs). The Chemical Manufacturers Association (CMA) and a number of companies affected by the regulations allege both procedural defects in their promulgation and substantive defects in various provisions, as well as defects in the application of specific provisions to particular plants. Intervening in some of the cases consolidated for review and appearing as amicus curiae in the others, the Natural Resources Defense Council (NRDC) also challenges the regulations, but on the different ground that they fail to require a sufficiently high degree of effluent pollution control. Although it contends that the regulations are invalid, the NRDC urges that they be enforced until more stringent standards can be adopted.

The case is of such complexity that the parties have submitted briefs totaling more than 3,000 pages and a joint appendix 9,000 pages long distilled from a 600,000-page administrative record. To enable us to render a decision as promptly as possible, the members of the panel have divided responsibility for preparing portions of this opinion, as the District of Columbia Circuit did in *Alabama Power Co. v. Costle.* Judge Garza prepared sections V, VI, and VII of this opinion, as well as all portions discussing issues raised by the NRDC; Judge Rubin prepared sections I and III; and Judge King prepared sections II and IV, except for those portions discussing issues raised by the NRDC.

[The excerpt below addresses the EPA's methodology for establishing NSPS, and the NRDC's challenge to the EPA's decision to promulgate, for certain chemical manufacturing source categories, NSPS that were identical to the existing source standards.]

RUBIN, GARZA and KING, CIRCUIT JUDGES Jointly.

* * *

V. New Source Performance Standards (NSPS) Issues

We now turn to the challenge presented by the NRDC that the EPA violated the Clean Water Act by basing New Source Performance Standards (NSPS) and Pretreatment Standards for New Sources (PSNS) upon BPT for conventional pollutants and upon BAT model technology for toxic discharges.

NRDC argues that effluent limitations for newly constructed dischargers represent the highest level of technology-based treatment under the Clean Water Act. In promulgating the New Source Performance Standards, according to NRDC, Congress intended that new facilities would be required to take advantage of the most current process and treatment innovations, irrespective of whether the cost of the new technologies is justified by any incremental degree of removal achieved by its application. The reason for dropping the cost-benefit analysis from the NSPS, according to NRDC, was the recognition by Congress that new facilities are not limited by cost and engineering constraints inherent in retrofitting existing plants. Congress also recognized that new sources are uniquely situated to push toward the outer envelope of pollution control technology in a way that will further progress toward the national goal of eliminating the discharge of all pollutants.

Instead of establishing effluent guidelines that would tend to achieve these legislative purposes, however, the EPA final rules set out standards for new sources identical to those for existing plants. This, the NRDC urges, violates section 306 of the Clean Water Act. * * *

1. The EPA's Cost Test in Establishing NSPS

First, NRDC asserts that the EPA used the same cost test for new and existing sources when Congress intended the Agency to use a "stricter cost test" for evaluating the efficacy of treatment technologies for new sources. According to NRDC, the EPA improperly compared "the costs of incremental pollution control technology against water quality benefits," thereby rejecting at least one new treatment technology on the basis of a cost-benefit analysis.

The EPA responds that the Act requires the Agency to "take into consideration the cost of achieving [NSPS] reduction, and any non-water quality environmental impact and energy requirements." This test, the EPA urges, is identical to the cost requirement for establishing BAT. The use of BPT and BAT costing methods to determine the cost of entirely new treatment systems for new sources was, according to EPA, entirely reasonable. The Agency denies that it compared these costs to the benefits accrued from compliance with NSPS.

We are not convinced that the EPA's costing methods for promulgating NSPS violated the Act. With respect to toxic pollutants, we agree that the statutory test for evaluating the costs of NSPS treatment is identical to that required for establishing BAT standards. In both cases, the Administrator must inquire into the initial and annual costs of applying the technology and make an affirmative determination that those costs can be reasonably borne by the industry. Congress may have contemplated that it would cost less to install new technologies in new plants than to retrofit old plants to accommodate new treatment systems. However, the determination whether that contemplation held true, in fact, with respect to any particular technology, was left by statute to the discretion of the Administrator.

For plants that discharge conventional pollutants, the EPA points out that new sources must install secondary clarifiers, biological treatment limits, equalization and other treatment technologies. BPT costing methods, according to the EPA, provide a framework for estimating the capital and operating costs of such systems. Given the legislative grant of discretion vested in the Administrator to determine the economic feasibility of costs under NSPS, we cannot say, on the basis of this record, that the methods used constitute a violation of the Act.

2.   NRDC's Challenge that the EPA Failed to Consider Technology Beyond BPT and BAT

The second reason presented to support NRDC's argument that the NSPS regulations violate the Clean Water Act is the assertion that the EPA failed to give serious consideration to better control technologies that could be used by new sources. Specifically, NRDC points to indications in the record that 26% of OCPSF plants are "zero or alternative discharge" plants and that 36 plants achieve zero discharge through recycling, a technology the EPA allegedly did not consider in its rulemaking.

The EPA argues that new technologies must be "demonstrated" to achieve more stringent limitations and that they must be "available" in the OCPSF industry before such technologies can form the basis for NSPS. The Agency claims to have considered and rejected technologies other than BPT and BAT. It found, for instance, that requiring filtration in addition to biological treatment for conventional pollutants had not been adequately demonstrated to accomplish better effluent results for the OCPSF industry. As another example, the Agency considered requiring the addition of activated carbon for further control of toxic pollutants but rejected it because of its high cost and because it had not been well-demonstrated to enhance treatment.

Intuitively, there is some force to the observation that Congress would not have devised a completely new statutory scheme for regulation of new sources if it intended that the effluent standards for such plants would be identical to those required for existing sources. This is especially true when one considers that the statute provides an exemption from more stringent standards of performance that the EPA may adopt under NSPS in the future.

The EPA asserts that, at this time, there exist no technologies that have been demonstrated to achieve a greater degree of effluent reduction than existing technologies that meet BPT and BAT standards. The key issue is the meaning attributable to the term "demonstrated." The EPA maintains that "best available demonstrated technology" means "those plant processes and control technology which, at the pilot plant, semi-works, or other level, has [sic] demonstrated both technological performance and economic viability at a level sufficient to reasonably justify the making of investments in such new facilities."

The Third Circuit has concluded, and we agree, that Congress did not intend the term "best available demonstrated control technology" to limit consideration of treatment systems only to those widely in use in the industry. Instead, the present availability of a particular technology may be "demonstrated" if even one plant utilizes the technology in question. NRDC asserts that 36 operating facilities achieve zero discharge by the use of recycling and that the EPA failed to consider this technology when it promulgated effluent limitations for new sources.

The EPA's only response is that NRDC failed to urge consideration of recycling during rulemaking and is therefore precluded from raising the issue on appeal. As to this, as we have previously pointed out, the failure of a petitioner to raise an issue before the Agency may cause us to view the contention less favorably but does not bar our consideration of it.

We frequently defer to the expertise of the EPA. We do this for good reason. Congress entertains the legitimate expectation that the various federal agencies, charged as they are with responsibility for promulgating highly detailed and technical regulations, will be aware of the events and breakthroughs on the technological frontiers that lie within the purview of the agencies' respective fields of expertise.

We do not require, however, that the EPA be fully cognizant of every innovation, wherever employed, that has the potential to achieve greater reductions in the discharge of pollutants into our environment. And we recognize that the purpose of a period of notice and comment during rulemaking is, at least in part, to allow interested parties to bring to the attention of the EPA relevant technologies that may assist the Agency in the discharge of its regulatory duties. Nevertheless, we consider that a treatment system employed by 36 plants in the OCPSF industry is sufficiently common that it is not unreasonable to expect the EPA to know about it. The NSPS statute directs that the "Administrator shall, from time to time, as technology and alternatives change," revise effluent standards for new point sources. We should be able to have confidence that the Administrator will do so, especially since he has chosen at this time to require no more stringent guidelines for new plants than for existing sources.

We know from the record that 36 plants in the industry use recycling and some of them achieve zero discharge. Thus, recycling easily fits the definition of an "available demonstrated technology" under § 306 of the Act. The failure of the EPA even to consider recycling, then, was arbitrary or capricious. We therefore remand these limitations to the EPA for consideration of whether zero discharge limits would be appropriate for new plants in the OCPSF industry because of the existence of recycling.

NOTE

Technology-based standards are meant to be dynamic. As technology improves, standards should ratchet up. In practice, however, the Act's elaborate system of phased standards may have virtually collapsed into a single stage of BPT. Commenting on the *CMA* case excerpted above, Houck observed:

> The attempt to set BAT for the organic chemicals, plastics, and synthetic materials category bottomed out, after years of administrative warfare, at a standard no better than BPT. Indeed, EPA concluded by proposing BAT for new sources in this industry, standards intended to be the toughest in the Clean Water Act, without consideration of recycling technologies that had already been adopted by thirty-six plants; twenty-six percent of the industry had already achieved *zero* discharge. These consequences are not unusual; one observer of the process concluded that, while the first-stage BPT inquiry was rigorous, subsequent BAT standards, in general, required little more.

Oliver A. Houck, Of Bats, Birds, and B-A-T: The Convergent Evolution of Environmental Law, 63 MISS. L.J. 403, 452 (1994). See also Jonathan K. Baum, Legislating Cost-Benefit Analysis: The Federal Water Pollution Control Act Experience, 9 COLUM. J. ENVTL. L. 75, 76 (1983) (arguing that separate cost tests applicable to BPT, BCT, BAT, and BDAT have become indistinguishable, and that this "blurring has resulted in ad hoc evaluations by [EPA] administrators, who treat all steps of the regulatory schedule the same, thus thwarting the goals of predictability and intellectual coherence in the law.").

f.   Publicly Owned Treatment Works

Publicly owned treatment works (POTWs) collect wastewater from homes, commercial buildings, and industrial facilities and transport it via a series of pipes, known as a collection system, to the treatment plant. The POTW removes harmful organisms and other contaminants from the sewage so it can be discharged safely into the receiving water body. Generally, POTWs are designed to treat domestic sewage only. However, they also receive wastewater from industrial (non-domestic) users. The Act requires industrial dischargers who send waste to POTWs to meet pretreatment standards to control pollutants which may pass through or interfere with POTW treatment processes, or which may contaminate sewage sludge. These standards are based on BAT.

Section 301 of the 1972 Amendments established standards for POTWs, requiring them to meet secondary treatment standards by 1977 and more stringent standards by 1983. In 1981, Congress amended the POTW provisions to extend the secondary treatment deadline to 1988 and to eliminate the advanced treatment requirement. Industrial dischargers sending waste to POTWs are required by § 307(b) to obtain pretreatment permits to ensure that their discharges (for which they are not required to obtain permits since the waste does not flow directly into surface waters) do not interfere with the POTW.

The 1972 Amendments also created a federal grant program to encourage the construction of POTWs. As a condition of receiving grants-in-aid, § 208 requires states to establish area-wide management agencies with both planning and regulatory functions for waste treatment. The grant program provided nearly $60 billion in federal funding to states, but in the 1987 Amendments, Congress stipulated that all direct federal grants for POTW construction would end as of 1990, and would be replaced by a new revolving loan program to be administered by the states. In 1998, this new fund had $26 billion in assets with approximately $3 billion distributed in new loans annually. "Since its beginning, the SRF [State Revolving Fund] has provided more than 5,700 loans throughout the United States and Puerto Rico. One of the benefits of the SRF is that it gives the states flexibility to provide funding for projects that address their highest priority water quality needs such as urban storm water and nonpoint source management practices, estuarine and groundwater protection programs, and sanitary sewer overflow control projects." OFFICE OF WASTEWATER MANAGEMENT, EPA, WATER POLLUTION CONTROL: 25 YEARS OF PROGRESS AND CHALLENGES FOR THE NEW MILLENNIUM 2 (1998).

g. Water Quality Standards (WQS)

Section 303(a) requires states and tribes to establish water quality standards for all intrastate waters and to review their standards every three years. State WQS are subject to EPA approval. § 303(c). Section 303(d) authorizes the EPA to issue standards for states that fail to submit their own or for state standards that fail to meet the requirements of the Act.

The Water Quality Standards Program consists of three major components: designated uses (DUs), water quality criteria (WQC), and an antidegradation policy. States determine DUs subject to EPA approval. The purpose of designating uses is to identify the activities the state expects the water body to support. Common DUs include the following:

drinking water, water-based recreation, fishing/eating, aquatic life, agriculture water supply, and industrial water supply. Although in some cases, the DUs have already been attained, in other cases, the current conditions in a water body do not support all the DUs. In cases like this, DUs might more accurately be thought of as *desired* uses. Generally, states assign different combinations of DUs not only to different water bodies, but to different portions of the same water body. A given segment will almost always be classified for more than one DU.

The second component of WQS is WQC. These are descriptions of the conditions in a water body necessary to support the DUs. WQC can be expressed numerically or in narrative terms. Numeric criteria are scientifically derived ambient concentrations, or other quantitative measures developed by the EPA or states, for various pollutants that adversely affect public health or aquatic life. These pollutants include such things as pH, turbidity units, temperature and toxicity units. WQC can also be narrative statements such as "no unreasonable interference with aquatic life" or "no toxic chemicals in toxic amounts." The EPA has provided states with three different methodologies for translating these criteria into numerical standards for permits. *See* American Paper Inst. v. EPA, 996 F.2d 346 (D.C. Cir. 1993). Economic factors can be considered when setting the DU for a water body but may not be considered when developing the WQC to protect a DU.

Section 304(a) of the Act requires the EPA to develop WQC. These serve as a point of reference for states to consider, though states frequently adopt more lenient standards and the EPA tends to approve them. Water quality standards could theoretically vary from state to state. However, state flexibility is limited by the requirement of EPA approval (even when states decline to follow EPA WQC), and by the EPA's antidegradation policy. This policy is designed to protect "existing uses" which are defined as those uses "actually attained in the water body on or after November 28, 1975, whether or not they are included in WQS." 40 C.F.R. § 131.3(e) (2002). The purpose of the antidegradation policy is to prevent backsliding from higher ambient water quality to lower ambient water quality. (The Prevention of Significant Deterioration provisions of the CAA function to similar effect.)

The respective roles of the federal and state governments in the water quality standards-setting process have not always been clear. In *Mississippi Commission on Natural Resources v. Costle*, 625 F.2d 1269 (5th Cir. 1980), the court attempted to clarify the EPA's relationship with the states. As the court understood the statute, the state's role is primarily to designate the appropriate *use* for a water body, while the EPA sets the criteria appropriate for various levels of use (fishable, swimmable, etc.). This coheres with the EPA's general hesitation to involve itself in the politically contentious question of desirable uses, while being more willing to intervene in the scientifically based process of setting water quality criteria. The court also upheld EPA's contention that economic factors are not relevant to setting the criteria. The *Mississippi Commission* opinion has been sharply criticized, however:

> Only one appellate decision has addressed the extent of EPA's authority to review a state's criteria judgments and use designations. In *Mississippi Commission on Natural Resources v. Costle,* the court found that intensive review by EPA of state use designation would amount to federal exercise of the zoning power Congress explicitly denied it. By contrast, EPA's review of the technical accuracy of state criteria judgments was perfectly proper. The court claimed to be accepting an EPA argument. In fact, however, EPA's regulatory program is approximately the reverse of the court's prescription. EPA's water quality standards rules assert a broad federal power to circumscribe the uses a state may choose for its water. The regulations declare that EPA will not approve state standards that allow water quality in a lake or stream to decline, no matter how compelling an argument might be made concerning local preferences or circumstances. Even if a state simply wants to maintain existing levels of water quality, EPA insists on a showing that improved water quality is unattainable by reasonable control measures.

William F. Pedersen, Jr., *Turning the Tide on Water Quality*, 15 ECOLOGY L.Q. 69, 93 (1988). Pedersen adds that the "legal soundness of these policies is highly debatable," but that Congress under the 1972 CWA effectively denied the EPA the authority and regulatory tools it needed to properly set and implement water quality standards or to ensure attainment of state WQS, such that WQS policy generally is a "muddle." *Id.* at 92–94. He further contends that the current use designations often are arbitrary. *Id.* at 94–95. As time goes on, progress using technology-based standards may slow, because such standards may become more difficult to enforce as they become more burdensome, and because they may be insufficient to assure adequate water quality in some areas. Water quality standards will attain greater significance, however, as it becomes increasingly difficult to make further progress using technology-based standards.

Water quality standards have a number of important consequences. For example, they may result in more stringent regulation of point sources that contribute pollutants to a water body that fails to achieve WQS. Section 301(b)(1)(c) requires the EPA to establish more stringent effluent limitations than § 301 would normally require, if necessary to achieve WQS. EPA regulations also require that permit writers translate state WQS into enforceable effluent controls. This can be challenging however, especially when WQS are expressed as narrative goals such as "no unreasonable interference with aquatic life." (As noted earlier, in order to address this problem, at least in part, Congress has required that states adopt numerical criteria for *toxic* pollutants that could interfere with attaining WQS.) How should this concretely affect the effluent limits imposed on a pulp and paper mill that contributes pollutants to that water body, especially when that mill is already subject to applicable BPT, BCT and BAT standards, which themselves require stringent end-of-pipe controls? What if nonpoint sources also contribute to the failure of a water body to achieve WQS? Should point sources, which alone are subject to NPDES requirements, bear the full burden? Is this fair? To some extent §§ 319 and 303(d) are meant to address this problem. We turn to them in Section D below.

In 2015, EPA updated WQ Criteria for 94 chemicals and set them at levels designed to protect human health. *See* U.S. EPA, EPA Updated Ambient Water Quality Criteria for the Protection of Human Health https://www.epa.gov/wqc/2015-epa-updated-ambient-water-quality-criteria-protection-human-health. This was an update to the 2002 *National Recommended Human Health Criteria*, https://www.epa.gov/wqc/2002-national-recommended-human-health-criteria. The updates come after EPA was criticized for falling behind in issuance of WQC. *See* GAO, WATER POLLUTION: EPA NEEDS TO SET PRIORITIES FOR WATER QUALITY CRITERIA ISSUES (1994). Individual state WQS can be found here: U.S. EPA, *State-Specific Water Quality Standards Effective Under the Clean Water Act (CWA)* https://www.epa.gov/wqs-tech/state-specific-water-quality-standards-effective-under-clean-water-act-cwa.

As with many of the major federal environmental statutes, environmental groups have been pushing—either via traditional lawsuits or agency petitions—to use the statutes to address climate change. The Clean Water Act is no exception. The Center for Biological Diversity has petitioned the EPA to address the problem of ocean acidification and its effect on water quality. Ocean acidification results from the ocean's absorption of carbon dioxide, the most prevalent of the greenhouse gases. Increasing amounts of $CO2$ absorption are leading to increases in the acidity of the oceans. Ocean acidification can have profoundly negative consequences for marine animals, including coral reefs, by impairing their ability to manufacturer and maintain their shells and skeletons. The Center's petition sought to have the agency establish more stringent PH standards for oceans. EPA denied the petition at the end of 2016. http://blogs2.law.columbia.edu/climate-change-litigation/wp-content/uploads/sites/16/case-documents/2016/20161214_docket-NA_response-to-petition-for-rulemaking.pdf.

If the EPA were to meet the Center's demand and increase the stringency of PH standards, states would presumably need to evaluate and designate water bodies that violate the PH standards as impaired. In turn states would then need to regulate those sources contributing to the increased acidity—sources of carbon dioxide emissions would be subject to regulation under the Clean Water Act. Can you imagine how such regulation might be carried out?

Water quality standards also play an important role in state certification under § 401 of the Act. This provision requires that federal agencies seeking to issue permits or licenses for activities that will discharge pollutants into waterways obtain state certification that the proposed activity will not violate water quality standards.

PUD No. 1 OF JEFFERSON COUNTY V. WASHINGTON DEPARTMENT OF ECOLOGY

Supreme Court of the United States, 1994.
511 U.S. 700, 114 S.Ct. 1900, 128 L.Ed.2d 716.

JUSTICE O'CONNOR delivered the opinion of the Court.

Petitioners, a city and a local utility district, want to build a hydroelectric project on the Dosewallips River in Washington State. We must decide whether respondent, the state environmental agency, properly conditioned a permit for the project on the maintenance of specific minimum stream flows to protect salmon and steelhead runs.

The principal dispute in this case concerns whether the minimum stream flow requirement that the State imposed on the Elkhorn project [to preserve salmon and trout runs] is a permissible condition of a § 401 certification under the Clean Water Act. To resolve this dispute we must first determine the scope of the State's authority under § 401. We must then determine whether the limitation at issue here, the requirement that petitioners maintain minimum stream flows, falls within the scope of that authority.

There is no dispute that petitioners were required to obtain a certification from the State pursuant to § 401. Petitioners concede that, at a minimum, the project will result in two possible discharges—the release of dredged and fill material during the construction of the project, and the discharge of water at the end of the tailrace after the water has been used to generate electricity. Petitioners contend, however, that the minimum stream flow requirement imposed by the State was unrelated to these specific discharges, and that as a consequence, the State lacked the authority under § 401 to condition its certification on maintenance of stream flows sufficient to protect the Dosewallips fishery.

If § 401 consisted solely of subsection (a), which refers to a state certification that a "discharge" will comply with certain provisions of the Act, petitioners' assessment of the scope of the State's certification authority would have considerable force. Section 401, however, also contains subsection (d), which expands the State's authority to impose conditions on the certification of a project. Section 401(d) provides that any certification shall set forth "any effluent limitations and other limitations * * * necessary to assure that any applicant" will comply with various provisions of the Act and appropriate state law requirements. The language of this subsection contradicts petitioners' claim that the State may only impose water quality limitations specifically tied to a "discharge." The text refers to the compliance of the applicant, not the discharge. Section 401(d) thus allows the State to impose "other limitations" on the project in general to assure compliance with various provisions of the Clean Water Act and with "any other appropriate requirement of State law." Although the dissent asserts that this interpretation of § 401(d) renders § 401(a)(1) superfluous, we see no such anomaly. Section 401(a)(1) identifies the category of activities subject to certification—namely those with discharges. And § 401(d) is most reasonably read as authorizing additional conditions and limitations on the activity as a whole once the threshold condition, the existence of a discharge, is satisfied. * * *

We agree with the State that ensuring compliance with § 303 is a proper function of the § 401 certification. Although § 303 is not one of the statutory provisions listed in § 401(d), the statute allows states to impose limitations to ensure compliance with § 301 of the Act, 33 U.S.C. § 1311. Section 301 in turn incorporates § 303 by reference. As a consequence, state water quality standards adopted pursuant to § 303 are among the "other limitations" with which a State may ensure compliance through the § 401 certification process. This interpretation is consistent with EPA's view of the statute. Moreover, limitations to assure compliance with state water quality standards are also permitted by § 401(d)'s reference to "any other appropriate requirement of State law." We do not speculate on what additional state laws, if any, might be incorporated by this language.[3] But at a minimum, limitations imposed pursuant to state water quality standards adopted pursuant to § 303 are "appropriate" requirements of state law. Indeed, petitioners appear to agree that the State's authority under § 401 includes limitations designed to ensure compliance with state water quality standards.

Having concluded that, pursuant to § 401, States may condition certification upon any limitations necessary to ensure compliance with state water quality standards or any other "appropriate requirement of State law," we consider whether the minimum flow condition is such a limitation. Under § 303, state water quality standards must "consist of the

---

[3] The dissent asserts that § 301 is concerned solely with discharges, not broader water quality standards. Although § 301 does make certain discharges unlawful, it also contains a broad enabling provision which requires states to take certain actions, to wit: "In order to carry out the objective of this chapter [viz. the chemical, physical, and biological integrity of the Nation's water] there shall be achieved * * * not later than July 1, 1977, any more stringent limitation, including those necessary to meet water quality standards * * * established pursuant to any State law or regulations." This provision of § 301 expressly refers to state water quality standards, and is not limited to discharges.

designated uses of the navigable waters involved and the water quality criteria for such waters based upon such uses." In imposing the minimum stream flow requirement, the State determined that construction and operation of the project as planned would be inconsistent with one of the designated uses of Class AA water, namely "[s]almonid [and other fish] migration, rearing, spawning, and harvesting." The designated use of the River as a fish habitat directly reflects the Clean Water Act's goal of maintaining the "chemical, physical, and biological integrity of the Nation's waters." Indeed, the Act defines pollution as "the man-made or man induced alteration of the chemical, physical, biological, and radiological integrity of water." Moreover, the Act expressly requires that, in adopting water quality standards, the State must take into consideration the use of waters for "propagation of fish and wildlife."

Petitioners assert, however, that § 303 requires the State to protect designated uses solely through implementation of specific "criteria." According to petitioners, the State may not require them to operate their dam in a manner consistent with a designated "use"; instead, say petitioners, under § 303 the State may only require that the project comply with specific numerical "criteria."

We disagree with petitioners' interpretation of the language of § 303(c)(2)(A). Under the statute, a water quality standard must "consist of the designated uses of the navigable waters involved and the water quality criteria for such waters based upon such uses." The text makes it plain that water quality standards contain two components. We think the language of § 303 is most naturally read to require that a project be consistent with both components, namely the designated use and the water quality criteria. Accordingly, under the literal terms of the statute, a project that does not comply with a designated use of the water does not comply with the applicable water quality standards. * * *

Washington's Class AA water quality standards are typical in that they contain several open-ended criteria which, like the use designation of the River as a fishery, must be translated into specific limitations for individual projects. For example, the standards state that "[t]oxic, radioactive, or deleterious material concentrations shall be less than those which may affect public health, the natural aquatic environment, or the desirability of the water for any use." Similarly, the state standards specify that "[a]esthetic values shall not be impaired by the presence of materials or their effects, excluding those of natural origin, which offend the senses of sight, smell, touch, or taste." We think petitioners' attempt to distinguish between uses and criteria loses much of its force in light of the fact that the Act permits enforcement of broad, narrative criteria based on, for example, "aesthetics." * * *

The State also justified its minimum stream flow as necessary to implement the "antidegradation policy" of § 303. When the Clean Water Act was enacted in 1972, the water quality standards of all 50 States had antidegradation provisions. These provisions were required by federal law. By providing in 1972 that existing state water quality standards would remain in force until revised, the Clean Water Act ensured that the States would continue their antidegradation programs. EPA has consistently required that revised state standards incorporate an antidegradation policy. And, in 1987, Congress explicitly recognized the existence of an "antidegradation policy established under [§ 303]." * * *

Petitioners contend that we should limit the State's authority to impose minimum flow requirements because FERC has comprehensive authority to license hydroelectric projects pursuant to the FPA, 16 U.S.C. § 791a et seq. In petitioners' view, the minimum flow requirement imposed here interferes with FERC's authority under the FPA. * * *

[T]he requirement for a state certification applies not only to applications for licenses from FERC, but to all federal licenses and permits for activities which may result in a discharge into the Nation's navigable waters. For example, a permit from the Army Corps of Engineers is required for the installation of any structure in the navigable waters which may interfere with navigation, including piers, docks, and ramps. Similarly, a permit must be obtained from the Army Corps of Engineers for the discharge of dredged or fill material, and from the Secretary of the Interior or Agriculture for the construction of reservoirs, canals and other water storage systems on federal land. We assume that a § 401 certification would also be required for some licenses obtained pursuant to these statutes. Because § 401's certification requirement applies to other statutes and regulatory schemes, and because any conflict with FERC's authority under the FPA is hypothetical, we are unwilling to read implied limitations into § 401. If FERC issues a license containing a stream flow condition with which petitioners disagree, they may pursue judicial remedies at that time.

In summary, we hold that the State may include minimum stream flow requirements in a certification issued pursuant to § 401 of the Clean Water Act insofar as necessary to enforce a designated use contained in a state water quality standard. The judgment of the Supreme Court of Washington, accordingly, is affirmed.

So ordered.

JUSTICE STEVENS, concurring.

While I agree fully with the thorough analysis in the Court's opinion, I add this comment for emphasis. For judges who find it unnecessary to go behind the statutory text to discern the intent of Congress, this is (or should be) an easy case. Not a single sentence, phrase, or word in the Clean Water

Act purports to place any constraint on a State's power to regulate the quality of its own waters more stringently than federal law might require. In fact, the Act explicitly recognizes States' ability to impose stricter standards.

JUSTICE THOMAS, with whom JUSTICE SCALIA joins, dissenting.

The Court today holds that a State, pursuant to § 401 of the Clean Water Act, may condition the certification necessary to obtain a federal license for a proposed hydroelectric project upon the maintenance of a minimum flow rate in the river to be utilized by the project. In my view, the Court makes three fundamental errors. First, it adopts an interpretation that fails adequately to harmonize the subsections of § 401. Second, it places no meaningful limitation on a State's authority under § 401 to impose conditions on certification. Third, it gives little or no consideration to the fact that its interpretation of § 401 will significantly disrupt the carefully crafted federal-state balance embodied in the Federal Power Act. Accordingly, I dissent. * * *

Although the Court notes in passing that "[t]he limitations included in the certification become a condition on any Federal license," it does not acknowledge or discuss the shift of power from FERC to the States that is accomplished by its decision. Indeed, the Court merely notes that "any conflict with FERC's authority under the FPA" in this case is "hypothetical" at this stage, because "FERC has not yet acted on petitioners' license application." We are assured that "it is quite possible * * * that any FERC license would contain the same conditions as the State § 401 certification."

The Court's observations simply miss the point. Even if FERC might have no objection to the stream flow condition established by respondents in this case, such a happy coincidence will likely prove to be the exception, rather than the rule. In issuing licenses, FERC must balance the Nation's power needs together with the need for energy conservation, irrigation, flood control, fish and wildlife protection, and recreation. State environmental agencies, by contrast, need only consider parochial environmental interests. Cf., e.g., Wash.Rev.Code § 90.54.010(2) (1992) (goal of State's water policy is to "insure that waters of the state are protected and fully utilized for the greatest benefit to the people of the state of Washington"). As a result, it is likely that conflicts will arise between a FERC-established stream flow level and a state-imposed level.

NOTES

1.   Note Justice Thomas's rather jaundiced view of environmental regulation by the states, which he considers to reflect only parochial local interests, as opposed to the national interests behind increased power generation.

2.   Consider the following assessment of the majority opinion:

After reflecting about the Supreme Court decision in *PUD No. 1*, I recalled my high school chemistry teacher who, after observing my inelegant experimental techniques, stated that the Jesuits used an old Latin expression in such circumstances—*non disputandum resultatem* [sic]. He roughly translated this to mean you don't argue with good results. * * *

In the area of statutory interpretation, unlike high-school chemistry experiments however, good technique is at least as important as good results. A good interpretive approach requires that courts consider more than mere text; they must carefully consider context as well. In the legal dispute at the heart of *PUD No. 1*, that context is defined not only by the CWA, but also by the FPA, the Court's interpretations of that statute, and how FERC and the state agencies have exercised the powers they believe have been delegated them. In enacting the FPA, Congress gave FERC the power to balance a variety of interests, including aesthetic, wildlife protection, recreation, preservation, and economic interests, against the need for energy. Congress also carved out an exception to FERC's authority and gave states the power to ensure that projects do not violate WQSs. Because, in conducting its balancing, FERC's concerns about the economic, development, and electric power factors have largely overwhelmed all other factors, courts, when they consider the interaction of the CWA and FPA, need to safeguard the single consideration that Congress has identified as beyond FERC's ability to balance out of existence. When interpreting these statutes, courts must also not view the in-state water quality factor so broadly that it alone overwhelms all other factors, at least some of which will have out-of-state impacts unlikely to be considered by the state when identifying its WQSs.

Michael P. Healy, *The Attraction and Limits of Textualism: The Supreme Court Decision in PUD No. 1 of Jefferson County v. Washington Department of Ecology*, 5 N.Y.U. ENVTL. L. J. 382, 441–43 (1996). *See also* Michael P. Healy, *Still Dirty After Twenty-Five Years: Water Quality Standard Enforcement and the Availability of Citizen Suits*, 24 ECOLOGY L.Q. 393 (1997) (considering "whether the Clean Water Act permits citizen suit enforcement of state WQSs and whether allowing such suits constitutes good public policy."). For an analysis of the unusual federalism arrangement Section 401 embodies and its implications for governance, *see* Ann E. Carlson and Andrew Meyer, *Reverse Preemption*, 40 ECOL. L. Q. 101 (2013).

3.   In *S.D. Warren Co. v. Maine Board of Envt'l Protection*, 547 U.S. 370 (2006), the U.S. Supreme Court held in an unanimous decision that a hydroelectric power company, in applying for renewal of a FERC license, was required to obtain Section 401 certification from the state of Maine for operating a series of dams on the Presumpscot River. S.D. Warren argued that a discharge of water from the dams did not constitute a discharge subject to Section 401 certification. The Supreme Court disagreed, analyzing the plain language of Section 401 and recognizing that dams alter water quality, can

change the movement and flow of a body of water, and can destroy natural habitat for fish and other aquatic life. *Id.*

4.   In an attempt to build on the *PUD* case and address the problem of nonpoint source pollution, a coalition of environmental groups challenged the U.S. Forest Service's issuance of grazing leases without first obtaining certification from the state of Oregon, pursuant to section 401 of the CWA, that the grazing would not cause violations of state water quality standards. On appeal, the court held that water quality certifications under section 401 are not required for nonpoint sources of pollution, apparently closing this avenue for addressing the nonpoint source problem. *See* Oregon Natural Desert Ass'n v. Dombeck, 172 F.3d 1092 (9th Cir. 1998), *cert. denied*, 528 U.S. 964 (1999).

5.   In October, 2000, in the wake of the 9th Circuit's rejection of the section 401 strategy in *Dombeck,* eight federal agencies jointly issued a Unified Federal Policy for a Watershed Approach to Federal Land and Resource Management. *See* 65 Fed. Reg. 62566–601. The policy, which describes how land management will be governed on 800 million acres of federal lands, calls for enhanced collaboration between federal land managers and state, tribal, and private landowners. The proposed policy may be the one of the most important tools for controlling nonpoint source pollution in the future. We take up the non-point source problem in Section D, below.

h.   Water Quality Standards and Interstate Pollution

The EPA has adopted the view that the water quality standards provisions of the Act can be used to regulate interstate water pollution, by requiring the upstream state's permit to be consistent with downstream water quality standards. The Supreme Court reviewed this policy in the following case.

ARKANSAS V. OKLAHOMA

Supreme Court of the United States, 1992.
503 U.S. 91, 112 S.Ct. 1046, 117 L.Ed.2d 239.

JUSTICE STEVENS delivered the opinion of the Court.

[An Arkansas sewage treatment plant received an EPA permit to discharge into a stream that ultimately flows (via some creeks) into the Illinois River 22 miles upstream of the Oklahoma border. The state of Oklahoma challenged the permit before an EPA hearing officer, on the ground that the discharge violated Oklahoma's water quality standards, which allow no degradation of water quality in that portion of the Illinois River. EPA granted the permit after concluding that the discharge would cause no detectable change in water quality. The Court of Appeals ruled, however, that a permit cannot be issued if the proposed discharge would contribute to an existing violation of water quality standards.]

The parties have argued three analytically distinct questions concerning the interpretation of the Clean Water Act. First, does the Act require the EPA, in crafting and issuing a permit to a point source in one State, to apply the water quality standards of downstream States? Second, even if the Act does not require as much, does the Agency have the statutory authority to mandate such compliance? Third, does the Act provide, as the Court of Appeals held, that once a body of water fails to meet water quality standards no discharge that yields effluent that reach the degraded waters will be permitted?

In this case, it is neither necessary nor prudent for us to resolve the first of these questions. In issuing the Fayetteville permit, the EPA assumed it was obligated by both the Act and its own regulations to ensure that the Fayetteville discharge would not violate Oklahoma's standards. As we discuss below, this assumption was permissible and reasonable and therefore there is no need for us to address whether the Act requires as much. Moreover, much of the analysis and argument in the briefs of the parties relies on statutory provisions that govern not only federal permits issued pursuant to §§ 401(a) and 402(a), but also state permits issued under § 402(b). It seems unwise to evaluate those arguments in a case such as this one, which only involves a federal permit.

Our decision not to determine at this time the scope of the Agency's statutory obligations does not affect our resolution of the second question, which concerns the Agency's statutory authority. Even if the Clean Water Act itself does not require the Fayetteville discharge to comply with Oklahoma's water quality standards, the statute clearly does not limit the EPA's authority to mandate such compliance.

Since 1973, EPA regulations have provided that an NPDES permit shall not be issued "[w]hen the imposition of conditions cannot ensure compliance with the applicable water quality requirements of all affected States." Those regulations—relied upon by the EPA in the issuance of the Fayetteville permit—constitute a reasonable exercise of the Agency's statutory authority. * * *

Notwithstanding this apparent reasonableness, Arkansas argues that our description in *Ouellette* [*supra,* page 584] of the role of affected States in the permit process and our characterization of the affected States' position as "subordinate," indicates that the EPA's application of the Oklahoma standards was error. We disagree. Our statement in *Ouellette* concerned only an affected State's input into the permit process; that input is clearly limited by the plain language of § 402(b). Limits on an affected State's direct participation in permitting decisions, however, do not in any way constrain the EPA's authority to require a point source to comply with downstream water quality standards.

Arkansas also argues that regulations requiring compliance with downstream standards are at odds with the legislative history of the Act and with the statutory scheme established by the Act. Although we agree with Arkansas that the Act's legislative history indicates that Congress intended to grant the Administrator discretion in his oversight of the issuance of NPDES permits, we find nothing in that history to indicate that Congress intended to preclude the EPA from establishing a general requirement that such permits be conditioned to ensure compliance with downstream water quality standards.

Similarly, we agree with Arkansas that in the Clean Water Act Congress struck a careful balance among competing policies and interests, but do not find the EPA regulations concerning the application of downstream water quality standards at all incompatible with that balance. Congress, in crafting the Act, protected certain sovereign interests of the States; for example, § 510 allows States to adopt more demanding pollution-control standards than those established under the Act. Arkansas emphasizes that § 510 preserves such state authority only as it is applied to the waters of the regulating State. Even assuming Arkansas's construction of § 510 is correct, that section only concerns state authority and does not constrain the EPA's authority to promulgate reasonable regulations requiring point sources in one State to comply with water quality standards in downstream States.

For these reasons, we find the EPA's requirement that the Fayetteville discharge comply with Oklahoma's water quality standards to be a reasonable exercise of the Agency's substantial statutory discretion.

The Court of Appeals construed the Clean Water Act to prohibit any discharge of effluent that would reach waters already in violation of existing water quality standards. We find nothing in the Act to support this reading.

The interpretation of the statute adopted by the court had not been advanced by any party during the agency or court proceedings. Moreover, the Court of Appeals candidly acknowledged that its theory "has apparently never before been addressed by a federal court." The only statutory provision the court cited to support its legal analysis was § 402(h), which merely authorizes the EPA (or a state permit program) to prohibit a publicly owned treatment plant that is violating a condition of its NPDES permit from accepting any additional pollutants for treatment until the ongoing violation has been corrected. Although the Act contains several provisions directing compliance with state water quality standards, the parties have pointed to nothing that mandates a complete ban on discharges into a waterway that is in violation of those standards. The statute does, however, contain provisions designed to remedy existing water quality violations and to allocate the burden of reducing undesirable discharges between existing sources and new sources. Thus, rather than establishing the categorical ban announced by the Court of Appeals—which might frustrate the construction of new plants that would improve existing conditions—the Clean Water Act vests in the EPA and the States broad authority to develop long-range, area-wide programs to alleviate and eliminate existing pollution. To the extent that the Court of Appeals relied on its interpretation of the Act to reverse the EPA's permitting decision, that reliance was misplaced. * * *

In sum, the Court of Appeals made a policy choice that it was not authorized to make. Arguably, as that court suggested, it might be wise to prohibit any discharge into the Illinois River, even if that discharge would have no adverse impact on water quality. But it was surely not arbitrary for the EPA to conclude—given the benefits to the River from the increased flow of relatively clean water and the benefits achieved in Arkansas by allowing the new plant to operate as designed—that allowing the discharge would be even wiser. It is not our role, or that of the Court of Appeals, to decide which policy choice is the better one, for it is clear that Congress has entrusted such decisions to the Environmental Protection Agency.

NOTES

1. *See also* City of Albuquerque v. Browner, 97 F.3d 415 (10th Cir. 1996) (finding that upstream state must respect water quality standards adopted by downstream Indian tribe acting under authority of section 518).

2. The Court leaves open the question of whether state-issued permits (as opposed to the EPA-approved permit in the case) must comply with the water quality standards of downstream states. Given the Court's deference to the EPA's regulations, however, there seems to be a strong case for extending the ruling to state permits. For some doubts about the efficacy of the Clean Water Act as construed in *Arkansas v. Oklahoma, see* Robert L. Glicksman, *Watching the River Flow: The Prospects for Improved Interstate Water Pollution Control*, 43 WASH. U. J. URB. & CONTEMP. L. 119 (1993).

3. 40 CFR 131.10(b) requires upstream states to "take into consideration the water quality standards of downstream waters and . . . ensure that its water quality standards provide for the attainment and maintenance of the water quality standards of downstream waters."

i. Total Maximum Daily Loads

Section 303(d) has emerged as the most promising provision of the Act for addressing the lingering problem of nonpoint source pollution. Under § 303(d), states are required to identify those waters within their boundaries that do not meet water quality standards, to establish TMDLs for those waters capable of achieving those standards, and to incorporate these pollutant loads into a state planning process. This provision of the law remained largely dormant until the EPA was driven by lawsuits to activate it in 1996. *See* Alaska Center for the Environment v. Browner, 20 F.3d 981 (9th Cir. 1994). The TMDL process adopts an ambient approach to regulating water quality, in concert with the use of water quality standards as a back-up to the technology-based thrust of the CWA. The TMDL process requires states to work backwards from effect to cause, in order to ensure that water bodies meet WQS. TMDLs have the potential to turn WQS into enforcement tools. While the TMDL provision does not directly mandate regulation of non-point sources, it does require state *planning* to impose effluent limitations on those sources.

The TMDL process is, however, severely constrained by the difficulties of implementation. Establishing TMDLs requires the states to identify the amounts of pollution that can be tolerated by individual water bodies before WQS will be violated. However, the statute does not dictate the means by which such load targets will be achieved, or by which sources of pollution, nor does it set deadlines by which WQS must be attained. The absence of legal mechanisms for implementing controls on nonpoint sources has created an equity problem because water bodies that do not meet WQS may result in more stringent NPDES permit limits for point sources, even when the failure to meet WQS is substantially the fault of nonpoint sources.

i.   Point Sources

The following case demonstrates that ambient water quality regulation in the form of WQS and TMDLs can lead the EPA to set effluent limits on point sources (here pulp and paper mills) that are more stringent than would apply under the traditional technology-based limits. As often is the case, however, the EPA was attacked in court by both environmentalists—arguing that the TMDLs were set too low in an arbitrary or capricious manner—and the regulated industry—arguing that the EPA lacked the statutory authority to regulate in line with TMDLs before it had determined if less costly technology-based effluent limits were inadequate to meet the states' WQS. The 9th Circuit rejected both challenges: It held that the EPA acted reasonably in setting the TMDLs at the level it chose, and that the EPA acted within its statutory authority by setting stricter ambient water quality effluent limits for point sources than would have applied under the usual technology-based limits.

DIOXIN/ORGANOCHLORINE CENTER V. EPA

United States Court of Appeals, Ninth Circuit, 1995.
57 F.3d 1517.

LEAVY, CIRCUIT JUDGE.

Appellants, environmental groups and paper and pulp mills, challenge on opposing grounds the district court's grant of summary judgment in favor of the Environmental Protection Agency ("EPA") on appellants' claims that the EPA violated the Clean Water Act ("Act"), by establishing total maximum daily load limits for the discharge of the toxic pollutant dioxin into the Columbia River. We affirm.

FACTS AND PRIOR PROCEEDINGS

In the late 1980's, a series of EPA-sponsored and independent biological studies revealed that high levels of 2,3,7,8—tetrachlorodibenzo-p-dioxin ("TCDD" or for the purposes of this appeal simply "dioxin") were accumulating in the tissue of fish located downstream from pulp and paper mills in the Columbia River Basin. These studies also confirmed that the mills themselves were a significant source of dioxin contamination as a result of their use of chlorine-based chemicals to bleach wood and other raw materials used in the paper production cycle.

Oregon, Washington, and Idaho had already adopted applicable water quality standards under state law for waters in the Columbia Basin including the Columbia, Snake, and Willamette Rivers. The EPA found that these water quality standards limited the permissible ambient concentration of dioxin to 0.013 parts per quadrillion ("ppq") as provided in the EPA's Quality Criteria for Water tables issued in 1986. Due in large part to the mills activity, the dioxin concentration in these waters exceeded the level permitted by the state standards.

Pursuant to 33 U.S.C. § 1314(l), the states listed the mills as particular point sources believed to be impairing the water quality. Section 1314 required the development of individual control strategies ("ICS") expressed as individual National Pollution Discharge Elimination System ("NPDES") permits which would result in the attainment of the applicable water quality standard within three years.

Oregon, Washington, and Idaho also identified the Columbia River as "water quality limited" pursuant to § 1313(d)(1)(A), finding that the levels of dioxin being discharged into the Columbia River violated the applicable state water quality standards. Once the states had made this finding under § 1313(d)(1)(A), the states, pursuant to § 1313(d)(1)(C), or, the EPA, pursuant to § 1313(d)(2), were required to establish a Total Maximum Daily Load ("TMDL") for dioxin.

A TMDL defines the specified maximum amount of a pollutant which can be discharged or "loaded" into the waters at issue from all combined sources. Thus a TMDL represents the cumulative total of all "load allocations" which are in turn best estimates of the discrete loading attributed to nonpoint sources, natural background sources, and individual wasteload allocations ("WLAs"), that is, specific portions of the total load allocated to individual point sources. When a TMDL and specific wasteload allocations for point sources have been established, any NPDES permits issued to a point source must be consistent with the terms of the TMDL and WLA.

The states decided against issuing TMDLs and WLAs on their own authority. Instead, after consultation and involvement in the development of the draft TMDL, the states requested the EPA to issue the proposed and final TMDL as a federal action under the authority of § 1313(d)(2). * * * On February 25, 1991, the EPA established the final TMDL for dioxin discharge into the Columbia River. * * *

[The environmental groups, Dioxin, Organochlorane Center and Columbia River United (DOC)] argues that the TMDL developed by the EPA fails to conform to the water quality standards adopted by the states because it is not stringent enough. DOC asserts that the TMDL was based on arbitrary or capricious decisions by the EPA constituting an abuse of discretion. The Mills, on the other hand, argue that the EPA violated the Clean Water Act by issuing a TMDL prior to establishing less burdensome technology-based limitations which the Mills assert are required by the Act before the EPA can establish TMDLs. * * *

B. Discussion

DOC contends that the TMDL fails to implement state water quality standards because it: 1) inadequately protects aquatic life and wildlife, 2) inadequately protects certain human subpopulations, and 3) fails to consider the cumulative effect of dioxin-related pollutants in the water system.

1. The TMDL: Aquatic Life and Wildlife

DOC maintains that the EPA abused its discretion by arbitrarily and capriciously considering only the risk to *human* life and failing to consider the effect of dioxin on *animal* life.

DOC first disputes the evidence relied upon by the district court to support its decision. In order to establish that it appropriately considered the effect of the TMDL on aquatic life and wildlife, the EPA filed in the district court an affidavit of Richard Albright. * * * In his affidavit Albright stated:

> During development of the TMDL, it was determined that an ambient concentration of [dioxin] of .013 ppq was necessary to protect human health. In addition, I concluded during development of the TMDL that an ambient concentration of .013 ppq would be protective of aquatic life and wildlife, and would therefore implement the state narrative water quality standards for aquatic life and wildlife protection.

> In reaching this conclusion, I was aware of the data and analyses regarding the dioxin toxicity to aquatic life and wildlife contained in the following documents. The Fish and Wildlife Service Dioxin Hazard Document, ... EPA's Background Document to the Integrated Risk Assessment for Dioxins and Furans from

Chlorine Bleaching in Pulp and Paper Mills, . . . and EPA's dioxin criteria guidance document, entitled "Ambient Water Quality Criteria for 2,3,7,8,-tetracholoro-dibenzo-p-diozin," dated 1984. . . . The TMDL was intended and designed to provide protection to humans aquatic life and wildlife.

DOC discounts the significance of Albright's affidavit and contends that the documents referred to do not support the conclusion that the EPA had adequately considered the effect of the TMDL on aquatic life and wildlife. We consider each of the documents cited by Albright in order to determine whether they provide sufficient evidence to support the EPA's setting of a TMDL at 0.013 ppq to protect aquatic biota and wildlife.

a.   EPA, Office of Water Regulations and Standards, *Ambient Water Quality Criteria for 2,3,7,8-Tetrachloro-dibenzo-p-dioxin* (Feb. 1984).

DOC asserts that this document does not support the conclusion that a dioxin level of 0.013 ppq would protect fish and other wildlife. DOC quotes the study itself:

> The data that are available concerning the effects of [dioxin] on aquatic organisms and their uses do not allow the calculation of an acute or chronic toxicity value for any freshwater animal species.

This report however indicates that the lowest level at which adverse effects on *aquatic life* had been noted was at 0.0001 micrograms per liter or 100 ppq. *Id.* B1–7. The ambient concentration of 0.013 ppq allows for a dioxin exposure only one ten-thousandth of that value.

b.   EPA, Office of Pesticides and Toxic Substances, *Background Document to the Integrated Risk Assessment for Dioxins and Furans from Chlorine Bleaching in Pulp and Paper Mills* (July 1990).

DOC argues that this document fails to establish that the TMDL was protective of aquatic life:

> Currently sufficient data are not available concerning the chronic effect of [dioxin] . . . on *aquatic* life to derive national water quality or sediment criteria for these contaminants.

The district court, however, found that this document, while not containing an estimate of the toxicity of dioxin for *aquatic* life, did justify the EPA's decision in regard to *wildlife*. This document indicates that the lowest concentration at which adverse effects had been observed in wildlife feeding upon aquatic life contaminated by dioxin was at dioxin concentrations of 3 parts per trillion ("ppt") in the consumed food items. The EPA estimates that the maximum fish tissue residues in food items expected under the TMDL are 0.07 ppt. This represents a level approximately 1/43rd of the level at which adverse effects had been observed.

c.   U.S. Fish and Wildlife Service, *Dioxin Hazards to Fish, Wildlife and Invertebrates: A Synoptic Review,* Contaminant Hazard Reviews Report No. 8 (May 1986).

The Fish and Wildlife Service ("FWS") published this report in 1986. In it the FWS asserted that, "the limited data suggest that [dioxin] concentrations in water should not exceed 0.01 *ppt* to protect aquatic life, or 10 to 12 ppt in food items of birds and other wildlife." DOC argues that since the *Background Document* (b. above) recommended a lower figure of 3 ppt for a safe dioxin concentration in food items, this *Dioxin Hazards* report was "outdated and refuted by all the other more current evidence in the record."

The purpose of this document, however, is to establish that an 0.013 *ppq* ambient concentration of dioxin is protective of *aquatic life* in that the level set by the EPA is one one-thousandth of the 0.01 *ppt* level advocated by the FWS. DOC's focusing on the FWS' high recommendation of the concentration of dioxin which could safely be allowed in wildlife food items, i.e., 10–12 ppt, is irrelevant given the 0.07 ppt residue level estimated to occur in food items under the 0.013 ppq water concentration set by the EPA. * * *

In sum, the EPA was required by § 1313(d)(2) to develop a TMDL for dioxin in the context of inconclusive and diverse scientific data regarding the toxicity of dioxin. * * * We reject DOC's claim that the EPA failed to consider the effect of the TMDL on aquatic life and wildlife, and its claim that the ambient concentration selected fails to protect animal life. We conclude that the EPA's decision is supported by substantial evidence.

2.   *The TMDL and Human Life on the Columbia*

Projecting that implementation of the TMDL would result in a 0.013 ppq ambient concentration of dioxin in the Columbia Basin, the EPA calculated that this figure would result in a bioaccumulation of dioxin in the tissue of freshwater fish equal to 65 picograms per kilo, i.e., approximately 0.07 ppt.

In order to calculate the quantity of dioxin that would in turn be consumed by humans, the EPA adopted as one of the relevant variables the national average total consumption rate for all freshwater and estuarine fish of 6.5 grams per day. Assuming a lifetime of consumption of this amount of fish per day, and assuming that all 6.5 grams were contaminated to the highest level possible under the TMDL, the agency determined that the average risk to health would still satisfy the general one-in-a-million risk level provided for by the state water quality standards.

DOC argues, however, that the EPA failed to consider the effect of this dioxin concentration level on certain human subpopulations which consume greater quantities of fish. DOC asserts that these subpopulations would not be protected to the one-in-a-million risk level.

While the EPA acknowledges that continuing scientific studies may indicate that subpopulations are not adequately protected by the TMDL, it states that its conclusion that the TMDL was adequately protective of human health was not at the time arbitrary or capricious. The EPA offers a variety of justifications for its decision:

> First, the EPA notes that the "potency factor" it adopted for dioxin was the most stringent in the world. Potency factors for dioxin used by other agencies or foreign governments would have resulted in numerical values between five and sixteen hundred times less stringent.

> Second, the EPA argues that it reasonably concluded that higher consumption of fish among subpopulations did not imply that the total quantity of fish consumed would be maximally contaminated. The EPA notes that no definitive study had established the quantity and variety of *contaminated* fish consumed by these subpopulations. Since much of the fish population in the Columbia Basin consists of anadromous fish, *e.g.,* salmon and steelhead trout, which spend only limited time in contaminated river waters, the EPA argues that it was reasonable to assume that not all the fish tissue consumed by the subpopulations would be contaminated. Further, even if the fish were contaminated, they would not necessarily be contaminated at the highest concentrations possible.

As a result of these uncertainties, the EPA estimated that the total consumption of 150 grams of fish by these subpopulations would lead to no greater dioxin ingestion than would occur by consuming 6.5 grams of fully contaminated fish. On this assumption the subpopulations would be adequately protected.

In addition, the EPA argues that even assuming consumption of 150 grams of fully contaminated fish, as claimed by DOC, the risk level would still be only 23 in a million. This level of risk protection is within levels historically approved by the EPA and upheld by courts. * * *

We hold that the EPA's decision to adopt a 0.013 ppq ambient dioxin concentration cannot be considered arbitrary or capricious with regard to the effect of dioxin on human subpopulations * * *.

3.   *The TMDL and Dioxin-Related Compounds*

DOC argues that limiting the amount of dioxin without consideration of the presence of other chemicals in the water which act in a similar fashion fails to achieve the level of safety mandated by the water quality standards of the states.

Nothing in the Clean Water Act requires TMDLs to be issued for all pollutants at once. In fact, regulations pertaining to TMDL implementation specifically provide that TMDLs may be developed on a specific pollutant basis, and the states bordering the Columbia River had decided to proceed on environmental cleanup according to a chemical-by-chemical priority. * * *

We hold that the EPA's decision to establish the dioxin TMDL at 0.013 ppq was within reasonable limits of its discretionary authority and reflected an adequate consideration of the facts. * * *

None of the bases asserted by the environmental groups provide sufficient grounds for overturning the EPA's decision as arbitrary or capricious. It appears that the EPA consistently took a conservative approach with a reasonably wide margin for safety. * * *

1.   The Mills' Argument

The Mills contend that the plain language of 33 U.S.C. § 1313(d)(1)(A) prohibits—prior to the application and proven ineffectiveness of less burdensome technology-based pollution controls—a body of water from being listed as "water quality limited" and from being regulated by TMDLs. The Mills assert that because no effluent limitations were developed for dioxin under § 1311(b)(1)(A) or (B), the states improperly listed, and the EPA improperly approved, such waters as water quality limited. Accordingly, neither could the states or the EPA move to the subsequent step of implementing TMDLs for those waters pursuant to § 1313(d)(1)(C) or (2).

The Mills focus particular attention on the present tense language of § 1313(d)(1)(A), *i.e.,* "the effluent limitations of § 1311 . . . *are not stringent enough* to implement any water quality standard applicable to such waters. . . ." The Mills argue that the "plain language" of the provision prohibits the EPA from developing TMDLs prior to the proven failure of technology-based limitations.

The Mills state that the procedure of first developing and applying technology-based limitations is mandated by the legislative history of the Clean Water Act. They claim that Congress intended that technology-based limitations be imposed prior to water-quality-based controls in a manner which "would balance the costs and the benefits of pollution control." * * *

2.   The EPA's Interpretation of § 1313(d)

The EPA argues that "we interpret section 1313(d) as requiring TMDLs where existing pollution controls will not lead to attainment of water quality standards." We take this as an assertion that when a state has listed a water as impaired by toxic pollutants, the EPA has authority to implement TMDLs for that toxic pollutant under § 1313(d) even before technological limitations have been developed and implemented pursuant to § 1311(b)(1)(A) or (B). We hold that the EPA's interpretation is reasonable and not contrary to congressional intent.

Section 1313(d)(1)(A) provides that states shall list waters as impaired when any technological limitations required by § 1311(b)(1)(A) and (B) fail to satisfy water quality standards. Section 1311(b)(1)(A) and (B), referred to in § 1313(d)(1)(A), require development of "effluent limitations for point sources . . . which shall require the application of the best practicable control technology currently available." Section 1311(b)(1)(A) and (B) therefore require development of technology-based effluent limitations only for those point sources that are discharging pollutants subject by the Act to best practicable technology limitations ("BPT limitations"). The Act is clear, however, that *toxic* pollutants, such as dioxin, are subject, not to BPT limitations, but rather to best *available* technology limitations ("BAT limitations"). Dioxin is not a conventional pollutant but a *toxic* pollutant and is therefore not subject to BPT limitations but BAT limitations. *See* §§ 1311(b)(2), 1317.

The Mills argue:

> Given that the Clean Water Act requires EPA to develop *BAT limitations* for toxic pollutants, the Mills acknowledge that a reasonable interpretation of the Act is to permit the establishment of TMDLs if BAT limitations are not stringent enough to achieve water quality standards, rather than interpreting the statute to require EPA to promulgate BPT limitations first in order to determine whether TMDLs are authorized. . . . Any other interpretation would inevitably lead to the conclusion the TMDLs are not authorized by toxic pollutants because BPT limitations are not established for toxic pollutants.

The Mills contend that the failure of § 1311(d)(1)(A) or (B) to require development of BPT limitations for the discharge of dioxin can only be interpreted to imply either that *BAT* limitations must first be developed and fail prior to listing the water as impaired under § 1313(d), or that TMDLs can never be issued under § 1313(d) for toxic pollutants. We agree with neither argument. * * *

We reject the Mills' claim that, prior to implementing TMDLs, § 1313(d) of the Act requires development and proven failure of BAT limitations for *toxic pollutants*. The Mills offer no authority for this interpretation and it is not supported by the language of the statute. BPT limitations are not required by § 1313(d) for dioxin because the limitations required by the provisions of § 1311 referred to in § 1313(d) are not applicable to toxic pollutants; thus any limitations required by those provisions of § 1311, as a matter of law, "are not stringent enough" to achieve established water quality standards. Nowhere does the Act prohibit the EPA from listing waters as impaired and implementing TMDLs for toxic pollutants pursuant to § 1313(d).

We conclude that § 1313(d) allows the EPA to establish TMDLs for waters contaminated with toxic pollutants without prior development of BAT limitations.* * *

* * * Federal and state governments should not be required to expend time-consuming effort on development and implementation of technology-based limitations when the issue is discharge of toxic pollutants. When only conventional pollutants are at issue, however, there is not the same pressing necessity to impose the burdens created by TMDLs:

Through [technological limitations], large numbers of pollutants and pollutant sources can be regulated, an initial and often preventative level of control can be achieved and economic impacts can be kept within reasonable limits *until such time as toxicity and exposure data are sufficient to justify more stringent control.*

See supra, A Legislative History of the Clean Water Act of 1977 at 1405 (1978) (emphasis added). * * *

We hold that the EPA's establishment of a TMDL for dioxin discharge into the Columbia River Basin is consistent with a reasonable interpretation and application of § 1313(d). * * *

Affirmed.

ii. Nonpoint Sources

Having established that the EPA may skip technology-based effluent limits and regulate point sources of pollution more stringently in order to meet TMDLs set to meet the states' ambient WQS, the next major question concerned the EPA's ability to regulate *nonpoint* sources of pollution, such as sediment run-off from forestry, under the TMDL scheme. In the following case, the EPA not only required California to set TMDLs for the Garcia River over California's objections (thus raising a 10th Amendment issue), but also required private landholders to include costly mitigation measures in their timber-harvesting permits in order to meet the TMDLs. Since there were no point sources of pollution on the stretch of the Garcia River where the logging was set to occur, the landowners argued that the EPA had exceeded its statutory authority because the TMDLs could only limit nonpoint sources of pollution on water bodies that were also polluted by point sources, and for which the existing point source effluent limitations were found to be inadequate to achieve water quality standards. As we shall see below, the 9th Circuit rejected the states' 10th Amendment argument, and held that the EPA's interpretation of the CWA is more reasonable than an interpretation that would exempt any water bodies only impacted by nonpoint sources of pollution from any regulation under the CWA.

PRONSOLINO V. NASTRI

United States Court of Appeals, Ninth Circuit, 2002.
291 F.3d 1123.

BERZON, CIRCUIT JUDGE.

[In 1998 the Pronsolinos and two other private landowners in the Garcia River watershed applied for timber harvesting permits from the California Department of Forestry (Forestry). Although there were no point sources of pollution along the stretch of the Garcia River near the planned logging, the EPA had set a TMDL for sediment that was 60% below historical loadings after entering a consent decree with environmental and fishermen's groups in earlier litigation. As a result, Forestry and the state's Regional Water Quality Control Board required the applicant landowners to incorporate mitigation measures in their logging permits to meet the Garcia River TMDL. The estimated combined loss of profits due to the mitigation measures was $12,314,000. The landowners challenged the EPA's authority under § 309(d) of the CWA to impose TMDLs on bodies of water polluted only by nonpoint sources. The District Court held for the EPA on a motion for summary judgment, and the Pronsolinos appealed.]

The United States Environmental Protection Agency ("EPA") required California to identify the Garcia River as a water body with insufficient pollution controls and, as required for waters so identified, to set so-called "total maximum daily loads" ("TMDLs")—the significance of which we explain later—for pollution entering the river. Appellants challenge the EPA's authority under the Clean Water Act ("CWA" or the "Act") § 303(d), to apply the pertinent identification and TMDL requirements to the Garcia River. The district court rejected this challenge, and we do as well.

CWA 303(d) requires the states to identify and compile a list of waters for which certain effluent limitations are not stringent enough to implement the applicable water quality standards for such waters. § 303(d)(1)(A). Effluent limitations pertain only to point sources of pollution; point sources of pollution are those from a discrete conveyance, such as a pipe or tunnel. Nonpoint sources of pollution are non-discrete sources; sediment run-off from timber harvesting, for example, derives from a nonpoint source. The Garcia River is polluted only by nonpoint sources. Therefore, neither the effluent limitations referenced in § 303(d) nor any other effluent limitations apply to the pollutants entering the Garcia River.

The precise statutory question before us is whether the phrase "are not stringent enough" triggers the identification requirement both for waters as to which effluent limitations apply [because there are point sources polluting them] but do not suffice to attain water quality standards and for waters as to which effluent limitations do not apply at all to the pollution sources impairing the water [because only nonpoint sources are polluting such waters]. We answer this question in the affirmative, a conclusion which triggers the application of the statutory TMDL requirement to waters such as the Garcia River. * * *

A.   The Major Goals and Concepts of the CWA

* * *

[The] CWA uses distinctly different methods to control pollution released from point sources and those that are traceable to nonpoint sources. The Act directly mandates technological controls to limit the pollution point sources may discharge into a body of water. On the other hand, the Act "provides no direct mechanism to control nonpoint source pollution but rather uses the 'threat and promise' of federal grants to the states to accomplish this task," (citations omitted), thereby "recognizing, preserving, and protecting the primary responsibilities and rights of States to prevent, reduce, and eliminate pollution, [and] to plan the development and use . . . of land and water resources. . . ." § 101(b).

B.   The Structure of CWA 303

1.   *Water Quality Standards*

Section 303 is central to the Act's carrot-and-stick approach to attaining acceptable water quality without direct federal regulation of nonpoint sources of pollution. Entitled Water Quality Standards and Implementation Plans, the provision begins by spelling out the statutory requirements for water quality standards: "Water quality standards" specify a water body's "designated uses" and "water quality criteria," taking into account the water's "use and value for public water supplies, propagation of fish and wildlife, recreational purposes, and agricultural, industrial, and other purposes. . . ." § 303(c)(2). The states are required to set water quality standards for *all* waters within their boundaries regardless of the sources of the pollution entering the waters. If a state does not set water quality standards, or the EPA determines that the state's standards do not meet the requirements of the Act, the EPA promulgates standards for the state. §§ 303(b), (c)(3)–(4).

2.   *Section 303(d): "Identification of Areas with Insufficient Controls; Maximum Daily Load"*

Section 303(d)(1)(A) requires each state to identify as "areas with insufficient controls" "those waters within its boundaries for which the effluent limitations required by section [301(b)(1)(A)] and section [301(b)(1)(B)] of this title are not stringent enough to implement any water quality standard applicable to such waters." *Id.* The CWA defines "effluent limitations" as restrictions on pollutants "discharged from point sources."

CWA § 502(11). Section 301(b)(1)(A) mandates application of the "best practicable control technology" effluent limitations for most point source discharges. * * *

For waters identified pursuant to § 303(d)(1)(A) (the § 303(d)(1) list), the states must establish the "total maximum daily load" ("TMDL") for pollutants identified by the EPA as suitable for TMDL calculation. § 303(d)(1)(C). "A TMDL defines the specified maximum amount of a pollutant which can be discharged or 'loaded' into the waters at issue from all combined sources." *Dioxin/Organochlorine Center v. Clarke*, 57 F.3d 1517, 1520 (9th Cir. 1995) The TMDL "shall be established at a level necessary to implement the applicable water quality standards. . . ." § 303(d)(1)(C).

Section 303(d)(2), in turn, requires each state to submit its § 303(d)(1) list and TMDLs to the EPA for its approval or disapproval. If the EPA approves the list and TMDLs, the state must incorporate the list and TMDLs into its continuing process, the requirements for which are set forth in § 303(e). § 303(d)(2). If the EPA disapproves either the § 303(d)(1) list or any TMDLs, the EPA must itself put together the missing document or documents. *Id*. The state then incorporates any EPA-set list or TMDL into the states continuing planning process. *Id*.

Each state must also identify all waters *not* placed on its § 303(d)(1) list (the "§ 303(d)(3) list") and "estimate" TMDLs for pollutants in those waters. § 303(d)(3). There is no requirement that the EPA approve the § 303(d)(3) lists or the TMDLs estimated for those waters. *Id*.

3. Continuing Planning Process

The final pertinent section of § 303, § 303(e), requiring each state to have a continuing planning process, gives some operational force to the prior information-gathering provisions. The EPA may approve a state's continuing planning process only if it "will result in plans for all navigable waters within such State" that include, inter alia, effluent limitations, TMDLs, areawide waste management plans for nonpoint sources of pollution, and plans for "adequate implementation, including schedules of compliance, for revised or new water quality standards." § 303(e)(3).

The upshot of this intricate scheme is that the CWA leaves to the states the responsibility of developing plans to achieve water quality standards if the statutorily-mandated point source controls will not alone suffice, while providing federal funding to aid in the implementation of the state plans. TMDLs are primarily informational tools that allow the states to proceed from the identification of waters requiring additional planning to the required plans. As such, TMDLs serve as a link in an implementation chain that includes federally-regulated point source controls, state or local plans for point and nonpoint source pollution reduction, and assessment of the impact of such measures on water quality, all to the end of attaining water quality goals for the nation's waters.

III. ANALYSIS

* * *

The EPA regulations pertinent to § 303(d)(1) lists and TMDLs focus on the attainment of water quality standards, whatever the source of any pollution. For instance, the EPA's regulations define TMDLs as the "sum of the individual WLAs [wasteload allocations] for point sources and LAs [load allocations] for nonpoint sources and natural background." 40 C.F.R. § 130.2(i). Section 130.2 also defines a "wasteload allocation" as the "portion of a receiving water's loading capacity that is allocated to one of its existing or future point sources of pollution," § 130.2(h), and a "load allocation" as the "portion of a receiving water's loading capacity that is attributed either to one of its existing or future nonpoint sources of pollution or to natural background sources," § 130.2(g). The load allocation regulation also advises that, if possible, "natural and nonpoint source loads should be distinguished." *Id*. No reason appears why, under this TMDL definition, the amount of either point source loads or nonpoint source loads cannot be zero. If the wasteload allocation is zero, then the TMDL would cover only the nonpoint sources and natural background sources. So read, the regulation provides that a TMDL can apply where there is no wasteload allocation for point source pollution.

Section 130.7 evinces the same understanding. That regulation directs states to identify those waters listed pursuant to § 303(d)(1) that still require the establishment of TMDLs if:

(i)   Technology-based effluent limitations required by sections 301(b), 306, 307, or other sections of the Act;

(ii)   More stringent effluent limitations (including prohibitions) required . . . and

(iii)   Other pollution control requirements (e.g., best management practices) required by local, States, or Federal authority are not stringent enough to implement any water quality standards . . . applicable to such waters.

§ 130.7(b)(1). "Best management practices" pertain to nonpoint sources of pollution. CWA § 208; CWA § 319. So, again, section 130.7 does not distinguish between sources of pollution for purposes of applying the TMDL requirement. Instead, control requirements applicable to either type of pollution receive equal treatment in the quest to achieve water quality standards.

Also consistent with application of the § 303(d)(1) listing and TMDL requirements to waters impaired only by nonpoint sources is the regulation addressing water quality standards. Section 130.3 explains that "such standards serve the dual purposes of establishing the water quality goals for a specific water body and serving as the regulatory basis for establishment of water quality-based treatment controls and strategies beyond the technology-based level of treatment required. . . ." 40 C.F.R. § 130.3. One purpose of water quality standards therefore—and not surprisingly—is to provide federally-approved goals to be achieved *both* by state controls and by federal strategies *other* than point-source technology-based limitations. This purpose pertains to waters impaired by both point and nonpoint source pollution. The regulations addressing states' water quality management plans, intended to attain the promulgated water quality standards, confirm this understanding. Such plans must include, among other things, TMDLs, effluent limitations, and "*nonpoint* source management and control." 40 C.F.R. § 130.6 (emphasis added).

In short, the EPA's regulations concerning § 303(d)(1) lists and TMDLs apply whether a water body receives pollution from point sources only, nonpoint sources only, or a combination of the two. The EPA has issued directives concerning the states' CWA § 303(d) requirements in conformity with this understanding of its regulations. * * * In light of the current regulations and the agency's understanding of those regulations, as well as the delegated authority of the EPA to interpret the CWA, the EPA's interpretation is entitled to *Chevron* deference. * * *

In short, Congress entrusted to the EPA the responsibility of approving or disapproving § 303(d)(1) lists, bestowing upon it the discretion that comes with such responsibility; the EPA has specialized experience regarding the CWA which this court lacks; and the agency has consistently interpreted the provisions at issue.

B. Plain Meaning and Structural Issues

1. *The Competing Interpretations*

Section 303(d)(1)(A) requires listing and calculation of TMDLs for "those waters within [the states] boundaries for which the effluent limitations required by section [301(b)(1)(A)] and section [301(b)(1)(B)] of this title *are not stringent enough to implement any water quality standard* applicable to such waters." § 303(d) (emphasis added). The precise statutory question before us is whether, as the Pronsolinos maintain, the term "not stringent enough to implement . . . water quality standards" as used in § 303(d)(1)(A) must be interpreted to mean *both* that application of effluent limitations will not achieve water quality standards *and* that the waters at issue are subject to effluent limitations. As only waters with point source pollution are subject to effluent limitations, such an interpretation would exclude from the § 303(d) listing and TMDL requirements waters impaired only by nonpoint sources of pollution.

The EPA, as noted, interprets "not stringent enough to implement . . . water quality standards" to mean "not adequate" or "not sufficient . . . to implement any water quality standard," and does not read the statute as implicitly containing a limitation to waters initially covered by effluent limitations. According to the EPA, if the use of effluent limitations will not implement applicable water quality standards, the water falls within § 303(d)(1)(A) regardless of whether it is point or nonpoint sources, or a combination of the two, that continue to pollute the water.

2. The Language and Structure of § 303(d)

Whether or not the appellants' suggested interpretation is entirely implausible, it is at least considerably weaker than the EPA's competing construction. The Pronsolinos' version necessarily relies upon: (1) understanding "stringent enough" to mean "strict enough" rather than "thoroughgoing enough" or "adequate" or "sufficient"; (2) reading the phrase "not stringent enough" in isolation, rather than with reference to the stated goal of implementing "any water quality standard applicable to such waters." Where the answer to the question "not stringent enough for what?" is "to implement any [applicable] water quality standard," the meaning of "stringent" should be determined by looking forward to the broad goal to be attained, not backwards at the inadequate effluent limitations. * * * Based on the language of the contested phrase alone, then, the more sensible conclusion is that the § 303(d)(1) list must contain any waters for which the particular effluent limitations will not be adequate to attain the statute's water quality goals. * * *

3. The Statutory Scheme as a Whole

The Pronsolinos' objection to this view of § 303(d), and of *Dioxin*, is, in essence, that the CWA as a whole distinguishes between the regulatory schemes applicable to point and nonpoint sources, so we must assume such a distinction in applying §§ 303(d)(1)(A) and (C). We would hesitate in any case to read into a discrete statutory provision something that is not there because it is contained elsewhere in the statute. But here, the premise is wrong: There is no such general division throughout the CWA.

Point sources are treated differently from nonpoint sources for many purposes under the statute, but not all. In particular, there is no such distinction with regard to the basic purpose for which the § 303(d) list and TMDLs are compiled, the eventual attainment of state-defined water quality standards. * * *

True, there are, as the Pronsolinos point out, two sections of the statute as amended, § 208 and § 319, that set requirements exclusively for nonpoint sources of pollution. But the structural inference we are asked to draw from those specialized sections—that no *other* provisions of the Act set requirements for waters polluted by nonpoint sources—simply does not follow. Absent some irreconcilable contradiction between the requirements contained in §§ 208 and 319, on the one hand, and the listing and TMDL requirements of § 303(d), on the other, both apply.

There is no such contradiction. Section 208 provides for federal grants to encourage the development of state areawide waste treatment management plans for areas with substantial water quality problems, §§ 208(a), (f), and requires that those plans include a process for identifying and controlling nonpoint source pollution "to the extent feasible" § 208(b)(2)(F). Section 319, added to the CWA in 1987, directs states to adopt "nonpoint source management programs;" provides grants for nonpoint source pollution reduction; and requires states to submit a report to the EPA that "identifies those navigable waters within the State which, without additional action to control nonpoint sources of pollution, cannot reasonably be expected to attain or maintain applicable water quality standards or the goals and requirements of this chapter." § 319(a)(1)(A). This report must also describe state programs for reducing nonpoint source pollution and the process "to reduce, to the maximum extent practicable, the level of pollution" resulting from particular categories of nonpoint source pollution. §§ 319(a)(1)(C), (D).

The CWA is replete with multiple listing and planning requirements applicable to the same waterways (quite confusingly so, indeed), so no inference can be drawn from the overlap alone. * * *

Essentially § 319 encourages the states to institute an approach to the elimination of nonpoint source pollution similar to the federally-mandated effluent controls contained in the CWA, while § 303 encompasses a water quality based approach applicable to all sources of water pollution. As various sections of the Act encourage different, and complementary, state schemes for cleaning up nonpoint source pollution in the nation's waterways, there is no basis for reading any of those sections—including § 303(d)—out of the statute. * * *

Looking at the statute as a whole, we conclude that the EPA's interpretation of § 303(d) is not only entirely reasonable but considerably more convincing than the one offered by the plaintiffs in this case.

C.   Federalism Concerns

The Pronsolinos finally contend that, by establishing TMDLs for waters impaired only by nonpoint source pollution, the EPA has upset the balance of federal-state control established in the CWA by intruding into the state's traditional control over land use. * * * The Garcia River TMDL identifies the maximum load of pollutants that can enter the Garcia River from certain broad categories of nonpoint sources if the river is to attain water quality standards. It does not specify the load of pollutants that may be received from particular parcels of land or describe what measures the state should take to implement the TMDL. Instead, the TMDL expressly recognizes that "implementation and monitoring" "are state responsibilities" and notes that, for this reason, the EPA did not include implementation or monitoring plans within the TMDL. Moreover, § 303(e) requires—separately from the § 303(d)(1) listing and TMDL requirements—that each state include in its continuing planning process "adequate implementation, including schedules of compliance, for revised or new water quality standards" "for all navigable waters within such State." § 303(e)(3). The Garcia River TMDL thus serves as an informational tool for the creation of the state's implementation plan, independently—and explicitly—required by Congress.

California chose both *if* and *how* it would implement the Garcia River TMDL. States must implement TMDLs only to the extent that they seek to avoid losing federal grant money; there is no pertinent statutory provision otherwise requiring implementation of § 303 plans or providing for their enforcement. * * *

We conclude that the Pronsolinos' federalism basis for reading § 303 against its own words and structure is unfounded.

IV. CONCLUSION

* * * We therefore hold that the EPA did not exceed its statutory authority in identifying the Garcia River pursuant to § 303(d)(1)(A) and establishing the Garcia River TMDL, even though the river is polluted only by nonpoint sources of pollution.

The decision of the district court is AFFIRMED.

The lawsuits that triggered the use of TMDLs—despite the fact that the TMDL process was included in the original 1972 amendments—set off a firestorm within EPA and among industry and trade groups potentially affected by them. Oliver Houck describes what happened.

OLIVER A. HOUCK, THE CLEAN WATER ACT TMDL PROGRAM V: AFTERSHOCK AND PRELUDE
32 ENVTL. L. REP. 10385 (2002).[1]

* * *

I.   The Showdown

The year 2000 saw a dramatic showdown between Congress and the executive branch over TMDLs. In retrospect, it was unavoidable. * * *

The showdown concerned EPA's first ever, comprehensive regulations for the TMDL program. The Agency and the states had been operating

---

[1]   Copyright © The Environmental Law Institute, 2002. Reprinted by permission. Oliver A. Houck is a Professor of Law at Tulane University.

under skeletal regulations originating in 1978 that repeated requirements of the statute but provided little additional guidance. As written earlier, the stage was set for underperformance, and underperformance happened.

Shocked into motion by citizen suits in the early 1990s, EPA struggled to get ahead of district court mandates with a flurry of TMDL guidance to the states that fleshed out preliminary requirements for impaired water listings and for the contents and schedules for TMDLs themselves. At the same time EPA convened a Federal Advisory Committee Act (FACA) committee with representation from state water agencies, agribusiness, timber, industrial point sources, municipal sources, environmentalists, Native Americans, academics, and, ex officio, EPA and the U.S. Department of Agriculture (USDA). Its mission was to forge a consensus on program regulations.

Consensus was not in the cards. At bottom, the timber and agriculture industries were not going to accept that CWA § 303(d) covered nonpoint sources or that, if it did, it required implementation plans. To these industries, the CWA's only lawful vehicle to abate their discharges was the voluntary, grant-in-aid program under § 319. TMDLs smacked of first ever regulation, a *causa belli.* * * *

EPA, for its part, could not let the issue slide. Environmental lawsuits were setting its agenda, case by case, state by state, with differing and at times highly demanding schedules for impaired waters listings and TMDLs. The Agency and the states were making decisions on the basis of guidance memoranda that had never been subjected to notice-and-comment rulemaking under the Administrative Procedure Act (APA) and that carried no force of law.

In July 1999, EPA proposed draft, comprehensive regulations for the TMDL program and launched a series of meetings, briefing sessions, and telethons in an attempt to calm the waters. This was to no avail. Most states and affected industries remained adamantly opposed. * * * [T]he Agency softened other aspects of its proposal, clarified that TMDL implementation plans could be satisfied through "voluntary means and education," lengthened the deadlines for TMDL submissions, and hoped for the best.

The rulemaking took a year. More than 34,000 comments were received, which, even discounting mass-mailings from industry trade associations, indicated no small controversy. At the same time, with little confidence in the administrative process, states and nonpoint industries turned up the heat and took their case to a very receptive Congress. Congressional committees held field hearings stocked with farmers and small woodlot owners afraid, and told, that EPA was going to require permits for the use of their land. Committees held hearings on Capitol Hill in which their mistrust of EPA was so marked that one took the unprecedented step of insisting that Agency witnesses provide their testimony under oath. Committee members accused EPA of "secret meetings" with environmentalists. Learning that an Undersecretary of Agriculture had cooperated with EPA in developing a timetable for nonpoint source TMDLs, a representative from Arkansas inserted a budget rider in the agriculture appropriations bill removing the Undersecretary from authority in the matter. The legislation passed.

By April 2000, battered by the House and Senate, EPA began adding concessions to its most vocal opponents. It would drop its proposal to include "threatened waters" in TMDLs despite its belief that attending to these waters early would save time and money later on. It would drop a requirement that gave waters used for human consumption and for endangered species priority attention despite its belief that these priorities were required by law. It would drop a process allowing the public to petition for review of TMDL decisions despite its belief that administrative review was preferable to litigation. It would promise flat out that forestry practices would not be subject to national pollutant discharge elimination system (NPDES) permitting "under any circumstances." And at seven congressional hearings, as if the white flag on these issues were not fully visible, the Agency stressed that it was trying to enhance flexibility and leave TMDL implementation to the states.

Too much flexibility, for some parties. Following publication of the proposed rules in 1999 and continuing into the early months of 2000, several environmental groups, including lead TMDL litigating groups, became disenchanted with EPA's concessions. They saw in the proposals a recipe for endless delay, well beyond the deadlines they were establishing through citizen suits. They also saw little assurance in implementation programs based on voluntary measures and education. On another side, however, were environmental groups that, having litigated over lists and TMDL schedules, were now engaged in their states on implementation issues. In their view, without regulations setting implementation standards, the rest of the TMDL process—listings, schedules of submissions etc.—even on accelerated schedules, led to no productive end. The environmental community split, some seeing the doughnut, others the hole.

In May 2000, the split broke open when six national environmental organizations wrote the EPA Administrator calling on her to scrap the regulations and go back to the drawing board. The letter could not have caught the Agency at a more vulnerable moment. Already under attack from the states, industry, and Congress, EPA was left without a single, unified constituency, while its opponents gained the argument that here was a rule that nobody liked.[34] * * *

* * * Congress hosted a competition of bills seeking to derail EPA's regulations. The lead vehicle, Senate Bill 2417, labeled with no apparent irony the "Water Pollution Program Enhancements Act of 2000," characterized the regulations as "hasty," "unscientific," "one-size-fits-all," and "unlikely to improve water quality." It would put the EPA program on hold pending studies on its supporting science and on the effectiveness of alternative, voluntary programs and their costs. Other bills would simply repeal the TMDL rules in full or exempt particular industries, e.g., forestry, from their scope.

Meanwhile, the Administration * * * began a race to beat the clock. Passing whatever bill Congress chose would take time. EPA accelerated its regulations review.

Outraged, now, by what appeared to be a stiff-arm of its concerns and an end-run on its authority, Congress looked for another vehicle to block the Administration. They found it in the Fiscal Year (FY) 2001 Military Constructions/FY 2000 Urgent Supplemental Appropriations Bill, an obscure funding bill that in neither House contained any mention of TMDLs. Overnight and without notice, Congress tacked on a provision that no funds would be used in FY 2000 or 2001 to "make a final determination on or implement any new rule relative" to EPA's regulations. It further mandated a study of the program by the National Academy of Sciences (NAS) to determine the adequacy of the scientific basis for the TMDL program. Among other things, the study would delay the program; even better, the study might derail it.

As appropriations for expenditures that were unavoidable and in some cases already expended, the supplemental appropriations bill was must-sign legislation. It was also, in a decade marked by environmental-legislation-by-appropriations-rider, a high watermark for this political art.[45] President William J. Clinton appeared check-mated; in order to cover, inter alia, monies spent for hurricane relief in Nicaragua, he would have to sign away the TMDL rule. A small window of opportunity remained, however, a gap of several days before which, with or without the president's signature, the bill would become law. The EPA Administrator signed off on the regulations on July 11. The final rule was published on July 13. The

---

[34] Sen. Max Baucus (D-Mont.), for example, vowing to "reverse the [TMDL] decision at the earliest opportunity," characterized the rules as "roundly criticized by states, environmental groups, business organizations, and agricultural interests."

[45] For a discussion of the use and abuse of appropriations riders, *see* Sandra A. Zellmer, *Sacrificing Legislative Integrity at the Altar of Appropriations Riders: A Constitutional Crisis*, 21 HARV. L. REV. 457 (1998). In this case, President William J. Clinton complimented Congress for dropping "several anti-environmental riders," without mention of its rider blocking the TMDL rule—which he knew he could finalize before he signed the rider. *See* H.R. 4425. Such is the language of politics. * * *

same day, the last available, President Clinton signed the appropriations bill prohibiting half of what his Administration had just done.

In the final regulations, EPA acknowledged the appropriations rider by delaying their effect until October 31, 2001, or until the expiration of the rider, whichever came first. As a practical matter, with a ban on funding program implementation, it would be delayed until whichever came second. In the meantime, EPA's skeletal regulations from the 1980s and subsequent guidance would remain in effect. The program would continue under the old rules. Environmentalists left the field bloodied but relieved that the TMDL program had not been repealed. The agriculture and timber industries left triumphant but insecure in their victory. The threat of TMDL-imposed requirements on nonpoint sources had been parried but it had not been eliminated.

II. The Aftermath

* * * The nonpoint source pollution that has swamped the nation's waters has many and diverse sources, but the lion's share are agricultural: crops and animals. More than 50% of water impairment nationally comes from agricultural runoff. In some western states dominated by cattle, the number reaches 90%. More than 80% of the eutrophication of the Gulf of Mexico dead zone is attributable to farm loadings over 500 river miles away. * * *

Agriculture is one of the largest industries in the United States, with a total production value of near $200 billion. Its principal field crops are corn, soybeans, hay, and wheat; it also produces on an annual basis 98 million cattle, 366 million egg-laying chickens, 6.75 billion meat chickens, and 61 million hogs. It spends $18 billion on agricultural chemicals a year, more than twice what it spends on gasoline and electricity. Its payroll reaches $16.9 billion in farm and contract employees. Its larger operations are industrial, look industrial, and are managed as any national or multinational corporation. * * *

With even this rudimentary understanding of the industry, the exemption of American agriculture from the CWA is either gross negligence or irresistible politics. Whichever, few of the reasons that have been given for exempting farm sources from the NPDES program obtain today. Far from being trivial, they are mammoth. Far from being site-specific and local, their impacts are multi-state, regional, and even international. Far from being without available control technologies, the control strategies for nonpoint source pollution, e.g., shelterbelts, cover crops, and cattle fences, are orders of magnitude less complex and less costly than other industry controls. To be sure, farms are diverse, but they are no more diverse by crop and production method than the many categories and subcategories of the pulp and paper industry, petrochemicals, metals, rubber, and other industries subject to the NPDES program. Nor is it a persuasive distinction that farm runoff does not emerge from a pipe. Construction, municipal, feedlot, and acid mine drainage do not emerge from pipes either. They all arise from identifiable technologies and practices. They all pollute. They should all share the burden of cleanup and this burden in America begins with adopting BAT. There is something wrong with a picture that regulates the discharges of small Pacific Coast canning factories while Boise Cascade, U.S. Sugar, and Archer Daniels Midland walk free. * * *

NOTES

1.   Houck's article on the future of the proposed TMDL program is, to put it mildly, not optimistic. He notes that the rule's effective date has been postponed several times by a hostile legislature. In 2003, the EPA withdrew the proposed rule. 68 Fed. Reg. 13607–614 (2003). The agency claimed that the National Academy of Sciences' National Research Council had suggested numerous improvements to the "new" rules that were not reflected in the July 2000 rules. If these are grounds to abandon regulations, could the EPA *ever* issue new rules? Notwithstanding the withdrawal of the rule, as of 2012 there were 40,000 TMDLs in existence. See Congressional Research Service, *Clean Water Act and Pollutant Total Maximum Daily Loads (TMDLs)* (Sept, 2012) at 9.

2.   Clearly, for the foreseeable future, the TMDL process is going to be where the action is under the CWA. As an exercise, put yourself in the position of: a) a member of Congress from a farm state; b) a state regulator in a state with both farming and heavy industry; c) a member of a national environmental organization and d) President of an agricultural trade association. From each of these perspectives, try to propose a TMDL action plan. Is there any alternative to the TMDL approach if we wish to address the lingering water pollution problems caused by unregulated sources? Specifically regarding the impacts of agriculture on the environment, *see* J.B. Ruhl, *Farms, Their Environmental Harms, and Environmental Law*, 27 ECOLOGY L.Q. 263 (2000). For an account of TMDL litigation, *see* James R. May, *The Rise and Repose of Assimilation-Based Water Quality: Part I: TMDL Litigation*, 34 Envt'l. L. Rep 10247 (2004).

j.   Area Planning for Non-Point Source Pollutants

The permits (and related effluent limitations and water quality requirements) that we have considered so far are required only for point sources. Yet most estimates suggest that nonpoint sources—particularly from agriculture—contribute a significant percentage of pollutants, including toxic pollutants, to the nation's waterways. And these pollutants are contributing to the failure of water bodies to meet WQS. The most recent National Water Quality Inventory Report to Congress, issued in 2017, concludes that "states identified a wide range of assessed waters as not fully supporting at least one of their designated uses * * * Mercury (primarily in fish tissue), pathogens, nutrients, PCBs, sediment, and organic enrichment/oxygen depletion were all cited as leading causes of impairment in assessed waters. Leading known sources included atmospheric deposition and agricultural activities." U.S. EPA, *National Water Quality Inventory, Report to Congress* (2017) at 2. The report contains survey results from a number of national surveys, concluding that 46 percent of the nation's river and stream length is in poor condition, 21 percent of the nation's lakes have excessive levels of nutrients, algae and plants; 18 percent of coastal waters and the Great Lakes are in poor biological condition with 14 percent with poor water quality; and 32 percent of wetlands are in poor shape. *Id* at 2.

As we described above, some of the sources one might consider to be non-point source pollution are now subject to the storm water provisions contained in Section 402 (p). Many other sources, particularly in non-urban areas, are not, however, well regulated. What is to be done about the failure of a substantial number of the nation's water bodies to meet WQS? The most significant remaining gap in the Act is the lack of regulation of runoff from agricultural water pollutants. The Act does provide in § 208 for the adoption of "areawide waste management plans" which may include controls on nonpoint sources, but these plans are unenforceable: the EPA cannot develop and implement a § 208 plan if the state fails to do so, or if the state plan is inadequate. See Jan G. Laitos & Heidi Ruckriegle, *the Clean Water Act and the Challenge of Agricultural Pollution*, 37 VERMONT L. REV 1033 (2013) for a good overview of the agricultural exemption and the limitations on pollutants from the agricultural sector. Historically, local governments have been especially resistant to area planning, which was a condition of federal grants for POTW construction:

> * * * Any community that strenuously objected to a section 208 areawide plan could delay POTW construction for years through recourse to judicial review and political lobbying, which would impede the statutory and EPA goal of achieving rapid water pollution control progress. If EPA found areawide or state plans inadequate, its only enforcement sanction was to withhold federal grants, which would delay pollution control progress and would not penalize the communities that resisted construction of large-scale POTWs.

Howard Latin, *Regulatory Failure, Administrative Incentives, and the New Clean Air Act*, 21 ENVTL. L. 1647, 1656 (1991). States are also required to put in place a "continuing planning process" as one requirement for obtaining approval of their permit programs under § 402, but the EPA has been reluctant to enforce regulation of nonpoint sources as a condition of approving state programs.

The 1987 Amendments to the CWA included a new attempt to regulate nonpoint source pollution in § 319, which requires states to identify waters that fail to achieve WQS because of nonpoint sources, and to develop comprehensive management plans, subject to EPA approval. These plans must include a process for identifying "best management practices" and other controls to reduce nonpoint source pollution. The EPA has no authority to prepare and implement nonpoint source controls, however, if the state's program is inadequate, or if the state refuses to produce a plan. *See* Jocelyn B. Garovoy, *"A Breathtaking Assertion of Power?" Not Quite. Pronsolino and the Still Limited Role of Federal Regulation of Nonpoint Source Pollution*, 30 ECOLOGY L Q 543 (2003).

This non-point source provision was part of the motivation for President Reagan's unsuccessful veto attempt on January 30, 1987:

> This new program threatens to become the ultimate whip hand for Federal regulators. For example, in participating States, if farmers have more run-off from their land than the Environmental Protection Agency decides is right, the Agency will be able to intrude into decisions such as how and where the farmers must plow their fields, what fertilizers they must use, and what kind of cover crops they must plant. To take another example, the Agency will be able to become a major force in local zoning decisions that will determine whether families can do such basic things as build a new home. That is too much power for anyone to have, least of all the Federal Government.

> * * * Let me repeat—controlling nonpoint source pollution has the potential to touch, in the most intimate ways, practically all of us as citizens, whether farmers, business people, or homeowners. I do not believe State programs should be subject to Federal control.

Contrary to President Reagan's dire prediction, however, § 319 has been said to have "not enough carrot, not enough stick, and too much of the same planning imperatives that characterized § 208." David Zaring, *Federal Legislative Solutions to Agricultural Nonpoint Source Pollution*, 26 ENVTL. L. REP. 10128, 10132 (1996). Section 319 seems to have "added little in the way of rigor to the Act's nonpoint source controls." Robert W. Adler, *Controlling Nonpoint Source Water Pollution: Is Help on the Way (From the Courts or EPA)?*, 31 ENVTL. L. REP. 10271 (2001). States may provide incentives to nonpoint sources to encourage the adoption of BMPs, but nothing in the statute makes the management plans enforceable against nonpoint sources themselves. The statute authorizes the EPA to provide technical and financial assistance to states to help with the development and implementation of management plans, with federal funds not to exceed 60 per cent of the costs of implementation. § 319(h)(3). Grants are also limited so that no one state can receive more than 15% of the total appropriated for this purpose. § 319(h)(4). Given the massive undertaking any state faces if it chooses to regulate nonpoint sources like agriculture, ranching, mining or forestry, the extent of federal support appears to be vanishingly small. Thus the section's reporting and planning mandate imposed on states by § 319 may prompt states to consider where the nonpoint source problems lie and how to address the nonpoint source problems through BMP plans, but it offers no penalties and very weak financial incentives to motivate meaningful state action. Either the states will undertake to regulate nonpoint sources on their own initiative or they won't, and there appears to be nothing the EPA can do but to cheer on the ambitious and chide the apathetic.

2. DEVELOPMENT RESTRICTIONS ON PRIVATE WETLANDS

Wetlands were once considered worthless swamps. Today, however, they are understood to have many valuable characteristics:

> Variously dry, wet, or anywhere between, wetlands are by their nature protean. Such constant change makes wetlands ecologically rich; they are often as diverse as rain forests. These shallow water-fed systems are central to the life cycle of many plants and animals, some of them endangered. They provide a habitat as well as spawning grounds for an extraordinary variety of creatures and nesting areas for migratory birds. Some wetlands even perform a global function. The northern peat lands of Canada, Alaska and Eurasia, in particular, may help moderate climatic change by serving as a sink for the greenhouse gas carbon dioxide.

> Wetlands also have commercial and utilitarian functions. They are sources of lucrative harvests of wild rice, fur-bearing animals, fish and shellfish. Wetlands limit the damaging effects of waves, convey and store floodwaters, trap sediment and reduce pollution—the last attribute has earned them the sobriquet "nature's kidneys."

Jon A. Kusler, et al., *Wetlands,* SCI. AM., Jan. 1994, at 64B. As a result of this shift in awareness, governmental policy has shifted from encouragement of draining and filling wetlands to support for preservation and restricted development. The federal government has taken the lead in protecting wetlands.

The catastrophic hurricane season in Louisiana and Mississippi in 2005 brought renewed attention to the importance of wetlands in protecting areas from flooding. For an interesting account of the history of flood planning and wetlands destruction *see* Oliver Houck, *Can We Save New Orleans?*, 19 TULANE ENVTL. L.J. 1 (2006).

Federal regulation of dredging and filling activities dates back to the Rivers and Harbors Appropriation Act of 1899. Section 13 of the Act prohibits discharge of "any refuse" other than liquid sewage into navigable waters. 33 U.S.C.A. § 407. The Supreme Court later construed this as a ban on water pollution.[2] Section 10 of the Act prohibits the creation of "any obstruction" to navigation, without permission from Congress. 33 U.S.C.A. § 403. At least since the passage of NEPA, issuance of a permit must be based on consideration of a broad range of environmental factors.

The permit program is now part of the Clean Water Act. Section 404 of the Clean Water Act establishes a separate permit system for discharges of dredged or fill materials into navigable waters. (Note that this covers discharges.) Unlike the rest of the Clean Water Act, however, the Army Corps of Engineers is the agency responsible for issuing Section 404 permits with guidance from the EPA. In *Coeur Alaska v. Southeast Alaska Conservation Council*, 129 S.Ct. 2458 (2009), the Supreme Court upheld a decision by the Army Corps and the EPA to classify slurry material from a gold mine as "dredge and fill" rather than as a discharge subject to Section 402 jurisdiction and to new source performance standards. What about draining? *See* United States v. Mango, 997 F.Supp. 264 (N.D.N.Y. 1998) (not covered). Courts have been vigorous in remedying violations of these provisions, even issuing orders for restoration of areas to their natural states. For a detailed overview of federal wetlands regulation, *see* Margaret N. Strand, *Federal Wetlands Law: Part I*, 23 ENVTL. L. REP. 10,185 (1993); Margaret N. Strand, *Federal Wetlands Law: Part II*, 23 ENVTL. L. REP. 10284 (1993).

There has been considerable controversy about the Clean Water Act's coverage of wetlands. Under the Rivers and Harbors Act, wetlands were not covered. Traditionally, the jurisdiction of the Army Corps of Engineers only extended to navigable waters. But the Clean Water Act is much more expansive. United States v. Ashland Oil and Transportation Co., 504 F.2d 1317 (6th Cir. 1974), holds that the Clean Water Act extends to any waters flowing into any navigable stream.[3] The court's discussion of the constitutional issue is noteworthy:

> Obviously water pollution is a health threat to the water supply of the nation. It endangers our agriculture by rendering water unfit for irrigation. It can end the public use and enjoyment of our magnificent rivers and lakes for fishing, for boating, and for

---

[2]   United States v. Standard Oil Co., 384 U.S. 224 (1966); United States v. Pennsylvania Indus. Chem. Corp., 411 U.S. 655 (1973). Section 402(a)(5) of the Clean Water Act terminates the permit program administered by the Army Corps of Engineers in the wake of these decisions.

[3]   The expansion of federal jurisdiction under the Clean Water Act has raised problems concerning the treatment of minor, routine changes in water use. When a farmer digs a ditch which connects to an existing drainage system, must he get a federal permit? The 1977 amendments to the Act exempt a number of "normal farming, silviculture, and ranching activities" from the § 404 permit requirement for dredging and filling, as well as authorizing use of general permits for other activities. Section 404(e)(1), (f)(1). The general permits are not blanket exemptions, but instead contain numerous qualifications and restrictions. *See* United States v. Marathon Dev. Corp., 867 F.2d 96 (1st Cir. 1989). * * *

swimming. These health and welfare concerns are, of course, proper subjects for congressional attention because of their many impacts upon interstate commerce generally. But water pollution is also a direct threat to navigation—the first interstate commerce system in this country's history and still a very important one.

We also know (and we take judicial notice) that two of the important rivers of this circuit, the Rouge River in Dearborn, Michigan, and the Cuyahoga River in Cleveland, Ohio, reached a point of pollution by flammable materials in the last ten years that they repeatedly caught fire. Such pollution is an obvious hazard to navigation which Congress has every right to seek to abate under its interstate commerce powers.

It would, of course, make a mockery of those powers if its authority to control pollution was limited to the bed of the navigable stream itself. The tributaries which join to form the river could then be used as open sewers as far as federal regulation was concerned. The navigable part of the river could become a mere conduit for upstream waste.

Such a situation would have vast impact on interstate commerce. States with cities and industries situated upstream on the nonnavigable tributaries of our great rivers could freely use them for dumping raw sewage and noxious industrial wastes upon their downstream neighboring states. There would be great pressure upon the upstream states to allow such usage. Reduced industrial costs and lower taxes thus resulting would tend to place industries, cities and states located on navigable rivers at a considerable competitive disadvantage in interstate commerce. In such a situation industrial frontage on a creek which flowed ultimately into a navigable stream would become valuable as an access point to an effectively unrestricted sewer.

Given this broad interpretation of the Act's coverage, application of the CWA to at least some wetlands was inevitable. During the Reagan Administration, the Corps' expansive jurisdiction over wetlands became a matter of political controversy, causing the Corps to vacillate in its commitment. *See* Frances L. McChesney, Comment, *Corps Recasts § 404 Permit Program, Braces for Political, Legal Skirmishes*, 13 ENVTL. L. REP. 10 128 (1983). As the next case demonstrates, the controversy spilled over into the courts.

UNITED STATES V. RIVERSIDE BAYVIEW HOMES, INC.

Supreme Court of the United States, 1985.
474 U.S. 121, 106 S.Ct. 455, 88 L.Ed.2d 419.

[A regulation of the Army Corps defines "waters of the United States" to include "freshwater wetlands" that are adjacent to other waters that themselves are subject to the CWA. Wetlands, in turn, are defined to include "those areas that are inundated or saturated by surface or ground water at a frequency and duration sufficient to support, and that under normal circumstances do support, a prevalence of vegetation typically adapted for life in saturated soil conditions." After Riverside Bayview Homes began fill operations on its property near a lake, the Corps filed suit in federal court for an injunction. The Court of Appeals construed the regulation to apply only to wetlands that are flooded by adjacent navigable waters often enough to support aquatic vegetation. The court's rationale was that a broader definition might constitute a taking.]

JUSTICE WHITE delivered the opinion for a unanimous Court.

The question whether the Corps of Engineers may demand that respondent obtain a permit before placing fill material on its property is primarily one of regulatory and statutory interpretation: we must determine whether respondent's property is an "adjacent wetland" within the meaning of the applicable regulation, and, if so, whether the Corps' jurisdiction over "navigable waters" gives it statutory authority to regulate discharges of fill material into such a wetland. In this connection, we first consider the Court of Appeals' position that the Corps' regulatory authority under the statute and its implementing regulations must be narrowly construed to avoid a taking without just compensation in violation of the Fifth Amendment.

We have frequently suggested that governmental land-use regulation may under extreme circumstances amount to a "taking" of the affected property. We have never precisely defined those circumstances, but our general approach [is] that the application of land-use regulations to a particular piece of property is a taking only "if the ordinance does not substantially advance legitimate state interests * * * or denies an owner economically viable use of his land." Moreover, we have made it quite clear that the mere assertion of regulatory jurisdiction by a governmental body does not constitute a regulatory taking. The reasons are obvious. A requirement that a person obtain a permit before engaging in a certain use of his or her property does not itself "take" the property in any sense: after all, the very existence of a permit system implies that permission may be granted, leaving the landowner free to use the property as desired. Moreover, even if the permit is denied, there may be other viable uses available to the owner. Only when a permit is denied and the effect of the denial is to prevent "economically viable" use of the land in question can it be said that a taking has occurred.

If neither the imposition of the permit requirement itself nor the denial of a permit necessarily constitutes a taking, it follows that the Court of Appeals erred in concluding that a narrow reading of the Corps' regulatory jurisdiction over wetlands was "necessary" to avoid "a serious taking problem." We have held that, in general, "[e]quitable relief is not available to enjoin an alleged taking of private property for a public use, duly authorized by law, when a suit for compensation can be brought against the sovereign subsequent to a taking." This maxim rests on the principle that so long as compensation is available for those whose property is in fact taken, the governmental action is not unconstitutional. For precisely the same reason, the possibility that the application of a regulatory program may in some instances result in the taking of individual pieces of property is no justification for the use of narrowing constructions to curtail the program if compensation will in any event be available in those cases where a taking has occurred. * * *

Purged of its spurious constitutional overtones, the question whether the regulation at issue requires respondent to obtain a permit before filling its property is an easy one. The regulation extends the Corps' authority under § 404 to all wetlands adjacent to navigable or interstate waters and their tributaries. Wetlands, in turn, are defined as lands that are "inundated *or saturated* by surface *or ground water* at a frequency and duration sufficient to support, and that under normal circumstances do support, a prevalence of vegetation typically adapted for life in saturated soil conditions." The plain language of the regulation refutes the Court of Appeals' conclusion that inundation or "frequent flooding" by the adjacent body of water is a *sine qua non* of a wetland under the regulation. Indeed, the regulation could hardly state more clearly that saturation by either surface or ground water is sufficient to bring an area within the category of wetlands, provided that the saturation is sufficient to and does support wetland vegetation. * * *

On a purely linguistic level, it may appear unreasonable to classify "lands," wet or otherwise, as "waters." Such a simplistic response, however, does justice neither to the problem faced by the Corps in defining the scope of its authority under § 404(a) nor to the realities of the problem of water pollution that the Clean Water Act was intended to combat. In determining the limits of its power to regulate discharges under the Act, the Corps must necessarily choose some point at which water ends and land begins. Our common experience tells us that this is often no easy task: the transition from water to solid ground is not necessarily or even typically an abrupt one. Rather, between open waters and dry land may lie shallows, marshes, mudflats, swamps, bogs—in short, a huge array of areas that are not wholly

aquatic but nevertheless fall far short of being dry land. Where on this continuum to find the limit of "waters" is far from obvious.

Faced with such a problem of defining the bounds of its regulatory authority, an agency may appropriately look to the legislative history and underlying policies of its statutory grants of authority. Neither of these sources provides unambiguous guidance for the Corps in this case, but together they do support the reasonableness of the Corps' approach of defining adjacent wetlands as "waters" within the meaning of § 404(a). Section 404 originated as part of the Federal Water Pollution Control Act Amendments of 1972, which constituted a comprehensive legislative attempt "to restore and maintain the chemical, physical, and biological integrity of the Nation's waters." CWA § 101. This objective incorporated a broad, systemic view of the goal of maintaining and improving water quality: as the House Report on the legislation put it, "the word 'integrity' * * * refers to a condition in which the natural structure and function of ecosystems is maintained." Protection of aquatic ecosystems, Congress recognized, demanded broad federal authority to control pollution, for "[w]ater moves in hydrologic cycles and it is essential that discharge of pollutants be controlled at the source."

In keeping with these views, Congress chose to define the waters covered by the Act broadly. Although the Act prohibits discharges into "navigable waters," the Act's definition of "navigable waters" as "the waters of the United States" makes it clear that the term "navigable" as used in the Act is of limited import. In adopting this definition of "navigable waters," Congress evidently intended to repudiate limits that had been placed on federal regulation by earlier water pollution control statutes and to exercise its powers under the Commerce Clause to regulate at least some waters that would not be deemed "navigable" under the classical understanding of that term.

This holds true even for wetlands that are not the result of flooding or permeation by water having its source in adjacent bodies of open water. The Corps has concluded that wetlands may affect the water quality of adjacent lakes, rivers, and streams even when the waters of those bodies do not actually inundate the wetlands. For example, wetlands that are not flooded by adjacent waters may still tend to drain into those waters. In such circumstances, the Corps has concluded that wetlands may serve to filter and purify water draining into adjacent bodies of water, and to slow the flow of surface runoff into lakes, rivers, and streams and thus prevent flooding and erosion. In addition, adjacent wetlands may "serve significant natural biological functions, including food chain production, general habitat, and nesting, spawning, rearing and resting sites for aquatic * * * species." In short, the Corps has concluded that wetlands adjacent to lakes, rivers, streams, and other bodies of water may function as integral parts of the aquatic environment even when the moisture creating the wetlands does not find its source in the adjacent bodies of water. Again, we cannot say that the Corps' judgment on these matters is unreasonable, and we therefore conclude that a definition of "waters of the United States" encompassing all wetlands adjacent to other bodies of water over which the Corps has jurisdiction is a permissible interpretation of the Act. Because respondent's property is part of a wetland that actually abuts on a navigable waterway, respondent was required to have a permit in this case.[9]

NOTES

1.   For approving commentary on the main case, *see* Kenneth L. Rosenbaum, Comment, *The Supreme Court Endorses A Broad Reading of Corps Wetland Jurisdiction Under FWPCA section 404*, 16 ENVTL. L. REP. 10,008 (1986). *Riverside* led several lower courts to uphold broad claims of jurisdiction on behalf of the Corps. *See* United States v. Banks, 115 F.3d 916 (11th Cir. 1997) (finding that wetlands were "adjacent" despite half-mile gap and debatable hydrological connection); United States v. Pozsgai, 999 F.2d 719 (3d Cir. 1993) (finding that wetlands covered by CWA because adjacent to tributaries of navigable stream).

2.   Controversy over wetlands jurisdiction has continued unabated. The next case narrowed EPA jurisdiction over wetlands.

SOLID WASTE AGENCY OF NORTHERN COOK COUNTY [SWANCC] v. UNITED STATES ARMY CORPS OF ENGINEERS

Supreme Court of the United States, 2001.
531 U.S. 159, 121 S.Ct. 675, 148 L.Ed.2d 576.

CHIEF JUSTICE REHNQUIST delivered the opinion of the Court.

[SWANCC, a consortium of Chicago suburbs, acquired an abandoned gravel pit, now containing several small ponds. The question before the Court was whether it needed to obtain a permit from the Army Corps of Engineers before filling the site. Section 404(a) of the Clean Water Act (CWA), which is discussed in more detail in Chapter 8, grants the Corps authority to issue permits for the discharge of dredged or fill material into navigable waters. The term "navigable waters" is defined under the Act as

---

[9]   Of course, it may well be that not every adjacent wetland is of great importance to the environment of adjoining bodies of water. But the existence of such cases does not seriously undermine the Corps' decision to define all adjacent wetlands as "waters." If it is reasonable for the Corps to conclude that in the majority of cases, adjacent wetlands have significant effects on water quality and the aquatic ecosystem, its definition can stand. That the definition may include some wetlands that are not significantly intertwined with the ecosystem of adjacent waterways is of little moment, for where it appears that a wetland covered by the Corps' definition is in fact lacking in importance to the aquatic environment—or where its importance is outweighed by other values—the Corps may always allow development of the wetland for other uses simply by issuing a permit.

"the waters of the United States, including the territorial seas." § 1362(7). The Corps has issued regulations defining the term "waters of the United States" to include "waters such as intrastate lakes, rivers, streams (including intermittent streams), mudflats, sandflats, wetlands, sloughs, prairie potholes, wet meadows, playa lakes, or natural ponds, the use, degradation or destruction of which could affect interstate or foreign commerce . . . " In 1986, the Corps stated that § 404(a) extends to intrastate waters which "are or would be used as habitat" by migratory birds that cross state lines. The Corp determined to exercise jurisdiction over the SWANCC site based on this Migratory Bird Rule. Approximately 121 bird species had been observed at the site, including several known to depend upon aquatic environments for a significant portion of their life requirements. SWANCC argued that the CWA did not cover nonnavigable, isolated, intrastate waters based upon the presence of migratory birds and, in the alternative, that Congress lacked the power under the Commerce Clause to grant such regulatory jurisdiction.]

This is not the first time we have been called upon to evaluate the meaning of § 404(a). In *United States v. Riverside Bayview Homes, Inc.* [page 682, *supra*] we held that the Corps had § 404(a) jurisdiction over wetlands that actually abutted on a navigable waterway. In so doing, we noted that the term "navigable" is of "limited import" and that Congress evidenced its intent to "regulate at least some waters that would not be deemed 'navigable' under the classical understanding of that term." But our holding was based in large measure upon Congress' unequivocal acquiescence to, and approval of, the Corps' regulations interpreting the CWA to cover wetlands adjacent to navigable waters. We found that Congress' concern for the protection of water quality and aquatic ecosystems indicated its intent to regulate wetlands "inseparably bound up with the 'waters' of the United States."

It was the significant nexus between the wetlands and "navigable waters" that informed our reading of the CWA in *Riverside Bayview Homes.* Indeed, we did not "express any opinion" on the "question of the authority of the Corps to regulate discharges of fill material into wetlands that are not adjacent to bodies of open water. . . ." In order to rule for respondents here, we would have to hold that the jurisdiction of the Corps extends to ponds that are not adjacent to open water. But we conclude that the text of the statute will not allow this.

[We] decline respondents' invitation to take what they see as the next ineluctable step after *Riverside Bayview Homes*: holding that isolated ponds, some only seasonal, wholly located within two Illinois counties, fall under § 404(a)'s definition of "navigable waters" because they serve as habitat for migratory birds. As counsel for respondents conceded at oral argument, such a ruling would assume that "the use of the word navigable in the statute . . . does not have any independent significance." We cannot agree that Congress' separate definitional use of the phrase "waters of the United States" constitutes a basis for reading the term "navigable waters" out of the statute. We said in *Riverside Bayview Homes* that the word "navigable" in the statute was of "limited effect" and went on to hold that § 404(a) extended to nonnavigable wetlands adjacent to open waters. But it is one thing to give a word limited effect and quite another to give it no effect whatever. The term "navigable" has at least the import of showing us what Congress had in mind as its authority for enacting the CWA: its traditional jurisdiction over waters that were or had been navigable in fact or which could reasonably be so made.

Respondents—relying upon all of the arguments addressed above—contend that, at the very least, it must be said that Congress did not address the precise question of § 404(a)'s scope with regard to nonnavigable, isolated, intrastate waters, and that, therefore, we should give deference to the "Migratory Bird Rule". We find § 404(a) to be clear, but even were we to agree with respondents, we would not extend Chevron deference here.

Where an administrative interpretation of a statute invokes the outer limits of Congress' power, we expect a clear indication that Congress intended that result. This requirement stems from our prudential desire not to needlessly reach constitutional issues and our assumption that Congress does not casually authorize administrative agencies to interpret a statute to push the limit of congressional authority. This concern is heightened where the administrative interpretation alters the federal-state framework by permitting federal encroachment upon a traditional state power. Thus, "where an otherwise acceptable construction of a statute would raise serious constitutional problems, the Court will construe the statute to avoid such problems unless such construction is plainly contrary to the intent of Congress."

Twice in the past six years we have reaffirmed the proposition that the grant of authority to Congress under the Commerce Clause, though broad, is not unlimited. *See* United States v. Morrison, 529 U.S. 598 (2000); United States v. Lopez, 514 U.S. 549 (1995). Respondents argue that the "Migratory Bird Rule" falls within Congress' power to regulate intrastate activities that "substantially affect" interstate commerce. They note that the protection of migratory birds is a "national interest of very nearly the first magnitude" [quoting *Missouri v. Holland*, page 222, *supra*], and that, as the Court of Appeals found, millions of people spend over a billion dollars annually on recreational pursuits relating to migratory birds. These arguments raise significant constitutional questions. For example, we would have to evaluate the precise object or activity that, in the aggregate, substantially affects interstate commerce. This is not clear, for although the Corps has claimed jurisdiction over petitioner's land because it contains water areas used as habitat by migratory birds, respondents now, *post litem motam*, focus upon the fact that the regulated activity is petitioner's municipal landfill, which is "plainly of a commercial nature." But this is a far cry, indeed, from the "navigable waters" and "waters of the United States" to which the statute by its terms extends.

These are significant constitutional questions raised by respondents' application of their regulations, and yet we find nothing approaching a clear statement from Congress that it intended § 404(a) to reach an abandoned sand and gravel pit such as we have here. Permitting respondents to claim federal jurisdiction over ponds and mudflats falling within the "Migratory Bird Rule" would result in a significant impingement of the States' traditional and primary power over land and water use. Rather than expressing a desire to readjust the federal-state balance in this manner, Congress chose to "recognize, preserve, and protect the primary responsibilities and rights of States . . . to plan the development and use . . . of land and water resources . . ." 33 U.S.C. § 1251(b). We thus read the statute as written to avoid the significant constitutional and federalism questions raised by respondents' interpretation, and therefore reject the request for administrative deference.

JUSTICE STEVENS, with whom JUSTICE SOUTER, JUSTICE GINSBURG, and JUSTICE BREYER join, dissenting. * * *

Because I am convinced that the Court's miserly construction of the statute is incorrect, I shall comment briefly on petitioner's argument that Congress is without power to prohibit it from filling any part of the 31 acres of ponds on its property in Cook County, Illinois. The Corps' exercise of its § 404 permitting power over "isolated" waters that serve as habitat for migratory birds falls well within the boundaries set by this Court's Commerce Clause jurisprudence.

In *United States v. Lopez*, 514 U.S. 549 (1995), this Court identified "three broad categories of activity that Congress may regulate under its commerce power": (1) channels of interstate commerce; (2) instrumentalities of interstate commerce, or persons and things in interstate commerce; and (3) activities that "substantially affect" interstate commerce. The migratory bird rule at issue here is properly analyzed under the third category. In order to constitute a proper exercise of Congress' power over intrastate activities that "substantially affect" interstate commerce, it is not necessary that each individual instance of the activity substantially affect commerce; it is enough that, taken in the aggregate, the *class of activities* in question has such an effect.

The activity being regulated in this case (and by the Corps' § 404 regulations in general) is the discharge of fill material into water. The Corps did not assert jurisdiction over petitioner's land simply because the waters were "used as habitat by migratory birds." It asserted jurisdiction because petitioner planned to *discharge fill* into waters "used as habitat by migratory birds." Had petitioner intended to engage in some other activity besides discharging fill (*i.e.*, had there been no activity to regulate), or, conversely, had the waters not been habitat for migratory birds (*i.e.*, had there been no basis for federal jurisdiction), the Corps would never have become involved in petitioner's use of its land. There can be no doubt that * * * the discharge of fill material into the Nation's waters is almost always undertaken for economic reasons. Moreover, no one disputes that the discharge of fill into "isolated" waters that serve as migratory bird habitat will, in the aggregate, adversely affect migratory bird populations. Nor does petitioner dispute that the particular waters it seeks to fill are home to many important species of migratory birds, including the second-largest breeding colony of Great Blue Herons in northeastern Illinois, and several species of waterfowl protected by international treaty and Illinois endangered species laws.

In addition to the intrinsic value of migratory birds, it is undisputed that literally millions of people regularly participate in birdwatching and hunting and that those activities generate a host of commercial activities of great value. The causal connection between the filling of wetlands and the decline of commercial activities associated with migratory birds is not "attenuated," it is direct and concrete. Finally, the migratory bird rule does not blur the "distinction between what is truly national and what is truly local." Justice Holmes cogently observed in *Missouri v. Holland* that the protection of migratory birds is a textbook example of a national problem. The destruction of aquatic migratory bird habitat, like so many other environmental problems, is an action in which the benefits (*e.g.*, a new landfill) are disproportionately local, while many of the costs (*e.g.*, fewer migratory birds) are widely dispersed and often borne by citizens living in other States. In such situations, described by economists as involving "externalities," federal regulation is both appropriate and necessary. Identifying the Corps' jurisdiction by reference to waters that serve as habitat for birds that migrate over state lines also satisfies this Court's expressed desire for some "jurisdictional element" that limits federal activity to its proper scope.

The power to regulate commerce among the several States necessarily and properly includes the power to preserve the natural resources that generate such commerce. Migratory birds, and the waters on which they rely, are such resources. Moreover, the protection of migratory birds is a well-established federal responsibility. As Justice Holmes noted in *Missouri v. Holland*, the federal interest in protecting these birds is of "the first magnitude." Because of their transitory nature, they "can be protected only by national action."

Whether it is necessary or appropriate to refuse to allow petitioner to fill those ponds is a question on which we have no voice. Whether the Federal Government has the power to require such permission, however, is a question that is easily answered. If, as it does, the Commerce Clause empowers Congress to regulate particular "activities causing air or water pollution, or other environmental hazards that may have effects in more than one State," there is no merit in petitioner's constitutional argument.

NOTES

1.   Notwithstanding *SWANCC*, the Ninth Circuit held that irrigation canals are subject to EPA jurisdiction even at times when they are isolated from navigable waters:

> Because the canals receive water from natural streams and lakes, and divert water to streams and creeks, they are connected as tributaries to other "waters of the United States." TID [the irrigation district] claims that the canals are not tributaries because, during the application of Magnacide H, the canals are a "closed system," isolated from natural streams by a system of closed waste gates . . . But even if TID succeeds, at certain times, in preventing the canals from exchanging any water with the local streams and lakes, that does not prevent the canals from being "waters of the United States" for which a permit is necessary. Even tributaries that flow intermittently are "waters of the United States." . . . The Clean Water Act is concerned with the pollution of tributaries as well as with the pollution of navigable streams, and "it is incontestable that substantial pollution of one not only may but very probably will affect the other."

Headwaters, Inc. v. Talent Irrigation Dist., 243 F.3d 526, 533–534 (9th Cir. 2001).

2.   Following *SWANCC*, EPA and the Corps issued a joint memorandum interpreting it, which reads the decision quite narrowly. The government's view is that the decision negates the "migratory bird" rule but does not eliminate other arguments for covering nonadjacent wetlands (for example, hydrological connections with navigable waters). EPA also decided not to issue any new wetlands rule in the wake of SWANCC. *See* EPA, EPA AND ARMY CORPS ISSUE WETLAND DECISION (2003), *available at* https://www.epa.gov/sites/production/files/2016-04/documents/swancc_guidance_jan_03.pdf.

3.   Although isolated wetlands may seem ecologically insignificant, scientists estimate that the *SWANCC* decision may affect almost 30 percent of the nation's wetlands. These wetlands are the source of enormous biodiversity. *See* Nature Serve, *Biodiversity Values of Geographically Isolated Wetlands in the United States* (2005), available at http://www.natureserve.org/conservation-tools/projects/biodiversity-values-geographically-isolated-wetlands-united-states at 41–42. In the wake of SWANCC and the case that follows, *Rapanos*, however, only six states have specific permitting programs for those waters excluded from federal jurisdiction by the cases. See Environmental Law Institute, *America's Vulnerable Waters: Assessing the Nation's Portfolio of Vulnerable Aquatic Resources Since Rapanos v. United*

States (2011), available at https://www.eli.org/sites/default/files/eli-pubs/d21-06.pdf.

4. Although the jurisdictional issues considered in *Riverside* and *SWANCC* are significant, other important questions involve the operation of the permitting program. The regulations prohibit filling wetlands if "there is a practicable alternative to the proposed discharge which would have less adverse impact on the aquatic ecosystem." There has been considerable controversy over how to determine the applicable alternatives. *See* Fund for Animals Inc. v. Rice, 85 F.3d 535 (11th Cir. 1996); Margaret N. Strand, *Federal Wetlands Law: Part II*, 23 ENVTL. L. REP. 10,284, 10,289–91 (1993).

5. SWANCC was not the last word from the Supreme Court on wetlands jurisdiction under the CWA:

RAPANOS V. UNITED STATES

Supreme Court of the United States, 2006.
547 U.S. 715, 126 S.Ct. 2208, 165 L.Ed.2d 159.

JUSTICE SCALIA delivered the judgment of the Court and delivered an opinion in which CHIEF JUSTICE ROBERTS, JUSTICE THOMAS and JUSTICE ALITO join. [JUSTICES ROBERTS and KENNEDY filed separate concurring opinion, excerpted below.]

* * *

In April 1989, petitioner John A. Rapanos backfilled wetlands on a parcel of land in Michigan that he owned and sought to develop. This parcel included 54 acres of land with sometimes-saturated soil conditions. The nearest body of navigable water was 11 to 20 miles away. Regulators had informed Mr. Rapanos that his saturated fields were "waters of the United States," 33 U. S. C. § 1362(7), that could not be filled without a permit. Twelve years of criminal and civil litigation ensued.

The burden of federal regulation on those who would deposit fill material in locations denominated "waters of the United States" is not trivial. In deciding whether to grant or deny a permit, the U. S. Army Corps of Engineers (Corps) exercises the discretion of an enlightened despot, relying on such factors as "economics," "aesthetics," "recreation," and "in general, the needs and welfare of the people," 33 CFR§ 320.4(a) (2004). The average applicant for an individual permit spends 788 days and $271,596 in completing the process, and the average applicant for a nationwide permit spends 313 days and $28,915—not counting costs of mitigation or design changes.

The enforcement proceedings against Mr. Rapanos are a small part of the immense expansion of federal regulation of land use that has occurred under the Clean Water Act—without any change in the governing statute—during the past five Presidential administrations. In the last three decades, the Corps and the Environmental Protection Agency (EPA) have interpreted their jurisdiction over "the waters of the United States" to cover 270 to 300 million acres of swampy lands in the United States— including half of Alaska and an area the size of California in the lower 48 States. And that was just the beginning. The Corps also asserted jurisdiction over virtually any parcel of land containing a channel or conduit—whether man-made or natural, broad or narrow, permanent or ephemeral—through which rainwater or drainage may occasionally or intermittently flow. On this view, the federally regulated "waters of the United States" include storm drains, roadside ditches, ripples of sand in the desert that may contain water once a year, and lands that are covered by floodwaters once every 100 years. Because they include the land containing storm sewers and desert washes, the statutory "waters of the United States" engulf entire cities and immense arid wastelands. In fact, the entire land area of the United States lies in some drainage basin, and an endless network of visible channels furrows the entire surface, containing water ephemerally wherever the rain falls. Any plot of land containing such a channel may potentially be regulated as a "water of the United States." * * *

* * * Section 1342(a) authorizes the Administrator of the EPA to "issue a permit for the discharge of any pollutant, . . . notwithstanding section 1311(a) of this title." Section 1344 authorizes the Secretary of the Army, acting through the Corps, to "issue permits . . . for the discharge of dredged or fill material into the navigable waters at specified disposal sites." § 1344(a), (d). It is the discharge of "dredged or fill material"—which, unlike traditional water pollutants, are solids that do not readily wash downstream—that we consider today. * * *

The Corps' current regulations interpret "the waters of the United States" to include, in addition to traditional interstate navigable waters, 33 CFR § 328.3(a)(1) (2004), "[a]ll interstate waters including interstate wetlands," § 328.3(a)(2); "[a]ll other waters such as intrastate lakes, rivers, streams (including intermittent streams), mudflats, sandflats, wetlands, sloughs, prairie potholes, wet meadows, playa lakes, or natural ponds, the use, degradation or destruction of which could affect interstate or foreign commerce," § 328.3(a)(3); "[t]ributaries of [such] waters," § 328.3(a)(5); and "[w]etlands adjacent to [such] waters [and tributaries] (other than waters that are themselves wetlands)," § 328.3(a)(7). The regulation defines "adjacent" wetlands as those "bordering, contiguous [to], or neighboring" waters of the United States. § 328.3(c). It specifically provides that "[w]etlands separated from other waters of the United States by man-made dikes or barriers, natural river berms, beach dunes and the like are 'adjacent wetlands.'" *Ibid.* * * *

Following our decision in *Riverside Bayview* [*supra* page 682], the Corps adopted increasingly broad interpretations of its own regulations under the Act. For example, in 1986, to "clarify" the reach of its jurisdiction, the Corps announced the so-called "Migratory Bird Rule," which purported to extend its jurisdiction to any intrastate waters "[w]hich are or would be used as habitat" by migratory birds. 51 Fed. Reg. 41217; see also *SWANCC* [*supra* page 685]. In addition, the Corps interpreted its own regulations to include "ephemeral streams" and "drainage ditches" as "tributaries" that are part of the "waters of the United States," see 33 CFR § 328.3(a)(5), provided that they have a perceptible "ordinary high water mark" as defined in § 328.3(e). 65 Fed. Reg. 12823 (2000). This interpretation extended "the waters of the United States" to virtually any land feature over which rainwater or drainage passes and leaves a visible mark—even if only "the presence of litter and debris." 33 CFR § 328.3(e). * * *

In *SWANCC*, * * * we held that "nonnavigable, isolated, intrastate waters,"—which, unlike the wetlands at issue in *Riverside Bayview*, did not "actually abu[t] on a navigable waterway,"—were not included as "waters of the United States."

Following our decision in *SWANCC*, the Corps did not significantly revise its theory of federal jurisdiction under § 1344(a). The Corps provided notice of a proposed rulemaking in light of *SWANCC*, 68 Fed. Reg. 1991 (2003), but ultimately did not amend its published regulations. Because *SWANCC* did not directly address tributaries, the Corps notified its field staff that they "should continue to assert jurisdiction over traditional navigable waters . . . and, generally speaking, their tributary systems (and adjacent wetlands)." 68 Fed. Reg. 1998. In addition, because *SWANCC* did not overrule *Riverside Bayview*, the Corps continues to assert jurisdiction over waters " 'neighboring' " traditional navigable waters and their tributaries. 68 Fed. Reg. 1997 (quoting 33 CFR § 328.3(c) (2003)).

Even after *SWANCC*, the lower courts have continued to uphold the Corps' sweeping assertions of jurisdiction over ephemeral channels and drains as "tributaries." * * *

These judicial constructions of "tributaries" are not outliers. Rather, they reflect the breadth of the Corps' determinations in the field. The Corps' enforcement practices vary somewhat from district to district because "the definitions used to make jurisdictional determinations" are deliberately left "vague." But district offices of the Corps have treated, as "waters of the United States," such typically dry land features as "arroyos, coulees, and washes," as well as other "channels that might have little water flow in a given year." They have also applied that definition to such manmade, intermittently flowing features as "drain tiles, storm drains systems, and culverts." * * *

In these consolidated cases, we consider whether four Michigan wetlands, which lie near ditches or man-made drains that eventually empty into traditional navigable waters, constitute "waters of the United

States" within the meaning of the Act. [T]he Rapanos and their affiliated businesses deposited fill material without a permit into wetlands on three sites near Midland, Michigan: the "Salzburg site," the "Hines Road site," and the "Pine River site." The wetlands at the Salzburg site are connected to a man-made drain, which drains into Hoppler Creek, which flows into the Kawkawlin River, which empties into Saginaw Bay and Lake Huron. The wetlands at the Hines Road site are connected to something called the "Rose Drain," which has a surface connection to the Tittabawassee River. And the wetlands at the Pine River site have a surface connection to the Pine River, which flows into Lake Huron. It is not clear whether the connections between these wetlands and the nearby drains and ditches are continuous or intermittent, or whether the nearby drains and ditches contain continuous or merely occasional flows of water. * * *

We have twice stated that the meaning of "navigable waters" in the Act is broader than the traditional understanding of that term, *SWANCC* and *Riverside Bayview*. We have also emphasized, however, that the qualifier "navigable" is not devoid of significance.

We need not decide the precise extent to which the qualifiers "navigable" and "of the United States" restrict the coverage of the Act. Whatever the scope of these qualifiers, the CWA authorizes federal jurisdiction only over "waters." The only natural definition of the term "waters," our prior and subsequent judicial constructions of it, clear evidence from other provisions of the statute, and this Court's canons of construction all confirm that "the waters of the United States" in § 1362(7) cannot bear the expansive meaning that the Corps would give it.

The Corps' expansive approach might be arguable if the CSA defined "navigable waters" as "water of the United States." But "the waters of the United States" is something else. The use of the definite article ("the") and the plural number ("waters") show plainly that § 1362(7) does not refer to water in general. In this form, "the waters" refers more narrowly to water "[a]s found in streams and bodies forming geographical features such as oceans, rivers, [and] lakes," or "the flowing or moving masses, as of waves or floods, making up such streams or bodies." Webster's New International Dictionary 2882 (2d ed. 1954) (hereinafter Webster's Second). On this definition, "the waters of the United States" include only relatively permanent, standing or flowing bodies of water.[5] The definition refers to water as found in "streams," "oceans," "rivers," "lakes," and "bodies" of water "forming geographical features." *Ibid.* All of these terms connote continuously present, fixed bodies of water, as opposed to ordinarily dry

---

[5] By describing "waters" as "relatively permanent," we do not necessarily exclude streams, rivers, or lakes that might dry up in extraordinary circumstances, such as drought. We also do not necessarily exclude *seasonal* rivers, which contain continuous flow during some months of the year but no flow during dry months—such as the 290-day, continuously flowing stream postulated by Justice Stevens' dissent (hereinafter the dissent). Common sense and common usage distinguish between a wash and seasonal river. * * *

channels through which water occasionally or intermittently flows. Even the least substantial of the definition's terms, namely "streams," connotes a continuous flow of water in a permanent channel especially when used in company with other terms such as "rivers," "lakes," and "oceans." None of these terms encompasses transitory puddles or ephemeral flows of water.

The restriction of "the waters of the United States" to exclude channels containing merely intermittent or ephemeral flow also accords with the commonsense understanding of the term. In applying the definition to "ephemeral streams," "wet meadows," storm sewers and culverts, "directional sheet flow during storm events," drain tiles, man-made drainage ditches, and dry arroyos in the middle of the desert, the Corps has stretched the term "waters of the United States" beyond parody. The plain language of the statute simply does not authorize this "Land Is Waters" approach to federal jurisdiction.

In addition, * * * [a]s we noted in *SWANCC*, the traditional term "navigable waters—even though defined as "the waters of the United States"—carries *some* of its original substance: "[I]t is one thing to give a word limited effect and quite another to give it no effect whatever." That limited effect includes, at bare minimum, the ordinary presence of water.

Our subsequent interpretation of the phrase "the waters of the United States" in the CWA likewise confirms this limitation of its scope. * * * [I]n both *Riverside Bayview* and *SWANCC*, we repeatedly described the "navigable waters" covered by the Act as "open water" and "open waters." Under no rational interpretation are typically dry channels described as "*open* waters."

Most significant of all, the CWA itself categorizes the channels and conduits that typically carry intermittent flows of water separately from "navigable waters," by including them in the definition of " 'point source.' " * * * It also defines " 'discharge of a pollutant' " as "any addition of any pollutant *to* navigable waters *from* any point source." § 1362(12)(A) (emphases added). * * *

Moreover, only the foregoing definition of "waters" is consistent with the CWA's stated "policy of Congress to recognize, preserve, and protect the primary responsibilities and rights of the States to prevent, reduce, and eliminate pollution, [and] to plan the development and use (including restoration, preservation, and enhancement) of land and water resources . . . ." § 1251(b). * * *

Even if the phrase "the waters of the United States" were ambiguous as applied to intermittent flows, our own canons of construction would establish that the Corps' interpretation of the statute is impermissible. As we noted in *SWANCC*, the Government's expansive interpretation would "result in a significant impingement of the States' traditional and primary power over land and water use." Regulation of land use, as through the issuance of the development permits sought by petitioners in both of these cases, is a quintessential state and local power. * * *

Likewise, just as we noted in *SWANCC*, the Corps' interpretation stretches the outer limits of Congress's commerce power and raises difficult questions about the ultimate scope of that power. * * *

In sum, on its only plausible interpretation, the phrase "the waters of the United States" includes only those relatively permanent, standing or continuously flowing bodies of water "forming geographic features" that are described in ordinary parlance as "streams[,] . . . oceans, rivers, [and] lakes." See Webster's Second 2882. The phrase does not include channels through which water flows intermittently or ephemerally, or channels that periodically provide drainage for rainfall. The Corps' expansive interpretation of the "the waters of the United States" is thus not "based on a permissible construction of the statute." [citing *Chevron*, casebook page 351].

* * * We * * * address in this Part whether a wetland may be considered "adjacent to" remote "waters of the United States," because of a mere hydrologic connection to them.

In *Riverside Bayview*, we * * * acknowledged * * * an inherent ambiguity in drawing the boundaries of any "waters": "[T]he Corps must necessarily choose some point at which water ends and land begins. * * * Where on this continuum to find the limit of 'waters' is far from obvious."

Because of this inherent ambiguity, we deferred to the agency's inclusion of wetlands "actually abut[ting]" traditional navigable waters. * * *

* * * [O]*nly* those wetlands with a continuous surface connection to bodies that are "waters of the United States" in their own right, so that there is no clear demarcation between "waters" and wetlands, are "adjacent to" such waters and covered by the Act. Wetlands with only an intermittent, physically remote hydrologic connection to "waters of the United States" do not implicate the boundary-drawing problem of *Riverside Bayview*, and thus lack the necessary connection to covered waters that we described as a "significant nexus" in *SWANCC*. Thus, establishing that wetlands such as those at the Rapanos and Carabell sites are covered by the Act requires two findings: First, that the adjacent channel contains a "wate[r] of the United States," (*i.e.*, a relatively permanent body of water connected to traditional interstate navigable waters); and second, that the wetland has a continuous surface connection with that water, making it difficult to determine where the "water" ends and the "wetland" begins.* * *

Respondents and their *amici* urge that such restrictions on the scope of "navigable waters" will frustrate enforcement against traditional water polluters under 33 U. S. C. §§ 1311 and 1342. Because the same definition of "navigable waters" applies to the entire statute, respondents contend that water polluters will be able to evade the permitting requirement of § 1342(a) simply by discharging their pollutants into noncovered intermittent watercourses that lie upstream of covered waters.

That is not so. * * * The Act does not forbid the "addition of any pollutant *directly* to navigable waters from any point source," but rather the "addition of any pollutant *to* navigable waters." § 1362(12)(A) (emphasis added); § 1311(a). Thus, from the time of the CWA's enactment, lower courts have held that the discharge into intermittent channels of any pollutant *that naturally washes downstream* likely violates § 1311(a), even if the pollutants discharged from a point source do not emit "directly into" covered waters, but pass "through conveyances" in between.* * *

In fact, many courts have held that such upstream, intermittently flowing channels themselves constitute "point sources" under the Act. We have held that the Act "makes plain that a point source need not be the original source of the pollutant; it need only convey the pollutant to 'navigable waters.' " * * *

In contrast to the pollutants normally covered by the permitting requirement of § 1342(a), "dredged or fill material," which is typically deposited for the sole purpose of staying put, does not normally wash downstream, and thus does not normally constitute an "addition . . . to navigable waters" when deposited in upstream isolated wetlands. §§ 1344(a), 1362(12). * * *

Finally, respondents and many *amici* admonish that narrowing the definition of "the waters of the United States" will hamper federal efforts to preserve the Nation's wetlands. It is not clear that the state and local conservation efforts that the CWA explicitly calls for, see 33 U. S. C. § 1251(b), are in any way inadequate for the goal of preservation. In any event, a Comprehensive National Wetlands Protection Act is not before us, and the "wis[dom]" of such a statute is beyond our ken. What is clear, however, is that Congress did not enact one when it granted the Corps jurisdiction over only "the *waters* of the United States." * * *

Absent a plausible ground in our case law for its sweeping position, the dissent relies heavily on "Congress' deliberate acquiescence in the Corps' regulations in 1977." * * * Congress takes no governmental action except by legislation. What the dissent refers to as "Congress' deliberate acquiescence" should more appropriately be called Congress's failure to express any opinion. * * *

Because the Sixth Circuit applied the wrong standard to determine if these wetlands are covered "waters of the United States," and because of the paucity of the record in both of these cases, the lower courts should determine, in the first instance, whether the ditches or drains near each wetland are "waters" in the ordinary sense of containing a relatively permanent flow; and (if they are) whether the wetlands in question are "adjacent" to these "waters" in the sense of possessing a continuous surface connection that creates the boundary-drawing problem we addressed in *Riverside Bayview*.* * *

We vacate the judgments of the Sixth Circuit and remand both cases for further proceedings. * * *

CHIEF JUSTICE ROBERTS, concurring.

Five years ago, this Court rejected the position of the Army Corps of Engineers on the scope of its authority to regulate wetlands under the Clean Water Act, in *SWANCC*. The Corps had taken the view that its authority was essentially limitless; this Court explained that such a boundless view was inconsistent with the limiting terms Congress had used in the Act.

In response to the *SWANCC* decision, the Corps and the Environmental Protection Agency (EPA) initiated a rulemaking to consider "issues associated with the scope of waters that are subject to the Clean Water Act (CWA), in light of the U. S. Supreme Court decision in [*SWANCC*]." 68 Fed. Reg. 1991 (2003). * * *

Agencies delegated rulemaking authority under a statute such as the Clean Water Act are afforded generous leeway by the courts in interpreting the statute they are entrusted to administer. See *Chevron* [*supra* page 351]. Given the broad, somewhat ambiguous, but nonetheless clearly limiting terms Congress employed in the Clean Water Act, the Corps and the EPA would have enjoyed plenty of room to operate in developing *some* notion of an outer bound to the reach of their authority.

The proposed rulemaking went nowhere. Rather than refining its view of its authority in light of our decision in *SWANCC*, and providing guidance meriting deference under our generous standards, the Corps chose to adhere to its essentially boundless view of the scope of its power. The upshot today is another defeat for the agency.* * *

JUSTICE KENNEDY, concurring in the judgment.

* * * In *SWANCC,* the Court held, under the circumstances presented there, that to constitute " 'navigable waters' " under the Act, a water or wetland must possess a "significant nexus" to waters that are or were navigable in fact or that could reasonably be so made. *Id.*, at 167, 172. In the instant cases neither the plurality opinion nor the dissent by Justice Stevens chooses to apply this test; and though the Court of Appeals recognized the test's applicability, it did not consider all the factors necessary to determine whether the lands in question had, or did not have, the requisite nexus. In my view the cases ought to be remanded to the Court of Appeals for proper consideration of the nexus requirement.

I

* * *

A

* * *

The statutory term to be interpreted and applied in the two instant cases is the term "navigable waters." The outcome turns on whether that phrase reasonably describes certain Michigan wetlands the Corps seeks to regulate. Under the Act "[t]he term 'navigable waters' means the waters of the United States, including the territorial seas." § 1362(7). In a regulation the Corps has construed the term "waters of the United States" to include * * * tributaries of those waters and, of particular relevance here, wetlands adjacent to those waters or their tributaries. 33 CFR §§ 328.3(a)(1), (5), (7) (2005). The Corps views tributaries as within its jurisdiction if they carry a perceptible "ordinary high water mark." § 328.4(c); 65 Fed. Reg. 12823 (2000). An ordinary high-water mark is a "line on the shore established by the fluctuations of water and indicated by physical characteristics such as clear, natural line impressed on the bank, shelving, changes in the character of soil, destruction of terrestrial vegetation, the presence of litter and debris, or other appropriate means that consider the characteristics of the surrounding areas." 33 CFR § 328.3(e).

Contrary to the plurality's description, wetlands are not simply moist patches of earth. They are defined as "those areas that are inundated or saturated by surface or ground water at a frequency and duration sufficient to support, and that under normal circumstances do support, a prevalence of vegetation typically adapted for life in saturated soil conditions. Wetlands generally include swamps, marshes, bogs, and similar areas." § 328.3(b). The Corps' Wetlands Delineation Manual, including over 100 pages of technical guidance for Corps officers, interprets this definition of wetlands to require: (1) prevalence of plant species typically adapted to saturated soil conditions, determined in accordance with the United States Fish and Wildlife Service's National List of Plant Species that Occur in Wetlands; (2) hydric soil, meaning soil that is saturated, flooded, or ponded for sufficient time during the growing season to become anaerobic, or lacking in oxygen, in the upper part; and (3) wetland hydrology, a term generally requiring continuous inundation or saturation to the surface during at least five percent of the growing season in most years. Under the Corps' regulations, wetlands are adjacent to tributaries, and thus covered by the Act, even if they are "separated from other waters of the United States by man-made dikes or barriers, natural river berms, beach dunes and the like." § 328.3(c). * * *

II

* * *

Riverside Bayview and *SWANCC* establish the framework for the inquiry in the cases now before the Court: Do the Corps' regulations, as applied to the wetlands in [this case], constitute a reasonable interpretation of "navigable waters" as in *Riverside Bayview* or an invalid construction as in *SWANCC?* * * * Absent a significant nexus, jurisdiction under the Act is lacking. * * *

A

* * *

From this reasonable beginning the plurality proceeds to impose two limitations on the Act; but these limitations, it is here submitted, are without support in the language and purposes of the Act or in our cases interpreting it. * * *

The plurality's first requirement—permanent standing water or continuous flow, at least for a period of "some months," and n. 5—makes little practical sense in a statute concerned with downstream water quality. The merest trickle, if continuous, would count as a "water" subject to federal regulation, while torrents thundering at irregular intervals through otherwise dry channels would not. Though the plurality seems to presume that such irregular flows are too insignificant to be of concern in a statute focused on "waters," that may not always be true. Areas in the western parts of the Nation provide some examples. The Los Angeles River, for instance, ordinarily carries only a trickle of water and often looks more like a dry roadway than a river. Yet it periodically releases water-volumes so powerful and destructive that it has been encased in concrete and steel over a length of some 50 miles. Though this particular waterway might satisfy the plurality's test, it is illustrative of what often-dry watercourses can become when rain waters flow. * * *

* * * In fact the *Riverside Bayview* opinion does not cite the dictionary definition on which the plurality relies, and the phrase "hydrographic features" could just as well refer to intermittent streams carrying substantial flow to navigable waters. See Webster's Second 1221 (defining "hydrography" as "[t]he description and study of seas, lakes, rivers, and other waters; specifically] . . . [t]he measurement of flow and investigation of the behavior of streams, esp[ecially] with reference to the control or utilization of their waters"). * * *

The plurality's second limitation—exclusion of wetlands lacking a continuous surface connection to other jurisdictional waters—is also unpersuasive. [T]he plurality is wrong to suggest that wetlands are "*indistinguishable*" from waters to which they bear a surface connection. Even if the precise boundary may be imprecise, a bog or swamp is different from a river. The question is what circumstances permit a bog, swamp, or other nonnavigable wetland to constitute a "navigable water" under the Act—as § 1344(g)(1), if nothing else, indicates is sometimes possible. *Riverside Bayview* addressed that question and its answer is inconsistent with the plurality's theory. There, in upholding the Corps' authority to regulate "wetlands adjacent to other bodies of water over which the Corps has jurisdiction," the Court deemed it irrelevant whether "the moisture creating the wetlands . . . find[s] its source in the adjacent bodies of water." The Court further observed that adjacency could serve as a valid basis for regulation even as to "wetlands that are not significantly intertwined with the ecosystem of adjacent waterways." "If it is reasonable," the Court explained, "for the Corps to conclude that in the majority of cases, adjacent wetlands have significant effects on water quality and the aquatic ecosystem, its definition can stand." * * *

As discussed above, the Act's prohibition on the discharge of pollutants into navigable waters, 33 U. S. C. § 1311(a), covers both the discharge of toxic materials such as sewage, chemical waste, biological material, and radioactive material and the discharge of dredged spoil, rock, sand, cellar dirt, and the like. All these substances are defined as pollutants whose discharge into navigable waters violates the Act. §§ 1311(a),1362(6), (12). One reason for the parallel treatment may be that the discharge of fill material can impair downstream water quality. The plurality argues otherwise, asserting that dredged or fill material "does not normally wash downstream." As the dissent points out, this proposition seems questionable as an empirical matter. It seems plausible that new or loose fill, not anchored by grass or roots from other vegetation, could travel downstream through waterways adjacent to a wetland; at the least this is a factual possibility that the Corps' experts can better assess than can the plurality. Silt, whether from natural or human sources, is a major factor in aquatic environments, and it may clog waterways, alter ecosystems, and limit the useful life of dams. * * *

Even granting, however, the plurality's assumption that fill material will stay put, Congress' parallel treatment of fill material and toxic pollution may serve another purpose. As the Court noted in *Riverside Bayview*, "the Corps has concluded that wetlands may serve to filter and purify water draining into adjacent bodies of water, 33 CFR § 320.4(b)(2)(vii) (1985), and to slow the flow of surface runoff into lakes, rivers, and streams and thus prevent flooding and erosion, see §§ 320.4(b)(2)(iv) and (v)." Where wetlands perform these filtering and runoff control functions, filling them may increase downstream pollution, much as a discharge of toxic pollutants would. Not only will dirty water no longer be stored and filtered but also the act of filling and draining itself may cause the release of nutrients, toxins, and pathogens that were trapped, neutralized, and perhaps amenable to filtering or detoxification in the wetlands. In many cases, moreover, filling in wetlands separated from another water by a berm can mean that flood water, impurities, or runoff that would have been stored or contained in the wetlands will instead flow out to major waterways. With these concerns in mind, the Corps' definition of adjacency is a reasonable one, for it may be the absence of an interchange of waters prior to the dredge and fill activity that makes protection of the wetlands critical to the statutory scheme. * * *

It bears mention also that the plurality's overall tone and approach from the characterization of acres of wetlands destruction as "backfilling . . . wet fields," to the rejection of Corps authority over "man-made drainage ditches" and "dry arroyos" without regard to how much water they periodically carry, to the suggestion, seemingly contrary to Congress' judgment, that discharge of fill material is inconsequential for adjacent waterways, seems unduly dismissive of the interests asserted by the United States in these cases. Important public interests are served by the Clean Water Act in general and by the protection of wetlands in particular. To give just one example, *amici* here have noted that nutrient-rich runoff from the Mississippi River has created a hypoxic, or oxygen-depleted, "dead zone" in the Gulf of Mexico that at times approaches the size of Massachusetts and New Jersey. * * *

B

* * *

When the Corps seeks to regulate wetlands adjacent to navigable-in-fact waters, it may rely on adjacency to establish its jurisdiction. Absent more specific regulations, however, the Corps must establish a significant nexus on a case-by-case basis when it seeks to regulate wetlands based on adjacency to nonnavigable tributaries. Given the potential overbreadth of the Corps' regulations, this showing is necessary to avoid unreasonable applications of the statute. Where an adequate nexus is established for a particular wetland, it may be permissible, as a matter of administrative convenience or necessity, to presume covered status for other comparable wetlands in the region. That issue, however, is neither raised by these facts nor addressed by any agency regulation that accommodates the nexus requirement outlined here. * * *

III

In both the consolidated cases before the Court the record contains evidence suggesting the possible existence of a significant nexus according to the principles outlined above. Thus the end result in these cases and many others to be considered by the Corps may be the same as that suggested by the dissent, namely, that the Corps' assertion of jurisdiction is valid. Given, however, that neither the agency nor the reviewing courts properly considered the issue, a remand is appropriate, in my view, for application of the controlling legal standard.

RAPANOS

As the dissent points out, in *Rapanos* an expert whom the District Court found "eminently qualified" and "highly credible," testified that the wetlands were providing "habitat, sediment trapping, nutrient recycling, and flood peak diminution, reduction flow water augmentation." Although the expert had "not studied the upstream drainage of these sites" and thus could not assert that the wetlands were performing important pollutant-trapping functions, he did observe: "we have a situation in which the flood water attenuation in that water is held on the site in the wetland . . . such that it does not add to flood peak. By the same token it would have some additional water flowing into the rivers during the drier periods, thus, increasing the low water flow. . . . By the same token on all of the sites to the extent that they slow the flow of water off of the site they will also accumulate sediment and thus trap sediment and hold nutrients for use in those wetlands systems later in the season as well."

In addition, in assessing the hydrology prong of the three-part wetlands test, the District Court made extensive findings regarding water tables and drainage on the parcels at issue. In applying the Corps' jurisdictional regulations, the District Court found that each of the wetlands bore surface water connections to tributaries of navigable-in-fact waters.

Much the same evidence should permit the establishment of a significant nexus with navigable-in-fact waters, particularly if supplemented by further evidence about the significance of the tributaries to which the wetlands are connected. * * *

In these consolidated cases I would vacate the judgments of the Court of Appeals and remand for consideration whether the specific wetlands at issue possess a significant nexus with navigable waters.

NOTES

1.   How are lower courts to determine what legal standard to apply in deciding whether Section 404 jurisdiction exists? The standard established in Justice Scalia's plurality opinion or the standard applied in Justice Kennedy's concurring opinion? *See* Marks v. United States, 430 U.S. 188, 193 (1977) ("When a fragmented Court decides a case and no single rationale explaining the result enjoys the assent of five Justices, the holding of the Court may be viewed as that position taken by those Members who concurred in the judgments on the narrowest grounds.") Courts to date have generally taken three different approaches. The 9th and 11th Circuits, for example, have held that Justice Kennedy's concurring opinion is controlling. *See Northern California River Watch v. City of Healdsburg*, 496 F.3d 993, 1000 (9th Cir.

2007); *see also United States v. Gerke Excavating*, 464 F.3d 723 (7th Cir. 2006) (same). The First Circuit, by contrast, has held that the U.S. can establish jurisdiction under Section 404 if the government can meet either the Kennedy standard or the standard set forth by the plurality. *United States v. Johnson*, 467 F.3d 56, 60 (1st Cir. 2006). And the 5th and 6th Circuits have refused to decide which test controls, holding that when both the plurality and concurring tests are met, jurisdiction is established. *United States v. Lucas*, 516 F.3d 316, 327 (5th Cir. 2008); *United States v. Cundiff*, 555 F.3d 200, 210–13 (6th Cir. 2009).

2. Can you square Chief Justice Roberts' concurring opinion with Justice Scalia's plurality opinion in which Roberts joined? Put a different way, suppose the Army Corps had in the wake of *SWANNC* issued a rulemaking that resulted in expansively defined jurisdiction that was nonetheless consistent with the ruling in SWANNC. Would Roberts uphold such a rule? He may have the opportunity to do so (or to reject it) given what has transpired since, described in the next paragraph.

3. In 2015, the Obama Administration issued a new rule—after extensive public comment, to clarify the federal government's jurisdiction over wetlands. 80 Fed Reg. 37054, https://19january2017snapshot.epa.gov/sites/production/files/2015-06/documents/epa-hq-ow-2011-0880-20862.pdf. Known as the "Waters of the United States" rule, or "WOTUS," the rule specifies waters that are categorically included in the definition (including traditional navigable waters, interstate waters, tributaries as long as they have a bed, bank, and high water mark, and adjacent waters). It also essentially codifies the "substantial nexus" test from *Rapanos* and delineates five categories of waters that should be subject to a case-by-case analysis to see if a substantial nexus exists between the water body and a "water of the United States." These five categories include Prairie potholes, Carolina and Delmarva bays, pocosins, western vernal pools in California, and Texas coastal prairie wetlands.

The Trump Administration made clear as soon as President Trump was elected that it would move to repeal the WOTUS rule. It began proceedings to do so in June of 2018 and temporarily replaced the WOTUS rule with pre-existing guidance documents. In December of 2018, EPA proposed a replacement rule, currently open for public comment. The replacement rule is much closer to Justice Scalia's dissent than to Justice Kennedy's substantial nexus test, repealing jurisdiction for ephemeral "features that flow only in respose to precipitation, and limiting jurisdiction by narrowing the scope of what constitutes a wetland adjacent to for wetlands adjacent to jurisdictional waters. *See* U.S. EPA, *Waters of the United. States (WOTUS) Rulemaking*, https://www.epa.gov/wotus-rule/proposed-revised-definition-wotus-factsheets. Once the rule is finalized, it will undoubtedly be challenged; the retirement of Justice Kennedy makes it hard to predict how a Supreme Court will react to the new rule.

While the Trump Administration ushers the proposed rule through the rulemaking process, different parts of the country are subject to different jurisdictional requirements. In *Nat'l Assn of Manufacturers v. Dept of Defense,* 583 U.S. ___, 138 S.Ct. 617 (2018), the Supreme Court held that challenges to the Obama WOTUS rule must be filed in federal district court, not in the federal courts of appeal. A number of challenges have been filed with differing outcomes; the result is that the Obama WOTUS rule is in effect in 22 states, the District of Columbia and U.S. territories; the remaining states are subject to the pre-2015 guidance.

4.   An internal memorandum at EPA concluded that a "significant portion" of enforcement efforts had been "adversely affected" by *Rapanos.* The memo says that between July, 2006 and December, 2007 jurisdictional concerns had led to decisions to drop 304 potential enforcement actions and to lower the priority of 147 others. The memo also says that lack of jurisdiction had been asserted in 61 cases as an affirmative defense. See *Internal EDPA Memo Finds Enforcement Decreased Following Rapanos Decision,* 30 ENV. REP. 1392 (July 11, 2008). A report by the House Oversight and Transportation Committee, *Decline of Clean Water Act Enforcement Program* (Dec. 16, 2008) found a "drastic deterioration" in post-Rapanos CWA enforcement as "hundreds of violations have not been pursued with enforcement actions and dozens of existing enforcement cases have become informal responses, have had civil penalties reduced, and have experienced significant delays. . . ." The difficulty in complying with *Rapanos* has been compounded by the staff time necessary to demonstrate Justice Kennedy's significant nexus test. Is there a way for the EPA to avoid these enforcement difficulties? Congress?

5.   John Rapanos did not escape liability. He settled the Clean Water Act case against him, paying a $150,000 civil penalty, agreeing to spend $750,000 to restore wetlands he had filled illegally and agreeing to preserve another 134 acres of wetlands on his property. *See* Environment News Service, *Rapanos Will Pay for Clean Water Act Violations* (Dec. 30, 2008), available at http://www.ens-newswire.com/ens/dec2008/2008-12-30-091.asp.

The following excerpt describes the government's efforts to reconcile land development and wetlands preservation. Increasingly, these efforts have focused on allowing for mitigation banking, which allows the restoration of one area of wetlands in exchange for the destruction of other wetlands under a § 404 permit. As of August, 2013, more than 1800 mitigation banks were registered as providing banking services. *See* U.S. EPA, *Section 404 of the Clean Water Act, Mitigation Banking Factsheet,* https://www.epa.gov/cwa-404/mitigation-banking-factsheet.

J.B. RUHL AND R. JUGE GREGG, INTEGRATING ECOSYSTEM SERVICES INTO ENVIRONMENTAL LAW: A CASE STUDY OF WETLANDS MITIGATION BANKING

20 STAN. ENVTL L. J. 365 (2001).[2]

The Corps' guidelines for administering wetlands mitigation require it to review 404 permit applications using a preference "sequencing" approach. The first preference is to require the applicant to avoid filling wetland resources; the second preference is to require minimization of adverse impacts that cannot reasonably be avoided; and the least desirable preference is to require the developer to provide compensatory mitigation for those unavoidable adverse impacts that remain after all minimization measures have been exercised. The least desirable option, compensatory mitigation, is the basis for wetlands trading.

Both EPA and the Corps traditionally have preferred on-site to off-site locations for the compensatory mitigation activity and have preferred in-kind mitigation to mitigation that uses a substantially different type of wetland. Regardless of location, EPA and the Corps prefer measures that restore prior wetland areas as the highest form of mitigation, followed by enhancement of low-quality wetlands, then creation of new wetlands, and, least favored of all, preservation of existing wetlands. . . . * * *

[D]uring the late 1980s the Corps and EPA started shifting compensatory activities increasingly from on-site to off-site mitigation, thus opening the door to the wetlands mitigation banking technique. This approach, its proponents argued, would prove advantageous both in terms of economic efficiency and ecological integrity, aggregating small wetlands threatened by development into larger restored wetlands in a different location. It is defined generally as "a system in which the creation, enhancement, restoration, or preservation of wetlands is recognized by a regulatory agency as generating compensation credits allowing the future development of other wetland sites." In its most basic form, wetlands mitigation banking allows a developer to protect wetlands at one site in advance of development and then draw down the resulting bank of mitigation "credits" as development is implemented and wetlands at another site are filled. Indeed, the concept has progressed beyond this personal bank model. Today, large commercial and public wetlands banks, not tied to a particular development, sell mitigation piecemeal to third-party developers in need of compensatory mitigation.

The Corps and EPA officially endorsed the mitigation banking approach in their 1995 Federal Guidance for the Establishment, Use and Operation of Mitigation Banks, setting out a standard review procedure for establishing and using wetlands banks in the 404 permit process.

---

[2]   Copyright © 2001, STANFORD ENVT'L L. J. Reprinted by Permission.

In 1995, five United States agencies published the Banking Guidance, as promised in the Mitigation Guidance, in order to detail the use and operation of mitigation banks The document's introduction declares that the "objective of a mitigation bank is to provide for the replacement of the chemical, physical, and biological functions of wetlands and other aquatic resources which are lost as a result of authorized impacts." This perspective is later broadened to acknowledge that "[t]he overall goal of a mitigation bank is to provide economically efficient and flexible mitigation opportunities, while fully compensating for wetland and other aquatic resource losses in a manner that contributes to the long-term ecological functioning of the watershed within which the bank is to be located." The Banking Guidance thus qualifies the goal of replacing ecological functioning by acknowledging economic realities. * * *

Because the crediting and debiting procedure forms the heart of a wetlands mitigation bank, the determination of what will be counted as "currency" is crucial. The Banking Guidance focuses initially on the use of "aquatic functions" as its banking currency—a currency that is easily "exchanged" or translated into service values. But the Banking Guidance then follows the lead of the Mitigation Guidance and allows acreage to be a surrogate measure if functional assessment is impractical. The Banking Guidance then takes one more step back from its vision and allows any "appropriate functional assessment methodology . . . acceptable to all signatories" to be used to quantify credits. Once again, therefore, the official guidance provides an opportunity, but not a requirement, to rely on ecosystem indicators as the assessment methodology. * * *

Ecosystem service valuation must be incorporated into wetlands mitigation banking decision making at two critical junctures: the wetlands assessment stage and the wetlands trading stage. The Environmental Law Institute's (ELI) groundbreaking 1993 study of wetlands mitigation banking describes these stages as raising the "credits defined and valued" issues, and recognizes that they are the most complex issues in mitigation banking. To fully capture ecosystem service values, the assessment method must consistently define the services and incorporate measurements of their value both for the wetlands to be lost and for those wetlands used for mitigation. Moreover, the trading ratio between wetlands lost and mitigated should reflect any differences in service population, service delivery type, and efficiency. It should also account for margins of error that may justify deviating from a fixed exchange rate. When function values and service populations are reliably measured and appropriately compared among sites, using a reasonable margin of error, ecosystem service valuation methods can be integrated into the assessment and trading stages of wetland mitigation banking.

In our survey of mitigation banks, however, we found no explicit use of this kind of ecosystem service valuation at either the assessment or

trading stages. Wetlands mitigation banking entities seem focused on using the most simple and expedient assessment method the relevant regulatory bodies would approve. Moreover, the regulatory bodies did not appear widely to require or even encourage a more sophisticated approach. These less refined valuation methods may work in situations involving an exchange of wetlands of basically similar attributes in the same watershed, because one can assume that similar wetlands provide similar functions to similar ecosystems. These basic valuation methods also suffice for trades based on gross comparisons between classes of wetlands—e.g., two acres of Type A are worth three acres of Type B. Trades based on wetland classes and fixed ratios thus dominate the wetlands mitigation banking practice.
* * *

Given the current state of affairs, there is little promise for the integration of ecosystem service valuation methods into wetlands mitigation banking until methods of wetland assessment are significantly improved. In the absence of widely available, readily applied methods for calculating and comparing ecosystem service values of the wetlands being traded, the Corps will likely put constraints on trading markets to compensate for ecosystem function losses not recognized by acre-based methods. These constraints significantly undercut the market and information advantages ecosystem service valuation would impart to wetlands mitigation banking in general, thus further reducing any incentive to apply such methods.

Hence, unless some way is developed to capture the ecosystem service value of wetlands without costly, time-consuming, and complicated valuation methods—e.g., by measurement of readily determinable indicators of ecosystem service value—wetlands mitigation banking is likely to rely most heavily on acre-based and narrow function-based methods and highly regulated "markets" for trades. Nevertheless, if such assessment methods can be developed, . . . the authority to require their use is implicit in the existing legal framework of the section 404 program. By using these new assessment methods, the wetlands mitigation banking program would surely come closer to meeting its environmental protection objectives.

NOTES

1.   Mitigation may allow development to proceed on at least part of a parcel in return for preservation or restoration efforts elsewhere. Thus, a mitigation requirement allows the regulator to avoid a complete, unconditional ban on use of property. This may have constitutional implications. The availability of mitigation banking may convert a complete ban on development, which would likely be found a per se taking under *Lucas*, into a conditional regulatory burden, which will be upheld under other Supreme Court takings cases involving development permits, *Nollan v. California Coastal Com'n*, 483

U.S. 825 (1987) and *Dolan v. City of Tigard*, 512 U.S. 374 (1994), described in more detail at page 269, *supra,* given the right factual basis. Presumably, it should not be difficult to show that there is a nexus between the loss of particular wetlands and the need to provide the same ecological services elsewhere, and any reasonably designed program should be able to survive *Dolan*'s rough proportionality test.

2.   What "currency" should be used to measure wetland value? By attempting to quantify wetland services, does the idea of ecosystem service value commodify nature in an inappropriate way?

3.   Would a well-developed market for wetlands mitigation have any significance with respect to Congress's regulatory power? Could Congress indirectly limit development of isolated wetlands by encouraging their use as mitigation for projects that do fall under its jurisdiction?

It is clear that the WQTP itself is *guidance* for states to *encourage voluntary* reductions in effluents:

> The purpose of this policy is to encourage states, interstate agencies and tribes to develop and implement water quality trading programs for nutrients, sediments and other pollutants where opportunities exist to achieve water quality improvements at reduced costs. More specifically, the policy is intended to encourage voluntary trading programs that facilitate implementation of TMDLs, reduce the costs of compliance with CWA regulations, establish incentives for voluntary reductions and promote watershed-based initiatives. A number of states are in various stages of developing trading programs. This policy provides guidance for states, interstate agencies and tribes to assist them in developing and implementing such programs.

68 Fed. Reg. 1608, 1609 (2003). Since the January 13, 2003 announcement of the new WQTP and claims that the EPA is giving states $800,000 for 11 pilot projects, it is quite clear that the agency's encouragement of state action is not financial, but more technical and aspirational.

In addition to the WQTP, wetlands mitigation banking offers another relatively new market-based approach to water quality regulation. *See* J. B. Ruhl & R. Juge Gregg, *Integrating Ecosystem Services into Environmental Law: A Case Study of Wetlands Mitigation Banking*, 20 STAN. ENVTL. L.J. 365 (2001).

CHAPTER 8

HAZARDOUS WASTE

■ ■ ■

As we have seen, in the early 1970s the federal government began its active involvement in the regulation of air and water pollution. In the latter half of the 1970s, Congress turned to a different problem, toxic and hazardous waste disposal. Congress faced the dual problems of dealing with the serious threats posed by many existing waste disposal sites and regulating future disposal activities so as not to multiply such threats. The result was the enactment of two enormously complex federal statutes, the Resource Conservation and Recovery Act of 1976 (RCRA), which regulates the handling and disposal of hazardous waste (and is hence largely forward-looking), and the Comprehensive Environmental Response, Compensation, and Liability Act of 1980 (CERCLA, also known as the Superfund law) which facilitates the cleanup of existing sites (and is hence largely backward-looking).

In establishing RCRA, Congress amended the Solid Waste Disposal Act, first passed in 1965 to address the regulation of landfills and dumps. RCRA emerged as Congress gradually became aware that toxics were seeping into groundwater through multiple pathways, including landfills, and posing a threat to human health. Part of this congressional awareness came through the issuance of an EPA report to Congress that had been required by the Solid Waste Disposal Act. The report documented a number of instances of groundwater contamination and human illness as a result of the mishandling of hazardous wastes. *See* Halina Szenjwald Brown, Brian J. Cook, Robert Krueger and Jo Anne Shatkin, *Reassessing the History of U.S. Hazardous Waste Disposal Policy—Problem Definitions, Expert Knowledge and Agenda-Setting*, 8 RISK: HEALTH, SAFETY & ENVIRONMENT 249 (Summer 1997), https://scholars.unh.edu/cgi/view content.cgi?article=1332&context=risk.

Not long after RCRA's passage, the issue of hazardous waste contamination made national headlines. In August 1978, President Carter declared a state of emergency in the Love Canal area of Niagara Falls, New York. Investigating serious health complaints by residents, the state health department found that toxic chemicals had leaked into the basements of many houses, and into the air, water, and soil. Indoor air pollution levels in some houses were far above maximum safe levels. In 1947, Hooker Chemical and Plastics Corporation had purchased an uncompleted waterway and used it as a depository for an estimated 352 million pounds of industrial wastes over the following six years. The land had then been used as a school site and a housing development. As a result, three decades later, over 1000 families were evacuated, $30 million in cleanup costs were required, and over $3 billion in damage claims were filed.[1]

Love Canal was not an isolated incident. For much of U.S. history, land was regarded as a "safe" repository for wastes that could not be disposed of in the air or water. Decades of uncontrolled dumping have led to contamination of land and of related ground and surface waters. Some of the most serious threats involve disposal or storage of wastes at sites where water contamination may occur, such as sites located in floodplains, over aquifers unprotected by impervious rock or soil, and in filled wetlands. Water filtering through such sites can leach chemicals into ground water, and runoff from rain and snowmelt can carry chemicals to nearby streams and rivers.

Love Canal had a significant effect on Congress and led to the passage of CERCLA. And though Love Canal and other high-profile incidents involved the past handling of hazardous wastes—and thus would become the focus of CERCLA cleanup efforts—they also re-focused congressional attention on the need to regulate the handling and disposal of hazardous waste to avoid the creation of new waste sites and led to significant amendments to RCRA in 1980 and 1984.

A. REGULATING THE TREATMENT, STORAGE, AND DISPOSAL OF HAZARDOUS WASTES: RCRA

1. BACKGROUND AND OVERVIEW

Although Congress enacted RCRA in 1976, the EPA moved very slowly in promulgating regulations to implement the statute. In part, this was because the task of issuing regulations was highly technical, and because the EPA was a relatively new agency with a number of complicated statutes to implement. Because of the delay, environmental groups sued the EPA, ultimately winning court victories forcing the agency to implement the statute. Yet the EPA continued to move slowly in the early

---

[1]   These facts are drawn from CEQ, ENVTL. QUALITY: TENTH ANN. REP., at 176–77 (1979); Mary Worobec, *An Analysis of the Resource Conservation and Recovery Act*, 11 ENV'T REP. 634–35 (1980).

In 1995, after sixteen years of litigation, the Clinton administration announced that Occidental Chemical Corp. had agreed to pay $129 million to the federal government for its costs of cleaning up the Love Canal neighborhood. $102 million was to go to EPA's Superfund to cover governmental cleanup costs. The other $27 million was to go to the Federal Emergency Management Agency, which undertook the initial evacuation and cleanup. Previously, in 1994, Occidental had entered into a $98 million settlement of claims by the state of New York related to Love Canal. *See* James Gerstenzang, *Firm Agrees to Settle Love Canal Suit*, L.A. TIMES, Dec. 22, 1995, at A43.

1980s, largely because of the Reagan Administration's opposition to implementing and enforcing hazardous waste laws. The administration had, after all, campaigned on a de-regulatory agenda, and viewed environmental, health and safety regulation as especially onerous. Eventually, in the face of publicity about Love Canal and other dangerous and highly contaminated sites, the Democratic Congress stepped in and amended RCRA in 1984 (the amendments are known as the Hazardous and Solid Waste Amendments). The 1984 amendments were much more specific and directive, and included provisions to clean up leaking underground storage tanks, expand liability for small generators of hazardous waste and ban land disposal of hazardous waste without treatment. The legislation also included "hammers" that would force industry groups to pressure EPA to meet various statutory deadlines or face much more draconian measures (such as the complete ban on land disposal). The intent of the congressional amendments was to remove much of EPA's discretion by providing detailed statutory provisions and hard deadlines. This example illustrates the institutional dynamic we have noted throughout the casebook: environmental policy is made in the push and pull between the branches. If the executive branch resists implementing environmental statutes, the legislative branch can always amend the law to force agency action. Caught in the middle, of course, are the agencies, which must abide by their statutory mandates and also respond to the legitimate political imperatives of the administration.

RCRA is designed to provide "cradle to grave" coverage for a large percentage of the hazardous waste generated by businesses and government. The statute covers approximately 37 million tons of hazardous wastes generated annually by more than 25,000 generators. *See* EPA, THE NATIONAL BIENNIAL RCRA HAZARDOUS WASTE REPORT (BASED ON 2017 DATA) https://rcrapublic.epa.gov/rcrainfoweb/action/modules/br/summary/ summarysearch. Chemical manufacturers produce the largest percentage of RCRA hazardous waste, followed by petroleum and coal products manufacturing. *Id.* Texas leads the country in generating RCRA waste, followed by Louisiana, Mississippi, and Ohio. *Id.*

RCRA's overarching theory is that if we know where the waste is during its life cycle—from the moment of generation through transport to its ultimate treatment, storage and disposal—then we can avoid the kinds of catastrophes at which CERCLA is aimed. RCRA is a highly prescriptive statute that employs a variety of regulatory strategies, including a permit system, design standards, performance standards, "good character" and capitalization requirements, information disclosure, liability provisions and absolute prohibitions on certain activities. Despite its highly prescriptive nature, RCRA's regulatory provisions apply almost exclusively to *hazardous* waste, which means that a great deal of waste that might nevertheless pose public health risks escapes RCRA regulation. RCRA also presents an opportunity to explore the difference between a "health-based" statute like the Clean Air Act, which sets national ambient air quality standards based on public health requirements, and a "technology based" statute that sets levels of pollution control based on what technology can achieve at an acceptable cost. As you read the materials, ask yourself: which kind of statute is RCRA?

RCRA contains ten separate subtitles, three of which contain the primary substantive features of RCRA: Subtitle C is the chapter that regulates hazardous waste; Subtitle D regulates and provides guidelines to states in their management of solid waste; and Subtitle I regulates underground storage tanks (USTs). We will focus most heavily on Subtitle C.

a.   Subtitle C: Hazardous Waste Management

Subtitle C is based on the simple premise that hazardous waste should be tracked from the time of its generation to the time of its disposal, and that it should not be disposed of in a manner that may create a danger to human health or to the environment. Naturally, however, the simplicity of the premise is belied by the complexity of the regulatory system. The central components of Subtitle C are as follows:

i.   *What Does RCRA Subtitle C Regulate? Solid Waste and Hazardous Waste*

Subtitle C covers material that must be both "solid waste" and "hazardous waste." Understandably, these definitional requirements lead to vigorous disputes over which activities and substances fall within the scope of the statute. As we saw in Chapter 5 with the Clean Water Act (which regulates almost exclusively point sources of water pollution and not non-point source run-off), definitions can function like "on-off" switches: activities that fall within the definitional reach of the statute are fully regulated, but those that fall outside the definitional categories can escape regulation altogether, even when the activities all pose some degree of risk to human health or the environment. Falling within RCRA's purview can be very burdensome and highly costly, and escaping coverage can have very significant implications for public health, which explains why the definitional battles over what constitutes solid waste and what constitutes hazardous waste have been so intense.

These definitional questions have occupied an enormous amount of regulatory energy. EPA has had difficulty identifying those wastes that ought to be considered hazardous, and struggled to define materials that should *not* be regarded as "waste" because they may be reused or recycled in the manufacturing process. In section 3001, Congress requires EPA to promulgate criteria for "identifying the characteristics" of hazardous waste, and for "listing" hazardous waste that should be subject to RCRA regulation. As discussed in more detail below, EPA has divided hazardous wastes into two separate categories, those that are "listed" and those that exhibit a particular characteristic—either toxicity, ignitability, corrosivity or reactivity (so called "characteristic" wastes)—that makes the waste hazardous. Generally speaking, listed wastes are subject to more rigorous regulation than characteristic wastes, though both listed and characteristic wastes must be tracked from cradle to grave.

ii. Who Does RCRA Subtitle C Regulate? Generators, Transporters, and TSD Facilities

RCRA applies separate regulatory standards to generators of hazardous wastes, transporters, and treatment, storage and disposal (TSD) facilities. The burden on generators and transporters is relatively lower than on TSDs, and consists primarily of labeling, tracking and reporting requirements. Because TSD requirements are more onerous, generators and transporters tend to take steps to avoid doing anything (such as treating the waste) that might trigger TSD status.

A.   Generators of Hazardous Wastes

Generators of hazardous waste occupy the "cradle" part of RCRA's "cradle-to-grave" system for regulating hazardous wastes. As the name suggests, generators are those entities whose activities generate hazardous waste. Subtitle C distinguishes between generators depending on the amount of hazardous waste they generate: large quantity generators are those producing 1000 kilograms or more of hazardous waste per month; small quantity generators are those producing between 100 and 1000 kilograms of hazardous waste per month; and very small quantity generators are those producing 100 kg or less of hazardous waste per month. The regulations for large and small quantity generators are quite similar. Very small quantity generators, however, are largely exempt from regulation under subtitle C. Businesses that generate hazardous waste must keep detailed records of the type, quantity and "disposition" of the waste and use a manifest system to ensure that the hazardous waste generated by the source is ultimately processed on-site or at a TSD facility with a § 3005 permit (a manifest is a list or invoice of cargo for a transporter, identifying the cargo and its intended destination.) If a generator's waste is disposed of offsite, the manifest must accompany the waste from the generator's site to the transporter and ultimately to the TSD facility and requires the inclusion of information about the type and quantity of waste being disposed of, along with how it is contained. The generator is responsible for ensuring that the manifest is properly filled out by transporters and TSD facilities. Generators are also subject to limitations on the amount of time they can store hazardous waste prior to shipment; if they store waste for too long (more than 90 days for large quantity generators and 180 days for small quantity generators) they are required to obtain a permit as a TSD facility. Because the regulatory burdens on TSD facilities are so much more onerous, most generators of hazardous waste ship their waste offsite for disposal.

B.   Transporters of Hazardous Waste

Transporters of hazardous waste are also subject to the manifest system and must comply with Department of Transportation regulations concerning the safe transport of hazardous wastes. 49 C.F.R. §§ 171–179 (2013). Transporters can become liable as generators of hazardous wastes if they mix dissimilar wastes; they also have reporting obligations in the event of a spill.

C.   Treatment, Storage, and Disposal Facilities

TSD facilities must obtain permits under RCRA § 3005 and are the most extensively regulated parties under the Act. Regulatory obligations include providing appropriate security, emergency planning, adequate employee training, groundwater monitoring, recordkeeping and proving adequate financial security in order to prevent the abandonment of the facility. RCRA also regulates the location, construction and operation of disposal sites. Common methods of disposing of hazardous waste include incinerating the waste; disposing liquid waste in surface impoundments; disposing treated waste on land; and injecting waste into underground storage wells in impermeable rock formations deep beneath the earth's surface.

The permit system established under § 3005 is the key enforcement provision for TSD facilities. EPA is given broad inspection powers (§ 3007) and the authority to issue administrative compliance orders (with violators subject to a civil penalty) or begin civil actions against violators of any requirement (§ 3008). Criminal penalties are also available for violation of the permit requirements or falsification of documents (§ 3008(d)).

iii. Federal Delegation to States for Implementation

As with many federal environmental statutes, RCRA embodies a version of "cooperative federalism." The statute delegates to states the authority to implement RCRA's regulatory requirements, subject to EPA oversight (§ 3006). Most states have been granted the authority to implement at least the basic RCRA programs. For more information on state delegation under RCRA *see* https://www.epa.gov/rcra/state-authorization-under-resource-conservation-and-recovery-act-rcra.   State laws less stringent than federal requirements are preempted. (§ 3009).

Although states play an important role in enforcing RCRA, the EPA sometimes steps in if a state is unable or unwilling to enforce the statute.

In a controversial decision, one federal appeals court has held that where EPA had authorized a state to administer and enforce a hazardous waste program, and a state court approved a no-penalty settlement between the state enforcement agency and a serious RCRA violator, § 3006(b) barred EPA from "overfiling," i.e., maintaining a separate action based on the same violations. *Harmon Industries, Inc. v. Browner*, 191 F.3d 894 (8th Cir. 1999). However, two other courts of appeals have rejected *Harmon* and held that EPA's authorization of a state hazardous waste program does not strip the United States of civil or criminal enforcement authority because RCRA contemplates that only the federal regulatory or permitting program is supplanted by authorized state programs. *United States v. Power Eng'g Co.*, 303 F.3d 1232 (10th Cir. 2002); *United States v. Elias*, 269 F.3d 1003 (9th Cir. 2001), *cert. denied,* 537 U.S. 812 (2002)

iv. Land Disposal Restrictions

In the 1984 Hazardous and Solid Waste Amendments, Public Law 98–616, 98 Stat. 3221, Congress shifted the focus of hazardous waste management away from safer land disposal to *treatment* alternatives. The 1984 amendments ban land disposal of hazardous wastes unless one of two conditions is satisfied: either the waste is treated to comply with standards promulgated by EPA under RCRA § 3004(m), or EPA determines that the hazardous constituents will not "migrate" from the disposal unit. RCRA § 3004(g)(5). As noted, the 1984 amendments also included so-called "hammer" provisions that would ban all land disposal if EPA did not meet certain deadlines in promulgating regulations. These provisions were designed to force a reluctant EPA, which had been slow to implement RCRA, to act, and to create incentives for industry to work together with the agency to develop acceptable treatment standards rather than to fight the EPA's every move, since without them the more draconian ban would apply.

b. Subtitle D: State or Regional Solid Waste Plans

Subtitle D of RCRA (§§ 4001 *et seq.*) requires states or regions, where appropriate, to submit solid waste plans to provide for the proper disposal of waste not defined as hazardous by Subtitle C. Subtitle D also provides criteria for sanitary landfills and the upgrading and closing of open dumps, and requires states to provide plans for handling household hazardous waste and small quantity generator waste. For several years in the late 1970s and 1980s RCRA also provided financial assistance to states and localities in developing solid waste plans. It is worth noting the contrast between RCRA's treatment of hazardous waste and all other solid waste. While Subtitle C establishes a detailed, onerous regulatory regime for all aspects of hazardous waste (from cradle to grave), Subtitle D is short and regulates only landfills and dumps.

c. Subtitle I: Underground Storage Tanks

As amended by Public Law 98–616, RCRA for the first time provided for regulation of *underground storage tanks* containing petroleum products and other hazardous liquids such as solvents and pesticides. RCRA §§ 9001–9010. The program is administered by EPA or by states with programs satisfying federal requirements. EPA regulations provide for detection and correction of leaks in existing tanks, and establish performance standards for new tanks. 40 CFR Part 280. In 2012, EPA proposed strengthening the regulations, with a focus on maintaining equipment, but as of press time the regulations have not been finalized. See U.S. EPA, *Proposal Revises Underground Storage Tank Regulations,* http://www.epa.gov/oust/fedlaws/proposedregs.html. The aim is to avoid groundwater pollution. Releases into the air of dangerous chemicals from underground tanks are not controlled directly by the 1984 RCRA amendments, which nevertheless may help to prevent such accidents. Section 112(r) of the Clean Air Act, added in 1990, authorizes EPA regulation of accidental releases of hazardous substances into the air.

For an overview of the federal UST program, *see* Laura J. Nagle, *RCRA Subtitle I: The Federal Underground Storage Tank Program*, 24 ENVTL. L. REP. 10057 (1994). Regulations adopted in 1988 gave owners of the nation's three million or so USTs ten years to either remove or upgrade them. The regulations covered tanks capable of holding at least 1,100 gallons. Smaller home heating oil tanks were exempted, though some states regulate them. By March of 2013, EPA reported there were about 582,000 regulated tanks still in the ground. Almost 1.8 million tanks have been closed since the program's inception in 1984. *See* U.S. EPA, Semiannual Report of UST Performance Measures Mid Fiscal Year 2013 (October 1, 2012–March 31, 2013), available at http://www.epa.gov/oust/cat/ca-13-12.pdf.

The 1986 amendments to RCRA established a $500 million Leaking Underground Storage Tank Trust Fund, derived from federal taxes on motor fuels and to be used for the correction of releases of petroleum where EPA cannot identify a solvent owner or operator of the tank who will undertake action properly. The amendments were contained in the Superfund Amendments and Reauthorization Act of 1986, Pub. L. No. 99–499, §§ 521–522, 100 Stat. 1613 (1986). The LUST fund, as it is known, is financed by a .01 cent tax per gallon of gasoline and provides about $100 million annually to EPA (paid from the interest on the balance in the fund) to disperse to states and tribes to clean up leaking tanks. In addition, the 2009 American Recovery and Reinvestment Act provided an additional one-time allocation of $200 million. *See* U.S. EPA, *Leaking Underground Storage Tank (LUST) Trust Fund,* http://www.epa.gov/oust/ltffacts.htm. From 1996–2009, the EPA and states that administer the program had confirmed over 488,000 leaks. As of the end of FY 2009, approximately 80 percent of leaking tanks had been cleaned up. Ten states were responsible for 61 percent of the remaining leaking tanks and EPA has launched an effort to try to reduce the backlog of necessary cleanups in those states. *See* U.S. EPA, *The National LUST Cleanup Backlog: A Study of Opportunities* (Sept. 2011), available at http://www.epa.gov/oust/pubs/backlog_national_chapter.pdf.

The next section details some of the more contentious issues the EPA has faced in implementing Subtitle C of RCRA. As noted in the introduction, the definition of solid and hazardous waste has proven to be quite difficult.

2. DEFINING "SOLID" AND "HAZARDOUS" WASTES

Much of the battle over RCRA involves defining what kind of material is "in" or "out" of the statute's reach. For example, solid waste is covered by RCRA with some exceptions; if a generator or handler of materials can define those materials out of the category of solid waste it can avoid the statute's requirements. And even if waste is defined as solid waste a generator can still avoid RCRA's onerous regulatory requirements if its waste is not considered "hazardous."

a. What Is a "Solid Waste"?

Before a waste can be "hazardous" and subject to RCRA's subtitle C regulations, it must first be a "solid waste" as defined in the statute and EPA regulations. This threshold determination is often more difficult than the subsequent question of whether the solid waste meets the definition of "hazardous waste." Much of the difficulty, as we will see, turns on whether the material in question has been "discarded" and thus can be considered part of the solid waste problem. RCRA defines "solid waste", in Section 1003(27):

> The term "solid waste" means any garbage, refuse, sludge from a waste treatment plant, water supply treatment plant, or air pollution control facility and other discarded material, including solid, liquid, semisolid, or contained gaseous material resulting from industrial, commercial, mining, and agricultural operations, and from community activities, but does not include solid or dissolved material in domestic sewage, or solid or dissolved materials in irrigation return flows or industrial discharges which are point sources subject to permits under [§ 402 of the Clean Water Act], or [certain radioactive wastes regulated under the Atomic Energy Act of 1954].

Despite the statutory definition of solid waste, EPA has struggled to clearly define which materials are subject to the definition. Ongoing questions regarding how to treat materials that are subject to reuse or recycling have generated significant litigation and led to an increasingly complex set of regulations defining solid waste. 40 C.F.R. § 261.2 contains the regulatory definition of solid waste.

Early EPA regulations defining "solid waste" provided that materials were solid waste if they were abandoned by being disposed of, burned, or incinerated; or stored, treated, or accumulated before or in lieu of those activities. 50 Fed. Reg. 614–01 (Jan. 4, 1985). The regulations also provided that certain materials used in recycling might be covered by RCRA, depending on the nature of the material and the recycling activity. The regulations were challenged by the mining and petroleum industries, which argued that materials intended for reuse were not "wastes" because they had not been discarded. The challenge resulted in the following decision.

AMERICAN MINING CONGRESS v. ENVIRONMENTAL PROTECTION AGENCY

United States Court of Appeals, District of Columbia Circuit, 1987.
824 F.2d 1177.

STARR, CIRCUIT JUDGE.

* * * Petitioners, trade associations representing mining and oil refining interests, challenge regulations promulgated by EPA that amend the definition of "solid waste" to establish and define the agency's authority to regulate secondary materials reused within an industry's ongoing production process. In plain English, petitioners maintain that EPA has exceeded its regulatory authority in seeking to bring materials that are not discarded or otherwise disposed of within the compass of "waste."

RCRA is a comprehensive environmental statute under which EPA is granted authority to regulate solid and hazardous wastes. * * *

Congress' "overriding concern" in enacting RCRA was to establish the framework for a national system to insure the safe management of hazardous waste. * * *

RCRA includes two major parts: one deals with nonhazardous solid waste management and the other with hazardous waste management. Under the latter, EPA is directed to promulgate regulations establishing a comprehensive management system. EPA's authority, however, extends only to the regulation of "hazardous waste." Because "hazardous waste" is defined as a subset of "solid waste," § 6903(5), the scope of EPA's jurisdiction is limited to those materials that constitute "solid waste." That pivotal term is defined by RCRA as

> any garbage, refuse, sludge from a waste treatment plant, water supply treatment plant, or air pollution control facility *and other discarded material,* including solid, liquid, semisolid or contained

gaseous material, resulting from industrial, commercial, mining, and agricultural operations, and from community activities. . .

42 U.S.C. § 6903(27) (emphasis added). As will become evident, this case turns on the meaning of the phrase, "and other discarded material," contained in the statute's definitional provisions.

EPA's interpretation of "solid waste" has evolved over time. On May 19, 1980, EPA issued interim regulations defining "solid waste" to include a material that is "a manufacturing or mining by-product and sometimes is discarded." 45 Fed. Reg. 33,119 (1980). This definition contained two terms needing elucidation: "by-product" and "sometimes discarded." In its definition of "a manufacturing or mining by-product," EPA expressly *excluded* "an intermediate manufacturing or mining product which results from one of the steps in a manufacturing or mining process and is typically processed through the next step of the process within a short time."

In 1983, the agency proposed narrowing amendments to the 1980 interim rule. The agency showed especial concern over *recycling* activities. In the preamble to the amendments, the agency observed that, in light of RCRA's legislative history, it was clear that "Congress indeed intended that materials being recycled or held for recycling can be wastes, and if hazardous, hazardous wastes." The agency also asserted that "not only can materials destined for recycling or being recycled be solid and hazardous wastes, but the Agency clearly has the authority to regulate recycling activities as hazardous waste management."

While asserting its interest in recycling activities (and materials being held for recycling), EPA's discussion left unclear whether the agency in fact believed its jurisdiction extended to materials recycled in an industry's on-going production processes, or only to materials disposed of and recycled as part of a waste management program. In its preamble, EPA stated that "the revised definition of solid waste sets out the Agency's view of its jurisdiction over the recycling of hazardous waste. . . . Proposed section 261.6 then contains exemptions from regulations for those hazardous waste recycling activities that we do not think require regulation." The amended regulatory description of "solid waste" itself, then, did not include materials "used or reused as effective substitutes for raw materials in processes using raw materials as principal feedstocks." EPA explained the exclusion as follows:

> [These] materials are being used essentially as raw materials and so ordinarily are not appropriate candidates for regulatory control. Moreover, when these materials are used to manufacture new products, the processes generally are normal manufacturing operations. . . . The Agency is reluctant to read the statute as regulating actual manufacturing processes.

This, then, seemed clear: EPA was drawing a line between discarding and ultimate recycling, on the one hand, and a continuous or ongoing manufacturing process with one-site "recycling," on the other. If the activity fell within the latter category, then the materials were not deemed to be "discarded."

After receiving extensive comments, EPA issued its final rule on January 4, 1985. Under the final rule, materials are considered "solid waste" if they are abandoned by being disposed of, burned, or incinerated; or stored, treated, or accumulated before or in lieu of those activities. In addition, certain recycling activities fall within EPA's definition. EPA determines whether a material is a RCRA solid waste when it is recycled by examining both the material or substance itself and the recycling activity involved. The final rule identifies five categories of "secondary materials" (spent materials, sludges, by-products, commercial chemical products, and scrap metal). These "secondary materials" constitute "solid waste" when they are disposed of; burned for energy recovery or used to produce a fuel; reclaimed; or accumulated speculatively. Under the final rule, if a material constitutes "solid waste," it is subject to RCRA regulation *unless* it is directly reused as an ingredient or as an effective substitute for a commercial product, or is returned as a raw material substitute to its original manufacturing process.[2] In the jargon of the trade, the latter category is known as the "closed-loop" exception. In either case, the material must not first be "reclaimed" (processed to recover a usable product or regenerated). EPA exempts these activities "because they are like ordinary usage of commercial products."

Petitioners, American Mining Congress ("AMC") and American Petroleum Institute ("API"), challenge the scope of EPA's final rule. Relying upon the statutory definition of "solid waste," petitioners contend that EPA's authority under RCRA is limited to controlling materials that are *discarded or intended for discard.* They argue that EPA's reuse and recycle rules, as applied to in-process secondary materials, regulate materials that have not been discarded, and therefore exceed EPA's jurisdiction.

[The court then describes how petroleum refineries use a complex retrieval system to recapture escaping hydrocarbons and return them to appropriate parts of the refining process. The court also states that mining facilities reprocess ore and recapture for reuse in the production process metal-and mineral-bearing dusts released during processing. The court

---

[2]   Specifically, the final rule excludes materials recycled by being: "(1) [u]sed or reused as ingredients in an industrial process to make a product, *provided the materials are not being reclaimed;* or (2) [u]sed or reused as effective substitutes for commercial products; or (3) [r]eturned to the original process from which they are generated, without first being reclaimed." Id. (emphasis added). In the third category, the material must be returned to the original manufacturing process as a substitute for raw material feedstock, and the process must use raw materials as principal feedstocks.

notes that the materials recaptured by petroleum refineries and mining facilities are considered "solid waste" under EPA's rule.] * * *

* * * Congress, it will be recalled, granted EPA power to regulate "solid waste." Congress specifically defined "solid waste" as "discarded material." EPA then defined "discarded material" to include materials destined for reuse in an industry's *ongoing* production processes. The challenge to EPA's jurisdictional reach is founded, again, on the proposition that in-process secondary materials are outside the bounds of EPA's lawful authority. Nothing has been *discarded,* the argument goes, and thus RCRA jurisdiction remains untriggered.

The first step in statutory interpretation is, of course, an analysis of the language itself. In pursuit of Congress' intent, we "start with the assumption that the legislative purpose is expressed by the ordinary meaning of the words used." Here, Congress defined "solid waste" as "discarded material." The ordinary plain-English meaning of the word "discarded" is "disposed of," "thrown away" or "abandoned." Encompassing materials retained for immediate reuse within the scope of "discarded material" strains, to say the least, the everyday usage of that term. * * *

The question we face, then, is whether, in light of the National Legislature's expressly stated objectives and the underlying problems that motivated it to enact RCRA in the first instance, Congress was using the term "discarded" in its ordinary sense—"disposed of" or "abandoned"—or whether Congress was using it in a much more open-ended way, so as to encompass materials no longer useful in their original capacity though destined for immediate reuse in another phase of the industry's ongoing production process.

For the following reasons, we believe the former to be the case. RCRA was enacted, as the congressional objectives and findings make clear, in an effort to help States deal with the ever-increasing problem of solid waste *disposal* by encouraging the search for and use of alternatives to existing methods of disposal (including recycling) and protecting health and the environment by regulating hazardous wastes. To fulfill these purposes, it seems clear that EPA need not regulate "spent" materials that are recycled and reused in an *ongoing* manufacturing or industrial process. These materials have not yet become part of the waste disposal problem; rather, *they are destined for beneficial reuse or recycling in a continuous process by the generating industry itself.* * * *

We are constrained to conclude that, in light of the language and structure of RCRA, the problems animating Congress to enact it, and the relevant portions of the legislative history, Congress clearly and unambiguously expressed its intent that "solid waste" (and therefore EPA's regulatory authority) be limited to materials that are "discarded" by virtue of being disposed of, abandoned, or thrown away. While we do not lightly

overturn an agency's reading of its own statute, we are persuaded that by regulating in-process secondary materials, EPA has acted in contravention of Congress' intent. Accordingly, the petition for review is granted.

MIKVA, CIRCUIT JUDGE, dissenting:

* * * In my opinion, the EPA's interpretation of solid waste is completely reasonable in light of the language, policies, and legislative history of RCRA. Congress had broad remedial objectives in mind when it enacted RCRA, most notably to "regulat[e] the treatment, storage, transportation, and disposal of hazardous wastes which have adverse effects on the environment." The disposal problem Congress was combatting encompassed more than just abandoned materials. RCRA makes this clear with its definition of the central statutory term "disposal":

> the discharge, deposit, injection, dumping, spilling, leaking, or placing of any solid waste or hazardous waste into or on any land or water so that such solid waste or hazardous waste or any constituent thereof may enter the environment or be emitted into the air or discharged into any waters, including ground waters.

42 U.S.C. § 6903(3). This definition clearly encompasses more than the everyday meaning of disposal, which is a "discarding or throwing away." Webster's Third International Dictionary 654 (2d ed. 1981). The definition is *functional:* waste is disposed under this provision if it is put into contact with land or water in such a way as to pose the risks to health and the environment that animated Congress to pass RCRA. Whether the manufacturer subjectively intends to put the material to additional use is irrelevant to this definition, as indeed it should be, because the manufacturer's state of mind bears no necessary relation to the hazards of the industrial processes he employs.

Faithful to RCRA's functional approach, EPA reasonably concluded that regulation of certain in-process secondary materials was necessary to carry out its mandate. The materials at issue in this case can pose the same risks as abandoned wastes, whether or not the manufacturer intends eventually to put them to further beneficial use. As the agency explained, "[s]imply because a waste is likely to be recycled will not ensure that it will not be spilled or leaked before recycling occurs." The storage, transportation, and even recycling of in-process secondary materials can cause severe environmental harm. Indeed, the EPA documented environmental disasters caused by the handling or storage of such materials. It also pointed out the risk of damage from spills or leaks when certain in-process secondary materials are placed on land or in underground product storage. * * *

* * * [I]n this case the EPA has interpreted solid waste in a manner that seems to expand the everyday usage of the word "discarded." Its conclusion, however, is fully supportable in light of the statutory scheme

and legislative history of RCRA. The agency concluded that certain on-site recycled materials constitute an integral part of the waste disposal problem. This judgment is grounded in the EPA's technical expertise and is adequately supported by evidence in the record. The majority nevertheless reverses the agency because it believes that the materials at issue "have not yet become part of the waste disposal problem." This declaration is nothing more than a substitution of the majority's own conclusions for the sound technical judgment of the EPA. The EPA's interpretation is a reasonable construction of an ambiguous statutory provision and should be upheld.

NOTES

1. Should the definition of "solid waste" be based upon whether materials have become a part of the waste disposal problem? Should the definition depend on whether a substance poses a risk warranting regulation? If such considerations are relevant, who—EPA or the courts—should weigh them and make a decision? Under the *Chevron* case, did the majority in *AMC* give sufficient deference to EPA's conclusion?

2. After the *AMC* decision, various industries claimed that numerous substances which EPA had regulated under subtitle C of RCRA were not "solid waste." Thus, the American Mining Congress claimed that EPA could not regulate sludge from wastewater, stored in a surface impoundment, if the sludge was to be reprocessed later for metals recovery. In *American Mining Congress v. EPA (AMC II)*, 907 F.2d 1179, 1186 (D.C. Cir. 1990), the court sided with EPA and sought to clarify its holding in the original AMC case:

> *AMC*'s holding concerned only materials that are "destined for *immediate reuse* in another phase of the industry's ongoing production process" (emphasis added), and that "have not yet become part of the waste disposal problem." Nothing in *AMC* prevents the agency from treating as "discarded" the wastes at issue in this case, which are managed in land disposal units that *are* part of wastewater treatment systems, which *have* therefore become "part of the waste disposal problem," and which are *not* part of ongoing industrial processes. Indeed, [we have] explicitly rejected the very claim that petitioners assert in this case, * * * namely, that under RCRA, potential reuse of a material prevents the agency from classifying it as "discarded."

3. If materials are in fact recycled, can they be considered wastes at the time of recycling? In reliance upon *AMC,* EPA determined that materials utilized in a metals reclamation process ceased to be solid wastes under RCRA when they arrived at a reclamation facility because they no longer were "discarded material." Environmentalists challenged this interpretation and prevailed in *American Petroleum Institute v. EPA,* 906 F.2d 729, 741 (D.C. Cir. 1990):

AMC is by no means dispositive of EPA's authority to regulate K061 slag [K061 slag is a listed hazardous waste]. Unlike the materials in question in *AMC,* K061 is indisputably "discarded" *before* being subject to metals reclamation. Consequently, it *has* "become part of the waste disposal problem"; that is why EPA has the power to require that K061 be subject to mandatory metals reclamation. Nor does anything in *AMC* require EPA to cease treating K061 as "solid waste" once it reaches the metals reclamation facility. K061 is delivered to the facility not as part of an "*ongoing* manufacturing or industrial process" within the generating industry, but as part of a mandatory waste treatment plan prescribed by EPA.

See also U.S. v. ILCO, 996 F.2d 1126, 1132 (11th Cir. 1993) (used lead batteries sent to a reclaimer have been "discarded once" by the entity that sent the battery to the reclaimer and are thus properly categorized as solid waste)). (*Owen Electric Steel Co. v. EPA,* 37 F.3d 146, 150 (4th Cir. 1994) (used slag held for six months could be solid waste even though subsequently recycled).

4.   As the cases mentioned in Note 3 indicate, EPA has struggled over the years to craft regulations that will encourage recycling of materials as a way to reduce the overall waste problem while ensuring that improper recycling activities do not result in "disposal" of wastes that creates new environmental problems. EPA's regulatory definition of solid waste defines some, but not all, recycled materials as "discarded" and therefore within the category of solid waste. In *Safe Food and Fertilizer v. EPA,* 350 F.3d 1263 (D.C. Cir. 2003) the court upheld an EPA rule that excludes certain recycled materials used to make fertilizer from the definition of solid waste provided the materials are handled in a way that meets certain reporting and handling conditions and contain below-threshold amounts of certain hazardous chemicals. The reasoning behind the fertilizer rule was based on a controversial theory that if certain market conditions exist, firms will have an incentive to engage in safe and responsible practices that can obviate the need for regulation.

After the case was decided, EPA proposed a rule to incorporate this novel "market theory" into the definition of solid waste more generally and received heavy criticism. EPA then commissioned several studies to evaluate the market theory and proposed a new set of recycling exclusions from the solid waste definition rule that incorporated the findings of the study. The final rule was adopted in 2008. *See EPA, Definition of Solid Waste,* Final Rule, 73 Fed. Reg. 64668 (Oct. 30, 2008). Generally speaking, the rule attempts to exempt materials where there is economic value in legitimately recycling the material, again on the theory that firms have an incentive to handle the material with care. It creates two specific exclusions for recycled materials from the definition of solid waste: (a) a generator-controlled exclusion that exempted hazardous secondary materials legitimately reclaimed under the control of the generator; and (b) a transfer-based exclusion that exempted hazardous secondary materials transferred to a third party for reclamation whom the generator had confirmed as legitimate.

The Sierra Club filed an administrative petition objecting to the 2008 rule. Among other things, the Sierra Club's challenge to the 2008 rule focused on the environmental justice implications of third-party recycling. Their concern was that the transfer-based exclusion did not allow for sufficient oversight of third-party recyclers and could result in over-accumulation and mismanagement of materials that might threaten neighboring communities. In response, EPA agreed to evaluate a number of the Sierra Club's claims and proposed a new rule in 2011. That rule was finalized in 2015, *See EPA, Definition of Solid Waste*, Final Rule, 80 Fed. Reg. 1694 (Jan. 13, 2015) and was the subject of the following case. The main issues in the case concerned (a) the four "legitimacy factors" that EPA developed to distinguish between "legitimate" and "sham" recycling; and (b) EPA's decision to replace the "transfer-based" exclusion for third-party recyclers with a new "verified recycler" exclusion.

AMERICAN PETROLEUM INSTITUTE V. EPA

United States Court of Appeals, District of Columbia Circuit, 2017.
862 F.3d 50.

PER CURIAM:

This case arises from the Environmental Protection Agency's latest effort to define the term "solid waste" under the Resource Conservation and Recovery Act. In 2015, EPA promulgated a final rule governing when certain hazardous materials qualify as "discarded" and hence are subject to the agency's regulatory authority. Environmental and Industry Petitioners have each petitioned for review of that rule, arguing that numerous aspects of it are unlawful and arbitrary and capricious. For the reasons explained, we grant the Industry petition for review with respect to Factor 4 of the legitimacy test and to the Verified Recycler Exclusion and we dismiss the Environmental petition for review.

I. Introduction

The Resource Conservation and Recovery Act ("RCRA") empowers EPA to manage solid and hazardous waste. The statute defines solid waste as "garbage, refuse, sludge . . . and other discarded material." Hazardous waste is a subset of solid waste that may pose a substantial threat to human health or the environment when improperly managed. If a material qualifies as hazardous waste, it is subject to regulation under RCRA Subtitle C, §§ 6921–6939g, which imposes comprehensive reporting and operating requirements. Material that is not solid waste, and therefore not hazardous waste, is exempt from Subtitle C.

Pursuant to its RCRA authority, EPA has promulgated a rule defining solid waste as "discarded material" not otherwise excluded from the agency's regulations. 40 C.F.R. § 261.2(a)(1). A separate regulation lists materials that fall outside the definition of solid waste. § 261.4. Central to the issues before us, EPA considers certain materials that are destined for recycling to be discarded and hence solid waste subject to RCRA regulation.

For our purposes, the relevant history begins in 2007, when EPA proposed a rule deregulating many hazardous secondary materials. Secondary materials are substances generated as the remainder of industrial processes; they include spent materials, byproducts, and sludges. EPA's proposed rule—which became a final rule in October 2008— excluded hazardous secondary materials from the definition of solid waste in two circumstances: first, if the company that generated the materials controlled the recycling of those materials; and second, if the generator transferred the materials to an off-site recycler it had audited to ensure compliance with proper recycling practices. These two exemptions were known, respectively, as the "Generator-Controlled Exclusion" and the "Transfer-Based Exclusion." To qualify for either, secondary materials had to be recycled "legitimately," a term EPA defined by reference to certain "legitimacy factors." EPA adopted this legitimacy requirement to distinguish "true" recycling from "sham" recycling in which companies claim to reuse materials they in fact discard.

Several organizations challenged the *2008 Rule*. One, the American Petroleum Institute, argued that the rule unlawfully regulated materials called spent petroleum refinery catalysts, which are byproducts of the oil refining process. Another group, the Sierra Club, asserted that the rule "was not sufficiently protective of human health and the environment," in violation of RCRA. * * *

Before this court heard oral argument, EPA entered a settlement agreement with the Sierra Club. Pursuant to that agreement, the Sierra Club withdrew its petition, and EPA agreed to propose a new solid waste rule. As promised, EPA published a notice of proposed rulemaking in July 2011. A year later, we held that API's challenge to the 2008 rule was unripe given the forthcoming final rule. * * *

EPA promulgated the *Final Rule* on solid waste—the one before us now—in January 2015. The 2015 *Final Rule* differs from the *2008 Rule* in several ways, four of which are relevant here. First, the *Final Rule* revises the definition of "legitimate" recycling and expands the scope of the legitimacy factors to cover all recycling. Second, it establishes that spent catalysts—which were ineligible for exclusions under the *2008 Rule*—could qualify for the exemptions in the 2015 regulation. Third, the rule defers a decision on whether to add conditions to 32 previously promulgated exclusions from the definition of solid waste, which EPA calls the "pre-2008" exclusions. Fourth and finally, the rule replaces the transfer-based exclusion with the "Verified Recycler Exclusion," a new standard governing when transferred materials qualify as solid waste. * * *

Multiple organizations petitioned for review of the 2015 rule. Their petitions, which are consolidated in this case, challenge the regulation on multiple fronts. Industry Petitioners argue that both the legitimacy test and the Verified Recycler Exclusion exceed EPA's RCRA authority. * * * Environmental Petitioners argue that the Verified Recycler Exclusion is too permissive and that EPA should have added containment and notification conditions to the 32 pre-2008 exclusions. We consider these challenges in turn.

II. Legitimacy Factors

Industry Petitioners first attack EPA's new legitimacy test. Before EPA can regulate a hazardous secondary material as hazardous waste, it must determine that the material has been "discarded" under 42 U.S.C. § 6903(27). Items recycled through "immediate reuse in" an "industry's ongoing production process," are not discarded within the meaning of that section and are outside EPA's hazardous waste regulations. See *American Mining Congress v. EPA*, 824 F.2d 1177, 1183–85 (D.C. Cir. 1987) ("*AMC*"); see also *Ass'n of Battery Recyclers, Inc. v. EPA*, 208 F.3d 1047, 1052–53 (D.C. Cir. 2000) (explaining that "immediate" in *AMC* means "direct," not instantaneous). But because EPA's waste disposal regulations are acknowledged to be very costly to meet, "there is an incentive for some handlers to claim they are recycling when, in fact, they are conducting . . . disposal." To prevent such evasion, EPA polices the line "between 'legitimate' (i.e., true) recycling and 'sham' (i.e., fake) recycling."

Until recently, EPA's policy on sham recycling existed chiefly in uncodified guidance, notably a memo issued in 1989 * * *. The memo discussed over a dozen factors for evaluating recycling, all aimed at determining "whether the secondary material is 'commodity-like,' " i.e., is it being handled like a valuable industrial input or like a worthless industrial byproduct.

The Final Rule updates and codifies this effort to draw the distinction between legitimate and sham recycling. It requires that all recycling of hazardous secondary materials meet a legitimacy test set forth in 40 C.F.R. § 260.43(a) or else be labeled "sham" and subjected to full RCRA regulation. Like the [1989] Memo, the rule is rooted in the assumption that legitimate recycling should involve some "recognizable benefit" independent of merely "avoid [ing] the requirements of" RCRA regulation.

To satisfy the legitimacy test for recycling of a particular material, firms must prevail on all of four factors, which are in addition to whatever elements a specific exclusion might require. First, the hazardous secondary material must "provide[ ] a useful contribution to the recycling process." Second, "[t]he recycling process must produce a valuable product or intermediate." Third, the persons controlling the secondary material must "manage the hazardous secondary material as a valuable commodity."

Fourth, "[t]he product of the recycling process must be comparable to a legitimate product or intermediate." Factors 1 and 3 address the process, Factors 2 and 4 the product.

Industry Petitioners do not attack EPA's authority to formulate and apply a legitimacy test, nor do they fault EPA's premise that legitimate recycling involves "valuable" materials being used for a "recognizable benefit." At that level of generality, EPA's policy seems to be a reasonable method for identifying materials that are "part of the waste disposal problem" and thus subject to EPA's RCRA authority over discarded materials. Industry Petitioners instead attack EPA's planned means to implement that policy. They complain that mandating Factors 3 and 4 across all recycling results in EPA's "unlawfully regulat[ing] non-discarded materials." * * *

> [the court found that EPA's requirements under Factor 3 were not unreasonable but that EPA's requirements under Factor 4 were unreasonable because of the "draconian character" of the procedures it imposed on recyclers seeking certain exceptions]

* * *

III. Verified Recycler Exclusion

The *Final Rule* also amended EPA's stance on "reclamation," a type of recycling that occurs when secondary materials are "processed to recover a usable product, or . . . regenerated." A dead battery is reclaimed, for example, by extracting the still-valuable lead from it. The other modes of recycling are "use[ ]" and "reuse[ ]," which occur when "[a] material is . . . [e]mployed as an ingredient . . . in an industrial process to make a product" or "[e]mployed . . . as an effective substitute for a commercial product." In the 1980s, EPA adopted a rule manifesting its belief that certain hazardous secondary materials are so "waste-like" that reclaiming them is equivalent to discard. The materials so classified are spent materials, listed sludges, listed byproducts, and scrap metal—although EPA has a specific exception for the latter. "Listed" means catalogued by EPA as hazardous in § 261.31 or § 261.32. Because processing something is hardly akin to throwing it away, we held that this reclamation rule improperly regulated materials that were "neither disposed of nor abandoned, but [were] passing in a continuous stream or flow from one production process to another."

* * * EPA sought to "implement the *AMC I* opinion" by adding exclusions for specific materials or processes. Materials-specific and process-specific exclusions form a large part of the pre-2008 exclusions discussed in the introduction to this opinion. Further, EPA adopted two general exclusions, which unlike almost all of the pre-2008 exclusions, depend on whether the recycling is performed by a third-party. The first general exclusion, the Generator-Controlled Exclusion, governs reclamation "under the control of the generator," and is not challenged

here. The other addresses reclamation of materials transferred to and reclaimed by a third-party, and has come in two successive editions. EPA adopted the first edition, the Transfer-Based Exclusion, as part of its *2008 Rule*, and replaced it with the current edition, the Verified Recycler Exclusion, in the *Final Rule*.

Under the Transfer-Based Exclusion, the party offloading the materials (the "generator") could send them to a reclaimer that possessed a RCRA permit (or interim status). Alternatively, the generator could send materials to a reclaimer that lacked such a permit or status, if the generator had made "reasonable efforts to ensure that [the chosen] reclaimer intends to properly and legitimately reclaim the hazardous secondary material and not discard it." The "reasonable efforts" involved investigating and "affirmatively answer[ing]" specific questions that the regulation posed about the reclaimer.

The Verified Recycler Exclusion is quite similar to its predecessor but makes two changes that Industry Petitioners challenge. First, the new exclusion requires the generator to meet special "emergency preparedness" standards in its custody of the materials before shipment. * * *

Second, the Verified Recycler Exclusion eliminates the "reasonable efforts" option afforded by the Transfer-Based Exclusion and requires that generators send their secondary materials to reclaimers who either have a RCRA permit (or interim status), as in the Transfer-Based Exclusion, or a RCRA variance—in effect an EPA (or state-level) approval of a firm to operate a third-party "reclamation facility."

The separate Generator-Controlled Exclusion carries the same emergency preparedness requirements, but it significantly does not mandate a permit, interim status, or variance. It instead asks generators to maintain a "written description of how the recycling meets all four [legitimacy] factors."

Industry Petitioners insist that EPA had no reason, in its 2015 shift to a Verified Recycler Exclusion, to tighten the conditions of its predecessor. Though EPA disagrees, it concedes that "withdrawing the transfer-based exclusion" entirely "would result in hazardous secondary material that is currently being legitimately recycled and not discarded being regulated as hazardous waste," in effect, regulation in excess of EPA's authority as defined in *AMC*. In this perhaps topsy-turvy universe, all spent materials, listed byproducts, and listed sludges being reclaimed are subject to *full* RCRA control unless affirmatively excluded. Because EPA chose to *retain* a rule that improperly treats as discarded materials that are "no longer useful in their original capacity though destined for immediate reuse," it has obliged itself to creating sufficient exceptions to counter that rule's overbreadth.

Given the parties' agreement that some general exclusion for third-party reclamation is necessary, the question before us is whether EPA acted reasonably in adding emergency preparedness requirements and in supplanting the reasonable efforts option with the variance procedure. * * *

[the court found that EPA acted reasonably in adding the emergency preparedness requirements]

* * * Under the Transfer-Based Exclusion, a generator could send materials to any reclaimer it chose, provided that, after making a reasonable investigation, it "affirmatively answer[ed]" five questions about the reclaimer. These asked if the reclaimer (1) was employing a legitimate recycling process; (2) had notified regulators of its operations and its financial stability; (3) had *not* been the subject of recent enforcement actions; (4) had adequate skill and equipment to perform the recycling safely; and (5) had adequate processes for disposing of any residual wastes generated during the recycling. *Id.* The rule required the generator to have met this obligation "in good faith" and to have based its analysis for each question on an "objectively reasonable belief." A generator that failed to meet that standard could be liable for a RCRA violation.

The new rule keeps the general framework for evaluating reclaimers but broadens the inquiry and assigns it to regulators, not the generator. If the reclaimer lacks a RCRA permit or interim status, it must secure a regulatory variance under from the EPA Administrator or applicable state regulator. And the questions, transmogrified into criteria for administrative grant, are expanded to include a sixth, requiring the reclaimer to "address the potential for risk to proximate populations from unpermitted releases of the hazardous secondary material." EPA asserts that this "additional oversight" is required "to ensure that [ ] hazardous secondary material is legitimately recycled and not discarded." Here again, EPA's "good reasons" and its claim for permissibility under the statute overlap, but not as persuasively as with the emergency preparation requirements.

Recall that EPA has a Generator-Controlled Exclusion which is targeted at the same types of material as the Verified Recycler Exclusion: hazardous secondary materials reclaimed in a manner that doesn't qualify for pre-2008 exclusions. EPA insists that these materials generally have little value as recycling inputs, a trait from which one can reasonably infer a greater susceptibility to illegitimate or improper recycling.

But this risk of discarding low-value materials would apply whether the reclamation occurs in-house or externally. And yet while the Generator-Controlled Exclusion and Verified Recycler Exclusion share some conditions, only the latter requires an administrative approval. Industry Petitioners charge that EPA has acted on the basis of an unreasonable presumption that transfer carries an undue risk of discard. Such a presumption would contradict our holding in *Safe Food* that "[a]s firms have ample reasons to avoid complete vertical integration, firm-to-firm transfers are hardly good indicia of a 'discard' " under RCRA.

EPA counters that its reasoning is more nuanced, that it rests not on transfer alone, but on the confluence of low-value materials and transfer. These factors combine to form "perverse incentives . . . to over-accumulate [ ] hazardous secondary materials" without recycling them. EPA's theory is certainly more clever than Industry Petitioners give it credit for, but EPA fails to provide sufficient linkage between theory, reality, and the result reached.

EPA's reasoning relies heavily on a theoretical study [the *Market Study*] predicting that when the value of a recycled product is low, or the market for it "weak or unstable," the "acceptance fee" generators pay when off-loading materials "may be an important component of the [reclaimer's] overall revenue." EPA asserts that this incentive leads "commercial third party recyclers to maximize the amount of hazardous secondary material they can accept to increase profits," thus creating risks of "over-accumulat[ion]" and "discard." But having found that some types of recycling are typified by transfers of materials low or unstable in value, and having surmised that those conditions could lead to "market failure," the study disclaims any analysis of whether such failures actually occur and to what degree: "limitations on the availability and quality of data prevented us from conducting [ ] empirical tests."

EPA is free to rely on theoretical or model-based approaches, as long as that reliance is reasonable in context. As our dissenting colleague points out, we long ago recognized that "[r]easoned decisionmaking can use an economic model to provide useful information about economic realities, provided there is a conscientious effort to take into account what is known as to past experience and what is reasonably predictable about the future." * * * Thus what we seek is some indication of a reasonable concurrence between model and reality. Here the *Market Study* * * * offers EPA reasons (based on seemingly sensible notions of market actors' incentives) to think that the incidence of discard might be somewhat higher in the presence of specific characteristics (e.g., low-value materials and third-party transfer) than in their absence. But it offers no data to support the view that the increased incidence actually exists nor to show how great the increase is. That type of information (or a sufficient explanation for its absence) is quite important in cases such as this, where EPA is determining that an activity nominally outside of its jurisdiction should be banned absent regulatory pre-approval. Thus EPA's reliance on the study, standing alone, does not provide a sufficient basis for the administrative approval provisions.

EPA claims to have the necessary support in its *Problems Study*. * * * Of the study's 250 instances of recycling gone awry, 238 involved third-party recycling as opposed to on-site recycling. Based on these "easy to find" cases, EPA inferred that discard could occur under the old Transfer-Based Exclusion unless "additional oversight" was imposed. But far from confirming the *Market Study*'s assumptions, the *Problems Study* is even more tentative in its treatment of third-party recycling. It cautions that the greater proportion of problems at off-site recyclers might be because "on-site recycling is simply a less common practice."

From the study, EPA concluded that "the vast majority of environmental damages—approximately 94%—occur at off-site commercial recyclers." But by focusing only on recycling gone wrong, that statistic tells us nothing about such episodes' overall likelihood in any particular setting. The dissent offers a helpful example: imagine that 94% of plane crashes are associated with Airline A; can we say that this airline is less safe than its competitors? Before we can land at that conclusion, we'd need first to know something about the distribution of flights among airlines. If Airline A performs 94% of the set of flights that happened to be studied, its crash-percentage would seem decidedly average. Or maybe Airline A flies only the most dangerous routes. Context gives clues. The *Problems Study* leaves us grasping.* * *

The *Market Study* and *Problems Study* at most support a belief, carried over from the Transfer-Based Exclusion, that third-party reclaimers present distinct risks compared to on-site reclaimers. These risks would accordingly justify special conditions, such as the variance criteria for which the Generator-Controlled Exclusion has no analogue. The first five of these criteria, which petitioners do not challenge, seem properly focused on whether the third-party reclaimer has the inclination and ability to recycle legitimately. We cannot readily say the same of the sixth, discussed below.

But the imposition of a requirement of advance administrative approval cannot be justified merely on the differences that EPA has identified between on-site and third-party reclamation. EPA must explain why the risk that purported third-party recyclers will in reality "discard" the materials is so high that reclamation under the Verified Recycler Exclusion may only proceed on the basis of prior agency approval. On this key aspect of third-party reclamation, EPA's *Problems* and *Market* studies say nothing useful.

EPA invokes yet another study, *An Assessment of Good Current Practices for Recycling of Hazardous Secondary Materials* (Nov. 22, 2006). This analysis, performed before adoption of the Transfer-Based Exclusion, discussed the extent to which generators voluntarily audited their third-party recyclers to ensure that "their materials are not mishandled." The study found that "auditing is being practiced by many responsible companies" but that "small generators do not audit as regularly as larger customers" and that smaller generators' audits may not be as thorough. In 2008, EPA evidently did not find much alarm in this data; it made the reasonable efforts option available for small and large generators alike. By 2015, EPA was less sanguine about the study's results, warning that "many smaller generators would not have the technical expertise or resources to" adequately assess third-party reclaimers. EPA is free to reasonably revise its interpretation of that study, but even this updated reasoning cannot support the *Final Rule*. EPA admits in the rulemaking that "many large companies do conduct environmental audits of recycling facilities." A risk that some smaller generators would misapply the reasonable efforts option does not explain why EPA should treat larger generators as prone to making inadequate assessments.

Along with their challenge to the variance procedure, Industry Petitioners also claim that the sixth variance criterion is, in substance, vague and unreasonable. This criterion involves something of a "cumulative" nuisance standard; it requires third-party reclaimers to account for how any "unpermitted releases" from their facilities might combine with "other nearby potential stressors" to create "risk[s] to proximate populations." The more environmental problems there already are in an area—such as "other industrial facilities, landfills, transportation-related air emissions, poor housing conditions (*e.g.*, lead-based paint), leaking underground tanks, pesticides, and incompatible land uses"—the less appropriate it might be for the reclaimer to add yet another stress.

Thus the criterion *assumes* discard, i.e., behavior regulable under RCRA, and seeks to constrain its environmental impact, rather than testing for discard's existence. It identifies one of the many *problems related to waste disposal*, but not whether the reclaimer is actually contributing to *the waste disposal problem*. Were we dealing with materials that were lawfully identified as hazardous waste, this test might be valid for some purposes. But the Verified Recycler Exclusion covers materials that might be labeled waste only because of a reclamation-equals-discard rule that EPA has all but conceded is overbroad. This criterion therefore cannot stand as a means of identifying discard. * * *

Having concluded that the Verified Recycler Exclusion is unreasonable, we need not address Environmental Petitioners' argument that the exclusion is too lenient. * * *

The *Final Rule* is upheld in part and vacated in part as consistent with this opinion. Briefly put: Factor 3 is upheld; Factor 4 is vacated insofar as it applies to all hazardous secondary materials via § 261.2(g); the Verified Recycler Exclusion is vacated except for its emergency preparedness provisions and its expanded containment requirement; and the Transfer-Based Exclusion is reinstated.

TATEL, CIRCUIT JUDGE, dissenting:

In the mid-1970s, as industrial and technological developments spurred the national economy, the United States faced "a rising tide of scrap, discarded, and waste materials." This mounting waste caused "serious financial, management, intergovernmental, and technical problems," and posed a grave threat "to human health and the environment." In response, Congress passed the Resource Conservation and Recovery Act (RCRA), a comprehensive scheme "to regulate hazardous wastes from cradle to grave in accordance with . . . rigorous safeguards and waste management procedures." Through RCRA, and central to this case, Congress sought to *prevent* environmental harm by ensuring that hazardous waste was "properly managed in the first instance thereby reducing the need for corrective action at a future date."

Congress gave the Administrator of the Environmental Protection Agency (EPA) broad authority to effectuate this goal. Selected by the President and confirmed by the Senate for his or her expertise in environmental issues, the Administrator may promulgate "such regulations as are necessary to carry out his [or her] functions." The judiciary, by contrast, has a limited role under RCRA. When reviewing rules issued by the Administrator, the courts, lacking environmental expertise and political accountability, are bound by two fundamental principles of judicial restraint.* * *

The key difference between the verified recycler exclusion and its predecessor—the transfer-based exclusion—is that the new rule shifts oversight of off-site recyclers from the industry to the Administrator. Whereas before waste generators audited off-site recyclers to ensure their legitimacy, now the Administrator or a state authority issues a variance confirming that a recycler's practices are sound. * * *

This approach finds ample support in the administrative record. When designing the verified recycler exclusion, the Administrator relied on multiple sources, including a report on market forces in the recycling industry and a study of the environmental problems associated with recycling hazardous secondary materials. The first of these, the market study, concluded that off-site commercial recyclers, which generate revenue primarily by receiving hazardous materials, have "economic incentives to accumulate waste beyond their ability to deal with it." The second report, the problems study, found that of 208 cases in which hazardous waste recycling led to serious environmental damage, 94 percent were attributable to "off-site third-party recyclers."

In the court's view, neither study justifies the rule. Although not impugning the market study on its merits, the court rejects it as lacking empirical analysis. But no rule of administrative law bars agencies from relying on studies that use economic models to assess market incentives.

In fact, EPA often relies on theoretical models—that is, studies without corroborating "data," and our court has long held that "[r]easoned decisionmaking can use an economic model to provide useful information about economic realities."

At any rate, the problems study provides plenty of empirical support for the conclusion that off-site recycling leads to discard. It surveyed cases since 1982 in which recyclers contaminated the environment by discarding hazardous waste, poisoning soil and groundwater "with remediation costs in some instances in the tens of millions of dollars." To identify these cases, EPA reviewed scores of sources, including the Superfund National Priorities List, national and state databases, comments from at least three different rulemakings, media reports, and information gleaned from contacts in EPA regional offices and state agencies. This thorough canvassing revealed that a full 94 percent of cases involving serious environmental damage could be attributed to off-site recycling.

The court condemns the problems study for "focus[ing] only on recycling gone wrong." As a result, the court reasons, the study "tells us nothing" about the relative risks of off-site recycling or the total damage caused by off-site recyclers. But this focuses on the wrong question. As the Administrator recognized, the salient question is not what percentage of all off-site recycling damages the environment, but rather what portion of serious damage from hazardous waste disposal is caused by off-site recyclers. The core issue here is whether EPA may target the very companies (off-site recyclers) most responsible for environmental damage. Given the agency's statutory obligation to prevent environmental harm from discarded hazardous waste, I see no reason why it cannot. Accordingly, that some off-site recycling is safe or that serious environmental damage is relatively unusual is beside the point.

Consider this issue in a different context. If there were 208 plane crashes and 94 percent were linked to one carrier, it would be eminently reasonable for an agency tasked with preventing plane crashes to require that carrier to demonstrate that its practices were safe, no matter how many flights the carrier completed or what percentage of total flights it performed. No one would argue that it was unreasonable to regulate the carrier because only a small percentage of its total flights crashed. Yet this court's approach would yield just that result.

In the end, the fundamental problem with the court's conclusion—that the Administrator needs more proof that off-site recycling is unsafe before requiring a variance—is that the court decides for itself a policy question Congress left to the Administrator. RCRA envisions a careful balance of authority between EPA and this court. Today the court upsets that balance.

NOTES

1.   Do you understand the key difference between the "transfer-based exclusion" and the "verified recycler exclusion"? Why do third-party recyclers create special concerns? What might guard against any perverse incentives they might have to over-accumulate materials and/or mismanage those materials?

2.   Much of the dispute over the "verified recycler exclusion" in this case turned on the evidence that EPA relied upon as the basis for the exclusion. In particular, EPA used three different studies: a Market Study, a Problems Study, and a Good Practices Study. What was the major difference between the majority and the dissent with respect to these different studies? Did you find any of these studies persuasive? What other evidence could EPA have relied upon?

3.   Why do you think EPA has struggled so hard with the issue of recycled materials? Should EPA take a more expansive approach to exempting recycled materials from RCRA's requirements?

4.   On May 30, 2018, EPA published a final rule responding to the API case above. The rule removes the 2015 verified recycler exclusion and reinstates the 2008 transfer based exclusion with modifications as directed by the court. *See Response to Vacatur of Certain Provisions of the Definition of Solid Waste Rule*, 83 Fed. Reg. 24664 (May 30, 2018).

5.   Various materials are excluded from classification as solid waste (and some are likewise excluded from classification as hazardous waste, discussed below). Materials excluded from classification as solid waste can be found at 40 C.F.R. § 261.4(a). Some of these are also explicitly identified in the statutory definition of solid waste, 42 U.S.C. § 6903(27), namely solid or dissolved materials in domestic sewage; solid or dissolved materials in irrigation return flows; and industrial point-source discharges regulated under the Clean Water Act's NPDES program; and various nuclear materials regulated under the Atomic Energy Act. In addition to these materials, the regulations at § 261.4(a) contain a long list of specific materials that are excluded from the solid waste classification.

b.   What Is a "Hazardous Waste"?

For generators of waste covered by RCRA, the next definitional battle is over whether the solid waste is *hazardous*. Subtitle C of RCRA provides for regulation of *hazardous* solid waste and is significantly more onerous than the regulation of *nonhazardous* solid waste, covered by subtitle D. One very important exemption from the definition of hazardous waste is for *household* waste. 40 C.F.R. section 261.4(b)(1). You should realize, therefore, that a material can be defined as hazardous when used by a business but is subject to no federal regulation when used at home.

RCRA does not indicate precisely how EPA is to determine which solid wastes are hazardous. "Hazardous waste" is defined in section 1004(5) of the statute:

The term "hazardous waste" means a solid waste, or combination of solid wastes, which because of its quantity, concentration, or physical, chemical, or infectious characteristics may—

(A) cause, or significantly contribute to an increase in mortality or an increase in serious irreversible, or incapacitating reversible, illness; or

(B) pose a substantial present or potential hazard to human health or the environment when improperly treated, stored, transported, or disposed of, or otherwise managed.

Under section 3001, EPA is to promulgate regulations identifying the *characteristics* of hazardous waste and *listing* particular hazardous wastes to be regulated under subtitle C, "taking into account toxicity, persistence, and degradability in nature, potential for accumulation in tissue, and other related factors such as flammability, corrosiveness, and other hazardous characteristics."

EPA regulations provide two principal ways in which solid waste may be deemed "hazardous": by exhibiting one of four hazardous characteristics (*"characteristic wastes"*) or by being identified and listed specifically as a hazardous waste by EPA (*"listed wastes"*). 40 C.F.R. section 261.3. EPA has established four general categories of listed wastes, the "F," "K," "P," and "U" lists. 40 C.F.R. sections 261.31–261.32. On the "P" list are acutely hazardous chemical products. The "U" list includes non-acutely hazardous chemical products. The "F" and "K" lists of waste mixtures and combinations include wastes that meet the criteria for the "P" and "U" lists or one of the four "characteristics" (*toxicity, ignitability, corrosivity, and reactivity*).

Listed wastes are treated differently from characteristic wastes in certain respects. Among other differences, listed wastes are considered hazardous regardless of the concentration of hazardous constituents within them, whereas a characteristic waste remains hazardous only as long as it exhibits the characteristic. Thus listed wastes remain hazardous even when mixed with other materials or when their composition is changed. Listed wastes are subject to two special rules, the "*mixture*" rule and the "*derived-from*" rule. The former provides that a mixture of a "listed" hazardous waste with another solid waste is also a hazardous waste. 40 C.F.R. sections 261.3(a)(2)(iv). The derived-from rule provides that any solid waste "generated from the treatment, storage, or disposal of a hazardous waste, including any sludge, spill, residue, ash, emission control dust, or leachate (but not including precipitation run-off)," is a hazardous waste. 40 CFR 261.3(c)(2)(i). The derived-from rule on its face thus seems to apply to all waste (listed and characteristic), but the regulations provide further that the derived-from rule does not apply to waste derived from characteristic wastes if that derived-from waste no longer exhibits one of the characteristics. Thus, a derived-from by-product from a solid waste exhibiting one of the four characteristics remains hazardous if it continues to exhibit the characteristic but is not considered hazardous if it no longer possesses the characteristic. Finally, listed hazardous wastes that are listed because they exhibit one of the first three characteristics (ignitibility, corrosivity, or reactivity) are treated as characteristic wastes for purposes of the mixture and derived-from rules. 40 C.F.R. § 261.3(g)

The following case illustrates the application of these rules for identifying hazardous wastes to be regulated under subtitle C of RCRA.

CHEMICAL WASTE MANAGEMENT, INC. v. ENVIRONMENTAL PROTECTION AGENCY

United States Court of Appeals, District of Columbia Circuit, 1989.
869 F.2d 1526.

WALD, CHIEF JUDGE.

* * *

The RCRA was recently modified by the Hazardous Solid Waste Amendments of 1984, which established sweeping restrictions on the land disposal of hazardous wastes. The EPA was required to establish a schedule dividing the hazardous wastes into "thirds," see 42 U.S.C. § 6924(g)(4); the agency promulgated the schedule in May of 1986. The division of the schedule into thirds was designed as a means of phasing in the land disposal restrictions. By August 8, 1988, the EPA was required to promulgate treatment standards for each of the first-third scheduled wastes; these wastes may not be land disposed unless they have been treated to meet the applicable standards or the disposal unit is one from which there will be no migration of hazardous constituents for as long as the waste remains hazardous. Similar land disposal restrictions for second-third and third-third wastes are scheduled to take effect on June 8, 1989 and May 8, 1990 * * *.

The present dispute concerns the rule-making in which the EPA established treatment standards for first-third wastes. * * * EPA issued treatment standards for the various wastes; in lengthy preambles to the notices, the agency discussed the interpretive principles which would guide its application of the standards. Three such principles merit discussion here.

One of these principles concerns the treatment standards applicable to leachate produced from hazardous waste. Leachate is produced when liquids, such as rainwater, percolate through wastes stored in a landfill.

The resulting fluid will contain suspended components drawn from the original waste. Proper leachate management involves the storage of wastes in lined containers so that leachate may be collected before it seeps into soil or groundwater. The leachate will periodically be pumped out of the container and subsequently treated.

An EPA regulation promulgated in 1980, known as the "derived-from rule," provided that "any solid waste generated from the treatment, storage, or disposal of a hazardous waste, including any sludge, spill residue, ash, emission control dust, or leachate (but not including precipitation run-off) is a hazardous waste." Thus, for some years prior to the 1988 rulemaking, it had been understood that leachate derived from a hazardous waste was itself a hazardous waste. In the 1988 preambles, the agency stated that leachate derived from multiple hazardous wastes would be deemed to contain each of the wastes from which it was generated, and that it must therefore be treated to meet the applicable treatment standards for each of the underlying wastes. This is known as the "waste code carry-through" principle.

The second interpretive principle at issue in this proceeding also involves the treatment requirements for hazardous waste leachate. In its preamble to the August rule, the agency stated that "[h]azardous waste listings are retroactive, so that once a particular waste is listed, all wastes meeting that description are hazardous wastes no matter when disposed." The implications of that statement center around wastes which were not deemed hazardous at the time they were disposed but which are subsequently listed as hazardous wastes. The RCRA does not require that such wastes be cleaned up or moved from the landfill, nor does the agency impose any retroactive penalty on the prior disposal of the waste. Under the August rule, however, the agency announced that leachate which is actively managed after the underlying wastes have been listed as hazardous will itself be deemed a hazardous waste and must be treated to the applicable standards. Under this approach, the fact that the original waste was not deemed hazardous at the time of disposal is simply irrelevant in determining the treatment requirements for the leachate.

Finally, the agency discussed the applicability of the treatment standards to contaminated environmental media such as soil and groundwater. The preamble stated that "[i]n these cases, the mixture is deemed to be the listed waste." Thus, when a listed hazardous waste (or hazardous waste leachate) is mixed with soil or groundwater—as may occur, for example, through spills or leaking—the soil or groundwater is subject to all the treatment standards or restrictions that would be applicable to the original waste.

The Present Litigation

* * *

Petitioners in this case raised a host of substantive and procedural challenges to the August rulemaking. * * *

Shortly before oral argument, * * * the parties filed an Emergency Joint Motion to Defer Oral Argument on Certain Leachate-Related Issues. That motion, which was granted by this court, covered the petitioners' challenge to the waste code carry-through principle—the requirement that derived-from wastes such as leachate would be deemed to contain each of the original wastes from which they were generated. * * * The explanation [was] that a negotiated settlement seemed likely on all issues pertaining to the waste code carry-through principle. Under the terms of the proposed settlement, all multiple-waste leachate would be rescheduled to the third-third, and a leachate treatability study would be undertaken so that appropriate treatment standards could be determined.

The issues argued to the court, and the issues that we decide today, are therefore limited to the following. First, did the agency improperly engage in retroactive rulemaking in ordering that its leachate regulations be made applicable to leachate derived from wastes which were not deemed hazardous at the time they were disposed? Second, did the agency act in an arbitrary or capricious manner by mandating that environmental media contaminated by hazardous wastes must themselves be treated as hazardous wastes? * * *

* * * Petitioners argue that the EPA lacks the authority to promulgate retroactive regulations, and they correctly observe that such regulations are disfavored. In our view, however, the crucial question is not whether the EPA is authorized to promulgate a retroactive rule. Rather, the crucial question is whether the challenged regulation in fact operates retroactively. We conclude that it does not.

* * * The agency has made no effort to impose a legal penalty on the disposal of waste which was not deemed hazardous at the time it was disposed. Nor, in fact, does this regulation require the cleanup of any newly listed hazardous wastes. The preamble to the final rule expressly provides that "these residues could become subject to the land disposal restrictions for the listed waste from which they derive *if they are managed actively after the effective date of the land disposal prohibition for the underlying waste.*" The rule has prospective effect only: treatment or disposal of leachate will be subject to the regulation only if that treatment or disposal occurs after the promulgation of applicable treatment standards.

As a practical matter, of course, a landfill operator has little choice but to collect and manage its leachate. Active management of leachate is sound environmental practice, and a panoply of regulations require it. * * *

Moreover, we find this aspect of the agency's interpretation of the derived-from rule to be eminently reasonable. The derived-from rule establishes a presumption: leachate generated from hazardous waste will be presumed hazardous unless it is proved nonhazardous or treated to applicable standards. The reasonableness of that presumption does not vary depending upon the time when the underlying waste was disposed. * * *

In reviewing the EPA's application of its 1980 rules to contaminated soil, we are guided by two fundamental principles. The first is that "[a]n agency's interpretation of its own regulations will be accepted unless it is plainly wrong." The second is that on "a highly technical question . . . courts necessarily must show considerable deference to an agency's expertise." * * *

The agency's rule, adopted in 1980, provides that "[a] hazardous waste will remain a hazardous waste" until it is delisted. The petitioners argue in essence that an agglomeration of soil and hazardous waste is to be regarded as a new and distinct substance, to which the presumption of hazardousness no longer applies. The agency's position is that hazardous waste cannot be presumed to change character when it is combined with an environmental medium, and that the hazardous waste restrictions therefore continue to apply to waste which is contained in soil or groundwater. * * *

The EPA's approach to contaminated environmental media is * * * consistent with the derived-from and mixture rules established in 1980. These rules provide that a hazardous waste will continue to be presumed hazardous when it is mixed with a solid waste, or when it is contained in a residue from treatment or disposal. The derived-from and mixture rules do not, it is true, apply by their own terms to contaminated soil or groundwater. They nevertheless demonstrate that the agency's rule on contaminated soil is part of a coherent regulatory framework. It is one application of a general principle, consistently adhered to, that a hazardous waste does not lose its hazardous character simply because it changes form or is combined with other substances. In promulgating the mixture rule, the agency did not presume that every mixture of listed wastes and other wastes would in fact present a hazard. Rather, the agency reasoned that "[b]ecause the potential combinations of listed wastes and other wastes are infinite, we have been unable to devise any workable, broadly applicable formula which would distinguish between those waste mixtures which are and are not hazardous." The EPA therefore concluded that it was fair to shift to the individual operator the burden of establishing (through the delisting process) that its own waste mixture is not hazardous. Precisely the same logic applies to combinations of hazardous waste and soil or groundwater. * * *

The EPA's interpretation is also buttressed by one provision of the Hazardous Solid Waste Amendments of 1984, 42 U.S.C. § 6924(e). Congress there provided that certain specified solvents and dioxins would be prohibited from land disposal. The statute further provided that, for a two-year period after the effective date of the ban, the prohibition "shall not apply to any disposal of contaminated soil or debris resulting from a response action taken under section 9604 or 9606 of this title or a corrective action required under this subchapter." This statutory exemption would of course have been superfluous unless contaminated soil would otherwise fall within the terms of the ban * * *.

We need not decide whether any of these factors, or all of them taken together, would *compel* the conclusion that soil or groundwater contaminated with hazardous waste is itself a hazardous waste as defined by EPA regulations. We do believe, however, that, given the agency's broad discretion to interpret its own rules, it was entirely reasonable for the EPA to arrive at that conclusion. We therefore must sustain the agency's position.

NOTES

1. In its long-delayed decision in *Shell Oil Co. v. EPA*, 950 F.2d 741 (D.C. Cir. 1991), the court held that EPA had failed to comply with the Administrative Procedure Act's notice-and-comment requirements when promulgating the mixture and derived-from rules in 1980. The court vacated the rules but suggested that EPA reenact them on an interim basis under the "good cause" exemption of 5 U.S.C.A. section 553(b)(3)(B), pending full notice and opportunity to comment. EPA took the suggestion and reissued the rules in 1992. The reinstated rules were challenged but upheld in *Mobil Oil Corp. v. EPA*, 35 F.3d 579 (D.C. Cir. 1994).

2. In 2001, EPA promulgated a new Hazardous Waste Identification Rule (HWIR), 66 Fed. Reg. 27,266 (Apr. 30, 2001). It replaced the 1992 interim regulations which reinstated the mixture and derived-from rules. The new regulation retains and amends the mixture and derived-from rules, narrowing their scope by (1) granting an expanded exclusion for wastes listed solely for their ignitability, corrosivity, and/or reactivity characteristics, and (2) establishing a new conditional exemption for "mixed" wastes, that is, wastes that are both hazardous and radioactive. The final rule was challenged and upheld in *American Chemistry Council v. EPA*, 337 F.3d 1060 (D.C. Cir. 2003).

3. As indicated in the case above, the mixture and derived-from rules do not address certain wastes generated at contaminated sites. In particular, how should contaminated soil be treated during the cleanup of such sites? The mixture rule does not apply because the hazardous waste was dumped on the soil and the soil itself is not a waste. Nor does the derived-from rule apply, given that the contaminated soil was not generated from the treatment of a hazardous waste. In order to address this situation, EPA created a "contained-

in policy" that applies to wastes generated during the remediation of contaminated sites. Under the policy, the waste resulting from the remediation of contaminated soil is considered hazardous if it exhibits one of the four characteristics or if it contains a listed hazardous waste at concentrations considered by EPA to exceed "health-based" levels. To date, EPA has not clarified the concentration of listed waste necessary to trigger a hazardous waste classification for the media in which it is contained.

4.   Generators are responsible for determining whether their solid wastes are also hazardous wastes. For listed hazardous wastes, this is relatively straightforward and involves checking with the waste is on one of the EPA lists. For characteristic wastes, the generator must either test the material according to specific instructions or use its "knowledge of process" (that is, its knowledge regarding the processes that generated the materials) to determine if the waste is a characteristic waste. Generators are responsible for maintaining records documenting their determinations. Errors in determinations can result in substantial liability under RCRA.

5.   Determining which wastes exhibit the toxicity characteristic has proved particularly challenging. EPA regulations currently provide that a waste exhibits the toxicity characteristic when an extract of the waste obtained using EPA's Toxicity Characteristic Leachate Procedure ("TCLP") contains one or more of 40 toxic substances at concentrations above their regulatory thresholds. The TCLP was designed to simulate the disposal of wastes in a municipal landfill under conditions that would cause toxic substances to leach out of the waste. A number of cases have raised questions about the appropriateness of the TCLP requirement to wastes that are not disposed of in municipal landfills or under conditions similar to such landfills. In *Edison Electric Inst. v. EPA*, 2 F.3d 438 (D.C. Cir. 1993), the court held that EPA had failed to justify application of TCLP to certain types of mineral processing wastes given that there was no evidence that such wastes had been disposed of in municipal landfills. In *Columbia Falls Aluminum Co. v. EPA*, 139 F.3d 914 (D.C. Cir. 1998), the court held that EPA's use of the TCLP to determine compliance with its treatment standard was arbitrary or capricious because the TCLP failed to predict the actual behavior of hazardous constituents in the leachate after a certain type of aluminum waste was treated and disposed in a landfill dedicated exclusively to this type of waste. Tests of the actual leachate showed concentrations of the hazardous constituents that were "orders of magnitude" different from the concentrations predicted by the TCLP. In *Association of Battery Recyclers v. EPA*, 208 F.3d 1047 (D.C. Cir. 2000), petitioners challenged EPA's application of the TCLP to 358 different types of mineral processing wastes generated by 41 different sectors of the mineral processing industry. With respect to 357 of the wastes, the court upheld EPA's use of the TCLP because evidence in the record showed that such wastes probably had been disposed of in municipal landfills. From an institutional perspective, how carefully should courts examine EPA's decisions to apply the TCLP to particular wastes?

6.   Because landfill space is scarce, many cities have built incinerators to dispose of municipal waste, often generating electricity in the process. Such incinerators generate millions of tons of ash. Ash residues include fly ash captured by emission control equipment, bottom ash, and the products of incomplete combustion. Heavy metals are present in the residues, especially in the fly ash. When tested using EPA's "toxicity characteristic leaching procedure" (TCLP), described in the *Edison Electric* case, fly ash and bottom ash from municipal incinerators frequently contain lead and cadmium at concentrations greater than the 5 and 1 milligram per liter cutoff levels for the toxicity characteristic.

Regulations adopted by EPA in 1980 provided that "[h]ousehold waste, including household waste that has been collected, transported, stored, treated, disposed, recovered (e.g., refuse-derived fuel) or reused" was not hazardous waste. Moreover, the preamble to the regulations stated that "residues remaining after treatment (e.g., incineration, thermal treatment) are not subject to regulation as a hazardous waste." 45 Fed.Reg. 33,099 (May 19, 1980). The regulations thus provided a "waste stream" exemption for household waste, covering it from generation through treatment to final disposal of residues. The regulations did not, however, exempt municipal incinerator ash from subtitle C coverage if the incinerator burned anything *in addition* to household waste, such as nonhazardous industrial waste. In that case, the facility would qualify as a hazardous waste *generator* if the ash it produced was sufficiently toxic—even though the incinerator still was not considered a subtitle C treatment or disposal facility, since all the waste it took in would be characterized as nonhazardous.

In 1984, as part of the Hazardous and Solid Waste Amendments to RCRA, Congress enacted section 3001(i), "Clarification of Household Waste Exclusion." Section 3001(i) provides that a "resource recovery facility" recovering energy from the burning of municipal solid waste "shall not be deemed to be treating, storing, disposing of, or otherwise managing hazardous wastes" for purposes of regulation under subtitle C, "if [the facility] receives and burns only * * * household waste * * * and solid waste from commercial or industrial sources that does not contain hazardous waste * * *."

City of Chicago v. Environmental Defense Fund, 511 U.S. 328 (1994), was a citizen suit by EDF under RCRA section 7002. Plaintiff alleged that the ash generated by defendant Chicago's incinerator—which burned both household waste and nonhazardous industrial waste—was toxic enough to qualify as "hazardous waste" under EPA's TCLP, and that defendant was not adhering to the requirements of subtitle C in disposing of the ash, which was being sent to landfills licensed to receive only nonhazardous waste. The city and EPA contended that under section 3001(i) the ash was excluded from the category of hazardous waste. (The city also claimed that treating the ash as hazardous waste could increase disposal costs by as much as ten times.) The Supreme Court held that although the *incinerator* was not subject to subtitle C regulation as a facility that treats, stores, disposes of, or manages hazardous waste, section 3001(i) did *not* contain any exclusion for the *ash* itself. The incinerator was a *generator* of hazardous waste; and while section 3001(i) states that the facility "shall not be deemed to be treating, storing, disposing of, or otherwise managing hazardous wastes," it "significantly omits from the catalogue" the word "generating." (Section 1004(7) defines "hazardous waste management" as "the systematic control of the collection, source separation, storage, transportation, processing, treatment, recovery, and disposal of hazardous wastes.") Therefore, Chicago was not entitled to the cost-saving waste stream exemption which it claimed.

7.   In addition to the household waste exclusion discussed in note 6, EPA regulations also exclude several other categories of wastes from classification as hazardous wastes. These exclusions are listed at 40 C.F.R. § 261.4(b). Some of the more important of these are wastes generated from growing crops or raising animals and returned to the soil as fertilizer; various process wastes associated with coal combustion; wastes generated from oil and gas exploration and production; and wastes generated from the extraction, crushing and separating, and storage of mineral ores.

3.   LAND DISPOSAL RESTRICTIONS

When it amended RCRA in 1984, Congress sought to discourage land disposal of hazardous waste. Section 1002(b)(7) announced a new national policy that, "to avoid substantial risk to human health and the environment, reliance on land disposal should be minimized or eliminated, and land disposal, particularly landfill and surface impoundment, should be the least favored method for managing hazardous wastes." Section 3004(d)(1) provided a staged prohibition on land disposal of *untreated* hazardous waste unless the EPA Administrator "determines the prohibition of one or more methods of land disposal of such waste is not required in order to protect human health and the environment for so long as the waste remains hazardous." In making these determinations, EPA was directed to take into account the characteristics of the waste, "the long-term uncertainties associated with land disposal," and the importance of encouraging proper management of hazardous waste initially. However, § 3004(d)(1), (e)(1), and (g)(5) limited EPA's discretion by specifying that a method of land disposal may not be determined to be protective of human health and the environment "unless, upon application by an interested person, it has been demonstrated to the Administrator, to a reasonable degree of certainty, that there will be *no migration* of hazardous constituents from the disposal unit or injection zone for as long as the wastes remain hazardous" (emphasis added).

Congress did not entirely ban the land disposal of wastes unable to meet this standard. It provided an exception for wastes treated to "substantially diminish the toxicity of the waste or substantially reduce the likelihood of migration of hazardous constituents from the waste so that short-term and long-term threats to human health and the environment are minimized" § 3004(m). The statute directed EPA to promulgate treatment standards specifying how waste otherwise subject to the "land ban" could satisfy the standard. Thus, the land disposal ban, in effect, applies to *untreated* hazardous wastes and authorizes EPA to require pre-treatment of wastes that cannot be shown to be capable of safe disposal on land in untreated form.

To prevent generators of hazardous wastes from frustrating the land ban by simply storing waste indefinitely, § 3004(j) prohibits the *storage* of wastes subject to the land disposal ban "unless such storage is solely for the purpose of the accumulation of such quantities of hazardous wastes as are necessary to facilitate proper recovery, treatment or disposal." In *Edison Electric Institute v. EPA*, 996 F.2d 326 (D.C. Cir. 1993), the court upheld an EPA rule making it unlawful to store hazardous waste indefinitely pending the development of adequate treatment techniques or disposal capacity. While the court expressed its sympathy with generators who had no treatment or disposal alternatives available, it emphasized that RCRA is "a highly prescriptive, technology-forcing statute * * * clearly intended to provide draconian incentives * * * for the rapid development of adequate treatment and storage capacity." If generators of hazardous wastes for which adequate treatment methods have not yet been developed could store those wastes indefinitely, the generators would have an incentive *not* to develop treatment technology—at least if the cost of storage was less than the probable sum of the costs of developing the technology and of treating and then disposing of the wastes. On the other hand, firms other than the generators still would have an economic incentive to devise new treatment methods.

The question of what standards should apply to the pre-treatment of hazardous wastes prior to their land disposal was addressed in *Hazardous Waste Treatment Council v. EPA*, 886 F.2d 355 (D.C. Cir. 1989). In that case, the court upheld EPA's decision to use technology-based standards (best demonstrated available technology) rather than specific risk-based standard in implementing the land disposal restrictions. But the case did not fully resolve the question of how much treatment (or how little) EPA should require for characteristic wastes under the land disposal restrictions. This was one of the issues raised in the following case. Environmental groups challenged EPA's decision not to require the use of "best demonstrated available technologies" (BDATs) in all situations, prior to land disposal, but to instead allow deactivation and dilution of certain characteristic wastes. Industry petitioners, on the other hand, were protesting regulations mandating levels of treatment which in some situations went beyond removal of the characteristic that led to the waste's classification as hazardous.

CHEMICAL WASTE MANAGEMENT, INC. v. EPA

United States Court of Appeals, District of Columbia Circuit, 1992.
976 F.2d 2, *cert. denied* 507 U.S. 1057, 113 S.Ct. 1961, 123 L.Ed.2d 664 (1993).

Before EDWARDS, BUCKLEY, and HENDERSON, CIRCUIT JUDGES.

Opinion PER CURIAM.

The Hazardous and Solid Waste Amendments of 1984 instituted a ban on the land disposal of classes of hazardous wastes unless certain conditions are met. Those amendments require the Environmental Protection Agency to follow a phased schedule for implementing the ban. In this case we consider various challenges to regulations implementing the final portion of this program, the so-called "third-third" rule, which largely covers the land disposal of wastes deemed hazardous because they possess certain defined characteristics.

Various petitioners raise multi-faceted challenges. A group of industry trade associations and companies (collectively, "industry petitioners") seek review of regulations mandating levels of treatment before land disposal that go beyond the removal of the attribute that led to the waste's classification as hazardous. These petitioners claim that the EPA lacked authority under the statute to require treatment to such levels. * * *

We deny each of these petitions for review. Sections 3004(g)(5) and (m) of [RCRA] give the EPA the statutory authority to mandate the treatment of wastes to levels beyond those at which the wastes present the characteristics that caused them to be deemed hazardous. * * *

Several environmental organizations, as well as the Hazardous Waste Treatment Council, an association representing companies that treat hazardous waste (collectively, "NRDC petitioners") * * * argued that * * * the new rule's "deactivation" treatment standard impermissibly allows the dilution, rather than treatment with specified technologies, of many characteristic wastes prior to land disposal. * * *.

* * * Under the statute, dilution of characteristic hazardous wastes may constitute treatment, but only if no hazardous constituents are present following dilution that would endanger human health or the environment. The EPA concedes that dilution will not attain this result for certain characteristic wastes. For others, it has not made clear that dilution will meet the requirements for treatment. The standard is therefore vacated as to those wastes. The dilution of wastes in Clean Water Act facilities is acceptable so long as the toxicity of the waste discharged from the facility is minimized or eliminated consistent with RCRA. Similarly, disposal of wastes in underground injection wells may occur as long as the hazardous characteristics have been eliminated and any health and environmental dangers posed by hazardous constituents of the wastes are minimized. * * *

I.   Statutory and Regulatory Background

[Under RCRA, wastes] are deemed hazardous in one of two ways: They possess one of the four hazardous characteristics identified by the EPA ("characteristic wastes"), or have been found to be hazardous as a result of an EPA rulemaking ("listed wastes").

The four characteristics identified as hazardous are ignitability, corrosivity, reactivity, and extraction procedure ("EP") toxicity. * * * Characteristic wastes comprise over fifty percent of all the hazardous wastes generated in the United States each year.

Although the EPA may list a waste if it possesses one of the four characteristics described above, in practice it will only list specific wastes that are either acutely hazardous or possess high levels of toxic constituents. A listed waste loses its hazardous status only after a petition for its "delisting" is approved by the EPA in a notice-and-comment rulemaking.

"Once a waste is listed or identified as hazardous, its subsequent management is regulated" under subtitle C of RCRA. * * * The management of a hazardous waste continues "until such time as it ceases to pose a hazard to the public."

* * * The Hazardous and Solid Waste Amendments of 1984 expressed a general policy preference that "reliance on land disposal should be minimized or eliminated." A prohibition on disposal would apply unless the waste is treated so as to minimize the short-term and long-term threats to human health and the environment posed by toxic and hazardous constituents, or unless the EPA finds that no migration of hazardous constituents from the facility will occur after disposal. * * *

II.   Treatment Standards for Characteristic Wastes

* * *

The EPA determined that for most ICR [ignitable, corrosive and reactive] wastes, treatment to characteristic levels would be sufficient. The Agency found upon review that

> [t]he environmental concerns from the properties of ignitability, corrosivity, and reactivity are different from the environmental concern from EP toxic wastes. Toxic constituents can pose a cumulative impact on land disposal even where waste is below the characteristic level. Where wastes pose an ascertainable toxicity concern * * * the Agency has developed treatment standards that address the toxicity concern and (in effect) require treatment below the characteristic level * * *. Otherwise, treatment that removes the properties of ignitability, corrosivity, and reactivity,

fully addresses the environmental concern from the properties themselves.

The EPA also retreated from its emphasis on technology-based treatment in the final regulations, altering its position on the use of dilution as a method of treatment:

> In all cases, the Agency has determined that for non-toxic hazardous characteristic wastes, it should not matter how the characteristic property is removed so long as it is removed. Thus, dilution is an acceptable treatment method for such wastes.

* * * Only in three subcategories of ICR wastes did the EPA mandate the use of technological treatment * * *.

Industry petitioners contend that RCRA does not provide authority for the EPA to mandate treatment of characteristic wastes after their ignitability, corrosiveness, reactivity, or EP toxicity has been addressed. They make a straightforward argument: Subtitle C regulations attach to a waste only when it is hazardous. The moment a waste ceases to meet the regulatory definition of a hazardous waste, the EPA loses its authority to regulate further. Thus, in industry petitioners' view, RCRA's cradle-to-grave system covers waste only if it remains hazardous throughout its life and at the moment of its burial. * * *

* * * EPA reiterates the rationales stated in its final rule: The key provisions of the land-ban program, sections 3004(g)(5) and (m), can be read as allowing the Agency to apply land disposal restrictions at any time it wishes; those provisions at a minimum contemplate activity that occurs before land disposal; section 3004(m)(1) requires treatment to avoid the prohibition on land disposal; and treatment must take place, by definition, before disposal occurs. * * * The Agency reasons that the subtitle C program can attach at the point of generation, and the broad language of section 3004(m)(1) allows additional treatment to remove risks posed by wastes beyond those inherent in the characteristic.

To succeed in their *Chevron* step one argument, industry petitioners must show that Congress "has directly spoken to the precise question at issue" and has "unambiguously expressed [its] intent." We find little support in the statute or our prior decisions for the notion that Congress mandated the line industry petitioners draw. These petitioners believe that the definition of a hazardous waste acts as a revolving regulatory door, allowing continual entrance and egress from RCRA's requirements. The key provisions of the statute support a contrary view—that hazardous waste becomes subject to the land disposal program as soon as it is generated. * * *

We conclude that, in combination, sections 3004(g)(5) and (m) provide the EPA with authority to bar land disposal of certain wastes unless they have been treated to reduce risks beyond those presented by the characteristics themselves. We also find the Agency's assertion of regulatory authority over the wastes from the moment they are generated to be "based on a permissible construction of the statute." *Chevron.*

NRDC petitioners ask this court to vacate the deactivation treatment standard as applied to ICR wastes because it authorizes the dilution of these wastes to eliminate their ignitability, corrosiveness, or reactivity rather than mandating use of technological treatment. * * * They claim that some form of technology must be used to treat wastes in all instances.

They also contend that dilution fails to satisfy the statutory requirement that treatment minimize short-term and long-term threats to human health and the environment, or to substantially diminish the toxicity of the waste. In their view, the removal of these characteristics through dilution only affects the short-term risk that the waste will manifest that property; it does not address the threats posed by the hazardous organic and inorganic constituents of those wastes. * * *

We believe that dilution can, in principle, constitute an acceptable form of treatment for ICR wastes. We do not read the 1984 Amendments as mandating the use of the best demonstrated available technologies ("BDAT") in all situations. To reiterate, section 3004(m)(1) directs the Administrator to

> specify[ ] those levels or methods of treatment, if any, which substantially diminish the toxicity of the waste or substantially reduce the likelihood of migration of hazardous constituents from the waste so that short-term and long-term threats to human health and the environment are minimized. * * *

We agree that the section imposes an exacting standard: It requires that treatment prior to land disposal "substantially diminish the toxicity of the waste or substantially reduce the likelihood of migration of hazardous constituents from the waste so that short-term and long-term threats to human health and the environment are minimized." But this provision does not bar dilution as a means of treating ICR wastes; instead, it defines the purposes that a method of treatment must achieve. Any treatment that meets those objectives is permissible. When read against RCRA's broad definition of treatment, we cannot say Congress clearly barred dilution as an acceptable methodology. * * *

[The Court also addressed the EPA's the application of the dilution rules to Clean Water Act treatment systems and deep injection wells; its ruling was subsequently overturned by the Land Disposal Flexibility Act of 1996, Public Law 104–119.]

NOTES

1. Why did EPA decide that "treatment to characteristic levels" would be sufficient for most "ICR wastes" but not for "EP toxic wastes?" How does that degree of treatment differ from treatment involving BDAT? Can the former involve only dilution?

2. The Hazardous Waste Treatment Council, an association representing companies that treat hazardous waste, joined with environmental organizations in pressing for more stringent treatment standards. Why do you think environmental and industry groups would join forces?

3. Does it make more policy sense to mandate the use of best demonstrated available technology ("BDAT") for or to require treatment to reduce toxicity to set concentration levels? What are the consequences of a BDAT standard for the development of new technologies to treat toxic wastes? Does BDAT spur innovation or lock certain technologies into place?

4. Chapter 2 describes various approaches to risk analysis and management. Does RCRA's approach strike the right balance between risk and safety?

5. Underground injection is used to dispose of a substantial part of the nation's hazardous wastes. Supposedly such disposal is allowed only where the waste will not mix with groundwater, e.g., because they will be separated by impermeable rock or soil. Can you imagine why this practice remains controversial?

4. LIABILITY AND ENFORCEMENT

Section 3008 of RCRA provides that for a violation of any requirement of subchapter III (concerning hazardous waste management), the EPA Administrator may issue a compliance order and assess a penalty that takes into account the seriousness of the violation and any good faith efforts to comply. EPA issued a formal policy on RCRA civil penalties in 2003, *see Resource Conservation and Recovery Act (RCRA) Civil Penalty Policy*, https:// www.epa.gov/enforcement/resource-conservation-and-recovery-act-rcra-civil-penalty-policy. Under the policy, civil penalties are calculated in part to eliminate the economic benefits of infractions. EPA rates violations according to their seriousness—major, moderate, or minor—based on "extent of deviation" from RCRA requirements and "potential for harm." Enforcement personnel are to calculate any economic gains from noncompliance, factor in the gravity component, and adjust the overall penalty to take into account the violator's past compliance record and good or bad faith.

Section 3008 also authorizes the federal government to file a civil action in federal district court for civil penalties, injunctive relief, and, in cases of 'knowing endangerment," criminal sanctions in response to violations of RCRA. The states also play a very important role in RCRA enforcement. EPA has delegated RCRA authority to every U.S. state, and one of the conditions of that delegation is a requirement that the state have authority to enforce against violations of its own state-adopted hazardous waste regulations.

In addition to these section 3008 enforcement authorities, EPA also has authority under sections 3007 and 3013 to order information disclosure and to enter facilities for investigation. Under section 7003, the federal government can also bring an action in federal district court to respond to situations that pose "an imminent and substantial endangerment to health or the environment" as a result past or present handling, storage, treatment, transportation, or disposal of any solid or hazardous waste. Section 7003 also applies to those who have "contributed" (or are "contributing") to the past or present handling, storage, treatment, transportation, or disposal of any solid or hazardous waste that may present an imminent and substantial endangerment. Thus, although RCRA is typically viewed as a prospective statute governing the handling of hazardous waste from cradle to grave, the statute also contains provisions for retroactive liability somewhat similar to CERCLA, though with important differences. The nature and scope of liability under section 7003, including liability for contributors, was addressed in *United States v. Northeastern Pharmaceutical & Chemical Co., Inc.*, 81 F.2d 726 (8th Cir., 1986). In that case, the court held (a) that RCRA § 7003 imposes strict liability upon past off-site generators of hazardous waste and upon past transporters of hazardous waste; and (b) that two corporate officers could be held individually liable as "contributors" because of active involvement by one in the conduct that created the imminent and substantial endangerment and overall supervisory authority by the other for the company's operations.

NOTES

1.   Is it fair to apply section 7003 to "past [i.e., pre-1976] non-negligent off-site generators and transporters" who acted lawfully at the time they "contributed" to disposal of the hazardous substances? Do you understand the court's rationale for concluding that this does not constitute "retroactive" application of RCRA? Would it be a denial of due process to apply the statute retroactively? In *Eastern Enterprises v. Apfel*, 524 U.S. 498 (1998), the Supreme Court found a federal law that imposed on a coal mining company a "severe retroactive liability" to pay health benefits for its former employees to be an unconstitutional "taking" of private property. Efforts to extend this reasoning to invalidate "retroactive" liability under RCRA and CERCLA have not been successful. *See, e.g., United States v. Dico, Inc.*, 266 F.3d 864 (8th Cir. 2001), *cert. denied*, 535 U.S. 1095 (2002).

2.   How important do you think it is for liability under section 7003 to extend to corporate officers and employees, as well as to the corporation itself?

3.   Issues like those in Notes 1 and 2 also arise in connection with CERCLA. Although much of the thrust of RCRA is prospective—directed at regulation of future waste treatment and disposal—section 7003 clearly is retrospective also. Thus it overlaps with CERCLA, which is concerned mainly with cleanups of past disposal sites. But there are important differences.

Sections 7002 (which authorizes citizen suits brought by private persons) and 7003 of RCRA apply to a different spectrum of substances than do sections 106 and 107 of CERCLA. It is common for public and private plaintiffs in these kinds of cases to rely on both RCRA and CERCLA.

4.   Although RCRA provides for liability for retrospective behavior, can a private party bring a RCRA cause of action for the costs of cleanup where a facility does not pose an immediate danger to human health or the environment? Section 7002 of RCRA authorizes citizen suits to be brought against any person alleged to be in violation of a RCRA permit or standard, but also against any person "who has contributed or who is contributing to the past or present handling, storage, treatment, transportation, or disposal of any solid or hazardous wastes which may present an imminent and substantial endangerment to health or the environment." The similarity to section 7003 is evident. However, in *Meghrig v. KFC Western, Inc.*, 516 U.S. 479 (1996), KFC brought suit against the prior owners of a parcel on which KFC operated a restaurant after finding petroleum contamination after KFC had spent more than $200,000 cleaning up the site. The Supreme Court held that RCRA does not authorize such a suit where no imminent threat exists. Because CERCLA exempts petroleum from its reach, *see* 42 U.S.C. section 9601(14), owners of sites contaminated with petroleum are limited to contributions to abate imminent harms, not for clean-up reimbursement. Why do you suppose the Court might interpret section 7003 to permit cost recovery after the imminent threat has passed, but not interpret section 7002 to do so? For a critique of *Meghrig* and an analysis of its practical consequences, *see* Jerome Organ, *Advice for Owners of Contaminated Land after Meghrig v. KFC Western, Inc.*, 26 ENVTL. L. REP. 10582 (1996).

5.   Enforcement of state hazardous waste laws (usually adopted pursuant to authority in RCRA) against federal facilities has been a problem. *See* Comment, *Lawmaker as Lawbreaker: Assessing Civil Penalties Against Federal Facilities Under RCRA*, 57 U. CHI. L. REV. 845 (1990). *Maine v. Navy Department,* 973 F.2d 1007 (1st Cir. 1992), held that the state of Maine could not recover civil penalties from the Navy Department for past violations of state hazardous waste laws at a Navy shipyard located in the state, because the Supreme Court previously had ruled in *United States Department of Energy v. Ohio,* 503 U.S. 607 (1992), that RCRA did not waive federal agencies' sovereign immunity from imposition of punitive civil penalties. A few weeks later, Congress approved the Federal Facility Compliance Act, Pub. L. No. 102–386 (1992), amending section 6001 of RCRA to allow state agencies and EPA to enforce hazardous waste laws at federal facilities. The law clarifies that federal sovereign immunity is waived to allow imposition and collection of civil and administrative penalties and fines, even if punitive or coercive, as well as reasonable, nondiscriminatory service charges for permits, review of plans, and inspection and monitoring of facilities.

5. WASTE MINIMIZATION AND
POLLUTION PREVENTION

The concept of waste reduction, or waste minimization, was incorporated into RCRA by the 1984 amendments. Section 1003(b) declares it to be national policy that "wherever feasible, the generation of hazardous waste is to be reduced or eliminated as expeditiously as possible." Section 1003(a)(6) announces the objective of "minimizing the generation of hazardous waste and the land disposal of hazardous waste by encouraging process substitution, materials recovery, properly conducted recycling and reuse, and treatment." Section 3002(a)(6) requires generators to report "efforts undertaken during the year to reduce the volume and toxicity of waste generated;" § 3002(b) requires generators to certify on their waste manifests that they have in place programs "to reduce the volume or quantity and toxicity of such waste to the degree determined by the generator to be economically practicable;" and § 3005(h) requires the same certification in connection with any new permit issued for the "treatment, storage, or disposal of hazardous waste."

In 1993, EPA announced that some 19,000 hazardous waste generators, including many that used incineration, would be asked to make their waste minimization plans public. *See* 24 ENV'T REP. 728 (1993). The agency also said that it planned to publish a list of the targeted generators, those required to certify on their hazardous wastes manifests that they have waste minimization programs in place. The response was that "industry in general will be unalterably opposed to making waste [minimization] plans public." The industry spokesperson denied any statutory authority for EPA to establish such a requirement.

In 1994, EPA released an update of its draft waste minimization guidance. *See* 25 ENV'T REP. 147 (1994). The update said that there should be specific waste reduction targets, short-term and long-term, though it did not specify what the percentage reduction rates should be. EPA sought comments on this matter. The agency said its goal was to achieve a national percentage reduction by 1997 of highly toxic and persistent hazardous wastes that are combusted. By the year 2000, EPA's goal was to achieve an overall reduction of RCRA hazardous waste through source reduction and recycling. However, the goals were not to be applied to individual facilities because EPA said it lacked statutory authority to impose such requirements.

In 2002, EPA established a "National Waste Minimization Partnership Program" to persuade industries to voluntarily reduce the amount of chemicals used in production processes. By 2006, the program— now called the National Partnership for Environmental Priorities, had enrolled 74 companies and federal and state facilities. Participants were asked to establish goals for chemical reduction and are to focus on "priority chemicals PBTs (persistent, bioaccumulative, and toxic chemicals)." The program was discontinued because of budget cuts.

In a related law, the Pollution Prevention Act of 1990, 42 U.S.C.A. §§ 13101–13109 (1990), Congress found that there are "significant opportunities for industry to reduce or prevent pollution at the source through cost-effective changes in production, operation, and raw materials use." Congress further found that opportunities for source reduction are "often not realized because existing regulations, and the industrial resources they require for compliance, focus upon treatment and disposal, rather than source reduction * * *." The Act provided that, as a first step in preventing pollution through source reduction, the EPA should establish a source reduction program which collects and disseminates information and provides financial assistance to states.

Besides providing for EPA matching grants to states for programs to promote the use of source reduction techniques by businesses, the Pollution Prevention Act provides that each owner or operator of a facility required to file an annual toxic chemical release form under the Emergency Planning and Community Right-to-Know Act (see Chapter 9, infra,) shall include with each such annual filing a toxic chemical source reduction and recycling report for the preceding calendar year. This report must cover each toxic chemical required to be reported in the annual toxic chemical release form. The toxic chemical source reduction and recycling report must explain, for each toxic chemical, the amount of that chemical which has been recycled; source reduction practices used with respect to that chemical; and the techniques used to identify source reduction opportunities. 42 U.S.C.A. § 13106 (1990). However, in 1994, EPA announced that a final rule detailing how companies should report pollution prevention data on the Toxic Release Inventory (TRI) reporting form was "on hold indefinitely," pending possible changes in the definitions of solid waste and other related terms under RCRA. See 25 ENV'T REP. 498 (1994).

In its 1991 Pollution Prevention Strategy, 56 Fed.Reg. 7849 (Feb. 26, 1991), EPA said studies have shown that pollution prevention can be "the most effective way to reduce risks by reducing or eliminating pollution at its source; it also is often the most cost-effective option because it reduces raw material losses, the need for expensive 'end-of-pipe' technologies, and long-term liability." In short, "pollution prevention offers the unique advantage of harmonizing environmental protection with economic efficiency." The strategy included a plan for targeting 15 to 20 high-risk chemicals that offered opportunities for prevention, and set a "voluntary goal of reducing total environmental releases of these chemicals by 33 percent by the end of 1992, and at least 50 percent by the end of 1995." (Hence the name "33/50 Program.") The strategy further provided that when EPA determined that specific regulatory actions were needed, it would investigate "flexible, cost-effective regulatory approaches that avoid prescriptive approaches and that rely on market-based incentives where practical and authorized by law."

A 1992 internal memorandum from the Deputy Administrator to all EPA personnel emphasized that "prevention is our first priority within an environmental management hierarchy that includes: 1) prevention, 2) recycling, 3) treatment, and 4) disposal or release." Henry F. Habicht II, Deputy Administrator, EPA, *Memorandum: EPA Definition of Pollution Prevention* (May 28, 1992), 1 ENV'T REP. (1992). The memorandum stated that pollution prevention means "source reduction," as defined in the Pollution Prevention Act, and other practices that reduce or eliminate the creation of pollutants through increased efficiency in the use of raw materials, energy, water or other resources, or through protection of natural resources by conservation. The Pollution Prevention Act defines "source reduction" to mean any practice which (i) reduces the amount of any hazardous substance, pollutant, or contaminant entering any waste stream or otherwise released into the environment prior to recycling, treatment, or disposal, and (ii) reduces the hazards to public health and the environment associated with the release of such substance, pollutants, or contaminants. Thus, under the Act, recycling, energy recovery, treatment, and disposal are not included within the definition of pollution prevention. However, some practices commonly described as "in-process recycling" may qualify as pollution prevention.

A 1994 study by a private environmental group concluded that EPA's voluntary pollution prevention program was a failure and should be replaced. The study said that many companies had cut their toxic waste at the source, but that for 83 percent of the projects the efforts already were under way before EPA's program was initiated in 1991. The critics said that EPA's industrial toxics project, the "33/50 Program," was "pollution prevention in name only," since "only under 33/50 are waste incineration, treatment, burning for energy recovery, recycling, and production cutbacks considered pollution prevention." *See* 25 ENV'T REP. 280 (1994).

A slightly more positive evaluation of the 33/50 Program is offered by Eric Orts, *Reflexive Environmental Law*, 89 NW. U. L. REV. 1227, 1284–87 (1995). As of 1994, EPA had invited over 8,000 companies to participate in the program, and 1,200 had agreed to do so. EPA's interim goal of 33% reductions by 1992 was exceeded: a 40% reduction from 1988 levels was achieved, and participating companies claimed to be on target for 50% reductions by 1995. Another author later reported that "the 1,300 participating facilities largely relied on end-of-pipe controls in successfully meeting the fifty percent reduction goal by 1994—one year earlier than planned." Michele Ochsner, *Pollution Prevention: An Overview of Regulatory Incentives and Barriers*, 6 N.Y.U. ENVTL L.J. 586, 592 (1998).

In addition to promoting voluntary pollution prevention actions by businesses, EPA also uses its leverage in enforcement negotiations to encourage such actions. In many cases, pollution prevention programs are required to redress violations and achieve compliance with environmental regulations, often as specific conditions of settlements. With increasing regularity, companies are mitigating cash fines and penalties by undertaking source reduction and similar techniques. *See* William Thomas et al., *Using Auditing, Pollution Prevention, and Management Systems to Craft Superior Environmental Enforcement Solutions*, 30 ENVTL. L. REP. 10299 (2000).

States have also instituted various pollution prevention programs, though as the National Pollution Prevention Roundtable suggests, these "efforts, due to poor funding, are still in their infancy." The Roundtable estimates nevertheless that state programs have achieved 167 billion pounds of pollution reduction from air, water and waste programs. *See* National Pollution Prevention Roundtable, An Ounce of Prevention is Worth Over 167 Billion Pounds of Cure (2003) (*available at* http://info house.p2ric.org/ref/26/25207.pdf).

For further discussion of waste minimization and pollution prevention, see James Salzman, *Sustainable Consumption and the Law*, 27 ENVTL. L. REP. 1243 (1997); Kurt Strasser, *Cleaner Technology, Pollution Prevention and Environmental Regulation*, 9 FORDHAM ENVTL. L.J. 1 (1997); Kurt Strasser, *Preventing Pollution*, 8 FORDHAM ENVTL. L.J. 1 (1996).

B. CLEAN-UP OF CONTAMINATED SITES: CERCLA

1. BACKGROUND AND OVERVIEW

As noted earlier, RCRA is primarily a forward-looking statute. Most of its provisions are aimed at creating a regulatory program to control future waste treatment, storage, and disposal activities. However, the statute is also retrospective, imposing civil liability for the handling, storage, treatment, transport, or disposal of solid or hazardous waste that presents an "imminent or substantial endangerment" to health or the environment.

CERCLA, by contrast, is primarily backward-looking. Its main thrust is to create broad civil liability for cleanup of contaminated sites, most of which were contaminated prior to the enactment of RCRA or CERCLA. However, CERCLA also includes some forward-looking elements. The statute contains provisions regulating the processes and standards governing clean up as well as requirements that persons in charge of facilities notify EPA of hazardous substance releases. More importantly, strict liability for cleanup of contaminated sites provides an important deterrent effect—encouraging proper behavior in the future by persons involved in the generation, transportation or disposal of hazardous wastes.

Nevertheless, CERCLA is not a prescriptive "command and control" statute like the Clean Air Act or the Clean Water Act. Rather, it is best viewed as a liability and financing regime.

As noted earlier, CERCLA was Congress's response to a number of high profile incidents—including the Love Canal debacle—that increased public awareness about the threat posed by improperly managed hazardous waste. Around the country, in defunct and abandoned plants, factories, mines and refineries, were pits, piles, drums and ditches full of dangerous, toxic substances poised to leach into water supplies, blow into the air and endanger public health and environment. One infamous example is the Stringfellow Acid Pits in Riverside, California, a granite quarry that served as the county's dumpsite starting in the 1950s. Over the years, companies big and small dumped millions of gallons and hundreds of different chemicals into huge, uncovered lagoons that the county periodically flushed into the town's open sewers. In 1983, the Stringfellow site became the first federal Superfund site in California and was designated the highest priority site in the state. In Northern Oklahoma, a century of intensive lead and zinc mining, to choose another example, has left a landscape littered with mountains of poisonous mine tailings that blow lead, cadmium and other metals onto properties and into heating ducts in the surrounding homes. Add to these stories the innumerable examples of decades of unregulated toxic dumping into the nation's waterways, burial of waste in leaky drums, and midnight dumping on abandoned properties, and you have the ingredients of a public health— and political—disaster.

CERCLA was initially a popular and bipartisan law. It passed at the end of the Carter administration, in a lame duck session of Congress, without significant debate. Yet it quickly became very controversial, as the reality of the costs of cleaning up hazardous waste sites, and the extent of CERCLA's liability regime, came into focus. CERCLA imposes strict, joint and several, and retroactive liability on a statutorily defined group of persons for the costs of cleaning up hazardous waste that may be "released" into the environment. Unlike the traditional tort system, imposition of this liability does not require that causation be proved under either the "but-for" or "substantial factor" test, and the waste released, or at risk of release into the environment, need not be "fingerprinted" or linked directly back to a particular party for that party to be responsible for cleanup costs.

According to one view, CERCLA is a necessary response to the serious threat posed by abandoned hazardous waste dumps and other contaminated sites. It is a law that largely affects those companies and persons who most profited from unregulated disposal practices in the past. According to another view, CERCLA is a draconian and overly broad effort to recover costs from "deep pocket" defendants for hazardous waste handling practices that were in many cases legal at the time they were used, and often encouraged, directly or indirectly, by government. As you read the materials below, ask yourself whether as a policymaker you might reform the statute and if so, how.

The following excerpt provides an early overview of CERCLA's main purposes.

U.S. COUNCIL ON ENVIRONMENTAL QUALITY, ENVIRONMENTAL QUALITY 1981: 12TH ANNUAL REPORT
99–101 (1981).

In December of 1980, the Comprehensive Environmental Response, Compensation, and Liability Act of 1980 (CERCLA), was signed into law. The goals of the legislation are to eliminate the threats from uncontrolled hazardous waste sites and to remove hazardous substance threats to public health and the environment in a cost-effective manner.

The act has four basic elements. First, it establishes an information-gathering and analysis system which will enable federal and state governments to characterize chemical dump site problems more accurately and to develop priorities for their investigation and response. Owners of hazardous waste sites were required to notify EPA by June 9, 1981, of the nature of the wastes buried at their sites. This notification data will help form the basis for a national list of uncontrolled sites to be used in planning appropriate responses.

Second, the act establishes federal authority to respond to hazardous substance emergencies and to clean up leaking chemical dump sites. Federal response actions are limited to cases in which the responsible party either cannot be found or does not take the required actions. The legislation mandates the revision of the National Contingency Plan currently published under Section 311 of the Clean Water Act to serve as a framework for such response actions.

Third, the act creates a hazardous substance response trust fund to pay for the removal, remedy, and cleanup of released hazardous substances and hazardous waste sites. * * * Most of the total * * * will be raised by an industry-based tax on manufacturers of petrochemical feedstocks and toxic organic chemicals, and importers of crude oil. The remaining portion * * * will come from general revenues.

Fourth, the act makes those persons responsible for hazardous substance release liable for cleanup and restitution costs. Thus, it creates a strong incentive both for prevention of releases and voluntary cleanup of releases by responsible parties. Furthermore, it replenishes the fund to assure that adequate response capability is available to mitigate environmental emergencies in the future.

CERCLA identifies two categories of federal response to releases of hazardous substances: removal activities (emergency response) and remedial activities (long-term solution). For a site or spill releasing hazardous substances into the environment, a preliminary assessment is made to determine the source and nature of the problem, the existence of an identifiable responsible party, and the appropriate type of response.

During the 1981 fiscal year, EPA responded to 33 emergency removal situations * * *.

In the remedial action category, EPA has compiled a list of 115 top priority sites that are targeted for Superfund action, i.e., enforcement action and/or federally financed cleanup. These sites will also be candidates for inclusion on the list of * * * national priority "response targets" that the Superfund law requires EPA to identify. * * *

The guiding policy behind these efforts is derived from CERCLA itself; private party cleanup, either voluntary or through enforcement action, is the preferred approach, but federally financed cleanup will be implemented when states and the federal government determine it is appropriate. * * *

A cornerstone of the CERCLA implementation program is the negotiation of cooperative agreements with the states under which they will take the lead responsibility for cleaning up hazardous waste sites. * * *

Where a responsible party is involved in the release of a hazardous substance, EPA works closely and expeditiously with the states to effect an adequate cleanup by that party. Where the responsible party cannot initially be found or is unable to provide cleanup measures, the Fund can be used to clean up and later recover the costs from the responsible party. In other cases, the states, or EPA in consultation with the Department of Justice, will negotiate agreements on the level of cleanup appropriate at a site.

2. LIABILITY

As noted above, CERCLA is primarily a liability statute, making it unlike any of the other major federal environmental laws. The statute is largely retrospective and uses tort-like liability to force a range of responsible parties to pay the costs of cleaning up contaminated sites. Whereas RCRA establishes a highly prescriptive, command-and-control regime aimed at ensuring that the handling of hazardous wastes will not create new environmental problems, CERCLA seeks to remedy environmental contamination caused in the past by improper waste handling practices and other activities. Not surprisingly, CERCLA's liability provisions have been the most controversial and the most litigated aspects of the statute.

a. Elements of Liability

Section 107(a) of CERCLA sets forth the basic elements of liability. The statute provides that where there is a release or threatened release of a hazardous substance from a vessel or a facility that causes the incurrence of response costs, responsible parties are liable for "(A) all costs of removal or remedial action incurred by the United States Government or a State or an Indian tribe not inconsistent with the national contingency plan; (B) any other necessary costs of response incurred by any other person consistent with the national contingency plan; (C) damages for injury to, destruction of, or loss of natural resources." Section 107(a) of the Act establishes four categories of responsible parties, which will be discussed further below:

(1)   the owner and operator of a vessel or a facility;

(2)   any person who at the time of disposal of any hazardous substance owned or operated the facility;

(3)   any person who by contract, agreement of otherwise arranged for disposal. . . or arranged with a transporter for . . . disposal . . . of hazardous substances owned or possessed by such person . . . ; and

(4)   any person who accepts . . . hazardous substances for transport to disposal . . . facilities or sites selected by such person.

Several of the elements of CERCLA liability are defined terms in the statute and it is important to pay careful attention to these definitions. Thus, the term "release" is defined very broadly in § 101(22) to mean "any spilling, leaking, pumping, pouring, emitting, emptying, discharging, injecting, escaping, leaching, dumping, or disposing into the environment (including the abandonment or discarding of barrels, containers, and other closed receptacles containing any hazardous substance or pollutant or contaminant)" but does not include releases within a workplace for which employees may have a claim against their employer, engine exhaust emissions from mobile sources, and releases of nuclear material.

Likewise, the term "hazardous substance" is defined in § 101(14) and incorporates by reference the substances designated as hazardous under section 112 of the Clean Air Act, sections 311(b)(2)(A) and 307(a) of the Clean Water Act, section 3001 of RCRA, and section 7 of TSCA. The term does *not* include petroleum; thus CERCLA is not applicable to oil spills, though it may apply to spills of oil contaminated with other hazardous substances. *United States v. Mexico Feed & Seed Co.*, 980 F.2d 478 (8th Cir. 1992). (Statutes that create liability for oil spills include the Outer Continental Shelf Lands Act amendments of 1978, 43 U.S.C. §§ 1841–1847, and the Oil Pollution Act of 1990, 33 U.S.C. §§ 2701–2761.)

Finally, the terms "facility" and "vessel" are also broadly defined in § 101(9) and § 101(28) respectively. In particular, "facility" is defined as

"(A) any building, structure, installation, equipment, pipe or pipeline (including any pipe into a sewer or publicly owned treatment works), well, pit, pond, lagoon, impoundment, ditch, landfill, storage container, motor vehicle, rolling stock, or aircraft, or (B) any site or area where a hazardous substance has been deposited, stored, disposed of, or placed, or otherwise come to be located; but does not include any consumer product in consumer use or any vessel."

b.   Standard of Liability

Section 107(a) of CERCLA establishes strict liability. *See Burlington Northern and Santa Fe Railroad Co. v. United States,* 556 U.S. 599, 608 (2009) ("CERCLA imposes strict liability for environmental contamination upon four broad classes of [potentially responsible parties]."). As enacted in 1980, the statute was silent on the issue of whether liability was also joint and several, or whether liability was restricted only to costs and damages caused by the conduct of one of the four classes of potentially responsible parties. Section 101(32) defines "liability" somewhat obscurely, by reference to § 311 the Clean Water Act (33 U.S.C. § 1321) which deals with liability for discharges of oil and hazardous substances" into the navigable waters of the United States. Courts had interpreted liability under this provision to be "joint and several." In the first case to address the issue under CERCLA, the court held, based on general tort law principles, that if two or more defendants cause an indivisible harm, "each is subject to liability for the entire harm." *See U.S. v. Chem-Dyne Corp.,* 572 F. Supp. 802, 810–11 (S.D. Ohio 1983). The court suggested, however, that costs might be apportioned among the defendants. Subsequent judicial decisions have adopted the approach in *Chem-Dyne.* In *Burlington Northern,* 556 U.S. at 613–19, the Supreme Court addressed this issue and upheld a trial court ruling that the railroad parties were responsible for only nine percent of the cleanup costs at a contaminated site. The Court held that apportionment is proper when "there is a reasonable basis for determining the contribution of each cause to a single harm." Given the facts in *Burlington Northern,* the Court found that it was reasonable for the district court to use the size of the leased parcel and the duration of the lease as the starting point for its analysis. The *Burlington Northern* decision is discussed further below in the sections on arranger liability at and apportionment.

Early judicial challenges to CERCLA's liability scheme argued that the imposition of retroactive liability for sites that were contaminated before the enactment of the statute violated due process. The courts have uniformly held that CERCLA's imposition of retroactive liability does not violate due process. *See, e.g., United States v. Monsanto,* 858 F.2d 160, 173 (4th Cir. 1988), excerpted in the section on arranger liability below.

In sum, CERCLA is based upon a default liability scheme that is strict, joint and several, and retroactive. For contaminated sites where the harm is divisible, defendants can argue for apportionment based on their relative contributions. But the practical result of CERCLA's liability scheme often means that the government can select a relatively small number of responsible parties as defendants from which to recover all of its costs for the clean-up of sites that were contaminated long before CERCLA was enacted. These defendants are then left with the burden of bringing actions for apportionment and for contribution against parties not named in the original action. Apportionment, contribution, and cost recovery will be discussed further below.

c.   Potentially Responsible Parties

Once the elements of CERCLA liability have been established for a particular site, the focus turns to who is responsible for the costs of cleaning it up. Consistent with the "polluter pays" principle, CERCLA seeks to ensure that a broad class of "responsible parties" will be held liable for these costs. Section 107(a) thus identifies four categories of potentially responsible parties or PRPs: (1) current owners and operators; (2) past owners and operators who owned or operated the facility "at the time of disposal" of hazardous substances; (3) any person who "arranged for" the disposal of hazardous substances at the facility; and (4) transporters of hazardous substances to the facility. The scope of each of these categories has been litigated, extensively in some cases. Since CERCLA was enacted, moreover, complex questions have emerged regarding liability under these four categories for various other parties, such as corporate parents, successor corporations, lenders, and governmental entities (among others). This section discusses each of the four categories of responsible parties as well as the relationship that these "other parties" have to one or more of the four categories.

i.   *Current Owners/Operators*

Current owners or operators of a facility from which there has been a release of a hazardous substance are liable under § 107(a)(1) of CERCLA. Current owners who hold title in fee simple clearly fit into this category and it does not matter if the activities at the facility leading to the release were undertaken by someone other than the owner (such as a lessee). More difficult cases of owner liability involve lesser interests in the property, such as those held by secured creditors, lessees, and corporate shareholders. Operator liability usually attaches to someone who has the legal authority to control the activities at the site and who actually exercises that control.

In *State of New York v. Shore Realty Corp.*, 759 F.2d 1032 (2d Cir. 1985), the state brought suit against Shore and its officer and shareholder,

LeoGrande, who had incorporated Shore solely for the purpose of purchasing and developing the Shore Road property. At the time of acquisition, LeoGrande—who directed and controlled all corporate decisions and actions—knew that hazardous waste was stored there, though neither Shore nor LeoGrande had participated in its generation or transportation. The court held that Shore and LeoGrande were jointly and severally liable under CERCLA for the state's response costs.

> We hold LeoGrande liable as an "operator" under CERCLA, 42 U.S.C. § 9607, for the State's response costs. Under CERCLA "owner or operator" is defined to mean "any person owning or operating" an onshore facility, id. § 9601(20)(A), and "person" includes individuals as well as corporations, id. § 9601(21). More important, the definition of "owner or operator" excludes "a person, who, without participating in the management of a * * * facility, holds indicia of ownership primarily to protect his security interest in the facility." Id. § 9601(20)(A). The use of this exception implies that an owning stockholder who manages the corporation, such as LeoGrande, is liable under CERCLA as an "owner or operator." That conclusion is consistent with that of other courts that have addressed the issue. In any event, LeoGrande is in charge of the operation of the facility in question, and as such is an "operator" within the meaning of CERCLA.

On the other hand, a "consultant" who also was the corporate secretary and chairman of the board, and who owned 85 percent of the company's stock, was held not to be an owner or operator under section 107 in *Riverside Market Development Corp. v. International Building Products, Inc.*, 931 F.2d 327 (5th Cir. 1991). The court of appeals found that plaintiffs had failed to produce any evidence showing that the individual personally participated in any conduct that violated CERCLA. He lived in New York and visited the New Orleans plant only two to four times a year, and his participation in plant operations was limited to reviewing financial statements and attending meetings of the officers. *See generally* Kathryn R. Heidt, *Liability of Shareholders Under the Comprehensive Environmental Response, Compensation and Liability Act (CERCLA)*, 52 OHIO ST. L.J. 133 (1991); Michael P. Healy, *Direct Liability for Hazardous Substance Cleanups Under CERCLA: A Comprehensive Approach*, 42 CASE W. RES. L. REV. 65 (1992).

In contrast, *United States v. Gurley*, 43 F.3d 1188 (8th Cir. 1994), imposed "operator" liability not only upon the principal shareholder and president of the corporate owner of a disposal site, but also upon his son who was an employee of the corporation. Citing trial court findings that the son "personally participated in the disposal of the hazardous substances" and that he "had extensive authority . . . to implement the policies and practices of the corporate entity, which included the disposal of these hazardous substances," the court of appeals concluded that the evidence clearly established that the son "had *authority* to determine [the corporation's] hazardous waste disposal activities and that he actually *exercised* that authority" (emphasis added). (Query: Would the son also be liable as an "arranger"?)

Even an "environmental contractor employed to investigate and assist in constructing a facility for remedying contamination already in the soils" could be held liable as an "operator" if he had control over monitoring wells that served to disperse the contamination. Geraghty & Miller, Inc. v. Conoco, Inc., 234 F.3d 917 (5th Cir. 2000), *cert. denied*, 533 U.S. 950 (2001).

Because section 107(a) extends liability for cleanup costs to all "owners" of contaminated properties, regardless of the circumstances of their ownership, parties who *involuntarily or innocently* acquired former disposal sites have been required to pay for clean-up, even when the cost exceeded the value of the land. Prompted by the perceived unfairness of such results, Congress in 1986 added a new defense to protect "innocent landowners." *See* Superfund Amendments and Reauthorization Act of 1986 (SARA), Pub. L. 99–499, 99th Cong., 2d Sess. (1986). (The defense will be discussed in greater detail in the defenses section, *infra*.) This new provision, and the adoption of a new contribution provision enabling PRPs to sue each other for contribution, and immunizing settling parties from contribution actions, were intended to soften the perceived unfairness in CERCLA's strict joint and several regime.

The Small Business Liability Relief and Brownfields Revitalization Act of 2002, Pub. L. No. 107–118, 115 Stat. 2356 altered the liability under section 107(a) not only of certain owners and operators but also of certain arrangers and transporters, as discussed in section (*ii*), *infra*. (The Act also added new provisions for settlements under section 122(g), discussed in the settlements section, *infra*, and new brownfields provisions, discussed in the brownfields section, *infra*.) The Act created two additional exclusions for owner/operator liability. New section 107(q) provides protection for the owner of property "contiguous" to land from which there is a hazardous substance release, and new section 107(r) exempts "bona fide prospective purchasers" (BFPPs) so long as they do not impede response actions or natural resource restoration.

Under section 107(q), an owner of land contaminated by a "contiguous property" is not considered to be an owner or operator under section 107(a) if that person (1) did not cause or contribute to the release of hazardous substances; (2) is not potentially liable or affiliated with any other person potentially liable for the release; (3) takes reasonable steps to stop or prevent any continuing or future release and to prevent or limit exposure to hazardous substances released on his own property; (4) provides full cooperation and access to persons authorized to undertake response action and natural resource restoration; (5) complies with all land use restrictions related to the response action; (6) does not impede any institutional controls related to the response action; (7) complies with all lawful information requests; (8) provides all legally required notices concerning discovery of the release; and (9) conducted "all appropriate inquiry" within the meaning of section 101(35) concerning "innocent landowners." If a person does not qualify for liability relief as a contiguous landowner because he knew of the contamination at the time of purchase, and therefore cannot satisfy item (9), he nevertheless may qualify for liability relief as a "bona fide prospective purchaser" under section 107(r).

Section 107(r) exempts "bona fide prospective purchasers" from owner or operator liability under section 107(a) so long as they do not impede a response action or natural resource restoration. The purpose of section 107(r) is to facilitate the acquisition, cleanup, and redevelopment of brownfields. Section 101(40) defines "bona fide prospective purchaser" as one who establishes that (1) all disposal on her land occurred before she purchased it; (2) she made "all appropriate inquiry" within the meaning of section 101(35); (3) she exercises appropriate care to stop or prevent any continuing or future release and prevent or limit exposure; (4) she provides full cooperation and access to persons authorized to undertake response actions or natural resource restoration; (5) she complies with land use restrictions, and does not impede institutional controls, related to the response action; and (6) she is not potentially liable or affiliated with any other person that is potentially liable for response costs through any familial, contractual, corporate, or financial relationship (other than the relationship created by the instruments by which title to the facility is conveyed or financed). The BFPP exemption is qualified by section 107(r)(2), which gives the United States a "windfall lien" on the property if EPA has incurred unrecovered response costs there and the response action increases the fair market value of the property.

ii. Past Owners/Operators

Past owners or operators of a facility can also be liable under CERCLA. Section 107(a)(2) provides that such owners or operators are liable if they owned or operated the facility "at the time of disposal" of hazardous substances. CERCLA § 101(29) adopts RCRA's broad definition of the term "disposal," which includes discharge, deposit, injection, spilling, leaking or placing. *United States v. Waste Industries, Inc.,* 734 F.2d 159, 164–65 (4th Cir. 1984) discusses that definition:

> The inclusion of "leaking" as one of the diverse definitional components of "disposal" demonstrates that Congress intended "disposal" to have a range of meanings, including conduct, a physical state, and an occurrence. Discharging, dumping, and injection (conduct), hazardous waste reposing (a physical state)

and movement of the waste after it has been placed in a state of repose (an occurrence) are all encompassed in the broad definition of disposal. "Leaking" ordinarily occurs when landfills are not constructed soundly or when drums and tank trucks filled with waste materials corrode, rust, or rot. Thus "leaking" is an occurrence included in the meaning of "disposal."

The district court's statutory analysis relied heavily upon the present-tense definition of "disposal" as indicative of an intent to restrain only ongoing human conduct. The Act, however, permits a court to order a responsible party to "stop" activities "*or to take such other action as may be necessary*" (emphasis added) to abate the endangerment. Such grammatical niceties as tense may be useful in arriving at a narrowly-sculpted meaning, but they are of little help in interpreting remedial statutes in which actions such as "may be necessary" are contemplated in order to abate gross dangers to a community. Since the term "disposal" is used throughout the Act, its definition in section 6903(3) must necessarily be broad and general to encompass both routine regulatory and the less common emergency situations. Thus it includes such diverse characteristics as "deposit, injection, dumping, spilling, leaking, or placing" wastes. We must assume that Congress included "leaking" as a definitional component of "disposal" for a purpose. We conclude that Congress made "leaking" a part of the definition of "disposal" to meet the need to respond to the possibility of endangerment, among other reasons.

Thus, persons who owned or operated a facility at the time of active disposal of hazardous substances clearly fit within § 107(a)(2). But what about persons who owned or operated the facility after the time that hazardous substances were "disposed" but before a CERCLA action was commenced? The courts are split on how to treat these so-called passive intervening landowners. In *Nurad, Inc. v. William E. Hooper & Sons Co.*, 966 F.2d 837 (4th Cir. 1992), the current owner of contaminated property brought an action against previous owners and previous tenants, seeking reimbursement of costs incurred in removing from the property underground storage tanks and their hazardous contents. The court held that § 107(a)(2) imposes liability not only for active involvement in the "dumping" or "placing" of hazardous wastes at the facility, but for ownership of the facility at a time that hazardous waste was "spilling" or "leaking." The previous owners were held liable to the plaintiff, but the claims against the tenants were dismissed on the ground that they lacked authority to control the storage tanks and therefore did not "operate" a facility under § 107(a). However, in *United States v. CDMG Realty Co.*, 96 F.3d 706 (3d Cir. 1996), the court rejected the view taken in *Nurad* and held that, "while 'leaking' and 'spilling' may not require affirmative human conduct, neither word denotes the gradual spreading of contamination." The court said that it is especially unjustified to stretch the meaning of "leaking" and "spilling" to encompass the passive migration that generally occurs in landfills in view of the fact that another word used in CERCLA, "release," shows that Congress "knew precisely how to refer to this spreading of waste." (A prior owner who owned a waste site at the time of "disposal" is liable under § 107(a) only in the event of a "release" or "threatened release." Section 101(22) defines "release" as "any spilling, leaking, . . . escaping, leaching. . . .") The court said that "[l]eaching of contaminants from rain and groundwater movement is a principal cause of contaminant movement in landfills," and that "leaching" is the word commonly used in the environmental context to describe the passive migration of contaminants. The court also said that because CERCLA conditions the innocent landowner defense on the defendant's having purchased the property "after the disposal" of hazardous waste there, "disposal" cannot consist of the constant spreading of contaminants. "Otherwise, the defense would almost never apply, as there would generally be no point 'after disposal'." *See* Michael Caplan, *Escaping CERCLA Liability: The Interim Owner Passive Migration Defense Gains Circuit Recognition*, 28 ENVTL. L. REP. 10121 (1998). The Ninth Circuit in *Carson Harbor Village, Ltd. v. Unocal Corp.*, 270 F.3d 863 (9th Cir. 2001) (en banc), held that "disposal" does "not include passive soil migration but . . . may include other passive migration [including leaking of contaminants out of underground barrels or storage tanks] that fits within the plain meaning of the terms used to define 'disposal'." For summaries of other authorities see the *Carson* opinion and James Periconi & Robert Roesener, *"Passive" Disposal Through Migration: Theory Still Alive and Kicking*, 32 ENV'T REP. 461 (2001).

iii. Arrangers

Arranger liability (also known as generator liability, since the arrangers are typically those who generated the hazardous substances) arises under CERCLA § 107(a)(3), which imposes strict liability upon "any person" who "arranged for" disposal or treatment, or transport for disposal or treatment, of hazardous substances "owned or possessed" by such person. CERCLA defines person in section 101(21) as "an individual, firm, corporation, association, partnership, consortium, joint venture, commercial entity, United States Government, State, municipality, commission, political subdivision of a State, or any interstate body."

Arranger liability thus extends to a very broad category of PRPs (by the largest of the four categories). As a result, the scope of arranger liability has been extensively litigated. The following case identifies the key elements of arranger liability (note that the decision uses the older term "generator" rather than "arranger" when referring to PRPs under § 107(a)(3)).

UNITED STATES V. MONSANTO CO.

United States Court of Appeals, Fourth Circuit, 1988.
858 F.2d 160, *cert. denied*, 490 U.S. 1106, 109 S.Ct. 3156, 104 L.Ed.2d 1019 (1989).

SPROUSE, CIRCUIT JUDGE.

Oscar Seidenberg and Harvey Hutchinson (the site-owners) and Allied Corporation, Monsanto Company, and EM Industries, Inc. (the generator defendants), appeal from the district court's entry of summary judgment holding them liable to the United States and the State of South Carolina (the governments) under section 107(a) of [CERCLA]. The court determined that the defendants were liable jointly and severally for $1,813,624 in response costs accrued from the partial removal of hazardous waste from a disposal facility located near Columbia, South Carolina. * * * We affirm the district court's liability holdings * * *.

[The site-owners had leased rural land to COCC and SCRDI, which between 1976 and 1980 accepted for disposal there 7,000 drums of chemical waste generated by third parties. The governments entered into settlement agreements under which twelve of the generators (but not defendants who were also third party generators) paid 75% of the cost of a surface cleanup at the site. The governments paid the other 25% and brought this action for reimbursement.]

II

* * * The generator defendants * * * repeat their arguments based on the governments' failure to establish a nexus between their specific waste and the harm at the site. They also claim that the trial court ignored material factual issues relevant to affirmative defenses to liability. * * *

In our view, the plain language of section 107(a) clearly defines the scope of intended liability under the statute and the elements of proof necessary to establish it. We agree with the overwhelming body of precedent that has interpreted section 107(a) as establishing a strict liability scheme. Further, in light of the evidence presented here, we are persuaded that the district court correctly held that the governments satisfied all the elements of section 107(a) liability as to both the site-owners and the generator defendants. * * *

B.   *Generator Defendants' Liability*

The generator defendants first contend that the district court misinterpreted section 107(a)(3) because it failed to read into the statute a requirement that the governments prove a nexus between the waste they sent to the site and the resulting environmental harm. They maintain that the statutory phrase "containing such hazardous substances" requires proof that the specific substances they generated and sent to the site were present at the facility at the time of release. The district court held, however, that the statute was satisfied by proof that hazardous substances "like" those contained in the generator defendants' waste were found at the site. We agree with the district court's interpretation.

Reduced of surplus language, sections 107(a)(3) and (4) impose liability on off-site waste generators who:

> "arranged for disposal . . . of hazardous substances . . . at any facility . . . *containing such hazardous substances* . . . from which there is a release . . . of a hazardous substance."

In our view, the plain meaning of the adjective "such" in the phrase "containing such hazardous substances" is "[a]like, similar, of the like kind." BLACK'S LAW DICTIONARY 1284 (5th ed. 1979). As used in the statute, the phrase "such hazardous substances" denotes hazardous substances alike, similar, or of a like kind to those that were present in a generator defendant's waste or that could have been produced by the mixture of the defendant's waste with other waste present at the site. It does not mean that the plaintiff must trace the ownership of each generic chemical compound found at a site. Absent proof that a generator defendant's specific waste remained at a facility at the time of release, a showing of chemical similarity between hazardous substances is sufficient.[15]

The overall structure of CERCLA's liability provisions also militates against the generator defendants' "proof of ownership" argument. In *Shore Realty,* the Second Circuit held with respect to site-owners that requiring proof of ownership at any time later than the time of disposal would go far toward rendering the section 107(b) defenses superfluous. *Shore Realty,* 759 F.2d at 1044. We agree with the court's reading of the statute and conclude that its reasoning applies equally to the generator defendants' contentions. As the statute provides—"[n]otwithstanding any other provision or rule of law"—liability under section 107(a) is "subject *only* to the defenses set forth" in section 107(b). Each of the three defenses[16] established in section 107(b) "carves out from liability an exception based on causation." *Shore Realty,* 759 F.2d at 1044. Congress has, therefore, allocated the burden of disproving causation to the defendant who profited from the generation and inexpensive disposal of hazardous waste. We

---

[15] CERCLA plaintiffs need not perform exhaustive chemical analyses of hazardous substances found at a disposal site. *See SCRDI,* 653 F.Supp. at 993 n. 6. They must, however, present evidence that a generator defendant's waste was shipped to a site and that hazardous substances similar to those contained in the defendant's waste remained present at the time of release. The defendant, of course, may in turn present evidence of an affirmative defense to liability.

[16] In addition to the limited third-party defense discussed above, sections 107(b)(1) and (2) respectively allow defendants to avoid liability by proving that the release and resulting damages were "caused solely" by an act of God or an act of war. 42 U.S.C. § 9607(b)(1), (2).

decline to interpret the statute in a way that would neutralize the force of Congress' intent.[17]

Finally, the purpose underlying CERCLA's liability provisions counsels against the generator defendants' argument. Throughout the statute's legislative history, there appears the recurring theme of facilitating prompt action to remedy the environmental blight of unscrupulous waste disposal.[18] In deleting causation language from section 107(a), we assume as have many other courts, that Congress knew of the synergistic and migratory capacities of leaking chemical waste, and the technological infeasibility of tracing improperly disposed waste to its source. In view of this, we will not frustrate the statute's salutary goals by engrafting a "proof of ownership" requirement, which in practice, would be as onerous as the language Congress saw fit to delete. * * *

IV

The generator defendants raise numerous constitutional challenges to the district court's interpretation and application of CERCLA. * * *

Many courts have concluded that Congress intended CERCLA's liability provisions to apply retroactively to pre-enactment disposal activities of off-site waste generators. They have held uniformly that retroactive operation survives the Supreme Court's tests for due process validity. We agree with their analyses. * * *

* * * While the generator defendants profited from inexpensive waste disposal methods that may have been technically "legal" prior to CERCLA's enactment, it was certainly foreseeable at the time that improper disposal could cause enormous damage to the environment. CERCLA operates remedially to spread the costs of responding to improper waste disposal among all parties that played a role in creating the hazardous conditions. * * *

In view of the above, the judgment of the district court as to the CERCLA liability of the site-owners and generator defendants is affirmed. * * *

---

[17] In fact, Congress specifically declined to include a similar nexus requirement in CERCLA. As the Second Circuit in *Shore Realty* observed, an early House version of what ultimately became section 107(a) limited liability to "any person who caused or contributed to the release or threatened release." 759 F.2d at 1044 (quoting H.R. Rep. 7020, 96th Cong., 2d Sess. § 307(a) (1980), *reprinted in* 2 A LEGISLATIVE HISTORY OF THE COMPREHENSIVE ENVIRONMENTAL RESPONSE, COMPENSATION AND LIABILITY ACT OF 1980 at 438. As ultimately enacted after House and Senate compromise, however, CERCLA "imposed liability on classes of persons without reference to whether they caused or contributed to the release or threat of release." *Shore Realty*, 759 F.2d at 1044. The legislature thus eliminated the element of causation from the plaintiff's liability case.

[18] The legislative history underlying the Superfund Amendments and Reauthorization Act of 1986 echoed this theme with even greater force than that underlying CERCLA's original enactment in 1980.

NOTES

1. Can you identify the four elements of "arranger liability" articulated by the court in *Monsanto*? Most courts have followed *Monsanto* in rejecting a requirement of proof that the arranger's waste is present at the site and have embraced the *Monsanto* court's four-element test: (a) the arranger disposed of hazardous substances at the site in question; (b) the site contains hazardous substances *like* those disposed of by the arranger; (c) there has been a release (or threat of release) of a hazardous substance from the site (though the substance that is released need not be the arranger's or even like the arranger's); and (4) the release (or threat of release) has caused the incurrence of response costs.

2. Compare the approach to causation in *Monsanto* to what would be required in a common law negligence suit. What is the rationale for creating such a different scheme here? Does it matter that the plaintiff in a section 107 action is pursuing cost recovery for clean-up and not personal injury damages? Note that CERCLA does not preclude such a common law action. *See, e.g.*, Anderson v. Cryovac, Inc., 862 F.2d 910 (1st Cir. 1988), *remanded to* Anderson v. Beatrice Foods Co., 127 F.R.D. 1 (D. Mass. 1989).

3. Notice how the *Monsanto* court reads the word "such" to refer to "chemically similar" waste. The Court refers to dictionary definitions as well as legislative history. Is this convincing? Isn't the more plausible reading that "such" refers specifically to the waste the defendant generator actually sent to the site? What would be the effect of this alternate reading?

4. Should it matter for arranger liability if the arranger acted with due care in arranging for its wastes to be shipped to a facility?

5. Should arranger liability extend to a company that supplies commercial chemicals to a customer whom the company knows (or should know) is improperly disposing of those chemicals? The U.S. Supreme Court addressed this question in the following case:

BURLINGTON NORTHERN & SANTA FE RAILWAY CO. v. UNITED STATES

Supreme Court of the United States, 2009.
556 U.S. 599; 129 S.Ct. 1870.

JUSTICE STEVENS delivered the opinion of the Court.

In 1980, Congress enacted the Comprehensive Environmental Response, Compensation, and Liability Act (CERCLA), in response to the serious environmental and health risks posed by industrial pollution. The Act was designed to promote the " 'timely cleanup of hazardous waste sites' " and to ensure that the costs of such cleanup efforts were borne by those responsible for the contamination. These cases raise the questions whether and to what extent a party associated with a contaminated site may be held responsible for the full costs of remediation.

I

In 1960, Brown & Bryant, Inc. (B & B), began operating an agricultural chemical distribution business, purchasing pesticides and other chemical products from suppliers such as Shell Oil Company (Shell). Using its own equipment, B & B applied its products to customers' farms. B & B opened its business on a 3.8 acre parcel of former farmland in Arvin, California, and in 1975, expanded operations onto an adjacent .9 acre parcel of land owned jointly by what is now known as the Burlington Northern and Santa Fe Railway Company and Union Pacific Railroad Company (Railroads). Both parcels of the Arvin facility were graded toward a sump and drainage pond located on the southeast corner of the primary parcel. Neither the sump nor the drainage pond was lined until 1979, allowing waste water and chemical runoff from the facility to seep into the ground water below.

During its years of operation, B & B stored and distributed various hazardous chemicals on its property. Among these were the herbicide dinoseb, sold by Dow Chemical, and the pesticides D-D and Nemagon, both sold by Shell. Dinoseb was stored in 55-gallon drums and 5-gallon containers on a concrete slab outside B & B's warehouse. Nemagon was stored in 30-gallon drums and 5-gallon containers inside the warehouse. Originally, B & B purchased D-D in 55-gallon drums; beginning in the mid1960's, however, Shell began requiring its distributors to maintain bulk storage facilities for D-D. From that time onward, B & B purchased D-D in bulk.[1]

When B & B purchased D-D, Shell would arrange for delivery by common carrier, f.o.b. destination.[2] When the product arrived, it was transferred from tanker trucks to a bulk storage tank located on B & B's primary parcel. From there, the chemical was transferred to bobtail trucks, nurse tanks, and pull rigs. During each of these transfers leaks and spills could—and often did—occur. Although the common carrier and B & B used buckets to catch spills from hoses and gaskets connecting the tanker trucks to its bulk storage tank, the buckets sometimes overflowed or were knocked over, causing D-D to spill onto the ground during the transfer process.

Aware that spills of D-D were commonplace among its distributors, in the late 1970's Shell took several steps to encourage the safe handling of its products. Shell provided distributors with detailed safety manuals and instituted a voluntary discount program for distributors that made improvements in their bulk handling and safety facilities. Later, Shell revised its program to require distributors to obtain an inspection by a qualified engineer and provide self-certification of compliance with

---

[1]   Because D-D is corrosive, bulk storage of the chemical led to numerous tank failures and spills as the chemical rusted tanks and eroded valves.

[2]   F.o.b. destination means "the seller must at his own expense and risk transport the goods to [the destination] and there tender delivery of them . . .

applicable laws and regulations. B & B's Arvin facility was inspected twice, and in 1981, B & B certified to Shell that it had made a number of recommended improvements to its facilities.

Despite these improvements, B & B remained a " '[s]loppy' [o]perator." Over the course of B & B's 28 years of operation, delivery spills, equipment failures, and the rinsing of tanks and trucks allowed Nemagon, D-D and dinoseb to seep into the soil and upper levels of ground water of the Arvin facility. In 1983, the California Department of Toxic Substances Control (DTSC) began investigating B & B's violation of hazardous waste laws, and the United States Environmental Protection Agency (EPA) soon followed suit, discovering significant contamination of soil and ground water. Of particular concern was a plume of contaminated ground water located under the facility that threatened to leach into an adjacent supply of potential drinking water.

Although B & B undertook some efforts at remediation, by 1989 it had become insolvent and ceased all operations. That same year, the Arvin facility was added to the National Priority List, see 54 Fed. Reg. 41027, and subsequently, DTSC and EPA (Governments) exercised their authority under 42 U. S. C. § 9604 to undertake cleanup efforts at the site. By 1998, the Governments had spent more than $8 million responding to the site contamination; their costs have continued to accrue.

In 1991, EPA issued an administrative order to the Railroads directing them, as owners of a portion of the property on which the Arvin facility was located, to perform certain remedial tasks in connection with the site. The Railroads did so, incurring expenses of more than $3 million in the process. Seeking to recover at least a portion of their response costs, in 1992 the Railroads brought suit against B & B.

II

CERCLA imposes strict liability for environmental contamination upon [Potentially Responsible Parties (PRP) as defined in] 42 U. S. C. § 9607(a).

Once an entity is identified as a PRP, it may be compelled to clean up a contaminated area or reimburse the Government for its past and future response costs.

In these cases, it is undisputed that the Railroads qualify as PRPs under both §§ 9607(a)(1) and 9607(a)(2) because they owned the land leased by B & B at the time of the contamination and continue to own it now. The more difficult question is whether Shell also qualifies as a PRP under § 9607(a)(3) by virtue of the circumstances surrounding its sales to B & B.

To determine whether Shell may be held liable as an arranger, we begin with the language of the statute. As relevant here, § 9607(a)(3) applies to an entity that "arrange[s] for disposal . . . of hazardous substances." It is plain from the language of the statute that CERCLA liability would attach under § 9607(a)(3) if an entity were to enter into a transaction for the sole purpose of discarding a used and no longer useful hazardous substance. It is similarly clear that an entity could not be held liable as an arranger merely for selling a new and useful product if the purchaser of that product later, and unbeknownst to the seller, disposed of the product in a way that led to contamination. Less clear is the liability attaching to the many permutations of "arrangements" that fall between these two extremes—cases in which the seller has some knowledge of the buyers' planned disposal or whose motives for the "sale" of a hazardous substance are less than clear. In such cases, courts have concluded that the determination whether an entity is an arranger requires a fact-intensive inquiry that looks beyond the parties' characterization of the transaction as a "disposal" or a "sale" and seeks to discern whether the arrangement was one Congress intended to fall within the scope of CERCLA's strict-liability provisions.

Although we agree that the question whether § 9607(a)(3) liability attaches is fact intensive and case specific, such liability may not extend beyond the limits of the statute itself. Because CERCLA does not specifically define what it means to "arrang[e] for" disposal of a hazardous substance, we give the phrase its ordinary meaning. In common parlance, the word "arrange" implies action directed to a specific purpose. See Merriam-Webster's Collegiate Dictionary 64 (10th ed. 1993) (defining "arrange" as "to make preparations for: plan[;] . . . to bring about an agreement or understanding concerning"). Consequently, under the plain language of the statute, an entity may qualify as an arranger under § 9607(a)(3) when it takes intentional steps to dispose of a hazardous substance.

The Governments do not deny that the statute requires an entity to "arrang[e] for" disposal; however, they interpret that phrase by reference to the statutory term "disposal," which the Act broadly defines as "the discharge, deposit, injection, dumping, spilling, leaking, or placing of any solid waste or hazardous waste into or on any land or water." The Governments assert that by including unintentional acts such as "spilling" and "leaking" in the definition of disposal, Congress intended to impose liability on entities not only when they directly dispose of waste products but also when they engage in legitimate sales of hazardous substances knowing that some disposal may occur as a collateral consequence of the sale itself. Applying that reading of the statute, the Governments contend that Shell arranged for the disposal of D-D within the meaning of § 9607(a)(3) by shipping D-D to B & B under conditions it knew would result in the spilling of a portion of the hazardous substance by the purchaser or common carrier. Because these spills resulted in wasted D-D, a result Shell anticipated, the Governments insist that Shell was properly found to have arranged for the disposal of D-D.

While it is true that in some instances an entity's knowledge that its product will be leaked, spilled, dumped, or otherwise discarded may provide evidence of the entity's intent to dispose of its hazardous wastes, knowledge alone is insufficient to prove that an entity "planned for" the disposal, particularly when the disposal occurs as a peripheral result of the legitimate sale of an unused, useful product. In order to qualify as an arranger, Shell must have entered into the sale of D-D with the intention that at least a portion of the product be disposed of during the transfer process by one or more of the methods described in § 6903(3). Here, the facts found by the District Court do not support such a conclusion.

Although the evidence adduced at trial showed that Shell was aware that minor, accidental spills occurred during the transfer of D-D from the common carrier to B & B's bulk storage tanks after the product had arrived at the Arvin facility and had come under B & B's stewardship, the evidence does not support an inference that Shell intended such spills to occur. To the contrary, the evidence revealed that Shell took numerous steps to encourage its distributors to reduce the likelihood of such spills, providing them with detailed safety manuals, requiring them to maintain adequate storage facilities, and providing discounts for those that took safety precautions. Although Shell's efforts were less than wholly successful, given these facts, Shell's mere knowledge that spills and leaks continued to occur is insufficient grounds for concluding that Shell "arranged for" the disposal of D-D within the meaning of § 9607(a)(3). Accordingly, we conclude that Shell was not liable as an arranger for the contamination that occurred at B & B's Arvin facility.

JUSTICE GINSBURG, dissenting.

Although the question is close, I would uphold the determinations of the courts below that Shell qualifies as an arranger within the compass of (CERCLA).

In the 1950s and early 1960s, Shell shipped most of its products to Brown and Bryant (B & B) in 55-gallon drums, thereby ensuring against spillage or leakage during delivery and transfer. Later, Shell found it economically advantageous, in lieu of shipping in drums, to require B & B to maintain bulk storage facilities for receipt of the chemicals B & B purchased from Shell. By the mid-1960s, Shell was delivering its chemical to B & B in bulk tank truckloads. As the Court recognizes, "bulk storage of the chemical led to numerous tank failures and spills as the chemical rusted tanks and eroded valves."

Shell furthermore specified the equipment to be used in transferring the chemicals from the delivery truck to B & B's storage tanks. In the process, spills and leaks were inevitable, indeed spills occurred every time deliveries were made.

The deliveries, Shell was well aware, directly and routinely resulted in disposals of hazardous substances (through spills and leaks) for more than 20 years. "[M]ere knowledge" may not be enough, but Shell did not simply know of the spills and leaks without contributing to them. Given the control rein held by Shell over the mode of delivery and transfer, the lower courts held and I agree, Shell was properly ranked an arranger.

I would return these cases to the District Court to give all parties a fair opportunity to address that court's endeavor to allocate costs. Because the Court's disposition precludes that opportunity, I dissent from the Court's judgment.

NOTES

1.   How much should intent matter when seeking to determine "arranger" liability? In *Burlington Northern*, the majority found that "mere knowledge" of leaks and spills was not enough; instead, Shell must have intended for some form of disposal to take place in order to trigger arranger liability. But as Justice Ginsburg argued in her dissent, Shell was far more involved in the operations at the site than merely knowing that spills and leaks were occurring during the transfer of its products. Should it matter to the Court's determination that Shell knew that chemicals were leaking upon transfer from Shell's tankers to B & B's storage tanks every time a delivery was made over a twenty-year timeframe? Could Shell have also been subject to operator liability?

2.   Several cases on arranger liability involve arrangements between different companies to handle hazardous substances. In *United States v. Aceto Agric. Chem. Corp.*, 872 F.2d 1373 (8th Cir. 1989), plaintiffs alleged that defendant pesticide manufacturers contracted with Aidex Corp. (a bankrupt company at the time of litigation) for the "formulation" of their technical grade pesticides into commercial grade pesticides; that inherent in the formulation process (involving mixture of the manufacturers' active ingredients with inert materials according to the manufacturers' specifications) was the generation and disposal of wastes containing defendants' hazardous substances; and that defendants retained ownership of their hazardous substances throughout the formulation process. The court held that these allegations were sufficient to establish—for purposes of defeating defendants' motion to dismiss—that defendants "arranged for" disposal of the hazardous waste under CERCLA section 107(a)(3). Defendants unsuccessfully sought to analogize the case to previous ones in which district courts had refused to impose liability where a "useful" substance was sold to another party who then incorporated it into a product which was later disposed of. *See also United States v. Hercules, Inc.*, 247 F.3d 706 (8th Cir. 2001).

3.   In 1999, Congress enacted the Superfund Recycling Equity Act, CERCLA section 127. The Act grants relief from liability under section 107(a)(3) and (4) to persons who "arranged for recycling of recyclable material." The term "recyclable material" means "scrap" paper, plastic, glass, textiles, rubber (other than whole tires) and metal, and "spent batteries." To qualify for relief, arrangers must prove that various requirements were met at the time of the transaction, e.g., that the arranger exercised "reasonable care" to determine that the recycling facility was in compliance with "substantive" federal, state and local environmental laws and regulations. Although several criteria for determining "reasonable care" are set forth in section 127(c)(6), scrap metal dealers and battery recyclers have asked EPA to issue guidance or a rule further clarifying what they must do to comply with the standard. 31 ENV'T REP. 1512 (2000). For examples of judicial application of the requirements and exemptions of section 127(c)(6), see Gould, Inc. v. A & M Battery and Tire Service, 176 F.Supp.2d 324 (M.D. Pa. 2001); United States v. Mountain Metal Co., 137 F.Supp.2d 1267 (N.D. Ala. 2001).

4.   Arranger liability also may be used to reach corporate officers and parent corporations. In *United States v. TIC Investment Corp.*, 68 F.3d 1082 (8th Cir. 1995), the questions were whether an officer and the corporate parents of a subsidiary corporation were liable as arrangers for disposal of hazardous wastes. With respect to the corporate officer, the court held that the proper standard would impose direct arranger liability on him if he had the authority to control and did in fact exercise actual or substantial control, directly or indirectly, over the arrangement for disposal or the off-site disposal of hazardous substances. The court found that the officer did not delegate authority and left no room for others to exercise any decisionmaking authority or judgment in any area of the business, including hazardous waste disposal. Thus, as a matter of law, he was liable as an arranger. With respect to the parent corporations, the court said that in order for them to incur direct arranger liability for a subsidiary's off-site disposal practices, "[T]here must be some causal connection or nexus between the parent corporation's conduct and the subsidiary's arrangement for disposal, or the off-site disposal itself." The court of appeals reversed the summary judgment against the parent corporations, saying that there were genuine issues of material fact concerning whether they not only had the authority to control but also "exercised actual or substantial control, directly or indirectly, over [the subsidiary's] waste disposal arrangement." (Compare to the test for "owner and operator" liability, discussed above.)

5.   The Small Business Liability Relief and Brownfields Revitalization Act of 2002 created new exclusions for the liability of arrangers and transporters as well as owners and operators. New section 107(o), the "de micromis exemption," protects a PRP from liability under section 107(a)(3) or (4) if he can demonstrate that (1) the total amount of the materials containing hazardous substances which he contributed was less than 110 gallons of liquid materials or 200 pounds of solid materials (or such greater or lesser amounts as the EPA may determine by regulation), and (2) all or part of the disposal,

treatment, or transport occurred before April 1, 2001. Several exceptions to the de micromis exemption are set forth in section 107(o)(2). The exemption does not apply where (a) the materials in question contribute significantly to the cost of the response action or natural resource restoration, (b) the person fails to comply with an information request or impedes the response action or restoration, or (c) the person has been convicted of a criminal violation for conduct to which the exemption would apply.

Another new section, 107(p), created an exemption from "arranger" liability for a person who is (1) an owner, operator, or lessee of residential property from which any "municipal solid waste" (MSW) (defined as waste generated by a household, or by a business or institutional entity to the extent that the waste is essentially the same as that normally generated by a household) is generated; (2) a business that employed on average not more than 100 full-time individuals (or equivalent) in the three tax years before notification of its potential liability, and is a "small business concern" (within the meaning of the Small Business Act, 15 U.S.C. section 631 et seq.); or (3) a "501(c)(3)" nonprofit organization that employed not more than 100 paid individuals during the preceding year at the location from which the MSW was generated. The exceptions to the MSW exemption are identical to exceptions (a) and (b) above, for the de micromis exemption.

iv. Transporters

The principal contested issue with respect to *transporter* liability has been the meaning of section 107(a)(4)'s requirement that the disposal or treatment facility be "selected by" the transporter. In *Tippins, Inc. v. USX Corp.*, 37 F.3d 87 (3d Cir. 1994), the court concluded that a person is liable as a transporter not only if it "ultimately selects" the disposal facility but also when it "actively participates in the disposal decision to the extent of having had substantial input" in the choice of disposal facility. Similarly, *United States v. Davis*, 261 F.3d 1 (1st Cir. 2001), held that transporter liability requires "substantial input" into the choice of the disposal facility.

United States v. USX Corp., 68 F.3d 811 (3d Cir. 1995), involved a claim against the principal shareholders and officers of a closely held corporation that transported hazardous substances. The United States argued that section 107(a)(4) was intended to impose liability on those who control the affairs of a responsible corporation, irrespective of whether those in control actually participated in the liability-creating conduct. The court rejected that argument, saying that liability may not be imposed solely on the basis of an officer's or shareholder's active involvement in the corporation's day-to-day affairs: "Instead, there must be a showing that the person sought to be held liable actually participated in the liability-creating conduct." However, liability is not limited to those who personally participate in the transportation of hazardous wastes, nor is it necessary that the officer participate in the selection of the disposal facility. "Liability may be imposed where the officer is aware of the acceptance of materials for transport and of his company's substantial participation in the selection of the disposal facility. An officer who has authority to control disposal decisions should not escape liability under section 107(a)(4) when he or she has actual knowledge that a subordinate has selected a disposal site and, effectively, acquiesces in the subordinate's actions."

In *American Cyanamid v. Capuano*, 381 F.3d 6 (1st Cir. 2004), the court held that the district court's finding that defendants were transporters was not clearly erroneous, on the basis of three factors. First, defendants had substantial input in the decision of where to dispose of the waste, often making the final determination of whether to allow the waste to be dumped at their own landfill or to send it to the disposal site. Second, the trucks carrying the hazardous waste would arrive at defendants' place of business only to be redirected by defendants to the disposal site. Third, although payments by defendants to the transportation drivers did not prove, in and of themselves, that defendants transported the waste, the court found that the payments did support the inference that defendants were involved with transportation of waste to the site.

v. *Other Parties: Parent Corporations, Successors, Lenders, and Governmental Entities*

As noted above and as should be evident from the some of the cases discussed in the notes accompanying the discussion of the four categories of PRPs, various corporate, financial, and governmental entities are often implicated in CERCLA actions, raising questions about whether they fit within one of the four categories.

A. Parent Corporations

Is a parent corporation necessarily the "owner or operator" of a hazardous waste facility owned by its wholly owned subsidiary? In *United States v. Bestfoods*, 524 U.S. 51 (1998), the Supreme Court framed the question as: "whether a parent corporation that actively participated in, and exercised control over, the operations of a subsidiary may, without more, be held liable as an operator of a polluting facility owned or operated by the subsidiary"? The Court continued: "We answer no, unless the corporate veil may be pierced. But a corporate parent that actively participated in, and exercised control over, the operations of the *facility itself* may be held directly liable in its own right [under CERCLA] as an operator of the facility" (emphasis added.) Under general corporate law, the corporate veil may be pierced and the parent held liable for the subsidiary's conduct when, e.g., the corporate form would otherwise be misused to accomplish wrongful purposes, most notably fraud, on the parent's behalf; or when stock ownership has been resorted to for the purpose of controlling a subsidiary company so that it may be used as a mere agency or instrumentality of the parent company. But under section 107(a) of

CERCLA, according to the Court, an "operator" is one who "directs the workings of, manages, or conducts the affairs of a facility." The operator— e.g., a parent corporation acting through an agent who is not an officer of the subsidiary—"must manage, direct, or conduct operations specifically related to pollution, that is, operations having to do with the leakage or disposal of hazardous waste, or decisions about compliance with environmental regulations." The critical question under section 107(a) is "whether, in degree and detail, actions directed to the facility by an agent of the parent alone are eccentric under accepted norms of parental oversight of a subsidiary's facility." Would a parent that satisfied this test also be liable as an "arranger"?

Carter-Jones Lumber Co. v. LTV Steel Co., 237 F.3d 745 (6th Cir. 2001), held that state, rather than federal, common law should apply in CERCLA "veil piercing" claims under *Bestfoods*. For further discussion of this issue, and of the definition of "operator" for purposes of assessing direct liability, *see* Lucia Silecchia, *Pinning the Blame & Piercing the Veil in the Mists of Metaphor: The Supreme Court's New Standards for the CERCLA Liability of Parent Companies and a Proposal for Legislative Reform*, 67 FORDHAM L. REV. 115 (1998).

B.   Successor Corporations

Based on the terms of CERCLA section 107(a), which allow for liability to be placed on any "person" who fits within the four categories of potentially responsible parties, federal courts have held that CERCLA allows for the imposition of liability on successor corporations. *See B.F. Goodrich v. Betkoski*, 99 F.3d 505, 518 (2d Cir. 1996). Beyond this general proposition, however, the decisions of which common law—federal or state—to apply and which factors to consider in setting liability have been somewhat less clear. In *Louisiana-Pacific Corp. v. Asarco, Inc.*, 909 F.2d 1260 (9th Cir. 1990), applying federal common law, the court held that CERCLA liability may be imposed upon "successors"—companies that purchase the stock or assets of hazardous waste disposers—under the narrow liability rules applied in most states. Under those rules an asset purchaser may be liable only if (1) it expressly or impliedly agreed to assume the predecessor's liabilities, (2) the transaction amounted to a "de facto" merger, (3) the successor is "merely a continuation" of the predecessor, or (4) the transaction involved fraud in an attempt to escape liability. The court left open the possible application of two more expansive successor liability rules, the "product line" rule and the "continuing business enterprise" rule. *See* Ronald R. Janke & Matthew L. Kuryla, *Environmental Liability Risks for Asset Purchasers*, 24 ENV'T REP. 2237 (1994); Alfred R. Light, *'Product Line' and 'Continuity of Enterprise' Theories of Corporation Successor Liability Under CERCLA*, 11 MISS. C. L. REV. 63 (1990).

Applying "evolving principles of federal common law" the court in *United States v. Carolina Transformer Co.,* 978 F.2d 832 (4th Cir. 1992), applied the continuing business enterprise rule (which it called the "continuity of enterprise" or "substantial continuity" rule) in a case that did not come within the "mere continuation" rule because there was no overlap of stock ownership between the seller and the buyer of a transformer construction business. The factors which the court considered in holding the purchaser liable under CERCLA were (1) retention of the same employees, (2) retention of the same supervisory personnel, (3) retention of the same production facilities in the same location, (4) production of the same product, (5) retention of the same name, (6) continuity of assets, (7) continuity of general business operations, and (8) successor's holding itself out as the continuation of the previous enterprise.

In *Atchison, Topeka & Santa Fe Railway Co. v. Brown & Bryant, Inc.,* 159 F.3d 358 (9th Cir. 1997), the Ninth Circuit expressed doubt about the correctness of its earlier view in *Louisiana-Pacific, supra,* that federal rather than state common law should govern successor liability under CERCLA. Citing intervening decisions by the Supreme Court in *O'Melveny & Myers v. FDIC,* 512 U.S. 79 (1994), and *Atherton v. FDIC,* 519 U.S. 213 (1997), neither of which involved CERCLA, the Ninth Circuit said that the Supreme Court had "rejected many of the very arguments that *Louisiana-Pacific* accepted in deciding CERCLA necessitated a set of uniform federal rules for successor liability." The court read *O'Melveny* to mean that when dealing with a "comprehensive and detailed" federal statutory regulation, a court should "presume that matters left unaddressed in such a scheme are subject to state law."

Later, in *United States v. Davis,* 261 F.3d 1 (1st Cir. 2001), the First Circuit followed the reasoning of the Ninth Circuit in *Atchison, Topeka* and concluded that state rather than federal common law should govern successor liability under CERCLA. The court chose to apply Connecticut's "mere continuation" test rather than the federal "substantial continuation" test, and consequently imposed successor liability on successor corporation Black & Decker.

The most important later development concerning successor liability is *United States v. General Battery Corp.,* 423 F.3d 294 (3d Cir. 2005), in which the court disagreed with *Davis,* holding that, based on the precedent of *Bestfoods* (discussed in the section on Parent Corporations, *supra*), a uniform *federal* standard should apply in determining successor liability. According to the court, although successor liability rests at "the intersection of tort and corporate law," both of which tend to rely on state law, applying a uniform federal standard—rather than the varying state standards—of successor liability better serves CERCLA's objectives of predictability, uniformity, encouraging settlements, and facilitating a market in brownfield assets.

Turning to the case at hand—in which defendant General Battery Corporation had acquired a defunct generator corporation and then merged with an existing corporation—the court applied the "fundamental" common-law principles of successor liability, as recommended by *Bestfoods*. Under these principles, a successor is not liable unless it meets one of four exceptions: (1) it assumes liability; (2) the transaction amounts to a consolidation or merger; (3) the transaction is fraudulent and intended to provide an escape from liability; or (4) the purchasing corporation is a mere continuation of the selling company. Noting that the case involved the "de facto merger" exception, the court then found that the transaction met all four elements of a de facto merger under the majority standard: (1) continuity of enterprise; (2) continuity of shareholders; (3) seller corporation ceased operation, liquidated, and dissolved as soon as possible; and (4) buyer assumed obligations ordinarily necessary for the uninterrupted continuation of normal business operations.

Both federal and state rules concerning the liability of successors may be modified by contract. Indemnification agreements are often used in transactions involving the acquisition of property to address environmental and other liabilities related to the assets and business transferred. Two key issues raised by CERCLA's language and judicial decisions concerning the enforceability of indemnification agreements are (1) whether indemnification agreements are barred by section 107(e), and, if not, (2) whether they nevertheless should be construed narrowly. Section 107(e)(1) provides:

> No indemnification, hold harmless, or similar agreement or conveyance shall be effective to transfer from the owner or operator of any vessel or facility or from any person who may be liable for a release or threat of release under this section, to any other person the liability imposed under this section. Nothing in this subsection shall bar any agreement to insure, hold harmless, or indemnify a party to such agreement for any liability under this section.

A majority of federal courts interpret section 107(e) as allowing indemnity agreements. As a result, indemnity agreements have become an integral part of real estate transactions. For example, in *Mardan Corp. v. C.G.C. Music, Ltd.*, 804 F.2d 1454 (9th Cir. 1986), a seller sold land on which it had manufactured musical instruments and deposited waste. As part of the sale, the purchaser agreed to release the seller from undisclosed environmental liabilities. After the EPA brought an enforcement action against the purchaser (which also had deposited waste upon the property), the purchaser sued the seller under section 107 for recovery of its cleanup costs. The court affirmed a summary judgment for the seller, stating that, while it is true that indemnification agreements cannot alter or excuse the underlying liability, they *can* change who ultimately pays for that liability.

Similarly, in *AM International v. International Forging Equipment Corp.,* 982 F.2d 989 (6th Cir. 1993), the court agreed that section 107(e) does not bar indemnification agreements, holding that the second sentence of section 107(e)(1) permits the shifting or allocation of the cost of liability between parties, so long as CERCLA liability for the cleanup itself is not diluted.

Concerning the construction of indemnification agreements, most courts have applied, either explicitly or implicitly, a rule that such arrangements can bar CERCLA liability between the parties only if there is clear language in the agreement anticipating and requiring such a result. *See Mobay Corp. v. Allied-Signal, Inc.,* 761 F.Supp. 345 (D.N.J. 1991); *Southland Corp. v. Ashland Oil, Inc., 696 F.Supp. 994* (D.N.J. 1988).

C. Lenders and Trustees

Section 101(20)(A) of CERCLA excludes from the definition of "owner or operator" any "person, who, without participating in the management of a * * * facility, holds indicia of ownership primarily to protect his security interest in the * * * facility." Financial institutions and other secured creditors were shocked by the decision in *United States v. Fleet Factors Corp.,* 901 F.2d 1550 (11th Cir. 1990), which held that it was not necessary to the imposition of liability that the creditor actually involve itself in day-to-day operations of the facility; it was enough if the involvement with management was "sufficiently broad to support the inference that it could affect hazardous waste decisions if it so chose." Prior district court decisions had permitted lenders to participate in the financial affairs of the borrowers without risking CERCLA liability, so long as the lenders did not become too involved in the borrowers' day-to-day operations.

Responding to the ensuing clamor from the banking community and to the federal government's increasing role as a secured creditor after taking over failed savings and loans, the EPA issued in 1992 a regulation that employed a framework of specific tests to provide clearer articulation of a lender's CERCLA liability. Lender Liability Under CERCLA, 57 Fed. Reg. 18,344, 18,382 (Apr. 29, 1992) (codified at 40 C.F.R. section 300.1100). The rule was vacated on procedural grounds in *Kelley v. Environmental Protection Agency,* 15 F.3d 1100 (D.C. Cir. 1994). But in 1996, Congress amended the lender liability provisions, essentially adopting the EPA's rule. The phrase "participate in management" is now defined in section 101(20)(E) to mean "actually participating in the management or operational affairs" of a facility, and "does not include merely having the capacity to influence, or the unexercised right to control," facility operations. *See* Public Law 104–208 (1996). Subsequently, *Monarch Tile, Inc. v. City of Florence,* 212 F.3d 1219 (11th Cir. 2000) held that a city that purchased land to foster private economic development thereon, leasing it to a private company and retaining title to secure payment of the development bonds that financed the property's acquisition, qualified for CERCLA's "secured creditor" liability exception.

Prior to 1996 there was uncertainty and litigation concerning the possible CERCLA liability of trustees when trust property is contaminated. Could a trustee be personally liable, beyond the extent of the trust assets, for cleanup costs? CERCLA was silent on the matter. The leading case was *City of Phoenix v. Garbage Services Co.*, 816 F.Supp. 564 (D. Ariz. 1993), in which the court held that the defendant trustee, a bank, would be liable under section 107(a)(2), without regard to the amount of trust assets available to indemnify it, if the plaintiff could prove at trial that hazardous substances were disposed of at the site when the bank held title.

In 1996, Congress enacted the Asset Conservation Act, amending section 107 of CERCLA to limit fiduciaries' personal liability. Under new section 107(n), the general rule is that a fiduciary's liability for the release or threatened release of a hazardous substance at a facility held in a fiduciary capacity shall not exceed the assets so held. The general rule does not apply, however, to the extent that a person is liable independently of his position or actions as a fiduciary, nor does it limit liability if the negligence of a fiduciary causes or contributes to the release or threatened release. Applying the negligence exception, the court in *Canadyne-Georgia Corp. v. NationsBank, N.A. (South)*, 183 F.3d 1269 (11th Cir. 1999), sustained a complaint against a bank that acted as a trustee for trusts whose assets included partnership interests in a company at the time the company allegedly contaminated certain property. The court looked to state law in determining that the bank could be deemed an "owner" for purposes of CERCLA liability. On remand, the trial court granted the trustee-bank's motion for summary judgment because plaintiff had presented no evidence that the bank "took particular negligent actions that caused or contributed to the release of hazardous substances." *Canadyne-Georgia Corp. v. Bank of America*, 174 F.Supp.2d 1360 (M.D. Ga. 2001).

D. Governmental Entities

Prior to the 1986 SARA amendments to CERCLA, the Third Circuit held in *United States v. Union Gas Co.*, 792 F.2d 372 (3d Cir. 1986), *vacated and remanded*, 479 U.S. 1025 (1987), that the Eleventh Amendment to the Constitution barred the imposition of cleanup liability against states because section 107 did not specifically identify states as liable parties. The court stated that, in order to overcome the Eleventh Amendment, the statute had to make clear that Congress consciously and directly focused on the issue of state sovereign immunity and chose to abrogate it. Subsequently, in 1986, Congress amended section 101(20), defining "owner or operator," to provide for state and local governmental liability under section 107. The Supreme Court then concluded that Congress did intend to subject states to suits for response costs if states caused or contributed to hazardous substance releases. *Pennsylvania v. Union Gas Co.*, 491 U.S. 1 (1989). In *Seminole Tribe of Florida v. Florida,* 517 U.S. 44 (1996), however, the Supreme Court overruled its decision in *Union Gas.* The Court held that the Commerce Clause does not authorize Congress to abrogate a state's Eleventh Amendment immunity to suit without its consent.

There has been much controversy about the CERCLA liability of municipal governments, many of which own or operate disposal or treatment facilities, transport wastes to such facilities, or arrange for disposal, treatment or transport. Municipalities, which are not protected by the Eleventh Amendment, hoped that the courts would interpret CERCLA narrowly to exclude them from section 107(a)'s list of "covered persons." However, federal courts consistently have interpreted the law broadly, holding that municipalities may be liable as owners and operators of hazardous waste sites as well as transporters and generators of hazardous waste. *See* Joseph M. Manko & Madeleine H. Cozine, *The Battle Over Municipal Liability Under CERCLA Heats Up: An Analysis of Proposed Congressional Amendments to Superfund,* 5 VILL. ENVTL. L.J. 23 (1994).

The most important case on this subject is *B.F. Goodrich Co. v. Murtha,* 958 F.2d 1192 (2d Cir. 1992). In holding that municipalities which send their residents' household waste to landfills can be liable under CERCLA, the court rejected the following arguments by the municipal defendants: (1) that a municipality cannot be liable under CERCLA for the disposal of hazardous substances since it is acting in its sovereign capacity; (2) that CERCLA's silence regarding municipal solid waste is evidence that Congress intended to exclude it from the definition of hazardous substances; (3) that the exemption for household hazardous waste under RCRA is incorporated into CERCLA's definition of hazardous substances; (4) that CERCLA's legislative history evinces an intent to exclude municipalities from liability for the disposal of municipal solid waste; and (5) that the EPA interpreted CERCLA as imposing no liability on municipalities for the disposal of municipal waste.

Under its 2003 "Interim Guidance on the Municipal Solid Waste Exemption Under § 107(p) (Aug. 20, 2003), https://www.epa.gov/enforcement/interim-guidance-municipal-solid-waste-exemption-under-superfund, EPA attempted to ameliorate the perceived harshness of CERCLA as applied to municipalities. Under this policy, EPA generally does not pursue municipalities under CERCLA as generators or transporters of MSW unless the waste contains hazardous substances derived from commercial, institutional or industrial activity. For municipal owners/operators of NPL sites that wish to resolve their potential CERCLA liability and obtain contribution protection pursuant to section 113(f), the policy establishes 20% of total estimated response costs for the site as a presumptive baseline settlement amount for an individual municipality. EPA may offer settlements varying upward or downward from this presumption, generally not to exceed 35%, based on site-specific factors.

With respect to hazardous waste facilities owned or operated by the federal government, section 120 of CERCLA provides that "[e]ach department, agency and instrumentality of the United States * * * shall be subject to * * * this chapter * * * to the same extent * * * as any nongovernmental entity, including liability under section [107]." Federal facilities are included on the NPL, but funds for cleanup must come from the budget of the responsible department or agency, not from the Superfund.

The greatest potential U.S. liability under section 120 appears to stem from contaminated military bases and nuclear weapons facilities. *See Cleaning Up Federal Facilities: Controversy Over an Environmental Peace Dividend*, 23 ENV'T REP. 2659 (1993). The facilities need not be owned by the federal government. In *FMC Corp. v. Department of Commerce*, 29 F.3d 833 (3d Cir. 1994) (en banc), a contribution suit by a private PRP, the court held that section 120 waives the federal government's immunity from CERCLA liability when the government engages in activities that would subject private parties to liability. The government was, therefore, liable under section 107 as "operator" of a private manufacturing facility over which the government "exerted considerable day-to-day control" during World War II to meet production goals for high-tenacity rayon. Rejecting the government's argument for a "*per se* rule that regulatory activities cannot constitute the basis for CERCLA liability," the court stated that "the government can be liable when it engages in regulatory activities extensive enough to make it an operator of a facility or an arranger of the disposal of hazardous wastes."

d. Defenses

CERCLA § 107(b) provides for a narrow set of defenses to liability. In particular, the defendant PRP must "establish by a preponderance of the evidence that the release or threat of release of a hazardous substance and the damages resulting therefrom were caused solely by—

(1) an act of God;

(2) an act of war;

(3) an act or omission of a third party other than an employee or agent of the defendant, or than one whose act or omission occurs in connection with a contractual relationship, existing directly or indirectly, with the defendant (except where the sole contractual arrangement arises from a published tariff and acceptance for carriage by a common carrier by rail), if the defendant establishes by a preponderance of the evidence

that (a) he exercised due care with respect to the hazardous substance concerned, taking into consideration the characteristics of such hazardous substance, in light of all relevant facts and circumstances, and (b) he took precautions against foreseeable acts or omissions of any such third party and the consequences that could foreseeably result from such acts or omissions; or

(4) any combination of the foregoing paragraphs.

42 U.S.C. § 9607.

In *Blasland, Bouck & Lee v. City of North Miami*, 283 F.3d 1286, 1302–05 (11th Cir. 2002), the court expressly affirmed the narrowness of the § 107(b) defenses, noting that, while it would appear that CERCLA sets out other defenses in parts of the statute other than section 107(b), there are only three potential defenses for PRPs.

The most prominent of the three defenses is section 107(b)(3), regarding acts or omissions by a third party. Congress attempted to address the perceived unfairness of section 107(a) in the SARA amendments of 1986 by adding a new defense for innocent landowners. While section 107(a)'s general liability standard for "owners and operators" was maintained, Congress expanded section 107(b)(3)'s third-party exception by redefining the term "contractual relationship" in section 101(35):

Section 101 (35) (A). The term "contractual relationship", for the purpose of section 9607(b)(3) of this title, includes, but is not limited to, land contracts, deeds, easements, leases, or other instruments transferring title or possession, unless the real property on which the facility concerned is located was acquired by the defendant after the disposal or placement of the hazardous substance on, in, or at the facility, and one of more of the circumstances described in clause (i), (ii), or (iii) is also established by the defendant by a preponderance of the evidence:

(i) At the time the defendant acquired the facility the defendant did not know and had no reason to know that any hazardous substance which is the subject of the release or threatened release was disposed of on, in, or at the facility.

(ii) The defendant is a government entity which acquired the facility by escheat, or through any other involuntary transfer or acquisition, or through the exercise of eminent domain authority by purchase or condemnation.

(iii) The defendant acquired the facility by inheritance of bequest.

42 U.S.C. § 9601(35)(A).

With respect to the "reason to know" limitation, section 101(35)(B)(i), after being further amended in 2002 by the Small Business Liability Relief and Brownfields Revitalization Act, provides in part:

> (B)(i)   * * * To establish that the defendant had no reason to know * * *, the defendant must demonstrate to a court that—

> (I)   * * * before [acquiring] the facility, the defendant carried out all appropriate inquiries [due diligence, pursuant to "standards and practices" to be established by EPA] into the previous ownership and uses of the facility in accordance with generally accepted good commercial and customary standards and practices; and

> (II) the defendant took reasonable steps to—

>> (aa)   stop any continuing release;

>> (bb)   prevent any threatened future release; and

>> (cc)   prevent or limit any human, environmental, or natural resource exposure to any previously released hazardous substance.

42 U.S.C. § 9601(35)(B).

All "innocent landowners," whether they acquired the land voluntarily or involuntarily, also must establish that they have cooperated fully with persons conducting any response actions and have complied with any land use restrictions or institutional controls related to the response actions.

The 2002 amendments also require that, within two years of the amendments' passage, EPA establish standards and practices for the purpose of fulfilling the 'all appropriate inquiries' requirement. On May 9, 2003, EPA promulgated these standards and practices, currently located at 40 C.F.R. Pt. 312. The text of the regulations is brief, stating simply that the procedures of the American Society for Testing and Materials ("ASTM") entitled "Standard Practice for Environmental Site Assessment: Phase 1 Environmental Site Assessment Process" shall satisfy the requirements for conducting all appropriate inquiry.

In *Franklin County Convention Facilities Authority v. American Premier Underwriters, Inc.*, 240 F.3d 534 (6th Cir. 2001), the court reversed the district court's holding that a PRP was entitled to the innocent landowner defense. Though the PRP played no role in placing the hazardous substance at the site—in this case, a buried box of creosote that the PRP's contractor accidentally split open while excavating—and the PRP could not be held liable for the "accidental and unavoidable" splitting open of the box, the PRP did not exercise due care after discovering the spill. Upon discovery, the PRP immediately ceased work and contacted an environmental contractor, but nevertheless allowed the spill to migrate forty-five feet through a sewer trench. Accordingly, the court held the PRP did not act with due care and, therefore, was not entitled to the innocent landowner defense.

In *Western Properties Service Corp. v. Shell Oil Co.*, 358 F.3d 678 (9th Cir. 2004), the Ninth Circuit rejected a claim requesting a broadening of the innocent landowner defense. The court's holding suggests that, though there is no legal basis for the broadening of the three section 107(b) defenses, the limits on what the court may consider in contribution actions under section 113(f) (discussed *infra*) are much less strict:

> There is some attraction, in certain circumstances, to a broad innocent-landowner rule for non-polluting landowners who are not statutorily innocent under section 101(35). The attractiveness is equitable, not textual, and the contribution statute already allows for equity to be taken into account. Suppose a person bought a lot on which to build a home, not knowing that some years ago a truck had overturned and spilled hazardous substances into the ground, which had seeped down into the water table. Suppose further that by due diligence he could have found out and is deemed to have had reason to know, so he is not a statutory innocent owner. In such a case, the district court would be able to consider the equities, as between the almost-innocent PRP landowner and the company whose truck had overturned, using its section 113(f)(1) authority to "allocate response costs among liable parties using such equitable factors as the court determines are appropriate."

Id. at 690. The court also discussed the proposition, noted also in *Blasland*, *supra*, and other circuits, that equitable defenses are barred under section 107(a) and therefore may not be admitted in a section 107 action. On the other hand, such equitable defenses may be considered in a contribution action under section 113(f).

Though section 107(b)(3) tends to be the most litigated of the three defenses, in *United States v. Shell Oil Co.*, 294 F.3d 1045 (9th Cir. 2002), defendant oil companies claimed a defense under section 107(b)(2), the "act of war" exception. In a suit under section 107(a), the United States and the State of California attempted to recover cleanup costs from oil companies that had produced aviation fuel for the federal government during World War II. Through the War Powers Clause of the Constitution, President Roosevelt had entered the U.S. into contractual agreements with the oil companies for their continued production of aviation fuel. While the U.S. provided low-cost loans for the production of facilities to increase production of the fuel, the companies ultimately retained ownership of the facilities. After the war, the federal government paid for the cleanup of "acid sludge" waste at the sites and subsequently brought a section 107 suit against the companies, who then claimed the act of war defense under section 107(b)(2). In rejecting the companies' claim, the court noted the dearth of case law and legislative history on the act of war defense. Based on the definition of "act of war" under international law and "dictum" from the Supreme Court, the court focused on the narrowness of the term and the logical division between unilateral acts and acts of mutual contract in wartime. The court held that the companies' "argument that any governmental act taken by authority of the War Powers Clause is an 'act of war' [swept] too broadly," and accordingly rejected the companies' defense.

e.   Apportionment and Allocation

As a general matter, while CERCLA does not dictate the imposition of joint and several liability, federal courts have held that the statute does allow for it. Indeed, most courts now impose some form of joint and several liability when dealing with multiple PRPs and indivisible harm. *United States v. Monsanto*, excerpted *supra*, is an instructive example of such a strict imposition. While joint and several liability is the norm for cases of indivisible harm, controversies and differences among courts begin to arise as to "the timing of the resolution of the divisibility question, whether equitable factors should be considered, and whether a defendant can avoid liability at all, or for only some portion, of the damages." *See In re Bell Petroleum Services, Inc., infra.* Because of the frequent commingling of wastes at dump sites, along with their potential to migrate and the fact that even small amounts of waste can be extremely dangerous, courts traditionally have rejected the notion that volume of waste alone should be a basis for apportionment. In general, courts resist considering equitable factors at the liability stage, refusing to apportion damages and instead leaving cost allocation for parties to sort out in the (inevitable) contribution actions that follow. Still, some courts have allowed the introduction of equitable factors as a consideration in the apportionment stage.

For example, in *United States v. A & F Materials Co.*, 578 F.Supp. 1249, 1256 (S.D. Ill. 1984), the court concluded that "a rigid application of the Restatement approach to joint and several liability is inappropriate" because such extensive liability would be unfair to a defendant who contributed only a small amount of waste to a site. The court preferred a "moderate approach" under which the court (a) had the power to impose joint and several liability whenever a defendant could not prove his contribution to an injury but (b) still could apportion damages according to the following factors contained in an unsuccessful amendment to CERCLA proposed by then Representative (later Vice President) Al Gore which became known as the "Gore factors":

(i)   the ability of the parties to demonstrate that their contribution to a discharge, release or disposal of a hazardous waste can be distinguished;

(ii) the amount of the hazardous waste involved;

(iii) the degree of toxicity of the hazardous waste involved;

(iv) the degree of involvement by the parties in the generation, transportation, treatment, storage, or disposal of the hazardous waste;

(v)   the degree of care exercised by the parties with respect to the hazardous waste concerned, taking into account the characteristics of such hazardous waste; and

(vi) the degree of cooperation by the parties with Federal, State, or local officials to prevent any harm to the public health or the environment.

Similarly, in *United States v. Alcan Aluminum Corp.*, 964 F.2d 252 (3d Cir. 1992), the court allowed the defendant to introduce evidence of apportionment. The government had argued that Alcan was jointly and severally liable for cleanup costs even though Alcan claimed that the only waste it had taken to the site was a non-hazardous, non-toxic emulsion with heavy metal fragments "orders of magnitude below ambient or naturally occurring background levels." The court of appeals vacated the judgment of the district court and remanded the case for "further factual development concerning the scope of Alcan's liability." Because of the "intensely factual nature of the 'divisibility' issue," the appeals court held that the district court erred in granting the United States summary judgment for its full claim against Alcan without benefit of a hearing. *Alcan* recognizes that proving divisibility will require "an assessment of the relative toxicity, migratory potential and synergistic capacity of the hazardous waste at issue."[2]

Some critics have argued that EPA often settles early with large defendants for amounts far below the actual costs incurred in cleaning up the wastes for which those defendants are responsible. Under joint and several liability, defendants that settle late or litigate bear the brunt of the EPA's failure to exact reasonable settlement amounts from the early

---

[2]   In a similar case also involving Alcan, the Second Circuit largely adopted the Third Circuit's reasoning. *United States v. Alcan Aluminum Corp.*, 990 F.2d 711 (2d Cir. 1993). "Alcan may escape liability for response costs if it either succeeds in proving that its oil emulsion, when mixed with other hazardous wastes, did not contribute to the release and the clean-up costs that followed, or contributed at most to only a divisible portion of the harm. Alcan as the polluter bears the ultimate burden of establishing a reasonable basis for apportioning liability." The court acknowledged that Alcan was being allowed to bring the issue of causation back into the case, "through the backdoor, after being denied entry at the frontdoor," but only to escape payment "where its pollutants did not contribute more than background contamination and also cannot concentrate."

settlors. *Alcan* is viewed as a vehicle for ameliorating inequitable results in such situations. *See* Daniel P. Harris & David M. Milan, *Avoiding Joint and Several Liability under CERCLA*, 23 ENV'T REP. 1726 (1992).

The dominant approach to apportionment and allocation is summed up in *In re Bell Petroleum Services, Inc.*, 3 F.3d 889 (5th Cir. 1993), which reversed a district court's judgment imposing joint and several liability upon each of three successive owners of a chrome-plating shop. Each owner had discharged rinse water onto the ground, causing the underlying aquifer to become contaminated with chromium. The court of appeals reviewed the *Chem-Dyne*-Restatement approach to joint and several liability adopted in *Monsanto, supra,* the "moderate approach" of *A & F Materials,* and the *Alcan* approach:

> The Fourth Circuit [in *Monsanto* rejected] the *A & F* moderate approach, stating that, while equitable factors are relevant in an action for contribution, "[t]hey are not pertinent to the question of joint and several liability, which focuses principally on the divisibility among responsible parties of the harm to the environment." 858 F.2d at 171 n.22. Other courts have similarly concluded that equitable factors, such as those listed in the Gore amendment, have no place in making the decision whether to impose joint and several liability, but are appropriate in an action for contribution among jointly and severally liable defendants. *See* Alcan, 964 F.2d at 270 n. 29. * * *
>
> * * * Under the *Restatement,* the plaintiff must first prove that the defendant's conduct was a substantial factor in causing the harm; the defendant may limit its liability by proving its contribution to the harm. In contrast, the *Alcan* approach suggests that a defendant may escape liability altogether if it can prove that its waste, even when mixed with other wastes at the site, did not cause the incurrence of response costs. * * *

Although these approaches are not entirely uniform, certain basic principles emerge. First, joint and several liability is not mandated under CERCLA; Congress intended that the federal courts impose joint and several liability only in appropriate cases, applying common-law principles. Second, all of the cases rely on the *Restatement* in resolving the issues of joint and several liability. The major differences among the cases concern the timing of the resolution of the divisibility question, whether equitable factors should be considered, and whether a defendant can avoid liability for all, or only some portion, of the damages. Third, even where commingled wastes of unknown toxicity, migratory potential, and synergistic effect are present, defendants are allowed an opportunity to attempt to prove that there is a reasonable basis for apportionment (although they rarely succeed); where such factors are not present, volume may be a reasonable means of apportioning liability.

With respect to the timing of the "divisibility" inquiry, we believe that an early resolution is preferable. We agree with the Second Circuit, however, that this is a matter best left to the sound discretion of the district court. We also agree with the majority view that equitable factors, such as those listed in the Gore amendment, are more appropriately considered in actions for contribution among jointly and severally liable parties, than in making the initial determination of whether to impose joint and several liability. We therefore conclude that the *Chem-Dyne* approach is an appropriate framework for resolving issues of joint and several liability in CERCLA cases. Although we express no opinion with respect to the *Alcan* approach, because it is not necessary with respect to the issues we are faced with in this case, we nevertheless recognize that the *Restatement* principles must be adapted, where necessary, to implement congressional intent with respect to liability under the unique statutory scheme of CERCLA.

In *United States v. Hercules, Inc.*, 247 F.3d 706 (8th Cir. 2001), the court clarified the difference between "distinct harms" and "divisibility of harm":

"Distinct harms" are those that may properly be regarded as separate injuries. Defendants may be able to demonstrate that harms are distinct based on geographical considerations, such as where a site consists of "non-contiguous" areas of soil contamination, or separate and distinct subterranean "plumes" of groundwater contamination.

Other cases, by contrast, involve a "single harm" that is nonetheless divisible because it is possible to discern the degree to which different parties contributed to the damage. The basis for division in such situations is that "it is clear that each [defendant] has caused a separate amount of harm, limited in time, and that neither has any responsibility for the harm caused by the other," such as where "two defendants, independently operating the same plant, pollute a stream over successive periods of time." *Bell*, 3 F.3d at 895. Single harms may also be "treated as divisible in terms of degree," based, for example, on the relative quantities of waste discharged into the stream. Divisibility of this type may be provable even where wastes have become cross-contaminated and commingled. . . . *Alcan II*, 990 F.2d at 772; *see also* Bell, 3 F.3d at 903.

Evidence supporting divisibility must be concrete and specific. The preliminary issue of whether the harm to the environment is capable of apportionment among two or more causes is a question of law. *Bell*, 3 F.3d at 902. Then, "[o]nce it has been determined that the harm is capable of being apportioned among the various causes of it, the actual apportionment of damages is a question of fact."

We also observe that the divisibility doctrine is conceptually distinct from contribution or allocation of damages. At the allocation phase, the only question is the extent to which a defendant's liability may be offset by the liability of another; the inquiry at this state is an equitable one and courts generally take into account the so-called "Gore factors." The divisibility of harm inquiry, by contrast, is guided not by equity—specifically, not by the Gore factors—but by principles of causation alone. Thus, where causation is unclear, divisibility is not an opportunity for courts to "split the difference" in an attempt to achieve equity.

The *Alcan* and *Bell* cases are discussed in Lynda Oswald, *New Directions in Joint and Several Liability under CERCLA?*, 28 U.C. DAVIS L. REV. 299 (1995). *See also* Richard White & John Butler, *Applying Cost Causation Principles in Superfund Allocation Cases*, 28 ENVTL. L. REP. 10067 (1998).

In the *Burlington Northern* case, discussed above in the section on arranger liability, the Supreme Court addressed the issue of apportionment with respect to the liability of the railroads:

BURLINGTON NORTHERN & SANTA FE RAILWAY CO. v. UNITED STATES

Supreme Court of the United States, 2009.
556 U.S. 599; 129 S.Ct. 1870.

[The facts of the case and the portion addressing arranger liability are excerpted in the section on arranger liability above.]

We must . . . determine whether the Railroads were properly held jointly and severally liable for the full cost of the Governments' response efforts. Apportionment is proper when "there is a reasonable basis for determining the contribution of each cause to a single harm." Restatement (Second) of Torts § 433A(1)(b), p. 434 (1963–1964).

Not all harms are capable of apportionment, however, and CERCLA defendants seeking to avoid joint and several liability bear the burden of proving that a reasonable basis for apportionment exists. When two or more causes produce a single, indivisible harm, "courts have refused to make an arbitrary apportionment for its own sake, and each of the causes is charged with responsibility for the entire harm."

The District Court calculated the Railroads' liability based on three figures. First, the court noted that the Railroad parcel constituted only 19% of the surface area of the Arvin site. Second, the court observed that the Railroads had leased their parcel to B & B for 13 years, which was only 45% of the time B & B operated the Arvin facility. Finally, the court found that the volume of hazardous substance-releasing activities on the B & B property was at least 10 times greater than the releases that occurred on the Railroad parcel, and it concluded that only spills of two chemicals, Nemagon and dinoseb (not D-D), substantially contributed to the contamination that had originated on the Railroad parcel and that those two chemicals had contributed to two-thirds of the overall site contamination requiring remediation. The court then multiplied .19 by .45 by .66 (two-thirds) and rounded up to determine that the Railroads were responsible for approximately 6% of the remediation costs. "Allowing for calculation errors up to 50%," the court concluded that the Railroads could be held responsible for 9% of the total CERCLA response cost for the Arvin site.

We conclude that the facts contained in the record reasonably supported the apportionment of liability. The District Court's detailed findings make it abundantly clear that the primary pollution at the Arvin facility was contained in an unlined sump and an unlined pond in the southeastern portion of the facility most distant from the Railroads' parcel and that the spills of hazardous chemicals that occurred on the Railroad parcel contributed to no more than 10% of the total site contamination, some of which did not require remediation. With those background facts in mind, we are persuaded that it was reasonable for the court to use the size of the leased parcel and the duration of the lease as the starting point for its analysis.

The Court of Appeals criticized the District Court's assumption that spills of Nemagon and dinoseb were responsible for only two-thirds of the chemical spills requiring remediation, observing that each PRP's share of the total harm was not necessarily equal to the quantity of pollutants that were deposited on its portion of the total facility. Although the evidence adduced by the parties did not allow the court to calculate precisely the amount of hazardous chemicals contributed by the Railroad parcel to the total site contamination or the exact percentage of harm caused by each chemical, the evidence did show that fewer spills occurred on the Railroad parcel and that of those spills that occurred, not all were carried across the Railroad parcel to the B & B sump and pond from which most of the contamination originated. The fact that no D-D spills on the Railroad parcel required remediation lends strength to the District Court's conclusion that the Railroad parcel contributed only Nemagon and dinoseb in quantities requiring remediation.

The District Court's conclusion that those two chemicals accounted for only two-thirds of the contamination requiring remediation finds less support in the record; however, any miscalculation on that point is harmless in light of the District Court's ultimate allocation of liability, which included a 50% margin of error equal to the 3% reduction in liability the District Court provided based on its assessment of the effect of the Nemagon and dinoseb spills. Had the District Court limited its apportionment calculations to the amount of time the Railroad parcel was in use and the percentage of the facility located on that parcel, it would have assigned the Railroads 9% of the response cost. By including a two-thirds reduction in liability for the Nemagon and dinoseb with a 50% "margin of error," the District Court reached the same result. Because the District Court's ultimate allocation of liability is supported by the evidence and comports with the apportionment principles outlined above, we reverse the Court of Appeals' conclusion that the Railroads are subject to joint and several liability for all response costs arising out of the contamination of the Arvin facility.

NOTE

How does the Supreme Court's conclusion that apportionment was possible and appropriate in the *Burlington Northern* case affect litigation strategies? If the railroads' share is limited to 9 percent and B & B is bankrupt, what happens going forward? If the federal government is left holding the bag for the remaining costs might it change the way it engages in the cleanup, searching, for example, for more cost-effective means or engaging in less thorough cleanup? Does this change the way we think about joint and several liability under CERCLA? Should it?

f.   Cost Recovery and Contribution

Section 107(a) provides for two different types of cost recovery: actions by the Government against PRPs to recover the response costs it has incurred in cleaning up contaminated sites and actions by private PRPs against other PRPs for costs they have incurred in cleaning up contaminated sites. Under the language of section 107(a), different standards apply to these two types of cost recovery:

[Persons covered by section 107(a)] shall be liable for—

(A) all costs of removal or remedial action incurred by the United States Government or a State or an Indian tribe not inconsistent with the national contingency plan;

(B) any other necessary costs of response incurred by any other person consistent with the national contingency plan.

42 U.S.C. 9607(a) (2000).

In *Monsanto, supra,* the court described the two standards in these terms:

> Appellants argue the district court erred in requiring them to prove the response costs were inconsistent with the NCP, not cost-effective or unnecessary. Appellants further argue the district court erred in assuming all costs that are consistent with the NCP are conclusively presumed to be reasonable. Appellants note that the information and facts necessary to establish consistency with the NCP are matters within the possession of the government.

> We believe the district court's analysis is correct. * * * The statutory language itself establishes an exception for costs that are inconsistent with the NCP, but appellants, as the parties claiming the benefit of the exception, have the burden of proving that certain costs are inconsistent with the NCP and, therefore, not recoverable. Contrary to appellants' argument, "not inconsistent" is not, at least for purposes of statutory construction and not syntax, the same as "consistent."

> The statutory scheme also supports allocation of the burden of proof of inconsistency with the NCP upon the defendants when the *government* seeks recovery of its response costs. As noted above, CERCLA § 107(a)(4)(A) provides that the federal government or a state can recover "all costs of removal or remedial action * * * not inconsistent with the [NCP]." In comparison, CERCLA § 107(a)(4)(B) provides that "any other person," referring to any "person" other than the federal government or a state, can recover "any other necessary costs of response * * * consistent with the [NCP]." That statutory language indicates that *non*-governmental entities must prove that their response costs are consistent with the NCP in order to recover them. The statutory scheme thus differentiates between governmental and non-governmental entities in allocating the burden of proof of whether response costs are consistent with the NCP.

> The statutory language also supports the district court's reasoning that under CERCLA § 107(a)(4)(A) "all costs" incurred by the government that are not inconsistent with the NCP are conclusively presumed to be reasonable. CERCLA does not refer to "all *reasonable* costs" but simply to "all costs." * * *

The key difference then between the government's burden and the burden for private parties is that the costs claimed by a private party must affirmatively be shown to be consistent with the National Contingency Plan, whereas costs incurred by the government will be presumed consistent unless shown to be inconsistent with the NCP.

But which private parties may recover response costs under section 107(a)? Local governments that conduct cleanups? The private owner of land adjacent to a leaking disposal site? The owner of the leaking disposal site? In *Jones v. Inmont Corp.*, 584 F.Supp. 1425 (S.D. Ohio 1984), the court held that under section 107(a)(4)(B) private parties owning land adjoining an illegal dump site were included within the phrase "any other person" and could recover their response costs from a past generator of hazardous waste deposited there. *See also Pinole Point Properties, Inc. v. Bethlehem Steel Corp.*, 596 F.Supp. 283 (N.D. Cal. 1984). In *City of Philadelphia v. Stepan Chemical Co.*, 544 F.Supp. 1135 (E.D. Pa. 1982), the court held that the city, which owned land on which hazardous industrial wastes were dumped illegally without its permission, was not precluded from recovering its actual cleanup costs from defendant generators, even though the city itself, as site owner, might be liable for any response costs later incurred by the state or federal government. The court said that Philadelphia qualified as "any other person" under § 107(a)(4)(B).

Costs recoverable by private plaintiffs do not include compensation for lost property value, income, or medical monitoring. *See Piccolini v. Simon's Wrecking*, 686 F.Supp. 1063 (M.D. Pa. 1988); *Lutz v. Chromatex, Inc.*, 718 F.Supp. 413 (M.D. Pa. 1989). Plaintiffs in *Daigle v. Shell Oil Co.,* 972 F.2d 1527 (10th Cir. 1992), were neighbors of the Rocky Mountain Arsenal, a federal chemical weapons facility generally regarded as one of the worst hazardous waste sites in the United States. Plaintiffs pointed out that CERCLA's definitions of "removal" and "remedial" actions both refer to "monitoring" necessary to protect "public health and welfare." Section 101(23)–(24). Plaintiffs argued that this language supported their claims for the costs of long term "medical monitoring" or "medical surveillance" designed to detect the onset of any latent disease that might be caused by exposure to toxic fumes released during cleanup of the arsenal. The court rejected the argument, saying that the definitions of removal and remedial actions are directed at containing and cleaning up hazardous substance releases. The court held that the monitoring contemplated by the statute is intended to prevent contact between contaminants and the public, and does not include long term health monitoring of the sort requested by plaintiffs. For a similar result, *see Price v. United States Navy*, 39 F.3d 1011 (9th Cir. 1994).

In *Key Tronic Corp. v. United States*, 511 U.S. 809 (1994), one of several parties responsible for contaminating a landfill settled a lawsuit filed by EPA and then brought an action against the Air Force and other responsible parties to recover a share of its cleanup costs, including *attorneys' fees* for legal services in connection with (1) the identification of other PRPs, (2) the preparation and negotiation of the consent decree with EPA, and (3) the prosecution of its action against the Air Force. Since CERCLA §§ 107 and 113(f) do not expressly mention attorneys' fees, in contrast to §§ 310(f) (citizen suits) and 106(b)(2)(E) (persons erroneously ordered to pay response costs), the issue was whether attorneys' fees may constitute "necessary costs of response" recoverable under § 107(a)(4)(B). The Court held that under the "American Rule", Key Tronic could not recover attorneys' fees for prosecuting its action against the Air Force. Neither was plaintiff allowed to recover for legal services in connection with the negotiations culminating in the consent decree with EPA. The Court viewed those services as "primarily protecting Key Tronic's interests as a defendant in the proceedings that established the extent of its liability," not as "necessary costs of response." However, "lawyers' work that is closely tied to the actual cleanup may constitute a necessary cost of response in and of itself," and the component of plaintiff's claim that covered work performed in identifying other PRPs was held to fall into this category. "Unlike the litigation services at issue in *Alyeska,* these efforts might well be performed by engineers, chemists, private investigators or other professionals who are not lawyers." (A court of appeals subsequently held, in *United States v. Chapman,* 146 F.3d 1166 (9th Cir. 1998), that response costs recoverable under § 107 by the EPA, in contrast to a private plaintiff, may include attorneys' fees for litigation and negotiations.)

In addition to seeking cost recovery under section 107, private parties can seek contribution from other PRPs. Under Section 113(f):

> Any person may seek contribution from any other person who is liable or potentially liable under [§ 107(a)], during or following any civil action under [§ 106 or 107(a)]. Such claims * * * shall be governed by Federal law. In resolving contribution claims, the court may allocate response costs among liable parties using such equitable factors as the court determines are appropriate.

42 U.S.C. § 9613(f).

Section 113(f) was among the additions to CERCLA in 1986 as part of the SARA amendments. Who can seek contribution under the section? Must a party have been party to an action under sections 106 or 107 in order to bring a contribution action, or may a party who has voluntarily cleaned a site seek contribution, too? The circuits were split on the resolution of this question until 2004, when the Supreme Court decided *Cooper Industries, Inc. v. Aviall Services, Inc.,* 543 U.S. 157 (2004). In that case, the Supreme Court held that PRPs engaged in voluntary cleanups could not seek contribution under § 113(f) because they had not been subject to a civil action under § 106 or § 107. The Court declined to answer the question whether such parties could seek cost recovery under section 107. The result was substantial uncertainty, and serious concerns about cost recovery, among PRPs engaged in voluntary cleanups. Three years later, the Supreme Court took up the question left open in *Cooper Industries* in the following case:

UNITED STATES V. ATLANTIC RESEARCH CORPORATION

Supreme Court of the United States, 2007.
551 U.S. 128; 127 S.Ct. 2331.

JUSTICE THOMAS delivered the opinion of the Court.

Two provisions of the Comprehensive Environmental Response, Compensation, and Liability Act of 1980 (CERCLA)—§§ 107(a) and 113(f)—allow private parties to recover expenses associated with cleaning up contaminated sites. In this case, we must decide a question left open in *Cooper Industries, Inc. v. Aviall Services, Inc.*, 543 U.S. 157, 161, 125 S.Ct. 577, 160 L.Ed.2d 548 (2004): whether § 107(a) provides so-called potentially responsible parties (PRPs), 42 U.S.C. §§ 9607(a)(1)–(4), with a cause of action to recover costs from other PRPs. We hold that it does.

I

A

Courts have frequently grappled with whether and how PRPs may recoup CERCLA-related costs from other PRPs. The questions lie at the intersection of two statutory provisions—CERCLA §§ 107(a) and 113(f). Section 107(a) defines four categories of PRPs, and makes them liable for, among other things:

"(A) all costs of removal or remedial action incurred by the United States Government or a State or an Indian tribe not inconsistent with the national contingency plan; [and]

"(B) any other necessary costs of response incurred by any other person consistent with the national contingency plan." §§ 9607(a)(4)(A)–(B).

Enacted as part of the Superfund Amendments and Reauthorization Act of 1986 (SARA), § 113(f) authorizes one PRP to sue another for contribution in certain circumstances.

Prior to the advent of § 113(f)'s express contribution right, some courts held that § 107(a)(4)(B) provided a cause of action for a private party to recover voluntarily incurred response costs and to seek contribution after having been sued. After SARA's enactment, however, some Courts of Appeals believed it necessary to "direc[t] traffic between" § 107(a) and § 113(f). As a result, many Courts of Appeals held that § 113(f) was the exclusive remedy for PRPs. But as courts prevented PRPs from suing under § 107(a), they expanded § 113(f) to allow PRPs to seek "contribution" even in the absence of a suit under § 106 or § 107(a).

In *Cooper Industries*, we held that a private party could seek contribution from other liable parties only after having been sued under § 106 or § 107(a). 543 U.S., at 161. This narrower interpretation of § 113(f) caused several Courts of Appeals to reconsider whether PRPs have rights under § 107(a)(4)(B), an issue we declined to address in, Cooper Industries, Id., at 168. After revisiting the issue, some courts have permitted § 107(a) actions by PRPs. However, at least one court continues to hold that § 113(f) provides the exclusive cause of action available to PRPs. Today, we resolve this issue.

B

In this case, respondent Atlantic Research leased property at the Shumaker Naval Ammunition Depot, a facility operated by the Department of Defense. At the site, Atlantic Research retrofitted rocket motors for petitioner United States. Using a high-pressure water spray, Atlantic Research removed pieces of propellant from the motors. It then burned the propellant pieces. Some of the resultant wastewater and burned fuel contaminated soil and ground water at the site.

Atlantic Research cleaned the site at its own expense and then sought to recover some of its costs by suing the United States under both §§ 107(a) and 113(f). After our decision in Cooper Industries foreclosed relief under § 113(f), Atlantic Research amended its complaint to seek relief under § 107(a) and federal common law. The United States moved to dismiss, arguing that § 107(a) does not allow PRPs (such as Atlantic Research) to recover costs. The District Court granted the motion to dismiss, relying on a case decided prior to our decision in Cooper Industries.

The Court of Appeals for the Eighth Circuit reversed. Recognizing that Cooper Industries undermined the reasoning of its prior precedent, the Court of Appeals joined the Second and Seventh Circuits in holding that § 113(f) does not provide "the exclusive route by which [PRPs] may recover cleanup costs." The court reasoned that § 107(a)(4)(B) authorized suit by any person other than the persons permitted to sue under § 107(a)(4)(A). Accordingly, it held that § 107(a)(4)(B) provides a cause of action to Atlantic Research. To prevent perceived conflict between §§ 107(a)(4)(B) and 113(f)(1), the Court of Appeals reasoned that PRPs that "have been subject to §§ 106 or 107 enforcement actions are still required to use § 113, thereby ensuring its continued vitality." We granted certiorari and now affirm.

II

A

The parties' dispute centers on what "other person[s]" may sue under § 107(a)(4)(B). The Government argues that "any other person" refers to any person not identified as a PRP in §§ 107(a)(1)–(4).2 In other words, subparagraph (B) permits suit only by non-PRPs and thus bars Atlantic Research's claim. Atlantic Research counters that subparagraph (B) takes its cue from subparagraph (A), not the earlier paragraphs (1)–(4). In accord with the Court of Appeals, Atlantic Research believes that subparagraph (B) provides a cause of action to anyone except the United States, a State, or an Indian tribe—the persons listed in subparagraph (A). We agree with Atlantic Research.

Statutes must "be read as a whole." Applying that maxim, the language of subparagraph (B) can be understood only with reference to subparagraph (A). The provisions are adjacent and have remarkably similar structures. Each concerns certain costs that have been incurred by certain entities and that bear a specified relationship to the national contingency plan.3 Bolstering the structural link, the text also denotes a relationship between the two provisions. By using the phrase "other necessary costs," subparagraph (B) refers to and differentiates the relevant costs from those listed in subparagraph (A).

In light of the relationship between the subparagraphs, it is natural to read the phrase "any other person" by referring to the immediately preceding subparagraph (A), which permits suit only by the United States, a State, or an Indian tribe. The phrase "any other person" therefore means any person other than those three. Consequently, the plain language of subparagraph (B) authorizes cost-recovery actions by any private party, including PRPs.

The Government's interpretation makes little textual sense. In subparagraph (B), the phrase "any other necessary costs" and the phrase "any other person" both refer to antecedents—"costs" and "person[s]"—located in some previous statutory provision. Although "any other necessary costs" clearly references the costs in subparagraph (A), the Government would inexplicably interpret "any other person" to refer not to the persons listed in subparagraph (A) but to the persons listed as PRPs in paragraphs (1)–(4). Nothing in the text of § 107(a)(4)(B) suggests an intent to refer to antecedents located in two different statutory provisions. Reading the statute in the manner suggested by the Government would destroy the symmetry of §§ 107(a)(4)(A) and (B) and render subparagraph (B) internally confusing.

Moreover, the statute defines PRPs so broadly as to sweep in virtually all persons likely to incur cleanup costs. Hence, if PRPs do not qualify as "any other person" for purposes of § 107(a)(4)(B), it is unclear what private party would. The Government posits that § 107(a)(4)(B) authorizes relief for "innocent" private parties—for instance, a landowner whose land has been contaminated by another. But even parties not responsible for contamination may fall within the broad definitions of PRPs in §§ 107(a)(1)–(4). The Government's reading of the text logically precludes all PRPs, innocent or not, from recovering cleanup costs. Accordingly, accepting the Government's interpretation would reduce the number of potential plaintiffs to almost zero, rendering § 107(a)(4)(B) a dead letter.

According to the Government, our interpretation suffers from the same infirmity because it causes the phrase "any other person" to duplicate work done by other text. In the Government's view, the phrase "any other necessary costs" "already precludes governmental entities from recovering under" § 107(a)(4)(B). Brief for United States 20. Even assuming the Government is correct, it does not alter our conclusion. The phrase "any other person" performs a significant function simply by clarifying that subparagraph (B) excludes the persons enumerated in subparagraph (A). In any event, our hesitancy to construe statutes to render language superfluous does not require us to avoid surplusage at all costs. It is appropriate to tolerate a degree of surplusage rather than adopt a textually dubious construction that threatens to render the entire provision a nullity.

B

The Government also argues that our interpretation will create friction between §§ 107(a) and 113(f), the very harm courts of appeals have previously tried to avoid. In particular, the Government maintains that our interpretation, by offering PRPs a choice between §§ 107(a) and 113(f), effectively allows PRPs to circumvent § 113(f)'s shorter statute of limitations. Furthermore, the Government argues, PRPs will eschew equitable apportionment under § 113(f) in favor of joint and several liability under § 107(a). Finally, the Government contends that our interpretation eviscerates the settlement bar set forth in § 113(f)(2).

We have previously recognized that §§ 107(a) and 113(f) provide two "clearly distinct" remedies. "CERCLA provide[s] for a right to cost recovery in certain circumstances, § 107(a), and separate rights to contribution in other circumstances, §§ 113(f)(1), 113(f)(3)(B)." The Government, however, uses the word "contribution" as if it were synonymous with any apportionment of expenses among PRPs. This imprecise usage confuses the complementary yet distinct nature of the rights established in §§ 107(a) and 113(f).

Section 113(f) explicitly grants PRPs a right to contribution. Contribution is defined as the "tortfeasor's right to collect from others responsible for the same tort after the tortfeasor has paid more than his or her proportionate share, the shares being determined as a percentage of fault." Black's Law Dictionary 353 (8th ed.2004). Nothing in § 113(f) suggests that Congress used the term "contribution" in anything other than this traditional sense. The statute authorizes a PRP to seek contribution "during or following" a suit under § 106 or § 107(a). Thus, § 113(f)(1) permits suit before or after the establishment of common liability. In either case, a PRP's right to contribution under § 113(f)(1) is contingent upon an inequitable distribution of common liability among liable parties.

By contrast, § 107(a) permits recovery of cleanup costs but does not create a right to contribution. A private party may recover under § 107(a) without any establishment of liability to a third party. Moreover, § 107(a) permits a PRP to recover only the costs it has "incurred" in cleaning up a site. When a party pays to satisfy a settlement agreement or a court judgment, it does not incur its own costs of response. Rather, it reimburses other parties for costs that those parties incurred.

Accordingly, the remedies available in §§ 107(a) and 113(f) complement each other by providing causes of action "to persons in different procedural circumstances." Section 113(f)(1) authorizes a contribution action to PRPs with common liability stemming from an action instituted under § 106 or § 107(a). And § 107(a) permits cost recovery (as distinct from contribution) by a private party that has itself incurred cleanup costs. Hence, a PRP that pays money to satisfy a settlement agreement or a court judgment may pursue § 113(f) contribution. But by reimbursing response costs paid by other parties, the PRP has not incurred its own costs of response and therefore cannot recover under § 107(a). As a result, though eligible to seek contribution under § 113(f)(1), the PRP cannot simultaneously seek to recover the same expenses under § 107(a). Thus, at least in the case of reimbursement, the PRP cannot choose the 6-year statute of limitations for cost-recovery actions over the shorter limitations period for § 113(f) contribution claims.

For similar reasons, a PRP could not avoid § 113(f)'s equitable distribution of reimbursement costs among PRPs by instead choosing to impose joint and several liability on another PRP in an action under § 107(a). The choice of remedies simply does not exist. In any event, a defendant PRP in such a § 107(a) suit could blunt any inequitable distribution of costs by filing a § 113(f) counterclaim. Resolution of a § 113(f) counterclaim would necessitate the equitable apportionment of costs among the liable parties, including the PRP that filed the § 107(a) action.

Finally, permitting PRPs to seek recovery under § 107(a) will not eviscerate the settlement bar set forth in § 113(f)(2). That provision prohibits § 113(f) contribution claims against "[a] person who has resolved its liability to the United States or a State in an administrative or judicially approved settlement . . . ." The settlement bar does not by its terms protect against cost-recovery liability under § 107(a). For several reasons, we doubt this supposed loophole would discourage settlement. First, as stated above, a defendant PRP may trigger equitable apportionment by filing a § 113(f) counterclaim. A district court applying traditional rules of equity would undoubtedly consider any prior settlement as part of the liability calculus. Cf. 4 Restatement (Second) of Torts § 886A(2), p. 337 (1977) ("No tortfeasor can be required to make contribution beyond his own equitable share of the liability"). Second, the settlement bar continues to provide significant protection from contribution suits by PRPs that have inequitably reimbursed the costs incurred by another party. Third, settlement carries the inherent benefit of finally resolving liability as to the United States or a State.

III

Because the plain terms of § 107(a)(4)(B) allow a PRP to recover costs from other PRPs, the statute provides Atlantic Research with a cause of action. We therefore affirm the judgment of the Court of Appeals.

It is so ordered.

NOTES

1.   As the Supreme Court made clear in *Atlantic Research Corp.*, § 107(a) and § 113(f) complement each other: § 113(f)(1) authorizes contribution actions by PRPs with common liability stemming from an action instituted under § 106 or § 107(a), while § 107(a) permits cost recovery (as distinct from contribution) by a private party that has itself incurred cleanup costs.

2.   Other questions remain about the operation of section 113(f). For example, what factors may be taken into account in contribution suits—the Gore factors alone? What is the plaintiff's burden of proof—is it the same as the government's burden in a section 107 cost recovery action? And what sort of liability can courts impose on parties to contribution suits? In *Environmental Transportation Systems, Inc. v. ENSCO, Inc.,* 969 F.2d 503 (7th Cir. 1992), defendant Northern States Power Co. had generated PCB-contaminated waste and hired defendant ENSCO to arrange for disposal. ENSCO hired plaintiff Environmental Transportation Systems (ETS) to transport the waste to a disposal facility. En route, the ETS truck overturned because it was driven at an excessive speed while the driver attempted to negotiate a highway access ramp. ETS paid for the cost of cleanup of the spill and sought contribution from ENSCO and Northern States under section 113(f) of CERCLA. Defendants moved for summary judgment. After concluding that ETS was responsible for all costs of cleanup because the accident was entirely ETS's fault, the district court granted defendants' motion. The district court held that, although ENSCO and Northern States would have been liable if sued under section 107, such liability does not necessarily lead to mandatory contribution for cleanup costs. The court of appeals affirmed the judgment of the district court, on the ground that Congress' intent in enacting section 113(f) was that the court should "equitably allocate costs of cleanup according to the relative culpability of the parties rather than an automatic equal shares rule." The court of appeals specifically mentioned that the legislative history of section 113(f) cites the *A & F Materials* criteria (the "Gore factors"), *supra*, as factors that a court may consider in deciding whether to grant apportionment in a contribution action.

In *Control Data Corp. v. S.C.S.C. Corp.,* 53 F.3d 930 (8th Cir. 1995), plaintiff sought contribution under section 113(f) after having cleaned up contamination caused by both plaintiff and defendant. Citing the "Gore factors," the court allocated one-third of the total cleanup costs to defendant because the chemical released by it—constituting only ten percent of the total contamination by volume—was much more toxic and difficult to remove than was the chemical released by plaintiff.

3.   Several cases have held that a defendant's potential liability under section 107(a) does not preclude a zero allocation of response costs to that defendant in a contribution suit under section 113(f). Thus, in *Kalamazoo River Study Group v. Rockwell International Corp.*, 274 F.3d 1043 (6th Cir. 2001), where the trial court found that defendant had released less than 20 pounds of PCBs into the river (in contrast to the hundreds of thousands of pounds released by plaintiffs), the appellate court affirmed the lower court's decision, made after a full trial, not to allocate any response costs to defendant. The court of appeals said that "a defendant's release of what, standing alone, would be a significant amount of such material might have no impact on the total cost of cleaning up a contaminated site." For further discussion of zero allocations of response costs, and additional citations, *see* Douglas McWilliams, *District Courts Can Inject Some Fairness Into CERCLA Liability Scheme*, 33 ENV'T REP. 663 (2002).

A few cases have considered specifically plaintiff's burden of proof in a contribution suit. In *Acushnet Co. v. Coaters, Inc.*, 937 F.Supp. 988 (D. Mass. 1996), the court granted a defendant's motion for summary judgment because plaintiff failed to prove that defendant's wastes had caused the incurrence of any response costs. In a later decision in the same case, 948 F.Supp. 128, 134–38 (1996), the court established a "threshold-of-significance standard," stating that "plaintiffs must proffer sufficient evidence as to a particular defendant to satisfy a minimum standard of significance of that defendant's responsibility as a source of one or more hazardous substances deposited at the site." However, the appellate court, though affirming the trial court's summary judgment for defendant, rejected the lower court's rationale:

> As we understand it, the district court ruled principally that the defendants deposited so little waste at the site that it could not reasonably be said that they caused plaintiffs to incur response costs. To the extent that the court's ruling may be interpreted to incorporate into CERCLA a causation standard that would require a polluter's waste to meet a minimum quantitative threshold, we disagree. Nevertheless, we conclude that the record was insufficient to permit a meaningful equitable allocation of remediation costs against any of the defendants under [section 113(f)].

Acushnet Co. v. Mohasco Corp., 191 F.3d 69, 72 (1st Cir. 1999).

One view of the appropriate standard in such a case is that the defendant in a contribution action ought to be entitled to summary judgment if it can demonstrate that, on the undisputed facts, (i) defendant is not liable under section 107(a) or is entitled to a defense under section 107(b), or (ii) it would not be equitable to require defendant to reimburse plaintiff for a portion of plaintiff's response costs. John Hyson, *The Plaintiff's Burden in CERCLA Contribution Actions: Unscrambling the First Circuit's Acushnet Decision*, 31 ENVTL. L. REP. 10180 (2001). For example, under (ii), even if defendant were shown to have been responsible for a small amount of hazardous substances which may have caused a small amount of plaintiff's response costs, a court might find that it would be inequitable to deny defendant summary judgment if it appeared that the public and private costs of conducting a full allocation hearing would exceed the amount of any likely reimbursement order.

In *New Jersey Turnpike Authority v. PPG Industries, Inc.*, 197 F.3d 96 (3d Cir. 1999), the court refused to apply a theory that would shift the burden of proof to defendants in a contribution suit. Relying on *Sindell v. Abbott Laboratories*, 26 Cal.3d 588, 607 P.2d 924 (1980), plaintiff argued that defendant chromium processors should bear the burden of proving that their wastes did not contaminate the New Jersey Turnpike. Contractors which built the highway had used chromate ore processing residue as fill material but maintained no records concerning the sources of the material. Defendants were the only chromium ore processors in New Jersey.

g. Settlement

Despite the massive amount of litigation that has occurred under CERCLA, most cleanup actions are accomplished through negotiation and settlement rather than litigation. Section 122 governs settlements and authorizes the Present to enter into settlements with any person to clean up a site. Among the tools authorized by section 122 to facilitate cost allocations, reduce transaction costs, and otherwise promote settlements, are (1) de minimis settlements—expedited settlements for small-volume waste contributors; (2) nonbinding preliminary allocations of responsibility ("NBARs") for cleanup costs—developed by EPA for PRPs; (3) mixed-funding agreements to share cleanup costs—permitting use of a combination of federal, state, and PRP funds; (4) covenants not to sue—protecting PRPs who settle from future liability to the United States related to the hazardous substance release addressed by a remedial action; and (5) alternative dispute resolution—the use of neutral third parties to help resolve liability and cost-allocation problems.

Section 122(g), concerning de minimis settlements, was amended in 2002 by the Small Business Liability Relief and Brownfields Revitalization Act. New subsection (7) provides for conditional expedited settlements between the United States and de minimis PRPs who demonstrate an "inability or a limited ability to pay response costs." In determining ability to pay, EPA shall consider whether the PRP can "pay response costs and still maintain its basic business operations."

Settling has significant benefits. In addition to securing some relative certainty about liability to the government, settlement also provides the benefit of immunity from contribution for matters "addressed in the settlement." The relevant provision is below:

§ 113(f)(2) A person who has resolved its liability to the United States or a State in an administrative or judicially approved settlement shall not be liable for claims for contribution regarding matters addressed in the settlement. Such settlement does not discharge any of the other potentially liable persons unless its terms so provide, but it reduces the potential liability of the others by the amount of the settlement.

Note that the last part of section 113(f)(2) ensures that the government cannot "double dip" by recovering from more than one party for the same costs.

Section 113(f)(2) provides that a settling PRP shall not be liable for claims for contribution "regarding matters addressed in the settlement." The meaning of this phrase was at issue in *Akzo Coatings, Inc. v. Aigner Corp.,* 30 F.3d 761 (7th Cir. 1994). In response to a section 106 administrative order by EPA, Akzo conducted certain "emergency removal activities" at the "Two-Line Road" facility, incurring costs of more than $1.2 million. Meanwhile, more than 200 other PRPs (including Aigner, but not Akzo) entered into a court-approved settlement with EPA concerning subsequent "remedial" activities to be performed by the settlors at the "Fisher-Calo site," of which the Two-Line Road facility was a part. Akzo then brought suit against Aigner, seeking contribution under section 113(f)(1) for the initial cleanup work which Akzo had performed at the behest of EPA as well as voluntary costs incurred in studying the long-term cleanup of the site with other PRPs. The trial court gave summary judgment for Aigner, finding that Akzo sought contribution for a "matter addressed" in the consent decree. In a split decision the Seventh Circuit reversed because Akzo's work "stands apart in kind, context, and time from the work envisioned by the consent decree." Akzo had engaged in "removal" work, while the settlement provided for the kind of "remedial" work needed to accomplish a complete cleanup of the site. The majority of the court perceived "no unfairness to Aigner" because Akzo's work was "over and done with by the time Aigner signed the consent decree." Thus, acknowledging a right to contribution did "not subject a settling PRP like Aigner to open-ended liability for contribution claims based on future, unanticipated remedial work." In a vigorous dissent, Judge Easterbrook said that the majority "plucks some language ["equitable factors"] from section 113(f)(1) and uses this language as a warrant to disregard the scope of the settlement." Judge Easterbrook expressed concern that the "[r]isk that in the name of equity a court will disregard the actual language of the parties' [settlement] bargain will lead potentially responsible parties to fight harder to avoid liability (and to pay less in settlements, reserving the residue to meet contribution claims), undermining the function of section 113(f)(2)."

The government and settling parties frequently enter into consent decrees that explicitly define the "matters addressed" therein in such a way as to attempt to bar all third-party contribution claims, even for voluntary private party cleanups not addressed in the decrees. James Brusslan, *Truth In Superfund Settlements: The Courts Strike Back on "Matters Addressed" Contribution Protection*, 27 ENV'T REP. 2522 (1997). For discussion of practical aspects of representing PRPs in the negotiation of CERCLA settlement agreements, *see* Peter E. Hapke & Andrew N. Davis, *Negotiating EPA Consent Orders and Consent Decrees: Steering Your Client Through the Shoals*, 24 ENVTL. L. REP. 10116 (1994).

In *Dravo Corp. v. Zuber,* 13 F.3d 1222 (8th Cir. 1994), a contribution suit, defendant PRPs had entered into a de minimis settlement agreement with EPA under CERCLA section 122(g). Paragraph (5) of that subsection provides that a party who "has resolved its liability to the United States under this subsection" shall not be liable for claims of contribution regarding matters addressed in the settlement. Plaintiff, which had incurred response costs, contended that defendants were not protected from contribution claims until after they fulfilled the obligations which they assumed by entering into the settlement agreement. The court held against plaintiffs on this contention. In the court's words, "[b]ecause Congress clearly * * * expressed its desire to minimize litigation by granting de minimis PRPs protection from contribution actions as soon as possible, and because this agreement expressly incorporates that mandate," defendants "are protected from contribution actions upon signing the agreement and will be protected so long as they comply with the agreement." Further, since section 122(a) says that "a decision of the President to use or not use the procedures in this section is not subject to judicial review," the court denied plaintiff's requests for discovery by which plaintiff wanted to determine whether—contrary to the EPA's conclusion—defendants had contributed to contamination of the site in more than a de minimis way. Because the settlement agreement was embodied in an administrative order under section 122(g)(4), rather than being entered as a consent decree, plaintiff's sole opportunity to block the de minimis agreement had been by filing comments with the EPA under section 122(i)(2) within 30 days after notice of the proposed settlement was published in the Federal Register.

Another important aspect of EPA settlement policy is the use of "supplemental environmental projects" (SEPs) as elements of some settlement agreements. A SEP is an "environmentally beneficial project" undertaken voluntarily in settlement of an enforcement action, in exchange for a decrease in the amount of the penalty. Approved SEPs have included environmental assessments and compliance audits as well as waste minimization and pollution prevention measures. *See also* William Thomas et al., *Using Auditing, Pollution Prevention, and Management Systems to Craft Superior Environmental Enforcement Solutions*, 30 ENVTL. L. REP. 10299, 10304–08 (2000).

EPA set forth the "Policy on the Use of Supplemental Environmental Projects in EPA Settlements" initially in 1991, and updated the policy effective May 1, 1998. The 1998 SEP policy requires that there be a nexus, or relationship, between the violation and the project. *See* Memorandum from Steven A. Herman, Assistant Administrator, to Regional Administrators (Apr. 10, 1998). In 2002, EPA reiterated the constraints of the 1998 policy (e.g., consistency with the statutory provisions, adequate nexus with the objectives of the environmental statutes) in order to ensure compliance by parties undertaking the SEPs. EPA was careful to note that the "constraints are intended to ensure compliance with statutory requirements and cannot be waived by Agency officials." On June 11, 2003, EPA issued a memorandum noting that it hoped to expand the use of SEPs in the settlement of enforcement action. As the expansion must still be constrained by the statutory nexus requirement, EPA announced plans to simplify its policy guidance and to initiate public dialogue. Subsequently, EPA has issued several new guidance documents for different areas of SEPs, including community involvement, the use of third parties, and green building. *See* Memorandum from Sylvia K. Lowrance, Acting Assistant Administrator, to Regional Administrators (Mar. 2, 2002); Memorandum from John Peter Suarez, Assistant Administrator, to Administrators and Enforcement Staff (Jun. 11, 2003). For EPA's current documents and policies, *see* EPA, Supplemental Environmental Projects, https://www.epa.gov/enforcement/supplemental-environmental-projects-seps.

3.   CLEANING UP CONTAMINATED SITES

Although we have focused thus far on the liability provisions of the statute, CERCLA also establishes a set of rules that govern the cleanup of contaminated sites. At complicated sites, the cleanup process can be lengthy and expensive, consuming many years and hundreds of millions of dollars.

a.   The National Priorities List

Section 105 of CERCLA establishes the basic process by which the EPA ranks and then lists sites on the "National Priorities List." The statute establishes a "Hazard Ranking System" which the agency uses to establish priorities for cleanup based on risks posed to human health. The original NPL listed 406 sites. *See Amendment to National Oil and Hazardous Substance Contingency Plan; National Priorities List*, 48 Fed. Reg. 40,658, 40,660 (Sept. 8, 1983) (codified at 40 C.F.R. pt. 300). This number was chosen because CERCLA originally required that, to the extent practicable, at least 400 sites be listed individually. *Id.* at 40,658. In order to reach that number of sites, EPA chose to list any site with a Hazard Ranking System ("HRS") score of above 28.50, along with all sites listed as states' top priorities. *Id.* at 40,659. As December 07, 2018, there are 1,338 sites on the National Priorities List (NPL) of hazardous waste sites eligible for long-term remedial action. Of these sites, 1,181 are non-federal and 157 are federal. *See Superfund: National Priorities List (NPL)*, https://www.epa. gov/superfund/superfund-national-priorities-list-npl (last visited January 12, 2019). New Jersey has the most of any state, at 114 NPL sites, followed by California (98 sites), Pennsylvania (92 sites), and New York (85 sites). *See* Environmental Protection Agency, *National Priorities List (NPL) Sites—by State*, https://www.epa.gov/superfund/national-priorities-list-npl-sites-state (last visited January 12, 2019). One GAO report from 2015 found that 39 million Americans lived within three miles of a nonfederal NPL site. *See* U.S. GOV'T ACCOUNTABILITY OFFICE, SUPERFUND: TRENDS IN FEDERAL FUNDING AND CLEANUP OF EPA'S NONFEDERAL NATIONAL PRIORITIES LIST SITES, GAO-15-812 (2015) at 9.

b. The National Contingency Plan

Section 105 of CERCLA also requires the EPA to produce the National Contingency Plan—essentially a blueprint document containing the standards, guidelines, and procedures that governs cleanups. 42 U.S.C. section 9605(a) (2000). EPA published its original section 105 National Contingency Plan (NCP) under court order in 1982. 47 Fed. Reg. 31,180 (July 16, 1982). The plan governs the use of Superfund monies in responding to hazardous substance spills and waste sites; it provides for determination of appropriate levels of response in individual situations, and for the establishment of priorities among spills and sites. The most recent major revisions to the plan were promulgated by the EPA in 1994. 59 Fed. Reg. 47,384, 47,440 (Sept. 15, 1994). The plan appears at 40 C.F.R. Pt. 300. Information on the National Contingency Plan is available at https://www.epa.gov/emergency-response/national-oil-and-hazardous-substances-pollution-contingency-plan-ncp-overview.

c. Response Actions

CERCLA defines two general types of responses to releases or threats of releases of hazardous substances. A *"removal action"* involves short-term activities (one year or less) aimed at stabilizing sites, cleaning up and removing hazardous substances, and (where possible) halting continued release and migration of hazardous substances. A *"remedial action"* involves long-term actions "consistent with permanent remedy taken instead of or in addition to removal actions * * *." 42 U.S.C. § 9601(23)–(24).

Section 104 authorizes the President to initiate or arrange for such responses—consistent with the National Contingency Plan, and subject to certain conditions—when a release or threatened release "may present an imminent and substantial danger to the public health or welfare." 42 U.S.C. § 9604.

In addition to authorizing the President to initiate cleanup of hazardous waste sites (section 104) and recover the government's costs (section 107), Congress authorized the President to compel PRPs to clean up contaminated sites. (These powers are delegated by the President to the EPA.) Thus, under section 106, when the EPA determines that a facility poses an "imminent and substantial endangerment to the public health or welfare or the environment because of an actual or threatened release of a hazardous substance," the agency may issue administrative orders directing PRPs to take response actions. The EPA may also seek injunctive or other equitable relief from a federal district court under § 106(a). For example, EPA could seek an injunction compelling one or more PRPs to take "removal" or "remedial" action, or to fence the site so as to prevent human exposure to the hazardous substance. The relevant statutory provisions appear below.

> Section 106 (a) * * * In addition to any other action taken by a State or local government, when the President determines that there may be an imminent and substantial endangerment to the public health or welfare or the environment because of an actual or threatened release of a hazardous substance from a facility, he may require the Attorney General of the United States to secure such relief as may be necessary to abate such danger or threat, and the district court of the United States in the district in which the threat occurs shall have jurisdiction to grant such relief as the public interest and the equities of the case may require. The President may also, after notice to the affected State, take other action under this section including, but not limited to, issuing such orders as may be necessary to protect public health and welfare and the environment.

> (b)(1) Any person who, without sufficient cause, willfully violates, or fails or refuses to comply with, any order of the President under subsection (a) may * * * be fined not more than $25,000 for each day in which such violation occurs or such failure to comply continues.

42 U.S.C. § 9606 (2000).

> Section 107 (c) (3) If any person who is liable for a release or threat of release of a hazardous substance fails without sufficient cause to properly provide removal or remedial action upon order of the President * * *, such person may be liable to the United States in an amount at least equal to, and not more than three times, the amount of any costs incurred by the Fund * * *.

42 U.S.C. § 9607(c)(3) (2000).

Failure to comply with a section 106 administrative order "without sufficient cause" can result in a fine of up to $25,000 per day under § 106 and, under § 107(c)(3), in liability for "punitive damages in an amount at least equal to, and not more than three times, the amount of any costs incurred by the Fund as a result of such failure to take proper action." *See* J. Wylie Donald, *Defending Against Daily Fines and Punitive Damages under CERCLA: The Meaning of "Without Sufficient Cause,"* 19 COLUM. J. ENVTL. L. 185 (1994). *Solid State Circuits, Inc. v. Environmental Protection Agency,* 812 F.2d 383 (8th Cir. 1987), upheld the constitutionality of section 107(c)(3). *United States v. Parsons,* 936 F.2d 526 (11th Cir. 1991), held that the federal government could recover *four times* the amount that EPA spent to clean up a site after defendants failed to comply with an administrative order by EPA to perform the cleanup. The government recovered its full response costs under section 107(a) and treble that amount under § 107(c)(3). Clearly, these provisions are very government-friendly—they encourage compliance with section 106 orders and allow for challenge after the fact. This is consistent with CERCLA's priority on making sure that sites are cleaned up, and that legal disputes do not delay response and remediation. Not surprisingly, however, the EPA's section 106 authority has been subject to challenge.

In *General Electric Co. v. Johnson,* 362 F.Supp.2d 327 (D.D.C. 2005), plaintiffs brought several constitutional challenges against CERCLA section 106, alleging, among other things, that section 106 violates the Due Process Clause of the Fifth Amendment because section 106 orders deprive PRPs of property without a meaningful hearing. The court granted EPA summary judgment, holding that PRPs are not deprived of meaningful hearings, as they can choose not to comply with a section 106 order or to challenge the order under the Administrative Procedure Act, thereby guaranteeing a judicial hearing.

Note the similarity of the "imminent and substantial endangerment" liability standard to that found in RCRA sections 7002(a)(1)(B) and 7003(a). Are different remedies available? Why might EPA prefer issuing a section 106 administrative order in lieu of cleaning up the site itself and pursuing cost recovery under section 107? Why might PRPs themselves prefer the administrative order? What would you advise a client PRP faced with a section 106 administrative order?

i.   Short-Term Removal Actions

As noted above, removal actions involve short-term activities aimed at assessing the contamination at the site, installing fences and warning signs, removing or cleaning up hazardous substances that pose an immediate threat, and stabilizing the site as a basis for longer term remedial actions. Section 104(c)(1) limits removal action to $2 million and/ or one year from the date of the initial response at the site.

ii. Long-Term Remedial Actions

Selection of an appropriate remedy for cleaning up a contaminated disposal site often is a difficult process involving complex scientific and technical questions as well as strong differences of opinion among federal, state and local officials, private PRPs, and neighboring landowners: The PRPs do not want to pay for excessively elaborate and expensive responses ("Cadillac cleanups"); neighbors may be concerned that the cleanup will be inadequate, or that it will exacerbate the situation by releasing contaminants that pose little current danger, or that it will be too disruptive of their lives for too long a time; state officials may want enforcement of state regulatory standards which are stricter than federal standards but which EPA believes should be waived; and local officials may be concerned about when and whether the site can be redeveloped and again be a source of jobs and tax revenues. As with the Hazard Ranking System, risk assessment is used for establishing a baseline for site cleanup, for determining the appropriate range of acceptable risk, and for choosing a response. *See* John S. Applegate, *The Perils of Unreasonable Risk: Information, Regulatory Policy, and Toxic Substances Control*, 91 COLUM. L. REV. 261, 284 n.119, 293 n.174 (1991).

Under the SARA amendments of 1986, Congress established schedules for response actions and preferences among types of responses. Section 121 establishes a preference (in remedial actions under section 104 or 106) for treatment which permanently and significantly reduces the volume, toxicity or mobility of the hazardous substances. Offsite transport and disposal of the hazardous substances or contaminated materials are least favored if "practical [onsite] treatment technologies" are available. Remedial actions are to be "cost-effective," considering total short-term and long-term costs. The actions taken are to attain a degree of cleanup and control of further releases which, at a minimum, "assures protection" of human health and the environment.

The following article analyzes the legal framework for remedy selection at CERCLA sites.

CASEY SCOTT PADGETT, SELECTING REMEDIES AT SUPERFUND SITES: HOW SHOULD 'CLEAN' BE DETERMINED?

18 VT. L. REV. 361, 367–70, 381–87, 391–405 (1994).[3]

The original Superfund statute failed to answer the following two questions: how clean is "clean" and how should "clean" be accomplished? Section 121 [enacted in 1986] was the congressional response to its earlier virtual silence on these issues. * * * While filling this void * * *, Congress

---

embedded a fundamental conflict into the foundation of CERCLA's remedy selection process. Remedies selected in accordance with section 121 were required to protect human health and the environment, attain compliance with ARARs, and be both "cost effective" and "permanent" through the use of treatment technologies to the "maximum extent practicable." The conflict inherent in these directives lies in the fact that, at nearly every Superfund site, a remedy that permanently eliminates the risks posed by the hazardous substances through the use of treatment technology will be far more costly than a remedy that reduces risks by containing or limiting human exposure to the hazardous substances. * * *

Section 121 established four basic objectives to guide the selection of remedial actions at Superfund sites. Remedial actions must:

> protect human health and the environment, attain applicable or relevant and appropriate requirements [ARARs], be cost effective, and utilize permanent solutions, and alternative treatment or resource recovery technologies, to the maximum extent practicable.

Specifically, section 121(b), which identifies "[g]eneral rules" for selecting remedies, provides that "[t]he President shall select a remedial action that is protective of human health and the environment, that is cost effective, and that utilizes permanent solutions and alternative treatment technologies or resource recovery technologies to the maximum extent practicable."

Subsection (d) of section 121, which establishes the "[d]egree of cleanup" required of remedial actions, reiterates the idea that remedial actions "shall attain a degree of cleanup of hazardous substances . . . and of control of further release at a minimum which assures protection of human health and the environment." In circumstances where any hazardous substance, pollutant, or contaminant will remain onsite, subsection (d) further specifies that remedial actions also must comply with any ARAR. Specifically, such remedial action must require "a level or standard of control for such hazardous substance or pollutant or contaminant which at least attains such legally applicable or relevant and appropriate standard, requirement, criteria, or limitation."

Although section 121 specifies that the use of treatment to reduce the volume, toxicity, or mobility of hazardous substances is a "preference," remedies which do not utilize such treatment may be selected if the President "publish[es] an explanation as to why a remedial action involving such reductions was not selected." In addition, the requirement that any particular ARAR be attained by a remedy may be waived by EPA under enumerated circumstances. * * *

Section 300.430 of the NCP establishes the regulatory parameters for identifying, developing, evaluating, and selecting a proposed remedy for cleaning up a CERCLA site. Section 300.430(e) identifies the requirement of a feasibility study ("FS") for developing and evaluating a range of remedial action alternatives. Section 300.430(f) defines the factors to be used in selecting a preferred remedy from among the range of alternatives developed in the FS. Together, these two subsections establish the heart of EPA's regulatory approach to implementing the remedy selection provisions of section 121 * * *.

* * * EPA translated the statutory requirements and preferences of section 121 into nine criteria for use in evaluating alternative remedies. Remedial alternatives that survive an initial screening are subject to a detailed comparative and objective assessment. Remedies are evaluated based on the following nine criteria:

1.   Overall protection of human health and the environment;

2.   Compliance with ARARs;

3.   Long-term effectiveness and permanence;

4.   Reduction of toxicity, mobility, or volume through treatment;

5.   Short-term effectiveness;

6.   Implementability;

7.   Cost;

8.   State acceptance; and

9.   Community acceptance.

EPA organized these criteria into three categories. The first two criteria, protectiveness and compliance with ARARs, are "[t]hreshold criteria," which an alternative must satisfy to be eligible for selection. The next five criteria are "[p]rimary balancing criteria." The final two criteria, state and community acceptance, are "[m]odifying criteria." * * *

To determine whether a remedy is cost effective, the NCP instructs:

> *Cost-effectiveness is determined by evaluating* the following three of the five balancing criteria . . . to determine *overall effectiveness:* long-term effectiveness and permanence, reduction of toxicity, mobility, or volume through treatment, and short-term effectiveness. *Overall effectiveness is then compared to cost* to ensure that the remedy is cost-effective. A remedy shall be cost-effective if its *costs are proportional to its overall effectiveness.*

In essence, the NCP offers a tautology to define cost effectiveness. A remedy is effective if, overall, it is effective, based on its long- and short-term effectiveness and the reduction of hazards posed by the hazardous substances. Further, the remedy is cost effective if its costs and effectiveness are "proportional."

The NCP defines a process for determining the maximum extent to which permanent treatment technologies are practicable that is similarly circular and ambiguous. The remedy will be found to utilize such treatment technologies to the maximum extent practicable if it

> provides the *best balance of trade-offs among alternatives* in terms of the five primary balancing criteria. . . . The balancing shall *emphasize* long-term effectiveness and reduction of toxicity, mobility, or volume through treatment. The balancing shall also *consider* the preference for treatment as a principal element and the bias against off-site land disposal of untreated waste.

Thus, pursuant to the NCP, a treatment technology, or remedy which employs such a technology, may be found *impracticable* if the "trade-offs" that arise from a consideration of the five balancing criteria are "worse" than those that arise from another remedy. Conversely, if the trade offs seem "better" than those trade offs posed by other remedial alternatives, a remedy that utilizes a permanent treatment technology may be determined to be practicable. Since the NCP requires that two of the balancing criteria be weighed in the balance initially, as well as given additional emphasis and consideration, remedies that incorporate treatment technologies may be more likely to be considered practicable. * * *

For the CERCLA remedy selection process to produce results that are better understood and that achieve greater acceptance among stakeholders, EPA or another lead agency should not be expected to balance the many ambiguous and subjective criteria inherent to remedy selection. Instead, a different approach should be developed that more effectively allows those whose interests are at stake to weigh the trade offs and strike the balance among competing objectives.

NOTES

1.   After the foregoing discussion, the author proposed changes in the EPA's remedy-selection process. The first question he would ask in each case is, "Why do we want to clean up the site?" That is, he believes that site-specific cleanup objectives must be based more explicitly on achieving defined future uses for that site, taking into account the uses and values of surrounding properties and natural resources which have been impacted by the release of hazardous substances at the site. In 1994, when the article was published, the EPA's remedy-selection process, in contrast, assumed that the future use of, and access to, the site would be unrestricted. Padgett urged that for the process to be more effective, all the "stakeholders"—the site owner, neighboring property owners, community residents, state and local government representatives, and other parties with a legitimate interest in the cleanup and future use of the site—"must become players in the process, not merely watchdogs over it."

2. In 1995, EPA announced a comprehensive program of 20 administrative reforms related to CERCLA and centered on the promise of smarter and more cost-effective cleanups. U.S. EPA, "Superfund Administrative Reforms: Reform Initiatives" (Oct. 2, 1995), discussed in Michael Steinberg & Joshua Swift, *EPA's New National Remedy Review Board Aims to Improve Superfund Decisions*, 26 ENV'T REP. 2353 (1996), and at 27 ENV'T REP. 2641 (1997). One of the most important reforms was creation of a new National Remedy Review Board to help control remedy costs by providing a cross-Regional, management-level review of high cost decisions on a site-specific basis.

Another important reform was a policy of updating previous remedy decisions at individual sites. This encouraged EPA Regional offices to examine and modify past remedy decisions when significant new factual, scientific, or technological information suggests that the same level of protectiveness of human health and the environment can be achieved at a lower cost. The importance of this reform was emphasized by a district court decision holding that cleanup cost overruns incurred because of EPA's failure to reconsider its selected site remedy, when changed circumstances fundamentally altered the estimated scope and cost of the remedy, were costs "inconsistent with the national contingency plan" for which PRPs were not liable under CERCLA section 107(a). *United States v. Broderick Inv. Co.*, 955 F.Supp. 1268 (D. Colo. 1997). *See* Timothy Malloy, *Second-Look Remedies: Strategies for Re-Evaluating Superfund Cleanups*, 26 ENV'T REP. 1420 (1995).

3. *Ohio v. EPA*, 997 F.2d 1520 (D.C. Cir. 1993), upheld several provisions of the NCP that had been challenged by various states and private parties as inconsistent with CERCLA. Among the provisions sustained were the definition of applicable or relevant and appropriate requirements (ARARs), various remedy selection provisions, and provisions concerning both the role of states in CERCLA cleanups and cost allocations between state and federal governments.

The court approved the NCP's restriction of state ARARs to "standards [that] are of general applicability and are legally enforceable." Although the Safe Drinking Water Act is cited in CERCLA section 121(d)(2)(A) as one of the federal laws containing ARARs for Superfund cleanups, the court upheld EPA's decision that Maximum Contaminant Level Goals ("MCLGs") established under the SDWA do not have to be attained for contaminants whose MCLG has been set at a level of zero. Under the SDWA, MCLGs are generally unenforceable goals that reflect the level for each contaminant at which "no known or anticipated adverse effects on the health of persons occur and which allows an adequate margin of safety." Many MCLGs for carcinogens are set at zero. The second type of standards, Maximum Contaminant Levels ("MCLs")—the actual maximum permissible concentration levels under the SWDA—must be set as close as "feasible" to their corresponding MCLGs, taking into account available technology and cost. While MCLGs are unenforceable under the SWDA, section 121(d)(2)(A) of CERCLA converts them into enforceable limits (ARARs) where they are "relevant and appropriate under the circumstances of the release or threatened release." In essence, the EPA made a categorical determination in the NCP that MCLGs set at a level of zero are *never* relevant and appropriate under the circumstances of a release because "it is impossible to detect whether 'true' zero has actually been attained."

Remedy-selection issues in *Ohio v. EPA* concerned the role of cost-benefit analysis in choosing remedies; the NCP's failure to require the selection of "permanent" remedies to the maximum extent practicable; the use of a cancer risk range between 1 in 10,000 and 1 in 1,000,000 (rather than a minimum risk of 1 in 1,000,000); and the requirement of five-year review of certain remedial actions. CERCLA section 121(b)(1) requires the President to select a remedial action "that is protective of human health and the environment, that is cost effective, and that utilizes permanent solutions * * * to the maximum extent practicable." The court upheld the NCP's classification of permanence as one of several "balancing criteria" rather than as "an overarching statutory principle."

4.   *United States v. Akzo Coatings of America, Inc.,* 949 F.2d 1409 (6th Cir. 1991), was an appeal by the state of Michigan from the entry of a consent decree between EPA and twelve PRPs, requiring the defendants to engage in remedial work at a contaminated site. The proposed remedial plan called for the excavation and incineration of surface soils contaminated with PCBs, lead, arsenic and other toxic materials, and the flushing of the subsurface soils contaminated with various volatile and semi-volatile organic compounds. The state challenged the effectiveness of soil flushing at the site in question, and the PRPs cross-appealed the district court's determination that the decree must comply with Michigan's groundwater antidegradation law. The court held that the record supported EPA's conclusion that the site was conducive to soil flushing; and that Michigan's antidegradation law was an ARAR because it was "of general applicability" and not too vague or lacking in a quantifiable standard to be "legally enforceable," as required by the NCP, and was "more stringent than any Federal standard, requirement, criteria or limitation," as required by CERCLA section 121(d)(2)(A)(ii).

5.   Suppose that the EPA, unable to reach a settlement with the PRPs, proposes to implement on its own, under CERCLA section 104, a more elaborate and expensive cleanup program than the PRPs believe is necessary. Knowing that EPA will come after them later for reimbursement under section 107, could the PRPs obtain judicial review of EPA's program before it is implemented, as a means of trying to limit their ultimate liability under CERCLA? Before the 1986 amendments to CERCLA, *Lone Pine Steering Committee v. EPA,* 777 F.2d 882 (3d Cir. 1985), held that the federal district court lacked jurisdiction to review plaintiff's challenge to the EPA's method of cleanup until the Agency brings suit to recover its cleanup costs. The court was concerned that such suits would frustrate Congress' intention that EPA act quickly to remedy problems posed by hazardous waste sites.

In 1986, Congress codified in section 113(h) the general denial of access to the courts to obtain pre-enforcement review of remedial action. Congress remained troubled, however, by the effect the rule might have on citizen groups wishing to challenge the adequacy of remedial action before cleanup was completed. Therefore, Congress created an exception authorizing the filing of citizen suits after a removal or remedial action has been taken under section 104 or secured under section 106. Congress encouraged liberal construction of the exception by explaining that such suits can be filed after the completion of "distinct and separate phases" of a remedial action, thus indicating that it is not necessary to wait until the entire action has been completed. The intent was to permit judicial review early enough so that the direction of a multi-stage cleanup could be modified, if necessary, prior to completion. *See* discussion of the conference report and other legislative history in *Superfund II: A New Mandate*, 17 ENV'T REP. 70–71 (1987).

In *McClellan Ecological Seepage Situation v. Perry*, 47 F.3d 325 (9th Cir. 1995), *cert. denied*, 516 U.S. 807 the court held that private citizens cannot circumvent the bar to judicial review of ongoing cleanups under CERCLA by suing under other federal and state environmental statutes. Hence, a federal district court lacked jurisdiction to hear a citizen suit claiming that the Defense Department's cleanup of an Air Force base violated state and federal environmental statutes, including RCRA and the Clean Water Act.[6] The case is discussed in Marianne Dugan, *Are Citizen Suits CERCLA section 113(h)'s Unintended Victims?*, 27 ENVTL. L. REP. 10003 (1997). Concerning section 113(h) generally, *see* Michael P. Healy, *Judicial Review and CERCLA Response Actions: Interpretive Strategies In the Face of Plain Meaning*, 17 HARV. ENVTL. L. REV. 1 (1993).

A novel approach to the application of section 113(h) to cleanups at federal facilities was taken in *Fort Ord Toxics Project, Inc. v. California Environ. Protect. Agency*, 189 F.3d 828 (9th Cir. 1999). The court held that section 113(h) did not bar private persons' suit challenging ongoing "remedial" action at a military base which was on EPA's National Priorities List. The court concluded that section 113(h) applies to both removal and remedial actions under § section 104 and 106, but that "remedial" (though not "removal") actions at federal facilities are governed solely by section 120, which is not mentioned in section 113(h). *See* Ingrid Wuerth, *Challenges to Federal Facility Cleanups and CERCLA Section 113(h)*, 8 TUL. ENVTL. L.J. 353, 370 (1995).

d. Brownfields

Brownfields are typically defined as vacant, contaminated, former industrial sites, often in inner cities. The EPA has estimated that there are

---

[6]   Similarly, in *Boarhead Corp. v. Erickson*, 923 F.2d 1011 (3d Cir. 1991), the court held that section 113(h) prevented a federal district court from reviewing a claim that CERCLA-related activities which EPA planned to conduct on a Pennsylvania farm would violate the National Historic Preservation Act. Even though the lack of review might harm Native-American artifacts on the farm, the court said that it must follow Congress' will that cleanups not be delayed by pre-enforcement challenges.

more than 450,000 brownfield sites nationwide. *See* Environmental Protection Agency, Brownfields, https://www.epa.gov/brownfields. Many of these sites are well located in relation to highways, rail facilities, public utilities, and workers in need of employment. However, because of potential CERCLA liabilities, businesses which could use these sites were reluctant to acquire and develop them. As a result, opportunities to create jobs and increase property tax revenues in the central cities were lost. City governments demanded a solution to this problem, and many states enacted voluntary cleanup laws or programs to address the brownfields problem. *See* the state-by-state summaries at 28 ENV'T REP. 2086, 2488 (1998).

The EPA developed a Brownfields Program in 1995, and Congress finally responded legislatively in 2002 with the Small Business Liability Relief and Brownfields Revitalization Act. With the passage of the Act, Congress hoped to incentivize cleanup and redevelopment of brownfields in three main ways: (1) increased federal funding for brownfields programs, (2) elimination of CERCLA liability for brownfields cleanups, and (3) a reduction of the federal government's role in administering brownfields sites. *See* Kelly J. Shira, Comment and Legislative Review, *Returning Common Sense to Cleanup? The Small Business Liability Relief and Brownfields Revitalization Act*, 34 ARIZ. ST. L.J. 991 (2002).

The Act defines brownfield sites to include "real property, the expansion, redevelopment, or reuse of which may be complicated by the presence or potential presence of a hazardous substance, pollutant, or contaminant." 42 U.S.C. section 9601(39). As discussed in greater detail, *supra*, the Act's liability provisions provide exemptions for owners of "contiguous properties" and for "bona fide prospective purchasers" (subsections 107(q) and (r)) a "de micromis" exemption for arrangers and transporters (subsection 107(o)), and expedited settlements for parties with an inability or a limited ability to pay response costs (subsection 122(g)(7)). With regard to funding, new subsection 104(k) provides substantial federal funding for brownfields redevelopment—an increase in funds from $98 million to $200 million annually for site assessment and cleanup. Entities eligible to receive brownfields funding include states, Indian tribes, local governments, land clearance authorities, regional councils, redevelopment agencies, other quasi-governmental entities created by states or local governments, and in limited circumstances private non-profit groups. In addition, new section 128 of CERCLA authorizes $50 million per year for grants to assist states and Indian tribes in the development of response programs. Addressing the reduced federal role in brownfields cleanup, subsection 128(b) restricts the EPA's authority, with limited exceptions, to take enforcement action under section 106(a), or to seek cost recovery under section 107(a), at eligible sites cleaned up in compliance with a state response program. The exceptions to this restriction include that the EPA will take response action if a state requests so or if the site contamination has migrated across state lines. Additionally, the EPA may act if new information about the site comes to light. *See* Flannary P. Collins, Note, *The Small Business Liability Relief and Brownfields Revitalization Act: A Critique*, 13 DUKE ENVTL. L. & POL'Y F. 303 (2003).

e.   The Superfund

In the original 1980 statute, Congress authorized a Trust Fund of $1.6 billion to fund cleanups of "orphan" sites on the NPL, emergencies, and longer-term cleanups. The 1986 SARA amendments increased this amount to $8.5 billion. This "Superfund," as the fund (and CERCLA) has come to be called, may pay for both cleanup costs and enforcement actions by EPA. The Superfund is also available to pay for certain natural resource damages, reimbursement of local governments, and claims by private parties.

The most important benefit of the Superfund is that it allows EPA to initiate response actions before a court determination of liability or a settlement. Later, when the liability is determined, the EPA can recover its response costs and the Superfund will be reimbursed. This ability to clean up first and collect later is one of the CERCLA's most important innovations. *See* ENVIRONMENTAL PROTECTION AGENCY, SUPERFUND 20TH ANNIVERSARY REPORT 9 (2000), (*available at* http://www.epa.gov/super fund/action/20years/20yrpt1.pdf).

The actual funding of the Superfund has come from a combination of general tax revenues, taxes of crude oil received at U.S. refineries, environmental taxes on corporations, recovery of response costs from responsible parties, taxes on imported petroleum products, and taxes on certain chemicals. The two main sources of the Fund were originally the taxes on crude oil and certain chemicals. ENVIRONMENTAL PROTECTION AGENCY, FISCAL YEAR 2004 SUPERFUND ANNUAL REPORT (2005), *available at* Authors: http://www.epa.gov/superfund/accomp/fy2004.htm. With the enactment of the SARA amendments in 1986, a third source of funding was added: the corporate environmental income tax. *See* SUPERFUND SUBCOMMITTEE OF THE NATIONAL ADVISORY COUNCIL FOR ENVIRONMENTAL POLICY AND TECHNOLOGY, FINAL REPORT 8 (2004).

These special taxes—excise taxes payable by petroleum and chemical industries, and an environmental income tax payable by corporations with annual profits of more than $2 million—which provided $4 million per day for the trust fund, expired in December 1995. In the absence of funding by the taxes, the Superfund continues to receive revenue from other sources, including cost recoveries, interest from investments, fines, and penalties. Recently, the Program has been increasingly funded through appropriations from general revenues.

According to a 2015 report from the General Accountability Office, annual federal appropriations to EPA's superfund program (which includes all of EPA's CERCLA related programs, not just funding for the trust fund) declined from about $2 billion to $1.1 billion between 1999 and 2013—a 45% decline (figures are in 2013 dollars). *See* U.S. GOV'T ACCOUNTABILITY OFFICE, SUPERFUND: TRENDS IN FEDERAL FUNDING AND CLEANUP OF EPA'S NONFEDERAL NATIONAL PRIORITIES LIST SITES, GAO-15-812 (2015) at 11–12. EPA expenditures from these federal appropriations on site-specific remedial activities at non-federal NPL sites declined during this period from about $700 million per year to about $400 million per year. *Id.* at 14–15. Less money has translated into slower cleanups. Between 1999 and 2013, the total number of nonfederal sites on the NPL increased slightly from 1,054 in FY1999 to 1,158 in FY2013. *Id.*, at 25. As noted above, as of December 2018, there were 1,181 nonfederal sites on the NPL slightly more than in 2013. Completions of remedial actions at nonfederal NPL sites during the 1999 to 2013 period actually declined by 37%. *Id.*, at 30.

CHAPTER 9

REGULATION OF TOXIC SUBSTANCES AND GENETICALLY MODIFIED ORGANISMS

■ ■ ■

Toxic chemicals and genetically modified organisms provoke significant controversy and fears over the widespread ecological and health damage they could wreak. But both also provide benefits: pesticides kill pests that can destroy agricultural crops, therefore increasing food supply (and hence have been called "economic poisons"); genetically modified organisms can, according to proponents, help feed an ever-increasing world population with healthier food but, critics fear, could cause major ecological disturbances by, for example, destroying native plants. How to weigh the costs and benefits of toxic chemicals and genetically modified organisms is the central question we examine in this chapter. Perhaps more than any other area of environmental law, this chapter faces head on the question of risk examined extensively in Chapter 2. Section A provides an overview of EPA's major responsibilities with respect to pesticides under the Federal Insecticide, Fungicide and Rodenticide Act (FIFRA) and the Federal Food, Drug and Cosmetic Act (FFDCA) as amended by the 1996 Food Quality Protection Act (FQPA). Section B discusses EPA's responsibilities regarding industrial chemicals under the Toxic Substances Control Act (TSCA), which was substantially amended in 2016. Section C describes and evaluates the federal program for the regulation of agricultural biotechnology and transgenic plants. Section D examines statutes that use information disclosure as a tool to regulate the use of chemicals, including the Emergency Planning and Community Right-to-Know Act (EPCRA) and the federal securities laws.

A. REGULATING PESTICIDES

1. THE PESTICIDE PROBLEM

In 1962, Rachel Carson published SILENT SPRING, a book that galvanized public concern regarding the environmental and human health harms of several widely used pesticides (the most prominent of which was DDT). As Carson dramatically described the pesticide problem: "For the first time in the history of the world, every human being I know is subjected to contact with dangerous chemicals, from the moment of conception until death."[1] Carson's fears about widespread contamination of the environment with pesticides have been well documented since she wrote. One 2006 government study that tested streams and groundwater across the country for the presence of pesticides found that every stream tested contained the residue of at least one pesticide. United States Geological Survey, *Pesticides in the Nation's Streams and Ground Water, 1992–2001, A Summary* (released March, 2006), available at http://pubs.usgs.gov/fs/2006/3028/. Many streams had concentrations unlikely to affect humans but that might affect fish and wildlife. *Id.* Biomonitoring data have also revealed the presence of pesticides and pesticide metabolites in the bodies of the vast majority of the American population. *See* Centers for Disease Control and Prevention, National Report on Human Exposure to Environmental Chemicals, Updated Tables, March 2018, https://www.cdc.gov/exposurereport/index.html. No one can, of course, deny that pesticides are toxic—their intent, after all, is to kill pests. But of course, pesticides also confer important benefits by dramatically increasing crop yield. These benefits can be of special importance in developing countries, with their acute need to feed their populace.

Pesticide usage remains widespread: in the United States, over 1.1 billion pounds of pesticides were used in 2012, accounting for 23 percent of total global pesticide use of 5.8 billion pounds. Nearly 90% of the total pesticide usage in the U.S. between 2005 and 2012 was in the agricultural sector, with herbicides accounting for close to 60% of the total. See EPA, *Pesticide Industry Sales and Usage: 2005–2012 Market Estimates* (2017) at 9–11, https://www.epa.gov/sites/production/files/2017-01/documents/pesticides-industry-sales-usage-2016_0.pdf. How to balance the benefits of pesticide usage against the very real harms these economic poisons can cause is the central quandary of pesticide regulation.

EPA has two major responsibilities with respect to pesticides: (1) regulating the sale and use of pesticides through the registration provisions of the Federal Insecticide, Fungicide, and Rodenticide Act (FIFRA); and (2) establishing tolerances for pesticide residues on food under the Federal Food, Drug and Cosmetic Act (FFDCA) as amended by the 1996 Food Quality Protection Act (FQPA). The following two parts discuss each of these in turn.

2. REGULATING THE SALE AND USE OF PESTICIDES

Pesticide use in the United States exploded after World War II, as a new class of synthetic organic pesticides, some of which had been developed as part of the war effort, became commercially available. In an effort to keep up with the growing sales of pesticides, Congress enacted FIFRA in 1947. The statute required that all pesticides (known as "economic

---

[1]   Rachel Carson, Silent Spring, 15 (1962).

poisons") be registered with the USDA before being sold in the United States, but it provided no authority for the government to ban individual pesticides on the basis of possible harm.

In 1972, in response to growing concerns with the environmental and human health effects of pesticides, Congress amended FIFRA to enact a much more comprehensive regulatory scheme. Among other things, the 1972 amendments transferred authority for pesticide registrations from USDA to EPA and established a new standard of "unreasonable risk" for the regulation of pesticides.

As amended, FIFRA, 7 U.S.C.A § 136, provides a framework for regulating the sale and distribution of pesticides within the United States. Under the statute, EPA may not approve a pesticide's introduction into commerce unless the Administrator finds that the pesticide "will not generally cause unreasonable adverse effects on the environment" when used in accordance with any EPA-imposed restrictions and "with widespread and commonly recognized practice." 7 U.S.C.A. § 136a(5)(D). "Unreasonable adverse effects on the environment" are defined to include "any unreasonable risk to man or the environment, taking into account the economic, social, and environmental costs and benefits of the use of any pesticide." § 136(bb). With few exceptions, FIFRA prohibits the sale, distribution, and professional use of unregistered pesticides. §§ 136a(a) & 136j(a)(1).

Because of the explicit requirement of a cost/benefit analysis, FIFRA's "unreasonable adverse effects" standard is unusual among federal environmental statutes: most others (except the Toxic Substances Control Act) employ risk-based standards softened only by the availability of control technologies. By disregarding the benefits of the regulated substances, these risk-based statutes provide more protection to health and the environment and less protection to industry than do FIFRA and TSCA.

As part of a registration, EPA must classify the pesticide for either "general" or "restricted" use. § 136a(d). Restrictions relate to such factors as methods of application, qualifications of applicators, amounts to be used, geographic areas of use, and species of targeted pests. EPA may "conditionally" register a pesticide if the pesticide and its proposed use are identical or substantially similar to any currently registered pesticide and use thereof, or differ only in ways that would not significantly increase the risk of unreasonable adverse effects on the environment. A pesticide containing an active ingredient not contained in any currently registered pesticide also may be conditionally registered for a period reasonably sufficient for the generation of required data. EPA may determine that use of the pesticide during such period will not cause any unreasonable adverse effects on the environment, and that use of the pesticide is in the public interest. § 136a(c)(7).

Once registered, pesticides are still subject to continuing scrutiny by EPA. § 136d. As amended by the 1996 FQPA, section 6 of FIFRA requires EPA to periodically review all pesticide registrations, with the goal of reviewing each pesticide's registration every 15 years. Section 6 of FIFRA also requires EPA to cancel a pesticide's registration after the first five years in which the registration has been effective (and at the conclusion of subsequent five year periods if the registration is renewed) "unless the registrant, or other interested person with the concurrence of the registrant, . . . requests . . . that the registration be continued in effect." § 136d(a). At any time, EPA may also propose cancellation of a registration and initiate elaborate cancellation proceedings if "it appears to the Administrator that a pesticide . . . does not comply with [FIFRA] or . . . generally causes unreasonable adverse effects on the environment. . . ." § 136d(b).

During the pendency of cancellation proceedings, the registration remains in effect unless the Administrator "suspend[s] the registration of the pesticide immediately." § 136d(c). But before suspending the pesticide, the Administrator must determine that an "imminent hazard" exists. Even then, FIFRA guarantees registrants the right to an expedited administrative hearing on that issue, and the pesticide's registration remains effective during this latter proceeding. § 136d(c)(2). Only if "the Administrator determines that an emergency exists that does not permit the Administrator to hold a hearing before suspending" may she prohibit commerce in the pesticide in advance of notification to the registrant. § 136d(c)(3).

While commerce in unregistered pesticides is generally prohibited, the Administrator may permit continued sale and use of existing stocks of pesticides whose registrations have been cancelled provided "he determines that such sale or use is not inconsistent with the purposes of this subchapter and will not have unreasonable adverse effects on the environment." § 136d(a)(1).

Viewed as a whole, two key features of FIFRA are worth emphasizing. First, pesticide sales are prohibited without a registration granted by EPA and the burden is on the applicant to demonstrate that the pesticide will not pose an unreasonable risk under the proposed uses. Second, as part of the registration process, the determination of unreasonable risk requires a balancing of the health and environmental risks of the pesticide against its economic and environmental benefits. In sum, FIFRA is a licensing statute based on risk-benefit balancing.

The following case illustrates the application of FIFRA's substantive standards in the context of suspension and cancellation proceedings for pesticides that had been registered under the pre-1972 version of the statute. Both heptachlor and chlordane were identified as pesticides of significant concern in *Silent Spring* and, along with DDT, Aldrin, and Dieldrin, were the subject of regulatory action by EPA using the Agency's new authorities under FIFRA.

ENVIRONMENTAL DEFENSE FUND, INC. V. ENVIRONMENTAL PROTECTION AGENCY [HEPTACHLOR AND CHLORDANE]

United States Court of Appeals, District of Columbia Circuit, 1976.
548 F.2d 998.

LEVENTHAL, CIRCUIT JUDGE.

This case involves the pesticides heptachlor and chlordane. Consolidated petitions seek review of an order of the Environmental Protection Agency (EPA) suspending the registration of those pesticides under the Federal Insecticide, Fungicide and Rodenticide Act (FIFRA) for certain uses. The Administrator of EPA issued an order on December 24, 1975. The order prohibited further production of these pesticides for the suspended uses, but permitted the pesticides' continued production and sale for limited minor uses. Even as to the suspended uses, the Order tempered its impact in certain respects: It delayed until August 1, 1976, the effective date of the prohibition of production for use on corn pests; and it permitted the continued sale and use of existing stocks of registered products formulated prior to July 29, 1975.

One petition to review was filed by Earl L. Butz, Secretary of Agriculture of the United States (U.S.D.A.). Secretary Butz and intervenor Velsicol Chemical Corporation, the sole manufacturer of heptachlor and chlordane, urge that the EPA order as to chlordane be set aside on both substantive and procedural grounds. They contend that substantial evidence does not support the Administrator's conclusion that continued use of chlordane poses an "imminent hazard" to human health, and that the Administrator made critical errors in assessing the burden of proof and in weighing the benefits against the risks of continued use of chlordane.

The other petition, filed by Environmental Defense Fund, urges that the Order did not go far enough to protect against the hazards of heptachlor and chlordane use. EDF sought an injunction against the provisions permitting continued production and use of the pesticides on corn pests until August 1, 1976. EDF also challenges the Administrator's decision to allow continued use of the stocks of the two pesticides existing as of July 29, 1975, contending that EPA should have provided for retrieval and controlled disposal of such stocks. EDF also contends that the Administrator erred in failing to suspend certain "minor uses" of chlordane and heptachlor. * * *

I.   STATUTORY FRAMEWORK AND STANDARD OF REVIEW

The issues posed by administrative action pursuant to FIFRA are not new to this court, and we have previously extensively described the statutory framework for such actions. What is involved here is a suspension of registration of two pesticides during the pendency of the more elaborate cancellation of registration proceeding, initiated in this case by a November 18, 1974, notice of intent to cancel. This 1974 notice stated that there existed "substantial questions of safety amounting to an unreasonable risk to man and the environment" from continued use of heptachlor and chlordane. Public cancellation hearings pursuant to that notice were not expected to commence for some time. On July 29, 1975, the Administrator issued a Notice of Intent to Suspend the registrations of most uses of the two pesticides. The Administrator then commented on that expected delay in completing the cancellation hearings, and cited "new evidence . . . which confirms and heightens the human cancer hazard posed by these pesticides." On August 4, 1975, registrant Velsicol Chemical Corporation requested an expedited adversary hearing on the suspension question pursuant to section 6 of FIFRA. Administrative Law Judge Herbert L. Perlman presided over the cancellation hearings beginning August 12. Evidence was limited to human health issues and the benefits of continued use of heptachlor and chlordane. The record was closed December 4, 1975, and on December 12, the ALJ recommended against suspension, stating that he was unable to find that "heptachlor and chlordane are conclusively carcinogens in laboratory animals." The Administrator reversed that decision on December 24, 1975, and suspended most uses of chlordane and heptachlor.

The Administrator is authorized to suspend the registration of a pesticide where he determines that an "imminent hazard" is posed by continued use during the time required for cancellation. Section 6(c) of FIFRA. An "imminent hazard" exists where continued use during the time required for the cancellation proceeding would be likely to result in "unreasonable adverse effects on the environment." Section 2(l) of FIFRA. The term "unreasonable adverse effects on the environment" is, in turn, defined as "any unreasonable risk to man or the environment, taking into account the economic, social, and environmental costs and benefits of the use of any pesticide." Section 2(bb) of FIFRA.

As in our previous suspension case involving aldrin/dieldrin, the primary challenge raised by Velsicol and USDA goes to the adequacy of the evidentiary basis of EPA's finding that the suspended pesticides present an imminent hazard during the time required for cancellation. The standard against which we test that challenge is defined in Section 16(b) of FIFRA:

The court shall consider all evidence of record. The order of the Administrator shall be sustained if it is supported by substantial evidence when considered on the record as a whole.

The standard of substantial evidence has been defined as:

> something less than the weight of the evidence ... (T)he possibility of drawing two inconsistent conclusions from the evidence does not prevent an administrative agency's finding from being supported by substantial evidence.

In applying this principle of review in the specific context of a suspension of pesticides, this court has reiterated that "the function of the suspension decision is to make a preliminary assessment of evidence, and probabilities, not an ultimate resolution of difficult issues. We cannot accept the proposition ... that the Administrator's findings ... (are) insufficient because controverted by respectable scientific authority. It (is) enough at this stage that the administrative record contain(s) respectable scientific authority supporting the Administrator."

These decisions of our court also point out that the Administrator is not required to establish that the product is unsafe in order to suspend registration, since FIFRA places "(t)he burden of establishing the safety of a product requisite for compliance with the labeling requirements . . . at all times on the applicant and registrant." Velsicol and USDA urge that this allocation of burden of proof relied on by the Administrator is inconsistent with the explicit terms of FIFRA. They rely on FIFRA's specific incorporation of subchapter II of the Administrative Procedure Act, which provides in relevant part that "Except as otherwise provided by statute, the proponent of a rule or order shall have the burden of proof." 5 U.S.C § 556(d).

The EPA regulation governing the burden of proof in suspension proceedings provides:

> At the hearing, the proponent of suspension shall have the burden of going forward to present an affirmative case for the suspension. However, the ultimate burden of persuasion shall rest with the proponent of the registration. 40 C.F.R. s 164.121(g) (1975).

Assuming that the Administrator is the "proponent" of a suspension order and is governed by § 556(d), the legislative history of that provision indicates that it allocates the burden of going forward rather than the burden of ultimate persuasion and is consistent with the EPA's apportionment of burden:

> That the proponent of a rule or order has the burden of proof means not only that the party initiating the proceeding has the general burden of coming forward with a prima facie case but that

other parties, who are proponents of some different result, also for that purpose have a burden to maintain.

This allocation of the burden of going forward structures evaluation of the factual evidence adduced for both the Administrator and the reviewing court, and is consistent with the traditional approach that this burden normally falls on the party having knowledge of the facts involved.

In urging that the ultimate burden of proof in a suspension proceeding rests on the Administrator, Velsicol and USDA assert that the suspension decision is a drastic step differing fundamentally from both the registration and cancellation decisions made under FIFRA. But we have already cautioned that the "imminent hazard" requisite for suspension is not limited to a concept of crisis: "It is enough if there is substantial likelihood that serious harm will be experienced during the year or two required in any realistic projection of the administrative process." "FIFRA confers broad discretion" on the Administrator to find facts and "to set policy in the public interest." Wellford v. Ruckelshaus, 142 U.S.App.D.C. 88, 91, 439 F.2d 598, 601 (1971). This broad discretion was conferred on the implicit assumption that interim action may be necessary to protect against the risk of harm to the environment and public health while a fuller factual record is developed in the cancellation proceeding. This avenue of protective relief would be effectively foreclosed if we accepted Velsicol's argument that the Administrator must prove imminent hazard apparently in some sense of weight of the evidence, going beyond substantial likelihood. But as we have already pointed out, the basic statutory directive requires affirmance of the Administrator's decision if supported by substantial evidence, and this requires "something less than the weight of the evidence." We reject that renewed invitation to exercise increased substantive control over the agency decision process, and turn to a consideration of whether the Administrator's decision to suspend most uses of heptachlor and chlordane is supported by substantial evidence.

II.   SUBSTANTIAL   EVIDENCE   SUPPORT   FOR   THE   ADMINISTRATOR'S DECISION

To evaluate whether use of a pesticide poses an "unreasonable risk to man or the environment," the Administrator engages in a cost-benefit analysis that takes "into account the economic, social, and environmental costs and benefits of the use of any pesticide." 7 U.S.C. 136(bb). We have previously recognized that in the "preliminary assessment of probabilities" involved in a suspension proceeding, "it is not necessary to have evidence on . . . a specific use or area in order to be able to conclude on the basis of substantial evidence that the use of (a pesticide) in general is hazardous." EDF v. EPA, 160 U.S.App.D.C. at 130, 489 F.2d at 1254, quoted in EDF v. EPA (Shell Chemical Co.), 167 U.S.App.D.C. at 80, 510 F.2d at 1301. "Reliance on general data, consideration of laboratory experiments on animals, etc." has been held a sufficient basis for an order cancelling or suspending the registration of a pesticide. Id. Once risk is shown, the responsibility to demonstrate that the benefits outweigh the risks is upon the proponents of continued registration. Conversely, the statute places a "heavy burden" of explanation on an Administrator who decides to permit the continued use of a chemical known to produce cancer in experimental animals. Applying these principles to the evidence adduced in this case, we conclude that the Administrator's decision to suspend most uses of heptachlor and chlordane and not to suspend others is supported by substantial evidence and is a rational exercise of his authority under FIFRA.

A. Risk Analysis Carcinogenicity of Heptachlor and Chlordane

Velsicol and USDA contend that the laboratory tests on mice and rats do not "conclusively" demonstrate that chlordane is carcinogenic to those animals; that mice are too prone to tumors to be used in carcinogenicity testing in any case; and that human exposure to chlordane is insufficient to create a cancer risk. They place strong reliance on the Administrative Law Judge's refusal to recommend suspension because he was "hesitantly unwilling at this time to find that heptachlor and chlordane are conclusively carcinogens in laboratory animals." (emphasis in original). The ALJ recognized however, that on the basis of the record made the Administrator "could determine that the pesticides involved pose potential or possible carcinogenic risk to man" and that he could "find that heptachlor and chlordane are conclusively carcinogenic in laboratory animals." While adopting the ALJ's factual findings, the Administrator concluded that the ALJ had applied an erroneous legal standard in requiring a conclusive rather than probable showing that the pesticides were animal carcinogens, and concluded in any case that the evidence showed heptachlor and chlordane to be animal carcinogens. We affirm.

1. Mice and Rat Studies

An ultimate finding in a suspension proceeding that continued use of challenged pesticides poses a "substantial likelihood of serious harm" must be supported by substantial, but not conclusive, evidence. In evaluating laboratory animal studies on heptachlor and chlordane there was sufficient "respectable scientific authority" upon which the Administrator could rely in determining that heptachlor and chlordane were carcinogenic in laboratory animals.

We start by rejecting Velsicol's argument that the "cancer principles" EPA relied on in structuring its analysis of the mice and rat studies improperly biased the agency's open-minded consideration of the evidence. In brief form, the principles accept the use of animal test data to evaluate human cancer risks; consider a positive oncogenic effect in test animals as sufficient to characterize a pesticide as posing a cancer risk to man;

recognize that negative results may be explained by the limited number and sensitivity of the test animals as compared to the general human population; note that there is no scientific basis for establishing a no-effect level for carcinogens; and view the finding of benign and malignant tumors as equally significant in determining cancer hazard to man given the increasing evidence that many "benign" tumors can develop into cancers. The Agency's reliance on these principles did not come as a surprise to Velsicol; they were included in the Administrator's Notice of Intent to Suspend; and * * * form part of the Agency's "scientific expertise." Velsicol was properly given an opportunity to put in evidence contesting those principles, but failed to demonstrate anything more than some scientific disagreement with respect to them. Velsicol's principal complaint that mice are inappropriate test animals was specifically rejected by the Administrator * * *.

2.   Extrapolation of Animal Data to Man

Human epidemiology studies so far attempted on chlordane and heptachlor gave no basis for concluding that the two pesticides are safe with respect to the issue of cancer. To conclude that they pose a carcinogenic risk to humans on the basis of such a finding of risk to laboratory animals, the Administrator must show a causal connection between the uses of the pesticides challenged and resultant exposure of humans to those pesticides. He made that link by showing that widespread residues of heptachlor and chlordane are present in the human diet and in human tissues. Their widespread occurrence in the environment and accumulation in the food chain is explained by their chemical properties of persistence, mobility and high solubility in lipids (the fats contained in all organic substances.) Residues of chlordane and heptachlor remain in soils and in air and aquatic ecosystems for long periods of time. They are readily transported by means of vaporization, aerial drift, and runoff of eroding soil particles. The residues have been consistently found in meat, fish, poultry and dairy products monitored in the FDA Market Basket Survey and are also frequent in components of animal feeds. This evidence supports a finding that a major route of human exposure is ingestion of contaminated foodstuffs. EPA's National Human Monitoring Survey data shows that heptachlor epoxide and oxychlordane, the principal metabolites of heptachlor and chlordane respectively, are present in the adipose tissue of over 90% of the U.S. population.

The population's exposure to these pesticides, in large part involuntary, can be divided into agricultural and nonagricultural related routes. Seven million pounds of heptachlor and chlordane were used as corn soil insecticide in 1975, producing residues which persist in the soil for several years after application. These residues are taken up by such food, feed, and forage crops as soybeans, barley, oats, and hays typically rotated with corn. By volatilization the pesticides contaminate corn and other plant leaves. And root crops like potatoes, carrots and beets directly absorb the pesticides from the soil. Other sources of agricultural-related residues include exposure to contaminated dust particles and agricultural runoff containing eroded soil particles.

Velsicol urges that the dietary exposure resulting from agricultural uses of the pesticides is insignificant, and that current exposure is well below "safe" dose levels as calculated by the Mantel-Bryan formula, or by the World Health Organization's Acceptable Daily Intake figures. Mantel himself criticized the use of the formula for a persistent pesticide, and the Administrator rejected the concept of a "safe" dose level defined by mathematical modeling because of "the incomplete assumptions made by the registrant's witnesses about the sources of human exposure in the environment, the natural variation in human susceptibility to cancer, the lack of any evidence relating the level of human susceptibility to cancer from heptachlor and chlordane as opposed to that of the mouse, and the absence of precise knowledge as to the minimum exposure to a carcinogen necessary to cause cancer." That explanation is within the reasonable bounds of the agency's expertise in evaluating evidence. And it is confirmed by the common sense recognition that reliance on average "safe" dietary levels fail to protect people with dietary patterns based on high proportional consumption of residue-contaminated foods (e.g., children who ingest greater quantities of milk than the general population).

There are several non-agricultural uses which involve a large volume of heptachlor and chlordane as well as significant human exposures. For example, the record shows that approximately six million pounds of chlordane are used annually on home lawns and gardens. The Administrator found that these uses involve high risks of human intake "due to the many avenues which exist for direct exposure, through improper handling and misuse, inhalation, and absorption through the skin from direct contact." Velsicol asserts that the mice studies showing carcinogenic effects after ingestion of chlordane do not warrant an inference about the carcinogenic effects of inhaling it or absorbing it through the skin, and that consequently nonagricultural routes of exposure cannot be considered to present a cancer risk. * * * [T]he FIFRA statutory scheme mandates explicit relief—the suspension of registration—when an unreasonable risk to health is made out. We have previously held that it is not necessary to have evidence on a specific use to be able to conclude that the use of a pesticide in general is hazardous. Once the initial showing of hazard is made for one mode of exposure in a suspension proceeding, and the pesticide is shown to be present in human tissues, the burden shifts to the registrant to rebut the inference that other modes of exposure may also pose a carcinogenic hazard for humans. Velsicol has totally failed to meet that burden here. Although it was put on notice in the Notice to Suspend of EPA's intent to rely on direct inhalation and dermal exposure as reasons to suspend household lawn and turf uses of chlordane, it failed to offer even a medical theory as to why the significant inhalation or dermal exposure associated with such uses would not pose a carcinogenic threat. In view of the general failure to understand the mechanics of carcinogenicity, the lack of hypothetical explanation may be based on Velsicol's own data that exposure to vapors of chlordane and heptachlor in the work place, leads (as dietary exposure leads) to storage of oxychlordane, heptachlor epoxide, and other components in the fat tissue, and to circulation of these compounds in the blood, with consequent exposure to other organs in the body. Nor did Velsicol focus on the individual user's intense inhalation exposure associated with lawn and turf uses in its response to the point made in the EPA Staff's exceptions to the ALJ recommended decision, that the evidence showed that an individual using these chemicals for lawn and turf applications is subjected to a marked intensity of inhalation. Instead Velsicol attacked as inconsistent with the minimal amounts of chlordane and heptachlor normally found in ambient air, the EPA Staff's proposed reliance on inhalation as a major route of human exposure for the general population. However, the Administrator did not proceed on this basis. And if Velsicol hypothesized that chlordane residues are safe so long as they reach the tissue only through inhalation (even intense inhalation) it should have presented witnesses expressing that hypothesis. Instead they argue, in general and procedural terms, that the evidence presented by the Administrator was not sufficient to meet his full burden, and this in our view seeks to impose a broader burden on the Administrator than is appropriate in a suspension proceeding.

B.   Benefits

Velsicol and USDA challenge the Administrator's finding that the benefits derived from the suspended uses of chlordane do not outweigh the harms done. EDF urges that the Administrator's decision to continue some uses was not justified by evidence that the risk of harm was outweighed by benefits from the continued uses.

1.   Use on Corn

Heptachlor and chlordane were used on an estimated 3.5% of the total corn acreage in the United States in 1975, largely in an effort to control black cutworm. Cutworms sporadically infest 2 to 8% of total U.S. corn farms, and occur most often in lowland, river bottom areas. Chlordane and heptachlor are used as preplant treatments to insure against possible infestations. The Administrator found, with record support, that no macro-economic impact will occur as a result of suspending those pesticides. He also found that crop surveillance or "scouting" for infestations during the early weeks of plant growth, together with application of post-emergence baits or sprays where necessary, provide an effective alternative to the more indiscriminate prophylactic use of chlordane and heptachlor. Velsicol urges that this approach is not as effective as the persistent protection provided by chlordane. Especially in the absence of proof of a serious threat to the nation's corn, there is no requirement that a pesticide can be suspended only if alternatives to its use are absolutely equivalent in effectiveness.

2.   Miscellaneous Agricultural Uses

The Administrator suspended a number of agricultural uses where the record was insufficient to support any finding that benefits outweigh costs of continued use of heptachlor or chlordane on these crops. Possibly the lack of benefits evidence reflected readily available alternatives, possibly a relative lack of interest in lesser-volume uses. In any event, the registrant's failure to carry its burden of adducing sufficient evidence on benefits in effect leaves the Administrator nothing to weigh in his cost-benefit analysis except the evidence that the use of the challenged pesticides in general is hazardous. That evidence of general hazard is sufficient to support a suspension of uses.

3.   Non-Agricultural Uses Suspended by the Administrator

Chlordane is a common household, lawn, garden, and ornamental turf insecticide, with over 7.5 million pounds (36% of total use) so employed in 1974. The ALJ and Administrator found on the basis of substantial evidence that the "efficaciousness of the substitutes for control of household and lawn insects is not really at issue" and that when lack of evidence of substantial benefits from continued use is weighed against the special hazards of exposure presented by the possibilities of inhalation, dermal absorption, and the increased dangers associated with improper handling, suspension of those uses was justified. Similarly, on the basis of evidence in the record, the Administrator could reasonably find that the residual capacity of chlordane was not necessary to control either structural pests or ticks and chiggers, given the existence of effective alternatives to each of those uses.

4.   The Administrator's Refusal to Suspend Certain Uses

EDF challenges the Administrator's refusal to suspend use of chlordane or heptachlor on strawberries, for seed treatment, pineapples, the white fringed beetle, Florida citrus, white grubs in Michigan, narcissi bulbs, harvester ants, imported fire ant, Japanese beetle quarantine, and black vine weevil quarantine in Michigan. Following the recommendations of the ALJ, the Administrator found that for each use the benefits outweighed the risks for the limited time under consideration, effective alternatives were generally not available, and that the exposure risk arising from the use was minimal. EDF counters that the total exposure resulting from these "minor" uses is in fact significant, and that the Administrator continued these uses whenever a "colorable" case of benefits had been made out.

Once the Administrator has found that a risk inheres in the use of a pesticide, he has an obligation to explain how the benefits of continued use outweigh that risk. We are satisfied that he has met that obligation here, and that substantial evidence supports his decision. We note, however, that we come to this conclusion in the context of a suspension proceeding where perforce the Administrator is engaged in making a "preliminary assessment" of the evidence; a more careful exploration of economic impact and available alternatives would be required to support continued registration in a cancellation proceeding.

C.   Continued Sale and Use of Existing Stocks of Chlordane and Heptachlor for Suspended Uses

Although we have no doubt that the Administrator has the power under FIFRA to exempt from a suspension order the use of existing stocks (in this case stocks existing as of July 29, 1975), the Administrator acted arbitrarily when he failed to even inquire into the amount of stocks left, and the problem of returning and disposing of them. Some evidence must be adduced before an exemption decision is made, and it is the responsibility of the registrant to provide it. It may be that the lapse of time has lessened the current significance of this issue but we are in no position to do other than remand for further consideration.

We affirm the Agency's suspension order of December 24, 1975, as clarified by the order of January 19, 1976, except for the exemption of the sale and use of existing stocks. The record is remanded for further consideration of that issue.

NOTES

1.   Note the court's approach to burden of proof, with specific attention to the problem of carcinogens. Is the presumption created by the court reasonable? Suppose the agency rejected the inference that a substance which causes cancer under one mode of exposure probably causes cancer under other modes. Should a court reverse based on its own view as to what presumption should apply?

In a law review article, Judge Leventhal maintained he had used "burden of proof" concepts in a different sense than the conventional usage in civil procedure. Instead, he said, burden of proof was used to refer to the burden of "adducing a reasoned presentation supporting [EPA's conclusions]." Leventhal, *Environmental Decisionmaking and the Role of the Courts*, 122 U. PA. L. REV. 509, 535–36 (1974). He also stated that burden of proof concepts are "nothing more or less than devices for controlling risks of error." *Id.* Do you find this to be a persuasive explanation of the pesticide cases? For further discussion, see Rodgers, *Benefits, Costs, and Risks: Oversight of Health and Environmental Decisionmaking*, 4 HARV. ENV. L. REV. 191, 219–24 (1980).

Which is preferable: Judge Leventhal's approach to burden of proof, or that of the plurality in the *Benzene* case as discussed in Chapter 2 *infra*?

2.   On denial of the petition for rehearing, the court issued a lengthy supplemental opinion rejecting the contention that the Administrative Procedure Act placed the burden of proof on the EPA throughout the proceeding. *EDF, Inc. v. EPA,* 548 F.2d 998, 1012–18 (D.C. Cir. 1976).

3.   Subsequent federal pesticide litigation has focused largely on deviations from the normal suspension/cancellation process discussed in the preceding case. *See Love v. Thomas,* 858 F.2d 1347 (9th Cir. 1988*), cert. denied,* 490 U.S. 1035 (1989) (right of pesticide users to judicial review of emergency suspension order when no registrant requests a hearing); *National Coalition Against the Misuse of Pesticides v. EPA,* 867 F.2d 636 (D.C. Cir. 1989) (authority of EPA to enter into agreement providing for voluntary cancellation of registration but allowing continued sale and use of existing stocks of cancelled pesticide).

4.   Stricter state and local regulation of pesticide use is permitted. In *People v. County of Mendocino,* 36 Cal.3d 476, 204 Cal.Rptr. 897, 683 P.2d 1150 (1984), the Supreme Court of California held that a county initiative ordinance prohibiting aerial application of phenoxy herbicides, including 2, 4, 5-T, Silvex, 2, 4-D and any matter containing dioxin, was not preempted by either state law or FIFRA. The court said that Congress, by providing in section 24(a) for further "State" regulation of federally registered pesticides, did not intend to preclude local regulation authorized under state law.

In *Wisconsin Public Intervenor v. Mortier,* 501 U.S. 597 (1991), the Supreme Court held that FIFRA does not preempt local pesticide-regulation ordinances.

5.   Section 136v(b) of FIFRA provides that a state "shall not impose or continue in effect any requirements for labeling or packaging in addition to or different from those required under this subchapter." In *Bates v. Dow Agrosciences,* 544 U.S. 431 (2005), the Supreme Court authorized a lawsuit brought under Texas law by Texas peanut farmers who alleged that their crops were damaged by a pesticide called "Strongarm." Dow moved to dismiss the case on the grounds that FIFRA preempted the state law claims. The Court found that as long as a state labeling law "is equivalent to, and fully consistent with, FIFRA's . . . provisions," the state cause of action can proceed. FIFRA requires that a pesticide label cannot contain "false or misleading statements;" as long as a state law contains a similar prohibition it can proceed. 125 S.Ct. at 1800. The Court effectively overruled a series of cases that had found state claims preempted, including *Etcheverry v. Tri-Ag Service, Inc.,* 993 P.2d 366 (Cal.2000) and *Arkansas-Platte & Gulf Partnership v. Van Waters & Rogers, Inc.,* 981 F.2d 1177 (10th Cir. 1993).

The California Safe Drinking Water and Toxic Enforcement Act of 1986 ("Proposition 65") requires California to *list* substances that it determines to be carcinogenic or reproductively toxic. Twelve months after a substance has been listed by the state, the manufacturers of products containing the listed substances must provide adequate *warnings* to the consuming public that their products pose a health risk. In *Chemical Specialties Manufacturers Ass'n v. Allenby,* 958 F.2d 941 (9th Cir. 1992), *cert. denied,* 506 U.S. 825 (1992), CSMA, a trade association of insecticide, disinfectant, and antimicrobial product manufacturers, contended that the adequate warning requirements of Proposition 65 were preempted as applied to products regulated under FIFRA. Proposition 65 provides that the required "warning" need not be provided separately to each exposed individual and may be provided by general methods "such as labels on consumer products, inclusion of notices in mailings to water customers, posting of notices, placing notices in the public news media, and the like, provided that the warning accomplished is clear and reasonable." CAL. HEALTH & SAFETY CODE section 25249.11(f). Relying on FIFRA's definitions of "label" and "labeling," the court rejected CSMA's position and found that point-of-sale warnings satisfying the requirements of Proposition 65 did not constitute additional labeling.

6. *Safe Alternatives for Fruit Fly Eradication v. Berryhill,* 1984 WL 178937 (C.D.Cal.1984), held that citizens living or working in the area of aerial spraying of the pesticide Malathion by a *state* agency to control the Mexican fruit fly lacked standing to seek an injunction against the spraying program because (a) FIFRA provided no private right of action, and (b) plaintiffs were foreclosed by *Middlesex County Sewerage Authority v. National Sea Clammers Ass'n,* 453 U.S. 1 (1981), from enforcing FIFRA rights under the Civil Rights Act of 1866, 42 U.S.C.A. section 1983.

7. *Headwaters, Inc. v. Talent Irrigation District,* 243 F.3d 526 (9th Cir. 2001), held that an irrigation district was liable under the Clean Water Act for discharging an aquatic herbicide into irrigation canals without an NPDES permit. The district contended that it did not require a CWA permit because the label approved for the herbicide by EPA under FIFRA did not mention a need for a CWA permit. The court of appeals rejected this contention, saying that the CWA and FIFRA serve different purposes. "FIFRA's labels are the same nationwide, and so the statute does not and cannot consider local environmental conditions. By contrast, the NPDES program under the CWA does just that." The spraying of herbicide on canals constituted a discharge of pollutants from a point source, and the canals were "waters of the United States" to which discharge permit requirements applied.

3. ESTABLISHING TOLERANCES FOR PESTICIDE RESIDUES ON FOOD

Pesticides in and on raw agricultural commodities are regulated under the Federal Food, Drug and Cosmetic Act (FFDCA), 21 U.S.C.A. section 301 et seq. EPA sets *tolerance* levels of pesticide concentrations in or on commodities consumed in the United States; the Food and Drug Administration monitors the actual pesticide *content* of commodities and has the authority to confiscate foods containing either excessive concentrations of registered pesticides or unsafe residues of unregistered pesticides. 21 U.S.C.A. sections 342, 346a. Under section 346a, the EPA Administrator is to consider, when establishing tolerances, "the necessity for the production of an adequate, wholesome, and economical food supply" as well as health effects.

Up until the mid-1990s, EPA determined tolerances for pesticide residues using the same risk-benefit balancing standard that the Agency used to register pesticides. Challenges emerged, however, in the case of pesticide residues that contained carcinogenic substances. For residues on raw foods or processed foods in cases where the processing did not result in a higher concentration of the pesticide, EPA continued to apply the risk-benefit balancing approach. But in cases where the pesticide concentrated during processing, it was then treated as a food additive under the FFDCA and thus subject to the much more restrictive Delaney Clause, which prohibited the use of any food additive that contained substances that had been shown to induce cancer in animals or humans. This became known as "the Delaney Paradox," given the uneven treatment of pesticide residues depending on whether they concentrated during processing or not. *See* NATIONAL RESEARCH COUNCIL, REGULATING PESTICIDES IN FOOD: THE DELANEY PARADOX (1987); JOHN WARGO, OUR CHILDREN'S TOXIC LEGACY: HOW SCIENCE AND LAW FAIL TO PROTECT US FROM PESTICIDES (2nd ed., 1998).

EPA sought to avoid strict application of the Delaney Clause to certain pesticides by using a *de minimis* risk standard. In 1993, however, the D.C. Circuit held that:

> The [FFDCA] unambiguously provides that pesticides which concentrate in processed foods are to be treated as food additives, and these are governed by the Delaney food additive provisions. * * * If pesticides which concentrate in processed foods induce cancer in humans or animals, they render the food adulterated and must be prohibited. * * * The EPA's refusal to revoke regulations permitting the use of benomyl, mancozeb, phosmet and trifluralin as food additives on the ground the cancer risk they pose is *de minimis* is contrary to the provisions of the Delaney clause prohibiting food additives that induce cancer. The EPA's final order is set aside.

Les v. Reilly, 968 F. 2d 985 (9th Cir. 1993).

As a result of the decision in *Les v. Reilly*, EPA began to revoke tolerances and cancel registrations for dozens of pesticides. Congress responded in 1996 with the Food Quality Protection Act (FQPA), which amended both FIFRA and the Federal Food, Drug and Cosmetic Act. Food Quality Protection Act of 1996, P. L. 104–170, 110 Stat 1489 (Aug. 3, 1996).

The amendments to the FFDCA created a new framework for regulating pesticide residues on food. Specifically, they did away with the distinction between raw and processed foods and established a single, new standard for safety—"reasonable certainty of no harm"—that would govern the setting of tolerances for pesticide residues in or on food. Under the new approach, EPA was directed to establish tolerances for residues in or on a food upon a determination that the tolerance was "safe," i.e., "that there is a reasonable certainty that no harm will result from aggregate exposure to the pesticide chemical residue, including all anticipated dietary exposures and all other exposures for which there is reliable information." 21 U.S.C. § 346a(b)(2)(A). The amendments also required that, in establishing a tolerance for a pesticide chemical residue, the Administrator (i) shall assess the risk of the residue based on available information about consumption patterns among infants and children, and about their special susceptibility to the residue, and (ii) shall ensure that there is a reasonable certainty that no harm will result to infants and children from aggregate exposure to the residue. "In the case of threshold effects, . . . an additional tenfold margin of safety for the pesticide chemical residue and other sources of exposure shall be applied for infants and children to take into account potential pre- and post-natal toxicity and completeness of the data with respect to exposure and toxicity to infants and children." 21 U.S.C. § 346a(b)(2)(C).

Assessment of cumulative exposures to pesticides and other chemicals with common mechanisms of toxicity is also required. 21 U.S.C § 346a(b)(2)(D). EPA was directed to review all pesticide tolerances that had been issued prior to enactment of the FQPA within ten years to ensure that they met the new safety standard. 21 U.S.C. § 346a(b)(2)(q). Finally, the FQPA also created a special category of "eligible pesticide chemical residues" for pesticides that did not meet the new safety standard but for which EPA determines that (a) use of the pesticide protects consumers from adverse health effects posing a greater risk or (b) use is necessary to avoid significant disruption of domestic production of an adequate, wholesome, and economic food supply and the risks posed by aggregate and lifetime exposure to the pesticide residue are below certain thresholds. 21 U.S.C. § 346a(b)(2)(B).

Although the FQPA's standard of "reasonable certainty of no harm" was viewed by many as an improvement over FIFRA's more lenient "unreasonable risk" standard as well as the Delaney Clause's zero-risk standard for carcinogens, it also imposed substantial analytical burdens on EPA. In particular, it required that EPA assess multiple exposure pathways as part of its assessment of the risks posed by particular pesticides. EPA has sometimes struggled to perform these assessments, leading to further delay in some cases. The following case addresses some of the challenges that EPA faces under the FQPA and the different tools it relies upon in assessing risk under the statute.

NORTHWEST COALITION FOR ALTERNATIVES TO PESTICIDES V. EPA

United States Court of Appeals, Ninth Circuit, 2008.
544 F.3d 1043.

PREGERSON, CIRCUIT JUDGE:

Petitioners are two environmental groups challenging the Environmental Protection Agency's ("EPA") establishment of tolerances for seven pesticides used mostly on fruit and vegetable crops. We grant the petition in part, deny it in part, and remand to the EPA.* * *

The EPA regulates pesticides under two statutes: The Federal Insecticide, Fungicide, and Rodenticide Act ("FIFRA") and the Federal Food, Drug, and Cosmetic Act ("FDCA").

Under FIFRA, pesticides sold in the United States must be registered by the EPA. The EPA may not register a pesticide unless the pesticide will perform its intended function without causing "any unreasonable adverse effects on the environment."

The FDCA authorizes the EPA to set "tolerances" for pesticide residues in food. "A tolerance is the maximum allowable amount of pesticide that may remain in or on a commodity." *Nader v. EPA*, 859 F.2d 747, 748 (9th Cir.1988). The EPA may "establish or leave in effect a tolerance for a pesticide chemical residue in or on a food only if [the EPA] determines that the tolerance is safe." The term "safe" is defined to mean that "there is a reasonable certainty that no harm will result from aggregate exposure to the pesticide chemical residue, including all anticipated dietary exposures and all other exposures for which there is reliable information." Any tolerance that is not "safe" must be modified or revoked.

Tolerances are established by rulemaking. Pesticide manufacturers initiate the rulemaking process by petitioning the EPA to set a tolerance. The EPA publishes notices of these petitions in the Federal Register. After reviewing a petition and any comments received on it, the EPA may issue: (1) a final rule establishing a tolerance, (2) a proposed rule, or (3) an order denying the petition. * * *

In 1996, Congress amended the FDCA by enacting the Food Quality Protection Act ("FQPA"), Pub.L. No. 104–170, 110 Stat. 1489. One of the key provisions of the FQPA requires the EPA to give special consideration to risks posed to infants and children when establishing pesticide tolerances. Specifically, the FQPA directs the EPA to use "an additional tenfold margin of safety . . . to take into account potential pre-and post-natal toxicity and completeness of the data with respect to exposure and toxicity to infants and children." This tenfold (or "10x") child safety factor is presumptively applied to all tolerances. Thus, in making tolerance decisions, the EPA must assume that the risk to children from the use of a particular pesticide on food is ten times greater than for adults. The EPA may "use a different margin of safety for the pesticide chemical residue *only if, on the basis of reliable data,* such margin will be safe for infants and children." (emphasis added).

Unfortunately, the FQPA does not define "reliable data." The dispute before us turns on the definition of this term.

Between December 2001 and April 2002, the EPA published seven regulations establishing tolerances for the pesticides acetamiprid, fenhexamid, halosulfuron-methyl, isoxadifen-ethyl, mepiquat, pymetrozine, and zetacypermethrin used on many foods, including fruits, vegetables, nuts, cereal grains, milk, and eggs. Each regulation was promulgated in response to an industry petition to establish tolerances.

The EPA did not apply the presumptive 10x child safety factor to any of these seven pesticides. The EPA reduced the 10x child safety factor to 3x for four of the pesticides (acetamiprid, fenhexamid, isoxadifen-ethyl, and pymetrozine). For the remaining three pesticides (halosulfuron, mepiquat, and zeta-cypermethrin), the EPA did not apply a child safety factor at all.

In 2002, Natural Resources Defense Council, Inc. ("NRDC") filed objections to each of the tolerances based on the EPA's decision to reduce or remove the child safety factor. NRDC argued that the EPA did not have "reliable data" allowing it to deviate from the child safety factor.

On August 10, 2005, the EPA issued its final order rejecting NRDC's objections. The Final Order upheld the 3x child safety factor for acetamiprid, fenhexamid, isoxadifenethyl, and pymetrozine, and a 1x child safety factor (i.e., *no* safety factor) for halosulfuron, mepiquat, and zetacypermethrin.

NRDC and the Northwest Coalition for Alternatives to Pesticides ("NCAP") each petitioned for review of the Final Order.* * *

ANALYSIS

Petitioners challenge seven tolerances (acetamiprid, fenhexamid, halosulfuron-methyl, isoxadifen-ethyl, mepiquat, pymetrozine, and zeta-cypermethrin) based on the EPA's failure to gather drinking water data as part of its exposure analysis. Petitioners also challenge three tolerances (acetamiprid, mepiquat, and pymetrozine) based on the absence of certain toxicity studies, and based on the EPA's failure to explain why it had reliable data in the absence of those toxicity studies. We address these challenges in turn.

I.

The FQPA directs the EPA to use an additional tenfold margin of safety to take into account completeness of data with respect to pesticide "*exposure* to infants and children."

As required by the FQPA, the EPA monitors whether infants and children will be exposed to unsafe levels of pesticides in drinking water. However, the EPA lacks sufficient drinking water exposure data for several pesticides, including the ones at issue in this case. Therefore, the EPA used computer modeling to determine drinking water exposure for the seven pesticides. Because the modeling results revealed little-to-no risk of pesticide exposure in drinking water, the EPA reduced or removed the child safety factor for each of the pesticide tolerances.

Petitioners argue that because the EPA used modeling instead of actual sampling data to determine drinking water exposure to these pesticides, the EPA does not have "reliable data" justifying its use of a lower than 10x margin of safety for the pesticide tolerances. In short, Petitioners argue that modeling results can never constitute reliable data within the meaning of the FQPA.

We disagree. Petitioners have presented no evidence that modeling does not yield reliable data. There is nothing inherently unreliable about the use of models in scientific assessments. *See, e.g., Small Refiner Lead Phase-Down Task Force v. EPA*, 705 F.2d 506, 535 (D.C.Cir.1983) ("[A]dministrative agencies have undoubted power to use predictive models."). Moreover, because of the difficulty in sampling the entire nation's water supply, modeling is necessary to determine whether drinking water has been contaminated by pesticides. Topography, geology, and hydrology differ greatly across the nation and constantly change. In many cases, computer modeling can more accurately incorporate these elements and provide more reliable data than actual water sampling data can provide.

Therefore, we are unwilling to adopt the narrow construction of "reliable data" that Petitioners advance. Although the FQPA does not define "reliable data," we are confident that modeling results can satisfy this statutory requirement.* * *

Accordingly, we conclude that the computer modeling used by the EPA to calculate the safety of drinking water was neither contrary to law nor arbitrary and capricious. We affirm this aspect of the Final Order.

II.

In addition to NRDC's challenge to the completeness of exposure data, Petitioners also raise two arguments regarding whether reliable toxicity data supported a reduction in the child safety factor.

A.

NRDC first challenges the EPA's failure to wait for the results of certain developmental neurotoxicity studies ("DNT studies") before establishing tolerances for acetamiprid, mepiquat, and pymetrozine. The EPA specifically required the registrants of these pesticides to conduct

DNT studies. However, the EPA did not wait for the results of the DNT studies before making its tolerance determinations.

Petitioners contend that DNT studies are essential for assessing pesticide effects. Petitioners explain that DNT studies are the best available studies for examining neurological effects in children because DNT studies are more sensitive than other studies, address areas that are not covered by other studies, and sometimes reveal developmental harm that is significant enough to require more stringent regulation. Petitioners argue that the EPA acted arbitrarily and capriciously by requesting DNT studies but failing to wait for the results of those studies before removing the child safety factor.* * *

[W]e reject Petitioner's argument that the EPA acted arbitrarily and capriciously by establishing the pesticide tolerances for acetamiprid, mepiquat, and pymetrozine before receiving the DNT studies. While Petitioners' concerns about the EPA's apparent change of heart are understandable, on such questions of scientific judgment, we are required to defer to the EPA.

B.

NRDC also disputes that the EPA's decision to deviate from the 10x presumptive child safety factor imposed by Congress was supported by reliable data establishing, with reasonable certainty, that the lower margin of safety for acetamiprid, mepiquat, and pymetrozine would not harm infants and children. Even though the EPA was not necessarily required to wait for the results of the DNT studies, the decision to reduce the 10x child safety factor for these three pesticides must still be based on reliable data. Moreover, the EPA must tell the public why its data are reliable.

The problem in this case is that the EPA's Final Order is vague, making it impossible for us to determine whether the EPA's deviations from the 10x child safety factor for acetamiprid, mepiquat, and pymetrozine were in fact supported by reliable data, even in the absence of the DNT studies.* * *

The Final Order recites that the "toxicological data" showed no evidence of increased sensitivity for developing fetuses or the "young." However, the Final Order does not explain the connection between the toxicological data and the 3x margin of safety selected by the EPA in place of the 10x standard. This same critique applies to the Final Order's reasoning with respect to acetamiprid and mepiquat. As a result, it is entirely unclear why the EPA chose safety factors of 3x for pymetrozine and acetamiprid, and 1x for mepiquat, as opposed to 4x or 5x or 8x or 9x. As far as we can tell from the record, it appears that the EPA chose these lower safety levels arbitrarily-to acknowledge certain concerns about each pesticide, but with no specific evidence that these lower safety factors would actually account for the risks to infants and children.

In sum, the Final Order does not provide enough information to demonstrate a rational connection between the factors that the EPA examined and the conclusions it reached. We are therefore unable to determine whether there was reliable data supporting the EPA's reductions of the 10x child safety factor. Although on remand the EPA may be able to explain why a 3x or 1x factor is appropriate, we cannot conclude it is appropriate on this record. To do so would abdicate our responsibility to ensure compliance with Congress's expressed desire to have a presumptive 10x child safety factor. Accordingly, we remand the tolerance regulations for acetamiprid, mepiquat, and pymetrozine to the EPA.

NOTES

1.   What do you think of the court's conclusion that the modeling EPA used to determine exposure constituted "reliable data" for purposes of adjusting the default safety factors required to account for special sensitivities of children and infants? Did EPA have an alternative? The use of safety factors as a way to account for uncertainty in risk assessments has a long history in U.S. health, safety, and environmental regulation. *See* William Boyd, *Genealogies of Risk: Searching for Safety, 1930s–1970s*, 39 ECOL. L. Q. 895, 928–33 (2012).

2.   The court notes that EPA had required the manufacturers to perform developmental neurotoxicity tests for the pesticides they were seeking to register but then finds that EPA's decision not to wait for the results of the tests before setting pesticide tolerances was a matter of "scientific judgment" left to the discretion of the Agency. Do you agree? Developmental neurotoxicity of certain pesticides and industrial chemicals has received increased attention since the passage of the FQPA in 1996. Some environmental health professionals argue that we are witnessing a "silent pandemic" of neurodevelopmental disorders such as autism, attention-deficit hyperactivity disorder, dyslexia, and other cognitive impairments as a result of exposure to pesticides and industrial chemicals. *See* Philippe Grandjean and Philip J. Landrigan, *Developmental Neurotoxicity of Industrial Chemicals*, 368 LANCET 2167 (2006); Philippe Grandjean and Philip J. Landrigan, *Neurobehavioral Effects of Developmental Toxicity*, 13 LANCET NEUROLOGY 330 (2014).

3.   Another class of potential harms associated with exposure to certain pesticides and industrial chemicals involves disruption of the endocrine system in humans and wildlife. Starting in the early-1990s, scientists began to report evidence that specific classes of pesticides could mimic hormones such as estrogen in the human body while others blocked the normal operation of hormonal signals. Possible human health effects of endocrine disruption include developmental and reproductive problems. These effects are subtle and are thought to result from exposure during particular windows of vulnerability rather than overall exposure. The 1996 FQPA directed EPA to create an Endocrine Disruptor Screening Program to screen pesticide chemicals for their potential to produce effects similar to those produced by the female hormones

(estrogen) in humans and gave EPA the authority to include other chemicals and endocrine effects in the program. 21 U.S.C. § 346a(p). In response, EPA has developed a program to screen pesticides, chemicals, and other environmental contaminants for their potential effect on estrogen, androgen and thyroid hormone systems. *See* EPA, Endocrine Disruptor Screening Program Overview https://www.epa.gov/endocrine-disruption/endocrine-disruptor-screening-program-edsp-overview.

4. The chlorpyrifos saga: In 2007, two environmental groups—the Pesticide Action Network North America (PANNA) and the Natural Resources Defense Council (NRDC) filed a petition requesting that EPA revoke the tolerances for chlorpyrifos. Chlorpyrifos is an organophosphate pesticide that was developed as a nerve gas during World War II. It was registered in the U.S. in 1965 for agricultural, residential, and commercial purposes. EPA had established chlorpyrifos residue tolerances for 80 different food crops, including fruits, nuts, and vegetables. The 2007 petition was based on scientific research showing that children and infants who had been exposed to low doses of chlorpyrifos suffer various neurodevelopmental harms such as reduced IQ, attention deficit disorder, and delayed motor development. After eight years of delay by EPA in responding to the 2007 petition, the 9th Circuit granted a request by PANNA and NRDC to issue a writ of mandamus ordering EPA to provide a final response to the 2007 petition by October 2015. *See In re PANNA*, 798 F.3d 809, 815 (9th Cir., 2015). EPA finally issued a proposed rule revoking all tolerances for chlorpyrifos in November 2015. *See Chlorpyrifos: Tolerance Revocations*, 80 Fed. Reg. 69,080 (Nov. 6, 2015). The 9th Circuit then ordered EPA to take final action on the proposed revocations by December 30, 2016. *See In re PANNA*, 808 F.3d 402 (9th Cir. 2015)—a deadline that was then extended by three months to March 2017. *In re PANNA*, 840 F.3d 1014, 1015 (9th Cir. 2016). In November 2016, EPA issued a risk assessment for chlorpyrifos concluding that estimated dietary exposure to chlorpyrifos at existing tolerances exceeded what was acceptable for all population groups, with the highest risks for your children. EPA found that the scientific literature on chlorpyrifos provided "evidence of long-lasting neurodevelopmental disorders" and concluded that the expected residues of chlorpyrifos under the existing tolerances "exceed the 'reasonable certainty of no harm' safety standard" under the FFDCA. *See Chlorpyrifos; Tolerance Revocations; Notice of Data Availability and Request for Comment*, 81 Fed. Reg. 81,049, 81,050 (Nov. 17, 2016). In April 2017, EPA reversed its position and denied the 2007 petition on the merits, leaving the chlorpyrifos tolerances in effect. *See Chlorpyrifos; Order Denying PANNA and NRDC's Petition to Revoke Tolerances*, 82 Fed. Reg. 16,581 (Apr. 5, 2017). EPA did not refute its previous scientific findings on chlorpyrifos or its conclusion that the chlorpyrifos tolerances violated the FFDCA safety standard. Instead, EPA based its decision on its view that "the science addressing neurodevelopmental effects remains unresolved." *Id.*, at 16,583. PANNA and NRDC, joined by several other groups and a number of states, petitioned the 9th Circuit to review EPA's 2017 Order denying the original 2007 petition. In August 2018, the 9th Circuit granted the petition for review, vacated EPA's 2017 order, and remanded the

case to EPA with "directions to revoke all tolerances and cancel all registrations for chlorpyrifos within 60 days." *See LULAC v. Wheeler*, 899 F.3d 814 (9th Cir. 2018). In September 2018, the Department of Justice requested that the 9th Circuit reconsider its decision. As this book goes to press, the 9th Circuit has not taken any action on the Justice Department's request. The saga continues.

5.   U.S. laws governing pesticides have paid very little attention to the promotion of alternative methods of pest control, such as Integrated Pest Management (IPM). For an argument that U.S. pesticide regulations should encourage alternative forms of pest control such as IPM, see Donald Hornstein, *Lessons from Federal Pesticide Regulation on the Paradigms and Politics of Environmental Law Reform*, 10 YALE J. REG. 369 (1993). The Food Quality Protection Act of 1996 did give a nod to adoption of IPM. The act added a new provision to FIFRA (7 U.S.C. § 136r–1) directed at promoting IPM:

> The Secretary of Agriculture, in cooperation with the [EPA] Administrator, shall implement research, demonstration, and education programs to support adoption of Integrated Pest Management. [IPM] is a sustainable approach to managing pests by combining biological, cultural, physical, and chemical tools in a way that minimizes economic, health, and environmental risks. The Secretary . . . and the Administrator shall make information on [IPM] widely available to pesticide users. . . . Federal agencies shall use [IPM] techniques in carrying out pest management activities and shall promote [IPM] through procurement and regulatory policies, and other activities.

6.   Another major risk of the improvident use of pesticides is widespread contamination of underground water sources, which are or may be tapped by wells to supply drinking water to individual homes and entire cities. For example, before it was banned in 1977 for causing sterility in humans and cancer in laboratory animals, the soil fumigant "DBCP" was used widely in California vineyards and orchards to combat root worms. During the 1990s, up and down the San Joaquin Valley, more than 100 municipal wells had to be shut down because of unsafe levels of DBCP. In 18 California counties, including Los Angeles, Riverside, San Bernardino, Orange, and San Diego, more than 1,700 public and private wells serving 200,000 people exceeded federal standards for exposure to DBCP. Between 1980 and 1995, the city of Fresno had to close 29 wells and install five carbon filtration systems at a cost of $800,000 each. *See* Mark Arax, *Banned DBCP Still Haunts San Joaquin Valley Water*, LOS ANGELES TIMES, June 12, 1995, at A1. Based on data from 2007 to 2017, 149 active and standby public water supply wells remain contaminated above federal levels. *See* California State Water Resources Control Board, GROUNDWATER INFORMATION SHEET Dibromochloropropane (DBCP) (November, 2017), https://www.waterboards.ca.gov/water_issues/programs/gama/docs/coc_dbcp.pdf.

7.   In addition to the risks they pose to public health, pesticides also threaten farm workers who apply the chemicals or work in affected fields. Since many of the workers are poor immigrants, these risks raise environmental justice issues. For extreme cases of thousands of farm workers in Latin America becoming sterile from unprotected exposure to pesticides manufactured in the United States and used on plantations owned by subsidiaries of U.S. corporations, *see Dow Chemical Co. v. Castro Alfaro*, 786 S.W.2d 674 (Tex.1990), *cert. denied*, 498 U.S. 1024 (1991); Diana Schemo, *Pesticide From U.S. Kills the Hopes of Fruit Pickers in the Third World*, N. Y. TIMES, Dec. 6, 1995, at A8, col. 4. A recent study of pesticide illness in the U.S. found more than 3000 cases of acute poisoning between 1998 and 2005, with women facing twice the risk of men. *See* GM Calvert, *et al., Acute Pesticide Poisoning Among Agricultural Workers in the United States, 1998–2005,* AM. J. IND. MED. (2008). The EPA does regulate the application of pesticides when workers are present, requiring training, protective equipment and restrictions on entering fields after the application of pesticides. *See* EPA, *Worker Protection Standard for Agricultural Pesticides*, https://www.epa.gov/pesticide-worker-safety/agricultural-worker-protection-standard-wps.   But   the   data about actual pesticide exposure and resultant harms remains problematic, as EPA itself recognizes. *See* EPA *Occupational Pesticide Handler Exposure Data*, https://www.epa.gov/pesticide-science-and-assessing-pesticide-risks/occupational-pesticide-handler-exposure-data.

8.   Some foods imported into the United States may contain unsafe pesticide residues, including residues of pesticides not registered here. In fact, many pesticides that are unlawful in the United States are exported for use abroad and may find their way back into the U.S. food stream via imported agriculture. Researchers estimate that between 2001–2003 U.S. companies exported 1.7 billion tons of pesticides to other countries. *See* Carl Smith, *et al., Pesticide Exports from U.S. Ports, 2001–03*, 14 INT. J. OCCUPATIONAL HEALTH 167 (2008). Section 17 OF FIFRA authorizes the export of pesticides so long as certain labeling and other conditions are met.

9.   As discussed in Chapter 3, GATT trade rules may affect domestic environmental regulations, as applied to imports. Section 346a(b)(2)(B)(iii) makes one of the conditions for a tolerance a finding that use is "necessary to avoid a significant disruption in domestic production." This provision may discriminate against foreign producers claiming a tolerance in order to avoid disruption in their production. Because of this discriminatory feature, the provision may be a prima facie violation of Article III of GATT. Other aspects of the provision, though facially neutral, might be found to have a disparate impact on foreign producers, also causing a potential GATT problem.

B. REGULATING INDUSTRIAL CHEMICALS

Congress enacted the Toxic Substances Control Act[3] (TSCA) in 1976 to prevent "unreasonable risks of injury to health or the environment"

---

3   90 Stat. 2003 (1976), 15 U.S.C.A. section 2601, et seq.

associated with the manufacture, processing, distribution, use or disposal of chemical substances other than drugs and pesticides. TSCA's emphasis is on regulating products—principally industrial chemicals—rather than pollution or wastes.[4] It was intended to fill a gap in the existing suite of federal environmental laws, providing a comprehensive approach to chemicals regulation. By virtually all accounts, however, TSCA has failed to deliver on its promise and is widely viewed as ineffectual.

After more than a decade of efforts to reform TSCA, the statute was overhauled in 2016, in a rare moment of bipartisan cooperation, by the Frank R. Lautenberg Chemical Safety for the 21st Century Act, P.L. 114–182, 130 Stat. 448 (2016). The new version of TSCA, which is discussed further below, contains several important changes intended to create a more effective regulatory program for industrial chemicals and to better protect public health and the environment. In particular, TSCA now provides EPA with enhanced authority to order the testing of chemicals. It also requires that EPA make an affirmative finding of safety before new chemicals (or significant new uses of existing chemicals) can be sold. And it establishes a new risk-based screening, prioritization, and evaluation process for existing chemicals and includes specific deadlines for moving chemicals through the screening and evaluation process.

Before discussing these new provisions in more detail, the next section provides some background on TSCA and the problems that plagued the statute for its first 40 years. In many ways, TSCA provides a cautionary lesson regarding how procedural burdens can overwhelm regulatory agencies and render the substantive, health-protective goals of a statute ineffective.

1. INFORMATION GAPS

Like FIFRA, TSCA employed a standard of "unreasonable risk" to govern whether and how EPA would regulate chemicals. Unlike FIFRA, TSCA placed the burden of producing the information needed to make a determination of unreasonable risk on EPA. While companies were required to submit any available health and safety data when filing premanufacture notices under section 5 of TSCA for new chemicals (or for significant new uses of existing chemicals), the statute did not require that the manufacturers perform any particular tests or submit specific types of data. EPA could order additional testing for these new chemicals under section 4, but it could only do so by rule after finding that the chemical posed an "unreasonable risk," which effectively put the burden on EPA to generate the required information to make such a finding except in the rare cases where the manufacturer provided sufficient information in its initial

---

4   For an extended discussion of TSCA and its implementation, *see* Hathaway, Hayes and Rawson, *A Practitioner's Guide to the Toxic Substances Control Act*, parts I–III, 24 ENVTL. L. REP. 10207, 10285, 10357 (1994).

submission. *See* Lyndon, *Information Economics and Chemical Toxicity: Designing Laws to Produce and Use Data*, 87 Mich. L. Rev. 1795, 1824 (1989). Because of these elaborate procedural requirements, EPA promulgated relatively few test rules under TSCA. *See* Applegate, *The Perils of Unreasonable Risk: Information, Regulatory Policy, and Toxic Substances Control*, 91 Colum. L. Rev. 261, 318–19 (1991).

For "existing" chemicals, defined as those chemicals that were in commerce at the time TSCA was enacted, there was no requirement that manufacturers submit any information or perform any testing in order to continue selling their products. In effect, these "existing" chemicals, estimated at 62,000 in 1976, were presumed to be safe and grandfathered under the statute. As with new chemicals, EPA could use its section 4 testing authority to compel companies to test, but only upon a finding of "unreasonable risk"—effectively putting the Agency in a Catch-22.

The result was a massive information gap regarding the health and safety of the vast majority of chemicals in commerce. This problem of "toxic ignorance," to quote the title of a 1997 report on the issue by the Environmental Defense Fund (EDF), has posed a major challenge to TSCA's effectiveness since its inception. *See* EDF, TOXIC IGNORANCE: THE CONTINUING ABSENCE OF BASIC HEALTH TESTING FOR TOPE SELLING CHEMICALS IN THE UNITED STATES (1997) https://www.edf.org/sites/default/files/243_toxicignorance_0.pdf. Several subsequent government reports have confirmed the basic problem. *See, e.g.,* U.S. GOV'T ACCOUNTABILITY OFFICE, CHEMICAL REGULATION: OPTIONS EXIST TO IMPROVE EPA'S ABILITY TO ASSESS HEALTH RISKS AND MANAGE ITS CHEMICAL REVIEW PROGRAM, GAO-05-458 (June 2005).

The problem was of particular concern for chemicals produced or imported into the United States in high volumes. EPA studies from the late 1990s assessed publicly available data on 2,863 chemicals produced and/or imported into the U.S. at over 1 million pounds per year. EPA found that a complete set of basic screening level data for six end points related to toxicity and environmental fate existed for only 7% of these chemicals. Only 50% of the chemicals had data for one to five of the end points and 43% had no data for any of the end points. *See* U.S. GOV'T ACCOUNTABILITY OFFICE, CHEMICAL REGULATION: OPTIONS EXIST TO IMPROVE EPA'S ABILITY TO ASSESS HEALTH RISKS AND MANAGE ITS CHEMICAL REVIEW PROGRAM, GAO-05-458 (June 2005) at 19–20. In an effort to deal with this problem, EPA initiated a voluntary program—the High Production Volume (HPV) Challenge—in 1998 to get chemical manufacturers and importers to provide basic health and safety information on chemicals produced in volumes of 1 million pounds or more per year. The HPV Challenge program proved to be ineffective, however, because of limited participation by the manufacturers. *See* EDF, HIGH HOPES, LOW MARKS: A FINAL REPORT CARD ON THE HIGH PRODUCTION CHEMICAL CHALLENGE (2007).

By the 2000s, very little progress had been made in solving the problem of toxic ignorance: comprehensive health and safety data existed for roughly two percent of the 85,000 chemicals that had been introduced into commerce before and after the enactment of TSCA in 1976. *See* Ellen K. Silbergeld, Daniele Mandrioli, and Carl F. Cranor, *Regulating Chemicals: Law, Science, and the Unbearable Burdens of Regulation*, 36 ANN. REV. PUB. HEALTH 175 (2015). A 2009 report by the Government Accountability Office (GAO) identified EPA's TSCA program as one of a handful of government programs that were sufficiently dysfunctional and important to require top-level intervention. The GAO explained that "EPA had not developed sufficient chemical assessment information under these programs to limit exposure to many chemicals that may pose substantial health risks." *See* U.S. GOV'T ACCOUNTABILITY OFFICE, GAO-09-271, HIGH RISK SERIES: AN UPDATE (2009).

2. REGULATORY GAPS

In addition to the problem of toxic ignorance, EPA also ran into problems in using its section 6 authority to regulate the handful of existing chemicals for which it did have sufficient information. Section 6(a) of TSCA provided that if the Administrator finds that there is "a reasonable basis to conclude" that the manufacture, processing, distribution in commerce, use, or disposal of a chemical substance or mixture "presents or will present an unreasonable risk of injury to health or the environment," he "shall by rule apply one or more of [seven specific] requirements * * * to the extent necessary to protect adequately against such risk *using the least burdensome requirements*" (emphasis added). The listed requirements include, among others, the prohibition of, or limitations on (e.g., total amount, maximum concentration, permissible uses) the manufacture, processing or distribution of such substance; regulation of the manner or method of use or disposal; and mandatory testing, record-keeping, and issuance of instructions, notices and warnings by manufacturers and processors. Section 6(c) prescribes criteria and procedures for promulgation of "subsection (a) rules."

Between 1978 and 1990, EPA successfully used its section 6 authority to regulate specific uses of four classes of chemical substances: halogenated chlorofluoroalkanes; 2,3,7,8-Tetrachlorodibenzo-p-dioxin (TCDD); three new chemical substances used in metalworking fluids; and hexavalent chromium. None of these rulemakings were challenged in court. In an effort to test its broader section 6 authority to regulate existing chemicals, EPA decided in 1979 to initiate an effort to regulate asbestos under TSCA. Asbestos seemed like an ideal candidate. It was widely used in the United States and elsewhere, although substitutes were available. It had been intensively studied for decades. It was a known human carcinogen, with well understood human exposure pathways. It had a so-called signature disease associated with it: mesothelioma. And it was killing a lot of people. In the mid 1980s, EPA estimated that between 3,330 and 12,000 new cancer cases were occurring every year because of past asbestos exposure, with many thousands more expected in the future. Starting in 1979, EPA spent ten years developing a 45,000 page record as a basis for its 1989 rule banning all uses of asbestos. *See Asbestos: Manufacture, Importation, Processing, and Distribution in Commerce Prohibitions*, 54 Fed. Reg. 29460 (July 12, 1989). That rule was the subject of the following case:

CORROSION PROOF FITTINGS V. ENVIRONMENTAL PROTECTION AGENCY

United States Court of Appeals, Fifth Circuit, 1991.
947 F.2d 1201.

JERRY E. SMITH, CIRCUIT JUDGE.

The Environmental Protection Agency (EPA) issued a final rule under section 6 of the Toxic Substances Control Act (TSCA) to prohibit the future manufacture, importation, processing, and distribution of asbestos in almost all products. Petitioners claim that the EPA's rulemaking procedure was flawed and that the rule was not promulgated on the basis of substantial evidence. * * *

Asbestos is a naturally occurring fibrous material that resists fire and most solvents. Its major uses include heat-resistant insulators, cements, building materials, fireproof gloves and clothing, and motor vehicle brake linings. Asbestos is a toxic material, and occupational exposure to asbestos dust can result in mesothelioma, asbestosis, and lung cancer. * * *

* * * Finding that asbestos constituted an unreasonable risk to health and the environment, the EPA promulgated a staged ban of most commercial uses of asbestos. The EPA estimates that this rule will save either 202 or 148 lives, depending upon whether the benefits are discounted, at a cost of approximately $450–800 million, depending upon the price of substitutes.* * *

Our inquiry into the legitimacy of the EPA rulemaking begins with a discussion of the standard of review governing this case. EPA's phase-out ban of most commercial uses of asbestos is a TSCA section 6(a) rulemaking. TSCA provides that a reviewing court "shall hold unlawful and set aside" a final rule promulgated under § 6(a) "if the court finds that the rule is not supported by substantial evidence in the rulemaking record . . . taken as a whole." * * *

"Under the substantial evidence standard, a reviewing court must give careful scrutiny to agency findings and, at the same time, accord appropriate deference to administrative decisions that are based on agency experience and expertise." As with consumer product legislation, "Congress put the substantial evidence test in the statute because it wanted the courts to scrutinize the Commission's actions more closely than an 'arbitrary or capricious' standard would allow."

The recent case of *Chemical Mfrs. Ass'n v. EPA*, 899 F.2d 344 (5th Cir. 1990), provides our basic framework for reviewing the EPA's actions. In evaluating whether the EPA has presented substantial evidence, we examine (1) whether the quantities of the regulated chemical entering into the environment are "substantial" and (2) whether human exposure to the chemical is "substantial" or "significant." An agency may exercise its judgment without strictly relying upon quantifiable risks, costs, and benefits, but it must "cogently explain why it has exercised its discretion in a given manner" and "must offer a 'rational connection between the facts found and the choice made.'"

We note that in undertaking our review, we give all agency rules a presumption of validity, and it is up to the challenger to any rule to show that the agency action is invalid. The burden remains on the EPA, however, to justify that the products it bans present an unreasonable risk, no matter how regulated. *See Industrial Union Dep't v. American Petroleum Inst.*, 448 U.S. 607, 662, 100 S.Ct. 2844, 2874, 65 L.Ed.2d 1010 (1980). Finally, as we discuss in detail *infra*, because TSCA instructs the EPA to undertake the least burdensome regulation sufficient to regulate the substance at issue, the agency bears a heavier burden when it seeks a partial or total ban of a substance than when it merely seeks to regulate that product. *See* 15 U.S.C. § 2605(a).

TSCA provides, in pertinent part, as follows:

(a) Scope of regulation.—If the Administrator finds that there is a *reasonable basis* to conclude that the manufacture, processing, distribution in commerce, use, or disposal of a chemical substance or mixture, or that any combination of such activities, presents or will present an *unreasonable risk of injury* to health or the environment, the Administrator shall by rule apply one or more of the following requirements to such substance or mixture to the extent necessary *to protect adequately* against such risk using the *least burdensome* requirements.

As the highlighted language shows, Congress did not enact TSCA as a zero-risk statute. The EPA, rather, was required to consider both alternatives to a ban and the costs of any proposed actions and to "carry out this chapter in a reasonable and prudent manner [after considering] the environmental, economic, and social impact of any action." 15 U.S.C. § 2601(c).

We conclude that the EPA has presented insufficient evidence to justify its asbestos ban. We base this conclusion upon two grounds: the failure of the EPA to consider all necessary evidence and its failure to give adequate weight to statutory language requiring it to promulgate the least burdensome, reasonable regulation required to protect the environment adequately. Because the EPA failed to address these concerns, and because the EPA is required to articulate a "reasoned basis" for its rules, we are compelled to return the regulation to the agency for reconsideration.

TSCA requires that the EPA use the least burdensome regulation to achieve its goal of minimum reasonable risk. This statutory requirement can create problems in evaluating just what is a "reasonable risk." Congress's rejection of a no-risk policy, however, also means that in certain cases, the least burdensome yet still adequate solution may entail somewhat more risk than would other, known regulations that are far more burdensome on the industry and the economy. The very language of TSCA requires that the EPA, once it has determined what an acceptable level of non-zero risk is, choose the least burdensome method of reaching that level.

In this case, the EPA banned, for all practical purposes, all present and future uses of asbestos—a position the petitioners characterize as the "death penalty alternative," as this is the *most* burdensome of all possible alternatives listed as open to the EPA under TSCA. TSCA not only provides the EPA with a list of alternative actions, but also provides those alternatives in order of how burdensome they are. The regulations [sic] thus provide for EPA regulation ranging from labeling the least toxic chemicals to limiting the total amount of chemicals an industry may use. Total bans head the list as the most burdensome regulatory option.

By choosing the harshest remedy given to it under TSCA, the EPA assigned to itself the toughest burden in satisfying TSCA's requirement that its alternative be the least burdensome of all those offered to it. Since, both by definition and by the terms of TSCA, the complete ban of manufacturing is the most burdensome alternative—for even stringent regulation at least allows a manufacturer the chance to invest and meet the new, higher standard—the EPA's regulation cannot stand if there is any other regulation that would achieve an acceptable level of risk as mandated by TSCA. * * *

The EPA considered, and rejected, such options as labeling asbestos products, thereby warning users and workers involved in the manufacture of asbestos-containing products of the chemical's dangers, and stricter workplace rules. EPA also rejected controlled use of asbestos in the workplace and deferral to other government agencies charged with worker and consumer exposure to industrial and product hazards, such as OSHA, the CPSC, and the MSHA. The EPA determined that deferral to these other agencies was inappropriate because no one other authority could address all the risks posed "throughout the life cycle" by asbestos, and any action by one or more of the other agencies still would leave an unacceptable residual risk.

Much of the EPA's analysis is correct, and the EPA's basic decision to use TSCA as a comprehensive statute designed to fight a multi-industry problem was a proper one that we uphold today on review. What concerns us, however, is the manner in which the EPA conducted some of its analysis. TSCA requires the EPA to consider, along with the effects of toxic substances on human health and the environment, "the benefits of such substance[s] or mixture[s] for various uses and the availability of substitutes for such uses," as well as "the reasonably ascertainable economic consequences of the rule, after consideration for the effect on the national economy, small business, technological innovation, the environment, and public health." *Id.* § 2605(c)(1)(C–D).

The EPA presented two comparisons in the record: a world with no further regulation under TSCA, and a world in which no manufacture of asbestos takes place. The EPA rejected calculating how many lives a less burdensome regulation would save, and at what cost. Furthermore the EPA, when calculating the benefits of its ban, explicitly refused to compare it to an improved workplace in which currently available control technology is utilized. This decision artificially inflated the purported benefits of the rule by using a baseline comparison substantially lower than what currently available technology could yield.

Under TSCA, the EPA was required to evaluate, rather than ignore, less burdensome regulatory alternatives. TSCA imposes a least-to-most-burdensome hierarchy. In order to impose a regulation at the top of the hierarchy—a total ban of asbestos—the EPA must show not only that its proposed action reduces the risk of the product to an adequate level, but also that the actions Congress identified as less burdensome also would not do the job. The failure of the EPA to do this constitutes a failure to meet its burden of showing that its actions not only reduce the risk but do so in the *least burdensome* fashion.

Thus it was not enough for the EPA to show, as it did in this case, that banning some asbestos products might reduce the harm that could occur from the use of these products. If that were the standard, it would be no standard at all, for few indeed are the products that are so safe that a complete ban of them would not make the world still safer.

This comparison of two static worlds is insufficient to satisfy the dictates of TSCA. While the EPA may have shown that a world with a complete ban of asbestos might be preferable to one in which there is only the current amount of regulation, the EPA has failed to show that there is not some intermediate state of regulation that would be superior to both the currently-regulated and the completely-banned world. Without showing that asbestos regulation would be ineffective, the EPA cannot discharge its TSCA burden of showing that its regulation is the least burdensome available to it.

Upon an initial showing of product danger, the proper course for the EPA to follow is to consider each regulatory option, beginning with the least burdensome, and the costs and benefits of regulation under each option. The EPA cannot simply skip several rungs, as it did in this case, for in doing so, it may skip a less-burdensome alternative mandated by TSCA. Here, although the EPA mentions the problems posed by intermediate levels of regulation, it takes no steps to calculate the costs and benefits of these intermediate levels. Without doing this it is impossible, both for the EPA and for this court on review, to know that none of these alternatives was less burdensome than the ban in fact chosen by the agency.

The EPA's offhand rejection of these intermediate regulatory steps is "not the stuff of which substantial evidence is made." While it is true that the EPA considered five different ban options, these differed solely with respect to their effective dates. The EPA did not calculate the risk levels for intermediate levels of regulation, as it believed that there was no asbestos exposure level for which the risk of injury or death was zero. Reducing risk to zero, however, was not the task that Congress set for the EPA in enacting TSCA. The EPA thus has failed "cogently [to] explain why it has exercised its discretion in a given manner," by failing to explore in more than a cursory way the less burdensome alternatives to a total ban.* * *

In addition to showing that its regulation is the least burdensome one necessary to protect the environment adequately, the EPA also must show that it has a reasonable basis for the regulation. To some extent, our inquiry in this area mirrors that used above, for many of the methodological problems we have noted also indicate that the EPA did not have a reasonable basis. We here take the opportunity to highlight some areas of additional concern.

Most problematical to us is the EPA's ban of products for which no substitutes presently are available. In these cases, the EPA bears a tough burden indeed to show that under TSCA a ban is the least burdensome alternative, as TSCA explicitly instructs the EPA to consider "the benefits of such substance or mixture for various uses and the availability of substitutes for such uses." These words are particularly appropriate where the EPA actually has decided to ban a product, rather than simply restrict its use, for it is in these cases that the lack of an adequate substitute is most troubling under TSCA. * * *

We also are concerned with the EPA's evaluation of substitutes even in those instances in which the record shows that they are available. The EPA explicitly rejects considering the harm that may flow from the increased use of products designed to substitute for asbestos, even where the probable substitutes themselves are known carcinogens. The EPA justifies this by stating that it has "more concern about the continued use and exposure to asbestos than it has for the future replacement of asbestos in the products subject to this rule with other fibrous substitutes." The agency thus concludes that any "[r]egulatory decisions about asbestos which poses well-recognized, serious risks should not be delayed until the risks of all replacement materials are fully quantified."

This presents two problems. First, TSCA instructs the EPA to consider the relative merits of its ban, as compared to the economic effects of its actions. The EPA cannot make this calculation if it fails to consider the effects that alternative substitutes will pose after a ban.

Second, the EPA cannot say with any assurance that its regulation will increase workplace safety when it refuses to evaluate the harm that will result from the increased use of substitute products. While the EPA may be correct in its conclusion that the alternate materials pose less risk than asbestos, we cannot say with any more assurance than that flowing from an educated guess that this conclusion is true.

Considering that many of the substitutes that the EPA itself concedes will be used in the place of asbestos have known carcinogenic effects, the EPA not only cannot assure this court that it has taken the least burdensome alternative, but cannot even prove that its regulations will increase workplace safety. Eager to douse the dangers of asbestos, the agency inadvertently actually may increase the risk of injury Americans face. The EPA's explicit failure to consider the toxicity of likely substitutes thus deprives its order of a reasonable basis.

Our opinion should not be construed to state that the EPA has an affirmative duty to seek out and test every workplace substitute for any product it seeks to regulate. TSCA does not place such a burden upon the agency. We do not think it unreasonable, however, once interested parties introduce credible studies and evidence showing the toxicity of workplace substitutes, or the decreased effectiveness of safety alternatives such as non-asbestos brakes, that the EPA then consider whether its regulations are even increasing workplace safety, and whether the increased risk occasioned by dangerous substitutes makes the proposed regulation no longer reasonable. . . .

The final requirement the EPA must satisfy before engaging in any TSCA rulemaking is that it only takes steps designed to prevent "unreasonable" risks. In evaluating what is "unreasonable," the EPA is required to consider the costs of any proposed actions and to "carry out this chapter in a reasonable and prudent manner [after considering] the environmental, economic, and social impact of any action." 15 U.S.C. § 2601(c). * * *

That the EPA must balance the costs of its regulations against their benefits further is reinforced by the requirement that it seek the least burdensome regulation. While Congress did not dictate that the EPA engage in an exhaustive, full-scale cost-benefit analysis, it did require the EPA to consider both sides of the regulatory equation, and it rejected the notion that the EPA should pursue the reduction of workplace risk at any cost. See *American Textile Mfrs. Inst.,* 452 U.S. at 510 n. 30, 101 S.Ct. at 2491 n. 30 ("unreasonable risk" statutes require "a generalized balancing of costs and benefits"). . . .

Even taking all of the EPA's figures as true, and evaluating them in the light most favorable to the agency's decision (non-discounted benefits, discounted costs, analogous exposure estimates included), the agency's analysis results in figures as high as $74 million per life saved. For example, the EPA states that its ban of asbestos pipe will save three lives over the next thirteen years, at a cost of $128–227 million ($43–76 million per life saved), depending upon the price of substitutes; that its ban of asbestos shingles will cost $23–34 million to save 0.32 statistical lives ($72–106 million per life saved); that its ban of asbestos coatings will cost $46–181 million to save 3.33 lives ($14–54 million per life saved); and that its ban of asbestos paper products will save 0.60 lives at a cost of $4–5 million ($7–8 million per life saved). Were the analogous exposure estimates not included, the cancer risks from substitutes such as ductile iron pipe factored in, and the benefits of the ban appropriately discounted from the time of the manifestation of an injury rather than the time of exposure, the costs would shift even more sharply against the EPA's position.

While we do not sit as a regulatory agency that must make the difficult decision as to what an appropriate expenditure is to prevent someone from incurring the risk of an asbestos-related death, we do note that the EPA, in its zeal to ban any and all asbestos products, basically ignored the cost side of the TSCA equation. The EPA would have this court believe that Congress, when it enacted its requirement that the EPA consider the economic impacts of its regulations, thought that spending $200–300 million to save approximately seven lives (approximately $30–40 million per life) over thirteen years is reasonable.

As we stated in the OSHA context, until an agency "can provide substantial evidence that the benefits to be achieved by [a regulation] bear a reasonable relationship to the costs imposed by the reduction, it cannot show that the standard is reasonably necessary to provide safe or healthful workplaces."

NOTES

1.   Environmentalists condemned the foregoing decision as a "death knell" for TSCA. One said that "if the agency can't use TSCA to ban asbestos, then it can't use Section 6 [to regulate any chemical] because the data base on adverse health effects of asbestos is one of the best." Another said, "The largely unworkable Section 6, which was unwieldly before, is now even more useless." *See* 22 ENV'T. REP. 1607 (1991).

Professor Thomas McGarity went to the legal heart of the matter, observing acidly that the Fifth Circuit's opinion

> is so lacking in deference to the agency's exercise of expertise and policy judgment, and so full of attempts to impose on the agency the judges' own views of the proper role of regulation in society, that it is virtually indistinguishable from the documents that OMB prepares in connection with its oversight of EPA rulemaking.

Thomas O. McGarity, Some Thoughts on 'Deossifying' the Rulemaking Process, 41 DUKE L.J. 1385, 1423 (1992).

2.   Are the estimated costs per life saved under EPA's asbestos regulations blatantly unreasonable, as the court seems to suggest at the end of the *Corrosion Proof Fittings* opinion? A study by Resources for the Future reviewed economic data used by EPA in support of its asbestos, pesticide, and carcinogenic air pollutant regulations. The study concluded that EPA implicitly had attached a value of $15 million to $45 million to the prevention of one case of cancer, much more than individuals appeared to be willing to spend to reduce their own risks of death. *See* Van Houtven and Cropper, *When Is a Life Too Costly to Save? The Evidence from Environmental Regulations*, RESOURCES, Winter 1994, at 6.

A subsequent study of regulatory costs of lives saved casts considerable doubt upon the validity of high estimates like those in *Corrosion Proof Fittings* and in the *Resources* article just cited. *See* Lisa Heinzerling, *Regulatory Costs of Mythic Proportions*, 107 YALE L.J. 1981 (1998). The author suggests that the same data relied upon in most prior studies indicate "a cost per life saved of less than $5 million" in most cases. "This means that . . . the costs per life saved . . . are below the range of current estimates of the monetary value of a human life based on studies of wage premiums for risky jobs. A figure of about $9 million is commonly reported today to be the preference-based value of life for nonmanual labor; for manual laborers, it is much lower, around $2.5 million. Another frequently cited range for the value of a human life is $3 million to $7 million." *Id.* at 2038–40.

3.   The court in *Corrosion Proof Fittings* also held that EPA must *discount* future benefits and that EPA's benefit-cost analysis gave too much weight to future deaths. For an exploration of the complexities of the choice of discount rates, with particular emphasis on the issue of discounting lives, *see* Farber and Hemmersbaugh, *The Shadow of the Future: Discount Rates, Later Generations, and the Environment*, 46 VAND. L. REV. 267 (1993). *See also* Richard Revesz, *Environmental Regulation, Cost-Benefit Analysis, and the Discounting of Human Lives*, 99 COL. L. REV. 941 (1999).

Professor Heinzerling, in her article cited in Note 2 *supra*, challenges the propriety of "discounting lives," i.e., lives saved in the future, in estimating the benefits of environmental regulation. She points out that the economic study most cited by persons claiming that regulatory costs are excessive in relation to benefits applied an annual discount rate of 10 percent in reducing lives saved in the future to present terms. Thus, 10 lives saved one year in the future are equivalent to 9 lives saved today, 10 lives saved two years in the future equal 8.3 lives saved today, and 10 lives saved 10 years in the future equal 3.9 lives saved today. *Id.* at 2018, 2043. Heinzerling argues that while discounting lives may be appropriate "as long as the value of a human life is measured in dollars" (though the proper discount *rate* may not be 10 percent), the case for discounting the future benefits of health regulation is "less straightforward" if one does not assign a monetary value to human life. She states the various arguments in support of such nonmonetary discounting and presents interesting counterarguments. *Id.* at 2044–56. Her case against discounting is presented more fully, and expanded to include not only fatal illnesses but also non-fatal mental and physical ailments during the "latency" period following toxic exposure, in Lisa Heinzerling, The *Temporal Dimension in Environmental Law*, 31 ENVTL L. REP. 11055 (2001).

4.   After the *Corrosion Proof Fittings* decision, EPA never again used its section 6 authority under TSCA. When combined with the general problem of toxic ignorance, EPA's inability to use its section 6 authority to regulate existing chemicals led to a growing chorus of calls for reform. The central criticisms behind these reform proposals focused on the various regulatory "gaps" under TSCA: a data gap because most chemicals can be sold without any disclosure of information about their risks; a safety gap because regulatory activity cannot take place given the absence of data; and a technology gap because of a lack of investment in alternative "green" chemistry. *See* UC CENTERS FOR OCCUPATIONAL AND ENVIRONMENTAL HEALTH, GREEN CHEMISTRY: CORNERSTONE TO A SUSTAINABLE CALIFORNIA (2008) at 8–9.

5.   In an effort to remedy the information gaps plaguing chemicals policy and to provide a more robust framework for regulation, the EU passed a regulation in 2006 known as Registration, Evaluation, Authorisation and Restriction of Chemicals (REACH). The core principle that motivates REACH is quite simple: "No Data, No Market." Before a firm can sell chemicals in the EU, it must provide basic safety information on those chemicals to regulators. Manufacturers and importers are required to gather information on the properties of their chemical substances, which will allow their safe handling, and to register the information in a central database maintained by the European Chemicals Agency in Helsinki. Based on this initial information, suspicious chemicals are subject to further evaluation and restrictions as needed. REACH also calls for the progressive substitution of the most dangerous chemicals (referred to as "substances of very high concern") when suitable alternatives have been identified. For background on REACH, including links to the regulation and other major documents, *see* http://ec. europa.eu/environment/chemicals/reach/reach_en.htm.

6.   In response to the shortcomings of TSCA, several states, including California, Maine and Washington, have sought to regulate chemicals more aggressively. For a description of some of these state efforts, see Richard A. Denison, *Ten Essential Elements in TSCA Reform,* 39 ELR 10020,10021, n. 10 (2009). These efforts, together with the EU's reforms under REACH and

ongoing recognition of the failure of TSCA, provided further impetus for reforming the statute.

3. TSCA 2.0: KEY PROVISIONS OF THE REVISED STATUTE

After more than a decade of legislative efforts to reform TSCA, Congress finally amended the statute in 2016. Signed into law on June 22, 2016, the Frank R. Lautenberg Chemical Safety for the 21st Century Act (Pub. L. 114–182, 130 Stat. 448) included significant changes to several core provisions of the statute. Most importantly, the new law seeks to remedy some of the problems created by the "grandfathering" of existing chemicals under TSCA and reduces some of the procedural burdens imposed on EPA before it can order testing and/or regulate chemicals.

Most of the definitions and the basic architecture of the statute are unchanged. TSCA continues to regulate "chemical substances" and "mixtures" and applies to manufacturers, processors, distributers, and importers of chemicals. 15 U.S.C. §§ 2602(2) and 2602(10). The 2016 amendments added a new term, "conditions of use," which describes the context that EPA must consider when screening and evaluating chemicals: "the circumstances . . . under which a chemical substance is intended, known, or reasonably foreseen to be manufactured, processed, distributed in commerce, used, or disposed of." 15 U.S.C. § 2602(4). The 2016 amendments also incorporate for the first time a definition of "potentially exposed or susceptible subpopulation," 15 U.S.C. § 2602(12), and requires that the risks posed by chemical substances to such subpopulations be accounted for when evaluating and regulating such chemicals. Finally, although the 2016 amendments continue to use "unreasonable risk" as the basic standard under TSCA, the new provisions explicitly exclude consideration of costs or other non-risk factors in assessing the risks of chemicals.

The most significant changes to the substantive sections of the statute include:

Section 4: Testing of Chemical Substances and Mixtures. EPA can now mandate new testing of chemicals by rule, order, or consent agreement, rather than exclusively by regulation as required under the old version of TSCA. EPA also no longer has to make a finding of "unreasonable risk" before requiring testing. 15 U.S.C. § 2603.

Section 5: Manufacturing and Processing Notices for New Chemicals and Significant New Uses. EPA must now make an affirmative finding that new chemicals or significant new uses of existing chemicals are "not likely to present an unreasonable risk of injury to health or the environment" before they can be commercialized. EPA is also directed to take regulatory action limiting or restricting the sale or use of such chemical substances "to the extent necessary" to provide protection against unreasonable risks, "without consideration of costs or other nonrisk factors, including an unreasonable risk to a potentially exposed subpopulation." 15 U.S.C. § 2604.

Section 6: Prioritization, Risk Evaluation, and Regulation of Chemical Substances and Mixtures. The changes to section 6 of TSCA are the most important changes added by the 2016 amendments and seek to deal with the long-standing problem of toxic ignorance, particularly with respect to existing chemicals, as well as with the impacts of the *Corrosion Proof Fittings* case on EPA's risk management options. The new section 6 creates a risk-based screening and prioritization process for all chemicals. EPA must now designate chemical substances as either high- or low-priority based on initial screening, with deadlines for moving chemicals through the screening process. Once identified, high-priority chemicals are subject to a risk evaluation (essentially, a risk assessment) conducted by EPA, also according to a specific schedule. Persistent bioaccumulative toxic substances (PBTs) are fast tracked for risk evaluations. And the risk evaluations must exclude consideration of costs and other non-risk factors and must consider risks to "susceptible and highly exposed subpopulations." Finally, the risk management option that EPA chooses when it decides to regulate a chemical substances are no longer required to be the "least burdensome" and EPA is now required to impose restrictions "to the extent necessary so that the chemical . . . no longer presents" an unreasonable risk. 15 U.S.C. § 2605.

Section 8: Reporting and Retention of Information. EPA is directed to require manufacturers or processors to submit information on those chemical substances that they have manufactured or processed during the ten years preceding the 2016 TSCA amendments. EPA is then directed to designate chemical substances as "active" or "inactive" and to use this as the basis for compiling and keeping current a list of all chemicals (the TSCA inventory) that are manufactured or processed in the U.S. These new provisions are intended to provide a comprehensive "reset" of the TSCA inventory of chemical substances that are actively in commerce in the U.S. 15 U.S.C. § 2607.

Section 18: Preemption. TSCA's preemption provisions were among the most contentious during the debates leading up to the 2016 amendments. As with pesticides and other commercial products (*e.g.*, new motor vehicles), TSCA preempts a broad range of state authority to regulate chemicals. As amended, however, the statute does provide several important carve-outs and exceptions for state regulations. In general, states can continue to regulate chemicals that EPA has not yet addressed. State regulations in existence at the time of the 2016 amendments are not preempted. And states are also allowed to continue regulating chemicals in the future under state laws adopted prior to August 31, 2003. If EPA determines through a risk evaluation that a chemical does not pose an unreasonable risk or when EPA takes final action to regulate a chemical, however, state regulations of that chemical are preempted. 15 U.S.C. § 2619.

One other provision that deserves mention is § 7, which allows EPA to obtain emergency judicial relief in case of "imminent hazards." The Act also contains the usual panoply of provisions on civil and criminal penalties, judicial enforcement, judicial review, and hybrid rule-making.

NOTES

1.   The revisions to section 5 of TSCA require that EPA make an affirmative finding of safety ("not likely to present an unreasonable risk of injury to health or the environment") before a new chemical (or significant new use of an existing chemical) can be commercialized. While this does not explicitly require manufacturers to come forward with health and safety information when submitting their pre-manufacture notices, does it change their incentives to do so when compared to the prior version of TSCA?

2.   Although TSCA 2.0 mandates risk assessments ("risk evaluations") for existing chemicals that are designated as "high priority" chemicals, the schedule it imposes on EPA for such assessments will not remedy the problem of toxic ignorance any time soon. Under the revised section 6 of TSCA, EPA is required to conduct risk evaluations for 20 high-priority chemicals within three and a half years of enactment. Once initiated, such risk evaluations must be completed within three years (with the possibility of a six-month extension. While this is an improvement over the previous version of TSCA, it pales in comparison to the vast numbers of chemicals in commerce for which there is little or no health and safety information. In addition, EPA has not received any new budgetary appropriation to implement the new risk evaluation requirements, although the legislation does allow EPA to impose up to $25 million in fees annually on chemical manufacturers and processors to help pay for the program.

3.   During the last days of the Obama administration, EPA proposed two "framework" rules setting out how it would prioritize and evaluate chemicals under the new provisions of TSCA. *See Procedures for Prioritization of Chemicals for Risk Evaluation Under the Toxic Substances Control Act*, Proposed Rule, 82 Fed. Reg. 4825 (Jan. 17, 2017); *Procedures for Chemical Risk Evaluation Under the Toxic Substances Control Act*, Proposed Rule, 82 Fed. Reg. 7562 (Jan. 19, 2017). Among other things, the proposed rules took an expansive approach to the interpretation of "conditions of use" of chemical substances as a basis for evaluating their risks. Specifically, the proposed rules viewed "conditions of use" as referring to all uses of a chemical substance, including past, present, and reasonably foreseeable uses. In June 2017, after the Trump administration took office, EPA changed course and issued final rules that took a much more restrictive approach to "conditions of use," asserting that EPA would identify the relevant conditions of use on a case-by-

case basis and would generally exclude past "legacy" uses of chemicals. *See Procedures for Prioritization of Chemicals for Risk Evaluation Under the Toxic Substances Control Act*, Final Rule, 82 Fed. Reg. 33753 (Jul. 20, 2017); *Procedures for Chemical Risk Evaluation Under the Toxic Substances Control Act*, Final Rule, 82 Fed. Reg. 33726 (Jul. 20, 2017). In August 2017, several environmental groups sued EPA over the new rules. This case will present the first opportunity for a court to interpret the 2016 TSCA amendments. Briefing was completed in December 2018. At the time that this book went to press, oral arguments had not yet been scheduled. *See Safer Chemicals, Healthy Families, et al. v. EPA*, Docket No. 17–72260, U.S. Court of Appeals for the Ninth Circuit.

C. REGULATING AGRICULTURAL BIOTECHNOLOGY AND TRANSGENIC PLANTS

1. REGULATING THE ENVIRONMENTAL EFFECTS OF AGRICULTURAL BIOTECHNOLOGY

FIFRA and TSCA were enacted before the widespread advances in biotechnology, though FIFRA in particular now plays a role in regulating certain aspects of biotechnology. The article below provides background about biotechnology regulation.

GREGORY N. MANDEL, GAPS, INEXPERIENCE, INCONSISTENCIES, AND OVERLAPS: CRISIS IN THE REGULATION OF GENETICALLY MODIFIED PLANTS AND ANIMALS
45 WM. & MARY L. REV. 2167 (2004).[2]

INTRODUCTION

Biotechnology may help ameliorate some of the greatest crises currently facing the United States and the world, including hunger and malnutrition, environmental degradation, and widespread disease. Genetically modifying crops through the use of biotechnology potentially allows for greater agricultural efficiency, increased nutritional content of food, and reduced environmental impacts. Genetically engineering animals may create cheaper food, reduce pressures on wild animal populations, and provide organs or tissues for human transplant. Modifying plants and animals to produce pharmaceuticals could provide for widespread, inexpensive dissemination of critical pharmaceuticals and vaccines throughout the United States and the world.

On the other hand, biotechnology could have harmful consequences. Potential problems include human health impacts resulting from the introduction of new allergens or toxins, widespread environmental and

---

[2]   Copyright © 2004. Reprinted by permission.

ecological damage resulting from the introduction of invasive species or loss of biodiversity, and unforeseen injury arising from the unintentional release of pharmaceuticals or industrial compounds into the food supply. * * *

CURRENT REGULATION OF GENETICALLY MODIFIED PLANTS AND ANIMALS

A. The Coordinated Framework

As the biotechnology industry developed in the early 1980s, it was recognized that regulation was necessary to protect human health and the environment from the potential deleterious effects of transgenic products. This recognition culminated in the promulgation of the federal government's Coordinated Framework for Regulation of Biotechnology by the White House Office of Science and Technology Policy in 1986. The Coordinated Framework instituted a "comprehensive federal regulatory policy for . . . biotechnology research and products." It specified that bioengineered products generally would be regulated under the then-existing statutory and regulatory structure. The foundation for this decision was a determination that the process of biotechnology was not inherently risky, and therefore, that only the products of biotechnology, not the process itself, required oversight. On this basis, the Coordinated Framework established that existing laws and regulations were sufficient to handle the products of biotechnology. This decision was based in part on a desire not to impose regulatory restrictions that could hamper the development of a promising and fledgling industry.

As a result of the Coordinated Framework, three administrative agencies are involved in the regulation of the genetically modified products discussed in this Article: The FDA is responsible for food safety issues for transgenic crop and food-animal varieties, and for drug safety issues for modified pharmaceutical-producing plants or animals; the EPA handles health and environmental effects of pest-protected plants; and the USDA regulates the effect of genetically modified plants on other plants and animals in both agricultural and nonagricultural environments. Because the Coordinated Framework would result in multiple agencies acting in closely related areas, two basic principles were delineated to guide regulatory policy. First, "[a]gencies should seek to adopt consistent definitions of those genetically engineered organisms subject to review to the extent permitted by their respective statutory authorities." Second, the "agencies should utilize scientific reviews of comparable rigor."

Implicit in the decision to regulate genetically modified products under preexisting statutes was the belief that bioengineered plants and animals were not significantly different from their conventional counterparts. This view was explicitly reiterated in a 1987 National Academy of Sciences report that reached three conclusions:

1.   There is no evidence that unique hazards exist either in the use of rDNA techniques or in the movement of genes between unrelated organisms.

2.   The risks associated with the introduction of rDNA-engineered organisms are the same in kind as those associated with the introduction of unmodified organisms and organisms modified by other methods.

3.   Assessment of the risks of introducing rDNA-engineered organisms into the environment should be based on the nature of the organism and the environment into which it is introduced, not on the method by which it was produced.

With the Coordinated Framework in place, the regulation of biotechnology was left to the administrative agencies.

B.   The Food and Drug Administration

The FDA is responsible for insuring that all food products on the market in the United States, other than meat and poultry, are safe. In furtherance of this goal, the FDA provides voluntary premarket consultations with food companies, seed companies, and plant developers regarding the safety of transgenic foods.

* * * No statutory provisions or FDA regulations expressly cover genetically modified foods. Pursuant to FDA regulations, plants modified through modern rDNA techniques are not treated any differently from conventionally modified plants.

Section 402(a)(1) of the FFDCA authorizes the FDA to regulate "adulterated foods," defined as food that "bears or contains any poisonous or deleterious substance which may render it injurious to health." In addition, section 409 of the FFDCA provides for the regulation of "food additives," which are substances that are intended for use in food, that may reasonably be expected to become a component of food, or that otherwise may affect the characteristics of food. A food additive must be approved by the FDA prior to being used in food. Manufacturers, however, do not need approval for a food additive if such substance is generally recognized as safe (GRAS) by experts. Thus, both the inserted gene of a transgenic plant and the product that it expresses are food additives, unless they are GRAS. With respect to genetically modified foods, the FDA has determined that "[i]n most cases, the substances expected to become components of food as a result of genetic modification of a plant will be the same as or substantially similar to substances commonly found in food, such as proteins, fats and oils, and carbohydrates," and therefore will be GRAS.

The food additive manufacturer determines whether a food additive is GRAS, not the FDA. A manufacturer does not need to report to the FDA that it has made a GRAS determination, but it may do so and may receive from the FDA an affirmation that the particular substance is GRAS. Thus, the FDA's regulatory requirements with respect to genetically modified food are primarily voluntary. This decision was explicitly made by the FDA based on its determination that "[a]ny genetic modification technique has the potential to alter the composition of food in a manner relevant to food safety, although, based on experience, the likelihood of a safety hazard is typically very low."

In 1995, the FDA conducted a safety review of the first genetically modified food product to be commercialized, the Flavr Savr tomato. This review was conducted at the request of the manufacturer, who was attempting to build public confidence. Since that time, the FDA has not conducted a safety review of any of the scores of other genetically modified food products that have been commercialized; however, the FDA believes that manufacturers have voluntarily consulted with it regarding each of these products.

The FDA does not require that genetically modified foods be labeled as such. The basis for this determination is the FDA's conclusion that genetically modified products do not differ materially from, or create greater safety concerns than, their conventional counterparts. To the extent that there are significant safety concerns or usage issues, such as substantial changes in composition or nutritive value, the FDA requires labeling.

The FDA explicitly has waived its regulatory authority over genetically modified pest-protected plants, so long as the plants have not also been modified to express other, nonpesticidal proteins. These plants are regulated by the EPA as pesticides, and are discussed below.

* * * The FDA asserts regulatory authority over genetically modified fish and other animals pursuant to the "new animal drug" provisions of the FFDCA. These provisions allow the FDA to evaluate the new animal drug's safety with "reference to the health of man or animal," which the FDA interprets to include environmental effects that directly or indirectly affect the health of humans or animals other than those intended to receive the new drug.

The FDA has regulatory authority over pharmaceuticals grown in genetically modified plants that are intended for use in humans pursuant to the Public Health Service Act and the FFDCA. * * * FDA regulations are similar to those governing transgenic plants used for food. In both cases, the FDA regulates the use of plants that might express an allergenic or toxic compound in the pharmaceutical, and protects against the introduction of nonfood material into food or feed. The FDA regulations governing human drugs and biologics and animal drugs do not specifically address biotechnology. The USDA shares regulatory authority over the growth of the genetically engineered pharmaceutical-producing plants, as discussed below.

C.   The Environmental Protection Agency

The EPA regulates genetically modified products through its authority to regulate pesticide use and pesticide residue in food products. All pesticides must be registered with the EPA prior to their distribution, sale, or use, pursuant to the Federal Insecticide, Fungicide, and Rodenticide Act (FIFRA). * * *

FIFRA was enacted to regulate chemical substances, not biotechnological products (it was enacted prior to Watson and Crick's discovery of the DNA molecule). Based on FIFRA's statutory definition of "pesticide," however, the EPA regulates the genetic material inserted into transgenic plants to express pesticidal products, as well as the expression products themselves, as pesticides. Thus, manufacturers of transgenic pest-protected plants must receive registration of the plants from the EPA prior to commercialization. * * *

In 1988, just prior to the widespread development of genetically engineered pest-protected plants, the EPA exempted plants and microorganisms with pesticidal properties from the requirements of FIFRA. This exemption was intended for plants, such as chrysanthemums, that are naturally pest-protected. Due to these regulations, the EPA does not regulate any plants themselves, including genetically modified ones. As discussed above, the EPA does regulate the inserted genetic material and the products it expresses.

The EPA is responsible for regulating both the environmental and human health impacts of plants genetically modified to produce their own pesticides, as the FDA has ceded regulatory authority over pest-protected plants to the EPA. Where use of a pesticide will result in any residue being left on food, the pesticide is subject to regulation by the EPA pursuant to the FFDCA. In these instances, the EPA establishes "tolerance" levels for the allowable amount of pesticide residue that can be left on food products. Currently, all FIFRA-registered, pest-protected plants are exempt from tolerance level requirements because tests of these transgenic plants have not revealed a human health risk.

The EPA does not regulate genetically engineered plants other than those modified to contain pesticides, and it does not regulate the environmental impacts or potential impacts of genetically engineered animals.

D.   The U.S. Department of Agriculture

The USDA is responsible for protecting and promoting American agriculture. On the principle that genetically modified plants could pose a risk to agricultural crops, the USDA oversees the agricultural safety of the movement, importation, and field testing of transgenic plants.

In order to grow transgenic plants outside of a laboratory, approval must be obtained from the Animal and Plant Health Inspection Service (APHIS) of the USDA. APHIS' authority to regulate genetically modified plants stems from the Plant Protection Act (PPA). The PPA was enacted in 2000, and thus, at first glance, appears to deviate from the trend of regulating biotechnology under ancient statutes. The PPA, however, essentially consolidated authority from two previous statutes that APHIS had used to regulate genetically modified organisms: the Federal Plant Pest Act (FPPA), enacted in 1957, and the Federal Plant Quarantine Act (PQA), enacted in 1912. Both the FPPA and PQA were originally enacted to regulate the introduction of nonindigenous plant species. APHIS regulations governing genetically modified plants under the PPA are simply those established pursuant to the FPPA and the PQA. No modification to APHIS' regulation of biotechnology products has been made pursuant to the PPA.

Pursuant to the PPA, APHIS has primary regulatory authority for all genetically modified plants except pest-protected ones. As APHIS is supposed to carry out its mandate while not impeding the growth of the biotechnology industry, critics have contended that an agency charged with promoting agriculture (including the biotechnology industry), "may not be able to objectively assess the safety of new products of agricultural biotechnology."

Under the PPA, anyone seeking to introduce (i.e., import, transport interstate, or release into the environment) a regulated article must receive authorization from APHIS. "Regulated article" includes [a]ny organism which has been altered or produced through genetic engineering. * * *

Prior to conducting a field trial of a new transgenic plant, a developer must perform a risk evaluation on the plant to determine whether the plant may be a plant pest. No consideration of any other risks, such as other human health or environmental risks, must be evaluated prior to the field test.

Authorization from APHIS can come via a notification or permitting process, each of which is aimed at ensuring that the transgenic organisms are grown and handled in a manner to prevent their escape into the environment. For most genetically modified plants, under certain conditions, simple notification of APHIS prior to release (without the requirement of receiving a permit) is sufficient. Nearly 99% of all field tests, importations, and interstate movement of genetically engineered plants take place under the notification system.

Permits are required for the movement, importation, and field testing of transgenic plants that do not qualify for notification, such as pharmaceutical-producing plants, and for plants denied notification. APHIS uses the permitting process to evaluate potential plant pest risk and to require prevention measures to reduce risk. The primary emphasis of the permitting process is confinement. * * *

APHIS regulates transgenic pharmaceutical-producing plants pursuant to the same authority under which it regulates other transgenic plants, such as "regulated articles" under the PPA. Thus, applicants must acquire a permit prior to the field test of transgenic pharmaceutical-producing plants, as such plants are specifically excluded from the notification process. Various measures must then be taken to confine the transgenic plants to the field site during the period of release, and to prevent the plants or their offspring from persisting in the environment subsequently.

With respect to biotechnology developments beyond plants, the Food Safety and Inspection Service (FSIS) of the USDA is responsible for the safety of food products prepared from domestic livestock and poultry. The Federal Meat Inspection Act (FMIA) and the Poultry Products Inspection Act (PPIA) require FSIS to inspect cattle, sheep, swine, goats, equines, poultry, and food products prepared from them, which are intended for use as human food. Pursuant to these acts, the FSIS has regulatory authority over genetically modified domestic livestock and poultry.

APHIS also has regulatory authority over the release of insects for pest management, and presumably would regulate the release of transgenic insects in the same manner. No agency regulates research and commercialization of transgenic insects other than for their intentional release, and no guidelines exist that govern their containment or the potential ecological risks posed by their release. * * *

2. TRANSGENIC PLANTS

In a report released in February 2002, a committee of the National Academies' National Research Council recommended that the public should be more involved in the review process of transgenic plants; that before making precedent-setting decisions regarding field-testing or deregulation, APHIS should solicit broad external scientific and public review well beyond use of the *Federal Register*; that the agency should convene a scientific advisory group before any changes in regulatory policy are made; and that ecological testing and monitoring should continue after commercial production of a transgenic plant has been approved. Excerpts from this report appear below.

While the report identifies some desirable regulatory changes, it does not condemn the 1986 Coordinated Framework for Regulation of Biotechnology as basically flawed and inadequate. For a more vigorous critique of the piecemeal approach of using mostly pre-1986 laws to regulate the environmental effects of biotechnology, *see* John Kunich, *Mother Frankenstein, Doctor Nature, and the Environmental Law of Genetic Engineering*, 74 S. CAL. L. REV. 807 (2001) (advocating enactment of a new, comprehensive "Transgenic Release Act").

NATIONAL RESEARCH COUNCIL, COMMITTEE ON ENVIRONMENTAL IMPACTS ASSOCIATED WITH COMMERCIALIZATION OF TRANSGENIC PLANTS, ENVIRONMENTAL EFFECTS OF TRANSGENIC PLANTS: THE SCOPE AND ADEQUACY OF REGULATION

9, 76, 176–77, 223–24, 229, 237, 246–49 (2002).[3]

. . . Plants that cannot be grown in the field, based on notification, include those that produce substances intended for use as pharmaceuticals and those that could affect non-target organisms. . . .

Non-Target Hazards

* * *

Non-target organisms are any species that is not the direct target of the transgenic crop. To date, the vast majority of the published studies that examine non-target hazards have focused on *Bt* [from the bacterium *Bacillus thuringiensis*] crops. For example, *Bt* corn is presently targeted to control the key pests, European corn borer . . . and southwestern corn borer . . . , and *Bt* rice is targeted against striped stem borer . . . and yellow stem borer. . . . Any other species affected by *Bt* corn or *Bt* rice is a non-target species; consequently, the list of potential non-target species is very long. These organisms can be grouped conveniently into five categories that are not mutually exclusive: (1) beneficial species, including natural enemies of pests (lacewings, ladybird beetles, parasitic wasps, and microbial parasites) and pollinators (bees, flies, beetles, butterflies and moths, birds and bats); (2) non-target pests; (3) soil organisms, which usually are difficult to study and identify to species; (4) species of conservation concern, including endangered species and popular, charismatic species (monarch butterfly); and (5) biodiversity, which may include the species richness in an area. * * *

Hazard of Resistance Evolution

Resistance evolution can occur in pests that are targeted for control by or associated with a transgenic crop. This is a potential environmental hazard because if the pest becomes resistant to control, alternative, more environmentally damaging controls may be used. In addition, new control tactics may be rushed into use before their environmental risks are

---

completely assessed. Insects, weeds, and microbial pathogens all have the potential to overcome most control tactics used against them. . . . * * *

GENERAL COMMENTS AND CONCERNS

Geopolitical Scale

The scope of APHIS oversight is limited to whether and how transgenic plants are moved and released in the United States. Although APHIS determinations sometimes include consideration of environmental impacts of deregulated genetically modified organisms outside the confines of the United States, the agency is under no obligation to do so. Indeed, relevant scientific data may be unavailable for many countries that are centers of diversity for wild relatives of a transgenic crop. Yet these locations might be the very places where environmental impacts might occur due to transgene flow into those populations. Also, once a transgenic plant is deregulated, descendants of that plant may find themselves intentionally or unintentionally transported far beyond the borders of the United States, to radically different environments. A transgenic crop variety developed to fit into U.S. systems of agriculture may cause changes in the agricultural systems of other countries that would cause environmental degradation.

One can imagine an argument being made by certain stakeholders, that if the U.S. government found a plant to be safe, that judgment should be good enough for a country without the resources to conduct its own environmental analysis. That would be wrong. Just because APHIS finds a transgenic plant to have no significant impact in the United States is not a guarantee that it will not have an impact elsewhere. To its credit, APHIS has held biosafety meetings in a number of developing countries to inform policymakers of the potential environmental effects of transgenic plants.

CBI in APHIS Decision Documents

Many people, including those generally supportive of biotechnology, decry the apparently large amount of data and information in submissions marked "CBI" (confidential business information). Under this CBI stamp, all manner of data are hidden from public view and even from independent scientific scrutiny. . . . This committee sometimes found that it could not provide an independent scientific assessment of APHIS rulings because of the broad use of CBI. . . . Without a transparent mechanism to evaluate and judge confidential data from applicants, APHIS appears to accept without question an applicant's assertion of what is CBI. Public credibility is eroded when the same information marked CBI in APHIS documents is not considered CBI and is open to public inspection in other jurisdictions, such as Canada or Europe. It must be understood that U.S. standards for what constitutes CBI are very broad. A company can claim that certain information is CBI as long as it can show there is any possibility that disclosure of the information could directly or indirectly harm its business. . . . * * *

THE NEXT TRANSGENIC CROPS

* * *

Improved Postharvest Processing

. . . The global demand for wood and wood products is growing along with the human population. To reduce pressure on existing forests, forest plantations that grow transgenic trees are expected to play an increasingly important role in meeting the demand for tree products. . . . [T]he first traits being genetically engineered into trees are herbicide tolerance and insect resistance, which are useful for establishing and maintaining young trees. Several traits are under development to better adapt trees to postharvest processing, and these may become commercially available in the near future. For example, there is research under way to modify the lignin content of certain tree species, in order to improve pulping, the process by which wood fibers are separated to make paper. Reduced lignin may improve the efficiency of paper production and may reduce environmental pollution from the paper production process. * * *

There is also interest in using genetic engineering technology to turn annual crop plants into factories that produce valuable chemicals. Plants have the capacity to synthesize a variety of complex molecules, given the simple inputs of a few minerals, carbon dioxide, water, and sunshine. It is widely thought that plants could provide a "green" renewable source of chemicals to replace those currently obtained from petroleum. . . . * * *

Mitigation of Environmental Pollution

In the future, transgenic plants may be grown for reasons other than commercialization. For example, it has been proposed that transgenic plants could contribute to removing or detoxifying heavy metal pollutants in contaminated soils ("phytoremediation"). A particular problem in some locations is mercury. Plants have already been created that can accumulate mercury. Thus, growing such plants is a potential solution for cleaning up mercury pollution at despoiled sites. * * *

FUTURE POLICY ISSUES

* * *

Agricultural Structure

Issues related to changing agricultural structure might have indirect environmental consequences. The socioeconomic considerations for evaluating transgenic crops have proven to be more volatile than was predicted only a few years ago. The desire of some consumers, both foreign and domestic, to avoid consumption of foods containing transgenes has led to the segmentation of markets for "genetically modified" ("GM") and "GM-free" crops. In the United States the creation of marketing standards for certified organic crops that do not contain transgenes or transgene products has established a market niche for producers. These forms of market segmentation create an opportunity for U.S. farmers to capture a price premium for nontransgenic crops. At the same time, the existence of a market for nontransgenic crops creates a new kind of environmental risk from transgenics: If they cannot be environmentally isolated, pollen and residues from transgenic crops can affect/influence the economic value of nontransgenic crop production. The development of market standards and international trade rules for nontransgenic crops will have economic implications for U.S. agriculture. In the worst-case scenario, U.S. producers may effectively be excluded from these emerging world markets. . . . * * *

REGULATORY ISSUES

* * *

U.S. and Global Capacity for Environmental Regulation

* * *

As noted above, some of the coming applications of biotechnology may involve the use of plants to produce pharmaceutical products, biologics, fuels, and other substances not intended for human food use. The introduction of such transgenes poses the potential for environmentally associated risks of a wholly different order than those associated with existing transgenic crops. If such a transgene moves into food crops, either through pollen transfer or physical contamination, there could be serious human safety risks. If such a transgene moves into a wild relative, there could be widespread environmental dissemination of the pharmaceutical substance or other nonfood substances that could have impacts on wildlife as well as microbial populations. * * *

The Precautionary Principle

At the same time that new products and applications of gene transfer are being applied in crop production, there has been discussion of new regulatory approaches. One important component of this discussion has been the "precautionary principle." . . . Language endorsing a precautionary principle and taking a precautionary approach in regulatory decision making is in the European Union's (EU) Directive 90/220 on biotechnology and its revision in 2001, the Cartagena Protocol on Biosafety, which was finalized in Montreal during 2000, under the Convention on Biological Diversity (CBD). The CBD has been ratified by many countries but not the United States. It is an international agreement to conserve and use sustainably biological diversity for the benefit of present and future generations. * * *

REGULATING AGRICULTURAL BIOTECHNOLOGY AND

The European discussion of the precautionary principle has occurred in the context of attempts to harmonize grades, standards, and regulatory approaches among member states. These discussions have occurred during a spate of food scares and failings in government oversight, most notably associated with transmissible bovine spongiform encephalopathy (Mad Cow Disease), that have rocked public confidence in government regulation of the food system. Although debate over the food safety and environmental risks of transgenic crops has figured prominently in Europe, European pronouncements on the precautionary principle neither offer a specific evaluation of transgenic crops nor provide language that would give regulators specific instructions on how to take a precautionary approach with respect to transgenic crops. The March 12, 2001, revision to EU Directive 90/220 states that the requirements of the Biosafety Protocol, including the precautionary principle, should be respected. The 2001 directive indicates that the precautionary principle was taken into account in the drafting of the directive and must be taken into account when implementing it. Consequently, the directive does not provide a statement of the precautionary principle but identifies regulatory processes that are precautionary. It is beyond the scope of this report to provide a detailed analysis of this new directive, but suffice it to say that the precautionary principle has been incorporated into at least the labeling and traceability standards, the monitoring standards, and the EU approval process. Much the same as in the Biosafety Protocol, the precautionary principle will be defined in Europe through its application to specific cases.

NOTES

1. Plants which are genetically engineered to produce their own pesticides are regulated not only by APHIS but also by EPA under FIFRA. *See* John Kunich, *Mother Frankenstein, Doctor Nature, and the Environmental Law of Genetic Engineering*, 74 S. CAL. L. REV. 807, 831–837 (2001).

2. The Coordinated Framework for the Regulation of Biotechnology discussed in the Mandel article, *supra*, was updated in January 2017—the first update in more than 20 years. Among other things, the 2017 update clarifies current roles and responsibilities of the major regulatory agencies, elaborates a long-term strategy to ensure that the federal biotechnology regulatory system is prepared for the future products of biotechnology, and commissions an expert analysis of the future landscape of biotechnology products to support these efforts. *See* EXECUTIVE OFFICE OF THE PRESIDENT, MODERNIZING THE REGULATORY SYSTEM FOR BIOTECHNOLOGY PRODUCTS: FINAL VERSION OF THE 2017 UPDATE TO THE COORDINATED FRAMEWORK FOR THE REGULATION OF BIOTECHNOLOGY (January 2017).

3. Directive 2001/18/EC and Regulation (EC) No 1829/2003 of the European Parliament regulate the introduction of genetically modified organisms into commerce in Europe. The regulations are significantly more stringent than U.S. law. No genetically modified products may be introduced

into commerce without prior approval and GMO products are subject to two post-introduction regulatory principles. First, GMO products must be labeled. Second, the EU is committed to the principle that GMO crops must be traceable in the market. Article 4 of Directive 2001/18/EC puts the precautionary principle at the heart of the EU approach to GMOs. Each notification of intent to undertake a deliberate release of a GMO must include a plan for monitoring its effects on human health or the environment (Article 6). For a detailed explanation *see* Damien Plan & Guy Van den Eede, *The EU Legislation on GMOs, available at* http://ihcp.jrc.ec.europa.eu/our_activities/gmo/eu-legislation-gmos/.

The EU regulation of GMOs has led to significant limitations on the importation of American agricultural products. American negotiators in bilateral trade talks are seeking to "harmonize" GMO rules between the two nations, which presumably would lead to the weakening of the much tougher EU rules. *See* Michael Birnbaum, *At Trade Talks, U.S., E.U., Ready for Fight on Genetically Modified Crops*, Wash. Post (May 13, 2013), http://www.washingtonpost.com/world/europe/at-trade-talks-us-eu-ready-for-fight-on-genetically-modified-crops/2013/05/17/8e61176a-bdb0-11e2-9b09-1638acc3942e_story.html.

4.   Consumer groups in the U.S. have led recent fights to require the labeling of genetically modified food, but lost a major ballot initiative in California in November, 2012. *See* Marc Lifsher, *California Voters Say No to Labeling Genetically Engineered Food,* L.A. Times (Nov 7, 2012), http://articles.latimes.com/2012/nov/07/business/la-fi-mo-genetically-engineered-food-labeling-20121107. More recently, Connecticut and Maine have both voted to require labeling, contingent upon other states in the area also passing labeling legislation. David Knowles, Maine Legislature easily passes GMO food labeling bill, a blow to Monsanto, New York Daily News, http://www.nydailynews.com/news/politics/maine-legislature-easily-passes-gmo-labeling-bill-article-1.1370871#ixzz2Z8l4h4b5 (June 12, 2013). The U.S. Senate voted down an amendment to the 2013 Farm Bill that would have required labeling.

5.   Biotech companies also are developing genetically modified *animals* for human consumption. They include pigs that produce leaner pork chops and less harmful manure, meatier chickens, disease-resistant shrimp, and fast-growing salmon and catfish. It is not clear how, and by whom, releases of such creatures will be regulated. With respect to the salmon, which are expected to be the first such modified animals to be marketed commercially, only the Food and Drug Administration seems to have asserted regulatory authority, which FDA claimed by designating the fish's foreign genes and the growth hormone they produce as a drug for animals. EPA and the Department of Agriculture bowed out, leaving critics concerned that while FDA may be rigorous in examining food safety, it is not qualified to evaluate the ecological risks posed by releases of transgenic salmon into oceans. Farmed salmon typically are grown in enclosures in the sea, known as net pens, which frequently are torn by waves or hungry wild animals. If the transgenic fish are grown in such pens and slip out, wild salmon could be devastated. According to one study, if wild

females preferred to mate with genetically engineered males, and if those matings produced offspring that did not survive well, wild populations could be wiped out—a result known as the "Trojan gene effect." In many species of fish, females prefer larger males as mates, setting the scene for an advantage for growth-enhanced fish. *See* Carol Yoon, *Altered Salmon Leading Way to Dinner Plates, but Rules Lag*, N. Y. TIMES, May 1, 2000, page A1, col. 1; Aaron Zitner, *Gene-Altered Catfish Raise Environmental, Legal Issues*, LOS ANGELES TIMES, Jan. 2, 2001, at A1, col. 1.

In 2001, FDA's Center for Veterinary Medicine asked the National Research Council's Committee on Agricultural Biotechnology, Health, and the Environment to convene an ad hoc committee of experts to identify and evaluate the science-based risks associated with animal biotechnology, prior to any regulatory review by FDA of the food and environmental safety of products resulting from such technology. A prepublication internet version of the ensuing report by the special Committee on Defining Science-Based Concerns Associated with Products of Animal Biotechnology, *Animal Biotechnology: Science-Based Concerns*, was released in August, 2002. Among the various topics considered, the effects on the environment were believed to have the greatest potential for long-term impact. The taxonomic groups presenting the greatest environmental concerns were found to be aquatic organisms and insects because their mobility poses serious containment problems and because, unlike domestic farm birds and mammals, they can easily become feral and compete with indigenous populations. Of immediate concern, the report said, is the release of transgenic fish and shellfish. The executive summary concluded as follows:

> The current regulatory framework might not be adequate to address unique problems and characteristics associated with animal biotechnologies. The responsibilities of federal agencies for regulating animal biotechnology are unclear. How each agency will deal with scientific uncertainty remains to be seen. The committee notes a particular concern about the lack of any established regulatory framework for the oversight of scientific research and commercial application of biotechnology to arthropods. In addition to the potential lack of clarity about regulatory responsibilities and data collection requirements, the committee also notes a concern about the legal and technical capacity of the agencies to address potential hazards, particularly in the environmental area.

D. MANDATORY DISCLOSURE OF INFORMATION CONCERNING CHEMICAL HAZARDS AND RELATED LIABILITIES

Parts A, B, and C of this chapter, as well as much of Chapters 6 and 7, have dealt with traditional "command and control" regulation. However, we also have explored, and will explore, alternate regulatory approaches. Chapter 2 contains important materials on economic incentive systems, such as effluent charges and marketable discharge permits, used increasingly as complements to traditional pollution regulation. Chapter 8 has examined the extensive civil liabilities—another type of economic incentive—created by RCRA, CERCLA, and the common law of "toxic torts." And the NEPA materials in Chapter 5 involve the most prominent example of mandating disclosure of information as a means of influencing both the behavior of the disclosers and the responses of the public and the political system.

This part of Chapter 9 discusses two other important examples of disclosure requirements. The first, arising from enactment in 1986 of the federal Emergency Planning and Community Right-to-Know Act (EPCRA), involves disclosure of the existence of physical conditions which pose potential chemical hazards as well as reporting on the release of listed toxic chemicals from industrial facilities. The second, stemming from reporting requirements under the federal securities laws, involves disclosure of potential corporate liabilities, especially liabilities of the types discussed in Chapter 8.

ROBERT F. BLOMQUIST, THE LOGIC AND LIMITS OF PUBLIC INFORMATION MANDATES UNDER FEDERAL HAZARDOUS WASTE LAW: A POLICY ANALYSIS
14 VT. L. REV. 559, 571–78 (1990).[4]

The Emergency Planning and Community Right-to-Know Act was passed by Congress as Title III to SARA.[54] The two general objectives of Title III are to encourage and support emergency planning efforts by local governments with regard to chemical hazards, and to provide citizens and local governments with information concerning potential community-based chemical hazards. Congress included three provisions within Title III to effectuate these objectives. The first concerns government emergency response planning. The second provision addresses emergency release notification by private industry. The third requires the compilation and reporting of information concerning chemical properties, manufacturing, usage, properties, and release.

The first provision of Title III requires the governors of the various states to have established a state emergency response commission by April 17, 1987. State commissions are also required to have established emergency planning districts no later than July 17, 1987, and to have appointed local emergency planning committees for each district by August 17, 1987.

---

[4]   Copyright 1990 by Vermont Law Review. Reprinted by permission.

[54] Superfund Amendment and Reauthorization Act of 1986 (SARA), Pub.L. No. 99–499, §§ 301–330, 100 Stat. 1613, 1729 (1986) (codified at 42 U.S.C. §§ 11001–11050 (Supp. V 1987)).

Each local committee is required to have completed preparation of an emergency response plan, no later than October 17, 1988, containing the following information:

1)   facilities within the district at which any one of numerous statutorily designated "extremely hazardous substances" at "threshold planning quantities" are present;

2)   methods and procedures for reporting a release of an extremely hazardous substance;

3)   names of community and facility coordinators;

4)   public notification procedures;

5)   methods for determining the occurrence of a release and the geographic area or population likely to be impacted;

6)   the available emergency equipment and facilities within the community;

7)   training programs; and

8)   evacuation plans.

"Congress intended the local planning process to be a truly community-based activity, and not simply an exercise carried out by a few representatives of industry and the government bureaucracy in a back room at city hall."

The second component of Title III—the emergency release notification provisions—requires the owner or operator of a "facility" to provide notification of a hazardous substance release within any affected area to the community emergency coordinator of the local committee and to the affected state's commission.[64] The statute mandates that the notification contain specific information. This information must include data about the chemical released, the estimated quantity of the hazardous substance, "the time and duration of the release," "[a]ny known or anticipated acute or chronic health risks associated with the emergency and, where appropriate, advice regarding medical attention necessary for exposed individuals," precautions to be taken in response to the release, and pertinent details regarding the contact person who can provide further information.

The final provision is perhaps the most important public environmental information mandate under Title III. This provision contains reporting requirements for chemical usage, chemical properties, manufacturing, and environmental releases. "In order to inform citizens about chemicals located in their communities, Title III requires the owners and operators of certain facilities to submit three types of information

---

[64]   SARA § 304(b)(1), 42 U.S.C. § 11004(b)(1) (Supp. V 1987); 40 C.F.R. § 355.40(b)(1) (1988).

concerning such chemicals to state and local authorities." This information entails: (a) material safety data sheets (MSDS) and hazardous chemical lists; (b) hazardous chemical inventory information; and (c) toxic chemical usage, manufacture, and release information.

All three components of Title III—government emergency response planning, emergency release notification procedures, and chemical inventory and usage reporting—are accessible to the public. Three specific public environmental information policies promote this accessibility: first, public participation requirements for local emergency response committees' formulation of emergency response plans; second, liberal public availability of local facility records (emergency response plans, follow-up emergency release notification, MSDS's, inventory forms, lists of hazardous chemicals, toxic chemical release forms); and, third, the EPA's development of a national computerized toxic chemical inventory database.[77] Moreover, citizen suit provisions create "the possibility of community self-help enforcement of SARA Title III by allowing suits against the facility owners or operators, state and local governments, or the EPA."[78] * * *

SARA's public information programs, particularly the Title III component, will promote six different policy goals. First, Title III will produce a baseline of

> data [that] can be used to characterize exposure levels, evaluate existing regulatory strategies and develop new ones, focus on specific locations of concern, identify important chemical releases and the types of operations they come from, compare permitted releases to reported releases, and aid in the development of waste minimization strategies.

Second, Title III holds promise for acting as "a valuable mechanism for effective emergency management, protecting environmental concerns, offering local citizens the opportunity to have a significant impact on the safety of their community, and for providing a structured forum in which industry, government, and citizens can work collectively on these issues."

Third, Title III should be applauded as "Congress' most significant experiment to involve the private sector and decentralize environmental problem solving. . . . [C]itizens [must] be informed about hazardous materials being stored, handled, or manufactured in their community, and local communities [must] have a coordinated emergency response plan to respond to chemical emergencies."

---

[77] SARA § 313(j), 42 U.S.C. § 11023(j) (Supp. V 1987). *See also* 53 Fed.Reg. 6567 (Mar. 9, 1988) (notice of public meeting to discuss options for making information available).

[78] Title III follows the "citizen as prosecutor" model by permitting citizen suits for civil penalties as well as injunctive relief. SARA § 326(c), 42 U.S.C. § 11046(c) (Supp. V 1987).

Fourth, while the information gathered in the Title III process should be viewed as preliminary, and subject to refinement, this public environmental information law will "provide Americans with at least two powerful pictures of the industries that put them at risk. Total annual discharges from the [*Toxic Release Inventory*, or "TRI"] data will be one picture. Another is the 'plume maps' or 'footprints' of potential chemical gas releases as they travel downwind or downstream." In a related way, the Toxic Release Inventory data generated by the imprimatur of section 313 will promote the better understanding of two major risk management problems: (a) identifying and specifying the "[m]any U.S. chemical plants [that] do not [currently] use the Best Achievable Control Technology (BACT) to minimize chemical discharges"; and (b) developing some rudimentary information "regarding chemical discharges once they have left the plant."

Fifth, the emergence of information regarding toxic chemical releases and mass balance inventories will, no doubt, serve as "strong public educational and motivational tools toward the improvement of chemical safety." Finally, Title III will facilitate the development of comparative emissions statistics of hazardous substances that will spur some industrial firms to take a leadership role by "openly communicating about risks" with the public in meetings that may reflect a "new era, and a new partnership." This industrial leadership has the potential of providing exemplary corporate models that will inspire other companies to respond to the competitive need to match the leaders' efforts.

NOTES

1.   EPA regulations concerning annual Toxic Release Inventory (TRI) reports by various industries are found at 40 C.F.R. Part 372. There are now more than 650 toxic chemicals and toxic chemical categories on the list of chemicals that must be reported to EPA and the states under the EPCRA/TRI Program. A facility must report to TRI if it meets the following three criteria:

a.   Conducts manufacturing operations within Standard Industrial Classification (SIC) codes 20 through 39; or, beginning in 1998, is in one of the following industry categories: metal mining, coal mining, electric utilities that burn coal or oil, chemical wholesale distributors, petroleum terminals and bulk storage facilities, RCRA hazardous waste TSD facilities, solvent recovery services, and federal facilities regardless of SIC codes.

b.   Has ten or more full-time employee equivalents.

c.   For all but certain persistent bioaccumulative toxic (PBT) chemicals, manufactures or processes more than 25,000 pounds or otherwise uses more than 10,000 pounds of any listed chemical during the calendar year. The reporting threshold for PBT chemicals is 100 pounds manufactured, processed, or used, except that for "highly persistent and highly bioaccumulative" chemicals it is 10 pounds.

2. The data disclosed by industries' annual TRI reports, and the reductions in releases seemingly attributable to EPCRA's disclosure requirements, have been remarkable. In 1988, the first reporting year, 18,500 companies disclosed that they had released 10.4 billion pounds of toxic chemicals in 1987: 3.9 billion into landfills, 3.3 billion to treatment and disposal facilities, 2.7 billion into the air, and 550 million into surface waters. These figures were far beyond EPA's expectations. *See* Weisskopf, *EPA Finds Pollution 'Unacceptably High'*, WASHINGTON POST, April 13, 1989, at A33. EPA subsequently revised the total of 10.4 billion pounds downward to 7 billion pounds because some mining companies which had reported were not required (prior to 1998) to do so. * * *

For 2016, 21,600 facilities reported 3.4 billion pounds of releases to air, water, and land—a 21% decline since 2006. Most of this decline occurred because of a 58% reduction in the release of hazardous air pollutants, with the largest reduction coming from the electric utility sector. The metal mining sector was responsible for the largest overall share of releases (66% of the total). Total releases reported under TRI have been declining steadily, from the initial 10.4 billion pounds in 1987 to 7.3 billion pounds in 1998 to the 3.4 billion pounds in 2016. For a national summary of the 2016 data, *see* EPA, Toxics Release Inventory (TRI) National Analysis https://www.epa.gov/trinationalanalysis. Of course, not all chemicals released into the environment are reported in the TRI; emissions from individuals, principally through driving, make up a large percentage of overall chemical releases. *See* Michael P. Vandenbergh, From Smokestack to SUV: The Individual as Regulated Entity in the New Era of Environmental Law, 57 VAND. L. REV. 515, 518 (2004).

The most complete and current TRI data and data release reports may be accessed through EPA's website at https://www.epa.gov/toxics-release-inventory-tri-program.

3. In *Atlantic States Legal Foundation v. Whiting Roll-Up Door Mfg. Corp.*, 1994 WL 236473 (W.D.N.Y.1994), plaintiffs brought a citizen's enforcement action under section 326 of EPCRA, alleging that defendant had failed to file timely hazardous chemical information with state and federal authorities under sections 311–313. Among other forms of relief, plaintiffs sought civil penalties, a permanent injunction prohibiting further EPCRA violations, and attorneys' fees and costs. Under a settlement agreement, plaintiffs were "prevailing parties" within the meaning of section 326(f), and the court therefore awarded them more than $32,000 in attorneys' fees and costs.

However, in *Steel Co. v. Citizens for a Better Environment*, discussed in an earlier chapter, the Supreme Court held that an environmental group *lacked standing* to bring a citizen suit under EPCRA for "purely past violations." In 1995, plaintiff sent a notice to defendant, to the EPA, and to Illinois authorities, alleging (accurately) that defendant had failed since 1988 (the first year of EPCRA's filing deadlines) to complete and to submit the requisite hazardous-chemical inventory and toxic-chemical release forms. Upon receiving the notice, defendant filed all of the overdue forms with the relevant agencies. EPA chose not to bring suit, e.g., to recover civil penalties; and when the 60-day, post-notice waiting period expired, plaintiff filed suit in the federal district court. The complaint asked for a declaratory judgment that defendant had violated EPCRA, an order requiring defendant to pay civil penalties of $25,000 per day for each EPCRA violation, and an award of plaintiff's attorney and expert witness fees. The Supreme Court held that the constitutional requirement of "redressability—a likelihood that the requested relief will redress the alleged injury"—was not satisfied because none of the items of relief sought "would serve to reimburse [plaintiff] for losses caused by the late reporting, or to eliminate any effects of that late reporting upon [plaintiff]." The penalties would be payable to the government, not to plaintiff, and "plaintiff cannot achieve standing to litigate a substantive issue by bringing suit for the cost of bringing suit."

Subsequently, in the *Laidlaw* decision, *supra*, the Court allowed a citizen suit for civil penalties where defendant's violations of the Clean Water Act continued until after the filing of plaintiff's complaint but ended prior to judgment by the district court.

MARK COHEN, INFORMATION AS A POLICY INSTRUMENT IN PROTECTING THE ENVIRONMENT: WHAT HAVE WE LEARNED?

31 ENVTL. L. REP. 10425, 10425–27 (2001).[5]

Since the introduction of the toxic release inventory (TRI) in 1988, there has been considerable interest in environmental information disclosure as a possible complement or substitute for traditional forms of regulation. Among the most important reasons for this growing interest are the following: (1) the TRI program led to a significant voluntary decrease in the total amount of TRI chemicals released in the United States, beyond any mandated levels; (2) information disclosure programs serve another very important social function—they satisfy the belief that the public has a "right to know" that they might be affected by third-party pollution; (3) new information technologies (both hardware and software) that facilitate the dissemination of environmental information in a meaningful way; (4) the fact that these programs are generally thought to cost the government far less than drafting and implementing industrywide regulations; and (5) these approaches are often politically more feasible to adopt since they are generally framed as "right to know" laws and thus not easily characterized as coercive new regulations. * * *

---

[5]   Copyright © 2001 by the Environmental Law Institute. Reprinted with permission.

Information Disclosure Programs Affect Firm Behavior

Empirically, it has been shown that mandatory disclosure programs such as TRI can have a significant effect on the environmental performance of firms. What is not fully understood, however, is the mechanism by which these programs induce firms to voluntarily reduce emissions beyond any legal requirement. For example, when the first such disclosure of TRI was made, there was a significant reduction in the market value for some publicly traded firms while other firms saw an increase in market value. Subsequently, firms dramatically reduced their emissions. However, the emissions reductions were not uniformly distributed across firms. One study found that firms with the largest negative stock price returns upon the initial announcement of TRI data were the firms that reduced emissions the most.

Thus, the important question remains as to why information disclosure may affect both stock prices of publicly traded companies and, ultimately, emissions of all firms subject to disclosure. Information about a firm's environmental performance—whether good or bad—may be of interest to shareholders or lenders for a variety of reasons. To the extent that the information concerns monetary sanctions or an announcement of an agreement to spend money on new pollution control equipment, we might expect these monetary outlays to reduce the expected value of the firm, thus reducing the share price and/or bond rating of the firm. It may also give lenders pause about risking more capital on that particular firm. Other costs of "bad information" might include future debarment from government contracts, targeted enforcement by environmental agencies, and lost sales to "green consumers." Some socially conscious investors might even shun the firm's stock, thereby depressing its value. Finally, it is possible that investors will update their assessment of the quality of management in the firm and view this information as a signal that the firm is not as well managed as they thought.

Aside from the stock market, there are other mechanisms through which information disclosure programs might ultimately result in improved environmental performance. In particular, there is empirical evidence that informal community pressure and social norms may play an important role in emissions and/or compliance. Not surprisingly, the ability of communities to play this role is an increasing function of income and education level as well as the degree of environmental activism by the local residents. * * *

Information Disclosure Programs Empower Local
Communities and Other Stakeholders

The increasing availability of environmental information has permitted stakeholder involvement to take on new, expanded roles. At the facility level, information can help empower a local community to take actions such as opposing a new permit or zoning application or beginning a meaningful dialogue on issues of concern with nearby industrial facilities. A recent study comparing TRI emissions across states found that states with higher membership levels of environmental organizations had larger TRI emission reductions, consistent with the theory that environmental group pressure can reduce emissions. * * *

Information Disclosure Programs Can Increase Cooperation between EPA and Regulated Industries

Many of these environmental information disclosure programs involve new channels of communication and cooperation between industry and the U.S. Environmental Protection Agency that can lead to both improved environmental performance and less costly methods of achieving these results. Instead of focusing the dialogue on technology standards, the health risks of varying regulatory standards, and other contentious issues, EPA and the regulated industry often find themselves in a new role of having common interests—how to find cost-effective methods of reducing emissions. The classic example of this was EPA's 33/50 Program, in which EPA invited firms to participate in a voluntary effort to reduce toxic emissions. Another example is EPA Region I's Environmental Leadership Program (known as StarTrack), which (among other things) rewards firms that regularly audit and disclose their environmental performance results with preferential treatment on compliance issues.

Benchmarking and Incentives to Go Beyond Compliance

The wide availability of environmental information due to current programs provides significant benchmarking opportunities, as firms are able to identify industry leaders in environmental performance. Numerous corporate environmental managers have told me that they closely watch the disclosures of their competitors to determine who the leaders and laggards are and how their company ranks. This information is useful in setting priorities and looking for areas where a company might be able to improve its environmental performance.

Coupled with the apparent desire of firms to be looked upon as environmental leaders (or at least not to be looked upon as among the worst environmental performers), information disclosure can take on many of the positive attributes of market-based regulatory mechanisms such as emission fees or marketable permits. Firms now have an incentive to go beyond compliance as long as the cost of doing so is less than the perceived benefit to the firm. Moreover, society is likely to benefit as these emission reductions are concentrated in companies that can do so at least cost.

In one very important way, information disclosure programs are more akin to emissions fees than to marketable permits. In a marketable permit regime, the government can set the level of emissions and knows in advance that it will be achieved (subject to adequate compliance). However,

emissions fees and information disclosure programs have no such guarantee. Although they have the added feature of encouraging beyond compliance behavior, they might not achieve any reduction at all. This has important implications when thinking about information disclosure as a *substitute* for regulation (as opposed to a complementary program). . . .
* * *

Disclosure Programs Must Take into Account Needs and Knowledge of Stakeholders

Current environmental information disclosure programs are generally designed to provide information to environmentally knowledgeable people rather than to the average citizen attempting to learn about the environment. Emissions information is generally disclosed without related hazard or risk content to place the information in a more meaningful context. This has the potential of misdirecting the attention of stakeholders toward lesser hazards or by focusing their attention on the wrong facilities. It also has the potential for confusing stakeholders about the extent to which they would support or oppose the existence of a polluting facility in their neighborhoods.

Although there is no easy solution to the potential misinformation on the part of the public, two programs could help alleviate this problem: (1) research on the information needs of stakeholders, and (2) expanded investment in educating the public (including children) about the meaning of the information being disseminated.

Although admittedly more knowledgeable than the average public, securities analysts and others in the financial markets currently have little use for environmental information disclosure programs. This is partly due to the fact that current programs do not provide information in a format that financial markets can use to accurately and effectively evaluate the environmental performance of firms. Once again, working with the financial community to assess their needs would potentially increase the value of these programs. One possibility is to ultimately standardize disclosure along the lines of financial statements monitored by the U.S. Securities and Exchange Commission.

MICHELLE CHAN-FISHEL, AFTER ENRON: HOW ACCOUNTING AND SEC REFORM CAN PROMOTE CORPORATE ACCOUNTABILITY WHILE RESTORING PUBLIC CONFIDENCE

32 ENVTL. L. REP. 10965, 10968–73 (2002).[6]

The SEC and Corporate Disclosure

Although the TRI is the best-known disclosure law in the environmental community, many publicly traded companies perceive the disclosure duties imposed by the SEC as their most rigorous and important reporting obligation. The SEC was created with the authority to require corporations to disclose any information that would benefit the interests of investors and/or the general public. * * *

Since 1998, the Corporate Sunshine Working Group (CSWG), an alliance of investors and public interest organizations, has worked to reform a key gatekeeper, the SEC, in an effort to broaden and deepen corporate nonfinancial disclosure rules to benefit investors, as well as the larger public interest. Members of this alliance include investors, asset managers, and public interest organizations who have submitted public comments to the SEC, produced case studies illustrating company noncompliance with existing SEC disclosure requirements, and advocated for broader, deeper, and more specific disclosure on nonfinancial matters, such as environmental performance, labor relations, and good governance. * * *

Current SEC Environmental Disclosure Regulations

Current SEC disclosure rules require publicly traded companies to disclose actual or potential environmental liabilities under Regulation S-K,[42] Items 101,[43] 103,[44] and 303.[45]

Item 101, governing the company's general description of business operations, requires disclosure of the material effects that complying with federal, state, and local environmental provisions may have upon the capital expenditures, earnings and competitive position of the registrant and its subsidiaries. The company is required to disclose any "material estimated capital expenditures for environmental control facilities for the remainder of its current fiscal year and its succeeding fiscal year and for such further periods as the registrant may deem material."

Item 103, governing the disclosure of legal proceedings, requires a company to disclose material environmentally related administrative or

---

[6]   Copyright © 2002 by the Environmental Law Institute. Reprinted with permission.

[42]   17 C.F.R. pt. 229.

[43]   Id. § 229.101.

[44]   Id. § 229.103.

[45]   Id. § 229.303.

judicial proceedings. The SEC provides two specific materiality thresholds which require disclosure if the proceeding involves a claim, sanction or expenditure that exceeds 10% of current assets, or if the proceeding involves a governmental authority seeking potential sanctions over $100,000.

Item 303, governing disclosure in the Management Discussion and Analysis section of a financial report, requires a registrant to disclose "where a trend, demand, commitment, event or uncertainty is both presently known to management and reasonably likely to have material effects on the registrant's financial condition or results of operation." Such trends can include environmental issues such as impending environmental regulation.

Companies' environmental disclosures are also subject to the anti-fraud provisions of SEC Rule 10b–5,[46] which prohibits a company from making false or misleading statements in SEC filings. The rule also prohibits a company from underreporting or omitting information that a reasonable investor would likely consider material given the total amount of information available to the investor.

The body of Generally Accepted Accounting Principles (GAAP) governing environmental and other types of accounting and disclosure are established through the SEC, the American Institute for Certified Public Accountants (AICPA), and the Financial Accounting Standards Board (FASB). GAAP is codified by the SEC through SEC Staff Accounting Bulletins (SAB), which reiterate and often provide interpretive guidance on SEC, AICPA, and FASB reporting and disclosure guidelines. * * *

Materiality

Disclosure of nonfinancial information, whether it be related to environmental liabilities, legal proceedings, or future trends, is triggered by the "materiality," or significance, of the data. Materiality has been defined with various levels of specificity by companies, private auditors, the SEC, and the accounting profession through the establishment of GAAP and through case law.

Many registrants and auditors use a general and quantitative definition of materiality that defines material disclosures as those data with financial impact exceeding 5%–10% of net income. Although the 5% threshold is widely used, the SEC points out that that materiality definition has no basis in accounting literature or law.[47]

On the contrary, the SEC's most recent (1999) pronouncement on materiality, SAB 99 clarifies that qualitative information can be material, and that "exclusive reliance on certain quantitative benchmarks to assess

---

[46]   52 Id. § 240.10b–5.

[47]   SEC, SAB–99–Materiality (Aug. 12, 1999).

materiality in preparing financial statements and performing audits of those financial statements is inappropriate; misstatements are not immaterial simply because they fall beneath a numerical threshold." The bulletin provides several cases in which disclosures that fall beneath the 5% threshold can in fact be material, such as when the disclosure refers to a company's regulatory compliance, or if it relates to an important portion of the registrant's business operations.

The FASB provided another definition of materiality in its Statement of Financial Accounting Concepts No. 2 (FAS 2), which takes a relatively expansive view. FAS 2 states that a disclosure should be made if its omission or correction would probably change or influence "the judgment of a reasonable person relying upon the report."

Case law is consistent with FASB's expansive definition of materiality. In 1976, the Supreme Court, in *TSC Industries, Inc. v. Northway, Inc.*[48] mirrored FAS 2's definition by concluding that a disclosure is material if there is "a substantial likelihood that the disclosure of the omitted fact would have been viewed by the reasonable investor as having significantly altered the total mix' of information available." In addition, the Court maintained that a disclosure it material if "there is a substantial likelihood that a reasonable shareholder would consider it important in deciding how to vote." * * *

A Pattern of Inadequate Nonfinancial Disclosure

Since 1997, individual members of the CSWG have monitored companies' disclosure of nonfinancial data, and notified the SEC of alleged misstatements or omissions of material environmental and social information. The complaints have been varied, with allegations of material misstatements of environmental, labor, and legal issues in several types of public filings, including annual reports, quarterly statements and registration documents. The group maintains that noncompliance with SEC environmental and social reporting requirements is a systemic problem, and that better enforcement is needed. * * *

Investor Lawsuits Alleging Inadequate Disclosure of Labor and Environmental Matters

In addition to the complaints filed with the SEC, shareholders have also recently filed lawsuits against companies for providing allegedly false or misleading information to investors, again illustrating a systemic problem of underreporting of environmental and social matters. * * *

In 1999, the shareholders of U.S. Liquids, Inc. filed a class action suit against the company for allegedly misleading shareholders about material environmental issues while raising capital through a public offering. In 1998, the company had claimed that its liquid waste management services

---

[48]   426 U.S. 438 (1976).

would generate 20% earnings per share growth in 1999. This claim allowed U.S. Liquids to raise $30 million through share offerings in 1998 and 1999, and inflated its stock to a Class Period high in early 1999. Several months later, the public learned that EPA and the Federal Bureau of Investigation were investigating illegal dumping activities at one of the company's most profitable sites. Share price dropped by 50%, and trading of the stock was halted after the company announced that earnings would be substantially lower than originally projected. The plaintiffs allege that the company deliberately misled the investing public by representing that it was in environmental compliance when the company either knew or was reckless in not knowing that illegal disposal of PCBs into the Detroit sewer system had occurred. The company has, in turn, sued its contractor. The lawsuit is still ongoing.

The SEC Responds to the Systemic Problem of Inadequate Disclosure

In 2001, EPA stepped up its efforts to educate companies of their SEC obligations regarding disclosure of environmental liabilities and enforcement actions. In 2001, the Agency publicly released a 1997 study which found that 74% of companies failed to report cases in which a national, state, or municipal agency is contemplating or has initiated an environmentally related legal proceeding that could result in monetary sanctions of over $100,000 (for which disclosure is required under Regulation S-K, Item 103). In fall 2001, the Agency issued an Enforcement Alert newsletter that notified companies of their SEC-mandated environmental disclosure duties. EPA is also preparing a guide to assist investors and the public on how to access environmental information on companies using EPA databases, some of which provide information on a facility rather than corporate basis.

INDEX

References are to Pages